REAL

REAL ORIGINAL

수능기출학력평가
7개년 기출 문제집

고3 영어 듣기

Contents

[모바일 영어 듣기 MP3 이용 방법]
① 스마트폰으로 QR 코드 스캔하기
② 입시플라이 or www.ipsifly.com 입력
모바일 홈페이지 [듣기 자료실] 이용

수능 모의고사 전문 출판

입시플라이

교재의 구성과 특징

실전은 연습처럼! 연습은 실전처럼! 「리얼 오리지널」

수능 시험장에 가면 낯선 환경과 긴장감 때문에 실력을 제대로 발휘 못하는 경우가 많습니다. 실전 연습은 여러분의 실력이 됩니다.

01 2026 수능 시험 + 학력평가 대비

2026 수능 시험과 전국 영어 듣기능력 평가 및 전국연합 학력평가를 대비할 수 있습니다.

❶ 영어 듣기 문제는 '기출이 답'이므로 **기출 문제를 많이 들어 보는 것과 많은 내용을 귀에 담는 연습이 결국 실력**이 됩니다.

❷ 전국 영어 듣기 평가와 수능 시험을 대비해 **기출 모의고사를 풀어 보면 영어 듣기는 만점**이 충분합니다.

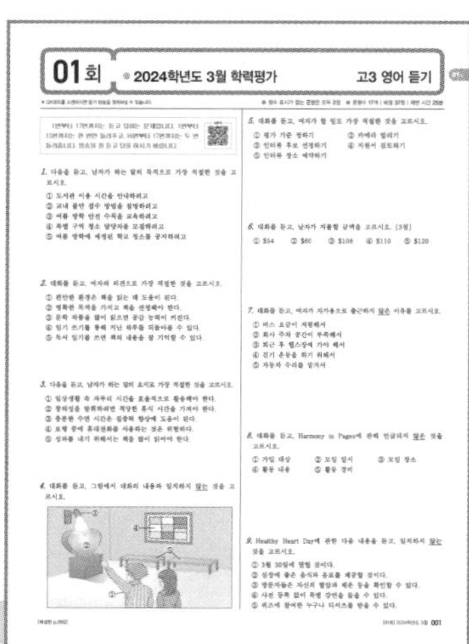

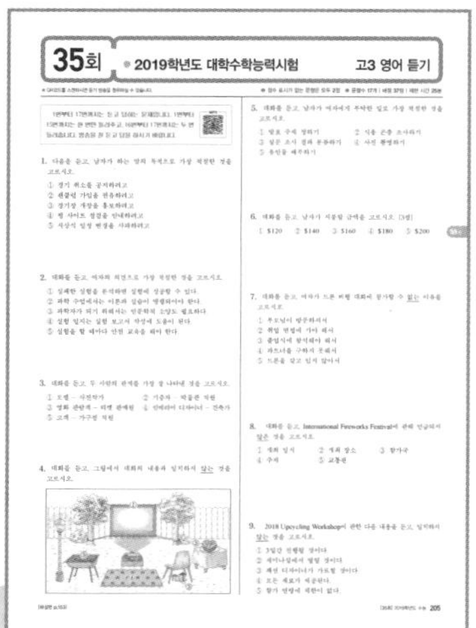

02 특별 부록 [파이널 모의고사] 3회

2026학년도 수능 시험과 6월·9월 모의평가를 대비한 파이널 모의고사 3회분을 특별 부록으로 **제공**합니다.

❶ 현직 **학교·학원 선생님들이 공동으로 출제한 파이널 모의고사 3회분을 제공해 학습 효과**를 최대한 높였습니다.

❷ 파이널 모의고사는 수록된 **35회분 듣기 문제를 모두 풀어 보고 2026 수능을 대비해 최종 점검으로 풀어** 보시면 됩니다.

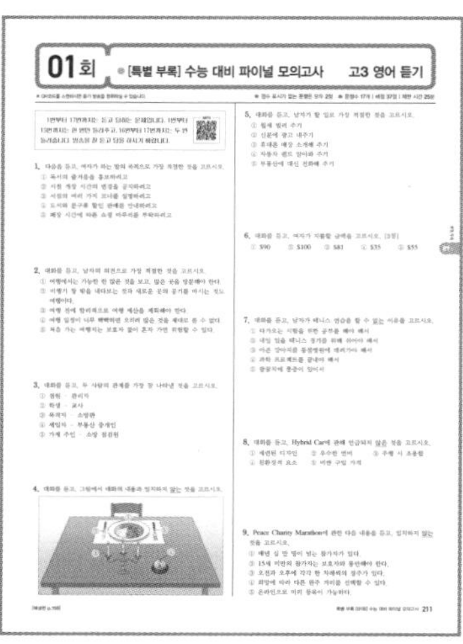

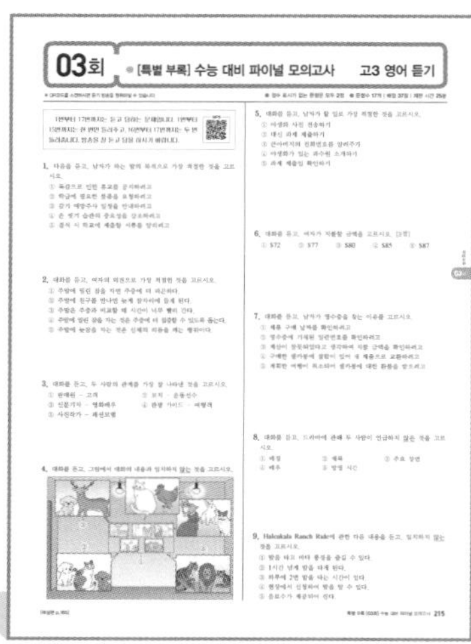

03 [문항 순서] 재배치 & 입체적 해설

최신 출제 경향에 맞추어 영어 듣기 [문항 순서]를 [재배치]했으며, 입체적 해설을 수록해 학습이 편리합니다.

❶ 최신 대학수학능력시험 듣기 **문항 순서 변경에 따라 출제 경향에 맞춰 전회차 [듣기 문항 순서]를 수정**했습니다.

❷ 해설편에 모든 **문제를 수록해 학습이 편리하며, 딕테이션에 한글 발문을 추가하고 친절한 입체적 해설을 수록**했습니다.

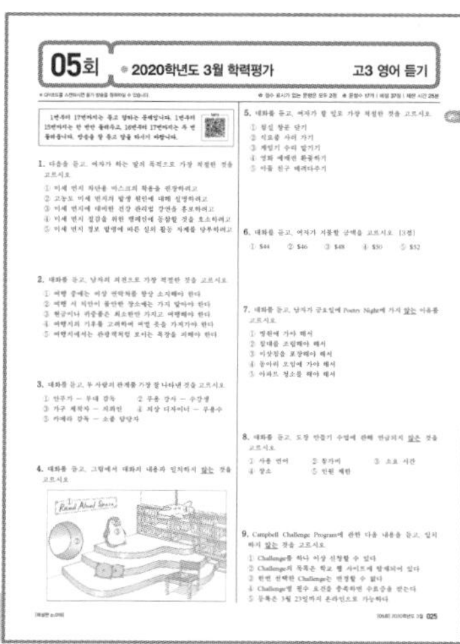

★ 모의고사를 실전과 똑같이 풀어보면
내 실력과 점수는 반드시 올라갈 수밖에 없습니다.

04

[딕테이션 TEST]로 만점 완성

영어 영역 듣기 파트에서 만점을 받을 수 있도록 [딕테이션]을 전회분 수록하여 학습 효과를 높였습니다.

❶ 영어 **듣기 대본에 한글 해석을 수록해 학습이 편리**하도록 했으며, 받아쓰는 문제를 통해 듣기 만점까지 가능합니다.

❷ **연음이나 핵심이 될 수 있는 중요 표현은 문항별로 빈칸에 ✪ 표기**하여 학습 효과를 높였습니다.

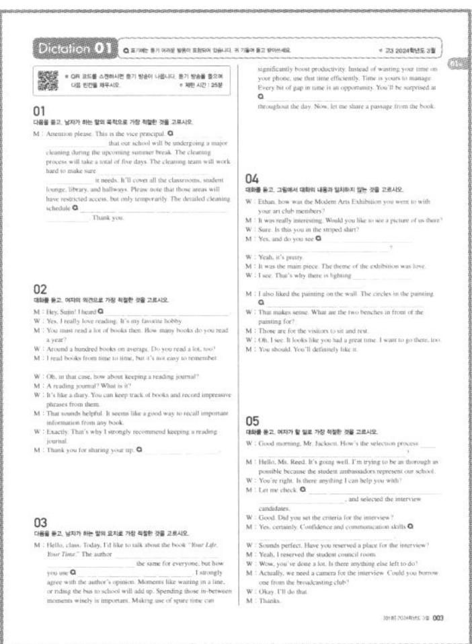

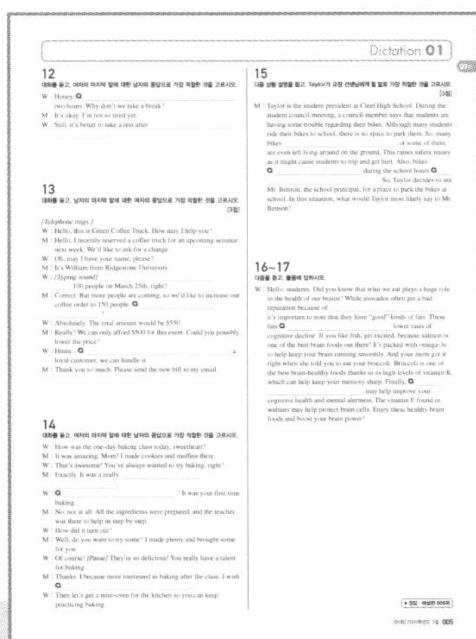

05

회차별 [VOCA LIST] 제공

회차별 문항 순서대로 쉬운 단어부터 어려운 단어까지 모두 정리한 [VOCA LIST]를 수록했습니다.

❶ **모의고사 회차별 문항 순서대로 어휘를 수록했으며 매회 문제편 뒤에 [VOCA LIST]를 제공**합니다.

❷ 듣기 문제로 학습한 후 듣기 딕테이션으로 중요 표현을 익히고 **[VOCA LIST]로 어휘를 복습하면 실력이 쑥쑥** 올라갑니다.

※ 모바일로 영단어를 학습할 수 있도록 VOCA 상단에 QR 코드를 제공합니다.

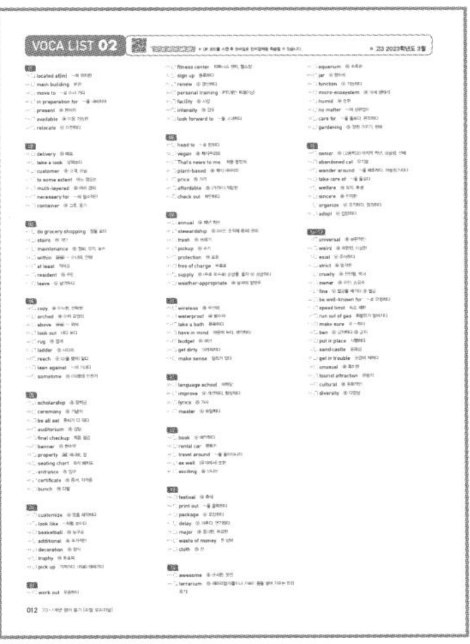

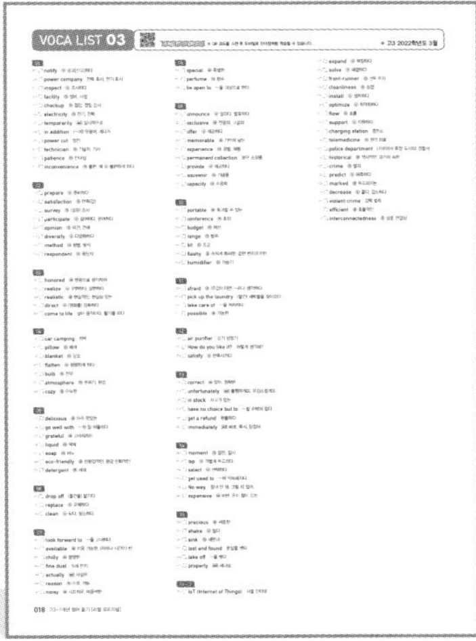

06

듣기 [QR 코드] 전회분 수록

영어 듣기는 매회 문제지와 딕테이션에 [듣기 QR 코드]를 모두 수록하여 학습이 편리하도록 했습니다.

❶ 영어 듣기 **전회차 문제지 상단에 듣기 QR 코드**를 수록하였으며, 듣기 **딕테이션 상단에도 수록**되어 있습니다.

❷ 홈페이지에서도 MP3 파일을 다운받을 수 있고, **일반배속, 1.25배속, 1.5배속, 1.75배속, 2배속으로 청취** 가능합니다.

※ QR 코드를 스캔 후 화면 우측에 있는 [⋮]을 클릭 후 재생 속도를 선택하세요.

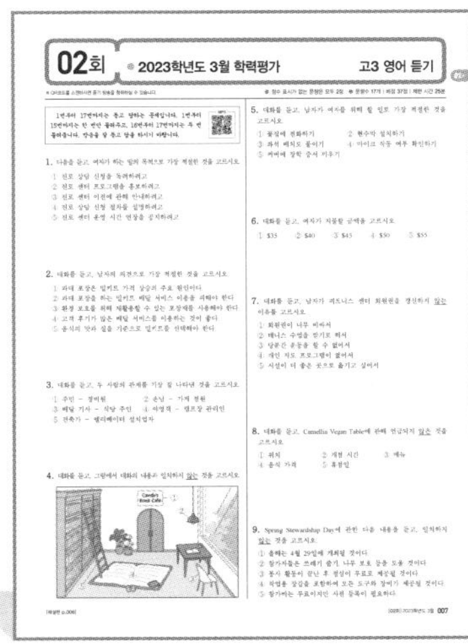

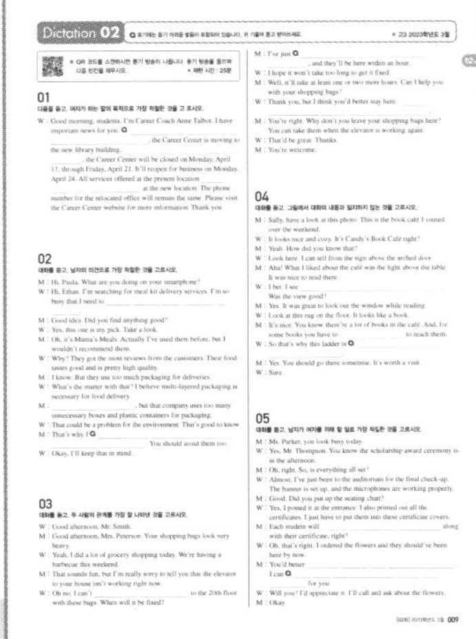

STUDY 플래너

● 영어 [듣기] | 학습 체크

회분	학습 날짜	학습 시간	채점 결과	틀린 문제	시간 부족 문제
01회 2024학년도 3월	월 일	시 분 ~ 시 분			
02회 2023학년도 3월	월 일	시 분 ~ 시 분			
03회 2022학년도 3월	월 일	시 분 ~ 시 분			
04회 2021학년도 3월	월 일	시 분 ~ 시 분			
05회 2020학년도 3월	월 일	시 분 ~ 시 분			
06회 2024학년도 5월	월 일	시 분 ~ 시 분			
07회 2023학년도 4월	월 일	시 분 ~ 시 분			
08회 2022학년도 4월	월 일	시 분 ~ 시 분			
09회 2021학년도 4월	월 일	시 분 ~ 시 분			
10회 2020학년도 4월	월 일	시 분 ~ 시 분			
11회 2025학년도 6월	월 일	시 분 ~ 시 분			
12회 2024학년도 6월	월 일	시 분 ~ 시 분			
13회 2023학년도 6월	월 일	시 분 ~ 시 분			
14회 2022학년도 6월	월 일	시 분 ~ 시 분			
15회 2021학년도 6월	월 일	시 분 ~ 시 분			
16회 2023학년도 7월	월 일	시 분 ~ 시 분			
17회 2022학년도 7월	월 일	시 분 ~ 시 분			
18회 2021학년도 7월	월 일	시 분 ~ 시 분			
19회 2020학년도 7월	월 일	시 분 ~ 시 분			
20회 2025학년도 9월	월 일	시 분 ~ 시 분			
21회 2024학년도 9월	월 일	시 분 ~ 시 분			
22회 2023학년도 9월	월 일	시 분 ~ 시 분			
23회 2022학년도 9월	월 일	시 분 ~ 시 분			
24회 2021학년도 9월	월 일	시 분 ~ 시 분			
25회 2023학년도 10월	월 일	시 분 ~ 시 분			
26회 2022학년도 10월	월 일	시 분 ~ 시 분			
27회 2021학년도 10월	월 일	시 분 ~ 시 분			
28회 2020학년도 10월	월 일	시 분 ~ 시 분			
29회 2025학년도 수능	월 일	시 분 ~ 시 분			
30회 2024학년도 수능	월 일	시 분 ~ 시 분			
31회 2023학년도 수능	월 일	시 분 ~ 시 분			
32회 2022학년도 수능	월 일	시 분 ~ 시 분			
33회 2021학년도 수능	월 일	시 분 ~ 시 분			
34회 2020학년도 수능	월 일	시 분 ~ 시 분			
35회 2019학년도 수능	월 일	시 분 ~ 시 분			

● [특별 부록] 파이널 모의고사

회분	학습 날짜	학습 시간	채점 결과	틀린 문제	시간 부족 문제
01회 파이널 모의고사	월 일	시 분 ~ 시 분			
02회 파이널 모의고사	월 일	시 분 ~ 시 분			
03회 파이널 모의고사	월 일	시 분 ~ 시 분			

01회 2024학년도 3월 학력평가 고3 영어 듣기

※ QR코드를 스캔하시면 듣기 방송을 청취하실 수 있습니다.

● 점수 표시가 없는 문항은 모두 2점 ● 문항수 17개 | 배점 37점 | 제한 시간 25분

1번부터 17번까지는 듣고 답하는 문제입니다. 1번부터 15번까지는 한 번만 들려주고, 16번부터 17번까지는 두 번 들려줍니다. 방송을 잘 듣고 답을 하시기 바랍니다.

MP3

1. 다음을 듣고, 남자가 하는 말의 목적으로 가장 적절한 것을 고르시오.

① 도서관 이용 시간을 안내하려고
② 교내 불만 접수 방법을 설명하려고
③ 여름 방학 안전 수칙을 교육하려고
④ 특별 구역 청소 담당자를 모집하려고
⑤ 여름 방학에 예정된 학교 청소를 공지하려고

2. 대화를 듣고, 여자의 의견으로 가장 적절한 것을 고르시오.

① 편안한 환경은 책을 읽는 데 도움이 된다.
② 명확한 목적을 가지고 책을 선정해야 한다.
③ 문학 작품을 많이 읽으면 공감 능력이 커진다.
④ 일기 쓰기를 통해 지난 하루를 되돌아볼 수 있다.
⑤ 독서 일기를 쓰면 책의 내용을 잘 기억할 수 있다.

3. 다음을 듣고, 남자가 하는 말의 요지로 가장 적절한 것을 고르시오.

① 일상생활 속 자투리 시간을 효율적으로 활용해야 한다.
② 창의성을 발휘하려면 적당한 휴식 시간을 가져야 한다.
③ 충분한 수면 시간은 집중력 향상에 도움이 된다.
④ 보행 중에 휴대전화를 사용하는 것은 위험하다.
⑤ 성과를 내기 위해서는 책을 많이 읽어야 한다.

4. 대화를 듣고, 그림에서 대화의 내용과 일치하지 않는 것을 고르시오.

5. 대화를 듣고, 여자가 할 일로 가장 적절한 것을 고르시오.

① 평가 기준 정하기
② 카메라 빌리기
③ 인터뷰 후보 선정하기
④ 지원서 검토하기
⑤ 인터뷰 장소 예약하기

6. 대화를 듣고, 남자가 지불할 금액을 고르시오. [3점]

① $54 ② $60 ③ $108 ④ $110 ⑤ $120

7. 대화를 듣고, 여자가 자가용으로 출근하지 않은 이유를 고르시오.

① 버스 요금이 저렴해서
② 회사 주차 공간이 부족해서
③ 퇴근 후 헬스장에 가야 해서
④ 걷기 운동을 하기 위해서
⑤ 자동차 수리를 맡겨서

8. 대화를 듣고, Harmony in Pages에 관해 언급되지 않은 것을 고르시오.

① 가입 대상 ② 모임 일시 ③ 모임 장소
④ 활동 내용 ⑤ 활동 경비

9. Healthy Heart Day에 관한 다음 내용을 듣고, 일치하지 않는 것을 고르시오.

① 3월 30일에 열릴 것이다.
② 심장에 좋은 음식과 음료를 제공할 것이다.
③ 방문자들은 자신의 혈압과 체온 등을 확인할 수 있다.
④ 사전 등록 없이 특별 강연을 들을 수 있다.
⑤ 퀴즈에 참여한 누구나 티셔츠를 받을 수 있다.

[해설편 p.002]

10. 다음 표를 보면서 대화를 듣고, 두 사람이 구매할 무선 마이크를 고르시오.

Wireless Microphones

	Model	Price	Color	Battery Life (hours)	LED light
①	A	$25	black	4	X
②	B	$40	white	4	O
③	C	$50	pink	6	O
④	D	$55	white	8	X
⑤	E	$75	pink	8	O

11. 대화를 듣고, 남자의 마지막 말에 대한 여자의 응답으로 가장 적절한 것을 고르시오.

① I'm sorry, but you can't use it as a credit card.
② Yes, I think it'd be great to take a group photo here.
③ No need. You can have your photo taken on the spot.
④ Fortunately, I found my ID card at the Lost and Found.
⑤ Right. The student services office doesn't reissue ID cards.

12. 대화를 듣고, 여자의 마지막 말에 대한 남자의 응답으로 가장 적절한 것을 고르시오.

① It wasn't easy. It took over three hours to get there.
② You're right. Let's pull over at the next rest area.
③ No problem. I got my car fixed before the trip.
④ Careful! You shouldn't go over the speed limit.
⑤ Okay. I can take over driving after the break.

13. 대화를 듣고, 남자의 마지막 말에 대한 여자의 응답으로 가장 적절한 것을 고르시오. [3점]

Woman: ____________________

① Sure. I will send it to you right away.
② I'm afraid we only have fruit juice and tea.
③ I'm sorry that you're not satisfied with our service.
④ Okay. I'll let you know the new date of our seminar.
⑤ Good. Let's order some drinks using the delivery service.

14. 대화를 듣고, 여자의 마지막 말에 대한 남자의 응답으로 가장 적절한 것을 고르시오.

Man: ____________________

① I'm sorry, but I'm not that interested in baking.
② Think twice. We already have an oven at home.
③ Fantastic! Then I can try more recipes at home.
④ Well, thank you for inviting me to your baking class.
⑤ Oh, no! I forgot to bring you some cookies and muffins.

15. 다음 상황 설명을 듣고, Taylor가 교장 선생님에게 할 말로 가장 적절한 것을 고르시오. [3점]

Taylor: ____________________

① Could you set up a bike parking station at school?
② Can we use the gym for the student council event?
③ Can you install a charging station for electric bikes?
④ Is it okay to include a bike tour during the field trip?
⑤ Could you repair the broken lockers inside the classrooms?

[16 ~ 17] 다음을 듣고, 물음에 답하시오.

16. 여자가 하는 말의 주제로 가장 적절한 것은?

① benefits of taking in raw foods
② the most globally used ingredients
③ dangers of consuming too much fat
④ different food cultures around the world
⑤ healthy foods for improving brain functions

17. 언급된 식품이 아닌 것은?

① avocado ② salmon ③ almond
④ broccoli ⑤ walnut

[해설편 p.004]

※ QR 코드를 스캔하시면 듣기 방송이 나옵니다. 듣기 방송을 들으며 다음 빈칸을 채우시오. ● 제한 시간 : 25분

01

다음을 듣고, 남자가 하는 말의 목적으로 가장 적절한 것을 고르시오.

M : Attention please. This is the vice principal. ✪ ____ ______ ___ ___________ ______ that our school will be undergoing a major cleaning during the upcoming summer break. The cleaning process will take a total of five days. The cleaning team will work hard to make sure _________ __________ _______ _____ ______________ it needs. It'll cover all the classrooms, student lounge, library, and hallways. Please note that those areas will have restricted access, but only temporarily. The detailed cleaning schedule ✪ ______ ____ ___________ ____ _____ ___________ ____________. Thank you.

02

대화를 듣고, 여자의 의견으로 가장 적절한 것을 고르시오.

M : Hey, Sujin! I heard ✪ _____ _____ __ ________ ________________.

W : Yes, I really love reading. It's my favorite hobby.

M : You must read a lot of books then. How many books do you read a year?

W : Around a hundred books on average. Do you read a lot, too?

M : I read books from time to time, but it's not easy to remember ________ __ ________ ________ __________.

W : Oh, in that case, how about keeping a reading journal?

M : A reading journal? What is it?

W : It's like a diary. You can keep track of books and record impressive phrases from them.

M : That sounds helpful. It seems like a good way to recall important information from any book.

W : Exactly. That's why I strongly recommend keeping a reading journal.

M : Thank you for sharing your tip. ✪ _____ _______ __ __ _____.

03

다음을 듣고, 남자가 하는 말의 요지로 가장 적절한 것을 고르시오.

M : Hello, class. Today, I'd like to talk about the book "*Your Life, Your Time*." The author __________________ ______ _____ _______ ________________ ___ the same for everyone, but how you use ✪ __ ___ _____________ ____ ___ ______. I strongly agree with the author's opinion. Moments like waiting in a line, or riding the bus to school will add up. Spending those in-between moments wisely is important. Making use of spare time can significantly boost productivity. Instead of wasting your time on your phone, use that time efficiently. Time is yours to manage. Every bit of gap in time is an opportunity. You'll be surprised at ✪ _______ _________ _______ ______ ________________ throughout the day. Now, let me share a passage from the book.

04

대화를 듣고, 그림에서 대화의 내용과 일치하지 않는 것을 고르시오.

W : Ethan, how was the Modern Arts Exhibition you went to with your art club members?

M : It was really interesting. Would you like to see a picture of us there?

W : Sure. Is this you in the striped shirt?

M : Yes, and do you see ✪ _____ ___________________ _______________ ______ _______________ ___?

W : Yeah, it's pretty.

M : It was the main piece. The theme of the exhibition was love.

W : I see. That's why there is lighting ____ _____ _______ _________ _____ ______________.

M : I also liked the painting on the wall. The circles in the painting ✪ _______________ _____ ____ ________ ____________.

W : That makes sense. What are the two benches in front of the painting for?

M : Those are for the visitors to sit and rest.

W : Oh, I see. It looks like you had a great time. I want to go there, too.

M : You should. You'll definitely like it.

05

대화를 듣고, 여자가 할 일로 가장 적절한 것을 고르시오.

W : Good morning, Mr. Jackson. How's the selection process _____ ____________ ____________________ __________?

M : Hello, Ms. Reed. It's going well. I'm trying to be as thorough as possible because the student ambassadors represent our school.

W : You're right. Is there anything I can help you with?

M : Let me check. ✪ ______ ____________ _______ _____________ _____ ___________________, and selected the interview candidates.

W : Good. Did you set the criteria for the interview?

M : Yes, certainly. Confidence and communication skills ✪ __________ ____ ________ ________________.

W : Sounds perfect. Have you reserved a place for the interview?

M : Yeah, I reserved the student council room.

W : Wow, you've done a lot. Is there anything else left to do?

M : Actually, we need a camera for the interview. Could you borrow one from the broadcasting club?

W : Okay. I'll do that.

M : Thanks.

Dictation 01

06

대화를 듣고, 남자가 지불할 금액을 고르시오. [3점]

[Telephone rings.]

W : Hello, this is StreamHub Services. How may I help you?

M : Hi, I'd like to subscribe to your video streaming service. ________ ________ ______ ______ ______?

W : We have two plans. The basic plan is 5 dollars a month, and the premium plan is 10 dollars a month.

M : What's the difference?

W : With the basic plan, you can only watch on one device at a time. But with the premium plan, you can watch on up to four.

M : I see. I'm going to use it with my family members, so I'll subscribe to the premium plan for one year.

W : In that case, we have a special deal. We offer a 10% discount on a 1-year subscription. But you have to pay for ✪ ____ ________ ________ ____ ______.

M : That's awesome! I'll pay for one year, now.

W : Great! Can you give me your credit card information?

M : Sure. ✪ ____ ____ ____ __.

07

대화를 듣고, 여자가 자가용으로 출근하지 않은 이유를 고르시오.

M : Kate, ✪ ______ ______ ________ ______ this morning. What happened?

W : Hi, Chris. I took a bus to work this morning. And ✪ __ ______ ____________ ______ ________.

M : But don't you usually drive? Oh, wait, you said your car broke down, didn't you?

W : Yes, but I had it fixed recently.

M : Then, were you trying to walk more and get some exercise?

W : No, these days I go to a fitness center. I'm already getting enough exercise.

M : Then why didn't you drive to work today?

W : Because parking has become a nightmare.

M : Really? Isn't there a parking lot for employees at our company?

W : True, but it's not enough. If you arrive a little late, there are no parking spaces left.

M : Ah, that must be annoying. I hope ______ ________ ______ ________ soon.

08

대화를 듣고, Harmony in Pages에 관해 언급되지 않은 것을 고르시오.

M : Mina, are you still looking for a club to join?

W : Yes. Do you have any suggestions?

M : I found a perfect club for you. It's called Harmony in Pages.

W : Harmony in Pages? What's that?

M : It's a book club. ________ ______ ______ ____ ______ ___ English is not their first language.

W : That would be great for international students like me. When do they meet?

M : They meet every Monday at 4 p.m.

W : Awesome. ✪ ____ ________ ____ Mondays.

M : And they meet near our campus, at the Arden Park Library.

W : That's good. I can go right after my last class.

M : ✪ ______ ________ ________? They also write book reviews in English with the help of native speakers as mentors.

W : Fantastic! Thanks for the information.

09

Healthy Heart Day에 관한 다음 내용을 듣고, 일치하지 않는 것을 고르시오.

W : Are you interested in staying healthy? ✪ ______ ________ ___ ________ your attention to our upcoming Healthy Heart Day. The Healthy Heart Day is a campaign to remind everyone to take care of their own heart. It will take place on March 30th at the public health center. We provide food and drinks that are good for your heart. You can check things ________ ___ ______ ______ ________, such as blood pressure, body temperature, and so on. You can also listen to a special lecture about a healthy heart, if you register in advance. Last but not least, there'll be a quiz for all visitors. Anyone ______ ____________ ___ ____ ______ can receive a T-shirt. We look forward to your visit. Please check our website for more information. Thank you.

10

다음 표를 보면서 대화를 듣고, 두 사람이 구매할 무선 마이크를 고르시오.

W : Honey, what are you looking at on your computer?

M : It's a website selling wireless microphones. I'm thinking of getting one for our son Jimmy's birthday present.

W : Oh, that sounds like a good idea. Do you ______ ____ __ ______ ______ ________ one?

M : Sure. There are five options here, and they all seem good.

W : Do you ✪ ________ ________ ___ ________?

M : Hmm... Let's not spend more than $60.

W : I agree. Which color should we choose? They come in three colors.

M : Well, anything but black. Jimmy ✪ ________ ______ ______ ___ ______ ones.

W : That's right. What about the battery life? I think 4 hours would be too short.

M : I agree. Let's buy one with a longer battery life.

W : Good idea. Now, we're down to two. This microphone has an LED light. I heard it creates a cool visual effect.

M : Really? Then, we should definitely get one with an LED light.

W : Okay. Let's go ahead and get this model.

11

대화를 듣고, 남자의 마지막 말에 대한 여자의 응답으로 가장 적절한 것을 고르시오.

M : Rachel, I heard you ____ ______ ________ ____ ______ ________.

W : Yeah, I ✪ ____ ____ ____ ____ ________. So I went to the student services office and got a new one.

M : Actually, I lost mine too, so I need to go there. Do I need to bring my photo for a new ID card?

12

대화를 듣고, 여자의 마지막 말에 대한 남자의 응답으로 가장 적절한 것을 고르시오.

W : Honey, ✪ __________ ________ ___________ _____ ________ two hours. Why don't we take a break?

M : It's okay. I'm not so tired yet.

W : Still, it's better to take a rest after _________ ______ _________ ___ ___________.

13

대화를 듣고, 남자의 마지막 말에 대한 여자의 응답으로 가장 적절한 것을 고르시오. [3점]

[Telephone rings.]

W : Hello, this is Green Coffee Truck. How may I help you?

M : Hello, I recently reserved a coffee truck for an upcoming seminar next week. We'd like to ask for a change.

W : Oh, may I have your name, please?

M : It's William from Ridgestone University.

W : *[Typing sound]* _______ _________ __ ___________________ _____ 100 people on March 25th, right?

M : Correct. But more people are coming, so we'd like to increase our coffee order to 150 people. ✪ ___________ _______ ____ ______________?

W : Absolutely. The total amount would be $550.

M : Really? We can only afford $500 for this event. Could you possibly lower the price?

W : Hmm... ✪ _________ ________ ___________ ______ ________ a loyal customer, we can handle it.

M : Thank you so much. Please send the new bill to my email.

14

대화를 듣고, 여자의 마지막 말에 대한 남자의 응답으로 가장 적절한 것을 고르시오.

W : How was the one-day baking class today, sweetheart?

M : It was amazing, Mom! I made cookies and muffins there.

W : That's awesome! You've always wanted to try baking, right?

M : Exactly. It was a really ________ _______________ _________________.

W : ✪ ___________ __ ___________________? It was your first time baking.

M : No, not at all. All the ingredients were prepared, and the teacher was there to help us step by step.

W : How did it turn out?

M : Well, do you want to try some? I made plenty and brought some for you.

W : Of course! *[Pause]* They're so delicious! You really have a talent for baking.

M : Thanks. I became more interested in baking after the class. I wish ✪ _____ ______ ____ ________ ___ _________.

W : Then let's get a mini-oven for the kitchen so you can keep practicing baking.

15

다음 상황 설명을 듣고, Taylor가 교장 선생님에게 할 말로 가장 적절한 것을 고르시오. [3점]

M : Taylor is the student president at Cleef High School. During the student council meeting, a council member says that students are having some trouble regarding their bikes. Although many students ride their bikes to school, there is no space to park them. So, many bikes _____ _______________ ___________, or some of them are even left lying around on the ground. This raises safety issues as it might cause students to trip and get hurt. Also, bikes ✪ _________ _____ _________ during the school hours ✪ ___ _________ _____ __________ ____. So, Taylor decides to ask Mr. Benson, the school principal, for a place to park the bikes at school. In this situation, what would Taylor most likely say to Mr. Benson?

16~17

다음을 듣고, 물음에 답하시오.

W : Hello, students. Did you know that what we eat plays a huge role in the health of our brains? While avocados often get a bad reputation because of _______ _______ ____ ___________, it's important to note that they have "good" kinds of fats. These fats ✪ ________ ________ ___________ ___ lower rates of cognitive decline. If you like fish, get excited, because salmon is one of the best brain foods out there! It's packed with omega-3s to help keep your brain running smoothly. And your mom got it right when she told you to eat your broccoli. Broccoli is one of the best brain-healthy foods thanks to its high levels of vitamin K, which can help keep your memory sharp. Finally, ✪ ______ __ ______ _____________ __ ______ may help improve your cognitive health and mental alertness. The vitamin E found in walnuts may help protect brain cells. Enjoy these healthy brain foods and boost your brain power!

▶ 정답 : 해설편 005쪽

VOCA LIST 01

회차별 영단어 QR 코드 ※ QR 코드를 스캔 후 모바일로 단어장처럼 학습할 수 있습니다.

● 고3 2024학년도 3월

01

001 □ vice principal 교감
002 □ inform ⓥ 알리다
003 □ undergo ⓥ 실시하다
004 □ cleaning ⓝ 청소
005 □ upcoming ⓐ 다가오는
006 □ hallway ⓝ 복도
007 □ restricted ⓐ 제한된
008 □ temporarily ad 일시적으로

02

009 □ enthusiast ⓝ 애호가
010 □ on average 평균적으로
011 □ journal ⓝ 일기
012 □ track ⓥ 추적하다
013 □ impressive ⓐ 인상적인
014 □ phrase ⓝ 절
015 □ recall ⓥ 기억하다
016 □ important ⓐ 중요한
017 □ recommend ⓥ 추천하다

03

018 □ emphasize ⓥ 강조하다
019 □ available ⓐ 이용 가능한, 이용할 수 있는
020 □ entirely ad 전적으로
021 □ wisely ad 현명하게
022 □ efficiently ad 효율적으로
023 □ accomplish ⓥ 성취하다
024 □ passage ⓝ 구절

04

025 □ exhibition ⓝ 전시회
026 □ striped ⓐ 줄무늬의
027 □ sculpture ⓝ 조형물
028 □ wall ⓝ 벽
029 □ definitely ad 분명히

05

030 □ ambassadors ⓝ 홍보대사
031 □ application ⓝ 지원서
032 □ reserve ⓥ 예약하다
033 □ borrow ⓥ 빌리다

06

034 □ subscribe ⓥ 구독하다
035 □ offer ⓥ 제공하다
036 □ device ⓝ 장치
037 □ at a time 한 번에
038 □ special deal 특가 상품
039 □ credit card 신용 카드

07

040 □ exhausted ⓐ 피곤한, 지친
041 □ jam-packed 가득 찬
042 □ break down ⓥ 고장 나다
043 □ fix ⓥ 고치다
044 □ recently ad 최근에
045 □ nightmare ⓝ 악몽
046 □ employee ⓝ 피고용인

08

047 □ suggestion ⓝ 추천, 제안
048 □ first language 모국어
049 □ international ⓐ 국제적인
050 □ meet ⓥ 만나다
051 □ native speaker 원어민

09

052 □ be delighted to ~해서 기쁘다
053 □ upcoming ⓐ 다가오는
054 □ remind ⓥ 상기시키다
055 □ public health center 보건소
056 □ blood pressure 혈압
057 □ body temperature 체온
058 □ lecture ⓝ 강의
059 □ register ⓥ 등록하다
060 □ in advance 사전에

10

061 □ wireless ⓐ 무선의
062 □ budget ⓝ 예산
063 □ bright ⓐ 밝은
064 □ dark ⓐ 어두운
065 □ visual effect 특수효과

11

066 □ reissue ⓥ 재발급하다
067 □ on the spot 현장에서

12

068 □ take a break 쉬다
069 □ tired ⓐ 피곤한

13

070 □ afford ⓥ 여유가 되다
071 □ price ⓝ 가격
072 □ loyal ⓐ 충성스러운
073 □ handle ⓥ 처리하다, 다루다
074 □ bill ⓝ 명세서

14

075 □ hands-on 실습의
076 □ ingredient ⓝ 재료
077 □ talent ⓝ 재능

15

078 □ park ⓥ 주차하다
079 □ randomly ad 무작위로
080 □ trip ⓥ 걸려 넘어지다
081 □ lie ⓥ 누워 있다

16~17

082 □ play a role 역할을 하다
083 □ reputation ⓝ 평판
084 □ content ⓝ 함량
085 □ cognitive ⓐ 인지적인
086 □ decline ⓝ 쇠퇴
087 □ sharp ⓐ 예리한
088 □ alertness ⓝ 각성
089 □ cell ⓝ 세포

02회 • 2023학년도 3월 학력평가 고3 영어 듣기

※ QR코드를 스캔하시면 듣기 방송을 청취하실 수 있습니다.

● 점수 표시가 없는 문항은 모두 2점 ● 문항수 17개 | 배점 37점 | 제한 시간 25분

1번부터 17번까지는 듣고 답하는 문제입니다. 1번부터 15번까지는 한 번만 들려주고, 16번부터 17번까지는 두 번 들려줍니다. 방송을 잘 듣고 답을 하시기 바랍니다.

MP3

1. 다음을 듣고, 여자가 하는 말의 목적으로 가장 적절한 것을 고르시오.

① 진로 상담 신청을 독려하려고
② 진로 센터 프로그램을 홍보하려고
③ 진로 센터 이전에 관해 안내하려고
④ 진로 상담 신청 절차를 설명하려고
⑤ 진로 센터 운영 시간 연장을 공지하려고

2. 대화를 듣고, 남자의 의견으로 가장 적절한 것을 고르시오.

① 과대 포장은 밀키트 가격 상승의 주요 원인이다.
② 과대 포장을 하는 밀키트 배달 서비스 이용을 피해야 한다.
③ 환경 보호를 위해 재활용할 수 있는 포장재를 사용해야 한다.
④ 고객 후기가 많은 배달 서비스를 이용하는 것이 좋다.
⑤ 음식의 맛과 질을 기준으로 밀키트를 선택해야 한다.

3. 대화를 듣고, 두 사람의 관계를 가장 잘 나타낸 것을 고르시오.

① 주민 – 경비원 ② 손님 – 가게 점원
③ 배달 기사 – 식당 주인 ④ 야영객 – 캠프장 관리인
⑤ 건축가 – 엘리베이터 설치업자

4. 대화를 듣고, 그림에서 대화의 내용과 일치하지 <u>않는</u> 것을 고르시오.

5. 대화를 듣고, 남자가 여자를 위해 할 일로 가장 적절한 것을 고르시오.

① 꽃집에 전화하기 ② 현수막 설치하기
③ 좌석 배치도 붙이기 ④ 마이크 작동 여부 확인하기
⑤ 커버에 장학 증서 끼우기

6. 대화를 듣고, 여자가 지불할 금액을 고르시오.

① $35 ② $40 ③ $45 ④ $50 ⑤ $55

7. 대화를 듣고, 남자가 피트니스 센터 회원권을 갱신하지 <u>않는</u> 이유를 고르시오.

① 회원권이 너무 비싸서
② 테니스 수업을 받기로 해서
③ 당분간 운동을 할 수 없어서
④ 개인 지도 프로그램이 없어서
⑤ 시설이 더 좋은 곳으로 옮기고 싶어서

8. 대화를 듣고, Camellia Vegan Table에 관해 언급되지 <u>않은</u> 것을 고르시오.

① 위치 ② 개점 시간 ③ 메뉴
④ 음식 가격 ⑤ 휴점일

9. Spring Stewardship Day에 관한 다음 내용을 듣고, 일치하지 <u>않는</u> 것을 고르시오.

① 올해는 4월 29일에 개최될 것이다.
② 참가자들은 쓰레기 줍기, 나무 보호 등을 도울 것이다.
③ 봉사 활동이 끝난 후 점심이 무료로 제공될 것이다.
④ 작업용 장갑을 포함하여 모든 도구와 장비가 제공될 것이다.
⑤ 참가비는 무료이지만 사전 등록이 필요하다.

영어 영역(듣기)

10. 다음 표를 보면서 대화를 듣고, 여자가 구매할 무선 방수 스피커를 고르시오.

Wireless Waterproof Speakers

	Model	Price	Playtime (hours)	FM Radio	Color
①	A	$35	8	×	Silver
②	B	$38	12	○	Blue
③	C	$40	15	○	Pink
④	D	$45	18	×	White
⑤	E	$55	24	○	Black

11. 대화를 듣고, 남자의 마지막 말에 대한 여자의 응답으로 가장 적절한 것을 고르시오.

① It's nice of you to help me read the lyrics of the songs.
② It took me so long to get to the language school.
③ I sing K-pop songs to master Korean.
④ I don't go to the Korean language school anymore.
⑤ I was able to read Korean lyrics in about three months.

12. 대화를 듣고, 여자의 마지막 말에 대한 남자의 응답으로 가장 적절한 것을 고르시오.

① I know, but I already rented a car.
② Good idea. Let's not rent a car this time.
③ Don't worry. The next bus is coming soon.
④ I'm sorry. I forgot to rent a car for our trip.
⑤ You're right. It'll be exciting to drive a luxury car.

13. 대화를 듣고, 남자의 마지막 말에 대한 여자의 응답으로 가장 적절한 것을 고르시오. [3점]

Woman: ______________________________

① No way. I'm still printing the banner.
② Yes, I'll let you know the new date soon.
③ But I've already sent them to your school.
④ No problem. I'll change the date on the banner.
⑤ Okay. I'll put them in when packaging the banner.

14. 대화를 듣고, 여자의 마지막 말에 대한 남자의 응답으로 가장 적절한 것을 고르시오. [3점]

Man: ______________________________

① I agree. Outdoor gardening is very good for health.
② Sounds great. I'll help the beginners with gardening.
③ Yeah. I already made a couple of terrarium gardens.
④ Thanks. Last weekend's terrarium workshop was helpful.
⑤ Sure. It'll be fun to create my own garden in a glass jar.

15. 다음 상황 설명을 듣고, Kate가 Ben에게 할 말로 가장 적절한 것을 고르시오. [3점]

Kate: ______________________________

① There're many things to consider when adopting a cat.
② Let's get advice from Sarah on how to start our club.
③ We should check with her if there's an animal club.
④ Why don't we join the school drama club instead?
⑤ How about helping Sarah organize a drama club?

[16 ~ 17] 다음을 듣고, 물음에 답하시오.

16. 남자가 하는 말의 주제로 가장 적절한 것은?

① surprising and unusual laws around the world
② the most visited tourist attractions in the world
③ universal laws and principles governing your life
④ necessity of improving laws on cultural diversity
⑤ what to consider when choosing a family tour program

17. 언급된 나라가 아닌 것은?

① Italy ② Germany ③ France
④ Greece ⑤ Spain

※ QR 코드를 스캔하시면 듣기 방송이 나옵니다. 듣기 방송을 들으며 다음 빈칸을 채우시오. ● 제한 시간 : 25분

01

다음을 듣고, 여자가 하는 말의 목적으로 가장 적절한 것을 고르시오.

W : Good morning, students. I'm Career Coach Anne Talbot. I have important news for you. ✪ ________ ________ ___ _____ ________ ________, the Career Center is moving to the new library building. ___ ________ _____ _____ ________, the Career Center will be closed on Monday, April 17, through Friday, April 21. It'll reopen for business on Monday, April 24. All services offered at the present location ______ ______ ____ ________ at the new location. The phone number for the relocated office will remain the same. Please visit the Career Center website for more information. Thank you.

02

대화를 듣고, 남자의 의견으로 가장 적절한 것을 고르시오.

M : Hi, Paula. What are you doing on your smartphone?

W : Hi, Ethan. I'm searching for meal kit delivery services. I'm so busy that I need to _______ _______ ______ _______ ___ _______.

M : Good idea. Did you find anything good?

W : Yes, this one is my pick. Take a look.

M : Oh, it's Mama's Meals. Actually I've used them before, but I wouldn't recommend them.

W : Why? They got the most reviews from the customers. Their food tastes good and is pretty high quality.

M : I know. But they use too much packaging for deliveries.

W : What's the matter with that? I believe multi-layered packaging is necessary for food delivery.

M : ____ ________ ________, but that company uses too many unnecessary boxes and plastic containers for packaging.

W : That could be a problem for the environment. That's good to know.

M : That's why I ✪ ________ _____ ____________ ________ ________. You should avoid them too.

W : Okay, I'll keep that in mind.

03

대화를 듣고, 두 사람의 관계를 가장 잘 나타낸 것을 고르시오.

W : Good afternoon, Mr. Smith.

M : Good afternoon, Mrs. Peterson. Your shopping bags look very heavy.

W : Yeah, I did a lot of grocery shopping today. We're having a barbecue this weekend.

M : That sounds fun, but I'm really sorry to tell you that the elevator to your house isn't working right now.

W : Oh no. I can't ________ ____ _____ ________ to the 20th floor with these bags. When will it be fixed?

M : I've just ✪ ________ _____ ____________ ________, and they'll be here within an hour.

W : I hope it won't take too long to get it fixed.

M : Well, it'll take at least one or two more hours. Can I help you with your shopping bags?

W : Thank you, but I think you'd better stay here. ________ ________ ______ ______ ______ ______.

M : You're right. Why don't you leave your shopping bags here? You can take them when the elevator is working again.

W : That'd be great. Thanks.

M : You're welcome.

04

대화를 듣고, 그림에서 대화의 내용과 일치하지 않는 것을 고르시오.

M : Sally, have a look at this photo. This is the book café I visited over the weekend.

W : It looks nice and cozy. It's Candy's Book Café right?

M : Yeah. How did you know that?

W : Look here. I can tell from the sign above the arched door.

M : Aha! What I liked about the café was the light above the table. It was nice to read there.

W : I bet. I see ______ ________ ____ _____ ________.
Was the view good?

M : Yes. It was great to look out the window while reading.

W : Look at this rug on the floor. It looks like a book.

M : It's nice. You know there're a lot of books in the café. And, for some books you have to _____ __ ________ to reach them.

W : So that's why this ladder is ✪ ________ ________ _____ ________.

M : Yes. You should go there sometime. It's worth a visit.

W : Sure.

05

대화를 듣고, 남자가 여자를 위해 할 일로 가장 적절한 것을 고르시오.

M : Ms. Parker, you look busy today.

W : Yes, Mr. Thompson. You know the scholarship award ceremony is in the afternoon.

M : Oh, right. So, is everything all set?

W : Almost. I've just been to the auditorium for the final check-up. The banner is set up, and the microphones are working properly.

M : Good. Did you put up the seating chart?

W : Yes, I posted it at the entrance. I also printed out all the certificates. I just have to put them into these certificate covers.

M : Each student will _____ __ ________ ____ ________ along with their certificate, right?

W : Oh, that's right. I ordered the flowers and they should've been here by now.

M : You'd better ________ ______ _____ ________ ______.
I can ✪ _____ _____ ____________ ______ _____ ________ for you.

W : Will you? I'd appreciate it. I'll call and ask about the flowers.

M : Okay.

06

대화를 듣고, 여자가 지불할 금액을 고르시오.

M : Hello, welcome to Jay's Cake Shop. How may I help you?
W : Hi, I'd like to ✪ ________ __ ________ ________ for my son's birthday.
M : Okay, we start from $30.
W : Good. Can you make it look like a basketball?
M : Sure, but you have to pay an additional $10.
W : That's reasonable.
M : Do you want to add any decorations to the cake? They're $5 each.
W : I'd like to have a trophy and a boy on top.
M : That means you're ✪ ________ ______ ________.
W : That's right. I want to get the cake this Saturday. Is that possible?
M : Yes, it is. Do you want to ________ __ ________? It'll cost $5.
W : No, I'll come pick it up. Here's my credit card.

07

대화를 듣고, 남자가 피트니스 센터 회원권을 갱신하지 않는 이유를 고르시오.

W : Jacob, are you still working out at the fitness center?
M : Yes, Laura. It's been almost a year since I signed up there. My one-year membership ends next week.
W : Are you going to renew it?
M : No, I decided not to.
W : Why? Is it because the membership is too expensive?
M : Not really. It's quite cheap if you ________ ________ ________ ________.
W : Then, are you going to move to another fitness center with better facilities?
M : No, I'm happy with the facilities now.
W : Then why aren't you renewing your membership?
M : Actually I'm going to ________ ________ ________ next month.
W : Cool. Tennis is ✪ __ ______ ______ ________ ________. You'll love it.
M : Yeah, I'm looking forward to it.

08

대화를 듣고, Camellia Vegan Table에 관해 언급되지 않은 것을 고르시오.

M : Hi, Cathy.
W : Hi, Matthew. Where are you heading to?
M : I'm going to Camellia Vegan Table for lunch.
W : Camellia Vegan Table? I've never heard of it. Where is it?
M : It's a new vegan restaurant on campus. It's on the first floor of the student union building.
W : That's news to me. ________ ______ __ ________?
M : It opened last month. You can eat ________ ________ ________ like plant-based tacos, burgers, and pizzas.
W : Sounds great. How about the price?
M : ✪ ________ ________. You can buy most of the dishes for less than $10. You should check it out.
W : Okay. I'll go there tomorrow.
M : Ah! It's closed every Wednesday. Try some other day.
W : All right. Thanks for letting me know.

09

Spring Stewardship Day에 관한 다음 내용을 듣고, 일치하지 않는 것을 고르시오.

M : Are you looking for volunteer programs this spring? Join us for our annual Spring Stewardship Day! This year, the Spring Stewardship Day will be held on Saturday, April 29 at Lakeside Park. Participants will assist with ✪ ________ ________, ________ ________ and more. This event is for volunteers aged 12 years and older. The volunteer work will run from 9 a.m. to noon, and lunch will be provided free of charge after work. We'll supply the necessary tools and supplies for you, but you should bring your own ________ ________ ______ ________ ________. Please wear weather-appropriate clothing. This event is free, but prior registration is required because ________ ______ ________. Please visit our website for more information.

10

다음 표를 보면서 대화를 듣고, 여자가 구매할 무선 방수 스피커를 고르시오.

W : Dad. Could you help me buy ✪ __ ________ ________ ________? I need one to listen to music while taking a bath.
M : Okay. Do you have anything in mind?
W : Yes, I want to choose one from these five models.
M : Let me see. Do you have a budget?
W : I'd like to keep it under $50.
M : Then this one is out. Oh, I wouldn't get this model, either. The playtime should be ________ ______ ____ ________.
W : I agree. Then I have to choose one of these three.
M : Why don't you go for one with FM radio? You often listen to the radio.
W : Good point. There are only two options left, but I like both of the colors.
M : I think ______ ______ _____ ______ ________.
W : That makes sense. I'll buy the other one.

11

대화를 듣고, 남자의 마지막 말에 대한 여자의 응답으로 가장 적절한 것을 고르시오.

M : Grandma, you still go to the Korean language school, right? Has your Korean improved a lot?
W : I guess so. Now I can ✪ ______ _____ ________ of my favorite K-pop songs.
M : Wow, that's cool. How long did it take you to ________ ______ ______?

12

대화를 듣고, 여자의 마지막 말에 대한 남자의 응답으로 가장 적절한 것을 고르시오.

W : Honey, ✪ ______ ______ __ ______ ______ for our trip to Jeju Island next month.

M : I've tried, but I couldn't. Car rental is too expensive these days.

W : Then why don't we ______ ______ ______ ____ ______? It'll be fun and cheap as well.

13

대화를 듣고, 남자의 마지막 말에 대한 여자의 응답으로 가장 적절한 것을 고르시오. [3점]

[Telephone rings.]

W : Star Printing. How may I help you?

M : Hi. I'm Alex Miller. I ordered a banner for our school festival a few days ago, but I wonder if I can ask for a change.

W : Let me check first. What's the name of your school?

M : It's Jackson High School.

W : Hang on. *[Typing sound]* I'm sorry, but it's already been printed out. It's going to ____ ______ ______ _____ ______.

M : Oh, no. Our school festival has been delayed. ______ ______ ______ ____ ______.

W : That sounds like a major change. I'm afraid you'll have to order a new one.

M : I don't want to do that. It's a waste of money. Do you have any other idea?

W : Well, you can write the new date on a piece of cloth and cover the old date.

M : All right. I'd appreciate it if you could ✪ ______ _____ ______ ______ ____ ______.

14

대화를 듣고, 여자의 마지막 말에 대한 남자의 응답으로 가장 적절한 것을 고르시오. [3점]

M : Hi, Jennifer. How was your weekend?

W : It was awesome. I had a great experience at a terrarium workshop.

M : What is a terrarium?

W : It's like an aquarium, but with plants instead of fish. It can be made in any glass container like a jar or bottle.

M : Simply put, you grow plants in glass containers, right?

W : Well, it's more than that. A good terrarium is a fully functioning micro-ecosystem.

M : Tell me more about it.

W : Terrariums are able to conserve water and ✪ ______ _____ ______ ______ no matter the weather outside. They're very ______ ___ ______ _____.

M : I see. They sound like a creative way to have your own mini garden.

W : Exactly. ______ ______ ______ _____ ______ ______? It won't be difficult, even for a beginner.

15

다음 상황 설명을 듣고, Kate가 Ben에게 할 말로 가장 적절한 것을 고르시오. [3점]

W : Ben and Kate are seniors at Eagle High School. They both love animals. Recently, they ✪ ______ ______ ______ ______ wandering around the school. Ben and Kate talk about what they can do to take care of them. Ben comes up with an idea to ✪ ______ ____ ______ ______ ______ at school. Kate thinks it's a good idea because students can work together with __ ______ ______ ___ ______ ______. But, they don't know how to get started because they've never organized a school club before. Kate remembers that her classmate, Sarah, started the school drama club last year. She wants to tell Ben that they should ask Sarah about it. In this situation, what would Kate most likely say to Ben?

16~17

다음을 듣고, 물음에 답하시오.

M : Hello, students. Laws may seem to be universal, yet every country's laws are different. In fact, ✪ ______ ____ ______ _____ ____ ______ that you may not believe they exist. In Italy, Rome has strict laws against animal cruelty. For example, if an owner does not walk their dog once a day, they could be fined €500. Germany's Autobahn is well-known for ______ ______ ______ ______ of more than 160 km per hour. But it's illegal to run out of gas on the Autobahn. When packing for a trip to Greece, make sure you have the right shoes. The country banned high heels at the Acropolis in 2009. The Greeks put this ban in place to ✪ ______ ____ ______ from damage caused by sharp shoes. Spain hates your attempts at making sand castles so much that you could be fined if caught building one. And the fines vary by location. On the island of Majorca, for example, you could pay €100. So, when you visit these countries, be careful! You certainly don't want to get in trouble!

▶ 정답 : 해설편 010쪽

VOCA LIST 02

회차별 영단어 QR 코드 ※ QR 코드를 스캔 후 모바일로 단어장처럼 학습할 수 있습니다.

● 고3 2023학년도 3월

01

001 □ located at[in] ~에 위치한
002 □ main building 본관
003 □ move to ~로 이사 가다
004 □ in preparation for ~을 대비하여
005 □ present ⓐ 현재의
006 □ available ⓐ 이용 가능한
007 □ relocate ⓥ 이전하다

02

008 □ delivery ⓝ 배송
009 □ take a look 살펴보다
010 □ customer ⓝ 고객, 손님
011 □ to some extent 어느 정도는
012 □ multi-layered ⓐ 여러 겹의
013 □ necessary for ~에 필수적인
014 □ container ⓝ 그릇, 용기

03

015 □ do grocery shopping 장을 보다
016 □ stairs ⓝ 계단
017 □ maintenance ⓝ 정비, 유지, 보수
018 □ within prep ~ 이내에, 안에
019 □ at least 적어도
020 □ resident ⓝ 주민
021 □ leave ⓥ 남겨두다

04

022 □ cozy ⓐ 아늑한, 안락한
023 □ arched ⓐ 아치 모양의
024 □ above prep ~ 위에
025 □ look out 내다 보다
026 □ rug ⓝ 깔개
027 □ ladder ⓝ 사다리
028 □ reach ⓥ (손을 뻗어) 닿다
029 □ lean against ~에 기대다
030 □ sometime ⓝ (미래의) 언젠가

05

031 □ scholarship ⓝ 장학금
032 □ ceremony ⓝ 기념식
033 □ be all set 준비가 다 되다
034 □ auditorium ⓝ 강당
035 □ final checkup 최종 점검
036 □ banner ⓝ 현수막
037 □ properly ad 제대로, 잘
038 □ seating chart 좌석 배치도
039 □ entrance ⓝ 입구
040 □ certificate ⓝ 증서, 자격증
041 □ bunch ⓝ 다발

06

042 □ customize ⓥ 맞춤 제작하다
043 □ look like ~처럼 보이다
044 □ basketball ⓝ 농구공
045 □ additional ⓐ 추가적인
046 □ decoration ⓝ 장식
047 □ trophy ⓝ 트로피
048 □ pick up 가져가다, (차로) 태워가다

07

049 □ work out 운동하다
050 □ fitness center 피트니스 센터, 헬스장
051 □ sign up 등록하다
052 □ renew ⓥ 갱신하다
053 □ personal training PT(개인 트레이닝)
054 □ facility ⓝ 시설
055 □ intensity ⓝ 강도
056 □ look forward to ~을 고대하다

08

057 □ head to ~로 향하다
058 □ vegan ⓐ 채식주의의
059 □ That's news to me. 처음 들었어.
060 □ plant-based ⓐ 채식 (위주)의
061 □ price ⓝ 가격
062 □ affordable ⓐ (가격이) 적당한
063 □ check out 확인하다

09

064 □ annual ⓐ 매년 하는
065 □ stewardship ⓝ (재산, 조직체 등의) 관리
066 □ trash ⓝ 쓰레기
067 □ pickup ⓝ 수거
068 □ protection ⓝ 보호
069 □ free of charge 무료로
070 □ supply ⓝ (주로 복수로) 공급품, 물자 ⓥ 공급하다
071 □ weather-appropriate ⓐ 날씨에 알맞은

10

072 □ wireless ⓐ 무선의
073 □ waterproof ⓐ 방수의
074 □ take a bath 목욕하다
075 □ have in mind 마음에 두다, 생각하다
076 □ budget ⓝ 예산
077 □ get dirty 더러워지다
078 □ make sense 일리가 있다

11

079 □ language school 어학당
080 □ improve ⓥ 개선되다, 향상되다
081 □ lyrics ⓝ 가사
082 □ master ⓥ 숙달하다

12

083 □ book ⓥ 예약하다
084 □ rental car 렌트카
085 □ travel around ~을 돌아다니다
086 □ as well (문미에서) 또한
087 □ exciting ⓐ 신나는

13

088 □ festival ⓝ 축제
089 □ print out ~을 출력하다
090 □ package ⓥ 포장하다
091 □ delay ⓥ 미루다, 연기하다
092 □ major ⓐ 중대한, 주요한
093 □ waste of money 돈 낭비
094 □ cloth ⓝ 천

14

095 □ awesome ⓐ 근사한, 멋진
096 □ terrarium ⓝ 테라리엄(식물이나 거북이 등을 넣어 기르는 유리 용기)
097 □ aquarium ⓝ 수족관
098 □ jar ⓝ 항아리
099 □ function ⓥ 기능하다
100 □ micro-ecosystem ⓝ 미세 생태계
101 □ humid ⓐ 습한
102 □ no matter ~에 상관없이
103 □ care for ~을 돌보다, 관리하다
104 □ gardening ⓝ 정원 가꾸기, 원예

15

105 □ senior ⓝ (고등학교) 마지막 학년, 상급생, 선배
106 □ abandoned cat 유기묘
107 □ wander around ~을 배회하다, 어슬렁거리다
108 □ take care of ~을 돌보다
109 □ welfare ⓝ 복지, 후생
110 □ sincere ⓐ 진지한
111 □ organize ⓥ 조직하다, 정리하다
112 □ adopt ⓥ 입양하다

16~17

113 □ universal ⓐ 보편적인
114 □ weird ⓐ 희한한, 이상한
115 □ exist ⓥ 존재하다
116 □ strict ⓐ 엄격한
117 □ cruelty ⓝ 잔인함, 학대
118 □ owner ⓝ 주인, 소유주
119 □ fine ⓥ 벌금을 매기다 ⓝ 벌금
120 □ be well-known for ~로 유명하다
121 □ speed limit 속도 제한
122 □ run out of gas 휘발유가 떨어지다
123 □ make sure 꼭 ~하다
124 □ ban ⓥ 금지하다 ⓝ 금지
125 □ put in place 시행하다
126 □ sand castle 모래성
127 □ get in trouble 곤경에 처하다
128 □ unusual ⓐ 특이한
129 □ tourist attraction 관광지
130 □ cultural ⓐ 문화적인
131 □ diversity ⓝ 다양성

03회 2022학년도 3월 학력평가 고3 영어 듣기

※ QR코드를 스캔하시면 듣기 방송을 청취하실 수 있습니다.

● 점수 표시가 없는 문항은 모두 2점 ● 문항수 17개 | 배점 37점 | 제한 시간 25분

1번부터 17번까지는 듣고 답하는 문제입니다. 1번부터 15번까지는 한 번만 들려주고, 16번부터 17번까지는 두 번 들려줍니다. 방송을 잘 듣고 답을 하시기 바랍니다.

1. 다음을 듣고, 여자가 하는 말의 목적으로 가장 적절한 것을 고르시오.

① 전기 절약의 필요성을 강조하려고
② 엘리베이터 안전 수칙을 알려 주려고
③ 전문 기술자 초청 강연을 공지하려고
④ 컴퓨터 데이터 복원 방법을 설명하려고
⑤ 전기 점검 관련 유의 사항을 안내하려고

2. 대화를 듣고, 남자의 의견으로 가장 적절한 것을 고르시오.

① 설문 방식을 다양화해야 응답자의 수를 늘릴 수 있다.
② 설문 문항은 가능한 한 쉽고 간결하게 제작해야 한다.
③ 온라인 설문은 응답을 수집하는 가장 편리한 방식이다.
④ 응답자의 익명을 보장해야 솔직한 의견을 얻을 수 있다.
⑤ 설문 참여를 높이려면 응답자에게 보상을 제공해야 한다.

3. 대화를 듣고, 두 사람의 관계를 가장 잘 나타낸 것을 고르시오.

① 영화감독 – 만화가
② 촬영 감독 – 영화배우
③ 방송 진행자 – 소설가
④ 출판사 직원 – 삽화가
⑤ 신문 기자 – 시나리오 작가

4. 대화를 듣고, 그림에서 대화의 내용과 일치하지 않는 것을 고르시오.

5. 대화를 듣고, 여자가 할 일로 가장 적절한 것을 고르시오.

① 설거지하기
② 와인 주문하기
③ 친환경 비누 만들기
④ 주방 세제 사 오기
⑤ 웹 사이트 링크 보내기

6. 대화를 듣고, 남자가 지불할 금액을 고르시오.

① $30 ② $40 ③ $45 ④ $55 ⑤ $60

7. 대화를 듣고, 여자가 야외 좌석을 원하지 않는 이유를 고르시오. [3점]

① 대화하기에 너무 시끄러워서
② 햇빛이 너무 강해 눈이 부셔서
③ 미세 먼지 때문에 공기 질이 나빠서
④ 기온이 낮아 감기에 걸릴까 걱정되어서
⑤ 야외에서 보는 전망이 마음에 들지 않아서

8. 대화를 듣고, Galland perfume workshop에 관해 언급되지 않은 것을 고르시오.

① 참가 연령
② 사용 언어
③ 시간
④ 예약 방법
⑤ 장소

9. Flashlight Tour에 관한 다음 내용을 듣고, 일치하지 않는 것을 고르시오.

① 미술관 폐장 후에 시작된다.
② 한 시간 동안 진행된다.
③ 성인 입장료는 10달러이다.
④ 손전등이 기념품으로 제공된다.
⑤ 참가 인원에 제한이 있다.

[해설편 p.010]

10. 다음 표를 보면서 대화를 듣고, 남자가 주문할 휴대용 가습기를 고르시오.

Best Portable Humidifiers

	Model	Price	Color	Capacity	Mood Light
①	A	$13	Gray	300 ml	×
②	B	$18	White	400 ml	○
③	C	$20	Orange	500 ml	○
④	D	$28	Black	700 ml	×
⑤	E	$35	White	900 ml	○

11. 대화를 듣고, 여자의 마지막 말에 대한 남자의 응답으로 가장 적절한 것을 고르시오.

① Thank you very much for picking me up.
② I'll finish the laundry as soon as possible.
③ I'm sorry. I won't be late for school again.
④ I'm not sure. I'll call you when I'm finished.
⑤ Never mind. I'll complete the project tomorrow.

12. 대화를 듣고, 남자의 마지막 말에 대한 여자의 응답으로 가장 적절한 것을 고르시오.

① I'm very satisfied. You should buy one.
② Right. The air quality today is not that bad.
③ Great. I want to buy an air purifier like yours.
④ Put it here near the window. It's the best place.
⑤ Okay. Let's open the window and get some fresh air.

13. 대화를 듣고, 여자의 마지막 말에 대한 남자의 응답으로 가장 적절한 것을 고르시오. [3점]

Man: ______________________________

① No. We had no choice but to send it to you.
② Sorry. There are no other colors available now.
③ Yes. I'd like to get a refund for the yellow one.
④ Okay. You can send the large size one back to us.
⑤ Sure. We'll send you a large size one immediately.

14. 대화를 듣고, 남자의 마지막 말에 대한 여자의 응답으로 가장 적절한 것을 고르시오. [3점]

Woman: ______________________________

① Of course. I don't need it any more.
② Don't worry. You'll get used to it soon.
③ Exactly! You need to buy a smartphone.
④ Right. I checked my text before sending it.
⑤ No way. Smartphones are not that expensive.

15. 다음 상황 설명을 듣고, Emily가 Randy에게 할 말로 가장 적절한 것을 고르시오.

Emily: ______________________________

① Do you know where the lost and found is?
② Can you tell me where you bought your watch?
③ Didn't you take off your watch in the bathroom?
④ Do you know how to wash your hands properly?
⑤ Didn't you visit the shop to have your watch fixed?

[16 ~ 17] 다음을 듣고, 물음에 답하시오.

16. 남자가 하는 말의 주제로 가장 적절한 것은?

① steps in planning an efficient smart city
② pros and cons of developing smart cities
③ problems of smart cities and why they arise
④ successful smart cities and how they operate
⑤ interconnectedness of smart cities around the world

17. 언급된 도시가 아닌 것은?

① Singapore ② San Diego ③ London
④ Dubai ⑤ New York

[해설편 p.012]

 ✪ 표기에는 듣기 어려운 발음이 포함되어 있습니다. 귀 기울여 듣고 받아쓰세요. ● 고3 2022학년도 3월

※ QR 코드를 스캔하시면 듣기 방송이 나옵니다. 듣기 방송을 들으며 다음 빈칸을 채우시오. ● 제한 시간 : 25분

01

다음을 듣고, 여자가 하는 말의 목적으로 가장 적절한 것을 고르시오.

W : Attention please, teachers and students. This is the vice principal. As we notified you last week, some workers from the power company are here today to ✪ _________ _________ _________ _________ _________. During the checkup, _________ _________ _________ _________ _________ in some offices and classrooms. In addition, the school elevators won't be available until the inspection is completed. In case of _________ _________ _________, I would like you to save your work and create back-up files while working on computers. The technicians will finish their work before lunch time ends. Thank you for your patience with any inconvenience.

02

대화를 듣고, 남자의 의견으로 가장 적절한 것을 고르시오.

M : What are you doing, Ms. Taylor?

W : I'm preparing a satisfaction survey for our community center.

M : I see. How are you going to do the survey?

W : I'll _________ _________ _________ to our members so that they can open it right on their smartphone.

M : Is that the only way for them to participate?

W : Yes. Is there a problem with that?

M : You may not ✪ _________ _________ _________ _________. I mean you can't get opinions from people who don't use a smartphone.

W : Oh, that's a good point.

M : I think you should diversify your survey methods to _________ _________ _________ _________ _________.

W : You're right. I'll add a paper-based survey. That'll cover a wider range of respondents.

03

대화를 듣고, 두 사람의 관계를 가장 잘 나타낸 것을 고르시오.

M : Hello, Ms. Russell. I'm honored to have you here.

W : Thank you for inviting me, Mr. Warren.

M : It was my pleasure to work with you. Did you enjoy my movie?

W : Yes. It was fantastic!

M : I'm glad to hear that.

W : Actually, I've never imagined that _________ _________ _________ _________ _________ _________ could be realized in a live action movie.

M : I liked the characters in your comic book so much that I wanted to ✪ _________ _________ _________ _________.

W : I'm wondering how you've put all the actions and scenes on the screen.

M : The computer graphics team did most of the work and my actors did their jobs very well as I directed.

W : Oh, I see. I'm so happy to see my characters _________ _________ _________ in the movie.

M : I'm happy you liked it.

04

대화를 듣고, 그림에서 대화의 내용과 일치하지 않는 것을 고르시오.

W : Hi, Logan. How was your weekend?

M : Hey, Lisa. I went car camping at Elf Lake. Look at this picture.

W : Did you sleep in a car?

M : Yeah, I put in a pillow and blanket on the ✪ _________ _________.

W : What are those hanging from the car trunk door?

M : They are string lights. It's beautiful when the bulbs light up.

W : The camping lantern on the table looks nice, too.

M : Right. It can ✪ _________ _________ _________ _________ at night.

W : You even set a tablecloth on the table. I like the checkered pattern.

M : I wanted to _________ _________ _________ _________ _________. Do you see the camping chair near the table?

W : Yeah, it looks good for sitting and relaxing with a cup of coffee.

05

대화를 듣고, 여자가 할 일로 가장 적절한 것을 고르시오.

M : Hannah, everything you made was delicious!

W : Thanks. The wine you brought went so well with the food.

M : I'm glad. I'll _________ _________ _________ for you.

W : If you do that, I'd be grateful.

M : By the way, where's the dishwashing liquid?

W : _________ _________ _________ _________ next to the sink is for dishwashing. I made it myself.

M : Oh, really?

W : Yes. It's more eco-friendly than ✪ _________ _________ _________ at the store.

M : How did you make it?

W : I followed a recipe from the Internet.

M : *[Pause]* Wow, this soap works so well. Can you _________ _________ _________ _________ to the website? I want to make one too.

W : Sure. I'll text you the link right away.

M : Okay. Thanks.

06

대화를 듣고, 남자가 지불할 금액을 고르시오.

W : Welcome to Bike Solutions. How may I help you?
M : Hello, I dropped off my bicycle yesterday. My name's Billy Hunter.
W : Let me check. *[Pause]* Here's your bicycle. We _________ _________ _________.
M : Oh, I see. What did you replace and how much is it?
W : We _________ _________ _________. Each tire is $15.
M : I see. Is that all?
W : No. We also replaced the brake pads for both wheels.
M : Good. How much is that?
W : We put a new pair of brake pads on each wheel. It's $10 for one pair.
M : You mean I need to pay for two pairs?
W : Right. And lastly, we _________ _________ _________. But that's free.
M : Thank you. Can I use this discount coupon?
W : Sure. You get ✪ _________________________________.
M : Thank you. Here's my credit card.

07

대화를 듣고, 여자가 야외 좌석을 원하지 않는 이유를 고르시오. [3점]

M : Alice, I've been really looking forward to eating at this restaurant.
W : Me too, Ryan. This is a hot spot on social media.
M : Right. Shall we sit outside?
W : Outside? You mean at a table on the terrace?
M : Yes. The view from the terrace is wonderful and it looks like there are still a few tables available.
W : I know, but I'd _________ _________ _________ _________, if you don't mind.
M : Why? Do you think it'd be ✪ _________ _________ _________ out there?
W : No. It's not as cold as I thought.
M : Then, is it _________ _________ _________ _________ _________? The air quality is actually pretty good today.
W : No, that's not the reason. It's _________ _________ _________ to talk comfortably.
M : Oh, I see. Let's eat inside, then.

08

대화를 듣고, Galland perfume workshop에 관해 언급되지 않은 것을 고르시오.

M : Honey, today's our last day in Paris. Is there anything special you want to do?
W : How about going to a perfume workshop? I've found some information about the Galland perfume workshop.
M : A perfume workshop?
W : Yes. The Galland perfume workshop is open to everyone ✪ _________ _________ _________ _________. We can make our own perfume there.
M : That sounds fun. Do they ✪ _________ _________ _________ _________ _________?
W : Yes. It starts at 1 p.m.
M : How long is the workshop?
W : Two hours.
M : I see. Then we'll have time to _________ _________ _________ after the workshop. Where's the workshop being held?
W : In the Saint Michel building. It's not far from our hotel.
M : Okay. Let's go.

09

Flashlight Tour에 관한 다음 내용을 듣고, 일치하지 않는 것을 고르시오.

M : Hello, visitors. Welcome to the Boledo Museum of Art. We're glad to announce our exclusive Flashlight Tour to you. The tour takes place every Thursday in April. After the Museum closes, _________ _________ _________ _________ _________ _________ _________ and the special flashlight tour will begin. This tour will offer you a unique and ✪ _________ _________ _________. It's a one-hour guided museum tour. During the tour, you'll enjoy our _________ _________ _________ _________ _________. Tickets are $15 for adults, and $10 for youth ages 5 to 17. Flashlights will be provided as a souvenir. This tour has a ✪ _________ _________ _________ _________, so book now. Thank you.

10

다음 표를 보면서 대화를 듣고, 남자가 주문할 휴대용 가습기를 고르시오.

W : Mr. Parker, what are you looking at on the computer?
M : Oh, Ms. Robinson. I'm looking at ✪ _________ _________ for a conference gift. Can you help me?
W : Sure. Let me see. You have five models to choose from. What's the budget range?
M : We can't spend more than $30 each.
W : Then this one's out. And orange doesn't seem like a good color. It's a bit flashy.
M : I agree. _________ _________ _________ _________?
W : I think 300 ml is too small.
M : Right. Then, there are two options left. Do you think a mood light is useful?
W : Yes. It can work as a bed lamp.
M : Okay. I'll order the model _________ _________ _________ _________. Thank you for your help.
W : You're welcome. It'll be a good gift.

11

대화를 듣고, 여자의 마지막 말에 대한 남자의 응답으로 가장 적절한 것을 고르시오.

[Cell phone rings.]
W : Hello, Lucas. What's up?
M : Hi, Mom. I have a group project meeting after school. I'm afraid ✪ _________ _________ _________ _________ _________ _________ on my way home.
W : No problem. I'll take care of it. What time do you think you'll be home?

12

대화를 듣고, 남자의 마지막 말에 대한 여자의 응답으로 가장 적절한 것을 고르시오.

M : Grace, is this an ✪ __________ __________?
W : Yeah. I bought it last week because __________ __________ __________ __________ __________ __________ these days.
M : How do you like it? I've been thinking about getting one for my office.

13

대화를 듣고, 여자의 마지막 말에 대한 남자의 응답으로 가장 적절한 것을 고르시오. [3점]

[Telephone rings.]
M : Joy's Clothing. How may I help you?
W : Hi. I'm Norah Davis. I ordered a T-shirt from your online store but I __________ __________ __________ __________.
M : I'm sorry to hear that. Can I have your order number, please?
W : Sure. It's P2203123.
M : Thanks. Let me check it for you. *[Typing sound]* You ordered a large size yellow T-shirt, correct?
W : Yes, that's right, but I got a medium one. Can you please send me the right size?
M : Oh, we're very sorry for the inconvenience. I'll check whether we have any large size ones ✪ __________ __________.
W : Okay.
M : *[Typing sound]* Unfortunately, we're __________ __________ __________ __________ __________ __________. We have larges in pink and white.
W : I see. Then can you send me __________ __________ __________?

14

대화를 듣고, 남자의 마지막 말에 대한 여자의 응답으로 가장 적절한 것을 고르시오. [3점]

M : Lydia, can you come here for a moment?
W : Sure. What is it, Grandpa?
M : I need some help with my cell phone.
W : Wow! You've got a smartphone!
M : Yes, but I don't know how to send a text message. Can you show me how to do it?
W : Okay. First, find the messaging icon and ✪ __________ __________.
M : Like this, right?
W : Yeah. Next, you need to __________ __________ __________ you want to text.
M : Select the person.... All right.
W : Now you can see the message box.
M : You mean the box here?
W : Yes. __________ __________ __________ __________ __________. And when you're done, hit 'Send.'
M : I got it. But using a smartphone still seems difficult.

15

다음 상황 설명을 듣고, Emily가 Randy에게 할 말로 가장 적절한 것을 고르시오.

W : Randy and Emily are very close friends and they go to school together. One day after school, on their way home, Randy notices that __________ __________ __________ __________ __________, which is very precious to him. Emily asks Randy when he last had his watch. Randy says it was during the last class. Emily remembers that she happened to see Randy come out from the bathroom __________ __________ __________ __________ __________. So, Emily thinks that Randy may have left his watch ✪ __________ __________ __________ __________ __________. Emily wants to ask Randy about this. In this situation, what would Emily most likely say to Randy?

16~17

다음을 듣고, 물음에 답하시오.

M : Hello, students. Last class, we talked about IoT home devices. Today, let's expand the topic and learn about smart cities. Smart cities use technology to provide services and solve various problems. Singapore is one of the front-runners in the race to __________ __________ __________ __________, with IoT cameras monitoring the condition of the city, including the cleanliness of public spaces. It also has systems to monitor energy use, waste management, and water use in real time. San Diego has installed 3,200 smart sensors to optimize traffic flow, and electric vehicles are supported by solar-to-electric charging stations. Traffic monitoring systems are also used in Dubai. This city has ✪ __________ __________ __________ __________ __________ as well as smart tourism options. In New York, the police department has tested web-based software that __________ __________ __________ __________ to predict and respond to crimes. The test has produced __________ __________ __________ in violent crimes in the city. Thanks to smart systems, many citizens around the world can improve their quality of life.

▶ 정답 : 해설편 014쪽

VOCA LIST 03

회차별 영단어 QR 코드 ※ QR 코드를 스캔 후 모바일로 단어장처럼 학습할 수 있습니다.

● 고3 2022학년도 3월

01
001 □ notify ⓥ 공고[신고]하다
002 □ power company 전력 회사, 전기 회사
003 □ inspect ⓥ 조사하다
004 □ facility ⓝ 설비, 시설
005 □ checkup ⓝ 점검, 정밀 검사
006 □ electricity ⓝ 전기, 전력
007 □ temporarily ad 일시적으로
008 □ in addition (~에) 덧붙여, 게다가
009 □ power cut 정전
010 □ technician ⓝ 기술자, 기사
011 □ patience ⓝ 인내심
012 □ inconvenience ⓝ 불편, 폐 ⓥ 불편하게 하다

02
013 □ prepare ⓥ 준비하다
014 □ satisfaction ⓝ 만족(감)
015 □ survey ⓝ (설문) 조사
016 □ participate ⓥ 참여하다, 관여하다
017 □ opinion ⓝ 의견, 견해
018 □ diversify ⓥ 다양화하다
019 □ method ⓝ 방법, 방식
020 □ respondent ⓝ 응답자

03
021 □ honored ⓐ 영광으로 생각하여
022 □ realize ⓥ 구현하다, 실현하다
023 □ realistic ⓐ 현실적인, 현실성 있는
024 □ direct ⓥ (영화를) 감독하다
025 □ come to life 살아 움직이다, 활기를 띠다

04
026 □ car camping 차박
027 □ pillow ⓝ 베개
028 □ blanket ⓝ 담요
029 □ flatten ⓥ 평평하게 하다
030 □ bulb ⓝ 전구
031 □ atmosphere ⓝ 분위기, 환경
032 □ cozy ⓐ 아늑한

05
033 □ delicious ⓐ 아주 맛있는
034 □ go well with ~와 잘 어울리다
035 □ grateful ⓐ 고마워하는
036 □ liquid ⓝ 액체
037 □ soap ⓝ 비누
038 □ eco-friendly ⓐ 친환경적인, 환경 친화적인
039 □ detergent ⓝ 세제

06
040 □ drop off (물건을) 맡기다
041 □ replace ⓥ 교체하다
042 □ clean ⓥ 닦다, 청소하다

07
043 □ look forward to ~을 고대하다
044 □ available ⓐ 이용 가능한, (자리나 시간이) 빈
045 □ chilly ⓐ 쌀쌀한
046 □ fine dust 미세 먼지
047 □ actually ad 사실은
048 □ reason ⓝ 이유, 까닭
049 □ noisy ⓐ 시끄러운, 떠들썩한

08
050 □ special ⓐ 특별한
051 □ perfume ⓝ 향수
052 □ be open to ~을 대상으로 한다

09
053 □ announce ⓥ 알리다, 발표하다
054 □ exclusive ⓐ 전용의, 고급의
055 □ offer ⓥ 제공하다
056 □ memorable ⓐ 기억에 남는
057 □ experience ⓝ 경험, 체험
058 □ permanent collection 영구 소장품
059 □ provide ⓥ 제공하다
060 □ souvenir ⓝ 기념품
061 □ capacity ⓝ 수용력

10
062 □ portable ⓐ 휴대할 수 있는
063 □ conference ⓝ 회의
064 □ budget ⓝ 예산
065 □ range ⓝ 범위
066 □ bit ⓝ 조금
067 □ flashy ⓐ 속되게 화려한, 겉만 번지르르한
068 □ humidifier ⓝ 가습기

11
069 □ afraid ⓐ (유감이지만) ~라고 생각하다
070 □ pick up the laundry (맡긴) 세탁물을 찾아오다
071 □ take care of ~을 처리하다
072 □ possible ⓐ 가능한

12
073 □ air purifier 공기 청정기
074 □ How do you like it? 어떻게 생각해?
075 □ satisfy ⓥ 만족시키다

13
076 □ correct ⓐ 맞는, 정확한
077 □ unfortunately ad 불행하게도, 유감스럽게도
078 □ in stock 재고가 있는
079 □ have no choice but to ~할 수밖에 없다
080 □ get a refund 환불하다
081 □ immediately ad 바로, 즉시, 당장에

14
082 □ moment ⓝ 잠깐, 잠시
083 □ tap ⓥ 가볍게 두드리다
084 □ select ⓥ 선택하다
085 □ get used to ~에 익숙해지다
086 □ No way. 절대 안 돼, 그럴 리 없어.
087 □ expensive ⓐ 비싼, 돈이 많이 드는

15
088 □ precious ⓐ 귀중한
089 □ shake ⓥ 털다
090 □ sink ⓝ 세면대
091 □ lost and found 분실물 센터
092 □ take off ~을 벗다
093 □ properly ad 제대로

16~17
094 □ IoT (Internet of Things) 사물 인터넷
095 □ expand ⓥ 확장하다
096 □ solve ⓥ 해결하다
097 □ front-runner ⓝ 선두 주자
098 □ cleanliness ⓝ 청결
099 □ install ⓥ 설치하다
100 □ optimize ⓥ 최적화하다
101 □ flow ⓝ 흐름
102 □ support ⓥ 지원하다
103 □ charging station 충전소
104 □ telemedicine ⓝ 원격 의료
105 □ police department (미국에서 특정 도시의) 경찰서
106 □ historical ⓐ 역사적인, 과거에 속한
107 □ crime ⓝ 범죄
108 □ predict ⓥ 예측하다
109 □ marked ⓐ 두드러지는
110 □ decrease ⓥ 줄다, 감소하다
111 □ violent crime 강력 범죄
112 □ efficient ⓐ 효율적인
113 □ interconnectedness ⓝ 상호 연결성

04회 ● 2021학년도 3월 학력평가 고3 영어 듣기

※ QR코드를 스캔하시면 듣기 방송을 청취하실 수 있습니다.

● 점수 표시가 없는 문항은 모두 2점 ● 문항수 17개 | 배점 37점 | 제한 시간 25분

1번부터 17번까지는 듣고 답하는 문제입니다. 1번부터 15번까지는 한 번만 들려주고, 16번부터 17번까지는 두 번 들려줍니다. 방송을 잘 듣고 답을 하시기 바랍니다.

1. 다음을 듣고, 남자가 하는 말의 목적으로 가장 적절한 것을 고르시오.

① 재활용 쓰레기 분리 배출 방법을 안내하려고
② 재활용 쓰레기 배출 시간 준수를 당부하려고
③ 재활용 쓰레기 분리수거 요일 변경을 공지하려고
④ 재활용 쓰레기 관련 주민 회의 결과를 알려주려고
⑤ 재활용 쓰레기 분리수거 관련 공청회 참석을 요청하려고

2. 대화를 듣고, 여자의 의견으로 가장 적절한 것을 고르시오.

① 적합한 조리 도구 사용은 요리를 쉽고 즐겁게 해 준다.
② 요리 동영상을 참고하면 누구나 요리를 할 수 있다.
③ 같은 재료라도 조리법에 따라 음식 맛이 달라진다.
④ 조리 도구는 훌륭한 인테리어 소품이 될 수 있다.
⑤ 조리 도구를 청결하게 관리하는 것이 중요하다.

3. 대화를 듣고, 두 사람의 관계를 가장 잘 나타낸 것을 고르시오.

① 꽃꽂이 강사 – 수강생 ② 택배 기사 – 수령인
③ 웨딩 플래너 – 예비 신부 ④ 꽃 판매 상인 – 사진작가
⑤ 인테리어 디자이너 – 건축가

4. 대화를 듣고, 그림에서 대화의 내용과 일치하지 않는 것을 고르시오.

5. 대화를 듣고, 여자가 남자를 위해 할 일로 가장 적절한 것을 고르시오.

① 물 가져가기 ② 안내 방송하기
③ 카메라 설치하기 ④ 배터리 충전하기
⑤ 구급상자 챙기기

6. 대화를 듣고, 남자가 지불할 금액을 고르시오. [3점]

① $117 ② $130 ③ $135 ④ $150 ⑤ $161

7. 대화를 듣고, 여자가 다른 주문처를 찾고 있는 이유를 고르시오.

① 더 좋은 품질을 원해서
② 더 빠른 배송을 원해서
③ 더 싼 가격을 원해서
④ 무료 배송을 원해서
⑤ 대량 주문을 원해서

8. 대화를 듣고, Delizia에 관해 언급되지 않은 것을 고르시오.

① 창업 연도 ② 창업자 ③ 예약 방법
④ 장소 협찬 영화 ⑤ 야외 정원

9. Nest Cave Boat Tour에 관한 다음 내용을 듣고, 일치하지 않는 것을 고르시오.

① 1시간 동안 진행된다.
② 보트당 최대 탑승 인원은 10명이다.
③ 동굴의 역사에 관해 들을 수 있다.
④ 동굴 내에서 사진 촬영을 할 수 있다.
⑤ 사전에 예약을 해야 한다.

10. 다음 표를 보면서 대화를 듣고, 두 사람이 주문할 사다리를 고르시오.

Stepladders

	Model	Price	Height (cm)	Load Capacity (kg)	Foldable
①	A	$55	90	80	○
②	B	$65	130	90	×
③	C	$75	150	110	○
④	D	$85	180	150	×
⑤	E	$105	210	200	○

11. 대화를 듣고, 여자의 마지막 말에 대한 남자의 응답으로 가장 적절한 것을 고르시오.

① Actually, it leads to the basement of the store.
② Please connect me with the marketing department.
③ No, the menswear is on the fifth floor of the store.
④ Well, the department store opens at 10 in the morning.
⑤ Not exactly. This is the direct number of the department.

12. 대화를 듣고, 남자의 마지막 말에 대한 여자의 응답으로 가장 적절한 것을 고르시오.

① Of course. She'll be very happy to see you.
② Thank you for the ride. Say hello to Daniel.
③ How nice! I'll call and thank her for the ride.
④ Never mind. I'll take a bus to the baseball field.
⑤ Hurry up. You'll be late for baseball practice again.

13. 대화를 듣고, 여자의 마지막 말에 대한 남자의 응답으로 가장 적절한 것을 고르시오. [3점]

Man: ____________________

① Great. It'll be really nice if we sing together.
② Thank you. I had a great time in your choir.
③ Think twice. It's not easy to sing in a choir.
④ Actually, I'm not a big fan of classical music.
⑤ Never mind. The choir practice has been canceled.

14. 대화를 듣고, 남자의 마지막 말에 대한 여자의 응답으로 가장 적절한 것을 고르시오. [3점]

Woman: ____________________

① I'm afraid I can't go with you this time.
② I'm glad you've done the farm work in time.
③ Unfortunately, there are no more apples to pick.
④ Thank you for the apples you sent me last week.
⑤ You'll enjoy it. It's hard work but very rewarding.

15. 다음 상황 설명을 듣고, Katrina가 Simon에게 할 말로 가장 적절한 것을 고르시오.

Katrina: ____________________

① Let's go bicycle riding as often as possible.
② Go to the hospital before the pain gets worse.
③ You shouldn't do risky things while riding a bicycle.
④ I'll let you know the repair shop that I often go to.
⑤ You're brave to ride a bicycle with no hands.

[16 ~ 17] 다음을 듣고, 물음에 답하시오.

16. 여자가 하는 말의 주제로 가장 적절한 것은?

① colors to help animals protect themselves
② English animal expressions and their meanings
③ animal sounds expressed in different languages
④ classroom animal games and activities for children
⑤ animals that appear frequently in children's stories

17. 언급된 동물이 아닌 것은?

① snail ② horse ③ hawk
④ monkey ⑤ snake

[해설편 p.017]

Dictation 04

✪ 표기에는 듣기 어려운 발음이 포함되어 있습니다. 귀 기울여 듣고 받아쓰세요. ● 고3 2021학년도 3월

※ QR 코드를 스캔하시면 듣기 방송이 나옵니다. 듣기 방송을 들으며 다음 빈칸을 채우시오. ● 제한 시간 : 25분

01

다음을 듣고, 남자가 하는 말의 목적으로 가장 적절한 것을 고르시오.

M : Hello, residents. This is Andy from the management office. We're currently ✪ _________ _________ _________ twice a week, on Wednesdays and Sundays, from 7 a.m. to 9 p.m. But we've had a lot of complaints from residents concerning the time, location, and smell. We're doing our best to _________ _________ _________ but it's been difficult to come up with satisfactory solutions. So, to deal with this matter effectively, we're going to _________ _________ _________ _________ at the community hall on Friday, March 26, at 8 p.m. We're asking everyone to attend the public hearing. Thank you in advance for your cooperation.

02

대화를 듣고, 여자의 의견으로 가장 적절한 것을 고르시오.

W : Eric, I made this pizza myself. Try some.
M : Thank you, Yujin. *[Pause]* Mmm.... It's delicious!
W : Is it? I watched a cooking video and followed the recipe from it.
M : You're a really good cook. Not everyone can just watch a video and make delicious food like you just did.
W : Well, I think it's all thanks to the cooking tools _________ _________ _________.
M : Cooking tools? You mean utensils?
W : Yes. ✪ _________ _________ _________ _________ makes cooking much easier.
M : You seem to be very happy with your utensils.
W : Yeah. They make cooking more enjoyable.
M : Oh, that's _________ _________ _________ _________ _________ these days!
W : Definitely.
M : Now I understand why chefs emphasize the importance of using the right utensils in cooking.

03

대화를 듣고, 두 사람의 관계를 가장 잘 나타낸 것을 고르시오.

M : Hi, Sofia. What did you do with the bouquet you made last Friday?
W : Hi, Brandon. I had it delivered to my friend. She was really happy to get it.
M : Did you tell her _________ _________ _________ _________?
W : Yes. I also told her that I made it in your class. She said she'd like to learn from you, too.
M : I'm glad to hear that. Why don't you _________ _________ _________ _________ _________ _________ sometime?
W : Yeah, I suggested signing up for the next one-day class together.
M : Good. You will get to spend quality time together.
W : I think so, too. I'll let her know how to register.
M : Thank you. Today you'll learn ✪ _________ _________ _________ _________ _________ in a vase. Look here. I've made this one in advance.
W : Wow, it looks gorgeous. I can't wait to make one myself.
M : Okay. Shall we get started?

04

대화를 듣고, 그림에서 대화의 내용과 일치하지 않는 것을 고르시오.

M : Rachel, I heard you adopted a puppy.
W : Yes. His name is Coco. I've rearranged the living room for him. Take a look at this picture.
M : Let's see. Oh, this must be Coco. He's playing with a ball.
W : Yes. It's his favorite toy.
M : I see. Is this striped tent for Coco?
W : Yeah. I bought it for him last week.
M : It looks cozy. You also _________ _________ _________ _________ _________ _________ _________ _________. What are they for?
W : They're pet steps to help Coco get on the sofa.
M : Ah, he can't jump onto it yet. Hey, Rachel, what's this elephant toy on the sofa?
W : It's another toy for Coco.
M : Well, _________ _________ _________ _________ _________?
W : Yes, he is. Do you see ✪ _________ _________ _________ _________ _________ _________ _________? I'm using them for his toilet training.
M : Good. Everything seems to be perfect for Coco.

05

대화를 듣고, 여자가 남자를 위해 할 일로 가장 적절한 것을 고르시오.

[Cell phone rings.]
M : Hi, Ms. Clark.
W : Mr. Dickson, where are you? The students' soccer final starts in 30 minutes.
M : I'm on the playing field, checking the ground conditions.
W : Well, _________ _________ _________ _________ _________ to the students about the match.
M : Thank you. I've already set up cameras to film the match.
W : Okay. How about extra batteries? Do you have them?
M : I checked. They're in the camera bag.
W : ✪ _________ _________ _________ _________ _________? We might need it during the game.
M : The school nurse will bring it before the game.
W : I see. Did you bring _________ _________ _________ _________ _________ _________ _________?
M : Oh, I forgot. Could you bring it for me? It's in the fridge.
W : Okay. I'll take it to the field right away.
M : Thanks.

06

대화를 듣고, 남자가 지불할 금액을 고르시오. [3점]

W : Welcome to Jo's Fragrance. How may I help you?

M : Hello. I want to buy a bottle of Wild Silverbell for my sister's birthday.

W : I see. It's a very popular perfume these days.

M : My sister really loves its scent. How much is it?

W : This small bottle is $80, and that larger one is $100.

M : I'll ✪ __________ __________ __________ __________.

W : Okay. We also sell __________ __________ __________ __________ __________ for $50 each.

M : Oh! My sister really likes scented candles. I'll take a candle, too.

W : Great. Since you're buying two items, you also get a 10% discount voucher. ✪ __________ __________ __________ __________ __________ __________ __________ __________ __________.

M : I see. Could you wrap them up, please?

W : Sure. Gift-wrapping is free, but we can tie a ribbon on it for an extra dollar.

M : I don't need a ribbon. Just gift-wrap them, please. Here's my credit card.

07

대화를 듣고, 여자가 다른 주문처를 찾고 있는 이유를 고르시오.

M : Ms. White, what are you doing on the Internet?

W : Oh, Mr. Brown. I'm looking for a store to order some file folders for my class.

M : Oh, I thought you already ordered them, didn't you?

W : Actually, I didn't. I thought I had found the right store, but now I changed my mind.

M : Did you find a store ✪ __________ __________ __________ __________?

W : No. The store I found was the cheapest and __________ __________ __________ __________.

M : Then, were the file folders sold out?

W : No. They have plenty in stock.

M : If so, why are you still searching for another store?

W : Because __________ __________ __________ __________ __________ __________ __________ __________ __________. I need the folders tomorrow.

M : I see. So, you're looking for a store with faster delivery, right?

W : Yes. The sooner, the better!

08

대화를 듣고, Delizia에 관해 언급되지 않은 것을 고르시오.

M : Hello, viewers! I'm currently at one of the popular restaurants, Delizia. I'm here with the manager of Delizia.

W : Hi, viewers. I'm Laura, the manager of Delizia.

M : Laura, Delizia is the oldest Italian restaurant in our city, isn't it?

W : Yes. It was founded in 1906.

M : Wow! Could you tell us __________ __________ __________?

W : Fabio Cannavaro. Today, his granddaughter runs it.

M : Oh, it's a family business. Tell us more about Delizia.

W : Our restaurant is famous not only for its food, but also ✪ __________ __________ __________ __________.

M : I see. I know Delizia was used as a location for some famous movies.

W : Right. The movie, *From Rome with Love*, was recently filmed in our restaurant.

M : Impressive! And Delizia has a very romantic outdoor garden, doesn't it?

W : Yeah. It's often used for weddings.

M : That's good. Now, __________ __________ __________ __________ __________ __________?

W : Sure. Come this way, please.

09

Nest Cave Boat Tour에 관한 다음 내용을 듣고, 일치하지 않는 것을 고르시오.

W : Hello, listeners. Are you looking for a special activity for the upcoming holidays? Nest Cave Boat Tour is here for you. You can explore the cave on a one-hour guided boat tour. __________ __________ __________ __________ are allowed on each boat. Along the way, you can hear about ✪ __________ __________ __________ __________ __________ __________ __________ __________. You can even see glowworms deep inside, but __________ __________ __________ __________ __________ __________ __________ __________. With your cameras off, just enjoy the mysterious light from the glowworms. For this wonderful cave tour, you need to make a reservation in advance. For reservation, please visit our website. Thank you.

10

다음 표를 보면서 대화를 듣고, 두 사람이 주문할 사다리를 고르시오.

W : Honey, what are you looking at on the computer?

M : I'm looking for a stepladder. We need one for when we do housework.

W : Good idea. Let me see. __________ __________ __________ __________ __________ look good.

M : Yes, but let's exclude this one. It's too much to spend over $100 for just a ladder.

W : I agree. What about the height?

M : __________ __________ __________, it should be at least 120 cm.

W : Okay. I think the weight a ladder can support is also important.

M : Oh, definitely. It should be able to hold more than 100 kg.

W : Right. Then we only have two options now.

M : Yes. Wouldn't it be better to buy a ladder that can fold?

W : Of course. It'll ✪ __________ __________ __________ __________ __________.

M : I agree. Let's order it now.

11

대화를 듣고, 여자의 마지막 말에 대한 남자의 응답으로 가장 적절한 것을 고르시오.

W : Excuse me. Can you tell me how I can get to Harriot Department Store?
M : Sure. Go straight ahead until you find exit 5.
W : Thank you. ✪ __________ __________ __________ __________ __________ __________ __________ __________?

12

대화를 듣고, 남자의 마지막 말에 대한 여자의 응답으로 가장 적절한 것을 고르시오.

M : Hi, Mom. I'm home.
W : Oh, you're back from your baseball practice early today.
M : Yeah. While I was waiting at the bus stop, Daniel's mom ✪ __________ __________ __________ __________ __________ __________ __________.

13

대화를 듣고, 여자의 마지막 말에 대한 남자의 응답으로 가장 적절한 것을 고르시오. [3점]

W : What's the tune you're humming, Kevin?
M : Ah, it's a song I sang in choir last week.
W : I didn't know you were in a choir!
M : It's just a small choir. We __________ __________ __________ __________ and sing together.
W : What kind of songs does the choir sing?
M : ✪ __________ __________ __________, __________. We do classical, jazz, pretty much anything you can think of.
W : That sounds fun.
M : You seem interested. How about joining our choir?
W : Well, I love music, but I'm not a good singer.
M : It doesn't matter. What matters is that __________ __________ __________ __________ __________.
W : Then I guess I'll __________ __________ __________ __________.

14

대화를 듣고, 남자의 마지막 말에 대한 여자의 응답으로 가장 적절한 것을 고르시오. [3점]

W : Hi, Lucas. How's it going?
M : Not bad, Sarah. Do you have any special plans for this weekend?
W : Yes, I'm going to visit my grandparents' farm. They're ✪ __________, __________ __________ __________ __________.
M : You mean you're going to do some farm work?
W : That's right.
M : What are you doing there?
W : Well, __________ __________ __________ __________ __________. If we don't pick them in time, we won't get a good price for them.
M : I see. I want to have a chance to pick apples.
W : Really? __________ __________ __________ __________ __________ __________ __________ this weekend?
M : I've never done any farm work, but I'd love to.

15

다음 상황 설명을 듣고, Katrina가 Simon에게 할 말로 가장 적절한 것을 고르시오.

M : Katrina and Simon are close friends in the neighborhood. Recently, they enjoy riding bicycles together. But Katrina often notices Simon's careless behavior while riding a bicycle. Although he is good at riding, there are some occasions where he almost falls over because he sometimes rides ✪ __________ __________ __________ __________ the handlebars. Furthermore, he __________ __________ __________ __________ while riding. Katrina is worried that __________ __________ __________ __________ __________ __________ __________ __________. So, Katrina wants to give Simon some safety advice. In this situation, what would Katrina most likely say to Simon?

16~17

다음을 듣고, 물음에 답하시오.

W : Okay, students. We just talked about idiomatic expressions related to color. As you know, idioms are creative descriptions. We use them to share an idea or feeling. Now, let's learn some animal idioms in English. The first idiom is "at a snail's pace," which means moving very slowly. This idiom is easy to understand because we all know __________ __________ __________ __________. The next one, "hold your horses," is a common way of telling someone to wait or slow down. If someone says "hold your horses," they're telling you to "wait a minute." And children often hear from their parents, "✪ __________ __________ __________ __________ __________ __________." This expression is often used to make sure that someone doesn't __________ __________ __________ __________ __________. The last idiom is "I'll be a monkey's uncle." People use this expression when __________ __________ __________ __________ __________. It's used in a comical way. These idioms may be confusing at first, but once you learn them, you'll have a fun new way of talking.

▶ 정답 : 해설편 019쪽

VOCA LIST 04

회차별 영단어 QR 코드 ※ QR 코드를 스캔 후 모바일로 단어장처럼 학습할 수 있습니다.

● 고3 2021학년도 3월

01

001 □ resident ⓝ (특정 지역의) 거주자[주민]
002 □ management ⓝ 경영진
003 □ currently ad 현재, 지금
004 □ collect ⓥ 모으다, 수집하다
005 □ recyclable ⓐ 재활용할 수 있는
006 □ garbage ⓝ 쓰레기
007 □ complaint ⓝ 불평, 항의
008 □ concerning prep ~에 관한[관련된]
009 □ address ⓥ (문제·상황 등에 대해) 고심하다[다루다]
010 □ come up with (해답 등을) 찾아내다
011 □ satisfactory ⓐ 만족스러운, 충분한
012 □ effectively ad 효과적으로
013 □ public hearing 공청회
014 □ attend ⓥ 참석하다
015 □ in advance 사전에, 미리
016 □ cooperation ⓝ 협력, 합동, 협조

02

017 □ recently ad 최근에
018 □ utensil ⓝ (가정, 특히 부엌에서 쓰는) 기구
019 □ enjoyable ⓐ 즐거운
020 □ totally ad 완전히, 전적으로
021 □ definitely ad 확실히, 그렇고 말고, 틀림없이
022 □ emphasize ⓥ 강조하다

03

023 □ bouquet ⓝ 부케, 꽃다발
024 □ deliver ⓥ 배달하다
025 □ sign up for ~에 등록[신청]하다
026 □ quality ⓐ 고급[양질]의
027 □ register ⓥ 신고하다, 등록하다
028 □ arrange ⓥ 정리하다, 배열하다
029 □ gorgeous ⓐ 아주 멋진

04

030 □ adopt ⓥ 입양하다
031 □ rearrange ⓥ 재배열[재배치]하다
032 □ cozy ⓐ 아늑한
033 □ jump onto ~에 뛰어오르다
034 □ potted plant 화초

05

035 □ final ⓝ 결승전
036 □ condition ⓝ 상태
037 □ announcement ⓝ 발표, 공표
038 □ extra ⓐ 여분의, 추가의
039 □ first-aid kit 비상약품 상자
040 □ fridge ⓝ 냉장고

06

041 □ popular ⓐ 인기 있는, 대중적인
042 □ perfume ⓝ 향수
043 □ voucher ⓝ 상품권, 할인권, 쿠폰
044 □ purchase ⓝ 구입, 구매
045 □ gift-wrapping ⓝ 선물 포장

07

046 □ order ⓥ 주문하다
047 □ file folder 서류철
048 □ actually ad 사실은, 실제로
049 □ sold out 매진된, 다 팔린
050 □ plenty ⓝ 풍부[충분]한 양
051 □ in stock 비축되어, 재고로

08

052 □ found ⓥ 설립하다, 세우다
053 □ run ⓥ (사업체 등을) 운영[경영]하다
054 □ architectural ⓐ 건축학[술]의
055 □ value ⓝ 가치
056 □ film ⓥ 촬영하다, 찍다
057 □ impressive ⓐ 인상적인, 인상[감명] 깊은
058 □ show A around (B) A에게 (B를) 구경시켜 주다

09

059 □ upcoming ⓐ 다가오는, 곧 있을
060 □ explore ⓥ 탐사[탐험]하다
061 □ cave ⓝ 동굴
062 □ up to ~까지
063 □ geological ⓐ 지질학의
064 □ feature ⓝ 특색, 특징
065 □ glowworm ⓝ 땅반딧불이
066 □ permit ⓥ 허용[허락]하다
067 □ mysterious ⓐ 이해[설명]하기 힘든, 신비한
068 □ make a reservation 예약하다

10

069 □ stepladder ⓝ 발판 사다리
070 □ exclude ⓥ 제외[배제]하다
071 □ considering prep ~을 고려[감안]하면
072 □ support ⓥ 지지하다, (넘어지지 않도록) 받치다
073 □ fold ⓥ 접히다, 포개지다
074 □ take up (공간 등을) 차지하다
075 □ storage ⓝ 저장, 보관

11

076 □ department store 백화점
077 □ exit ⓝ 출구
078 □ connect A with B A를 B와 연결하다
079 □ menswear ⓝ 남성복

12

080 □ give ~ a ride ~를 태워주다

13

081 □ tune ⓝ 곡, 선율
082 □ hum ⓥ 콧노래를 부르다, (노래를) 흥얼거리다
083 □ choir ⓝ 합창단, 성가대
084 □ mix ⓝ 혼합체, 섞인 것
085 □ pretty ad 아주, 매우
086 □ matter ⓥ 중요하다, 문제되다
087 □ give ~ a try ~을 한번 해보다
088 □ not a big fan of ~을 그다지 좋아하지 않는

14

089 □ farm ⓝ 농장
090 □ short-handed ⓐ 일손이 부족한
091 □ pick ⓥ (과일 등을) 따다
092 □ in time 시간 맞춰, 늦지 않게
093 □ rewarding ⓐ 보람 있는

15

094 □ close ⓐ 가까운, 친밀한
095 □ careless ⓐ 부주의한
096 □ occasion ⓝ 때, 경우
097 □ fall over 넘어지다
098 □ handlebar ⓝ (자전거·오토바이의) 핸들
099 □ serious ⓐ 심각한
100 □ risky ⓐ 위험한

16~17

101 □ idiomatic ⓐ 관용구[숙어]가 든
102 □ expression ⓝ 표현
103 □ related to ~와 관련 있는
104 □ idiom ⓝ 관용구, 숙어
105 □ creative ⓐ 창조적인, 창의적인
106 □ at a snail's pace 달팽이 같은 속도로, 느릿느릿
107 □ hold your horses (주로 명령문으로) 흥분부터 하지 말라
108 □ common ⓐ 흔한, 공동의
109 □ slow down 천천히 하다, 속도를 늦추다
110 □ I'm watching you like a hawk. 나는 너를 엄중히 감시하고 있다.
111 □ make sure 반드시 ~하도록 하다
112 □ misbehave ⓥ 못된[버릇없는] 짓을 하다
113 □ unexpected ⓐ 예기치 않은, 예상 밖의
114 □ unlikely ⓐ 있음 직하지[있을 것 같지] 않은
115 □ comical ⓐ 웃기는, 재미있는
116 □ confuse ⓥ 혼란시키다

05회 ● 2020학년도 3월 학력평가 고3 영어 듣기

※ QR코드를 스캔하시면 듣기 방송을 청취하실 수 있습니다.

● 점수 표시가 없는 문항은 모두 2점 ● 문항수 17개 | 배점 37점 | 제한 시간 25분

1번부터 17번까지는 듣고 답하는 문제입니다. 1번부터 15번까지는 한 번만 들려주고, 16번부터 17번까지는 두 번 들려줍니다. 방송을 잘 듣고 답을 하시기 바랍니다.

1. 다음을 듣고, 여자가 하는 말의 목적으로 가장 적절한 것을 고르시오.

① 미세 먼지 차단용 마스크의 착용을 권장하려고
② 고농도 미세 먼지의 발생 원인에 대해 설명하려고
③ 미세 먼지에 대비한 건강 관리법 강연을 홍보하려고
④ 미세 먼지 절감을 위한 캠페인에 동참할 것을 호소하려고
⑤ 미세 먼지 경보 발령에 따른 실외 활동 자제를 당부하려고

2. 대화를 듣고, 남자의 의견으로 가장 적절한 것을 고르시오.

① 여행 중에는 비상 연락처를 항상 소지해야 한다.
② 여행 시 치안이 불안한 장소에는 가지 말아야 한다.
③ 현금이나 귀중품은 최소한만 가지고 여행해야 한다.
④ 여행지의 기후를 고려하여 여벌 옷을 가져가야 한다.
⑤ 여행지에서는 관광객처럼 보이는 복장을 피해야 한다.

3. 대화를 듣고, 두 사람의 관계를 가장 잘 나타낸 것을 고르시오.

① 안무가 — 무대 감독 ② 무용 강사 — 수강생
③ 가구 제작자 — 의뢰인 ④ 의상 디자이너 — 무용수
⑤ 카메라 감독 — 소품 담당자

4. 대화를 듣고, 그림에서 대화의 내용과 일치하지 <u>않는</u> 것을 고르시오.

5. 대화를 듣고, 여자가 할 일로 가장 적절한 것을 고르시오.

① 침실 창문 닫기
② 식료품 사러 가기
③ 게임기 수리 맡기기
④ 영화 예매권 환불하기
⑤ 아들 친구 데려다주기

6. 대화를 듣고, 여자가 지불할 금액을 고르시오. [3점]

① $44 ② $46 ③ $48 ④ $50 ⑤ $52

7. 대화를 듣고, 남자가 금요일에 Poetry Night에 가지 <u>않는</u> 이유를 고르시오.

① 병원에 가야 해서
② 침대를 조립해야 해서
③ 이삿짐을 포장해야 해서
④ 동아리 모임에 가야 해서
⑤ 아파트 청소를 해야 해서

8. 대화를 듣고, 도장 만들기 수업에 관해 언급되지 <u>않은</u> 것을 고르시오.

① 사용 언어 ② 참가비 ③ 소요 시간
④ 장소 ⑤ 인원 제한

9. Campbell Challenge Program에 관한 다음 내용을 듣고, 일치하지 <u>않는</u> 것을 고르시오.

① Challenge를 하나 이상 신청할 수 있다.
② Challenge의 목록은 학교 웹 사이트에 탑재되어 있다.
③ 한번 선택한 Challenge는 변경할 수 없다.
④ Challenge별 필수 요건을 충족하면 수료증을 받는다.
⑤ 등록은 3월 23일까지 온라인으로 가능하다.

[해설편 p.019]

10. 다음 표를 보면서 대화를 듣고, 두 사람이 선택한 비디오 스트리밍 상품을 고르시오.

Video Streaming Subscription Plans

		Number of Screens	Screen Quality	Monthly Fee
①	Basic	1 at once	SD (standard definition)	$10
②	Standard	2 at once	HD (high definition)	$14
③	Premium	3 at once	HD (high definition)	$15
④	VIP	3 at once	UHD (ultra-high definition)	$17
⑤	VVIP	4 at once	UHD (ultra-high definition)	$18

11. 대화를 듣고, 여자의 마지막 말에 대한 남자의 응답으로 가장 적절한 것을 고르시오.

① Hurry up, or you'll be late for school.
② Sure, why not? Let's go pick up your dad.
③ I'm sorry but the school bus has already left.
④ Okay. I'll drive you to school tomorrow morning.
⑤ Well, he's too busy working so he couldn't make it.

12. 대화를 듣고, 남자의 마지막 말에 대한 여자의 응답으로 가장 적절한 것을 고르시오.

① Of course. This is the latest model.
② Really? Then, I need to get it fixed.
③ Don't worry. Here's a bandage for you.
④ Right. You should have been more careful.
⑤ Let me pay for the repair. It's all my fault.

13. 대화를 듣고, 남자의 마지막 말에 대한 여자의 응답으로 가장 적절한 것을 고르시오. [3점]

Woman: ______________________________

① Sorry. I don't know much about biology.
② I doubt I can come. Africa is too far away.
③ Exactly. That's an advantage of team teaching.
④ That's true. Some students prefer to study alone.
⑤ Not yet. I'm not ready to try the teaching model.

14. 대화를 듣고, 여자의 마지막 말에 대한 남자의 응답으로 가장 적절한 것을 고르시오. [3점]

Man: ______________________________

① Me, neither. I'm not into cooking videos.
② Okay. I'll keep uploading videos on my channel.
③ I'd rather not. It's too late to start a new project.
④ Thanks for your offer. I'm happy to work with you.
⑤ You've got a point. I'll try to reduce my screen time.

15. 다음 상황 설명을 듣고, Scott이 Jane에게 할 말로 가장 적절한 것을 고르시오.

Scott: ______________________________

① Being well prepared will help you overcome your fear.
② Come on. You can make up for the mistake next time.
③ It was an excellent presentation. I'm quite impressed.
④ Remember that a long speech can bore the audience.
⑤ You should take the psychology class this semester.

[16 ~ 17] 다음을 듣고, 물음에 답하시오.

16. 여자가 하는 말의 주제로 가장 적절한 것은?

① recycling household plastic items
② reducing microplastics in the house
③ extensive use of plastic in medicine
④ technologies to remove plastic waste
⑤ environmental impact of microplastics

17. 언급된 물건이 아닌 것은?

① carpets ② toys ③ toothpastes
④ air purifier ⑤ bottled water

[해설편 p.021]

Dictation 05

✪ 표기에는 듣기 어려운 발음이 포함되어 있습니다. 귀 기울여 듣고 받아쓰세요.

● 고3 2020학년도 3월

※ QR 코드를 스캔하시면 듣기 방송이 나옵니다. 듣기 방송을 들으며 다음 빈칸을 채우시오. ● 제한 시간 : 25분

01

다음을 듣고, 여자가 하는 말의 목적으로 가장 적절한 것을 고르시오.

W : Good morning, everybody. This is your principal Alexandra Hamilton. Our field trip last week was canceled __________ __________ __________ __________ __________ __________. Many students were disappointed and so was I. Since there will be many days with high levels of fine dust this spring, we should learn how to take care of ourselves. So, our school is holding __________ __________ __________ __________ __________ __________. Famous doctor and TV show host Dr. Linda Han will come and show you ✪ __________ __________ __________ __________ __________ __________ of fine dust in everyday life. It'll be held at 4 p.m., Wednesday. This lecture is open to all students and parents. Every attendee will be given free dust masks. __________ __________ __________ __________ __________ __________ __________!

02

대화를 듣고, 남자의 의견으로 가장 적절한 것을 고르시오.

M : Rebecca, I hear that you're planning a trip to France.

W : Yeah. I'm very excited. It's my first trip abroad.

M : That's exciting. Where in France are you going?

W : Paris. I'll visit many tourist spots there. I'm thinking of buying some clothes for the trip.

M : Well, __________ __________ __________, can I give you some advice?

W : Sure. What is it?

M : If you __________ __________ __________ __________ __________ there, you'll be an easy target for pickpockets.

W : Oh, I didn't know that. Then, what should I wear?

M : If I were you, ✪ __________ __________ __________ that the locals would not wear.

W : I see. What clothes would make me look like a tourist in Paris?

M : As far as I know, the locals __________ __________ __________ __________ __________ __________ __________ on the street.

W : Thanks. I'll keep that in mind.

03

대화를 듣고, 두 사람의 관계를 가장 잘 나타낸 것을 고르시오.

M : Hey, Kimmy. Do you have a minute? I have something to say about the stage.

W : Okay. I'm listening.

M : Last evening, I went on the stage and tried the dance moves myself.

W : Did everything go well?

M : Pretty well, but we need to change some things.

W : Just a second. Let me ✪ __________ __________ __________ __________ __________ __________. *[Pause]* Go ahead.

M : While I was doing the turns, I bumped into the bench. We need to move it.

W : Well, I was told to place it in the center of the stage.

M : True. But __________ __________ __________ __________ so that the dancers make bigger turns. That means we need more room.

W : I see. I'll push the bench to the back.

M : Thanks. And please fix the bench to the floor. I created a move where the dancers __________ __________ __________ __________.

W : All right. I'll fix it nice and tight.

04

대화를 듣고, 그림에서 대화의 내용과 일치하지 <u>않는</u> 것을 고르시오.

W : Mr. Thompson. Can we talk about the design for the Read Aloud Space?

M : Sure. Oh, is this a photo from another school?

W : Yes. I thought we could borrow some ideas.

M : I'm sure we can. I can see the sign "Read Aloud Space" on the wall.

W : __________ __________ __________ __________ __________ like that, too. And they put a big round hole in the wall.

M : It's brilliant. Kids would enjoy going through the hole.

W : What do you think about this penguin between the hole and the bookcases?

M : We should absolutely have something like that. Kids __________ __________ __________.

W : The airplane ✪ __________ __________ __________ __________ __________ looks pretty, doesn't it?

M : It looks lovely. Kids will like looking at it.

W : Yeah. And I see a table on the floor. Maybe it's for the teacher.

M : I guess so.

05

대화를 듣고, 여자가 할 일로 가장 적절한 것을 고르시오.

W : Sean, did you close your bedroom windows? The rain will start any minute.

M : Yes, Mom. I've already closed all the windows.

W : Good. A storm is coming. So, __________ __________ __________ __________. Are you going out tonight?

M : No. I was planning to go to the movies, but I'm staying home.

W : Good idea. What will you do?

M : Can I invite Eric to our house? I want to play video games with him.

W : Okay. __________ __________ __________ __________ __________ __________ for you two boys?

M : That'd be great. Eric loves your chicken stew.

W : All right. ✪ __________ __________ __________ __________ before it rains hard.

M : Do you want me to come with you?

W : No, that's okay. I'll grab a few things and be right back.

06

대화를 듣고, 여자가 지불할 금액을 고르시오. [3점]

M : Hi. Welcome to Korean Table. What would you like to order?
W : I'd like to ✪ __________ __________ __________ __________. What would you recommend?
M : What about the Korean BBQ Combo? It comes with *bulgogi*, rice and a soda.
W : Sounds good. How much is it?
M : It's $18. And if you pay an extra $2, you can size up.
W : I want two combos but I __________ __________ __________ __________ __________.
M : Sure. What do you want for your soda, Coke or lemonade?
W : Lemonade for both combos, please. Do you also have dumplings?
M : Yes. We have fried dumplings and steamed dumplings. Fried are $14 for a plate, and steamed are $12.
W : I'll have ✪ __________ __________ __________ __________. Here's my credit card.
M : Okay. Your take-out will be ready in ten minutes.

07

대화를 듣고, 남자가 금요일에 Poetry Night에 가지 않는 이유를 고르시오.

W : Hey, Neil. How's your new apartment?
M : It's fantastic. Thanks for helping me move in.
W : No problem. __________ __________ __________ __________ __________ __________ __________.
M : Of course. By the way, I can't go to Poetry Night this Friday.
W : Really? All the club members will be expecting you.
M : I know. But I need to take care of some other stuff.
W : What do you need to do?
M : ✪ __________ __________ __________ __________ __________ __________ __________ __________. I have to assemble it myself.
W : I see. But can't you assemble the bed on the weekend?
M : The thing is, I've been sleeping on the sofa for a week so __________ __________ __________. I really want to sleep in a bed.
W : Well, if you say so. See you later.

08

대화를 듣고, 도장 만들기 수업에 관해 언급되지 않은 것을 고르시오.

W : Hi, Rick. What are you doing tomorrow afternoon?
M : I'm ✪ __________ __________ __________ __________ for __________ __________ __________. You can come along if you want.
W : Sounds interesting. I'm in. Will the class be conducted in English?
M : The instructor will speak Korean, but there'll be an English translator.
W : Good. How much is the participation fee?
M : It's 10,000 won per person. You can __________ __________ __________ __________ after class.
W : That's reasonable. How long is the class?
M : It'll start at two and __________ __________ __________ __________. Let's have lunch together before the class.
W : Okay. Where's the class being held?
M : It's taking place at the City Art Center.
W : Wonderful. I'll meet you in front of the Art Center at 1 p.m.
M : Cool. See you there.

09

Campbell Challenge Program에 관한 다음 내용을 듣고, 일치하지 <u>않는</u> 것을 고르시오.

M : Hello, students of Campbell High School. I'm happy to introduce our new program — the Campbell Challenge Program. It'll provide opportunities for students to __________ __________ __________ __________ __________ __________ such as academics, sports, arts, and computers. __________ __________ __________, choose one or more Challenges every year and work on them throughout the year. The list of Challenges you can choose from __________ __________ __________ on our school website. The Challenges you choose can be changed one time during the year. Students who ✪ __________ __________ __________ of their selected Challenges will receive a certificate at the end of the year. You can sign up for the program online until March 23. Ask your teacher for more information.

10

다음 표를 보면서 대화를 듣고, 두 사람이 선택한 비디오 스트리밍 상품을 고르시오.

W : Kevin, have you heard of *The Two Suspects*? It's a really popular drama.
M : Yes, but I ✪ __________ __________ __________ __________ to watch it yet.
W : Me, neither. Why don't we subscribe to a video streaming service? We can share an ID.
M : Good idea. Let's find one online. *[Pause]* Here, we can choose from these five plans.
W : Since we'll be using one ID together, __________ __________ __________ __________ __________ should be two or more at once.
M : Of course. What about screen quality?
W : UHD is higher quality than HD. But is UHD available on your device?
M : No, it's not. What about yours?
W : __________ __________ __________ __________ __________. But I'm fine with HD.
M : Good. Then we'll go with HD. So we should choose between these two.
W : If we choose this one, it'll be easier to __________ __________ __________. Besides, it's cheaper.
M : Perfect. Let's subscribe to that one.

11
대화를 듣고, 여자의 마지막 말에 대한 남자의 응답으로 가장 적절한 것을 고르시오.

W : Grandpa! I didn't expect to see you here!
M : Hi, Molly. I came to pick you up. How was school?
W : Great, but where's Dad? I thought ✪ _________ _________ _________ _________ _________ today.

12
대화를 듣고, 남자의 마지막 말에 대한 여자의 응답으로 가장 적절한 것을 고르시오.

M : Jamie, the screen of your phone is cracked. You should get it fixed.
W : Well, the screen works just fine. I'll use it as is.
M : But you may ✪ _________ _________ _________ _________ _________ _________ _________.

13
대화를 듣고, 남자의 마지막 말에 대한 여자의 응답으로 가장 적절한 것을 고르시오. [3점]

M : Ms. Smith. How was the teacher training course about team teaching?
W : It was very helpful. Would you like to _________ _________ _________ _________ _________?
M : Sure. I've always wanted to try that. Do you have any topic in mind?
W : I'm planning to teach about the plants and animals in Africa in my biology class.
M : Okay. In my social studies class, students can learn about the economies of African countries.
W : Great. Afterwards we can give the students _________ _________ _________ _________ what they've learned.
M : It could be in the form of a team project or a discussion.
W : From that point on, we can lead the class together.
M : Good idea. If we're both in the classroom, students will be able to ✪ _________ _________ _________ _________ _________ _________ _________.

14
대화를 듣고, 여자의 마지막 말에 대한 남자의 응답으로 가장 적절한 것을 고르시오. [3점]

M : Kate, do you have a minute? I need your advice on something.
W : Okay. What is it?
M : I've recently started my online video channel.
W : That's cool. What's it about?
M : Mainly, it's about cooking. Since your video channel is so popular, I wanted to ask you how to attract more people to my channel.
W : Then _________ _________ _________ _________ _________.
M : So tell me. What can I do to make my channel popular?
W : First of all, _________ _________ _________ _________ _________ _________ _________. You don't really know which video will attract people.
M : I can do that. But I always feel disappointed when my videos _________ _________ _________ _________ _________ _________ _________.
W : Well, if you put up a lot of videos, there's a better chance that some of them ✪ _________ _________ _________ _________.

15
다음 상황 설명을 듣고, Scott이 Jane에게 할 말로 가장 적절한 것을 고르시오.

M : Scott and Jane are college sophomores. This semester Jane is taking a psychology class. The class ✪ _________ _________ _________ _________. The problem for Jane is that she is _________ _________ _________ _________ in front of other students. She finds it hard to breathe just thinking about it. Jane asks Scott for help. Scott thinks that her lack of confidence is the problem. In his opinion, the best way to gain confidence is to be _________ _________ _________ _________ _________. He wants to advise Jane to fully understand her topic and practice several times before the big day. In this situation, what would Scott most likely say to Jane?

16~17
다음을 듣고, 물음에 답하시오.

W : Tiny pieces of plastic, or microplastics, are everywhere. According to recent findings, the concentration of microplastics in the air is higher indoors than outdoors. Considering that we spend about 90 percent of our time indoors, this may _________ _________ _________ _________. Here are some tips on ✪ _________ _________ _________ _________ at your home. First, remove carpets, which trap plastic fibers and particles. Also, do not buy toys made of plastic. Rather, choose ✪ _________ _________ _________ _________ _________ instead. There are many daily products that contain microplastics such as cosmetic products and toothpastes. If the label on the product says PP, PE, or PET, that means there are microplastics in it. It's better to choose microplastic-free products. It's also a good idea to put an air purifier in your house. Certain models are _________ _________ _________ _________ _________. Scientists are still unsure what specific dangers microplastics may pose to our health. Even so, we can never be too careful about our health.

▶ 정답 : 해설편 023쪽

VOCA LIST 05

회차별 영단어 QR 코드 ※ QR 코드를 스캔 후 모바일로 단어장처럼 학습할 수 있습니다.

● 고3 2020학년도 3월

01

001 □ **fine dust** 미세 먼지
002 □ **alert** ⓝ 경계경보
003 □ **personal** ⓐ 개인의, 개인적인
004 □ **healthcare** ⓝ 건강관리, 보건
005 □ **minimize** ⓥ 최소화하다
006 □ **attendee** ⓝ 참석자

02

007 □ **speaking of** ~에 관해서 말한다면
008 □ **typical** ⓐ 전형적인, 대표적인
009 □ **pickpocket** ⓝ 소매치기
010 □ **outfit** ⓝ 옷, 복장
011 □ **local** ⓝ 주민, 현지인
012 □ **as far as I know** 내가 아는 바로는
013 □ **hiking jacket** 등산복
014 □ **keep in mind** ~을 명심하다

03

015 □ **pull out** ~을 꺼내다
016 □ **layout sheet** 배치도
017 □ **bump into** ~에 부딪치다
018 □ **room** ⓝ 공간
019 □ **tight** [ad] 단단히, 꽉

04

020 □ **read aloud** 소리 내어 읽다
021 □ **put up** (포스터 등을) 붙이다
022 □ **brilliant** ⓐ 훌륭한, 멋진
023 □ **absolutely** [ad] 정말로, 전적으로
024 □ **stuffed animal** 동물 (봉제) 인형
025 □ **ceiling** ⓝ 천장
026 □ **guess** ⓥ 추측하다

05

027 □ **(at) any minute** 당장에라도, 금방이라도
028 □ **go grocery shopping** 식료품을 사러 가다
029 □ **grab** ⓥ 잡아채다, 거머쥐다

06

030 □ **recommend** ⓥ 추천하다
031 □ **come with** ~이 딸려 있다
032 □ **extra** ⓐ 여분의, 추가의
033 □ **dumpling** ⓝ 만두
034 □ **steam** ⓥ (음식을) 찌다

07

035 □ **fantastic** ⓐ 환상적인, 멋진
036 □ **poetry** ⓝ (집합적으로) 시, 시가
037 □ **deliver** ⓥ 배달하다
038 □ **assemble** ⓥ 조립하다
039 □ **the thing is** 사실은, 문제는
040 □ **If you say so.** 하는 수 없지.

08

041 □ **hand-carved** ⓐ 손으로 조각한[새긴]
042 □ **stamp** ⓝ 도장, 우표
043 □ **come along** 함께 가다[오다]
044 □ **conduct** ⓥ (특정한 활동을) 하다
045 □ **instructor** ⓝ 강사, 지도자
046 □ **translator** ⓝ 통역사, 번역가
047 □ **participation** ⓝ 참가
048 □ **fee** ⓝ 요금, 수수료
049 □ **reasonable** ⓐ (가격이) 적정한, 너무 비싸지 않은
050 □ **take place** 개최되다, 일어나다

09

051 □ **take on** (일 등을) 맡다, (책임을) 지다
052 □ **academic** ⓝ 학문
053 □ **work on** ~에 노력을 들이다, ~에 착수하다
054 □ **certificate** ⓝ 수료증, 증명서, 증서
055 □ **sign up for** ~을 신청하다

10

056 □ **subscribe to** ~을 구독하다
057 □ **screen quality** 화질
058 □ **available** ⓐ 이용 가능한
059 □ **device** ⓝ 기기
060 □ **compatible with** ~와 호환되는
061 □ **split** ⓥ 나누다, 쪼개다
062 □ **besides** [ad] 게다가

11

063 □ **expect** ⓥ 기대하다, 예상하다
064 □ **pick up** ~를 (차에) 태우러 가다

12

065 □ **crack** ⓥ 갈라지게[금이 가게] 하다
066 □ **cut one's finger** ⓥ 손을 베이다
067 □ **sharp** ⓐ 날카로운
068 □ **edge** ⓝ 가장자리, 모서리
069 □ **repair** ⓝ 수리
070 □ **fault** ⓝ 잘못, 책임

13

071 □ **have in mind** ~을 염두에 두다
072 □ **biology** ⓝ 생물학
073 □ **economy** ⓝ 경제
074 □ **afterwards** [ad] 나중에, 그 뒤에
075 □ **combine** ⓥ 결합하다
076 □ **perspective** ⓝ 관점, 시각
077 □ **doubt** ⓥ 확신하지 못하다, 의심하다
078 □ **advantage** ⓝ 장점

14

079 □ **mainly** [ad] 주로, 대부분
080 □ **attract** ⓥ 마음을 끌다
081 □ **disappointed** ⓐ 실망한
082 □ **catch one's attention** ~의 관심을 끌다
083 □ **be into** ~에 관심이 많다
084 □ **You've got a point.** 네 말은 일리가 있어. 네 말이 맞아.
085 □ **screen time** (전자 기기) 화면 (사용) 시간

15

086 □ **sophomore** ⓝ 2학년생
087 □ **semester** ⓝ 학기, 임기
088 □ **individual** ⓐ 개인의
089 □ **lack** ⓝ 부족, 결핍
090 □ **confidence** ⓝ 자신감
091 □ **overcome** ⓥ 극복하다
092 □ **make up for** (실수 등을) 벌충[만회]하다, (손실 등을) 보상하다, 보전하다
093 □ **impressed** ⓐ 감명 깊은
094 □ **bore** ⓥ 지루하게 하다

16~17

095 □ **microplastic** ⓝ 미세 플라스틱
096 □ **recent** ⓐ 최근의
097 □ **concentration** ⓝ 집중, 농도
098 □ **considering** [prep] ~을 고려하면
099 □ **pose a risk** 해를 끼치다
100 □ **trap** ⓥ 끌어모으다, 모아 두다
101 □ **particle** ⓝ 입자, 조각
102 □ **toothpaste** ⓝ 치약
103 □ **air purifier** 공기청정기
104 □ **filter out** ~을 걸러 내다
105 □ **extensive** ⓐ 아주 넓은[많은], 대규모의

06회 ● 2024학년도 5월 학력평가 고3 영어 듣기

※ QR코드를 스캔하시면 듣기 방송을 청취하실 수 있습니다.

● 점수 표시가 없는 문항은 모두 2점 ● 문항수 17개 | 배점 37점 | 제한 시간 25분

1번부터 17번까지는 듣고 답하는 문제입니다. 1번부터 15번까지는 한 번만 들려주고, 16번부터 17번까지는 두 번 들려줍니다. 방송을 잘 듣고 답을 하시기 바랍니다.

1. 다음을 듣고, 남자가 하는 말의 목적으로 가장 적절한 것을 고르시오.

① 내년에 새로 개설되는 과목을 홍보하려고
② 영상 제작 시 유의해야 할 사항을 안내하려고
③ 교육 과정 박람회의 변경된 일정을 공지하려고
④ 학교 홍보 영상의 온라인 제출 방법을 설명하려고
⑤ 교육 과정 박람회를 위한 자원봉사자를 모집하려고

2. 대화를 듣고, 여자의 의견으로 가장 적절한 것을 고르시오.

① 서늘한 곳에 화장품을 보관해야 한다.
② 유효 기간 내 화장품을 사용해야 한다.
③ 화장품 구매 시 성분을 확인해야 한다.
④ 화장 도구를 정기적으로 세척해야 한다.
⑤ 자외선 차단제를 사계절 내내 발라야 한다.

3. 다음을 듣고, 남자가 하는 말의 요지로 가장 적절한 것을 고르시오.

① 어려운 일을 먼저 처리하면 생산성을 향상시킬 수 있다.
② 적절한 휴식은 업무 진행의 효율성을 증진시킬 수 있다.
③ 성공을 위해서는 과제를 완수하려는 태도가 필요하다.
④ 매일 실천하는 작은 일이 평생 지속되는 습관이 된다.
⑤ 할 일 목록 작성은 체계적인 일 처리에 도움이 된다.

4. 대화를 듣고, 그림에서 대화의 내용과 일치하지 않는 것을 고르시오.

5. 대화를 듣고, 여자가 할 일로 가장 적절한 것을 고르시오.

① 촬영 자세 검색하기 ② 문자 메시지 보내기
③ 조원들 분장시키기 ④ 의상 대여하기
⑤ 소품 주문하기

6. 대화를 듣고, 남자가 지불할 금액을 고르시오. [3점]

① $45 ② $50 ③ $55 ④ $60 ⑤ $65

7. 대화를 듣고, 여자가 프리 다이빙 체험을 할 수 없는 이유를 고르시오.

① 물을 무서워해서
② 가족여행을 가야 해서
③ 체육 보고서를 써야 해서
④ 체험권에 당첨되지 않아서
⑤ 야구 경기를 관람해야 해서

8. 대화를 듣고, Fusion of Code and Canvas 전시회에 관해 언급되지 않은 것을 고르시오.

① 작품 수 ② 장소 ③ 휴관일
④ 전시 기간 ⑤ 입장료

9. 2024 May Dog Festival에 관한 다음 내용을 듣고, 일치하지 않는 것을 고르시오.

① 2021년에 처음 개최되었다.
② 시청 앞 광장에서 열릴 것이다.
③ 놀이터 입장 시 주인이 반려견과 함께해야 한다.
④ 무료 셀프 사진 부스가 마련되어 있을 것이다.
⑤ 벼룩시장에서 수제 개 장난감을 구매할 수 없다.

10. 다음 표를 보면서 대화를 듣고, 남자가 주문할 마사지 도구를 고르시오.

Massage Tools

	Product	Price	Target-Use Body Part	Material	Free Gift
①	A	$8	Head	Metal	Pouch
②	B	$10	Face	Ceramic	Aroma oil
③	C	$12	Feet	Rubber	Pouch
④	D	$16	Back	Wood	Aroma oil
⑤	E	$22	Whole body	Plastic	Massage cream

11. 대화를 듣고, 여자의 마지막 말에 대한 남자의 응답으로 가장 적절한 것을 고르시오.

① No problem. You can leave it to me.
② Too late. The meeting is already over.
③ Of course. You can use free wi-fi in the room.
④ I'm sorry. We have no record of your reservation.
⑤ Not really. It takes two hours for us to get there.

12. 대화를 듣고, 남자의 마지막 말에 대한 여자의 응답으로 가장 적절한 것을 고르시오.

① Why not? The area is a popular tourist destination.
② Not yet. We haven't decided where to go on a trip.
③ My mistake. I'll change the tickets for the correct date.
④ That's okay. I can get to the train station by myself.
⑤ I apologize. All the tickets for today are sold out.

13. 대화를 듣고, 여자의 마지막 말에 대한 남자의 응답으로 가장 적절한 것을 고르시오. [3점]

Man: ______________________________

① I agree. I have to make a complaint.
② You're right. Let's learn to ride a bicycle.
③ That's true. I'm still waiting for it to be found.
④ Good idea. I'll give it a shot and see if it helps.
⑤ Absolutely. That's why you should bike to work.

14. 대화를 듣고, 남자의 마지막 말에 대한 여자의 응답으로 가장 적절한 것을 고르시오.

Woman: ______________________________

① Awesome. Let's go to the shop and get a hanbok.
② Look at me. It seems hanbok really suits me well.
③ One moment. Let's find out how to download a travel app.
④ No worries. I'll look for ways to get a discount for the class.
⑤ Right. This is the clothing the royal family wore in the past.

15. 다음 상황 설명을 듣고, Ms. Kim이 Taylor에게 할 말로 가장 적절한 것을 고르시오. [3점]

Ms. Kim: ______________________________

① You need to keep your audience focused during a show.
② You'd better practice harder to be on the school stage.
③ You should apply for an audition on a TV talent show.
④ Why don't you memorize the song for the audition?
⑤ How about singing in the upcoming school festival?

[16 ~ 17] 다음을 듣고, 물음에 답하시오.

16. 여자가 하는 말의 주제로 가장 적절한 것은?

① impacts of cultural traits on conflict situations
② traits that attract readers in heroic characters
③ strategies for teaching character traits in literature
④ reasons why personality traits matter in writing an epic
⑤ changes to traits that have defined heroes through history

17. 언급된 특성이 <u>아닌</u> 것은?

① courage ② strength ③ leadership
④ intelligence ⑤ selflessness

[해설편 p.026]

※ QR 코드를 스캔하시면 듣기 방송이 나옵니다. 듣기 방송을 들으며 다음 빈칸을 채우시오. ● 제한 시간 : 25분

01

다음을 듣고, 남자가 하는 말의 목적으로 가장 적절한 것을 고르시오.

[Chime bell rings.]

M : Hello, third graders. This is your school career counselor, Michael Cliff. As you know, the School Curriculum Expo ✪ _______ ____ _______ next month and many freshmen are excited to learn about the school curriculum and various subjects. So, we're ✪ ____________ _____ ________________ for the expo. Since third graders have already studied many subjects, I believe you can support the freshmen as mentors. Volunteers will create videos about different subjects, and these videos will be shown in the school lobby during the expo. This will _______ _____ ______________ ___________ the subjects that are right for them. If you're interested, please visit the school website and apply for a volunteer position by this Friday. Thank you.

02

대화를 듣고, 여자의 의견으로 가장 적절한 것을 고르시오.

W : Honey, what are you doing?

M : I'm looking for the sunscreen before I go hiking.

W : Oh, here it is. *[Pause]* Wait, you'd better not use this.

M : What's the matter?

W : The sunscreen is expired. I bought it __ _________ ______. Cosmetics should be used before the expiration date.

M : Why is that? They're not even food.

W : It's not safe to keep using them after ✪ _____ _______ ____ _____ _______. Bacteria can grow over time.

M : Oh, that could cause problems, I suppose.

W : Exactly. It increases the risk of developing skin problems. Plus, when it comes to sunscreen, expired ones might not protect your skin.

M : I guess I should check on my cosmetic products.

W : Absolutely. It's important to use cosmetics ✪ __________ _______ ______________ ________ to maintain their freshness and effectiveness.

M : Thanks for letting me know. I'll be more mindful of that now.

03

다음을 듣고, 남자가 하는 말의 요지로 가장 적절한 것을 고르시오.

M : Good afternoon, listeners! This is *Brian's Daily Management Tips.* Many people these days ✪ ______ ____________________ ____ their to-do lists. They have many things to do every day and struggle with making progress. If that's your case, doing _____ ________ ____________ _______ first can help you improve productivity. Have you ever heard of the saying "✪ _____ _____ _______ _______"? It means starting with the hardest task. Once that's out of the way, the rest of your work will feel like a piece of cake. Are you interested in boosting your productivity? Dealing with the most challenging task first is a simple but powerful tool to help you get there. We'll catch up with you after this short break!

04

대화를 듣고, 그림에서 대화의 내용과 일치하지 않는 것을 고르시오.

M : Kate, I ✪ _______ __ ___________ of the school library. My art club is drawing a wall painting there.

W : Let me have a look. *[Pause]* That's awesome. There's a book tree on the wall.

M : All the club members worked together on it. Do you see the ____________________ _______ _________ the door? I designed it.

W : Superb! I love the slogan on the sign. Oh, I also like the flower-patterned rug.

M : I like it, too. It fits the setting well.

W : Will the brush under the ladder be used to color the background?

M : Yes. When the painting is complete, it'll come to life even more.

W : Absolutely! And those two light bulbs above the clock ✪ ______ ___ _____ ________________.

M : Right. I hope you're looking forward to seeing the finished painting.

05

대화를 듣고, 여자가 할 일로 가장 적절한 것을 고르시오.

M : Molly, can you believe it's time for our graduation photo shoot? It's coming next week.

W : I know. Shall we check if everything's ready?

M : Sure. Did you ✪ ___________ _____ ______________?

W : Yes, I already did.

M : Well done! I've searched for a few group poses to match those costumes.

W : Cool. Did you remind our team members to ✪ ________ ________ _________________ _________ to pose with?

M : Oh, I was supposed to send a text message to them. I completely forgot.

W : Don't worry. I'll do it. The items will help us recall our high school life.

M : Right. What do you think of the ____________ ________ _______ from the photos John sent?

W : I like it! It's __ ___________ _________ for our team's concept.

M : I agree. I think we're all set now.

06

대화를 듣고, 남자가 지불할 금액을 고르시오. [3점]

W : Welcome to Darcy's Drug Store. How may I help you today?

M : Hello. I'm looking for a health supplement. I'm feeling a bit low on energy lately.

W : I see. How about a multivitamin? It contains a ✪ ____________ ___ ________ ________ in one pill.

M : That sounds convenient. How much does it cost?

W : It's $15 per bottle.

M : Then I'll take one bottle.

W : Okay. Anything else?

M : I heard probiotics help ✪ ________ ___ ________ ______. Do you have any?

W : Sure. I recommend this one. It's $25 per bottle.

M : Perfect. I'll take two bottles.

W : So, one multivitamin and two probiotics, correct?

M : That's right. Will you check if I have a coupon? Here's my loyalty card.

W : Let me check. *[Beep sound]* You have a $5 ________ ________ for the total purchase. Do you want to use it?

M : Yes, please. And I'll pay in cash.

07

대화를 듣고, 여자가 프리 다이빙 체험을 할 수 없는 이유를 고르시오.

M : Stella, have you heard about the new free-diving center in town?

W : Yeah, I went there for a P.E. report. Their training programs were really impressive.

M : You did! And you won't believe this. I got two one-day ✪ ________ ________ ______!

W : Congratulations! That's exciting news!

M : Thanks. It's next Saturday, and I can bring a friend. Would you like to join me?

W : I'd love to, but I don't think _ ____ ______ __.

M : Why not? Are you afraid of water or something?

W : Not at all. I'm practically a seal.

M : Oh, then are you going to go watch the Baseball All-Star Game?

W : Yes, but that's next Sunday.

M : So, can you tell me why?

W : I'm ✪ ________ ________ that day to celebrate my parents' wedding anniversary.

M : How nice! Then, I'll find another friend to come with me.

08

대화를 듣고, Fusion of Code and Canvas 전시회에 관해 언급되지 않은 것을 고르시오.

M : Lily, what are you up to?

W : Hi, Dad. I'm looking at art created by artificial intelligence! Isn't it amazing?

M : Fascinating. You know what? The AI art exhibition, Fusion of Code and Canvas, will open soon.

W : Are the ✪ ______ ________ ____________?

M : Exactly. They'll showcase 14 works.

W : Interesting. So, is the exhibition held online?

M : No, it's at the Quantum Art Museum.

W : Oh, I've been there before. The ____________ ___ ____ ________ is really impressive. When will the exhibition start?

M : The website says it starts on May 10th and runs for a month.

W : It would be great to visit this weekend.

M : Let's do that. There will be not just paintings but also photographs and media arts.

W : That's really something! How much is ✪ ___ ____________ ____?

M : It's free. But, the earnings from the gift shop will be donated to charity.

W : Wow, AI is making a donation!

09

2024 May Dog Festival에 관한 다음 내용을 듣고, 일치하지 않는 것을 고르시오.

W : Hello, dog lovers! This is Lisa from Pet Pals Podcast. If you're wondering where to go with your dogs on Merry Dog Day, how about going to the 2024 May Dog Festival? It was first held in 2021 and continues to be loved by many dog lovers. Starting on May 17th, it'll ✪ ________ ___ ____ ______. It'll take place at the square in front of City Hall. A dog playground will be divided into two areas for small and large dogs to ensure safe play. When entering the playground, ________ ______ ____ ______ their dogs. Also, to capture memorable moments with your companion animal, there will be a free self-service photo booth. But that's not all. You can ✪ ________ ________ ____ ______ at the flea market. Come and make lasting memories with your furry friends!

10

다음 표를 보면서 대화를 듣고, 남자가 주문할 마사지 도구를 고르시오.

W : Shawn, what are you looking at on your phone?

M : Hi, Chloe. I'm ✪ ________ __ ________ ______ for my mom. Can you help me choose a good one?

W : My pleasure. So, are these the top five best sellers?

M : Yes. But I can't afford more than $20 because I'm on a tight budget.

W : All right. Options ____ __________ ______.
Have you considered where your mom would want a massage?

M : Hmm, I think any product except the one for the face would be fine. She already has one.

W : Okay. Does she have ✪ ____ ____________ ____ ________?

M : I don't believe she likes the cold feeling of metal.

W : That's not the right choice, then. Now, there are two options left.

M : Oh, they come with a free gift. I think she'd prefer an aroma oil. I'll go with that one.

W : Great choice.

M : Thanks for helping me. I'll order it now.

11
대화를 듣고, 여자의 마지막 말에 대한 남자의 응답으로 가장 적절한 것을 고르시오.

W : Mr. Cooper, you said you ✪ ___________ _____ ___________ ________ only for two hours. Now our time is almost up.
M : Oh, we still have some ___________ ___ ___________. I think we have to extend the time.
W : Agreed. Since you made the reservation, could you _______ _______ ___ ______ for us?

12
대화를 듣고, 남자의 마지막 말에 대한 여자의 응답으로 가장 적절한 것을 고르시오.

M : Honey, our trip ___ ___________ _______. Did you buy our train tickets?
W : Yes, I did. Here are _____ __________ __________. Paris, Saturday the 11th, right?
M : Oh! The ✪ ______________ ___ ___________, but they're for the wrong Saturday!

13
대화를 듣고, 여자의 마지막 말에 대한 남자의 응답으로 가장 적절한 것을 고르시오. [3점]

W : Ben, I heard you finally __________ _______ __________ ___________. Congratulations!
M : Thanks, Amy. But I haven't received the bicycle yet.
W : How come? Are there any issues?
M : Yes, there's an issue with ✪ _____ ____________________ ___________. It's going to take a few more weeks.
W : I'm sorry to hear that. You must be pretty frustrated.
M : Yeah, it's disappointing. I'm trying to stay patient, but it's not easy.
W : How about searching for some bicycle routes?
M : What do you mean?
W : I mean you may turn this lemon of ✪ __ ____________ ______ _____________. You can find fantastic roads for cycling before the bicycle arrives.
M : I hadn't thought of that, but I like the idea of turning this situation around.
W : You could even create your own bicycle tour by using a route planner. I'm sure it'll be worth the wait.

14
대화를 듣고, 남자의 마지막 말에 대한 여자의 응답으로 가장 적절한 것을 고르시오.

M : Claire, we've finally arrived.
W : It's my first time visiting a Korean royal palace. I'm really excited!
M : Me, too. My friends in Korean class highly recommended this place. It has a lot of positive reviews on the _________ ______ ___ _______.
W : Great. Let's quickly buy the tickets and go inside.
M : Wait! Normally, ✪ _____ ____________ _____ is $2, but if you wear a hanbok, it's free.
W : Hanbok? What's that?
M : Look at the clothes those people are wearing. It's ✪ _____ ____________ ____________ ____________.
W : It's so beautiful. I want to wear it, too. Can we try it on?
M : I think so. I saw some hanbok rental shops on the app.
W : Really? Let's pick one with good reviews and head for the store right now.
M : Hmm... How about this one? It has high ratings and it's just a short walk from here.

15
다음 상황 설명을 듣고, Ms. Kim이 Taylor에게 할 말로 가장 적절한 것을 고르시오. [3점]

M : Taylor is a high school student who wants to become a singer. He spends a lot of time practicing to ✪ _________ _____ ____ ____________ on a TV talent show. However, whenever he thinks about being on stage, he still feels anxious. He asks his music teacher Ms. Kim for advice because she has a lot of stage experience. Ms. Kim believes Taylor is talented and can ✪ ______________ _____ ________ _________ by singing in front of a smaller and more familiar audience. So Ms. Kim wants to suggest to Taylor that he give a performance in the __________ __________ _______ _________. In this situation, what would Ms. Kim most likely say to Taylor?

16~17
다음을 듣고, 물음에 답하시오.

W : Hello, future writers. In our last session, we learned about ____________ _______ __________, from mythology to modern stories. Today, we're going to __________ _____ ________ ________ that make such characters so attractive to readers of literature. First, one of the primary traits is courage. These heroes ✪ ______________ _______ _______________ and their courage inspires others to overcome their own difficulties. You can see it in Harry Potter. Second, strength is an essential trait. Take Beowulf as an example. He has the unbelievable strength of thirty men in his arm alone. Next, let's take a look at the intelligence trait. Epic heroes ✪ ____________ _________ _____________ and solve mysteries. Sherlock Holmes, for example, is a genius detective with extraordinary intelligence. Lastly, selflessness is a key trait. Heroes often sacrifice their well-being for the greater good. This is evident in Prometheus, who stole fire for humans and was punished. This selflessness makes readers love him. All of these traits make heroic characters stand out and turn them into captivating figures. Now, let's create your hero and craft a story.

▶ 정답 : 해설편 028쪽

VOCA LIST 06

회차별 영단어 QR 코드 ※ QR 코드를 스캔 후 모바일로 단어장처럼 학습할 수 있습니다.

● 고3 2024학년도 5월

01

001 □ career counselor 진로 상담사
002 □ Curriculum Expo 교육과정 박람회
003 □ freshmen ⓝ 신입생
004 □ subject ⓝ 학과, 과목
005 □ volunteer ⓝ 자원봉사자
006 □ support ⓥ 지원하다
007 □ mentor ⓝ 멘토
008 □ lobby ⓝ 로비, 현관
009 □ different ⓐ 다른
010 □ interested ⓐ (…에) 흥미를 가진, 관심이 있는
011 □ apply ⓥ 신청하다, 지원하다
012 □ position ⓝ 직책, 자리

02

013 □ expiration date 유효 기간
014 □ bacteria ⓝ 박테리아, 세균
015 □ develop ⓥ 생기다
016 □ protect ⓥ 보호하다
017 □ effectiveness ⓝ 효과
018 □ mindful ⓐ 주의 깊은, 신경 쓰는
019 □ cosmetic products 화장품
020 □ sunscreen ⓝ 자외선 차단제
021 □ hiking ⓝ 하이킹, 등산
022 □ freshness ⓝ 신선함

03

023 □ overwhelmed ⓐ 압도된
024 □ to-do list 할 일 목록
025 □ productivity ⓝ 생산성
026 □ eat the frog first 가장 어려운 일을 먼저 하다 (비유적 표현)
027 □ a piece of cake 식은 죽 먹기 (아주 쉬운 일)
028 □ boost ⓥ 증가시키다, 향상시키다
029 □ challenging ⓐ 도전적인
030 □ manage ⓥ 관리하다
031 □ efficiently ad 효율적으로
032 □ forget ⓥ 잊다
033 □ start ⓥ 시작하다

04

034 □ wall painting 벽화
035 □ slogan ⓝ 슬로건, 구호
036 □ patterned ⓐ 무늬가 있는
037 □ fit the setting 환경에 잘 어울리다
038 □ come to life 생기를 띠다
039 □ atmosphere ⓝ 분위기
040 □ looking forward to ~을 기대하다

05

041 □ graduation photo shoot 졸업 사진 촬영
042 □ costume ⓝ 의상
043 □ group poses 그룹 포즈
044 □ memorable items 기억에 남는 물건
045 □ recall ⓥ 기억하다
046 □ makeup style ⓝ 메이크업 스타일
047 □ concept ⓝ 개념
048 □ text message 문자 메시지
049 □ remind ⓥ 상기시키다
050 □ all set 모든 준비가 완료된

06

051 □ loyalty card 적립 카드
052 □ discount ⓝ 할인
053 □ total purchase 총 구매 액
054 □ cash ⓝ 현금
055 □ check ⓥ 확인하다
056 □ pay ⓥ 지불하다

07

057 □ report ⓝ 보고서
058 □ training ⓝ 훈련
059 □ impressive ⓐ 인상적인
060 □ experience ⓝ 체험, 경험
061 □ exciting ⓐ 신나는
062 □ join ⓥ 참여하다
063 □ be afraid of ~을 무서워하다
064 □ practically ad 사실상
065 □ seal ⓝ 물개
066 □ celebrate ⓥ 축하하다

08

067 □ create ⓥ 창작하다
068 □ artificial ⓐ 인공적인
069 □ exhibition ⓝ 전시회
070 □ intelligence ⓝ 지능
071 □ hold ⓥ 개최하다
072 □ impressive ⓐ 인상적인
073 □ photograph ⓝ 사진
074 □ admission fee ⓝ 입장료
075 □ earning ⓝ 수익
076 □ donation 기부

09

077 □ wonder ⓥ 고민하다
078 □ continue ⓥ 계속되다
079 □ run ⓥ 운영하다
080 □ take place 개최되다
081 □ divide into ~로 나뉘다
082 □ area ⓝ 영역
083 □ owner ⓝ 주인
084 □ capture ⓥ 잡다
085 □ memorable ⓐ 기억할 만한
086 □ companion ⓝ 동료
087 □ purchase ⓥ 구매하다

10

088 □ tool ⓝ 도구
089 □ afford ⓥ 여유가 되다
090 □ option ⓝ 옵션, 선택권
091 □ narrow down 좁혀 내려가다
092 □ consider ⓥ 생각하다
093 □ except ⓥ 기대하다
094 □ preference ⓝ 선호
095 □ material ⓝ 재료
096 □ choice ⓝ 선택
097 □ order ⓥ 주문하다

11

098 □ book ⓥ 예약하다
099 □ meeting room 회의실
100 □ time is up 시간이 다 되다
101 □ extend ⓥ 연장하다
102 □ reservation ⓝ 예약
103 □ take care sth ~을 처리하다

12

104 □ ticket ⓝ 표
105 □ mobile ⓝ 휴대폰
106 □ destination ⓝ 목적지
107 □ wrong ⓐ 잘못된

13

108 □ receive ⓥ 받다
109 □ issue ⓝ 문제
110 □ manufacture ⓥ 제조하다
111 □ process ⓝ 과정
112 □ frustrated ⓐ 실망한
113 □ search ⓥ 찾다
114 □ turn the lemon into lemonade 위기를 기회로 바꾸다
115 □ worth ⓝ 가치

14

116 □ arrive ⓥ 도착하다
117 □ visit ⓥ 방문하다
118 □ royal ⓐ 왕족
119 □ palace ⓝ 궁전
120 □ recommend ⓥ 추천하다
121 □ entrance ⓝ 입장
122 □ traditional ⓐ 전통적인
123 □ try on 입어 보다
124 □ rating ⓝ 평가, 별점

15

125 □ spend ⓥ 소비하다
126 □ practice ⓥ 연습하다
127 □ apply ⓥ 지원하다
128 □ audition ⓝ 오디션
129 □ whenever conj 언제든
130 □ experience ⓝ 경험
131 □ believe ⓥ 믿다
132 □ audience ⓝ 관중
133 □ suggest ⓥ 제안하다
134 □ situation ⓝ 상황
135 □ likely to ~할 확률이 높다

16~17

136 □ epic hero 서사적 영웅
137 □ mythology ⓝ 신화
138 □ trait ⓝ 특성
139 □ courage ⓝ 용기
140 □ inspire ⓥ 영감을 주다
141 □ strength ⓝ 힘
142 □ unbelievable ⓐ 믿기 어려운
143 □ navigate ⓥ 헤쳐 나가다
144 □ tricky ⓐ 까다로운
145 □ extraordinary ⓐ 비범한
146 □ selflessness ⓝ 이타심
147 □ sacrifice ⓥ 희생하다
148 □ greater good ⓝ 더 큰 선

07회 • 2023학년도 4월 학력평가 고3 영어 듣기

※ QR코드를 스캔하시면 듣기 방송을 청취하실 수 있습니다.

● 점수 표시가 없는 문항은 모두 2점 ● 문항수 17개 | 배점 37점 | 제한 시간 25분

1번부터 17번까지는 듣고 답하는 문제입니다. 1번부터 15번까지는 한 번만 들려주고, 16번부터 17번까지는 두 번 들려줍니다. 방송을 잘 듣고 답을 하시기 바랍니다.

MP3

1. 다음을 듣고, 여자가 하는 말의 목적으로 가장 적절한 것을 고르시오.

① 행사에 참여하는 회사 명단을 공개하려고
② 참가자에게 박람회 장소 변경을 공지하려고
③ 자기소개서 작성 시 유의 사항을 전달하려고
④ 신입 사원 채용을 위한 면접 절차를 설명하려고
⑤ 취업 박람회에 가지고 가야 할 것을 안내하려고

2. 대화를 듣고, 남자의 의견으로 가장 적절한 것을 고르시오.

① 자원 낭비를 줄이기 위해 옷을 재활용해야 한다.
② 옷장 정리 시 잘 입지 않는 옷을 처분해야 한다.
③ 유행을 덜 타는 디자인의 옷을 구매해야 한다.
④ 자주 입는 옷을 옷장 문 쪽에 배치해야 한다.
⑤ 비슷한 색깔끼리 옷을 정리해야 한다.

3. 대화를 듣고, 두 사람의 관계를 가장 잘 나타낸 것을 고르시오.

① 건축가 - 의뢰인 ② 집주인 - 사진사
③ 임대인 - 세입자 ④ 기자 - 잡지사 편집장
⑤ 고객 - 이삿짐센터 직원

4. 대화를 듣고, 그림에서 대화의 내용과 일치하지 <u>않는</u> 것을 고르시오.

5. 대화를 듣고, 여자가 할 일로 가장 적절한 것을 고르시오.

① 방송 부탁하기 ② 간식 주문하기
③ 포스터 게시하기 ④ 지원서 출력하기
⑤ QR 코드 제작하기

6. 대화를 듣고, 여자가 지불할 금액을 고르시오. [3점]

① $30 ② $36 ③ $40 ④ $45 ⑤ $50

7. 대화를 듣고, 남자가 반려동물 박람회에 갈 수 <u>없는</u> 이유를 고르시오.

① 가족 여행을 떠나야 해서
② 반려동물을 입양해야 해서
③ 액세서리를 사러 가야 해서
④ 과학 프로젝트에 참여해야 해서
⑤ 반려견에게 예방 접종을 해야 해서

8. 대화를 듣고, International Game Conference에 관해 언급되지 <u>않은</u> 것을 고르시오.

① 기간 ② 장소 ③ 강의 주제
④ 티켓 가격 ⑤ 기념품

9. Superhero Museum에 관한 다음 내용을 듣고, 일치하지 <u>않는</u> 것을 고르시오.

① 7만 권이 넘는 만화책을 보유하고 있다.
② 시립 도서관 옆에 위치하고 있다.
③ 슈퍼히어로 의상을 대여해 준다.
④ 취학 연령 미만의 아동에게 무료 입장권을 준다.
⑤ 생일에 방문한 고객에게 음료 쿠폰을 제공한다.

[해설편 p.028]

10. 다음 표를 보면서 대화를 듣고, 두 사람이 주문할 손 세정제를 고르시오.

Hand Soap

	Product	Price	Form	Fragrance	Tested on Animals
①	A	$4	bar	lemon	×
②	B	$7	bar	lavender	○
③	C	$10	bar	vanilla	×
④	D	$15	liquid	rosemary	○
⑤	E	$22	liquid	tea tree	×

11. 대화를 듣고, 여자의 마지막 말에 대한 남자의 응답으로 가장 적절한 것을 고르시오.

① The soccer match is going to start in 30 minutes.
② I'm disappointed that all the chicken was sold out.
③ No matter how much we hurry, it'll take about an hour.
④ Seating is available on a first come, first served basis.
⑤ Your order was cancelled due to a delivery problem.

12. 대화를 듣고, 남자의 마지막 말에 대한 여자의 응답으로 가장 적절한 것을 고르시오.

① No problem. I can do that for you.
② Sorry. I'm not able to give you a ride.
③ Definitely. He's already arrived there.
④ Sure. You can take him to the ice rink.
⑤ Cheer up. Your presentation will be great.

13. 대화를 듣고, 여자의 마지막 말에 대한 남자의 응답으로 가장 적절한 것을 고르시오. [3점]

Man: ______________________________

① All right. Then I'll wait for him to return.
② Stay calm. I know where he might be now.
③ Believe me. He'll come back before the deadline.
④ Never mind. He's already registered for the class.
⑤ No worries. The results of the consultation were fine.

14. 대화를 듣고, 남자의 마지막 말에 대한 여자의 응답으로 가장 적절한 것을 고르시오.

Woman: ______________________________

① I'm sorry. I'm tired of having music practice every day.
② Okay. I'll try to find something new to challenge myself.
③ Absolutely. You'll be good at playing the ukulele one day.
④ You're right. I'd better stay away from relationship stress.
⑤ I agree. You should put more effort into the work you're doing.

15. 다음 상황 설명을 듣고, Emma가 Tom에게 할 말로 가장 적절한 것을 고르시오. [3점]

Emma: ______________________________

① Could you check whether I got double charged?
② Can I get a discount coupon via message again?
③ Would it be okay for me to use your cell phone?
④ Did you insert your credit card to the card reader?
⑤ Is it possible to get a refund through a bank transfer?

[16 ~ 17] 다음을 듣고, 물음에 답하시오.

16. 여자가 하는 말의 주제로 가장 적절한 것은?

① practical methods of conflict management
② socially acceptable ways to express anger
③ various behaviors to trigger social conflict
④ communicative skills for customer satisfaction
⑤ situations causing conflict between generations

17. 언급된 전략이 <u>아닌</u> 것은?

① accommodating ② compromising ③ competing
④ assessing ⑤ avoiding

[해설편 p.030]

※ QR 코드를 스캔하시면 듣기 방송이 나옵니다. 듣기 방송을 들으며 다음 빈칸을 채우시오. ● 제한 시간 : 25분

01

다음을 듣고, 여자가 하는 말의 목적으로 가장 적절한 것을 고르시오.

W : Hello, students. I'm Olivia Watson, manager of the Yellowhill College Student Job Fair. This event is a great opportunity because more than 50 companies will visit in search of new qualified employees. For participants to be fully prepared, I'd like to tell you ________ ________ ______ ___________ ________. First, you must show your student ID card since it'll be used as the entrance ticket. Second, ✪ ________ _______ __________. Most interviewers will require it to get a deeper understanding of your experiences and skills. Finally, if you have ✪ ______ ____________ ____ __________ ________, please print a few copies to share with companies. Don't forget to bring the items that I mentioned and you'll have a better chance at success. Thank you.

02

대화를 듣고, 남자의 의견으로 가장 적절한 것을 고르시오.

M : What are you doing, Jessie?
W : I'm cleaning out my closet. It's too small to hold all my clothes.
M : Well, the closet looks big enough. Did you ______ _______ _____ __________?
W : Not yet. I'm trying to arrange all of them by color now.
M : Oh, dear. You need to get rid of clothes you don't really wear.
W : But when it comes to fashion, _________ ________ ______ ____, and often come back again. I can wear them later.
M : Well, nobody knows when a trend might come back.
W : I guess that makes sense.
M : And the colors will fade if you keep them for too long.
W : You're right. I have lots of old clothes whose colors are already gone.
M : You see? When arranging your closet, you should ✪ __________ ___ __________ ______ ________ __________ _______.
W : Okay. I think that's good advice.

03

대화를 듣고, 두 사람의 관계를 가장 잘 나타낸 것을 고르시오.

[Door bell rings.]
W : You must be Mr. Cooper. Nice to meet you. Come on in.
M : Hello, Ms. Wood. You have a really beautiful home.
W : Thank you. Let me show you around.
M : Okay. *[Pause]* Wow, I can see ________ _______ ________ _______ ________________ for house of the month. Such elegant modern style!
W : I'm glad to hear that. My husband and I _____ ______ ___ ________ ______ ______________. Where do you want to start shooting?
M : I'd like to take pictures in the living room, and then move to the bedroom and bathroom.
W : Sounds good.
M : As you know, ✪ _____ ___________ _________ _________ ______ ____ _______________ in *Family Home Magazine*.
W : Yes, in next month's issue, right?
M : Well, actually I'm not sure, but if you ask the editor, you'll get an answer.
W : I see. In case you need help, please give me a shout.
M : All right. I'll let you know when everything's done.

04

대화를 듣고, 그림에서 대화의 내용과 일치하지 않는 것을 고르시오.

M : Hi, Alice. Did you move to your new art studio?
W : Yes, I did. Here's the picture of it. Take a look.
M : Okay. You ✪ _____ ____ ________ _______ _____ ____________.
W : Yeah. I usually paint as I look out the window. And I put ______ ________ ____________ ___ _____ __________.
M : That'll make it easy to take them out and use them. And I like the sculpture of a head on the table. It adds to the atmosphere.
W : Thanks. Look at the heart-shaped vase on the shelf. It was a gift from my family to __________________ _____ ____ _____ _______ ________.
M : They're so thoughtful. Did you paint the picture hanging on the wall?
W : Yes, I did.
M : Wow. You're so talented. Show me later what else you're working on.
W : Of course.

05

대화를 듣고, 여자가 할 일로 가장 적절한 것을 고르시오.

W : Oscar, the club recruitment period begins soon. Let's check how well we've prepared so far.
M : Good idea. Did you ask Mr. Kim to inform students about ✪ _____ _______ _________________?
W : Of course. He'll broadcast the information to the students.
M : Good. By the way, how's it going with ____________ ______ ______ __________?
W : I finished it this morning. Do you want to take a look at it?
M : Sure. *[Pause]* It's wonderful! I like the QR code in the corner.
W : Thanks. Students can scan this QR code and complete the application form online.
M : Awesome. That way we don't need to print out application forms.
W : Yeah. Did you order snacks for the applicants?
M : Oh, I forgot. I'll do that right away.
W : Great. Then I'll _____ ____ _____ ___________ in the main hallway.

Dictation 07

06

대화를 듣고, 여자가 지불할 금액을 고르시오. [3점]

M : Stacey, we need to ________ __ ____________ ________ for band rehearsal.

W : Okay. Let's make a reservation online. *[Typing sound]* This rehearsal studio looks good.

M : I think so, too. The studio has two kinds of rooms. The standard room costs $15 per hour and the expert room costs $20 per hour.

W : They say that only one keyboard comes with the standard room. We'll definitely need the other room.

M : You're right. ✪ ________ ________ _____ ________ ________ _____ _____ ________.

W : Good. Do they provide a recording service?

M : Of course, they do. It costs $5 per song.

W : That's a reasonable price. Let's record two songs.

M : Sounds good. Then we'll rent the expert room for two hours and use the recording service for two songs, right?

W : Yes. Look. They provide a 10% discount to students.

M : Oh, __ ____________ ________ ___ ___. It's only for teenagers.

W : All right. I'll pay with my credit card.

07

대화를 듣고, 남자가 반려동물 박람회에 갈 수 없는 이유를 고르시오.

W : Hi, Leon. I haven't seen you since you went on your family trip.

M : Hi, Emilia. We just got back yesterday. What a lovely dog! Is this Lucy?

W : Yes. She's a bit shy.

M : Oh. *[Pause]* Is she wearing a ribbon around her neck? It's so cute. I'd like to ✪ ______ ______ __________ ________ ____________ like Lucy's.

W : So, you have a puppy, too?

M : Yes. __ ____________ ____________ ______. He's really adorable.

W : Good for you. Then why don't we go to the Pet Expo together? It'll be held downtown this Saturday.

M : This Saturday? I'm sorry but I can't.

W : Are you still working on your science project?

M : No. I've already done it.

W : Then why can't you come?

M : Actually, I'm going to ✪ ____________ ______ ______ on that day.

W : Okay. Nothing is more important than good health. Maybe next time.

08

대화를 듣고, International Game Conference에 관해 언급되지 않은 것을 고르시오.

[Cell phone rings.]

M : Hermia, what's up?

W : Miles, did you hear that? The International Game Conference is going to take place soon.

M : Oh, we've been waiting for so long! When is it held?

W : It starts on May 4th, and lasts for 3 days. Do you want to join me?

M : ______ ______ __________ ______? I'm already all set. Is it held at the same place as last year?

W : Yes. It's at the Central Convention Center.

M : Good. It's definitely within walking distance. Could you ______ ______ ______ ___ ______ __________?

W : Okay. *[Pause]* Check it out.

M : Wow. The speakers are all well known in the game industry. Did you see the topics of their lectures?

W : Yeah. They'll talk about the metaverse, virtual reality, and mobile games.

M : Amazing! And a ticket only costs $30. It's quite reasonable.

W : I agree. We can ✪ ________ ________ ________ ______ ________ we want during the conference.

M : Great. I can't wait.

09

Superhero Museum에 관한 다음 내용을 듣고, 일치하지 않는 것을 고르시오.

M : Hello, Animation World podcast listeners! Are you ✪ __ ________ _____ ___ ____________ __________ ______ __________? Then, why don't you visit our Superhero Museum and meet your favorite characters? Our museum holds over 70,000 comic books and 40,000 films as well as over 10,000 toys. All of these fantastic pieces are on display in our museum __________ ______ ___ _____ ______ ________. And we provide a superhero costume rental service for adults as well as kids. To enjoy all the fun, the admission fee is only $8, and we offer ______ ________ ___ ____ ________ ________ ______ ______. Also, customers who visit our museum on their birthday will get a special piece of cake in our cafeteria. For more information, please visit our website. Come and be a superhero with us!

10

다음 표를 보면서 대화를 듣고, 두 사람이 주문할 손 세정제를 고르시오.

M : Honey, we're almost out of hand soap.

W : Oh, I was just looking for some online. Will you choose with me?

M : Sure. Let's see. How about choosing one of these for less than $20?

W : I agree. I don't want to spend too much for hand soap, either. Which form of hand soap do you want?

M : You know, ________ ________ ___ ________ ___ ______ but produces more plastic waste.

W : Yeah. Then why don't we choose from among the bar soaps?

M : Good. ✪ ________ ________ _____ ____________? Do you have a preference?

W : I'd like anything but lemon. We've used lemon for a long time. Let's make a change this time.

M : Okay. There are two options left, then.

W : Oh, this one is _____ ________ _____ __________. I believe testing on living animals is not ethical.

M : I agree. Let's order it now.

11

대화를 듣고, 여자의 마지막 말에 대한 남자의 응답으로 가장 적절한 것을 고르시오.

W : Hello. Can I order a fried chicken to go please?

M : Yes, but ✪ _____ ___________ ________ _________ ____ because of the big soccer match tonight. Is it okay for you to wait?

W : Oh, I should have come much earlier. _________ ____ ______ ________ _____ ____________ _____ ________?

12

대화를 듣고, 남자의 마지막 말에 대한 여자의 응답으로 가장 적절한 것을 고르시오.

M : Sweetie, do you have any plans this Saturday?

W : Nothing special. Why, Dad?

M : Well, I _______ __ ______________ ____________ that morning. So I need somebody to ✪ _______ _______ ___________ __ ______ to ice hockey practice.

13

대화를 듣고, 여자의 마지막 말에 대한 남자의 응답으로 가장 적절한 것을 고르시오. [3점]

W : Hello, Kevin. What brings you to my office today?

M : Hello, Ms. Smith. I'd like to take the computer coding class, but I heard that _____ ____________ ________ ___________.

W : You're right. Far more students wanted to sign up for the class than we expected.

M : Oh, no. I was really looking forward to it.

W : Then _______ ________ ______ _______ __ __________? Our school also offers an online coding class.

M : Lucky me. But I've never taken an online class.

W : I'm sure Mr. Brown can give you more information. He's in charge of students taking online classes.

M : Okay. Where's his office?

W : Well, he's on a business trip. You'll be able to see him this coming Thursday.

M : Hmm. I'm afraid that'll be too late to register for the class.

W : Don't worry. ✪ ___________________ ___ ______ _______ __________. Before deciding whether to take the class, you should consult with Mr. Brown first.

14

대화를 듣고, 남자의 마지막 말에 대한 여자의 응답으로 가장 적절한 것을 고르시오.

M : Molly, how have you been?

W : Hi, Ron. To tell you the truth, I've been feeling a little bit down lately. ✪ ______ ______ __________ ____ _______________.

M : I see. I've felt that way before, myself.

W : Really? You've had this experience, too?

M : Of course. Last year, I felt like my life was ____ ______ ____ ______ ____________.

W : I didn't know that. How did you overcome?

M : For me, learning to play the ukulele helped a lot. Why don't you try learning a new hobby? That might _______ _________ ________ _________.

W : Interesting. But learning something new also causes stress, doesn't it?

M : Yes, but in a positive way. I gained more energy in my life by pushing myself to try a new activity.

W : That makes sense. Do you think it'll work for me, too?

M : Well, it did for me. I think it might do you good.

15

다음 상황 설명을 듣고, Emma가 Tom에게 할 말로 가장 적절한 것을 고르시오. [3점]

M : Emma has lots of friends. One day, she plans to invite some close friends to her house and treat them to a home-cooked meal. On the way home, she ________ ___ _____ ____________ ________ and puts foods and beverages in her cart. She stands at the counter and meets Tom, who works at the store as a cashier. ✪ _______ ___ __ ________________ ________ ________, he has to swipe Emma's credit card two times. After paying the bill, she checks the payment confirmation messages on her cell phone, and finds out she got two messages about the same amount of money. So she wants to ask Tom to see __ _____ ____________ ______ _________ ________. In this situation, what would Emma most likely say to Tom?

16~17

다음을 듣고, 물음에 답하시오.

W : Good morning, students. It's good to see you again. Last time, we talked about how to express your anger in a healthy way. Today, I'm going to tell you some useful ways to manage conflict situations. First, ✪ _____ _____ ______________________ ____________. Simply accept the opponent's argument and you'll see that small disagreements can be handled quickly and easily with a minimum of effort. Second, you can use compromising strategy. To reach agreement, each party sometimes needs to _______ ____ _______________ ______ _______ ________. Through finding the middle ground, both parties can feel they've been listened to. Next, competing strategy is helpful when you decide to hold to your principles. When it comes to moral judgment, you can reject compromise. Sometimes it's best to ✪ ________ ___ ________ ______ ____________ ___ __________. Finally, avoiding strategy is another type of conflict management. This style aims to reduce conflict by ignoring it. That can give you time to calm down and analyze the situation based on a more objective point of view. Now, let's watch a few videos and think about how to handle each situation.

▶ 정답 : 해설편 032쪽

VOCA LIST 07

회차별 영단어 QR 코드 ※ QR 코드를 스캔 후 모바일로 단어장처럼 학습할 수 있습니다.

● 고3 2023학년도 4월

01

001 □ **job fair** 취업 박람회
002 □ **opportunity** ⓝ 기회
003 □ **qualified** ⓐ 자격 있는
004 □ **in search of** ~을 찾아서
005 □ **fully prepared** 만반의 준비를 갖춘
006 □ **student ID card** 학생증
007 □ **entrance** ⓝ 입장, 출입
008 □ **résumé** ⓝ 이력서
009 □ **certificate** ⓝ 자격증

02

010 □ **clean out** 청소하다
011 □ **sort** ⓥ 분류하다, 정리하다
012 □ **arrange** ⓥ 정리하다, 배치하다
013 □ **get rid of** ~을 버리다
014 □ **when it comes to** ~에 관해서라면
015 □ **come and go** 생겼다 없어지다, 변하다
016 □ **make sense** 일리가 있다
017 □ **fade** ⓥ (색이) 옅어지다
018 □ **dispose of** ~을 처분하다

03

019 □ **show around** (~에게) 둘러보도록 안내하다
020 □ **elegant** ⓐ 우아한
021 □ **put effort into** ~에 노력을 들이다
022 □ **living room** 거실
023 □ **publish** ⓥ 게재하다, 출판하다
024 □ **issue** ⓝ (잡지 등 정기 간행물의) 호
025 □ **in case** ~에 대비하여, ~할 경우
026 □ **give A a shout** A에게 말해주다

04

027 □ **art studio** 화실
028 □ **easel** ⓝ 이젤
029 □ **look out** 내다보다
030 □ **take out** 꺼내다
031 □ **sculpture** ⓝ 조각
032 □ **add to the atmosphere** 분위기를 더해주다
033 □ **vase** ⓝ 꽃병
034 □ **congratulate** ⓥ 축하하다
035 □ **thoughtful** ⓐ 사려 깊은
036 □ **talented** ⓐ 재능 있는

05

037 □ **recruitment** ⓝ 모집
038 □ **broadcast** ⓥ 방송하다
039 □ **by the way** 그나저나
040 □ **take a look at** ~을 보다
041 □ **in the corner** 구석에, 귀퉁이에
042 □ **scan** ⓥ 스캔하다, 찍다
043 □ **application form** 신청서, 지원서
044 □ **print out** 출력하다
045 □ **put up** 게시하다, 붙이다

06

046 □ **book** ⓥ 예약하다
047 □ **standard** ⓝ 일반, 표준
048 □ **expert** ⓝ 전문가
049 □ **definitely** ad 꼭, 반드시
050 □ **recording** ⓝ 녹음
051 □ **discount** ⓝ 할인
052 □ **apply to** ~에게 적용되다, 해당되다

07

053 □ **go on a trip** 여행을 가다
054 □ **shy** ⓐ 수줍어하는
055 □ **adopt** ⓥ 입양하다
056 □ **adorable** ⓐ 사랑스러운
057 □ **vaccinate** ⓥ 예방 접종하다

08

058 □ **Are you kidding me?** 장난해? 말이라고 해?
059 □ **be all set** 준비가 다 되다
060 □ **within walking distance** 걸어서 갈 수 있는 거리인
061 □ **industry** ⓝ 업계
062 □ **lecture** ⓝ 강의
063 □ **metaverse** ⓝ 메타버스, 사이버 공간
064 □ **reasonable** ⓐ (값이) 적당한, 싼, 합리적인
065 □ **I can't wait.** 몹시 기대돼.

09

066 □ **huge fan** 열성팬
067 □ **comic** ⓝ 만화
068 □ **on display** 전시 중인
069 □ **costume** ⓝ 의상
070 □ **rental** ⓝ 대여
071 □ **A as well as B** B뿐만 아니라 A도
072 □ **fee** ⓝ 요금
073 □ **school age** 취학 연령

10

074 □ **be[run] out of** ~이 다 떨어지다
075 □ **hand soap** 손 세정제, 핸드워시
076 □ **form** ⓝ 형태 ⓥ 형성하다
077 □ **waste** ⓝ 쓰레기
078 □ **fragrance** ⓝ 향기
079 □ **anything but** ~만 제외하고
080 □ **ethical** ⓐ 윤리적인

11

081 □ **to go** (매장에서 먹지 않고) 가져갈, 포장할
082 □ **pile up** 쌓이다, 밀리다
083 □ **because of** ~ 때문에
084 □ **receive** ⓥ 받다, 수령하다
085 □ **sold out** 품절된, 다 팔린
086 □ **first come, first served** 선착순(의)
087 □ **no matter how** 아무리 ~하더라도

12

088 □ **business meeting** 업무 미팅
089 □ **give a ride** (차로) 태워다주다
090 □ **ice hockey** 아이스하키
091 □ **Cheer up.** 힘내.
092 □ **presentation** ⓝ 발표

13

093 □ **What brings you to ~?** ~에는 무슨 일이니?
094 □ **fully booked** 예약이 다 찬
095 □ **sign up for** ~에 등록하다
096 □ **look forward to** ~을 고대하다
097 □ **Lucky me.** 잘됐네요. 저는 운이 좋네요.
098 □ **be in charge of** ~을 담당하다, 책임지다
099 □ **business trip** 출장
100 □ **register for** ~에 등록하다
101 □ **due** ⓐ 예정인, 마감이 다 된
102 □ **consult with** ~와 상의하다
103 □ **consultation** ⓝ 상담, 진찰

14

104 □ **How have you been?** 어떻게 지냈어?
105 □ **to tell you the truth** 솔직히 말하면
106 □ **feel down** 마음이 울적하다
107 □ **repetitive** ⓐ 반복적인
108 □ **full of** ~로 가득한
109 □ **dull** ⓐ 지루한, 따분한
110 □ **overcome** ⓥ 극복하다
111 □ **gain** ⓥ 얻다
112 □ **work for** ~에게 효과가 있다
113 □ **do good** (~에게) 도움이 되다
114 □ **be tired of** ~에 질리다
115 □ **stay away from** ~에서 멀어지다, 떨어지다

15

116 □ **on the way home** 집에 오는 길에, 귀갓길에
117 □ **beverage** ⓝ 음료
118 □ **work at** ~에서 일하다
119 □ **cashier** ⓝ 계산대 점원
120 □ **temporary** ⓐ 일시적인
121 □ **swipe** ⓥ (신용 카드 등을 단말기에) 대다, 읽히다
122 □ **confirmation** ⓝ (사실이라는) 확인
123 □ **make (a) payment** 지불하다
124 □ **charge** ⓥ (요금을) 청구하다
125 □ **bank transfer** 계좌 이체

16~17

126 □ **anger** ⓝ 화
127 □ **conflict** ⓝ 갈등
128 □ **accommodate** ⓥ 수용하다, (필요에) 대응하다
129 □ **accept** ⓥ 받아들이다
130 □ **opponent** ⓝ 상대방, 적수
131 □ **argument** ⓝ 주장, 논거, 논쟁
132 □ **disagreement** ⓝ 불일치, 다툼
133 □ **minimum** ⓝ 최소
134 □ **compromise** ⓥ 타협하다
135 □ **reach agreement** 합의에 이르다
136 □ **middle ground** 타협안, 절충안
137 □ **hold to** ~을 고수하다
138 □ **stick to** ~을 고수하다
139 □ **ignore** ⓥ 무시하다
140 □ **point of view** 관점, 시각
141 □ **communicative** ⓐ 의사소통의

08회 ● 2022학년도 4월 학력평가 고3 영어 듣기

※ QR코드를 스캔하시면 듣기 방송을 청취하실 수 있습니다.

● 점수 표시가 없는 문항은 모두 2점 ● 문항수 17개 | 배점 37점 | 제한 시간 25분

1번부터 17번까지는 듣고 답하는 문제입니다. 1번부터 15번까지는 한 번만 들려주고, 16번부터 17번까지는 두 번 들려줍니다. 방송을 잘 듣고 답을 하시기 바랍니다.

MP3

1. 다음을 듣고, 여자가 하는 말의 목적으로 가장 적절한 것을 고르시오.

① 자선 경매 행사를 위한 자원봉사자를 모집하려고
② 지역 아동을 위한 자선 물품 기부를 독려하려고
③ 봉사 활동 확인서 발급 절차를 안내하려고
④ 아동 병원 설립의 필요성을 강조하려고
⑤ 자원봉사 사전 교육 일정을 공지하려고

2. 대화를 듣고, 남자의 의견으로 가장 적절한 것을 고르시오.

① 교사의 칭찬은 학생의 불안감을 낮출 수 있다.
② 예술 교육은 학생의 사회성 발달을 촉진시킨다.
③ 어휘를 배우는 것은 독해력 향상에 필수적이다.
④ 노래는 학생이 어휘를 쉽게 기억하도록 도와준다.
⑤ 음악 감상을 통해 학생의 창의력을 향상시킬 수 있다.

3. 대화를 듣고, 두 사람의 관계를 가장 잘 나타낸 것을 고르시오.

① 운전자 – 주차 관리 요원
② 동물 보호소 직원 – 기부자
③ 인테리어 디자이너 – 의뢰인
④ 건물 관리인 – 청소업체 직원
⑤ 애견용품 판매점 주인 – 손님

4. 대화를 듣고, 그림에서 대화의 내용과 일치하지 <u>않는</u> 것을 고르시오.

5. 대화를 듣고, 남자가 할 일로 가장 적절한 것을 고르시오.

① 테이블 설치하기
② 스피커 점검하기
③ 포스터 제작하기
④ 배지 배송 확인하기
⑤ 무선 마이크 가져오기

6. 대화를 듣고, 여자가 지불할 금액을 고르시오.

① $108 ② $110 ③ $120 ④ $162 ⑤ $180

7. 대화를 듣고, 남자가 영화를 보러 갈 수 <u>없는</u> 이유를 고르시오.

① 면접 준비를 해야 해서
② 아르바이트를 해야 해서
③ 요가 수업을 들어야 해서
④ 건강 검진을 받아야 해서
⑤ 동아리 모임에 참석해야 해서

8. 대화를 듣고, Spring Walking Challenge에 관해 언급되지 <u>않은</u> 것을 고르시오.

① 운영 기간
② 참가 대상
③ 우승 상금
④ 주최 기관
⑤ 신청 방법

9. International Beatbox Championship에 관한 다음 내용을 듣고, 일치하지 <u>않는</u> 것을 고르시오.

① 5월 10일부터 시작한다.
② 단독 공연과 단체 공연이 있다.
③ 전년도 우승자들이 심사 위원으로 참여한다.
④ 결승전은 온라인으로 생중계된다.
⑤ 표는 현장 구매가 가능하다.

영어 영역(듣기)

10. 다음 표를 보면서 대화를 듣고, 두 사람이 대여할 정수기를 고르시오.

Water Purifiers

	Product	Monthly Rental Fee	Hot Water	Filter Replacement	Color
①	A	$25	X	self	black
②	B	$30	O	self	black
③	C	$35	O	self	white
④	D	$38	O	service visit	white
⑤	E	$42	X	service visit	gray

11. 대화를 듣고, 여자의 마지막 말에 대한 남자의 응답으로 가장 적절한 것을 고르시오.

① It wasn't easy to discover my new hobby.
② I began taking drum lessons in middle school.
③ It was very hard to practice drums every day.
④ I brought them from my home for this festival.
⑤ I used to enjoy listening to modern rock music.

12. 대화를 듣고, 남자의 마지막 말에 대한 여자의 응답으로 가장 적절한 것을 고르시오.

① No worries. His school grades will get better.
② Sure. I'll adjust my schedule to join the event.
③ Wonderful. Your parents must be proud of you.
④ Hurry up. You're really late for the school event.
⑤ Absolutely. I'm happy to invite your teacher here.

13. 대화를 듣고, 여자의 마지막 말에 대한 남자의 응답으로 가장 적절한 것을 고르시오. [3점]

Man: ______________________________

① No problem. I can help him find his future career.
② I got it. I'll send you the website about promising jobs.
③ Don't worry. I won't be late for the counseling next time.
④ Of course. I'll keep the appointment with my homeroom teacher.
⑤ Thanks. I'll check it out and book a meeting with the counselor.

14. 대화를 듣고, 남자의 마지막 말에 대한 여자의 응답으로 가장 적절한 것을 고르시오. [3점]

Woman: ______________________________

① I'm sorry. I can't imagine living without new technology.
② Cheer up. You'll find more information from digital resources.
③ You get it. I'm sure it'll help reduce your digital device usage.
④ That makes sense. We're more productive using smartphones.
⑤ I agree. You can get more rest by giving up your painting time.

15. 다음 상황 설명을 듣고, Amy가 Terry에게 할 말로 가장 적절한 것을 고르시오. [3점]

Amy: ______________________________

① We'll do great since we've worked so hard.
② I signed up for the contest, so don't worry.
③ We need more practice to win the dance contest.
④ If you're nervous, I'll cancel the rehearsal for you.
⑤ You should follow my moves to correct your mistakes.

[16 ~ 17] 다음을 듣고, 물음에 답하시오.

16. 남자가 하는 말의 주제로 가장 적절한 것은?

① methods of obtaining nutrition by marine creatures
② causes of dramatic decrease in sea animal populations
③ ways for creatures in the ocean to protect themselves
④ difficulties in observing ocean animals' hunting patterns
⑤ importance of adapting to new surroundings for sea creatures

17. 언급된 해양 생물이 아닌 것은?

① penguins ② sea horses ③ jellyfish
④ whales ⑤ oysters

[해설편 p.035]

※ QR 코드를 스캔하시면 듣기 방송이 나옵니다. 듣기 방송을 들으며 다음 빈칸을 채우시오. ● 제한 시간 : 25분

01

다음을 듣고, 여자가 하는 말의 목적으로 가장 적절한 것을 고르시오.

W : Hello, citizens of Grandsville. I'm your mayor, Clara Bennett. As you know, our city is going to ✪ _________ _________ _________ _________ for the local children's hospital. I'm sure that many citizens are paying attention to this special event, so we're _________ _________ _________ for the event. The volunteers are going to take care of _________ _________ _________ and cleaning up the event hall. I hope you can make a truly memorable contribution to our community. If you're interested, please visit www.grandsville.gov and fill out the volunteer application. Thank you for your help in advance.

02

대화를 듣고, 남자의 의견으로 가장 적절한 것을 고르시오.

[Door knocks.]

M : Come on in, Ms. Dale. Take a seat.

W : Good afternoon, Mr. Harrison. Thank you for your time.

M : No problem. I'm happy to share my teaching experience with you. How can I help?

W : Well, students in my class are having a hard time memorizing vocabulary. Do you have any ideas on how to make it easier for them?

M : Hmm, _________ _________ _________ _________? Songs are helpful for remembering vocabulary easily.

W : Do you really think so?

M : Yes. The repetition of the ✪ _________ _________ _________ in a song can help them remember words for longer periods of time.

W : That makes sense.

M : Also, you can see students enjoy _________ _________ _________ _________. Learning is easier when it's fun.

W : Sounds good. I should try that.

M : I'm sure songs will help your students to _________ _________ _________.

W : Thank you for your advice.

03

대화를 듣고, 두 사람의 관계를 가장 잘 나타낸 것을 고르시오.

W : Hello, Mr. Ryan. It's been a while.

M : You're right, Ms. Brown. It's been a year since I visited here.

W : Did you notice some changes around the place?

M : Yeah. The facilities look _________ _________ _________.

W : Due to the increasing concerns about ✪ _________ _________, more donations were made, which allowed us to renovate.

M : That's good. It looks like the number of workers in this shelter has increased as well.

W : That's true. There were only _________ _________ _________ _________ _________ _________, but now there are five.

M : I see. Well, as I told you on the phone, I _________ _________ _________ _________ _________.

W : Thank you so much. Your donations have always been a great help for our animals.

M : I'm glad to hear that. Then I'll bring the food from my car.

W : Can I help you?

M : Thank you. Let's go to the parking lot together.

04

대화를 듣고, 그림에서 대화의 내용과 일치하지 않는 것을 고르시오.

M : Mindy, you prepared a lot for ✪ _________ _________ _________ _________ _________. How did it go?

W : Dad, Mr. Peters loved it so much. Do you want to see a picture of it?

M : Sure. *[Pause]* Oh, you _________ _________ _________ on the banner.

W : Yeah. He used to play the violin in front of us. Look at the picture on the wall. It's a picture of the music club members.

M : Looks lovely. By the way, what are those two boxes next to the plant for?

W : Those are the gifts we prepared for Mr. Peters. And, do you see the cake on the table?

M : Yes. Is that the cake you were baking last night? He _________ _________ _________ _________.

W : He sure did. Also, we played the piano for Mr. Peters.

M : Oh, I can see a piano under the clock.

W : Right. I hope he had a great time with us.

05

대화를 듣고, 남자가 할 일로 가장 적절한 것을 고르시오.

W : John, the Earth Day event is in an hour. Let's do a ✪ _________ _________.

M : Okay, Kelly. The table for registration is nicely set in that booth.

W : Wonderful. The earth-shaped badges we're going to give out to visitors were delivered in the morning.

M : Perfect. I hope people will like them.

W : I'm sure they will. And the materials for ✪ _________ _________ _________ are in this box.

M : Good. And I've already checked the speakers we're going to use for the broadcast. They work well.

W : Great. By the way, where's the wireless microphone?

M : Oh, I _________ _________ _________ _________ from the school auditorium. I'll get it right away.

W : Thanks. Then I'll put the Earth Day poster on the front of the table.

Dictation 08

06

대화를 듣고, 여자가 지불할 금액을 고르시오.

M : Welcome to King Wave Surfing.
W : Hello. I'd like to sign up for a surfing lesson with my husband.
M : Sure. Which program do you want to register for?
W : Hmm, is there a beginners' lesson available this Friday for two people?
M : Let me check. *[Typing sound]* Yes, we have a private lesson and a ✪ _________ _________ on that day. The private lesson costs $80 per person, and the group lesson costs $50 per person.
W : I'd like to _________ _________ _________ _________ for two people.
M : All right. How about ✪ _________ _________ _________? They're $10 per person.
W : Yeah, I think we need to rent two of them.
M : Okay. So that's two people for the group lesson and two suits, right?
W : Yes. Oh, can I use this coupon? I got it from the hotel where I'm staying.
M : Let me see. Sure, you get 10% off the total.
W : Great. Here's my credit card.

07

대화를 듣고, 남자가 영화를 보러 갈 수 없는 이유를 고르시오.

[Cell phone rings.]
W : Hello, Ted.
M : Hi, Kristine. Have you finished your yoga class?
W : Yes, it has just finished. I'm on my way to a club meeting. What's up?
M : Guess what? _________ _________ _________ into the internship program.
W : Congratulations! You must have made ✪ _________ _________ during the interview.
M : Thanks. But that's not the only reason I called you.
W : Then why did you call me?
M : Well, I have to tell you that I can't go to see the movie this Friday. I'm really sorry.
W : Didn't you say that you ✪ _________ _________ _________ _________?
M : Yes, I stopped working there last month.
W : Then why can't you come?
M : Actually, I _________ _________ _________ _________ for the internship on that day.
W : I see. Maybe next time.

08

대화를 듣고, Spring Walking Challenge에 관해 언급되지 않은 것을 고르시오.

M : Bella, did you see ✪ _________ _________ about Spring Walking Challenge?
W : Walking Challenge? I've never heard of that.
M : It's about _________ _________ _________ _________ _________ _________ and deciding who walks the longest distance with the Challenge Tracker app.
W : Interesting. When is it?
M : It's held from April 17th to May 1st.
W : I see. Oh, the challenge is open to any community member.
M : Good. Then a lot of people can participate.
W : I think it'll be a fun experience.
M : Absolutely. And $500 will be given to the winner.
W : Really? I want to participate in it. How can I sign up for the challenge?
M : Just _________ _________ _________ _________ and fill in the application form on the website.
W : Thanks. I'll do that now.

09

International Beatbox Championship에 관한 다음 내용을 듣고, 일치하지 않는 것을 고르시오.

M : Hello, listeners. I'm Jay Cloud, director of the International Beatbox Championship. I'm so thrilled to invite you to our upcoming championship. It'll be a five-day event ✪ _________ _________ _________ _________ in Miami. There will be solo performances and group performances. And guess what? _________ _________ _________ _________ _________ will participate as judges. The finals will be broadcast live on our website. Tickets are only _________ _________ _________, but seats will be assigned on a first come, first served basis. For more information, visit www.beatboxchamps.org. Join us and feel the rhythm with your whole body.

10

다음 표를 보면서 대화를 듣고, 두 사람이 대여할 정수기를 고르시오.

M : Honey, what are you doing?
W : I'm looking at this catalogue of ✪ _________ _________ we can rent. Why don't we choose one together?
M : Sure. How much can we spend on the _________ _________ _________?
W : We can't afford more than $40.
M : Then let's cross this out. Do you think we should get one with hot water?
W : Yes. I drink a lot of hot tea, so a water purifier with hot water will be more convenient.
M : All right. What about the filter replacement? We can ask service engineers to visit our home to change the filters or do that by ourselves.
W : Well, which one is better?
M : Hmm, _________ _________ _________ _________ _________ doesn't seem difficult. Let's choose the self replacement option.
W : Okay. Now, there are only two options left. Which color do you like?
M : I prefer _________ _________ _________ since it'll match with our kitchen better.
W : I agree. Then let's rent this.

11

대화를 듣고, 여자의 마지막 말에 대한 남자의 응답으로 가장 적절한 것을 고르시오.

W : Jeremy, I was surprised to see you play the drums at the school festival. You were incredible.

M : ✪ __________ __________, Ms. Anderson. I play them as a hobby.

W : Really? When did you __________ __________ __________ __________?

12

대화를 듣고, 남자의 마지막 말에 대한 여자의 응답으로 가장 적절한 것을 고르시오.

M : Mom, take a look at this ✪ __________ __________.

W : Hmm, there's an Easter egg hunt. That looks like an exciting event.

M : My teacher said __________ __________ __________ __________ __________. And I really hope you come.

13

대화를 듣고, 여자의 마지막 말에 대한 남자의 응답으로 가장 적절한 것을 고르시오. [3점]

W : What are you doing, Jake?

M : Hi, Diane. I'm reading a book about ✪ __________ __________ in the future.

W : Great. What kind of future career are you interested in?

M : Well, I don't have any specific career in mind.

W : Oh, I see. So you're getting ideas from that book.

M : Yes. This book is really helpful, but I need more detailed information related to my preferences and interests.

W : Well, how about talking with __________ __________ __________ __________?

M : I didn't think about that.

W : He has given me lots of information in finding my future career through some counseling sessions.

M : Sounds good. Then I should talk to him today.

W : Hold on. You have to __________ __________ __________ __________.

M : How can I do that?

W : __________ __________ __________ __________ on our school website. You should look at it and make an appointment online.

14

대화를 듣고, 남자의 마지막 말에 대한 여자의 응답으로 가장 적절한 것을 고르시오. [3점]

M : Honey, what time is it now?

W : It's already 2 o'clock. You've been looking at your smartphone for two hours.

M : Oh, I didn't realize that it was that long.

W : I'm worried that you've been spending too much time on your smartphone. Why don't you __________ __________ __________ __________?

M : What's that?

W : It's voluntarily avoiding the use of digital devices like smartphones for a certain amount of time.

M : But it'll be hard to just stop using them so suddenly.

W : Well, how about doing more ✪ __________ __________ instead? By focusing on other activities, you won't think of using digital devices.

M : Okay, you have a point. Once I __________ __________ __________ __________ __________, I may not think about digital devices.

W : Right. You can do anything you want during that time. Why don't you start painting again?

M : Good idea. It'll __________ __________ __________ __________ from smart devices.

15

다음 상황 설명을 듣고, Amy가 Terry에게 할 말로 가장 적절한 것을 고르시오. [3점]

W : Amy and Terry are members in the same dance club. They come to know that there will be a dance contest for high school students. Amy asks Terry to apply for it ✪ __________ __________ __________, and he agrees. From that day, they have practiced really hard for the contest. Finally, the day of the contest comes, and they meet to rehearse one last time. However, Terry __________ __________ __________, even for the dance moves that he used to do easily. Amy asks Terry what's going on with him, and he tells her that it's because he's really __________ __________ __________ __________. Amy wants to assure him that since they have ✪ __________ __________ __________ __________ __________ in, they will do amazingly on the stage. In this situation, what would Amy most likely say to Terry?

16~17

다음을 듣고, 물음에 답하시오.

M : Good morning, students. Last class, we talked about how animals in the ocean live together. Today, I'm going to tell you how ✪ __________ __________ __________ __________. First, many ocean inhabitants use large groups to protect themselves from predators. For example, penguins often enter the water in groups in an attempt to confuse predators. Second, one form of concealment animals use is disguising themselves to __________ __________ __________ __________ __________. Sea horses act like coral by clinging to it with their tails so a predator may not notice them. Third, many forms of sea life use poisons to drive off predators. Jellyfish have stinging body parts, which not only paralyze their food but also provide protection from predators. Lastly, some marine creatures ✪ __________ __________ __________ that prevent predators from attacking them. Oysters have thick and hard covers that protect them. Isn't that interesting? Now, let's watch a video to help you understand better.

▶ 정답 : 해설편 037쪽

01

001 □ mayor ⓝ 시장(市長)
002 □ charity ⓝ 자선
003 □ auction ⓝ 경매
004 □ pay attention to ~에 관심을 갖다, 주의를 기울이다
005 □ volunteer ⓝ 자원 봉사자
006 □ categorize ⓥ 분류하다
007 □ make a contribution 기여하다, 이바지하다
008 □ fill out (양식을) 작성하다

02

009 □ have a hard time ~ing ~하는 데 어려움을 겪다
010 □ vocabulary ⓝ 어휘(단어)
011 □ helpful ⓐ 도움이 되는
012 □ repetition ⓝ 반복
013 □ period ⓝ 기간, 시기(時期)
014 □ make sense 일리가 있다, 이해가 되다

03

015 □ facility ⓝ (편의) 시설
016 □ renovate ⓥ 보수하다
017 □ concern ⓝ 우려, 걱정
018 □ abandoned animal 유기 동물
019 □ shelter ⓝ 보호소, 쉼터

04

020 □ prepare ⓥ 준비하다
021 □ farewell ⓝ 작별

05

022 □ do a final check 마지막으로 점검하다
023 □ registration ⓝ 등록
024 □ nicely ad 잘, 좋게
025 □ give out 나눠주다
026 □ deliver ⓥ 배달하다
027 □ decorate ⓥ 장식하다, 꾸미다
028 □ reusable ⓐ 재사용 가능한
029 □ broadcast ⓝ 방송
030 □ wireless ⓐ 무선의
031 □ right away 즉시, 곧, 바로

06

032 □ sign up for ~에 등록하다
033 □ husband ⓝ 남편
034 □ register ⓥ 등록하다
035 □ beginner ⓝ 초보자
036 □ available ⓐ 이용할 수 있는
037 □ private ⓐ 개인의
038 □ surfing suit 서핑복

07

039 □ finish ⓥ 끝내다
040 □ get accepted into ~에 합격하다
041 □ internship ⓝ 인턴사원 근무, 인턴직
042 □ make a good impression 좋은 인상을 주다
043 □ interview ⓝ 면접
044 □ part-time job 시간제 근무, 아르바이트
045 □ medical check-up 건강 검진

08

046 □ leaflet ⓝ 전단
047 □ track ⓥ 추적하다
048 □ decide ⓥ 결정하다, 결정을 내리다
049 □ distance ⓝ 거리
050 □ participate ⓥ 참여하다, 참가하다
051 □ fill in (서식을) 작성하다, 채우다
052 □ application form 신청서

09

053 □ director ⓝ 책임자
054 □ upcoming ⓐ 다가오는, 곧 있을
055 □ performance ⓝ 공연
056 □ judge ⓝ 심사위원
057 □ purchase ⓥ 구입하다, 구매하다
058 □ on a first come, first served basis 선착순으로

10

059 □ catalogue ⓝ (상품자료의) 목록, 카탈로그
060 □ water purifier 정수기
061 □ rental fee 대여료
062 □ afford ⓥ 여유가 있다
063 □ convenient ⓐ 편리한
064 □ replacement ⓝ 교체
065 □ prefer ⓥ ~을 좋아하다
066 □ match with ~와 어울리다, 부합하다

11

067 □ incredible ⓐ 놀라운, 훌륭한, 대단한, 굉장한
068 □ I'm flattered. 과찬이에요.
069 □ hobby ⓝ 취미
070 □ discover ⓥ 발견하다
071 □ practice ⓥ 연습하다

12

072 □ Easter egg 부활절 달걀
073 □ adjust ⓥ 조정하다

13

074 □ promising ⓐ 유망한
075 □ career ⓝ 직업
076 □ detailed ⓐ 상세한, 자세한
077 □ preference ⓝ 선호
078 □ interest ⓝ 관심
079 □ counseling session 상담 시간
080 □ keep an appointment 약속을 지키다
081 □ homeroom teacher 담임 선생님

14

082 □ realize ⓥ 알아차리다
083 □ digital detox 디지털 디톡스(전자기기를 일부러 잠시 꺼두는 시간)
084 □ voluntarily ad 자발적으로
085 □ avoid ⓥ 피하다
086 □ device ⓝ 장치, 기기(機器)
087 □ suddenly ad 갑자기
088 □ activity ⓝ 활동
089 □ You have a point. 일리가 있어요.
090 □ resource ⓝ 자원
091 □ reduce ⓥ 줄이다
092 □ usage ⓝ 사용

15

093 □ apply ⓥ 신청하다
094 □ mistake ⓝ 실수
095 □ nervous ⓐ (…을 앞두고) 긴장한, 초조한
096 □ competition ⓝ 대회, 경쟁
097 □ assure ⓥ 장담하다
098 □ put in effort 노력을 기울이다
099 □ amazingly ad 놀랄 만큼, 굉장하게
100 □ correct ⓥ 바로잡다

16~17

101 □ sea creature 해양 생물, 바다 생물
102 □ defend ⓥ 방어하다
103 □ inhabitant ⓝ 서식 동물, 거주민
104 □ protect ⓥ 보호하다, 지키다
105 □ predator ⓝ 포식자
106 □ concealment ⓝ 은폐, 숨김
107 □ disguise ⓥ 위장하다
108 □ blend in ~에 섞이다
109 □ surroundings ⓝ 환경
110 □ coral ⓝ 산호
111 □ cling ⓥ 달라붙다, 매달리다
112 □ poison ⓝ 독, 독약
113 □ drive off 물리치다
114 □ jellyfish ⓝ 해파리
115 □ sting ⓥ (침을) 쏘다, 따갑게 하다
116 □ paralyze ⓥ 마비시키다
117 □ protective ⓐ 보호하는, 보호용의
118 □ prevent ⓥ (…의 발생을) 막다
119 □ oyster ⓝ 굴
120 □ nutrition ⓝ 영양
121 □ method ⓝ 방법
122 □ obtain ⓥ 얻다
123 □ pattern ⓝ (정형화된) 양식, 패턴
124 □ importance ⓝ 중요성
125 □ adapt ⓥ 적응하다

09회 2021학년도 4월 학력평가 고3 영어 듣기

※ QR코드를 스캔하시면 듣기 방송을 청취하실 수 있습니다.

● 점수 표시가 없는 문항은 모두 2점 ● 문항수 17개 | 배점 37점 | 제한 시간 25분

1번부터 17번까지는 듣고 답하는 문제입니다. 1번부터 15번까지는 한 번만 들려주고, 16번부터 17번까지는 두 번 들려줍니다. 방송을 잘 듣고 답을 하시기 바랍니다.

MP3

1. 다음을 듣고, 남자가 하는 말의 목적으로 가장 적절한 것을 고르시오.

① 아파트 입주민 회의 참여를 독려하려고
② 아파트 입주민을 위한 앱을 소개하려고
③ 아파트 관리비 납부 방법 변경을 알리려고
④ 아파트 시설 보수 공사 계획을 안내하려고
⑤ 아파트 단지 내 승강기 점검 일정을 공지하려고

2. 대화를 듣고, 여자의 의견으로 가장 적절한 것을 고르시오.

① 근력 운동은 관절 강화에 효과적이다.
② 스트레칭을 통해 자세 교정이 가능하다.
③ 몸 상태에 따라 운동량을 조절할 필요가 있다.
④ 규칙적인 운동은 스트레스 완화에 도움이 된다.
⑤ 바른 자세로 운동하는 것은 부상 위험을 줄인다.

3. 대화를 듣고, 두 사람의 관계를 가장 잘 나타낸 것을 고르시오.

① 음악 교사 – 학생
② 학생회장 – 졸업생
③ 진로 상담사 – 학부모
④ 콘서트 진행자 – 관객
⑤ 드럼 연주자 – 악기점 주인

4. 대화를 듣고, 그림에서 대화의 내용과 일치하지 않는 것을 고르시오.

5. 대화를 듣고, 남자가 여자에게 부탁한 일로 가장 적절한 것을 고르시오.

① 회의 참석하기
② 티켓 출력하기
③ 저녁 준비하기
④ 유니폼 가져오기
⑤ 자동차 수리하기

6. 대화를 듣고, 여자가 지불할 금액을 고르시오. [3점]

① $90 ② $99 ③ $108 ④ $110 ⑤ $120

7. 대화를 듣고, 여자가 Katie Wood의 책 사인회에 갈 수 없는 이유를 고르시오.

① 요리 수업을 들어야 해서
② 사촌 결혼식에 참석해야 해서
③ 중국어 시험공부를 해야 해서
④ 도서관 봉사 활동을 해야 해서
⑤ 에세이 쓰기 대회에 참가해야 해서

8. 대화를 듣고, Summer Computer Coding Program에 관해 언급되지 않은 것을 고르시오.

① 장소
② 운영 기간
③ 수강료
④ 수업 시간
⑤ 신청 마감일

9. Rescue the Animals에 관한 다음 내용을 듣고, 일치하지 않는 것을 고르시오.

① 시청 광장에서 열릴 것이다.
② 20개가 넘는 부스가 있을 것이다.
③ 구조된 동물들의 사진들이 전시될 것이다.
④ 기부자들에게 동물 모양의 열쇠고리를 줄 것이다.
⑤ 시청 옆 공터는 주차장으로 사용될 것이다.

[해설편 p.037]

10. 다음 표를 보면서 대화를 듣고, 두 사람이 선택할 음악 축제를 고르시오.

Music Festivals

	Festival	Date	Genre	Place	Pet-friendly
①	A	April 24	Rock	Union Square	O
②	B	May 8	Jazz	Limestone Island	O
③	C	May 22	Rock	Olympic Stadium	X
④	D	June 5	Jazz	Grand Park	O
⑤	E	June 12	Classical	Fitzroy Garden	X

11. 대화를 듣고, 남자의 마지막 말에 대한 여자의 응답으로 가장 적절한 것을 고르시오.

① I should be there by the end of this month.
② Working on the marketing team isn't easy.
③ I have to go to Canada for a job interview.
④ They haven't hired a new manager yet.
⑤ My family is going to travel with me.

12. 대화를 듣고, 여자의 마지막 말에 대한 남자의 응답으로 가장 적절한 것을 고르시오.

① Excuse me. I can't find where my baggage is.
② Hurry up. We might miss the train to the airport.
③ Okay. I'd like to buy a ticket for the earlier flight.
④ Really? I'm sorry that there are no seats available today.
⑤ I see. I'll let you know when we arrive at the destination.

13. 대화를 듣고, 남자의 마지막 말에 대한 여자의 응답으로 가장 적절한 것을 고르시오.

Woman: ______________________________

① Right. That's why I always check customers' reviews.
② I'd rather not. It's too late to get a refund for the laptop bag.
③ Thanks for your tip. I can save money by using a rental service.
④ That makes sense. I should read the reviews to make a decision.
⑤ Don't worry. The item I ordered online will be delivered soon.

14. 대화를 듣고, 여자의 마지막 말에 대한 남자의 응답으로 가장 적절한 것을 고르시오. [3점]

Man: ______________________________

① That's true. I received an acceptance letter from the university.
② You're right. I'll think about the internship in a more positive way.
③ I agree. The experience helped me a lot in getting a job.
④ No problem. I can take the fashion class next semester.
⑤ Thank you. I've dreamed of working in your company.

15. 다음 상황 설명을 듣고, Ms. Brown이 Andrew에게 할 말로 가장 적절한 것을 고르시오. [3점]

Ms. Brown: ______________________________

① How about reading Spanish books on a regular basis?
② I recommend you read more science books for yourself.
③ What do you think of taking an extra class to get a good score?
④ You'd better write book reports to improve your writing skills.
⑤ Why not try books with different themes to grow your vocabulary?

[16 ~ 17] 다음을 듣고, 물음에 답하시오.

16. 여자가 하는 말의 주제로 가장 적절한 것은?

① materials used for writing before paper
② difficulties of processing natural materials
③ ways raw materials were stored in the past
④ writing materials that affected printing techniques
⑤ common characteristics of eco-friendly materials

17. 언급된 재료가 <u>아닌</u> 것은?

① clay ② papyrus ③ stone
④ animal skins ⑤ silk

[해설편 p.039]

Dictation 09

✪ 표기에는 듣기 어려운 발음이 포함되어 있습니다. 귀 기울여 듣고 받아쓰세요. ● 고3 2021학년도 4월

※ QR 코드를 스캔하시면 듣기 방송이 나옵니다. 듣기 방송을 들으며 다음 빈칸을 채우시오. ● 제한 시간 : 25분

01
다음을 듣고, 남자가 하는 말의 목적으로 가장 적절한 것을 고르시오.

M : Hello, residents. I'm Harry Robinson from the Sunnyville apartment management office. Our apartment staff has made a lot of effort to provide high-quality services for our residents. One of the things we did was to ✪ __________ __________ __________ __________ __________ __________ __________. With the app, you can easily check the monthly maintenance fee and important notices like elevator maintenance schedules or residents' meetings. Also, when you have any requests about your apartment, you can __________ __________ __________ __________ __________ __________ __________. Please download the app and enjoy a more convenient life in Sunnyville apartment. Thank you.

02
대화를 듣고, 여자의 의견으로 가장 적절한 것을 고르시오.

W : Hello, Daniel. Did you finish the warm-up exercise?
M : Hi, Kelly. I did. I'm ready for today's workout.
W : Great. Let's start with squats.
M : Okay. I'll try.
W : Hmm, you're doing good, but __________ __________ __________ __________ __________ __________ __________.
M : Oh, I should be more careful.
W : Yes. Working out with the correct posture is important because it can ✪ __________ __________ __________ __________ __________.
M : I'm aware of that, but it's hard.
W : But if you continue to exercise in the wrong position, you're more likely to get hurt by placing too much stress on your joints and muscles.
M : Oh, that might cause an injury.
W : That's right. That's why I always __________ __________ __________ __________ __________ __________ __________.
M : Okay. I'll pay more attention to my workout posture.
W : Good. Let's try it again.

03
대화를 듣고, 두 사람의 관계를 가장 잘 나타낸 것을 고르시오.

[Door knocks.]
M : Come on in, Lily.
W : Hello, Mr. Thompson. Thank you for seeing me.
M : No problem. You said you needed some advice, right?
W : Yes. I want to be a drummer, but these days I think ✪ __________ __________ __________ __________ __________.
M : Oh, I disagree with that. You've been doing great in my music class.
W : Even though I practice a lot, I feel my performance in the band isn't improving.
M : Lily, I can see your progress. You did a great job at the last school festival.
W : But I don't know exactly what to do to __________ __________ __________ __________.
M : Hmm, what about meeting Elton, a drummer who graduated from our high school? He called me to say he would visit the school next Friday.
W : Really? That would be great.
M : He __________ __________ __________ when I taught him. He can give you some advice.
W : Thank you, Mr. Thompson.

04
대화를 듣고, 그림에서 대화의 내용과 일치하지 않는 것을 고르시오.

M : Jane, what are you looking at?
W : Hi, David. This is a picture of the film club room. We redecorated it last week.
M : Let me see. *[Pause]* Oh, you __________ __________ __________ __________ on the wall. I like that phrase 'LIFE IS LIKE A MOVIE.'
W : Actually, it's a line from our first movie.
M : Wonderful. And the computer under the clock must be for editing movies.
W : You're right. Look at the telephone __________ __________ __________ __________ in the middle of the room.
M : Is it the one you mentioned before? You said you bought it at the antique market.
W : Right. We're going to use it in our next movie.
M : Good. By the way, what's __________ __________ __________ __________ __________ __________ for?
W : We put the costumes for our next movie in that box.
M : Cool. Oh, there are ✪ __________ __________ __________ __________ __________.
W : Yeah. We won them at university film festivals.
M : Great. I hope your club continues making good movies.
W : Thanks.

05
대화를 듣고, 남자가 여자에게 부탁한 일로 가장 적절한 것을 고르시오.

[Cell phone rings.]
W : Hello, honey. What's up?
M : I'm sorry, honey. I think I'll be late for today's soccer match. The meeting just ended.
W : Really? Hmm, I also heard there was a car accident near the stadium.
M : Oh, I'll take the subway, then. By the way, __________ __________ __________ __________ __________ __________?
W : Yeah. I did it this morning. What should we do about dinner?
M : Hmm, let's buy some food at the snack bar in the stadium.
W : Okay. Oh, the ticket says people who wear uniforms will get a free drink at the snack bar.
M : Then, __________ __________ __________ __________ __________? I think ✪ __________ __________ __________ __________ __________.
W : Sure. I'll do that.
M : Thanks. See you soon.

09회

Dictation 09

06

대화를 듣고, 여자가 지불할 금액을 고르시오. [3점]

M : Hello. Welcome to Adventure Camping Supplies. How can I help you?

W : Hi. Can you recommend a children's tent?

M : Okay. Could you follow me? *[Pause]* These two are the best selling models.

W : They both look nice. How much are they?

M : The blue tent is $80, and the red tent is $70. _________ _________ _________ _________ _________ _________ _________.

W : Well, I have two boys. So, ✪ _________ _________ _________ _________. I'll take one blue tent.

M : Okay. Anything else?

W : How much is that children's camping chair?

M : It's $20. It's really popular because of _________ _________ _________ _________ _________.

W : That's my kids' favorite character. I'll buy two.

M : I'm sure your kids will love them.

W : Oh, can I use this discount coupon?

M : Of course. You'll get 10% off the total price.

W : Thank you. Here's my credit card.

07

대화를 듣고, 여자가 Katie Wood의 책 사인회에 갈 수 없는 이유를 고르시오.

[Cell phone rings.]

W : Hello, Chris.

M : Hi, Mindy. Is your cooking class over?

W : Yes, it's just finished. What's up?

M : Have you heard about Katie Wood's _________ _________ _________?

W : No, I haven't. She's one of my favorite essay writers! When is it?

M : It's next Saturday at 2 p.m. I saw a poster while volunteering at the library. Let's go together.

W : Next Saturday? Oh, no. I can't go then.

M : Oh, do you still have to prepare for the Chinese speaking test?

W : No, I took the test last week.

M : Okay. Then, why can't you go?

W : I'm ✪ _________ _________ _________ _________ on that day.

M : Oh, I see. If possible, I'll _________ _________ _________. Have a wonderful time at the wedding.

W : That would be great. Thanks.

08

대화를 듣고, Summer Computer Coding Program에 관해 언급되지 않은 것을 고르시오.

M : Mom, what are you looking at?

W : Look at this leaflet, Paul. It's for a Summer Computer Coding Program. Why don't you try this during summer vacation?

M : Sounds interesting. I've wanted to learn computer coding.

W : It'll be held at Greendale Community College. It's near our house.

M : Oh, yeah! I know where that is. _________ _________ _________ _________ _________ _________?

W : It lasts ✪ _________ _________ _________ _________ _________ _________. Are you okay with that?

M : Yes. By the way, it says the class starts at 9 a.m. and finishes at 11 a.m. I think _________ _________ _________ _________.

W : You might think so, but you're going to have so much fun.

M : Okay, Mom. I'll sign up for it.

W : Good. By the way, the registration for the program _________ _________ _________ _________ by June 25th.

M : I'll do that now. Thanks, Mom.

09

Rescue the Animals에 관한 다음 내용을 듣고, 일치하지 않는 것을 고르시오.

W : Hello, citizens! I'm Rachel Hawkins, mayor of Campbell City. This year, our city is going to hold a meaningful event called Rescue the Animals on May 15th. It'll be held at City Hall Square from 10 a.m. to 5 p.m. The aim of this event is to _________ _________ _________ _________ _________. There will be more than twenty booths which will sell ✪ _________ _________ _________ _________ _________ _________ _________. Also, a variety of photos of rescued animals will be on display. For people who want to contribute, there will be a donation box, and _________ _________ _________ _________ _________ _________ to people who donate. For your convenience, the empty space next to City Hall will be used as a parking lot. Please come and enjoy the event and _________ _________ _________ _________. Thank you.

10

다음 표를 보면서 대화를 듣고, 두 사람이 선택할 음악 축제를 고르시오.

W : Honey, did you see this brochure?

M : What's this?

W : It's about music festivals. What about going to one of them?

M : That sounds fun. Oh, there are five different music festivals.

W : Yeah. Didn't you say your company's new project finishes at the end of April?

M : Right. So, I'd prefer a festival in May or June.

W : Okay. We went to a classical concert last time, so I want to _________ _________ _________ _________ _________ _________.

M : Me, too. Hmm, isn't Limestone Island too far? It takes three hours by car.

W : Yeah. I don't want to spend hours _________ _________ _________.

M : Then, we can choose between these two festivals.

W : Oh, why don't we go to this festival? ✪ _________ _________ _________, we can go there with our dog, Willy.

M : Cool! We can make a special memory with Willy. Let's buy tickets for that festival.

11

대화를 듣고, 남자의 마지막 말에 대한 여자의 응답으로 가장 적절한 것을 고르시오.

M : Jessica, I've just heard about your job promotion. Congratulations!

W : Thanks, Sean. I'm going to be ✪ __________ __________ __________ __________ __________ __________ __________ in Canada.

M : You've wanted that position for a long time. __________ __________ __________ __________ __________ __________ __________ __________?

12

대화를 듣고, 여자의 마지막 말에 대한 남자의 응답으로 가장 적절한 것을 고르시오.

W : Welcome to Blue Bird Airline. How may I help you, sir?

M : I just missed my flight to Boston. __________ __________ __________ __________ __________ __________ __________ __________?

W : Let me check. *[Typing sound]* We have ✪ __________ __________ __________ __________. One departs at 5 p.m., and the other one at 8:30 p.m.

13

대화를 듣고, 남자의 마지막 말에 대한 여자의 응답으로 가장 적절한 것을 고르시오.

M : Anna, what are you doing?

W : Hi, Jeremy. I'm looking for a laptop bag online, but it's hard to decide which one to buy.

M : Oh, do you need help?

W : Yes, please. Look at these models. I'm thinking of buying one of them.

M : Wow, there are too many types of bags.

W : Yeah, it's hard to pick one.

M : Hmm, __________ __________ __________ __________ __________ __________? When I shop online, I always read them.

W : Really? I haven't done that before.

M : It's helpful because some customers ✪ __________ __________ __________ __________ __________ __________.

W : I see, but are those reviews reliable?

M : I believe so because those are the opinions of customers __________ __________ __________ __________ __________.

14

대화를 듣고, 여자의 마지막 말에 대한 남자의 응답으로 가장 적절한 것을 고르시오. [3점]

W : Phillip, do you have a minute?

M : Yes, Professor Jones.

W : Did you hear about the fashion internship program in France? How about applying for it?

M : I heard. I know it's a great opportunity, but I have some concerns.

W : Why? I know you really want to __________ __________ __________ __________ __________ __________ __________.

M : That's right, but I'm nervous about living alone in France.

W : I understand, but the company will __________ __________ __________ __________ __________ __________. So, you don't have to worry too much.

M : Oh, really? I didn't know that. That's good.

W : Most of all, the experience you'll have there can't be acquired in a classroom.

M : I understand what you mean.

W : I'm sure that the experience there will be ✪ __________ __________ __________ __________ __________ __________ __________.

15

다음 상황 설명을 듣고, Ms. Brown이 Andrew에게 할 말로 가장 적절한 것을 고르시오. [3점]

M : Ms. Brown is a Spanish teacher and Andrew is one of her students. Ms. Brown has given reading lessons __________ __________ __________ __________ __________ __________ and write book reports. When Ms. Brown checks students' book reports, she finds out Andrew only reads science-related books. She thinks if he reads books about other topics, he can __________ __________ __________ __________ __________. So, Ms. Brown wants to suggest that Andrew read books dealing with other subjects ✪ __________ __________ __________ __________ __________. In this situation, what would Ms. Brown most likely say to Andrew?

16~17

다음을 듣고, 물음에 답하시오.

W : Hello, students. Last class, we learned about how writing first began in history. Today, we'll discuss ✪ __________ __________ __________ __________ __________ __________ before paper was invented. First, in the river plains of Mesopotamia that are now part of Iraq, clay was an easily available material. People dried clay in the sun and used it to write on. Second, papyrus was the first paper-like medium in Egypt. Since the papyrus plant __________ __________ __________ near the Nile River, people laid it out and pressed it together to create sheets. Third, people in ancient Greece used animal skins to write on. Animal skins had great advantages __________ __________ __________ __________ __________ __________ __________ enough for making books. Lastly, silk was used as writing material in ancient China. It was durable and __________ __________ __________ __________. So, people there used it to make a writing surface that could be used for scrolls. Isn't it interesting? Now, let's talk about the development of the printing technology.

▶ 정답 : 해설편 041쪽

VOCA LIST 09

회차별 영단어 QR 코드 ※ QR 코드를 스캔 후 모바일로 단어장처럼 학습할 수 있습니다.

● 고3 2021학년도 4월

01

001 □ **make an effort** 노력하다
002 □ **convenience** ⓝ 편의
003 □ **maintenance** ⓝ 유지, 관리

02

004 □ **extend** ⓥ 뻗어나오다, 확장되다
005 □ **injure** ⓥ 다치게 하다, 부상 입히다
006 □ **place stress on** ~에 무리를 주다, ~을 강조하다
007 □ **joint** ⓝ 관절
008 □ **emphasize** ⓥ 강조하다
009 □ **pay attention to** ~에 주의를 기울이다

03

010 □ **talented** ⓐ 재능 있는
011 □ **improve** ⓥ 나아지다, 향상시키다
012 □ **progress** ⓝ 진전
013 □ **concern** ⓝ 걱정, 우려 ⓥ 걱정하다

04

014 □ **redecorate** ⓥ 재단장하다
015 □ **edit** ⓥ 편집하다
016 □ **antique** ⓝ 골동품
017 □ **costume** ⓝ 의상

05

018 □ **car accident** 교통사고
019 □ **stadium** ⓝ 경기장
020 □ **snack bar** 매점
021 □ **by the way** 그나저나, 그런데
022 □ **closet** ⓝ 옷장

06

023 □ **camping supplies** 캠핑 용품
024 □ **recommend** ⓥ 추천하다, 권하다
025 □ **a bit** 조금, 다소

07

026 □ **book signing** 책 사인회
027 □ **be supposed to** ~하기로 되어 있다, ~해야 하다
028 □ **attend** ⓥ 참석하다
029 □ **signature** ⓝ 사인, 서명

08

030 □ **last** ⓥ 지속되다
031 □ **sign up for** ~에 등록하다, ~을 신청하다
032 □ **registration** ⓝ 등록

09

033 □ **rescue** ⓥ 구조하다
034 □ **raise money** 모금하다
035 □ **a wide range of** 매우 다양한
036 □ **on display** 전시 중인
037 □ **contribute** ⓥ 기부하다, 기여하다

10

038 □ **prefer** ⓥ 선호하다
039 □ **stuck in** ~에 갇힌
040 □ **pet-friendly** ⓐ 반려동물에 친화적인

11

041 □ **promotion** ⓝ 승진
042 □ **by the end of** ~의 끝무렵에

12

043 □ **available** ⓐ 이용 가능한
044 □ **depart** ⓥ 출발하다
045 □ **baggage** ⓝ 짐, 수하물
046 □ **destination** ⓝ 목적지

13

047 □ **attach** ⓥ 첨부하다, 부착하다
048 □ **reliable** ⓐ 믿을 만한
049 □ **get a refund** 환불 받다

14

050 □ **apply for** ~에 지원하다
051 □ **concern** ⓝ 걱정거리
052 □ **dormitory** ⓝ 기숙사
053 □ **acquire** ⓥ 얻다, 습득하다
054 □ **stepping stone** 발판, 디딤돌
055 □ **acceptance** ⓝ 수락, 합격

15

056 □ **book report** 독후감, 서평
057 □ **deal with** ~을 다루다
058 □ **broaden** ⓥ 확장하다
059 □ **on a regular basis** 꾸준히, 규칙적으로
060 □ **improve** ⓥ 향상시키다

16~17

061 □ **material** ⓝ 소재, 재료
062 □ **invent** ⓥ 발명하다
063 □ **river plain** 평야
064 □ **medium** ⓝ 매체, 수단
065 □ **abundant** ⓐ 풍부한
066 □ **lay out** 펼치다
067 □ **portable** ⓐ 들고 다닐 수 있는, 휴대용의
068 □ **scroll** ⓝ 두루마리
069 □ **development** ⓝ 발달, 전개
070 □ **characteristic** ⓝ 특징

※ QR코드를 스캔하시면 듣기 방송을 청취하실 수 있습니다.

● 점수 표시가 없는 문항은 모두 2점 ● 문항수 17개 | 배점 37점 | 제한 시간 25분

1번부터 17번까지는 듣고 답하는 문제입니다. 1번부터 15번까지는 한 번만 들려주고, 16번부터 17번까지는 두 번 들려줍니다. 방송을 잘 듣고 답을 하시기 바랍니다.

1. 다음을 듣고, 남자가 하는 말의 목적으로 가장 적절한 것을 고르시오.

① 글쓰기 특강 참여를 독려하려고
② 보고서 작성 지침을 안내하려고
③ 발표 대회 유의 사항을 전달하려고
④ 모둠 프로젝트의 주제를 발표하려고
⑤ 학술 연구 공모전 일정을 공지하려고

2. 대화를 듣고, 두 사람이 하는 말의 주제로 가장 적절한 것을 고르시오.

① 개인 정보 자료 유출의 심각성
② 반려동물 등록제의 장점
③ 동물원 환경 개선의 필요성
④ 멸종 위기 동물 보호 방안
⑤ 생명 윤리 교육의 중요성

3. 대화를 듣고, 두 사람의 관계를 가장 잘 나타낸 것을 고르시오.

① 꽃집 직원 – 고객 ② 식물학자 – 기자
③ 숲 해설사 – 학생 ④ 의사 – 환자
⑤ 전자 제품 판매원 – 택배원

4. 대화를 듣고, 그림에서 대화의 내용과 일치하지 않는 것을 고르시오.

5. 대화를 듣고, 여자가 할 일로 가장 적절한 것을 고르시오.

① 의자 배열하기 ② 조명 확인하기
③ 카메라 설치하기 ④ 프로젝터 연결하기
⑤ 배터리 가져오기

6. 대화를 듣고, 남자가 지불할 금액을 고르시오. [3점]

① $40 ② $63 ③ $66 ④ $70 ⑤ $72

7. 대화를 듣고, 여자가 재즈 콘서트에 갈 수 없는 이유를 고르시오.

① 피아노 레슨을 받아야 해서
② 취업 면접을 보러 가야 해서
③ 아르바이트를 해야 해서
④ 남동생들을 돌봐야 해서
⑤ 결혼식에 참석해야 해서

8. 대화를 듣고, Hampton Soccer Program에 관해 언급되지 않은 것을 고르시오.

① 장소 ② 기간 ③ 강사
④ 모집 인원 ⑤ 참가 비용

9. Auburn Green City Festival에 관한 다음 내용을 듣고, 일치하지 않는 것을 고르시오.

① 5월 29일부터 6월 1일까지 열릴 것이다.
② 올해의 주제는 재활용이다.
③ 개막식에서 유명한 음악가들이 공연할 것이다.
④ 다양한 체험 활동이 준비되어 있다.
⑤ 야간에도 행사가 있을 것이다.

[해설편 p.042]

10. 다음 표를 보면서 대화를 듣고, 두 사람이 수강할 서핑 강좌를 고르시오.

One Day Surfing Lesson

	Lesson	Beach	Level	Group Size	Suit Rental
①	A	Sunrise	Beginner	5	○
②	B	Manson	Intermediate	2	×
③	C	Longport	Intermediate	2	○
④	D	Northwest	Advanced	5	○
⑤	E	Greenpoint	Advanced	2	×

11. 대화를 듣고, 남자의 마지막 말에 대한 여자의 응답으로 가장 적절한 것을 고르시오.

① No. He won't be able to come.
② Exactly. That's why I'm on a diet.
③ Of course. That would be so great.
④ I agree. Baking is difficult to learn.
⑤ I'm sorry. The cookies are all sold out.

12. 대화를 듣고, 여자의 마지막 말에 대한 남자의 응답으로 가장 적절한 것을 고르시오.

① It took me two months to learn to drive.
② I'm at the parking lot of the city library.
③ I don't know how much fuel I need.
④ You could rent this blue car.
⑤ I'll arrive there by 10 a.m.

13. 대화를 듣고, 여자의 마지막 말에 대한 남자의 응답으로 가장 적절한 것을 고르시오.

Man: ______________________________

① Don't worry. I've already made some amazing friends here.
② You're right. I think I should join the campus newspaper.
③ Trust me. I can teach you how to write a good article.
④ Correct. You shouldn't go to too many school events.
⑤ Sorry. Our school newspaper team is already full.

14. 대화를 듣고, 남자의 마지막 말에 대한 여자의 응답으로 가장 적절한 것을 고르시오. [3점]

Woman: ______________________________

① Exactly. It's important for you to take pictures more often.
② Yes. You'll get a college graduation photo album next week.
③ Sure. You'll be able to win an award for nature photography.
④ Right. I'll hire the same professional photographer as last year.
⑤ Thanks. She can help me to learn about majoring in photography.

15. 다음 상황 설명을 듣고, David가 Jenny에게 할 말로 가장 적절한 것을 고르시오. [3점]

David: ______________________________

① You should use fun activities to get the kids to participate in class.
② You don't have to do too many extracurricular activities in school.
③ You need to know that playing games is not helpful for kids.
④ Why don't you motivate the kids to study by themselves?
⑤ How about encouraging kids to respect each other more?

[16 ~ 17] 다음을 듣고, 물음에 답하시오.

16. 여자가 하는 말의 주제로 가장 적절한 것은?

① foods to celebrate birthdays around the world
② mistaken ideas about global birthday traditions
③ traditional dessert recipes around the globe
④ common traits of holiday foods worldwide
⑤ histories of world famous healthy dishes

17. 언급된 나라가 <u>아닌</u> 것은?

① Australia ② Russia ③ Sweden
④ China ⑤ England

[해설편 p.044]

※ QR 코드를 스캔하시면 듣기 방송이 나옵니다. 듣기 방송을 들으며 다음 빈칸을 채우시오. ● 제한 시간 : 25분

01
다음을 듣고, 남자가 하는 말의 목적으로 가장 적절한 것을 고르시오.

M : Hello, students. So far you've done a great job on your science project. Now there's one last task to do. You must submit the report of your project by next Friday. Let me give you __________ __________ __________ __________ __________ __________. First, you need to follow this basic structure: introduction, body, result, and discussion. Second, always stick to your data and evidence. You should make conclusions supported by them. Third, give ✪ __________ __________ __________ references. If not, you can be __________ __________ __________ __________ __________ __________. Lastly, the layout, tables, and graphs should be easy to understand. It'll help you convey your ideas to the readers. If you have any further questions about these guidelines, please ask me after class.

02
대화를 듣고, 두 사람이 하는 말의 주제로 가장 적절한 것을 고르시오.

W : Hey, Simon. Did you see the news about pet registration?
M : I did. I think it's good that the government is beginning ✪ __________ __________ __________ __________.
W : Right. After watching the news, I've been thinking it has a lot of benefits.
M : Yes. It'll help pet owners find their lost pets more easily.
W : That's right. It's because __________ __________ __________ __________ __________ __________.
M : Also, I think the owners will have more responsibility thanks to this system.
W : Yeah. People will think twice before abandoning their pets.
M : In addition, animal rescue workers can easily see who is responsible for the pet.
W : It'll help them track down those bad people and __________ __________ __________ __________.
M : By doing so, we'll have fewer abandoned pets.
W : Yeah. The pet registration system seems good for both pets and pet owners!
M : You can say that again.

03
대화를 듣고, 두 사람의 관계를 가장 잘 나타낸 것을 고르시오.

W : Hi. What can I do for you?
M : Hi. I'm looking for something good for purifying the air in my house.
W : You came to the right place. At our flower shop you can buy plants too.
M : Could you show me some popular ones?
W : Of course. Here are the best-selling indoor plants that ✪ __________ __________ __________ __________ __________ __________.
M : Hmm... I've never grown any plants before.
W : Okay. Then, this one might be perfect for you.
M : It looks good. Is it easy to take care of?
W : Yes. All you have to do is __________ __________ __________ __________ __________.
M : I like it. Is this the right price on this tag? It's ✪ __________ __________ __________ __________.
W : That's right. It's on sale now.
M : Great. I'll take it.

04
대화를 듣고, 그림에서 대화의 내용과 일치하지 <u>않는</u> 것을 고르시오.

M : Hi, Ms. Clark. I'm James Beck. I'm here to look around your day care center __________ __________ __________ __________ __________ __________.
W : Welcome, Mr. Beck. We talked on the phone yesterday, right? Let me show you this room first.
M : That'll be great. I like the banner that says Happy Children's Day on the wall.
W : Thanks. We also ✪ __________ __________ __________ __________ under the banner for Children's Day next week.
M : The kids will love it. What's the picture next to the door?
W : It's __________ __________ __________ __________ __________ __________.
M : Great. There are boxes on the table. What are they for?
W : We put toys in the boxes so the kids can play with them. Does your son like reading books?
M : Actually, he does. Oh, I see the bookshelf under the window.
W : Yes. It has various kinds of books children would like.
M : How nice! My son would love this place.
W : __________ __________ __________ __________.

05
대화를 듣고, 여자가 할 일로 가장 적절한 것을 고르시오.

W : Hey, Chris. I'm so excited for the student-teacher talk show today.
M : Me, too. Since it's a live video streaming at the gym, we should be perfectly prepared.
W : Absolutely. Let's __________ __________ __________ __________ in the checklist one by one.
M : Okay. First, we've already arranged the chairs for the audience, right?
W : Yes, we have. Did you check the stage lights?
M : They worked perfectly. I'll turn them on right before the show starts.
W : Next, cameras. __________ __________ __________ __________ __________ __________ __________ __________?
M : Yeah. I've just set them up as you told me. How about the projector?
W : Don't worry. I've ✪ __________ __________ __________ __________ __________.
M : Good. Is there anything else left to do?
W : You brought the wireless microphones, right?
M : Yes. *[Pause]* Oh, no! I __________ __________ __________ __________ __________ for them.
W : Really? Let me go get the batteries right away.
M : Thanks a lot.

Dictation 10

06

대화를 듣고, 남자가 지불할 금액을 고르시오. [3점]

W : Welcome to Westlake Bird Museum. How may I help you?
M : Hello, I'd like to buy admission tickets. My twin daughters are very interested in birds.
W : Okay. Admission tickets are $20 for an adult and $10 for a child.
M : I'll take one adult ticket and two child tickets. What's this? A guided museum tour?
W : It's a tour where the guide gives excellent explanations about ✪ __________ __________ __________ __________ __________ __________ __________ __________.
M : Nice. How much is it?
W : It's $10 per person. The tour starts soon. You can book it now.
M : Okay. I'll do that for the three of us.
W : So, one adult and two child admission tickets and __________ __________.
M : Yes. Can I use this coupon?
W : Sure. You can get 10% off the total price with the coupon.
M : That's great. I'll pay by credit card.

07

대화를 듣고, 여자가 재즈 콘서트에 갈 수 없는 이유를 고르시오.

M : Rachel. What are you doing?
W : Hey, Jeremy. I'm watching a video clip of jazz pianists.
M : You like jazz! Do you go to jazz concerts often?
W : No. I've never been to one.
M : Well, my brother gave me two jazz concert tickets because __________ __________ __________ __________ __________ that day. So, do you want to go with me?
W : That's amazing! When is the concert?
M : It's next Saturday. Are you available?
W : I'm afraid I'm not.
M : Oh, right! You said you started a part time job on weekends.
W : No. It's only on Sundays. I have to __________ __________ __________ __________ __________ that day.
M : Why do you have to do that?
W : My parents asked me because they're celebrating ✪ __________ __________ __________.
M : I see. I hope we can go together next time.

08

대화를 듣고, Hampton Soccer Program에 관해 언급되지 않은 것을 고르시오.

M : Honey, we need to find a soccer program for Kevin.
W : Right. I brought a brochure about Hampton Soccer Program from the community center.
M : Good. Let me see. The program will be held __________ __________ __________ __________ in Riverside Park.
W : Isn't that good? The park is near our house.
M : Right. It says the program starts on May 2nd, and __________ __________ __________ __________ __________ __________ __________.
W : Yeah. He'll play and practice for three hours a day.
M : Wow. It's a tough schedule.
W : Yes. But he'll improve his skills a lot. Look. The instructor is Aaron Smith. He's a well-known soccer coach in this town.
M : Really? He must be good at teaching. What about the participation fee for the program?
W : It's $400. Do you think it's expensive?
M : It's not bad ✪ __________ __________ __________ __________ __________ __________.
W : Right. Kevin will be happy to hear about this.
M : I'm sure he'll be.

09

Auburn Green City Festival에 관한 다음 내용을 듣고, 일치하지 <u>않는</u> 것을 고르시오.

W : Hello, listeners. I'm Lily Johnson, festival manager. I'm happy to announce the Auburn Green City Festival. It'll be held from May 29th to June 1st. The location will be City Hall Square. This year's theme is recycling. The festival provides various recycling events and activities. At the opening ceremony, famous musicians will perform. To spread the message of recycling, they'll __________ __________ __________ __________ __________ __________. Also, ✪ __________ __________ __________ are prepared. You can experience turning trash into treasure in activities like 'making a shopping bag out of old clothes' and 'creating a recycled art wall'. The festival runs from 9 a.m. to 5 p.m. There'll be __________ __________ __________ __________. We're looking forward to seeing you.

10

다음 표를 보면서 대화를 듣고, 두 사람이 수강할 서핑 강좌를 고르시오.

M : Amelia, do you want to take a one day surfing lesson this weekend?
W : Sure. Let's look for the information online.
M : *[Typing sound]* Look. I found __________ __________ __________ __________ __________.
W : Hmm... do you want to go to Manson beach again?
M : Manson beach is too far from here. Let's try another place.
W : Okay. What about the level? I don't think we have to __________ __________ __________ __________ as we took lessons several times.
M : Right. ✪ __________ __________ __________ __________ seem fine.
W : Yes. And the group size. Should we take a lesson with others or only two of us?
M : We can each get more attention from the instructor if we choose the lesson for two.
W : You're right. Then we have two options left.
M : __________ __________ __________ __________ __________ __________. Let's rent the suits.
W : Okay. Good thinking.
M : Great. Let's take this lesson.

11
대화를 듣고, 남자의 마지막 말에 대한 여자의 응답으로 가장 적절한 것을 고르시오.

M : The cookies smell so good, mom. But _________ _________ _________ _________ _________ _________ _________ _________?

W : These are ✪ _________ _________ _________ _________ for Charity Night tomorrow.

M : I see. I have no plans tomorrow. Can I come and help you?

12
대화를 듣고, 여자의 마지막 말에 대한 남자의 응답으로 가장 적절한 것을 고르시오.

[Phone rings.]

W : Hello. This is Rodney's Car Repair Shop. How may I help you?

M : My car has a problem. It doesn't start. Can you send someone to help me?

W : No problem. ✪ _________ _________ _________ _________ _________ _________ _________.

13
대화를 듣고, 여자의 마지막 말에 대한 남자의 응답으로 가장 적절한 것을 고르시오.

[Cell phone rings.]

W : Hi, Noah. It's been a while. How's your first year of college going?

M : It's so nice to talk to you, Cathy. Making new friends here is very hard.

W : I understand. It's not like high school.

M : I don't know what to do.

W : Well, if you're looking for friends, _________ _________ _________ _________ _________.

M : But I'm not sure about ✪ _________ _________ _________ _________ _________.

W : How about the campus newspaper? You wrote some newspaper articles in high school.

M : Yes. I enjoyed it even when I had to stay up all night.

W : See? You have a passion for writing.

M : I guess it would be fun to join a club I like.

W : And you can get involved in events with other reporters.

M : True. I can have more chances to spend time with them regularly while covering stories.

W : Yeah. It'll allow you to _________ _________ _________ _________ _________ _________ _________ at the campus newspaper.

14
대화를 듣고, 남자의 마지막 말에 대한 여자의 응답으로 가장 적절한 것을 고르시오. [3점]

M : Stephanie, I saw your photos of the school scenery in the lobby. They were amazing!

W : Thanks, Mr. Brown. I'm really glad that people like my photos.

M : Did you learn ✪ _________ _________ _________ _________ _________?

W : Not really. I learned it by myself, searching for information online.

M : How smart! Are you going to _________ _________ _________ _________ _________?

W : I think so. But I don't know much about how to prepare for all that.

M : Do you know anyone who is majoring in that field?

W : Not really. I wish I knew someone who could give me some advice on how to prepare.

M : Hmm... oh! There's Julia Watson. She was one of my students, and she is now a famous photographer.

W : Really? Do you _________ _________ _________ _________ her?

M : Yes. If you want, I'll set up a meeting for you.

15
다음 상황 설명을 듣고, David가 Jenny에게 할 말로 가장 적절한 것을 고르시오. [3점]

M : David has a lot of volunteering experience in teaching children, and Jenny has just started the same volunteering. Jenny imagines that kids will learn many things and focus on her class, but her first class doesn't go as well as she has expected. Jenny tries to teach what she knows as much as possible. However, the kids get bored easily and ✪ _________ _________ _________ _________ _________ _________. Jenny feels frustrated and she asks David for advice. After hearing Jenny's problem, David thinks she should include more interesting activities that would help children _________ _________ _________ _________ _________. So, he wants to tell Jenny that she needs to provide children with _________ _________ _________ _________ _________ _________ _________. In this situation, what would David most likely say to Jenny?

16~17
다음을 듣고, 물음에 답하시오.

W : Hello, students. Last time we talked about traditional holiday foods. Today, let's talk about traditional birthday foods around the world. Food is a big part of _________ _________ _________ _________ _________ _________ _________. First, in Australia, Fairy Bread is a must-have birthday dessert. It's a buttered piece of bread covered with sprinkles all over, and people ✪ _________ _________ _________ _________ _________. Second, in Russia, people get a special message on their birthday, not from a card _________ _________ _________ _________ _________. The message is carved into the dough on top of the pie. Third, eating a bowl of noodles on one's birthday is a deeply rooted tradition in China. It symbolizes the birthday person's long life. Lastly, people in England bake fortune-telling cakes with certain symbolic small things inside on their birthday. For example, if someone bites a coin in their piece of cake, it means _________ _________ _________ _________ _________ _________. Now let's watch a video about these foods.

▶ 정답 : 해설편 046쪽

회차별 영단어 QR 코드 ※ QR 코드를 스캔 후 모바일로 단어장처럼 학습할 수 있습니다.

01

001 □ submit ⓥ 제출하다
002 □ guideline ⓝ 지침
003 □ discussion ⓝ 논의
004 □ stick to ⓥ ~에 충실하다, ~을 고수하다
005 □ reference ⓝ 참조 (문헌)
006 □ be accused of ⓥ ~로 비난받다, 기소되다
007 □ convey ⓥ 전달하다

02

008 □ registration ⓝ 등록
009 □ government ⓝ 정부
010 □ abandon ⓥ 버리다
011 □ fine ⓝ 벌금
012 □ You can say that again. 정말 그래. 전적으로 동의해.

03

013 □ purify ⓥ 정화하다
014 □ pollutant ⓝ 오염원
015 □ take care of ⓥ ~을 돌보다

04

016 □ day care center ⓝ 어린이집, 탁아소
017 □ sign up ⓥ 등록하다, 신청하다
018 □ bet ⓥ 장담하다, 내기하다

05

019 □ live video streaming ⓝ 실시간 영상 송출
020 □ mark off ⓥ (선을 그어) 표시하다
021 □ arrange ⓥ 배열하다, 준비하다

06

022 □ exhibit ⓝ 전시물, 전시회
023 □ habitat ⓝ 서식지

07

024 □ celebrate ⓥ 축하하다, 기념하다
025 □ wedding anniversary ⓝ 결혼기념일

08

026 □ improve ⓥ 향상시키다
027 □ instructor ⓝ 강사
028 □ participation fee ⓝ 참가비
029 □ considering prep ~을 생각하면, 고려하면

09

030 □ recycling ⓝ 재활용
031 □ made of ~로 만들어진
032 □ hands-on ⓐ 체험의, 직접 해보는
033 □ turn A into B ⓥ A를 B로 바꾸다

10

034 □ intermediate ⓐ 중급의
035 □ suit ⓝ (특정한 활동을 위해 입는) 복장 ⓥ 어울리다
036 □ Good thinking. 좋은 생각이야.

11

037 □ baking ⓝ (오븐에) 굽기
038 □ sold out (가게에서 특정 상품이) 다 팔린

12

039 □ start ⓥ 시동이 걸리다, 시동을 걸다
040 □ parking lot 주차장
041 □ fuel ⓝ 연료
042 □ rent ⓥ 대여하다, 빌리다

13

043 □ article ⓝ 기사
044 □ stay up all night ⓥ 밤을 새다
045 □ get involved in ⓥ ~에 참여하다, 엮이다
046 □ regularly ad 정기적으로
047 □ connect with ⓥ ~와 어울리다, 연결되다

14

048 □ scenery ⓝ 풍경
049 □ professionally ad 전문적으로
050 □ major in ⓥ ~을 전공하다
051 □ keep in touch with ⓥ ~와 연락하다

15

052 □ pay attention to ⓥ ~에 주의를 기울이다
053 □ frustrated ⓐ 좌절한
054 □ take part in ⓥ ~에 참여하다
055 □ engage A in B ⓥ A를 B에 참여시키다
056 □ extracurricular ⓐ 교과 외의

16~17

057 □ celebrate ⓥ 축하하다, 기념하다
058 □ personalize ⓥ 개인의 필요에 맞추다
059 □ carve ⓥ 새기다, 조각하다
060 □ symbolize ⓥ 상징하다
061 □ bite ⓥ 깨물다
062 □ trait ⓝ 특성

11회 ● 2025학년도 6월 모의평가 고3 영어 듣기

※ QR코드를 스캔하시면 듣기 방송을 청취하실 수 있습니다.

● 점수 표시가 없는 문항은 모두 2점 ● 문항수 17개 | 배점 37점 | 제한 시간 25분

1번부터 17번까지는 듣고 답하는 문제입니다. 1번부터 15번까지는 한 번만 들려주고, 16번부터 17번까지는 두 번 들려줍니다. 방송을 잘 듣고 답을 하시기 바랍니다.

MP3

1. 다음을 듣고, 여자가 하는 말의 목적으로 가장 적절한 것을 고르시오.

① 계절별 꽃의 종류를 소개하려고
② 꽃꽂이 동호회 가입을 독려하려고
③ 정기적인 꽃 배송 서비스를 홍보하려고
④ 꽃을 신선하게 관리하는 법을 알리려고
⑤ 전문적으로 꽃을 가꾸는 사람을 모집하려고

2. 대화를 듣고, 남자의 의견으로 가장 적절한 것을 고르시오.

① 자녀의 인터넷 사용 시간을 제한해야 한다.
② 소셜 미디어는 자녀의 학업에 도움이 된다.
③ 소셜 미디어를 통한 영화 홍보는 효과적이다.
④ 온라인에서 사생활을 공유하는 것은 위험하다.
⑤ 소셜 미디어를 통해 자녀를 더 잘 이해할 수 있다.

3. 다음을 듣고, 여자가 하는 말의 요지로 가장 적절한 것을 고르시오.

① 적성에 맞는 업무를 맡으면 직장에 대한 만족도가 높아진다.
② 세미나에 참여하는 것은 팀워크 향상에 효과가 있다.
③ 동료의 피드백은 업무 능력 향상에 도움이 된다.
④ 동료와의 과도한 경쟁은 업무 효율성을 떨어뜨린다.
⑤ 프로젝트를 잘 수행하기 위해서는 사전 계획이 필수적이다.

4. 대화를 듣고, 그림에서 대화의 내용과 일치하지 않는 것을 고르시오.

5. 대화를 듣고, 남자가 할 일로 가장 적절한 것을 고르시오.

① 회의실 예약하기
② 참가 인원 확인하기
③ 유인물 복사하기
④ 음료 주문하기
⑤ 점심 메뉴 정하기

6. 대화를 듣고, 여자가 지불할 금액을 고르시오.

① $54 ② $60 ③ $72 ④ $80 ⑤ $90

7. 대화를 듣고, 남자가 Prime Travel Writing Contest에 참가할 수 없는 이유를 고르시오.

① 여행이 계획되어 있어서
② 결혼식에 참석해야 해서
③ 글쓰기 수업을 들어야 해서
④ 다른 대회에 참가해야 해서
⑤ 대회를 준비할 시간이 없어서

8. 대화를 듣고, Starry Family Reading Night 행사에 관해 언급되지 않은 것을 고르시오.

① 주제 ② 시작 시간 ③ 장소
④ 신청 방법 ⑤ 참가비

9. Wondrous Tastes 행사에 관한 다음 내용을 듣고, 일치하지 않는 것을 고르시오.

① 3일 동안 진행된다.
② 한 개의 매장에서만 열린다.
③ 새로운 다섯 종류 도넛의 샘플이 제공된다.
④ 모든 방문객은 무료로 커피를 받는다.
⑤ 도넛 한 상자를 구매한 사람들은 할인 쿠폰을 받는다.

[해설편 p.046]

10. 다음 표를 보면서 대화를 듣고, 여자가 주문할 연필꽂이를 고르시오.

Pencil Holders

	Model	Price	Material	Shape	Phone Stand
①	A	$10	plastic	elephant	×
②	B	$10	metal	bear	○
③	C	$15	metal	elephant	○
④	D	$20	wood	bear	×
⑤	E	$25	wood	bear	○

11. 대화를 듣고, 남자의 마지막 말에 대한 여자의 응답으로 가장 적절한 것을 고르시오. [3점]

① I agree. Let's look for another resort.
② How disappointing! The rooms are fully booked.
③ Congratulations! You did a good job at the conference.
④ That's okay. I'm sure we can reschedule the conference.
⑤ What a relief! Now I don't need to change the reservation.

12. 대화를 듣고, 여자의 마지막 말에 대한 남자의 응답으로 가장 적절한 것을 고르시오.

① I'm sorry. You're on the wrong train.
② Good point. I'll check the train schedule.
③ Don't worry. The concert lasts less than one hour.
④ Hurry up! You'd better take a taxi rather than a train.
⑤ No problem. I'm glad to give you a ride to the concert.

13. 대화를 듣고, 남자의 마지막 말에 대한 여자의 응답으로 가장 적절한 것을 고르시오.

Woman: ______________________

① Why not? You can take my math class.
② I hope so. I'll send him an email right away.
③ Probably not. He should've checked his message.
④ Certainly. Thanks for choosing me to be your guest.
⑤ That's right. We've already invited a mathematician.

14. 대화를 듣고, 여자의 마지막 말에 대한 남자의 응답으로 가장 적절한 것을 고르시오. [3점]

Man: ______________________

① I see. Then I'll come back with it later.
② Oh, no. I can't find a pharmacy nearby.
③ That's terrible. I hope you get well soon.
④ Of course. Relaxing is good for your eyes.
⑤ I'm not sure. You'd better try another medicine.

15. 다음 상황 설명을 듣고, Jason이 Kathy에게 할 말로 가장 적절한 것을 고르시오. [3점]

Jason: ______________________

① Thanks for buying me a new pair of pants.
② You need to wash your car as quickly as possible.
③ Get the dust off your clothes before getting in the car.
④ Can you first take off your jacket when we get home?
⑤ Don't forget to put on warm clothes before you go hiking.

[16～17] 다음을 듣고, 물음에 답하시오.

16. 남자가 하는 말의 주제로 가장 적절한 것은?

① practical use of photography in various fields
② importance of choosing a practical field for research
③ applications of high-speed cameras in academic fields
④ sudden decline of photography in the contemporary era
⑤ how to take photographs effectively in specialized fields

17. 언급된 분야가 아닌 것은?

① space science ② biology ③ medicine
④ psychology ⑤ education

[해설편 p.048]

※ QR 코드를 스캔하시면 듣기 방송이 나옵니다. 듣기 방송을 들으며 다음 빈칸을 채우시오. ● 제한 시간 : 25분

01

다음을 듣고, 여자가 하는 말의 목적으로 가장 적절한 것을 고르시오.

W : Hello, viewers! Are you too busy to visit a flower shop but want to experience the happiness that comes from flowers? Happy Florette can save you time and energy while you enjoy the benefits of fresh flowers. You can have them delivered weekly, every other week, or monthly ___ __ ______________ ________. The beautiful seasonal flowers are selected by our professional florists, and they are regularly delivered ✪ ________ __________ ___ ________ ________ _________ __________. Plus, for new customers, we send ✪ __ ____________ _______ ____ __ ______. Don't miss out on our regular flower delivery service, and bring the beauty of the season into your house.

02

대화를 듣고, 남자의 의견으로 가장 적절한 것을 고르시오.

M : Honey, you look worried.

W : Yeah. __ _________ _________ ___________ _______________ in our son Dave's life since we don't talk much these days.

M : I felt the same way. But using social media ✪ _________ _____ ________________ _______ _________.

W : What do you mean?

M : I follow him on his favorite social media service, and it allows me to know him more deeply.

W : Honestly, I'm not a fan of social media.

M : I know. *[Tapping sound]* But look at this. Dave often posts his thoughts and feelings on it.

W : Wow, he posts so many things about himself.

M : Yes. You can see ✪ ________ __________ ______ ___________ _______ _______________ ___. I think if parents use social media like me, they will understand their children better.

W : Hmm. I guess I should start using it.

03

다음을 듣고, 여자가 하는 말의 요지로 가장 적절한 것을 고르시오.

W : Good morning, everyone. I'm Sharon Parker from the Lenyard Consulting Company. ______ ______________ ___ ____ ________ for the employee training seminar. I've heard many of you are struggling to get your projects done well. However, there's one simple and effective way to improve your work performance. Ask your co-workers ✪ ___ _______ _______ _______________ ____ ________ _________. They may have fresh perspectives and be able to find creative solutions ✪ ______ ______ ____________ _____________ ___. Furthermore, this feedback helps identify your strong and weak points at work. So, you should seek your colleagues' feedback, which will help you to perform better in the workplace. Give it a try and see the difference.

04

대화를 듣고, 그림에서 대화의 내용과 일치하지 <u>않는</u> 것을 고르시오.

M : Hey, Rachel. How was your weekend?

W : Hi, Liam. I had fun with my kids on my rooftop. Here's a picture.

M : It looks nice. *[Pause]* Wow. I like the round pool.

W : Yeah. It's perfect for my kids to play in. Do you see this stripe-patterned chair?

M : Yes. I love it. You can sit in the chair and watch your kids.

W : You're right. I just ✪ ___________ _____ ______ ___ _________ _____ ________. Isn't she cute?

M : Oh, she's so lovely. I also see there are three beach balls on the bench. Your kids must love playing with them.

W : Yes, they do. They're gifts from their grandmother.

M : Look at the "NO RUNNING" sign on the wall. _________ __ ____________ _______ ________ __________?

W : Yes, it does. I'm glad ✪ __ ______ __ _____ _________. Why don't you bring your kids next weekend?

M : Sounds great!

05

대화를 듣고, 남자가 할 일로 가장 적절한 것을 고르시오.

W : Steve, __________ ________ ______________ on the Greener Path Workshop for a few weeks. It's just around the corner.

M : Right. I really want to make this workshop successful. We should ✪ ____ _______ _____ _________________.

W : Sure. Let's start with the conference room. I've got the confirmation that the room is for 100 people. Is that okay?

M : Of course. Around 80 people are expected to come, so it'll be large enough. How about the presentation handouts?

W : I got them from Mr. Lee and made copies of them.

M : Great. I'm sure that they'll be helpful for the audience. Also, I've confirmed that ✪ _________ _______ ____ ___________ _______ ________ _____ ___________________.

W : Good. One last thing. Did you order drinks?

M : Not yet. Thanks for reminding me. I'll take care of it.

W : Perfect! It seems like everything will be ready in time.

06

대화를 듣고, 여자가 지불할 금액을 고르시오.

M : Welcome to ✪ _________ _____ _____ ___ *Secrets in Paris.* How may I help you?
W : Hi, I'd like to buy admission tickets.
M : Certainly, admission tickets are $20 per adult and $10 per child.
W : I need two adult tickets and one child ticket.
M : All right. Do you want the family photo service?
W : I'm not sure. What is it?
M : We take family photos at each special filming location and provide you with a book of the photos.
W : How interesting! How much is it?
M : It's $30.
W : Then, ✪ ________ _____ ______ ___ _______.
M : Okay. So that's tickets for two adults and one child along with the family photo service, right?
W : Yes. Are there any discounts available?
M : Sure. You'll get a 10% discount off the total __________ ________ ___ __ ____________.
W : Great. Here is my credit card.

07

대화를 듣고, 남자가 Prime Travel Writing Contest에 참가할 수 없는 이유를 고르시오.

[Cell phone rings.]
W : Hello, Brian.
M : Hello, Kate. What's up?
W : I heard about the Prime Travel Writing Contest, and I thought ______ ________ ____ ____________.
M : Oh, I know about it. But I can't participate.
W : Really? You love writing. Are you planning to attend a different contest?
M : Not at all. There ✪ _________ ______ ________ ____________ at that time.
W : Why not then? You have almost one month to prepare because the contest will be on July 13th.
M : Well, I don't have a problem preparing by then.
W : That's good. Hmm. Is it because you have vacation plans?
M : No, I'm not traveling.
W : Then, why ✪ ________ ______ _______________?
M : The simple truth is that I'm attending my sister's wedding that day.
W : Oh, now I understand. Tell her congratulations for me.
M : Of course, I'll let her know.

08

대화를 듣고, Starry Family Reading Night 행사에 관해 언급되지 않은 것을 고르시오.

M : Honey, Tony's school is going to have the Starry Family Reading Night.
W : Oh, isn't it the event where we read and share about books?
M : Yes. The ✪ _________ ___ _____ _________ _________ is "Female Adventurers."
W : That sounds interesting. When is the event?
M : It'll be held next Friday night.
W : I see. I have an important meeting that afternoon. ________ _______ ______ _______?
M : It starts at 8 p.m. Can you make it?
W : Yes, I'm sure I can. Do you know ✪ _________ __ ______ ___? I heard the school library is being remodeled.
M : Actually, it was finished last week. So the reading night is going to be in the library.
W : Oh, I didn't know that. How can we sign up?
M : We can sign up on the school's website. I'll do it tomorrow.
W : Terrific! It's going to be a great night.

09

Wondrous Tastes 행사에 관한 다음 내용을 듣고, 일치하지 않는 것을 고르시오.

M : Hello, listeners. This is John Brady from Creamery Doughnut. I'm pleased to introduce the event, Wondrous Tastes, where you can taste our new doughnuts. This event will be held for three days from June 21st to 23rd. So ________ ______ ___ ________ your calendar. Wondrous Tastes will take place at all of our stores. You can find the closest store to you on our website. At the event, samples of five new kinds of doughnuts will be provided. These doughnuts have special flavored creams and toppings. Also, all visitors to the event will receive a free coffee. And you know, ✪ _________ _____ _____ ______ ___ __. Those who buy a box of doughnuts ✪ ______ _____ __ ___________ _________. Come and enjoy the wonderful tastes of our new doughnuts.

10

다음 표를 보면서 대화를 듣고, 여자가 주문할 연필꽂이를 고르시오.

W : Hi, Ben. Could you help me buy a pencil holder for my nephew?
M : Sure, Jessie. ✪ ________ ______ _________ _________ some online?
W : Yes, and I ✪ _____________ ________ _________ ___ these five models.
M : Let me see. I think a 25-dollar pencil holder is too expensive.
W : You're right. Hmm, they come in several materials. Which one would be good?
M : I don't recommend plastic. Since it's light, _____ _____ _________ ____________ _______.
W : That's true. You know, the bear ones look cuter than the elephant ones. Plus, bears are my nephew's favorite.
M : Well, you have two options left. Do you think your nephew needs one with a phone stand?
W : Of course. It'll be convenient for him.
M : Then you should go with this one.
W : Thanks for helping me. I'll order it now.

11

대화를 듣고, 남자의 마지막 말에 대한 여자의 응답으로 가장 적절한 것을 고르시오. [3점]

M : Honey, what are you doing?
W : ______ _________ ___ ___________ the date for our booking at the resort. You told me you need to attend a conference on that day, right?
M : Oh, I forgot to tell you. The conference ✪ _____ ________ ______________, so I'll be completely free then.

12

대화를 듣고, 여자의 마지막 말에 대한 남자의 응답으로 가장 적절한 것을 고르시오.

W : Hello, Andy. Do you have plans tonight?
M : Hi, Lisa. I'm going to a jazz concert in Midtown City. ✪ ________ _______ ________ __ _______ ___ get there by car? I need to be there by 7.
W : Usually, one hour. But today's Friday, so the traffic will be horrible. ________ _________ _______ _______ __ ________ that works for you?

13

대화를 듣고, 남자의 마지막 말에 대한 여자의 응답으로 가장 적절한 것을 고르시오.

[Cell phone rings.]
M : Hello, Ms. Miller. Did you see the message I sent this morning?
W : Hi, Mr. Peterson. No, I didn't. I ______ ________ ____ ______________. What's it about?
M : It's about our math club activity on the last Friday of next month. I was thinking we could invite a ✪ ________________________ ___ _____ ___________ ________.
W : Oh, I see. Can you tell me more?
M : Students would hear about a mathematician's life and work experiences. I think it would further inspire those who are interested in mathematics.
W : Hmm, that makes sense. Actually, there are several students who want to be mathematicians in the future. So, let's do it.
M : Okay, but I can't ✪ _________ ___ ______ _________________________ ___ _________.
W : I know someone I can contact. I met him at the math workshop I attended.
M : Really? I wonder if he's available on that day.

14

대화를 듣고, 여자의 마지막 말에 대한 남자의 응답으로 가장 적절한 것을 고르시오. [3점]

W : Good afternoon. May I help you?
M : Yes. I'm looking for eye drops.
W : We ________ _____________ _________. Do you have something in mind?
M : Not really. What would you recommend?
W : It depends on your symptoms.
M : My eyes are dry and red.
W : Hmm. ✪ ________ ________ ________ ______ ______ those symptoms?
M : I've had them for around one week.
W : Have you used these eye drops to relieve your symptoms?
M : Yes, I'm using those eye drops now. They help but the problem isn't going away.
W : In that case, people usually take stronger eye drops.
M : Can I get those? I really want ✪ ___ _____ _________ ___ ________ ___ _____________.
W : I'm sorry. But to get the stronger eye drops, you need a prescription from a doctor.

15

다음 상황 설명을 듣고, Jason이 Kathy에게 할 말로 가장 적절한 것을 고르시오. [3점]

W : Jason has a new car and tries to keep it from getting dirty. On one weekend, Jason and his daughter Kathy take a camping trip together. During the trip, they go fishing, hiking and rock climbing. Due to the intense activities, their jackets and pants ✪ _____________ _____________ _______ _______. Now it's time to go home. Jason shakes the dust off from his clothes before he gets into the car because he wants to keep his car clean. However, Kathy ✪ _______ ________________ _________ the dust on her jacket and pants. So Jason wants to tell her to remove the dust from her clothes before _____ _____ ___ _____ _____. In this situation, what would Jason most likely say to Kathy?

16~17

다음을 듣고, 물음에 답하시오.

M : Hello, students. Do you know ✪ _______ __________________ ___________________ __ ___ _____ ______________________ _____? Today, I'd like to talk about the practical applications of photography. It's commonly used in several areas. Here are some examples. First, people use photography to look out into space. Photographs are used in space science to study other planets in our solar system and even distant stars. Second, photography ___ ____________ ________ ___ _____________ to show what cannot be seen with the naked eye. Biologists often use photographic images to study life forms that are extremely small. Third, photography is used extensively in medicine. X-ray film ✪ ____________ ______________ _________ ________________, which helps doctors to choose the best treatment. Lastly, photography provides a useful tool for education. Photographs allow learners to visualize unfamiliar concepts and abstract ideas in clear and concrete ways. Various uses of photography are constantly being developed in the modern era. Now let's watch a video about how photography is applied for practical purposes.

▶ 정답 : 해설편 050쪽

VOCA LIST 11

회차별 영단어 QR 코드 ※ QR 코드를 스캔 후 모바일로 단어장처럼 학습할 수 있습니다.

● 고3 2025학년도 6월

01

001 □ experience ⓝ 경험
002 □ benefit ⓝ 혜택
003 □ reasonable ⓐ 합리적인
004 □ seasonal ⓐ 제철의
005 □ regularly ad 정기적으로
006 □ vase ⓝ 꽃병

02

007 □ allow ⓥ 허락하다
008 □ deeply ad 깊게
009 □ be a fan of ~를 좋아하다
010 □ post ⓥ 올리다
011 □ thought ⓝ 생각

03

012 □ employee ⓝ 직원
013 □ struggle ⓥ 애쓰다
014 □ effective ⓐ 효과적인
015 □ improve ⓥ 향상하다
016 □ performance ⓝ 성과
017 □ perspective ⓝ 관점
018 □ identify ⓥ 확인하다
019 □ seek ⓥ 구하다
020 □ colleague ⓝ 동료

04

021 □ rooftop ⓝ 옥상
022 □ stripe-patterned 줄무늬의
023 □ careful ⓐ 조심하는
024 □ put up ~를 게시하다

05

025 □ preparation ⓝ 준비
026 □ go over ~를 점검하다
027 □ confirmation ⓝ 확인
028 □ audience ⓝ 청중
029 □ remind ⓥ 상기시키다
030 □ in time 제 시간에

06

031 □ admission ⓝ 입장
032 □ interesting ⓐ 흥미로운
033 □ weekday 평일
034 □ credit card 신용 카드

07

035 □ participate ⓥ 참석하다
036 □ attend ⓥ 참가하다
037 □ vacation ⓝ 휴가

08

038 □ theme ⓝ 주제
039 □ library ⓝ 도서관
040 □ sign up 신청하다

09

041 □ wondrous ⓐ 경이로운
042 □ taste ⓥ 맛보다
043 □ mark ⓥ 표시하다
044 □ take place 열리다
045 □ flavored 맛이 나는

10

046 □ pencil holder 연필꽂이
047 □ nephew ⓝ 조카
048 □ narrow ⓥ 좁히다
049 □ recommend ⓥ 추천하다
050 □ light ⓐ 가벼운
051 □ knock over 넘어지다
052 □ convenient ⓐ 편리한

11

053 □ booking ⓝ 예약
054 □ conference ⓝ 회의
055 □ completely ad 완전히
056 □ relief ⓐ 안도하는
057 □ reservation ⓝ 예약

12

058 □ be going to ~할 예정이다
059 □ usually ad 보통
060 □ horrible ⓐ 끔찍한

13

061 □ mathematician ⓝ 수학자
062 □ further ad 더
063 □ inspire ⓥ 영감을 주다
064 □ interested in ~에 관심이 있다
065 □ make sense 일리가 있다
066 □ invite ⓥ 초대하다
067 □ contact ⓥ 연락하다
068 □ wonder ⓥ 궁금하다

14

069 □ eye drops 안약
070 □ various ⓐ 다양한
071 □ dry ⓐ 건조한
072 □ symptom ⓝ 증상
073 □ relieve ⓥ 완화하다
074 □ prescription ⓝ 처방전

15

075 □ intense ⓐ 격렬한
076 □ be concerned about ~에 신경 쓰다

16~17

077 □ widespread ⓐ 널리 퍼진
078 □ contemporary ⓐ 현대의
079 □ practical ⓐ 실용적인
080 □ application ⓝ 이용
081 □ look out into ~을 내다보다
082 □ naked eye 맨눈
083 □ extremely ad 극도의
084 □ extensively ad 광범위하게
085 □ reveal ⓥ 드러내다
086 □ treatment ⓝ 치료
087 □ visualize ⓥ 시각화하다
088 □ unfamiliar ⓐ 생소한
089 □ abstract ⓐ 추상적인
090 □ concrete ⓐ 구체적인
091 □ constantly ad 끊임없이

12회 • 2024학년도 6월 모의평가 고3 영어 듣기

※ QR코드를 스캔하시면 듣기 방송을 청취하실 수 있습니다.

● 점수 표시가 없는 문항은 모두 2점 ● 문항수 17개 | 배점 37점 | 제한 시간 25분

1번부터 17번까지는 듣고 답하는 문제입니다. 1번부터 15번까지는 한 번만 들려주고, 16번부터 17번까지는 두 번 들려줍니다. 방송을 잘 듣고 답을 하시기 바랍니다.

1. 다음을 듣고, 남자가 하는 말의 목적으로 가장 적절한 것을 고르시오.

① 수족관 직원 채용 광고를 하려고
② 수족관 내 기념품 상점을 홍보하려고
③ 수족관 내부 사진 촬영 금지를 안내하려고
④ 수족관 물고기에게 먹이를 주지 말 것을 당부하려고
⑤ 수족관 수조의 유리벽을 두드리지 말 것을 요청하려고

2. 대화를 듣고, 여자의 의견으로 가장 적절한 것을 고르시오.

① 아기용 선물은 깨끗이 소독해야 한다.
② 아기의 체온 유지에 모자가 도움이 된다.
③ 실내에서는 모자를 벗는 것이 바람직하다.
④ 아기의 방은 적절한 온도 유지가 중요하다.
⑤ 에어컨 사용 시 주기적인 환기가 필요하다.

3. 다음을 듣고, 남자가 하는 말의 요지로 가장 적절한 것을 고르시오.

① 생각을 비울 수 있는 취미가 필요하다.
② 악기 연주는 감수성 발달에 도움이 된다.
③ 작문 능력 향상에는 생각의 정리가 중요하다.
④ 올바른 자세를 위해 운동을 꾸준히 해야 한다.
⑤ 메시지를 명확하게 전달하는 습관을 길러야 한다.

4. 대화를 듣고, 그림에서 대화의 내용과 일치하지 <u>않는</u> 것을 고르시오.

5. 대화를 듣고, 여자가 할 일로 가장 적절한 것을 고르시오.

① 청소 업체 예약하기
② 인터넷 설치 신청하기
③ 아들의 새 학교에 연락하기
④ 버릴 의자에 스티커 붙이기
⑤ 이사 업체에 이사 날짜 확인하기

6. 대화를 듣고, 남자가 지불할 금액을 고르시오. [3점]

① $36 ② $40 ③ $45 ④ $50 ⑤ $54

7. 대화를 듣고, 여자가 독서 모임에 참석하지 <u>못한</u> 이유를 고르시오.

① 고객과의 대화가 계획보다 오래 걸려서
② 아이를 돌봐 줄 사람을 찾지 못해서
③ 공상 과학 장르를 이해하지 못해서
④ 신제품을 온라인에 출시해야 해서
⑤ 모임 날짜를 전달받지 못해서

8. 대화를 듣고, Now-and-Then Tech Showcase에 관해 언급되지 <u>않은</u> 것을 고르시오.

① 목적 ② 시작일 ③ 장소
④ 관람 시간 ⑤ 입장료

9. Found 211에 관한 다음 내용을 듣고, 일치하지 <u>않는</u> 것을 고르시오.

① H-rail 기차에서 분실한 물건에 대한 정보를 제공한다.
② 웹사이트 회원이 아니어도 사용할 수 있다.
③ 분실한 물건 발견 시 문자 메시지로 통지한다.
④ 다양한 언어로 외국어 서비스가 제공된다.
⑤ 모바일 앱에서도 사용할 수 있다.

[해설편 p.051]

10. 다음 표를 보면서 대화를 듣고, 여자가 구매할 쿠키 커터 세트를 고르시오.

Cookie Cutter Sets

	Type	Shape	Price	Material	Color
①	A	Heart	$11	Metal	Yellow
②	B	Circle	$11	Plastic	Red
③	C	Heart	$14	Silicone	Yellow
④	D	Star	$14	Metal	Red
⑤	E	Circle	$20	Silicone	Yellow

11. 대화를 듣고, 여자의 마지막 말에 대한 남자의 응답으로 가장 적절한 것을 고르시오.

① Sorry. I forgot to invite him to my birthday party last week.
② That's too bad. I'll let him know the meeting is cancelled.
③ That's weird. He took all the pictures away with him.
④ Alright. Please say thanks to Mr. Williams for them.
⑤ I'd be happy to. He'll love to have the pictures.

12. 대화를 듣고, 남자의 마지막 말에 대한 여자의 응답으로 가장 적절한 것을 고르시오.

① What do you mean? The trip was last week.
② I'm sorry to hear that. I hope he'll get better soon.
③ That's a relief. I'm glad that he's doing well in school.
④ Pardon me? I completely forgot the festival tomorrow.
⑤ It's no big deal. I'll check the opening day for the festival.

13. 대화를 듣고, 여자의 마지막 말에 대한 남자의 응답으로 가장 적절한 것을 고르시오. [3점]

Man: ______________________________

① Of course. He'll be grateful for my valuable tips.
② I hope not. You don't have enough time to study psychology.
③ Good idea. I can definitely get information on that from him.
④ What a shame! I should've invited the former graduates.
⑤ No wonder. They didn't show up yesterday.

14. 대화를 듣고, 남자의 마지막 말에 대한 여자의 응답으로 가장 적절한 것을 고르시오.

Woman: ______________________________

① No problem. I can walk him and get some exercise too.
② Certainly. He can help me with my assignment this weekend.
③ Absolutely! You can join me on my business trip tomorrow.
④ Keep it up! You can take care of yourself by working out.
⑤ Not at all. I don't mind walking you to your house.

15. 다음 상황 설명을 듣고, Kate가 Professor Lee에게 할 말로 가장 적절한 것을 고르시오. [3점]

Kate: ______________________________

① Do you mind if I change my topic for the writing contest?
② I was wondering why my presentation was postponed.
③ I'm looking forward to awarding you the first prize.
④ I'm afraid you're not allowed to attend the ceremony.
⑤ Could I switch my presentation date with another student's?

[16~17] 다음을 듣고, 물음에 답하시오.

16. 여자가 하는 말의 주제로 가장 적절한 것은?

① the communication patterns of insects
② the reasons why insects dry their wings
③ the ways insects protect their eggs in the rain
④ the behavior of various insects on a rainy day
⑤ the significance of insects' role in the food chain

17. 언급된 곤충이 <u>아닌</u> 것은?

① cockroaches ② beetles ③ mosquitos
④ ants ⑤ flies

[해설편 p.053]

※ QR 코드를 스캔하시면 듣기 방송이 나옵니다. 듣기 방송을 들으며 다음 빈칸을 채우시오. ● 제한 시간 : 25분

01

다음을 듣고, 남자가 하는 말의 목적으로 가장 적절한 것을 고르시오.

M : Visitors, may I have your attention please? This is Anderson Thompson, manager of Benjiville Aquarium. While enjoying your time at our aquarium, we kindly request that ✪ ______ ______ ______ ______ ______ ______ of the aquarium tanks. ______ ______ ______ can be quite loud for the fish in the water. The vibrations from the knocking can make the fish stressed, and they might become sick. So, to ______ ______ ______ ______, we ask you not to hit the glass walls of the aquarium tanks. Thank you for your cooperation.

02

대화를 듣고, 여자의 의견으로 가장 적절한 것을 고르시오.

M : Hey, Laura. Mom asked me what we're going to buy for our newborn baby cousin.
W : Oh, yeah. What should we get? Did Mom suggest anything?
M : She said a hat might be a good choice.
W : That sounds good. ✪ ______ ______ ______ __ ______, wearing a hat helps maintain babies' body temperature.
M : It's the beginning of summer, though. Do you think the baby will really need one?
W : Yes. Without a hat on, the baby might get cold when the air conditioning is on.
M : I didn't consider that. Now I understand why I've seen so many babies ______ ______ ______ in the summer.
W : Right. Hats help to ✪ ______ ______ ______ ______ ______.
M : Okay. Let's find the cutest hat in the world for our baby cousin!
W : Absolutely.

03

다음을 듣고, 남자가 하는 말의 요지로 가장 적절한 것을 고르시오.

M : Hello, listeners. This is Claude's Radio Advice Show. One of our listeners sent me a message. It says that she's having a hard time these days because she ______ __ ______ ______ ______ ______. I think many of you may be having a similar problem. If this is true for you, you ______ __ ______ that can help clear your mind. For example, you can try going camping, gardening, or playing a musical instrument. And any kind of exercise, such as hiking, can also be good. How about ✪ ______ ______ ______ with one of these hobbies? We'll be right back after the break with more tips. Stay tuned!

04

대화를 듣고, 그림에서 대화의 내용과 일치하지 <u>않는</u> 것을 고르시오.

W : Arthur, how did the rehearsal for your drama club go?
M : It went well. Oh, I have a picture of it on my smartphone. Do you want to see it?
W : Sure. Let me have a look. *[Pause]* ✪ ______ ______ ______ ______ ______ in front of the window.
M : Yeah. That's me.
W : You look so cool in the costume.
M : Thanks. Do you see the two paintings on the wall? I painted them myself.
W : Wow, they look great. I also like ______ ______ ______ ______ ______ ______. Where did you get that?
M : I bought it at a flea market. I also got the flower-patterned rug at the market.
W : They all ______ ______ ______ well. Oh, there's a cat under the chair. I think it's so cute.
M : I agree. By the way, you're going to come and see my play, right?
W : Of course! I'm looking forward to seeing you perform.

05

대화를 듣고, 여자가 할 일로 가장 적절한 것을 고르시오.

W : Honey, our moving day is coming up in two weeks.
M : Yeah. I think we need to check our to-do list again.
W : Okay. We ✪ ______ ______ ______ from the moving company for the date, right?
M : Yes, we did. Did you sign up for the Internet at our new place?
W : Uh-huh, I did. It should be connected by the move-in date. And I already put stickers on the chairs we will throw away.
M : Great. Oh, I still have to ______ ______ ______ ______.
W : That's okay. You have time. Did you call our son's new school? Did they tell you what he needs to take with him on his first day?
M : Yes, he has to ______ ______ ______ for his gym class. Oh, we forgot to make a reservation with the cleaning company.
W : No worries. I'll do it right now.
M : Thanks.

06

대화를 듣고, 남자가 지불할 금액을 고르시오. [3점]

W : Welcome to the Fresh Salad Store. What would you like to have?
M : Hi. I'm not sure. What do you recommend?
W : The beef salad is pretty popular. And some people like the chicken salad too.
M : Okay. How much are they?
W : It's $20 for the beef salad and $15 for the chicken salad.
M : Then, I'll take ______ ______ ______ ______ ______ ______ ______.
W : Good choice.
M : ___ ______ ______ with the salads?
W : Yes. All salads come with lemon dressing for free. But if you want a different kind of dressing, you need to pay $5 extra for each.
M : I'll just take the lemon dressing. Can I use this 10% discount coupon?
W : Yes, you can. So, that's one beef salad and two chicken salads. ✪ ______ ______ ______ ______?
M : Yes. Here's my coupon and credit card.

Dictation 12

07

대화를 듣고, 여자가 독서 모임에 참석하지 못한 이유를 고르시오.

M : Sandra, I didn't see you at the company book club meeting yesterday.
W : Yeah, I really wanted to go, but I ________ ________ ___.
M : You missed a really interesting discussion about our science fiction novel. That's ✪ ________.
W : It is. But I had to take care of something.
M : What was that? You couldn't find a babysitter for your son like last time?
W : No. My husband was with him.
M : Well, then was it because ✪ ________ ________ online yesterday?
W : No, I wasn't involved with that.
M : Then, why couldn't you come to the meeting?
W : A conversation with a client took longer than I had planned.
M : Oh, I see. I was worried about you. I hope everything went well.
W : Yes, it did. Thanks for asking.

08

대화를 듣고, Now-and-Then Tech Showcase에 관해 언급되지 않은 것을 고르시오.

M : Hannah, I saw a poster at the library that you might be interested in.
W : What's it about, Dad?
M : It says the Now-and-Then Tech Showcase is coming to our city soon. The purpose of the showcase is to ________ ________ ________ ________ that local companies have developed.
W : Great! When does it start?
M : It'll open from Saturday, June 24th.
W : Good! I think I can go then. Do you remember where it's going to be held?
M : Yes, at Golden Maples Field Stadium.
W : ✪ ________ ________! I can walk there. ___ ___ ___ ________ ____?
M : Um... I don't remember. Maybe you can check that online.
W : Yeah. Just a second. *[Tapping sounds]* Oh, the admission fee is $12 per person.
M : Sounds good. You should go.
W : Definitely. Thanks for telling me about it.

09

Found 211에 관한 다음 내용을 듣고, 일치하지 않는 것을 고르시오.

W : Attention, H-rail train passengers. We would like to introduce a new website called Found 211 to ________ ______ ______ ________ ___ ____ ________. Found 211 provides information about items you've lost on H-rail trains. To use Found 211, you first ________ ___ ____ __ ________ of the website. Then, you need to post the details of your lost items to the website. If your lost items are found, Found 211 will inform you by a text message. In addition, foreign language services are provided in various languages, including French, Spanish and Chinese. You can also use Found 211 ✪ ________ _____ ________ ________. We hope you have a pleasant trip to your destination. Thank you.

10

다음 표를 보면서 대화를 듣고, 여자가 구매할 쿠키 커터 세트를 고르시오.

M : Ellie, what are you looking at on your tablet PC?
W : I'm looking for a set of ______ ______ ________. Can you help me pick a new set out from among these five?
M : Sure. There are many shapes to choose from. Do you have one in mind?
W : The star-shaped cutters look cool.
M : They do, but I've heard it's difficult to ✪ ______ _____ ________ _____ ___ ________.
W : Really? Then, I don't want to get the star-shaped ones.
M : That makes sense. How much do you want to spend?
W : I'd like to spend less than $20.
M : I see. ________ ______ ______ ___ ________ ________?
W : I've been using metal cutters. But I want to use a different kind this time.
M : Okay, then you have two options left.
W : Yellow is my favorite color, so I'll buy the yellow set.

11

대화를 듣고, 여자의 마지막 말에 대한 남자의 응답으로 가장 적절한 것을 고르시오.

W : Grandpa, I took some pictures at your birthday party last week. And your best friend Mr. Williams was in a few of them.
M : Oh, really? That's great. I'm meeting him today, and he might want those pictures.
W : Well, I can ✪ ______ _____ _____ ________ now. Would you like to ______ ________ ___ ______?

12

대화를 듣고, 남자의 마지막 말에 대한 여자의 응답으로 가장 적절한 것을 고르시오.

[Cell phone rings.]
M : Hello, Ms. Davis. This is Kevin's father. His class is visiting the Pop Art Culture Festival tomorrow, right?
W : Yes. We're going to ✪ ____ ___ ________. Is there anything wrong?
M : Actually, Kevin ______ __ ________, so I don't think he can go tomorrow.

13

대화를 듣고, 여자의 마지막 말에 대한 남자의 응답으로 가장 적절한 것을 고르시오. [3점]

W : Liam, have you decided what you want to study at college?
M : Not yet, Mom. Yesterday, ✪ _________ ___________ _______________ came to our school and gave us some tips on choosing a major.
W : Great. What did they say?
M : They told us that we should first think about what we are most interested in.
W : That's good advice. Are there ______ _______________ _____________ that you like?
M : I like children very much, so I'd like to study something related to children.
W : How about studying early childhood education?
M : That sounds interesting, but I'm also interested in psychology.
W : Then, you might want to ✪ __________ ___ __________________ and become a counselor for children.
M : I've never thought of that. But I'm not sure about which colleges have a psychology major.
W : Me, neither. But your teacher, Mr. Scott, might be able to help you find out more about that.

14

대화를 듣고, 남자의 마지막 말에 대한 여자의 응답으로 가장 적절한 것을 고르시오.

[Cell phone rings.]
M : Hello, Claire.
W : Hi, Uncle Louis. How are you doing?
M : I'm good. Are you busy this weekend?
W : Not really. I'll be home ✪ _________ _____ _________________.
Do you need anything?
M : Yeah, I was wondering if you could take care of my dog for the weekend.
W : Sure. He's such a good dog. Are you going somewhere?
M : Yes. I have ____ __________________ ______________ ______.
W : I see. Are you going to _______ ______ _____ at my house tomorrow?
M : Sorry, I can't. I have a few things to do before the trip. Could you come and get him this evening?
W : Yes, I can. Is there anything I need to know to take care of him?
M : Actually, he's on a diet. Do you think you can take him for a walk once a day?

15

다음 상황 설명을 듣고, Kate가 Professor Lee에게 할 말로 가장 적절한 것을 고르시오. [3점]

M : Kate is taking Professor Lee's East Asian history class. She is given an assignment to make an individual presentation on Monday of the following week. However, she finds out that she won the first prize in a national essay writing contest, and she is asked to ✪ __________ _____ ____________ ______________. She's happy to hear the good news and really wants to go to the ceremony to receive her award. But she's not sure about whether she can go because the awards ceremony and the presentation are _______ ________________ _____ _____ ________ _______. So, she wants to ask Professor Lee if it is possible for her to __________ _____ _______ of the presentation with another student in the class. In this situation, what would Kate most likely say to Professor Lee?

16~17

다음을 듣고, 물음에 답하시오.

W : Hello, students. Have you ever thought about what's happening in the insect world when it's raining? Today, we're going to talk about what insects do on a rainy day. Some insects come outside from their home. For example, cockroaches living in drains have to __________ ________ ________ ___ ____________ when it rains. It's because their homes get flooded easily. They leave, so they ✪ ______ _____ __________. To give another example, mosquitos come out in the rain to lay eggs. Rainy days are the best time since newborn mosquitos need water to grow. However, other insects have to hide to stay alive. For instance, some types of ants hide themselves to _____ _________ ________ _____ ______ because their body temperature drops when it rains. If they get cold during a rainy day, their bodies can freeze and they could die. Also, some kinds of flies go underground to avoid the rain. When their wings get wet, they can't fly, so they have to find some place to stay dry. As we can see, the rain affects various insects' behavior in different ways. Now, let's watch a video.

▶ 정답 : 해설편 055쪽

VOCA LIST 12

회차별 영단어 QR 코드 ※ QR 코드를 스캔 후 모바일로 단어장처럼 학습할 수 있습니다.

● 고3 2024학년도 6월

01

001 □ attention ⓝ 주의, 주목
002 □ aquarium ⓝ 수족관
003 □ request ⓥ 요청하다
004 □ wall ⓝ 벽
005 □ loud ⓐ 시끄러운
006 □ vibration ⓝ 진동
007 □ stressed ⓐ 스트레스를 받은
008 □ cooperation ⓝ 협조, 협력

02

009 □ newborn baby 신생아
010 □ suggest ⓥ 제안하다
011 □ hat ⓝ 모자
012 □ as far as I know 내가 알기로는
013 □ maintain ⓥ 유지하다
014 □ temperature ⓝ 온도, 체온
015 □ beginning ⓝ 시작
016 □ air conditioning 에어컨
017 □ indoors ad 실내에서
018 □ steady ⓐ 일정한, 꾸준한

03

019 □ have a hard time 힘들어하다
020 □ true for ~에 해당하는
021 □ gardening ⓝ 정원 가꾸기
022 □ musical instrument 악기
023 □ exercise ⓝ 운동
024 □ clear one's mind 마음을 비우다
025 □ stay tuned (명령문으로) 채널 고정하세요

04

026 □ rehearsal ⓝ 리허설, 예행연습
027 □ have a look 살펴보다
028 □ knight ⓝ 기사
029 □ costume ⓝ 의상
030 □ tea pot 찻주전자
031 □ flea market 벼룩시장
032 □ rug ⓝ 깔개
033 □ fit ⓥ 어울리다, 적합하다
034 □ by the way 그건 그렇고, 그나저나
035 □ look forward to ~을 기대하다
036 □ perform ⓥ 공연하다

05

037 □ come up 다가오다
038 □ to-do list 할 일 목록
039 □ confirmation ⓝ (맞다는) 확인
040 □ moving company 이삿짐 회사
041 □ date ⓝ 날짜
042 □ sign up for ~을 가입하다
043 □ throw away 버리다
044 □ wrap ⓥ 싸다, 포장하다
045 □ vase ⓝ 꽃병
046 □ uniform ⓝ 제복, 유니폼
047 □ gym class 체육 수업

06

048 □ recommend ⓥ 추천하다
049 □ beef ⓝ 소고기
050 □ dressing ⓝ (샐러드 등에 얹는) 드레싱
051 □ come with ~이 딸려오다
052 □ for free 무료로
053 □ discount ⓝ 할인
054 □ Will that be all? 다 되셨나요?

07

055 □ book club 독서 모임
056 □ make it (시간 맞춰) 가다
057 □ interesting ⓐ 흥미로운
058 □ discussion ⓝ 논의, 토론
059 □ science fiction 공상 과학
060 □ novel ⓝ 소설
061 □ genre ⓝ 장르
062 □ take care of ~을 처리하다
063 □ department ⓝ 부서
064 □ launch ⓥ 출시하다
065 □ be involved with ~에 관여하다

08

066 □ library ⓝ 도서관
067 □ purpose ⓝ 목적
068 □ local ⓐ 지역의
069 □ develop ⓥ 개발하다
070 □ awesome ⓐ 멋진
071 □ admission fee 입장료
072 □ tap ⓥ 가볍게 두드리다
073 □ Definitely. (동의하며) 물론이죠, 그러게요.

09

074 □ introduce ⓥ 소개하다
075 □ lost item 분실물
076 □ member ⓝ 회원
077 □ post ⓥ 게시하다
078 □ detail ⓝ 세부사항
079 □ text message 문자 메시지
080 □ foreign language 외국어
081 □ various ⓐ 다양한
082 □ including prep ~을 포함해서
083 □ pleasant ⓐ 즐거운, 유쾌한
084 □ destination ⓝ 목적지

10

085 □ pick out ~을 고르다
086 □ among prep ~ 중에서
087 □ shape ⓝ 모양
088 □ choose from ~ 중에서 고르다
089 □ have in mind 마음에 두다
090 □ take out of ~에서 꺼내다
091 □ make sense 말이 되다, 이해가 되다
092 □ material ⓝ 소재, 재료
093 □ metal ⓐ 금속의
094 □ favorite ⓐ 가장 좋아하는

11

095 □ birthday party 생일 파티
096 □ best friend 가장 친한 친구
097 □ cancel ⓥ 취소하다
098 □ take away 가지고 가다, 제거하다, 치우다
099 □ say thanks to ~에게 고맙다고 하다

12

100 □ as scheduled 예정대로
101 □ have a fever 열이 나다
102 □ trip ⓝ 여행, 이동
103 □ get well (병 등이) 낫다
104 □ That's a relief. 다행이네요, 안심이네요.
105 □ no big deal 대단한 일이 아니다
106 □ opening day 개막일

13

107 □ decide ⓥ 결정하다
108 □ graduate ⓝ 졸업생 ⓥ 졸업하다
109 □ advice ⓝ 조언
110 □ particular ⓐ 특정한
111 □ subject ⓝ 과목
112 □ related to ~와 관련된
113 □ early childhood education 유아교육
114 □ psychology ⓝ 심리학
115 □ major in ~을 전공하다
116 □ counselor ⓝ 상담사
117 □ grateful for ~을 고마워하는
118 □ valuable ⓐ 귀중한
119 □ What a shame! 유감이네요! 안타깝네요!
120 □ No wonder. 당연하죠.
121 □ show up 나타나다, 모습을 보이다

14

122 □ busy ⓐ 바쁜, 분주한
123 □ unexpected ⓐ 예상치 못한
124 □ business trip 출장
125 □ drop off (차로) 내려주다
126 □ on a diet 다이어트 중인
127 □ take A for a walk A을 데리고 산책 나가다
128 □ Keep it up! 계속 그렇게 하세요!
129 □ work out 운동하다
130 □ Not at all. (Do you mind ~? 형태의 부탁에 수락의 의미로) 좋아요, 물론이죠.

15

131 □ professor ⓝ 교수
132 □ East Asian history 동아시아사
133 □ assignment ⓝ 과제
134 □ make a presentation 발표하다
135 □ individual ⓐ 개인의 ⓝ 개인, 개체
136 □ win the first prize 1등상을 타다
137 □ essay contest 글짓기 대회
138 □ awards ceremony 시상식
139 □ receive ⓥ 받다
140 □ switch ⓥ 바꾸다

16~17

141 □ insect ⓝ 곤충
142 □ rainy ⓐ 비가 오는
143 □ cockroach ⓝ 바퀴벌레
144 □ drain ⓝ 하수구 ⓥ 배수시키다
145 □ escape from ~에서 탈출하다
146 □ flood ⓥ 넘치다, 범람하다
147 □ drown ⓥ 익사하다
148 □ mosquito ⓝ 모기
149 □ lay an egg 알을 낳다
150 □ hide ⓥ 숨다
151 □ stay alive 살아남다
152 □ get away from ~을 피하다
153 □ underground ad 지하로
154 □ significance ⓝ 중요성, 의의

13회 • 2023학년도 6월 모의평가 고3 영어 듣기

※ QR코드를 스캔하시면 듣기 방송을 청취하실 수 있습니다.

● 점수 표시가 없는 문항은 모두 2점 ● 문항수 17개 | 배점 37점 | 제한 시간 25분

1번부터 17번까지는 듣고 답하는 문제입니다. 1번부터 15번까지는 한 번만 들려주고, 16번부터 17번까지는 두 번 들려줍니다. 방송을 잘 듣고 답을 하시기 바랍니다.

MP3

1. 다음을 듣고, 남자가 하는 말의 목적으로 가장 적절한 것을 고르시오.

① 저작권 위반 사례를 소개하려고
② 홈페이지 점검 시간을 공지하려고
③ 보안 시스템 업그레이드를 권장하려고
④ 웹사이트 제작 프로그램을 홍보하려고
⑤ 조립식 컴퓨터 구매 방법을 설명하려고

2. 대화를 듣고, 여자의 의견으로 가장 적절한 것을 고르시오.

① 매일 다양한 색의 채소를 섭취해야 한다.
② 채소의 종류에 따라 세척 방법이 달라야 한다.
③ 채소는 수확 시기에 따라 맛이 달라질 수 있다.
④ 채소는 냉장 보관하면 비타민 파괴를 늦출 수 있다.
⑤ 익혀서 조리하는 것이 건강에 더 좋은 채소가 있다.

3. 대화를 듣고, 두 사람의 관계를 가장 잘 나타낸 것을 고르시오.

① 공연 기획자 – 연극배우
② 패션 디자이너 – 사진작가
③ 예술가 – 전시회 관람객
④ 건축가 – 인테리어 업체 직원
⑤ 보안 요원 – 기념품 판매원

4. 대화를 듣고, 그림에서 대화의 내용과 일치하지 않는 것을 고르시오.

5. 대화를 듣고, 남자가 할 일로 가장 적절한 것을 고르시오.

① 배드민턴 레슨 등록하기
② 신입 회원에게 행사 공지하기
③ 홍보 포스터 제작하기
④ 소셜 미디어 계정 만들기
⑤ 안내문 게시하기

6. 대화를 듣고, 여자가 지불할 금액을 고르시오. [3점]

① $40 ② $45 ③ $50 ④ $55 ⑤ $65

7. 대화를 듣고, 남자가 과학 보고서 대회에서 상을 받지 못한 이유를 고르시오.

① 실험 사진을 포함시키지 않아서
② 마감 기한을 지키지 못해서
③ 주제가 창의적이지 않아서
④ 부정확한 정보를 사용해서
⑤ 제시된 분량을 초과해서

8. 대화를 듣고, 2022 Technology Fair에 관해 언급되지 않은 것을 고르시오.

① 주제 ② 참여 업체 ③ 장소
④ 입장료 ⑤ 종료일

9. Junior Money Smart Course에 관한 다음 내용을 듣고, 일치하지 않는 것을 고르시오.

① 강사는 경제학 교수이다.
② 고등학생만을 대상으로 한다.
③ 월요일부터 금요일까지 진행될 것이다.
④ 7월에 등록이 시작된다.
⑤ 등록자 전원에게 선물을 제공할 것이다.

13회

영어 영역(듣기)

10. 다음 표를 보면서 대화를 듣고, 여자가 구입할 책상용 태블릿 거치대를 고르시오.

Tablet Stands for Desks

	Model	Price	Material	Foldable	Color
①	A	$11	Plastic	×	White
②	B	$12	Plastic	○	Silver
③	C	$14	Wood	○	Black
④	D	$16	Aluminum	×	Silver
⑤	E	$21	Aluminum	○	Black

11. 대화를 듣고, 여자의 마지막 말에 대한 남자의 응답으로 가장 적절한 것을 고르시오.

① No problem. I'll put it in the refrigerator.
② Of course. I'll check tomorrow's weather.
③ Okay. We can buy it at the store after work.
④ Great. Let's order from a seafood restaurant.
⑤ Never mind. I don't care if it's delivered late.

12. 대화를 듣고, 남자의 마지막 말에 대한 여자의 응답으로 가장 적절한 것을 고르시오.

① Absolutely. I'm proud of my son.
② Fantastic. He'll really enjoy the ride.
③ Too bad. He should have come earlier.
④ It's all right. The line is getting shorter.
⑤ I'm sorry. Then he's not allowed to ride.

13. 대화를 듣고, 여자의 마지막 말에 대한 남자의 응답으로 가장 적절한 것을 고르시오. [3점]

Man: ______________________________

① Don't worry. I'll check the date for you.
② Oh, no. We don't have time to print it out.
③ I see. I'll put the bread back in the package.
④ I agree. We need to buy more cream cheese.
⑤ Good. I'll bring some bread to the neighbors.

14. 대화를 듣고, 남자의 마지막 말에 대한 여자의 응답으로 가장 적절한 것을 고르시오.

Woman: ______________________________

① No, thanks. We already have enough eco-bags.
② That's a relief. Then we can prepare more presents.
③ That's true. Last year's festival was a great success.
④ I appreciate that. That's why I've won the quiz event.
⑤ Right. The book you recommended was so interesting.

15. 다음 상황 설명을 듣고, Tom이 Alice에게 할 말로 가장 적절한 것을 고르시오. [3점]

Tom: ______________________________

① You should take advantage of negative reviews for your business.
② You'd better take an online class to get a degree in marketing.
③ Don't forget the negative effects of enlarging your business.
④ Why don't you put up an advertisement for your products?
⑤ How about starting a new online business together?

[16～17] 다음을 듣고, 물음에 답하시오.

16. 여자가 하는 말의 주제로 가장 적절한 것은?

① how birds cooperate to collect nesting materials
② why birds use certain materials in nest building
③ natural substances that are harmful to bird nests
④ shortage of birds' nesting materials in urban areas
⑤ industrial building materials inspired by bird nests

17. 언급된 재료가 아닌 것은?

① feathers ② mud ③ spiderwebs
④ leaves ⑤ stones

※ QR 코드를 스캔하시면 듣기 방송이 나옵니다. 듣기 방송을 들으며 다음 빈칸을 채우시오. ● 제한 시간 : 25분

01
다음을 듣고, 남자가 하는 말의 목적으로 가장 적절한 것을 고르시오.

M : Hello, everyone. Are you looking for an easier way to create your own website? Then use Dream Website Wizard, __________ __________ __________ __________ __________ __________. With Dream Website Wizard, no technical skills are needed to build a well-designed website that fits your needs. This program has a variety of designer templates for you to choose from. You'll also find hundreds of images and video backgrounds __________ __________ __________. You can use them for your own website without worrying about ✪ __________ __________. Download the program for a 30-day free trial and start making your own website today.

02
대화를 듣고, 여자의 의견으로 가장 적절한 것을 고르시오.

M : Hi, honey. I bought these carrots on my way home.
W : Great. We can add roasted carrots to our dinner.
M : Well, isn't it healthier to eat vegetables raw rather than cooked?
W : Not necessarily. ✪ __________ __________ __________ __________ for us when cooked.
M : What do you mean?
W : For example, by __________ __________ __________ __________, it helps us to receive more substances that are good for our health.
M : Oh, really? What other vegetables are better when cooked?
W : When we steam broccoli and cabbage, they ✪ __________ __________ __________ that helps to prevent certain types of cancer.
M : I see. That's why you always put steamed broccoli in our salad.
W : Exactly. Cooking can be a good way to increase some vegetables' health benefits.
M : Okay. Then I'll prepare the roasted carrots.

03
대화를 듣고, 두 사람의 관계를 가장 잘 나타낸 것을 고르시오.

W : Hi, are you enjoying the exhibition?
M : Yes. It's the most unique art exhibition that I've ever been to.
W : Thanks. I'm glad that you like my ✪ __________ __________ __________.
M : Oh, you must be Karen Edwards. I can't believe I'm getting the chance to meet you in front of your artwork.
W : Well, I'll be here for the first three days of my exhibition. Is this your first time visiting this gallery?
M : Yeah. I'm especially impressed with this paper sculpture. __________ __________ __________ __________, though?
W : I intended to __________ __________ __________ when I created it.
M : How's that?
W : By putting different pieces of paper together, it becomes complete just like a family.
M : Wow, I can __________ __________ __________ even more after your explanation. I'm so lucky that I visited this gallery today.
W : Good to hear that. Thanks for coming.

04
대화를 듣고, 그림에서 대화의 내용과 일치하지 않는 것을 고르시오.

M : Kate, I heard __________ __________ __________ __________ has been remodeled. How did it turn out?
W : It's great. All our club members are excited about it. Here, check out this picture.
M : Wow, it's much better than I imagined. There's even an ON AIR sign above the clock.
W : Isn't it cool? That's my favorite part of this studio.
M : Awesome. Oh, ✪ __________ __________ __________ in the corner.
W : We're going to __________ __________ __________ in it. What do you think of the world map on the wall?
M : That's perfect for the background. I also like this stripe-patterned rug on the floor.
W : Yeah, it makes the place feel so cozy.
M : I agree. Oh, there are three cameras. They give the studio __________ __________ __________.
W : I know. I can't wait to start broadcasting the school news.

05
대화를 듣고, 남자가 할 일로 가장 적절한 것을 고르시오.

W : Jason, you look worried. Is something wrong?
M : Well, you know our badminton club has been losing members recently.
W : That's right. We may need something to promote our club.
M : How about a special event like offering one-on-one ✪ __________ __________?
W : I don't think we have enough members for that. Hmm, __________ __________ __________ __________ instead?
M : Good idea. Do you want to try creating the poster?
W : Well, I'm not sure. I'm not good at design.
M : Then I'll make the poster. I'll try my best to ✪ __________ __________ __________.
W : Thanks. Once you're done, I'll put the posters up around the school and on social media as well.
M : Good. I hope this will get many students to join our club.

Dictation 13

06

대화를 듣고, 여자가 지불할 금액을 고르시오. [3점]

M : Welcome to Spring Road Garden. May I help you?
W : Hi. I'm thinking of putting some flowers in the living room. What would you recommend?
M : How about carnations or tulips in flowerpots? They're popular for home decoration.
W : I like them. How much are they?
M : A pot of carnations is $20, and a pot of tulips is $30.
W : I'll take two pots of carnations.
M : Good choice. I also recommend ✪ _________ _________ _________ _________ to water your flowers.
W : Oh, I was thinking of buying one. How much is it?
M : It's normally $10, but I'll give you a ✪ _________ _________ _________ _________.
W : Thanks. I'll buy one.
M : So, two pots of carnations and one spray bottle. _________ _________ _________ _________ _________? It's only $5.
W : No, thanks. I brought my car.
M : Okay. How would you like to pay?
W : I'll pay with cash.

07

대화를 듣고, 남자가 과학 보고서 대회에서 상을 받지 못한 이유를 고르시오.

W : Hi, Dave. Come in.
M : You wanted to see me, Ms. Adams?
W : Yes. It's about the ✪ _________ _________ _________. You must be disappointed that you didn't get a prize.
M : Well, I tried my best until the last minute, so I was wondering why.
W : Actually, your topic was creative and interesting.
M : How about the length? Was my report too long?
W : No, the length ✪ _________ _________ _________ _________.
M : Then, did I use any incorrect information?
W : Not at all. It seemed that you _________ _________ _________ _________.
M : Yes. I tried to use reliable sources from the Internet and books.
W : Good. However, you _________ _________ _________ _________ _________ in your report.
M : Really? I thought I put them in my report.
W : Unfortunately, you didn't. That's the reason why you didn't get a prize.
M : Oh, I see. I won't make the same mistake next time.

08

대화를 듣고, 2022 Technology Fair에 관해 언급되지 않은 것을 고르시오.

M : Rosa, did you find anything interesting on the community board?
W : Hey, James. Look. The 2022 Technology Fair is going on right now.
M : Let me see. It says the theme of this fair is "AI and the Fourth Industrial Revolution."
W : Yeah, AI technology is the topic for our group presentation.
M : Right. I bet we could _________ _________ _________ _________ _________ _________ there. Hmm, do you see where it's taking place?
W : Yes, look here. It's being held at the civic center downtown. It's ✪ _________ _________ _________ from here.
M : Perfect. And the admission fee is $10 for students. Should we go?
W : Definitely. How about _________ _________ _________?
M : No, we have to go this weekend. The fair ends on June 15th.
W : Okay. Let's look into getting tickets.

09

Junior Money Smart Course에 관한 다음 내용을 듣고, 일치하지 않는 것을 고르시오.

W : Hello, parents. Do you want your children to learn how to be smart with their money? Then, sign them up for the Junior Money Smart Course. The instructor of this course is an economics professor, who will teach your children basic accounting principles and _________ _________ _________. This course is only for high school students. It'll be held at the Shellburne Community Center from Monday to Friday in the afternoon. Registration can be done on our website ✪ _________ _________ _________ _________. Please note that _________ _________ _________ _________ _________. Everyone who signs up will _________ _________ _________ as a gift. Set your children on the right path for their ✪ _________ _________. For more information, visit our website, www.juniormoneysmart.com.

10

다음 표를 보면서 대화를 듣고, 여자가 구입할 책상용 태블릿 거치대를 고르시오.

M : Emily, what are you shopping for on your computer?
W : I'm looking at these tablet stands for desks. Can you help me choose one?
M : Sure. Let me take a look. *[Pause]* Hmm, these five models all look pretty good. How much do you want to spend?
W : I'd like to keep it under $20.
M : Okay. Oh, it seems they _________ _________ _________ _________ _________. Do you have any preference?
W : Well, I don't like ✪ _________ _________ _________ _________. The other materials are fine, though.
M : I see. And I think you should consider a ✪ _________ _________ because it's easier to carry around.
W : But I'll mainly use it at home, so I don't _________ _________ _________ _________. Plus, it seems less stable.
M : Then there are two options left. Which one do you like?
W : _________ _________ _________ _________ _________.
M : I agree.
W : Okay. I'll buy this one then. Thanks for your help.

11

대화를 듣고, 여자의 마지막 말에 대한 남자의 응답으로 가장 적절한 것을 고르시오.

[Cell phone rings.]

W : Honey, did you get home from work yet? The fish I ordered yesterday has just arrived, but I'll be home late today.

M : Oh, I'll be home in two hours. ✪ _________ _________ _________ _________ because the weather is so hot?

W : I hope not. Can you store the fish _________ _________ _________ _________ _________ _________?

12

대화를 듣고, 남자의 마지막 말에 대한 여자의 응답으로 가장 적절한 것을 고르시오.

M : Hello, my son would love to ride on ✪ _________ _________ _________. Can he?

W : Well, he must be at least 130 cm tall to ride it. How tall is he?

M : Oh, my son is _________ _________ _________ _________.

13

대화를 듣고, 여자의 마지막 말에 대한 남자의 응답으로 가장 적절한 것을 고르시오. [3점]

M : Grandma, I'm home. What are you making?

W : Hi, Kevin. I'm about to bake some cream cheese bread. I know how much you love it.

M : Of course, I do. It's really soft and delicious.

W : Oh, sweetheart, you're too kind.

M : No, really. It's the best. Is there anything I can help you with?

W : That'd be lovely. Can you get the butter from the refrigerator?

M : Sure. *[Pause]* Here it is. What should I do next?

W : Wait. The butter ✪ _________ _________ _________. Do you remember when we bought it?

M : Probably a few months ago. But usually butter lasts a long time, so it should be okay.

W : Yeah, but it's important to always check ✪ _________ _________ _________ before cooking.

M : I guess you're right. It's better to be safe.

W : Let me take a look. *[Pause]* Oh, dear. The print on the package is _________ _________ _________ _________ _________ _________.

14

대화를 듣고, 남자의 마지막 말에 대한 여자의 응답으로 가장 적절한 것을 고르시오.

W : Hi, Mr. Taylor.

M : Hi, Christie. How is the preparation for the school's Eco-Festival going?

W : Well, our club is planning to hold a quiz event during the festival.

M : Sounds interesting. What is the quiz about?

W : It'll be on the best-selling book, *An Eco-Friendly Way of Life*.

M : I've read that book. It's ✪ _________ _________ _________.

W : Yeah. I think the students will be really into it. Plus, as a present, each participant will receive an eco-bag made from recycled materials.

M : Oh, that's why you asked me to order the eco-bags. How many students have signed up for the quiz event so far?

W : _________ _________ _________ _________ _________.

M : That's great news!

W : Yeah, but I'm really concerned because we didn't prepare enough eco-bags.

M : Don't worry. I'll _________ _________ _________ _________ _________. We still have funds that can be used for the festival.

15

다음 상황 설명을 듣고, Tom이 Alice에게 할 말로 가장 적절한 것을 고르시오. [3점]

M : Alice runs an online shopping mall. Recently, some of her customers ✪ _________ _________ _________ about her products. She's worried that these comments will cause customers to _________ _________ _________ _________ _________. She visits her friend Tom, who also runs an online shopping mall, and asks for his advice. Tom thinks that those negative comments can be useful, as they can help owners to better understand consumers' needs and to improve the quality of the products. He believes this can contribute to ✪ _________ _________ _________ in the end. So, Tom wants to tell Alice that she needs to _________ _________ _________ _________ _________ to improve her business. In this situation, what would Tom most likely say to Alice?

16~17

다음을 듣고, 물음에 답하시오.

W : Hello, students. We all know birds are ✪ _________ _________ _________. So today, we'll learn about the reasons that some materials are used in bird nests. Firstly, many types of birds incorporate different kinds of materials to keep their nests warm. Particularly, feathers are commonly used for this purpose. Secondly, some bird species build their nests along the side of ✪ _________ _________ _________, which requires sticky substances. These birds use mud because it _________ _________ _________ _________ _________. Next, some tiny birds normally build small cup-like nests with light materials, so they need an additional material to bind them. They often use spiderwebs to fasten these nesting materials together. Lastly, some species of birds that live in cold environments use certain objects to protect their eggs. These birds gather stones for their nests to _________ _________ _________ _________. This keeps their eggs above ground level, which reduces the danger of flooding from melting ice. Now, let's watch a short video clip about these fascinating bird nests.

▶ 정답 : 해설편 059쪽

VOCA LIST 13

회차별 영단어 QR 코드 ※ QR 코드를 스캔 후 모바일로 단어장처럼 학습할 수 있습니다.

● 고3 2023학년도 6월

01

001 □ create ⓥ 창조하다, 만들어 내다
002 □ easy-to-use ⓐ 사용하기 편한
003 □ well-designed ⓐ 잘 설계된
004 □ fit one's needs 필요에 맞추다
005 □ template ⓝ 견본, 본보기
006 □ at one's fingertips 즉시 이용할 수 있는
007 □ copyright ⓝ 저작권
008 □ trial ⓝ 체험, 시험

02

009 □ roast ⓥ 굽다
010 □ vegetable ⓝ 채소, 야채
011 □ raw ⓐ 익히지 않은, 날것의
012 □ rather than ~보다는
013 □ not necessarily 반드시[꼭] ~은 아닌
014 □ receive ⓥ 받다, 받아들이다
015 □ substance ⓝ 물질
016 □ release ⓥ 방출하다, 배출하다
017 □ compound ⓝ 화합물
018 □ certain ⓐ 특정한, 일정한
019 □ cancer ⓝ 암
020 □ steam ⓥ (음식을) 찌다
021 □ increase ⓥ 증가하다

03

022 □ exhibition ⓝ 전시회
023 □ unique ⓐ 독특한
024 □ sculpture ⓝ 조각
025 □ artwork ⓝ 미술품, 공예품
026 □ gallery ⓝ 미술관
027 □ especially ad 특히
028 □ impressed ⓐ 감명 받은
029 □ symbolize ⓥ (상징으로) 나타내다
030 □ intend ⓥ 의도하다
031 □ represent ⓥ 표현하다, 나타내다
032 □ appreciate ⓥ 이해하다, 감상하다
033 □ explanation ⓝ 설명

04

034 □ broadcasting studio 방송실
035 □ remodel ⓥ 개조하다, 리모델링하다
036 □ imagine ⓥ 상상하다
037 □ turn out (~라고) 판명되다
038 □ on air 방송 중
039 □ favorite ⓐ 아주 좋아하는, 마음에 드는
040 □ bookshelf ⓝ 책장
041 □ script ⓝ 대본
042 □ stripe-patterned ⓐ 줄무늬의
043 □ rug ⓝ 양탄자
044 □ cozy ⓐ 아늑한

05

045 □ promote ⓥ 홍보하다
046 □ one-on-one ⓐ 일대일의
047 □ promotional ⓐ 홍보의
048 □ eye-catching ⓐ (단번에) 시선을 끄는
049 □ put up ~을 게시하다

06

050 □ recommend ⓥ 추천하다
051 □ flowerpot ⓝ 화분
052 □ decoration ⓝ 장식품, 장식
053 □ spray bottle 분무기

07

054 □ competition ⓝ 대회, 경쟁
055 □ disappoint ⓥ 실망하다
056 □ prize ⓝ 상, 상품
057 □ wonder ⓥ 궁금해 하다
058 □ actually ad 사실은
059 □ length ⓝ 길이
060 □ incorrect ⓐ 부정확한
061 □ thoroughly ad 철저하게
062 □ reliable ⓐ 믿을 만한
063 □ include ⓥ 포함시키다
064 □ experiment ⓝ 실험
065 □ unfortunately ad 불행하게도, 유감스럽게도

08

066 □ AI 인공 지능(= artificial intelligence)
067 □ industrial revolution 산업 혁명
068 □ useful ⓐ 유용한, 도움이 되는, 쓸모 있는
069 □ civic ⓐ 시민의
070 □ within walking distance 걸어갈 수 있는 거리에 있는
071 □ admission fee 입장료
072 □ definitely ad 확실히, 분명히
073 □ look into ~을 살펴보다, 조사하다

09

074 □ smart with money 돈 관리를 잘하는
075 □ sign up for ~에 등록하다
076 □ instructor ⓝ 강사
077 □ economics ⓝ 경제학
078 □ accounting ⓝ 회계
079 □ management skill 관리기술
080 □ registration ⓝ 등록
081 □ on-site ⓐ 현장의
082 □ financial security 재정적인 안정

10

083 □ stand ⓝ 거치대
084 □ material ⓝ 소재, 자재
085 □ preference ⓝ 선호
086 □ texture ⓝ 질감
087 □ consider ⓥ 잘 생각해 보다, 고려하다
088 □ foldable ⓐ 접을 수 있는
089 □ carry around 운반하다
090 □ stable ⓐ 안정적인
091 □ fancy ⓐ 멋진

11

092 □ order ⓥ 주문하다, 시키다
093 □ store ⓥ 보관하다
094 □ deliver ⓥ 배달하다

12

095 □ ride on ~에 타다
096 □ at least 적어도, 최소한

13

097 □ be about to ~하려던 참이다
098 □ delicious ⓐ 맛있는
099 □ refrigerator ⓝ 냉장고
100 □ slightly ad 약간
101 □ last ⓥ 지속되다
102 □ expiration date 유효 기간
103 □ package ⓝ 포장지
104 □ neighbour ⓝ 이웃

14

105 □ preparation ⓝ 준비
106 □ hold ⓥ 열다, 개최하다
107 □ eco-friendly ⓐ 친환경적인, 환경 친화적인
108 □ educational ⓐ 교육적인
109 □ fascinating ⓐ 대단히 흥미로운
110 □ be into ~에 푹 빠지다
111 □ participant ⓝ 참가자
112 □ recycle ⓥ 재활용하다
113 □ expect ⓥ 예상하다
114 □ prepare ⓥ 준비하다
115 □ fund ⓝ 자금, 기금
116 □ relief ⓝ 안도, 안심

15

117 □ recently ad 최근에
118 □ customer ⓝ 고객
119 □ negative ⓐ 부정적인
120 □ review ⓝ 비평
121 □ product ⓝ 제품
122 □ comment ⓝ 언급, 논평
123 □ turn away from ~을 외면하다, ~로부터 돌아서다
124 □ ask for ~을 구하다
125 □ improve ⓥ 개선하다, 향상하다
126 □ contribute to ~에 이바지하다
127 □ in the end 결국
128 □ make use of ~을 이용하다, 활용하다
129 □ take advantage of ~을 이용하다
130 □ degree ⓝ 학위
131 □ enlarge ⓥ 확장하다, 확대하다
132 □ advertisement ⓝ 광고

16~17

133 □ expert ⓐ 전문적인
134 □ nest ⓝ 둥지
135 □ incorporate ⓥ (~의 일부로) 포함하다
136 □ particularly ad 특히
137 □ feather ⓝ 깃털
138 □ commonly ad 흔히, 보통
139 □ species ⓝ 종(種)
140 □ require ⓥ 필요하다, 필요로 하다
141 □ sticky ⓐ 끈적거리는
142 □ attach ⓥ 붙다, 부착하다
143 □ vertical ⓐ 수직의
144 □ tiny ⓐ 매우 작은
145 □ normally ad 보통
146 □ bind ⓥ 묶다
147 □ spiderweb ⓥ 거미줄로 덮다
148 □ fasten ⓥ 고정하다, (단단히) 잠그다
149 □ gather ⓥ 모으다
150 □ ground level 지표면
151 □ melt ⓥ 녹다
152 □ fascinating ⓐ 매혹적인
153 □ harmful ⓐ 해로운
154 □ shortage ⓝ 부족, 결핍
155 □ inspire ⓥ 영감을 주다

14회 ● 2022학년도 6월 모의평가 고3 영어 듣기

※ QR코드를 스캔하시면 듣기 방송을 청취하실 수 있습니다.

● 점수 표시가 없는 문항은 모두 2점 ● 문항수 17개 | 배점 37점 | 제한 시간 25분

1번부터 17번까지는 듣고 답하는 문제입니다. 1번부터 15번까지는 한 번만 들려주고, 16번부터 17번까지는 두 번 들려줍니다. 방송을 잘 듣고 답을 하시기 바랍니다.

MP3

1. 다음을 듣고, 남자가 하는 말의 목적으로 가장 적절한 것을 고르시오.

① 댄스 동아리 가입 조건을 안내하려고
② 동아리 개설 신청 기간을 홍보하려고
③ 동아리 만족도 설문 조사 참여를 당부하려고
④ 댄스 동아리 활동 장소 폐쇄 이유를 설명하려고
⑤ 댄스 동아리 회원 모집 인원 증원을 공지하려고

2. 대화를 듣고, 여자의 의견으로 가장 적절한 것을 고르시오.

① 불필요한 쓰레기를 줄이기 위해 과도한 포장을 지양해야 한다.
② 환경 보호를 위해 쓰레기 분리배출을 철저히 해야 한다.
③ 선물을 고를 때는 받는 사람의 취향을 고려해야 한다.
④ 사용 빈도가 높지 않은 물건은 상자에 보관해야 한다.
⑤ 선물 종류에 따라 포장 방법을 달리해야 한다.

3. 대화를 듣고, 두 사람의 관계를 가장 잘 나타낸 것을 고르시오.

① 잡지 기자 – 시나리오 작가 ② 아나운서 – 작사가
③ 라디오 진행자 – 음악 평론가 ④ 영화감독 – 배우
⑤ 신문 기자 – 모델

4. 대화를 듣고, 그림에서 대화의 내용과 일치하지 <u>않는</u> 것을 고르시오.

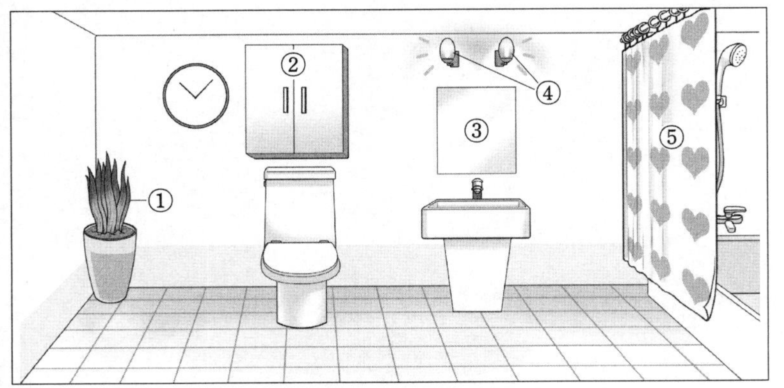

5. 대화를 듣고, 여자가 남자를 위해 할 일로 가장 적절한 것을 고르시오.

① 경제학 과제 자료 조사하기 ② 자원봉사 신청서 제출하기
③ 환경 캠페인 포스터 만들기 ④ 학생회관 가는 길 알려 주기
⑤ 마라톤 코스 답사하기

6. 대화를 듣고, 여자가 지불할 금액을 고르시오. [3점]

① $30 ② $36 ③ $40 ④ $45 ⑤ $50

7. 대화를 듣고, 남자가 컴퓨터 프로그래밍 강좌를 신청하지 <u>않은</u> 이유를 고르시오.

① 수업이 30분 일찍 시작되어서
② 다른 도시로 이사를 가게 되어서
③ 컴퓨터 프로그래밍에 흥미를 잃어서
④ 퇴근 후에 수업 듣는 것이 너무 피곤해서
⑤ 컴퓨터 프로그래밍이 자신의 경력과 무관해서

8. 대화를 듣고, Samuel's Woodworking Class에 관해 언급되지 <u>않은</u> 것을 고르시오.

① 장소 ② 시간 ③ 복장
④ 등록비 ⑤ 모집 인원

9. 2021 Lakeside Essay Contest에 관한 다음 내용을 듣고, 일치하지 <u>않는</u> 것을 고르시오.

① 주제는 여름으로부터의 메시지이다.
② Lakeside High School 전교생이 참가할 수 있다.
③ 에세이 분량은 3페이지를 넘으면 안 된다.
④ 제출 마감은 다음 주 금요일이다.
⑤ 상위 10편의 에세이는 학교 웹 사이트에 게시될 예정이다.

14회

영어 영역[듣기]

10. 다음 표를 보면서 대화를 듣고, 남자가 주문할 자전거를 고르시오.

Bicycles for Commuters

	Model	Color	Price	Frame Size	Foldable
①	A	Black	$190	Small	×
②	B	Yellow	$210	Medium	×
③	C	Silver	$270	Large	×
④	D	White	$290	Large	○
⑤	E	Blue	$320	Medium	○

11. 대화를 듣고, 여자의 마지막 말에 대한 남자의 응답으로 가장 적절한 것을 고르시오.

① Sure. Let me call him now.
② Not at all. My hair is really long.
③ Yes. I really like my new hairstyle.
④ Why not? I'll text the number to you.
⑤ Not really. I don't need to check your schedule.

12. 대화를 듣고, 남자의 마지막 말에 대한 여자의 응답으로 가장 적절한 것을 고르시오.

① Fine. I'll look for another band.
② Great! You can be our drummer.
③ Sorry. I can't offer you the position.
④ Really? It'll be great to play in your band.
⑤ What a surprise! I didn't know you play drums.

13. 대화를 듣고, 여자의 마지막 말에 대한 남자의 응답으로 가장 적절한 것을 고르시오. [3점]

Man: ____________________

① No problem. You'll get your refund.
② Of course. That's why I canceled my order.
③ Excellent. I'll exchange it with a bigger size.
④ Good. I'm glad to hear you received the package.
⑤ Okay. We'll send the gray skirt to you right away.

14. 대화를 듣고, 남자의 마지막 말에 대한 여자의 응답으로 가장 적절한 것을 고르시오.

Woman: ____________________

① All right. I'll check if it's in the jacket and call you back.
② Don't worry. I'll visit the lost and found for you.
③ Too bad. Let me have my credit card replaced.
④ I see. I'll buy a new jacket if you can't find it.
⑤ Thank you. Pick me up at the grocery store.

15. 다음 상황 설명을 듣고, Rachel이 Kevin에게 할 말로 가장 적절한 것을 고르시오. [3점]

Rachel: ____________________

① Is it necessary to exercise every day?
② Why don't you work out at the closer one?
③ I recommend the one with good facilities.
④ You should choose the one within your budget.
⑤ What about looking for a better place to work at?

[16～17] 다음을 듣고, 물음에 답하시오.

16. 여자가 하는 말의 주제로 가장 적절한 것은?

① decline in employment opportunities due to drones
② regulations for using drones in various fields
③ job skills necessary for drone development
④ workplace accidents caused by drone use
⑤ various uses of drones in different jobs

17. 언급된 직업이 아닌 것은?

① farmers ② photographers ③ soldiers
④ police officers ⑤ firefighters

[해설편 p.062]

※ QR 코드를 스캔하시면 듣기 방송이 나옵니다. 듣기 방송을 들으며 다음 빈칸을 채우시오. ● 제한 시간 : 25분

01

다음을 듣고, 남자가 하는 말의 목적으로 가장 적절한 것을 고르시오.

M : Good afternoon, students of Robinson High School. This is Mr. Anderson, coach of the school dance club. I'd like to announce that we'll be __________ __________ __________ __________ for our school dance club. Previously we were looking for 10 new club members, and many students showed interest in joining. Luckily, ✪ __________ __________ __________ __________ __________ __________ __________ than expected. Now we're allowed to accept five additional new members to __________ __________ __________ __________ __________ __________.
Once again, I'm happy to inform you that our school dance club has increased the number of new members to recruit. Thank you for your interest.

02

대화를 듣고, 여자의 의견으로 가장 적절한 것을 고르시오.

W : Hey, Connor. What are you doing with all of these gift boxes?
M : Mom, I'm wrapping a scarf for Grandma. You know, her birthday is in a week.
W : Great. But do you really need these three boxes for just one scarf?
M : Yes. The boxes are all different sizes, and I'll put each one inside the other.
W : Well, don't you feel bad about wasting all of those boxes?
M : What do you mean? I just wanted the gift to look fancy and interesting.
W : I understand. However, the boxes will __________ __________ __________ __________ __________, right?
M : So, you mean it's overpackaging? Oh, I didn't know I was wasting boxes.
W : Yeah. I think ✪ __________ __________ __________ __________ __________ __________ __________ __________.
M : You're right. I'll use one box for now and save the others for later.
W : Good idea. No matter how it looks, Grandma will love your gift.

03

대화를 듣고, 두 사람의 관계를 가장 잘 나타낸 것을 고르시오.

M : Hello, Ms. Lee. It's an honor to meet you in person.
W : Oh, thank you for interviewing me, Mr. Wilson. I'm __________ __________ __________ __________ __________ __________.
M : Thanks. People love your movie *Short Days*. I was wondering who picked out the title.
W : Well, it was basically my idea and the movie director agreed.
M : It really __________ __________ __________ __________ __________ __________. Why do you think people love your stories?
W : When writing film scripts, I always try to ✪ __________ __________ __________ __________ __________ __________ __________.
M : Maybe that's why people feel stronger connections to them. What inspires you when you write your scripts?
W : Often, my own life experiences help create many of the scenes in my scripts.
M : I see. Thank you. The readers of our magazine will appreciate you sharing your time with us.
W : My pleasure. Could you please email me the article?
M : No problem.

04

대화를 듣고, 그림에서 대화의 내용과 일치하지 않는 것을 고르시오.

W : Honey, today I went to the house we'll be moving in to. I really liked the bathroom renovations.
M : Oh, really? Did you take a picture of the bathroom?
W : Of course. Here it is. How's the plant in the corner? I bought it on the way to the house.
M : Excellent choice. The cabinet next to the clock is perfect for our family.
W : Yeah, it'll be useful for __________ __________ __________ __________ __________.
M : You're right. And look at this round mirror over the bathroom sink. It's very modern.
W : Yes. That's my favorite part. And I also like the two lights on the wall.
M : Me, too. __________ __________ __________?
W : Absolutely. What do you think about ✪ __________ __________ __________ __________ __________ __________ __________?
M : The kids will definitely love it.
W : I agree. I'm excited to move in to our new house this weekend.

05

대화를 듣고, 여자가 남자를 위해 할 일로 가장 적절한 것을 고르시오.

W : Hey, Brandon. Have you seen this poster?
M : What's this? Oh, it's the Earth Hour Marathon.
W : Yeah, it's ✪ __________ __________ __________ __________ about protecting the environment.
M : That sounds like a great campaign. Are you participating in it?
W : Actually, I'm a staff member of the event and I'm looking for volunteers.
M : Oh, is that so? Then, what's the role of a volunteer?
W : A volunteer hands out water to the runners during the race.
M : That sounds good. When does it take place?
W : It's next Saturday at City Hall. Are you interested?
M : Sure. __________ __________ __________ __________ __________ __________ __________ __________?
W : Here. You must submit this application form to the student center by 5 o'clock today.
M : Oh! I have economics class in 10 minutes, and it finishes at 6 o'clock.
W : Just write your name and phone number. __________ __________ __________ __________ __________ for you.
M : Thanks. *[Writing sound]* Here you go.

Dictation 14

06

대화를 듣고, 여자가 지불할 금액을 고르시오. [3점]

M : Welcome to Family Pet Shop. May I help you?
W : Hi, I'm looking for dog food.
M : Let me show you.
W : Thanks. How much is it for a bag of dog food?
M : That depends on your dog's age.
W : Oh, ✪ _________ _________ _________ _________ _________?
M : Yes. It costs $15 per bag for little puppies and $20 per bag for adult dogs.
W : My dogs are all grown up. So, I'll get two bags of dog food for adult dogs.
M : All right. Do you need anything else?
W : Well, _________ _________ _________ _________ _________?
M : Oh, how about this one? It's very popular among our customers and only costs $10.
W : Perfect. I'll take one.
M : Good. So you want two bags of dog food for adult dogs and one brush, right?
W : Yes. Can I use this discount coupon?
M : Let me see. *[Pause]* Yes, you can get 10% off the total with this coupon.
W : Great. I'll pay in cash.

07

대화를 듣고, 남자가 컴퓨터 프로그래밍 강좌를 신청하지 않은 이유를 고르시오.

W : Hey, Blake. It's the last day of the class. Did you sign up for the next computer programming class?
M : No, Angela. I cannot take the class anymore.
W : Oh, I thought you enjoyed the programming class.
M : Yeah. I found it _________ _________ _________ _________ _________, too.
W : Then, what's the reason? Are you ✪ _________ _________ _________ _________ _________ after work?
M : Not at all. The class is quite exciting.
W : Is it because the new class starts 30 minutes earlier?
M : No. That's actually better for my schedule. The problem is that I have to _________ _________ _________ _________.
W : Oh, you're moving?
M : Yes. So, I don't think I can make it.
W : I'm sorry to hear that. It was nice taking the class with you.
M : Same here. Let's keep in touch.

08

대화를 듣고, Samuel's Woodworking Class에 관해 언급되지 않은 것을 고르시오.

M : Gina, come check out this flyer.
W : What's this, Ted? *[Pause]* Oh, Samuel's Woodworking Class. Looks interesting.
M : It's a one-time class ✪ _________ _________ _________ _________ _________ _________ _________ _________. I think you'd like it, too.
W : Absolutely! Look, we can _________ _________ _________ _________ making a pencil case or a wooden plate.
M : Yes! The class will be held from 7 p.m. to 9 p.m. next Friday.
W : I'll be available then. Do you want to take the class together?
M : Sure. I think I'm going to make a pencil case. What about you?
W : I'd like to make a wooden plate. How much is the registration fee?
M : It's only $40 per person.
W : That's a good price. Does it say how we can register?
M : Here. We can register on the community center website.
W : Yes, and look. _________ _________ _________ _________ _________. We'd better hurry.
M : Let's sign up now.

09

2021 Lakeside Essay Contest에 관한 다음 내용을 듣고, 일치하지 않는 것을 고르시오.

W : Okay, class. Before I let you go, I'd like to remind you about the 2021 Lakeside Essay Contest. As you know, the theme of this year is "messages from summer." Last year, the contest was _________ _________ _________ _________. But this year, all students at Lakeside High School can participate. You can submit your essay to me by email. Don't forget your essay ✪ _________ _________ _________ _________ _________ _________. Please start writing your essay today because _________ _________ _________ _________ _________. You can check the results of the contest on July 3rd. The top 10 essays will be posted on our school website. I hope many of you participate in this contest! All right, everyone. See you next time.

10

다음 표를 보면서 대화를 듣고, 남자가 주문할 자전거를 고르시오.

M : Hey, Olivia. You know a lot about bicycles. Would you help me choose one from this list?
W : Sure. Let me see. *[Pause]* Oh, you're looking at bicycles for commuters. Well, I don't recommend the black one for your safety at night.
M : You're right. It won't be safe when it's dark. Then I'll _________ _________ _________ _________ _________.
W : Good idea. What's your budget?
M : I can spend up to $300.
W : Okay. Now you need to choose a frame size.
M : Should I choose a medium-sized frame?
W : No. Because you're tall, you'll need a bigger one.
M : Okay. I'll get one of these then. Do you think I need a foldable bicycle?
W : Hmm, it depends on _________ _________ _________ _________ _________ transportation.
M : I ✪ _________ _________ _________ _________, so I guess I don't need a foldable one.
W : Then, this model is the best choice for you.
M : Great. I'll order it now. Thanks.

11

대화를 듣고, 여자의 마지막 말에 대한 남자의 응답으로 가장 적절한 것을 고르시오.

W : Honey, your hair's getting pretty long.
M : Yeah. I was thinking about getting a haircut today. _________ _________ _________ _________ _________ _________ _________?
W : He's good, but you should call him first and ✪ _________ _________ _________ _________. Do you want the phone number?

12

대화를 듣고, 남자의 마지막 말에 대한 여자의 응답으로 가장 적절한 것을 고르시오.

M : Hey, Lauren. Are you still looking for _________ _________ _________ _________ _________ _________?
W : Yes, but I haven't found one yet. Your band is still my first choice, but I know you already have a drummer.
M : Actually, our drummer had to quit for personal reasons. We want you ✪ _________ _________ _________ _________ _________ _________.

13

대화를 듣고, 여자의 마지막 말에 대한 남자의 응답으로 가장 적절한 것을 고르시오. [3점]

[Cell phone rings.]
W : Hello.
M : Good afternoon. This is S&G Clothing Company. Can I speak to Ms. Thompson, please?
W : Yes, speaking.
M : I'm calling to tell you about the order you placed.
W : Oh, is there a problem?
M : Yes. Unfortunately, the black skirt you ordered is _________ _________ _________ _________ _________ _________.
W : Oh, no. I need it for my graduation ceremony this weekend.
M : We're very sorry for the inconvenience.
W : Okay. Then, what are my options?
M : You may cancel your order and get a full refund. Or we could send you the same skirt, but _________ _________ _________ _________.
W : Hmm... What colors do you have?
M : We currently have only gray in stock. If we send it out today, ✪ _________ _________ _________ _________.
W : Well, I like the design of the skirt, so gray's fine.

14

대화를 듣고, 남자의 마지막 말에 대한 여자의 응답으로 가장 적절한 것을 고르시오.

[Cell phone rings.]
W : Hi, honey. What's up?
M : Where are you right now?
W : I just parked my car. I'll be home in a minute. How about you?
M : I'm at the grocery store, but I've just realized _________ _________ _________ _________ _________ _________ _________.
W : Really? You should call the credit card company and cancel your card right away.
M : I will. But before I do that, _________ _________ _________ _________ _________ _________ _________ _________, please?
W : Okay. Which jacket do you want me to check?
M : It's the brown one. I wore it yesterday.
W : You mean the one I bought for you last spring?
M : That's right. It's in the living room. Meanwhile, I'll ✪ _________ _________ _________ _________ _________ just in case I dropped the card.

15

다음 상황 설명을 듣고, Rachel이 Kevin에게 할 말로 가장 적절한 것을 고르시오. [3점]

M : Kevin is looking for a place to work out every day. He has found two fitness centers with good facilities. The first one is a 5-minute walk from home, and the second one is a 30-minute walk. Kevin likes the first fitness center because it's closer to home. However, he also thinks that the second fitness center can be a good choice because it _________ _________ _________ _________ for new members. Kevin cannot decide which one to choose and asks his sister, Rachel, for advice. Rachel remembers that he ✪ _________ _________ _________ _________ _________ because the fitness centers were far from home. She thinks that Kevin should choose a fitness center _________ _________ _________, not cost. So, Rachel wants to suggest to Kevin that he should choose the fitness center near home. In this situation, what would Rachel most likely say to Kevin?

16~17

다음을 듣고, 물음에 답하시오.

W : Hello, students. Last time, you learned about the people who invented drones. As technology develops, ✪ _________ _________ _________ _________ _________ _________ around the world. So, today, we'll talk about how they're used in different jobs. First, drones help farmers _________ _________ _________ _________. For example, drones are used to spread seeds that may be difficult to plant. They also spray chemicals to protect plants from harmful insects. Second, photographers use drones to easily access areas that are _________ _________ _________. Specifically, nature and wildlife photographers no longer need to go through dangerous jungles and rainforests. Next, drones are useful for police officers when they control traffic. Drones could provide updates on traffic flow and accidents, and even help identify anyone driving dangerously. Last, drones aid firefighters. Firefighters use drones that drop tanks of special chemicals to prevent the spread of fire. Now, let's watch an incredible video of drones in action.

▶ 정답 : 해설편 064쪽

VOCA LIST 14

회차별 영단어 QR 코드 ※ QR 코드를 스캔 후 모바일로 단어장처럼 학습할 수 있습니다.

● 고3 2022학년도 6월

01

001 □ announce ⓥ 발표하다, 알리다
002 □ recruit ⓥ 모집하다
003 □ previously ad 이전에
004 □ luckily ad 운 좋게, 다행히도
005 □ assign ⓥ 배정하다
006 □ expected ⓐ 예상되는
007 □ accept ⓥ 받아들이다
008 □ inform ⓥ 알리다

02

009 □ wrap ⓥ 포장하다
010 □ waste ⓥ 낭비하다 ⓝ 쓰레기
011 □ fancy ⓐ 멋진
012 □ throw away ~을 버리다
013 □ overpackage ⓥ 과대 포장하다
014 □ reduce ⓥ 줄이다
015 □ unnecessary ⓐ 불필요한

03

016 □ wonder ⓥ 궁금하다
017 □ pick out ~을 선택하다
018 □ basically ad 기본적으로
019 □ director ⓝ (영화·연극의) 감독
020 □ catch ⓥ 정확히 보여주다
021 □ theme ⓝ 주제, 테마
022 □ script ⓝ 대본
023 □ realistic ⓐ 현실적인
024 □ connection ⓝ 연관성
025 □ scene ⓝ (영화·연극·책의) 장면
026 □ article ⓝ (신문 등의) 기사

04

027 □ move in 이사 오다
028 □ renovation ⓝ 수리, 개조
029 □ cabinet ⓝ 수납장
030 □ store ⓥ 저장[보관]하다
031 □ sink ⓝ 세면대
032 □ absolutely ad 전적으로

05

033 □ raise ⓥ 올리다, 높이다
034 □ awareness ⓝ 의식, 관심
035 □ staff ⓝ 직원
036 □ volunteer ⓝ 자원봉사자
037 □ take place (예정된 행사가) 열리다[개최되다]
038 □ apply ⓥ 신청하다, 지원하다
039 □ submit ⓥ 제출하다
040 □ application ⓝ 지원, 신청
041 □ economics ⓝ 경제학

06

042 □ depend on ~에 달려 있다
043 □ cost ⓥ (비용이) ~이다[들다]
044 □ adult ⓐ 다 자란
045 □ recommend ⓥ 추천하다
046 □ customer ⓝ 고객

07

047 □ anymore ad 더 이상은
048 □ career ⓝ 직업, 직장 생활
049 □ attend ⓥ 참석하다
050 □ quite ad 꽤
051 □ earlier ⓐ 예상보다 일찍
052 □ actually ad 사실은
053 □ make it (어떤 곳에 간신히) 시간 맞춰 가다
054 □ keep in touch 연락하고 지내다

08

055 □ check out ~을 살펴보다
056 □ flyer ⓝ (광고·안내용) 전단
057 □ woodwork ⓝ 목공예
058 □ hands-on 직접 해 보는
059 □ plate ⓝ 접시
060 □ hold ⓥ (회의·시합 등을) 하다[열다]
061 □ registration ⓝ 등록
062 □ register ⓥ 등록하다

09

063 □ remind ⓥ 상기시키다
064 □ freshman ⓝ (대학·고등학교의) 신입생
065 □ deadline ⓝ 기한
066 □ result ⓝ 결과
067 □ post ⓥ 게시하다

10

068 □ commuter ⓝ 통근자
069 □ budget ⓝ 예산
070 □ up to ~까지
071 □ frame ⓝ 뼈대
072 □ foldable ⓐ 접을 수 있는
073 □ transportation ⓝ 교통 수단
074 □ guess ⓥ 추측하다

11

075 □ pretty ad 꽤, 아주
076 □ text ⓥ 문자를 보내다

12

077 □ quit ⓥ 그만하다
078 □ personal ⓐ 개인적인
079 □ reason ⓝ 이유
080 □ offer ⓥ 제안하다
081 □ position ⓝ (일)자리, 직위

13

082 □ place ⓥ (주문·지시·명령 등을) 하다
083 □ unfortunately ad 불행하게도
084 □ out of stock 품절인, 재고가 떨어진
085 □ at the moment 지금으로서는
086 □ inconvenience ⓝ 불편
087 □ option ⓝ 선택(할 수 있는 것)
088 □ cancel ⓥ 취소하다
089 □ refund ⓝ 환불(금)
090 □ currently ad 현재, 지금
091 □ in stock 재고가 있는
092 □ exchange ⓥ 교환하다
093 □ package ⓝ 소포

14

094 □ park ⓥ 주차하다
095 □ in a minute 금방
096 □ grocery ⓝ 식료품
097 □ realize ⓥ 깨닫다, 알아차리다
098 □ credit card 신용 카드
099 □ missing ⓐ 없어진
100 □ right away 곧바로, 즉시
101 □ meanwhile ad 그동안에
102 □ lost and found 분실물 보관소
103 □ replace ⓥ 대신[대체]하다

15

104 □ work out 운동하다
105 □ facility ⓝ ((*pl.*)) (생활의 편의를 위한) 시설
106 □ likely ⓐ ~할 것 같은
107 □ necessary ⓐ 필요한

16~17

108 □ spread ⓥ 퍼뜨리다
109 □ plant ⓥ (나무·씨앗 등을) 심다
110 □ spray ⓥ 살포하다
111 □ chemical ⓝ 화학 물질
112 □ insect ⓝ 곤충
113 □ access ⓥ 접근하다, 입수[이용]하다
114 □ area ⓝ 지역, 구역
115 □ reach ⓥ ~에 이르다
116 □ specifically ad 구체적으로 말하면
117 □ wildlife ⓝ 야생 동물
118 □ rainforest ⓝ (열대) 우림
119 □ flow ⓝ 흐름
120 □ identify ⓥ 찾다, 발견하다
121 □ prevent ⓥ 막다, 예방하다
122 □ incredible ⓐ 믿을 수 없는
123 □ in action 활동[작동]을 하는
124 □ decline ⓝ 감소
125 □ employment ⓝ 취업, 고용
126 □ opportunity ⓝ 기회
127 □ due to ~ 때문에
128 □ regulation ⓝ 규정
129 □ various ⓐ 여러 가지의
130 □ field ⓝ 분야
131 □ development ⓝ 성장, 개발
132 □ workplace ⓝ 직장
133 □ cause ⓥ 초래하다, 야기하다

15회 ● 2021학년도 6월 모의평가 고3 영어 듣기

※ QR코드를 스캔하시면 듣기 방송을 청취하실 수 있습니다.

● 점수 표시가 없는 문항은 모두 2점 ● 문항수 17개 | 배점 37점 | 제한 시간 25분

1번부터 17번까지는 듣고 답하는 문제입니다. 1번부터 15번까지는 한 번만 들려주고, 16번부터 17번까지는 두 번 들려줍니다. 방송을 잘 듣고 답을 하시기 바랍니다.

1. 다음을 듣고, 남자가 하는 말의 목적으로 가장 적절한 것을 고르시오.

① 발명 대회 참가 신청 마감일 변경을 안내하려고
② 수업 과제의 온라인 제출 방법을 설명하려고
③ 학교 홈페이지 운영 도우미를 모집하려고
④ 발명 아이디어 우수 사례를 소개하려고
⑤ 발명가 초청 특별 강연을 홍보하려고

2. 대화를 듣고, 여자의 의견으로 가장 적절한 것을 고르시오.

① 보고서 주제는 구체적이어야 한다.
② 도표 활용은 자료 제시에 효과적이다.
③ 설문 대상에 따라 질문을 달리해야 한다.
④ 설문 조사자를 위한 사전 교육이 필요하다.
⑤ 보고서 작성 시 도표 제시 순서에 유의해야 한다.

3. 대화를 듣고, 두 사람의 관계를 가장 잘 나타낸 것을 고르시오.

① 화가 – 기자 ② 작곡가 – 가수
③ 시인 – 교사 ④ 영화감독 – 배우
⑤ 무용가 – 사진작가

4. 대화를 듣고, 그림에서 대화의 내용과 일치하지 않는 것을 고르시오.

5. 대화를 듣고, 여자가 남자를 위해 할 일로 가장 적절한 것을 고르시오.

① 저작권 확인하기 ② 포스터 인쇄하기
③ 프린터 구매하기 ④ 파일 전송하기
⑤ 만화 그리기

6. 대화를 듣고, 남자가 지불할 금액을 고르시오. [3점]

① $54 ② $55 ③ $60 ④ $63 ⑤ $70

7. 대화를 듣고, 동아리 봉사 활동이 연기된 이유를 고르시오.

① 기부받은 옷 정리 시간이 더 필요해서
② 동아리 홍보 동영상을 제작해야 해서
③ 중간고사 기간이 얼마 남지 않아서
④ 동아리 정기 회의를 개최해야 해서
⑤ 기부 행사 참가자가 부족해서

8. 대화를 듣고, Annual Charity Baseball Game에 관해 언급되지 않은 것을 고르시오.

① 참가 선수 ② 일시 ③ 입장료
④ 기념품 ⑤ 장소

9. Kaufman Special Exhibition에 관한 다음 내용을 듣고, 일치하지 않는 것을 고르시오.

① 1995년에 처음 개최되었다.
② 월요일에는 열리지 않는다.
③ 올해의 주제는 예술과 기술의 결합이다.
④ 일일 관람객 수를 100명으로 제한한다.
⑤ 예매를 통해 할인을 받을 수 있다.

[해설편 p.064]

10. 다음 표를 보면서 대화를 듣고, 여자가 등록할 강좌를 고르시오.

Community Center Classes in July

	Class	Fee	Location	Start Time
①	Graphic Design	$50	Greenville	5 p.m.
②	Coding	$70	Greenville	7 p.m.
③	Photography	$80	Westside	7 p.m.
④	Flower Art	$90	Westside	5 p.m.
⑤	Coffee Brewing	$110	Greenville	8 p.m.

11. 대화를 듣고, 남자의 마지막 말에 대한 여자의 응답으로 가장 적절한 것을 고르시오.

① I'll be back tomorrow.
② You liked the food there.
③ I go to the gym every day.
④ You should be here by six.
⑤ We finished dinner already.

12. 대화를 듣고, 여자의 마지막 말에 대한 남자의 응답으로 가장 적절한 것을 고르시오.

① All right. I'll take the bus then.
② No. My bicycle is broken again.
③ No problem. I'll give you a ride.
④ Don't worry. I'm already at school.
⑤ Indeed. I'm glad it's getting warmer.

13. 대화를 듣고, 남자의 마지막 말에 대한 여자의 응답으로 가장 적절한 것을 고르시오. [3점]

Woman: ______________________________

① Absolutely. I was impressed after reading this script.
② No doubt. I think I acted well in the last comedy.
③ Great. I'll write the script for your new drama.
④ I'm sorry. I'm not able to direct the movie.
⑤ Okay. I'll let you know my decision soon.

14. 대화를 듣고, 여자의 마지막 말에 대한 남자의 응답으로 가장 적절한 것을 고르시오. [3점]

Man: ______________________________

① That's okay. You can reserve another place.
② I see. I should hurry to join your company event.
③ Why not? My company has its own sports facilities.
④ I agree. We should wait until the remodeling is done.
⑤ Thanks. I'll call now to see if they're available that day.

15. 다음 상황 설명을 듣고, Mary가 Steve에게 할 말로 가장 적절한 것을 고르시오.

Mary: ______________________________

① Why don't you take leave today and look after yourself?
② Your interests should be the priority in your job search.
③ You'd better actively support your teammates' ideas.
④ Let's find a way to increase sales of health products.
⑤ How about changing the details of the contract?

[16~17] 다음을 듣고, 물음에 답하시오.

16. 여자가 하는 말의 주제로 가장 적절한 것은?

① reasons why chemicals are harmful to plants
② ways that plants protect themselves from danger
③ difficulties in preventing plants from overgrowing
④ tips for keeping dangerous insects away from plants
⑤ importance of recognizing poisonous plants in the wild

17. 언급된 식물이 <u>아닌</u> 것은?

① roses ② tomato plants ③ clovers
④ cherry trees ⑤ walnut trees

[해설편 p.066]

Dictation 15

✪ 표기에는 듣기 어려운 발음이 포함되어 있습니다. 귀 기울여 듣고 받아쓰세요.

● 고3 2021학년도 6월

※ QR 코드를 스캔하시면 듣기 방송이 나옵니다. 듣기 방송을 들으며 다음 빈칸을 채우시오. ● 제한 시간 : 25분

01

다음을 듣고, 남자가 하는 말의 목적으로 가장 적절한 것을 고르시오.

M : Good morning, Hotwells High School students. This is your science teacher, Mr. Moore, with an announcement about our invention contest. I know you all have creative invention ideas, and I'm excited to see them. As you know, we were accepting applications until July 8th through the school website. However, the deadline has been changed _________ _________ _________ _________ on July 7th and 8th. So, I'd like to inform you that ✪ _________ _________ _________ _________ _________ _________ _________. Thank you for understanding, and please don't forget the changed deadline. If you have questions, please visit me in my office. Thank you.

02

대화를 듣고, 여자의 의견으로 가장 적절한 것을 고르시오.

M : Ms. Lee. Can you help me with my sociology report?

W : Sure, Alex. You surveyed teens ✪ _________ _________ _________ _________, right?

M : Yes, I did. I've collected data, but I'm not sure how to present the numbers effectively.

W : Let's see. Oh, you just listed all the numbers. Why don't you use charts or graphs, instead? They _________ _________ _________ _________.

M : Okay. What kind can I use?

W : For example, you can use pie charts or bar graphs.

M : Oh, I didn't think about that.

W : Yeah. Charts and graphs can be helpful. They can _________ _________ _________ _________ _________ _________.

M : That's good.

W : Also, they can help people see the relationship between numbers quickly.

M : So, charts and graphs can make data easy to understand.

W : Right. Using those can be effective in presenting data.

M : I got it. Thanks for your help.

03

대화를 듣고, 두 사람의 관계를 가장 잘 나타낸 것을 고르시오.

[Cell phone rings.]

W : Hi, Mr. Parker.

M : Hi, Ms. Jones. I'm so glad _________ _________ _________ _________ _________ _________ _________ to my literature class.

W : My pleasure. You said you have 20 students. Is there anything special you'd like me to do?

M : Well, they've read your poems in my class. Could you _________ _________ _________ and explain their meaning?

W : Sure thing. I could explain my writing process, too.

M : Great. Also, my students wrote poems. Maybe you could hear some of them.

W : Absolutely. And I'd like to give ✪ _________ _________ _________ _________ _________ _________ _________ _________ to each of your students.

M : Oh, thank you. That would be such a meaningful gift.

W : So, when should I arrive at your high school?

M : Could you come by 3 p.m.? I'll meet you in the lobby.

W : Okay. I'll be there.

04

대화를 듣고, 그림에서 대화의 내용과 일치하지 않는 것을 고르시오.

M : Hello, Susan. How was the pet cafe you visited yesterday?

W : Hi, Sam. It was wonderful. Look at this picture I took there.

M : Okay. Oh, the dog next to the counter looks sweet. Is it yours?

W : No. He's the cafe owner's.

M : I'd love to play with the dog.

W : Yeah, we should go together. _________ _________ _________ _________ _________ _________ _________. Isn't it beautiful?

M : It really is. And I see many good photo spots here.

W : You know my favorite spot? It's the mug sculpture ✪ _________ _________ _________ _________ _________ on it.

M : I like it. It makes the cafe unique. Hmm, what are these balls in the basket?

W : People can _________ _________ _________ _________ _________ with their dogs.

M : Sounds fun. By the way, there are only two tables. Don't they need more?

W : Well, they need space so pets can run around.

M : I see. It looks like a great place to visit.

05

대화를 듣고, 여자가 남자를 위해 할 일로 가장 적절한 것을 고르시오.

W : Hi, Ted. How are you doing with the poster for the Student Dance Festival?

M : Hello, Ms. Wood. Here, take a look at my monitor. It's the final draft of the poster.

W : Let's see. Wow, you did a great job. It looks like you're all done.

M : Thank you, Ms. Wood.

W : Oh, I like the cartoon at the bottom. Did you _________ _________ _________?

M : No, I downloaded the image. I checked the copyright and it's free to use.

W : That's great. Are you ready to print the poster, then?

M : Yes, but ✪ _________ _________ _________ _________, so I can't print it now.

W : Don't worry. I can do it for you in the teachers' lounge.

M : That'd be great.

W : How many copies of the poster do you need?

M : _________ _________ _________ _________ _________.

W : No problem. Just send me the file.

M : Thank you so much.

15회

06

대화를 듣고, 남자가 지불할 금액을 고르시오. [3점]

M : Good afternoon.
W : Hi, welcome to the gift shop. How was the soap art exhibition?
M : It was amazing. I never imagined ✪ __________ __________ __________ __________ __________ __________.
W : Many visitors say that. And you know what? We're having a promotion this week. All items are 10% off.
M : That's great. I like this handmade soap. How much is it?
W : It's $20 for one set.
M : Good. I'll buy two sets. Oh, is this a soap flower?
W : Uh-huh. You can use it __________ __________ __________ __________. The large one is $10, and the small one is $5.
M : It smells really nice. I'll take three large ones, please.
W : Okay. Anything else?
M : No, thanks. That's it.
W : So, here are two sets of handmade soap, and three large soap flowers. And __________ __________ __________, __________ __________ __________ __________.
M : Thanks. Here's my credit card.

07

대화를 듣고, 동아리 봉사 활동이 연기된 이유를 고르시오.

W : Hi, John. We just finished the volunteer club meeting.
M : Hi, Alice. Sorry, I'm late. __________ __________ __________?
W : Well, we ✪ __________ __________ __________ __________ at the homeless shelter until next week.
M : Why? Is it because midterm exams are coming up?
W : No. That's not a problem. All of our members still want to participate.
M : Then, why did we postpone?
W : You know we posted a video online about our club last week, right?
M : Sure. I helped make the video. It was a big hit.
W : Well, since then, we've received __________ __________ __________.
M : Oh, that's great news. But it sounds like a lot of work.
W : Yes. We need more time to __________ __________ __________ __________ __________ __________. That's why we postponed.
M : I get it. When will we start?
W : We're going to start organizing them tomorrow morning.
M : Okay. I'll see you then.

08

대화를 듣고, Annual Charity Baseball Game에 관해 언급되지 않은 것을 고르시오.

M : Hey, Clara. What are you looking at on your phone?
W : Hi, Harry. I'm looking at information about the Annual Charity Baseball Game.
M : Oh, I went to see the game last year. It was so fun. __________ __________ __________ __________ __________?
W : The actors from the movie *Heroes from Mercury* are playing. Let's go together.
M : Great idea. When is it?
W : It's at 3 p.m. ✪ __________ __________ __________.
M : Okay. Then, __________ __________ __________ __________ __________ __________.
W : You're right. Tickets are $30 each. Isn't it a little expensive?
M : Maybe. But all ticket sales will be __________ __________ __________ __________.
W : Yeah, that's true. And the game is going to be held here in town.
M : Oh, is it at Clifton Baseball Stadium again?
W : That's right. I'll book the tickets now.

09

Kaufman Special Exhibition에 관한 다음 내용을 듣고, 일치하지 않는 것을 고르시오.

W : Hi, DSNB listeners! This is Olivia Wilson with *One Minute Culture News*. I'd like to introduce the upcoming Kaufman Special Exhibition. This event was first held in 1995 and continues to be loved by the art community. Starting August 1st, __________ __________ __________ __________ __________ __________ __________ __________, every day except Mondays. You can experience the exhibition in the West Hall of Timothy Kaufman Gallery. This year's theme is ✪ __________ __________ __________ __________ __________ __________. You can see unique artwork created __________ __________ __________ __________ __________. The number of daily visitors is limited to 300 to avoid crowding. You can buy tickets on site, but __________ __________ __________ gets you a 20% discount. To learn more, please visit their website. Next is weather with Sean. Stay tuned.

10

다음 표를 보면서 대화를 듣고, 여자가 등록할 강좌를 고르시오.

M : Hi, can I help you?
W : Hi. I'd like to see which classes your community center is offering in July.
M : Here. Take a look at this flyer.
W : Hmm... I'm interested in all five classes, but I shouldn't take this one. I'm ✪ __________ __________ __________ __________.
M : Oh, that's too bad. Well, now you've got four options.
W : I see __________ __________ __________ __________ __________ __________. I don't want to spend more than $100, though.
M : All right. And how about the location? Do you care which location you go to?
W : Yeah. Greenville is __________ __________ __________ __________, so I'd prefer my class to be there.
M : Okay. What time is good for you?
W : Well, I'm busy until 6 p.m., so I'll take a class after that.
M : I see. There's just one left then. It's a really popular class.
W : Great. Sign me up.

11

대화를 듣고, 남자의 마지막 말에 대한 여자의 응답으로 가장 적절한 것을 고르시오.

M : Honey, I'm going to the gym now.
W : Don't forget our neighbors are coming to have dinner with us. _________ _________ _________ _________ _________ _________ _________.
M : I know. What time do you ✪ _________ _________ _________ _________?

12

대화를 듣고, 여자의 마지막 말에 대한 남자의 응답으로 가장 적절한 것을 고르시오.

W : Michael, you're going to take the school bus today, right?
M : ✪ _________ _________ _________ than yesterday, I'm going to take my bicycle, Mom. Why?
W : It's much colder and windier today. _________ _________ _________ _________ _________ _________.

13

대화를 듣고, 남자의 마지막 말에 대한 여자의 응답으로 가장 적절한 것을 고르시오. [3점]

M : Hey, Sylvia. I saw your new movie a few days ago. You played the character beautifully.
W : Thanks, Jack. I _________ _________ _________ _________ _________ in that movie.
M : I'm sure you did. Sylvia, I'm going to be directing a new movie. You'd be perfect for the lead role.
W : Oh, really? What's the movie about?
M : It's ✪ _________ _________ _________ _________ _________ who just moved to a new town.
W : That sounds interesting, and I'd like to be in your movie. But I'm not sure _________ _________ _________ _________ _________ _________ _________.
M : Why do you say that?
W : Well, I haven't acted in a comedy before.
M : Don't worry. _________ _________ _________ _________.
W : That's kind of you. Can I read the script and then decide?
M : Sure. I'll send you a copy of the script. I'll be waiting to hear from you.

14

대화를 듣고, 여자의 마지막 말에 대한 남자의 응답으로 가장 적절한 것을 고르시오. [3점]

W : Jason, I heard you're planning a sports day for your company.
M : Yeah, it's next Saturday. But the problem is that I haven't been able to reserve a place yet.
W : Oh, really? Have you looked into Portman Sports Center?
M : I have. _________, _________ _________ _________.
W : That's too bad. It's perfect for sports events.
M : I know. Well, I've been looking everywhere, but every place I've called is booked.
W : Oh, no. Can you postpone the event until they finish remodeling?
M : No, we can't. The company has a busy schedule after that day.
W : Hmm... How about Whelford High School? They have great sports facilities.
M : Really? _________ _________ _________ _________ _________ _________?
W : Sure, they are. We rented them for a company event last month.
M : _________ _________ _________ _________ _________ _________ _________.
W : Yes, it is. But ✪ _________ _________ _________ _________, so you'd better hurry up.

15

다음 상황 설명을 듣고, Mary가 Steve에게 할 말로 가장 적절한 것을 고르시오.

M : Mary is leading a sales team at a company. Her team is working hard on a proposal for a very important contract. In the morning, Mary notices that Steve, one of her team members, is ✪ _________ _________ _________ _________ _________ _________. Mary asks Steve if he is feeling okay. Steve says that he has been feeling pain in his shoulder for the last few days, but he also says that he is okay to continue working. Mary is concerned that if Steve continues to work despite his pain, _________ _________ _________ _________ _________. She believes that his health should be the first priority. So, she wants to suggest to Steve that _________ _________ _________ _________ _________ and take care of himself. In this situation, what would Mary most likely say to Steve?

16~17

다음을 듣고, 물음에 답하시오.

W : Good morning, students. Previously, we learned about various environments in which plants grow. Today, we'll discuss how plants defend themselves from threat. Even though plants cannot run away from danger, they know how to keep themselves safe. First, many plants, like roses, _________ _________ _________. When animals get too close, these thorns cut them, warning them to stay away. Also, plants can create _________ _________ _________ _________ _________ _________. When insects attack, for example, tomato plants release chemicals, making their leaves taste bad. Next, some plants ✪ _________ _________ _________ _________. For instance, some cherry trees attract ants by making a sweet liquid. The ants guard the tree from enemies to keep this food source safe. Finally, there are plants that generate a poison to protect themselves. For example, certain walnut trees see other nearby trees as a danger, so they produce a poison to prevent the other trees from growing. Now, let's watch a video about these incredible plants.

▶ 정답 : 해설편 068쪽

01

- 001 □ **invention** ⓝ 발명
- 002 □ **contest** ⓝ 대회
- 003 □ **application** ⓝ 신청서
- 004 □ **deadline** ⓝ 마감일, 마감 기한
- 005 □ **due to** ~로 인해

02

- 006 □ **sociology** ⓝ 사회학
- 007 □ **preference** ⓝ 선호
- 008 □ **effectively** ad 효과적으로

03

- 009 □ **literature** ⓝ 문학
- 010 □ **poem** ⓝ 시
- 011 □ **read aloud** 낭독하다, 소리 내어 읽다
- 012 □ **process** ⓝ 과정
- 013 □ **absolutely** ad 그럼, 물론이지 (강한 동의·허락을 나타냄)
- 014 □ **meaningful** ⓐ 의미 있는

04

- 015 □ **flowerbed** ⓝ 화단
- 016 □ **photo spot** 사진 찍기에 좋은 장소
- 017 □ **mug** ⓝ 머그잔, 손잡이가 있는 컵
- 018 □ **sculpture** ⓝ 조각상
- 019 □ **play catch** 잡기 놀이를 하다

05

- 020 □ **final draft** 최종안
- 021 □ **copyright** ⓝ 저작권
- 022 □ **lounge** ⓝ 휴게실, 대합실
- 023 □ **copy** ⓝ (책·신문 등의) 한 부

06

- 024 □ **impressive** ⓐ 인상적인
- 025 □ **promotion** ⓝ 판촉
- 026 □ **air freshener** 방향제

07

- 027 □ **postpone** ⓥ 연기하다
- 028 □ **homeless shelter** 노숙자 보호소[쉼터]
- 029 □ **midterm** ⓐ 중간의
- 030 □ **donation** ⓝ 기부
- 031 □ **organize** ⓥ 정리하다

08

- 032 □ **annual** ⓐ 연례의, 매년의
- 033 □ **charity** ⓝ 자선 (단체)
- 034 □ **donate** ⓥ 기부하다
- 035 □ **local** ⓐ 지역의
- 036 □ **in town** 시내에서

09

- 037 □ **exhibition** ⓝ 전시회
- 038 □ **community** ⓝ (종교·직업 등이 같은 사람들의) 공동체[사회]
- 039 □ **combination** ⓝ 결합
- 040 □ **unique** ⓐ 독특한
- 041 □ **with the help of** ~의 도움으로
- 042 □ **limit** ⓥ 제한하다
- 043 □ **crowding** ⓝ 혼잡
- 044 □ **on site** 현장에서
- 045 □ **in advance** 사전에, 미리

10

- 046 □ **community center** 주민 센터
- 047 □ **flyer** ⓝ 전단
- 048 □ **allergic to** ~에 알레르기가 있는
- 049 □ **option** ⓝ 선택권
- 050 □ **fee** ⓝ 수업료
- 051 □ **location** ⓝ 장소, 위치
- 052 □ **care** ⓥ 상관하다, 신경을 쓰다
- 053 □ **close to** ~에 가까운
- 054 □ **prefer** ⓥ 선호하다

11

- 055 □ **gym** ⓝ 체육관
- 056 □ **neighbor** ⓝ 이웃
- 057 □ **make sure** 반드시 ~하다

12

- 058 □ **had better** ~하는 게 낫다
- 059 □ **ride** ⓥ (차량·자전거 등을) 타다 ⓝ 타기, 타고 가기

13

- 060 □ **character** ⓝ 등장인물
- 061 □ **beautifully** ad 멋지게
- 062 □ **direct** ⓥ 감독하다
- 063 □ **lead role** 주연
- 064 □ **dreamer** ⓝ 몽상가
- 065 □ **natural** ⓐ 타고난
- 066 □ **impressed** ⓐ 감명을 받은
- 067 □ **script** ⓝ 대본
- 068 □ **No doubt.** 당연하죠.

14

- 069 □ **reserve** ⓥ 예약하다
- 070 □ **remodel** ⓥ 개조 공사하다
- 071 □ **book** ⓥ 예약하다
- 072 □ **facility** ⓝ 시설
- 073 □ **open to the public** 대중에 개방된
- 074 □ **rent** ⓥ 빌리다

15

- 075 □ **proposal** ⓝ 제안, 계획
- 076 □ **frequently** ad 수시로, 자주
- 077 □ **take a day off** 하루 휴가를 내다
- 078 □ **look after** ~을 돌보다

16~17

- 079 □ **previously** ad 먼젓번에, 지난 시간에
- 080 □ **various** ⓐ 다양한
- 081 □ **defend** ⓥ 방어하다
- 082 □ **threat** ⓝ 위협, 협박
- 083 □ **run away from** ~에게서 도망치다
- 084 □ **thorn** ⓝ 가시
- 085 □ **stay away** 떨어져 있다, 거리를 두다
- 086 □ **substance** ⓝ 물질
- 087 □ **insect** ⓝ 곤충
- 088 □ **form** ⓥ 형성하다
- 089 □ **partnership** ⓝ 동반자 관계
- 090 □ **liquid** ⓝ 액체
- 091 □ **guard** ⓥ 지키다, 보호하다
- 092 □ **generate** ⓥ 만들어 내다
- 093 □ **nearby** ⓐ 주변의
- 094 □ **incredible** ⓐ 놀라운, 믿기 힘든
- 095 □ **overgrow** ⓥ (식물 등이) 무성하게 자라다
- 096 □ **poisonous** ⓐ 독성이 있는

16회 • 2023학년도 7월 학력평가 고3 영어 듣기

※ QR코드를 스캔하시면 듣기 방송을 청취하실 수 있습니다.

● 점수 표시가 없는 문항은 모두 2점 ● 문항수 17개 | 배점 37점 | 제한 시간 25분

1번부터 17번까지는 듣고 답하는 문제입니다. 1번부터 15번까지는 한 번만 들려주고, 16번부터 17번까지는 두 번 들려줍니다. 방송을 잘 듣고 답을 하시기 바랍니다.

MP3

1. 다음을 듣고, 남자가 하는 말의 목적으로 가장 적절한 것을 고르시오.

① 발코니 사용 수칙을 안내하려고
② 화재 시 대피 방법을 설명하려고
③ 발코니 보수공사 동의를 요청하려고
④ 아파트 안전 점검 계획을 공지하려고
⑤ 아파트 주민 친목 행사를 홍보하려고

2. 대화를 듣고, 여자의 의견으로 가장 적절한 것을 고르시오.

① 언어 교육은 일찍 시작할수록 효과적이다.
② 외국어 학습 시 구체적인 목표를 설정해야 한다.
③ 외국어 교육을 위한 다양한 학습 방법 개발이 필요하다.
④ 외국어 말하기 연습 시 실수를 두려워하지 않아야 한다.
⑤ 언어를 통해 그 언어 사용자들의 문화를 이해할 수 있다.

3. 대화를 듣고, 두 사람의 관계를 가장 잘 나타낸 것을 고르시오.

① 방송 작가 – 애견 훈련사
② 고객 – 애견 미용사
③ 달력 디자이너 – 인쇄소 직원
④ 자원봉사자 – 수의사
⑤ 사진작가 – 유기견보호소 직원

4. 대화를 듣고, 그림에서 대화의 내용과 일치하지 않는 것을 고르시오.

5. 대화를 듣고, 남자가 할 일로 가장 적절한 것을 고르시오.

① 공항에 마중 나가기
② 안내 학생 선정하기
③ 안내 학생 이름표 만들기
④ 학교 방문단 사진 찍기
⑤ 학교 방문단 점심 준비하기

6. 대화를 듣고, 여자가 지불할 금액을 고르시오. [3점]

① $68 ② $75 ③ $81 ④ $86 ⑤ $95

7. 대화를 듣고, 남자가 스쿨버스를 놓친 이유를 고르시오.

① 늦잠을 자서
② 병원에 다녀와서
③ 아침 운동을 오래 해서
④ 수업 발표 자료를 두고 와서
⑤ 아파트 엘리베이터가 고장 나서

8. 대화를 듣고, Translators For All에 관해 언급되지 않은 것을 고르시오.

① 지원 자격
② 근무 장소
③ 급여
④ 채용 인원
⑤ 지원 방법

9. Firefly Walk에 관한 다음 내용을 듣고, 일치하지 않는 것을 고르시오.

① 곤충 전문가가 안내한다.
② 일일 최대 참여 인원은 12명이다.
③ 사전에 예약을 해야 한다.
④ 기부금만으로 운영된다.
⑤ 비가 오면 다른 행사로 대체된다.

[해설편 p.069]

영어 영역[듣기]

10. 다음 표를 보면서 대화를 듣고, 두 사람이 주문할 베개를 고르시오.

Pillows

	Model	Price	Thickness (inches)	Filling Material	Machine Wash
①	A	$60	4	Goose Down	×
②	B	$62	5	Cotton	○
③	C	$80	6	Goose Down	○
④	D	$85	6	Cotton	×
⑤	E	$110	7	Cotton	○

11. 대화를 듣고, 여자의 마지막 말에 대한 남자의 응답으로 가장 적절한 것을 고르시오.

① That painting won't be displayed in this exhibition.
② I'll pack all my paintings for delivery to the gallery.
③ I should start learning to paint like you.
④ I've already met some of the other painters.
⑤ It was sold on the first day of the gallery exhibition.

12. 대화를 듣고, 남자의 마지막 말에 대한 여자의 응답으로 가장 적절한 것을 고르시오.

① Of course. When are you available?
② No worries. Your package is the cheapest one.
③ Sure. The package is refundable if you don't open it.
④ Absolutely. I'm happy to contact you before you leave.
⑤ Be careful. You should get enough information on the trip.

13. 대화를 듣고, 여자의 마지막 말에 대한 남자의 응답으로 가장 적절한 것을 고르시오. [3점]

Man: ______________________________

① Great. A powerful stroke is my strongest point in tennis.
② I see. Is there any lighter racket I can borrow from you?
③ I agree. Try to practice your stroke more with this racket.
④ That's true. I'll be a respectful tennis player from now on.
⑤ Okay. I should drop by a shop to see which racket suits me.

14. 대화를 듣고, 남자의 마지막 말에 대한 여자의 응답으로 가장 적절한 것을 고르시오.

Woman: ______________________________

① That's why I changed all of my glass cups to plastic.
② I'll try to look for a delivery restaurant to save time.
③ There's a reason that restaurant is popular with people.
④ You really made me think again about using food delivery.
⑤ I hope people know how important it is to eat fresh food.

15. 다음 상황 설명을 듣고, Nicky가 Chris에게 할 말로 가장 적절한 것을 고르시오. [3점]

Nicky: ______________________________

① You need to stick to your musical identity.
② Can you invite me to your band's performance?
③ Think about becoming a professional musician later.
④ Why don't we accept the proposal to try something new?
⑤ Let's keep practicing so we win instead of that other team.

[16 ~ 17] 다음을 듣고, 물음에 답하시오.

16. 남자가 하는 말의 주제로 가장 적절한 것은?

① animal-related terms in the financial sector
② what animals symbolize by country
③ aggressive tendencies of animals
④ how humans have domesticated animals
⑤ risks and benefits of livestock industry investment

17. 언급된 동물이 아닌 것은?

① bulls ② sheep ③ cats
④ pigs ⑤ chicken

[해설편 p.071]

Dictation 16

✪ 표기에는 듣기 어려운 발음이 포함되어 있습니다. 귀 기울여 듣고 받아쓰세요. ● 고3 2023학년도 7월

※ QR 코드를 스캔하시면 듣기 방송이 나옵니다. 듣기 방송을 들으며 다음 빈칸을 채우시오. ● 제한 시간 : 25분

01

다음을 듣고, 남자가 하는 말의 목적으로 가장 적절한 것을 고르시오.

M : Hello, residents. This is an announcement from the maintenance office. Last week, we ✪ _______________ __ __________ _______________ of the apartments and found some inappropriate uses of the balconies. Please be aware of ✪ _____ _______ _____ _________ _______________ as follows. First, balconies should not be used for the storage of goods, such as barbecue fuel materials which can cause a fire. Second, lightweight outdoor furniture should be removed when winds are strong because the objects can be blown off of the balcony. Lastly, please avoid watering plants too much ✪ ___ ___________ _____________. Thank you for your cooperation for your safe and pleasant residence.

02

대화를 듣고, 여자의 의견으로 가장 적절한 것을 고르시오.

M : Grace, I'm thinking about learning Korean. But I don't know where to start.
W : Why do you want to learn it?
M : I'm interested in Korean culture, so I'm curious about the language.
W : Well, if you've decided to learn a foreign language, you need to ✪ _____ _ __________ _______.
M : A specific goal? What's that?
W : It's something that you hope to achieve by learning a foreign language. For example, watching dramas without subtitles.
M : That sounds interesting.
W : ______ ________ ___________ _______ _______, the better you can choose your learning methods.
M : I see. Now I have a better idea of what I have to do.
W : Yeah. Also, a specific goal will keep you _______________ ______ ___________.
M : All right! I'll clarify what I want to achieve.
W : Good luck!

03

대화를 듣고, 두 사람의 관계를 가장 잘 나타낸 것을 고르시오.

[Cell phone rings.]
M : Ms. Evans! Hi, how are you?
W : I'm good, Mr. Johnson. Actually, our shelter's dog calendar sold really well. The photos you took for it were great.
M : Thanks. I hope it helped your shelter and ✪ _____ _______ ___ ________________ _______.
W : It definitely did. Thanks to the calendar, we had more visitors ______________ ___ _____________ __ ______.
M : I'm glad to hear that.
W : So we've decided to make a calendar for next year, too. Would you take pictures for us again?
M : I'd love to! I'm happy to help those homeless dogs to find a home!
W : Thanks so much! When do you think you'll be available?
M : I'm taking pictures for another client this week I'll be available right after it's done.
W : Great. So is there something we should prepare differently this time?
M : Could you just ✪ _____ _____ _______ _________ like last year?
W : Sure, I'll wash and brush them.
M : Perfect! I'll visit your shelter soon to get ready.
W : Great, thanks! I look forward to more of your amazing pictures!

04

대화를 듣고, 그림에서 대화의 내용과 일치하지 않는 것을 고르시오.

W : Honey, look at this! I've found one of our baby shower photos!
M : Oh, it's been a long time since I saw this! It was just a month before Amy was born!
W : You remember the heart balloon under the banner? You really ✪ _______________ ___ ________ __ ____.
M : Right, _ _______ ____ _________ after doing it.
W : I loved those three notes on the message board. But your note was the sweetest.
M : Thank you, dear. Oh! Is that Kiki the rabbit on the sofa?
W : Yes! It's amazing that rabbit doll has been Amy's best friend for years.
M : But, most of all, you were so beautiful in _______ __________ ________.
W : That dress was one of my favorites. I was grateful that I received so many presents that day.
M : I was happy, too. Just look at the gift boxes beside you.
W : It was really a great celebration for our whole family!

05

대화를 듣고, 남자가 할 일로 가장 적절한 것을 고르시오.

M : Ms. Valentine, is everything ready for the students from Thailand to visit?
W : Almost. Our students are all excited about our ✪ ______ __________________ ___________.
M : Are you picking them up at the airport? Shall I go with you?
W : Thanks, but I'll greet them with Mr. Howard.
M : All right! What time will you get back?
W : Probably at about 1 o'clock. We're all having lunch together in the school cafeteria.
M : That'll be lovely. Who will guide the Thai students on the campus tours?
W : Some students already volunteered for that. I have a list of their names.
M : Good! Would it be helpful if the guides ________ _________ ______?
W : That's a great idea. But I'm leaving soon, so could you make the tags?
M : Absolutely! And how about __________ ___________ ___ _____ ___________ ________?
W : I already asked some students from the photography club to do that.
M : Perfect. I can't wait to meet our international guests!

16회

Dictation 16

06

대화를 듣고, 여자가 지불할 금액을 고르시오. [3점]

M : Ms. Anderson, for our staff meeting today, how about we order some sandwiches?

W : Good idea! I'll order them from Jolly Sandwiches right now.

M : We can use a delivery app.

W : Sounds good. *[Pause]* How about tuna sandwiches or chicken sandwiches?

M : How much are they?

W : Tuna sandwiches are $8 each and chicken sandwiches are $6 each.

M : Let's have _____ _____ _____.

W : Okay, I'll add ten of them to our order. We also need beverages.

M : Sure. I think _____ _____ _____ _____ _____ for everyone.

W : They're $1 each. I'll add ten bottles.

M : Please check if they have a delivery fee.

W : It says it's $5. Oh, we can use a 10% off coupon for our order, but ✪ _____ _____ _____ _____ _____ _____.

M : All right, so the discount is only for the food and drinks.

W : Correct. I'll place the order and pay.

07

대화를 듣고, 남자가 스쿨버스를 놓친 이유를 고르시오.

W : Hi, Steve. I didn't see you on the school bus today.

M : Yes, I missed it.

W : I saw you running in the park early this morning. So you didn't wake up late.

M : Not at all. I'm working out to improve my health after I caught a cold.

W : But _____ _____ _____. Did you see a doctor this morning?

M : Not yet.

W : Then why did you miss the bus?

M : Actually, I left home as usual, but ✪ _____ _____ _____ _____.

W : Wait... Don't you live on a pretty high floor?

M : Yeah. I ran down the stairs as quickly as I could, but the bus drove away right before my eyes.

W : I'm sorry that you had a tough morning. How did you get to school?

M : The subway. Fortunately, it was quite empty, so I could ✪ _____ _____ _____ _____ for history class.

08

대화를 듣고, Translators For All에 관해 언급되지 않은 것을 고르시오.

W : David, what are you doing on your smartphone?

M : I'm researching internship programs to join. This one looks quite interesting.

W : What is it?

M : It's called Translators For All. The interns participate in ✪ _____ _____ _____ _____.

W : That is pretty cool. Could I apply, too?

M : Definitely. It says here they want college students _____ _____ _____.

W : Sounds like a good fit for both of us!

M : Absolutely. And what I like most about it is we can _____ _____ _____.

W : That's fantastic! But how much does the job pay?

M : Usually $500 a month.

W : Wow! Okay, so how do I apply?

M : We just have to fill out this online application form.

W : I'll get my smartphone and apply as well. It'll be a great experience.

09

Firefly Walk에 관한 다음 내용을 듣고, 일치하지 않는 것을 고르시오.

W : Hello, listeners! Lakeside Park invites you to the Firefly Walk this summer. You'll see the magical world of fireflies on a two-hour walk _____ _____ _____ _____. This event will be held from August 19th to 27th, open to a maximum of 12 participants per day. To join this event, you should make reservations in advance on our website. We're happy to offer this wonderful experience ✪ _____ _____ _____ _____. However, we operate the Firefly Walk based only on donations, so we would greatly appreciate ✪ _____ _____ _____. We'll hold the event even if it rains because it does not affect the firefly viewing. So join us for this unforgettable adventure at Lakeside Park!

10

다음 표를 보면서 대화를 듣고, 두 사람이 주문할 베개를 고르시오.

W : Honey, it looks like our pillows are pretty old. Why don't we buy new ones online?

M : All right. *[Typing sound]* I found the top five pillow recommendations on the online store.

W : Great! Let's see... I don't think I want to pay more than $100 for just one pillow.

M : I agree. So how thick would you like the pillows?

W : I guess four inches would be _____ _____ _____ _____ _____, right?

M : Probably. Something thicker than that would be better. Now, let's choose _____ _____ _____.

W : We've always used goose down. But how about picking another material instead of goose down this time?

M : Good point. Shall we ✪ _____ _____ _____ again?

W : Yes, but this time I want to get ones with a machine-wash option.

M : Definitely! Let's order them now!

11

대화를 듣고, 여자의 마지막 말에 대한 남자의 응답으로 가장 적절한 것을 고르시오.

W : Andy, your exhibition is coming up soon. Are the preparations going well?
M : Yeah, almost done. I finally ____________ _____ _____ ____________ for the exhibition yesterday.
W : Great! I ✪ ________ ________ ___ _____ your work. What do you have to do next for the exhibition?

12

대화를 듣고, 남자의 마지막 말에 대한 여자의 응답으로 가장 적절한 것을 고르시오.

M : Hi. I'd like to cancel the trip package I booked. Here's my reservation number.
W : Sure. *[Typing sound]* I'm sorry but we ✪ __________ _______ ______ __ __________ because you bought the special discounted package.
M : Oh, in that case, I wonder if I can __________ _____ ________ of the trip.

13

대화를 듣고, 여자의 마지막 말에 대한 남자의 응답으로 가장 적절한 것을 고르시오. [3점]

M : Thanks for today's tennis lesson, Ms. Rossini.
W : Oh, Mr. Chen, you did great with your backhand stroke today.
M : It's ____ __________ ___ ______. I couldn't even hit the ball at first!
W : Just remember to ✪ ____________ _______ _________ ______ ____________ when you strike.
M : I try to, but it's not easy.
W : Really? Can I see your racket?
M : Sure, here it is.
W : The head size is good for you, but this is too light.
M : Well... it's what my older sister used.
W : ✪ ________ __________ ________ __ _______________ to put force on the ball when striking. I think an around 300-gram racket is fit for you.
M : Oh, so a heavier racket makes it easier for me to control the ball?
W : That's right. Choosing the right racket for you is essential.

14

대화를 듣고, 남자의 마지막 말에 대한 여자의 응답으로 가장 적절한 것을 고르시오.

W : Jason, do you know any good Indian restaurants that deliver?
M : Oh, I don't use food delivery, so I'm not sure.
W : Really? I can get food delivered right to my front door with my smartphone.
M : Sure, it's convenient, but delivery food makes a lot of waste from all its packaging.
W : Well, unless we cook at home all the time, delivery is easier.
M : Have you thought about how many plastic containers are used in just one order?
W : Oh, that's true... I always put them in the recycling after, though.
M : That's not always enough. When I don't cook, I go to the restaurant and get the food served in _____ _______ _____________ _____________.
W : I've never thought about that. What a responsible way to _________ _________ ______!
M : People need to be aware of what ✪ _____ _________________ ___ _______ ___________ will be in the future.

15

다음 상황 설명을 듣고, Nicky가 Chris에게 할 말로 가장 적절한 것을 고르시오. [3점]

W : Chris is ✪ _____ ________________ _________ of an electronic music band at his university. His band is pretty good, close to professional level when it comes to electronic music. Then one day, another band on his campus, which plays classical music, offers his band _____ __________ ___ ___________ ____________ at the upcoming campus festival. Chris hesitates to respond because classical music feels quite unfamiliar to him. But Nicky, another member of his band, thinks if they work with musicians of the seemingly distant genre, they'd be able to present a different side of their music. So, Nicky wants to suggest to Chris that their team ✪ _______ _____ ________ ___ _________________ in an attempt to play music they've never done before. In this situation, what would Nicky most likely say to Chris?

16~17

다음을 듣고, 물음에 답하시오.

M : Hello, students. Have you ever heard a market analyst or an investment banker use animal references? It's because such expressions give you some ✪ __________ ______ _____ _____________ ____________. I'll introduce some examples of what animals represent in the market. Let's start with bulls. You've probably seen them raising their horns when they attack. So a 'bull market' represents a period when _________ _____ _____________ _________. The next one is sheep. As they move in a herd, the 'sheep-flock effect' means a bias that influences the decisions of investors, often causing irrational reactions. Pigs are also fairly common in finance-speak. They are used to define ✪ ______________ _______ _____ __________ and take high risks in anticipation of making huge profits. Finally, chicken indicates investors who are reluctant to take risks and prefer a safer approach. From these few examples, you can get an idea of the variety of financial vocabulary. Why don't you look for other examples and find your favorite one?

▶ 정답 : 해설편 073쪽

VOCA LIST 16

회차별 영단어 QR 코드 ※ QR 코드를 스캔 후 모바일로 단어장처럼 학습할 수 있습니다.

● 고3 2023학년도 7월

01

001 □ announcement ⓝ 안내
002 □ maintenance office 관리 사무소
003 □ conduct ⓥ 실시하다
004 □ inspection ⓝ 점검, 조사
005 □ inappropriate ⓐ 부적절한
006 □ be aware of ~을 인지하다, 알다
007 □ as follows 다음과 같은
008 □ storage ⓝ 보관
009 □ material ⓝ 재료
010 □ lightweight ⓐ 가벼운, 경량의
011 □ remove ⓥ 치우다
012 □ blow off (바람에) 불어 날리다
013 □ prevent ⓥ 방지하다
014 □ pleasant ⓐ 쾌적한, 즐거운

02

015 □ be interested in ~에 관심이 있다
016 □ curious ⓐ 호기심 많은
017 □ foreign language 외국어
018 □ set a goal 목표를 설정하다
019 □ specific ⓐ 구체적인
020 □ achieve ⓥ 성취하다
021 □ subtitle ⓝ 자막 ⓥ 자막 처리하다
022 □ detailed ⓐ 세부적인
023 □ motivated ⓐ 의욕을 가진, 동기 부여된
024 □ clarify ⓥ 분명히 하다, 명확히 하다

03

025 □ shelter ⓝ 보호소
026 □ calendar ⓝ 달력
027 □ abandon ⓥ 버리다, 유기하다
028 □ definitely ad 당연히, 물론
029 □ adopt ⓥ 입양하다
030 □ homeless ⓐ 집 잃은
031 □ available ⓐ (사람이) 여유가 있는
032 □ differently ad 달리
033 □ bathe ⓥ 목욕시키다
034 □ brush ⓥ 빗질하다

04

035 □ baby shower 베이비 샤워(출산을 앞둔 임신부에게 아기용 선물을 주는 파티)
036 □ balloon ⓝ 풍선
037 □ banner ⓝ 현수막
038 □ struggle to ~하느라 고생하다
039 □ dizzy ⓐ 어지러운
040 □ sweet ⓐ 사랑스러운, 상냥한
041 □ most of all 무엇보다도
042 □ grateful ⓐ 고마운

05

043 □ international ⓐ 국제의, 외국의
044 □ greet ⓥ 맞이하다, 인사하다
045 □ about ad 대략, 약
046 □ have lunch 점심을 먹다
047 □ guide ⓥ 안내하다 ⓝ 가이드
048 □ photography ⓝ 사진
049 □ can't wait to ~하기를 몹시 기대하다

06

050 □ staff meeting 직원 회의
051 □ tuna ⓝ 참치
052 □ add ⓥ 더하다
053 □ beverage ⓝ 음료
054 □ bottled water 물병
055 □ check ⓥ 확인하다, 점검하다
056 □ fee ⓝ 요금

07

057 □ school bus 스쿨버스, 통학 버스
058 □ wake up 일어나다
059 □ late ad 늦게
060 □ cough ⓥ 기침하다
061 □ see a doctor 진찰을 받다, 병원에 가다
062 □ as usual 평소대로
063 □ out of order 고장 난
064 □ stairs ⓝ 계단
065 □ get to school 학교에 오다[가다]
066 □ presentation ⓝ 발표

08

067 □ internship ⓝ 인턴십
068 □ join ⓥ 참여하다
069 □ quite ad 꽤
070 □ translator ⓝ 번역가
071 □ participate in ~에 참여하다
072 □ apply ⓥ 지원하다, 신청하다, 적용하다
073 □ work from home 재택 근무하다
074 □ fill out 작성하다
075 □ form ⓝ (서류) 양식
076 □ as well 또한
077 □ experience ⓝ 경험 ⓥ 경험하다

09

078 □ invite ⓥ 초대하다
079 □ firefly ⓝ 반딧불이
080 □ maximum ⓝ 최대
081 □ in advance 미리, 사전에
082 □ wonderful ⓐ 멋진
083 □ at no cost 무료로
084 □ based on ~에 바탕을 둔
085 □ donation ⓝ 기부(금)
086 □ appreciate ⓥ 고마워하다
087 □ generous ⓐ 관대한
088 □ contribution ⓝ 기부, 기여
089 □ unforgettable ⓐ 잊지 못할

10

090 □ pillow ⓝ 베개
091 □ recommendation ⓝ 추천, 권장
092 □ thick ⓐ 두꺼운
093 □ neck ⓝ 목
094 □ filling material 속재료
095 □ Good point. 좋은 지적이에요.
096 □ machine-wash ⓥ 세탁기로 빨다

11

097 □ exhibition ⓝ 전시(회)
098 □ preparation ⓝ 준비, 대비
099 □ painting ⓝ 그림
100 □ display ⓥ 전시하다
101 □ pack ⓥ (짐을) 싸다
102 □ painter ⓝ 화가

12

103 □ give a refund 환불해주다
104 □ discount ⓥ 할인하다 ⓝ 할인
105 □ wonder ⓥ 궁금하다
106 □ refundable ⓐ 환불 가능한

13

107 □ stroke ⓝ 스트로크, (공을 치는) 타법
108 □ thanks to ~ 덕분에
109 □ remember to ~을 명심하다
110 □ stability ⓝ 안정성
111 □ strike ⓥ 치다, 타격하다
112 □ older sister 누나, 언니
113 □ challenging ⓐ 어려운, 까다로운
114 □ respectful ⓐ 공손한
115 □ from now on 지금부터
116 □ drop by ~에 들르다
117 □ suit ⓥ 적합하다

14

118 □ Indian ⓐ 인도의
119 □ front door 현관
120 □ waste ⓝ 쓰레기 ⓥ 낭비하다, 버리다
121 □ unless conj ~하지 않는다면
122 □ container ⓝ 용기, 그릇
123 □ consequence ⓝ 결과, 영향
124 □ that's why 그래서 ~하다, 그것이 ~한 이유이다
125 □ think again 재고하다, 다시 생각하다

15

126 □ passionate ⓐ 열정 넘치는
127 □ close to ~에 가까운, 근접한
128 □ when it comes to ~에 관해서
129 □ perform ⓥ 연주하다, 공연하다
130 □ upcoming ⓐ 다가오는
131 □ hesitate ⓥ 망설이다
132 □ unfamiliar ⓐ 생소한, 낯선
133 □ seemingly ad 겉보기에
134 □ distant ⓐ 동떨어진, 먼
135 □ present ⓥ 보여주다, 제시하다, 발표하다
136 □ in an attempt to ~하기 위해서
137 □ stick to ~을 고수하다

16~17

138 □ investment banker 증권 인수업자
139 □ insight ⓝ 통찰력
140 □ financial ⓐ 금융의
141 □ industry ⓝ 업계
142 □ represent ⓥ 나타내다, 표현하다
143 □ bull ⓝ 황소
144 □ raise ⓥ 치켜들다, 올리다
145 □ horn ⓝ 뿔
146 □ herd ⓝ 무리, 떼
147 □ flock ⓝ 무리, 떼 ⓥ 모이다
148 □ bias ⓝ 편견
149 □ irrational ⓐ 불합리한
150 □ fairly ad 꽤
151 □ greedy ⓐ 탐욕스러운
152 □ anticipation ⓝ 기대
153 □ reluctant ⓐ 꺼리는, 마지못해 하는
154 □ sector ⓝ 부문
155 □ domesticate ⓥ 길들이다, 사육하다

17회 2022학년도 7월 학력평가 고3 영어 듣기

※ QR코드를 스캔하시면 듣기 방송을 청취하실 수 있습니다.

● 점수 표시가 없는 문항은 모두 2점 ● 문항수 17개 | 배점 37점 | 제한 시간 25분

1번부터 17번까지는 듣고 답하는 문제입니다. 1번부터 15번까지는 한 번만 들려주고, 16번부터 17번까지는 두 번 들려줍니다. 방송을 잘 듣고 답을 하시기 바랍니다.

1. 다음을 듣고, 여자가 하는 말의 목적으로 가장 적절한 것을 고르시오.

① 환경보호 표어 대회 참여를 독려하려고
② 학교 생태정원 이름짓기 공모를 안내하려고
③ 학교 시설 보수공사 기간 연장을 공지하려고
④ 학생회장 선출을 위한 온라인 투표 방법을 알리려고
⑤ 생태정원 가꾸기 활동을 위한 자원봉사자를 모집하려고

2. 대화를 듣고, 남자의 의견으로 가장 적절한 것을 고르시오.

① 학생 간 동료 피드백은 온라인 수업에 효과적이다.
② 수업 전 학생들과의 대화로 친밀감을 형성할 수 있다.
③ 온라인 자료를 수업에 활용할 때 저작권에 유의해야 한다.
④ 긍정적인 격려로 학생들에게 자신감을 심어 주는 것이 좋다.
⑤ 학생의 다양한 수준을 고려하여 온라인 수업을 계획해야 한다.

3. 대화를 듣고, 두 사람의 관계를 가장 잘 나타낸 것을 고르시오.

① 사진작가 – 학생　② 화가 – 잡지사 기자
③ 미술 교사 – 학부모　④ 전시회 기획자 – 의뢰인
⑤ 큐레이터 – 인쇄물 제작업자

4. 대화를 듣고, 그림에서 대화의 내용과 일치하지 <u>않는</u> 것을 고르시오.

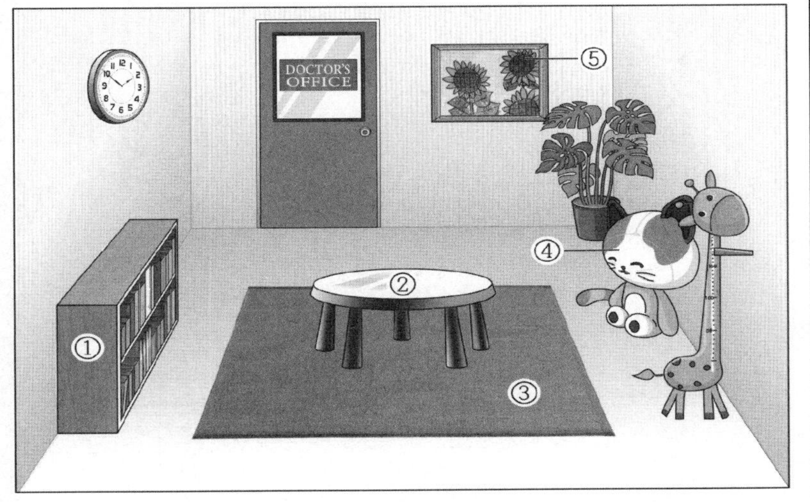

5. 대화를 듣고, 남자가 할 일로 가장 적절한 것을 고르시오.

① 영화 고르기　② 스피커 설치하기
③ 간식 만들기　④ 담요 가지고 오기
⑤ 쿠션 빌려오기

6. 대화를 듣고, 여자가 지불할 금액을 고르시오. [3점]

① $225　② $250　③ $255　④ $280　⑤ $315

7. 대화를 듣고, 여자가 벼룩시장 운영을 연기한 이유를 고르시오.

① 공원 긴급 보수 작업이 계획되어서
② 행사 당일 폭우가 예상되어서
③ 행사 물품 배송이 지연되어서
④ 다른 행사와 시간이 겹쳐서
⑤ 참가 인원이 적어서

8. 대화를 듣고, Young Edison Science Program에 관해 언급되지 <u>않은</u> 것을 고르시오.

① 장소　② 주제　③ 참여 가능 인원
④ 운영 시간　⑤ 준비물

9. Flash Fiction Contest에 관한 다음 내용을 듣고, 일치하지 <u>않는</u> 것을 고르시오.

① 출품작의 단어 수에 제한이 있다.
② 참가자는 다수의 작품을 제출할 수 있다.
③ 제출 마감일은 7월 15일이다.
④ 심사는 학년별로 이루어진다.
⑤ 입상작은 학교 신문에 게재된다.

10. 다음 표를 보면서 대화를 듣고, 남자가 주문할 아웃도어용 시계를 고르시오.

Outdoor Watches

	Model	Price	GPS tracking	Material	Feature
①	A	$200	×	Plastic	Waterproof
②	B	$240	○	Plastic	Waterproof
③	C	$260	○	Plastic	Solar charging
④	D	$290	○	Metal	Waterproof
⑤	E	$320	○	Metal	Solar charging

11. 대화를 듣고, 여자의 마지막 말에 대한 남자의 응답으로 가장 적절한 것을 고르시오.

① Let's ask where Monica's classroom is.
② I'll take her a bit earlier than usual then.
③ Okay. I'll ask her teacher when they close.
④ No problem. My meeting ended successfully.
⑤ Thank you. I'll take care of the client instead.

12. 대화를 듣고, 남자의 마지막 말에 대한 여자의 응답으로 가장 적절한 것을 고르시오.

① Sorry. I can't remember my script at all.
② With your help, the repairman fixed the copier.
③ Let's try a different copier on the second floor.
④ I was impressed by your presentation last time.
⑤ Don't panic. You can finish your script next week.

13. 대화를 듣고, 여자의 마지막 말에 대한 남자의 응답으로 가장 적절한 것을 고르시오. [3점]

Man: ______________________________

① It's better to get dance training this time.
② Why don't you try auditioning to join our team?
③ Okay. I'll be sure to make the post by tomorrow.
④ Good job! The audition was tough, but we made it!
⑤ Offline performances are more fun than online ones.

14. 대화를 듣고, 남자의 마지막 말에 대한 여자의 응답으로 가장 적절한 것을 고르시오. [3점]

Woman: ______________________________

① Of course. I'll practice making Japanese dishes with you.
② Right. You'll build confidence through continual practice.
③ Great! I'm so proud of you for passing the test.
④ Well, you need to be careful while cooking.
⑤ I agree. Empathy is the key to success.

15. 다음 상황 설명을 듣고, Clara가 Jacob에게 할 말로 가장 적절한 것을 고르시오.

Clara: ______________________________

① You'll have more followers soon, so don't worry.
② Be more responsible when posting to social media.
③ It's essential to actively interact with your followers.
④ How about putting away your smartphone at bedtime?
⑤ You should disable social media notifications during dinner.

[16~17] 다음을 듣고, 물음에 답하시오.

16. 남자가 하는 말의 주제로 가장 적절한 것은?

① sounds and roles of string instruments in an orchestra
② ways to tune different types of string instruments
③ importance of playing in harmony in an orchestra
④ stage positions of various orchestral instruments
⑤ origins of the names of musical instruments

17. 언급된 악기가 <u>아닌</u> 것은?

① violin ② viola ③ double bass
④ cello ⑤ harp

[해설편 p.075]

Dictation 17

✪ 표기에는 듣기 어려운 발음이 포함되어 있습니다. 귀 기울여 듣고 받아쓰세요. ● 고3 2022학년도 7월

※ QR 코드를 스캔하시면 듣기 방송이 나옵니다. 듣기 방송을 들으며 다음 빈칸을 채우시오. ● 제한 시간 : 25분

01

다음을 듣고, 여자가 하는 말의 목적으로 가장 적절한 것을 고르시오.

W : Good afternoon, students. This is Vice Principal Webster. As you know, our school's new eco garden will open next month. I'm very happy to have a new school garden. Completing construction is thanks to your help. However, our new eco garden _________ _________ _________ _________ _________ yet. So, we're holding a school garden naming contest. I'm sure you'll be proud of yourself if you suggest the winning name. You can participate in this naming contest by clicking the banner on our school website. The deadline is next Tuesday. We'll select the top three submissions and _________ _________ _________ _________ next Friday. The name with the most votes wins. We're looking forward to seeing ✪ _________ _________ _________ _________ _________ for the garden name!

02

대화를 듣고, 남자의 의견으로 가장 적절한 것을 고르시오.

M : Have you finished class for today?
W : Yeah. But it's really hard for me to manage my online classes.
M : Why? I thought ✪ _________ _________ _________ _________ _________.
W : I'm comfortable with teaching. The problem is that students have a hard time _________ _________ _________ _________.
M : I see. *[Pause]* In my case, I encourage students to _________ _________ _________. It's very effective during online class.
W : What do you mean by "peer review"?
M : During class, I get students to review each other's work and to provide meaningful feedback. It helps encourage students to interact.
W : How do they give each other feedback?
M : I usually use chatrooms. It allows students to talk with one another.
W : Hmm.... That makes sense. Plus, that can help them _________ _________ _________.
M : Exactly. Having students give peer feedback makes my online classes much more effective.
W : Okay. I'll give it a try for my online classes.

03

대화를 듣고, 두 사람의 관계를 가장 잘 나타낸 것을 고르시오.

M : Welcome to the exhibition!
W : Thank you for putting together such an amazing show. _________ _________ _________ _________ _________.
M : All the works here are watercolor paintings, so you can clearly feel the painters' moods.
W : I can't believe they were made by students. The canvases featuring flowers are especially colorful and detailed.
M : They ✪ _________ _________ _________ with different brush sizes to develop their skills. That's the most important part of _________ _________ _________ _________.
W : It was really helpful. How my daughter uses color is better than before. She enjoys your class a lot.
M : Oh, really? It's a great pleasure to see our high school's students improve.
W : Can I take some pictures of the works?
M : Absolutely. There's also more information about the artworks in the leaflets at the entrance.
W : I'll be sure to pick up a leaflet before I go.

04

대화를 듣고, 그림에서 대화의 내용과 일치하지 <u>않는</u> 것을 고르시오.

M : Hi, Grace. Congratulations on opening your hospital. It looks amazing.
W : Thanks for coming. Feel free to look around.
M : You prepared children's books. The bookcase with two shelves displays them perfectly.
W : Right. The children can reach the books easily.
M : Oh, they can read books at the table in the middle of the room.
W : I chose the round one for their safety.
M : Good thinking. I love _________ _________ _________ _________ _________. It looks very cozy.
W : Sure. Children can sit on it comfortably.
M : Wow, look at the big cat doll between _________ _________ _________ _________ and the plant. It's so cute!
W : Children really love it because it's so soft. What do you think about the painting on the wall?
M : I like it. The picture of the rainbow is very ✪ _________ _________ _________.
W : _________ _________ _________ _________. She's excited that all our visitors get to see her art.
M : It goes well with your children's hospital.

05

대화를 듣고, 남자가 할 일로 가장 적절한 것을 고르시오.

M : Honey, the backyard looks fantastic. You did a great job.
W : Thanks! I tried to decorate it like a little theater.
M : I'm very excited to _________ _________ _________ _________, especially for Lauren and her friends.
W : Did you pick out a movie for the kids?
M : I chose *My Little Dragon*, Lauren's favorite musical.
W : Perfect. I just _________ _________ _________ _________, and they sound amazing.
M : Good quality sound is essential, especially for a musical film!
W : Totally! I prepared some popcorn, drinks, and candy for the kids as well. Do we need anything else?
M : Oh, I forgot to check the weather for tonight.
W : Let's check it now. *[Pause]* Well, they say it might be ✪ _________ _________ _________ _________ tonight.
M : I'll _________ _________ _________ for the kids then.
W : That's very thoughtful. I'll prepare some comfortable cushions.
M : Great. This movie night is going to be terrific.

17회

06

대화를 듣고, 여자가 지불할 금액을 고르시오. [3점]

M : Lamps Plus Lighting! How may I help you?

W : Hi, I'm looking for pendant lights for my kitchen. How much are the ones __________?

M : The pendant light with the metal shade is 100 dollars and the one with the glass shade is 150 dollars.

W : Hmm.... Both look great, but the metal one will go better with my kitchen. I'll take __________ __________.

M : All right. Can I help you with anything else?

W : I need some lightbulbs for the pendant lights. What is the best kind for these lights?

M : We have many options, but I recommend LED lightbulbs for energy efficiency. They're 10 dollars each.

W : Okay. I'll take five LED lightbulbs.

M : So, that's two pendant lights and five lightbulbs. By the way, for our store's 10th anniversary, you'll receive a 10% discount from the total price.

W : Sounds great.

M : Do you need help ✪ __________ __________ __________? We offer an installation service for 30 dollars.

W : No, thanks. I can install them myself. Here's my credit card.

07

대화를 듣고, 여자가 벼룩시장 운영을 연기한 이유를 고르시오.

M : Rosie, how's organizing the flea market going?

W : Good, I'm pretty __________ __________ __________ __________ that were delivered today.

M : I heard a lot of people have signed up for the market.

W : Yes. Thirty-six people so far.

M : That's amazing! It'll be held at Sunkist Park this Saturday afternoon, right?

W : Unfortunately, the market ✪ __________ __________ __________ one week. But it'll be held at the same place.

M : Why? Is there another event scheduled at the park?

W : No. Only our market was supposed to be held during that time.

M : Is it __________ __________ __________ __________? I've heard that it's supposed to rain.

W : It'll only rain a little, so I'm not worried about that. Actually, the park scheduled urgent repair work for Saturday. So, we __________ __________ __________ __________ __________.

M : I'm sorry to hear that. Well, I'm still planning to go.

W : Thanks. I'll see you at the market!

08

대화를 듣고, Young Edison Science Program에 관해 언급되지 않은 것을 고르시오.

W : Adam, I can't find an exciting place for my club's field trip.

M : I'm reading about the Young Edison Science Program at the Discovery Science Museum. I think that would be a great field trip.

W : Oh, I've heard about that program. What's ✪ __________ __________ __________ __________?

M : It's a group experience program about the intersection of art and technology.

W : Sounds cool. When we built __________ __________ __________ __________ in science class, everyone was really into it.

M : It says the maximum number of daily participants is 60. How about both our clubs go together?

W : Really? That would be wonderful!

M : Okay, let's make a reservation. It says the program only takes place in the morning from 9 to 12. Does that work for you?

W : That's fine. The other club members are usually busy in the afternoon, so __________ __________ __________ __________ __________ __________.

M : All right. Is August 3rd at 9 a.m. okay?

W : Perfect. My club members will love it.

09

Flash Fiction Contest에 관한 다음 내용을 듣고, 일치하지 않는 것을 고르시오.

M : Good morning. I'm Mr. Thomas from the English department. I'm excited to be hosting our Flash Fiction Contest. Writing a very short story can be a great way to ✪ __________ __________ __________ __________ __________ __________. You can write on any topic. Entries must be no more than 600 words in length. __________ __________ __________ __________ __________ __________ and be your original work. Entries must be written by only one writer. Each participant is allowed to submit only one story. Entries will be accepted July 11th through July 15th. __________ __________ __________ stories will be judged in three different grade groups: first, second, and third grades. The winning stories from each grade will be published in the school newspaper. For more information, visit our school website. Don't miss this fun event!

10

다음 표를 보면서 대화를 듣고, 남자가 주문할 아웃도어용 시계를 고르시오.

W : Hey, Simon. What are you doing?

M : I'm looking at a brochure for outdoor watches. I need one for when I go hiking.

W : Great idea. You can use it when you go to Halla Mountain this summer.

M : Exactly. Can you help me choose one?

W : Sure. How much do you want to spend on it?

M : I think paying more than $300 for a watch isn't reasonable.

W : All right. *[Pause]* Oh! GPS tracking is __________ __________ __________. You should get an outdoor watch that has it.

M : You're right. I think it'll be very useful. What about the material?

W : __________ __________ __________ would be better for hiking. You should go with the plastic one.

M : I agree. Hmm, I think the waterproof feature is ✪ __________ __________ __________ __________ __________.

W : Good point. You never know when it'll rain while you're on a mountain.

M : Okay. This watch is perfect. I'll order it.

11

대화를 듣고, 여자의 마지막 말에 대한 남자의 응답으로 가장 적절한 것을 고르시오.

W : Honey, can you take Monica ✪ _________ _________ tomorrow morning?

M : I have a client meeting at 10 a.m. What time should I _________ _________ _________?

W : She usually goes to daycare around 10, but it opens at 8.

12

대화를 듣고, 남자의 마지막 말에 대한 여자의 응답으로 가장 적절한 것을 고르시오.

M : Emma! Can you help me out? This copier isn't working.

W : Ryan, your presentation starts in 5 minutes. Why are you making copies now?

M : I changed something, so I need to ✪ _________ _________ _________ _________ _________. What should I do?

13

대화를 듣고, 여자의 마지막 말에 대한 남자의 응답으로 가장 적절한 것을 고르시오. [3점]

W : Erik, did you enjoy the Seoul Dance Festival yesterday?

M : I did. Phantom Dance Group's performance was the best.

W : I agree. I was so excited to see their new hip hop performance.

M : I found a video of their performance online today. Why don't we learn their dance for our school's dance festival?

W : Sounds great. I think it'll be good for the festival.

M : But their dance is for five people. Our club has only four members.

W : We should _________ _________ _________ _________. Do you have any ideas for how we can find one?

M : Well, how about posting on the school website? And we ✪ _________ _________ _________ _________ next week.

W : That's a good idea. I'll prepare the audition _________ _________ _________ _________ _________ _________ _________.

14

대화를 듣고, 남자의 마지막 말에 대한 여자의 응답으로 가장 적절한 것을 고르시오. [3점]

M : Hi, Chef. Can I get some advice?

W : Sure. Is it about your performance test for Western food next month?

M : Yeah. Actually, I'm afraid I won't pass.

W : What's the issue?

M : I'm supposed to make two dishes in an hour, but I'm not sure if I can do it.

W : I think you're _________ _________ _________ _________ _________ _________.

M : But when it comes to making both dishes within the time limit, I've succeeded only twice. I'm losing confidence.

W : Don't worry. Everybody fails at first and _________ _________ _________ _________ _________.

M : Did you ever have a difficult time like I'm having?

W : Of course. It was ✪ _________ _________ for me to get my license for Japanese food. But the more I practiced, _________ _________ _________ _________ _________.

M : I see. So you mean I just need more practice?

15

다음 상황 설명을 듣고, Clara가 Jacob에게 할 말로 가장 적절한 것을 고르시오.

W : Clara has noticed that her son, Jacob, spends all his time checking his social media accounts. Recently, Jacob started to ✪ _________ _________ _________ _________ _________ for his followers to see, so he thinks it's important to read and _________ _________ _________ right away. With every sound, buzz, or flash from the notification light, he immediately checks his phone, even while having dinner with the family. Although Clara knows interacting with his followers is important to him, she thinks spending time with the family is more important than checking social media and that it's not appropriate to _________ _________ _________ _________ _________ _________. So, Clara wants to tell Jacob that he needs to turn off notifications while the family is eating dinner. In this situation, what would Clara most likely say to Jacob?

16~17

다음을 듣고, 물음에 답하시오.

M : Hello, class. We discussed the four main instrument sections of an orchestra last week. Today, I'll tell you about _________ _________ _________ _________ and what they play in an orchestra. The first is the violin. The violin is the baby of the string family, and like babies, it makes the highest sounds. Violins often play the melody in an orchestra. Next is the viola. Violas produce _________ _________, _________ _________ than the violin, and they almost always play the harmony in an orchestra. The third is the cello. Of all the string instruments, cellos sound the most like a human voice, and they can make a wide variety of tones, from warm, low pitches to bright, higher notes. They play both harmony and melody. Lastly, the harp is different from the other string instruments. The sound of the harp _________ _________ _________, almost like a ✪ _________ _________. It plays both melody and harmony. Now, shall we listen to the sound of each instrument to learn the differences?

▶정답 : 해설편 077쪽

VOCA LIST 17

회차별 영단어 QR 코드 ※ QR 코드를 스캔 후 모바일로 단어장처럼 학습할 수 있습니다.

● 고3 2022학년도 7월

01

001 □ construction ⓝ 건설, 공사
002 □ proper ⓐ 적당한
003 □ proud ⓐ 자랑스러워하는, 자랑스러운
004 □ suggest ⓥ 제안하다
005 □ participate ⓥ 참가하다
006 □ deadline ⓝ 기한, 마감 시간
007 □ submission ⓝ 제출물
008 □ vote ⓝ 투표
009 □ brilliant ⓐ 훌륭한, 멋진

02

010 □ manage ⓥ 관리하다
011 □ be accustomed to ~에 적응하다
012 □ comfortable ⓐ 편한, 편안한
013 □ have a hard time ~ing ~하기 어려워하다
014 □ encourage ⓥ 격려하다
015 □ peer review 동료 심사(평가)
016 □ effective ⓐ 효과적인
017 □ provide ⓥ 제공하다
018 □ meaningful ⓐ 의미 있는
019 □ feedback ⓝ 피드백, 반응, 의견, 감상
020 □ achieve ⓥ 해내다, 잘 해내다
021 □ give it a try 시도해 보다

03

022 □ exhibition ⓝ 전시회
023 □ put together 준비하다, 모으다
024 □ watercolor painting 수채화
025 □ clearly ad 명확히, 확실히
026 □ especially ad 특히
027 □ colorful ⓐ 다채로운
028 □ detailed ⓐ 상세한
029 □ practice ⓥ 연습하다
030 □ helpful ⓐ 도움이 되는
031 □ daughter ⓝ 딸, 여식
032 □ improve ⓥ 나아지다, 개선되다
033 □ leaflet ⓝ (안내) 책자, 전단

04

034 □ feel free to 편하게 ~하다
035 □ look around 둘러보다
036 □ prepare ⓥ 준비하다
037 □ perfectly ad 완벽하게, 멋지게
038 □ reach ⓥ (손을) 뻗다, ~에 이르다
039 □ safety ⓝ 안전
040 □ cozy ⓐ 포근한, 아늑한
041 □ comfortably ad 편안하게
042 □ giraffe ⓝ 기린
043 □ measuring stick 키 재는 막대

05

044 □ backyard ⓝ 뒷마당
045 □ decorate ⓥ 꾸미다, 장식하다
046 □ theater ⓝ 극장
047 □ especially ad 특히
048 □ pick out 고르다, 선택하다
049 □ musical film 뮤지컬 영화
050 □ chilly ⓐ 쌀쌀한
051 □ blanket ⓝ 담요
052 □ thoughtful ⓐ 사려 깊은
053 □ terrific ⓐ 아주 좋은, 멋진, 훌륭한

06

054 □ shade ⓝ (전등의) 갓, 그늘, 그림자
055 □ lightbulb ⓝ 전구
056 □ option ⓝ 선택권
057 □ recommend ⓥ 추천하다
058 □ efficiency ⓝ 효율
059 □ anniversary ⓝ 기념일
060 □ install ⓥ 설치하다

07

061 □ organize ⓥ 준비하다
062 □ flea market 벼룩시장
063 □ sort ⓥ 분류하다
064 □ supply ⓝ 용품, 비품
065 □ unfortunately ad 불행하게도, 유감스럽게도
066 □ delay ⓥ 연기하다
067 □ urgent ⓐ 긴급한, 다급한
068 □ repair ⓝ 수리, 보수, 수선
069 □ put off 미루다, 연기하다

08

070 □ field trip 현장 학습
071 □ experience ⓝ 체험, 경험
072 □ intersection ⓝ 교차로
073 □ be into ~에 빠지다, ~에 관심이 있다
074 □ participant ⓝ 참가자
075 □ reservation ⓝ 예약

09

076 □ department ⓝ 과, 부서
077 □ host ⓥ 주최하다
078 □ topic ⓝ 화제, 주제
079 □ entry ⓝ 출품작
080 □ length ⓝ 길이
081 □ original work 창작물, 원저작물
082 □ allow ⓥ 인정하다, 허용하다
083 □ submit ⓥ 제출하다
084 □ accept ⓥ 받아 주다
085 □ flash fiction 짧은 단편
086 □ judge ⓥ 심사하다
087 □ publish ⓥ 게재하다, 싣다

10

088 □ brochure ⓝ (안내·광고용) 책자
089 □ pay ⓥ 지출하다
090 □ reasonable ⓐ 합리적인
091 □ track ⓥ 추적하다 ⓝ 추적
092 □ function ⓝ 기능
093 □ useful ⓐ 유용한, 도움이 되는
094 □ material ⓝ 소재
095 □ waterproof ⓐ 방수의
096 □ solar ⓐ 태양의
097 □ practical ⓐ 실용적인

11

098 □ take A to B A를 B에 데려다주다
099 □ daycare ⓥ 탁아소에 맡기다
100 □ client ⓝ 고객
101 □ meeting ⓝ 회의
102 □ drop off ~을 (차에서) 내려주다
103 □ bit ⓝ 조금, 약간
104 □ successfully ad 성공적으로
105 □ instead ad 대신에

12

106 □ copier ⓝ 복사기
107 □ print out 출력하다
108 □ script ⓝ 대본
109 □ different ⓐ 다른
110 □ repairman ⓝ 수리공, 수리기사
111 □ fix ⓥ 수리하다
112 □ impress ⓥ 감명을 주다

13

113 □ performance ⓝ 공연
114 □ hold an audition 오디션을 열다
115 □ make the post 포스팅을 하다, 게시물을 올리다

14

116 □ performance test 기능 시험, 직능 검사
117 □ afraid ⓐ 두려워하는
118 □ dish ⓝ 요리
119 □ time limit 제한 시간
120 □ license ⓝ 면허증, 허가증, 자격증
121 □ lose confidence 자신감을 잃다
122 □ continual ⓐ 지속적인, 계속되는
123 □ empathy ⓝ 공감, 감정 이입

15

124 □ account ⓝ 계정, 계좌
125 □ respond ⓥ 대답하다
126 □ right away 즉시, 곧
127 □ notification ⓝ 알림
128 □ immediately ad 즉시, 즉각
129 □ interact ⓥ 소통하다
130 □ appropriate ⓐ 적절한
131 □ attention ⓝ 관심
132 □ disable ⓥ (기기나 소프트웨어의 기능을) 억제하다

16~17

133 □ discuss ⓥ 논의하다, 상의하다
134 □ instrument ⓝ 악기, 기구
135 □ a wide variety of 폭넓은
136 □ pitch ⓝ 음높이
137 □ dreamlike ⓐ 꿈같은
138 □ fairy tale 동화

18회 • 2021학년도 7월 학력평가 고3 영어 듣기

※ QR코드를 스캔하시면 듣기 방송을 청취하실 수 있습니다.

● 점수 표시가 없는 문항은 모두 2점 ● 문항수 17개 | 배점 37점 | 제한 시간 25분

1번부터 17번까지는 듣고 답하는 문제입니다. 1번부터 15번까지는 한 번만 들려주고, 16번부터 17번까지는 두 번 들려줍니다. 방송을 잘 듣고 답을 하시기 바랍니다.

1. 다음을 듣고, 남자가 하는 말의 목적으로 가장 적절한 것을 고르시오.

① 학교 정원 관리 봉사자를 모집하려고
② 식물원 체험 학습 일정을 공지하려고
③ 봉사 활동 확인서 신청 방법을 안내하려고
④ 학교 정원에 심을 모종 기부를 부탁하려고
⑤ 정원의 잡초를 제거하는 요령을 설명하려고

2. 대화를 듣고, 여자의 의견으로 가장 적절한 것을 고르시오.

① 자신의 체력 수준에 맞게 운동 계획을 세우는 것이 좋다.
② 과도한 운동은 심리적 불안정을 초래할 수 있다.
③ 운동 일지 작성이 체력 관리에 도움이 된다.
④ 근력 운동과 유산소 운동을 병행하는 것이 유익하다.
⑤ 운동 중 부상 예방을 위해 적절한 장비를 착용해야 한다.

3. 대화를 듣고, 두 사람의 관계를 가장 잘 나타낸 것을 고르시오.

① 기자 – 농업 연구원　② 콜센터 직원 – 고객
③ 방송 연출가 – 작가　④ 홈 쇼핑 쇼 호스트 – 농부
⑤ 식료품 가게 직원 – 조리사

4. 대화를 듣고, 그림에서 대화의 내용과 일치하지 않는 것을 고르시오.

5. 대화를 듣고, 남자가 여자를 위해 할 일로 가장 적절한 것을 고르시오.

① 이미지 검색하기　② 발표 대본 검토하기
③ 면접 예상 질문 만들기　④ 포트폴리오 우편 발송하기
⑤ 발표 연습 영상 촬영하기

6. 대화를 듣고, 여자가 지불할 금액을 고르시오.

① $30　② $32　③ $35　④ $39　⑤ $40

7. 대화를 듣고, 남자가 연구 주제를 변경한 이유를 고르시오.

① 관련 데이터를 찾기 어려워서
② 지도 교수를 구하지 못해서
③ 희망하는 진로가 바뀌어서
④ 연구 지원금을 확보하지 못해서
⑤ 다른 학생과 연구 주제가 겹쳐서

8. 대화를 듣고, Mobile Throwing Championship에 관해 언급되지 않은 것을 고르시오.

① 최초 개최 연도　② 개최 목적　③ 참가비
④ 우승 상품　⑤ 심사 기준

9. 다음 표를 보면서 대화를 듣고, 두 사람이 주문할 휴대용 사진 인화기를 고르시오.

Portable Photo Printers

	Model	Price	Power	Bluetooth Connection	Free Photo Paper (sheets)
①	A	$139	plug-in	X	20
②	B	$149	built-in battery	○	20
③	C	$169	built-in battery	○	40
④	D	$189	built-in battery	X	40
⑤	E	$219	plug-in	○	30

18회

영어 영역[듣기]

10. 2021 International Violin Making Competition에 관한 다음 내용을 듣고, 일치하지 <u>않는</u> 것을 고르시오.

① 참가 신청서에 바이올린 사진을 첨부하여 제출해야 한다.
② 5월 1일까지 등록하면 등록비가 할인된다.
③ 바이올린을 우편으로 제출할 수 있다.
④ 유명 바이올린 연주자가 심사 위원에 포함된다.
⑤ 우승자는 10,000유로를 받는다.

11. 대화를 듣고, 남자의 마지막 말에 대한 여자의 응답으로 가장 적절한 것을 고르시오.

① Why don't you put off visiting the doctor?
② Let's ask David if we can reschedule.
③ How about inviting David to our club?
④ I'll go to the bookstore without you both.
⑤ We should find a place for today's meeting.

12. 대화를 듣고, 여자의 마지막 말에 대한 남자의 응답으로 가장 적절한 것을 고르시오.

① No worries. I've already got your file.
② Right. There's no assignment today.
③ Sorry. Your file has been deleted.
④ Yes. You can send it to me by email.
⑤ Sure. Try downloading it from our website.

13. 대화를 듣고, 남자의 마지막 말에 대한 여자의 응답으로 가장 적절한 것을 고르시오. [3점]

Woman: ____________________

① I'll find out who directed them for you.
② I'll give you a list of his best films then.
③ That's why I prefer watching popular movies.
④ They didn't leave a lasting impression on me.
⑤ You shouldn't worry about getting bad reviews.

14. 대화를 듣고, 여자의 마지막 말에 대한 남자의 응답으로 가장 적절한 것을 고르시오. [3점]

Man: ____________________

① I see. I'll take a break more often to increase concentration.
② Okay. I should avoid playing games during study breaks.
③ Certainly. You'll enjoy playing mobile games, too.
④ All right. I'd rather study alone to prepare for my exam.
⑤ Interesting. I thought mobile games do more harm than good.

15. 다음 상황 설명을 듣고, Nancy가 Jake에게 할 말로 가장 적절한 것을 고르시오. [3점]

Nancy: ____________________

① We'd rather stay with our original design.
② Why don't we design the poster by ourselves?
③ Don't forget to apply for the contest this time.
④ How about going outdoors to take photos for a change?
⑤ We should ask your friends if it's okay to use their photo.

[16~17] 다음을 듣고, 물음에 답하시오.

16. 여자가 하는 말의 주제로 가장 적절한 것은?

① natural materials traditionally used for skincare
② how to store natural skincare products properly
③ differences in the cultural perception of skincare
④ ways to prevent skin troubles caused by facial masks
⑤ examples of natural substances with harmful properties

17. 언급된 나라가 <u>아닌</u> 것은?

① India ② Iran ③ Poland
④ China ⑤ Greece

[해설편 p.080]

Dictation 18

✪ 표기에는 듣기 어려운 발음이 포함되어 있습니다. 귀 기울여 듣고 받아쓰세요.

● 고3 2021학년도 7월

※ QR 코드를 스캔하시면 듣기 방송이 나옵니다. 듣기 방송을 들으며 다음 빈칸을 채우시오. ● 제한 시간 : 25분

01

다음을 듣고, 남자가 하는 말의 목적으로 가장 적절한 것을 고르시오.

M : Hello, students. This is the president of the student council, Jason Miller, with an announcement about our school garden. The school garden is very special to us _________ _________ _________ _________ _________. So, we're recruiting students who can do volunteer work for our school garden. Volunteering is done twice a week, mainly by ✪ _________ _________ _________ _________ _________. If you're interested, please stop by the student council room by next Friday. We're _________ _________ _________ _________ _________ _________ _________ to maintain our school garden. Please participate in this wonderful opportunity to contribute to our school.

02

대화를 듣고, 여자의 의견으로 가장 적절한 것을 고르시오.

W : Justin, you look tired. What happened?

M : I made a plan to run five miles a day. I went running this morning, so I'm exhausted.

W : Isn't that too much to run in one day?

M : It's challenging, but I believe the harder I work out, the better result I'll get.

W : Not always. What's important is to plan your exercise routine to ✪ _________ _________ _________ _________ _________.

M : Why is that?

W : Exercising beyond your fitness level _________ _________ _________, or even sickness.

M : That makes sense. How can I know my fitness level?

W : Well, you could measure how long it takes for you to run one mile and _________ _________ _________ _________ _________ _________ on the Internet.

M : Oh, that sounds simple.

W : I'm sure that planning your exercise routine based on your physical fitness level will definitely be beneficial.

M : I agree. Thanks for your advice.

03

대화를 듣고, 두 사람의 관계를 가장 잘 나타낸 것을 고르시오.

W : Michael, look! They're almost sold out! Everybody who ordered, thank you so much!

M : Wow! Thank you Lisa, for the great explanations and comments on my potatoes!

W : ✪ _________ _________ _________ _________ _________ _________ when we showed how to cook them.

M : Right, I wanted to show the viewers all the delicious ways to enjoy my potatoes.

W : Also, our viewers loved hearing from you since you actually grew the product.

M : I'm just happy to appear on your home-shopping channel. I _________ _________ _________ _________ _________ _________ _________. I'm so proud of these premium organic potatoes.

W : You should be! Everyone at home, you don't want to miss this. Great potatoes at a great price.

M : I guarantee these are the best potatoes you'll ever eat.

W : _________ _________ _________ _________ _________ _________! So order right now, and get a free recipe book.

M : I know you'll enjoy the potatoes. Please leave a lot of good reviews!

04

대화를 듣고, 그림에서 대화의 내용과 일치하지 <u>않는</u> 것을 고르시오.

W : Honey, look. I changed this room into a workout space while you were on a business trip, like we talked about before.

M : Wow, it's fantastic! We can work out at home now.

W : Right. Did you notice the two exercise balls under the clock? I bought them for us.

M : Great. I heard exercise balls are good for stretching. I see a pair of shoes on the shelf.

W : Yeah. It's important to _________ _________ _________ _________ _________ when exercising indoors.

M : Good point. And you put a fan in the corner.

W : It'll _________ _________ _________ _________ after exercising hard.

M : Okay. What's the laptop on the table for?

W : We can play exercise videos and follow along. And ✪ _________ _________ _________ _________ _________ _________ on the floor. Doesn't it look nice?

M : It sure does. Thank you for doing all this while I was away.

18회

05

대화를 듣고, 남자가 여자를 위해 할 일로 가장 적절한 것을 고르시오.

W : Bob, I got a call from the company I applied to last week. I'm one of the final candidates for the assistant manager position.

M : Great! What do you have to do next?

W : I have to do a presentation based on a set of questions.

M : It'd be helpful to record a video of yourself to practice.

W : Okay, I'll try it. I'm going to write a script first, and then make the presentation slides.

M : You should ✪ _________ _________ _________ _________ _________ _________ to show your message clearly.

W : Yes. But it takes quite long _________ _________ _________ _________ _________.

M : Definitely. You must be very busy.

W : Yeah. Actually, I still need to _________ _________ _________ _________ _________ for another company, but I don't have time to go to the post office.

M : Oh, let me do it for you.

W : Really? Then I'll bring it to you. Thank you so much.

M : It's my pleasure.

Dictation 18

06

대화를 듣고, 여자가 지불할 금액을 고르시오.

M : Welcome to the Jurassic Adventure Fair. How can I help you?
W : I'd like to buy tickets for the event. How much are they?
M : It's 15 dollars for adults and ten dollars for children under ten.
W : Then one ticket for me and one for my son, please. He's eight years old.
M : Okay. Would you like to __________ __________ __________ __________ to enjoy the fair even more?
W : A VR headset? What can I do with that?
M : You can see the dinosaurs move and ✪ __________ __________ __________ __________ __________ __________ while you walk around the fair.
W : Wow, my son would love that. How much is the rental fee?
M : It's seven dollars for one headset, but if you rent two or more, it's five dollars each.
W : That's great. I'll rent two VR headsets.
M : __________ __________ __________ __________. How would you like to pay?
W : I'll pay in cash.

07

대화를 듣고, 남자가 연구 주제를 변경한 이유를 고르시오.

W : Hey, how's the science research going? I like your idea about dream recording technology.
M : Well, I changed my topic, so I'm pretty __________ __________ __________ __________.
W : Really? Aren't you interested in that field anymore?
M : I am. I still want to become a neuroscientist.
W : Then why did you change it? Did your professor ask you to?
M : No. Actually, she said it could be an interesting topic because many people are curious about this new technology.
W : It is very new, so I was wondering __________ __________ __________ __________ __________ __________.
M : That's the problem. The topic was so new that it was ✪ __________ __________ __________ __________ __________. So, I decided to do research on brain scanning technology instead.
W : Oh, I see. What are you going to do for that?
M : I'm thinking of applying for research funding.
W : I hope you'll get it. Good luck.

08

대화를 듣고, Mobile Throwing Championship에 관해 언급되지 않은 것을 고르시오.

M : Rachael, there'll be a competition called the Mobile Throwing Championship next month. Why don't we join it?
W : Mobile Throwing Championship? I've never heard of it.
M : It's been around quite long. It was first held in 2000 in Finland, and is now held around the world.
W : What's the purpose of holding the contest?
M : It's to give people a chance to __________ __________ __________ __________ even for a moment.
W : Oh, I see. Sometimes I just want to throw my phone away, too! So, do I have to bring a phone to participate in the contest?
M : No. The organizers will provide one to each participant. If you win, you get a fancy new phone as a prize.
W : Really? __________ __________ __________ __________ __________?
M : Participants are judged for ✪ __________ __________ __________ __________ __________ __________ __________.
W : Sounds fun! Let's sign up for the competition.
M : Okay, I'll do it now online.

09

다음 표를 보면서 대화를 듣고, 두 사람이 주문할 휴대용 사진인화기를 고르시오.

M : Honey, what are you doing on your computer?
W : I'm looking for __________ __________ __________ __________. If we buy one, we can easily print pictures that are on our phones.
M : Great idea. Let's order one together.
W : Sure. These five models look good, but I don't want to spend more than 200 dollars.
M : Me, neither. And I think ✪ __________ __________ __________ __________ __________ __________ would be inconvenient. What do you think?
W : I agree. I'd like one with a built-in battery.
M : Great. Do you think we need a Bluetooth connection?
W : Yeah. With that function, we can print pictures directly from our phones without cables.
M : You're right. Then we have these two options left.
W : Hmm... they both look good, so the one that __________ __________ __________ __________ __________ __________ is better.
M : I think so, too. Let's order this one then.

10

2021 International Violin Making Competition에 관한 다음 내용을 듣고, 일치하지 않는 것을 고르시오.

W : Are you interested in showing the world your own original violin? Then enter the 2021 International Violin Making Competition. This year, it will be held in Vienna, Austria, from July 13th to 16th. To enter, submit an application form __________ __________ __________ __________ __________ __________ __________ by June 1st. The enrollment fee is 90 euros, but you can get a 30% discount if you register by May 1st. We will not accept any violins sent by post, so you must be present in Vienna with your instruments during the competition. A number of famous violinists ✪ __________ __________ __________ __________ __________ __________ will serve as judges for the competition. The winner will receive 10,000 euros. For more details, visit www.2021VMC.org.

11

대화를 듣고, 남자의 마지막 말에 대한 여자의 응답으로 가장 적절한 것을 고르시오.

M : Jenny, I'm afraid I cannot make it to our book club today. So, will you and David meet without me?
W : Well... I have to miss it, too. I ✪ __________ __________ __________ __________.
M : That means only David will be there. __________ __________ __________ __________ __________ __________. What should we do?

12

대화를 듣고, 여자의 마지막 말에 대한 남자의 응답으로 가장 적절한 것을 고르시오.

W : Professor Smith, I'm _________ _________ _________ _________ _________ _________ _________ to our online course website.

M : Maybe it's because your file is too big. It has to be less than ten megabytes.

W : Oh, mine is bigger than that. I wonder if there's another way ✪ _________ _________ _________ _________.

13

대화를 듣고, 남자의 마지막 말에 대한 여자의 응답으로 가장 적절한 것을 고르시오. [3점]

W : _________ _________ _________ _________ _________ _________ I recommended?

M : I really enjoyed it! The story was so refreshing. I've never seen anything like it before.

W : It's an independent film, so it was possible for the director to try new and creative things.

M : Yeah. And he created remarkable scenes using impressive color and sound effects.

W : I agree. _________ _________ _________ _________ _________ _________ _________?

M : They were really different compared to what we see in popular movies.

W : Yes. The director is famous for _________ _________ _________. And the film received ✪ _________ _________ _________ _________ _________.

M : I can see why! People should be more interested in his films.

W : Absolutely. I really enjoy his other works as well.

M : Oh, I'd really like to watch them, too!

14

대화를 듣고, 여자의 마지막 말에 대한 남자의 응답으로 가장 적절한 것을 고르시오. [3점]

W : Hi, John. Oh, you're playing a mobile game.

M : Yes, it's so fun. Do you want to join me?

W : Not right now. I have to prepare for the math exam. Did you finish studying?

M : Not yet. I'm taking a break now after two hours of studying. I play games during study breaks to relax.

W : Playing games to relax? That's not a good idea.

M : How come? It's important to rest ✪ _________ _________ _________ _________.

W : That's true. But while playing games, _________ _________ _________ _________ _________. I read that in an article.

M : Really? I thought I'd be able to get refreshed when playing games.

W : Actually, your brain is still working while you're playing.

M : Maybe that's _________ _________ _________ _________ after I came back from my breaks.

W : Exactly. Playing games may not have allowed you to rest fully.

15

다음 상황 설명을 듣고, Nancy가 Jake에게 할 말로 가장 적절한 것을 고르시오. [3점]

M : Nancy and Jake are students at an arts high school. They plan to participate in a graphic design poster contest. They want to ✪ _________ _________ _________ _________ _________ _________ on their poster. Jake shows Nancy a photo of his classmates taken _________ _________ _________ _________ _________. Jake says the photo would look good with their design, so he wants to include it on their poster. Nancy agrees, but she thinks Jake's classmates should first _________ _________ _________ _________ _________ _________. So, Nancy decides to tell Jake that they should get his friends' permission to use the photo for the poster. In this situation, what would Nancy most likely say to Jake?

16~17

다음을 듣고, 물음에 답하시오.

W : Hello, students. Last time, we learned about various natural substances used by our ancestors in medicine. Today, we'll discuss some natural ingredients that have been used for skincare purposes throughout history. First, coconut oil has been loved as a moisturizer for a very long time in India. It has a high moisture retaining capacity, so it acts as an excellent moisturizer for our skin. Secondly, rose water has been in use for thousands of years and is still easily found in the market today. It's thought to have originated in Iran, and is known to _________ _________ _________ _________ _________ _________. Next, pearl powder has long been used in China to brighten skin. It helps to remove dead skin naturally and ✪ _________ _________ _________ _________ _________. Finally, in Greece, people have used yogurt as a facial mask for centuries. Greeks even used yogurt on their skin to _________ _________ _________ _________ _________. Now, I'll show you a video about how these natural ingredients are used.

▶ 정답 : 해설편 082쪽

01

001 ☐ **student council** 학생회
002 ☐ **recruit** ⓥ 모집하다
003 ☐ **weed** ⓝ 잡초
004 ☐ **contribute to** ~에 기여하다, 이바지하다

02

005 ☐ **challenging** ⓐ 어려운, 도전적인
006 ☐ **work out** 운동하다
007 ☐ **important** ⓐ 중요한
008 ☐ **exercise** ⓝ 운동
009 ☐ **physical fitness** 체력
010 ☐ **injury** ⓝ 부상
011 ☐ **scale** ⓝ 척도
012 ☐ **definitely** ad 확실히, 분명히
013 ☐ **beneficial** ⓐ 이로운

03

014 ☐ **sold out** 매진된
015 ☐ **flood in** 쇄도하다
016 ☐ **put devotion into** ~에 공을 들이다, 헌신하다
017 ☐ **in stock** 재고로, 비축되어

04

018 ☐ **business trip** 출장
019 ☐ **injury** ⓝ 부상
020 ☐ **follow along** 따라가다

05

021 ☐ **candidate** ⓝ 후보자
022 ☐ **assistant manager** 부팀장, 대리
023 ☐ **appropriate** ⓐ 적절한

06

024 ☐ **dinosaur** ⓝ 공룡
025 ☐ **virtual reality** 가상현실
026 ☐ **regret** ⓝ 후회
027 ☐ **pay in cash** 현금 결제하다

07

028 ☐ **be busy ~ing** ~하느라 바쁘다
029 ☐ **neuroscientist** ⓝ 신경 과학자
030 ☐ **curious** ⓐ 호기심이 많은
031 ☐ **relevant** ⓐ 관련된, 적절한
032 ☐ **apply for** ~에 지원하다, ~을 신청하다

08

033 ☐ **purpose** ⓝ 목적
034 ☐ **feel free from** ~로부터 해방감을 느끼다
035 ☐ **criterion** 기준 (*pl.* criteria)
036 ☐ **sign up for** ~에 등록하다, 신청하다

09

037 ☐ **portable** ⓐ 휴대용의
038 ☐ **plug-in power** 플러그인 전원
039 ☐ **inconvenient** ⓐ 불편한
040 ☐ **built-in** ⓐ 내장된

10

041 ☐ **application form** 참가 신청서
042 ☐ **attach** ⓥ 부착하다
043 ☐ **enrollment fee** 등록비
044 ☐ **serve as** ~의 역할을 하다

11

045 ☐ **make it** (약속에) 가다, (일을) 성공하다, 해내다
046 ☐ **put off** 미루다
047 ☐ **reschedule** ⓥ 일정을 조정하다

12

048 ☐ **have trouble ~ing** ~하는 데 문제가 있다, 애를 먹다
049 ☐ **assignment** ⓝ 과제, 숙제
050 ☐ **submit** ⓥ 제출하다

13

051 ☐ **How do you like~?** ~은 어때?
052 ☐ **refreshing** ⓐ 신선한
053 ☐ **remarkable** ⓐ 놀랄 만한, 주목할 만한
054 ☐ **impressive** ⓐ 인상적인
055 ☐ **enthusiastic** ⓐ 열렬한, 열광적인
056 ☐ **lasting** ⓐ 오래가는, 지속적인

14

057 ☐ **in between** 중간에, 사이사이에
058 ☐ **article** ⓝ 기사
059 ☐ **concentration** ⓝ 집중(력)
060 ☐ **do more harm than good** 백해무익하다
061 ☐ **fully** ad 온전히, 완전히, 충분히

15

062 ☐ **participate in** ~에 참여하다
063 ☐ **outdoor field trip** 야외 현장 학습
064 ☐ **agree to** ~에 동의하다
065 ☐ **permission** ⓝ 허락, 허가
066 ☐ **for a change** 기분 전환으로
067 ☐ **by oneself** 혼자서, 직접
068 ☐ **apply for** ~에 지원하다

16~17

069 ☐ **substance** ⓝ 물질
070 ☐ **ingredient** ⓝ 재료
071 ☐ **retain** ⓥ 보유하다
072 ☐ **capacity** ⓝ 능력, 용량
073 ☐ **originate** ⓥ 기원하다
074 ☐ **promote** ⓥ 촉진하다
075 ☐ **restoration** ⓝ 회복, 복구
076 ☐ **traditionally** ad 전통적으로
077 ☐ **properly** ad 적절히
078 ☐ **harmful** ⓐ 해로운
079 ☐ **property** ⓝ 특성, 속성

19회 ● 2020학년도 7월 학력평가 고3 영어 듣기

※ QR코드를 스캔하시면 듣기 방송을 청취하실 수 있습니다.

● 점수 표시가 없는 문항은 모두 2점 ● 문항수 17개 | 배점 37점 | 제한 시간 25분

1번부터 17번까지는 듣고 답하는 문제입니다. 1번부터 15번까지는 한 번만 들려주고, 16번부터 17번까지는 두 번 들려줍니다. 방송을 잘 듣고 답을 하시기 바랍니다.

1. 다음을 듣고, 남자가 하는 말의 목적으로 가장 적절한 것을 고르시오.

① 개조 공사 중 박물관 운영에 대해 안내하려고
② 박물관 시설 안전 점검 계획을 공지하려고
③ 박물관 개관식 참석을 요청하려고
④ 전시관 관람 시 안전 질서 유지를 당부하려고
⑤ 시설 파손에 따른 불편에 대해 양해를 구하려고

2. 대화를 듣고, 여자의 의견으로 가장 적절한 것을 고르시오.

① 자원 재활용 교육을 강화해야 한다.
② 일상생활에서 플라스틱 소비를 줄여야 한다.
③ 친환경 플라스틱 제품 개발을 확대해야 한다.
④ 해양 생태계 보존을 위한 기금 마련이 필요하다.
⑤ 일회용품 사용 규제를 위한 법률 제정이 시급하다.

3. 대화를 듣고, 두 사람의 관계를 가장 잘 나타낸 것을 고르시오.

① 교사 – 체험농장 운영자 ② 관광객 – 버스 운전기사
③ 수강생 – 요리학원 강사 ④ 학생 – 동물원 사육사
⑤ 고객 – 키즈 카페 직원

4. 대화를 듣고, 그림에서 대화의 내용과 일치하지 않는 것을 고르시오.

5. 대화를 듣고, 남자가 할 일로 가장 적절한 것을 고르시오.

① 선물 포장하기 ② 파티 의상 찾아오기
③ 축하 영상 편집하기 ④ 생일 케이크 주문하기
⑤ 카메라 배터리 충전하기

6. 대화를 듣고, 남자가 지불할 금액을 고르시오. [3점]

① $60 ② $63 ③ $70 ④ $72 ⑤ $80

7. 대화를 듣고, 여자가 응시할 스페인어 시험이 연기된 이유를 고르시오.

① 졸업 시험과 날짜가 겹쳐서
② 수업 진도를 다 마치지 못해서
③ 수강생들이 시험 연기를 요청해서
④ 강사가 해외 세미나에 참석해야 해서
⑤ 수강생 중 다수가 구직 면접을 보러 가서

8. 대화를 듣고, Classic Myanmar Tour에 관해 언급되지 않은 것을 고르시오.

① 기간 ② 방문 도시 ③ 이동 수단
④ 비용 ⑤ 최대 참가 인원

9. 2020 Student Infographic Contest에 관한 다음 내용을 듣고, 일치하지 않는 것을 고르시오.

① 모든 학년의 학생이 참여할 수 있다.
② 주제는 자유롭게 선택 가능하다.
③ 출품작을 이미지 파일로 제출해야 한다.
④ 수상자는 상품으로 영화 관람권을 받을 것이다.
⑤ 수상작은 한 달 동안 전시될 것이다.

[해설편 p.082]

영어 영역[듣기]

10. 다음 표를 보면서 대화를 듣고, 남자가 구매할 눈 마사지기를 고르시오.

Eye Massagers

	Model	Price	Heat Setting	Number of Massage Modes	Music Function
①	A	$90	×	2	×
②	B	$120	×	3	×
③	C	$150	○	5	×
④	D	$190	○	3	○
⑤	E	$210	○	6	○

11. 대화를 듣고, 남자의 마지막 말에 대한 여자의 응답으로 가장 적절한 것을 고르시오.

① In fact, I'm not sure what the problem is.
② Well, you'd better ice your sprained ankle.
③ You're right. I'd rather stay at home and rest.
④ One week or so, but I have to see how it heals.
⑤ Terrible. I should have worn a cast for two weeks.

12. 대화를 듣고, 여자의 마지막 말에 대한 남자의 응답으로 가장 적절한 것을 고르시오.

① Great. Let's go shopping together.
② No. I haven't decided on my survey topic.
③ Okay. Please send me the link to the survey.
④ Yes. I've finished writing the survey questions.
⑤ I see. I'll take the marketing class online today.

13. 대화를 듣고, 여자의 마지막 말에 대한 남자의 응답으로 가장 적절한 것을 고르시오. [3점]

Man: ______________________________

① Sure, you can take the boxes home if you want.
② Well, my children have lost interest in smartphones.
③ I agree. Storing the phones in a box isn't the answer.
④ Actually, we need to update our phones on a regular basis.
⑤ Definitely. I'll get a box and see if it works for my family.

14. 대화를 듣고, 남자의 마지막 말에 대한 여자의 응답으로 가장 적절한 것을 고르시오. [3점]

Woman: ______________________________

① Great. Let's ask her if she can help us with the interview.
② Sure. I'll look at the questions and tell you what I think.
③ Don't worry. I'll recommend a good translator for her.
④ Wow! I didn't know you are that good at Chinese.
⑤ Right. Mr. Chen is fluent in both languages.

15. 다음 상황 설명을 듣고, Alex가 Carol에게 할 말로 가장 적절한 것을 고르시오.

Alex: ______________________________

① I think you need to take a break right now.
② Why not sign up for the presentation contest?
③ Don't be afraid if you're selected as a representative.
④ You'd better set aside your routine activities for a while.
⑤ How about setting a daily plan to prepare for the contest?

[16~17] 다음을 듣고, 물음에 답하시오.

16. 여자가 하는 말의 주제로 가장 적절한 것은?

① positive effects of regular exercise on flexibility
② using ordinary household items for home exercise
③ physical benefits of doing household chores
④ maintaining workout equipment properly
⑤ useful tips on buying home appliances

17. 언급된 물건이 아닌 것은?

① chair ② towel ③ broomstick
④ basket ⑤ water bottle

[해설편 p.084]

Dictation 19

✪ 표기에는 듣기 어려운 발음이 포함되어 있습니다. 귀 기울여 듣고 받아쓰세요. ● 고3 2020학년도 7월

※ QR 코드를 스캔하시면 듣기 방송이 나옵니다. 듣기 방송을 들으며 다음 빈칸을 채우시오. ● 제한 시간 : 25분

01

다음을 듣고, 남자가 하는 말의 목적으로 가장 적절한 것을 고르시오.

M : Can I have your attention, please? This is an announcement for visitors of our museum. There will be renovations to the Dumbarton Museum from November 23rd through the end of 2020. During this period, __________ __________ __________ __________ __________ __________ __________ will be closed. So, we ✪ __________ __________ __________ __________ __________ __________ __________ of the museum. However, the special art exhibition for children will continue on the first floor. The gardens will be open, and the Museum Shop will move to the greenhouse in the gardens. More information can be found on our website. We're sorry for the inconvenience caused by the renovations, and we look forward to seeing you at the newly renovated museum.

02

대화를 듣고, 여자의 의견으로 가장 적절한 것을 고르시오.

W : Honey, look at these horrific photographs!
M : It looks like these animals are suffering a lot.
W : Yes, it's our fault! Many marine animals are __________ __________ __________ __________ that we throw away.
M : I didn't know it was that serious. But isn't it impossible to live entirely without plastic?
W : True, but as a result of our current plastic use, millions of tons of plastics have ended up in the sea, damaging the environment. We should ✪ __________ __________ __________ __________ __________ __________ in our daily routine.
M : But plastics are very useful and convenient. How can we live with less plastic in our lives?
W : We can start by minimizing the use of disposable plastic. Instead, we can use things like refillable water bottles and reuseable shopping bags.
M : You mean that we should __________ __________ __________ __________ for our environment?
W : Exactly!

03

대화를 듣고, 두 사람의 관계를 가장 잘 나타낸 것을 고르시오.

W : Mr. Johns, we had such a wonderful time here today. Thank you so much.
M : It's been my pleasure, Ms. Parker.
W : I think my students had a lot of fun doing all the hands-on activities you had planned.
M : I'm glad they enjoyed them.
W : They were especially excited about ✪ __________ __________ __________ and ✪ __________ __________ __________.
M : I could tell that from their faces. They also worked hard to __________ __________ __________ __________ __________.
W : Yeah. When we go back to school, we'll do some cooking activities with the vegetables they collected today.
M : That's a great idea. I hope they'll __________ __________ __________ __________ __________.
W : I'm sure they will. Before we get on the bus, can you take a picture of us in front of the farmhouse?
M : Of course. Please tell me when you're ready.
W : Okay. Thanks.

04

대화를 듣고, 그림에서 대화의 내용과 일치하지 <u>않는</u> 것을 고르시오.

[Telephone rings.]
M : Hello, Mom!
W : Oh, Peter! Dad and I are just looking at the picture you sent.
M : The picture I took of my dormitory room?
W : Yeah. I see two beds in there. Is the room for two people?
M : Yes. Do you see ✪ __________ __________ __________ __________ __________ __________ __________ __________? That's my roommate, Jack.
W : I see. The room looks cozy because of the striped rug on the floor.
M : Jack brought it. He's __________ __________ __________ __________ __________.
W : How kind of him! Did he also bring the shelf under the clock?
M : Yes. It's full of our books. I didn't realize we would need that many books for our classes.
W : It seems you've got a lot of work to do.
M : Right. And I __________ __________ __________ __________ __________ __________ __________ over my bed. It's a good decoration.
W : Great. I'm glad you're doing well there.

05

대화를 듣고, 남자가 할 일로 가장 적절한 것을 고르시오.

W : Jason, let's check everything that we need for Dad's 70th birthday party.
M : Okay. I've packed the camera and lenses for taking pictures.
W : Good. How about the battery?
M : I've fully charged it and also prepared an extra one.
W : All right. Did you finish ✪ __________ __________ __________ __________?
M : Yes, I did. I'm sure Dad will be touched when he sees it.
W : I'm looking forward to watching it.
M : Oh, wait! Did you order a birthday cake?
W : Yes, I placed a special order for one.
M : Great. Then what else do we have to do?
W : Hmm.... We should __________ __________ __________ __________ __________ from the rental shop and wrap the gifts for the guests.
M : I think we should divide the work.
W : Okay. I'll __________ __________ __________.
M : In that case, I'll go to the rental shop.

06

대화를 듣고, 남자가 지불할 금액을 고르시오. [3점]

W : Welcome to the Band Teen Spirit's Goods House. May I help you?
M : Thanks. I've come here all the way from America to watch the band's concert and visit this store. ________ ________ ________ ________ ________ ________?
W : This poster set and that T-shirt. The poster set is 14 dollars and the T-shirt is 24 dollars.
M : I already have the poster set. I love that T-shirt! I'll take one.
W : All right. Do you want anything else?
M : Yes, ________ ________ ________ ________ ________ ________ ________.
W : Here they are. They cost eight dollars each.
M : There are seven members, so I'll take one for each of them.
W : Okay, one T-shirt and seven key rings. Do you need anything else?
M : No, but can I use the coupon ✪ ________ ________ ________ ________ ________?
W : Of course. You can get a 10% discount.
M : Great. I'll use my smart pay.

07

대화를 듣고, 여자가 응시할 스페인어 시험이 연기된 이유를 고르시오.

M : Natalie, you seem to be working hard for your Spanish exam.
W : Yes, it's ________ ________ ________ ________ with my class instructor.
M : Haven't you just finished taking your graduation exam? With all of these exams, you must feel quite stressed.
W : In a way, but I'm thinking of it as an opportunity to prepare for my job interviews after graduation.
M : Good. Then, when is the Spanish exam?
W : It's on June 24th.
M : Really? Aren't most exams scheduled between June 15th and 19th?
W : Yes, my speaking exam was supposed to take place on June 17th, but it was ________ ________ ________ ________ ________.
M : Did your class ask for a delay?
W : No, we didn't. Our instructor has to ✪ ________ ________ ________ ________ on the original test day.
M : I think this could work out better for you. You have one extra week to prepare.
W : Yeah. I'll try my best.

08

대화를 듣고, Classic Myanmar Tour에 관해 언급되지 않은 것을 고르시오.

W : David, I heard you're traveling to Myanmar this summer.
M : Right. I'm going with a tour program named the Classic Myanmar Tour.
W : Actually, I'm planning to travel around Myanmar this summer, too.
M : Really? Then, you might be interested in this tour I'm taking.
W : Sure. ________ ________ ________ ________ ________?
M : It's seven days, from July 10th to 16th.
W : Good. Does the tour visit Yangon? I'd really like to go there.
M : Yes. The tour also ________ ________ ________ ________ ________, such as Mandalay.
W : Great. What kind of transportation do you use during the tour?
M : We'll take trains between cities and use buses in cities. We'll also ✪ ________ ________ ________ ________ ________.
W : That sounds fun. Can I still sign up for the tour?
M : If you want to, you have to hurry! The tour has a limit of ten people.
W : I'll contact the travel agency. Thank you for the information.

09

2020 Student Infographic Contest에 관한 다음 내용을 듣고, 일치하지 않는 것을 고르시오.

W : Hello, everyone. This is Ms. Harris, your social studies teacher. I'm glad to announce the 2020 Student Infographic Contest. As you know, an infographic is a ________ ________ ________ ________ ________ ________ ________ that makes it easier to understand. The contest is open to students of all grades. To enter the contest, ✪ ________ ________ ________ on the topic of your choice and turn it in by November 15th. Please be sure to ________ ________ ________ ________ ________ ________. There will be three winners and they'll each receive two movie tickets as a prize. Winning entries will be on display in the library for the first week of December. For questions or more information, please come to my office. Thank you.

10

다음 표를 보면서 대화를 듣고, 남자가 구매할 눈 마사지기를 고르시오.

M : Jessica, I'm thinking of buying one of these eye massagers. Can you help me choose one?
W : Sure. The cheapest one here is the one I have. It's not bad, but I don't think it's ________ ________ ________.
M : Okay. I won't buy it then.
W : Do you need a heat setting?
M : Yes. It probably relaxes the muscles and ✪ ________ ________ ________ ________ ________ ________.
W : All right. Then, you may also want different massage modes. They help to ease eye fatigue with their different vibration functions.
M : Great. I'll get one that ________ ________ ________ ________ ________. Hmm, what's a music function?
W : With that function, you can listen to calming music through built-in speakers.
M : That sounds interesting, but I don't think it's necessary.
W : Then, this one is perfect for you.
M : Okay, I'll buy it.

11

대화를 듣고, 남자의 마지막 말에 대한 여자의 응답으로 가장 적절한 것을 고르시오.

M : Hey, Sally, why are you __________ __________ __________ on your foot?

W : I tripped over a rock yesterday and ✪ __________ __________ __________.

M : That sounds bad. How long do you have to wear your cast?

12

대화를 듣고, 여자의 마지막 말에 대한 남자의 응답으로 가장 적절한 것을 고르시오.

W : Steve, I'm conducting a survey for my marketing class. __________ __________ __________ __________ __________ __________ __________.

M : Sure, I'd be happy to help. What's the survey about?

W : It's about ✪ __________ __________ __________ __________. You can do it online by visiting the survey website.

13

대화를 듣고, 여자의 마지막 말에 대한 남자의 응답으로 가장 적절한 것을 고르시오. [3점]

W : Stanley, you look very concerned.

M : Well, I'm worried about my children's smartphone use. They won't put their phones down, even at the family dinner table.

W : I can imagine. Smartphones are useful, but they often distract us and take away precious family time.

M : I totally agree. How can I make my children __________ __________ __________ __________ __________ __________?

W : You can do that by first setting a good example. Your children will change if you start limiting your own phone time.

M : Good point. But isn't it too tempting to be on your phone when you have it nearby?

W : Of course. For that reason, many parents have started to __________ __________ __________ __________ __________ __________ __________ __________ at home and have asked their children to do the same.

M : Great idea. If we don't see our phones, we'll ✪ __________ __________ __________.

W : Yes, maybe you should consider trying this at home.

14

대화를 듣고, 남자의 마지막 말에 대한 여자의 응답으로 가장 적절한 것을 고르시오. [3점]

W : Andrew, guess what? I've just got an email saying that Mr. Chen agreed to give an interview for our student magazine.

M : The Chinese CEO? That's such good news.

W : The email says he hopes his business success will ✪ __________ __________ __________ __________ __________ __________ __________.

M : How nice of him! So when is he available for the interview?

W : Next Friday afternoon.

M : Okay. We'll have to talk about __________ __________ __________ __________ __________. Is there anything else we should prepare?

W : There's one important thing that should be taken care of.

M : What is it?

W : While doing research for the interview, I found out that Mr. Chen doesn't speak English that well. So I think we should find someone __________ __________ __________ __________ __________.

M : Hmm.... Doesn't Julia speak Chinese fluently? I think she can translate our questions into Chinese and tell us Mr. Chen's responses in English.

15

다음 상황 설명을 듣고, Alex가 Carol에게 할 말로 가장 적절한 것을 고르시오.

M : Carol is going to enter a presentation contest in a month as the school representative. She feels anxious even when going about her daily life because she doesn't think she can __________ __________ __________ __________ __________ __________ and still have time to prepare for the contest. But her classmate Alex thinks Carol doesn't have to feel so stressed, because a month is actually plenty of time to prepare for it. Alex thinks that if she ✪ __________ __________ __________ __________ __________ into what she can do each day, she'll be better able to prepare while still having time for her other activities. So Alex wants to suggest to Carol that she __________ __________ __________ __________ to accomplish each day for her preparation. In this situation, what would Alex most likely say to Carol?

16~17

다음을 듣고, 물음에 답하시오.

W : Hello, listeners. Welcome to Fitness Expert Radio Broadcast! Is a gym membership or fancy equipment necessary to get in shape? No. Luckily, there are some objects around your home that are perfect for __________ __________ __________ __________. First, a chair is a good tool for your at-home workouts. Consider using one to do your aerobics, leg raises and incline push-ups. Next, one person's towel is another person's resistance band! Try stretching with one. You can also do shoulder stretches with a broomstick. A broomstick can help __________ __________ __________ __________ __________ __________ by keeping your spine in line. Lastly, use filled water bottles. One in each hand can be used for aerobic exercises. Most water bottles are designed to be gripped, ✪ __________ __________ __________ __________ __________ __________. Now, are you ready to try these at home? For more fitness tips, please visit our website www.fitnessexpert.com. We can't wait to help you feel the burn!

19회

▶ 정답 : 해설편 086쪽

VOCA LIST 19

회차별 영단어 QR 코드 ※ QR 코드를 스캔 후 모바일로 단어장처럼 학습할 수 있습니다.

● 고3 2020학년도 7월

01

001 □ **renovation** ⓝ 개조 공사
002 □ **accommodate** ⓥ (시설 등에) 수용하다
003 □ **exhibition** ⓝ 전시

02

004 □ **entirely** ad 전적으로
005 □ **end up** ⓥ 결국 ~하게 되다
006 □ **consumption** ⓝ 소비
007 □ **minimize** ⓥ 최소화하다
008 □ **disposable** ⓐ 일회용의, 사용 후 버릴 수 있는
009 □ **refillable** ⓐ 리필 가능한, 다시 채울 수 있는
010 □ **reuseable** ⓐ 재사용 가능한
011 □ **inconvenience** ⓝ 불편

03

012 □ **feed** ⓥ 먹이를 주다
013 □ **harvest** ⓥ 수확하다

04

014 □ **dormitory** ⓝ 기숙사
015 □ **cozy** ⓐ 아늑한
016 □ **be willing to** ⓥ 기꺼이 ~하다

05

017 □ **pack** ⓥ 챙기다, (짐을) 싸다
018 □ **celebration** ⓝ 축하, 기념
019 □ **costume** ⓝ 의상
020 □ **divide** ⓥ 나누다

06

021 □ **key ring** ⓝ 열쇠고리
022 □ **official** ⓐ 공식적인

07

023 □ **oral interview** ⓝ 구술시험
024 □ **graduation** ⓝ 졸업
025 □ **postpone** ⓥ 연기하다
026 □ **overseas** ⓐ 해외의 ad 해외로

08

027 □ **transportation** ⓝ 교통 수단
028 □ **sign up for** ⓥ ~에 등록하다
029 □ **information** ⓝ 정보

09

030 □ **present** ⓥ 제시하다
031 □ **grade** ⓝ 학년
032 □ **turn in** ⓥ ~을 제출하다
033 □ **entry** ⓝ 출품작
034 □ **on display** 전시 중인

10

035 □ **blood circulation** ⓝ 혈액순환
036 □ **fatigue** ⓝ 피로
037 □ **vibration** ⓝ 진동
038 □ **calming** ⓐ 마음을 편안하게 해주는, 진정시키는

11

039 □ **cast** ⓝ 깁스(붕대)
040 □ **trip** ⓥ 걸려 넘어지다
041 □ **sprain** ⓥ (발목·손목 등을) 삐다
042 □ **ankle** ⓝ 발목

12

043 □ **conduct** ⓥ 실시하다
044 □ **survey** ⓝ 설문조사
045 □ **wonder** ⓥ 궁금해 하다
046 □ **decide on** ⓥ ~에 대해 결정하다

13

047 □ **concerned** ⓐ 걱정하는
048 □ **distract** ⓥ 산만하게 하다, 주의를 흩뜨리다
049 □ **precious** ⓐ 소중한, 귀중한
050 □ **tempting** ⓐ 유혹적인, 솔깃한
051 □ **on a regular basis** 주기적으로

14

052 □ **inspire** ⓥ 영감을 주다
053 □ **take care of** ⓥ ~을 처리하다
054 □ **do research** ⓥ 조사하다
055 □ **interpret** ⓥ 통역하다, 해석하다, 이해하다
056 □ **fluently** ad 유창하게
057 □ **translate** ⓥ 번역하다, 통역하다

15

058 □ **representative** ⓝ 대표 ⓐ (특정 단체를) 대표하는
059 □ **anxious** ⓐ 불안해하는, 걱정하는
060 □ **routine** ⓐ 일상적인
061 □ **plenty of** 많은
062 □ **specific** ⓐ 구체적인
063 □ **accomplish** ⓥ 달성하다
064 □ **set aside** ⓥ (다른 더 중요한 일들 때문에) ~을 고려하지 않다

16~17

065 □ **get in shape** ⓥ 몸매를 가꾸다, 건강해지다
066 □ **incline** ⓝ 경사(면), 비탈
067 □ **broomstick** ⓝ 빗자루
068 □ **grip** ⓥ 잡다, 쥐다
069 □ **substitute** ⓝ 대체품
070 □ **properly** ad 적절히
071 □ **home appliance** ⓝ 가전제품

20회 ● 2025학년도 9월 모의평가 고3 영어 듣기

※ QR코드를 스캔하시면 듣기 방송을 청취하실 수 있습니다.

● 점수 표시가 없는 문항은 모두 2점 ● 문항수 17개 | 배점 37점 | 제한 시간 25분

1번부터 17번까지는 듣고 답하는 문제입니다. 1번부터 15번까지는 한 번만 들려주고, 16번부터 17번까지는 두 번 들려줍니다. 방송을 잘 듣고 답을 하시기 바랍니다.

1. 다음을 듣고, 여자가 하는 말의 목적으로 가장 적절한 것을 고르시오.

① 새로 부임한 교직원을 소개하려고
② 시설 안전 포스터 공모전을 홍보하려고
③ 학교 복도에서 뛰지 말 것을 당부하려고
④ 학교 엘리베이터 수리 일정을 공지하려고
⑤ 엘리베이터 사용 실태 조사를 안내하려고

2. 대화를 듣고, 남자의 의견으로 가장 적절한 것을 고르시오.

① 과도한 양의 단백질 섭취는 건강에 좋지 않다.
② 칼슘 보충을 위해 채소를 많이 섭취해야 한다.
③ 회사 구내식당에서 식사하는 것이 경제적이다.
④ 갑작스러운 운동량 변화는 신체에 부담이 된다.
⑤ 도시락을 싸 오면 음식물 쓰레기를 줄일 수 있다.

3. 다음을 듣고, 여자가 하는 말의 요지로 가장 적절한 것을 고르시오.

① 학생에게 실생활에 필요한 역량을 키워 줄 필요가 있다.
② 학생 인성 교육을 위해 충분한 상담 지식을 갖추어야 한다.
③ 학생을 잘 이해하려면 그 학생의 관심사를 파악해야 한다.
④ 효과적인 수업을 하려면 교사 간의 많은 대화가 필수적이다.
⑤ 학생 이름을 부르는 것은 그 학생과의 좋은 관계 형성에 기여한다.

4. 대화를 듣고, 그림에서 대화의 내용과 일치하지 않는 것을 고르시오.

5. 대화를 듣고, 남자가 할 일로 가장 적절한 것을 고르시오.

① 유인물 만들기 ② 점심 주문하기
③ 버스 대절하기 ④ 입장권 예약하기
⑤ 문자 메시지 보내기

6. 대화를 듣고, 여자가 지불할 금액을 고르시오.

① $45 ② $50 ③ $54 ④ $63 ⑤ $70

7. 대화를 듣고, 여자가 Kenton Biotech Career Fair에 갈 수 없는 이유를 고르시오.

① 마케팅 특강을 들어야 해서
② 생명과학 실험을 해야 해서
③ 요양원 자원봉사를 해야 해서
④ 역사 시험 공부를 해야 해서
⑤ 뮤지컬 오디션에 가야 해서

8. 대화를 듣고, Dallers City Sharks의 우승 축하 행사에 관해 언급되지 않은 것을 고르시오.

① 날짜 ② 장소 ③ 경품
④ 입장료 ⑤ 반입 금지 물품

9. Williamton Hotel Internship에 관한 다음 내용을 듣고, 일치하지 않는 것을 고르시오.

① 8주간 이어질 것이다.
② 근무 시간 동안 유니폼을 입고 있어야 한다.
③ 회의가 월요일 아침마다 있을 것이다.
④ 업무에는 음식 서비스와 테이블 세팅이 포함될 것이다.
⑤ 종료 후 참가 인턴 중 절반이 호텔에 고용될 것이다.

[해설편 p.087]

10. 다음 표를 보면서 대화를 듣고, 남자가 주문할 전자 도어 록을 고르시오.

Electronic Door Locks

	Model	Price	Case Material	Color	Fingerprint Recognition
①	A	$100	Plastic	Red	×
②	B	$120	Steel	Gold	×
③	C	$170	Aluminum	Black	×
④	D	$190	Plastic	Blue	○
⑤	E	$220	Aluminum	Silver	○

11. 대화를 듣고, 여자의 마지막 말에 대한 남자의 응답으로 가장 적절한 것을 고르시오.

① No problem. The dentist recommended this toothbrush.
② Thanks. I'll be able to get to my appointment on time.
③ Sounds great. I'll make an appointment for 3 o'clock.
④ How unfortunate. The clinic is closed for lunch.
⑤ Never mind. You can pay the parking fee later.

12. 대화를 듣고, 남자의 마지막 말에 대한 여자의 응답으로 가장 적절한 것을 고르시오. [3점]

① Good idea. That way, we won't forget to buy what we need.
② All right. Keep a daily record of how many calories you eat.
③ Too bad. Next time, bring a bag when you buy groceries.
④ Sorry. I should've checked where the onions were from.
⑤ That's true. We need to clean out the refrigerator often.

13. 대화를 듣고, 여자의 마지막 말에 대한 남자의 응답으로 가장 적절한 것을 고르시오.

Man: ____________________

① Excuse me. You're not allowed to cook here.
② Thanks for refunding my class registration fee.
③ Excellent. Everyone's going to like your videos.
④ Okay. I'll wait until then to sign up for that class.
⑤ I prepared some Italian food for my students last week.

14. 대화를 듣고, 남자의 마지막 말에 대한 여자의 응답으로 가장 적절한 것을 고르시오. [3점]

Woman: ____________________

① Don't worry. You'll learn to ride a bike quickly.
② That'll be nice. I hope that'll enhance my confidence.
③ Yes. You haven't been physically active at all these days.
④ Terrific. I'm glad you got a good score on the presentation.
⑤ Not really. I prefer watching team sports to individual sports.

15. 다음 상황 설명을 듣고, Roger가 Monica에게 할 말로 가장 적절한 것을 고르시오. [3점]

Roger: ____________________

① We'd better take our dogs for a check-up on a regular basis.
② You'll have to spend a lot of money on feeding the puppies.
③ I must ask my roommate if it's okay for me to adopt a puppy.
④ I'll gladly look after your pets while you're on your trip.
⑤ You should get to know the dogs before adopting them.

[16~17] 다음을 듣고, 물음에 답하시오.

16. 남자가 하는 말의 주제로 가장 적절한 것은?

① features that allow certain animals to achieve high speeds
② effects of environmental changes on animal behaviors
③ difficulties that the fastest animals have in common
④ reasons for certain species' faster growth over others
⑤ hunting patterns of animals genetically close to humans

17. 언급된 동물이 <u>아닌</u> 것은?

① cheetah ② falcon ③ iguana
④ swordfish ⑤ dragonfly

[해설편 p.089]

※ QR 코드를 스캔하시면 듣기 방송이 나옵니다. 듣기 방송을 들으며 다음 빈칸을 채우시오. ● 제한 시간 : 25분

01

다음을 듣고, 여자가 하는 말의 목적으로 가장 적절한 것을 고르시오.

W : Hello, everyone at Philston High School. This is Principal Jackson. This announcement is ___ ___________ _____________ ______ _______ of the school elevator repair schedule. As you know, the school elevator stopped working yesterday. It's ✪ ____________ ___ ____ ___________ __________ at 1 p.m. this afternoon. The repair is expected to take about 3 hours. In the meantime, you'll have to continue using the stairs. Once again, please ✪ _____ ________ ______ the school elevator will be undergoing repairs from 1 p.m. to about 4 p.m. today. We'll announce when the elevator is running again. Sorry for the inconvenience.

02

대화를 듣고, 남자의 의견으로 가장 적절한 것을 고르시오.

M : Oh, Susan. You're eating lunch here in the office.

W : Hi, Aaron. ✪ ______ ________ ____________ my own lunch.

M : That's why I haven't seen you in the company cafeteria recently. Wait. That's a lot of chicken breast for one meal!

W : Yeah. I've been eating a lot of protein for each meal these days because I want to build bigger muscles.

M : Well, it seems that you're eating too much protein. Overconsuming protein is unhealthy.

W : Don't we need __ ____ ____ ___________ ____ _______ bigger muscles?

M : Yes, but too much protein can cause stomachaches.

W : Oh, that's probably why I've felt uncomfortable after each meal lately.

M : Besides, eating too much protein ✪ _______ ________ __________ ______. It can lead to poor bone health.

W : Really? I didn't know that.

M : So, taking in too much protein is harmful for your health.

W : I see. Then I'll cut down on the amount of protein I eat.

03

다음을 듣고, 여자가 하는 말의 요지로 가장 적절한 것을 고르시오.

W : Hello, fellow teachers. Welcome back to my video channel, *Ms. Freeman's Teaching Tips*. Do you have ____________ _____________ ______ _____________ _______ your students? I understand ✪ ______ _____ _____ _____ __________. Here's a tip. Calling your students by their names can help you develop a good relationship with them. It'll show the students that you're interested in them, and they'll feel more comfortable with you. Then, the students will be more likely to open up to you. So, call your students by their names, and ✪ _____ ____________ ___ __________ a good relationship with them. Thanks for watching and don't forget to subscribe.

04

대화를 듣고, 그림에서 대화의 내용과 일치하지 않는 것을 고르시오.

M : Ellen, yesterday I visited the ______ ______ _____ _________ ________ _____ ________.

W : Really? Is it nice?

M : Yes, it is. Look. Here's a picture of the café

W : It seems lovely. There's a leaf-shaped mirror on the wall!

M : Right, it's so unique. What do you think about the painting between the windows?

W : ✪ ___________ __________ __ __ really talented. I also like the two flowerpots on the shelf. They're so pretty.

M : They really ✪ ___________ ____ _____ ________. And do you see the star-patterned table cloth?

W : Yes, it's eye-catching. Oh, the round rug is really neat.

M : It creates a comfortable mood.

W : Yeah, I feel the same way. I'll definitely visit the cafćwhen I have the chance.

05

대화를 듣고, 남자가 할 일로 가장 적절한 것을 고르시오.

W : Andy, our art club's visit to the Waneville Art Museum is just a week away.

M : Right, Ms. Peterson. Our club members are really excited to see the Jonathan
Vinston exhibit. He's so popular on social media nowadays.

W : Great. For transportation, I ✪ ___________ _____ __ _____ ___ ______ us there. Have you and
the other students decided what we'll eat for lunch?

M : Yes. Yesterday, I ordered 25 sandwiches.

W : Excellent. Do our members know about the meeting time and place?

M : Not yet. Do you _______ _____ ___ _____ ________ _____ ________?

W : No, I'll do that.

M : Thank you. Have you booked the admission tickets?

W : Of course. I've received the online confirmation. Oh, it might be good to provide the members with ✪ ___________ ________ _____ _______ ____________.

M : Okay. I'll make a handout about him right away.

W : Thanks. I'm sure everyone will enjoy the visit.

Dictation 20

06

대화를 듣고, 여자가 지불할 금액을 고르시오.

M : Welcome to Winsley's Drugstore. How may I help you?
W : Hi. I need some foot cream for my hiking trip.
M : What size _____ _____ _____________ _____? The small size is $10 and the regular size is $20.
W : That small size would be handy. I'll take two.
M : Good. Anything else?
W : I also need lip balm.
M : Is there any ✪ ______________ _________ ______ _______ ___ ________?
W : Not really.
M : Then, this one is quite popular. It's only $5.
W : All right. I'll take six. I'll give them out to my fellow hikers. And, that's all.
M : Okay. So, two small size foot creams and six lip balms, right?
W : Yes. And I heard there's a sales event this week.
M : Right. ✪ __________________ _________ ______ the total.
W : Great. Here's my credit card.

07

대화를 듣고, 여자가 Kenton Biotech Career Fair에 갈 수 없는 이유를 고르시오.

M : Jane, have you heard about the Kenton Biotech Career Fair this Saturday?
W : Yes, Daniel. It's a one-day event that covers biotechnology, health care, and marketing, right?
M : Yeah. There'll ✪ ________ ______ ____________ ___________ ____ the subjects. Would you like to go?
W : I'd like to, but I'm afraid I can't.
M : Oh, are Saturdays when you're volunteering at the nursing home?
W : No, that's on Sundays.
M : Then, do you have to study for your history exam?
W : I took it last week. Actually, ____ ___ ___ ___ __ ________ ________ an audition for a musical.
M : Really? That's awesome! I ✪ ______________ ______ __________.
W : Thanks. I hope I get the part.

08

대화를 듣고, Dallers City Sharks의 우승 축하 행사에 관해 언급되지 않은 것을 고르시오.

W : Dad, I can't believe our Dallers City Sharks won the National Baseball League Championship.
M : Yeah. This is the first championship in their 27-year history. The city's going wild.
W : There'll be a big celebration to honor this historic victory.
M : Right. Look. There's ✪ ____ ________________ _________ __ ____ the team's website. It'll be held on Friday, November 1st.
W : There's no way I'm going to miss it. It says the celebration will take place at Dallers City Sharks Stadium.
M : I'm sure ______ _____________. Oh, there's an admission fee.
W : Yeah, it's $20 per person. Do you want to go with me, Dad?
M : Sure. Oh, look. There's a list of ✪ _________ ______ _____ ___________. We're not allowed to bring fireworks or drones.
W : That makes sense. They can be dangerous in a stadium. Anyway, I can't wait to take part in the celebration!

09

Williamton Hotel Internship에 관한 다음 내용을 듣고, 일치하지 않는 것을 고르시오.

M : Welcome to the Williamton Hotel Internship. I'm Matthew Collins, the hotel manager. Let me provide some general guidelines for your internship. This internship ✪ ___________ _____ ________ starting today. You'll be working weekdays from 9 a.m. to 6 p.m. You _________ ____ ____________ ___ your uniform during working hours. Also, you should remember that there'll be a meeting each Monday morning at 9 in this seminar room, where you'll receive your tasks for the week. Your duties will involve food service and table setting. Our staff will be sharing all the details with you about ✪ ______ ____ ____________ _______ _________ and how you'll be evaluated. After this internship, the top 10% of the interns will be employed by the hotel. Thank you.

10

다음 표를 보면서 대화를 듣고, 남자가 주문할 전자 도어 록을 고르시오.

W : Honey, we need to change the electronic door lock on the front door.
M : Yeah. So ______ ________ ___________ online to find a replacement.
W : Have you found any good options?
M : These five look promising. Take a look. What do you think?
W : Well, I don't want to spend more than $200.
M : Okay. How about the case material?
W : ✪ ____________ _____ ________ _______ ______. It looks old-fashioned.
M : I agree. And, I don't like the red one.
W : Yeah, ✪ __ ___________ _____ _______ with our door.
M : Now, we're down to these two. Do you think we need the fingerprint recognition feature?
W : I don't think we'll use it much. Let's choose the one without it.
M : Sounds like a good choice. I'll order this one.

11

대화를 듣고, 여자의 마지막 말에 대한 남자의 응답으로 가장 적절한 것을 고르시오.

W : Josh, it's already 3 o'clock! ________ ________ ___________ ___________________ at 3:30 today?
M : Oh, no. Mom, we've been chatting for so long! I think I'm going to be late. Can you ✪ _______ _____ __ ______?
W : Sure, I can do that. I'm free this afternoon.

12

대화를 듣고, 남자의 마지막 말에 대한 여자의 응답으로 가장 적절한 것을 고르시오. [3점]

M : Honey, I don't see any onions in the shopping bags.
W : Let me check. *[Pause]* Oh, we __________ ___ ______ ________ again. And we also didn't remember to buy milk.
M : Well, how about ✪ _____________ __ _____________ _____ before we go shopping next time?

13

대화를 듣고, 여자의 마지막 말에 대한 남자의 응답으로 가장 적절한 것을 고르시오.

[Telephone rings.]
W : Hello, Benjamin Cooking Academy. How can I help you?
M : Hi, ✪ _____ ______ ___ ____________ for Chef Antonio's Italian cooking class for beginners.
W : All right. Chef Antonio teaches that class on two different days.
M : When are they?
W : He has __ _______________ ________ on Tuesdays and a weekend class on Saturdays.
M : I'll take the weekend class because I can't do weekdays.
W : *[Mouse clicking sound]* Oh, I'm sorry. That class is full this month.
M : Oh, no. I really want to learn from Chef Antonio. ✪ ______ __ _____ ______ ___ his online cooking videos. Will he teach the same class next month?
W : Yes, that's correct.
M : Can I register for that class now?
W : Sorry. Registration starts next Monday.

14

대화를 듣고, 남자의 마지막 말에 대한 여자의 응답으로 가장 적절한 것을 고르시오. [3점]

M : Kristen, you seem worried. What's wrong?
W : Well, Grandpa. I'm feeling down these days. I ✪ _____ ____________ ___ ____ __________ _____________ last week even though I'd prepared really hard.
M : It's all right. It happens to everyone.
W : It's not only that. I have a chemistry presentation coming up, and I'm afraid I'm going ✪ ___ _________ ______ ____, too.
M : You've been working so hard on it that I'm sure you'll do great. Maybe you just need to boost your confidence.
W : But I don't know how.
M : How about getting involved in physical activities? You can go for a bike ride.
W : How does riding a bike help boost my confidence?
M : It causes the release of endorphins, which can lead to a boost in confidence.
W : Okay, I'll give it a try. But I _________ _________ ___ ______ _________.
M : Why don't you join me? You know I ride a bike every evening.

15

다음 상황 설명을 듣고, Roger가 Monica에게 할 말로 가장 적절한 것을 고르시오. [3점]

W : Roger and Monica are close friends. Monica has two dogs, and ✪ ______ ____ _________ ________ ________ ___ four puppies recently. Now, she's looking for someone to adopt one of the puppies because she cannot ✪ ________ ____ ____ ________ ____ __________. She asks Roger if he can adopt one. Roger's been thinking about raising a dog himself. He knows how to take care of dogs since he's spent a lot of time with Monica's dogs. However, he's currently living with one of his co-workers. So, Roger __________ ___ _____ ____________ that he needs to first make sure that his roommate agrees with him adopting a puppy. In this situation, what would Roger most likely say to Monica?

16~17

다음을 듣고, 물음에 답하시오.

M : Good morning, students. Today, we're going to learn about the key characteristics that enable some animals to reach high speeds. First, there's no animal faster on land than the cheetah. Its flexible backbone and joints allow for extreme extension, ______________ __ ___ ___________ its legs very far and push off its back legs with great force like a spring. Second, the falcon is one of the fastest birds. Its large breastbone ✪ ___________ ________ ____________ ___ ____ ______________ to it, so it can beat its wings with greater power. Third, the swordfish is among the fastest fish in the sea. It releases a special, slippery oil from its head that coats the front of its body, enabling it to swim with less resistance. Lastly, the dragonfly is considered the world's fastest flying insect. It has ✪ _____ ___________ ___________ ___ _____________ ________ its wings as they swing down, causing a small tornado-like wind that gives it a boost of speed. Now, let's watch a video of nature's speedsters.

20회

▶ 정답 : 해설편 090쪽

VOCA LIST 20

회차별 영단어 QR 코드 ※ QR 코드를 스캔 후 모바일로 단어장처럼 학습할 수 있습니다.

● 고3 2025학년도 9월

01

001 □ **vice principal** 교감
002 □ **inform** ⓥ 알리다
003 □ **undergo** ⓥ 실시하다
004 □ **upcoming** ⓐ 다가오는
005 □ **hallway** ⓝ 복도

02

006 □ **breast** ⓝ 가슴
007 □ **protein** ⓝ 단백질
008 □ **overconsume** ⓥ 과잉 섭취하다

03

009 □ **frustrating** ⓐ 좌절감을 주는
010 □ **contribute to** ~에 도움이 되다, 기여하다
011 □ **subscribe** ⓥ 구독하다

04

012 □ **flowerpot** ⓝ 화분
013 □ **eye-catching** 시선을 사로잡는
014 □ **neat** ⓐ 깔끔한

05

015 □ **arrange** ⓥ 준비하다
016 □ **admission** ⓝ 입장
017 □ **confirmation** ⓝ 확인
018 □ **beforehand** ad 미리

06

019 □ **handy** ⓐ 편리한
020 □ **have ~ in mind** ~을 마음에 두다
021 □ **quite** ⓐ 꽤
022 □ **fellow** ⓝ 동료

07

023 □ **cover** ⓥ 다루다
024 □ **subject** ⓝ 주제
025 □ **volunteer** ⓥ 자원봉사를 하다
026 □ **awesome** ⓐ 멋진

08

027 □ **historic** ⓐ 역사적인
028 □ **admission fee** 입장료
029 □ **ban** ⓥ 금지하다
030 □ **stadium** ⓝ 경기장

09

031 □ **guideline** ⓝ 지침
032 □ **duty** ⓝ 업무
033 □ **perform** ⓥ 수행하다
034 □ **task** ⓝ 업무
035 □ **evaluate** ⓥ 평가하다
036 □ **employ** ⓥ 고용하다

10

037 □ **electronic** ⓐ 전자의
038 □ **replacement** ⓝ 대체품
039 □ **promising** ⓐ 좋을 것 같은
040 □ **old-fashioned** ⓐ 구식의
041 □ **go well with** ~와 잘 어울리다
042 □ **fingerprint** ⓝ 지문
043 □ **recognition** ⓝ 인식

11

044 □ **dentist** ⓝ 치과 의사
045 □ **appointment** ⓝ 예약
046 □ **give ~ a ride** 차로 ~를 태워다 주다

12

047 □ **grocery** ⓝ 식료품

13

048 □ **register** ⓥ 등록하다
049 □ **beginner** ⓝ 초보
050 □ **weekday** ⓝ 평일

14

051 □ **competition** ⓝ 대회
052 □ **mess up** ~을 망치다
053 □ **boost** ⓥ 높이다 ⓝ 상승
054 □ **give ~ a try** ~을 해보다
055 □ **ride** ⓥ 타다
056 □ **enhance** ⓥ 올라가다, 강화하다

15

057 □ **give birth to** ~을 낳다
058 □ **currently** ad 현재
059 □ **adopt** ⓥ 입양하다

16~17

060 □ **loyalty** ⓝ 충심
061 □ **exclusive** ⓐ 독점의
062 □ **depart** ⓥ 출발하다
063 □ **specialty** ⓝ 특별
064 □ **abroad** ad 승선하여, 해외로
065 □ **journey** ⓝ 여행

21회 • 2024학년도 9월 모의평가 고3 영어 듣기

※ QR코드를 스캔하시면 듣기 방송을 청취하실 수 있습니다.

● 점수 표시가 없는 문항은 모두 2점 ● 문항수 17개 | 배점 37점 | 제한 시간 25분

1번부터 17번까지는 듣고 답하는 문제입니다. 1번부터 15번까지는 한 번만 들려주고, 16번부터 17번까지는 두 번 들려줍니다. 방송을 잘 듣고 답을 하시기 바랍니다.

1. 다음을 듣고, 여자가 하는 말의 목적으로 가장 적절한 것을 고르시오.

① 멸종 위기 동물을 소개하려고
② 동물원 관람 예절을 안내하려고
③ 어린이 동물 캠프를 홍보하려고
④ 신입 동물 훈련사를 모집하려고
⑤ 야생 동물 보호를 독려하려고

2. 대화를 듣고, 남자의 의견으로 가장 적절한 것을 고르시오.

① 점심시간에 운동하는 것은 활력과 집중력을 높인다.
② 개인의 건강 상태에 따라 운동 강도를 조절해야 한다.
③ 부상 방지를 위해 올바른 자세로 운동하는 것이 중요하다.
④ 규칙적인 운동은 정서 안정에 도움을 줄 수 있다.
⑤ 과도한 아침 운동은 업무에 방해가 될 수 있다.

3. 다음을 듣고, 여자가 하는 말의 요지로 가장 적절한 것을 고르시오.

① 정기적인 학습 상담은 학습 능률을 높여 줄 수 있다.
② 메모하는 것은 과제를 관리하는 데 효율적인 방법이다.
③ 자신만의 암기법을 활용하면 성적을 향상시킬 수 있다.
④ 두뇌의 균형적인 발달은 메모하는 습관으로 촉진된다.
⑤ 실천 가능한 계획 수립이 과제 해결의 출발점이다.

4. 대화를 듣고, 그림에서 대화의 내용과 일치하지 않는 것을 고르시오.

5. 대화를 듣고, 여자가 할 일로 가장 적절한 것을 고르시오.

① 간식 준비하기
② 유인물 출력하기
③ 학교 체육관 예약하기
④ 강사에게 연락하기
⑤ 배너 배송 일정 확인하기

6. 대화를 듣고, 남자가 지불할 금액을 고르시오. [3점]

① $60 ② $63 ③ $70 ④ $75 ⑤ $80

7. 대화를 듣고, 여자가 콘서트에 갈 수 없는 이유를 고르시오.

① 콘서트 티켓을 예매하지 못해서
② 과학 토론 대회에 참가해야 해서
③ 아르바이트 대체 근무자를 찾지 못해서
④ 부모님과 함께 여행을 가야 해서
⑤ 축구 경기에 출전해야 해서

8. 대화를 듣고, Raven Elliott의 책 사인회에 관해 언급되지 않은 것을 고르시오.

① 날짜 ② 장소 ③ 시작 시간
④ 기념품 ⑤ 신청 방법

9. Grandhill Park Cleanup 행사에 관한 다음 내용을 듣고, 일치하지 않는 것을 고르시오.

① 9월 30일에 열릴 것이다.
② 참가자들은 둘이서 짝을 이루어 쓰레기를 주울 것이다.
③ 유명 인사들이 참가할 것이다.
④ 모든 참가자들은 에코백을 받을 것이다.
⑤ 참가자들은 쓰레기봉투와 장갑을 가져와야 한다.

영어 영역[듣기]

10. 다음 표를 보면서 대화를 듣고, 여자가 수강할 스포츠 프로그램을 고르시오.

After-school Sports Programs

	Program	Sport	Grade	Day	Equipment provided
①	A	Volleyball	All	Monday	○
②	B	Baseball	All	Tuesday	○
③	C	Soccer	3rd	Wednesday	×
④	D	Badminton	1st & 2nd	Thursday	×
⑤	E	Table tennis	2nd & 3rd	Friday	○

11. 대화를 듣고, 남자의 마지막 말에 대한 여자의 응답으로 가장 적절한 것을 고르시오.

① Why don't you download the app first?
② I agree! We can open a new pizza place.
③ Really? I wonder why they don't deliver.
④ That's great! Can you order the pizza now?
⑤ Okay. I'll attend the meeting in person then.

12. 대화를 듣고, 여자의 마지막 말에 대한 남자의 응답으로 가장 적절한 것을 고르시오.

① That's a good idea. You'd better take it.
② Sorry, but you're not allowed to go outside.
③ Cheer up. We'll take a trip to the mountains.
④ That's true. We saw a shooting star last night.
⑤ Don't worry. I can give you a ride to your school.

13. 대화를 듣고, 남자의 마지막 말에 대한 여자의 응답으로 가장 적절한 것을 고르시오.

Woman: ______________________________

① Excellent! I'll see you at 7 p.m. on Sunday.
② I'd appreciate it if you could do that for me.
③ Why not? I want to pick them up right now.
④ Please remember to fix the zipper on time.
⑤ Well done! The repaired pants fit me well.

14. 대화를 듣고, 여자의 마지막 말에 대한 남자의 응답으로 가장 적절한 것을 고르시오.

Man: ______________________________

① I know what you mean. You can stay home.
② Absolutely. I would never go barefoot walking.
③ Sounds good to me. Let's try it this weekend!
④ It's my fault. I should've booked the event earlier.
⑤ I had a nice time there. You should do it.

15. 다음 상황 설명을 듣고, Jack이 Amy에게 할 말로 가장 적절한 것을 고르시오. [3점]

Jack: ______________________________

① No problem. We can reschedule our meeting.
② Don't be upset. I'll record the interview for you.
③ Calm down. Did you call the computer service center?
④ I see. We can exchange your laptop for a new one.
⑤ No way. Are you done editing the video clips?

[16～17] 다음을 듣고, 물음에 답하시오.

16. 여자가 하는 말의 주제로 가장 적절한 것은? [3점]

① survival strategies of endangered animals
② impacts of environmental changes on animals' diet
③ methods animals adopt to make up for lack of sleep
④ hunting patterns used by animals in the wild
⑤ factors that affect animals' sleep patterns

17. 언급된 동물이 아닌 것은?

① elephants ② bats ③ sheep
④ lions ⑤ flamingos

[해설편 p.093]

※ QR 코드를 스캔하시면 듣기 방송이 나옵니다. 듣기 방송을 들으며 다음 빈칸을 채우시오. ● 제한 시간 : 25분

01

다음을 듣고, 여자가 하는 말의 목적으로 가장 적절한 것을 고르시오.

W : Hello, viewers! Are you looking for a fun activity for your kids to enjoy on the weekend? Then, come and join _____ __________ __________ _____ ______. Happy Animal Friends Camp will be held every weekend in September. We'll ✪ __________ ______________ ______________ with a wide variety of animals such as rabbits, turtles, and parrots. Your kids will learn how to care for and interact with the animals under the guidance of experienced trainers. If your children like ____________ _______ ________ ___________, sign them up for the Happy Animal Friends Camp! You can find more information on our website. Don't miss this great opportunity!

02

대화를 듣고, 남자의 의견으로 가장 적절한 것을 고르시오.

W : Hey, Kevin! Where are you going?

M : I'm going to take _____ ______ _________ __________.

W : Oh, is it the 25-minute lunch break workout that the company is offering?

M : That's right. I find that exercising at lunch time boosts my energy and helps me focus on my work.

W : Really? I think it would ________ _____ ________ _______. I usually just want to take a rest.

M : I did, too. But I actually feel more energized after the lunch break workout. It even ✪ ____________ _____ ______________.

W : You mean you have more energy and can focus better when you get back to your desk?

M : Exactly. It's been very helpful for me.

W : Okay. Maybe I'll join. Thanks for the information.

M : My pleasure.

03

다음을 듣고, 여자가 하는 말의 요지로 가장 적절한 것을 고르시오.

W : Good morning, students. I'm Ms. Thompson, your learning consultant for today's workshop. Many of you have expressed concerns that you're having ✪ ____________ ______________ _______ ______________ ____ _______. But you know what? Making a memo is an efficient way to __________ _______ ______________. You can't only rely on your memory. You need to make a note about what to do and when to do it so that you don't forget. Writing a memo might be ____________ ___ ______, but you'll get used to it in no time. With a memo, you can organize your assignments better. Now, we're going to see some good examples of students' memos. Let's look at the screen.

04

대화를 듣고, 그림에서 대화의 내용과 일치하지 않는 것을 고르시오.

M : Clara, I took a picture of the new reading room at our community center. Come and take a look!

W : Okay, Dad. Let me see. *[Pause]* Oh, look at the table in front of the window! There are three chairs at the table.

M : You're right. So we can enjoy reading books together. How about the lamp ____________ ___ _____ _____ __________?

W : Cool! It looks much taller than me. Wow, I love ✪ _____ ___________________ _____ under the bookshelf.

M : It's nice, isn't it?

W : Yeah, we can also read books sitting on the rug.

M : And look! There's a heart-shaped cushion on the sofa.

W : It's so cute. Hmm... Dad, what's the board under the clock for?

M : That's for ________________ ______ _________ at the community center.

W : I see. I want to go soon.

05

대화를 듣고, 여자가 할 일로 가장 적절한 것을 고르시오.

M : Ms. Jackson, the traffic safety education is just one week away.

W : You're right, Mr. Kim. I think it'll be helpful for our 1st graders since many of them are starting to walk to school.

M : Shall we check if everything's ready?

W : Sure. Let's see... Did you ✪ __________ _____ _________ _______?

M : Yes, I did it yesterday.

W : How about the traffic safety handouts?

M : I've already printed them out. Ah, do you know when the banner will be delivered?

W : Yeah, I checked it already. It'll arrive tomorrow.

M : Okay. ______ ______ ______ _____ ____________?

W : That's right! _ __________ ________. I'll contact him this afternoon.

M : Great. And I'm going to prepare some snacks for the students.

W : Good idea! The kids will love it.

06

대화를 듣고, 남자가 지불할 금액을 고르시오. [3점]

W : Hello, welcome to the Monet Art Museum. What can I do for you?

M : Hi, I'd like to purchase admission tickets.

W : Sure. Tickets are $30 for adults, and $15 for children under 12.

M : My sons are both under 12. So, I'll get one adult and two child tickets.

W : Okay.

M : We're also interested in the kids' oil painting program. How much is it?

W : It's $5 per child, and parents are ____________ ___ ______ _____ ______.

M : That's great. Then, two tickets for the program as well.

W : Okay. Do you want to join ✪ _____ ___________ __________? It's only $10, and you'll receive our monthly art magazine.
M : No, thank you. ______ _____ __________, please.
W : Alright. So, that's admission tickets for one adult and two children. And, two oil painting program tickets, right?
M : Perfect. Here's my credit card.

07

대화를 듣고, 여자가 콘서트에 갈 수 없는 이유를 고르시오.

M : Hey, Stella. Aren't you a fan of Miracle Girls?
W : I sure am. Any good news?
M : They're going to _______ __ _______________ ___________ in our city next month.
W : Nice. I've been waiting so long to see them perform. When is the concert?
M : It's on October 6th.
W : Oh, no! I can't make it.
M : Why not? Is it because you have to work at your part-time job?
W : No, it's not that. I could easily change my schedule with another person.
M : What is it then? Don't tell me you have to play soccer.
W : No. Actually, I have to join __ ____ ________ __________________ that day.
M : Science debate competition? That's amazing! I'll ✪ _______ _____ ______.
W : Thanks. I hope I can make it next time.

08

대화를 듣고, Raven Elliott의 책 사인회에 관해 언급되지 않은 것을 고르시오.

[Cell phone rings.]
W : What's up, James?
M : Hey, Amanda. What are you doing this Friday?
W : Not much. Why?
M : Raven Elliott's book signing event is on Friday.
W : Really? That's November 3rd, right?
M : That's right. The event will be held at Pineway bookstore. You know, _____ ___________ _____ ______ _______.
W : Yes, I know. I heard it's really good. What time does the event start?
M : It starts at 7 p.m. Do you want to go?
W : Definitely! Do we need to sign up?
M : Yeah, I just did it. I'll send you the link to the form. You should _____ __ _____ and submit it soon.
W : Thanks. I'll do it today.
M : ✪ _________ ________ ________! It's limited to only 100 people.
W : Got it.

09

Grandhill Park Cleanup 행사에 관한 다음 내용을 듣고, 일치하지 않는 것을 고르시오.

M : Hello, listeners. I'm John Anderson, president of Greenism, an environmental volunteering group. We'll be holding the Grandhill Park Cleanup event on September 30th. Come and help ______ ____ _____ ______ _______! In this event, participants will pick up trash in pairs. It'll be good for the environment and our community. ✪ _______ ____ ____________ will join in our event, including local influencers and entertainers. I'm sure you'll have a meaningful time enjoying the beautiful scenery. At the end of the event, all participants ______ ____ ________ _____ _____ _____ made from recycled materials. You don't need to bring trash bags and gloves. We'll provide them! I look forward to seeing you all there!

10

다음 표를 보면서 대화를 듣고, 여자가 수강할 스포츠 프로그램을 고르시오.

M : Anna, what are you doing on your tablet?
W : I'm checking out the list of _______________ _________ _____________. Did you pick one?
M : No, I'm learning computer programming this time. Do you want some help?
W : Sure.
M : Which sports do you like?
W : ✪ ____________ _____ ___________. I don't like baseball that much.
M : Okay. This one is out. Some programs are limited to certain grades.
W : Yeah. We're in 2nd grade, so I cannot take this one.
M : ________ ______ _____ ______?
W : Hmm... I have a piano lesson on Mondays, so that day doesn't work for me.
M : Now you have two options.
W : Well, the school provides equipment for this program but not for the other one.
M : Which one do you like more?
W : I like this program better, and the school provides equipment for it. So I'll take this one.

11

대화를 듣고, 남자의 마지막 말에 대한 여자의 응답으로 가장 적절한 것을 고르시오.

M : Honey, shall we go to the new pizza place that you keep talking about?
W : I'd really love to. But I have to stay home to _________ ____ _________ ____________ soon. Do they deliver?
M : Let me check the delivery app. *[Tapping sound]* Yep, they have delivery service. Oh, ✪ _______ _______ _________ ________, your favorite.

12

대화를 듣고, 여자의 마지막 말에 대한 남자의 응답으로 가장 적절한 것을 고르시오.

W : Dad, I'm so excited. It's my first time to go on a school trip to the mountains in the fall.

M : Right. It'll be especially great to look at the stars outside. Maybe you'll need something to ________ ____________ _________ because it's getting colder at night.

W : So, do you think I should ✪ _________ _____ _______ ___________?

13

대화를 듣고, 남자의 마지막 말에 대한 여자의 응답으로 가장 적절한 것을 고르시오.

[Cell phone rings.]

W : Hello?

M : Good afternoon, Ms. Ford. This is Fine Line ____________ ________ _______.

W : Oh, hi.

M : I'm calling to let you know that your pants are ready to be picked up.

W : The pants with the broken zipper? Wow! You fixed them earlier than expected.

M : Yes. Do you want to stop by and pick them up sometime today?

W : Actually, I'm ✪ _____ ___ ________ on a business trip, but I'll be back on Sunday. I can come in then.

M : I'm sorry, but we're closed on Sundays.

W : I see. Then, how late are you open this coming Monday?

M : We're open until 7 p.m.

W : Hmm, I finish work at 6:30 p.m. I'm afraid _ _________ ____ _ _______ ____ _____.

M : It's alright. I can wait until you arrive.

14

대화를 듣고, 여자의 마지막 말에 대한 남자의 응답으로 가장 적절한 것을 고르시오.

W : Honey, do we have any plans this weekend?

M : Nothing special. Why?

W : I saw an interesting event in a brochure.

M : Oh, yeah? What's that?

W : Barefoot walking in the woods. Have you heard of it?

M : You mean ____________ ____________ ________? That doesn't sound comfortable. Why would people want to do that?

W : According to the brochure, it's effective for _____________ _______ _______.

M : Really? My feet have been a little bit sore these days. How does it work?

W : It works like a foot massage.

M : Aha! Walking in bare feet probably ✪ _____________ ________ _______________.

W : Yes. Plus, it can help you reduce stress.

M : It seems like barefoot walking will be good for both body and mind.

W : Exactly. I think we should do it.

15

다음 상황 설명을 듣고, Jack이 Amy에게 할 말로 가장 적절한 것을 고르시오. [3점]

M : Jack and Amy are members of their high school orchestra club. They're creating a video to introduce their club ✪ ___ _____ ____________ _________________ next month. Jack records the orchestra during practice and interviews some members. Amy says she'll edit the video clips so they can review them in their meeting tomorrow. However, she cannot finish the work because her laptop suddenly stops working. She takes her laptop to the computer service center, but it'll _______ ______ _______ ___ ____. Amy feels bad that she cannot complete the work by tomorrow and calls Jack to explain. Jack thinks that they have enough time to finish the video. So Jack wants to let Amy know that it's okay and offer to ___________ _______ ____________ _______. In this situation, what would Jack most likely say to Amy?

16~17

다음을 듣고, 물음에 답하시오.

W : Hello, students. As you know, sleep is common to all animals, but their sleep patterns vary in many ways. Today, we'll learn what makes ____________ ________ ________________.
First, what animals eat can impact their sleep patterns. As grass has much fewer calories than meat, large grass-eating animals sleep only a few hours and spend the majority of their time eating. Elephants sleep only three to four hours a day. Second, temperature affects animals' sleep patterns. High temperatures can cause ✪ ________ ____________ ___ _____________.
Thus, bats sleep during the day to avoid overheating. Next, another factor is the fear of dangerous meat-eating animals. For protection against these hunters, sheep generally sleep closely together. Finally, the living environment. Flamingos live in shallow waters that contain high amounts of salt. In such a harmful environment, there's no place _____ ________ ___ ____ ________. This is a reason why flamingos sleep standing up.
Now, let's watch a video clip.

▶ 정답 : 해설편 095쪽

VOCA LIST 21

회차별 영단어 QR 코드 ※ QR 코드를 스캔 후 모바일로 단어장처럼 학습할 수 있습니다.

● 고3 2024학년도 9월

01

001 □ weekend ⓝ 주말
002 □ hands-on ⓐ 직접 하는
003 □ a wide variety of 매우 다양한
004 □ turtle ⓝ 거북이
005 □ parrot ⓝ 앵무새
006 □ care for ~을 관리하다, 돌보다
007 □ interact with ~와 상호 작용하다
008 □ guidance ⓝ 지도
009 □ experienced ⓐ 숙련된
010 □ sign up ~을 등록시키다

02

011 □ staff ⓝ 직원
012 □ fitness ⓝ 건강, 적합성
013 □ lunch break 점심 시간
014 □ workout ⓝ 운동
015 □ offer ⓥ 제공하다
016 □ focus on ~에 집중하다
017 □ tired ⓐ 피곤한
018 □ take a rest 휴식을 취하다
019 □ energized ⓐ 활력이 넘치는
020 □ concentration ⓝ 집중
021 □ get back to ~로 돌아오다

03

022 □ consultant ⓝ 컨설턴트, 자문 위원
023 □ concern ⓝ 걱정, 우려
024 □ have difficulty ~ing ~하는 데 어려움이 있다
025 □ on time 제때
026 □ make a note 메모하다
027 □ efficient ⓐ 효율적인
028 □ assignment ⓝ 숙제
029 □ annoying ⓐ 성가신
030 □ get used to ~에 익숙하다
031 □ organize ⓥ 정리하다

04

032 □ community center 주민센터
033 □ take a look 살펴보다
034 □ in front of ~ 앞에
035 □ rug ⓝ 깔개
036 □ heart-shaped ⓐ 하트 모양의

05

037 □ traffic ⓝ 교통
038 □ safety ⓝ 안전
039 □ helpful ⓐ 도움이 되는, 유용한
040 □ reserve ⓥ 예약하다
041 □ gym ⓝ 체육관
042 □ handout ⓝ 배부 자료, 유인물
043 □ banner ⓝ 현수막
044 □ instructor ⓝ 강사
045 □ contact ⓥ 연락하다
046 □ snack ⓝ 간식

06

047 □ art museum 미술관
048 □ purchase ⓥ 구매하다
049 □ admission ⓝ 입장
050 □ oil painting 유화
051 □ for free 무료로
052 □ annual ⓐ 매년의
053 □ monthly ⓐ 월례의

07

054 □ perform ⓥ 공연하다
055 □ make it (시간에 맞게) 가다, 성공하다
056 □ part-time job 아르바이트
057 □ easily ad 쉽게
058 □ debate ⓝ 토론
059 □ competition ⓝ 대회, 경쟁
060 □ amazing ⓐ 굉장한, 멋진, 근사한
061 □ I'll keep my fingers crossed. 행운을 빌어줄게.

08

062 □ What's up? 잘 지내? 무슨 일이야?
063 □ signing event 사인회
064 □ bookstore ⓝ 서점
065 □ release ⓥ 출시하다
066 □ novel ⓝ 소설
067 □ Definitely! 물론이지!
068 □ form ⓝ (서류) 양식
069 □ fill out (서류를) 작성하다
070 □ limited to ~에 한정된, 제한된

09

071 □ clean up ~을 치우다
072 □ local ⓐ 지역의, 현지의
073 □ trash ⓝ 쓰레기
074 □ in pairs 짝지어서
075 □ celebrity ⓝ 유명 인사
076 □ meaningful ⓐ 유의미한
077 □ scenery ⓝ 경치
078 □ made from ~로 만들어진
079 □ recycle ⓥ 재활용하다

10

080 □ after-school ⓐ 방과 후의
081 □ anything but ~만 빼고 전부
082 □ certain ⓐ 특정한
083 □ grade ⓝ 학년
084 □ work for ~에 적합하다
085 □ equipment ⓝ 장비

11

086 □ deliver ⓥ 배달하다
087 □ delivery ⓝ 배달, 배송
088 □ shrimp ⓝ 새우
089 □ wonder ⓥ 궁금해하다
090 □ in person 직접

12

091 □ school trip 수학여행, 소풍
092 □ especially ad 특히
093 □ warm ⓐ 따뜻한
094 □ blanket ⓝ 담요
095 □ Cheer up. 기운 내.
096 □ shooting star 별똥별

13

097 □ clothing ⓝ 의류
098 □ repair ⓝ 수선 ⓥ 고치다, 수리하다
099 □ ready to ~할 준비가 된
100 □ pick up 수거하다
101 □ broken ⓐ 고장난, 부서진
102 □ stop by ~에 들르다
103 □ sometime ⓝ 언젠가
104 □ out of town 타지에 있는
105 □ business trip 출장
106 □ appreciate ⓥ 감사하다, 감상하다

14

107 □ brochure ⓝ 홍보 책자
108 □ barefoot ⓐ 맨발의 ad 맨발로
109 □ comfortable ⓐ 불편한
110 □ according to ~에 따르면
111 □ effective ⓐ 효과적인
112 □ relieve ⓥ 완화하다
113 □ sore ⓐ 아픈, 따가운
114 □ massage ⓝ 마사지
115 □ blood circulation 혈액순환
116 □ fault ⓝ 잘못

15

117 □ freshman ⓝ 신입생
118 □ practice ⓝ 연습, 관행
119 □ edit ⓥ 편집하다
120 □ review ⓥ 검토하다
121 □ laptop ⓝ 노트북
122 □ feel bad 속상하다, (몸이) 불편하다, 유감이다
123 □ complete ⓥ 완수하다
124 □ enough ⓐ 충분한
125 □ reschedule ⓥ (~의 일정을) 재조정하다

16~17

126 □ common ⓐ 흔한
127 □ vary ⓥ 다양하다, 다르다
128 □ differently ad 다르게
129 □ impact ⓥ 영향을 끼치다 ⓝ 영향, 여파, 충격
130 □ grass-eating ⓐ 초식의, 풀을 먹는
131 □ majority ⓝ 대다수
132 □ temperature ⓝ 온도
133 □ overheat ⓥ 과열되다
134 □ meat-eating ⓐ 육식의
135 □ protection ⓝ 보호
136 □ closely ad 가까이
137 □ shallow ⓐ 얕은
138 □ amount ⓝ 양
139 □ harmful ⓐ 해로운
140 □ lie down 눕다
141 □ endangered ⓐ 멸종 위기에 처한
142 □ make up for ~을 보상하다
143 □ factor ⓝ 요인

22회 ● 2023학년도 9월 모의평가 고3 영어 듣기

※ QR코드를 스캔하시면 듣기 방송을 청취하실 수 있습니다.

● 점수 표시가 없는 문항은 모두 2점 ● 문항수 17개 | 배점 37점 | 제한 시간 25분

1번부터 17번까지는 듣고 답하는 문제입니다. 1번부터 15번까지는 한 번만 들려주고, 16번부터 17번까지는 두 번 들려줍니다. 방송을 잘 듣고 답을 하시기 바랍니다.

MP3

1. 다음을 듣고, 남자가 하는 말의 목적으로 가장 적절한 것을 고르시오.

① 비상 시 대피 장소를 안내하려고
② 버스 출발 시간 변경을 공지하려고
③ 차량 운행 중 안전벨트 착용을 당부하려고
④ 버스 내 휴대 전화 통화 자제를 요청하려고
⑤ 차량 내 무선 인터넷 연결 방법을 설명하려고

2. 대화를 듣고, 여자의 의견으로 가장 적절한 것을 고르시오.

① 라디오를 듣는 것은 행복감을 높여 준다.
② 인터넷 발달은 라디오의 대중화에 기여한다.
③ 노년층을 위한 멀티미디어 교육이 필요하다.
④ 대화할 때는 상대방의 말을 경청하는 것이 중요하다.
⑤ 라디오 프로그램 편성 시 청취 연령을 고려해야 한다.

3. 대화를 듣고, 두 사람의 관계를 가장 잘 나타낸 것을 고르시오.

① 건축가 ― 건물 주인
② 코딩 강사 ― 수강생
③ 영양사 ― 과일 도매상
④ 음식 평론가 ― 요리사
⑤ 홍보 회사 직원 ― 과일 농장 주인

4. 대화를 듣고, 그림에서 대화의 내용과 일치하지 <u>않는</u> 것을 고르시오.

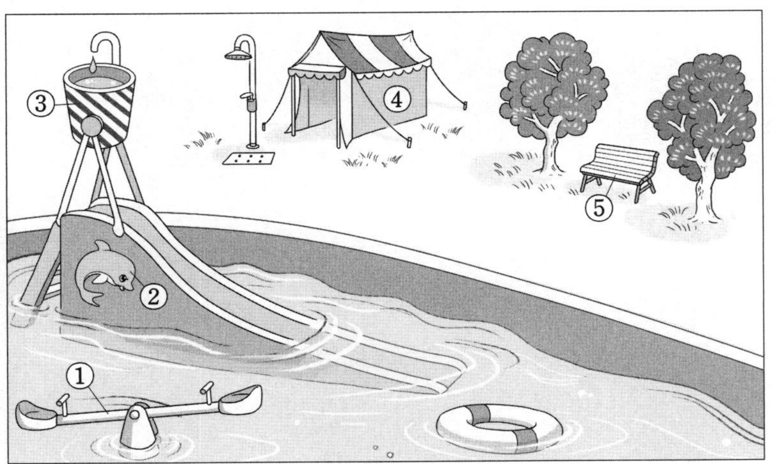

5. 대화를 듣고, 여자가 할 일로 가장 적절한 것을 고르시오.

① 현수막 걸기
② 의자 배치하기
③ 카메라 설치하기
④ 디제이 일정 조율하기
⑤ 마이크 상태 확인하기

6. 대화를 듣고, 남자가 지불할 금액을 고르시오. [3점]

① $45 ② $54 ③ $63 ④ $65 ⑤ $70

7. 대화를 듣고, 여자가 밴드 오디션에 참가하지 <u>않은</u> 이유를 고르시오.

① 기타에 문제가 생겨서
② 몸 상태가 좋지 않아서
③ 졸업 시험을 치러야 해서
④ 취업 면접 일정과 겹쳐서
⑤ 가족 행사에 참여해야 해서

8. 대화를 듣고, Kint Chocolate Museum에 관해 언급되지 <u>않은</u> 것을 고르시오.

① 위치
② 개관 시간
③ 입장료
④ 선물 가게
⑤ 휴관일

9. Endangered Animals Photo Exhibition에 관한 다음 내용을 듣고, 일치하지 <u>않는</u> 것을 고르시오.

① 3주 동안 지속된다.
② 멸종 위기 동물들의 사진 100장이 전시된다.
③ 사진 속 동물들이 멸종 위기에 처한 이유가 설명되어 있다.
④ 수익금 전액은 동물 보호 센터에 기부될 것이다.
⑤ 멸종 위기 동물 포스터를 무료로 제공할 것이다.

[해설편 p.095]

영어 영역(듣기)

10. 다음 표를 보면서 대화를 듣고, 두 사람이 주문할 기내 휴대용 가방을 고르시오.

Carry-On Bags for Kids

	Model	Price	Height (inches)	Color	Material
①	A	$35	14	Red	Plastic
②	B	$50	16	Blue	Plastic
③	C	$70	16	Pink	Fabric
④	D	$95	18	Black	Fabric
⑤	E	$110	18	Purple	Aluminum

11. 대화를 듣고, 남자의 마지막 말에 대한 여자의 응답으로 가장 적절한 것을 고르시오.

① Sorry. I broke the bottles by accident.
② Sure. Let's remove the labels together.
③ You shouldn't. Your hands are still dirty.
④ I agree. Recycled paper bags are cheaper.
⑤ No problem. I'm going to order some bottles.

12. 대화를 듣고, 여자의 마지막 말에 대한 남자의 응답으로 가장 적절한 것을 고르시오.

① Sounds wonderful! That fits our budget.
② Terrific! I'm glad we're done with the project.
③ Too bad. There's no ticket available for your trip.
④ Okay. I'll reschedule the meeting and let you know.
⑤ Thanks for offering. I'll be happy to join your team.

13. 대화를 듣고, 남자의 마지막 말에 대한 여자의 응답으로 가장 적절한 것을 고르시오.

Woman: ______________________

① Of course. I accept the instructor position.
② Great. Let me sign up for the 8 p.m. class, then.
③ Please write your name down on the waiting list.
④ Thanks for the refund of my class registration fee.
⑤ Sounds exciting. Good luck on your ballet performance.

14. 대화를 듣고, 여자의 마지막 말에 대한 남자의 응답으로 가장 적절한 것을 고르시오. [3점]

Man: ______________________

① Thanks for telling me. I'll call her and apologize.
② Good idea. Don't forget to bring your tennis shoes.
③ Not really. The match wasn't as good as I expected.
④ Fine. Promise me you'll do your best to win the match.
⑤ I understand. I'll give you more time to finish the series.

15. 다음 상황 설명을 듣고, Randy가 Angela에게 할 말로 가장 적절한 것을 고르시오. [3점]

Randy: ______________________

① Why don't you find members to form a drone racing club?
② I think you should become friends with the transfer student.
③ Practice more if you want to participate in the next race.
④ Safety comes first when it comes to flying drones.
⑤ How about buying a drone of your own?

[16～17] 다음을 듣고, 물음에 답하시오.

16. 여자가 하는 말의 주제로 가장 적절한 것은?

① positive effects of plants on insects
② diverse purposes of plant communication
③ different methods for controlling toxic chemicals
④ key aspects of non-verbal human communication
⑤ important roles of plants in balancing the food chain

17. 언급된 식물이 아닌 것은?

① cotton plants ② mustard plants ③ pine trees
④ tomato plants ⑤ walnut trees

[해설편 p.097]

Dictation 22

✪ 표기에는 듣기 어려운 발음이 포함되어 있습니다. 귀 기울여 듣고 받아쓰세요. ● 고3 2023학년도 9월

※ QR 코드를 스캔하시면 듣기 방송이 나옵니다. 듣기 방송을 들으며 다음 빈칸을 채우시오. ● 제한 시간 : 25분

01

다음을 듣고, 남자가 하는 말의 목적으로 가장 적절한 것을 고르시오.

M : Good afternoon, Bolden Express Bus passengers. My name is Logan Campbell, and I'll be your bus driver today. ✪ _________ _________, I'd like to ask you to _________ _________ _________ _________ _________ on the bus. Loud conversations on the phone may bother the other passengers. We kindly ask you to wait until you've reached your destination to talk on the phone. If you must answer a call, please keep it short and _________ _________ _________ while speaking on the phone. Thank you for your cooperation.

02

대화를 듣고, 여자의 의견으로 가장 적절한 것을 고르시오.

M : Hi, Grandma. What are you doing?

W : I'm listening to the radio. I really like it.

M : I wonder why some people love the radio. _________ _________ _________.

W : You may think so. But listening to the radio can increase your sense of happiness.

M : I don't understand.

W : Well, by listening to a radio talk show, for example, you often feel like you're part of the conversation.

M : Hmm... That makes sense.

W : Then, you feel ✪ _________ _________ _________ _________ _________.

M : And that can eventually make you happy, right?

W : That's correct. Also, when you feel down, listening to the radio brings you joy and good laughs.

M : Wow. I never thought that the radio has this much power.

W : See? Listening to the radio _________ _________ _________.

M : Now I understand why you love the radio so much.

03

대화를 듣고, 두 사람의 관계를 가장 잘 나타낸 것을 고르시오.

[Telephone rings.]

W : Good morning. Cathy Sullivan speaking.

M : Hello, Ms. Sullivan. This is Josh Gordon from Gordon's Fresh Fruits.

W : Hi, Mr. Gordon! How's this year's fruit harvest?

M : This has been the best year since I started my farm. I've already begun packaging the summer fruits for sale.

W : That's good to hear. How may I help you today?

M : Well, I'd like to promote my fruit farm more actively on the Internet.

W : In that case, we can _________ _________ _________ _________ and display it on personal blogs and social networking sites.

M : That sounds like a good idea.

W : Our advertisements will definitely help you _________ _________ _________ and increase your fruit sales.

M : Sounds wonderful. When can you start ✪ _________ _________ _________?

W : I'll ask my boss and call you back.

M : Great. Thank you.

04

대화를 듣고, 그림에서 대화의 내용과 일치하지 <u>않는</u> 것을 고르시오.

M : Honey, let's take Jack to the outdoor pool at the park across the road.

W : Does the park have a pool?

M : Yes. Check out this picture I found on the Internet. Look! There's a see-saw in the pool.

W : I'm sure he'd want to go on it with you. And I see a ✪ _________ _________ _________ _________ on the slide.

M : Jack loves dolphins. I bet he'll _________ _________ _________ _________ _________ _________ all day.

W : I think so, too. There's a ✪ _________ _________ at the top of the slide. What's that for?

M : Hmm... I think it pours out water every few minutes. Look at the two tents near the shower.

W : Those must be _________ _________ _________.

M : That's convenient. Oh, I see a bench between the trees.

W : We could sit there while Jack plays in the pool.

M : Yeah. That'll be nice. Let's get ready to go.

05

대화를 듣고, 여자가 할 일로 가장 적절한 것을 고르시오.

W : Hi, Mr. Kane. How's the preparation going for tomorrow's outdoor school concert?

M : Hi, Ms. Anderson. I've been working on it all morning, and I just finished confirming the schedule with the DJ.

W : Would you like me to help you with anything?

M : That would be great. There are still a few more things that need to be done.

W : Okay. Do you want me to _________ _________ _________ for the audience?

M : No. That's not necessary. I have volunteers to do that this afternoon.

W : I see. How about ✪ _________ _________ _________ _________? I don't see them anywhere.

M : I'll take care of it when they arrive. Actually, it would be helpful if you _________ _________ _________ _________ on the stage.

W : Sure. I'll do that.

M : Great! The camera is on that table. Thank you.

Dictation 22

06

대화를 듣고, 남자가 지불할 금액을 고르시오. [3점]

W : Welcome to the Mentonberg Paper Art Gallery. How may I help you?
M : Hi. I need four admission tickets. How much do they cost?
W : It's $15 per adult and $10 per child under the age of 13.
M : My twin daughters are only 10 years old, so I'll get __________ __________ __________ __________ __________ __________ __________.
W : Okay. So, you want four tickets.
M : Yes. We're also interested in your special program. How much is it?
W : You mean the "Traditional Paper-Making" program? It's $5 per person.
M : Good. All four of us ✪ __________ __________ __________ __________ in the program.
W : All right. So, __________ __________ __________. Admission tickets for two adults and two children. Plus, four special program tickets, right?
M : That's right. Can I get the 10% resident discount off the total price?
W : Sure. Do you have your IDs with you?
M : Yeah. Here are our IDs and my credit card.

07

대화를 듣고, 여자가 밴드 오디션에 참가하지 않은 이유를 고르시오.

M : Hi, Nancy. How are you today? I heard you were sick last week.
W : Hello, Scott. Yes. I had a stomachache but I'm all right now.
M : I'm glad to hear that. So, __________ __________ __________ __________ __________ yesterday?
W : Actually, I didn't go to the audition.
M : Really? Why not? Did you have to do something with your family?
W : Not at all. It had nothing to do with my family.
M : Was there a problem with your guitar again?
W : No. My guitar works just fine.
M : Then, why didn't you go to the audition?
W : I __________ __________ __________ __________ with a company I want to work for. Unfortunately, it was at the same time as the audition.
M : Well, you were worried about what you should do ✪ __________ __________ __________. How did the interview go?
W : __________ __________ __________ __________. Thanks for asking.

08

대화를 듣고, Kint Chocolate Museum에 관해 언급되지 않은 것을 고르시오.

M : Ms. Brown. Have you decided where you're taking the students on the school trip next month?
W : Yes, Principal Thompson. We're going to the Kint Chocolate Museum.
M : Oh, I've heard about that museum. It's located in the center of Queen's City, right?
W : That's right. We're going to leave at 9 a.m. from the school because the museum opens at 10 a.m.
M : I didn't know it takes an hour to get there.
W : It doesn't. But we wanted to make sure that __________ __________ __________.
M : ✪ __________ __________! How about the admission fee?
W : Each entry ticket costs $12 and includes a chocolate-tasting event.
M : The students will love it. I'm sure they'll want to buy some chocolates.
W : Absolutely. The museum is __________ __________ __________ __________ __________, and it has various chocolate-related items.
M : Sounds great!

09

Endangered Animals Photo Exhibition에 관한 다음 내용을 듣고, 일치하지 않는 것을 고르시오.

W : Hello, listeners. If you're ✪ __________ __________ __________ __________, don't miss the Endangered Animals Photo Exhibition at the Kenton Cultural Center. It starts on December 2nd, and continues for three weeks. Wildlife photographer, Richard Burrow, has taken pictures of many endangered species around the world. The exhibition displays 100 pictures of endangered animals, including birds and fish. Under the photographs, there are explanations for why the animals in the photos are ✪ __________ __________ __________ __________. Admission will be $20, and all the profits from the exhibition will be donated to an animal-protection center. At the end of the exhibition hall, __________ __________ __________ __________ __________ will be for sale at $5 each. For more information, please visit the website, www.kentonculturalcenter.com.

10

다음 표를 보면서 대화를 듣고, 두 사람이 주문할 기내 휴대용 가방을 고르시오.

W : Honey. Could you come here and help me __________ __________ __________ __________ for Sarah?
M : Of course. She's old enough to have her own carry-on bag for our family trip next month.
W : Right. Look at this website. There are five models to choose from.
M : Hmm... How much should we spend?
W : Let's not spend more than $100.
M : That sounds reasonable. What about the size? How tall should it be?
W : The one that's 14 inches in height isn't big enough. She always likes to __________ __________ __________ __________ __________ with her.
M : Okay. Do you think she'd like the black one?
W : No. She doesn't like the color black. So, there are only two options left.
M : I don't think ✪ __________ __________ __________ __________ __________. It'll easily get dirty.
W : I agree. Let's order the other one.

11

대화를 듣고, 남자의 마지막 말에 대한 여자의 응답으로 가장 적절한 것을 고르시오.

M : Rachel, we have too many plastic bottles to throw away. Let's take them to the recycling area.

W : Okay, Dad. But wait. There are ✪ _________ _________ _________ _________ _________. They need to be removed first.

M : Oh, you're right! Then, could you give me a hand?

12

대화를 듣고, 여자의 마지막 말에 대한 남자의 응답으로 가장 적절한 것을 고르시오.

W : Daniel, I'm sorry but can we ✪ _________ _________ _________ _________? I cannot attend it tomorrow.

M : Oh. It's impossible to have this meeting without your presentation, Ms. Robinson. May I ask what the problem is?

W : Well, there was _________ _________ _________ _________ to my business trip schedule. I'll be available any day after next Monday.

13

대화를 듣고, 남자의 마지막 말에 대한 여자의 응답으로 가장 적절한 것을 고르시오.

M : Good afternoon. Welcome to Swan Palace Ballet Studio.

W : Hello. I'm here to register for one of your classes.

M : Great. We offer three levels of classes from beginner to advanced. Which class do you want to take?

W : I'd like to take the advanced class.

M : Okay. Do you have any particular instructor in mind?

W : Actually, I do. I heard Gina Miller _________ _________ _________ _________ _________.

M : Indeed. She's a popular instructor. She has _________ _________ _________ on Wednesdays, one at 7 p.m. and one at 8 p.m.

W : I think the 7 p.m. class would be good.

M : Sure. Let me check if there are ✪ _________ _________ _________. *[Typing sound]* Oh, her 7 p.m. class is full. Sorry.

W : Hmm... Then, what about the 8 p.m. class? I really want to take her class.

M : One moment, please. *[Pause]* Yes, there's _________ _________ _________.

14

대화를 듣고, 여자의 마지막 말에 대한 남자의 응답으로 가장 적절한 것을 고르시오. **[3점]**

[Cell phone rings.]

M : Hello, Clara. What's up?

W : Hi, Brian. I've been trying to reach you all morning. Why didn't you answer your phone?

M : Sorry. I just woke up. What's the matter?

W : Jane had her tennis match early this morning. We promised her that we would come and cheer for her.

M : Oh, right! That was this morning! I forgot.

W : Oh, no. How could you forget?

M : I _________ _________ _________ _________ watching a fascinating TV series. I guess Jane's tennis match completely ✪ _________ _________ _________.

W : Well, after the match, Jane told me that she was disappointed because you didn't come.

M : Oh, I feel _________ _________ _________ _________ _________.

W : I think it would be good if you told her that you didn't mean to miss it.

15

다음 상황 설명을 듣고, Randy가 Angela에게 할 말로 가장 적절한 것을 고르시오. **[3점]**

M : Angela transferred to a new school a few months ago. She has adjusted to life at the new school and has made many new friends. However, there's one thing that she isn't happy about. Her previous school had _________ _________ _________ _________, but her new school doesn't. One day, she meets Randy, one of her old club members, and talks about how much she ✪ _________ _________ _________ _________. Randy thinks that there could be some students in Angela's new school who would love racing drones. So, Randy wants to suggest to Angela that she _________ _________ _________ to start a drone racing club. In this situation, what would Randy most likely say to Angela?

16~17

다음을 듣고, 물음에 답하시오.

W : Good morning, students. Did you know that plants can send out messages? Today, we're going to learn about the various reasons that plants communicate. First, plants communicate to _________ _________ _________. When cotton plants are attacked by bugs, these plants send out a chemical signal to attract the bugs' natural enemy that eats them. Second, plants communicate to ✪ _________ _________ _________. When mustard plants recognize their family members by exchanging chemical signals, they grow shorter roots to avoid competing with one another. Third, some plants communicate with other plant species to ✪ _________ _________ _________. For example, tomato plants use low vibrating sounds to attract other plants that produce a smell, which is unpleasant to insects. Last, plants communicate to warn other plants and defend their territory. Walnut trees spread toxic chemicals to hurt or kill plants nearby. It's their way of saying, "Stay away from me." Now, let's watch some related videos.

▶ 정답 : 해설편 099쪽

VOCA LIST 22

회차별 영단어 QR 코드 ※ QR 코드를 스캔 후 모바일로 단어장처럼 학습할 수 있습니다.

● 고3 2023학년도 9월

01

001 □ passenger ⓝ 승객
002 □ depart ⓥ 출발하다, 떠나다
003 □ avoid ⓥ 피하다
004 □ loud ⓐ 큰, 시끄러운
005 □ conversation ⓝ 대화
006 □ bother ⓥ 귀찮게 하다, 성가시게 하다
007 □ destination ⓝ 목적지
008 □ answer a call 전화를 받다
009 □ lower ⓥ 낮추다

02

010 □ boring ⓐ 지루한
011 □ sense of happiness 행복감
012 □ feel like ~처럼 느끼다
013 □ make sense 일리가 있다
014 □ emotionally ad 감정적으로, 정서적으로
015 □ lonely ⓐ 외로운
016 □ boost ⓥ 증진하다, 높이다

03

017 □ harvest ⓝ 수확 ⓥ 수확하다
018 □ farm ⓝ 농장
019 □ package ⓥ 포장하다
020 □ promote ⓥ 홍보하다
021 □ display ⓥ 보여주다, 전시하다
022 □ advertisement ⓝ 광고
023 □ attract ⓥ (고객을) 유치하다, 매혹시키다
024 □ call back (전화를) 회신하다

04

025 □ dolphin ⓝ 돌고래
026 □ slide ⓝ 미끄럼틀 ⓥ 미끄러지다
027 □ bucket ⓝ 양동이
028 □ at the top of ~의 위에
029 □ pour ⓥ 붓다
030 □ every few minutes 몇 분마다
031 □ change clothes 옷을 갈아입다
032 □ convenient ⓐ 편리한
033 □ get ready to ~할 준비를 하다

05

034 □ preparation ⓝ 준비, 대비
035 □ confirm ⓥ (맞음을) 확인하다
036 □ place ⓥ 배치하다, 놓다
037 □ audience ⓝ 관객, 청중
038 □ necessary ⓐ 필요한
039 □ volunteer ⓝ 자원봉사자
040 □ hang up 걸다
041 □ set up 설치하다
042 □ stage ⓝ 무대

06

043 □ admission ticket 입장권
044 □ cost ⓥ ~의 비용이 들다
045 □ adult ⓝ 성인, 어른
046 □ twin ⓝ 쌍둥이
047 □ interested in ~에 관심이 있는
048 □ resident ⓝ 주민, 거주자

07

049 □ have a stomachache 배가 아프다
050 □ audition ⓝ 오디션
051 □ have nothing to do with ~와 관련이 없다
052 □ work fine 잘 작동하다
053 □ job interview 일자리 면접
054 □ work for ~에서 일하다
055 □ worried ⓐ 걱정하는
056 □ graduate ⓥ 졸업하다
057 □ go well 잘 진행되다

08

058 □ trip ⓝ 여행
059 □ museum ⓝ 박물관
060 □ be located in ~에 위치하다
061 □ in the center of ~의 중심부에
062 □ make sure 확실히 ~하다
063 □ admission fee 입장료
064 □ entry ⓝ 입장
065 □ famous for ~로 유명한
066 □ various ⓐ 다양한

09

067 □ wildlife ⓝ 야생 동물
068 □ endangered ⓐ 멸종 위기에 처한
069 □ explanation ⓝ 설명
070 □ in danger of ~의 위험에 처한
071 □ extinction ⓝ 멸종
072 □ profit ⓝ 수익(금)
073 □ donate ⓥ 기부하다
074 □ protection ⓝ 보호
075 □ at the end of ~의 끝에
076 □ for sale 팔려고 내놓은

10

077 □ carry-on bag 기내용 휴대 가방
078 □ spend ⓥ 소비하다, 쓰다
079 □ reasonable ⓐ 적당한, 합리적인
080 □ height ⓝ 높이
081 □ fabric ⓝ 천, 직물
082 □ practical ⓐ 실용적인
083 □ easily ad 쉽게
084 □ get dirty 더러워지다

11

085 □ bottle ⓝ 병
086 □ recycling ⓝ 재활용
087 □ remove ⓥ 제거하다
088 □ give a hand 도와주다
089 □ break ⓥ 깨다, 부수다
090 □ by accident 실수로, 우연히
091 □ cheap ⓐ 값싼
092 □ No problem. 문제 없어요.

12

093 □ reschedule ⓥ (일정을) 재조정하다
094 □ attend ⓥ 참석하다
095 □ impossible ⓐ 불가능한
096 □ presentation ⓝ 발표
097 □ last minute change 막바지 변경 사항
098 □ business trip 출장
099 □ available ⓐ (사람에게) 시간이 있는
100 □ fit ⓥ 맞다, 적합하다
101 □ budget ⓝ 예산
102 □ terrific ⓐ 멋진, 대단한
103 □ be done with ~을 끝내다

13

104 □ register for ~에 등록하다
105 □ beginner ⓝ 초급자 ⓐ 초급의
106 □ advanced ⓐ 고급의
107 □ have in mind ~을 염두에 두다
108 □ instructor ⓝ 강사
109 □ popular ⓐ 인기 있는
110 □ spot ⓝ (특정한) 장소, 자리
111 □ sign up for ~에 등록하다

14

112 □ reach ⓥ ~에게 연락하다
113 □ match ⓝ 시합
114 □ stay up all night 밤을 새다
115 □ fascinating ⓐ 대단히 흥미로운, 매력적인
116 □ slip one's mind 잊어버리다
117 □ disappointed ⓐ 실망한
118 □ awful ⓐ 끔찍한, 지독한
119 □ apologize ⓥ 사과하다

15

120 □ transfer to ~로 옮기다
121 □ adjust ⓥ 적응하다
122 □ previous ⓐ 이전의
123 □ drone ⓝ 드론, 무인 항공기
124 □ form ⓥ 만들다, 형성하다
125 □ safety ⓝ 안전
126 □ when it comes to ~에 관해서는
127 □ How about ~ing ~? ~하는 게 어때?

16~17

128 □ send out 내보내다
129 □ call for help 도움을 청하다
130 □ attack ⓥ 공격하다 ⓝ 공격
131 □ natural enemy 천적
132 □ recognize ⓥ 인식하다, 알아보다
133 □ relative ⓝ 친척
134 □ exchange ⓥ 교환하다
135 □ compete with ~와 경쟁하다
136 □ scare away ~을 겁주어 쫓아버리다
137 □ unpleasant ⓐ 불쾌한
138 □ defend ⓥ 지키다, 방어하다
139 □ stay away from ~에게서 떨어지다
140 □ non-verbal ⓐ 비언어적인

23회 • 2022학년도 9월 모의평가 고3 영어 듣기

※ QR코드를 스캔하시면 듣기 방송을 청취하실 수 있습니다.

● 점수 표시가 없는 문항은 모두 2점 ● 문항수 17개 | 배점 37점 | 제한 시간 25분

1번부터 17번까지는 듣고 답하는 문제입니다. 1번부터 15번까지는 한 번만 들려주고, 16번부터 17번까지는 두 번 들려줍니다. 방송을 잘 듣고 답을 하시기 바랍니다.

1. 다음을 듣고, 남자가 하는 말의 목적으로 가장 적절한 것을 고르시오.

① 학생회장 선거 투표 결과를 공지하려고
② 음악 경연 대회 참가 신청을 권장하려고
③ 홈 쇼핑 가전제품 구매 방법을 설명하려고
④ 새로운 음악 프로그램 방송 일정을 안내하려고
⑤ 노래 경연 우승자 선정을 위한 투표를 독려하려고

2. 대화를 듣고, 여자의 의견으로 가장 적절한 것을 고르시오.

① 아이들은 집안일을 함으로써 자존감을 높일 수 있다.
② 아이들의 나이에 맞는 균형 잡힌 식단 관리가 필요하다.
③ 집안일을 통해 아이들에게 경제관념을 심어 줄 수 있다.
④ 적절한 보상은 아이들의 독서 습관 형성에 도움이 된다.
⑤ 여행을 통해 아이들에게 가족의 중요성을 일깨워 줄 수 있다.

3. 대화를 듣고, 두 사람의 관계를 가장 잘 나타낸 것을 고르시오.

① 정원사 – 파티 플래너
② 꽃집 점원 – 식당 주인
③ 꽃꽂이 강사 – 수강생
④ 식물학 교수 – 행정실 직원
⑤ 잡지 편집장 – 음식 칼럼니스트

4. 대화를 듣고, 그림에서 대화의 내용과 일치하지 않는 것을 고르시오.

5. 대화를 듣고, 남자가 할 일로 가장 적절한 것을 고르시오.

① 필터 주문하기
② 어항 물 갈기
③ 체리 주스 만들기
④ 세탁물 맡기기
⑤ 히터 온도 조절하기

6. 대화를 듣고, 여자가 지불할 금액을 고르시오.

① $50 ② $60 ③ $65 ④ $75 ⑤ $85

7. 대화를 듣고, 남자가 Career Day 행사 장소를 변경하려는 이유를 고르시오.

① 초청 강사의 요청이 있어서
② 다른 행사와 장소가 겹쳐서
③ 신청 학생이 예상보다 많아서
④ 보수 공사 소음이 시끄러워서
⑤ 세미나실 프로젝터가 고장 나서

8. 대화를 듣고, Digital Publishing Workshop에 관해 언급되지 않은 것을 고르시오.

① 목적
② 대상
③ 날짜
④ 등록 방법
⑤ 준비물

9. 2021 Playground in the Park에 관한 다음 내용을 듣고, 일치하지 않는 것을 고르시오.

① 라디오 방송국이 주최한다.
② 다섯 개의 놀이 구역이 있다.
③ 최대 60명의 아이들이 참여할 수 있다.
④ 행사장에서 음식을 구입할 수 없다.
⑤ 비가 오면 일정이 조정된다.

[해설편 p.100]

영어 영역[듣기]

10. 다음 표를 보면서 대화를 듣고, 여자가 구매할 블루투스 이어폰을 고르시오.

Bluetooth Earphones

	Model	Battery Life	Wireless Charging	Price	Case Cover Material
①	A	2 hours	×	$49.99	Silicone
②	B	3 hours	○	$69.99	Silicone
③	C	3 hours	×	$79.99	Leather
④	D	4 hours	○	$89.99	Leather
⑤	E	5 hours	○	$109.99	Leather

11. 대화를 듣고, 여자의 마지막 말에 대한 남자의 응답으로 가장 적절한 것을 고르시오.

① Yes. I only communicate face-to-face.
② Me, too. Don't put me in the chat room.
③ Right. We don't have biology class today.
④ No. We've already finished our group project.
⑤ Sure. I'll open a chat room and invite everyone.

12. 대화를 듣고, 남자의 마지막 말에 대한 여자의 응답으로 가장 적절한 것을 고르시오.

① Thank you. I'm relieved to hear that.
② It's terrible. I'll go check if it's ready.
③ That's great. It's good to be back home.
④ Okay. You're free to read in the living room.
⑤ No way. Turn off the lights when you go to bed.

13. 대화를 듣고, 여자의 마지막 말에 대한 남자의 응답으로 가장 적절한 것을 고르시오. [3점]

Man: ______________________

① Too bad. I hope you'll feel better soon.
② Of course. I'm sure you'll win the race.
③ I see. I've never been a cycling champion.
④ All right. I'll be just fine at the competition.
⑤ Terrific. I'm also looking forward to the camp.

14. 대화를 듣고, 남자의 마지막 말에 대한 여자의 응답으로 가장 적절한 것을 고르시오.

Woman: ______________________

① No problem. I can email you the details of our program.
② No worries. I'll let you know what day is available.
③ That's right. I need to get more students.
④ That's true. It's difficult to explain scientific principles.
⑤ Brilliant. I can recommend a good science fiction movie.

15. 다음 상황 설명을 듣고, Megan이 Philip에게 할 말로 가장 적절한 것을 고르시오. [3점]

Megan: ______________________

① You can sign up for our membership and get a discount.
② I regret to say that I can't find your membership number.
③ Unfortunately, the poster you're looking for is not for sale.
④ Congratulations on the successful release of your new book.
⑤ I'm afraid the members' discount doesn't apply to this book.

[16~17] 다음을 듣고, 물음에 답하시오.

16. 여자가 하는 말의 주제로 가장 적절한 것은? [3점]

① what issues arise from abandoned pets
② how city growth affected wildlife diversity
③ why wild animals came to flourish in cities
④ ways to make cities environmentally friendly
⑤ problems between humans and animals in cities

17. 언급된 도시가 <u>아닌</u> 것은?

① Paris ② London ③ Delhi
④ Bangkok ⑤ New York City

[해설편 p.102]

※ QR 코드를 스캔하시면 듣기 방송이 나옵니다. 듣기 방송을 들으며 다음 빈칸을 채우시오. ● 제한 시간 : 25분

01
다음을 듣고, 남자가 하는 말의 목적으로 가장 적절한 것을 고르시오.

M : Welcome back to the final episode of *Tomorrow's Singer*. We hope you enjoyed the performances of our two finalists. Now, it's time to ✪ __________ __________ __________ __________ __________ __________ __________. Vote now by __________ __________ __________ __________ __________ __________ __________ to the number at the bottom of your TV screen. This is your last chance to help your favorite contestant become a super star. You can also win exciting prizes just by voting. Remember voting closes in only five minutes. So, __________ __________ __________ now and decide who'll be tomorrow's singer. We'll be right back after a short commercial break.

02
대화를 듣고, 여자의 의견으로 가장 적절한 것을 고르시오.

M : Honey, I just saw Amy folding laundry in the living room. Did you ask her to do it?
W : Well, she said she wanted to help with the housework.
M : That's fine. But don't you think she's too young to do housework? She's just six years old.
W : Maybe. But I think doing housework ✪ __________ __________ __________ __________ __________.
M : Why do you think so?
W : I read in a book that __________ __________ __________ __________ __________, they feel like they're more important to the family.
M : Hmm, that makes sense.
W : Besides, children often __________ __________ __________ __________ __________ from completing household tasks.
M : Oh, and maybe it could help Amy to feel proud of herself, too.
W : Exactly. That's why children who do housework often have higher self-esteem.
M : You're right. Then let's think about other kinds of housework Amy would enjoy.
W : Sounds good.

03
대화를 듣고, 두 사람의 관계를 가장 잘 나타낸 것을 고르시오.

W : Hello, Mr. Miller. __________ __________ __________ __________. How's your business?
M : The restaurant is doing pretty good. Jessica, I'd like to buy some purple flowers.
W : I'm sorry. We don't have any purple flowers right now. Why are you looking for that specific color?
M : I need that color to decorate my restaurant. My customer is ✪ __________ __________ __________ __________ __________, and its logo is purple.
W : I see. When do you need the flowers?
M : This Friday.
W : Okay. Shall I ask my boss to __________ __________ __________?
M : That'd be perfect. I didn't know there were purple lilies.
W : They're rare and __________ __________ __________ __________ __________. They'd be a great fit for this event in your restaurant.
M : Great to know. And I could put notes about the flower's meaning on the tables.
W : Good idea. My boss will call you with the details.
M : Thanks for all your help.

04
대화를 듣고, 그림에서 대화의 내용과 일치하지 않는 것을 고르시오.

M : Hi, Jane. What are you doing?
W : Hi, Sam. I'm reading a blog about that book cafe we used to visit.
M : Oh, I heard that ✪ __________ __________ __________ __________.
W : Right. Take a look at this picture of the first floor. I love the stairs next to the windows.
M : Yeah, the view from the stairs is amazing.
W : For sure. Do you remember the square clock on the wall?
M : Of course. It's been there since we first visited. Oh, there are __________ __________ __________ __________ __________ now.
W : Fantastic. I love to listen to music while I read.
M : That's the best. And look at the stripe-patterned cushion on the chair. I love it.
W : So do I. I actually have the same one at home.
M : Cool. Hey, __________ __________ __________ __________ on the table.
W : Yeah, it'll be easier to read now. I really like how the book cafe has been remodeled.

05
대화를 듣고, 남자가 할 일로 가장 적절한 것을 고르시오.

W : Hi, honey. How was school today?
M : Fine, Mom. But I spilled some cherry juice on my shirt.
W : Don't worry. I'll take it to the dry cleaner's later.
M : Thanks. By the way, what are you doing?
W : I was just about to __________ __________ __________ in the fish tank.
M : Do you need some help?
W : No, it's okay. But thanks for asking.
M : Okay. Be careful with the water heater. You almost broke it last time.
W : I'm not going to make the same mistake twice. Oh, we need to ✪ __________ __________ __________ in the tank with a new one.
M : Really? But we're __________ __________ __________. Should I order some online right now?
W : Great.
M : Okay, I'll do it. I think they'll arrive in about two days.

Dictation 23

06

대화를 듣고, 여자가 지불할 금액을 고르시오.

M : Hello. May I help you?

W : Yes. I need a badminton racket for my son. He's starting lessons next week.

M : How old is your son?

W : Seven. What's a good one?

M : How about this one? It's only $20 and perfect for children that age.

W : Okay. I'll take it.

M : What about ________ ________ ________ in case you want to play with your son?

W : Oh, that's a great idea.

M : I recommend these two. This is $30 and the other is $55. But the $55 racket is much lighter.

W : I really like the lighter one, but ✪ ________ ________ ________.

M : Well, if you buy the lighter one, I can ________ ________ ________ ________ worth $10 for free. You'll need shuttlecocks anyway.

W : That's a good deal. Then I'll get the lighter one.

M : Okay. So, the rackets for you and your son. And of course, the free shuttlecocks.

W : Thank you. Here's my credit card.

07

대화를 듣고, 남자가 Career Day 행사 장소를 변경하려는 이유를 고르시오.

W : Mr. Bresnan, how's the preparation for this month's Career Day going?

M : Pretty well, Ms. Potter. This time, a local baker is visiting our school to speak with our students.

W : It'll be good for our students to learn about what bakers do. The event will be held in the seminar room tomorrow, right?

M : Well, I think I have to ________ ________ ________ ________ ________ ________.

W : Why? Is there another event scheduled in that room?

M : No, I already checked.

W : Then is it ________ ________ ________ ________ ________ going on next door?

M : That's not an issue. It starts after school.

W : So, why do you want to change the place?

M : Actually, ✪ ________ ________ ________ ________ than I expected.

W : Oh, I see. How about using the conference room, then? It has more space.

M : Great idea. I'll go check if it's available and let the students know.

08

대화를 듣고, Digital Publishing Workshop에 관해 언급되지 않은 것을 고르시오.

[Cell phone rings.]

M : Hey, Charlotte. What's up?

W : Hi, Chris. I'm looking at information about an online course called Digital Publishing Workshop. How about taking it with me?

M : Sounds interesting. Tell me more.

W : The purpose of the workshop is to provide guidelines for ________ ________ ________ ________ ________. What do you think?

M : Actually, I've been dreaming about publishing my own e-books. But, is it okay if I ________ ________ ________ ________?

W : Of course. It's ✪ ________ ________ ________ ________ who're just starting out.

M : Great. Then when is the workshop?

W : It's held for three days from October 27th to 29th.

M : Excellent. Midterm exams will be over by then. Do we need to register?

W : Yes. We can do it online. There's a link to the registration page on our library's website.

M : Okay. Let's sign up.

09

2021 Playground in the Park에 관한 다음 내용을 듣고, 일치하지 않는 것을 고르시오.

W : Hello, listeners. Would you like your kids to have a good time in a park ________ ________ ________ ________ ________ ________? Then there's an exciting event for all of you. Our radio station is hosting the 2021 Playground in the Park. This event will be on Saturday, September 25th from 10 a.m. to 3 p.m. at the Queens Quarter Park. There are five play zones, including giant seesaws, tree houses, and elephant-shaped slides. Hurry and sign up now because ________ ________ ________ ________ ________ can participate in this event. There'll be food trucks, so you can ✪ ________ ________ ________ ________ ________ at the event site. This is an outdoor event, so the event will be rescheduled if it rains. Visit our website for more information.

10

다음 표를 보면서 대화를 듣고, 여자가 구매할 블루투스 이어폰을 고르시오.

M : Welcome to Aiden's Electronics. What can I do for you?

W : Hi. I'm looking for bluetooth earphones.

M : Okay. These are the five models we carry. Do you have any particular brand in mind?

W : No, but I want earphones with a battery that ________ ________ ________ ________ ________. It takes me more than two hours to go to work.

M : All right. Are you interested in wireless charging?

W : Yes. It'd be nice to charge my earphones ✪ ________ ________ ________ ________ ________ ________.

M : Got it. What about the price?

W : I definitely don't want to spend more than $100.

M : No problem. Then you are down to these two. This model comes with a silicone case cover, and that one comes with a leather case cover.

W : Well, I don't like the feel of the silicone. ________ ________ ________.

M : Then, this is the model for you.

W : Perfect. I'll take it.

11

대화를 듣고, 여자의 마지막 말에 대한 남자의 응답으로 가장 적절한 것을 고르시오.

W : Andy, it's hard to get together for our biology group project. All our group members seem busy.

M : I know. Why don't we ✪ __________ __________ __________ __________ __________ __________? Then, we can communicate easily without face-to-face meetings.

W : That's a wonderful idea. Could you do it for us?

12

대화를 듣고, 남자의 마지막 말에 대한 여자의 응답으로 가장 적절한 것을 고르시오.

M : I'm excited to go on this trip. Honey, did you fasten your seatbelt?

W : Yes. *[Pause]* Oh, wait. I'm not sure __________ __________ __________ __________ __________ __________ in the living room when I left the house.

M : Don't worry. I turned them off. And I ✪ __________ __________ __________ __________ __________, too.

13

대화를 듣고, 여자의 마지막 말에 대한 남자의 응답으로 가장 적절한 것을 고르시오. [3점]

W : Hi, Uncle James. I'm back from the cycling camp.

M : Hey, Clara. How was it?

W : It was great. __________ __________ __________ __________ __________. I want to be a national cycling champion just like you.

M : I know you will. You're participating in the national youth cycling competition next month, right?

W : Yeah, but I'm a little bit nervous because it's my first national competition.

M : I felt the same way. But once you start racing, you'll forget about being nervous.

W : I hope so. I really want to __________ __________ __________.

M : Well, you did set the record at the city competition this year.

W : That's true. And I've trained really hard all year.

M : See, I know you're ready.

W : Thank you. I hope ✪ __________ __________ __________ __________ __________ __________. Wish me luck.

14

대화를 듣고, 남자의 마지막 말에 대한 여자의 응답으로 가장 적절한 것을 고르시오.

[Phone rings.]

W : Ashton Science Museum. How can I help you?

M : Hi. I'm planning __________ __________ __________ for my students, and I was wondering if your museum had any programs for high school students.

W : Yes, we have one. It's named Teen Science Adventure. When is the field trip?

M : It's October 14th. I'm bringing about 50 students. Is it available that day?

W : Let me check. *[Mouse clicking sound]* It's available in the afternoon.

M : Perfect. Can you __________ __________ __________ __________?

W : Sure. It includes workshops, hands-on activities, and AI robot demonstrations.

M : Amazing.

W : And the highlight of this program is the VR Escape Room ✪ __________ __________ __________ __________ __________ __________ __________ using scientific knowledge.

M : It sounds fun and educational. My students would love that.

W : Would you like to make a reservation then?

M : It'd be nice if you could __________ __________ __________ __________ today, so I can discuss it with my principal.

15

다음 상황 설명을 듣고, Megan이 Philip에게 할 말로 가장 적절한 것을 고르시오. [3점]

M : Philip goes to a bookstore to buy a recently published book titled *The Psychology of Everyday Affairs*. While Philip is looking for the book, he happens to see an advertisement poster on the wall. It says that if people __________ __________ __________ __________ __________, they can get a 10% discount on books. At the counter, he meets Megan, who works at the bookstore. He tells her that he wants to become a bookstore member to get a discount on the book. However, Megan knows that the membership discount is only for books ✪ __________ __________ __________ __________ __________ __________ __________ __________. Even though Megan doesn't want to disappoint Philip, she has to tell him that he __________ __________ __________ __________ on the book he wants to buy. In this situation, what would Megan most likely say to Philip?

16~17

다음을 듣고, 물음에 답하시오.

W : Hello, students. I'm sure you've encountered some wild animals in cities. Let's look at some reasons that wild animals have done well and __________ __________ __________ __________ in cities. First, pigeons were rare in cities like Paris, but now you can easily find them. Urban expansion reduced the number of animals hunting them, and food waste in cities has been a great food source for them. And, while London is not by the sea, it has many seagulls. This is because nesting on the roofs of buildings __________ __________ __________ __________ __________. Next, Delhi is home to about 30,000 monkeys. Experts say that monkeys' high intelligence and comfort with humans __________ __________ __________ in the city. Lastly, in the 19th century, there was a small population of squirrels in New York City. Squirrels were seen as public pets, so the city ✪ __________ __________ __________ as their food source. This increased their population in the city. Let's watch a video about these animals' city lives.

▶ 정답 : 해설편 104쪽

VOCA LIST 23

회차별 영단어 QR 코드 ※ QR 코드를 스캔 후 모바일로 단어장처럼 학습할 수 있습니다.

● 고3 2022학년도 9월

01

001 □ finalist ⓝ 결승전 진출자
002 □ competition ⓝ (경연) 대회
003 □ contestant ⓝ 참가자
004 □ bottom ⓝ 맨 아래 (부분)
005 □ commercial break 광고 시간

02

006 □ fold ⓥ 접다, 개키다
007 □ laundry ⓝ 세탁물
008 □ self-esteem ⓝ 자존감
009 □ participate in ~에 참여하다
010 □ make sense 타당하다
011 □ achievement ⓝ 성취

03

012 □ specific ⓐ 특정한
013 □ decorate ⓥ 장식하다
014 □ anniversary ⓝ 기념일
015 □ lily ⓝ 백합
016 □ stand for ~을 상징하다
017 □ pride ⓝ 자부심

04

018 □ recently ad 최근에
019 □ take a look at ~을 보다
020 □ stair ⓝ ((*pl.*)) 계단
021 □ bookcase ⓝ 책장
022 □ stripe-patterned ⓐ 줄무늬의
023 □ check out ~을 (살펴) 보다

05

024 □ spill ⓥ 쏟다
025 □ dry cleaner 세탁소
026 □ fish tank 어항
027 □ replace A with B A를 B로 교체하다
028 □ be out of ~이 다 떨어지다
029 □ arrive ⓥ 도착하다

06

030 □ in case ~할 경우를 대비하여
031 □ recommend ⓥ 추천하다
032 □ light ⓐ 가벼운
033 □ a bit 조금
034 □ dozen ⓝ 12개짜리 한 묶음
035 □ worth ⓐ ~의 가치가 있는

07

036 □ preparation ⓝ 준비
037 □ pretty ad 꽤
038 □ local ⓐ 현지의
039 □ repair ⓝ 수리
040 □ sign up 신청하다
041 □ expect ⓥ 예상하다
042 □ conference room 회의실
043 □ available ⓐ 이용할 수 있는

08

044 □ purpose ⓝ 목적
045 □ target ⓥ 대상으로 하다
046 □ midterm exam 중간고사
047 □ register ⓥ 등록하다

09

048 □ host ⓥ 주최하다
049 □ include ⓥ 포함하다
050 □ slide ⓝ 미끄럼틀
051 □ up to ~까지
052 □ a variety of 다양한
053 □ reschedule ⓥ 일정을 조정하다

10

054 □ electronics ⓝ 전자 제품
055 □ particular ⓐ 특정한
056 □ last ⓥ 지속되다
057 □ at least 적어도
058 □ wireless ⓐ 무선의
059 □ connect to ~에 연결하다
060 □ charging cable 충전 케이블
061 □ leather ⓝ 가죽
062 □ weird ⓐ 이상한

11

063 □ get together 모이다
064 □ biology ⓝ 생물학
065 □ face-to-face ⓐ 대면하는

12

066 □ go on a trip 여행을 떠나다
067 □ fasten ⓥ 매다
068 □ seatbelt ⓝ 안전벨트
069 □ be free to 자유롭게 ~하다

13

070 □ improve ⓥ 향상되다
071 □ national ⓐ 전국적인
072 □ youth ⓝ 청(소)년
073 □ nervous ⓐ 불안해하는
074 □ set the record 기록을 수립하다
075 □ terrific ⓐ 멋진
076 □ look forward to ~을 기대하다

14

077 □ field trip 현장 학습
078 □ briefly ad 간단히
079 □ hands-on ⓐ 직접 해 보는
080 □ demonstration ⓝ 시연
081 □ escape room 방 탈출
082 □ solve ⓥ 해결하다
083 □ virtual ⓐ 가상의
084 □ challenge ⓝ 도전
085 □ knowledge ⓝ 지식
086 □ reservation ⓝ 예약
087 □ principle ⓝ 원리
088 □ brilliant ⓐ 훌륭한
089 □ science fiction 공상과학

15

090 □ publish ⓥ 출간하다
091 □ happen to-v 우연히 ~하다
092 □ advertisement ⓝ 광고
093 □ get a discount on ~을 할인 받다
094 □ disappoint ⓥ 실망시키다
095 □ regret ⓥ 유감스럽게 생각하다
096 □ release ⓝ 발표, 출간

16~17

097 □ population ⓝ 개체 수
098 □ pigeon ⓝ 비둘기
099 □ expansion ⓝ 팽창
100 □ reduce ⓥ 줄어들다
101 □ seagull ⓝ 갈매기
102 □ nest ⓥ 둥지를 틀다
103 □ protect A from B A를 B로부터 보호하다
104 □ chick ⓝ 새끼 새
105 □ intelligence ⓝ 지능
106 □ comfort ⓝ 편안
107 □ flourish ⓥ 번성하다
108 □ squirrel ⓝ 다람쥐
109 □ nut-bearing ⓐ 견과류가 열리는
110 □ arise ⓥ 발생하다
111 □ abandoned ⓐ 유기된
112 □ affect ⓥ 영향을 미치다

24회 ● 2021학년도 9월 모의평가 고3 영어 듣기

※ QR코드를 스캔하시면 듣기 방송을 청취하실 수 있습니다.

● 점수 표시가 없는 문항은 모두 2점 ● 문항수 17개 | 배점 37점 | 제한 시간 25분

1번부터 17번까지는 듣고 답하는 문제입니다. 1번부터 15번까지는 한 번만 들려주고, 16번부터 17번까지는 두 번 들려줍니다. 방송을 잘 듣고 답을 하시기 바랍니다.

MP3

1. 다음을 듣고, 여자가 하는 말의 목적으로 가장 적절한 것을 고르시오.

① 등교 시간 변경을 알리려고
② 학교 매점의 영업 재개를 안내하려고
③ 체육관 신축 공사 일정을 예고하려고
④ 교실 의자와 책상 교체 계획을 공지하려고
⑤ 학교 급식 만족도 조사 참여를 독려하려고

2. 대화를 듣고, 남자의 의견으로 가장 적절한 것을 고르시오.

① 등산 전에는 과식을 삼가는 것이 좋다.
② 야생동물에게 먹이를 주지 말아야 한다.
③ 야외 활동은 가족 간의 유대를 돈독히 한다.
④ 산에서 야생동물을 만났을 때는 침착해야 된다.
⑤ 반려동물을 키우는 것은 정서 안정에 도움이 된다.

3. 대화를 듣고, 두 사람의 관계를 가장 잘 나타낸 것을 고르시오.

① 스타일리스트 − 기상 캐스터 ② 연출가 − 극작가
③ 매니저 − 뮤지컬 배우 ④ 해군 장교 − 항해사
⑤ 디자이너 − 신문 기자

4. 대화를 듣고, 그림에서 대화의 내용과 일치하지 않는 것을 고르시오.

5. 대화를 듣고, 여자가 할 일로 가장 적절한 것을 고르시오.

① 프로젝터와 스크린 챙기기 ② 담요 가져오기
③ 영화 선택하기 ④ 접이식 의자 구매하기
⑤ 짐을 차에 싣기

6. 대화를 듣고, 남자가 지불할 금액을 고르시오. [3점]

① $126 ② $130 ③ $140 ④ $144 ⑤ $150

7. 대화를 듣고, 여자가 송별회 장소를 변경한 이유를 고르시오.

① 참석 인원에 변경 사항이 생겨서
② 예약한 레스토랑의 평이 안 좋아서
③ 모임 장소로 가는 교통편이 불편해서
④ 송별회 주인공이 다른 메뉴를 원해서
⑤ 해산물 알레르기가 있는 동료들이 있어서

8. 대화를 듣고, Run with Your Dog 행사에 관해 언급되지 않은 것을 고르시오.

① 목적 ② 날짜 ③ 복장
④ 장소 ⑤ 참가비

9. Bluemont Salt Mine의 특별 행사에 관한 다음 내용을 듣고, 일치하지 않는 것을 고르시오.

① 10월 10일부터 10월 16일까지 진행된다.
② 가장 깊은 구역에 입장이 허용된다.
③ 사진 촬영이 가능하다.
④ 입장료는 무료이다.
⑤ 방문객들에게 선물을 준다.

10. 다음 표를 보면서 대화를 듣고, 두 사람이 주문할 크레용 세트를 고르시오.

Crayon Sets

	Set	Number of Crayons	Price	Washable	Free Gift
①	A	24	$9	×	coloring book
②	B	24	$11	○	sharpener
③	C	36	$15	×	sharpener
④	D	36	$17	○	coloring book
⑤	E	48	$21	○	coloring book

11. 대화를 듣고, 남자의 마지막 말에 대한 여자의 응답으로 가장 적절한 것을 고르시오.

① I think so. I should be fine by then.
② I'm sorry. I forgot to bring my racket.
③ Of course. Keep me posted on his recovery.
④ I'm afraid not. The doctor's schedule is full today.
⑤ Good idea. Let's watch the tennis match at my house.

12. 대화를 듣고, 여자의 마지막 말에 대한 남자의 응답으로 가장 적절한 것을 고르시오.

① I remember where I left my uniform.
② We can't participate in P.E. class now.
③ You should hurry before the cafeteria closes.
④ You can leave it with me and I'll find the owner.
⑤ I hope someone will bring it with your belongings.

13. 대화를 듣고, 남자의 마지막 말에 대한 여자의 응답으로 가장 적절한 것을 고르시오. [3점]

Woman: ______________________________

① I'll give it a try. What time shall we meet?
② Not yet. We need to wait for the food to be ready.
③ I don't know. Do you want me to send the recipe?
④ Absolutely. I'll stress the importance of education.
⑤ Cheer up. We can relax after our homework is done.

14. 대화를 듣고, 여자의 마지막 말에 대한 남자의 응답으로 가장 적절한 것을 고르시오.

Man: ______________________________

① Not now. It'll be easier to park there late at night.
② Sounds good. I'm glad to hear that you'll arrive soon.
③ Sure. I'll check the app for a spot and make a reservation.
④ One moment. The kids should be back from the museum.
⑤ No problem. I'll remove the app for the children's safety.

15. 다음 상황 설명을 듣고, Jane이 Andrew에게 할 말로 가장 적절한 것을 고르시오. [3점]

Jane: ______________________________

① Make sure everybody is prepared for next week.
② I think you should wear this jacket for the festival.
③ Thank you for keeping all your things in perfect shape.
④ How about choosing just the items that are in a good state?
⑤ Why don't you buy secondhand items instead of new ones?

[16～17] 다음을 듣고, 물음에 답하시오.

16. 남자가 하는 말의 주제로 가장 적절한 것은?

① positive effects of plants on insects
② benefits of insects to human beings
③ various methods of insect reproduction
④ relationship between diseases and insects
⑤ ways to prevent insects from damaging crops

17. 언급된 곤충이 <u>아닌</u> 것은?

① honeybees ② grasshoppers ③ silkworms
④ fruit flies ⑤ ladybugs

[해설편 p.106]

Dictation 24

✪ 표기에는 듣기 어려운 발음이 포함되어 있습니다. 귀 기울여 듣고 받아쓰세요.

● 고3 2021학년도 9월

※ QR 코드를 스캔하시면 듣기 방송이 나옵니다. 듣기 방송을 들으며 다음 빈칸을 채우시오. ● 제한 시간 : 25분

01

다음을 듣고, 여자가 하는 말의 목적으로 가장 적절한 것을 고르시오.

W : Hello, students. This is your principal, Ms. Carson. I'm sure you've all been looking forward to the __________ __________ __________ __________ __________. I'm very happy to announce that after some improvements the store will finally open again tomorrow. Based on your comments and requests, we ✪ __________ __________ __________ __________ __________ __________ __________ and replaced the chairs and tables. So now, the school store has become a better place for you to relax and enjoy your snacks. The store's operating hours will remain the same as before. Once again, our school store __________ __________ __________. I hope you will all enjoy it.

02

대화를 듣고, 남자의 의견으로 가장 적절한 것을 고르시오.

M : Cathy, it feels so great to be out in the mountains, doesn't it?
W : Yes, Dad. Look at that tree. There's a squirrel.
M : Oh, there's also a bird on the branch.
W : I want to feed them. Is it okay if I share my sandwich with them?
M : Hmm... I don't think __________ __________ __________ __________ __________.
W : Why do you think so, Dad? Isn't giving food to them helpful?
M : No. If people feed wild animals, they'll stop looking for wild food and they could __________ __________ __________ __________ in nature.
W : I didn't know that.
M : Also, ✪ __________ __________ __________ __________ __________ __________ __________ to some animals. This is another reason why we shouldn't feed wild animals.
W : I guess giving food to wildlife is not as helpful as I thought.
M : That's right.
W : I'll keep that in mind.

03

대화를 듣고, 두 사람의 관계를 가장 잘 나타낸 것을 고르시오.

W : Jack, I've been waiting with these clothes for you. You're going on air in 30 minutes.
M : Sorry, Amy. It took longer than usual to __________ __________ __________ __________ __________ __________ __________ __________ for the weather broadcast.
W : I was worried you might be late for the live weather report.
M : I'm ready. What am I wearing today?
W : I suggest this gray suit with a navy tie.
M : Okay. I'll go get dressed.
W : Wait. Put on these glasses, too. They'll give you a more professional look.
M : Whatever you say. I can always count on you __________ __________ __________ __________ __________ __________ __________.
W : That's what I'm here for. By the way, thanks to your weather forecast yesterday, I was ✪ __________ __________ __________ __________ __________ this morning.
M : I did say there was an 80% chance of rain in the morning.
W : Yes, you did. Now, go get changed.

04

대화를 듣고, 그림에서 대화의 내용과 일치하지 않는 것을 고르시오.

W : Hi, David. How was your picnic with your family on the weekend?
M : It was good. Do you want to see a picture I took?
W : Sure. *[Pause]* Wow, ✪ __________ __________ __________ __________ __________ __________.
M : He sure has. He just turned 11 years old.
W : Time flies. __________ __________ __________ __________ __________ __________ __________ must be his.
M : Yeah. He brings it with him everywhere.
W : I see. Oh, there are three bicycles.
M : Yes. We love riding bicycles these days.
W : That's good. I like that checkered-patterned mat.
M : That's my wife's favorite pattern. Do you recognize that heart-shaped cushion?
W : Of course. We each got that cushion from our company last year.
M : Right. My wife loves it.
W : Me, too. Oh, I guess your wife __________ __________ __________ __________ on the canvas.
M : Uh-huh. We all had a great time.

05

대화를 듣고, 여자가 할 일로 가장 적절한 것을 고르시오.

M : Honey, I'm so excited about going camping tomorrow.
W : Me, too. I especially like our plan of __________ __________ __________ __________ __________ __________ __________.
M : Absolutely! I think it's a great idea.
W : It's going to be so romantic. Did you pack the projector and screen?
M : Of course. I've put them in the car.
W : Great. Thanks.
M : Shall we take some blankets just in case it gets cold in the evening?
W : I've already packed them in our luggage.
M : Good. Oh, we haven't decided which movie we're going to watch tomorrow. Could you pick one?
W : Sure. I'll choose a movie.
M : Thanks. Do you know __________ __________ __________ __________ __________?
W : I think I last saw them in the trunk.
M : Alright. I'll check when I'm ✪ __________ __________ __________ in the car.
W : Great. I cannot wait for tomorrow!

Dictation 24

06
대화를 듣고, 남자가 지불할 금액을 고르시오. [3점]

W : Welcome to Vestian Electronics. How can I help you?
M : Hi. I need webcams for my son and daughter for their online classes. Which one would you recommend?
W : This one is really _________ _________ _________. It has a great design and picture quality.
M : That model seems good. How much is it?
W : The original price was $70, but it's on sale. It's $60 now.
M : Nice! I'll take two.
W : Anything else?
M : I also need a wireless speaker.
W : I recommend this one. The sound quality is good and it's only $20.
M : Perfect. Then I'll take that as well.
W : Do you also need two of these?
M : No. Just one is enough. _________ _________ _________ _________ _________ _________ _________.
W : Okay. Also, this week, we're ✪ _________ _________ _________ _________. With any purchase of $100 or more, we're giving a $10 discount to customers.
M : Great! Here's my credit card.

07
대화를 듣고, 여자가 송별회 장소를 변경한 이유를 고르시오.

M : Hey, Laura. What's up?
W : You know we're having a farewell party for our boss, Miranda, next Friday, right?
M : Yes. The party is at 7 p.m. at the seafood restaurant downtown, isn't it?
W : That was the original plan. But _________ _________ _________ _________.
M : Oh, really? Didn't you say that restaurant is known for ✪ _________ _________ _________ _________ _________ _________?
W : Yeah. That's why I booked a table there. But I changed the place to the Italian restaurant near the seafood restaurant.
M : I guess you did that because Miranda loves Italian food.
W : She does, but she also really likes seafood.
M : Then, why did you change the place?
W : I found out that _________ _________ _________ _________ _________ _________ _________.
M : Oh, that's why. By the way, Janet from the sales department said she wanted to come.
W : Great! I'm sure Miranda will be happy to see her.

08
대화를 듣고, Run with Your Dog 행사에 관해 언급되지 않은 것을 고르시오.

W : Hey, Lucas. What are you doing?
M : Hi, Erica. I'm reading an email about a charity event called Run with Your Dog.
W : I've never heard about that before. What is it for?
M : This event is to ✪ _________ _________ _________ _________ _________ in the neighborhood.
W : That sounds like a really good cause. Are you going to sign up?
M : Yes. Are you interested?
W : Maybe. When is it?
M : It's on Saturday, September 19th. The event will run from 7 a.m. to 10 a.m.
W : That's good. I'm free, then. _________ _________ _________ _________ _________?
M : It'll take place at Magic River Park.
W : Oh, I often walk my dog there. Is there a participation fee?
M : Yes. It's $5. If you would like to join, I'll send you the link to the website, which _________ _________ _________ _________.
W : Yes, please. I want to participate in the event, too.
M : Good. I expect to see you there.

09
Bluemont Salt Mine의 특별 행사에 관한 다음 내용을 듣고, 일치하지 않는 것을 고르시오.

M : Hello, listeners. I'm Bernard Reed from Bluemont Salt Mine. I'm pleased to announce that we're having a special event from October 10th to October 16th. It's to celebrate the 500th anniversary of the salt mine's opening. During this event, visitors will be allowed to ✪ _________ _________ _________ _________ _________ _________ _________ _________. Also, you'll have the chance to dress up in our traditional miner's clothes. _________ _________ _________ _________ _________ to remember your visit. But that's not all. There will be a 50% discount on the admission fee for all visitors. Last but not least, _________ _________ _________ _________ to all visitors. It's a badge with the Bluemont logo on it. For more information, please visit our website.

10
다음 표를 보면서 대화를 듣고, 두 사람이 주문할 크레용 세트를 고르시오.

W : Honey, what should we get for our granddaughter, Emily, for her birthday?
M : Well, I've been looking up crayon sets on the Internet. Do you want to see?
W : Sure. *[Pause]* How many crayons do you think are enough?
M : I think _________ _________ _________ _________ _________ for a six year old.
W : I agree. But I also want to spend more than $10 on our granddaughter's present.
M : Definitely. Do you think ✪ _________ _________ _________ _________?
W : Yes. That way Emily can wash off crayon marks if she gets them on her hands.
M : I see. Look. Each set comes with a free gift.
W : Oh, that's right. Which one is better for her, _________ _________ _________ _________ _________ _________?
M : I think the coloring book is better because she likes to collect all kinds of coloring books.
W : Right. I really think she's going to love our present.
M : Then, it's settled. Let's order this one.

11

대화를 듣고, 남자의 마지막 말에 대한 여자의 응답으로 가장 적절한 것을 고르시오.

[Cell phone rings.]

M : Hello, Chloe. How's your leg?

W : Hey, Sean. It still hurts, but the doctor said I'll be fully recovered in a few days.

M : I'm glad to hear that. Then, will you be able to ✪ _________ _________ _________ _________ _________ next weekend as scheduled?

12

대화를 듣고, 여자의 마지막 말에 대한 남자의 응답으로 가장 적절한 것을 고르시오.

W : Mr. Brown, I brought this P.E. uniform that somebody left in the cafeteria.

M : That's very considerate of you. Is the student's name on the uniform?

W : Yes, but the student is ✪ _________ _________ _________ _________ _________. The uniform must belong to a student in another class.

13

대화를 듣고, 남자의 마지막 말에 대한 여자의 응답으로 가장 적절한 것을 고르시오. [3점]

[Cell phone rings.]

M : Hi, Stacy. What are you doing this afternoon?

W : Hi, Ben. I hope to finish my math homework around noon, and after that I don't have any plans. Why?

M : I was thinking about going to a cooking class at 5 p.m. Do you want to come?

W : A cooking class? Isn't cooking difficult? I'm already _________ _________ _________ _________ _________ _________.

M : Well, actually, I recently read an article that said cooking is very effective in relieving stress.

W : What do you mean?

M : When you cook, the smell from the food you're making can help you feel relaxed.

W : I can see that. The smell of a freshly-cooked meal ✪ _________ _________ _________.

M : That's what I mean. Also, when you eat the delicious food you make, you'll feel happy.

W : That does sound appealing. Perhaps it'll help me _________ _________ _________ _________ _________.

M : Exactly. You should definitely come with me.

14

대화를 듣고, 여자의 마지막 말에 대한 남자의 응답으로 가장 적절한 것을 고르시오.

M : Honey, what time are we visiting the museum?

W : We should be able to get to the museum at around 2 p.m. after having lunch at Nanco's Restaurant.

M : Okay. Are we taking the bus?

W : We have two kids with us and the museum is pretty far from the restaurant. Let's drive.

M : But it'll be hard to find a parking space at the museum today. There are so many visitors on the weekend.

W : How about using an app to search for parking lots near the museum?

M : Is there an app for that?

W : Yes. The app is called Parking Paradise. It helps you ✪ _________ _________ _________ _________ _________ _________.

M : That's cool! Have you tried it?

W : No. But I heard that it's _________ _________ _________.

M : It sounds handy. Let me find the app and download it.

W : Okay. Can you find a parking space while I _________ _________ _________ _________?

24회

15

다음 상황 설명을 듣고, Jane이 Andrew에게 할 말로 가장 적절한 것을 고르시오. [3점]

W : Andrew is preparing to sell his used things at his school festival next week. Andrew gathers all the stuff that he wants to sell and asks his mother, Jane, _________ _________ _________ _________ _________ _________. Jane ✪ _________ _________ the items and notices that some of them are _________ _________ _________ _________ _________. She thinks that Andrew shouldn't take such worn-out things to the festival because people won't be interested in buying them. So, Jane wants to suggest that Andrew should only pick out the ones that are in fine condition. In this situation, what would Jane most likely say to Andrew?

16~17

다음을 듣고, 물음에 답하시오.

M : Hello, students. Last class, we discussed the harm caused by insects. Today, we're going to learn about the advantages that insects can bring us. First, honeybees _________ _________ _________ _________ _________ _________ _________ _________ of plants by helping them to produce seeds. In the U.S., the honeybees' assistance in this process accounts for about $20 billion in crops per year, including fruits and vegetables. Second, insects like grasshoppers are a major food source in the world because they're ✪ _________ _________ _________ _________ _________ _________ _________. In Mexico, for example, you can easily find fried grasshoppers sold in village markets. Next, silkworms are responsible for producing most of the world's silk, which is recognized as a valuable product. In China, silkworms produce approximately 30,000 tons of raw silk annually. Finally, fruit flies have been used by many researchers in genetic studies. Fruit flies are practical test subjects for such studies _________ _________ _________ _________ _________. Now, let's watch some video clips to help you understand better.

▶ 정답 : 해설편 108쪽

VOCA LIST 24

회차별 영단어 QR 코드 ※ QR 코드를 스캔 후 모바일로 단어장처럼 학습할 수 있습니다.

● 고3 2021학년도 9월

01

001 □ **principal** ⓝ 교장
002 □ **announce** ⓥ 발표하다
003 □ **comment** ⓝ 의견, 논평, 언급
004 □ **replace** ⓥ 교체하다
005 □ **operating hour** 운영 시간
006 □ **remain** ⓥ 계속[여전히] ~이다

02

007 □ **squirrel** ⓝ 다람쥐
008 □ **branch** ⓝ 나뭇가지
009 □ **feed** ⓥ 먹이를 주다
010 □ **wildlife** ⓝ 야생 생물
011 □ **survival** ⓝ 생존
012 □ **certain** ⓐ (분명히 명시하지 않고) 어떤
013 □ **nutrient** ⓝ 영양소
014 □ **harmful** ⓐ 해로운
015 □ **reason** ⓝ 이유, 까닭
016 □ **keep ~ in mind** ~을 명심하다

03

017 □ **go on air** 방송하다
018 □ **organize** ⓥ 정리하다
019 □ **script** ⓝ 대본
020 □ **live** ⓐ 생방송의, 생중계의
021 □ **weather report** 일기 예보
022 □ **suit** ⓝ 정장
023 □ **navy** ⓐ 짙은 남색의
024 □ **professional** ⓐ 전문적인, 직업적인
025 □ **count on** ~을 믿다, ~에 의지하다
026 □ **when it comes to** ~에 관해서
027 □ **thanks to** ~ 덕분에
028 □ **sudden** ⓐ 갑작스러운
029 □ **shower** ⓝ 소나기
030 □ **chance** ⓝ 가능성

04

031 □ **turn** ⓥ (어떤 나이·시기가) 되다
032 □ **drone** ⓝ 드론, 무인 항공기
033 □ **checkered-patterned** ⓐ 체크 무늬의

05

034 □ **outdoors** ad 야외[옥외]에서
035 □ **pack** ⓥ (짐을) 챙기다, 싸다
036 □ **projector** ⓝ 영사기, 프로젝터
037 □ **blanket** ⓝ 담요
038 □ **luggage** ⓝ 짐, 수하물
039 □ **folding chair** 접이식 의자
040 □ **last** ad 가장 최근에, 마지막으로

06

041 □ **recommend** ⓥ 추천하다, 권하다
042 □ **youngster** ⓝ 청소년, 젊은이
043 □ **picture quality** 화질
044 □ **wireless** ⓐ 무선의
045 □ **as well** 또한, 역시
046 □ **autumn** ⓝ 가을
047 □ **purchase** ⓝ 구매

07

048 □ **farewell party** 송별회
049 □ **reasonable** ⓐ (가격이) 적당한
050 □ **coworker** ⓝ 동료
051 □ **department** ⓝ 부서

08

052 □ **charity** ⓝ 자선
053 □ **raise** ⓥ (기금을) 모으다
054 □ **shelter** ⓝ (학대 받는 동물들의) 보호소
055 □ **neighborhood** ⓝ 지역, 이웃
056 □ **sign up** (참가) 신청하다, 등록하다
057 □ **run** ⓥ (얼마의 기간 동안) 계속되다
058 □ **free** ⓐ 다른 계획[약속]이 없는, 한가한
059 □ **take place** 개최되다, 일어나다
060 □ **walk** ⓥ (동물을) 걷게 하다[산책시키다]
061 □ **fee** ⓝ 요금, 수수료
062 □ **detailed** ⓐ 상세한

09

063 □ **mine** ⓝ 광산
064 □ **celebrate** ⓥ 기념하다, 축하하다
065 □ **anniversary** ⓝ 기념일
066 □ **admission fee** 입장료
067 □ **give away** (공짜로) 주다

10

068 □ **look up** (참고 자료·컴퓨터 등에서 정보를) 찾아보다
069 □ **definitely** ad 분명히[틀림없이]
070 □ **washable** ⓐ 물에 씻기는
071 □ **wash off** ~을 씻어 없애다[지우다]
072 □ **mark** ⓝ 자국
073 □ **sharpener** ⓝ 연필깎이
074 □ **coloring book** 색칠놀이 책
075 □ **collect** ⓥ 모으다, 수집하다
076 □ **settle** ⓥ 결정하다

11

077 □ **fully** ad 완전히, 충분히
078 □ **recover** ⓥ 회복하다
079 □ **as scheduled** 예정대로
080 □ **Keep me posted.** 계속 소식 들려줘.

12

081 □ **P.E. uniform** 체육복
082 □ **cafeteria** ⓝ 구내식당
083 □ **considerate** ⓐ 사려 깊은
084 □ **leave ~ with ...** ~을 …에게 맡기다
085 □ **belonging** ⓝ 소지품

13

086 □ **stressed out** 스트레스가 쌓인, 스트레스를 받는
087 □ **actually** ad 사실은, 실은
088 □ **article** ⓝ (신문 등의) 기사
089 □ **effective** ⓐ 효과적인
090 □ **relieve** ⓥ (긴장 등을) 풀게 하다
091 □ **relaxed** ⓐ 느긋한, 편안한
092 □ **freshly-cooked** ⓐ 갓 요리한
093 □ **calm down** 진정시키다, 진정하다
094 □ **appealing** ⓐ 매력적인
095 □ **take one's mind off** ~에서 관심을 돌리다, 머리를 식히다
096 □ **stress** ⓥ 강조하다

14

097 □ **pretty** ad 꽤, 상당히
098 □ **parking lot** 주차장
099 □ **reserve** ⓥ 예약하다
100 □ **user-friendly** ⓐ 사용자 친화적인
101 □ **convenient** ⓐ 편리한
102 □ **handy** ⓐ 편리한, 유용한
103 □ **remove** ⓥ 제거하다, 없애다

15

104 □ **prepare** ⓥ 준비하다
105 □ **used** ⓐ 중고의
106 □ **gather** ⓥ 모으다
107 □ **stuff** ⓝ 물품
108 □ **selection** ⓝ 선발[선택]된 사람[것]들
109 □ **look through** ~을 훑어보다
110 □ **notice** ⓥ 알아차리다
111 □ **poor** ⓐ (질적으로) 좋지 못한
112 □ **worn-out** ⓐ 낡아빠진, 닳아 해진
113 □ **pick out** ~을 가려내다[선택하다]
114 □ **secondhand** ⓐ 중고의

16~17

115 □ **advantage** ⓝ 이점
116 □ **play a role in** ~에 역할을 하다
117 □ **crucial** ⓐ 중대한
118 □ **reproductive** ⓐ 생식의, 번식의
119 □ **seed** ⓝ 씨앗
120 □ **assistance** ⓝ 도움, 원조
121 □ **account for** ~을 차지하다
122 □ **crop** ⓝ ((*pl.*)) 농작물
123 □ **grasshopper** ⓝ 메뚜기
124 □ **major** ⓐ 주된, 주요한
125 □ **protein** ⓝ 단백질
126 □ **silkworm** ⓝ 누에
127 □ **responsible** ⓐ 책임지고[책임 맡고] 있는
128 □ **valuable** ⓐ 귀중한
129 □ **approximately** ad 대략
130 □ **raw** ⓐ 생[날]것의, 가공하지 않은
131 □ **practical** ⓐ 유용한, 실용적인
132 □ **subject** ⓝ 실험 대상
133 □ **lifespan** ⓝ 수명
134 □ **prevent A from B** A가 B하지 못하게 하다

25회 • 2023학년도 10월 학력평가 고3 영어 듣기

※ QR코드를 스캔하시면 듣기 방송을 청취하실 수 있습니다.

● 점수 표시가 없는 문항은 모두 2점 ● 문항수 17개 | 배점 37점 | 제한 시간 25분

1번부터 17번까지는 듣고 답하는 문제입니다. 1번부터 15번까지는 한 번만 들려주고, 16번부터 17번까지는 두 번 들려줍니다. 방송을 잘 듣고 답을 하시기 바랍니다.

1. 다음을 듣고, 여자가 하는 말의 목적으로 가장 적절한 것을 고르시오.

① 놀이공원 운영 시간 연장을 공지하려고
② 새로 생긴 실내 놀이 기구를 홍보하려고
③ 놀이공원 내 공연 장소의 변경을 알리려고
④ 놀이 기구 탑승 시 안전 수칙 준수를 당부하려고
⑤ 야외 놀이 기구의 일시적 운행 중단을 안내하려고

2. 대화를 듣고, 남자의 의견으로 가장 적절한 것을 고르시오.

① 온라인 계정 비밀번호는 주기적으로 바꿔야 한다.
② 중요한 비밀번호는 메모해 두어야 한다.
③ 소셜 미디어 사용 시간을 줄여야 한다.
④ 보안 프로그램은 수시로 업데이트해야 한다.
⑤ 소셜 미디어에서 개인 정보 노출에 유의해야 한다.

3. 다음을 듣고, 여자가 하는 말의 요지로 가장 적절한 것을 고르시오.

① 상대방의 부탁을 거절할 때는 이유를 제시해야 한다.
② 무리한 부탁은 처음부터 거절하는 것이 바람직하다.
③ 부탁을 들어 준 상대방에게 감사 인사를 해야 한다.
④ 친한 사이일수록 예의를 지켜서 부탁하는 것이 좋다.
⑤ 부탁을 하기 전에 상대방의 상황을 확인하는 것이 필요하다.

4. 대화를 듣고, 그림에서 대화의 내용과 일치하지 <u>않는</u> 것을 고르시오.

5. 대화를 듣고, 남자가 할 일로 가장 적절한 것을 고르시오.

① 후원 업체 구하기
② 행사장 예약하기
③ 등록 현황 파악하기
④ 지역 예술가 섭외하기
⑤ 자원봉사자 모집하기

6. 대화를 듣고, 여자가 지불할 금액을 고르시오. [3점]

① $62 ② $65 ③ $70 ④ $82 ⑤ $85

7. 대화를 듣고, 남자가 학교 정원 음악회에 참가할 수 <u>없는</u> 이유를 고르시오.

① 아직 손목이 낫지 않아서
② 첼로 대회에 참가해야 해서
③ 첼로 연습을 오랫동안 쉬어서
④ 함께 연주할 사람을 찾지 못해서
⑤ 대학 입학 면접 준비를 해야 해서

8. 대화를 듣고, 컴퓨터 수업에 관해 언급되지 <u>않은</u> 것을 고르시오.

① 장소 ② 내용 ③ 기간
④ 준비물 ⑤ 신청 방법

9. Sunnyville Coffee Expo에 관한 다음 내용을 듣고, 일치하지 <u>않는</u> 것을 고르시오.

① 11월 18일과 19일에 개최될 것이다.
② 티켓당 무료 머그잔을 하나씩 받게 된다.
③ 올해의 주제는 'From Bean to Brew'이다.
④ 커피를 생산하는 10개국의 커피를 맛볼 수 있다.
⑤ 일찍 예매하면 할인을 받을 수 있다.

10. 다음 표를 보면서 대화를 듣고, 여자가 구매할 SIM 카드를 고르시오.

SIM Cards for Australia

	Plan	Days	Data (GB)	Free International Calls	Price
①	A	5	10	○	$20
②	B	10	15	×	$25
③	C	15	20	○	$30
④	D	20	30	×	$35
⑤	E	30	50	○	$50

11. 대화를 듣고, 남자의 마지막 말에 대한 여자의 응답으로 가장 적절한 것을 고르시오.

① I'm not sure where they are now.
② My aunt is expecting her baby soon.
③ My aunt and the baby are both in good health.
④ I'm on my way to the hospital for a health checkup.
⑤ I don't know whether they'll like the gift and flowers.

12. 대화를 듣고, 여자의 마지막 말에 대한 남자의 응답으로 가장 적절한 것을 고르시오.

① Exactly. That's why I gave up swimming.
② Right. It's cheaper to buy a monthly pass.
③ Not at all. The pool is warm enough to swim in.
④ I don't think so. We're not allowed to dive into the pool.
⑤ Good point. Swimming is an exercise for the whole body.

13. 대화를 듣고, 남자의 마지막 말에 대한 여자의 응답으로 가장 적절한 것을 고르시오. [3점]

Woman: ______________________________

① I'm sorry. I can't go to the lab with you now.
② I totally agree. We should wash vegetables thoroughly.
③ Sure. It'll be nice to study for the biology exam together.
④ Yeah. Vegetables like broccoli are good for our health.
⑤ Indeed. I can't wait to do the broccoli cell experiment.

14. 대화를 듣고, 여자의 마지막 말에 대한 남자의 응답으로 가장 적절한 것을 고르시오.

Man: ______________________________

① Thanks. Donating books is a way to help those in need.
② My pleasure. My customers will love your books.
③ Me too. Joining the book club is worth it.
④ I'd love to. But we don't buy old books anymore.
⑤ That's right. So I've ordered those novels for you.

15. 다음 상황 설명을 듣고, Lydia가 Mr. Robinson에게 할 말로 가장 적절한 것을 고르시오. [3점]

Lydia: ______________________________

① I'd like to enter the brochure competition next time.
② I'm afraid you forgot to put my name on the brochure.
③ I'm deeply disappointed that I didn't win the competition.
④ You haven't shown me the first draft of the brochure.
⑤ You should've informed me about the competition.

[16 ~ 17] 다음을 듣고, 물음에 답하시오.

16. 남자가 하는 말의 주제로 가장 적절한 것은?

① the average life expectancy of animals
② similarities between humans and animals
③ animals that stay longer with their mothers
④ independent animals that travel and live alone
⑤ different roles of mothers and fathers in parenting

17. 언급된 동물이 <u>아닌</u> 것은?

① chimpanzees ② elephants ③ kangaroos
④ giraffes ⑤ polar bears

[해설편 p.111]

Dictation 25

✪ 표기에는 듣기 어려운 발음이 포함되어 있습니다. 귀 기울여 듣고 받아쓰세요. ● 고3 2023학년도 10월

※ QR 코드를 스캔하시면 듣기 방송이 나옵니다. 듣기 방송을 들으며 다음 빈칸을 채우시오. ● 제한 시간 : 25분

01

다음을 듣고, 여자가 하는 말의 목적으로 가장 적절한 것을 고르시오.

W : Attention, please. Welcome to the Wonderland Amusement Park. We ________ ________ ________ ___ providing you with thrilling rides, shows, and attractions. However, we regret to inform you that due to the bad weather, ✪ ____________ ________ ______ ____ ________________ __________. We'll monitor the weather and reopen outdoor rides as soon as conditions permit. In the meantime, please enjoy our exciting indoor rides, shows, and interactive exhibits. We kindly request that you cooperate, as your safety is ✪ _____ _____ ___________. We apologize for any inconvenience. Thank you.

02

대화를 듣고, 남자의 의견으로 가장 적절한 것을 고르시오.

M : Jennifer, what are you doing?

W : I'm checking an email. It says that I should change my password on my social media account.

M : When was the last time you changed your password?

W : Actually I've never changed it since I created my account.

M : You mean you've been ________ _____ ________ ____________ all this time?

W : Yes. I haven't changed any of my passwords on my online accounts. I forget my passwords easily.

M : That's too risky! It's important to change your passwords regularly to ✪ ___________ ______________ ____________ ____________.

W : That makes sense. How often should I change my passwords?

M : Experts recommend changing passwords ________ ________ ___ _____ __________.

W : I'll keep that in mind. Thanks.

03

다음을 듣고, 여자가 하는 말의 요지로 가장 적절한 것을 고르시오.

W : Hello, listeners! I'm Jessica, your host from Happy Days. Today, we're going to explore the art of ✪ ______________ ______________ ________________ __________. The key to this is ____________ __ _______ _________ __________ ____. By doing so, we create understanding, prevent any potential misunderstandings, and strengthen our connections with others. Of course, there may be exceptions, but in general, giving an explanation can truly make a big difference. It shows that we care about the other person's feelings while still being ✪ __________ __________ _____ _______ ____________. We'll be back with more tips after the break. Stay tuned.

04

대화를 듣고, 그림에서 대화의 내용과 일치하지 않는 것을 고르시오.

W : Ted, what are you looking at on your smartphone?

M : Hi, Nancy, it's a photo of the food truck that my brother Tom recently opened. Take a look.

W : Okay. Oh, I love this teddy bear on top of the truck. It's very cute.

M : Right. Do you see the sign on the truck?

W : Yes, it says Tom's Organic Food. Your brother is __________ ____________ _______. Nice!

M : Yeah. This man inside the truck is my brother.

W : He looks cool ✪ ___________ _____ __________ _____!

M : Look at this standing signboard for the menu. Isn't it pretty?

W : Absolutely. I like that it's decorated with flowers.

M : And my brother set up this table with a parasol for the customers.

W : Yeah, _____ ____________________ ___________ looks good. I'd like to visit the food truck someday.

M : Sure. Let's go there together.

05

대화를 듣고, 남자가 할 일로 가장 적절한 것을 고르시오.

M : Hey, Stella! How's everything going with ✪ _____ ______ ______ ____ __________ ________________?

W : Hi, Anthony! It's going well. Many local artists are excited to join.

M : That's fantastic news! Have you ✪ ___________ ______ ____________ for the event?

W : Yes, two local businesses have agreed to sponsor the market.

M : Wonderful! Have you found a suitable location?

W : Sure, I've already reserved the town square.

M : You're doing an amazing job! Is there anything I can do to help?

W : On the market day, we'll need some volunteers to help with setup and registration. Do you think you could find some?

M : Of course! I'll recruit volunteers ✪ ____________ __ ________________ _____________ on my social media.

W : That'd be great. Thank you so much!

06

대화를 듣고, 여자가 지불할 금액을 고르시오. [3점]

M : Honey, what are you doing on the Internet?

W : I'm shopping for ✪ __ __________ __________ ____________ for Jason's birthday party.

M : That's a good idea. Jason will love it.

W : Sure. I'm having difficulty choosing between these two options, though. One is $50, and the other is $70.

M : I think the $70 one will be better. Look, __ _____ _________ __________.

W : I agree. I'll go for it.

M : Don't we need packs of sugar powder for the cotton candy, too?

W : You're right. Let's buy some. *[Clicking sound]* How about these? They're $5 per pack.
M : Good. Hang on. If we buy three packs, we can get $3 off the total price.
W : Great, ______ ______ ________ ________ ________. I'll place the order now.
M : Go ahead.

07

대화를 듣고, 남자가 학교 정원 음악회에 참가할 수 없는 이유를 고르시오.

W : Hi, Brenden. Long time no see! How have you been?
M : Hi, Laura. I had some trouble with my wrist, but now I'm feeling much better.
W : I didn't know that. So you're back in the music room today to practice the cello?
M : Yeah, I missed being here a lot.
W : I was wondering if you'd like to join me for the school garden music concert.
M : I'd love to. When is it?
W : It's on Friday, November 24th. We'll have ✪ ________ ________ ___ ________.
M : Well, I'm afraid I won't be able to make it then.
W : Ah, you're entering the cello contest around that time, right?
M : __ ________ ______ ___. I have to focus on preparing for ___ ________ ________ ________ ________.
W : Oh, when is it?
M : It's the day after the garden concert. That's why I can't participate in the concert.
W : I understand. Good luck with your interview!

08

대화를 듣고, 컴퓨터 수업에 관해 언급되지 않은 것을 고르시오.

M : Grandma, look at this leaflet. It was in your postbox.
W : What is it, sweetheart?
M : It's about free computer classes ✪ ________________ ________ _____ _____ ________. Are you interested?
W : Sure. Let me have a look. Oh, they take place in the Cromby community center. That's quite convenient.
M : Right. Volunteers from the college will come to teach older people like you.
W : Cool. What kind of things will they teach us?
M : Many things, including sending emails and ________ ________ ________.
W : Perfect. And the classes will ______ ______ ________ ________, starting on October 16th.
M : Yeah, they'll be held every Monday and Wednesday.
W : That's great timing. How do I sign up for them?
M : You can simply call the community center and register.
W : I see.

09

Sunnyville Coffee Expo에 관한 다음 내용을 듣고, 일치하지 않는 것을 고르시오.

M : Coffee lovers, listen up! The Sunnyville Coffee Expo is back. It'll be held on November 18th and 19th at the Jefferson Convention Center. For just $20 per day, you can be part of this fantastic event with famous coffee experts. And here's the best part — you get ________ ________ ________ ________ ________. This year's theme is "From Bean to Brew," which means you'll learn everything about coffee, from the cultivation of the beans to ✪ ______ ______ ______ ______. Plus, you'll be able to taste coffee from six coffee-producing countries, including Brazil and Vietnam. You can get a discount ___ ______ ________ ________. Visit our website for more information. See you there!

10

다음 표를 보면서 대화를 듣고, 여자가 구매할 SIM 카드를 고르시오.

W : Paul, I need to buy a SIM card for my upcoming trip to Australia. Do you know any good website?
M : Yes. I'll show you one on my smartphone. *[Pause]* Here it is. Have a look.
W : Okay. Hmm, I don't think this plan will work for me since I'll be traveling for ________ ______ ___ ________.
M : Then you can choose one from these four. How about this one?
W : I'm afraid the data is not enough for me. I need at least 20GB. I'm ________ ________ ________ ________.
M : I see. ✪ ________ ________ ________ ______ ________. I recommend one with free international calls.
W : Right. I'll make a lot of calls to my family and friends.
M : Now you have two options left. Which one do you prefer?
W : This one seems expensive to me. I'll go for the other one.
M : Good choice.

11

대화를 듣고, 남자의 마지막 말에 대한 여자의 응답으로 가장 적절한 것을 고르시오.

M : Hey, Sonia, where are you going with that gift box and flowers?
W : Hi, Ethan! I'm ________ ______ ______ ________ to visit my aunt Lisa. She had a baby yesterday.
M : ✪ ________ ________ ________! Congratulations! How are they doing?

12

대화를 듣고, 여자의 마지막 말에 대한 남자의 응답으로 가장 적절한 것을 고르시오.

W : Mark, I remember that you learned how to swim last year. Do you still go swimming?
M : Of course. I ________ ________ ________ the swimming pool at least three times a week.
W : Good for you. But ✪ ________ __ ______ ________ ___ ________ these days?

13

대화를 듣고, 남자의 마지막 말에 대한 여자의 응답으로 가장 적절한 것을 고르시오. [3점]

M : Gina, do you know what experiment we're doing in biology class today?

W : Sure. We're going to ✪ ______ __ ________________ to observe broccoli cells.

M : That's pretty cool. Have you ever had a chance to do this kind of experiment before?

W : No, it's my first time getting a close look at plant cells.

M : Same here. I've only seen ✪ ________________ ___ ________ in the textbook.

W : Me too! I wonder what real plant cells look like.

M : I guess we'll find out soon.

W : Yeah. Oh, _____ ________ ___ __________ ___ _______.
Let's head to the lab quickly.

M : Okay. We'll have a lot of fun in the lab, exploring a hidden world within a vegetable.

14

대화를 듣고, 여자의 마지막 말에 대한 남자의 응답으로 가장 적절한 것을 고르시오.

M : Good afternoon. How may I help you?

W : Hi. I heard that your bookstore buys old books from customers. Is that true?

M : Yes. We buy and sell old books here.

W : That's great. Actually, I have a bag of classic novels that you might be interested in.

M : Good! Show me what you have.

W : Here they are.

M : *[Pause]* Wow, these are ✪ ____ ________________ __________.
I'd love to purchase them. How about $50 for the whole lot?

W : Okay. I'm happy with that.

M : Perfect. Your books ________________ ___ _____ ___________ ________________ in our store. Thank you for bringing them in.

W : You're welcome. It feels great to sell my old books to ✪ ______________ _______ __________________ ________.

15

다음 상황 설명을 듣고, Lydia가 Mr. Robinson에게 할 말로 가장 적절한 것을 고르시오. [3점]

W : Lydia is a talented high school student who dreams of ________________ ____ ____ ___________. This year, she decides to enter the school festival brochure competition. She is eager to win because the winning artist's name will be included on the brochure. Lydia works hard to create a beautiful design and submits it to Mr. Robinson, the person responsible for the brochure. ✪ ______ _______ ________ ________ _____ when she wins the competition. She excitedly looks forward to seeing her name alongside her artwork on the brochure. However, when Mr. Robinson shows her the first draft of the brochure, Lydia notices that _____ _________ ___ ____________. She wants to point out the problem to Mr. Robinson. In this situation, what would Lydia most likely say to Mr. Robinson?

16~17

다음을 듣고, 물음에 답하시오.

M : Hello, class! Let's continue talking about animals today. Most animals become independent quite early, some even shortly after they're born. However, some animals really enjoy staying with their mothers for a long time. Chimpanzees live with their mothers ✪ _____ ____ _______________ __________ ____ _______. They are reported to stay with their mothers until they are teenagers. Elephants are also known to live with their mothers for up to 16 years, and sometimes even a lifetime. Giraffes typically ________ _____ _______________ ___ _______ ___________ for up to two years. Occasionally female giraffes travel with their mothers until the parent dies. Lastly, polar bears remain with their mothers until they are two and a half years old. During this period, they ________ ________________ _____________ ________ necessary for living in the Arctic environment. Now, let's watch a video clip about these animals.

▶ 정답 : 해설편 112쪽

VOCA LIST 25

회차별 영단어 QR 코드 ※ QR 코드를 스캔 후 모바일로 단어장처럼 학습할 수 있습니다.

● 고3 2023학년도 10월

01

001 □ take great pride in ~에 자부심을 갖다
002 □ regret to ~하게 되어 유감이다
003 □ due to ~ 때문에
004 □ outdoor ⓐ 실외의
005 □ ride ⓝ 놀이 기구, 탈것
006 □ temporarily ad 임시로
007 □ permit ⓥ 허락하다
008 □ in the meantime 그 동안
009 □ interactive ⓐ 상호 작용의, 대화식의, 양방향의
010 □ inconvenience ⓝ 불편

02

011 □ password ⓝ 비밀번호
012 □ account ⓝ 계정
013 □ easily ad 쉽게
014 □ risky ⓐ 위험한
015 □ regularly ad 주기적으로
016 □ potential ⓐ 잠재적인
017 □ attempt ⓝ 시도
018 □ recommend ⓥ 권장하다
019 □ keep in mind 염두에 두다, 명심하다

03

020 □ host ⓝ 진행자
021 □ explore ⓥ 탐구하다, 탐색하다
022 □ offer ⓥ 제시하다
023 □ say no 거절하다
024 □ misunderstanding ⓝ 오해
025 □ strengthen ⓥ 강화하다
026 □ exception ⓝ 예외
027 □ in general 일반적으로
028 □ explanation ⓝ 설명
029 □ make a difference 차이를 만들다

04

030 □ food truck 푸드 트럭
031 □ recently ad 최근에
032 □ on top of ~ 위에
033 □ cute ⓐ 귀여운
034 □ organic ⓐ 유기농의
035 □ signboard ⓝ 간판
036 □ decorate ⓥ 장식하다
037 □ set up 설치하다
038 □ parasol ⓝ 파라솔

05

039 □ craft ⓝ 공예
040 □ preparation ⓝ 준비, 대비
041 □ local ⓐ 지역의, 현지의
042 □ be excited to ~하기를 기대하다
043 □ fantastic ⓐ 멋진, 환상적인
044 □ secure ⓥ 확보하다
045 □ agree to ~하기로 동의하다
046 □ suitable ⓐ 적절한, 알맞은
047 □ square ⓝ 광장
048 □ volunteer ⓝ 자원봉사자
049 □ registration ⓝ 등록, 신청
050 □ promotional ⓐ 홍보의

06

051 □ cotton candy 솜사탕
052 □ have difficulty ~ing ~하는 데 애를 먹다
053 □ review ⓝ 평, 검토
054 □ Hang on. 잠깐만, 가만 있어봐.
055 □ pack ⓝ 묶음, 꾸러미
056 □ place an order 주문하다
057 □ Go ahead. 그렇게 하세요. 먼저 하세요.

07

058 □ wrist ⓝ 손목
059 □ practice ⓥ 연습하다
060 □ miss ⓥ 그리워하다
061 □ plenty of 많은
062 □ college entrance 대학 입학
063 □ interview ⓝ 면접
064 □ Good luck with ~. ~에 행운을 빌어.

08

065 □ postbox ⓝ 우편함
066 □ specifically ad 특별히
067 □ the elderly 어르신
068 □ take place 열리다
069 □ community center 주민센터
070 □ convenient ⓐ 편리한
071 □ surf the web 웹 서핑하다
072 □ sign up for ~에 등록하다
073 □ simply ad 단지, 그저

09

074 □ Listen up! 잘 들어주세요!
075 □ expert ⓝ 전문가
076 □ mug ⓝ 머그잔
077 □ theme ⓝ 주제
078 □ cultivation ⓝ 재배
079 □ art ⓝ 기술, 예술
080 □ brew ⓥ 끓이다, (커피를) 내리다
081 □ taste ⓥ 맛보다, 시음하다
082 □ get a discount 할인 받다
083 □ book ⓥ 예약하다

10

084 □ upcoming ⓐ 다가오는
085 □ work for ~에게 효과가 있다, 좋다
086 □ enough ⓐ 충분한
087 □ heavy user 많이 사용하는 사람, 헤비 유저
088 □ eliminate ⓥ 제외하다, 없애다
089 □ international ⓐ 국제의
090 □ expensive ⓐ 비싼

11

091 □ gift box 선물 상자
092 □ head to ~로 향하다
093 □ have a baby 아기를 낳다
094 □ amazing ⓐ 놀라운
095 □ expect a baby 임신하다
096 □ in good health 건강한
097 □ health checkup 건강 검진

12

098 □ go swimming 수영하러 가다
099 □ make sure to 반드시 ~하다
100 □ give up 포기하다
101 □ cheap ⓐ 값싼
102 □ monthly pass 한 달 정기권
103 □ dive into ~에 뛰어들다
104 □ whole body 전신

13

105 □ biology ⓝ 생물학
106 □ microscope ⓝ 현미경
107 □ observe ⓥ 관찰하다
108 □ cell ⓝ 세포
109 □ have a chance to ~할 기회를 갖다
110 □ illustration ⓝ 삽화, 예시
111 □ textbook ⓝ 교과서
112 □ be about to ~할 참이다
113 □ lab (laboratory) ⓝ 실험실
114 □ thoroughly ad 꼼꼼히, 철저히

14

115 □ bookstore ⓝ 서점
116 □ old book 헌책
117 □ classic ⓐ 고전적인
118 □ remarkable ⓐ 드문, 놀라운, 주목할 만한
119 □ purchase ⓥ 구매하다
120 □ lot ⓝ 전부, 많음, 다수
121 □ contribute to ~에 기여하다
122 □ appreciate ⓥ 진가를 알다, 인정하다
123 □ My pleasure. 천만에요. 제가 감사하죠.
124 □ those in need 어려운[도움이 필요한] 사람들

15

125 □ talented ⓐ 재능 있는
126 □ attend ⓥ 다니다
127 □ art college 미술 대학
128 □ brochure ⓝ 홍보 책자, 브로셔
129 □ competition ⓝ 대회, 경쟁
130 □ be eager to 몹시 ~하고 싶어하다
131 □ submit ⓥ 제출하다
132 □ responsible for ~을 담당하는, 책임지는
133 □ excitedly ad 설레며, 신나서
134 □ look forward to ~을 고대하다
135 □ first draft 초안
136 □ missing ⓐ 빠진
137 □ point out 지적하다
138 □ disappointed ⓐ 실망한
139 □ inform ⓥ 알려주다

16~17

140 □ independent ⓐ 독립적인
141 □ shortly after 직후에
142 □ extended ⓐ 장기간의
143 □ teenager ⓝ 십대
144 □ lifetime ⓝ 평생
145 □ typically ad 보통, 대체로
146 □ Arctic ⓐ 북극의
147 □ necessary for ~에 필요한
148 □ video clip 영상
149 □ life expectancy 기대 수명
150 □ similarity ⓝ 유사점, 공통점
151 □ parenting ⓝ 양육

26회 • 2022학년도 10월 학력평가 고3 영어 듣기

※ QR코드를 스캔하시면 듣기 방송을 청취하실 수 있습니다.

● 점수 표시가 없는 문항은 모두 2점 ● 문항수 17개 | 배점 37점 | 제한 시간 25분

1번부터 17번까지는 듣고 답하는 문제입니다. 1번부터 15번까지는 한 번만 들려주고, 16번부터 17번까지는 두 번 들려줍니다. 방송을 잘 듣고 답을 하시기 바랍니다.

MP3

1. 다음을 듣고, 남자가 하는 말의 목적으로 가장 적절한 것을 고르시오.

① 동영상 편집 강좌를 홍보하려고
② 학교 홍보 영상 출연자를 모집하려고
③ 교내 댄스 동아리 가입을 권유하려고
④ 웹 사이트 제작 경연 대회를 안내하려고
⑤ 신입생 환영 행사 아이디어를 공모하려고

2. 대화를 듣고, 여자의 의견으로 가장 적절한 것을 고르시오.

① 장시간의 컴퓨터 작업은 위장 활동을 저해한다.
② 엎드려 자는 자세는 목에 통증을 유발할 수 있다.
③ 잠자기 전 가벼운 스트레칭은 숙면에 도움을 준다.
④ 올바른 자세를 위해 모니터 높이를 조절해야 한다.
⑤ 잠자는 자세를 보면 그 사람의 성격을 알 수 있다.

3. 대화를 듣고, 두 사람의 관계를 가장 잘 나타낸 것을 고르시오.

① 소설가 – 편집자 ② 환경미화원 – 관광객
③ 기자 – 프로듀서 ④ 방송 작가 – 환경 운동가
⑤ 사진작가 – 낚시꾼

4. 대화를 듣고, 그림에서 대화의 내용과 일치하지 않는 것을 고르시오.

5. 대화를 듣고, 남자가 할 일로 가장 적절한 것을 고르시오.

① 튜브에서 바람 빼기 ② 수영복 챙기기
③ 숙박 시설 검색하기 ④ 식당 예약하기
⑤ 퇴실 시간 문의하기

6. 대화를 듣고, 여자가 지불할 금액을 고르시오. [3점]

① $54 ② $60 ③ $63 ④ $70 ⑤ $75

7. 대화를 듣고, 남자가 학생회 자선 행사에 갈 수 없는 이유를 고르시오.

① 뮤지컬을 보러 가야 해서
② 병원 진료를 받아야 해서
③ 농구 시합에 출전해야 해서
④ 기말고사 준비를 해야 해서
⑤ 자원봉사를 하러 가야 해서

8. 대화를 듣고, Kimchi Dish Contest에 관해 언급되지 않은 것을 고르시오.

① 경연 과제 ② 주최 기관 ③ 우승 상금
④ 시작 연도 ⑤ 참가 자격

9. Full Day City Tour에 관한 다음 내용을 듣고, 일치하지 않는 것을 고르시오.

① 호텔 투숙객에게 특가로 제공한다.
② 매일 오전 10시에 버스가 출발한다.
③ 여섯 곳의 주요 관광 명소에 들른다.
④ 전문 여행 가이드가 동행한다.
⑤ 점심 식사를 무료로 제공한다.

[해설편 p.113]

10. 다음 표를 보면서 대화를 듣고, 남자가 구입할 캔들 워머 램프를 고르시오.

Candle Warmer Lamp

	Model	Price	Shade Color	Base Material	Timer
①	A	$65	gold	metal	○
②	B	$52	white	marble stone	○
③	C	$45	black	marble stone	×
④	D	$40	pink	marble stone	○
⑤	E	$37	white	metal	×

11. 대화를 듣고, 여자의 마지막 말에 대한 남자의 응답으로 가장 적절한 것을 고르시오.

① I'm glad to hear you enjoyed your food today.
② We've run out of ingredients to make the dish.
③ Thank you for bringing your home-cooked food.
④ I'll let you know when your seats are available.
⑤ I'll recommend the special creamy salmon pasta.

12. 대화를 듣고, 남자의 마지막 말에 대한 여자의 응답으로 가장 적절한 것을 고르시오.

① I'm afraid that I can't get this stain out.
② Sorry. I'll take it to the dry cleaner's now.
③ No way. You should organize the closet today.
④ You should have worn the suit at the presentation.
⑤ Don't worry. I'm going to pick it up this afternoon.

13. 대화를 듣고, 여자의 마지막 말에 대한 남자의 응답으로 가장 적절한 것을 고르시오. [3점]

Man: ______________________________

① Hurry up. Her birthday is coming soon.
② Sounds great. I'm sure it'll make her feel better.
③ Sure. You should have bought her another model.
④ No worries. This keyboard is what I want to have.
⑤ A belated happy birthday to you. This gift is for you.

14. 대화를 듣고, 남자의 마지막 말에 대한 여자의 응답으로 가장 적절한 것을 고르시오. [3점]

Woman: ______________________________

① Right. He's been away from work for five days.
② No problem. I'll send you an engineer right away.
③ Okay. He'll call you before he makes the visit tomorrow.
④ Sure. You can use the Internet service anywhere at home.
⑤ Sorry. You need to change your Internet service provider.

15. 다음 상황 설명을 듣고, Sofia가 Hannah에게 할 말로 가장 적절한 것을 고르시오.

Sofia: ______________________________

① I think our costume preparation is way behind schedule.
② Please put the leading actor in the middle of the poster.
③ Let's pick a color that makes the main character noticeable.
④ I'll recommend someone to take over my position next year.
⑤ More comfortable clothing will be better for the character.

[16 ~ 17] 다음을 듣고, 물음에 답하시오.

16. 여자가 하는 말의 주제로 가장 적절한 것은?

① tools used to study animal behaviors
② animals that make clever use of tools
③ cooperation between humans and animals
④ types of communication between animals
⑤ disadvantages of animals living in the wild

17. 언급된 동물이 <u>아닌</u> 것은?

① crows ② monkeys ③ elephants
④ beavers ⑤ octopuses

[해설편 p.115]

Dictation 26

✪ 표기에는 듣기 어려운 발음이 포함되어 있습니다. 귀 기울여 듣고 받아쓰세요.

● 고3 2022학년도 10월

※ QR 코드를 스캔하시면 듣기 방송이 나옵니다. 듣기 방송을 들으며 다음 빈칸을 채우시오. ● 제한 시간 : 25분

01

다음을 듣고, 남자가 하는 말의 목적으로 가장 적절한 것을 고르시오.

M : Hello, students. This is your vice principal, Mr. Smith. Our school is going to _________ _________ _________ _________ for future freshmen. It'll be a music video with students doing dances. The famous dance director, Kiera Turner, will help us. She'll be ✪ _________ _________ _________ in the auditorium on Tuesday, October 25th. If you want to participate and _________ _________ _________ _________, just sign up using the QR code posted on the school bulletin board by this Friday. We'll upload the video on our school website after it's been completed, so please don't miss out on this wonderful opportunity to contribute to our school.

02

대화를 듣고, 여자의 의견으로 가장 적절한 것을 고르시오.

W : Owen, why are you massaging your neck?

M : Hey, Karen. My neck feels stiff.

W : That's too bad. When did it start?

M : ✪ _________ _________ _________ for a while, but it's gotten worse lately. I think it might be because my monitor is too low.

W : The height seems fine. Umm... Do you _________ _________ _________ _________, by any chance?

M : How did you know that? Yes, I'm a stomach sleeper.

W : Well... Sleeping on your stomach may lead to some pretty bad pain in your neck.

M : Are you saying that my neck pain came from my sleeping position?

W : Right. _________ _________ _________ _________ to one side when you sleep on your stomach. It can cause neck pain.

M : That makes sense. I'll try changing my sleeping position, then.

W : Yeah. I'm sure it'll help.

03

대화를 듣고, 두 사람의 관계를 가장 잘 나타낸 것을 고르시오.

M : Ms. Lopez, I'm pleased to meet you.

W : Hello, Mr. Stewart. You are preparing scripts for a documentary TV show, right?

M : Yes, so I need your story. You've been fighting to _________ _________ _________ for 20 years?

W : Yes. I can't believe it's been that long.

M : What made you start ✪ _________ _________ _________ _________ _________ in the first place?

W : Actually, it started from a simple accident.

M : Really? What happened?

W : A friend of mine _________ _________ _________ _________ _________ while walking barefoot on the beach with me.

M : Ouch! A careless fisherman must have left it after fishing.

W : Right. I saw all kinds of waste materials around me and organized my first beach clean-up. That was the beginning of my career.

M : I see. I'd like to use your story when I write the introductory scene for the show.

04

대화를 듣고, 그림에서 대화의 내용과 일치하지 않는 것을 고르시오.

W : The shooting starts soon. Are you ready, Jackson?

M : Yes. I'm adjusting the camera angles for the set.

W : I like the floor lamp on the left. It goes well with the set.

M : Yeah. There are three different chairs around the table. Are they for our guests?

W : Yes. Look at the ✪ _________ _________ on one of the chairs. The star represents our program's title, StarMaking.

M : Good. I see the piano next to the plant. Is someone going to play the piano?

W : Of course, our guests are all musicians. I want to _________ _________ _________ _________ to the piano.

M : Great. The audience will enjoy their performance. There are bottles of water _________ _________ _________. Are they from our program's sponsor?

W : Yes. _________ _________ _________ _________ _________ _________ when the guests drink them.

M : Okay. I'll take care of it.

05

대화를 듣고, 남자가 할 일로 가장 적절한 것을 고르시오.

W : Honey, I can't believe it's our last day at this resort.

M : Yeah, but it was nice to relax _________ _________ _________ here.

W : Right. I liked the swimming pool the most.

M : So did I. It was great to swim every day. Anyway, what's the checkout time?

W : By 11 a.m. Why don't we have lunch at Del Casa after checkout?

M : Good. Should I make a reservation?

W : Actually, they don't accept reservations.

M : Don't they? _________ _________ _________ _________. Did you put our swimsuits in the bag?

W : Yes, I already did. We also need to ✪ _________ _________ _________ _________ _________ _________ _________ _________.

M : Okay. I'll do it right away.

W : Thanks. In the meantime, I'll do a final check.

Dictation 26

06

대화를 듣고, 여자가 지불할 금액을 고르시오. [3점]

M : Welcome to Purple Bike Rental Shop. How may I help you?
W : Hi. I want to rent some bikes.
M : We have regular bikes and electric bikes.
W : Okay. How much do they cost to rent for a day?
M : Regular bikes are $25 each, and electric bikes are $30 each.
W : Then, I'll rent two electric bikes. Does the rental __________ __________ __________?
M : It sure does.
W : Very good. Do you offer __________ __________ __________ __________?
M : Yes, but ✪ __________ __________ __________ __________. It costs $5 for one bike.
W : I'll use the collection service for the two bikes. Can I use this discount coupon?
M : Sure. You'll get a 10% discount off the total.
W : Good. Here's my credit card.

07

대화를 듣고, 남자가 학생회 자선 행사에 갈 수 없는 이유를 고르시오.

W : Scott, the Student Council Charity Event is this Saturday at the gym, right?
M : No. It's next Saturday.
W : Really? I thought it's this Saturday.
M : ✪ __________ __________ __________ __________. There's a basketball match scheduled this Saturday.
W : I see. Then, why don't we go to the charity event together next Saturday?
M : I'm afraid I can't.
W : Oh, I forgot you sometimes __________ __________ __________ at the hospital on Saturday.
M : Yes, but I'm not doing it next Saturday.
W : Then why can't you go to the charity event?
M : I promised to __________ __________ __________ with my younger brother. I couldn't spend much time with him recently because of the final exams.
W : No problem. I hope you have a good time with your brother.

08

대화를 듣고, Kimchi Dish Contest에 관해 언급되지 않은 것을 고르시오.

M : Hey, Clara. Guess what I did last weekend.
W : I heard you won the Kimchi Dish Contest. Congratulations!
M : Thank you. I'm happy to be this year's winner.
W : I didn't know that there's a kimchi-themed cooking contest. Is it ✪ __________ __________ __________, then?
M : Yes. Every year, all participants are required to make a fusion dish using kimchi. I made kimchi pizza.
W : Sounds good. __________ __________ __________ __________?
M : It's the Institute of Korean Food and Culture.
W : I see. How long has it been running for?
M : The first contest was held in 2015.
W : That's __________ __________ __________ __________. I want to participate myself next year. Are there any special requirements for me to participate?
M : __________ __________ __________ __________ __________ can compete.
W : Great. I'll give it a try.

09

Full Day City Tour에 관한 다음 내용을 듣고, 일치하지 않는 것을 고르시오.

W : Good evening, Central Hotel guests. We are happy to inform you about __________ __________ __________ for the Full Day City Tour. This tour normally costs $90 but is offered to our hotel guests at a special price of just $55. Leaving at 10 a.m. every morning, a luxury coach bus __________ __________ __________ __________ __________. It stops at six major tourist attractions, including the waterfront and the Museum of Art History. Professional tour guides are with you __________ __________ __________ __________ __________, answering questions and ✪ __________ __________ __________. There is also a stop so that you can buy lunch. Please come to the reception desk if you're interested in signing up. Thank you.

10

다음 표를 보면서 대화를 듣고, 남자가 구입할 캔들 워머 램프를 고르시오.

M : Hey, Emily. Would you help me choose a candle warmer lamp for my sister's birthday gift?
W : Sure. *[Pause]* These five models look pretty good. What's your budget?
M : I can spend up to $60.
W : Okay. The lamp shades come in different colors. Does your sister have ✪ __________ __________ __________?
M : She doesn't like pink. I think the other colors will be okay.
W : Got it. I recommend the ones with __________ __________ __________ __________. They're strong and beautiful.
M : Great. They can also be used as a beautiful home decoration.
W : Then these two are the best options.
M : Right. Do you think the candle warmer lamp with a timer is better?
W : With that function, your sister doesn't need to worry about __________ __________ __________ __________.
M : Then, I'll buy the one with a timer. Thanks.

11

대화를 듣고, 여자의 마지막 말에 대한 남자의 응답으로 가장 적절한 것을 고르시오.

W : Excuse me. I'd like to order the special ✪ __________ __________ __________.
M : We're very sorry. We __________ __________ __________ __________ __________ __________ right now.
W : Why not? I've come here especially to eat that pasta.

12

대화를 듣고, 남자의 마지막 말에 대한 여자의 응답으로 가장 적절한 것을 고르시오.

M : Have you seen my gray suit, Mom? It was in the closet a week ago, but I can't find it now.

W : I took it to the dry cleaner's because ✪ __________ __________ __________ __________ __________.

M : Oh, my! I need to wear it to an important presentation tomorrow.

13

대화를 듣고, 여자의 마지막 말에 대한 남자의 응답으로 가장 적절한 것을 고르시오. [3점]

M : You look down. What's wrong, Jennifer?

W : Dad, you know my best friend Betty? Her birthday was the day before yesterday, but I totally forgot about it.

M : Oh dear. She must have been ✪ __________ __________.

W : Absolutely. Now I understand why __________ __________ __________ __________ __________ __________ __________ since yesterday.

M : It would have been nice if she had told you in advance that her birthday was coming.

W : Well... I think so too.

M : Why don't you __________ __________ __________ __________ __________ even though it's late?

W : That's exactly what I'm thinking.

M : Do you have anything good in mind?

W : I'm going to buy her a bluetooth keyboard. She has always wanted to get one.

14

대화를 듣고, 남자의 마지막 말에 대한 여자의 응답으로 가장 적절한 것을 고르시오. [3점]

[Telephone rings.]

W : Gladmax Broadband. How may I help you?

M : Hello, my name is Morris Davis. I called yesterday.

W : Hold on, please. *[Typing sound]* Yes, you called us ✪ __________ __________ __________ __________ __________ __________.

M : Yes. An engineer is supposed to come to my house at 3 p.m. today.

W : Right. Is there any problem?

M : Can you __________ __________ __________? I won't be home at that time.

W : Okay. What time would be better for you?

M : __________ __________ __________ __________ for around 1 p.m. tomorrow?

W : Let me check. *[Pause]* I'm afraid that the engineer has already been scheduled for that time. But he's available after 4 p.m.

M : Good. I'll be home around that time.

15

다음 상황 설명을 듣고, Sofia가 Hannah에게 할 말로 가장 적절한 것을 고르시오.

M : Sofia and Hannah are members of the school drama club. They are ✪ __________ __________ __________ __________ __________ for this year's play. Sofia is the head, and Hannah is quite new on the costume team. They have sketched some costume ideas and now it's time to choose colors for the costumes. Hannah suggests yellow for their leading role's costume. However, Sofia thinks that yellow is not a good idea because the __________ __________ will also be mostly yellow. She wants to tell Hannah to choose a color different from that of the set to __________ __________ __________ __________ __________ __________. In this situation, what would Sofia most likely say to Hannah?

16~17

다음을 듣고, 물음에 답하시오.

W : Hello, students. Do you think only humans are __________ __________ __________ __________ __________? Absolutely not. Today, we'll learn about animals using tools available to them. It's no secret that ✪ __________ __________ __________ __________ using tools. Their clever tricks include manipulating sticks to extract insects from logs and dropping walnuts in front of moving cars to crack them. Elephants also have problem solving abilities. They use branches for scratching parts of their body that their tail and trunk cannot reach. They also chew on bark and use it as a sponge to __________ __________ __________ __________. Clever animals are observed in water, too. Beavers construct dams to __________ __________ __________ __________. They build these by cutting down trees and packing them with mud and stones. Some octopuses have been observed carrying two halves of a shell. Threatened by predators, they close the shells over themselves to hide. Now, let's watch a video clip about these intelligent animals.

▶ 정답 : 해설편 117쪽

회차별 영단어 QR 코드 ※ QR 코드를 스캔 후 모바일로 단어장처럼 학습할 수 있습니다.

● 고3 2022학년도 10월

01

001 □ **vice principal** 교감
002 □ **promotional** ⓐ 홍보의
003 □ **freshman** ⓝ 신입생
004 □ **applicant** ⓝ 지원자
005 □ **auditorium** ⓝ 강당
006 □ **show off** ~을 선보이다, 자랑하다
007 □ **miss out on** ~을 놓치다

02

008 □ **stiff** ⓐ 뻣뻣한
009 □ **get worse** 나빠지다, 심해지다
010 □ **sleep on one's stomach** 엎드려 자다
011 □ **by any chance** (의문문에서) 혹시
012 □ **twist** ⓥ 구부리다, 비틀다
013 □ **make sense** 일리가 있다

03

014 □ **fight** ⓥ 싸우다, 분투하다
015 □ **save the environment** 환경을 보호하다
016 □ **activist** ⓝ 운동가, 활동가
017 □ **in the first place** 처음에, 애초에
018 □ **fishhook** ⓝ 낚시바늘
019 □ **barefoot** ad 맨발로
020 □ **careless** ⓐ 조심성 없는
021 □ **introductory** ⓐ 도입의, 서두의

04

022 □ **shooting** ⓝ 촬영
023 □ **adjust** ⓥ 조정하다, 맞추다
024 □ **go well with** ~와 잘 어울리다
025 □ **sing along to** ~에 맞추어 노래하다
026 □ **take care of** ~을 처리하다

05

027 □ **checkout** ⓝ 체크아웃, 퇴실, 반납
028 □ **make a reservation** 예약하다
029 □ **accept** ⓥ 접수하다, 받다
030 □ **pack** ⓥ 짐을 싸다
031 □ **let out** ~을 빼다
032 □ **in the meantime** 그동안, 한편
033 □ **do a final check** 최종 점검을 하다

06

034 □ **rent** ⓥ 빌리다, 대여하다
035 □ **electric** ⓐ 전기의
036 □ **cost** ⓥ (비용이) ~이다
037 □ **collection** ⓝ 수거, 모음
038 □ **additional** ⓐ 추가적인
039 □ **charge** ⓝ 비용 ⓥ 부과하다

07

040 □ **charity event** 자선행사
041 □ **You must be mistaken.** 너 오해했나보다. 착각했나 보다.
042 □ **match** ⓝ 시합, 경기
043 □ **do volunteer work** 자원봉사를 하다
044 □ **final exam** 기말고사

08

045 □ **annual** ⓐ 연마다 하는
046 □ **be required to** ~해야 하다
047 □ **fusion dish** 퓨전 요리
048 □ **institute** ⓝ (교육) 기관
049 □ **requirement** ⓝ 요구사항

09

050 □ **promotion** ⓝ 홍보
051 □ **coach bus** 대형 버스
052 □ **tourist attraction** 관광 명소
053 □ **waterfront** ⓝ 해안가
054 □ **fascinating** ⓐ 대단히 흥미로운

10

055 □ **candle warmer lamp** 캔들 워머 램프
056 □ **budget** ⓝ 예산
057 □ **marble** ⓝ 대리석
058 □ **overheat** ⓥ 과열하다

11

059 □ **salmon** ⓝ 연어
060 □ **take an order** 주문을 받다
061 □ **run out of** ~이 다 떨어지다
062 □ **home-cooked** ⓐ 집에서 요리한

12

063 □ **suit** ⓝ 정장
064 □ **closet** ⓝ 옷장
065 □ **stain** ⓝ 얼룩

13

066 □ **You look down.** 우울해 보이네.
067 □ **disappointed** ⓐ 실망한
068 □ **birthday gift** 생일 선물
069 □ **belated** ⓐ 뒤늦은

14

070 □ **connection** ⓝ 연결
071 □ **engineer** ⓝ 기사, 수리공
072 □ **reschedule** ⓥ 일정을 조정하다
073 □ **make a visit** 방문하다

15

074 □ **drama club** 연극부
075 □ **in charge of** ~을 담당하는
076 □ **costume** ⓝ 의상
077 □ **stand out** 돋보이다, 두드러지다
078 □ **noticeable** ⓐ 눈에 띄는
079 □ **take over** ~을 이어받다, 대체하다

16~17

080 □ **clever** ⓐ 똑똑한
081 □ **extract** ⓥ 꺼내다, 추출하다
082 □ **crack** ⓥ 깨다
083 □ **branch** ⓝ 나뭇가지
084 □ **scratch** ⓥ 긁다
085 □ **absorb** ⓥ 흡수하다
086 □ **disadvantage** ⓝ 불리한 점, 난점

27회 ● 2021학년도 10월 학력평가 고3 영어 듣기

※ QR코드를 스캔하시면 듣기 방송을 청취하실 수 있습니다.

● 점수 표시가 없는 문항은 모두 2점 ● 문항수 17개 | 배점 37점 | 제한 시간 25분

1번부터 17번까지는 듣고 답하는 문제입니다. 1번부터 15번까지는 한 번만 들려주고, 16번부터 17번까지는 두 번 들려줍니다. 방송을 잘 듣고 답을 하시기 바랍니다.

MP3

1. 다음을 듣고, 남자가 하는 말의 목적으로 가장 적절한 것을 고르시오.

① 사진 동아리 부원을 모집하려고
② 동물원 견학 프로그램을 홍보하려고
③ 동물 사진을 찍는 요령을 알려 주려고
④ 동물원 관람 시 유의 사항을 안내하려고
⑤ 새로 출시된 카메라의 사용법을 설명하려고

2. 대화를 듣고, 여자의 의견으로 가장 적절한 것을 고르시오.

① 개인 이메일 계정을 업무용으로 사용하지 말아야 한다.
② 환경을 보호하기 위해 종이 우편물을 줄일 필요가 있다.
③ 출처가 불분명한 이메일의 첨부 파일을 열어서는 안 된다.
④ 탄소 배출량 감소를 위해 불필요한 이메일을 삭제해야 한다.
⑤ 개인 정보 유출을 방지하기 위해 휴면 계정을 정리해야 한다.

3. 대화를 듣고, 두 사람의 관계를 가장 잘 나타낸 것을 고르시오.

① 환경 운동가 – 기자 ② 고객 – 청소업체 직원
③ 집주인 – 실내 디자이너 ④ 건축가 – 건축 자재 판매자
⑤ 지역 주민 – 건설 현장 직원

4. 대화를 듣고, 그림에서 대화의 내용과 일치하지 않는 것을 고르시오.

5. 대화를 듣고, 남자가 할 일로 가장 적절한 것을 고르시오.

① 무대 조명 점검하기 ② 사회자에게 연락하기
③ 피아노 위치 조정하기 ④ 무선 마이크 가져가기
⑤ 참가자에게 공연 순서 알리기

6. 대화를 듣고, 여자가 지불할 금액을 고르시오. [3점]

① $26 ② $28 ③ $30 ④ $34 ⑤ $36

7. 대화를 듣고, 남자가 전자책을 사려는 이유를 고르시오.

① 글자 크기를 조절할 수 있어서
② 종이책 재고가 부족해서
③ 휴대하기가 편리해서
④ 종이책보다 가격이 저렴해서
⑤ 서점에 가지 않고 구매할 수 있어서

8. 대화를 듣고, Central Flower Market에 관해 언급되지 않은 것을 고르시오.

① 운영 시간 ② 위치 ③ 휴무 요일
④ 주차 요금 ⑤ 입점 매장 수

9. 2021 Robinson Fishing Contest에 관한 다음 내용을 듣고, 일치하지 않는 것을 고르시오.

① 10월 22일부터 23일까지 개최된다.
② 대회 장소는 Silver Cloud 호수이다.
③ 1등 상품은 고급 낚싯대 한 세트이다.
④ 잡은 물고기의 수를 기준으로 심사한다.
⑤ 대회가 끝난 후에 호수를 청소하는 행사가 있다.

[해설편 p.117]

10. 다음 표를 보면서 대화를 듣고, 두 사람이 주문할 와플 메이커를 고르시오.

Waffle Makers

	Model	Price	Plates	Waffle Shape	Audible Alert
①	A	$20	Fixed	Square	×
②	B	$33	Removable	Round	×
③	C	$48	Fixed	Round	×
④	D	$52	Removable	Round	○
⑤	E	$70	Removable	Square	○

11. 대화를 듣고, 여자의 마지막 말에 대한 남자의 응답으로 가장 적절한 것을 고르시오.

① Thank you. Please let me know if you find it.
② Don't worry. I can find your house by myself.
③ Why don't you try it on? It'll look nice on you.
④ I'm sorry. I don't think I can make it to your party.
⑤ I think you're right. The baseball cap doesn't fit me.

12. 대화를 듣고, 남자의 마지막 말에 대한 여자의 응답으로 가장 적절한 것을 고르시오.

① Be careful. You might get an electric shock.
② Oh, I see. Then I'll go get some new ones now.
③ Great. The bathroom is much brighter than before.
④ All right. I'll replace the garage light bulb right now.
⑤ Never mind. I'll come back when the items are in stock.

13. 대화를 듣고, 여자의 마지막 말에 대한 남자의 응답으로 가장 적절한 것을 고르시오. [3점]

Man: ______________________________

① I'm sorry I can't join the design project this time.
② Traditional culture can be a great source of creativity.
③ Our preference should be quality over brand and price.
④ I'll change the pattern of the dress as you suggested.
⑤ We should have handed in the assignment on time.

14. 대화를 듣고, 남자의 마지막 말에 대한 여자의 응답으로 가장 적절한 것을 고르시오. [3점]

Woman: ______________________________

① Great. I can't wait to open the boxes myself.
② Right. I'll ask about replacing it with a new one.
③ Yes. You should return the product within a week.
④ Sorry. The delivery will be a little later than usual.
⑤ No problem. I've already moved all the boxes for you.

15. 다음 상황 설명을 듣고, Sarah가 Emily에게 할 말로 가장 적절한 것을 고르시오.

Sarah: Emily, ______________________________

① you should rinse plastic containers before recycling them.
② I want you to do your laundry by yourself more often.
③ our recycling center requires us to remove the labels.
④ we need to refill these containers with some fruits.
⑤ you have to wipe the table right after you eat.

[16 ~ 17] 다음을 듣고, 물음에 답하시오.

16. 여자가 하는 말의 주제로 가장 적절한 것은?

① the origins of national sports teams' nicknames
② the ways countries choose their capital cities
③ city nicknames and how they came to be
④ commonly confused capital cities in the world
⑤ famous tourist attractions and their economic value

17. 언급된 도시가 <u>아닌</u> 것은?

① Rome　② Paris　③ Singapore
④ Sydney　⑤ Seattle

[해설편 p.119]

※ QR 코드를 스캔하시면 듣기 방송이 나옵니다. 듣기 방송을 들으며 다음 빈칸을 채우시오. ● 제한 시간 : 25분

01

다음을 듣고, 남자가 하는 말의 목적으로 가장 적절한 것을 고르시오.

M : Hello, students of the Live Photography Club. I'm glad to see you at East Hills Zoo today. Before we start, I want to share some tips for taking good photos of animals. First, be patient. Take your time until the animal is ________ ________ ________ ________ ________. Second, try to ________ ________ ________ ________ on your camera. The flash impacts some of the shadows that natural light creates, making the picture look "flat" and less interesting. Lastly, I also recommend you try using burst mode. Burst mode allows you to ✪ ________ ________ ________ ________ ________ ________ and capture action shots of animals. Now, let's split up and try to get the best animal pictures.

02

대화를 듣고, 여자의 의견으로 가장 적절한 것을 고르시오.

M : Olivia, what are you doing on your computer?
W : Hi, Jason. I'm clearing out old emails from my inbox.
M : Why are you deleting them?
W : Because deleting old, unnecessary emails can be a step to saving the planet by ________ ________ ________ ________.
M : What do you mean by that?
W : You know emails you never deleted are stored in data centers, right?
M : Yeah, I know that.
W : The data centers consume quite a lot of electricity. A lot of electricity is still generated by burning fossil fuels.
M : You mean ________ ________ ________ ________ helps save electricity?
W : Right. We need to delete unneeded emails to reduce carbon emissions.
M : Now I understand ✪ ________ ________ ________ ________ ________ ________. I'll check my own inbox now.

03

대화를 듣고, 두 사람의 관계를 가장 잘 나타낸 것을 고르시오.

W : Excuse me.
M : Hello. How may I help you?
W : Hi. I'm here ________ ________ ________ ________ ________ ________. Who should I talk to about it?
M : I'm in charge. You can talk to me.
W : Okay. Your construction site is ________ ________ ________ ________ ________.
M : Oh, really? We've already set up a dust screen.
W : I know, but I live right across the street from here, and I still can't open the windows in my house.
M : Oh, we're very sorry for your inconvenience.
W : I'd like you to ✪ ________ ________ ________ to solve this problem.
M : All right. We'll have a meeting and try to find a better solution as soon as possible.
W : Okay. Thank you.

04

대화를 듣고, 그림에서 대화의 내용과 일치하지 않는 것을 고르시오.

M : Silvia, guess what I did last weekend.
W : Sounds like you did something special.
M : Yes, I went on a family picnic. Look at this picture.
W : It looks great! Who is this girl in the boat? She's ________ ________ ________ ________.
M : She's my younger sister, Jenny. She likes to wear that hat outside.
W : Oh, you're ________ ________ ________. Wasn't it hard work?
M : Yeah, it was a little hard, but my sister really enjoyed the boat ride.
W : You're such a good brother. And what is this in front of your boat?
M : It's a duck. Its head is under the surface of the water.
W : I guess it's trying to get some food in the water.
M : The man ✪ ________ ________ ________ ________ ________ ________ is my father. He's relaxing.
W : I see. The two hot air balloons in the sky look awesome.
M : Yeah, it was my first time seeing real hot air balloons.
W : Cool! You must have had a really great weekend.

05

대화를 듣고, 남자가 할 일로 가장 적절한 것을 고르시오.

W : Hi, Mr. White. The school concert starts in the afternoon.
M : Yeah, I know. I think we need to check ________ ________ ________ ________ ________.
W : Good idea.
M : Did you call Henry this morning? He's the student MC for the concert.
W : I told him to come to the auditorium by 10 a.m. for the rehearsal.
M : Good. The participants know the order of their performances, right?
W : I told them all about it. Ah, we should also ✪ ________ ________ ________ of the piano on the stage.
M : Don't worry. I already did it yesterday afternoon.
W : Thank you, Mr. White. Then now I think all we have to do is check the stage lighting and get some wireless microphones ready.
M : The wireless microphones are in the broadcasting room. I'll go and take them to the auditorium.
W : Okay. Then, I'll go to the auditorium and ________ ________ ________.
M : All right. See you there in a minute.

06

대화를 듣고, 여자가 지불할 금액을 고르시오. [3점]

M : Welcome to Lynn's Garden Center. How may I help you?
W : Hi, I'm looking for some gardening tools. Do you have any shovels?
M : Of course. We have two types of shovel.
W : What's the difference between the two types?
M : One has a plastic handle, and the other has a wooden handle.
W : Well, wooden handles are __________ __________ __________ __________. I'll buy a shovel with a wooden handle. How much is it?
M : Originally they cost $20 each, but all shovels are 10% off this week.
W : Great! I also need __________ __________ __________.
M : Okay. I recommend these rubber-coated gloves. A pair of them cost $8, but two pairs cost only $12.
W : Oh, I'll buy two pairs.
M : Good. So you want ✪ __________ __________ __________ __________ __________ and two pairs of gardening gloves, right?
W : Yes, that's all. Here's my credit card.

07

대화를 듣고, 남자가 전자책을 사려는 이유를 고르시오.

M : Hi, Nicole. What are you reading?
W : Hi, Danny. I'm reading the newly released book, *London Ever After*.
M : Oh, I want to buy that book, too.
W : You can get a copy of its limited hardcover edition at Jackson's bookstore.
M : I know, but I'm going to buy its eBook version, instead.
W : Is there any reason you prefer eBooks? Are they cheaper?
M : Well, __________ __________ __________ __________ in the price.
W : Is that so? Then, is it because eBooks are more convenient to carry around?
M : Well, that's not the reason, either. Actually, you can __________ __________ __________ __________ while reading eBooks.
W : You mean you're able to ✪ __________ __________ __________ __________?
M : Exactly. That's why I want to buy the eBook version.
W : I see.

08

대화를 듣고, Central Flower Market에 관해 언급되지 않은 것을 고르시오.

M : Lauren, what are all these flowers?
W : Hi, Brian. I bought them at Central Flower Market this morning.
M : Is that ✪ __________ __________ __________ __________?
W : Yes. I often buy flowers there. I have to go there very early in the morning, though.
M : When does the flower market open?
W : It opens as early as 4 a.m. and closes around 10 a.m.
M : They start quite early. __________ __________ __________ __________ __________?
W : Near Central Station on 6th Street.
M : It's not that far from here. Is it open on weekends?
W : Yes, but it's __________ __________ __________.
M : Okay. Does it have a lot of parking spaces?
W : Of course. The parking lot is large and the parking fee is only two dollars per hour.
M : Sounds good. I'll take some time to go there next week.

09

2021 Robinson Fishing Contest에 관한 다음 내용을 듣고, 일치하지 않는 것을 고르시오.

M : Hello, fishermen. I'm Bruce Miller, the president of Robinson Fishing Association. You've been waiting for a long time, but now I'm happy to announce that we're hosting the '2021 Robinson Fishing Contest.' It'll be held from the 22nd to the 23rd of October. The contest is taking place at Lake Silver Cloud this year. The first place winner will be awarded a set of ✪ __________ __________ __________ and the second place winner will __________ __________ __________ __________ __________. Judges will not count the number of fish you catch. Only the length of the fish matters! After the contest, we're also having __________ __________ __________ __________. We strongly encourage you to join the event. You can sign up for the contest on our website. Thank you very much.

10

다음 표를 보면서 대화를 듣고, 두 사람이 주문할 와플 메이커를 고르시오.

M : Honey, look at this website. There are five waffle maker models on sale now.
W : Oh, I was thinking of buying one.
M : Should we buy the cheapest one?
W : No. I've heard of this model, and its reviews aren't that good.
M : Then, we won't buy it. Hmm..., some of the waffle makers ✪ __________ __________ __________ __________, but the others don't.
W : The ones with fixed plates are __________ __________ __________.
M : Then the ones with fixed plates are out. What about the waffle shape?
W : I like round waffles better than square ones.
M : All right. Let's choose from the ones that make round waffles.
W : Great. Do you think we need __________ __________ __________? It goes off when the waffles are done.
M : Well, I'm afraid the sound might __________ __________ __________ __________ while he's sleeping.
W : Good point. Let's order the one without it.
M : Perfect!

11
대화를 듣고, 여자의 마지막 말에 대한 남자의 응답으로 가장 적절한 것을 고르시오.

[Cell phone rings.]

W : Hello, Jake. What's up?

M : Hi, Kate. I had a great time at your party last night, but I think I left my baseball cap at your house. Have you seen it?

W : Oh, I'm afraid not. I'll search for it while ✪ __________ __________ __________ __________.

12
대화를 듣고, 남자의 마지막 말에 대한 여자의 응답으로 가장 적절한 것을 고르시오.

M : Honey, __________ __________ __________ __________ __________ now. I guess it's time to change the light bulb.

W : You're right. Don't we have an extra light bulb?

M : Well, I used it when I ✪ __________ __________ __________ __________ __________ __________ __________. We don't have any at home.

13
대화를 듣고, 여자의 마지막 말에 대한 남자의 응답으로 가장 적절한 것을 고르시오. [3점]

W : Hi, Minsu. How's it going with the clothing design assignment?

M : Hey, Jessica. I'm almost done with it. How about you?

W : I'm not doing well. As you know, our professor always ✪ __________ __________ __________ __________ __________, but I can't come up with any ideas.

M : I know what you mean. It wasn't easy for me, either.

W : Minsu, if you don't mind, can I see __________ __________ __________?

M : Sure. Look at my sketch.

W : Wow, it's an evening dress. Its pattern looks very unique.

M : Thanks. I got the idea from *hanbok*.

W : You mean traditional Korean clothes, right?

M : That's right. I designed this dress __________ __________ __________ __________ of *hanbok*.

W : Awesome! I've never thought I could create something new from something old.

14
대화를 듣고, 남자의 마지막 말에 대한 여자의 응답으로 가장 적절한 것을 고르시오. [3점]

W : Excuse me, sir.

M : Yes, ma'am.

W : What are those boxes?

M : These are the goods __________ __________ __________ __________ __________ on the 7th floor.

W : Well, I'm afraid you can't stack those boxes there.

M : I'll deliver them to each office soon.

W : I'm sorry, but all the emergency doorways must be __________ __________ __________ at all times.

M : Oh, is this an emergency exit?

W : Actually, there is a sign here saying "Emergency Exit."

M : I didn't notice it. I'll move the boxes right away.

W : Thanks. It's not surprising you didn't notice the sign. It's very old.

M : It'd be better if the sign were ✪ __________ __________ __________ __________.

15
다음 상황 설명을 듣고, Sarah가 Emily에게 할 말로 가장 적 절한 것을 고르시오.

W : Sarah has lived by herself since last year, when she started working at a company. This year, her sister Emily moved in because she entered a college near Sarah's house. Now they __________ __________ __________. Emily usually prepares breakfast, and Sarah cooks dinner after work. Emily does the laundry, and Sarah takes out the recycling. One day Sarah finds Emily puts plastic food containers which are still dirty into their recycling bin. Sarah knows that the local recycling center does not ✪ __________ __________ __________. She wants to tell Emily to __________ __________ __________ __________ with water before putting them into the bin. In this situation, what would Sarah most likely say to Emily?

16~17
다음을 듣고, 물음에 답하시오.

W : Okay, students. We just learned about the ten most popular visitor destinations in the world. Did you know that many cities have an alternative way of referring to them? You may have heard of some of these famous nicknames, but you might not know __________ __________ __________. Rome's nickname, "The Eternal City" can be traced far back to Ancient Rome! Citizens of this original settlement believed the city would never fall and __________ __________ __________. Paris came to be called "The City of Light." One origin of this nickname is that by the 19th century Paris used gas street lighting and Europeans who passed through Paris spread the reputation of Paris as "The City of Light." As for Singapore, it's known as "The Lion City." The city earned this name when an ancient prince spotted a lion __________ __________ __________ __________ __________. Lastly, Seattle is ✪ __________ __________ __________ __________. With all of its forestry, it's no surprise that Seattle is known as "The Emerald City." Interesting, isn't it? You can find more city nicknames and their origins in the following video clip. Now, let's watch it together.

▶ 정답 : 해설편 121쪽

VOCA LIST 27

회차별 영단어 QR 코드 ※ QR 코드를 스캔 후 모바일로 단어장처럼 학습할 수 있습니다.

● 고3 2021학년도 10월

01

001 ☐ **patient** ⓐ 인내심 있는
002 ☐ **impact** ⓥ 영향을 끼치다 ⓝ 영향
003 ☐ **burst mode** 연속 촬영
004 ☐ **sequence** ⓝ 연속, 차례
005 ☐ **capture** ⓥ 포착하다

02

006 ☐ **clear out** (~을 없애고) 청소하다
007 ☐ **inbox** ⓝ 받은편지함
008 ☐ **carbon footprint** 탄소 발자국
009 ☐ **consume** ⓥ 소비하다
010 ☐ **unneeded** ⓐ 불필요한

03

011 ☐ **building construction** 건설 현장
012 ☐ **be in charge** 책임지다, 담당하다
013 ☐ **inconvenience** ⓝ 불편, 폐
014 ☐ **take measures** 조치를 취하다

04

015 ☐ **family picnic** 가족 소풍
016 ☐ **row** ⓥ 노를 젓다
017 ☐ **surface** ⓝ 표면, 수면
018 ☐ **hot air balloon** 열기구

05

019 ☐ **auditorium** ⓝ 강당
020 ☐ **adjust** ⓥ 조정하다
021 ☐ **broadcasting room** 방송실

06

022 ☐ **gardening tool** 원예 도구
023 ☐ **shovel** ⓝ 삽
024 ☐ **rubber-coated** ⓐ 고무로 도포된

07

025 ☐ **release** ⓥ 출시하다
026 ☐ **convenient** ⓐ 편리한
027 ☐ **adjust** ⓥ 조절하다

08

028 ☐ **wholesale** ⓝ 도매 ⓐ 도매의
029 ☐ **quite** ad 아주
030 ☐ **parking lot** 주차장

09

031 ☐ **association** ⓝ 협회
032 ☐ **announce** ⓥ 발표하다, 알리다
033 ☐ **fishing rod** 낚싯대
034 ☐ **sign up for** ~에 등록하다

10

035 ☐ **removable** ⓐ 분리 가능한, 떼어낼 수 있는
036 ☐ **fixed** ⓐ 고정된
037 ☐ **audible** ⓐ 들을 수 있는, 가청의
038 ☐ **go off** (알람 등이) 울리다

11

039 ☐ **baseball cap** 야구 모자
040 ☐ **tidy up** ~을 치우다, 정리하다
041 ☐ **make it** (시간 맞춰) 가다, 해내다, 성공하다
042 ☐ **fit** ⓥ 어울리다

12

043 ☐ **blink** ⓥ 깜박이다
044 ☐ **get an electric shock** 감전되다
045 ☐ **in stock** 재고가 있는

13

046 ☐ **emphasize** ⓥ 강조하다
047 ☐ **originality** ⓝ 독창성
048 ☐ **come up with** ~을 떠올리다
049 ☐ **preference** ⓝ 선호
050 ☐ **hand in** ~을 제출하다

14

051 ☐ **stack** ⓥ 쌓다
052 ☐ **accessible** ⓐ 접근 가능한
053 ☐ **noticeable** ⓐ 눈에 띄는
054 ☐ **replace A with B** A를 B로 교체하다

15

055 ☐ **do the laundry** 세탁하다
056 ☐ **container** ⓝ 그릇, 용기
057 ☐ **recycling bin** 재활용 쓰레기통
058 ☐ **contaminate** ⓥ 오염시키다
059 ☐ **wipe** ⓥ (먼지나 물기를 없애려고) 닦다

16~17

060 ☐ **visitor destination** 관광지
061 ☐ **alternative** ⓐ 대안의
062 ☐ **originate** ⓥ 기원하다
063 ☐ **trace back to** ~의 기원이 …까지 거슬러 올라가다
064 ☐ **settlement** ⓝ 정착지
065 ☐ **thrive** ⓥ 번성하다
066 ☐ **reputation** ⓝ 명성, 평판
067 ☐ **forestry** ⓝ 숲, 산림

28회 ● 2020학년도 10월 학력평가 고3 영어 듣기

※ QR코드를 스캔하시면 듣기 방송을 청취하실 수 있습니다.

● 점수 표시가 없는 문항은 모두 2점 ● 문항수 17개 | 배점 37점 | 제한 시간 25분

1번부터 17번까지는 듣고 답하는 문제입니다. 1번부터 15번까지는 한 번만 들려주고, 16번부터 17번까지는 두 번 들려줍니다. 방송을 잘 듣고 답을 하시기 바랍니다.

MP3

1. 다음을 듣고, 남자가 하는 말의 목적으로 가장 적절한 것을 고르시오.

① 반려견을 위한 공원 시설 개선 아이디어를 공모하려고
② 반려견과의 공원 산책 시 준수 사항을 안내하려고
③ 반려견의 감염병 발병 시 대처법을 소개하려고
④ 반려견을 동반한 공원 출입 자제를 요청하려고
⑤ 공원 시설 수리를 위한 휴관을 공지하려고

2. 대화를 듣고, 여자의 의견으로 가장 적절한 것을 고르시오.

① 의뢰인의 취향을 존중하여 인테리어를 디자인해야 한다.
② 인테리어 작업은 전문가에게 맡기는 것이 좋다.
③ 인테리어 공사는 예산 안에서 진행해야 한다.
④ 집안의 색이 가족의 기분에 영향을 미친다.
⑤ 주기적으로 가구를 재배치하는 것이 좋다.

3. 대화를 듣고, 두 사람의 관계를 가장 잘 나타낸 것을 고르시오.

① 자전거 수리공 - 고객 ② 스포츠 기자 - 사이클 선수
③ 건물 청소부 - 입주민 ④ 골동품 감정사 - 의뢰인
⑤ 농기구 판매상 - 농장주

4. 대화를 듣고, 그림에서 대화의 내용과 일치하지 않는 것을 고르시오.

5. 대화를 듣고, 여자가 남자를 위해 할 일로 가장 적절한 것을 고르시오.

① 요리 강습 신청하기 ② 김치 조리법 전송하기
③ 김치 시식 후기 쓰기 ④ 채식 도시락 주문하기
⑤ 요리 재료 구매하기

6. 대화를 듣고, 남자가 지불할 금액을 고르시오. [3점]

① $25 ② $30 ③ $35 ④ $40 ⑤ $45

7. 대화를 듣고, 남자가 화상 회의에 참석하지 못한 이유를 고르시오.

① 회의 시간을 착각해서
② 휴대 전화가 고장 나서
③ 접속 비밀번호를 잊어서
④ 인터넷 접속이 불안정해서
⑤ 다른 회의에 참석해야 해서

8. 대화를 듣고, Jazz Guitar Contest에 관해 언급되지 않은 것을 고르시오.

① 주최 단체 ② 개최 장소 ③ 개최 시기
④ 우승 상금 ⑤ 참가비

9. The 10th International Hot Air Balloon Fiesta에 관한 다음 내용을 듣고, 일치하지 않는 것을 고르시오.

① 다음 주 월요일부터 2주간 개최된다.
② 열기구 탑승 시각은 매일 오전 10시와 오후 5시이다.
③ 첫날 열기구 탑승권은 20% 할인된다.
④ 열기구는 다양한 국기로 장식된다.
⑤ 웹 사이트에서 실시간으로 스트리밍된다.

10. 다음 표를 보면서 대화를 듣고, 여자가 구매할 캣 트리를 고르시오.

Multi-Level Cat Trees

	Model	Price	No. of Levels	Size	Assembly Required
①	A	$65	5	Medium	○
②	B	$85	4	Medium	×
③	C	$75	5	Large	○
④	D	$95	5	Large	×
⑤	E	$105	4	X-Large	○

11. 대화를 듣고, 여자의 마지막 말에 대한 남자의 응답으로 가장 적절한 것을 고르시오.

① Thanks. That would be a great help.
② Really? You'd better leave school early.
③ Okay. Then, let me call my doctor later.
④ I know how you feel. It must hurt a lot.
⑤ Oh, no. You should have been more careful.

12. 대화를 듣고, 남자의 마지막 말에 대한 여자의 응답으로 가장 적절한 것을 고르시오.

① Definitely. Don't forget to wash it after emptying it.
② Look at the expiration date! We shouldn't buy this.
③ Yes. It's cheaper to buy it from an online store.
④ No. We shouldn't put too much ketchup on the food.
⑤ Sure. We can keep the ketchup at room temperature.

13. 대화를 듣고, 여자의 마지막 말에 대한 남자의 응답으로 가장 적절한 것을 고르시오.

Man: ______________________________

① That's a good idea. I'll sign up for a booth.
② I disagree. Camping equipment is overpriced.
③ Yes. I'm looking for a two-bedroom apartment.
④ I see it differently. Selling offline is much easier.
⑤ Thanks. But I can manage the packing on my own.

14. 대화를 듣고, 남자의 마지막 말에 대한 여자의 응답으로 가장 적절한 것을 고르시오. [3점]

Woman: ______________________________

① Oh, really? Good luck with your book search.
② I don't think so. Reading is not for everybody.
③ Hold on. Let me bring the books you requested.
④ Not at all. You should respect his taste in books.
⑤ Okay. I hope my son enjoys reading books there.

15. 다음 상황 설명을 듣고, Josh가 Lily에게 할 말로 가장 적절한 것을 고르시오. [3점]

Josh: ______________________________

① It's too bad that your phone is not working.
② Just turn off your phone when you go to bed.
③ Did you check out the latest model at the shop?
④ You're not allowed to use your phone during class.
⑤ Why don't you switch your phone to one like mine?

[16 ~ 17] 다음을 듣고, 물음에 답하시오.

16. 여자가 하는 말의 주제로 가장 적절한 것은?

① chemical compositions of fatty acids
② benefits of various vegetable cooking oils
③ tips for choosing fresh vegetable cooking oils
④ roles of fatty acids in delaying the aging process
⑤ advantages of vegetable oils as a flavor enhancer

17. 언급된 기름이 <u>아닌</u> 것은?

① coconut oil ② olive oil ③ avocado oil
④ grapeseed oil ⑤ walnut oil

[해설편 p.124]

Dictation 28

✪ 표기에는 듣기 어려운 발음이 포함되어 있습니다. 귀 기울여 듣고 받아쓰세요. ● 고3 2020학년도 10월

※ QR 코드를 스캔하시면 듣기 방송이 나옵니다. 듣기 방송을 들으며 다음 빈칸을 채우시오. ● 제한 시간 : 25분

01

다음을 듣고, 남자가 하는 말의 목적으로 가장 적절한 것을 고르시오.

M : Hello, visitors! I'm Henry Stratton, Manager of Wellington Park. I'd like to ask you to keep in mind a few things when you're walking your dog in the park. First of all, please __________ __________ __________ __________ __________. No one likes to step on dog waste, and it can ✪ __________ __________ __________ to other dogs or even to people. Cleaning up after your dog is the price of walking your dog in this beautiful park. There is one more thing. Always make sure to __________ __________ __________ __________ __________ __________. We're getting more complaints about unleashed dogs these days. Please watch your dog and keep it under control at all times. Your neighbors will appreciate your thoughtfulness. Thank you.

02

대화를 듣고, 여자의 의견으로 가장 적절한 것을 고르시오.

W : Honey, are you reading that magazine on interior design?

M : Yes. We talked about making some changes around the house. Remember?

W : Of course. I can't wait to __________ __________ __________ __________ __________ __________.

M : I'm thinking of changing the color of the walls and replacing the old tiles and doors.

W : Good idea. Do you know any good interior designers?

M : Well, I thought we could save money if we did it ourselves.

W : I disagree. If we're not happy ✪ __________ __________ __________ __________ __________, we'll eventually have to hire someone to fix it.

M : Hmm.... In that case, we could end up spending more money.

W : Also, think of all the time and energy we'll have to put in. __________ __________ __________ __________ __________ __________ __________ for us.

M : You're right. We can discuss what we want with them.

W : There's a reason people hire professionals to renovate their house.

M : Okay. I'll ask around and find someone.

03

대화를 듣고, 두 사람의 관계를 가장 잘 나타낸 것을 고르시오.

M : Hello, Ms. Sandburg. I'm glad you made it here. Please come on in.

W : Good morning. Thanks for meeting me so early in the morning.

M : No problem. Is this the bike you mentioned on the phone?

W : Yes. This is my mom's old bike.

M : It's a beautiful classic road bicycle. Let me take a look. *[Pause]* It looks like it hasn't been used for a long time.

W : Right. It's been kept in the garage at my parents' farmhouse for years.

M : Still it's __________ __________ __________ __________, but some parts need to be replaced.

W : I figured. Can you __________ __________ __________ __________ for this model?

M : I'll try. But if I can't, I'll be able to find other ones that could work.

W : Okay. It ✪ __________ __________ __________ __________ __________. Do you do that, too?

M : Of course. The cleaning will take another day or two.

W : Thanks. Give me a call when you're finished.

04

대화를 듣고, 그림에서 대화의 내용과 일치하지 <u>않는</u> 것을 고르시오.

W : Hey, Ben. I hear you're back from Surf School. How was it?

M : It was tough, but I had so much fun. This is a photo of the school's main lobby.

W : Let me see. *[Pause]* Oh, there are __________ __________ __________ __________ __________ __________.

M : The bigger ones are for beginners, and the smaller ones are ✪ __________ __________ __________ __________.

W : Interesting. The wetsuits are hanging under the sign that says SURF SCHOOL. Are those for rent?

M : Yes. People can put on their wetsuits in the changing room. See the door next to the wetsuits?

W : Yeah. What's __________ __________ __________ __________ on the floor for?

M : It's for people to return their used wetsuits.

W : Who is the surfer in the poster on the left wall?

M : He's __________ __________ __________ __________.

W : Wow. I would love to go to Surf School someday.

05

대화를 듣고, 여자가 남자를 위해 할 일로 가장 적절한 것을 고르시오.

W : Hi, Eric. I didn't expect to see you here at the bookstore.

M : Hi, Kimmy. I'm ✪ __________ __________ __________ __________ __________. I need some fresh ideas for my writing.

W : What are you writing?

M : It's a book based on my life as a vegan.

W : That's great. When you finish writing, I'd love to read it. I'm a vegan, too.

M : Okay, I'll send you a copy. I think you'll like the special section that __________ __________ __________ __________.

W : That'd be useful. It's not easy to find those.

M : That's what I mean. I'm looking for some good vegan kimchi recipes.

W : Oh, I happen to have a vegan kimchi recipe. It uses soy sauce __________ __________ __________ __________.

M : Sounds interesting. Could you send me the recipe? Maybe I can add it to my book.

W : Sure. I'll email it to you.

06

대화를 듣고, 남자가 지불할 금액을 고르시오. [3점]

M : Good morning. I'd like to buy tickets to the ice rink.
W : Okay. Tickets are $10 per adult, and $5 per child under 12.
M : I need tickets for one adult and two children. Both kids are under 12.
W : Sure. Do you want to rent some skates as well?
M : No, thanks. _____ _____ _____ _____ _____.
W : Good. Do your children need a private skating lesson?
M : Oh, I didn't know you had private lessons.
W : We do, actually. It's a one-hour session for children.
M : I think my younger one needs a lesson. He is _____ _____ _____ _____ _____ yet.
W : Good choice. So you're ✪ _____ _____ _____ _____ _____ _____ for just one of your children.
M : That's right. How much is the lesson fee?
W : It's $15. How would you like to pay?
M : I'll pay with my credit card.

07

대화를 듣고, 남자가 화상 회의에 참석하지 못한 이유를 고르시오.

M : Hey, Diane. I'm sorry I couldn't attend the video conference this morning.
W : That's okay. I just assumed you were ✪ _____ _____ _____ _____.
M : Not exactly. I was on the train coming back from my business trip.
W : Oh, I guess you had a problem accessing the Internet on the train.
M : No, the Internet was fine and the train had wifi.
W : Then, were you too busy and _____ _____ _____ _____?
M : No. When I took out my phone to join, the person next to me hit my hand with his bag.
W : Oh, no! Did you drop your phone?
M : Yes. _____ _____ _____ _____, and my phone wasn't working anymore.
W : I'm so sorry to hear that.
M : So, there was no way I could join the conference.
W : I understand. I'll share the details of the morning conference later.

08

대화를 듣고, Jazz Guitar Contest에 관해 언급되지 않은 것을 고르시오.

W : Hey, Tim. What are you doing on your phone?
M : Oh, Cathy. I'm applying for the Jazz Guitar Contest.
W : You mean the contest hosted by the World Guitarist Association?
M : Yes. It's a huge event that ✪ _____ _____ _____ _____ every year. I'm signing up early so I can focus on my practice.
W : Great. I hope you'll have enough time to practice.
M : It's held during the first week of December. So I have two months.
W : What are the prizes for the winners?
M : The first place winner will receive $10,000, and the top three winners _____ _____ _____ _____ _____ to New Orleans.
W : It'd be great if you won the contest. Is there an entry fee?
M : Yes, it's $50.
W : You're an excellent guitarist. I'm sure you _____ _____ _____ _____ _____.
M : Thanks for saying so.

09

The 10th International Hot Air Balloon Fiesta에 관한 다음 내용을 듣고, 일치하지 않는 것을 고르시오.

W : Hello, ballooning fans! The 10th International Hot Air Balloon Fiesta is coming! This Fiesta _____ _____ _____ _____ _____ _____ from around the world since 2011. Starting next Monday, the Fiesta will ✪ _____ _____ a magical world of balloons for two weeks at Titan National Park. Anybody can enjoy a hot air balloon ride. Boarding times are 10 a.m. and 5 p.m. every day. Ticket prices for the ride are 50% off on the first day of the Fiesta. This year's theme is "National Flags," so the balloons will be _____ _____ _____ _____ _____. This event _____ _____ _____ _____ on the Fiesta website. If you cannot make it to Titan National Park, you can enjoy the vibrant balloons floating in the sky on your screen!

10

다음 표를 보면서 대화를 듣고, 여자가 구매할 캣 트리를 고르시오.

W : Neil, I'm looking for a cat tree for my cats. Would you help me choose a good one?
M : Okay. Hmm.... You're going to choose _____ _____ _____ _____ _____, right?
W : Yes, but I don't want to buy this one. I'd like to stay under $100.
M : I see. How about we take a look at these four?
W : Yeah. How many levels would you recommend?
M : Usually, _____ _____ _____ _____ _____.
W : Then I'll go with something that has five levels.
M : Now, you should choose the size. How big are your cats?
W : My cats are young and small now, but they'll grow bigger soon. I'd rather buy a large one.
M : Good choice. You'll be able to use it longer.
W : Now I have two options left. Is it okay to get something that requires assembly?
M : It's ✪ _____ _____ _____ _____. Why don't you get the cheaper one?
W : Okay. I'll take your advice and order this one.

11

대화를 듣고, 여자의 마지막 말에 대한 남자의 응답으로 가장 적절한 것을 고르시오.

W : Jake, you have a cast on your leg. What happened?
M : I fell down the stairs. I'm __________ __________ __________ __________.
W : Do you want me to go to the cafeteria with you at lunch? I can ✪ __________ __________ __________ __________ __________ __________.

12

대화를 듣고, 남자의 마지막 말에 대한 여자의 응답으로 가장 적절한 것을 고르시오.

M : Honey, this ketchup is ✪ __________ __________ __________ __________ __________. But there's still some left in the bottle.
W : Oh, what a waste! __________ __________ __________ __________ __________.
M : Okay. Do I have to empty the bottle before putting it into the recycling bin?

13

대화를 듣고, 여자의 마지막 말에 대한 남자의 응답으로 가장 적절한 것을 고르시오.

W : Liam, you're moving in a month. How's everything going?
M : Pretty well, but I __________ __________ __________ __________.
W : You have a lot of camping equipment. It must be hard to pack it all.
M : It is. I'm trying to __________ __________ __________ __________ __________.
W : Are you trying to sell them online?
M : Yeah. Since I'm moving to a smaller apartment, I need to downsize.
W : You know you can sell them offline, too.
M : Do you know a good place to sell?
W : The community flea market is being held next weekend. You can get a booth there.
M : Cool! Do you have any ideas on how I can __________ __________ __________ __________ __________?
W : Set up a camping tent and display your ✪ __________ __________. It'll surely draw attention.

14

대화를 듣고, 남자의 마지막 말에 대한 여자의 응답으로 가장 적절한 것을 고르시오. [3점]

W : Nate, my son doesn't seem to enjoy reading. How can I get him to read more?
M : When I think about my children, they love to take their books to their reading nook.
W : What's a reading nook?
M : It's ✪ __________ __________ __________ __________ __________. It's also called a reading corner.
W : Oh, I thought that children should always read at a desk.
M : Let me put it this way. When you're in a relaxing environment, you can concentrate better.
W : My mom likes to read in her armchair. Is that her reading nook?
M : Maybe. And it'd be even better if __________ __________ __________ __________.
W : I see. I'll set up a reading corner for my son. Is there anything else I should consider?
M : Yes. The place should be quiet and __________ __________ __________.

15

다음 상황 설명을 듣고, Josh가 Lily에게 할 말로 가장 적절한 것을 고르시오. [3점]

M : Josh and Lily are friends. Josh notices that Lily looks tired at school these days. Josh is worried about Lily and asks her if she's okay. Lily says she's using her phone too much. She finds it hard to put her smartphone down late at night, watching videos and playing games. Josh wants to offer her a solution to __________ __________ __________ __________. That is, __________ __________ __________ __________ __________ __________ __________. He's using one himself, and he's happy with it. It has limited functions, so he uses his phone only for phone calls and text messages. Using a feature phone helps him ✪ __________ __________ __________ __________ __________ __________. Josh wants to recommend that Lily use the same kind of phone as his. In this situation, what would Josh most likely say to Lily?

16~17

다음을 듣고, 물음에 답하시오.

W : Last class we learned about the origins of different cooking oils. Today, I'd like to focus on vegetable oils and what good characteristics they have. First, coconut oil. Fats from coconut oil __________ __________ __________ __________. They help boost metabolism and aid in weight loss. Second, olive oil. It contains natural vitamins and minerals and of course, it's a nutritious staple of the Mediterranean diet. Next, sesame oil. It's loaded with antioxidants that __________ __________ __________ __________. It's also known to lower blood pressure and reduce wrinkles. If you find these three oils rather expensive, ✪ __________ __________ __________ __________, which is grapeseed oil. This is a great source of essential fatty acids and vitamin E. Its high smoking point works well for any cooking method such as roasting and frying. Before we move on, I'd like to mention one more oil. Walnut oil contains omega-3 fatty acids and minerals like iron and zinc. Its rich flavor can __________ __________ __________ __________ __________ __________. Now, let's look into each of these oils in detail.

▶ 정답 : 해설편 126쪽

VOCA LIST 28

회차별 영단어 QR 코드 ※ QR 코드를 스캔 후 모바일로 단어장처럼 학습할 수 있습니다.

● 고3 2020학년도 10월

01

001 □ pick up after ~의 뒤처리를 하다
002 □ transfer ⓥ (병을) 옮기다, 전염시키다
003 □ infectious ⓐ 감염성의
004 □ leash ⓝ (개 등을 매어두는) 줄
005 □ thoughtfulness ⓝ 배려, 사려 깊음

02

006 □ replace ⓥ (낡은 것·손상된 것 등을) 바꾸다, 교체하다
007 □ eventually ad 결국
008 □ end up ~ing 결국 ~하다
009 □ professional ⓝ 전문가
010 □ renovate ⓥ 개조하다

03

011 □ make it 도착하다
012 □ in good shape 상태가 좋은
013 □ thorough ⓐ 꼼꼼한, 철저한

04

014 □ lean on ~에 기대다
015 □ skilled ⓐ 숙련된
016 □ wetsuit ⓝ 잠수복
017 □ rent ⓝ 대여
018 □ legendary ⓐ 전설적인

05

019 □ expect ⓥ 예상하다, 기대하다
020 □ browse ⓥ 둘러보다, 훑어보다
021 □ inspiration ⓝ 영감
022 □ vegan ⓝ (완전) 채식주의자
023 □ soy sauce 간장
024 □ ferment ⓥ 발효시키다
025 □ add A to B A를 B에 추가하다

06

026 □ as well (문미에서) 또한
027 □ private ⓐ 사적인
028 □ session ⓝ (강의, 회의 등의) 시간
029 □ confident ⓐ 자신 있는
030 □ sign up for ~에 등록하다

07

031 □ video conference 화상 회의
032 □ be occupied with ~로 바쁘다, ~에 열중하다
033 □ business trip 출장
034 □ lose track of time 시간 가는 줄 모르다
035 □ crack ⓥ 깨지다, 부서지다

08

036 □ apply for ~에 신청하다
037 □ host ⓥ (행사를) 주최하다
038 □ huge ⓐ 거대한
039 □ entry fee 참가비
040 □ have a strong chace of ~할 가능성이 크다

09

041 □ ballooning ⓝ 열기구 여행
042 □ present ⓥ (특정한 방식으로) 선보이다, 나타내다
043 □ ride ⓥ 타다, 달리다
044 □ make it to ~에 오다
045 □ vibrant ⓐ (색깔이) 강렬한, 선명한

10

046 □ take a look at ~을 살펴보다
047 □ level ⓝ (건물의) 층
048 □ recommend ⓥ 추천하다
049 □ assembly ⓝ 조립

11

050 □ have a cast 깁스하다
051 □ fall down 넘어지다
052 □ have trouble ~ing ~하기가 어렵다
053 □ food tray 식판

12

054 □ expiration date 유통기한
055 □ recycling bin 재활용품 통
056 □ room temperature 상온

13

057 □ time-consuming ⓐ 시간이 많이 걸리는
058 □ equipment ⓝ 장비
059 □ get rid of ~을 치우다, 없애다
060 □ downsize ⓥ (규모를) 줄이다, 축소하다
061 □ flea market 벼룩시장
062 □ draw attention 이목을 끌다
063 □ overprice ⓥ 값을 비싸게 매기다

14

064 □ nook ⓝ 자리, 장소, 구석
065 □ cozy ⓐ 안락한
066 □ Let me put it this way. 이렇게 말해 보죠.
067 □ free from ~로부터 벗어난
068 □ distraction ⓝ 주의를 산만하게 하는 것

15

069 □ break a habit 습관을 버리다
070 □ limited ⓐ 제한된
071 □ be allowed to ~하도록 허용되다
072 □ switch A to B A를 B로 바꾸다

16~17

073 □ convert ⓥ 전환하다
074 □ metabolism ⓝ 신진대사
075 □ nutritious ⓐ 영양가 풍부한
076 □ staple ⓝ 주식
077 □ antioxidant ⓝ 항산화 물질
078 □ be loaded with ~로 가득 차다
079 □ essential ⓐ 필수적인
080 □ add a kick to ~에 짜릿함을 더하다
081 □ composition ⓝ 구성 (요소)
082 □ flavor enhancer 화학 조미료

29회 • 2025학년도 대학수학능력시험 고3 영어 듣기

※ QR코드를 스캔하시면 듣기 방송을 청취하실 수 있습니다.

● 점수 표시가 없는 문항은 모두 2점 ● 문항수 17개 | 배점 37점 | 제한 시간 25분

1번부터 17번까지는 듣고 답하는 문제입니다. 1번부터 15번까지는 한 번만 들려주고, 16번부터 17번까지는 두 번 들려줍니다. 방송을 잘 듣고 답을 하시기 바랍니다.

1. 다음을 듣고, 여자가 하는 말의 목적으로 가장 적절한 것을 고르시오.

① 학교 종소리 교체 계획을 알리려고
② 학교 수업 시간 단축을 공지하려고
③ 등교 시간 변경을 안내하려고
④ 학부모 상담 신청서 제출을 독려하려고
⑤ 학교 행사 후 교실 정리 정돈을 당부하려고

2. 대화를 듣고, 남자의 의견으로 가장 적절한 것을 고르시오.

① 드라마 캠프는 효율적인 여가 시간 활용 수단이다.
② 좋은 연기를 하려면 다른 사람과의 협력이 중요하다.
③ 드라마에는 독특한 개성을 가진 등장인물이 필요하다.
④ 원만한 교우 관계를 위해 친구의 말에 귀 기울여야 한다.
⑤ 드라마 캠프 참여는 다양한 시각을 갖는 데 도움이 된다.

3. 다음을 듣고, 여자가 하는 말의 요지로 가장 적절한 것을 고르시오.

① 예술가에 관해 알면 작품을 더 잘 이해할 수 있다.
② 지역 사회는 예술가에 대한 지원을 확대해야 한다.
③ 예술 작품을 전시할 때 조명 효과를 고려해야 한다.
④ 정기적인 미술관 방문은 작품 감상 능력을 높여 준다.
⑤ 예술 작품은 보는 사람에 따라 다양한 해석이 가능하다.

4. 대화를 듣고, 그림에서 대화의 내용과 일치하지 않는 것을 고르시오.

5. 대화를 듣고, 남자가 할 일로 가장 적절한 것을 고르시오.

① 트로피 가져오기 ② 사진 출력하기
③ 이메일 확인하기 ④ 스티커 주문하기
⑤ 게시판 사용 허락받기

6. 대화를 듣고, 여자가 지불할 금액을 고르시오.

① \$100 ② \$150 ③ \$180 ④ \$200 ⑤ \$220

7. 대화를 듣고, 남자가 Streamline Broadcasting Workshop에 갈 수 없는 이유를 고르시오.

① 동아리 공연에 참여해야 해서
② 교내 방송 준비를 해야 해서
③ 야구 경기를 보러 가야 해서
④ 생일 파티에 참석해야 해서
⑤ 선물을 사러 가야 해서

8. 대화를 듣고, Outstanding Octopuses 행사에 관해 언급되지 않은 것을 고르시오.

① 목적 ② 프로그램 ③ 후원 기관
④ 입장료 ⑤ 기간

9. 2024 Grand Butterfly Circus에 관한 다음 내용을 듣고, 일치하지 않는 것을 고르시오.

① 5일 동안 진행될 것이다.
② 마술 쇼를 포함한다.
③ 2세 미만의 아이는 무료로 입장한다.
④ 할인 쿠폰을 웹사이트에서 다운로드할 수 있다.
⑤ 지정석이 있다.

[해설편 p.126]

10. 다음 표를 보면서 대화를 듣고, 여자가 구입할 식물 씨앗 키트를 고르시오.

Plant Seed Kits

	Kit	Price	Plant Varieties	Pot Material	Plant Growing Guide
①	A	$40	3	Plastic	×
②	B	$45	4	Wood	○
③	C	$45	5	Metal	×
④	D	$50	5	Ceramic	○
⑤	E	$60	6	Glass	○

11. 대화를 듣고, 남자의 마지막 말에 대한 여자의 응답으로 가장 적절한 것을 고르시오. [3점]

① Great idea! Let's ask him to come to the party.
② That's okay. I'll check if I can change the order.
③ I can't believe it! We finally won a tennis match.
④ No thanks. I don't really like cakes with nuts on them.
⑤ No problem. I won't eat foods that cause allergic reactions.

12. 대화를 듣고, 여자의 마지막 말에 대한 남자의 응답으로 가장 적절한 것을 고르시오.

① In that case, let's give it a try.
② I don't know. It's a bit expensive.
③ That's the best class we've ever taken.
④ I'd be happy to teach yoga to beginners.
⑤ You're right. The hotel's view is amazing.

13. 대화를 듣고, 남자의 마지막 말에 대한 여자의 응답으로 가장 적절한 것을 고르시오.

Woman: ______________________

① Too bad. I hope you can find your lost bike.
② Good job. You'll get used to riding a bike soon.
③ Awesome! Thank you for lending me your new bike.
④ I'm sorry. I'm afraid our auction has already finished.
⑤ Excellent! I'm sure your donation will be appreciated.

14. 대화를 듣고, 여자의 마지막 말에 대한 남자의 응답으로 가장 적절한 것을 고르시오. [3점]

Man: ______________________

① Sure. I hope you'll be able to judge the competition.
② Well done. You've advanced to the final round.
③ Great. Text me the dates of the competition.
④ Don't worry. We'll announce the winners shortly.
⑤ I understand. It's hard to be fair when judging others.

15. 다음 상황 설명을 듣고, Sophia가 Jack에게 할 말로 가장 적절한 것을 고르시오. [3점]

Sophia: ______________________

① I think it'll be better to stick to your plan.
② Let's head out for the concert far in advance.
③ We can ask for a seat change so we can sit together.
④ Don't you think we need to rehearse one more time?
⑤ How about leaving the concert early to avoid traffic?

[16~17] 다음을 듣고, 물음에 답하시오.

16. 여자가 하는 말의 주제로 가장 적절한 것은?

① desirable conditions to store food
② importance of having a nutritious diet
③ suitable foods to solve future food shortages
④ popular dishes made from unusual ingredients
⑤ future technologies to cope with food shortages

17. 언급된 음식이 아닌 것은?

① seaweed ② beans ③ pumpkins
④ potatoes ⑤ mushrooms

[해설편 p.128]

※ QR 코드를 스캔하시면 듣기 방송이 나옵니다. 듣기 방송을 들으며 다음 빈칸을 채우시오. ● 제한 시간 : 25분

01

다음을 듣고, 여자가 하는 말의 목적으로 가장 적절한 것을 고르시오.

W : Good morning, students. This is your vice principal, Ms. Morris. I want to inform you that each class period will be reduced from 50 minutes to 40 minutes next Tuesday. __________ ___ _____ ______________________ conferences that will beheld on that day, school will end one hour earlier than usual. You'll still take the same classes that you normally would on that day. The starting and ending bells will ring according to the ✪ ____________ ________ ________ ____________. Once again, __________ ________ ___ ________ that next Tuesday's class periods will be shortened by 10 minutes each. Thank you.

02

대화를 듣고, 남자의 의견으로 가장 적절한 것을 고르시오.

M : Honey, I was thinking about asking our daughter to sign up for drama camp this winter. What do you think?

W : Hmm. Why do you want her to _________________ ___ __________ _________?

M : I think drama camp is helpful for gaining diverse perspectives.

W : How will the camp help her with that?

M : In the camp, she'll play different types of characters. This can help her see ✪ __________ ________ ___________ ____________________.

W : That makes sense.

M : Also, she'll be expected to listen to other kids _________ _____________________ _______ _______.

W : Oh, that could help her broaden her views.

M : Right. So, participating in drama camp is helpful for obtaining various perspectives.

W : Okay. Then let's suggest it to her.

03

다음을 듣고, 여자가 하는 말의 요지로 가장 적절한 것을 고르시오.

W : Hello, viewers! I'm Kate and welcome back to my channel, Art Pier 25. Have you ever felt like you couldn't _________________ _____ ____________ in a museum? If so, here's a simple tip for understanding artists' work better. ______________ __________ _____ _________ can deepen your appreciation of their work. Art is often a reflection of their feelings and thoughts. Therefore, by exploring their lives and experiences, you can see what influenced their work. So, the next time you go to an art museum, why not ✪ ____________ _____ ___________ ____________________ first? Once you know about the artists, you'll be able to have a better understanding of their work. I hope this helps.

04

대화를 듣고, 그림에서 대화의 내용과 일치하지 않는 것을 고르시오.

M : Hi, Sarah. What are you doing?

W : I'm looking at a picture that I took last weekend. Do you want to take a look?

M : Sure. I see a flea market sign hanging from the tree.

W : I was selling some of my old stuff at the flea market.

M : Oh, I like the crown-shaped balloon the girl is holding.

W : She's my daughter. Hey, do you remember ______ ________________________ ______?

M : Of course. That's the one I gave you. Oh, there are three vases on the table.

W : Unfortunately, I wasn't able to sell them.

M : I guess people weren't interested in them.

W : Yeah. People ✪ ________ _________ ________________ ___ the speaker on the chair even though it wasn't for sale. I __________ ____ __________ ___ __________ customers.

M : I see. Looks like you had a busy weekend.

05

대화를 듣고, 남자가 할 일로 가장 적절한 것을 고르시오.

W : Hey, Brian. The Playful Cat Photo Contest is only two days away.

M : That's right, Lisa. Many students are excited about our club's contest.

W : Yeah. Let's check the preparations we've done so far.

M : Alright. I checked our email and confirmed that all the ✪ __________________ ______ ________________ their photos.

W : Great. I'll print them out tomorrow.

M : Okay. What about the ____________ __________ ___ the school lobby? We'll need it to post the photos on.

W : Don't worry. I already got __________________ ___ ______ __. Have you ordered stickers yet?

M : Yes, I ordered enough for everyone to use when voting for their favorite photos.

W : Good. What about the trophy for the winner?

M : It's at my house. I'll bring it tomorrow.

W : Thanks, I think we're all set.

06

대화를 듣고, 여자가 지불할 금액을 고르시오.

M : Welcome to Camoo Traditional Village. How can I help you?
W : Hi. I'd like to ✪ ________ my family. Is there a discount for senior citizens?
M : Yes. Regular tickets are $30 each, and senior tickets are $20 each for people over 65 years old.
W : Good. My parents are in their 70s. So I'll take two regular tickets and two senior tickets.
M : Great. Would you also like lunch tickets? We ________ ________ ________ ________. It's $25 per person.
W : I'd love that. Is the ________ ________ ________ for senior citizens?
M : No. I'm sorry. It's the same price.
W : Ah, okay. I'll buy four lunch tickets as well.
M : Alright. So you want two regular tickets and two senior tickets with four lunch tickets, right?
W : That's right. Here's my credit card.

07

대화를 듣고, 남자가 Streamline Broadcasting Workshop에 갈 수 없는 이유를 고르시오.

W : Hey, John. Come and look at this poster.
M : Hi, Sharon. The Streamline Broadcasting Workshop? What's that?
W : It's a student workshop that offers an ✪ ________ ___ ________ ________ experts in broadcasting. How about going together?
M : Oh, it's on Friday. I wish I could, but I can't.
W : Why not? Is your dance club's performance on that day?
M : No, the performance is next month.
W : Then, is your little brother's birthday party on Friday?
M : No, it was last week. I got him a ________ ___ ___ ________.
W : So why can't you go to the workshop?
M : Actually, I'm going to ________ ___ ________ ________ on that day. I have tickets for that game.
W : Oh, I see. I hope your team wins.

08

대화를 듣고, Outstanding Octopuses 행사에 관해 언급되지 않은 것을 고르시오.

M : Honey, did you hear that the ________ ________ ___ ________ an event called Outstanding Octopuses?
W : Outstanding Octopuses? What's it for?
M : The purpose of the event is to ________ ________ ________ ________.
W : Sounds interesting. What programs does the event have?
M : There are several programs. They ✪ ________ ________ ________ from the Pacific Ocean and showing a documentary about how to protect them.
W : Really? Let me search for more information on my phone. *[Pause]* Oh, it's sponsored by the Aqua Life Council.
M : I'm glad that they're helping people realize how remarkable these creatures are.

W : I agree. The event started on October 4th and will end on December 8th.
M : Good. We still have a lot of time to visit.
W : You're right. Let's make plans to go soon.

09

2024 Grand Butterfly Circus에 관한 다음 내용을 듣고, 일치 하지 않는 것을 고르시오.

M : Hello, listeners. Are you looking for something fun to do with your family? Well, we're pleased to announce that the 2024 Grand Butterfly Circus is coming to town. It'll run for five days from November 15th to 19th. The circus starts at 8 p.m. each night at City Square. It includes ✪ ___ ________ ________ ________, high-rope walking, and juggling. Admission tickets are $35 per person, and children under 2 years old are admitted for free. ________ ___ ________ ________ as well as on site. You can download a discount coupon on the circus website. If you want the best seats, please come early because there are no assigned seats. Join us for a ________ ________ ________ ___ ________ for you and your family!

10

다음 표를 보면서 대화를 듣고, 여자가 구입할 식물 씨앗 키트를 고르시오.

W : Jason, what's that in your hand?
M : It's a flyer from the neighborhood flower shop, Mom.
W : Oh, they're selling plant seed kits! I want one. Can you help me choose?
M : Sure. I don't think you need the most expensive kit since it's your first try.
W : Right. But I'd like some variety. So, at least four kinds of plants would be nice.
M : Okay. What about the pots? They ✪ ________ ___ ________ ________.
W : I don't want the ceramic one. It'll be too heavy for me.
M : Good point. I think the one that comes with ___ ________ ________ ________ would be helpful for you.
W : Yes, I can ________ ________ ________ how to grow plants.
M : Then this seed kit is perfect for you.
W : Thanks for helping me. I'll buy that one.

11

대화를 듣고, 남자의 마지막 말에 대한 여자의 응답으로 가장 적절한 것을 고르시오. [3점]

M : Jane, ________ ________ ________ a cake for our tennis coach's farewell party next week?
W : Yes, I ordered a walnut cake with ________ ________ ___ ________. I'll pick it up next Wednesday afternoon from the bakery.
M : Oh, no. I should have told you that he's ✪ ________ ___ ___ ________ of nuts.

12

대화를 듣고, 여자의 마지막 말에 대한 남자의 응답으로 가장 적절한 것을 고르시오.

W : Honey, the hotel ________ __ ______ _______ class on the beach to the guests. Do you want to go with me tomorrow morning?

M : Oh, really? I ✪ ____________ _______ ___ _____ yoga, but I'm afraid we might be the only beginners.

W : Don't worry. This class is for _____ ____________ ______ have never done yoga before. So why don't we take it?

13

대화를 듣고, 남자의 마지막 말에 대한 여자의 응답으로 가장 적절한 것을 고르시오.

[Cell phone rings.]

M : Hi, Rachel. What's up?

W : Hi, Kevin. Do you have any plans for next weekend?

M : No, I'm free. Why do you ask?

W : The City Transportation Office is ✪ _________ __ ______ _________ at their parking lot. Do you want to check it out together?

M : Sounds like fun. Are they selling new bicycles?

W : No, they're selling used bikes. People ______ _________ ______ for a good cause.

M : What's the cause?

W : I heard all the money they raise will ___ ______ ___ _________ youth sports clubs.

M : Oh, really? Then, I'd like to contribute to the auction. Actually, I have a bike that I don't ride anymore.

W : That's great. Just make sure it's in a good enough condition to be sold.

M : Not to worry. It's only been used two or three times.

14

대화를 듣고, 여자의 마지막 말에 대한 남자의 응답으로 가장 적절한 것을 고르시오. [3점]

[Telephone rings.]

W : Hello, Dr. Wilson speaking.

M : Hello, this is Glenn Scott ✪ ______ ____ ___________ ___________ of the National Science Talent Competition.

W : Hi, Mr. Scott. How can I help you?

M : I'm calling to see if you would be a judge for this year's competition.

W : Thanks. I'd be happy to take part in it again. When is the competition?

M : It starts on December 9th and continues for three days.

W : Oh, no. I have __ __________ ___ _______ on December 9th.

M : Is there any chance that you can change the date of your meeting? I really want to have you as a judge.

W : I'm _______ __ ______ _________ that right now.

M : When can you let me know? I can wait a couple of days.

W : I'll let you know by the end of the day.

15

다음 상황 설명을 듣고, Sophia가 Jack에게 할 말로 가장 적절한 것을 고르시오. [3점]

M : Sophia and Jack are sister and brother. They're going to their favorite singer's concert tonight. The concert starts at 7 p.m., and since it takes an hour to get to the concert, Jack proposes that they leave their house at 6 p.m. While this is Jack's first time going to a concert, Sophia has ✪ ______ ___ ________ __________. She knows that even after they arrive at the concert site, it takes a long time to go through the security line and get to their seats. Also, she wants to _____ ________ _____ _____ ___ the gift shops before the concert. So, Sophia wants to suggest to Jack that _____ ________ _______ ____ the concert much earlier than he proposed. In this situation, what would Sophia most likely say to Jack?

16~17

다음을 듣고, 물음에 답하시오.

W : Hello, students. As you know, we may be facing serious food shortages down the road. So, today let's talk about foods that are ✪ ______________ ____ _________ ______ food shortages in the future. First, seaweed is cost-efficient because it doesn't take up land or need to be watered. It not only contains lots of minerals and vitamins but also can be used to make diverse types of dishes. Second, beans are adapted to growing in a wide range of ________________ ______ _______ ________ to mountain slopes. Plus, they offer us a rich source of fiber and protein. Third, pumpkins grow large and their leaves and flowers can be consumed as well. These precious parts are often thrown away, but they are a good source of nutrients and flavor. Finally, mushrooms grow ___ ______ ________ and where many other foods would not. They are very affordable and rich in various nutrients. Now let's watch a video demonstrating the value of these foods.

▶정답 : 해설편 130쪽

VOCA LIST 29

회차별 영단어 QR 코드 ※ QR 코드를 스캔 후 모바일로 단어장처럼 학습할 수 있습니다.

● 고3 2025학년도 수능

01

001 □ inform ⓥ 알리다
002 □ reduce ⓥ 줄이다
003 □ conference ⓝ 협의회, 회의
004 □ normally ad 평소에
005 □ ring ⓥ 울리다
006 □ shorten ⓥ 단축하다

02

007 □ sign up ~에 등록하다
008 □ diverse ⓐ 다양한
009 □ perspective ⓝ 시각
010 □ character ⓝ 등장인물
011 □ collaborate ⓥ 협력하다
012 □ broaden ⓥ 넓히다

03

013 □ deepen ⓥ 깊게 하다
014 □ appreciation ⓝ 이해
015 □ reflection ⓝ 반영한 것
016 □ influence ⓥ 영향을 주다
017 □ explore ⓥ 탐구하다
018 □ background ⓝ 배경

04

019 □ flea market ⓝ 벼룩시장
020 □ hang ⓥ 매달다
021 □ crown-shaped ⓐ 왕관 모양의
022 □ stripe-patterned ⓐ 줄무늬의
023 □ attract ⓥ 끌다

05

024 □ preparation ⓝ 준비 사항, 준비
025 □ participant ⓝ 참가자
026 □ submit ⓥ 제출하다
027 □ bulletin board ⓝ 게시판
028 □ permission ⓝ 허락, 허가
029 □ vote ⓥ 투표하다

06

030 □ admission ticket ⓝ 입장권
031 □ senior citizen ⓝ 고령자, 어르신
032 □ local ⓐ 현지의
033 □ cheap ⓐ 싸다
034 □ credit ⓐ 신용의

07

035 □ expert ⓝ 전문가
036 □ broadcasting ⓝ 방송
037 □ performance ⓝ 공연
038 □ ticket ⓝ 표
039 □ hope ⓥ 희망하다

08

040 □ aquarium ⓝ 수족관
041 □ octopus ⓝ 문어
042 □ sponsor ⓥ 후원하다
043 □ realize ⓥ 깨닫다
044 □ remarkable ⓐ 눈에 띄는

09

045 □ spectacular ⓐ 화려한, 볼 만한
046 □ juggling ⓝ 저글링, 곡예
047 □ admission ⓝ 입장
048 □ assigned ⓐ 지정된, 할당된
049 □ breathtaking ⓐ 숨 막히는

10

050 □ flyer ⓝ 전단
051 □ variety ⓝ 다양성
052 □ ceramic ⓐ 도자기의
053 □ easily ad 쉽게
054 □ guide ⓥ 이끌다

11

055 □ farewell party ⓝ 송별 파티
056 □ walnut ⓝ 호두
057 □ pistachio ⓝ 피스타치오
058 □ order ⓥ 주문하다
059 □ allergic ⓐ 알레르기가 있는

12

060 □ definitely ad 꼭, 반드시
061 □ tomorrow ⓝ 내일
062 □ morning ⓝ 아침
063 □ free ⓐ 공짜의
064 □ offer ⓥ 제공하다

13

065 □ transportation ⓝ 교통
066 □ auction ⓝ 경매
067 □ donate ⓥ 기증하다
068 □ cause ⓝ 목적, 대의
069 □ contribute ⓥ 기증하다

14

070 □ organizing committee ⓝ 조직 위원회
071 □ competition ⓝ 대회
072 □ judge ⓝ 심사위원
073 □ afraid ⓥ 두려워하다
074 □ meeting ⓝ 회의

15

075 □ propose ⓥ 제안하다
076 □ stop by ~에 들르다
077 □ gift shop ⓝ 기념품 가게
078 □ arrive ⓥ 도착하다
079 □ security ⓝ 보안

16~17

080 □ seaweed 해초
081 □ beans 콩
082 □ pumpkins 호박
083 □ mushrooms 버섯
084 □ potatoes 감자
085 □ face ⓥ 직면하다
086 □ food shortage ⓝ 식량 부족
087 □ down the road 장래에
088 □ appropriate ⓐ 적합한
089 □ cost-efficient ⓐ 비용 효율적인
090 □ water ⓥ 물을 주다
091 □ slope ⓝ (산)비탈
092 □ fiber ⓝ 섬유질
093 □ precious ⓐ 소중한, 가치가 있는
094 □ nutrient ⓝ 영양소
095 □ affordable ⓐ (가격이) 적정한
096 □ rich ⓐ 풍부한
097 □ demonstrate ⓥ 보여 주다

30회 • 2024학년도 대학수학능력시험 고3 영어 듣기

※ QR코드를 스캔하시면 듣기 방송을 청취하실 수 있습니다.

● 점수 표시가 없는 문항은 모두 2점 ● 문항수 17개 | 배점 37점 | 제한 시간 25분

1번부터 17번까지는 듣고 답하는 문제입니다. 1번부터 15번까지는 한 번만 들려주고, 16번부터 17번까지는 두 번 들려줍니다. 방송을 잘 듣고 답을 하시기 바랍니다.

MP3

1. 다음을 듣고, 여자가 하는 말의 목적으로 가장 적절한 것을 고르시오.

① 축구 경기장 사용 수칙을 설명하려고
② 지역 아동 병원의 개원을 홍보하려고
③ 자선 축구 경기의 변경된 일정을 공지하려고
④ 축구 경기 티켓의 구매 사이트를 소개하려고
⑤ 자선 축구 경기 자원봉사자 모집을 안내하려고

2. 대화를 듣고, 남자의 의견으로 가장 적절한 것을 고르시오.

① 상대방이 말할 때는 말을 끊지 말아야 한다.
② 회의 발언은 주제에서 벗어나지 않아야 한다.
③ 적절한 제스처는 대화의 전달력을 높일 수 있다.
④ 회의를 진행할 때는 개인적인 감정을 배제해야 한다.
⑤ 자신의 의견을 주장할 때는 충분한 근거를 들어야 한다.

3. 다음을 듣고, 여자가 하는 말의 요지로 가장 적절한 것을 고르시오.

① 일정한 실내 온도 유지는 건강에 중요한 역할을 한다.
② 충분한 햇빛 노출은 수면 호르몬 분비를 촉진한다.
③ 정서 안정을 위해서는 양질의 수면이 필요하다.
④ 수면 안대를 착용하면 잠드는 데 도움이 될 수 있다.
⑤ 적당한 밝기의 조명은 일의 능률을 향상시킬 수 있다.

4. 대화를 듣고, 그림에서 대화의 내용과 일치하지 않는 것을 고르시오.

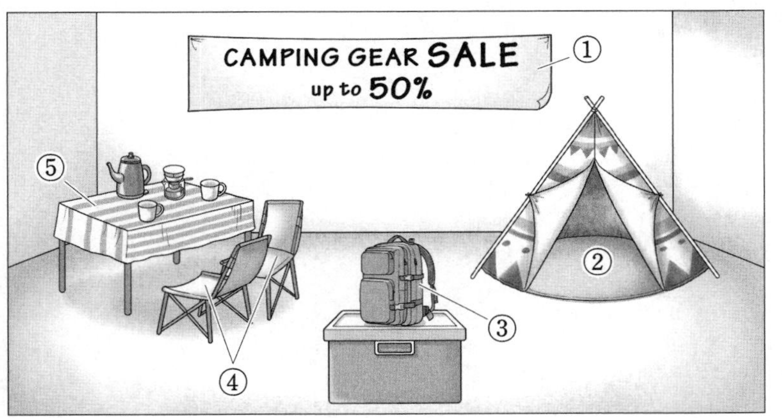

5. 대화를 듣고, 여자가 할 일로 가장 적절한 것을 고르시오.

① 신입 회원 선물 준비하기
② 대회 일정 인쇄하기
③ 음악 재생 목록 만들기
④ 식당 예약하기
⑤ 문자 메시지 보내기

6. 대화를 듣고, 남자가 지불할 금액을 고르시오. [3점]

① $63 ② $70 ③ $72 ④ $78 ⑤ $80

7. 대화를 듣고, 여자가 산책을 할 수 없는 이유를 고르시오.

① 얇은 재킷을 입어서
② 회의 준비를 해야 해서
③ 알레르기 증상이 심해서
④ 경찰서에 방문해야 해서
⑤ 병원 진료를 받아야 해서

8. 대화를 듣고, 남자가 예약할 연극 공연에 관해 언급되지 않은 것을 고르시오.

① 제목 ② 날짜 ③ 출연자
④ 입장료 ⑤ 시작 시각

9. *Golden Palette* Walking Tour에 관한 다음 내용을 듣고, 일치하지 않는 것을 고르시오.

① 11월에 매일 진행된다.
② 안내 책자가 무료로 제공된다.
③ 오전 10시 30분에 시작한다.
④ 출발 지점은 Central Studio의 남쪽 문이다.
⑤ 참가자 전원은 선물을 받을 것이다.

[해설편 p.131]

10. 다음 표를 보면서 대화를 듣고, 남자가 주문할 접이식 카트를 고르시오.

Foldable Carts

	Model	Price	Weight Limit	Color	Handle Material
①	A	$38	30kg	Black	Silicone
②	B	$42	40kg	Green	Silicone
③	C	$44	45kg	Blue	Metal
④	D	$48	50kg	White	Metal
⑤	E	$53	45kg	Red	Rubber

11. 대화를 듣고, 여자의 마지막 말에 대한 남자의 응답으로 가장 적절한 것을 고르시오.

① Right. We should've watched them.
② Why not? Just put the mat on the shelf.
③ Great. We can store some snacks at home.
④ I'm sorry. I can't find the parking lot.
⑤ No problem. I'll take care of it.

12. 대화를 듣고, 남자의 마지막 말에 대한 여자의 응답으로 가장 적절한 것을 고르시오.

① That's too bad. I was looking forward to seeing you there.
② Thank you. I'm so glad you could make it to the party.
③ That's okay. The birthday party has already finished.
④ Sure. I'll arrange the business trip for you and your team.
⑤ Don't worry. My boss will return from the trip this Monday.

13. 대화를 듣고, 여자의 마지막 말에 대한 남자의 응답으로 가장 적절한 것을 고르시오. [3점]

Man: ______________________________

① Don't give up! You've inspired me to be a painter.
② Cheer up! The fashion market is open to everybody.
③ You have a point. I don't have any fashion sense at all.
④ I agree. You should make a balance between work and life.
⑤ Be positive. You can start pursuing your dream at any time.

14. 대화를 듣고, 남자의 마지막 말에 대한 여자의 응답으로 가장 적절한 것을 고르시오.

Woman: ______________________________

① No worries. I can go pick it up now.
② All right. Just be sure to return it tomorrow.
③ That's okay. We can fix the system next week.
④ Sorry to hear that. You can buy it next time.
⑤ Never mind. I'll bring a new copy for you.

15. 다음 상황 설명을 듣고, Jake가 Yuna에게 할 말로 가장 적절한 것을 고르시오. [3점]

Jake: ______________________________

① Could you please take my picture again with the rock in it?
② I'd appreciate it if you could come to the mountain with me.
③ You shouldn't take any photos while climbing the rock.
④ I'm wondering if you can pose in front of the rock.
⑤ Why don't you take a selfie in the national park?

[16~17] 다음을 듣고, 물음에 답하시오.

16. 여자가 하는 말의 주제로 가장 적절한 것은?

① various natural materials as a source of building supplies
② how upcycling is used in architecture across the globe
③ strategic use of upcycled plastics in different countries
④ impact of architectural waste on the global environment
⑤ why nations should employ eco-friendly shipping methods

17. 언급된 나라가 아닌 것은?

① Singapore ② Mexico ③ Australia
④ Indonesia ⑤ France

[해설편 p.133]

※ QR 코드를 스캔하시면 듣기 방송이 나옵니다. 듣기 방송을 들으며 다음 빈칸을 채우시오. ● 제한 시간 : 25분

01

다음을 듣고, 여자가 하는 말의 목적으로 가장 적절한 것을 고르시오.

W : Hello, Timberglade High School students. This is your P.E. teacher, Ms. Larsen. I'd like to announce that we're __________ ____ ______________ to help with the charity soccer match next month. As you know, our best players will ✪ __________ ________ ____ ____________ at Ebanwood Stadium. Volunteers will show the audience to their seats and ______ ____ ______ ____ ________. All the money from the ticket sales will get donated to the local children's hospital. This will be a great opportunity to get involved in helping children. Please don't hesitate to apply for this volunteer work at our charity soccer match. For more information, you can check the school website. Thank you.

02

대화를 듣고, 남자의 의견으로 가장 적절한 것을 고르시오.

M : Ellie, you seem down. What's on your mind?
W : Well, Dad, Tiffany and I got into an argument at school.
M : You two are so close. What happened?
W : During our student council meeting, she was taking ____ ______ ___ ________ ____ _______, so I had to jump in to finish her sentence.
M : Oh, no. You ✪ __________ __________ __________ when they're in the middle of speaking.
W : I know. But she kept talking about so many details.
M : Still, that's not polite. How would you feel if you were her?
W : I'd probably be upset.
M : Exactly. That's why when somebody's talking, you shouldn't cut them off.
W : You're right. I guess I didn't see things from her point of view.
M : So, how about ________ ________ ________ what they're saying next time?
W : Okay. Thanks, Dad. I'll apologize to her tomorrow.

03

다음을 듣고, 여자가 하는 말의 요지로 가장 적절한 것을 고르시오.

W : Hello, listeners. This is *Dr. Graham's One-minute Health Tips*. Getting a good night's sleep is important for your health. But recently, more and more people are experiencing __________ ________ ________. If that's your case, __________ ____ ____ ________ for sleeping can help you fall asleep. If your room doesn't get dark enough, it'll be difficult to fall asleep. This is because light ✪ ______________ ______ ____ ________ ___ ____ ____________ that makes you sleepy. An eye mask can block the light, which makes it easier for you to fall asleep. Why not try one tonight? I'll be back with more tips next time!

04

대화를 듣고, 그림에서 대화의 내용과 일치하지 않는 것을 고르시오.

M : Ms. Blake, I've finished decorating the camping gear section to look like a campsite.
W : Thanks, Chris. It's much nicer than what's represented in our sales plan. I like that banner on the wall.
M : I think it'll attract our customers' attention. And I set up the cone-shaped tent as you suggested before.
W : Good. That Native American-style tent is quite popular these days.
M : Yes, it is. Also, the backpack ______ ___ _____ ______ is currently our best-selling item.
W : That's true. I love its design. Oh, those two chairs look comfortable. I'd like to sit on one of them and ________ ________ ________ ________.
M : Me, too. And isn't ✪ _____ __________ ____________ really eye-catching?
W : It certainly is. Everything looks really good. You did an excellent job!

05

대화를 듣고, 여자가 할 일로 가장 적절한 것을 고르시오.

W : Oliver, I'm so excited about the party for the new members of our tennis club this Friday.
M : Me, too. Let's go through the to-do list. I want it to be perfect.
W : Agreed. Did you reserve the Mexican restaurant downtown for the party?
M : Yes, I did. ✪ ______ ____________ ___ ____________, so it's perfect for a party like ours.
W : Plus, the food there is terrific. And you prepared gifts for the new members, right?
M : Yeah, they're in my car. Did you remind the members about the party?
W : I've just sent a text message to everyone.
M : Great. What about the tennis competition schedule? ________ ______ __________ __ ______?
W : Oh, _ __________ ________. I'll do it tonight. Um, is the music ready?
M : Uh-huh. I made a playlist last night.
W : That's great. I think we're good to go!

Dictation 30

06

대화를 듣고, 남자가 지불할 금액을 고르시오. [3점]

W : Welcome to Jamie's Gift Shop! What can I do for you?

M : Hi. I need to get Christmas gifts for my friends. Is there anything you can recommend?

W : Sure. How about this photo tumbler? You can ________ __ ________ ___ ________ __________ into the tumbler to decorate it.

M : Ooh, my friends will love it. How much is it?

W : It's $30.

M : It seems a bit pricey, but I like it. I'll take two of them.

W : Okay. Anything else?

M : These Christmas key chains look cute. Oh, they're $5 each.

W : Yes. They're ✪ ________ ________ ______ ________.

M : Are they? I'll take four then. I think that's all.

W : So, that's ________ ________ ________ ________ ________.

M : That's right.

W : And you get 10% off the total cost for our Christmas promotion.

M : Great. Here's my credit card.

07

대화를 듣고, 여자가 산책을 할 수 없는 이유를 고르시오.

W : It was nice having lunch outside the office.

M : Yes. It feels so good now that _____ ___ _____ _____. Shall we take a walk as usual before going back to the office?

W : I'd love to, but I can't today.

M : Is it too cold? Your jacket does look thin.

W : No, I'm okay. This jacket is warmer than it looks.

M : Then, are your allergy symptoms bothering you again?

W : Not really. I ✪ ______ __ ________ ________, but I've already seen a doctor. It's okay now.

M : So, why not today?

W : Actually, I need to ______ _____ ________ ________. I got a text message saying that my new driver's license is ready.

M : I see. Then I'll just go back to prepare for the afternoon meeting.

W : Okay. See you at the office.

08

대화를 듣고, 남자가 예약할 연극 공연에 관해 언급되지 않은 것을 고르시오.

M : Hi, this is William Parker from Breezeville Senior Center.

W : Oh, Mr. Parker. You called yesterday about ___________ ________ ___________ to see the play.

M : Yes. Before I book, I'd like to ✪ __________ __________ ______ ______. It's *The Shiny Moments*, right?

W : That's right. Have you decided on the date?

M : Yes. Could I reserve seats for 25 people on December 27th?

W : Absolutely. But in that case, you'll need to pay today.

M : Okay. You said admission tickets for seniors are $30 each.

W : That's correct. I'll send you the link for the payment.

M : Thank you. I'll pay tonight.

W : That'll be fine. The play starts at 3 p.m., but ________ ________ ____ ________ ________.

M : No problem. See you then.

09

***Golden Palette* Walking Tour에 관한 다음 내용을 듣고, 일치하지 않는 것을 고르시오.**

M : Hello, viewers. Are you looking for an interesting experience? How about joining the *Golden Palette* Walking Tour? You'll get the chance to see some of ✪ ______ ________ ________ ______ from the movie Golden Palette. This tour runs every day in November. It's __ ________ ______ ________ ______ with one of our professional guides. Also, brochures are provided for free, and you can find additional information about the filming sites there. The tour begins at 10:30 a.m. and takes you to six locations from the movie. The starting point is at the north gate of Central Studio. The price for this tour is $40 per person. All participants will ________ __ __________ ___ ______. Book it now on our website!

10

다음 표를 보면서 대화를 듣고, 남자가 주문할 접이식 카트를 고르시오.

W : Honey, what are you doing on your laptop?

M : I'm trying to choose one of these foldable carts. You know our cart broke yesterday.

W : Oh, that's right. Let me see the ones you're looking at.

M : Sure. There are these five. They all look good, but let's not spend more than $50.

W : All right. How about the weight limit? Our last one was 30 kilograms.

M : Hmm, ________ ________ ________ __________.

W : Okay. Then, this one won't be any good.

M : Yeah. Do you have any color preference?

W : The old one was blue. Why don't we _____ __ ________ ______ this time?

M : Good idea. Now, there are two options left. ✪ ________ ________ ________ do you like better?

W : Well, metal gets too cold in winter.

M : Good point. Then, let's get the other model. I'll order it now.

11

대화를 듣고, 여자의 마지막 말에 대한 남자의 응답으로 가장 적절한 것을 고르시오.

W : Dad, we should leave soon to ________ ______ ________ in the park. Shall we bring something to eat?

M : Yeah, we might get hungry. Oh, we also need the picnic mat to sit on. I think I ✪ _____ __ ____ ______ ____ _____ ________ in the storage room, but I'm not sure.

W : Then, could you find the mat while I pack some snacks and soft drinks?

12

대화를 듣고, 남자의 마지막 말에 대한 여자의 응답으로 가장 적절한 것을 고르시오.

M : Hey, Tina. I have something to tell you about ________ ______________ ________ this Saturday.

W : Oh, Clark. You're coming, right? I'd really love it if you could come. All our friends will be there.

M : ✪ ______ __________ __ ________ ________ __ this time. I have to go on a business trip with my boss this weekend.

13

대화를 듣고, 여자의 마지막 말에 대한 남자의 응답으로 가장 적절한 것을 고르시오. [3점]

W : Shaun, you really ✪ ___________ _____ ____________ as a senior fashion model yesterday!

M : Thanks for coming to my first show, Grace.

W : My pleasure. You'll be an inspiration to many people our age.

M : I'm so flattered.

W : It's amazing that you ✪ ____________________ ______________ ___________.

M : Thank you. My dream has finally come true.

W : It couldn't have been easy to realize your dream in your 60s.

M : It wasn't. But I've always believed in myself, and age was never an issue for me.

W : You make me think of my old passion to be a painter, but I _____ __ _____ _____ _____ _______.

M : Now is the time to give it a try.

W : I think it's too late for that.

14

대화를 듣고, 남자의 마지막 말에 대한 여자의 응답으로 가장 적절한 것을 고르시오.

W : Excuse me. Can you tell me where the non-fiction books are?

M : Sure. They're right over here. Are you looking for anything in particular?

W : I want to buy the latest book by Harriot Braun.

M : You mean *Follow Your Own Trail*?

W : Yes, that's the book.

M : Sorry. We ✪ ________ _______ ______ __________ _____ at the moment.

W : I can't believe it. It just came out three weeks ago.

M : The book is so popular that __ _______ _____ _______ ____________. Do you want me to find out if any of our other stores has a copy?

W : Yes, please. I really need to buy one for my book club meeting tomorrow. Could you check the store downtown? It's on my way home.

M : Certainly. Let me look it up in our system. *[Typing sound]* Oh, there's one copy left there, but unfortunately _____ ________ _______ __ _____ ______.

15

다음 상황 설명을 듣고, Jake가 Yuna에게 할 말로 가장 적절한 것을 고르시오. [3점]

M : Jake and Yuna are members of a climbing club. Today, they're visiting a national park with other club members. At the top of the mountain, Jake sees a beautiful rock. He ✪ _________ __________ __________ with it. When Yuna sees Jake, she offers to take photos for him. Jake finds a great spot to take a photo with the rock and gives Yuna his smartphone. After Yuna takes some photos of him, Jake looks at the photos and notices that _____ ________ ___ _____ ___ ________. So Jake wants to ask Yuna to _____ ___________ _______ ___ ______ and this time include the rock. In this situation, what would Jake most likely say to Yuna?

16~17

다음을 듣고, 물음에 답하시오.

W : Hello, students. Last week, we learned about upcycling, the process of reusing old materials to _________ __ _______ __________ _________ ______________ than the original pieces. Today, I'll focus on how this eco-friendly practice is ✪ ________________ ___ ___________________ around the world. Our first example is a community center in Singapore, called Enabling Village. Its buildings are famous for being made from old shipping containers. Second, we have a hotel in Mexico, called Tubohotel. The capsule-style rooms of this hotel were built using huge upcycled concrete pipes. Next, Microlibrary Bima is a small local library located in Indonesia. The building was constructed by arranging 2,000 plastic ice cream buckets. Finally, there's the Circular Pavilion in France. It is known for its exterior design which consists of 180 reused wooden doors. Each of these examples shows how upcycling is applied in architecture globally to ✪ _______________ _____ _____________________ ______________. Now, let's watch a video showing how these buildings were made.

▶정답 : 해설편 135쪽

VOCA LIST 30

회차별 영단어 QR 코드 ※ QR 코드를 스캔 후 모바일로 단어장처럼 학습할 수 있습니다.

● 고3 2024학년도 수능

01

001 □ P.E. (physical education) ⓝ 체육
002 □ announce ⓥ 발표하다, 알리다
003 □ volunteer ⓝ 자원봉사자
004 □ charity ⓝ 자선
005 □ compete against ~와 겨루다
006 □ graduate ⓝ 졸업생
007 □ audience ⓝ 관중
008 □ tidy up ~을 깔끔하게 정리하다
009 □ donate ⓥ 기부하다
010 □ apply ⓥ 신청하다
011 □ Don't hesitate to ~ 망설이지 말고 ~하세요

02

012 □ get into an argument 논쟁하다
013 □ close ⓐ 가까운, 친밀한
014 □ student council 학생회
015 □ jump in (대화에) 불쑥 끼어들다
016 □ interrupt ⓥ 가로막다, 방해하다
017 □ polite ⓐ 공손한, 예의 바른
018 □ cut off ~을 끊다
019 □ point of view 관점, 시각
020 □ apologize ⓥ 사과하다

03

021 □ get a good night's sleep 숙면을 취하다
022 □ fall asleep 잠들다
023 □ eye mask 안대
024 □ interfere with ~을 방해하다
025 □ release ⓝ 분비 ⓥ 내보내다, 방출하다
026 □ block ⓥ 차단하다

04

027 □ decorate ⓥ 꾸미다, 장식하다
028 □ gear ⓝ 장비
029 □ campsite ⓝ 캠핑장
030 □ represent ⓥ 나타내다, 제시하다
031 □ banner ⓝ 현수막
032 □ attract ⓥ (관심을) 끌다, 매혹하다
033 □ set up 설치하다
034 □ cone ⓝ 원뿔
035 □ Native American 북미 원주민(의)
036 □ currently ad 현재
037 □ comfortable ⓐ 편안한
038 □ tablecloth ⓝ 식탁보
039 □ eye-catching ⓐ 눈길을 끄는
040 □ certainly ad 확실히
041 □ excellent ⓐ 탁월한

05

042 □ go through 검토하다
043 □ to-do list 할 일 목록
044 □ reserve ⓥ 예약하다
045 □ spacious ⓐ (공간이) 넓은
046 □ terrific ⓐ 훌륭한
047 □ remind ⓥ 상기시키다
048 □ print out 출력하다

06

049 □ gift shop 선물 가게
050 □ recommend ⓥ 추천하다
051 □ insert ⓥ 넣다, 삽입하다
052 □ pricey ⓐ 비싼
053 □ key chain 열쇠고리
054 □ available ⓐ 이용할 수 있는
055 □ promotion ⓝ 판촉, 홍보

07

056 □ take a walk 산책하다
057 □ thin ⓐ 얇은
058 □ symptom ⓝ 증상
059 □ bother ⓥ 괴롭히다
060 □ have a runny nose 콧물이 흐르다
061 □ driver's license 운전 면허증

08

062 □ senior ⓝ 노인, 어르신
063 □ book ⓥ 예약하다
064 □ double check 재확인하다
065 □ decide on ~을 정하다
066 □ admission ⓝ 입장
067 □ payment ⓝ 지불

09

068 □ filming site 영화 현장
069 □ run ⓥ 운영되다, (위험 등을) 감수하다, 무릅쓰다
070 □ brochure ⓝ 안내 책자
071 □ additional ⓐ 추가적인
072 □ location ⓝ 위치
073 □ starting point 출발점
074 □ postcard ⓝ 엽서

10

075 □ foldable ⓐ 접이식의
076 □ weight ⓝ 무게
077 □ limit ⓝ 한도
078 □ strong ⓐ 튼튼한
079 □ preference ⓝ 선호, 호불호
080 □ metal ⓝ 금속
081 □ Good point. 좋은 지적이네요.

11

082 □ firework ⓝ 불꽃놀이, 폭죽
083 □ picnic mat 야외용 돗자리
084 □ shelf ⓝ 선반
085 □ storage ⓝ 보관
086 □ pack ⓥ 챙기다, 싸다
087 □ soft drink 청량음료
088 □ take care of ~을 처리하다

12

089 □ make it (시간 맞춰) 가다, 해내다
090 □ go on a business trip 출장 가다
091 □ That's too bad. 안됐네, 아쉽네.
092 □ look forward to ~을 고대하다
093 □ arrange ⓥ 정리하다, 배치하다, 배열하다
094 □ return ⓥ 돌아오다, 반품하다

13

095 □ rock ⓥ 뒤흔들다
096 □ My pleasure. 천만에요.
097 □ inspiration ⓝ 영감, 자극
098 □ switch careers 전업하다
099 □ realize ⓥ (꿈을) 실현하다
100 □ passion ⓝ 열정
101 □ put off ~을 미루다
102 □ give it a try 시도하다
103 □ You have a point. 당신 말이 일리가 있네요.
104 □ make a balance 균형을 맞추다
105 □ pursue ⓥ 추구하다

14

106 □ non-fiction ⓝ 논픽션, 실화
107 □ in particular 특히
108 □ trail ⓝ 길, 자국, 자취
109 □ at the moment 지금
110 □ come out 나오다, 출간되다
111 □ on one's way home 집에 가는 길에
112 □ look up 찾아보다
113 □ unfortunately ad 안타깝게도
114 □ be sure to 꼭 ~하다
115 □ Never mind. 신경 쓰지 마세요.

15

116 □ climbing ⓝ 등산
117 □ national park 국립공원
118 □ at the top of ~의 꼭대기에
119 □ selfie ⓝ 셀피
120 □ spot ⓝ 장소 ⓥ 찾아내다
121 □ appreciate ⓥ 고마워하다

16~17

122 □ upcycling ⓝ 업사이클링
123 □ reuse ⓥ 재사용하다
124 □ valuable ⓐ 가치 있는
125 □ original ⓐ 원래의
126 □ eco-friendly ⓐ 친환경적인
127 □ practice ⓝ 관행
128 □ employ ⓥ 사용하다
129 □ architecture ⓝ 건축
130 □ famous for ~로 유명한
131 □ shipping ⓝ 선적, 해운
132 □ huge ⓐ 거대한
133 □ construct ⓥ 짓다, 건축하다
134 □ bucket ⓝ 통, 양동이
135 □ exterior ⓐ 외부의
136 □ wooden ⓐ 나무로 만든
137 □ minimize ⓥ 최소화하다
138 □ environmental footprint 환경 발자국, 환경에 악영향을 미친 범위
139 □ supplies ⓝ 용품, 자재
140 □ strategic ⓐ 전략적인

31회 ● 2023학년도 대학수학능력시험 고3 영어 듣기

※ QR코드를 스캔하시면 듣기 방송을 청취하실 수 있습니다.

● 점수 표시가 없는 문항은 모두 2점 ● 문항수 17개 | 배점 37점 | 제한 시간 25분

1번부터 17번까지는 듣고 답하는 문제입니다. 1번부터 15번까지는 한 번만 들려주고, 16번부터 17번까지는 두 번 들려줍니다. 방송을 잘 듣고 답을 하시기 바랍니다.

1. 다음을 듣고, 남자가 하는 말의 목적으로 가장 적절한 것을 고르시오.

① 도서관의 변경된 운영 시간을 안내하려고
② 독후감 쓰기 대회의 일정을 공지하려고
③ 책갈피 디자인 대회 참가를 독려하려고
④ 기한 내 도서 반납을 촉구하려고
⑤ 전자책 이용 방법을 설명하려고

2. 대화를 듣고, 여자의 의견으로 가장 적절한 것을 고르시오.

① 사과를 먹으면 장운동이 원활해진다.
② 사과 껍질은 피부 상태 개선에 도움이 된다.
③ 충분한 수면은 건강한 피부 유지에 필수적이다.
④ 사과를 먹기 전에 껍질을 깨끗이 씻어야 한다.
⑤ 주기적인 수분 섭취는 피부 노화를 늦춘다.

3. 대화를 듣고, 두 사람의 관계를 가장 잘 나타낸 것을 고르시오.

① 평론가 – 영화감독 ② 심판 – 수영 선수
③ 작가 – 수영 코치 ④ 서점 주인 – 유치원 교사
⑤ 잡지사 편집장 – 광고주

4. 대화를 듣고, 그림에서 대화의 내용과 일치하지 않는 것을 고르시오.

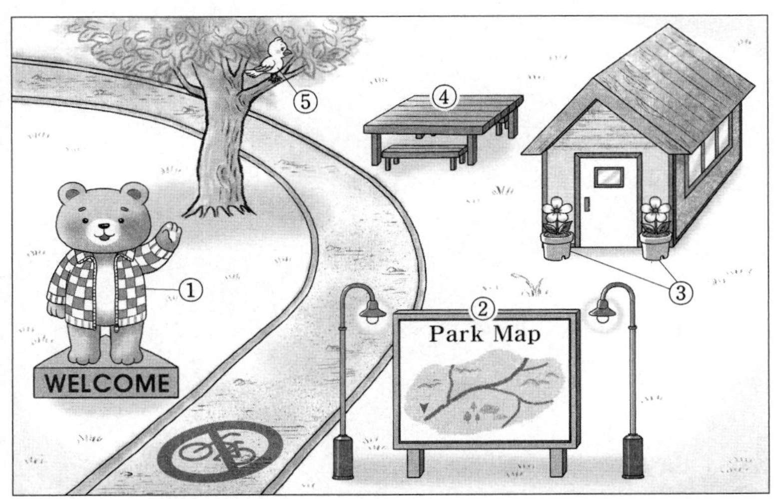

5. 대화를 듣고, 남자가 할 일로 가장 적절한 것을 고르시오.

① 음식 재료 주문하기 ② 와인 잔 포장하기
③ 추가 메뉴 선정하기 ④ 초대 문자 메시지 보내기
⑤ 노래 목록 확인하기

6. 대화를 듣고, 여자가 지불할 금액을 고르시오.

① $55 ② $63 ③ $70 ④ $81 ⑤ $90

7. 대화를 듣고, 남자가 K-Trend Festival에 갈 수 없는 이유를 고르시오.

① 영화관에서 일해야 해서
② 유학 설명회에 참석해야 해서
③ 경제학 시험공부를 해야 해서
④ 태권도 시합에 출전해야 해서
⑤ 동생을 공항에 데려다줘야 해서

8. 대화를 듣고, 졸업 사진 촬영에 관해 언급되지 않은 것을 고르시오.

① 날짜 ② 장소 ③ 복장
④ 참여 학생 수 ⑤ 소요 시간

9. Greenville Houseplant Expo에 관한 다음 내용을 듣고, 일치하지 않는 것을 고르시오.

① 3일 동안 진행될 것이다.
② 식물 관리 방법에 관한 강의가 매일 있을 것이다.
③ 희귀종을 포함한 다양한 식물을 구입할 수 있다.
④ 티켓 구입은 온라인으로만 가능하다.
⑤ 에메랄드 컨벤션 센터에서 열릴 것이다.

10. 다음 표를 보면서 대화를 듣고, 여자가 구매할 첼로 케이스를 고르시오.

Hard Cello Cases

	Model	Price	Interior Material	Length (inches)	Wheels
①	A	$140	Nylon	51	×
②	B	$160	Cotton	49	○
③	C	$175	Velvet	53	×
④	D	$190	Cotton	52	○
⑤	E	$215	Cotton	55	×

11. 대화를 듣고, 남자의 마지막 말에 대한 여자의 응답으로 가장 적절한 것을 고르시오.

① Never mind. I'm selling my old helmet.
② All right. I'll buy a bigger one that fits you.
③ No way. You should not ride a bicycle at night.
④ Great. I think it matches your bicycle perfectly.
⑤ No. We don't have to worry about the tight schedule.

12. 대화를 듣고, 여자의 마지막 말에 대한 남자의 응답으로 가장 적절한 것을 고르시오.

① Okay. Let's go and look at his career options together.
② Don't worry. There's no admission fee for the fair.
③ Too bad. The career fair doesn't suit my purpose.
④ Why not? He can join the firm as a freelancer.
⑤ Awesome! Good luck with your new career.

13. 대화를 듣고, 남자의 마지막 말에 대한 여자의 응답으로 가장 적절한 것을 고르시오. [3점]

Woman: ______________________________

① Not really. It's better to speak in simple sentences.
② Yes. Try to memorize words by learning the root words.
③ That's right. I'm glad you've studied the proper examples.
④ Exactly. That way you can use the proper words in context.
⑤ I don't think so. Always use an Italian-to-Italian dictionary.

14. 대화를 듣고, 여자의 마지막 말에 대한 남자의 응답으로 가장 적절한 것을 고르시오. [3점]

Man: ______________________________

① I had the photos from our trip printed out yesterday.
② The problem is that I already put out the campfire.
③ I gladly accept his invitation to the fishing camp.
④ Then I'll ask him to come with me on this trip.
⑤ Remember not to set up your tent near a river.

15. 다음 상황 설명을 듣고, Katie가 Jacob에게 할 말로 가장 적절한 것을 고르시오. [3점]

Katie: ______________________________

① You should check how many nursing homes there are.
② Why don't you reuse the activity you prepared last time?
③ How about preparing multiple activities for your next visit?
④ You need to gain more practical knowledge about nursing.
⑤ You'd better speak to the residents of the neighborhood.

[16~17] 다음을 듣고, 물음에 답하시오.

16. 여자가 하는 말의 주제로 가장 적절한 것은?

① how metals advanced human civilization
② how techniques applied to metals improved
③ where most precious metals originated from
④ why metals were used in the fashion industry
⑤ why ancient civilizations competed for metals

17. 언급된 금속이 아닌 것은?

① gold ② silver ③ iron
④ aluminum ⑤ nickel

[해설편 p.137]

※ QR 코드를 스캔하시면 듣기 방송이 나옵니다. 듣기 방송을 들으며 다음 빈칸을 채우시오. ● 제한 시간 : 25분

01

다음을 듣고, 남자가 하는 말의 목적으로 가장 적절한 것을 고르시오.

M : Hello, Lockwood High School students. This is your school librarian, Mr. Wilkins. I'm sure you're aware that our school library is hosting a bookmark design competition. I encourage students of _________ _________ _________ _________ _________ _________ _________. The winning designs will be made into bookmarks, which will be distributed to library visitors. We're also giving out a variety of other prizes. So don't let this great opportunity ✪ _________ _________. Since the registration period for the bookmark design competition ends this Friday, make sure you visit our school library to submit your application. Come and _________ _________ _________ _________ _________ and talents.

02

대화를 듣고, 여자의 의견으로 가장 적절한 것을 고르시오.

M : Honey, do you want some apples with breakfast?

W : Sounds great. Can you ✪ _________ _________ _________ _________ _________ _________?

M : Why? What do you want them for?

W : I'm going to use them to make a face pack. Apple peels are _________ _________ _________ _________ _________.

M : Where did you hear about that?

W : I recently read an article about their benefits for our skin.

M : Interesting. What's in them?

W : It said apple peels are rich in vitamins and minerals, so they _________ _________ _________ _________ _________ skin glow.

M : That's good to know.

W : Also, they remove oil from our skin and have a cooling effect.

M : Wow! Then I shouldn't throw them away.

W : Right. Apple peels can help improve our skin condition.

M : I see. I'll save them for you.

03

대화를 듣고, 두 사람의 관계를 가장 잘 나타낸 것을 고르시오.

W : Hello, Mr. Roberts. I appreciate you taking the time to share your experience and knowledge.

M : My pleasure, Ms. Lee. I've enjoyed all your bestselling books. So, I'm excited to help you.

W : Thanks. Since I'm writing about ✪ _________ _________, I wanted to hear how you've trained children who became Olympic swimming champions.

M : Then we should start with what I observe on the first day of my swimming classes.

W : Do some children stand out right away?

M : Yes. Some kids are able to pick up _________ _________ _________ _________ _________.

W : I see. So did many of those kids go on to become Olympic champions?

M : Well, practicing is much more important. Those who _________ _________ _________ _________ _________ _________ became champions.

W : This is good insight I can use in my book.

M : I hope it helps.

04

대화를 듣고, 그림에서 대화의 내용과 일치하지 않는 것을 고르시오.

M : Hi, Jane. What are you looking at on your phone?

W : Hi, Brian. It's a picture I took at Grand Boulder National Park. I went hiking there last weekend.

M : Let me see. I like the _________ _________ _________ _________ _________ _________ jacket.

W : It's cute, right?

M : Yeah. There's a park map between the lights. It seems to include useful information.

W : It helps me pick a different trail each time I go hiking. Do you see the _________ _________ _________ _________ _________ _________ _________?

M : Yes. They look beautiful. Oh, there's a round table by the path.

W : I had lunch there.

M : What a nice place to enjoy lunch! Look at the bird ✪ _________ _________ _________ _________.

W : Isn't it lovely? I love going there and being close to nature.

05

대화를 듣고, 남자가 할 일로 가장 적절한 것을 고르시오.

W : Honey, I'm so excited for our restaurant's reopening event tomorrow.

M : So am I. Let's see. We've ✪ _________ _________ _________, right?

W : I think so. We need to remind our loyal customers of the event.

M : I already sent text messages.

W : Good. I hope people like the new menu items that we added.

M : Don't worry. We have a great chef. So I'm sure the new dishes will be a hit.

W : What about the live music? Did you _________ _________ _________ _________ _________ the band?

M : Not yet. And we also need to _________ _________ _________ to give as gifts for the customers.

W : Okay. Could you wrap them?

M : Sure. I'll do it now.

W : Great! Then I'll contact the band.

06

대화를 듣고, 여자가 지불할 금액을 고르시오.

M : Hello, are you enjoying your time here at Magic Unicorn Children's Farm?

W : Yes, thank you. I'd like to buy some snacks to feed the animals.

M : Sure. We sell two kinds of food for the animals, ✪ __________ __________ __________ __________ __________.

W : How much do they cost?

M : It's $5 for a pack of vegetable sticks and $10 for a pack of sliced fruits.

W : I'll take four packs of vegetable sticks. Are there any other activities?

M : We offer horseback riding. A ticket for a ride around the farm is $25.

W : Oh, my __________ __________ __________ __________ __________ __________. Two tickets, please.

M : So, four packs of vegetable sticks and __________ __________ __________ __________, correct?

W : Right. And I heard you're offering a 10% discount as an autumn promotional event.

M : I'm sorry. That event ended last week.

W : I see. Here's my credit card.

07

대화를 듣고, 남자가 K-Trend Festival에 갈 수 없는 이유를 고르시오.

W : Sam, do you want to go to the K-Trend Festival with me this Saturday?

M : Hi, Olivia. Is that the festival held at Central Square?

W : Yeah, that's it. There'll be many ✪ __________ __________ __________ __________ __________ __________ K-pop dance moves.

M : Really? Sounds cool! What time does it start?

W : It starts at 5 p.m. Will you be working at the movie theater at that time?

M : No, I'm not working this Saturday. But I can't come to the festival.

W : Too bad. Do you have to __________ __________ __________ __________ __________?

M : Actually, I already took the exam yesterday.

W : Then, what's the matter?

M : I have to take my younger sister __________ __________ __________ on Saturday evening.

W : Where's she going?

M : She's going to Canada to study abroad.

W : That's awesome. I hope she has a good experience there.

08

대화를 듣고, 졸업 사진 촬영에 관해 언급되지 않은 것을 고르시오.

[Telephone rings.]

W : Hello, Jennifer Porter speaking.

M : Hi, Ms. Porter. This is Steve Jackson from Lifetime Photo Studio.

W : Oh, how are you?

M : Good. I'm ✪ __________ __________ __________ __________ __________ __________ photos on Wednesday, November 23rd. So, I'm __________ __________ __________ __________ __________.

W : Sure. As we previously discussed, the place will be Lily Pond Park.

M : Okay. Could you tell me the exact number of students taking part in the photo session?

W : Let me check. *[Pause]* Well, it'll be 180 students.

M : I see. The same as you said before.

W : That's right. How long will it __________ __________ __________ __________ __________?

M : It'll take almost three hours. We should finish by noon.

W : Great. Is there any other information you need?

M : No, I'm all set. Bye.

09

Greenville Houseplant Expo에 관한 다음 내용을 듣고, 일치하지 않는 것을 고르시오.

W : Hello, listeners. I'm Melinda Jones from the organizing committee of the Greenville Houseplant Expo. I'm here to announce that the expo will run for three days starting on March 17th, 2023. Just on the opening day, there'll be ✪ __________ __________ __________ __________ __________ __________. This lecture will be given by Dr. Evans, host of the TV show *Plants Love You*. Most importantly, you can buy a variety of plants, including rare species, exhibited in the expo. Due to its popularity, you'd better get your tickets early. Tickets are __________ __________ __________ __________ __________. If you're a plant lover, come to the expo, which will take place at the Emerald Convention Center, and refresh your ✪ __________ __________.

10

다음 표를 보면서 대화를 듣고, 여자가 구매할 첼로 케이스를 고르시오.

M : Welcome to Uptown Music Shop. How can I help you?

W : Hi, I'm __________ __________ __________ __________ __________ __________.

M : All right. Here's our catalog. These are the __________ __________ __________ __________ __________. How much are you willing to spend?

W : I can spend up to $200.

M : Okay. How about the ✪ __________ __________? Do you have a preference?

W : Well, I don't want the velvet one. It __________ __________ __________ __________ __________ __________.

M : Right. Then how about the length?

W : I have a full-size cello, so I want a case that's at least 50 inches long.

M : Now you have two options left. Do you need wheels on your case?

W : No, I don't need them. I won't carry it around a lot.

M : Then this is the one for you.

W : Thank you. I'll take it.

11

대화를 듣고, 남자의 마지막 말에 대한 여자의 응답으로 가장 적절한 것을 고르시오.

M : Mom, I'd like to get a new bicycle helmet. Can you buy me one?
W : I'll buy you a new helmet if you need it. But what's the problem with the one you have now?
M : ✪ _________ _________ _________ _________ _________. It hurts my head.

12

대화를 듣고, 여자의 마지막 말에 대한 남자의 응답으로 가장 적절한 것을 고르시오.

W : Honey, are you free on Saturday afternoon? Our son said he's going to a career fair and asked if we can come along.
M : Great, I'm free. I've been ✪ _________ _________ _________ _________ _________ _________ might suit him.
W : Me, too. Then why don't we join him?

13

대화를 듣고, 남자의 마지막 말에 대한 여자의 응답으로 가장 적절한 것을 고르시오. [3점]

M : Can I come in, Professor Rossini?
W : Of course. Come on in, Ben. What brings you here?
M : I came to ask for advice on studying Italian.
W : Is there anything specific you're having trouble with?
M : Yes. I'm ✪ _________ _________ _________ _________ _________. Could I get some tips?
W : Sure. First, let me ask how you use your dictionary.
M : Well, I use it to look up words that I don't know the meanings of.
W : Dictionaries ✪ _________ _________ _________ _________ _________ _________. Do you read them, too?
M : No, I don't pay attention to the example sentences.
W : Knowing the meaning of words is important, but you should also understand _________ _________ in which the words are properly used.
M : I see. So you're suggesting that I study the example sentences as well, right?

14

대화를 듣고, 여자의 마지막 말에 대한 남자의 응답으로 가장 적절한 것을 고르시오. [3점]

W : Dad, I found these old photos of our camping trip from 25 years ago.
M : Oh, I remember this trip. You were about the _________ _________ _________ _________ _________, Peter.
W : Right. It was a really fun trip.
M : Yeah. I still go camping often, but that's the most ✪ _________ _________.
W : I agree. I want Peter to have that experience, too. But he always refuses to go.
M : Why doesn't he want to go camping?
W : He just wants to stay home and spend all his time on his smartphone.
M : Don't worry. I'm sure Peter will _________ _________ _________ _________ _________ how fun it is.
W : You're probably right. Dad, when is the next time you're going camping?
M : This weekend. We should all go together.
W : That'd be great. Peter _________ _________ _________ _________ _________ _________ _________ grandpa invites him.

15

다음 상황 설명을 듣고, Katie가 Jacob에게 할 말로 가장 적절한 것을 고르시오. [3점]

M : Jacob just started volunteering at a nursing home and is planning his next visit. He recalls that not every resident in the nursing home _________ _________ _________ _________ _________ _________ last time. To avoid this situation, he tries to find an activity that all residents in the nursing home can enjoy. But he ✪ _________ _________ _________ _________ one that everyone would like. He asks his friend Katie for advice because she has lots of _________ _________ _________ _________ _________. Katie thinks there's no single activity that can interest all the residents. So Katie wants to suggest to Jacob that next time he should plan more than one activity. In this situation, what would Katie most likely say to Jacob?

16~17

다음을 듣고, 물음에 답하시오.

W : Hello, students. Perhaps no material on earth has been more important in human history than metal. Today, we're going to discuss the contribution of metals to the development of civilization. First, gold was considered the most valuable metal due to ✪ _________ _________ _________ _________. Because of its visual appeal and ability to be easily shaped, it's been used to _________ _________ _________ _________ _________. Second, silver was mainly prized for being the shiniest of all metals. It's been one of the main forms of currency since it was the chief metal used for making coins. Next, iron became widely used once humans _________ _________ _________ _________ _________. This metal was fashioned into tools that revolutionized farming, and later, machines that industrialized the world. Finally, aluminum is the most abundant metal in the world and is also lightweight. That's why it's been essential to countless industries in modern society from _________ _________ _________ _________ _________. Now, let's watch a short related video.

▶ 정답 : 해설편 139쪽

회차별 영단어 QR 코드 ※ QR 코드를 스캔 후 모바일로 단어장처럼 학습할 수 있습니다.

01

001 □ librarian ⓝ (도서관의) 사서
002 □ host ⓥ 개최하다 ⓝ 진행자
003 □ aware ⓐ 알고 있는
004 □ bookmark ⓝ 책갈피
005 □ competition ⓝ 대회, 경연, 경쟁
006 □ encourage ⓥ 권장하다
007 □ grade ⓝ 학년
008 □ participate ⓥ 참여하다, 참가하다
009 □ distribute ⓥ 배부하다
010 □ a variety of 다양한
011 □ prize ⓝ 상, 상품
012 □ slip away 사라지다, 훌쩍 지나가 버리다
013 □ registration ⓝ 등록
014 □ submit ⓥ 제출하다
015 □ creativity ⓝ 창의성

02

016 □ peel ⓝ (과일 등의) 껍질 ⓥ 껍질을 벗기다
017 □ effective ⓐ 효과적인
018 □ improve ⓥ 개선하다, 향상시키다
019 □ condition ⓝ 상태
020 □ recently ad 최근에
021 □ article ⓝ 기사
022 □ benefit ⓝ 이점
023 □ moisturize ⓥ 수분을 공급하다
024 □ enhance ⓥ 개선하다
025 □ glow ⓝ 윤기, 빛
026 □ throw away ~을 버리다

03

027 □ appreciate ⓥ 감사하다
028 □ knowledge ⓝ 지식
029 □ excited ⓐ 신나는, 설레는
030 □ athlete ⓝ 운동선수
031 □ observe ⓥ 관찰하다
032 □ stand out 두드러지다, 눈에 띄다
033 □ instruction ⓝ 지시, 가르침
034 □ consistently ad 일관되게, 계속해서, 꾸준히
035 □ make an improvement 개선되다

04

036 □ go hiking 하이킹을 가다
037 □ statue ⓝ 조각상
038 □ trail ⓝ (작은) 길
039 □ flowerpot ⓝ 화분
040 □ cabin ⓝ 오두막
041 □ branch ⓝ 나뭇가지

05

042 □ reopening ⓝ 재개업
043 □ order ⓥ 주문하다
044 □ ingredient ⓝ 재료
045 □ live music 라이브 음악
046 □ wrap ⓥ 포장하다
047 □ customer ⓝ 고객

06

048 □ feed ⓥ 먹이를 주다, 먹이다
049 □ slice ⓥ 자르다, 쪼개다
050 □ cost ⓥ ~의 비용이 들다, 희생시키다
051 □ horseback riding 승마
052 □ promotional ⓐ 홍보의, 판촉의
053 □ credit card 신용 카드

07

054 □ attraction ⓝ 볼거리, 명물
055 □ incorporate ⓥ 결합하다, 통합하다
056 □ dance move 안무
057 □ economics ⓝ 경제학
058 □ take an exam 시험을 치다
059 □ take A to B A를 B에 데려다 주다
060 □ study abroad 유학하다
061 □ awesome ⓐ 멋진, 근사한, 기막히게 좋은

08

062 □ be scheduled to ~할 예정이다
063 □ shoot ⓥ 촬영하다
064 □ graduation ⓝ 졸업
065 □ confirm ⓥ (맞는지) 확인하다
066 □ previously ad 이전에
067 □ exact ⓐ 정확한
068 □ be all set 다 준비되다

09

069 □ committee ⓝ 위원회
070 □ lecture ⓝ 강의
071 □ method ⓝ 방법
072 □ importantly ad 중요하게
073 □ rare ⓐ 희귀한
074 □ exhibit ⓥ 전시하다
075 □ popularity ⓝ 인기

10

076 □ have in stock 재고가 있다
077 □ be willing to 기꺼이 ~하다
078 □ interior ⓐ 내부의
079 □ preference ⓝ 선호
080 □ wheel ⓝ 바퀴
081 □ carry around 들고 다니다, 휴대하다

11

082 □ helmet ⓝ 헬멧
083 □ tight ⓐ 꽉 끼는, 조이는
084 □ hurt ⓥ 아프게 하다, 아프다
085 □ Never mind. 신경 쓰지 마.
086 □ match ⓥ ~와 맞다, 어울리다

12

087 □ career fair 직업 박람회
088 □ come along 함께 가다
089 □ emerging ⓐ 떠오르는, 생겨나는, 신흥의
090 □ suit ⓥ ~에 적합하다
091 □ admission fee 참가비
092 □ freelancer ⓝ 프리랜서

13

093 □ What brings you here? 어쩐 일이니?
094 □ ask for ~을 요청하다
095 □ have trouble with ~에 문제가 있다
096 □ properly ad 적절히, 알맞게
097 □ dictionary ⓝ 사전
098 □ look up (사전이나 책 등에서) ~을 찾아보다
099 □ context ⓝ 맥락
100 □ memorize ⓥ 암기하다, 외우다

14

101 □ about ad 약, 대략
102 □ memorable ⓐ 기억에 남는
103 □ refuse ⓥ 거부하다
104 □ print out 인쇄하다
105 □ put out (불을) 끄다
106 □ gladly ad 기쁘게
107 □ set up a tent 텐트를 치다

15

108 □ nursing home 요양원
109 □ recall ⓥ 회상하다
110 □ resident ⓝ 거주민
111 □ reuse ⓥ 다시 사용하다
112 □ multiple ⓐ 여럿의, 다수의
113 □ practical ⓐ 실용적인

16~17

114 □ contribution ⓝ 기여, 이바지
115 □ civilization ⓝ 문명
116 □ valuable ⓐ 가치 있는
117 □ scarcity ⓝ 희소성
118 □ appeal ⓝ 매력
119 □ decorate ⓥ 꾸미다, 장식하다
120 □ religious ⓐ 종교적인
121 □ be prized for ~로 귀하게 여겨지다
122 □ currency ⓝ 화폐
123 □ strengthen ⓥ 강화하다
124 □ fashion ⓥ (~로) 만들다
125 □ revolutionize ⓥ ~에 혁명을 일으키다
126 □ industrialize ⓥ 산업화하다
127 □ abundant ⓐ 풍부한, 많은
128 □ countless ⓐ 수많은
129 □ automotive ⓝ 자동차 부품 ⓐ 자동차의

32회 ● 2022학년도 대학수학능력시험 고3 영어 듣기

※ QR코드를 스캔하시면 듣기 방송을 청취하실 수 있습니다.

● 점수 표시가 없는 문항은 모두 2점 ● 문항수 17개 | 배점 37점 | 제한 시간 25분

1번부터 17번까지는 듣고 답하는 문제입니다. 1번부터 15번까지는 한 번만 들려주고, 16번부터 17번까지는 두 번 들려줍니다. 방송을 잘 듣고 답을 하시기 바랍니다.

1. 다음을 듣고, 여자가 하는 말의 목적으로 가장 적절한 것을 고르시오.

① 조련사 자격증 취득 방법을 설명하려고
② 동물 병원 확장 이전을 공지하려고
③ 새로 출시된 개 사료를 소개하려고
④ 반려동물 입양 절차를 안내하려고
⑤ 개 훈련 센터를 홍보하려고

2. 대화를 듣고, 남자의 의견으로 가장 적절한 것을 고르시오.

① 여행 전에 합리적으로 예산을 계획해야 한다.
② 여행 가서 할 것을 너무 많이 계획하면 안 된다.
③ 인생에서 자신의 원칙을 고수하는 것이 중요하다.
④ 여행은 사고의 폭을 확장시켜 사람을 성장하게 한다.
⑤ 보호자 없이 학생끼리 여행하는 것은 안전하지 않다.

3. 대화를 듣고, 두 사람의 관계를 가장 잘 나타낸 것을 고르시오.

① 라디오 쇼 진행자 – 제빵사 ② 리포터 – 과수원 주인
③ 광고주 – 요리사 ④ 방송 작가 – 경제학자
⑤ 유통업자 – 농부

4. 대화를 듣고, 그림에서 대화의 내용과 일치하지 않는 것을 고르시오.

5. 대화를 듣고, 남자가 할 일로 가장 적절한 것을 고르시오.

① 리본 가져오기 ② 선글라스 주문하기
③ 사진사 섭외하기 ④ 설문 조사 실시하기
⑤ 졸업 연설문 작성하기

6. 대화를 듣고, 여자가 지불할 금액을 고르시오. [3점]

① $36 ② $45 ③ $50 ④ $54 ⑤ $60

7. 대화를 듣고, 남자가 탁구 연습을 할 수 없는 이유를 고르시오.

① 학교 도서관에 자원봉사를 하러 가야 해서
② 과학 퀴즈를 위한 공부를 해야 해서
③ 연극부 모임에 참가해야 해서
④ 역사 숙제를 제출해야 해서
⑤ 어깨에 통증이 있어서

8. 대화를 듣고, Little Readers' Class에 관해 언급되지 않은 것을 고르시오.

① 장소 ② 시간 ③ 대상 연령
④ 모집 인원 ⑤ 등록 방법

9. 2021 Family Science Festival에 관한 다음 내용을 듣고, 일치하지 않는 것을 고르시오.

① 12월 7일부터 일주일 동안 진행된다.
② 8개의 프로그램이 제공될 것이다.
③ 어린이 과학 잡지를 판매할 것이다.
④ 11세 미만의 어린이들은 성인을 동반해야 한다.
⑤ 참가를 위해 미리 등록해야 한다.

[해설편 p.140]

10. 다음 표를 보면서 대화를 듣고, 두 사람이 예약할 스터디룸을 고르시오.

Study Rooms

	Room	Capacity (persons)	Available Times	Price (per hour)	Projector
①	A	2-3	9 a.m. − 11 a.m.	$10	×
②	B	4-6	9 a.m. − 11 a.m.	$16	○
③	C	4-6	2 p.m. − 4 p.m.	$14	×
④	D	6-8	2 p.m. − 4 p.m.	$19	○
⑤	E	6-9	4 p.m. − 6 p.m.	$21	×

11. 대화를 듣고, 여자의 마지막 말에 대한 남자의 응답으로 가장 적절한 것을 고르시오.

① Just give me about ten minutes.
② It took an hour for us to get back home.
③ I think you need to focus on your work.
④ It was nice of you to invite my co-workers.
⑤ Call me when you finish sending the email.

12. 대화를 듣고, 남자의 마지막 말에 대한 여자의 응답으로 가장 적절한 것을 고르시오.

① Excellent. I like the camera you bought for me.
② Good. I'll stop by and get it on my way home.
③ Never mind. I'll drop off the camera tomorrow.
④ I see. Thanks for taking those pictures of me.
⑤ No way. That's too expensive for the repair.

13. 대화를 듣고, 여자의 마지막 말에 대한 남자의 응답으로 가장 적절한 것을 고르시오. [3점]

Man: ______________________________

① No worries. Stress is not always as bad as you think.
② Don't forget to bring a charger whenever you go out.
③ Great. That'll be a good way to take time for yourself.
④ I think working out too much will burn all your energy.
⑤ Fantastic. Let's enjoy ourselves at the exhibition with the kids.

14. 대화를 듣고, 남자의 마지막 말에 대한 여자의 응답으로 가장 적절한 것을 고르시오.

Woman: ______________________________

① Please check it again. The hotel can't be fully booked.
② Too bad. I should've checked out as early as possible.
③ Sure. I'm very satisfied with your cleaning service.
④ I'm sorry. You can't switch your room with mine.
⑤ Perfect. That's high enough to avoid the smell.

15. 다음 상황 설명을 듣고, Jason이 Sarah에게 할 말로 가장 적절한 것을 고르시오. [3점]

Jason: ______________________________

① Good luck. I hope you finish your work in time.
② Okay. Let's meet to discuss the changes to the sculpture.
③ That's terrible. I'm sorry that the reopening was postponed.
④ Hurry up. You have to send the final design immediately.
⑤ Don't worry. I can get the job done before the deadline.

[16～17] 다음을 듣고, 물음에 답하시오.

16. 남자가 하는 말의 주제로 가장 적절한 것은?

① effects of incorporating painting into math education
② mathematical analysis of the art industry's growth
③ application of mathematics in different types of art
④ historical review of important concepts in the arts
⑤ challenges of harmonizing mathematics and art

17. 언급된 예술 분야가 <u>아닌</u> 것은?

① music ② painting ③ photography
④ dance ⑤ cinema

Dictation 32

✪ 표기에는 듣기 어려운 발음이 포함되어 있습니다. 귀 기울여 듣고 받아쓰세요.

● 고3 2022학년도 수능

※ QR 코드를 스캔하시면 듣기 방송이 나옵니다. 듣기 방송을 들으며 다음 빈칸을 채우시오. ● 제한 시간 : 25분

01

다음을 듣고, 여자가 하는 말의 목적으로 가장 적절한 것을 고르시오.

W : Hello, dog lovers. Does your dog chew up your shoes or ________ ________ ________ ________ at times? Is it hard to control your dog during walks? You no longer have to worry. We'll help you solve these problems. At the Chester Dog Training Center, we have five ✪ ________ ________ ________ who will ________ ________ ________ ________. We also teach you how to understand your dog and what to do when it misbehaves. Leave it to the Chester Dog Training Center. We'll train your dog to become a well-behaved pet. Call us at 234-555-3647 or visit our website at www.chesterdogs.com.

02

대화를 듣고, 남자의 의견으로 가장 적절한 것을 고르시오.

M : Monica. Have you made plans for your trip to Busan?

W : Yes, Dad. I'm going to the beach and visiting an aquarium in the morning. Then I'll eat lunch at a fish market and go hiking.

M : Hold on! ________ ________ ________ ________.

W : You know, it's my first trip after starting college.

M : I understand, but I think you shouldn't ✪ ________ ________ ________ ________ ________ ________ for a trip.

W : Well, I only have one day, and I want to experience as much as possible.

M : You'll ________ ________ ________ if you stick to your plan. Also, consider the time it takes to move to each place.

W : I guess you're right. And there could be a long waiting line at some places.

M : Right. That's why you shouldn't fill your trip plan with too many things.

W : Okay. I'll revise my plan.

03

대화를 듣고, 두 사람의 관계를 가장 잘 나타낸 것을 고르시오.

W : Hello, Mr. Newton. Welcome to the *Delicacies Show*.

M : Thanks for inviting me.

W : I want to first start talking about your famous apple bread. Can you briefly introduce it to our radio show listeners?

M : Sure. Instead of sugar, I use ________ ________ ________ when I bake bread.

W : That's interesting. What inspired the recipe?

M : Well, one day, I saw a news report about local apple farmers. They were experiencing difficulty due to ✪ ________ ________ ________.

W : So you created this new recipe to help the local economy.

M : Yes. I also thought that ________ ________ ________ could add a special flavor.

W : Sounds delicious. I'll definitely go to your bakery and try some of your bread.

M : Actually, I brought some for you and your radio show staff.

W : Oh, thank you. We'll be back after a commercial break.

04

대화를 듣고, 그림에서 대화의 내용과 일치하지 않는 것을 고르시오.

M : Wow, Ms. Peters! It looks like everything is ready for the exchange student welcoming ceremony.

W : Almost, Mr. Smith. What do you think?

M : It looks great. There's a basket beside the stairs. What is it for?

W : We're going to put flowers in it for the exchange students.

M : That'll be nice. I like ________ ________ ________ ________ ________ ________. It makes the table look fancy.

W : Yeah, I'm going to put water bottles there. What do you think about the balloons next to the welcome banner?

M : They really ✪ ________ ________ ________ ________. Oh, look at the bear on the flag. It's cute.

W : Yes. It's the symbol of the exchange students' school.

M : I see. And you ________ ________ ________ ________.

W : It's because there'll be two MCs.

M : Good idea. Everything looks perfect.

05

대화를 듣고, 남자가 할 일로 가장 적절한 것을 고르시오.

W : Brian. I'm so excited about our school club photo this Friday.

M : Me, too. The photo will be included in our graduation album. Let's check our preparations for it.

W : All right. I'm going to ✪ ________ ________ ________ ________ ________ ________.

M : You said you'll bring some from home, right?

W : Yes. When is the photographer coming?

M : The photographer is coming after lunch.

W : Great. That gives us time to get ready. You know I surveyed our club members about ________ ________ ________ ________ ________ ________.

M : Right. What were the results?

W : Most of our members wanted to wear heart-shaped sunglasses. Now all that's left is to ________ ________ ________ ________ ________.

M : I know a good online store. I can order the sunglasses.

W : Could you? That'll be great.

M : No problem. I'll take care of that.

06

대화를 듣고, 여자가 지불할 금액을 고르시오. [3점]

M : Welcome to Daisy Valley Restaurant.
W : Hi. I'd like to order some food to go. How much is the shrimp pasta and the chicken salad?
M : The shrimp pasta is $20, and the chicken salad is $10.
W : I'll take two shrimp pastas and one chicken salad, please.
M : Sure. ________ ________ ________ ________ ________, too?
W : Yes. What do you recommend?
M : The mini cheese cake is ✪ ________ ________ ________ ________ ________ in our restaurant. It's $5 each.
W : Great! I'll order two of them.
M : Okay. Let me ________ ________ ________. Two shrimp pastas, one chicken salad, and two mini cheese cakes. Is that correct?
W : Yes. And I have ________ ________ ________ here. Can I use it?
M : Let me see. *[Pause]* Yes. You can get a 10% discount off the total.
W : Terrific. I'll use this coupon. Here's my credit card.

07

대화를 듣고, 남자가 탁구 연습을 할 수 없는 이유를 고르시오.

W : Hey, Mike. How's your shoulder? ________ ________ ________?
M : No, I feel totally fine, Emily. I should be ready for the table tennis tournament.
W : That's good to hear. Then do you want to practice with me now?
M : I'm sorry but I can't right now.
W : Why not? Do you have to work on your history homework?
M : No, I ✪ ________ ________ ________ to Mr. Jackson.
W : Oh, then I guess you have to study for the science quiz, right?
M : I think I'm ready for it. Actually, I'm ________ ________ ________ ________ ________ at the school library.
W : I see. Then, don't forget about our drama club meeting tomorrow.
M : Of course not. See you there.

08

대화를 듣고, Little Readers' Class에 관해 언급되지 않은 것을 고르시오.

M : Christine, I heard your daughter Jennifer loves reading. Unfortunately, my daughter doesn't.
W : Actually, Jennifer didn't enjoy reading until she took the Little Readers' Class. It ✪ ________ ________ ________ ________ ________.
M : Really? It might be good for my daughter, too. Where's it held?
W : It's held at the Stonefield Library. I have a picture of the flyer somewhere in my phone. *[Pause]* Here.
M : Oh. The class is from 4 p.m. to 5 p.m. every Monday.
W : Is that time okay for her?
M : Yeah, she's ________ ________ ________ ________.
W : Great. The class is for children ________ ________ ________ ________. Your daughter is eight years old, right?
M : Yes, she can take it. So, to register, I should send an email to the address on the flyer.
W : That's right. I hope the class ________ ________ ________ ________ ________.

09

2021 Family Science Festival에 관한 다음 내용을 듣고, 일치하지 않는 것을 고르시오.

M : Hello, WBPR listeners. Are you looking for a chance to enjoy quality family time? Then, we invite you to the 2021 Family Science Festival. It starts on December 7th and ________ ________ at the Bermont Science Museum located near City Hall. Eight programs will be offered for parents and children to enjoy together, ✪ ________ ________ ________ ________ ________ ________.
We'll also give out a children's science magazine for free. This event is open to anyone, but remember that all children under age 11 must be ________ ________ ________ ________.
There's no admission fee, but to participate, you must register in advance. Come and learn about the exciting world of science with your family. For more information, visit our website, www.wbpr.com.

10

다음 표를 보면서 대화를 듣고, 두 사람이 예약할 스터디룸을 고르시오.

M : Megan, did you ________ ________ ________ ________ for our group project meeting tomorrow?
W : I'm looking at a website to book a room. Let's book it together.
M : Sure. *[Pause]* Oh, only these rooms are available.
W : Yeah. Hmm, this one is too small for us.
M : Right. We need a room big enough to ✪ ________ ________ ________ ________.
W : Okay. Now, let's look at the times. We all agreed to meet after 1 p.m., right?
M : Yes. Then let's skip this one.
W : ________ ________ ________ ________ ________ on the study room?
M : Since we're meeting for two hours, I don't think we can spend more than $20 per hour. It's beyond our budget.
W : Then, there are two options left. Should we choose a study room with a projector?
M : Absolutely. We'll need it to practice for our presentation.
W : Then let's reserve this one.

11

대화를 듣고, 여자의 마지막 말에 대한 남자의 응답으로 가장 적절한 것을 고르시오.

W : Honey, I'm going out for a walk. Do you want to join me?
M : Sure. But can you wait for a moment? I have to ✪ ________ ________ ________ to one of my co-workers right now.
W : No problem. How long do you think it'll take?

12
대화를 듣고, 남자의 마지막 말에 대한 여자의 응답으로 가장 적절한 것을 고르시오.

[Telephone rings.]

M : Hello, this is Bob's Camera Shop.

W : Hi, this is Clara Patterson. I'm calling to see _________ _________ _________ _________ _________ _________ _________ today.

M : Let me check. *[Clicking sound]* Yes. ✪ _________ _________ _________ your camera. It's ready to go.

13
대화를 듣고, 여자의 마지막 말에 대한 남자의 응답으로 가장 적절한 것을 고르시오. [3점]

W : Honey, I'm home.

M : Is everything all right? You seem low on energy.

W : I am. I'm ✪ _________ _________ _________.

M : It's no wonder. You've been so stressed out from work these days.

W : Yeah, I can't remember the last time that I really got to enjoy myself.

M : You need to recharge your batteries. Why don't you spend some time alone this weekend?

W : Maybe you're right. I might need my own personal time.

M : Yes. And don't worry about the kids. I'll take care of them.

W : Sounds good. Then let me think about what I can do.

M : You can go to the theater, ride your bike along the river, or _________ _________ _________ _________ _________ _________.

W : Well, there's an exhibition that I've been interested in.

14
대화를 듣고, 남자의 마지막 말에 대한 여자의 응답으로 가장 적절한 것을 고르시오.

[Telephone rings.]

M : Front desk. How may I help you?

W : I'm in Room 201. I specifically booked a non-smoking room, but I smell cigarette smoke in my room.

M : We're sorry about that. Let me check that for you. *[Typing sound]* You're Wendy Parker, right?

W : Yes, that's correct.

M : Hmm, the record says ✪ _________ _________ _________ _________ _________ _________.

W : Then why do I smell cigarette smoke here?

M : Well, since your room is _________ _________ _________ _________ _________, cigarette smoke must have come in from outside. Sorry for the inconvenience. Would you like to switch rooms?

W : Yes, please. The smell is really bothering me.

M : Let me first check if there are any rooms available.

W : If it's possible, I'd like to _________ _________ _________ _________ _________. Maybe higher than the 5th floor?

M : Okay. *[Typing sound]* Oh, we have one. Room 908 on the 9th floor is available.

15
다음 상황 설명을 듣고, Jason이 Sarah에게 할 말로 가장 적절한 것을 고르시오. [3점]

W : Jason is a sculptor and Sarah is the head of a local library. A few days ago, Sarah hired Jason ✪ _________ _________ _________ _________ _________ _________ _________ _________ by the end of next month. This morning, Sarah received the final design of the sculpture from Jason. She likes his design, but it _________ _________ _________ to her. She's worried whether he can finish in time, so she calls him to express her concern. However, Jason thinks that he has _________ _________ _________ _________ _________ since he has worked on these types of sculptures before. So Jason wants to tell Sarah that he can finish it in time and that she doesn't have to be concerned. In this situation, what would Jason most likely say to Sarah?

16~17
다음을 듣고, 물음에 답하시오.

M : Good morning, students. You might think that math is all about boring formulas, but actually it involves much more. Today, we'll learn how mathematics is used in the arts. First, let's take music. Early mathematicians found that ✪ _________ _________ _________ _________ _________ created different musical notes. Many musicians started applying this mathematical concept to make harmonized sounds. Second, painting frequently uses math concepts, particularly the "Golden Ratio." Using this, great painters created masterpieces that ✪ _________ _________ _________. The *Mona Lisa* is well-known for its accurate proportionality. Photography is another example of using mathematical ideas. Photographers divide their frames into 3 by 3 sections and place their subjects along the lines. By doing so, the photo becomes balanced, thus more pleasing. Lastly, dance applies mathematics to position dancers on the stage. In ballet, dancers calculate distances between themselves and other dancers, and adjust to the size of the stage. This gives _________ _________ _________ _________ _________. I hope you've gained a new perspective on mathematics.

▶ 정답 : 해설편 144쪽

VOCA LIST 32

회차별 영단어 QR 코드 ※ QR 코드를 스캔 후 모바일로 단어장처럼 학습할 수 있습니다.

● 고3 2022학년도 수능

01

001 □ **chew** ⓥ (음식을) 씹다, 깨물다
002 □ **bark** ⓥ (개·여우 등이) 짖다, 고함치다
003 □ **professional** ⓐ 전문적인, 직업[직종]의
004 □ **certified** ⓐ 자격증을 가진
005 □ **behavior** ⓝ 행동, 태도
006 □ **misbehave** ⓥ 잘못된 행동을 하다
007 □ **train** ⓥ (사람·짐승을) 훈련하다, 몸을 단련하다
008 □ **well-behaved** ⓐ 얌전한, 예의 바른

02

009 □ **plan** ⓝ 계획, 방안 ⓥ 계획을 세우다
010 □ **beach** ⓝ 해변, 바닷가
011 □ **aquarium** ⓝ 수족관, 수조
012 □ **demanding** ⓐ 벅찬, 지나치게 요구하는
013 □ **worn out** (힘든 노동·운동으로) 매우 지친, 닳고 닳은
014 □ **revise** ⓥ 수정하다

03

015 □ **delicacy** ⓝ 맛있는 것, 별미
016 □ **briefly** [ad] 간략하게, 간단히
017 □ **introduce** ⓥ 소개하다
018 □ **bake** ⓥ (음식을) 굽다
019 □ **inspire** ⓥ 영감을 주다, (자신감·열의를 갖도록) 고무[격려]하다
020 □ **local** ⓐ 지역의, 현지의
021 □ **consumption** ⓝ (에너지·식품·물질의) 소비[소모](량)
022 □ **economy** ⓝ (국가의) 경제 (활동[상태])
023 □ **sweetness** ⓝ 단맛
024 □ **flavor** ⓝ 풍미, 맛
025 □ **definitely** [ad] 분명히, 틀림없이
026 □ **commercial break** (텔레비전·라디오의) 광고 (방송)

04

027 □ **exchange student** 교환학생
028 □ **ceremony** ⓝ (행사를 치르는) 의식, 식
029 □ **beside** [prep] ~ 옆에
030 □ **striped** ⓐ 줄무늬의
031 □ **fancy** ⓐ 화려한, 고급의
032 □ **banner** ⓝ 현수막, 플래카드
033 □ **brighten** ⓥ 밝아 보이게 하다
034 □ **flag** ⓝ 깃발, (국가·단체의) 기(旗)
035 □ **symbol** ⓝ 상징(물), 기호

05

036 □ **include** ⓥ 포함하다
037 □ **graduation** ⓝ 졸업(식)
038 □ **preparation** ⓝ 준비, 대비
039 □ **decorate** ⓥ 꾸미다, (집이나 방에) 실내 장식을 하다
040 □ **survey** ⓥ (설문) 조사하다
041 □ **result** ⓝ 결과
042 □ **take care of** ~을 돌보다[처리하다], ~의 책임을 지다

06

043 □ **food to go** 포장 음식
044 □ **shrimp** ⓝ 새우
045 □ **recommend** ⓥ 추천하다, (행동 등을) 권장하다
046 □ **confirm** ⓥ 확인해 주다, 확정[공식화]하다
047 □ **discount** ⓝ 할인(액)
048 □ **terrific** ⓐ 아주 좋은, (양·정도가) 엄청난

07

049 □ **totally** [ad] 완전히, 모두
050 □ **table tennis** 탁구
051 □ **practice** ⓥ 연습[훈련]하다, 실행하다
052 □ **submit** ⓥ (제안서·서류 등을) 제출하다
053 □ **on one's way to** ~하러 가는 길이다
054 □ **volunteer** ⓥ (힘든 일 등을) 자진[자원]해서 하다

08

055 □ **unfortunately** [ad] 유감스럽게도, 안타깝게도
056 □ **provide** ⓥ 제공하다, 주다
057 □ **various** ⓐ 다양한, 많은
058 □ **activity** ⓝ (취미·목적을 위한) 활동
059 □ **hold** ⓥ (모임·식 등이) 열리다
060 □ **flyer** ⓝ (광고·안내용) 전단
061 □ **somewhere** [ad] 어딘가에(서[로]), (수량·정도 등이) 대략
062 □ **free** ⓐ 다른 계획[약속]이 없는, 자유로운
063 □ **register** ⓥ 등록하다
064 □ **get A into B** A가 B에 흥미를 갖게 하다

09

065 □ **locate** ⓥ (건물 등이) 위치하다, 위치[장소]를 알아내다
066 □ **offer** ⓥ 제공하다, 제안하다
067 □ **simulation** ⓝ 모의실험, 시뮬레이션
068 □ **give out** 나눠주다, 배포하다
069 □ **admission** ⓝ 입장, 가입
070 □ **in advance** 미리, 사전에

10

071 □ **reserve** ⓥ 예약하다
072 □ **accommodate** ⓥ (건물 등이 사람을) 수용하다, 공간을 제공하다
073 □ **skip** ⓥ 생략하다, 넘어가다
074 □ **option** ⓝ 선택(지)
075 □ **absolutely** [ad] (강한 동의·허락을 나타내어) 그럼, 물론이지

11

076 □ **go out for a walk** 산책 가다
077 □ **co-worker** ⓝ 동료, 협력자
078 □ **get back** (특히 자기 집에) 돌아오다

12

079 □ **pick up** 찾아오다, 태워오다
080 □ **stop by** (도중에) 들르다
081 □ **mind** ⓥ 신경을 쓰다, 꺼리다
082 □ **drop off** ~을 갖다 놓다
083 □ **repair** ⓝ 수리, 보수

13

084 □ **low on energy** 에너지가 부족한
085 □ **burnt out** 극도로 피곤한, 다 타버린
086 □ **stressed out** 스트레스를 받는
087 □ **enjoy oneself** 즐기다, 즐겁게 보내다
088 □ **recharge** ⓥ (휴식으로) 재충전하다, (전지를) 충전하다
089 □ **personal** ⓐ 개인적인, 개개인을 위한
090 □ **along** [prep] ~을 따라, ~의 끝에서 끝까지 쭉
091 □ **exhibition** ⓝ 전시(회)
092 □ **charger** ⓝ 충전기
093 □ **work out** 운동하다

14

094 □ **specifically** [ad] 특별히, 분명히
095 □ **book** ⓥ (방·좌석 등을) 예약하다
096 □ **cigarette** ⓝ 담배
097 □ **record** ⓝ 기록
098 □ **assign** ⓥ 배정하다
099 □ **level** ⓝ (건물의) 층
100 □ **inconvenience** ⓝ 불편, 폐
101 □ **switch** ⓥ 바꾸다
102 □ **bother** ⓥ 신경 쓰이게 하다, 괴롭히다
103 □ **available** ⓐ 이용할 수 있는
104 □ **fully booked** 예약이 다 찬
105 □ **satisfy** ⓥ 만족시키다, 충족시키다
106 □ **avoid** ⓥ (회)피하다, 모면하다

15

107 □ **sculptor** ⓝ 조각가
108 □ **head** ⓝ (집단의) 지도자
109 □ **hire** ⓥ 고용하다
110 □ **sculpture** ⓝ 조각품, 조형물
111 □ **receive** ⓥ 받다, 받아들이다
112 □ **quite** [ad] 꽤, 완전히
113 □ **complicated** ⓐ 복잡한
114 □ **in time** 제 시간에, 때맞춰
115 □ **express** ⓥ 표현하다[나타내다]
116 □ **concern** ⓝ 우려, 관심사 ⓥ 걱정하다, 관여하다
117 □ **discuss** ⓥ 상의[논의]하다, 토론하다
118 □ **terrible** ⓐ 끔찍한
119 □ **postpone** ⓥ 미루다, 연기하다
120 □ **immediately** [ad] 즉시
121 □ **deadline** ⓝ 최종 기한, 마감

16~17

122 □ **formula** ⓝ 공식
123 □ **mathematician** ⓝ 수학자
124 □ **multiply** ⓥ 곱하다
125 □ **frequency** ⓝ 주파수
126 □ **note** ⓝ ((음악)) 음(표)
127 □ **apply** ⓥ 적용하다
128 □ **harmonize** ⓥ 조화를 이루다, 어울리다
129 □ **ratio** ⓝ 비율, 비(比)
130 □ **masterpiece** ⓝ 걸작, 일품
131 □ **proportion** ⓝ 부분, 비율
132 □ **proportionality** ⓝ 비례, 균형
133 □ **subject** ⓝ (그림·사진 등의) 대상[소재], 주제, 과목
134 □ **balance** ⓥ 균형을 유지하다
135 □ **pleasing** ⓐ 즐거운, 만족스러운
136 □ **position** ⓥ (특정한 위치에) 두다[배치하다]
137 □ **calculate** ⓥ 계산하다, 추정하다
138 □ **adjust** ⓥ 조정[조절]하다, 적응하다
139 □ **impression** ⓝ (사람·사물로부터 받는) 인상[느낌], 감명
140 □ **harmonious** ⓐ 조화를 이루는
141 □ **incorporate A into B** A를 B에 통합시키다
142 □ **analysis** ⓝ 분석

33회 ● 2021학년도 대학수학능력시험 고3 영어 듣기

※ QR코드를 스캔하시면 듣기 방송을 청취하실 수 있습니다.

● 점수 표시가 없는 문항은 모두 2점 ● 문항수 17개 | 배점 37점 | 제한 시간 25분

1번부터 17번까지는 듣고 답하는 문제입니다. 1번부터 15번까지는 한 번만 들려주고, 16번부터 17번까지는 두 번 들려줍니다. 방송을 잘 듣고 답을 하시기 바랍니다.

1. 다음을 듣고, 남자가 하는 말의 목적으로 가장 적절한 것을 고르시오.

① 헬스클럽 할인 행사를 안내하려고
② 동영상 업로드 방법을 설명하려고
③ 스포츠 중계방송 중단을 예고하려고
④ 체육관 보수 공사 일정 변경을 공지하려고
⑤ 운동 방법에 관한 동영상 채널을 홍보하려고

2. 대화를 듣고, 여자의 의견으로 가장 적절한 것을 고르시오.

① 별 관찰은 아이들이 수학 개념에 친숙해지도록 도와준다.
② 아이들은 별 관찰을 통해 예술적 영감을 얻는다.
③ 야외 활동이 아이들의 신체 발달에 필수적이다.
④ 아이들은 자연을 경험함으로써 인격적으로 성장한다.
⑤ 수학 문제 풀이는 아이들의 논리적 사고력을 증진시킨다.

3. 대화를 듣고, 두 사람의 관계를 가장 잘 나타낸 것을 고르시오.

① 학생 – 건축가 ② 신문 기자 – 화가
③ 탐험가 – 환경 운동가 ④ 건물 관리인 – 정원사
⑤ 교사 – 여행사 직원

4. 대화를 듣고, 그림에서 대화의 내용과 일치하지 않는 것을 고르시오.

5. 대화를 듣고, 남자가 여자를 위해 할 일로 가장 적절한 것을 고르시오.

① 사진 전송하기 ② 그림 그리기
③ 휴대 전화 찾기 ④ 생물 보고서 제출하기
⑤ 야생화 개화 시기 검색하기

6. 대화를 듣고, 여자가 지불할 금액을 고르시오.

① $180 ② $190 ③ $200 ④ $210 ⑤ $230

7. 대화를 듣고, 남자가 텐트를 반품하려는 이유를 고르시오.

① 크기가 작아서
② 캠핑이 취소되어서
③ 운반하기 무거워서
④ 설치 방법이 어려워서
⑤ 더 저렴한 제품을 찾아서

8. 대화를 듣고, Bradford Museum of Failure에 관해 언급되지 않은 것을 고르시오.

① 전시품 ② 설립 목적 ③ 개관 연도
④ 입장료 ⑤ 위치

9. National Baking Competition에 관한 다음 내용을 듣고, 일치하지 않는 것을 고르시오.

① 해마다 열리는 행사이다.
② 올해의 주제는 건강한 디저트이다.
③ 20명이 결선에 진출할 것이다.
④ 수상자들의 조리법이 잡지에 실릴 것이다.
⑤ 웹 사이트에서 생중계될 것이다.

10. 다음 표를 보면서 대화를 듣고, 여자가 주문할 재사용 빨대 세트를 고르시오.

Reusable Straw Sets (3 pieces)

	Set	Material	Price	Length (inches)	Carrying Case
①	A	Bamboo	$5.99	7	×
②	B	Glass	$6.99	7	○
③	C	Glass	$7.99	8	×
④	D	Silicone	$8.99	8	○
⑤	E	Stainless Steel	$11.99	9	○

11. 대화를 듣고, 남자의 마지막 말에 대한 여자의 응답으로 가장 적절한 것을 고르시오.

① I don't feel like going out today.
② You must get to the airport quickly.
③ How about going to the cafe over there?
④ I didn't know you wanted to go sightseeing.
⑤ Why didn't you wear more comfortable shoes?

12. 대화를 듣고, 여자의 마지막 말에 대한 남자의 응답으로 가장 적절한 것을 고르시오.

① I see. Then I'll park somewhere else.
② It's all right. I'll bring your car over here.
③ No thanks. I don't want my car to be painted.
④ Never mind. I'll pay the parking fee later.
⑤ Okay. I'll choose another car instead.

13. 대화를 듣고, 남자의 마지막 말에 대한 여자의 응답으로 가장 적절한 것을 고르시오. [3점]

Woman: ______________________________

① Sorry. I don't think I can wait until tomorrow for this one.
② I agree. The displayed one may be the best option for me.
③ Oh, no. It's too bad you don't sell the displayed model.
④ Good. Call me when my washing machine is repaired.
⑤ Exactly. I'm glad that you bought the displayed one.

14. 대화를 듣고, 여자의 마지막 말에 대한 남자의 응답으로 가장 적절한 것을 고르시오. [3점]

Man: ______________________________

① Don't worry. I already found his briefcase.
② Of course. You deserve to receive the award.
③ Don't mention it. I just did my duty as a citizen.
④ Definitely. I want to go to congratulate him myself.
⑤ Wonderful. It was the best ceremony I've ever been to.

15. 다음 상황 설명을 듣고, Ben이 Stacy에게 할 말로 가장 적절한 것을 고르시오. [3점]

Ben: ______________________________

① Feel free to take the tomatoes from my backyard.
② Tell me if you need help when planting tomatoes.
③ Do you want the ripe tomatoes I picked yesterday?
④ Why don't we grow tomatoes in some other places?
⑤ Let me take care of your tomatoes while you're away.

[16~17] 다음을 듣고, 물음에 답하시오.

16. 남자가 하는 말의 주제로 가장 적절한 것은?

① color change in nature throughout seasons
② various colors used in traditional English customs
③ differences in color perceptions according to culture
④ why expressions related to colors are common in English
⑤ how color-related English expressions gained their meanings

17. 언급된 색깔이 <u>아닌</u> 것은?

① blue ② white ③ green
④ red ⑤ yellow

[해설편 p.146]

Dictation 33

✪ 표기에는 듣기 어려운 발음이 포함되어 있습니다. 귀 기울여 듣고 받아쓰세요. ● 고3 2021학년도 수능

※ QR 코드를 스캔하시면 듣기 방송이 나옵니다. 듣기 방송을 들으며 다음 빈칸을 채우시오. ● 제한 시간 : 25분

01

다음을 듣고, 남자가 하는 말의 목적으로 가장 적절한 것을 고르시오.

M : Hello, viewers. Thank you for clicking on this video. I'm Ronnie Drain, and I've been _________ _________ _________ _________ for over 15 years. Today, I'd like to tell you about my channel, *Build Your Body*. On my channel, you can watch videos showing you ✪ _________ _________ _________ _________ _________ _________ _________ that you can do at home or at your office. If _________ _________ _________ _________ _________, my videos can provide easy guidelines and useful resources on exercise routines. New videos will be uploaded every Friday. Visit my channel and build a stronger, healthier body.

02

대화를 듣고, 여자의 의견으로 가장 적절한 것을 고르시오.

W : Good morning, Chris.

M : Good morning, Julie. How was your weekend?

W : It was wonderful. I went to an event called Stargazing Night with my 7-year-old son.

M : Oh, so you went outdoors to _________ _________ _________ _________. Your son must have had a great time.

W : Yes. And I think it helped my son become familiar with mathematical concepts.

M : Interesting! How does it do that?

W : _________ _________ _________ _________ _________, my son had a chance to practice counting to high numbers.

M : Ah, that makes sense.

W : Also, he enjoyed ✪ _________ _________ _________ _________ _________ that stars form together.

M : Sounds like you had a magical and mathematical night!

W : Absolutely. I think looking at stars is a good way for kids to get used to mathematical concepts.

M : Maybe I should take my daughter to the event next time.

03

대화를 듣고, 두 사람의 관계를 가장 잘 나타낸 것을 고르시오.

M : Hello, Ms. Watson. Thank you for accepting my interview request.

W : My pleasure. You must be Michael from Windmore High School.

M : Yes. I'm honored to interview the person who _________ _________ _________ _________ _________.

W : Thank you. I'm very proud of that design.

M : What was the concept behind it?

W : When planning the design of the school building, I wanted to ✪ _________ _________ _________ _________ _________ _________.

M : I see. Did you apply this concept in any other building designs?

W : Yes. Skyforest Tower. My design included mini gardens for each floor and a roof-top garden, making the building look like a rising forest.

M : That's impressive. Actually, my art teacher is taking us on a field trip there next week.

W : Really? Make sure to _________ _________ _________ _________ on the 32nd floor. The view is spectacular.

M : Thanks. I'll check it out with my classmates.

04

대화를 듣고, 그림에서 대화의 내용과 일치하지 않는 것을 고르시오.

W : Wow, Sam. You turned the student council room into a hot chocolate booth.

M : Yes, Ms. Thompson. We're ready to sell hot chocolate to _________ _________ _________ _________ _________ _________.

W : Excellent. What are you going to put on the bulletin board under the clock?

M : I'll post information letting people know where the profits will go.

W : Good. I like the banner on the wall.

M : Thanks. I designed it myself.

W : Awesome. Oh, I'm glad you put ✪ _________ _________ _________ on the table.

M : Thanks for letting us use it. Did you notice the snowman drawing that's hanging on the tree?

W : Yeah. I remember it was _________ _________ _________ _________ _________ _________ last year. By the way, there are three boxes on the floor. What are they for?

M : We're going to fill those up with donations of toys and books.

W : Sounds great. Good luck.

05

대화를 듣고, 남자가 여자를 위해 할 일로 가장 적절한 것을 고르시오.

M : Hi, Mary. You look worried. What's the matter?

W : Hi, Steve. Remember the report about wildflowers I've been working on?

M : Of course. That's for your biology class, right?

W : Yeah. I was able to get pictures of all the wildflowers in my report ✪ _________ _________ _________.

M : I see. Can't you submit your report without pictures of daisies?

W : No. I really need them. I even tried to take pictures of daisies myself, but I found out that _________ _________ _________ _________ _________ _________ _________.

M : You know what? This spring, I went hiking with my dad and took some pictures of wildflowers.

W : Do you have them on your phone? Can I see them?

M : Sure. Have a look.

W : Oh, the flowers in the pictures are daisies! These will be great for my report.

M : Really? Then I'll _________ _________ _________ _________.

W : Thanks. That would be very helpful.

33회

06

대화를 듣고, 여자가 지불할 금액을 고르시오.

M : Welcome to the Chestfield Hotel. How may I help you?

W : Hi, I'm Alice Milford. I made a reservation for me and my husband.

M : *[Typing sound]* Here it is. You reserved one room for one night at the regular rate of $100.

W : Can I use this 10% discount coupon?

M : Sure, you can.

W : Fantastic. And is it possible to stay one more night?

M : Let me check. *[Mouse clicking sound]* Yes, the same room is available for tomorrow.

W : Good. Do I _________ _________ _________ _________ _________ _________ _________, too?

M : Sorry. The coupon ✪ _________ _________ _________ _________ _________ _________. It'll be $100. Do you still want to stay an extra night?

W : Yes, I do.

M : Great. _________ _________ _________ _________ _________ _________ _________? It's $10 per person for each day.

W : No thanks. We'll be going out early to go shopping. Here's my credit card.

07

대화를 듣고, 남자가 텐트를 반품하려는 이유를 고르시오.

W : Honey, I'm home.

M : How was your day?

W : Alright. Hey, did you order something? There's a large box outside the door.

M : It's the tent we bought online for our camping trip. I'm returning it.

W : _________ _________ _________ _________ _________ _________? I remember you said it might be a little small to fit all of us.

M : Actually, when I set up the tent, it seemed big enough to hold us all.

W : Then, did you find a cheaper one on another website?

M : No, price is not the issue.

W : Then, why are you returning the tent?

M : It's ✪ _________ _________ _________ _________ _________. We usually have to walk a bit to get to the campsite.

W : I see. Is someone coming to pick up the box?

M : Yes. I already _________ _________ _________.

08

대화를 듣고, Bradford Museum of Failure에 관해 언급되지 <u>않은</u> 것을 고르시오.

M : Hey, Kelly. Have you been to the Bradford Museum of Failure?

W : I've never even heard of it.

M : Well, I went there yesterday and it was amazing.

W : What does the museum exhibit?

M : It exhibits ✪ _________ _________ _________ from the world's best-known companies.

W : Interesting. That makes me curious about the purpose of founding the museum.

M : It was founded to deliver the message that we need to _________ _________ _________ _________ _________ _________.

W : That's quite a message, and it makes a lot of sense. Did it just open?

M : No, it opened in 2001.

W : How come I've never heard of it?

M : I guess many people don't know about it. But visiting the museum was _________ _________ _________.

W : Where is it?

M : It's located in Greenfalls, Hillside.

W : That's not too far from here. I'll be sure to visit it.

09

National Baking Competition에 관한 다음 내용을 듣고, 일치하지 <u>않는</u> 것을 고르시오.

W : Hello, listeners. I'm Carla Jones from the National Baking Association. I'm glad to announce that we're hosting the National Baking Competition on December 20th. It's an annual event _________ _________ _________ _________ _________ a talent and passion for baking. This year, the theme of the competition is "healthy desserts." We had the most applicants in the history of this competition, and ✪ _________ _________ _________ _________ _________ to the final round. The top three will win the grand prize of $10,000 each, and the recipes of the winners will appear in our magazine. You can enjoy watching the entire competition from home. It'll be broadcast live on our website starting from 9 a.m. If you're a food lover, you _________ _________ _________ _________ _________ this event.

10

다음 표를 보면서 대화를 듣고, 여자가 주문할 재사용 빨대 세트를 고르시오.

M : Hi, Nicole. What are you doing?

W : Hi, Jack. I'm trying to ✪ _________ _________ _________ _________ _________ on the Internet. Do you want to see?

M : Sure. *[Pause]* These bamboo ones seem good. They're made from natural materials.

W : That's true, but I'm worried they may not dry quickly.

M : Okay. Then let's look at straws made from other materials. _________ _________ _________ _________ _________ _________ _________ on a set of straws?

W : I don't want to spend more than $10.

M : That's reasonable. How about length?

W : _________ _________ _________ _________ _________, eight or nine inches should be perfect.

M : Then you're down to these two. A carrying case would be very useful when going out.

W : Good point. I'll take your recommendation and order this set now.

11

대화를 듣고, 남자의 마지막 말에 대한 여자의 응답으로 가장 적절한 것을 고르시오.

M : Lisa, are you okay from all the walking we did today?

W : Actually, Dad, my feet are __________ __________ __________ __________ __________. Also, I'm thirsty because the weather is so hot out here.

M : Oh, then let's go somewhere inside and ✪ __________ __________ __________ __________. Where should we go?

12

대화를 듣고, 여자의 마지막 말에 대한 남자의 응답으로 가장 적절한 것을 고르시오.

W : Excuse me, sir. I'm from the management office. You cannot park here because we're __________ __________ __________ __________ this section of the parking lot.

M : Why? What's going on here?

W : We're going to ✪ __________ __________ __________ __________ __________ __________. If there are cars parked here, we cannot start our work.

13

대화를 듣고, 남자의 마지막 말에 대한 여자의 응답으로 가장 적절한 것을 고르시오. [3점]

W : Hi. Can I get some help over here?

M : Sure. What can I help you with?

W : I'm thinking of buying this washing machine.

M : Good choice. It's our best-selling model.

W : I really like its design and it has a lot of useful features. I'll take it.

M : Great. However, you'll have to wait for two weeks. We're __________ __________ __________ __________ right now.

W : Oh, no. I need it today. My washing machine broke down yesterday.

M : Then how about __________ __________ __________ __________ __________?

W : Oh, I didn't know I could ✪ __________ __________ __________ __________.

M : Sure, you can. We can deliver and install it today.

W : That's just what I need, but it's not a new one.

M : Not to worry. It's never been used. Also, like with the new ones, you can __________ __________ __________ __________ __________ for up to three years.

W : That's good.

M : We can also give you a 20% discount on it. It's a pretty good deal.

14

대화를 듣고, 여자의 마지막 말에 대한 남자의 응답으로 가장 적절한 것을 고르시오. [3점]

[Cell phone rings.]

M : Hello, Joe Burrow speaking.

W : Hello. This is Officer Blake from the Roselyn Police Station.

M : Oh, it's good to speak to you again.

W : Nice to speak to you, too. Do you remember the boy __________ __________ __________ __________ and brought it here?

M : Sure. I wanted to give him a reward. But he wouldn't accept it.

W : I remember you saying that before.

M : Yeah. I'd still like to ✪ __________ __________ __________ __________ __________ __________.

W : Good. That's why I'm calling you. Are you available next Friday at 10 a.m.?

M : Yes. I'm free at that time. Why?

W : The boy will receive the Junior Citizen Award for what he's done for you.

M : That's great news!

W : There'll be a ceremony for him at the police station, and he __________ __________ __________ __________ __________. I was wondering if you can make it.

15

다음 상황 설명을 듣고, Ben이 Stacy에게 할 말로 가장 적절한 것을 고르시오. [3점]

W : Ben and Stacy are neighbors. Ben ✪ __________ __________ __________ __________ in his backyard for several years. Ben shares his tomatoes with Stacy every year because she loves his fresh tomatoes. Today, Ben notices that his tomatoes will be __________ __________ __________ __________ in about a week. However, he leaves for a month-long business trip tomorrow. He's worried that there'll be __________ __________ __________ __________ in his backyard by the time he comes back. He'd like Stacy to have them while they are fresh and ripe. So, Ben wants to tell Stacy that she can come and get the tomatoes from his backyard whenever she wants. In this situation, what would Ben most likely say to Stacy?

16~17

다음을 듣고, 물음에 답하시오.

M : Hello, students. Last time, I gave you a list of English expressions containing color terms. Today, we'll learn how these expressions got their meanings. The first expression is "__________ __________ __________ __________," meaning something happens unexpectedly. It came from the phrase "a lightning bolt out of the blue," which expresses the idea that it's __________ __________ __________ __________ when there's a clear blue sky. The next expression, "white lie," means a harmless lie to protect someone from a harsh truth. This is because the color white ✪ __________ __________ __________. Another expression, "green thumb," refers to __________ __________ __________ __________ __________ __________. Planting pots were often covered with tiny green plants, so those who worked in gardens had green-stained hands. The last expression, "to see red," means to suddenly get very angry. Its origin possibly comes from the belief that bulls get angry and attack when a bullfighter waves a red cape. I hope this lesson helps you remember these phrases better.

▶ 정답 : 해설편 148쪽

회차별 영단어 QR 코드 ※ QR 코드를 스캔 후 모바일로 단어장처럼 학습할 수 있습니다.

01

001 □ personal fitness trainer 개인 헬스 트레이너
002 □ build a body 신체를 단련하다, 몸을 만들다
003 □ a variety of 다양한
004 □ exercise ⓝ 운동
005 □ regularly ad 규칙적으로
006 □ resource ⓝ 자원, 재료
007 □ routine ⓝ (늘 하도록 정해진) 루틴, 습관

02

008 □ stargazing ⓝ 별 보기, 천문학
009 □ familiar with ~에 친숙한
010 □ mathematical ⓐ 수학적인
011 □ concept ⓝ 개념
012 □ trace ⓥ (추적하여) 찾아내다, 밝혀내다
013 □ magical ⓐ 황홀한, 아주 멋진
014 □ get used to ~에 익숙해지다

03

015 □ request ⓝ 요구, 요청
016 □ attend ⓥ 참석하다, (~에) 다니다
017 □ proud of ~을 자랑으로 여기는
018 □ incorporate A into B A를 B에 포함시키다, 통합하다
019 □ element ⓝ 요소, 성분
020 □ rise ⓥ 오르다, 올라가다[오다]
021 □ impressive ⓐ 인상적인
022 □ observation deck 전망대
023 □ spectacular ⓐ 장관인, (경치가) 멋진

04

024 □ student council 학생회
025 □ raise money 모금하다
026 □ in need 불우한, 도움이 필요한
027 □ bulletin board 게시판
028 □ profit ⓝ 수익
029 □ banner ⓝ 플래카드, 현수막
030 □ tablecloth ⓝ 식탁보, 테이블보
031 □ fill up 채우다

05

032 □ wildflower ⓝ 야생화
033 □ work on ~을 작업하다
034 □ biology ⓝ 생물학
035 □ except prep ~을 제외하고, ~ 외에
036 □ bloom ⓥ (꽃이) 피다, 개화하다

06

037 □ make a reservation 예약하다
038 □ regular ⓐ 일반적인, 보통의, 평상시의
039 □ available ⓐ 구할[이용할] 수 있는, 시간[여유]이 있는
040 □ apply to ~에 적용되다
041 □ extra ⓐ 추가의

07

042 □ fit ⓥ ~에 맞다, 적합하다
043 □ set up 설치하다
044 □ issue ⓝ (걱정거리가 되는) 문제, 주제, 안건
045 □ a bit 조금, 다소, 약간
046 □ schedule ⓥ 일정[시간 계획]을 잡다, 예정하다

08

047 □ amazing ⓐ 멋진, 놀라운
048 □ exhibit ⓥ 전시하다
049 □ purpose ⓝ 목적, 용도
050 □ found ⓥ 설립하다
051 □ admit ⓥ 인정하다
052 □ quite ad 꽤, 상당히
053 □ guess ⓥ 추측[짐작]하다
054 □ eye-opening ⓐ 경이로운, 놀랄 만한

09

055 □ association ⓝ 협회, 조합
056 □ announce ⓥ 발표하다, 알리다
057 □ aim ⓥ 목표로 하다
058 □ discover ⓥ 발견하다, 찾다
059 □ talent ⓝ 재능, 재주
060 □ passion ⓝ 열정
061 □ competition ⓝ 대회, 시합, 경쟁
062 □ applicant ⓝ 지원자
063 □ participant ⓝ 참가자
064 □ advance ⓥ 진출하다, 나아가다
065 □ appear ⓥ 언급되다, (글 속에) 나오다
066 □ entire ⓐ 전체의
067 □ broadcast ⓥ 방송[방영]하다

10

068 □ reusable ⓐ 재사용 가능한
069 □ straw ⓝ 빨대
070 □ bamboo ⓝ 대나무
071 □ be made from ~로 만들어지다
072 □ material ⓝ (물건의) 재료
073 □ be willing to ~할 의향이 있다
074 □ reasonable ⓐ 적정한, 너무 비싸지 않은
075 □ length ⓝ 길이
076 □ recommendation ⓝ 추천

11

077 □ be tired from ~로 피곤하다
078 □ sightseeing ⓝ 관광
079 □ feel like ~ing ~하고 싶지 않다
080 □ comfortable ⓐ 편한, 편안한

12

081 □ management office 관리사무소
082 □ park ⓥ 주차하다
083 □ close off 폐쇄하다
084 □ parking lot 주차장

13

085 □ washing machine 세탁기
086 □ feature ⓝ 기능, 특징
087 □ break down 고장 나다
088 □ on display 진열 중인, 전시 중인
089 □ install ⓥ 설치하다
090 □ repair ⓥ 수리하다
091 □ up to ~까지
092 □ pretty ad 꽤, 아주
093 □ deal ⓝ 거래, 합의

14

094 □ briefcase ⓝ 서류 가방
095 □ reward ⓝ 보상, 사례
096 □ accept ⓥ 받아들이다, 수락하다
097 □ somehow ad 어떻게든, 왠지
098 □ in person 직접
099 □ make it 참석하다, 해내다
100 □ deserve ⓥ ~할 가치[자격]가 있다

15

101 □ pick in (빨래 등을) 거두어들이다
102 □ ripe ⓐ 다 익은
103 □ Feel free to ~. 마음껏 ~하세요, 편하게 ~하세요.
104 □ take care of ~을 돌보다, 처리하다

16~17

105 □ expression ⓝ 표현, 표출
106 □ meaning ⓝ 뜻, 의미
107 □ out of the blue 난데없이, 갑자기
108 □ unexpectedly ad 예기치 않게
109 □ lightning ⓝ 번개
110 □ unlikely ⓐ ~할[일] 것 같지 않은
111 □ white lie 선의의 거짓말
112 □ harmless ⓐ 무해한
113 □ protect ⓥ 보호하다, 지키다
114 □ harsh ⓐ 가혹한
115 □ traditionally ad 전통적으로
116 □ symbolize ⓥ 상징하다
117 □ innocence ⓝ 결백
118 □ green thumb 원예의 재능
119 □ cultivate ⓥ 재배하다, 기르다
120 □ tiny ⓐ 아주 작은
121 □ stained ⓐ 얼룩진
122 □ see red 붉으락푸르락하다, 화를 벌컥 내다
123 □ bull ⓝ 황소
124 □ bullfighter ⓝ 투우사
125 □ cape ⓝ 망토

34회 ● 2020학년도 대학수학능력시험 고3 영어 듣기

※ QR코드를 스캔하시면 듣기 방송을 청취하실 수 있습니다.

● 점수 표시가 없는 문항은 모두 2점 ● 문항수 17개 | 배점 37점 | 제한 시간 25분

1번부터 17번까지는 듣고 답하는 문제입니다. 1번부터 15번까지는 한 번만 들려주고, 16번부터 17번까지는 두 번 들려줍니다. 방송을 잘 듣고 답을 하시기 바랍니다.

1. 다음을 듣고, 남자가 하는 말의 목적으로 가장 적절한 것을 고르시오.

① 백화점 주말 특별 행사를 안내하려고
② 백화점 층별 신규 매장을 소개하려고
③ 주차장 이용 요금 변경을 공지하려고
④ 고객 만족도 조사 참여를 요청하려고
⑤ 백화점 회원 가입 방법을 설명하려고

2. 대화를 듣고, 여자의 의견으로 가장 적절한 것을 고르시오.

① 왼쪽 신체의 잦은 사용은 두뇌 활동을 촉진한다.
② 수면 시간과 심장 기능은 밀접한 관련이 있다.
③ 왼쪽으로 누워 자는 것은 건강에 도움이 된다.
④ 규칙적인 운동은 소화 불량 개선에 필수적이다.
⑤ 숙면은 정신 건강을 유지하는 데 중요한 요인이다.

3. 대화를 듣고, 두 사람의 관계를 가장 잘 나타낸 것을 고르시오.

① 곤충학자 – 학생
② 동물 조련사 – 사진작가
③ 농부 – 잡지기자
④ 요리사 – 음식 평론가
⑤ 독자 – 소설가

4. 대화를 듣고, 그림에서 대화의 내용과 일치하지 않는 것을 고르시오.

5. 대화를 듣고, 여자가 할 일로 가장 적절한 것을 고르시오.

① 간식 가져오기
② 책 기부하기
③ 점심 준비하기
④ 설거지하기
⑤ 세탁실 청소하기

6. 대화를 듣고, 여자가 지불할 금액을 고르시오. [3점]

① $72 ② $74 ③ $76 ④ $78 ⑤ $80

7. 대화를 듣고, 남자가 요리 대회 참가를 포기한 이유를 고르시오.

① 다친 팔이 낫지 않아서
② 조리법을 완성하지 못해서
③ 다른 대회와 일정이 겹쳐서
④ 입학시험 공부를 해야 해서
⑤ 대회 전에 유학을 떠나야 해서

8. 대화를 듣고, Ten Year Class Reunion Party에 관해 언급되지 않은 것을 고르시오.

① 장소
② 날짜
③ 회비
④ 음식
⑤ 기념품

9. *Green Ocean* 영화 시사회에 관한 다음 내용을 듣고, 일치하지 않는 것을 고르시오.

① 100명을 초대할 예정이다.
② 다음 주 토요일 오후 4시에 시작할 것이다.
③ 영화 출연 배우와 사진을 찍을 수 있다.
④ 입장권을 우편으로 보낼 예정이다.
⑤ 초대받은 사람은 극장에서 포스터를 받을 것이다.

10. 다음 표를 보면서 대화를 듣고, 두 사람이 예약할 항공편을 고르시오.

Flight Schedule to New York City Area

	Flight	Ticket Price	Departure Time	Arrival Airport	Stops
①	A	$600	6:00 a.m.	JFK	1 stop
②	B	$625	10:00 a.m.	Newark	Nonstop
③	C	$700	11:30 a.m.	JFK	1 stop
④	D	$785	2:30 p.m.	JFK	Nonstop
⑤	E	$810	6:30 p.m.	Newark	1 stop

11. 대화를 듣고, 남자의 마지막 말에 대한 여자의 응답으로 가장 적절한 것을 고르시오.

① Okay. I'll send the address to your phone.
② Yes. I'll have your dress cleaned by noon.
③ Of course. I'll open the shop tomorrow.
④ No. I'm not moving to a new place.
⑤ Too late. I'm already back at home.

12. 대화를 듣고, 여자의 마지막 말에 대한 남자의 응답으로 가장 적절한 것을 고르시오.

① Unbelievable. I'm really going to be on stage today.
② Absolutely. I'm so eager to see him sing in person.
③ Not really. He wasn't as amazing as I expected.
④ Sure. I'll find someone else to perform instead.
⑤ Oh, no. You shouldn't have missed his performance.

13. 대화를 듣고, 여자의 마지막 말에 대한 남자의 응답으로 가장 적절한 것을 고르시오.

Man: ______________________________

① It's worthwhile to spend money on my suit.
② It would be awesome to borrow your brother's.
③ Your brother will have a fun time at the festival.
④ I'm looking forward to seeing you in a new suit.
⑤ You're going to build a great reputation as an MC.

14. 대화를 듣고, 남자의 마지막 말에 대한 여자의 응답으로 가장 적절한 것을 고르시오. [3점]

Woman: ______________________________

① Definitely! This book isn't as interesting as yours.
② Terrific! I'll check right away if there are any nearby.
③ Never mind. I won't take that course next semester.
④ Really? I didn't know you have a degree in philosophy.
⑤ Why not? You can join my philosophy discussion group.

15. 다음 상황 설명을 듣고, Brian의 어머니가 Brian에게 할 말로 가장 적절한 것을 고르시오. [3점]

Brian's mother: ______________________________

① Make sure to call me whenever you go somewhere new.
② School trips are good opportunities to make friends.
③ I believe traveling broadens your perspective.
④ How about carrying the luggage on your own?
⑤ Why don't you pack your bag by yourself for the trip?

[16～17] 다음을 듣고, 물음에 답하시오.

16. 남자가 하는 말의 주제로 가장 적절한 것은?

① animals used in delivering mail in history
② difficulty of training animals from the wild
③ animals' adaptation to environmental changes
④ endangered animals in different countries
⑤ ways animals sent each other messages

17. 언급된 동물이 아닌 것은?

① horses ② pigeons ③ eagles
④ dogs ⑤ camels

[해설편 p.151]

※ QR 코드를 스캔하시면 듣기 방송이 나옵니다. 듣기 방송을 들으며 다음 빈칸을 채우시오. ● 제한 시간 : 25분

01
다음을 듣고, 남자가 하는 말의 목적으로 가장 적절한 것을 고르시오.

M : Shoppers, may I have your attention please? Thank you for visiting Miracle Department Store. We'd like to __________ __________ __________ __________ __________ __________ going on through this weekend. First, we're offering a 50 percent discount on certain electronics and sporting goods on the seventh floor. Second, we're __________ __________ __________ __________ at our coffee shop on the first floor to shoppers who spend over $50. Third, we're also ✪ __________ __________ __________ __________ __________ to all shoppers who spend over $100. Last but not least, you don't have to worry about parking fees this weekend. Parking is free. We hope you enjoy this weekend's special events at our department store.

02
대화를 듣고, 여자의 의견으로 가장 적절한 것을 고르시오.

W : Hi, Sam. How are you?
M : Fine. How about you, Christine?
W : I feel really good.
M : Wow! What happened to you? You usually say you're tired.
W : Well, I changed how I sleep. I started __________ __________ __________ __________ __________, and it has improved my health.
M : Really?
W : Yeah. I've done it for a week, and my digestion has got better.
M : I didn't know how we sleep __________ __________ __________ __________ __________.
W : It does. Sleeping on your left side helps ✪ __________ __________ __________ because your stomach is on the left.
M : I can see that. But does improving digestion make you that much healthier?
W : Sleeping on the left side does more than that. I think it's good for health because it also __________ __________ __________ to the heart.
M : That makes sense. I guess I should try it.

03
대화를 듣고, 두 사람의 관계를 가장 잘 나타낸 것을 고르시오.

M : Hello, I'm Ted Benson. You must be Ms. Brown.
W : Hi, Mr. Benson. Thank you for sparing time for this interview. I've wanted to meet you since you won the "Best Rice Award."
M : I'm honored. I'm __________ __________ __________ __________ __________ __________. The articles are very informative.
W : Thank you. Can you tell me the secret to your success?
M : I grow rice __________ __________ __________ __________ to kill harmful insects. It's organic.
W : How do you do that?
M : I ✪ __________ __________ __________ __________ __________, and they eat the insects.
W : So that's how you grew the best rice in the country. What a great idea!
M : Yeah, that's the know-how I've got from my 30 years of farming life.
W : Well, it's amazing. May I take a picture of you __________ __________ __________ __________ __________ __________ for my magazine article?
M : Go ahead.

04
대화를 듣고, 그림에서 대화의 내용과 일치하지 않는 것을 고르시오.

W : What are you looking at, honey?
M : Aunt Mary sent me a picture. She's already set up a room for Peter.
W : Wow! She's excited for him to stay during the winter vacation, isn't she?
M : Yes, she is. I like the ✪ __________ __________ __________ __________ __________ on the bed.
W : I'm sure it must be very warm. Look at the chair below the window.
M : It looks comfortable. He could sit there and read.
W : Right. I guess that's why Aunt Mary put the bookcase next to it.
M : That makes sense. Oh, there's __________ __________ __________ __________ __________ __________.
W : It looks real. I think it's a gift for Peter.
M : Yeah, I remember she mentioned it. And do you see __________ __________ __________ __________ __________?
W : It's nice. It looks like the one Peter has here at home.
M : It does. Let's show him this picture.

05
대화를 듣고, 여자가 할 일로 가장 적절한 것을 고르시오.

M : Good morning, Jane.
W : Good morning, Mr. Smith.
M : Thanks for volunteering to __________ __________ __________ __________ __________ __________ again.
W : I'm happy to help. And I brought some snacks for the elderly.
M : ✪ __________ __________ __________ __________! Last time you donated some books. Everyone really enjoyed reading them.
W : It was my pleasure. So, what am I supposed to do today? Should I __________ __________ __________ __________ __________ __________?
M : There are some other volunteers today, and they'll do that work.
W : Good. Then what would you like me to do?
M : Well, you could do the dishes or clean the laundry room.
W : I'm good at washing dishes. So I'll do that.
M : Great. We'll __________ __________ __________ __________ __________ __________ __________.

Dictation 34

06

대화를 듣고, 여자가 지불할 금액을 고르시오. [3점]

M : Welcome to the Science and Technology Museum. How can I help you?

W : Hi. I want to buy admission tickets.

M : Okay. They're $20 for adults and $10 for children.

W : Good. Two adult tickets and two child tickets, please. And I'm a member of the National Robot Club. __________ __________ __________ __________ __________?

M : Yes. You get 10 percent off all of those admission tickets with your membership.

W : Excellent.

M : We also have the AI Robot program. You can __________ __________ __________ __________ __________ and take pictures with them.

W : That sounds interesting. How much is it?

M : It's just $5 per person. But ✪ __________ __________ __________ __________ __________ __________ to this program.

W : Okay. I'll take four tickets.

M : So two adult and two child admission tickets, and four AI Robot program tickets, right?

W : Yes. Here are my credit card and membership card.

07

대화를 듣고, 남자가 요리 대회 참가를 포기한 이유를 고르시오.

W : Hi, Michael.

M : Hi, Sarah. Did you apply for the cooking contest?

W : I did. I've already finished developing a recipe.

M : That's great. Actually, I __________ __________ __________ __________ __________.

W : Why? Is your arm still hurt?

M : No, ✪ __________ __________ __________.

W : Is your recipe not ready yet?

M : I already created a unique recipe for the contest.

W : Then, what made you give up the contest?

M : You know __________ __________ __________ __________ __________. The cooking school in Italy just informed me that I've been accepted. The problem is __________ __________ __________ __________ __________ __________ __________ __________.

W : I'm sorry you'll miss the contest. But it's good for you since you've always wanted to study in Italy.

M : I think so, too. I wish you luck in the contest.

W : Thanks. I'll do my best.

08

대화를 듣고, Ten Year Class Reunion Party에 관해 언급되지 않은 것을 고르시오.

W : Hi, Ross. How's everything going for our Ten Year Class Reunion Party?

M : I think we're done, Jennifer.

W : Then let's __________ __________ __________ __________ __________.

M : I already booked the Silver Corral Restaurant for the party.

W : Good. It must have been very difficult to get a reservation because our party is on December 24th.

M : Yeah, we were lucky.

W : What food will they serve?

M : Their steak, spaghetti, and pizza are famous, so __________ __________ __________ __________.

W : Sounds delicious. And the ✪ __________ __________ __________ __________ are ready, too.

M : You ordered mugs for souvenirs, right?

W : Yes, I did. I'll bring them that day.

M : Perfect. It's going to be a great party.

09

***Green Ocean* 영화 시사회에 관한 다음 내용을 듣고, 일치하지 않는 것을 고르시오.**

W : Hello, listeners. Welcome to *Good Day Movie*. We'd like to let you know about a great chance to __________ __________ __________ __________ __________ __________ *Green Ocean* by Feather Pictures. One hundred people will be invited to the event. It'll begin at the Glory Theater at 4 p.m. next Saturday. After watching the movie, you can meet and take pictures with the actors of the movie. If you're interested, apply for admission tickets on the *Green Ocean* homepage, and the tickets will be __________ __________ __________ __________ to the first 100 people who apply. Those who are invited ✪ __________ __________ __________ __________ __________ at the theater. Hurry up and don't miss this chance to watch *Green Ocean* in advance. Now we'll be back after the commercial break. So stay tuned.

10

다음 표를 보면서 대화를 듣고, 두 사람이 예약할 항공편을 고르시오.

M : Ms. Roberts, we're going on a business trip to New York City next week. Why don't we book the flight on this website?

W : Okay, Mr. White. Let's take a look at the flight schedule.

M : Sure. How much can we spend on the flight?

W : __________ __________ __________ __________ __________ __________ to spend more than $800 per ticket.

M : I see. And what about the departure time? I have to take my daughter to daycare early in the morning that day.

W : Then how about choosing a flight after 9 a.m.?

M : That'll be great. __________ __________ __________ __________ __________ __________?

W : JFK is closer to the company we're visiting.

M : Oh, you're right. Let's go there.

W : Then we have two options left, nonstop or one stop.

M : I don't want to ✪ __________ __________ __________ __________ __________ __________ __________.

W : Me, neither. We should choose the nonstop flight.

M : Okay. Let's book the flight now.

11

대화를 듣고, 남자의 마지막 말에 대한 여자의 응답으로 가장 적절한 것을 고르시오.

[Cell phone rings.]

M : Honey, I've just left work. I'll be home in half an hour.

W : Good. Is it possible for you to __________ __________ __________ __________ __________ __________ and pick up my dress?

M : Sure. Can you tell me ✪ __________ __________ __________ __________ __________?

12

대화를 듣고, 여자의 마지막 말에 대한 남자의 응답으로 가장 적절한 것을 고르시오.

W : David, look at this advertisement! Jason Stevens is going to sing at the opening of City Concert Hall next Saturday.

M : Wow! You know I'm __________ __________ __________ __________ __________, Mom. Luckily, I don't have anything scheduled that day.

W : Great. ✪ __________ __________ __________ on your calendar, so you don't miss his performance.

13

대화를 듣고, 여자의 마지막 말에 대한 남자의 응답으로 가장 적절한 것을 고르시오.

W : Hi, Justin. I heard you're going to be the MC at the school festival.

M : Yes, I am, Cindy.

W : Do you have everything ready?

M : Mostly. I __________ __________ __________ __________ __________ and I've practiced a lot.

W : I'm sure you'll do a great job.

M : I hope so, too. But there's one thing I'm worried about.

W : What is it?

M : I need a suit, so I'm thinking of buying one. But it's expensive, and I don't think I'll wear it after the festival.

W : Well, if you want, I can ask my older brother to ✪ __________ __________ __________ __________ __________ __________. He has a lot of them.

M : Could you please?

W : I'd be happy to.

M : Thanks. But will his suit be my size?

W : It will. You and my brother __________ __________ __________ __________ __________ __________.

14

대화를 듣고, 남자의 마지막 말에 대한 여자의 응답으로 가장 적절한 것을 고르시오. [3점]

M : Amy, what are you reading?

W : Dad, it's a book for my philosophy course.

M : Let me take a look. Wow! It's a book by Kant.

W : Yeah. It's very difficult to understand.

M : You're right. His books take a lot of effort to read since __________ __________ __________ __________ __________ __________ __________.

W : I think so, too. Do you have any ideas for me to understand the book better, Dad?

M : Well, why don't you __________ __________ __________ __________ __________? You can find one in our area.

W : Are there discussion groups for philosophy? That sounds interesting.

M : Yeah. You can share ideas with others in the group about the book you're reading.

W : You mean I can understand Kant's book more clearly by discussing it?

M : Absolutely. Plus, you can ✪ __________ __________ __________ __________ in the group as well.

15

다음 상황 설명을 듣고, Brian의 어머니가 Brian에게 할 말로 가장 적절한 것을 고르시오. [3점]

W : Brian is a high school student. He has only traveled with his family before. Until now his mother __________ __________ __________ __________ __________ __________ __________ __________, so he doesn't have any experience preparing it himself. This weekend, Brian is supposed to go on a school trip with his friends. He asks his mother to get his stuff ready for his trip this time, too. However, she believes Brian is ✪ __________ __________ __________ __________ __________ __________ __________, and she thinks this time is a great opportunity for him to learn to be more independent. So, she wants to tell Brian that he should get his things ready and put them in his bag __________ __________ __________. In this situation, what would Brian's mother most likely say to Brian?

16~17

다음을 듣고, 물음에 답하시오.

M : How did people send mail before they had access to cars and trains? There were simple options out there, __________ __________ __________ __________. Horses were frequently utilized in delivery of letters and messages. In the 19th century, a mail express system that used horses serviced a large area of the United States. Pigeons may be seen as a problem by many people today. However, in ancient Greece, they were used to mail people the results of the Olympics between cities. Alaska and Canada are known for their cold winters. In their early days, dogs were utilized to deliver mail because they've ✪ __________ __________ __________ __________ __________ __________ __________. Maybe the most fascinating of all delivery animals is the camel. Australia imported camels from the Middle East and utilized them to transfer mail across vast deserts. They were __________ __________ __________ __________ __________ because they can go without water for quite a while. Fortunately, we've developed faster and more reliable delivery systems, but we should not ignore the important roles these animals played in the past.

▶ 정답 : 해설편 153쪽

VOCA LIST 34

회차별 영단어 QR 코드 ※ QR 코드를 스캔 후 모바일로 단어장처럼 학습할 수 있습니다.

● 고3 2020학년도 수능

01

001 ☐ **inform** ⓥ 알리다
002 ☐ **certain** ⓐ 특정한
003 ☐ **electronics** ⓝ 전자제품
004 ☐ **beverage** ⓝ 음료
005 ☐ **gift certificate** 상품권

02

006 ☐ **improve** ⓥ 향상시키다
007 ☐ **digestion** ⓝ 소화
008 ☐ **have something to do with** ~와 관련이 있다
009 ☐ **stomach** ⓝ 위(소화 기관)
010 ☐ **blood circulation** 혈액 순환
011 ☐ **make sense** 일리가 있다, 의미가 통하다

03

012 ☐ **spare** ⓥ (시간·돈 등을) 할애하다[내다]
013 ☐ **award** ⓝ 상
014 ☐ **reader** ⓝ 구독자
015 ☐ **article** ⓝ 기사, 글
016 ☐ **informative** ⓐ 유익한
017 ☐ **harmful** ⓐ 해로운
018 ☐ **know-how** ⓝ 비결

04

019 ☐ **stay** ⓥ 머무르다
020 ☐ **checkered pattern** 체크무늬
021 ☐ **comfortable** ⓐ 안락한, 편한
022 ☐ **bookcase** ⓝ 책장, 책꽂이
023 ☐ **mention** ⓥ 말하다

05

024 ☐ **volunteer** ⓥ 자원봉사하다
025 ☐ **bring** ⓥ 가져오다
026 ☐ **considerate** ⓐ 사려 깊은
027 ☐ **donate** ⓥ 기부하다
028 ☐ **prepare** ⓥ 준비하다
029 ☐ **do the dishes** 설거지를 하다
030 ☐ **laundry room** 세탁실

06

031 ☐ **discount** ⓝ 할인
032 ☐ **apply to** ~에 적용되다

07

033 ☐ **develop** ⓥ 개발하다
034 ☐ **recipe** ⓝ 조리법
035 ☐ **participate** ⓥ 참가하다
036 ☐ **hurt** ⓥ 아프다
037 ☐ **unique** ⓐ 독특한
038 ☐ **abroad** ad 해외에서

08

039 ☐ **class reunion** 반 동창회
040 ☐ **go over** ~을 검토[점검]하다
041 ☐ **book** ⓥ 예약하다
042 ☐ **reservation** ⓝ 예약
043 ☐ **serve** ⓥ (식당에서 음식을) 제공하다
044 ☐ **souvenir** ⓝ 기념품

09

045 ☐ **preview** ⓝ 시사회
046 ☐ **admission ticket** 입장권
047 ☐ **apply** ⓥ 신청하다
048 ☐ **in advance** 미리, 사전에
049 ☐ **commercial break** 광고 시간

10

050 ☐ **go on a business trip** 출장을 가다
051 ☐ **policy** ⓝ 정책
052 ☐ **allow** ⓥ 허락하다
053 ☐ **departure** ⓝ 출발
054 ☐ **daycare** ⓝ 어린이집
055 ☐ **connecting flight** 연결 항공편

11

056 ☐ **stop by** ~에 잠시 들르다
057 ☐ **pick up** (어디에서) ~을 찾다[찾아오다]

12

058 ☐ **advertisement** ⓝ 광고
059 ☐ **mark** ⓥ 표시하다

13

060 ☐ **introduction** ⓝ 도입
061 ☐ **practice** ⓥ 연습하다
062 ☐ **suit** ⓝ 정장
063 ☐ **lend** ⓥ 빌려주다
064 ☐ **build** ⓝ 체구
065 ☐ **awesome** ⓐ 좋은, 엄청난
066 ☐ **reputation** ⓝ 명성, 평판

14

067 ☐ **philosophy** ⓝ 철학
068 ☐ **include** ⓥ 포함하다
069 ☐ **discussion** ⓝ 토론
070 ☐ **share** ⓥ 공유하다
071 ☐ **discuss** ⓥ 토론하다
072 ☐ **absolutely** ad (강한 동의·허락을 나타내어) 그럼, 물론이지
073 ☐ **critical** ⓐ 비판적인
074 ☐ **as well** 또한
075 ☐ **definitely** ad (강한 긍정을 나타내어) 그렇고 말고, 확실히
076 ☐ **mind** ⓥ 상관하다, 신경을 쓰다

15

077 ☐ **experience** ⓝ 경험
078 ☐ **stuff** ⓝ 물건
079 ☐ **opportunity** ⓝ 기회
080 ☐ **independent** ⓐ 독립적인

16~17

081 ☐ **have access to** ~을 이용할 수 있다
082 ☐ **delivery** ⓝ 배달
083 ☐ **utilize** ⓥ 활용하다
084 ☐ **service** ⓥ (서비스를) 제공하다
085 ☐ **pigeon** ⓝ 비둘기
086 ☐ **adapt** ⓥ 적응하다
087 ☐ **import** ⓥ 수입하다
088 ☐ **transfer** ⓥ 옮기다
089 ☐ **desert** ⓝ 사막
090 ☐ **ideally** ad 이상적으로
091 ☐ **reliable** ⓐ 믿을 만한

35회 ● 2019학년도 대학수학능력시험 고3 영어 듣기

※ QR코드를 스캔하시면 듣기 방송을 청취하실 수 있습니다.

● 점수 표시가 없는 문항은 모두 2점 ● 문항수 17개 | 배점 37점 | 제한 시간 25분

1번부터 17번까지는 듣고 답하는 문제입니다. 1번부터 15번까지는 한 번만 들려주고, 16번부터 17번까지는 두 번 들려줍니다. 방송을 잘 듣고 답을 하시기 바랍니다.

1. 다음을 듣고, 남자가 하는 말의 목적으로 가장 적절한 것을 고르시오.

① 경기 취소를 공지하려고
② 팬클럽 가입을 권유하려고
③ 경기장 개장을 홍보하려고
④ 웹 사이트 점검을 안내하려고
⑤ 시상식 일정 변경을 사과하려고

2. 대화를 듣고, 여자의 의견으로 가장 적절한 것을 고르시오.

① 실패한 실험을 분석하면 실험에 성공할 수 있다.
② 과학 수업에서는 이론과 실습이 병행되어야 한다.
③ 과학자가 되기 위해서는 인문학적 소양도 필요하다.
④ 실험 일지는 실험 보고서 작성에 도움이 된다.
⑤ 실험을 할 때마다 안전 교육을 해야 한다.

3. 대화를 듣고, 두 사람의 관계를 가장 잘 나타낸 것을 고르시오.

① 모델 − 사진작가　② 기증자 − 박물관 직원
③ 영화 관람객 − 티켓 판매원　④ 인테리어 디자이너 − 건축가
⑤ 고객 − 가구점 직원

4. 대화를 듣고, 그림에서 대화의 내용과 일치하지 <u>않는</u> 것을 고르시오.

5. 대화를 듣고, 남자가 여자에게 부탁한 일로 가장 적절한 것을 고르시오.

① 발표 주제 정하기　② 식용 곤충 조사하기
③ 설문 조사 결과 분류하기　④ 사진 촬영하기
⑤ 유인물 배부하기

6. 대화를 듣고, 남자가 지불할 금액을 고르시오. [3점]

① $120　② $140　③ $160　④ $180　⑤ $200

7. 대화를 듣고, 여자가 드론 비행 대회에 참가할 수 <u>없는</u> 이유를 고르시오.

① 부모님이 방문하셔서
② 취업 면접에 가야 해서
③ 졸업식에 참석해야 해서
④ 파트너를 구하지 못해서
⑤ 드론을 갖고 있지 않아서

8. 대화를 듣고, International Fireworks Festival에 관해 언급되지 <u>않은</u> 것을 고르시오.

① 개최 일시　② 개최 장소　③ 참가국
④ 주제　⑤ 교통편

9. 2018 Upcycling Workshop에 관한 다음 내용을 듣고, 일치하지 <u>않는</u> 것을 고르시오.

① 3일간 진행될 것이다.
② 세미나실에서 열릴 것이다.
③ 패션 디자이너가 가르칠 것이다.
④ 모든 재료가 제공된다.
⑤ 참가 연령에 제한이 없다.

[해설편 p.153]

10. 다음 표를 보면서 대화를 듣고, 여자가 구매할 도마를 고르시오.

Cutting Boards at Camilo's Kitchen

	Model	Material	Price	Handle	Size
①	A	plastic	$25	×	medium
②	B	maple	$35	○	small
③	C	maple	$40	×	large
④	D	walnut	$45	○	medium
⑤	E	walnut	$55	○	large

11. 대화를 듣고, 남자의 마지막 말에 대한 여자의 응답으로 가장 적절한 것을 고르시오.

① No. You can't study with us.
② Okay. I'll do the report by myself.
③ Sure. I'll call you when I'm done.
④ Yes. I'm pleased to join your team.
⑤ Sorry. You have to finish by tomorrow.

12. 대화를 듣고, 여자의 마지막 말에 대한 남자의 응답으로 가장 적절한 것을 고르시오.

① Be careful. The roads are slippery.
② I agree. The seats are very comfortable.
③ Wonderful. Let's attend the program together.
④ Great. I'll register my son for the program.
⑤ I'm sorry. Your son has to wait longer.

13. 대화를 듣고, 여자의 마지막 말에 대한 남자의 응답으로 가장 적절한 것을 고르시오. [3점]

Man: ______________________________

① Absolutely! You should go and see a doctor.
② No problem. I'll visit you on my business trip.
③ Sure. You can check the directions before driving.
④ Okay. I'll ask my team so I can take the medicine.
⑤ Right. Taking a trip is a great way to relieve stress.

14. 대화를 듣고, 남자의 마지막 말에 대한 여자의 응답으로 가장 적절한 것을 고르시오.

Woman: ______________________________

① I agree. The actors performed well in the musical.
② You're right. Let's wait for the reviews of the musical.
③ Good. Now, we should rewrite the script of the musical.
④ Great. I need a new musical instrument for our performance.
⑤ Thanks. Then, I'll read the novel before I watch the musical.

15. 다음 상황 설명을 듣고, Steve가 Cathy에게 할 말로 가장 적절한 것을 고르시오. [3점]

Steve: ______________________________

① You should highlight your volunteer experience as a translator.
② How about volunteering together for the translation club?
③ Why don't you help me write a self-introduction letter?
④ You need to spend more time practicing translation.
⑤ You'd better become more qualified as a volunteer.

[16~17] 다음을 듣고, 물음에 답하시오.

16. 여자가 하는 말의 주제로 가장 적절한 것은?

① why traditional foods are popular
② misconceptions about organic foods
③ unexpected origins of common foods
④ when foods spread across countries
⑤ importance of eating fresh foods

17. 언급된 음식이 아닌 것은?

① Caesar salad ② bagels ③ kiwis
④ potatoes ⑤ buffalo wings

[해설편 p.155]

※ QR 코드를 스캔하시면 듣기 방송이 나옵니다. 듣기 방송을 들으며 다음 빈칸을 채우시오. ● 제한 시간 : 25분

01
다음을 듣고, 남자가 하는 말의 목적으로 가장 적절한 것을 고르시오.

M : Attention, Whittenberg Dragons and Westbrook Whales fans. This is an announcement about today's game at Estana Stadium. Today's baseball game ✪ ________ ________ ________ ________ ________ ________ ________. But it started raining one hour ago, and has not stopped. According to the forecast, the weather will only get worse. Because of this, we ________ ________ ________ ________ ________ ________. Tickets you purchased for today's event will be fully refunded. And information about the make-up game will be updated on our website soon. Once again, today's game has been canceled ________ ________ ________ ________. Thank you for visiting our stadium, and we hope to see you again at our next game.

02
대화를 듣고, 여자의 의견으로 가장 적절한 것을 고르시오.

W : Andrew, you look unhappy. What's wrong?
M : Hi, Ms. Benson. I've been trying this chemical reaction experiment again and again, but it's not working.
W : Why isn't it working?
M : I don't know. Maybe I don't have much talent for chemistry.
W : ________ ________ ________ ________ ________ ________.
M : So what should I do?
W : I believe that the path to success is ✪ ________ ________ ________.
M : Analyzing failure? What do you mean?
W : By examining what went wrong in your experiment, you can do it right.
M : Hmm. You mean that even though my experiment didn't work, I can learn something from failure?
W : Exactly. If you figure out how and why it didn't work, you can succeed at your experiment.
M : Now I understand. I'll ________ ________ ________. Thanks.

03
대화를 듣고, 두 사람의 관계를 가장 잘 나타낸 것을 고르시오.

[Cell phone rings.]
W : Hello.
M : Hello, Ms. Monroe. This is John Brown. I'm calling to invite you to a special event.
W : Oh, thank you for calling. What's the event?
M : Our museum will ________ ________ ________ ________ ________ ________, including the old pictures and tools you donated, under the theme *Life in the 1800s*.
W : That's wonderful. When is it?
M : It'll be from December 3rd to 7th. And ________ ________ ________ ________ ________ ________ like you.
W : It's my pleasure. I want my donation to help people learn about the past.
M : Thank you. The antique items you donated have really improved our collection.
W : I'm glad to hear that. I'm looking forward to visiting the exhibition.
M : I'll send you the invitation letter soon.
W : Great. I'll be waiting for it.
M : Again, ✪ ________ ________ ________ ________ ________, we appreciate your donation.

04
대화를 듣고, 그림에서 대화의 내용과 일치하지 <u>않는</u> 것을 고르시오.

M : Mom, I think ________ ________ ________ ________ ________ Dad's birthday party.
W : Really? Let's see.
M : *[Pause]* I hung a screen between the trees.
W : That's nice.
M : I think he'll enjoy watching our old family videos there.
W : I'm sure he will. Oh, did you ________ ________ ________ ________ on the table?
M : Yes. I got it from Dad's favorite bakery.
W : He'll love it. What are the two boxes under the chair?
M : They're gifts from Grandma and Grandpa.
W : ________ ________ ________ ________. Hmm. I think ✪ ________ ________ ________ on the grass is too small. We cannot all sit there.
M : You're right. I'll bring more chairs.
W : Good idea. And you put the grill next to the garden lamp.
M : Yeah. As you know, Dad loves barbecue.
W : Right. We're almost ready for the party.

05
대화를 듣고, 남자가 여자에게 부탁한 일로 가장 적절한 것을 고르시오.

W : Jim, are you doing a presentation for the science fair?
M : Yes. I'm really nervous because it's ________ ________ ________ ________ ________ ________.
W : Don't worry. You'll do well. What's the topic?
M : Eating insects as food.
W : Sounds interesting. Why did you choose that?
M : Because it's a possible solution to future food problems.
W : So what are you going to do in your presentation?
M : I'll introduce some insect-based recipes and share my survey results on people's opinions about eating insects.
W : ________ ________ ________ ________ ________. I'll take some pictures for you since it's your first public presentation.
M : Thank you. But my brother Tom is going to take pictures.
W : Okay. Is there anything I can help you with?
M : Sure. Could you help with ✪ ________ ________ ________ ________ ________?
W : Yes, I'll do that.
M : Thank you.

Dictation 35

06

대화를 듣고, 남자가 지불할 금액을 고르시오. [3점]

W : Good afternoon. _________ _________ _________ _________ _________ _________, sir?

M : I'm looking for inline skates for my twins.

W : I see. We have beginner skates and advanced skates. A pair of beginner skates is $60 and a pair of advanced skates is $80.

M : My boys will start learning next week.

W : Then you need the beginner skates.

M : Right. I'll buy two pairs in size 13.

W : Okay. And I think _________ _________ _________ _________ _________ _________.

M : They already have ✪ _________ _________ _________ _________. So, they only need helmets. How much are helmets?

W : They originally cost $20 each. But we _________ _________ this week. So, you will get a 50 percent discount on each helmet.

M : That's nice. I'll buy two helmets.

W : Do you want anything else?

M : No, that's all. Here's my credit card.

07

대화를 듣고, 여자가 드론 비행 대회에 참가할 수 없는 이유를 고르시오.

[Cell phone rings.]

M : Hey, Rebecca. I have good news.

W : Hi, Michael. What is it?

M : I saw _________ _________ _________ _________ _________ _________. Why don't we enter the competition as a team?

W : Great! I recently got a new drone as a graduation present. Is there anything we need to enter the competition?

M : No, _________ _________ _________ _________ our own drones.

W : Good. My new drone flies much faster and longer than the old one. When is the competition?

M : It's next Friday afternoon.

W : Friday? ✪ _________ _________ _________ _________ _________ _________.

M : Oh! I forgot. You said that your parents are visiting.

W : Actually, they came yesterday.

M : Then, why can't you go?

W : I have to go to a job interview.

M : I see. Good luck on the interview. I'll try to find another partner.

08

대화를 듣고, International Fireworks Festival에 관해 언급되지 않은 것을 고르시오.

M : Honey, what are you looking at?

W : I'm looking at the International Fireworks Festival website. You know I love fireworks.

M : Okay, then we should go. When is it?

W : It's on Saturday, November 24th and starts at 8 p.m. It's also _________ _________ _________ _________ _________ _________ _________.

M : Ah! It'll be held at Green Dove Park again?

W : Yes. And the website says four countries are going to participate this year.

M : Great. Which countries?

W : Korea, Spain, China and the U.S. will take part.

M : Our children loved the festival last year. Let's take them again.

W : Of course. But last year, there were _________ _________ _________ _________ _________ near the park.

M : If we don't drive, how should we get there?

W : The festival ✪ _________ _________ _________ _________ _________ from Town Hall Station.

M : Really? Then, let's take the shuttle bus.

09

2018 Upcycling Workshop에 관한 다음 내용을 듣고, 일치하지 않는 것을 고르시오.

W : Attention, please. I'm Jenny Stone, the manager of the community center. I'm going to tell you about the 2018 Upcycling Workshop. ✪ _________ _________ _________ _________. It gives new life to old objects. The workshop will last three days, from November 23rd to 25th. It'll run from 1 to 4 p.m. The workshop will be held in the seminar room. And we _________ _________ _________ _________ this time. The famous fashion designer, Elizabeth Thompson, will teach you in the workshop. You'll learn many upcycling methods from her. For example, you'll remake plastic bags into rugs and old shirts into hats. All materials are provided. And there's _________ _________ _________. The workshop is open to people 18 and older. We're looking forward to seeing you.

10

다음 표를 보면서 대화를 듣고, 여자가 구매할 도마를 고르시오.

M : Welcome to Camilo's Kitchen.

W : Hello. I'm looking for a cutting board.

M : Let me show you our five top-selling models, ✪ _________ _________ _________ _________. Do you have a preference for any material? We have plastic, maple, and walnut cutting boards.

W : I don't want the plastic one because I think ✪ _________ _________ _________ _________.

M : I see. What's your budget range?

W : No more than $50.

M : Okay. Do you prefer one _________ _________ _________ _________ _________?

W : I think a cutting board with a handle is easier to use. So I'll take one with a handle.

M : Then, which size do you want? You have two models left.

W : Hmm. A small-sized cutting board isn't convenient when I cut vegetables. I'll buy the other model.

M : Great. Then this is the cutting board for you.

11

대화를 듣고, 남자의 마지막 말에 대한 여자의 응답으로 가장 적절한 것을 고르시오.

M : Amy, you said you're going to study at Donna's house tonight, right?

W : Yes, Dad. We have to __________ __________ __________ __________ online by midnight.

M : I think you'll be quite late. ✪ __________ __________ __________ __________ __________?

12

대화를 듣고, 여자의 마지막 말에 대한 남자의 응답으로 가장 적절한 것을 고르시오.

W : Thank you for waiting, sir. How can I help you?

M : My son wants to join the road safety program. Are there ✪ __________ __________ __________ __________?

W : It's your lucky day! Somebody just canceled. So your son can have that seat.

13

대화를 듣고, 여자의 마지막 말에 대한 남자의 응답으로 가장 적절한 것을 고르시오. [3점]

W : Honey, what did the doctor say about your neck?

M : She said that it's not too bad. I just need to __________ __________ __________ and get enough rest.

W : I'm relieved that it's not so serious.

M : But there's a problem. The doctor said I __________ __________ __________ __________ __________ __________. It can make me very sleepy.

W : Oh, no. What about your business trip on Monday?

M : Exactly. I'm supposed to drive my team members since I know the area.

W : You cannot drive. It would be very dangerous.

M : Maybe I'll skip the medicine before I drive.

W : ✪ __________ __________ __________ __________ __________ and even make your neck pain worse?

M : Yeah. I do need to take the medicine regularly.

W : Then one solution would be to see if somebody else in your team can drive instead of you.

14

대화를 듣고, 남자의 마지막 말에 대한 여자의 응답으로 가장 적절한 것을 고르시오.

M : Hey, Jessica. You got here early.

W : You too, Mike. What are you reading?

M : I'm reading a magazine article about the musical *Spring Empire*.

W : Oh, *Spring Empire*? I'm going to see it next week. What does the article say?

M : It mentions that ✪ __________ __________ __________ __________ __________ and that the musical is going to be so popular.

W : Wow, I really can't wait to see it.

M : Actually, I've seen it already. Since you haven't watched the musical, __________ __________ __________ __________ __________ __________ __________ first.

W : Why do you say that?

M : The storyline is complicated. In my case, reading the novel first helped me fully understand and __________ __________ __________ __________.

W : Then, I need to get a copy of the book.

M : I have one. I can lend it to you if you want.

15

다음 상황 설명을 듣고, Steve가 Cathy에게 할 말로 가장 적절한 것을 고르시오. [3점]

M : Cathy is starting high school and is looking to join a club. She's interested in translation and ✪ __________ __________ __________ __________ __________ __________. So she's happy when she finds a translation club at her school. To enter the club, she must write a self-introduction letter. However, she's not satisfied with the letter she wrote. She remembers that her older brother Steve __________ __________ __________ __________ __________ __________ __________. Cathy asks him for advice about her self-introduction letter. Steve thinks the letter doesn't focus enough on what she did as a volunteer translator. So Steve wants to suggest to Cathy that __________ __________ __________ __________ __________ related to translation. In this situation, what would Steve most likely say to Cathy?

16~17

다음을 듣고, 물음에 답하시오.

W : Hello, students. Previously, we discussed traditional foods in different countries. Today, I'll talk about surprising birthplaces of everyday foods. First, people believe the Caesar salad is named after a Roman emperor. But a well-known story is that the name came from a chef in Mexico. He created it by putting together some basic ingredients __________ __________ __________ __________ __________. Second, bagels are a famous New York food. But they're likely from central Europe. A widely repeated story says that they were first made in Vienna to celebrate the ✪ __________ __________ __________ __________ __________. Third, many people think kiwis are from New Zealand. It's probably because a small flightless bird from New Zealand has the same name. In fact, the food is from China. Last, if there's __________ __________ __________ __________ __________, it's Ireland. That's because crop failures of this food caused extreme hunger in Ireland in the 19th century. However, the food __________ __________ __________ __________ __________ South America. Now, we'll watch a short video about these foods.

▶ 정답 : 해설편 157쪽

VOCA LIST 35

회차별 영단어 QR 코드 ※ QR 코드를 스캔 후 모바일로 단어장처럼 학습할 수 있습니다.

● 고3 2019학년도 수능

01

001 □ announcement ⓝ 발표, 소식
002 □ be supposed to ~할 예정이다, ~하기로 되어있다
003 □ forecast ⓝ (일기의) 예보, 예측
004 □ decided ⓐ 결정한, 분명한
005 □ purchase ⓝ 구매, 구입
006 □ be fully refunded 전액 환불되다
007 □ make-up game 재경기
008 □ due to ~ 때문에

02

009 □ chemical reaction 화학 반응
010 □ experiment ⓝ 실험
011 □ again and again 되풀이해서
012 □ talent ⓝ 재능
013 □ chemistry ⓝ 화학
014 □ Don't be so hard on yourself. 너무 자책하지 마.
015 □ path ⓝ 길
016 □ figure out ~을 이해하다[알아내다]
017 □ succeed at ~에 성공하다
018 □ review ⓥ 다시 살펴보다, 검토하다

03

019 □ exhibition ⓝ 전시회
020 □ antique item 골동품
021 □ donate ⓥ 기증하다
022 □ thanks to ~의 덕분인
023 □ generous ⓐ 관대한, 후한, 넉넉한
024 □ donation ⓝ 기증(품)
025 □ improve ⓥ (~의 가치를) 높여주다, 향상시키다
026 □ collection ⓝ 소장품, 수집품
027 □ invitation letter 초대장
028 □ on behalf of ~을 대표하여, 대신하여
029 □ appreciate ⓥ 감사하다, 고마워하다

04

030 □ backyard ⓝ 뒷마당
031 □ heart-shaped 하트 모양의
032 □ striped ⓐ 줄무늬의
033 □ ready for ~할 준비가 된

05

034 □ presentation ⓝ 발표
035 □ fair ⓝ 박람회
036 □ in public 사람들 앞에서, 공개적으로
037 □ insect ⓝ 곤충
038 □ introduce ⓥ 소개하다
039 □ share ⓥ 함께 나누다
040 □ survey ⓝ 설문 조사
041 □ opinion ⓝ 의견, 생각, 여론
042 □ distribute ⓥ 배부하다
043 □ hand-out ⓝ 유인물
044 □ audience ⓝ 관객, 청중

06

045 □ advanced ⓐ 상급의, 고급의
046 □ safety equipment 안전 장비
047 □ elbow ⓝ 팔꿈치
048 □ knee ⓝ 무릎

07

049 □ advertisement ⓝ 광고
050 □ competition ⓝ 경연대회, 경쟁
051 □ graduation ⓝ 졸업
052 □ present ⓝ 선물
053 □ enter ⓥ 출전하다
054 □ make it (시간 맞춰) 참석하다, 가다, 해내다, 성공하다

08

055 □ firework ⓝ 불꽃놀이, 폭죽
056 □ take part 참가하다, 참여하다
057 □ provide ⓥ 제공하다

09

058 □ upcycling ⓝ 새활용
059 □ creative ⓐ 창의적인
060 □ give life to ~에 생명을 주다, 생기를 불어넣다
061 □ object ⓝ 물건
062 □ special treat 특별한 사항, 특별한 대접
063 □ method ⓝ 방법
064 □ participation fee 참가비

10

065 □ cutting board 도마
066 □ affordable ⓐ (가격이) 적당한, 알맞은, 저렴한
067 □ preference ⓝ 선호
068 □ maple ⓝ 단풍나무
069 □ walnut ⓝ 호두나무
070 □ environmentally friendly 환경 친화적인
071 □ range ⓝ 범위
072 □ handle ⓝ 손잡이
073 □ convenient ⓐ 편리한

11

074 □ submit ⓥ 제출하다
075 □ midnight ⓝ 자정

12

076 □ available ⓐ 이용[사용]할 수 있는
077 □ cancel ⓥ 취소하다
078 □ slippery ⓐ 미끄러운
079 □ comfortable ⓐ 안락한, 쾌적한
080 □ register A for B A를 B에 등록시키다

13

081 □ pill ⓝ 알약
082 □ relieved ⓐ 다행인, 안도한
083 □ business trip 출장
084 □ skip ⓥ 생략하다, 건너뛰다
085 □ delay ⓥ 지연시키다, 늦추다
086 □ regularly [ad] 규칙적으로
087 □ solution ⓝ 해결책

14

088 □ article ⓝ 기사
089 □ mention ⓥ 언급하다, 말하다
090 □ leading actor 주연 배우
091 □ recommend ⓥ 추천하다, 권하다
092 □ original novel 원작 소설
093 □ storyline ⓝ 줄거리
094 □ complicated ⓐ 복잡한

15

095 □ translation ⓝ 번역, 통역
096 □ volunteer ⓥ 자원봉사하다 ⓝ 자원봉사자
097 □ self-introduction letter 자기소개서
098 □ satisfied ⓐ 만족스러운
099 □ emphasize ⓥ 강조하다
100 □ highlight ⓥ 강조하다
101 □ qualified ⓐ 자격을 갖춘, 자격이 있는

16~17

102 □ birthplace ⓝ 탄생지, 출생지
103 □ emperor ⓝ 황제
104 □ be named after ~의 이름을 따서 짓다
105 □ ingredient ⓝ 재료
106 □ run out of ~이 다 떨어지다
107 □ invading army 침략군
108 □ flightless ⓐ (새가) 날지 못하는
109 □ crop failure 흉작
110 □ hunger ⓝ 기아, 기근
111 □ misconception ⓝ 오해, 잘못된 견해
112 □ spread ⓥ 전파되다, 퍼지다, 흩뜨리다

01회 ● [특별 부록] 수능 대비 파이널 모의고사 고3 영어 듣기

※ QR코드를 스캔하시면 듣기 방송을 청취하실 수 있습니다.

● 점수 표시가 없는 문항은 모두 2점 ● 문항수 17개 | 배점 37점 | 제한 시간 25분

1번부터 17번까지는 듣고 답하는 문제입니다. 1번부터 15번까지는 한 번만 들려주고, 16번부터 17번까지는 두 번 들려줍니다. 방송을 잘 듣고 답을 하시기 바랍니다.

1. 다음을 듣고, 여자가 하는 말의 목적으로 가장 적절한 것을 고르시오.

① 독서의 즐거움을 홍보하려고
② 서점 개장 시간의 변경을 공지하려고
③ 서점의 여러 가지 코너를 설명하려고
④ 도서와 문구류 할인 판매를 안내하려고
⑤ 폐장 시간에 따른 쇼핑 마무리를 부탁하려고

2. 대화를 듣고, 남자의 의견으로 가장 적절한 것을 고르시오.

① 여행에서는 가능한 한 많은 것을 보고, 많은 곳을 방문해야 한다.
② 비행기 창 밖을 내다보는 것과 새로운 곳의 공기를 마시는 것도 여행이다.
③ 여행 전에 합리적으로 여행 예산을 계획해야 한다.
④ 여행 일정이 너무 빡빡하면 오히려 많은 것을 제대로 볼 수 없다.
⑤ 처음 가는 여행지는 보호자 없이 혼자 가면 위험할 수 있다.

3. 대화를 듣고, 두 사람의 관계를 가장 잘 나타낸 것을 고르시오.

① 점원 – 관리자
② 학생 – 교사
③ 목격자 – 소방관
④ 세입자 – 부동산 중개인
⑤ 가게 주인 – 소방 점검원

4. 대화를 듣고, 그림에서 대화의 내용과 일치하지 않는 것을 고르시오.

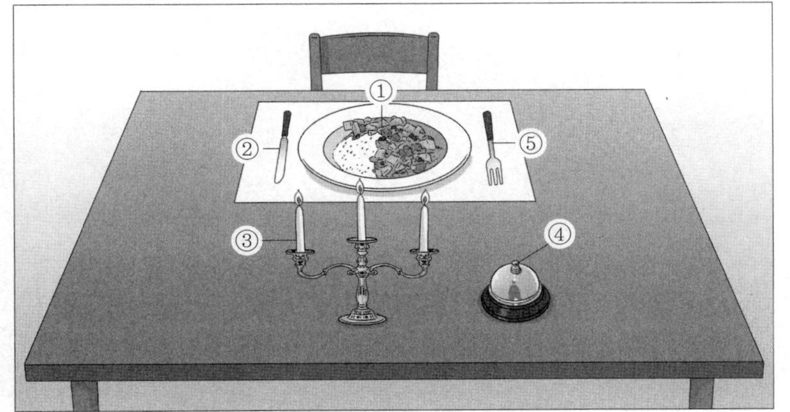

5. 대화를 듣고, 남자가 할 일로 가장 적절한 것을 고르시오.

① 월세 빌려 주기
② 신문에 광고 내주기
③ 휴대폰 매장 소개해 주기
④ 자동차 렌트 알아봐 주기
⑤ 부동산에 대신 전화해 주기

6. 대화를 듣고, 여자가 지불할 금액을 고르시오. [3점]

① $90 ② $100 ③ $81 ④ $35 ⑤ $55

7. 대화를 듣고, 남자가 테니스 연습을 할 수 없는 이유를 고르시오.

① 다가오는 시험을 위한 공부를 해야 해서
② 내일 있을 테니스 경기를 위해 쉬어야 해서
③ 아픈 강아지를 동물병원에 데려가야 해서
④ 과학 프로젝트를 끝내야 해서
⑤ 팔꿈치에 통증이 있어서

8. 대화를 듣고, Hybrid Car에 관해 언급되지 않은 것을 고르시오.

① 세련된 디자인 ② 우수한 연비 ③ 주행 시 조용함
④ 친환경적 요소 ⑤ 비싼 구입 가격

9. Peace Charity Marathon에 관한 다음 내용을 듣고, 일치하지 않는 것을 고르시오.

① 매년 십 만 명이 넘는 참가자가 있다.
② 15세 미만의 참가자는 보호자와 동반해야 한다.
③ 오전과 오후에 각각 한 차례씩의 경주가 있다.
④ 희망에 따라 다른 완주 거리를 선택할 수 있다.
⑤ 온라인으로 미리 등록이 가능하다.

[해설편 p.158]

10. 다음 표를 보면서 대화를 듣고, 여자가 구매할 의자를 고르시오.

	Model	Price	Weight	Wheels	Color
①	A	$85	60 pounds	×	brown
②	B	$90	40 pounds	×	beige
③	C	$120	35 pounds	○	blue
④	D	$82	55 pounds	○	red
⑤	E	$88	40 pounds	○	green

11. 대화를 듣고, 남자의 마지막 말에 대한 여자의 응답으로 가장 적절한 것을 고르시오.

① He got a new job there.
② Sure, he lives there alone.
③ I hope he will visit Korea soon.
④ I know moving is a stressful job.
⑤ Why not? Seattle is a beautiful city.

12. 대화를 듣고, 여자의 마지막 말에 대한 남자의 응답으로 가장 적절한 것을 고르시오.

① Don't worry about it. I wouldn't miss it.
② Yes, I'm thinking about changing classes.
③ No way! In that case, I have to pay late fee.
④ Sure, I'd like to study together in the library.
⑤ No problem. I can check out the book you need.

13. 대화를 듣고, 남자의 마지막 말에 대한 여자의 응답으로 가장 적절한 것을 고르시오. [3점]

Woman: ______________________________

① You can do it. You'll do well at the second interview.
② No problem. These days there are lots of vacancies at hotels.
③ I hope it goes well. I'd love it if you came to this area to work.
④ I wish you the best of luck. I want you to be promoted to manager.
⑤ Cheer up! You'd better have pride in your being selected among 16.

14. 대화를 듣고, 여자의 마지막 말에 대한 남자의 응답으로 가장 적절한 것을 고르시오.

Man: ______________________________

① Sure. I like American dramas, too.
② Right. We need to cut down on them.
③ No way. We need subtitles watching them.
④ I know what you mean. You are a big fan of that.
⑤ I don't think so. Watching them has lots of benefits.

15. 다음 상황 설명을 듣고, Jieun이가 아버지에게 할 말로 가장 적절한 것을 고르시오. [3점]

Jieun: Dad, ______________________________

① my teacher advises me to major in law.
② I'm proud that you are a wonderful lawyer.
③ I am more interested in English than becoming a lawyer.
④ I am going to persuade my teacher to modify my future job.
⑤ I prefer participating in the speech contest to the essay contest.

[16~17] 다음을 듣고, 물음에 답하시오.

16. 여자가 하는 말의 주제로 가장 적절한 것은?

① how handy AI can be in the future
② why we should compete with AI
③ professions AI will never be able to replace
④ what AI is capable of career-wise
⑤ various industries where AI is wanted

17. AI가 대체할 직업으로 언급되지 않은 것은?

① judges ② translators ③ pharmacists
④ drivers ⑤ teachers

[해설편 p.159]

02회 [특별 부록] 수능 대비 파이널 모의고사 고3 영어 듣기

※ QR코드를 스캔하시면 듣기 방송을 청취하실 수 있습니다.

● 점수 표시가 없는 문항은 모두 2점 ● 문항수 17개 | 배점 37점 | 제한 시간 25분

1번부터 17번까지는 듣고 답하는 문제입니다. 1번부터 15번까지는 한 번만 들려주고, 16번부터 17번까지는 두 번 들려줍니다. 방송을 잘 듣고 답을 하시기 바랍니다.

1. 다음을 듣고, 남자가 하는 말의 목적으로 가장 적절한 것을 고르시오.

① 소화불량의 원인을 보고하려고
② 정기적인 비타민 C 섭취를 권장하려고
③ 비타민 C의 감기 예방 효과를 설명하려고
④ 필요한 정보를 선별하는 방법을 안내하려고
⑤ 비타민 C 과다 복용의 부작용을 경고하려고

2. 대화를 듣고, 여자의 의견으로 가장 적절한 것을 고르시오.

① 주방 세제 대신 달걀껍데기를 사용하면 환경을 보호할 수 있다.
② 친환경 주방 세제는 일반 주방 세제보다 세정력이 우수하다.
③ 달걀껍데기는 일상생활에서 유용하게 쓰인다.
④ 아침 식사로 달걀을 섭취하는 것은 건강에 도움이 된다.
⑤ 달걀껍데기는 주방 세제보다 물병 세척에 탁월하다.

3. 대화를 듣고, 두 사람의 관계를 가장 잘 나타낸 것을 고르시오.

① 잡지 기자 – 운동선수
② 교통 경찰관 – 운전자
③ 운전 강사 – 수강생
④ 자동차 수리공 – 고객
⑤ 관광 가이드 – 여행객

4. 대화를 듣고, 그림에서 대화의 내용과 일치하지 않는 것을 고르시오.

5. 대화를 듣고, 여자가 할 일로 가장 적절한 것을 고르시오.

① 좌석 예매하기 ② 피자 주문하기
③ 과학 과제 도와주기 ④ 상영 시간 알아보기
⑤ 뮤지컬 연습 도와주기

6. 대화를 듣고, 남자가 지불할 금액을 고르시오. [3점]

① $15 ② $19 ③ $20 ④ $21 ⑤ $24

7. 대화를 듣고, 여자가 사이클 대회에 참가할 수 없는 이유를 고르시오.

① 파트너를 구하지 못해서
② 취업 면접에 가야 해서
③ 남동생의 병문안을 가야 해서
④ 사이클을 갖고 있지 않아서
⑤ 조카의 졸업식에 참석해야 해서

8. 대화를 듣고, Days Inn에 관해 언급되지 않은 것을 고르시오.

① 주차장 ② 전망 ③ 대중교통
④ 인터넷 접속 ⑤ 수영장

9. Auburn Stadium에 관한 다음 내용을 듣고, 일치하지 않는 것을 고르시오.

① 경기장 대관에 관심이 있으면 1번을 누른다.
② 미식축구 경기에 관한 정보를 알고 싶으면 3번을 누른다.
③ 매표소 운영 시간이 궁금하면 4번을 누른다.
④ 다시 듣고 싶으면 9번을 누른다.
⑤ 아무것도 누르지 않으면 교환원과 연결된다.

10. 다음 표를 보면서 대화를 듣고, 두 사람이 예약할 항공편을 고르시오.

Flight Schedule to Japan

	Flight	Ticket Price	Departure Time	Arrival Airport	Stops
①	A	$480	6:00 a.m.	Haneda	nonstop
②	B	$420	10:00 a.m.	Narita	nonstop
③	C	$455	12:30 p.m.	Narita	nonstop
④	D	$490	1:00 p.m.	Haneda	one stop
⑤	E	$510	3:20 p.m.	Narita	one stop

11. 대화를 듣고, 남자의 마지막 말에 대한 여자의 응답으로 가장 적절한 것을 고르시오.

① You're right. I can't wait to go there today.
② I see. I will buy them online this afternoon.
③ I'm sorry to hear they are already sold out.
④ Sure. Busan is one of the most beautiful cities.
⑤ Good job. It was good to purchase them before.

12. 대화를 듣고, 여자의 마지막 말에 대한 남자의 응답으로 가장 적절한 것을 고르시오.

① Then we'll have to arrange another supplier.
② I'm glad they came in ahead of our schedule.
③ Don't worry. I can come to the place on time.
④ Actually, we didn't order the products from them.
⑤ I'm sorry, but we should have ordered them last week.

13. 대화를 듣고, 남자의 마지막 말에 대한 여자의 응답으로 가장 적절한 것을 고르시오.

Woman: ______________________

① I'd like to say you should focus on reality.
② I will not put my parents in an old-people's facility.
③ It is natural for parents to take care of their children.
④ It is better for senior citizens to live in the rural area.
⑤ I think these facilities should spread all over the country.

14. 대화를 듣고, 여자의 마지막 말에 대한 남자의 응답으로 가장 적절한 것을 고르시오. [3점]

Man: ______________________

① Now you are talking. I'm a party mania.
② Actually, I'm going to the party using my father's car.
③ In my case, I prefer to meet people in small groups.
④ Sure, I love hanging around with people everywhere.
⑤ At the party, I've met many interesting people to mingle with.

15. 다음 상황 설명을 듣고, Janet이 David에게 할 말로 가장 적절한 것을 고르시오. [3점]

Janet: ______________________

① Will you forward articles that I might like via email?
② You can read my morning paper while I am gone if you want.
③ Can you check if a newspaper delivery man actually comes every day?
④ Why don't we share the morning paper and split the bill?
⑤ Can you take in my morning paper while I am away?

[16~17] 다음을 듣고, 물음에 답하시오.

16. 여자가 하는 말의 주제로 가장 적절한 것은?

① origins of animal-related English expressions
② various animals in relation to English expressions and meanings
③ how colors and animals appeared in English expressions
④ why making English expressions using animals is common
⑤ hidden meanings of some frequently used English idioms

17. 언급된 동물이 아닌 것은?

① dog ② horse ③ sheep ④ goose ⑤ elephant

[해설편 p.163]

03회 ● [특별 부록] 수능 대비 파이널 모의고사 고3 영어 듣기

※ QR코드를 스캔하시면 듣기 방송을 청취하실 수 있습니다.

● 점수 표시가 없는 문항은 모두 2점 ● 문항수 17개 | 배점 37점 | 제한 시간 25분

1번부터 17번까지는 듣고 답하는 문제입니다. 1번부터 15번까지는 한 번만 들려주고, 16번부터 17번까지는 두 번 들려줍니다. 방송을 잘 듣고 답을 하시기 바랍니다.

MP3

1. 다음을 듣고, 남자가 하는 말의 목적으로 가장 적절한 것을 고르시오.

① 독감으로 인한 휴교를 공지하려고
② 학급에 필요한 물품을 요청하려고
③ 감기 예방주사 일정을 안내하려고
④ 손 씻기 습관의 중요성을 강조하려고
⑤ 결석 시 학교에 제출할 서류를 알리려고

2. 대화를 듣고, 여자의 의견으로 가장 적절한 것을 고르시오.

① 주말에 밀린 잠을 자면 주중에 더 피곤하다.
② 주말에 친구를 만나면 늦게 잠자리에 들게 된다.
③ 주말은 주중과 비교할 때 시간이 너무 빨리 간다.
④ 주말에 밀린 잠을 자는 것은 주중에 더 집중할 수 있도록 돕는다.
⑤ 주말에 늦잠을 자는 것은 신체의 리듬을 깨는 행위이다.

3. 대화를 듣고, 두 사람의 관계를 가장 잘 나타낸 것을 고르시오.

① 판매원 – 고객 ② 코치 – 운동선수
③ 신문기자 – 영화배우 ④ 관광 가이드 – 여행객
⑤ 사진작가 – 패션모델

4. 대화를 듣고, 그림에서 대화의 내용과 일치하지 않는 것을 고르시오.

5. 대화를 듣고, 남자가 할 일로 가장 적절한 것을 고르시오.

① 야생화 사진 전송하기
② 대신 과제 제출하기
③ 큰아버지의 전화번호를 알려주기
④ 야생화가 있는 과수원 소개하기
⑤ 과제 제출일 확인하기

6. 대화를 듣고, 여자가 지불할 금액을 고르시오. [3점]

① $72 ② $77 ③ $80 ④ $85 ⑤ $87

7. 대화를 듣고, 남자가 영수증을 찾는 이유를 고르시오.

① 제품 구매 날짜를 확인하려고
② 영수증에 기재된 일련번호를 확인하려고
③ 계산이 잘못되었다고 생각하여 지불 금액을 확인하려고
④ 구매한 셀카봉에 결함이 있어 새 제품으로 교환하려고
⑤ 계획한 여행이 취소되어 셀카봉에 대한 환불을 받으려고

8. 대화를 듣고, 드라마에 관해 두 사람이 언급하지 않은 것을 고르시오.

① 배경 ② 제목 ③ 주요 장면
④ 배우 ⑤ 방영 시간

9. Haleakala Ranch Ride에 관한 다음 내용을 듣고, 일치하지 않는 것을 고르시오.

① 말을 타고 바다 풍경을 즐길 수 있다.
② 1시간 넘게 말을 타게 된다.
③ 하루에 2번 말을 타는 시간이 있다.
④ 현장에서 신청하여 말을 탈 수 있다.
⑤ 음료수가 제공되어 진다.

특별 부록 03회

10. 다음 표를 보면서 대화를 듣고, 여자가 구매할 도마를 고르시오.

Cutting board at Dominion's Kitchen

	Type	Price	Material	Handle	Hole
①	A	$52	plastic	○	○
②	B	$60	soft wood	×	×
③	C	$55	soft wood	○	×
④	D	$75	hard wood	×	○
⑤	E	$64	hard wood	○	×

11. 대화를 듣고, 남자의 마지막 말에 대한 여자의 응답으로 가장 적절한 것을 고르시오.

① Well, he didn't show up.
② Have you seen him before?
③ Yes, he attended the meeting.
④ No, the meeting was excellent.
⑤ He greeted me with a warm attitude.

12. 대화를 듣고, 여자의 마지막 말에 대한 남자의 응답으로 가장 적절한 것을 고르시오.

① She is eighty years old, but very healthy.
② That's fine with me. Anyone can make a mistake.
③ You're right. She should have gone to your party.
④ You can say that again. The doctor was really kind.
⑤ She was not good at one time, but is recovering now.

13. 대화를 듣고, 남자의 마지막 말에 대한 여자의 응답으로 가장 적절한 것을 고르시오.

Woman: ____________________

① My pleasure. I think it's lucky for you to be in my class.
② Good for you. You will help the chairman at every event.
③ Cheer up. Next time you'll get a lot of support from friends.
④ Not at all. I was glad to compete with you in the election.
⑤ Don't worry. Losing in the election doesn't mean a failure.

14. 대화를 듣고, 여자의 마지막 말에 대한 남자의 응답으로 가장 적절한 것을 고르시오. [3점]

Man: ____________________

① They don't belong to me. Actually, they are yours.
② Sure, cleaning always makes me happy and refreshed.
③ Before cleaning up, I want to get rid of my old books.
④ They look useless to you, but they are precious to me.
⑤ I see. I'll try to clean the bookshelf more often from now on.

15. 다음 상황 설명을 듣고, Hyunwoo가 친구들에게 할 말로 가장 적절한 것을 고르시오. [3점]

Hyunwoo: ____________________

① Thank you for giving me a ride to the airport.
② Of course. I love to go shopping with you.
③ I'd love to, but I have a previous engagement.
④ I'm sorry, but I have to leave for America now.
⑤ That's a good idea. I'll follow you wherever you go.

[16~17] 다음을 듣고, 물음에 답하시오.

16. 여자가 하는 말의 주제로 가장 적절한 것은?

① how some foods spread across countries
② why traditional foods are popular
③ misconceptions about well-known foods
④ unexpected origins of common foods
⑤ how some foods got their names

17. 언급된 음식이 아닌 것은?

① croissants ② nachos ③ gim
④ french fries ⑤ kiwis

[해설편 p.166]

SPEED 정답 체크

수능기출 학력평가 7개년 기출 문제집 | 고3·영어 듣기

01회 2024학년도 03월

01 ⑤ 02 ⑤ 03 ① 04 ④ 05 ②

06 ③ 07 ② 08 ⑤ 09 ④ 10 ③

11 ③ 12 ② 13 ① 14 ③ 15 ①

16 ⑤ 17 ③

02회 2023학년도 03월

01 ③ 02 ② 03 ① 04 ③ 05 ⑤

06 ④ 07 ② 08 ② 09 ④ 10 ②

11 ⑤ 12 ② 13 ⑤ 14 ⑤ 15 ②

16 ① 17 ③

03회 2022학년도 03월

01 ⑤ 02 ① 03 ① 04 ④ 05 ⑤

06 ③ 07 ① 08 ④ 09 ③ 10 ②

11 ④ 12 ① 13 ⑤ 14 ② 15 ③

16 ④ 17 ③

04회 2021학년도 03월

01 ⑤ 02 ① 03 ① 04 ④ 05 ①

06 ④ 07 ② 08 ③ 09 ④ 10 ③

11 ① 12 ③ 13 ① 14 ⑤ 15 ③

16 ② 17 ⑤

05회 2020학년도 03월

01 ③ 02 ⑤ 03 ① 04 ⑤ 05 ②

06 ③ 07 ② 08 ⑤ 09 ③ 10 ②

11 ⑤ 12 ② 13 ③ 14 ② 15 ①

16 ② 17 ⑤

06회 2024학년도 05월

01 ⑤ 02 ② 03 ① 04 ④ 05 ②

06 ④ 07 ② 08 ③ 09 ⑤ 10 ④

11 ① 12 ③ 13 ④ 14 ① 15 ⑤

16 ② 17 ③

07회 2023학년도 04월

01 ⑤ 02 ② 03 ② 04 ④ 05 ③

06 ⑤ 07 ⑤ 08 ⑤ 09 ⑤ 10 ③

11 ③ 12 ① 13 ① 14 ② 15 ①

16 ① 17 ④

08회 2022학년도 04월

01 ① 02 ④ 03 ② 04 ③ 05 ⑤

06 ① 07 ④ 08 ④ 09 ⑤ 10 ③

11 ② 12 ② 13 ⑤ 14 ③ 15 ①

16 ③ 17 ④

09회 2021학년도 04월

01 ② 02 ⑤ 03 ① 04 ⑤ 05 ④

06 ③ 07 ② 08 ③ 09 ④ 10 ④

11 ① 12 ③ 13 ④ 14 ② 15 ⑤

16 ① 17 ③

10회 2020학년도 04월

01 ② 02 ② 03 ① 04 ④ 05 ⑤

06 ② 07 ④ 08 ④ 09 ⑤ 10 ③

11 ③ 12 ② 13 ② 14 ⑤ 15 ①

16 ① 17 ③

11회 2025학년도 06월

01 ③ 02 ⑤ 03 ③ 04 ④ 05 ④

06 ③ 07 ② 08 ⑤ 09 ② 10 ②

11 ⑤ 12 ② 13 ② 14 ① 15 ③

16 ① 17 ④

12회 2024학년도 06월

01 ⑤ 02 ② 03 ① 04 ⑤ 05 ①

06 ③ 07 ① 08 ④ 09 ② 10 ③

11 ⑤ 12 ② 13 ③ 14 ① 15 ⑤

16 ④ 17 ②

13회 2023학년도 06월

01 ④ 02 ⑤ 03 ③ 04 ⑤ 05 ③

06 ② 07 ① 08 ② 09 ④ 10 ④

11 ① 12 ⑤ 13 ① 14 ② 15 ①

16 ② 17 ④

14회 2022학년도 06월

01 ⑤ 02 ① 03 ① 04 ③ 05 ②

06 ④ 07 ② 08 ③ 09 ④ 10 ③

11 ① 12 ④ 13 ⑤ 14 ① 15 ②

16 ⑤ 17 ③

15회 2021학년도 06월

01 ① 02 ② 03 ③ 04 ③ 05 ②

06 ④ 07 ① 08 ④ 09 ④ 10 ②

11 ④ 12 ① 13 ⑤ 14 ⑤ 15 ①

16 ② 17 ③

16회 2023학년도 07월

01 ① 02 ② 03 ⑤ 04 ④ 05 ③

06 ④ 07 ⑤ 08 ④ 09 ⑤ 10 ②

11 ② 12 ① 13 ⑤ 14 ④ 15 ④

16 ① 17 ③

17회 2022학년도 07월

01 ② 02 ① 03 ③ 04 ⑤ 05 ④

06 ① 07 ① 08 ⑤ 09 ② 10 ②

11 ② 12 ③ 13 ③ 14 ② 15 ⑤

16 ① 17 ③

18회 2021학년도 07월

01 ① 02 ① 03 ④ 04 ⑤ 05 ④

06 ③ 07 ① 08 ③ 09 ③ 10 ③

11 ② 12 ④ 13 ② 14 ② 15 ⑤

16 ① 17 ③

19회 2020학년도 07월

01 ① 02 ② 03 ① 04 ④ 05 ②

06 ④ 07 ④ 08 ④ 09 ⑤ 10 ③

11 ④ 12 ③ 13 ⑤ 14 ① 15 ⑤

16 ② 17 ④

20회 2025학년도 09월

01 ④ 02 ① 03 ⑤ 04 ⑤ 05 ①

06 ① 07 ⑤ 08 ③ 09 ⑤ 10 ③

11 ② 12 ① 13 ④ 14 ② 15 ③

16 ① 17 ③

21회 2024학년도 09월

01 ③ 02 ① 03 ② 04 ③ 05 ④

06 ③ 07 ② 08 ④ 09 ⑤ 10 ⑤

11 ④ 12 ① 13 ② 14 ③ 15 ①

16 ⑤ 17 ④

22회 2023학년도 09월

01 ④ 02 ① 03 ⑤ 04 ④ 05 ③

06 ③ 07 ④ 08 ⑤ 09 ⑤ 10 ②

11 ② 12 ④ 13 ② 14 ① 15 ①

16 ② 17 ③

23회 2022학년도 09월

01 ⑤ 02 ① 03 ② 04 ③ 05 ①

06 ④ 07 ③ 08 ⑤ 09 ④ 10 ④

11 ⑤ 12 ① 13 ② 14 ① 15 ⑤

16 ③ 17 ④

24회 2021학년도 09월

01 ② 02 ② 03 ① 04 ⑤ 05 ③

06 ② 07 ⑤ 08 ③ 09 ④ 10 ④

11 ① 12 ④ 13 ① 14 ③ 15 ④

16 ② 17 ⑤

25회 2023학년도 10월

01 ⑤ 02 ① 03 ① 04 ⑤ 05 ⑤

06 ④ 07 ⑤ 08 ④ 09 ④ 10 ③

11 ③ 12 ③ 13 ⑤ 14 ② 15 ②

16 ③ 17 ③

26회 2022학년도 10월

01 ② 02 ② 03 ④ 04 ⑤ 05 ①

06 ③ 07 ① 08 ③ 09 ⑤ 10 ②

11 ② 12 ⑤ 13 ② 14 ③ 15 ③

16 ② 17 ②

27회 2021학년도 10월

01 ③ 02 ④ 03 ⑤ 04 ③ 05 ④

06 ③ 07 ① 08 ⑤ 09 ④ 10 ②

11 ① 12 ② 13 ② 14 ② 15 ①

16 ③ 17 ④

28회 2020학년도 10월

01 ② 02 ② 03 ① 04 ④ 05 ②

06 ③ 07 ② 08 ② 09 ③ 10 ③

11 ① 12 ① 13 ① 14 ⑤ 15 ⑤

16 ② 17 ③

29회 2025학년도 수능

01 ② 02 ⑤ 03 ① 04 ③ 05 ①

06 ④ 07 ③ 08 ④ 09 ⑤ 10 ②

11 ② 12 ① 13 ⑤ 14 ① 15 ②

16 ③ 17 ④

30회 2024학년도 수능

01 ⑤ 02 ① 03 ④ 04 ③ 05 ②

06 ③ 07 ④ 08 ③ 09 ④ 10 ②

11 ⑤ 12 ① 13 ⑤ 14 ① 15 ①

16 ② 17 ③

31회 2023학년도 수능

01 ③ 02 ② 03 ③ 04 ④ 05 ②

06 ③ 07 ⑤ 08 ③ 09 ② 10 ①

11 ② 12 ① 13 ④ 14 ④ 15 ③

16 ① 17 ⑤

32회 2022학년도 수능

01 ⑤ 02 ② 03 ① 04 ④ 05 ②

06 ④ 07 ① 08 ④ 09 ③ 10 ④

11 ① 12 ② 13 ③ 14 ⑤ 15 ⑤

16 ③ 17 ⑤

33회 2021학년도 수능

01 ⑤ 02 ① 03 ① 04 ⑤ 05 ①

06 ② 07 ③ 08 ④ 09 ③ 10 ④

11 ③ 12 ① 13 ② 14 ④ 15 ①

16 ⑤ 17 ⑤

34회 2020학년도 수능

01 ① 02 ③ 03 ③ 04 ④ 05 ④

06 ② 07 ⑤ 08 ③ 09 ④ 10 ④

11 ① 12 ② 13 ② 14 ② 15 ⑤

16 ① 17 ③

35회 2019학년도 수능

01 ① 02 ① 03 ② 04 ④ 05 ⑤

06 ② 07 ② 08 ④ 09 ⑤ 10 ④

11 ③ 12 ④ 13 ④ 14 ⑤ 15 ①

16 ③ 17 ⑤

01회 [특별 부록] 파이널 모의고사

01 ⑤ 02 ② 03 ⑤ 04 ⑤ 05 ⑤

06 ① 07 ③ 08 ③ 09 ③ 10 ⑤

11 ① 12 ① 13 ③ 14 ② 15 ③

16 ④ 17 ⑤

02회 [특별 부록] 파이널 모의고사

01 ⑤ 02 ⑤ 03 ③ 04 ⑤ 05 ②

06 ④ 07 ⑤ 08 ② 09 ③ 10 ③

11 ② 12 ① 13 ② 14 ③ 15 ⑤

16 ② 17 ④

03회 [특별 부록] 파이널 모의고사

01 ② 02 ④ 03 ② 04 ② 05 ③

06 ② 07 ② 08 ① 09 ④ 10 ④

11 ① 12 ⑤ 13 ① 14 ④ 15 ③

16 ④ 17 ②

※ 절취선을 따라 잘라서 쓰실 수 있습니다.

리얼 오리지널

REAL

575만권 베스트셀러
리얼 오리지널 시리즈 누적 판매
2006~2024

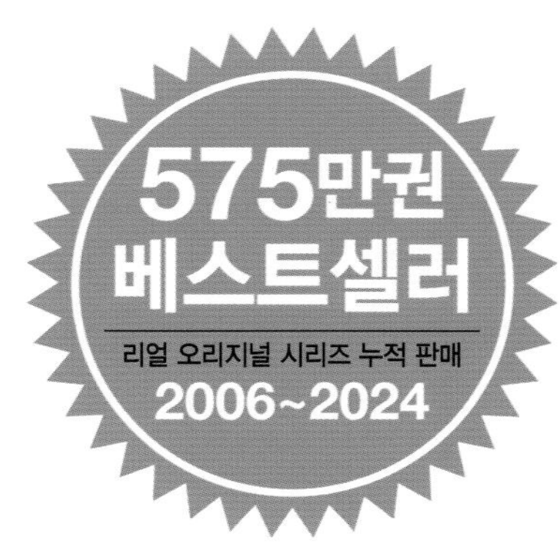

대학수학능력시험완벽대비

수능기출 학력평가 7개년 기출문제집

38회 [6·9 모평·수능 17회 학평 18회+파이널 3회]

- 최신 7개년 [3·4·7·10월 학평]+[6·9·수능] 기출 35회
- 학교·학원 선생님이 새롭게 출제한 파이널 모의고사 3회
- 실력 향상과 점수를 올려주는 [딕테이션 테스트] 수록
- 대본에 [한글 해석] 및 듣기 어려운 발음에 ✪ 표기
- 듣기 파일 5종 [정배속·1.25배속·1.5배속·1.75배속·2배속]
- 회차별 [SPEED 정답 체크표·STUDY 플래너·정답률]
- 문제지와 딕테이션에 QR 코드 수록 & MP3 파일 제공
- [특별 부록] 회차별 영단어

3회분 파이널 모의고사 수록

고3 영어 듣기

모바일로 학습하는 회차별 영단어 QR 코드 제공

•해설편•

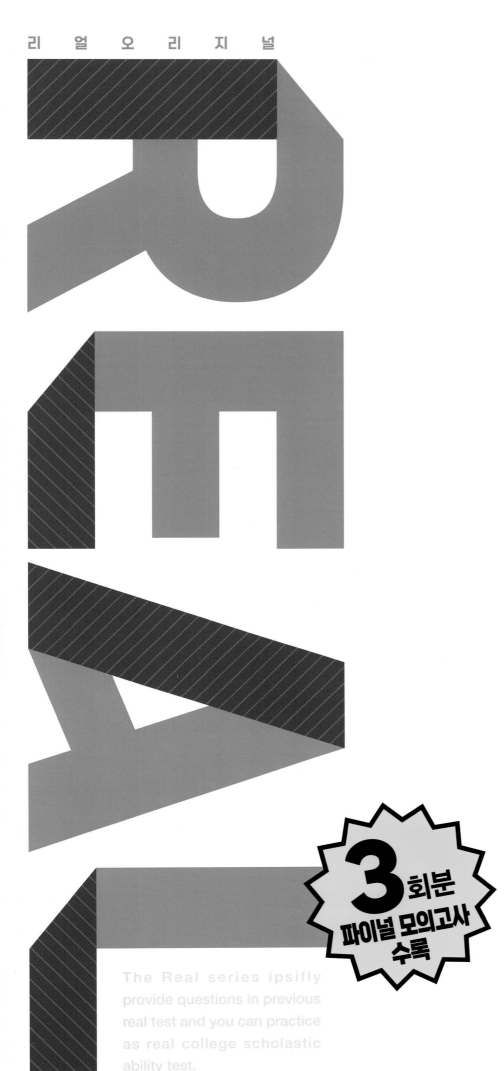

The Real series ipsifly provide questions in previous real test and you can practice as real college scholastic ability test.

수능 모의고사 전문 출판
입시플라이

SPEED 정답 체크

수능기출 학력평가 7개년 기출 문제집 | 고3·영어 듣기

01회 2024학년도 03월

01 ⑤ 02 ⑤ 03 ① 04 ④ 05 ②

06 ③ 07 ② 08 ⑤ 09 ④ 10 ③

11 ③ 12 ② 13 ① 14 ③ 15 ①

16 ⑤ 17 ③

02회 2023학년도 03월

01 ③ 02 ② 03 ① 04 ③ 05 ⑤

06 ④ 07 ② 08 ② 09 ④ 10 ②

11 ⑤ 12 ② 13 ⑤ 14 ⑤ 15 ②

16 ① 17 ③

03회 2022학년도 03월

01 ⑤ 02 ① 03 ① 04 ④ 05 ⑤

06 ③ 07 ① 08 ④ 09 ③ 10 ②

11 ④ 12 ① 13 ⑤ 14 ② 15 ③

16 ④ 17 ③

04회 2021학년도 03월

01 ⑤ 02 ① 03 ① 04 ④ 05 ①

06 ④ 07 ② 08 ③ 09 ④ 10 ③

11 ① 12 ③ 13 ① 14 ⑤ 15 ③

16 ② 17 ⑤

05회 2020학년도 03월

01 ③ 02 ⑤ 03 ① 04 ⑤ 05 ②

06 ③ 07 ② 08 ⑤ 09 ③ 10 ②

11 ⑤ 12 ② 13 ③ 14 ② 15 ①

16 ② 17 ⑤

06회 2024학년도 05월

01 ⑤ 02 ② 03 ① 04 ④ 05 ②

06 ④ 07 ② 08 ③ 09 ⑤ 10 ④

11 ① 12 ③ 13 ④ 14 ① 15 ⑤

16 ② 17 ③

07회 2023학년도 04월

01 ⑤ 02 ② 03 ② 04 ④ 05 ③

06 ⑤ 07 ⑤ 08 ⑤ 09 ⑤ 10 ③

11 ③ 12 ① 13 ① 14 ② 15 ①

16 ① 17 ④

08회 2022학년도 04월

01 ① 02 ④ 03 ② 04 ③ 05 ⑤

06 ① 07 ④ 08 ④ 09 ⑤ 10 ③

11 ② 12 ② 13 ⑤ 14 ③ 15 ①

16 ③ 17 ④

09회 2021학년도 04월

01 ② 02 ⑤ 03 ① 04 ⑤ 05 ④

06 ③ 07 ② 08 ③ 09 ④ 10 ④

11 ① 12 ③ 13 ④ 14 ② 15 ⑤

16 ① 17 ③

10회 2020학년도 04월

01 ② 02 ② 03 ① 04 ④ 05 ⑤

06 ② 07 ④ 08 ④ 09 ⑤ 10 ③

11 ③ 12 ② 13 ② 14 ⑤ 15 ①

16 ① 17 ③

11회 2025학년도 06월

01 ③ 02 ⑤ 03 ③ 04 ④ 05 ④

06 ③ 07 ② 08 ⑤ 09 ② 10 ②

11 ⑤ 12 ② 13 ② 14 ① 15 ③

16 ① 17 ④

12회 2024학년도 06월

01 ⑤ 02 ② 03 ① 04 ⑤ 05 ①

06 ③ 07 ① 08 ④ 09 ② 10 ③

11 ⑤ 12 ② 13 ③ 14 ① 15 ⑤

16 ④ 17 ②

13회 2023학년도 06월

01 ④ 02 ⑤ 03 ③ 04 ⑤ 05 ③

06 ② 07 ① 08 ② 09 ④ 10 ④

11 ① 12 ⑤ 13 ① 14 ② 15 ①

16 ② 17 ④

14회 2022학년도 06월

01 ⑤ 02 ① 03 ① 04 ③ 05 ②

06 ④ 07 ② 08 ③ 09 ④ 10 ③

11 ① 12 ④ 13 ⑤ 14 ① 15 ②

16 ⑤ 17 ③

15회 2021학년도 06월

01 ① 02 ② 03 ③ 04 ③ 05 ②

06 ④ 07 ① 08 ④ 09 ④ 10 ②

11 ④ 12 ① 13 ⑤ 14 ⑤ 15 ①

16 ② 17 ③

16회 2023학년도 07월

01 ① 02 ② 03 ⑤ 04 ④ 05 ③

06 ④ 07 ⑤ 08 ④ 09 ⑤ 10 ②

11 ② 12 ① 13 ⑤ 14 ④ 15 ④

16 ① 17 ③

17회 2022학년도 07월

01 ② 02 ① 03 ③ 04 ⑤ 05 ④

06 ① 07 ① 08 ⑤ 09 ② 10 ②

11 ② 12 ③ 13 ③ 14 ② 15 ⑤

16 ① 17 ③

18회 2021학년도 07월

01 ① 02 ① 03 ④ 04 ⑤ 05 ④

06 ③ 07 ① 08 ③ 09 ③ 10 ③

11 ② 12 ④ 13 ② 14 ② 15 ⑤

16 ① 17 ③

19회 2020학년도 07월

01 ① 02 ② 03 ① 04 ④ 05 ②

06 ④ 07 ④ 08 ④ 09 ⑤ 10 ③

11 ④ 12 ③ 13 ⑤ 14 ① 15 ⑤

16 ② 17 ④

20회 2025학년도 09월

01 ④ 02 ① 03 ⑤ 04 ⑤ 05 ①

06 ① 07 ⑤ 08 ③ 09 ⑤ 10 ③

11 ② 12 ① 13 ④ 14 ② 15 ③

16 ① 17 ③

21회 2024학년도 09월

01 ③ 02 ① 03 ② 04 ③ 05 ④

06 ③ 07 ② 08 ④ 09 ⑤ 10 ⑤

11 ④ 12 ① 13 ② 14 ③ 15 ①

16 ⑤ 17 ④

22회 2023학년도 09월

01 ④ 02 ① 03 ⑤ 04 ④ 05 ③

06 ③ 07 ④ 08 ⑤ 09 ⑤ 10 ②

11 ② 12 ④ 13 ② 14 ① 15 ①

16 ② 17 ③

23회 2022학년도 09월

01 ⑤ 02 ① 03 ② 04 ③ 05 ①

06 ④ 07 ③ 08 ⑤ 09 ④ 10 ④

11 ⑤ 12 ① 13 ② 14 ① 15 ⑤

16 ③ 17 ④

24회 2021학년도 09월

01 ② 02 ② 03 ① 04 ⑤ 05 ③

06 ② 07 ⑤ 08 ③ 09 ④ 10 ④

11 ① 12 ④ 13 ① 14 ③ 15 ④

16 ② 17 ⑤

25회 2023학년도 10월

01 ⑤ 02 ① 03 ① 04 ⑤ 05 ⑤

06 ④ 07 ⑤ 08 ④ 09 ④ 10 ③

11 ③ 12 ③ 13 ⑤ 14 ② 15 ②

16 ③ 17 ③

26회 2022학년도 10월

01 ② 02 ② 03 ④ 04 ⑤ 05 ①

06 ③ 07 ① 08 ③ 09 ⑤ 10 ②

11 ② 12 ⑤ 13 ② 14 ③ 15 ③

16 ② 17 ②

27회 2021학년도 10월

01 ③ 02 ④ 03 ⑤ 04 ③ 05 ④

06 ③ 07 ① 08 ⑤ 09 ④ 10 ②

11 ① 12 ② 13 ② 14 ② 15 ①

16 ③ 17 ④

28회 2020학년도 10월

01 ② 02 ② 03 ① 04 ④ 05 ②

06 ③ 07 ② 08 ② 09 ③ 10 ③

11 ① 12 ① 13 ① 14 ⑤ 15 ⑤

16 ② 17 ③

29회 2025학년도 수능

01 ② 02 ⑤ 03 ① 04 ③ 05 ①

06 ④ 07 ③ 08 ④ 09 ⑤ 10 ②

11 ② 12 ① 13 ⑤ 14 ① 15 ②

16 ③ 17 ④

30회 2024학년도 수능

01 ⑤ 02 ① 03 ④ 04 ③ 05 ②

06 ③ 07 ④ 08 ③ 09 ④ 10 ②

11 ⑤ 12 ① 13 ⑤ 14 ① 15 ①

16 ② 17 ③

31회 2023학년도 수능

01 ③ 02 ② 03 ③ 04 ④ 05 ②

06 ③ 07 ⑤ 08 ③ 09 ② 10 ①

11 ② 12 ① 13 ④ 14 ④ 15 ③

16 ① 17 ⑤

32회 2022학년도 수능

01 ⑤ 02 ② 03 ① 04 ④ 05 ②

06 ④ 07 ① 08 ④ 09 ③ 10 ④

11 ① 12 ② 13 ③ 14 ⑤ 15 ⑤

16 ③ 17 ⑤

33회 2021학년도 수능

01 ⑤ 02 ① 03 ① 04 ⑤ 05 ①

06 ② 07 ③ 08 ④ 09 ③ 10 ④

11 ③ 12 ① 13 ② 14 ④ 15 ①

16 ⑤ 17 ⑤

34회 2020학년도 수능

01 ① 02 ③ 03 ③ 04 ④ 05 ④

06 ② 07 ⑤ 08 ③ 09 ④ 10 ④

11 ① 12 ② 13 ② 14 ② 15 ⑤

16 ① 17 ③

35회 2019학년도 수능

01 ① 02 ① 03 ② 04 ④ 05 ⑤

06 ② 07 ② 08 ④ 09 ⑤ 10 ④

11 ③ 12 ④ 13 ④ 14 ⑤ 15 ①

16 ③ 17 ⑤

01회 [특별 부록] 파이널 모의고사

01 ⑤ 02 ② 03 ⑤ 04 ⑤ 05 ⑤

06 ① 07 ③ 08 ③ 09 ③ 10 ⑤

11 ① 12 ① 13 ③ 14 ② 15 ③

16 ④ 17 ⑤

02회 [특별 부록] 파이널 모의고사

01 ⑤ 02 ⑤ 03 ③ 04 ⑤ 05 ②

06 ④ 07 ⑤ 08 ② 09 ③ 10 ③

11 ② 12 ① 13 ② 14 ③ 15 ⑤

16 ② 17 ④

03회 [특별 부록] 파이널 모의고사

01 ② 02 ④ 03 ② 04 ② 05 ③

06 ② 07 ② 08 ① 09 ④ 10 ④

11 ① 12 ⑤ 13 ① 14 ④ 15 ③

16 ④ 17 ②

REAL

R E A L O R I G I N A L

수능기출학력평가 7개년 기출 문제집

고3 영어 듣기 해설편

Contents

※ 수록된 정답률은 실제와 차이가 있을 수 있습니다. 문제 난도를 파악하는데 참고용으로 활용하시기 바랍니다.

수능 모의고사 전문 출판
입시플라이

| 정답과 해설 |

회 | 2024학년도 3월 학력평가 고3

• 정답 •

01 ⑤ 02 ⑤ 03 ① 04 ④ 05 ② 06 ③ 07 ② 08 ⑤ 09 ④ 10 ③ 11 ③ 12 ② 13 ① 14 ③ 15 ① 16 ⑤ 17 ③

01 대청소 공지

정답률 89% | 정답 ⑤

다음을 듣고, 남자가 하는 말의 목적으로 가장 적절한 것을 고르시오.

① 도서관 이용 시간을 안내하려고
② 교내 불만 접수 방법을 설명하려고
③ 여름 방학 안전 수칙을 교육하려고
④ 특별 구역 청소 담당자를 모집하려고
✔ 여름 방학에 예정된 학교 청소를 공지하려고

M : Attention please.
주목해 주세요.
This is the vice principal.
교감입니다.
I'd like to inform you that our school will be undergoing a major cleaning during the upcoming summer break.
다가오는 여름방학 기간 동안 우리 학교에서 대대적인 청소를 실시하게 되었음을 알립니다.
The cleaning process will take a total of five days.
청소 과정은 총 5일이 소요될 것입니다.
The cleaning team will work hard to make sure every corner gets the cleaning it needs.
청소 팀은 모든 모서리에 청소가 필요한지 확인하기 위해서 열심히 해야 할 것입니다.
It'll cover all the classrooms, student lounge, library, and hallways.
이는 교실, 학생 라운지, 도서관, 복도도 포함합니다.
Please note that those areas will have restricted access, but only temporarily.
해당 지역은 일시적으로 출입이 제한될 예정입니다.
The detailed cleaning schedule will be posted on the school website.
자세한 청소 일정은 학교 홈페이지에 게시될 예정입니다.
Thank you.
감사합니다.

Why? 왜 정답일까?

여름방학 동안에 대청소를 실시한다고 알리고(**I'd like to inform you that our school will be undergoing a major cleaning during the upcoming summer break.**) 있으므로, 남자가 하는 말의 목적으로 가장 적절한 것은 ⑤ '여름 방학에 예정된 학교 청소를 공지하려고'이다.

- **vice principal** 교감
- **undergo** ⓥ 실시하다
- **upcoming** ⓐ 다가오는
- **restricted** ⓐ 제한된
- **inform** ⓥ 알리다
- **cleaning** ⓝ 청소
- **hallway** ⓝ 복도
- **temporarily** ad 일시적으로

02 책 내용을 기억하는 팁

정답률 94% | 정답 ⑤

대화를 듣고, 여자의 의견으로 가장 적절한 것을 고르시오.

① 편안한 환경은 책을 읽는 데 도움이 된다.
② 명확한 목적을 가지고 책을 선정해야 한다.
③ 문학 작품을 많이 읽으면 공감 능력이 커진다.
④ 일기 쓰기를 통해 지난 하루를 되돌아볼 수 있다.
✔ 독서 일기를 쓰면 책의 내용을 잘 기억할 수 있다.

M : Hey, Sujin! I heard you are a book enthusiast.
안녕, Sujin! 네가 책 애호가라고 들었어.
W : Yes, I really love reading. It's my favorite hobby.
응, 난 독서를 정말 좋아해. 내가 제일 좋아하는 취미야.
M : You must read a lot of books then. How many books do you read a year?
그럼 책을 많이 읽겠네. 1년에 몇 권의 책을 읽어?
W : Around a hundred books on average. Do you read a lot, too?
평균적으로 약 100권 정도. 너도 많이 읽어?
M : I read books from time to time, but it's not easy to remember what I read from books.
난 가끔 책을 읽지만, 책에서 읽은 것을 기억하는 건 쉽지 않아.
W : Oh, in that case, how about keeping a reading journal?
오, 그렇다면, 독서 일기를 쓰는 건 어때?
M : A reading journal? What is it?
독서 일기? 그게 뭐야?
W : It's like a diary. You can keep track of books and record impressive phrases from them.
일기 같은 거야. 책을 추적하고 인상적인 문구를 기록할 수 있어.
M : That sounds helpful. It seems like a good way to recall important information from any book.
도움이 될 것 같네. 책에서 중요한 정보를 기억할 수 있는 좋은 방법인 것 같아.
W : Exactly. That's why I strongly recommend keeping a reading journal.
그렇지. 내가 독서 일기를 쓰는 것을 매우 추천하는 이유야.
M : Thank you for sharing your tip. I'll give it a try.
팁을 공유해 줘서 고마워. 한번 해 볼게.

Why? 왜 정답일까?

독서 일기를 쓰면 책을 추적하고 인상적인 문구를 기억할 수 있다(**You can keep track of books and record impressive phrases from them.**)고 이야기하고 있으므로, 여자의 의견으로 가장 적절한 것은 ⑤ '독서 일기를 쓰면 책의 내용을 잘 기억할 수 있다.'이다.

- **enthusiast** ⓝ 애호가
- **journal** ⓝ 일기
- **impressive** ⓐ 인상적인
- **on average** 평균적으로
- **track** ⓥ 추적하다
- **phrase** ⓝ 절
- **recall** ⓥ 기억하다
- **recommend** ⓥ 추천하다
- **important** ⓐ 중요한

03 자투리 시간 활용

정답률 92% | 정답 ①

다음을 듣고, 남자가 하는 말의 요지로 가장 적절한 것을 고르시오.

✔ 일상생활 속 자투리 시간을 효율적으로 활용해야 한다.
② 창의성을 발휘하려면 적당한 휴식 시간을 가져야 한다.
③ 충분한 수면 시간은 집중력 향상에 도움이 된다.
④ 보행 중에 휴대전화를 사용하는 것은 위험하다.
⑤ 성과를 내기 위해서는 책을 많이 읽어야 한다.

M : Hello, class. Today, I'd like to talk about the book "*Your Life, Your Time.*"
안녕하세요, 수강생 여러분. 오늘은 '*당신의 인생, 당신의 시간*'이라는 책에 대해 이야기 해 보겠습니다.
The author emphasizes that the time available is the same for everyone, but how you use it is entirely up to you.
작가는 누구에게나 사용할 수 있는 시간은 다 똑같지만 어떻게 사용하는지는 전적으로 여러분께 달려있다고 강조하고 있습니다.
I strongly agree with the author's opinion.
전 작가의 의견에 매우 동의합니다.
Moments like waiting in a line, or riding the bus to school will add up.
줄을 기다리거나 학교에 가는 버스를 기다리는 순간들이 늘어날 것입니다.
Spending those in-between moments wisely is important.
이런 사이의 순간들을 현명하게 사용하는 것이 중요합니다.
Making use of spare time can significantly boost productivity.
여분 시간을 사용하는 것은 생산성을 크게 높일 수 있습니다.
Instead of wasting your time on your phone, use that time efficiently.
핸드폰으로 여러분의 시간을 낭비하는 것 대신, 시간을 효율적으로 사용하세요.
Time is yours to manage. Every bit of gap in time is an opportunity.
시간은 당신이 관리합니다. 시간 내의 모든 틈은 기회입니다.
You'll be surprised at how much you can accomplish throughout the day.
여러분은 하루 내내 여러분이 얼마나 성취할 수 있는지 놀랄 것입니다.
Now, let me share a passage from the book.
이제, 책의 구절을 공유해 드리겠습니다.

Why? 왜 정답일까?

여분 시간을 사용하면 생산성을 크게 높일 수 있다(**Making use of spare time can significantly boost productivity.**)고 이야기 하므로, 남자가 하는 말의 요지로 가장 적절한 것은 ① '일상생활 속 자투리 시간을 효율적으로 활용해야 한다.'이다.

- **emphasize** ⓥ 강조하다
- **entirely** ad 전적으로
- **efficiently** ad 효율적으로
- **passage** ⓝ 구절
- **available** ⓐ 이용 가능한, 이용할 수 있는
- **wisely** ad 현명하게
- **accomplish** ⓥ 성취하다

04 현대 미술 전시회 관람

정답률 89% | 정답 ④

대화를 듣고, 그림에서 대화의 내용과 일치하지 않는 것을 고르시오.

W : Ethan, how was the Modern Arts Exhibition you went to with your art club members?
Ethan, 미술 동아리 회원들과 같이 간 현대 미술 전시회는 어땠어?
M : It was really interesting. Would you like to see a picture of us there?
정말 흥미로웠어. 거기에 있는 우리 사진 한 장 볼래?
W : Sure. Is this you in the striped shirt?
물론. 줄무늬 셔츠 입은 사람이 너야?
M : Yes, and do you see the heart-shaped sculpture I'm pointing at?
응. 그리고 여기 내가 가리키고 있는 하트 모양의 조형물 보여?
W : Yeah, it's pretty.
응. 예쁘다.
M : It was the main piece. The theme of the exhibition was love.
이게 메인 작품이었어. 전시의 주제가 사랑이었거든.
W : I see. That's why there is lighting on the wall above the sculpture.
그렇구나. 그래서 이 조형물 위에 조명이 있는 거구나.
M : I also liked the painting on the wall. The circles in the painting reminded me of soap bubbles.
벽에 걸린 그림도 좋았어. 그림의 원이 비누 거품을 떠오르게 했거든.
W : That makes sense. What are the two benches in front of the painting for?
말이 되네. 그림 앞에 있는 두 개의 벤치는 무엇을 위한 거야?
M : Those are for the visitors to sit and rest.
그것들은 방문객들이 앉아서 쉬기 위한 거야.
W : Oh, I see. It looks like you had a great time. I want to go there, too.
오, 알겠어. 좋은 시간을 보낸 것 같네. 나도 거기 가고 싶어.
M : You should. You'll definitely like it.
가 봐. 분명 좋아할 거야.

Why? 왜 정답일까?

대화에서 벽에 걸린 그림에 원이 있다(**I also liked the painting on the wall. The circles in the painting reminded me of soap bubbles.**)고 했는데, 그림 속에는 사각형이 있다. 따라서 그림에서 대화의 내용과 일치하지 않는 것은 ④이다.

- **exhibition** ⓝ 전시회
- **sculpture** ⓝ 조형물
- **definitely** ad 분명히
- **striped** ⓐ 줄무늬의
- **wall** ⓝ 벽

[문제편 p.001]

05 학생 홍보대사 선발 준비
정답률 94% | 정답 ②

대화를 듣고, 여자가 할 일로 가장 적절한 것을 고르시오.

① 평가 기준 정하기
② 카메라 빌리기
③ 인터뷰 후보 선정하기
④ 지원서 검토하기
⑤ 인터뷰 장소 예약하기

W : Good morning, Mr. Jackson. How's the selection process for student ambassadors going?
좋은 아침입니다, Jackson씨. 학생 홍보대사 선발 절차는 어떻게 되어 가고 있나요?
M : Hello, Ms. Reed. It's going well. I'm trying to be as thorough as possible because the student ambassadors represent our school.
안녕하세요, Reed씨. 잘 진행되고 있습니다. 학생 홍보대사는 우리 학교를 대표하기 때문에 최대한 철저하게 하려고 노력하고 있습니다.
W : You're right. Is there anything I can help you with?
맞아요. 제가 도울 건 없을까요?
M : Let me check. I've already read through the applications, and selected the interview candidates.
확인해 볼게요. 이미 지원서를 읽고 면접 후보자를 선정했습니다.
W : Good. Did you set the criteria for the interview?
좋아요. 면접 기준은 정했나요?
M : Yes, certainly. Confidence and communication skills would be most important.
네, 물론입니다. 자신감과 커뮤니케이션 능력이 가장 중요할 것입니다.
W : Sounds perfect. Have you reserved a place for the interview?
완벽하네요. 면접 장소는 예약했나요?
M : Yeah, I reserved the student council room.
네, 학생회실을 예약했습니다.
W : Wow, you've done a lot. Is there anything else left to do?
와, 정말 많이 하셨네요. 다른 남은 할 일이 있나요?
M : Actually, we need a camera for the interview. Could you borrow one from the broadcasting club?
사실 면접을 위한 카메라가 필요합니다. 방송부에서 빌려주실 수 있나요?
W : Okay. I'll do that.
네, 제가 할게요.
M : Thanks.
감사합니다.

Why? 왜 정답일까?
두 사람은 학생 선발대회를 위해 준비 중인데 남자가 면접을 위한 카메라를 빌려 달라(**Actually, we need a camera for the interview. Could you borrow one from the broadcasting club?**)고 요청한다. 따라서 여자가 할 일로 가장 적절한 것은 ② '카메라 빌리기'이다.

- **ambassadors** ⓝ 홍보대사
- **application** ⓝ 지원서
- **reserve** ⓥ 예약하다
- **borrow** ⓥ 빌리다

06 동영상 스트리밍 서비스 구독
정답률 86% | 정답 ③

대화를 듣고, 남자가 지불할 금액을 고르시오. [3점]

① $54 ② $60 ③ $108 ④ $110 ⑤ $120

[Telephone rings.]
[전화가 울린다.]
W : Hello, this is StreamHub Services. How may I help you?
안녕하세요, StreamHub Services입니다. 무엇을 도와드릴까요?
M : Hi, I'd like to subscribe to your video streaming service. What options do you offer?
안녕하세요, 동영상 스트리밍 서비스를 구독하고 싶어요. 어떤 옵션이 있나요?
W : We have two plans. The basic plan is 5 dollars a month, and the premium plan is 10 dollars a month.
두 가지 요금제가 있습니다. 베이직 요금제는 월 5달러, 프리미엄 요금제는 월 10달러입니다.
M : What's the difference?
뭐가 다른가요?
W : With the basic plan, you can only watch on one device at a time. But with the premium plan, you can watch on up to four.
베이직 요금제는 한 번에 하나의 기기에서만 시청할 수 있습니다. 하지만 프리미엄 요금제는 최대 4대까지 시청 가능합니다.
M : I see. I'm going to use it with my family members, so I'll subscribe to the premium plan for one year.
알겠습니다. 가족과 함께 사용할 예정이니, 1년간 프리미엄 요금제를 구독하겠습니다.
W : In that case, we have a special deal. We offer a 10% discount on a 1-year subscription. But you have to pay for all twelve months at once.
이 경우 특별 할인이 있습니다. 1년 구독 시 10% 할인을 제공하고 있습니다. 하지만 12개월분을 한 번에 결제해야 합니다.
M : That's awesome! I'll pay for one year, now.
좋네요. 지금 바로 1년 치 결제할게요.
W : Great! Can you give me your credit card information?
좋습니다! 신용 카드 정보를 주시겠어요?
M : Sure. I'll go get it.
네, 가서 가져올게요.

Why? 왜 정답일까?
대화에 따르면 남자는 가족과 함께 사용하기 위해 프리미엄 요금제를 1년 동안 구독하기로 하였다. 월 10달러이므로 1년간 120달러이며 10% 할인 혜택을 받아 남자가 지불할 금액은 ③ '$108'이다.

- **subscribe** ⓥ 구독하다
- **offer** ⓥ 제공하다
- **at a time** 한 번에
- **credit card** 신용 카드

07 사내 주차 공간 문제
정답률 94% | 정답 ②

대화를 듣고, 여자가 자가용으로 출근하지 않은 이유를 고르시오.

① 버스 요금이 저렴해서
② 회사 주차 공간이 부족해서
③ 퇴근 후 헬스장에 가야 해서
④ 걷기 운동을 하기 위해서
⑤ 자동차 수리를 맡겨서

M : Kate, you look exhausted this morning. What happened?
Kate, 오늘 아침 피곤해 보이네요. 무슨 일 있어요?
W : Hi, Chris. I took a bus to work this morning. And it was jam-packed with people.
안녕하세요, Chris. 아침에 버스를 타고 출근했어요. 근데 사람들로 가득 찼었어요.
M : But don't you usually drive? Oh, wait, you said your car broke down, didn't you?
그런데 평소에는 운전을 하지 않나요? 오, 잠깐만요, 차가 고장 났다고 하셨었죠?
W : Yes, but I had it fixed recently.
네, 하지만 최근에 고쳤습니다.
M : Then, were you trying to walk more and get some exercise?
그럼, 더 많이 걷고 운동을 하려고 했나요?
W : No, these days I go to a fitness center. I'm already getting enough exercise.
아뇨, 요즘 헬스장에 갑니다. 이미 충분히 운동을 하고 있어요.
M : Then why didn't you drive to work today?
그럼 오늘 왜 차를 끌고 출근하지 않았나요?
W : Because parking has become a nightmare.
왜냐면 주차가 악몽이 되었기 때문이에요.
M : Really? Isn't there a parking lot for employees at our company?
정말요? 우리 회사에 직원들을 위한 주차장이 있지 않나요?
W : True, but it's not enough. If you arrive a little late, there are no parking spaces left.
네, 근데 충분하지 않아요. 만약 조금이라도 늦게 도착하면, 남은 주차공간이 없습니다.
M : Ah, that must be annoying. I hope your situation gets better soon.
아, 그거 정말 짜증나겠네요. 상황이 금방 나아지길 바라요.

Why? 왜 정답일까?
여자가 자가용으로 출근하지 않은 이유는 주차 공간이 충분하지 않기(**True, but it's not enough. If you arrive a little late, there are no parking spaces left.**) 때문이다. 따라서 답은 ② '회사 주차 공간이 부족해서'이다.

- **exhausted** ⓐ 피곤한, 지친
- **jam-packed** 가득 찬
- **nightmare** ⓝ 악몽

08 책 동아리 가입
정답률 96% | 정답 ⑤

대화를 듣고, Harmony in Pages에 관해 언급되지 않은 것을 고르시오.

① 가입 대상 ② 모임 일시 ③ 모임 장소
④ 활동 내용 ⑤ 활동 경비

M : Mina, are you still looking for a club to join?
Mina, 아직 가입할 동아리를 찾고 있어?
W : Yes. Do you have any suggestions?
응, 추천할 만한 게 있어?
M : I found a perfect club for you. It's called Harmony in Pages.
너를 위해 완벽한 동아리를 찾았어. Harmony in Pages라는 동아리야.
W : Harmony in Pages? What's that?
Harmony in Pages? 그게 뭔데?
M : 『It's a book club. Anyone can join as long as English is not their first language.』 ①의 근거 일치
책 동아리야. 영어가 모국어가 아니라면 누구나 가입할 수 있어.
W : That would be great for international students like me. When do they meet?
나 같은 유학생한테 정말 좋은 것 같은데. 언제 만나?
M : 『They meet every Monday at 4 p.m.』 ②의 근거 일치
매주 월요일 4시에 만나.
W : Awesome. I'm available on Mondays.
굉장해. 나 월요일에 가능해.
M : 『And they meet near our campus, at the Arden Park Library.』 ③의 근거 일치
그리고 캠퍼스 근처 Arden 공원 도서관에서 만나.
W : That's good. I can go right after my last class.
좋다. 마지막 수업이 끝나면 바로 갈 수 있어.
M : 『You know what? They also write book reviews in English with the help of native speakers as mentors.』 ④의 근거 일치
그거 알아? 그들은 원어민 멘토의 도움을 받아서 영어로 서평을 작성하기도 해.
W : Fantastic! Thanks for the information.
훌륭해! 정보 고마워.

Why? 왜 정답일까?
대화에서 남자와 여자는 행사에 관해 '가입 대상, 모임 일시, 모임 장소, 활동 내용'을 언급하므로, 언급되지 않은 것은 ⑤ '활동 경비'이다.

- **suggestion** ⓝ 추천, 제안
- **first language** 모국어
- **international** ⓐ 국제적인
- **meet** ⓥ 만나다
- **native speaker** 원어민

09 Healthy Heart Day
정답률 91% | 정답 ④

Healthy Heart Day에 관한 다음 내용을 듣고, 일치하지 않는 것을 고르시오.

① 3월 30일에 열릴 것이다.
② 심장에 좋은 음식과 음료를 제공할 것이다.
③ 방문자들은 자신의 혈압과 체온 등을 확인할 수 있다.
④ 사전 등록 없이 특별 강연을 들을 수 있다.
⑤ 퀴즈에 참여한 누구나 티셔츠를 받을 수 있다.

W : Are you interested in staying healthy?
건강을 유지하는 데 관심이 있나요?
I'm delighted to bring your attention to our upcoming Healthy Heart Day.
다가오는 Healthy Heart Day에 관심을 가져 주셔서 기쁩니다.
The Healthy Heart Day is a campaign to remind everyone to take care of their own heart. It will take place on March 30th at the public health center.
Healthy Heart Day는 모든 사람에게 자신의 심장을 돌보라고 상기시키는 캠페인입니다. 이는 3월 30일 보건소에서 개최됩니다.
We provide food and drinks that are good for your heart.
심장에 좋은 음식과 음료를 제공합니다.
You can check things related to your heart health, such as blood pressure, body temperature, and so on.
혈압, 체온 등 심장 건강과 관련된 것들을 확인할 수 있습니다.
You can also listen to a special lecture about a healthy heart, if you register in advance.
또한, 사전 등록하면 건강한 심장에 대한 특별 강연도 들을 수 있습니다.

[문제편 p.001]

Last but not least, there'll be a quiz for all visitors.
마지막으로, 모든 방문객을 위한 퀴즈가 있습니다.

Anyone who participates in the quiz can receive a T-shirt. We look forward to your visit.
퀴즈에 참여하는 사람은 누구나 티셔츠를 받을 수 있습니다. 여러분의 방문을 기대합니다.

Please check our website for more information.
자세한 내용은 웹사이트를 확인하세요.

Thank you.
감사합니다.

Why? 왜 정답일까?

사전에 등록하면 특별한 강연을 들을 수 있다(**You can also listen to a special lecture about a healthy heart, if you register in advance.**)고 이야기하고 있으므로, 내용과 일치하지 않는 것은 ④ '사전 등록 없이 특별 강연을 들을 수 있다.'이다.

- **be delighted to** ~해서 기쁘다
- **remind** ⓥ 상기시키다
- **upcoming** ⓐ 다가오는
- **in advance** 사전에

10 무선 마이크 고르기

정답률 90% | 정답 ③

다음 표를 보면서 대화를 듣고, 두 사람이 구매할 무선 마이크를 고르시오.

Wireless Microphones

	Model	Price	Color	Battery Life (hours)	LED light
①	A	$25	black	4	×
②	B	$25	white	4	○
✔③	C	$50	pink	6	○
④	D	$55	white	8	×
⑤	E	$75	pink	8	○

W : Honey, what are you looking at on your computer?
자기야, 컴퓨터에서 뭐 찾고 있어?

M : It's a website selling wireless microphones. I'm thinking of getting one for our son Jimmy's birthday present.
이건 무선 마이크를 판매하는 웹사이트야. 아들 Jimmy 생일 선물로 하나 살까 생각 중이야.

W : Oh, that sounds like a good idea. Do you want me to help you choose one?
오, 좋은 생각 같아 보이네. 내가 하나 골라 줄까?

M : Sure. There are five options here, and they all seem good.
물론. 여기 다섯 개의 옵션이 있는데, 다 좋아 보여.

W : Do you have a budget in mind?
생각해 둔 예산 있어?

M : 「Hmm... Let's not spend more than $60.」 근거1 Price 조건
음... 60달러 이상 쓰진 말자.

W : I agree. Which color should we choose? They come in three colors.
동의해. 어떤 색을 고를까? 세 가지 색이 나온대.

M : 「Well, anything but black. Jimmy prefers bright colors to dark ones.」 근거2 Color 조건
음, 검정 빼고 아무거나. Jimmy는 어두운 색보다 밝은 걸 선호해.

W : 「That's right. What about the battery life? I think 4 hours would be too short.」
맞아. 배터리 수명은 어때? 내 생각에 4시간은 많이 짧은 것 같은데. 근거3 Battery Life 조건

M : I agree. Let's buy one with a longer battery life.
동의해. 배터리 수명이 긴 걸 사자.

W : Good idea. Now, we're down to two. This microphone has an LED light. I heard it creates a cool visual effect.
좋은 생각이야. 이제 두 개로 줄였네. 이 마이크는 LED 불빛이 있어. 듣기로는 멋진 시각 효과를 만들어 낸다던데.

M : 「Really? Then, we should definitely get one with an LED light.」 근거4 LED light 조건
정말? 그럼, 반드시 LED 불빛이 있는 걸 사야겠네.

W : Okay. Let's go ahead and get this model.
그래. 그럼 이 모델로 하자.

Why? 왜 정답일까?

대화에 따르면 남자와 여자는 60달러 미만의, 검은색을 제외한, 배터리 수명이 4시간보다 길고, LED 불빛이 있는 마이크를 골랐다. 따라서 그들이 주문할 무선 마이크는 ③ 'C'이다.

- **wireless** ⓐ 무선의
- **bright** ⓐ 밝은
- **visual effect** 특수효과
- **budget** ⓝ 예산
- **dark** ⓐ 어두운

11 학생증 재발급 받기

정답률 65% | 정답 ③

대화를 듣고, 남자의 마지막 말에 대한 여자의 응답으로 가장 적절한 것을 고르시오.

① I'm sorry, but you can't use it as a credit card.
미안하지만 이걸 신용카드처럼 쓸 수 없어요.
② Yes, I think it'd be great to take a group photo here.
응, 내 생각에 여기서 단체 사진을 찍기 좋을 것 같아.
✔③ No need. You can have your photo taken on the spot.
필요 없어. 현장에서 사진을 찍을 수 있어.
④ Fortunately, I found my ID card at the Lost and Found.
운 좋게도, 분실물센터에서 학생증을 찾았어.
⑤ Right. The student services office doesn't reissue ID cards.
맞아. 학생 사무실에서는 학생증을 재발급해 주지 않아.

M : Rachel, I heard you got your student ID card reissued.
Rachel, 학생증을 재발급 받았다고 들었어.

W : Yeah, I lost my old one somewhere. So I went to the student services office and got a new one.
응, 어디에선가 예전 걸 잃어버렸어. 그래서 학생 사무실에 가서 새 걸 얻었어.

M : Actually, I lost mine too, so I need to go there. Do I need to bring my photo for a new ID card?
사실, 나도 잃어버렸어. 그래서 그 곳에 가야 해. 새 학생증을 받으려면 사진을 갖고 가야 할까?

W : No need. You can have your photo taken on the spot.
필요 없어. 현장에서 사진을 찍을 수 있어.

Why? 왜 정답일까?

남자도 **Rachel**처럼 학생증을 잃어버려서 재발급 받아야 하는 상황이다. 새 학생증을 받기 위해 사진을 가져가야 하는(**Actually, I lost mine too, so I need to go there. Do I need to bring my photo for a new ID card?**) 물어보고 있으므로, 여자의 응답으로 가장 적절한 것은 ③ '필요 없어. 현장에서사진을 찍을 수 있어.'이다.

- **reissue** ⓥ 재발급하다
- **on the spot** 현장에서

12 운전 중 휴식

정답률 53% | 정답 ②

대화를 듣고, 여자의 마지막 말에 대한 남자의 응답으로 가장 적절한 것을 고르시오.

① It wasn't easy. It took over three hours to get there. – 그건 쉽지 않아. 가는데 세 시간이 걸렸어.
✔② You're right. Let's pull over at the next rest area. – 맞아. 다음 휴게소에 차를 세우자.
③ No problem. I got my car fixed before the trip. – 문제없어. 여행 전에 차를 고쳤어.
④ Careful! You shouldn't go over the speed limit. – 조심해! 속도 제한을 넘으면 안 돼.
⑤ Okay. I can take over driving after the break. – 좋아. 휴식 다음에 내가 운전 할게.

W : Honey, you've been driving for over two hours. Why don't we take a break?
여보, 두 시간 넘게 운전 중이야. 쉬는 게 어때?

M : It's okay. I'm not so tired yet.
괜찮아. 아직 피곤하진 않아.

W : Still, it's better to take a rest after every two hours of driving.
그래도, 운전할 때 두 시간마다 휴식을 취하는 것이 좋아.

M : You're right. Let's pull over at the next rest area.
맞아. 다음 휴게소에 차를 세우자.

Why? 왜 정답일까?

여자는 남자에게 운전한 지 두 시간이 넘었으므로 쉴 것을 제안(**Still, it's better to take a rest after every two hours of driving.**)하고 있다. 따라서 남자의 응답으로 가장 적절한 것은 ② '맞아. 다음 휴게소에 차를 세우자.'이다.

- **take a break** 쉬다
- **tired** ⓐ 피곤한

13 세미나를 위한 커피 주문

정답률 91% | 정답 ①

대화를 듣고, 남자의 마지막 말에 대한 여자의 응답으로 가장 적절한 것을 고르시오. [3점]

Woman: ____________

✔① Sure. I will send it to you right away.
네, 바로 보내드리겠습니다.
② I'm afraid we only have fruit juice and tea.
유감이지만 과일 주스랑 차만 있습니다.
③ I'm sorry that you're not satisfied with our service.
서비스에 만족하지 못하셨다니 죄송합니다.
④ Okay. I'll let you know the new date of our seminar.
네, 세미나의 새 날짜를 알려드릴게요.
⑤ Good. Let's order some drinks using the delivery service.
좋아요. 배달 서비스를 이용해서 음료를 주문합시다.

[Telephone rings.]
[전화가 울린다.]

W : Hello, this is Green Coffee Truck. How may I help you?
안녕하세요, Green Coffee Truck입니다. 무엇을 도와드릴까요?

M : Hello, I recently reserved a coffee truck for an upcoming seminar next week. We'd like to ask for a change.
안녕하세요, 최근 다음 주에 있을 세미나를 위해 커피 트럭을 예약했습니다. 변경을 요청하고 싶습니다.

W : Oh, may I have your name, please?
아, 이름을 말씀해 주시겠어요?

M : It's William from Ridgestone University.
Ridgestone 대학의 William입니다.

W : *[Typing sound]* You made a reservation for 100 people on March 25th, right?
[타자치는 소리] 3월 25일에 100명 예약하셨죠?

M : Correct. But more people are coming, so we'd like to increase our coffee order to 150 people. Would that be possible?
맞습니다. 하지만 더 많은 사람이 오기 때문에 커피 주문을 150명으로 늘리고 싶습니다. 가능할까요?

W : Absolutely. The total amount would be $550.
물론입니다. 총 550달러입니다.

M : Really? We can only afford $500 for this event. Could you possibly lower the price?
정말요? 우리는 이 행사를 위해 500달러만 쓸 수 있어요. 가격을 낮춰 주실 수 있나요?

W : Hmm... Since your school has been a loyal customer, we can handle it.
음... 당신의 학교는 충성 고객이기 때문에, 저희가 처리할 수 있습니다.

M : Thank you so much. Please send the new bill to my email.
감사합니다. 이메일로 새 청구서를 보내주세요.

W : Sure. I will send it to you right away.
네, 바로 보내드리겠습니다.

Why? 왜 정답일까?

남자는 세미나를 위해 준비한 커피 주문을 늘리고 새 청구서를 받고자(**Thank you so much. Please send the new bill to my email.**)한다. 따라서 여자의 응답으로 가장 적절한 것은 ① '네, 바로 보내드리겠습니다.'이다.

- **afford** ⓥ 여유가 되다
- **handle** ⓥ 처리하다, 다루다
- **loyal** ⓐ 충성스러운

14 일일 베이킹 수업

정답률 89% | 정답 ③

대화를 듣고, 여자의 마지막 말에 대한 남자의 응답으로 가장 적절한 것을 고르시오.

Man: ____________

① I'm sorry, but I'm not that interested in baking.
죄송하지만 베이킹에 흥미가 없어요.
② Think twice. We already have an oven at home.
두 번 생각해 보세요. 이미 집에 오븐이 있잖아요.
✔③ Fantastic! Then I can try more recipes at home.
멋진데요! 그럼 제가 집에서 레시피를 더 시도해 볼게요.
④ Well, thank you for inviting me to your baking class.
음, 베이킹 수업에 초대해 주셔서 감사합니다.
⑤ Oh, no! I forgot to bring you some cookies and muffins.
안돼요! 쿠키랑 머핀을 갖고 오는 걸 깜빡했어요.

[문제편 p.002]

W : How was the one-day baking class today, sweetheart?
오늘 일일 베이킹 수업은 어땠니, 아가?
M : It was amazing, Mom! I made cookies and muffins there.
정말 좋았어요, 엄마! 거기서 쿠키랑 머핀을 만들었어요.
W : That's awesome! You've always wanted to try baking, right?
정말 놀랍구나! 항상 베이킹을 해 보고 싶어 했잖아, 그렇지?
M : Exactly. It was a really good hands-on experience.
네, 정말 좋은 실습 경험이었어요.
W : Wasn't it challenging? It was your first time baking.
어렵진 않았니? 베이킹은 처음이었잖아.
M : No, not at all. All the ingredients were prepared, and the teacher was there to help us step by step.
아뇨, 전혀요. 모든 재료가 준비되어 있었고, 거기 계신 선생님이 하나씩 우리를 도와주셨어요.
W : How did it turn out?
어떤 결과가 나왔니?
M : Well, do you want to try some? I made plenty and brought some for you.
음, 좀 드셔보실래요? 엄마를 위해 많이 만들어서 가지고 왔어요.
W : Of course! *[Pause]* They're so delicious! You really have a talent for baking.
물론! *[일시정지]* 정말 맛있구나! 베이킹에 정말 재능이 있네.
M : Thanks. I became more interested in baking after the class. I wish we had an oven at home.
감사해요. 수업 이후에 베이킹에 대해 관심이 더 많아졌어요. 집에 오븐이 있었으면 좋겠어요.
W : Then let's get a mini-oven for the kitchen so you can keep practicing baking.
그럼 베이킹 연습을 계속할 수 있게 주방에 미니 오븐을 사자!
M : Fantastic! Then I can try more recipes at home.
멋진데요! 그럼 제가 집에서 레시피를 더 시도해 볼게요.

Why? 왜 정답일까?

처음 일일 베이킹 수업에 다녀온 남자는 이후 베이킹에 관심을 더 가지고 있다. 이에 여자는 연습을 위해 미니 오븐을 사자고 제안한다(**Then let's get a mini-oven for the kitchen so you can keep practicing baking.**). 남자의 응답으로 가장 적절한 것은 ③ '멋진데요! 그럼 제가 집에서 레시피를 더 시도해 볼게요.'이다.

- **hands-on** 실습의
- **ingredient** ⓝ 재료

15 학생 회의 의제 정답률 88% | 정답 ①

다음 상황 설명을 듣고, Taylor가 교장 선생님에게 할 말로 가장 적절한 것을 고르시오. [3점]

Taylor: ______________________

✔ Could you set up a bike parking station at school?
학교에 자전거 주차장을 설치해 주시겠습니까?
② Can we use the gym for the student council event?
학생회 행사를 위해 체육관을 사용해도 될까요?
③ Can you install a charging station for electric bikes?
전기 자전거를 위한 충전소를 설치해 주실 수 있나요?
④ Is it okay to include a bike tour during the field trip?
현장학습에 자전거 투어를 포함해도 될까요?
⑤ Could you repair the broken lockers inside the classrooms?
교실 내 망가진 사물함을 수리해 주시겠어요?

M : Taylor is the student president at Cleef High School.
Taylor는 Cleef 고등학교의 학생회장입니다.
During the student council meeting, a council member says that students are having some trouble regarding their bikes.
학생 회의에서, 학생회 회원이 학생들이 자전거에 관해 문제를 가지고 있다고 말했습니다.
Although many students ride their bikes to school, there is no space to park them.
많은 학생들이 학교에 자전거를 타고 오지만, 그것들을 주차할 공간이 없습니다.
So, many bikes are randomly parked, or some of them are even left lying around on the ground.
그래서, 많은 자전거들이 무작위로 주차되어 있거나 땅에 누워있습니다.
This raises safety issues as it might cause students to trip and get hurt.
이로 인해 학생들이 넘어져 다칠 수 있기 때문에 안전 문제가 발생할 수 있습니다.
Also, bikes might get stolen during the school hours as they're not locked up.
또한, 자전거가 잠겨 있지 않아, 학교 수업 내에 도난당할 수도 있습니다.
So, Taylor decides to ask Mr. Benson, the school principal, for a place to park the bikes at school.
그래서, Taylor는 학교 교장선생님인 Benson에게 학교에 자전거를 주차할 공간에 대해 물어보기로 결심했습니다.
In this situation, what would Taylor most likely say to Mr. Benson?
이 상황에서, Taylor는 Benson 선생님에게 뭐라고 말할 가능성이 가장 높을까요?
Taylor : Could you set up a bike parking station at school?
학교에 자전거 주차장을 설치해 주시겠습니까?

Why? 왜 정답일까?

상황에 따르면 학생회장인 **Taylor**는 학생들을 대표하여 학교 내 자전거 주차 공간이 없는 것에 대해 교장 선생님께 건의하고자(**So, Taylor decides to ask Mr. Benson, the school principal, for a place to park the bikes at school.**) 한다. 따라서 **Taylor**가 **Benson**에게 할 말로 가장 적절한 것은 ① '학교에 자전거 주차장을 설치해 주시겠습니까?'이다.

- **park** ⓥ 주차하다
- **lie** ⓥ 누워 있다

16-17 뇌에 좋은 음식들

W: Hello, students.
안녕하세요, 학생 여러분.
「Did you know that what we eat plays a huge role in the health of our brains?」
우리가 먹는 음식이 뇌 건강에 큰 역할을 한다는 사실을 알고 있나요? 16번의 근거
「While avocados often get a bad reputation because of their high fat content, it's important to note that they have "good" kinds of fats.」 17번 ①의 근거 일치
아보카도는 지방 함량이 높아서 종종 나쁜 평판을 받지만, 아보카도에는 "좋은" 지방이 있다는 점에 유의하는 것이 중요합니다.
These fats have been shown to lower rates of cognitive decline.
이러한 지방은 인지 기능의 저하율을 낮추는 것으로 나타났습니다.
「If you like fish, get excited, because salmon is one of the best brain foods out there!」
만약 생선을 좋아한다면 기뻐하세요. 왜냐하면 연어는 최고의 두뇌음식 중 하나이기 때문이죠! 17번 ②의 근거 일치
It's packed with omega-3s to help keep your brain running smoothly.
오메가 3가 함유되어 있어서 두뇌가 원활하게 움직이는 데 도움이 됩니다.
「And your mom got it right when she told you to eat your broccoli.」 17번 ④의 근거 일치
그리고 당신에게 브로콜리를 먹으라고 하는 당신의 엄마가 옳았습니다.
Broccoli is one of the best brain-healthy foods thanks to its high levels of vitamin K, which can help keep your memory sharp.
브로콜리는 기억력을 선명하게 유지하는 데 도움이 되는 비타민 K의 함량이 높아, 최고의 뇌 건강식품 중 하나입니다.
「Finally, just a few walnuts a day may help improve your cognitive health and mental alertness.」 17번 ⑤의 근거 일치
마지막으로, 하루에 호두 몇 개만 섭취하는 것은 인지 건강과 정신적 각성을 개선하는 데 도움이 될 수 있습니다.
The vitamin E found in walnuts may help protect brain cells.
호두에서 발견되는 비타민 E는 뇌 세포를 보호하는 데 도움이 될 수 있습니다.
Enjoy these healthy brain foods and boost your brain power!
건강한 두뇌 음식을 즐기고 두뇌 능력을 향상시키세요!

- **play a role** 역할을 하다
- **reputation** ⓝ 평판
- **content** ⓝ 함량
- **cognitive** ⓐ 인지적인
- **alertness** ⓝ 각성

16 주제 파악 정답률 94% | 정답 ⑤

여자가 하는 말의 주제로 가장 적절한 것은?

① benefits of taking in raw foods – 날 음식 섭취의 이점
② the most globally used ingredients – 가장 세계적으로 사용되는 재료
③ dangers of consuming too much fat – 너무 많은 지방을 섭취하는 것의 위험성
④ different food cultures around the world – 전 세계의 다양한 음식 문화
✔ healthy foods for improving brain functions – 뇌 기능을 개선하기 위한 건강한 음식

Why? 왜 정답일까?

여자는 뇌 건강에 좋은 음식에 대해 이야기하고자(**Did you know that what we eat plays a huge role in the health of our brains?**) 하며 다양한 예시를 언급하고 있다. 따라서 여자가 하는 말의 주제로 가장 적절한 것은 ⑤ '뇌 기능을 개선하기 위한 건강한 음식'이다.

17 언급 유무 파악 정답률 86% | 정답 ③

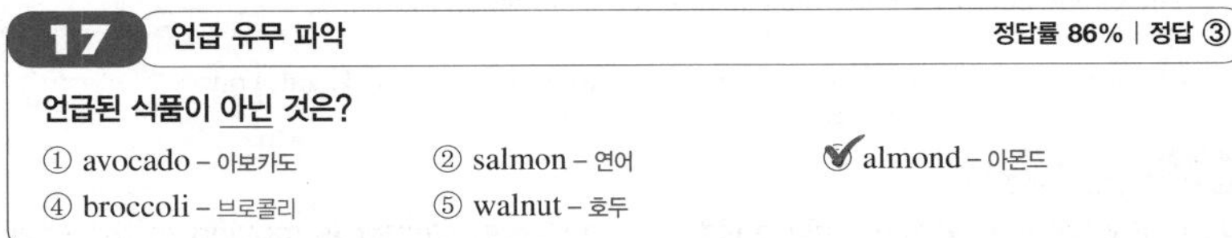

언급된 식품이 아닌 것은?

① avocado – 아보카도 ② salmon – 연어 ✔ almond – 아몬드
④ broccoli – 브로콜리 ⑤ walnut – 호두

Why? 왜 정답일까?

담화에서 여자는 뇌에 좋은 음식에 대한 예시로 '아보카도, 연어, 브로콜리, 호두'를 언급하고 있으며, 언급되지 않은 것은 ③ '아몬드'이다.

Why? 왜 오답일까?

① '**While avocados often get a bad reputation because of their high fat content, it's important to note that they have "good" kinds of fats.**'에서 '아보카도'가 언급되었다.
② '**If you like fish, get excited, because salmon is one of the best brain foods out there!**'에서 '연어'가 언급되었다.
④ '**And your mom got it right when she told you to eat your broccoli.**'에서 '브로콜리'가 언급되었다.
⑤ '**Finally, just a few walnuts a day may help improve your cognitive health and mental alertness.**'에서 '호두'가 언급되었다.

Dictation 01

문제편 003쪽

01 I'd like to inform you / every corner gets the cleaning / will be posted on the school website
02 you are a book enthusiast / what I read from books / I'll give it a try
03 emphasizes that the time available is / it is entirely up to you / how much you can accomplish
04 the heart-shaped sculpture I'm pointing at / on the wall above the sculpture / reminded me of soap bubbles
05 for student ambassadors going / I've already read through the applications / would be most important
06 What options do you offer / all twelve months at once / I'll go get it
07 you look exhausted / it was jam-packed with people / your situation gets better
08 Anyone can join as long as / I'm available on / You know what
09 I'm delighted to bring / related to your heart health / who participates in the quiz
10 want me to help you choose / have a budget in mind / prefers bright colors to dark
11 got your student ID card reissued / lost my old one somewhere
12 you've been driving for over / every two hours of driving
13 You made a reservation for / Would that be possible / Since your school has been
14 good hands-on experience / Wasn't it challenging / we had an oven at home
15 are randomly parked / might get stolen / as they're not locked up
16-17 their high fat content / have been shown to / just a few walnuts a day

| 정답과 해설 |

02 회 | 2023학년도 3월 학력평가 고3

• 정답 •

01 ③ 02 ② 03 ① 04 ③ 05 ⑤ 06 ④ 07 ② 08 ② 09 ④ 10 ② 11 ⑤ 12 ② 13 ⑤ 14 ⑤ 15 ② 16 ① 17 ③

01 진로 센터 이전 안내

정답률 85% | 정답 ③

다음을 듣고, 여자가 하는 말의 목적으로 가장 적절한 것을 고르시오.

① 진로 상담 신청을 독려하려고
② 진로 센터 프로그램을 홍보하려고
✔ 진로 센터 이전에 관해 안내하려고
④ 진로 상담 신청 절차를 설명하려고
⑤ 진로 센터 운영 시간 연장을 공지하려고

W : Good morning, students. I'm Career Coach Anne Talbot.
안녕하세요, 학생 여러분. 저는 진로 상담 교사 Anne Talbot입니다.
I have important news for you.
여러분을 위한 중요 뉴스가 있습니다.
Currently located at the main building, the Career Center is moving to the new library building.
현재 본관에 위치한 진로 센터가 새로운 도서관 건물로 이전할 예정입니다.
In preparation for the move, the Career Center will be closed on Monday, April 17, through Friday, April 21.
이사 준비를 위해, 진로 센터는 4월 17일 월요일부터 4월 21일 금요일까지 폐관합니다.
It'll reopen for business on Monday, April 24.
4월 24일 월요일에 다시 문을 열 것입니다.
All services offered at the present location will still be available at the new location.
현재 위치에서 제공되는 서비스는 새로운 위치에서도 여전히 이용 가능합니다.
The phone number for the relocated office will remain the same.
이사하는 사무실의 전화번호도 그대로 유지됩니다.
Please visit the Career Center website for more information. Thank you.
더 많은 정보를 얻으려면, 진로 센터 웹 사이트를 방문해 주세요. 고맙습니다.

Why? 왜 정답일까?

'**Currently located at the main building, the Career Center is moving to the new library building.**'에서 여자는 원래 본관에 있던 진로 센터가 도서관 건물로 이전할 예정임을 공지하고 있다. 따라서 여자가 하는 말의 목적으로 가장 적절한 것은 ③ '진로 센터 이전에 관해 안내하려고'이다.

• in preparation for ~을 대비하여
• available ⓐ 이용 가능한

02 과대 포장 밀키트 업체 피하기

정답률 81% | 정답 ②

대화를 듣고, 남자의 의견으로 가장 적절한 것을 고르시오.

① 과대 포장은 밀키트 가격 상승의 주요 원인이다.
✔ 과대 포장을 하는 밀키트 배달 서비스 이용을 피해야 한다.
③ 환경 보호를 위해 재활용할 수 있는 포장재를 사용해야 한다.
④ 고객 후기가 많은 배달 서비스를 이용하는 것이 좋다.
⑤ 음식의 맛과 질을 기준으로 밀키트를 선택해야 한다.

M : Hi, Paula. What are you doing on your smartphone?
안녕, Paula. 너 스마트폰으로 뭐 해?
W : Hi, Ethan. I'm searching for meal kit delivery services. I'm so busy that I need to save time and effort to cook.
안녕, Ethan. 난 밀키트 배송 서비스를 검색하고 있어. 너무 바빠서 요리할 시간과 노력을 아껴야 하거든.
M : Good idea. Did you find anything good?
좋은 생각이네. 뭐 좋은 거 찾았어?
W : Yes, this one is my pick. Take a look.
어, 이게 내가 고른 거야. 한번 봐봐.
M : Oh, it's Mama's Meals. Actually I've used them before, but I wouldn't recommend them.
오, 여기 Mama's Meals잖아. 사실 나 전에 써봤는데, 여기 추천하지 않아.
W : Why? They got the most reviews from the customers. Their food tastes good and is pretty high quality.
왜? 고객 평이 제일 많던데. 음식이 맛있고 꽤 품질이 좋대.
M : I know. But they use too much packaging for deliveries.
알지. 그런데 거긴 배송에 포장재를 너무 많이 써.
W : What's the matter with that? I believe multi-layered packaging is necessary for food delivery.
그게 무슨 문제야? 음식 배송에 여러 겹 포장은 필수라고 생각해.
M : To some extent, but that company uses too many unnecessary boxes and plastic containers for packaging.
어느 정도야 그렇지. 그런데 이 회사는 불필요한 상자와 플라스틱 용기를 포장에 너무 많이 써.
W : That could be a problem for the environment. That's good to know.
그건 환경에 문제가 될 수 있겠네. 알게 돼서 다행이야.
M : That's why I don't use over-packaged delivery services. You should avoid them too.
그래서 내가 과포장 배송 서비스를 이용하지 않는 거지. 너도 피하는 게 좋을 거야.
W : Okay, I'll keep that in mind.
알겠어. 명심할게.

Why? 왜 정답일까?

남자는 여자가 주문할 예정이었던 밀키트 배달 업체를 추천하지 않는다면서 그 이유로 과대 포장을 언급하고 있다(~ **that company uses too many unnecessary boxes and plastic containers for packaging. / You should avoid them too.**). 따라서 남자의 의견으로 가장 적절한 것은 ② '과대 포장을 하는 밀키트 배달 서비스 이용을 피해야 한다.'이다.

• multi-layered ⓐ 여러 겹의
• container ⓝ 그릇, 용기

03 엘리베이터 고장 알려주기

정답률 84% | 정답 ①

대화를 듣고, 두 사람의 관계를 가장 잘 나타낸 것을 고르시오.

✔ 주민 – 경비원
② 손님 – 가게 점원
③ 배달 기사 – 식당 주인
④ 야영객 – 캠프장 관리인
⑤ 건축가 – 엘리베이터 설치업자

W : Good afternoon, Mr. Smith.
안녕하세요, Smith 씨.
M : Good afternoon, Mrs. Peterson. Your shopping bags look very heavy.
안녕하세요, Peterson 씨. 장바구니가 엄청 무거워 보이네요.
W : Yeah, I did a lot of grocery shopping today. We're having a barbecue this weekend.
네, 오늘 장을 많이 봤어요. 이번 주말에 저희 바비큐를 해 먹거든요.
M : That sounds fun, but I'm really sorry to tell you that the elevator to your house isn't working right now.
재미있겠네요. 그런데 정말 죄송하지만 댁까지 가는 엘리베이터가 지금 작동을 안 해요.
W : Oh no. I can't walk up the stairs to the 20th floor with these bags. When will it be fixed?
오 이런. 이 가방을 다 들고 20층까지 갈 순 없어요. 언제 고쳐지나요?
M : I've just called the maintenance service, and they'll be here within an hour.
정비 서비스에 방금 전화를 했고, 한 시간 안에 온대요.
W : I hope it won't take too long to get it fixed.
수리하는 데 얼마 안 걸렸으면 좋겠네요.
M : Well, it'll take at least one or two more hours. Can I help you with your shopping bags?
음, 적어도 한두 시간 넘게 걸릴 거예요. 제가 장바구니 좀 들어드릴까요?
W : Thank you, but I think you'd better stay here. Other residents may need your help.
고맙습니다만 여기 계시는 게 좋을 거 같아요. 다른 주민이 당신의 도움을 받아야 할지도 모르니까요.
M : You're right. Why don't you leave your shopping bags here? You can take them when the elevator is working again.
맞는 말씀이네요. 여기다 장바구니를 두고 가시는 게 어떨겠어요? 엘리베이터가 다시 작동하면 가져가시고요.
W : That'd be great. Thanks.
좋네요. 감사합니다.
M : You're welcome.
천만에요.

Why? 왜 정답일까?

'**I'm really sorry to tell you that the elevator to your house isn't working right now.**', '**I can't walk up the stairs to the 20th floor with these bags.**', '**I've just called the maintenance service, ~**', '**~ you'd better stay here. Other residents may need your help.**' 등에서 20층 주민인 여자에게 경비원인 남자가 엘리베이터 고장을 알리고 필요한 도움을 제안하고 있음을 알 수 있다. 따라서 두 사람의 관계로 가장 적절한 것은 ① '주민 – 경비원'이다.

• do grocery shopping 장을 보다
• maintenance ⓝ 정비, 유지, 보수

04 북카페 사진 구경하기

정답률 88% | 정답 ③

대화를 듣고, 그림에서 대화의 내용과 일치하지 않는 것을 고르시오.

M : Sally, have a look at this photo. This is the book café I visited over the weekend.
Sally, 이 사진 좀 봐. 여긴 내가 주말에 들렀던 북카페야.
W : It looks nice and cozy. It's Candy's Book Café right?
근사하고 아늑해 보이네. 여기 Candy's Book Café지?
M : Yeah. How did you know that?
맞아. 어떻게 알았어?
W : Look here. 「I can tell from the sign above the arched door.」 ①의 근거 일치
여기 봐. 여기 아치 모양 문 위에 있는 간판을 보면 알지.
M : Aha! 「What I liked about the café was the light above the table.」 It was nice to read there. ②의 근거 일치
아하! 내가 이 카페에서 좋았던 건 테이블 위 조명이야. 거기서 책을 읽기 좋더라고.
W : I bet. 「I see two chairs by the window.」 Was the view good?
그러게. 창문 옆에 의자 두 개도 있네. 전망 좋았어? ③의 근거 불일치
M : Yes. It was great to look out the window while reading.
응. 독서하면서 창밖을 보니 좋더라.
W : 「Look at this rug on the floor. It looks like a book.」 ④의 근거 일치
바닥에 있는 이 러그 좀 봐. 책처럼 생겼어.
M : It's nice. You know there're a lot of books in the café. And, for some books you have to use a ladder to reach them.
멋지네. 너도 알다시피 카페 안에 책이 많더라고. 그리고, 어떤 책은 꺼내려면 사다리를 써야 해.
W : 「So that's why this ladder is leaning against the bookcase.」 ⑤의 근거 일치
그래서 여기 이 사다리가 책장에 기대어져 있구나.
M : Yes. You should go there sometime. It's worth a visit.
응. 언제 한번 가봐. 가볼 만해.
W : Sure.
그래.

Why? 왜 정답일까?

대화에 따르면 창문 옆에 의자가 두 개 있다(**I see two chairs by the window.**)고 하는데, 그림 속 의자는 한 개뿐이다. 따라서 그림에서 대화의 내용과 일치하지 않는 것은 ③이다.

• cozy ⓐ 아늑한, 안락한
• arched ⓐ 아치 모양의
• ladder ⓝ 사다리
• lean against ~에 기대다

[문제편 p.007]

05 장학금 수여식 준비하기

정답률 78% | 정답 ⑤

대화를 듣고, 남자가 여자를 위해 할 일로 가장 적절한 것을 고르시오.

① 꽃집에 전화하기
② 현수막 설치하기
③ 좌석 배치도 붙이기
④ 마이크 작동 여부 확인하기
⑤ 커버에 장학 증서 끼우기

M : Ms. Parker, you look busy today.
Parker 선생님, 오늘 바빠 보이시네요.
W : Yes, Mr. Thompson. You know the scholarship award ceremony is in the afternoon.
네, Thompson 선생님. 아시다시피 장학금 수여식이 오늘 오후에 있어요.
M : Oh, right. So, is everything all set?
오, 그러네요. 준비 다 되셨나요?
W : Almost. I've just been to the auditorium for the final check-up. The banner is set up, and the microphones are working properly.
거의 다 됐어요. 마지막 점검을 하려고 방금 강당에 다녀왔어요. 현수막이 설치됐고, 마이크도 잘 작동하고 있어요.
M : Good. Did you put up the seating chart?
좋네요. 좌석 배치도를 놔두셨어요?
W : Yes, I posted it at the entrance. I also printed out all the certificates. I just have to put them into these certificate covers.
네, 입구에 붙여놨어요. 그리고 장학 증서도 다 출력해 뒀어요. 이 커버 안에 끼워넣기만 하면 돼요.
M : Each student will get a bunch of flowers along with their certificate, right?
학생들 모두 장학 증서와 함께 꽃다발을 받게 되는 거죠, 맞죠?
W : Oh, that's right. I ordered the flowers and they should've been here by now.
오, 맞아요. 제가 꽃을 시켜놔서 지금쯤 왔어야 하는데요.
M : You'd better check with the flower shop. I can put the certificates into the covers for you.
꽃집에 확인해보시는 게 좋겠어요. 제가 증서들을 커버에 끼워둘게요.
W : Will you? I'd appreciate it. I'll call and ask about the flowers.
그래주실래요? 고마워요. 전 전화해서 꽃 좀 물어볼게요.
M : Okay.
알겠어요.

Why? 왜 정답일까?

장학금 수여식을 준비 중인 여자가 아직 배달되지 않은 꽃의 행방을 확인하는 사이 남자는 여자를 대신해 장학 증서를 커버 안에 끼우고 있겠다(**I can put the certificates into the covers for you.**)고 말한다. 따라서 남자가 할 일로 가장 적절한 것은 ⑤ '커버에 장학 증서 끼우기'이다.

- **scholarship** ⓝ 장학금
- **auditorium** ⓝ 강당
- **certificate** ⓝ 증서, 자격증
- **be all set** 준비가 다 되다
- **entrance** ⓝ 입구

06 맞춤 케이크 주문하기

정답률 85% | 정답 ④

대화를 듣고, 여자가 지불할 금액을 고르시오.

① $35 ② $40 ③ $45 ④ $50 ⑤ $55

M : Hello, welcome to Jay's Cake Shop. How may I help you?
Jay's Cake Shop에 잘 오셨습니다. 무엇을 도와드릴까요?
W : Hi, I'd like to order a customized cake for my son's birthday.
안녕하세요, 제 아들 생일을 위해 맞춤 케이크를 주문하려고요.
M : Okay, we start from $30.
그러시군요, 금액은 30달러부터 시작합니다.
W : Good. Can you make it look like a basketball?
좋네요. 농구공 모양으로 만들어주실 수 있나요?
M : Sure, but you have to pay an additional $10.
물론이죠, 하지만 추가 금액 10달러를 지불하셔야 합니다.
W : That's reasonable.
적당한 가격이네요.
M : Do you want to add any decorations to the cake? They're $5 each.
케이크에 장식 추가도 원하시나요? 하나에 5달러입니다.
W : I'd like to have a trophy and a boy on top.
위쪽에 트로피랑 남자아이 하나를 넣겠어요.
M : That means you're adding two decorations.
그러면 장식을 두 개 추가하시는 거군요.
W : That's right. I want to get the cake this Saturday. Is that possible?
맞아요. 케이크는 이번 주 토요일에 받고 싶어요. 가능할까요?
M : Yes, it is. Do you want to have it delivered? It'll cost $5.
네. 배송해 드릴까요? 5달러입니다.
W : No, I'll come pick it up. Here's my credit card.
아니요, 제가 와서 가져갈게요. 여기 제 신용카드요.

Why? 왜 정답일까?

남자는 아들의 생일을 위해 30달러부터 시작하는 맞춤 케이크를 주문하는데, 농구공 모양으로 제작을 의뢰해서 10달러, 하나당 5달러짜리 장식을 2개 추가해서 10달러가 각각 추가되었다. 5달러짜리 배송 서비스는 이용하지 않았다. 이를 식으로 나타내면 '$30+10+(5\times2)=50$'이므로, 남자가 지불할 금액은 ④ '$50'이다.

- **customize** ⓥ 맞춤 제작하다

07 피트니스 센터 회원권을 갱신하지 않는 이유

정답률 94% | 정답 ②

대화를 듣고, 남자가 피트니스 센터 회원권을 갱신하지 않는 이유를 고르시오.

① 회원권이 너무 비싸서
② 테니스 수업을 받기로 해서
③ 당분간 운동을 할 수 없어서
④ 개인 지도 프로그램이 없어서
⑤ 시설이 더 좋은 곳으로 옮기고 싶어서

W : Jacob, are you still working out at the fitness center?
Jacob, 너 여전히 피트니스 센터에서 운동해?
M : Yes, Laura. It's been almost a year since I signed up there. My one-year membership ends next week.
응, Laura. 내가 거기 등록한 지 거의 1년이 다 됐어. 내 1년 회원권이 다음 주에 끝나.
W : Are you going to renew it?
갱신할 거야?
M : No, I decided not to.
아니, 안 그러기로 했어.
W : Why? Is it because the membership is too expensive?
왜? 회원권이 너무 비싸서?
M : Not really. It's quite cheap if you don't get personal training.
그건 아냐. PT를 받지 않으면 꽤 싸.
W : Then, are you going to move to another fitness center with better facilities?
그럼, 시설이 더 나은 다른 피트니스 센터로 옮길 계획인 거야?
M : No, I'm happy with the facilities now.
아니, 지금 시설에 만족해.
W : Then why aren't you renewing your membership?
그럼 왜 회원권을 갱신하지 않는 거야?
M : Actually I'm going to take tennis lessons next month.
사실 다음 달에 테니스 수업을 받으려고.
W : Cool. Tennis is a fun and high-intensity sport. You'll love it.
멋지다. 테니스는 즐겁고 강도 높은 운동이지. 넌 되게 좋아할 거야.
M : Yeah, I'm looking forward to it.
그래, 기대하고 있어.

Why? 왜 정답일까?

피트니스 센터 회원권을 갱신하지 않기로 했다는 남자는 그 이유로 다음 달에 테니스 수업을 받기로 했다(**Actually I'm going to take tennis lessons next month.**)고 말한다. 따라서 남자가 피트니스 센트 회원권을 갱신하지 않는 이유로 가장 적절한 것은 ② '테니스 수업을 받기로 해서'이다.

- **work out** 운동하다
- **facility** ⓝ 시설
- **renew** ⓥ 갱신하다
- **intensity** ⓝ 강도

08 새로 생긴 채식주의 식당

정답률 56% | 정답 ②

대화를 듣고, Camellia Vegan Table에 관해 언급되지 않은 것을 고르시오.

① 위치 ② 개점 시간 ③ 메뉴 ④ 음식 가격 ⑤ 휴점일

M : Hi, Cathy.
안녕, Cathy.
W : Hi, Matthew. Where are you heading to?
안녕, Matthew. 어디 가고 있어?
M : I'm going to Camellia Vegan Table for lunch.
점심 먹으러 Camellia Vegan Table에 가고 있어.
W : Camellia Vegan Table? I've never heard of it. 『Where is it?
Camellia Vegan Table이라고? 한 번도 못 들어봤어. 그거 어디 있어?
M : It's a new vegan restaurant on campus. It's on the first floor of the student union building.』 ①의 근거 일치
캠퍼스에 새로 생긴 비건 식당이야. 학생회관 건물 1층에 있어.
W : That's news to me. When did it open?
처음 들었네. 언제 열었어?
M : It opened last month. 『You can eat delicious vegan dishes like plant-based tacos, burgers, and pizzas.』 ③의 근거 일치
지난달에 열었어. 채식 타코, 버거, 피자와 같이 맛있는 비건 요리를 먹을 수가 있어.
W : Sounds great. 『How about the price?
근사하겠네. 가격은 어때?
M : Quite affordable. You can buy most of the dishes for less than $10.』 You should check it out. ④의 근거 일치
꽤 괜찮아. 10달러 밑으로 대부분의 음식을 살 수 있어. 너도 한번 가서 봐.
W : Okay. I'll go there tomorrow.
알겠어. 내가 내일 가볼게.
M : Ah! 『It's closed every Wednesday.』 Try some other day. ⑤의 근거 일치
아! 거기 수요일마다 닫는다. 다른 날 가 봐.
W : All right. Thanks for letting me know.
알겠어. 알려줘서 고마워.

Why? 왜 정답일까?

대화에서 남자와 여자는 **Camellia Vegan Table**의 위치, 메뉴, 음식 가격, 휴점일에 관해 언급하므로, 언급되지 않은 것은 ② '개점 시간'이다.

Why? 왜 오답일까?

① '**It's on the first floor of the student union building.**'에서 '위치'가 언급되었다.
③ '**You can eat delicious vegan dishes like plant-based tacos, burgers, and pizzas.**'에서 '메뉴'가 언급되었다.
④ '**You can buy most of the dishes for less than $10.**'에서 '음식 가격'이 언급되었다.
⑤ '**It's closed every Wednesday.**'에서 '휴점일'이 언급되었다.

- **vegan** ⓐ 채식주의의
- **plant-based** ⓐ 채식 (위주)의
- **That's news to me.** 처음 들었어.
- **affordable** ⓐ (가격이) 적당한

09 공원 관리 자원봉사

정답률 86% | 정답 ④

Spring Stewardship Day에 관한 다음 내용을 듣고, 일치하지 않는 것을 고르시오.

① 올해는 4월 29일에 개최될 것이다.
② 참가자들은 쓰레기 줍기, 나무 보호 등을 도울 것이다.
③ 봉사 활동이 끝난 후 점심이 무료로 제공될 것이다.
④ 작업용 장갑을 포함하여 모든 도구와 장비가 제공될 것이다.
⑤ 참가비는 무료이지만 사전 등록이 필요하다.

M : Are you looking for volunteer programs this spring?
이번 봄 자원봉사 프로그램을 찾고 계신가요?
Join us for our annual Spring Stewardship Day!
매년 하는 저희 Spring Stewardship Day에 참여하세요!
『This year, the Spring Stewardship Day will be held on Saturday, April 29 at Lakeside Park.』 ①의 근거 일치
올해 Spring Stewardship Day는 Lakeside Park에서 4월 29일 토요일에 개최됩니다.

「Participants will assist with trash pickup, tree protection and more.」 ②의 근거 일치
참가자들은 쓰레기 줍기, 나무 보호 등을 돕게 됩니다.
This event is for volunteers aged 12 years and older.
이 행사는 12세 이상의 자원봉사자를 대상으로 합니다.
The volunteer work will run from 9 a.m. to noon, and 「lunch will be provided free of charge after work.」 ③의 근거 일치
자원봉사 작업은 오전 9시부터 정오까지 진행되며, 활동이 끝난 후 점심이 무료로 제공됩니다.
「We'll supply the necessary tools and supplies for you, but you should bring your own water bottle and work gloves.」 ④의 근거 불일치
필요한 도구와 장비는 제공할 예정이지만, 물병과 작업용 장갑은 지참하셔야 합니다.
Please wear weather-appropriate clothing.
날씨에 알맞은 옷을 입어주세요.
「This event is free, but prior registration is required because spaces are limited.」
본 행사는 무료이지만, 공간이 한정되어 있어 사전 등록이 필요합니다. ⑤의 근거 일치
Please visit our website for more information.
더 많은 정보를 얻으시려면 저희 웹 사이트를 방문해 주세요.

Why? 왜 정답일까?

'We'll supply the necessary tools and supplies for you, but you should bring your own water bottle and work gloves.'에서 물병과 작업용 장갑은 따로 직접 준비해야 한다고 하므로, 내용과 일치하지 않는 것은 ④ '작업용 장갑을 포함하여 모든 도구와 장비가 제공될 것이다.'이다.

Why? 왜 오답일까?

① 'This year, the Spring Stewardship Day will be held on Saturday, April 29 at Lakeside Park.'의 내용과 일치한다.
② 'Participants will assist with trash pickup, tree protection and more.'의 내용과 일치한다.
③ '~ lunch will be provided free of charge after work.'의 내용과 일치한다.
⑤ 'This event is free, but prior registration is required because spaces are limited.'의 내용과 일치한다.

- annual ⓐ 매년 하는
- stewardship ⓝ (재산, 조직체 등의) 관리
- trash ⓝ 쓰레기
- free of charge 무료로
- weather-appropriate ⓐ 날씨에 알맞은

10 무선 방수 스피커 사기 정답률 83% | 정답 ②

다음 표를 보면서 대화를 듣고, 여자가 구매할 무선 방수 스피커를 고르시오.

Wireless Waterproof Speakers

	Model	Price	Playtime(hours)	FM Radio	Color
①	A	$35	8	×	Silver
✔②	B	$38	12	○	Blue
③	C	$40	15	○	Pink
④	D	$45	18	×	White
⑤	E	$55	24	○	Black

W : Dad. Could you help me buy a wireless waterproof speaker? I need one to listen to music while taking a bath.
아빠, 무선 방수 스피커 사는 것 좀 도와주실래요? 목욕하면서 음악을 듣게 하나 필요해서요.
M : Okay. Do you have anything in mind?
알겠어. 생각해 둔 게 있니?
W : Yes, I want to choose one from these five models.
네, 이 다섯 개 제품 중 하나를 고르려고요.
M : Let me see. 「Do you have a budget?
어디 보자. 예산은 있어?
W : I'd like to keep it under $50.」 근거1 Price 조건
50달러 밑으로 하려고요.
M : Then this one is out. Oh, I wouldn't get this model, either. 「The playtime should be longer than 10 hours.」 근거2 Playtime 조건
그럼 이건 빠져야겠네. 오, 나라면 이 제품도 안 사겠어. 재생 시간은 10시간은 넘어야 해.
W : I agree. Then I have to choose one of these three.
맞는 말이에요. 그럼 이 세 개 중 하나를 골라야겠어요.
M : 「Why don't you go for one with FM radio? You often listen to the radio.
FM 라디오가 있는 걸로 고르면 어때? 너 라디오를 자주 듣잖아. 근거3 FM Radio 조건
W : Good point.」 There are only two options left, but I like both of the colors.
좋은 지적이세요. 선택권이 두 개밖에 안 남았는데, 색상이 둘 다 마음에 드네요.
M : 「I think pink will get dirty easily.」 근거4 Color 조건
내 생각에 분홍색은 쉽게 더러워질 것 같아.
W : That makes sense. I'll buy the other one.
일리 있는 말씀이에요. 그럼 다른 것을 살래요.

Why? 왜 정답일까?

대화에 따르면 여자는 가격이 50달러 이하이면서, 재생 시간은 10시간 이상이고, FM 라디오 기능이 있으면서, 분홍색이 아닌 스피커를 사려고 한다. 따라서 여자가 구매할 무선 방수 스피커는 ② 'B'이다.

- have in mind 마음에 두다, 생각하다
- budget ⓝ 예산
- make sense 일리가 있다

11 한국어 공부 기간 묻기 정답률 69% | 정답 ⑤

대화를 듣고, 남자의 마지막 말에 대한 여자의 응답으로 가장 적절한 것을 고르시오.

① It's nice of you to help me read the lyrics of the songs.
내가 가사 읽는 것을 도와주다니 친절하구나.
② It took me so long to get to the language school.
내가 어학당까지 가는 게 너무 오래 걸렸어.
③ I sing K-pop songs to master Korean.
난 한국어를 마스터하기 위해 케이팝 노래를 불러.
④ I don't go to the Korean language school anymore.
난 더 이상 한국어학당에 다니지 않는단다.
✔⑤ I was able to read Korean lyrics in about three months.
3달 정도 지나서 한국어 가사를 읽을 수 있게 되었어.

M : Grandma, you still go to the Korean language school, right? Has your Korean improved a lot?
할머니, 한국어학당 아직 계속 다니시죠, 그렇죠? 한국어 많이 느셨어요?
W : I guess so. Now I can read the lyrics of my favorite K-pop songs.
그런 거 같아. 이제 내가 제일 좋아하는 케이팝 노래 가사도 읽을 수 있어.
M : Wow, that's cool. How long did it take you to develop such skill?
와, 근사해요. 그런 실력을 키우는 데 얼마나 걸리셨어요?
W : I was able to read Korean lyrics in about three months.
3달 정도 지나서 한국어 가사를 읽을 수 있게 되었어.

Why? 왜 정답일까?

할머니인 여자가 한국어 가사를 읽을 수 있게 되었다는 말에 남자는 그렇게 되기까지 얼마나 걸렸는지 질문하고 있다(How long did it take you to develop such skill?). 따라서 여자의 응답으로 가장 적절한 것은 ⑤ '3달 정도 지나서 한국어 가사를 읽을 수 있게 되었어.(I was able to read Korean lyrics in about three months.)'이다.

- lyrics ⓝ 가사

12 여행 때 이용할 교통수단 정하기 정답률 84% | 정답 ②

대화를 듣고, 여자의 마지막 말에 대한 남자의 응답으로 가장 적절한 것을 고르시오.

① I know, but I already rented a car. – 나도 아는데, 난 이미 차를 예약했어요.
✔② Good idea. Let's not rent a car this time. – 좋은 생각이에요. 이번에는 차를 렌트하지 말죠.
③ Don't worry. The next bus is coming soon. – 걱정 마요. 다음 버스가 곧 와요.
④ I'm sorry. I forgot to rent a car for our trip. – 미안해요. 우리 여행을 위해 차를 빌리는 걸 깜빡했어요.
⑤ You're right. It'll be exciting to drive a luxury car. – 당신 말이 맞아요. 고급 차를 몰면 신날 거예요.

W : Honey, let's book a rental car for our trip to Jeju Island next month.
여보, 다음 달 우리 제주도 여행을 위해 렌트카를 예약하죠.
M : I've tried, but I couldn't. Car rental is too expensive these days.
시도해 봤는데, 못 했어요. 렌트카 요새 너무 비싸요.
W : Then why don't we travel around there by bus? It'll be fun and cheap as well.
그럼 버스로 돌아다니는 게 어때요? 그것은 재미있고 비용도 쌀 거예요.
M : Good idea. Let's not rent a car this time.
좋은 생각이에요. 이번에는 차를 렌트하지 말죠.

Why? 왜 정답일까?

렌트카가 너무 비싸서 대여하지 못했다는 남자에게 여자는 그럼 대신 버스를 타고 돌아다니자고 제안하고 있다(Then why don't we travel around there by bus?). 따라서 남자의 응답으로 가장 적절한 것은 ② '좋은 생각이에요. 이번에는 차를 렌트하지 말죠.(Good idea. Let's not rent a car this time.)'이다.

- book ⓥ 예약하다
- as well (문미에서) 또한

13 현수막 글자 수정 문의 정답률 70% | 정답 ⑤

대화를 듣고, 남자의 마지막 말에 대한 여자의 응답으로 가장 적절한 것을 고르시오. [3점]

Woman: ______________________

① No way. I'm still printing the banner. – 절대 안 돼요. 전 아직 현수막을 인쇄하고 있단 말이에요.
② Yes, I'll let you know the new date soon. – 네, 새 날짜를 곧 알려드리겠습니다.
③ But I've already sent them to your school. – 하지만 이미 그것을 학교로 보내드렸습니다.
④ No problem. I'll change the date on the banner. – 문제 없습니다. 현수막에 있는 날짜를 고쳐드릴게요.
✔⑤ Okay. I'll put them in when packaging the banner. – 알겠습니다. 현수막을 포장할 때 넣어드리겠습니다.

[Telephone rings.]
[전화벨이 울린다.]
W : Star Printing. How may I help you?
Star Printing입니다. 무엇을 도와드릴까요?
M : Hi. I'm Alex Miller. I ordered a banner for our school festival a few days ago, but I wonder if I can ask for a change.
안녕하세요, 저는 Alex Miller입니다. 며칠 전에 저희 학교 축제 때문에 현수막을 주문했는데요, 변경을 요청해도 될지 궁금해서요.
W : Let me check first. What's the name of your school?
확인 먼저 하겠습니다. 학교명이 어떻게 되시죠?
M : It's Jackson High School.
Jackson 고등학교입니다.
W : Hang on. *[Typing sound]* I'm sorry, but it's already been printed out. It's going to be packaged soon for delivery.
잠시만 기다려주세요. *[타자 치는 소리]* 죄송한데 이미 출력이 완료되었습니다. 곧 배송될 수 있도록 포장될 거예요.
M : Oh, no. Our school festival has been delayed. The date should be changed.
오, 이런. 학교 축제가 연기되었어요. 날짜가 변경돼야 해요.
W : That sounds like a major change. I'm afraid you'll have to order a new one.
그건 중대 수정 같군요. 죄송하지만 새로 현수막을 주문하셔야 할 것 같습니다.
M : I don't want to do that. It's a waste of money. Do you have any other idea?
그렇게는 하고 싶지 않군요. 돈 낭비잖아요. 다른 방법은 없나요?
W : Well, you can write the new date on a piece of cloth and cover the old date.
음, 천 조각에 새 날짜를 쓰셔서 기존 날짜에 덮으시면 됩니다.
M : All right. I'd appreciate it if you could send me some pieces of cloth.
알겠습니다. 천 조각을 좀 보내주시면 고맙겠습니다.
W : Okay. I'll put them in when packaging the banner.
알겠습니다. 현수막을 포장할 때 넣어드리겠습니다.

Why? 왜 정답일까?

현수막에 적힌 축제 날짜를 수정하려 했던 남자는 이미 인쇄가 완료되어 새로 주문해야 한다는 여자의 말에 다른 방법이 없을지 묻고, 여자는 천 조각에 날짜를 새로 써서 덮으라고 조언하고 있다. 이에 남자는 천 조각이 있으면 좀 보내달라고 부탁하고 있으므로(I'd appreciate it if you could send me some pieces of cloth.), 여자의 응답으로 가장 적절한 것은 ⑤ '알겠습니다. 현수막을 포장할 때 넣어드리겠습니다.(Okay. I'll put them in when packaging the banner.)'이다.

- festival ⓝ 축제
- print out ~을 출력하다
- delay ⓥ 미루다, 연기하다

[문제편 p.008]

14 테라리엄 권유하기

정답률 73% | 정답 ⑤

대화를 듣고, 여자의 마지막 말에 대한 남자의 응답으로 가장 적절한 것을 고르시오. [3점]

Man: ______________________

① I agree. Outdoor gardening is very good for health.
동의해. 실외 정원 가꾸기는 건강에 아주 좋아.
② Sounds great. I'll help the beginners with gardening.
근사할 거 같다. 난 정원 가꾸기에 초보인 사람들을 돕겠어.
③ Yeah. I already made a couple of terrarium gardens.
그래. 난 이미 테라리엄 정원을 몇 개 만들었어.
④ Thanks. Last weekend's terrarium workshop was helpful.
고마워. 지난 주 테라리엄 워크숍은 유용했어.
✔ Sure. It'll be fun to create my own garden in a glass jar.
그래. 나만의 정원을 유리 항아리 안에서 키우는 건 재미있겠어.

M : Hi, Jennifer. How was your weekend?
안녕, Jennifer. 주말 잘 보냈어?
W : It was awesome. I had a great experience at a terrarium workshop.
근사했지. 테라리엄 워크숍에서 멋진 경험을 했어.
M : What is a terrarium?
테라리엄이 뭔데?
W : It's like an aquarium, but with plants instead of fish. It can be made in any glass container like a jar or bottle.
수족관 같은 건데, 물고기 대신 식물이 있는 거야. 항아리나 병처럼 아무 유리 그릇이든 그 안에 만들 수 있어.
M : Simply put, you grow plants in glass containers, right?
쉽게 말하면, 유리 그릇 안에 식물을 키우는 거구나, 맞지?
W : Well, it's more than that. A good terrarium is a fully functioning micro-ecosystem.
음, 그 이상이야. 좋은 테라리엄은 완전히 기능하는 미세 생태계거든.
M : Tell me more about it.
좀 더 말해줘.
W : Terrariums are able to conserve water and keep the environment humid no matter the weather outside. They're very easy to care for.
테라리엄은 물을 아껴주고, 바깥 날씨에 상관없이 환경을 습하게 유지해줘. 관리하기 아주 편하지.
M : I see. They sound like a creative way to have your own mini garden.
그렇구나. 너만의 미니 정원을 갖는 창의적인 방법 같네.
W : Exactly. Why don't you try making one? It won't be difficult, even for a beginner.
바로 그거지. 너도 해보면 어때? 어렵지 않을 거야, 초보자한테도.
M : Sure. It'll be fun to create my own garden in a glass jar.
그래. 나만의 정원을 유리 항아리 안에서 키우는 건 재미있겠어.

Why? 왜 정답일까?

여자는 테라리엄이 단순히 유리병 안에서 식물을 키우는 것 이상의 의미를 갖는다면서, 남자에게도 어렵지 않을 테니 해볼 것을 권하고 있다(**Why don't you try making one?**). 따라서 남자의 응답으로 가장 적절한 것은 ⑤ '그래. 나만의 정원을 유리 항아리 안에서 키우는 건 재미있겠어.(**Sure. It'll be fun to create my own garden in a glass jar.**)'이다.

- **awesome** ⓐ 근사한, 멋진
- **terrarium** ⓝ 테라리엄(식물이나 거북이 등을 넣어 기르는 유리 용기)
- **micro-ecosystem** ⓝ 미세 생태계
- **humid** ⓐ 습한
- **care for** ~을 돌보다, 관리하다

15 동아리 조직 방법 물어보기

정답률 77% | 정답 ②

다음 상황 설명을 듣고, Kate가 Ben에게 할 말로 가장 적절한 것을 고르시오. [3점]

Kate: ______________________

① There're many things to consider when adopting a cat.
고양이를 입양할 때는 생각해야 할 게 많아.
✔ Let's get advice from Sarah on how to start our club.
Sarah한테 우리 동아리를 어떻게 시작할지 조언을 구해보자.
③ We should check with her if there's an animal club.
동물 동아리가 있는지 그 애랑 함께 확인해 봐야 해.
④ Why don't we join the school drama club instead?
대신 연극 동아리에 들면 어때?
⑤ How about helping Sarah organize a drama club?
Sarah가 연극 동아리 조직하는 걸 도우면 어때?

W : Ben and Kate are seniors at Eagle High School.
Ben과 Kate는 Eagle 고등학교 3학년이다.
They both love animals.
그들은 둘 다 동물을 좋아한다.
Recently, they found some abandoned cats wandering around the school.
최근에 그들은 학교를 배회하는 유기묘 몇 마리를 발견했다.
Ben and Kate talk about what they can do to take care of them.
Ben과 Kate는 그들을 돌보기 위해 무엇을 할 수 있을지 이야기를 나눴다.
Ben comes up with an idea to start an animal welfare club at school.
Ben은 학교에서 동물 복지 동아리를 시작해보자는 아이디어를 떠올린다.
Kate thinks it's a good idea because students can work together with a sincere interest in animal protection.
Kate는 학생들이 동물 보호에 진지한 관심을 갖고 함께 노력해볼 수 있기에 그것이 좋은 아이디어라고 생각한다.
But, they don't know how to get started because they've never organized a school club before.
하지만 그들은 전에 학교 동아리를 조직해본 적이 없어 어떻게 시작해야 할지 모른다.
Kate remembers that her classmate, Sarah, started the school drama club last year.
Kate는 자기 반 친구 Sarah가 작년에 학교 연극 동아리를 시작했던 것을 기억해 낸다.
She wants to tell Ben that they should ask Sarah about it.
그녀는 Sarah에게 그것을 물어보자고 Ben에게 말하고 싶다.
In this situation, what would Kate most likely say to Ben?
이 상황에서, Kate는 Ben에게 뭐라고 말할 것인가?
Kate : Let's get advice from Sarah on how to start our club.
Sarah한테 우리 동아리를 어떻게 시작할지 조언을 구해보자.

Why? 왜 정답일까?

상황에 따르면 동아리를 만들어본 경험이 없는 Kate는 연극 동아리를 시작해본 적이 있는 Sarah에게 방법을 물어보자고 제안하고 싶어 한다(**She wants to tell Ben that they should ask Sarah about it.**). 따라서 Kate가 Ben에게 할 말로 가장 적절한 것은 ② 'Sara한테 우리 동아리를 어떻게 시작할지 조언을 구해보자.(**Let's get advice from Sarah on how to start our club.**)'이다.

- **senior** ⓝ (고등학교) 마지막 학년, 상급생, 선배
- **abandoned cat** 유기묘
- **wander around** ~을 배회하다, 어슬렁거리다
- **welfare** ⓝ 복지, 후생

16-17 세계 곳곳의 특이한 법률

M : Hello, students.
안녕하세요, 학생 여러분.
「Laws may seem to be universal, yet every country's laws are different.
법은 보편적으로 보일 수 있지만, 모든 나라의 법은 다릅니다.
In fact, some of them are so weird that you may not believe they exist.」 16번의 근거
사실, 어떤 법은 너무 희한해서 여러분은 그런 게 있다고 믿지 않을지도 모릅니다.
「In Italy, Rome has strict laws against animal cruelty.」 17번 ①의 근거 일치
이탈리아의 로마는 동물 학대에 대해 엄격한 법을 가지고 있습니다.
For example, if an owner does not walk their dog once a day, they could be fined €500.
예를 들어, 어떤 주인이 개를 하루에 한 번 산책시키지 않으면, 그들은 500유로의 벌금에 처해질 수 있습니다.
「Germany's Autobahn is well-known for having dynamic speed limits of more than 160 km per hour.」 17번 ②의 근거 일치
독일의 Autobahn은 시속 160km 이상이라는 역동적인 속도 제한을 둔 곳으로 유명합니다.
But it's illegal to run out of gas on the Autobahn.
하지만 Autobahn에서 휘발유가 떨어지면 불법입니다.
「When packing for a trip to Greece, make sure you have the right shoes.」
그리스에 가려고 짐을 쌀 때에는, 꼭 알맞은 신발을 넣도록 하세요. 17번 ④의 근거 일치
The country banned high heels at the Acropolis in 2009.
2009년에 이 나라는 아크로폴리스에서 하이힐을 (신지 못하게) 금지했습니다.
The Greeks put this ban in place to protect its ruins from damage caused by sharp shoes.
그리스 사람들은 날카로운 신발로 인해 유적지에 손상이 가해지는 것을 막기 위해 이러한 금지 조항을 시행했습니다.
「Spain hates your attempts at making sand castles so much that you could be fined if caught building one.」 17번 ⑤의 근거 일치
스페인에서는 사람들이 모래성을 만들려고 하는 것을 너무도 싫어해서, 여러분이 만들다가 잡히면 벌금에 처해질 수도 있습니다.
And the fines vary by location.
그리고 벌금은 지역마다 다릅니다.
On the island of Majorca, for example, you could pay €100.
예컨대, Majorca의 섬에서는 100유로를 낼 수 있습니다.
So, when you visit these countries, be careful!
그러니 이 국가들을 방문할 때 주의하세요!
You certainly don't want to get in trouble!
여러분은 분명 곤경에 처하고 싶지 않을 테니까요!

- **strict** ⓐ 엄격한
- **cruelty** ⓝ 잔인함, 학대
- **fine** ⓥ 벌금을 매기다 ⓝ 벌금
- **run out of gas** 휘발유가 떨어지다
- **ban** ⓥ 금지하다 ⓝ 금지
- **put in place** 시행하다
- **tourist attraction** 관광지

16 주제 파악

정답률 74% | 정답 ①

남자가 하는 말의 주제로 가장 적절한 것은?

✔ surprising and unusual laws around the world – 세계 곳곳의 놀랍고 특이한 법률
② the most visited tourist attractions in the world – 세계에서 방문자가 가장 많은 관광지
③ universal laws and principles governing your life – 여러분의 삶을 지배하는 보편적인 법과 원칙들
④ necessity of improving laws on cultural diversity – 문화적 다양성에 관한 법을 개선할 필요성
⑤ what to consider when choosing a family tour program – 가족 여행 프로그램을 고를 때의 고려 사항

Why? 왜 정답일까?

'**Laws may seem to be universal, yet every country's laws are different. In fact, some of them are so weird that you may not believe they exist.**'에서 남자는 세계 각국의 법률이 서로 다르며, 특히 어떤 법들은 존재한다고 믿기지 않을 정도로 특이하다는 화제를 제시한다. 따라서 남자가 하는 말의 주제로 가장 적절한 것은 ① 세계 곳곳의 놀랍고 특이한 법률(**surprising and unusual laws around the world**)'이다.

17 언급 유무 파악

정답률 89% | 정답 ③

언급된 나라가 아닌 것은?

① Italy – 이탈리아 ② Germany – 독일 ✔ France – 프랑스
④ Greece – 그리스 ⑤ Spain – 스페인

Why? 왜 정답일까?

담화에서 남자는 특이한 법률을 둔 나라의 예시로 이탈리아, 독일, 그리스, 스페인을 언급하므로, 언급되지 않은 것은 ③ '프랑스'이다.

Why? 왜 오답일까?

① '**In Italy, Rome has strict laws against animal cruelty.**'에서 '이탈리아'가 언급되었다.
② '**Germany's Autobahn is well-known for having dynamic speed limits of more than 160 km per hour.**'에서 '독일'이 언급되었다.
④ '**When packing for a trip to Greece, make sure you have the right shoes.**'에서 '그리스'가 언급되었다.
⑤ '**Spain hates your attempts at making sand castles so much that you could be fined if caught building one.**'에서 '스페인'이 언급되었다.

[문제편 p.008]

Dictation 02

문제편 009쪽

01 Currently located at the main building / In preparation for the move / will still be available
02 save time and effort to cook / To some extent / don't use over-packaged delivery services
03 walk up the stairs / called the maintenance service / Other residents may need your help
04 two chairs by the window / use a ladder / leaning against the bookcase
05 get a bunch of flowers / check with the flower shop / put the certificates into the covers
06 order a customized cake / adding two decorations / have it delivered
07 don't get personal training / take tennis lessons / a fun and high-intensity sport
08 When did it open / delicious vegan dishes / Quite affordable
09 trash pickup, tree protection / water bottle and work gloves / spaces are limited
10 a wireless waterproof speaker / longer than 10 hours / pink will get dirty easily
11 read the lyrics / develop such skill
12 let's book a rental car / travel around there by bus
13 be packaged soon for delivery / The date should be changed / send me some pieces of cloth
14 keep the environment humid / easy to care for / Why don't you try making one
15 found some abandoned cats / start an animal welfare club / a sincere interest in animal protection
16-17 some of them are so weird / having dynamic speed limits / protect its ruins

03회 | 2022학년도 3월 학력평가

| 정답과 해설 | 고3

• 정답 •

01⑤ 02① 03① 04④ 05⑤ 06③ 07① 08④ 09③ 10② 11④ 12① 13⑤ 14② 15③ 16④ 17③

01 전기 점검 관련 유의 사항 안내

정답률 84% | 정답 ⑤

다음을 듣고, 여자가 하는 말의 목적으로 가장 적절한 것을 고르시오.

① 전기 절약의 필요성을 강조하려고
② 엘리베이터 안전 수칙을 알려 주려고
③ 전문 기술자 초청 강연을 공지하려고
④ 컴퓨터 데이터 복원 방법을 설명하려고
✔ 전기 점검 관련 유의 사항을 안내하려고

W : Attention please, teachers and students.
주목해 주세요, 교사 및 학생 여러분.
This is the vice principal.
저는 교감입니다.
As we notified you last week, some workers from the power company are here today to inspect the school's electric facilities.
지난 주에 공지했듯이, 전기 회사 직원 몇몇 분이 오늘 교내 전기 설비를 점검하러 와 계십니다.
During the checkup, electricity might temporarily go out in some offices and classrooms.
점검 동안, 일부 사무실 및 교실에 전기가 일시적으로 나갈 수도 있습니다.
In addition, the school elevators won't be available until the inspection is completed.
추가로, 점검이 끝날 때까지 학교 엘리베이터는 사용 불가할 예정입니다.
In case of unexpected power cuts, I would like you to save your work and create back-up files while working on computers.
예기치 못한 정전을 대비해, 컴퓨터 작업 도중 작업물을 저장해 두시고 백업 파일을 만들어 두세요.
The technicians will finish their work before lunch time ends.
기술자 분들은 점심 시간이 끝나기 전에 작업을 마치실 것입니다.
Thank you for your patience with any inconvenience.
불편을 참아주셔서 고맙습니다.

Why? 왜 정답일까?

전기 기술자가 전기 설비를 점검하기 위해 와 있다(~ **some workers from the power company are here today to inspect the school's electric facilities.**)는 말 뒤로 전기 점검 도중 정전이 일어날 수 있으며, 엘리베이터는 사용 불가할 것이라는 점 등이 안내되고 있다. 따라서 남자가 하는 말의 목적으로 가장 적절한 것은 ⑤ '전기 점검 관련 유의 사항을 안내하려고'이다.

- **notify** ⓥ 공고[신고]하다
- **inspect** ⓥ 조사하다
- **electricity** ⓝ 전기, 전력
- **in addition** (~에) 덧붙여, 게다가
- **technician** ⓝ 기술자, 기사
- **inconvenience** ⓝ 불편, 폐 ⓥ 불편하게 하다
- **power company** 전력 회사, 전기 회사
- **facility** ⓝ 설비, 시설
- **temporarily** ad 일시적으로
- **power cut** 정전
- **patience** ⓝ 인내심

02 주민 센터 만족도 조사

정답률 76% | 정답 ①

대화를 듣고, 남자의 의견으로 가장 적절한 것을 고르시오.

✔ 설문 방식을 다양화해야 응답자의 수를 늘릴 수 있다.
② 설문 문항은 가능한 한 쉽고 간결하게 제작해야 한다.
③ 온라인 설문은 응답을 수집하는 가장 편리한 방식이다.
④ 응답자의 익명을 보장해야 솔직한 의견을 얻을 수 있다.
⑤ 설문 참여를 높이려면 응답자에게 보상을 제공해야 한다.

M : What are you doing, Ms. Taylor?
뭐 하고 계세요, Taylor 씨?
W : I'm preparing a satisfaction survey for our community center.
우리 주민 센터에 대한 만족도 조사를 준비하고 있어요.
M : I see. How are you going to do the survey?
그러시군요. 설문을 어떻게 진행하실 예정인가요?
W : I'll send a link to our members so that they can open it right on their smartphone.
스마트폰에서 바로 열어볼 수 있도록 우리 주민 분들께 링크를 보낼 거예요.
M : Is that the only way for them to participate?
그게 유일한 참여 방법인가요?
W : Yes. Is there a problem with that?
네, 문제가 있나요?
M : You may not get a large sample. I mean you can't get opinions from people who don't use a smartphone.
큰 표본을 구하지 못할 수도 있어요. 제 말은 스마트폰을 안 쓰는 사람들의 의견은 구할 수 없다는 거죠.
W : Oh, that's a good point.
오, 좋은 지적이네요.
M : I think you should diversify your survey methods to increase the number of respondents.
응답자 수를 증가시키기 위해 설문 방식을 다양화해야 할 것 같아요.
W : You're right. I'll add a paper-based survey. That'll cover a wider range of respondents.
맞는 말씀이에요. 서면 조사를 추가하겠어요. 그럼 더 다양한 응답자가 포함될 거예요.

Why? 왜 정답일까?

남자는 응답자 수를 키우기 위해 설문 방식을 다각화해야 한다고 말하고 있으므로(**I think you should diversify your survey methods to increase the number of respondents.**), 남자의 의견으로 가장 적절한 것은 ① '설문 방식을 다양화해야 응답자의 수를 늘릴 수 있다.'이다.

- **prepare** ⓥ 준비하다
- **satisfaction** ⓝ 만족(감)

[문제편 p.013]

- survey ⓝ (설문) 조사
- opinion ⓝ 의견, 견해
- respondent ⓝ 응답자
- participate ⓥ 참여하다, 관여하다
- diversify ⓥ 다양화하다

03 영화 감독과 원작 만화가의 대화 정답률 90% | 정답 ①

대화를 듣고, 두 사람의 관계를 가장 잘 나타낸 것을 고르시오.

① 영화감독 – 만화가 ② 촬영 감독 – 영화배우
③ 방송 진행자 – 소설가 ④ 출판사 직원 – 삽화가
⑤ 신문 기자 – 시나리오 작가

M : Hello, Ms. Russell. I'm honored to have you here.
안녕하세요, Russell 씨. 모시게 되어 영광입니다.
W : Thank you for inviting me, Mr. Warren.
초대 감사합니다, Warren 씨.
M : It was my pleasure to work with you. Did you enjoy my movie?
당신과 함께 작업해서 무척 기뻤습니다. 제 영화를 즐겁게 보셨나요?
W : Yes. It was fantastic!
네. 환상적이었어요!
M : I'm glad to hear that.
그 말씀을 들으니 기쁘네요.
W : Actually, I've never imagined that the characters from my comic book could be realized in a live action movie.
사실, 제 만화책 속 주인공들이 실사 액션 영화로 구현될 수 있을 거라고 상상해보지 못했어요.
M : I liked the characters in your comic book so much that I wanted to make them super realistic.
당신의 만화 속 캐릭터가 너무도 마음에 들어서 그들을 아주 현실적으로 만들고 싶었답니다.
W : I'm wondering how you've put all the actions and scenes on the screen.
그 모든 액션과 장면을 화면에 어떻게 다 담아내셨는지 궁금해요.
M : The computer graphics team did most of the work and my actors did their jobs very well as I directed.
컴퓨터 그래픽 팀에서 거의 모든 일을 해줬고 저희 배우들은 제가 감독하는 대로 일을 아주 잘해줬죠.
W : Oh, I see. I'm so happy to see my characters come to life in the movie.
오, 그렇군요. 제 캐릭터들이 영화에서 살아 움직이는 걸 봐서 몹시 기뻐요.
M : I'm happy you liked it.
마음에 드셨다니 기쁩니다.

Why? 왜 정답일까?

'Did you enjoy my movie?', 'The computer graphics team did most of the work and my actors did their jobs very well as I directed.' 등에서 남자가 영화감독임을 알 수 있고, 'Actually, I've never imagined that the characters from my comic book could be realized in a live action movie.' 등에서 여자가 만화가임을 알 수 있다. 따라서 두 사람의 관계로 가장 적절한 것은 ① '영화감독 – 만화가'이다.

- realize ⓥ 구현하다, 실현하다
- direct ⓥ (영화를) 감독하다
- realistic ⓐ 현실적인, 현실성 있는
- come to life 살아 움직이다, 활기를 띠다

04 차박 사진 구경하기 정답률 90% | 정답 ④

대화를 듣고, 그림에서 대화의 내용과 일치하지 않는 것을 고르시오.

W : Hi, Logan. How was your weekend?
안녕, Logan. 주말 잘 보냈어?
M : Hey, Lisa. I went car camping at Elf Lake. Look at this picture.
안녕, Lisa. 난 Elf Lake에서 차박을 했어. 이 사진을 봐.
W : Did you sleep in a car?
차에서 잔 거야?
M : 「Yeah, I put in a pillow and blanket on the flattened backseats.」 ①의 근거 일치
응, 뒷좌석을 눕혀서 그 위에 베개와 담요를 뒀지.
W : 「What are those hanging from the car trunk door?
차 트렁크 문에 달려있는 건 뭐야?
M : They are string lights.」 It's beautiful when the bulbs light up. ②의 근거 일치
줄로 연결된 전구야. 불이 들어오면 예뻐.
W : 「The camping lantern on the table looks nice, too.」 ③의 근거 일치
탁자 위에 있는 캠핑 랜턴도 근사해 보이네.
M : Right. It can make a romantic atmosphere at night.
맞아. 밤에 낭만적인 분위기를 만들어 줘.
W : 「You even set a tablecloth on the table. I like the checkered pattern.」 ④의 근거 불일치
탁자에 식탁보도 깔았구나. 체크무늬가 마음에 들어.
M : I wanted to create my own cozy campsite. 「Do you see the camping chair near the table?」 ⑤의 근거 일치
나만의 아늑한 캠핑장을 만들고 싶었어. 탁자 주변에 캠핑 의자 보여?
W : Yeah, it looks good for sitting and relaxing with a cup of coffee.
응, 커피 한 잔 들고 앉아서 쉬기 좋겠다.

Why? 왜 정답일까?

대화에서 탁자 위에 깔린 식탁보가 체크무늬라고 하는데(You even set a tablecloth on the table. I like the checkered pattern.), 그림 속의 식탁보는 도트 무늬이다. 따라서 그림에서 대화의 내용과 일치하지 않는 것은 ④이다.

- car camping 차박
- flatten ⓥ 평평하게 하다
- atmosphere ⓝ 분위기, 환경
- pillow ⓝ 베개
- bulb ⓝ 전구
- cozy ⓐ 아늑한

05 주방용 비누 제조법 링크 보내주기 정답률 94% | 정답 ⑤

대화를 듣고, 여자가 할 일로 가장 적절한 것을 고르시오.

① 설거지하기 ② 와인 주문하기 ③ 친환경 비누 만들기
④ 주방 세제 사 오기 ⑤ 웹 사이트 링크 보내기

M : Hannah, everything you made was delicious!
Hannah, 네가 만든 거 다 맛있었어!
W : Thanks. The wine you brought went so well with the food.
고마워. 네가 가져온 와인이 음식하고 잘 어울렸어.
M : I'm glad. I'll do the dishes for you.
기쁘다. 내가 설거지할게.
W : If you do that, I'd be grateful.
해주면 고맙지.
M : By the way, where's the dishwashing liquid?
그나저나, 설거지용 세제는 어딨어?
W : That bar of soap next to the sink is for dishwashing. I made it myself.
싱크대 옆에 있는 그 비누가 설거지용이야. 내가 직접 만들었어.
M : Oh, really?
오, 진짜?
W : Yes. It's more eco-friendly than the liquid detergent at the store.
응. 가게에서 파는 액상 세제보다 더 친환경적이야.
M : How did you make it?
어떻게 만들었어?
W : I followed a recipe from the Internet.
인터넷에 있는 제조법대로 했어.
M : *[Pause]* Wow, this soap works so well. Can you send me the link to the website? I want to make one too.
[잠시 멈춤] 와, 이 비누 효과 정말 좋네. 그 웹 사이트 링크 나한테 보내줄 수 있어? 나도 하나 만들고 싶어.
W : Sure. I'll text you the link right away.
물론이지. 내가 문자로 바로 링크를 보내줄게.
M : Okay. Thanks.
그래. 고마워.

Why? 왜 정답일까?

남자는 여자가 만든 주방 비누에 관심을 보이며 여자가 보고 따라서 만들었다는 제조법 링크를 보내달라고 말하고, 여자는 즉시 문자로 보내주겠다(I'll text you the link right away.)고 답한다. 따라서 여자가 할 일로 가장 적절한 것은 ⑤ '웹 사이트 링크 보내기'이다.

- delicious ⓐ 아주 맛있는
- grateful ⓐ 고마워하는
- soap ⓝ 비누
- detergent ⓝ 세제
- go well with ~와 잘 어울리다
- liquid ⓝ 액체
- eco-friendly ⓐ 친환경적인, 환경 친화적인

06 맡긴 자전거 찾기 정답률 72% | 정답 ③

대화를 듣고, 남자가 지불할 금액을 고르시오.

① $30 ② $40 ③ $45 ④ $55 ⑤ $60

W : Welcome to Bike Solutions. How may I help you?
Bike Solutions에 잘 오셨습니다. 무엇을 도와드릴까요?
M : Hello, I dropped off my bicycle yesterday. My name's Billy Hunter.
안녕하세요, 전 어제 제 자전거를 맡겼어요. 제 이름은 Billy Hunter예요.
W : Let me check. *[Pause]* Here's your bicycle. We replaced some parts.
확인해 보겠습니다. *[잠시 멈춤]* 여기 자전거가 있습니다. 부품 몇 개를 교체했어요.
M : Oh, I see. What did you replace and how much is it?
오, 그렇군요. 어떤 것을 교체하셨고 비용은 얼마죠?
W : We changed both tires. Each tire is $15.
타이어를 둘 다 갈았습니다. 타이어 하나당 15달러이고요.
M : I see. Is that all?
그렇군요. 그게 전부인가요?
W : No. We also replaced the brake pads for both wheels.
아니요. 두 바퀴 브레이크 패드도 모두 갈았어요.
M : Good. How much is that?
좋네요. 얼마인가요?
W : We put a new pair of brake pads on each wheel. It's $10 for one pair.
바퀴마다 브레이크 패드를 새로 한 쌍씩 설치했습니다. 한 쌍에 10달러이구요.
M : You mean I need to pay for two pairs?
그럼 제가 두 쌍 가격을 지불해야 한다는 말씀인가요?
W : Right. And lastly, we cleaned the chain. But that's free.
맞습니다. 그리고 마지막으로, 체인도 세척했습니다. 하지만 이건 무료예요.
M : Thank you. Can I use this discount coupon?
고맙습니다. 이 할인 쿠폰을 써도 될까요?
W : Sure. You get $5 off the total.
물론입니다. 총 가격에서 5달러 할인을 받으시게 됩니다.
M : Thank you. Here's my credit card.
감사합니다. 여기 제 신용 카드요.

Why? 왜 정답일까?

대화에 따르면 남자는 자전거 수리점에서 15달러짜리 바퀴 두 개, 한 쌍에 10달러인 브레이크 패드 두 쌍을 새로 갈고, 총 가격에서 5달러를 할인받았다. 체인 세척에는 돈이 들지 않았다. 이를 식으로 나타내면 '$(15\times2+10\times2)-5=45$'이므로, 남자가 지불할 총 금액은 ③ '$45'이다.

- drop off (물건을) 맡기다
- clean ⓥ 닦다, 청소하다
- replace ⓥ 교체하다

07 식당 자리 선택하기 정답률 94% | 정답 ①

대화를 듣고, 여자가 야외 좌석을 원하지 않는 이유를 고르시오. [3점]

[문제편 p.013]

✔ 대화하기에 너무 시끄러워서
② 햇빛이 너무 강해 눈이 부셔서
③ 미세 먼지 때문에 공기 질이 나빠서
④ 기온이 낮아 감기에 걸릴까 걱정되어서
⑤ 야외에서 보는 전망이 마음에 들지 않아서

M : Alice, I've been really looking forward to eating at this restaurant.
Alice, 난 이 식당에서 밥을 먹기를 무척 손꼽아 기다렸어.
W : Me too, Ryan. This is a hot spot on social media.
나도, Ryan. 여기 소셜 미디어에서 인기 많은 곳이야.
M : Right. Shall we sit outside?
맞아. 우리 밖에 앉을래?
W : Outside? You mean at a table on the terrace?
밖에? 테라스에 있는 자리 말하는 거야?
M : Yes. The view from the terrace is wonderful and it looks like there are still a few tables available.
응. 테라스에서 보이는 경치가 근사하고, 보기에 아직 몇 자리가 비어 있는 것 같아.
W : I know, but I'd prefer to sit inside, if you don't mind.
알아, 그런데 난 네가 괜찮으면 안쪽에 앉는 게 더 좋아서.
M : Why? Do you think it'd be a bit chilly out there?
왜? 바깥에 좀 쌀쌀할 것 같아서?
W : No. It's not as cold as I thought.
아니. 내가 생각했던 것만큼 춥진 않아.
M : Then, is it because of the fine dust? The air quality is actually pretty good today.
그럼, 미세 먼지 때문에 그래? 공기 질은 오늘 사실 꽤 좋아.
W : No, that's not the reason. It's too noisy outside to talk comfortably.
아니, 그것 때문이 아냐. 밖은 너무 시끄러워서 편하게 얘기할 수가 없어.
M : Oh, I see. Let's eat inside, then.
아, 그렇구나. 그럼 안에서 먹자.

Why? 왜 정답일까?

여자는 밖에 앉으면 너무 시끄러워서 편하게 얘기할 수 없으니(It's too noisy outside to talk comfortably.) 안에 있자고 말하므로, 여자가 야외 좌석을 원하지 않는 이유로 가장 적절한 것은 ① '대화하기에 너무 시끄러워서'이다.

- look forward to ~을 고대하다
- chilly ⓐ 쌀쌀한
- actually ad 사실은
- noisy ⓐ 시끄러운, 떠들썩한
- available ⓐ 이용 가능한, (자리나 시간이) 빈
- fine dust 미세 먼지
- reason ⓝ 이유, 까닭

08 향수 워크숍

정답률 91% | 정답 ④

대화를 듣고, Galland perfume workshop에 관해 언급되지 않은 것을 고르시오.

① 참가 연령 ② 사용 언어 ③ 시간
✔ 예약 방법 ⑤ 장소

M : Honey, today's our last day in Paris. Is there anything special you want to do?
여보, 오늘이 파리에서의 마지막 날이에요. 뭐 특별한 거 하고 싶은 거 있어요?
W : How about going to a perfume workshop? I've found some information about the Galland perfume workshop.
향수 워크숍에 가는 거 어때요? Galland perfume workshop에 관해서 몇 가지 정보를 찾았어요.
M : A perfume workshop?
향수 워크숍이라고요?
W : Yes. 「The Galland perfume workshop is open to everyone ages 12 and over.」 We can make our own perfume there. ①의 근거 일치
네. Galland perfume workshop은 12세 이상인 누구나 참여할 수 있대요. 거기서 우리만의 향수도 만들 수 있어요.
M : That sounds fun. 「Do they have a workshop in English? ②의 근거 일치
재미있겠네요. 영어로 하는 워크숍이 있어요?
W : Yes.」 It starts at 1 p.m.
네. 오후 1시에 시작해요.
M : 「How long is the workshop?
워크숍은 얼마나 오래 해요?
W : Two hours.」 ③의 근거 일치
두 시간이요.
M : I see. Then we'll have time to get afternoon tea after the workshop. 「Where's the workshop being held?
그렇군요. 그럼 워크숍이 끝나고 애프터눈 티를 마실 시간이 있겠어요. 워크숍이 어디서 열리나요?
W : In the Saint Michel building.」 It's not far from our hotel. ⑤의 근거 일치
Saint Michel 건물에서요. 우리 호텔에서 멀지 않아요.
M : Okay. Let's go.
알겠어요. 갑시다.

Why? 왜 정답일까?

대화에서 남자와 여자는 Galland perfume workshop의 참가 연령, 사용 언어, 시간, 장소에 관해 언급하므로, 언급되지 않은 것은 ④ '예약 방법'이다.

Why? 왜 오답일까?

① 'The Galland perfume workshop is open to everyone ages 12 and over.'에서 '참가 연령'이 언급되었다.
② 'Do they have a workshop in English? / Yes.'에서 '사용 언어'가 언급되었다.
③ 'Two hours.'에서 '시간'이 언급되었다.
⑤ 'In the Saint Michel building.'에서 '장소'가 언급되었다.

- perfume ⓝ 향수
- be open to ~을 대상으로 한다

09 미술관 특별 투어

정답률 92% | 정답 ③

Flashlight Tour에 관한 다음 내용을 듣고, 일치하지 않는 것을 고르시오.

① 미술관 폐장 후에 시작된다.
② 한 시간 동안 진행된다.
✔ 성인 입장료는 10달러이다.
④ 손전등이 기념품으로 제공된다.
⑤ 참가 인원에 제한이 있다.

M : Hello, visitors. Welcome to the Boledo Museum of Art.
안녕하세요, 방문객 여러분. Boledo 미술관에 잘 오셨습니다.
We're glad to announce our exclusive Flashlight Tour to you.
저희 전용 Flashlight Tour에 대해 안내드리려고 합니다.
The tour takes place every Thursday in April.
이 투어는 4월 매주 목요일에 진행됩니다.
「After the Museum closes, all the lights will be turned off and the special flashlight tour will begin.」 ①의 근거 일치
미술관이 폐장하고 나면, 모든 불빛이 꺼지고 특별한 손전등 투어가 시작됩니다.
This tour will offer you a unique and memorable gallery experience.
이 투어는 독특하고 기억에 남는 갤러리 체험을 제공할 것입니다.
「It's a one-hour guided museum tour.」 ②의 근거 일치
이것은 가이드가 있는 한 시간짜리 미술관 투어입니다.
During the tour, you'll enjoy our permanent collections and special exhibitions.
투어 도중, 여러분은 저희의 영구 소장품과 특별 전시를 즐기시게 됩니다.
「Tickets are $15 for adults, and $10 for youth ages 5 to 17.」 ③의 근거 불일치
티켓은 성인 15달러, 5세부터 17세까지의 어린이는 10달러입니다.
「Flashlights will be provided as a souvenir.」 ④의 근거 일치
손전등은 기념품으로 제공될 예정입니다.
「This tour has a limited capacity of 20, so book now.」 Thank you. ⑤의 근거 일치
이 투어는 20명이 제한 원인이므로, 지금 예약하세요. 고맙습니다.

Why? 왜 정답일까?

'Tickets are $15 for adults, and $10 for youth ages 5 to 17.'에서 성인 입장료는 15달러라고 하므로, 내용과 일치하지 않는 것은 ③ '성인 입장료는 10달러이다.'이다.

Why? 왜 오답일까?

① 'After the Museum closes, ~ the special flashlight tour will begin.'의 내용과 일치한다.
② 'It's a one-hour guided museum tour.'의 내용과 일치한다.
④ 'Flashlights will be provided as a souvenir.'의 내용과 일치한다.
⑤ 'This tour has a limited capacity of 20, so book now.'의 내용과 일치한다.

- announce ⓥ 알리다, 발표하다
- memorable ⓐ 기억에 남는
- provide ⓥ 제공하다
- capacity ⓝ 수용력
- exclusive ⓐ 전용의, 고급의
- permanent collection 영구 소장품
- souvenir ⓝ 기념품

10 휴대용 가습기 구입하기

정답률 84% | 정답 ②

다음 표를 보면서 대화를 듣고, 남자가 주문할 휴대용 가습기를 고르시오.

Best Portable Humidifiers

	Model	Price	Color	Capacity	Mood Light
①	A	$13	Gray	300 ml	×
✔	B	$18	White	400 ml	○
③	C	$20	Orange	500 ml	○
④	D	$28	Black	700 ml	×
⑤	E	$35	White	900 ml	○

W : Mr. Parker, what are you looking at on the computer?
Parker 씨, 컴퓨터로 뭘 보고 계세요?
M : Oh, Ms. Robinson. I'm looking at portable humidifiers for a conference gift. Can you help me?
오, Robinson 씨. 회의 선물로 휴대용 가습기를 사려고 보고 있어요. 저 좀 도와주실래요?
W : Sure. Let me see. You have five models to choose from. 「What's the budget range?
그래요. 살펴볼게요. 고를 만한 제품이 다섯 개 있군요. 예산 범위는 얼마예요?
M : We can't spend more than $30 each.」 근거1 Price 조건
하나에 30달러 이상은 쓸 수 없어요.
W : Then this one's out. 「And orange doesn't seem like a good color.」 It's a bit flashy.
그럼 이건 빼야겠네요. 그리고 주황색은 괜찮은 색이 아닌 것 같아요. 좀 펑해요. 근거2 Color 조건
M : I agree. 「How about the capacity?
동의해요. 용량은 얼마나 돼야 할까요?
W : I think 300 ml is too small.」 근거3 Capacity 조건
300ml는 너무 작은 것 같아요.
M : Right. Then, there are two options left. 「Do you think a mood light is useful?
맞아요. 그럼 두 개 선택지가 남네요. 무드등이 유용할 거라고 생각하세요?
W : Yes. It can work as a bed lamp.」 근거4 Mood Light 조건
네. 침대 등으로도 쓸 수 있어요.
M : Okay. I'll order the model with the mood light. Thank you for your help.
알겠어요. 그럼 무드등이 있는 제품으로 주문하겠어요. 도와주셔서 고마워요.
W : You're welcome. It'll be a good gift.
천만에요. 좋은 선물이 될 거예요.

Why? 왜 정답일까?

대화에 따르면 남자는 가격이 30달러를 넘지 않으면서, 색은 주황색이 아니고, 용량은 300ml 이상에, 무드등이 있는 가습기를 사려고 한다. 따라서 남자가 주문할 휴대용 가습기는 ② 'B'이다.

- budget ⓝ 예산
- bit ⓝ 조금
- humidifier ⓝ 가습기
- range ⓝ 범위
- flashy ⓐ 속되게 화려한, 겉만 번지르르한

11 귀가 일정 알리기

정답률 78% | 정답 ④

대화를 듣고, 여자의 마지막 말에 대한 남자의 응답으로 가장 적절한 것을 고르시오.

① Thank you very much for picking me up. – 절 태우러 와 주셔서 고마워요.
② I'll finish the laundry as soon as possible. – 제가 최대한 빨리 세탁을 끝낼게요.
③ I'm sorry. I won't be late for school again. – 죄송해요. 전 다시는 학교에 늦지 않을게요.

[문제편 p.013]

✓ I'm not sure. I'll call you when I'm finished. – 잘 모르겠어요. 끝나면 전화 드릴게요.
⑤ Never mind. I'll complete the project tomorrow. – 신경 쓰지 마세요. 내일 프로젝트를 끝낼 거예요.

[Cell phone rings.]
[휴대전화 벨이 울린다.]

W : Hello, Lucas. What's up?
여보세요, Lucas, 무슨 일이니?

M : Hi, Mom. I have a group project meeting after school. I'm afraid I can't pick up the laundry on my way home.
안녕, 엄마. 저 학교 끝나고 그룹 프로젝트 회의가 있어요. 집 가는 길에 세탁물을 못 찾아갈 것 같아요.

W : No problem. I'll take care of it. What time do you think you'll be home?
괜찮아. 내가 알아서 할게. 집에 몇 시에 올 거 같니?

M : I'm not sure. I'll call you when I'm finished.
잘 모르겠어요. 끝나면 전화 드릴게요.

Why? 왜 정답일까?

팀 프로젝트 회의를 언제쯤 마치고 올 것 같냐는 여자의 물음(**What time do you think you'll be home?**)에 대한 남자의 응답으로 가장 적절한 것은 ④ '잘 모르겠어요. 끝나면 전화 드릴게요.'이다.

- **afraid** ⓐ (유감이지만) ~라고 생각하다
- **pick up the laundry** (맡긴) 세탁물을 찾아오다
- **take care of** ~을 처리하다
- **possible** ⓐ 가능한

12 공기 청정기 구매하기

정답률 58% | 정답 ①

대화를 듣고, 남자의 마지막 말에 대한 여자의 응답으로 가장 적절한 것을 고르시오.

✓ I'm very satisfied. You should buy one. – 난 되게 만족해. 너도 하나 사.
② Right. The air quality today is not that bad. – 맞아. 오늘 공기 질은 별로 안 나빠.
③ Great. I want to buy an air purifier like yours. – 훌륭해. 나도 네 것 같은 공기 청정기를 하나 사고 싶어.
④ Put it here near the window. It's the best place. – 그걸 여기 창가에 놔. 여기가 적격이야.
⑤ Okay. Let's open the window and get some fresh air. – 그래. 창문을 열어서 환기를 시키자.

M : Grace, is this an air purifier?
Grace, 이거 공기 청정기야?

W : Yeah. I bought it last week because the air quality is so bad these days.
응. 요새 공기 질이 너무 나빠서 지난주에 그걸 샀어.

M : How do you like it? I've been thinking about getting one for my office.
이거 어때? 난 사무실에 하나 들일까 생각 중이야.

W : I'm very satisfied. You should buy one.
난 되게 만족해. 너도 하나 사.

Why? 왜 정답일까?

공기 청정기를 산 여자에게 남자는 자신도 하나 살 생각인데 어떤지 묻고 있으므로(**How do you like it? I've been thinking about getting one for my office.**), 여자의 응답으로 가장 적절한 것은 ① '난 되게 만족해. 너도 하나 사.'이다.

- **air purifier** 공기 청정기
- **How do you like it?** 어떻게 생각해?
- **satisfy** ⓥ 만족시키다

13 티셔츠 다시 받기

정답률 80% | 정답 ⑤

대화를 듣고, 여자의 마지막 말에 대한 남자의 응답으로 가장 적절한 것을 고르시오. [3점]

Man: ______________________

① No. We had no choice but to send it to you.
아니요. 그걸 고객님께 보내드리는 수밖에 없었네요.
② Sorry. There are no other colors available now.
죄송합니다. 지금 이용 가능한 다른 색이 없어요.
③ Yes. I'd like to get a refund for the yellow one.
네. 노란색 티셔츠를 환불 받고 싶어요.
④ Okay. You can send the large size one back to us.
네. 라지 사이즈는 저희한테 다시 보내주세요.
✓ Sure. We'll send you a large size one immediately.
알겠습니다. 라지 사이즈로 하나 바로 보내드리겠습니다.

[Telephone rings.]
[전화벨이 울린다.]

M : Joy's Clothing. How may I help you?
Joy's Clothing입니다. 무엇을 도와드릴까요?

W : Hi. I'm Norah Davis. I ordered a T-shirt from your online store but I received the wrong size.
안녕하세요. Norah Davis라고 합니다. 귀사의 온라인 매장에서 티셔츠를 하나 주문했는데 사이즈를 잘못 받아서요.

M : I'm sorry to hear that. Can I have your order number, please?
말씀 들으니 송구합니다. 주문 번호를 알려주시겠어요?

W : Sure. It's P2203123.
네. P2203123이에요.

M : Thanks. Let me check it for you. *[Typing sound]* You ordered a large size yellow T-shirt, correct?
고맙습니다. 제가 확인해 보겠습니다. *[타자 치는 소리]* 노란색 티셔츠를 라지 사이즈로 주문하셨죠, 맞습니까?

W : Yes, that's right, but I got a medium one. Can you please send me the right size?
네, 맞아요. 그런데 전 미듐 사이즈를 받았어요. 제대로 된 사이즈를 보내주실래요?

M : Oh, we're very sorry for the inconvenience. I'll check whether we have any large size ones in stock.
오, 불편을 끼쳐 정말 죄송합니다. 라지 사이즈가 재고에 있나 확인해 보겠습니다.

W : Okay.
알겠습니다.

M : *[Typing sound]* Unfortunately, we're all out of larges in yellow. We have larges in pink and white.
[타자 치는 소리] 안타깝게도, 노란색 라지 사이즈는 재고가 없습니다. 라지 사이즈로는 분홍색과 흰색이 있어요.

W : I see. Then can you send me a pink one?
알겠습니다. 그럼 분홍색으로 보내주실래요?

M : Sure. We'll send you a large size one immediately.
알겠습니다. 라지 사이즈로 하나 바로 보내드리겠습니다.

Why? 왜 정답일까?

대화에 따르면 여자가 주문한 노란색 라지 사이즈 티셔츠는 재고가 다 떨어졌고, 분홍색과 흰색만 재고가 남아 있다. 이에 여자는 분홍색으로 하나 보내달라고 하므로(**Then can you send me a pink one?**), 남자의 응답으로 가장 적절한 것은 ⑤ '알겠습니다. 라지 사이즈로 하나 바로 보내드리겠습니다.'이다.

- **correct** ⓐ 맞는, 정확한
- **unfortunately** ad 불행하게도, 유감스럽게도
- **in stock** 재고가 있는
- **have no choice but to** ~할 수밖에 없다
- **get a refund** 환불하다

14 스마트폰 사용법 알려드리기

정답률 94% | 정답 ②

대화를 듣고, 남자의 마지막 말에 대한 여자의 응답으로 가장 적절한 것을 고르시오. [3점]

Woman: ______________________

① Of course. I don't need it any more. – 물론이죠. 전 더 이상 그게 필요 없어요.
✓ Don't worry. You'll get used to it soon. – 걱정 마세요. 곧 익숙해지실 거예요.
③ Exactly! You need to buy a smartphone. – 바로 그거예요! 스마트폰을 하나 사셔야 해요.
④ Right. I checked my text before sending it. – 맞아요. 전 제 문자를 보내기 전에 확인했어요.
⑤ No way. Smartphones are not that expensive. – 절대 아녜요. 스마트폰은 그렇게 비싸지 않아요.

M : Lydia, can you come here for a moment?
Lydia, 잠깐 이리 와줄 수 있니?

W : Sure. What is it, Grandpa?
물론이죠. 무슨 일이세요, 할아버지?

M : I need some help with my cell phone.
핸드폰 때문에 도움이 필요하단다.

W : Wow! You've got a smartphone!
와! 스마트폰 사셨네요!

M : Yes, but I don't know how to send a text message. Can you show me how to do it?
응, 그런데 문자를 어떻게 보내는지 모르겠어. 어떻게 하는지 알려줄래?

W : Okay. First, find the messaging icon and tap it.
네. 먼저, 메시지 아이콘을 찾아서 누르세요.

M : Like this, right?
이렇게 말이지?

W : Yeah. Next, you need to select the person you want to text.
네. 다음으로, 문자를 보내고 싶은 사람을 선택하셔야 해요.

M : Select the person.... All right.
사람을 선택하라... 알겠어.

W : Now you can see the message box.
이제 메시지 상자가 보이시죠.

M : You mean the box here?
여기 상자 말하는 거니?

W : Yes. Type your message in it. And when you're done, hit 'Send.'
네. 거기다 메시지를 쓰세요. 그리고 다 쓰시면, '전송' 버튼을 누르세요.

M : I got it. But using a smartphone still seems difficult.
알겠어. 하지만 스마트폰 사용은 여전히 어려운 것 같구나.

W : Don't worry. You'll get used to it soon.
걱정 마세요. 곧 익숙해지실 거예요.

Why? 왜 정답일까?

메시지 사용을 배운 후 아직 스마트폰을 쓰는 것은 어렵다(**But using a smartphone still seems difficult.**)는 남자의 말에 대한 여자의 응답으로 가장 적절한 것은 ② '걱정 마세요. 곧 익숙해지실 거예요.'이다.

- **moment** ⓝ 잠깐, 잠시
- **tap** ⓥ 가볍게 두드리다
- **select** ⓥ 선택하다
- **get used to** ~에 익숙해지다
- **No way.** 절대 안 돼, 그럴 리 없어.
- **expensive** ⓐ 비싼, 돈이 많이 드는

15 잃어버린 시계 찾기

정답률 87% | 정답 ③

다음 상황 설명을 듣고, Emily가 Randy에게 할 말로 가장 적절한 것을 고르시오.

Emily: ______________________

① Do you know where the lost and found is? – 너 분실물 센터가 어디 있는지 알아?
② Can you tell me where you bought your watch? – 네 시계를 어디서 샀는지 말해줄래?
✓ Didn't you take off your watch in the bathroom? – 너 화장실에서 시계를 풀어놓지 않았어?
④ Do you know how to wash your hands properly? – 너 손을 제대로 씻는 방법을 아니?
⑤ Didn't you visit the shop to have your watch fixed? – 너 시계 고치려고 수리점에 가지 않았어?

W : Randy and Emily are very close friends and they go to school together.
Randy와 Emily는 아주 친한 친구 사이이고 학교에 같이 다닌다.
One day after school, on their way home, Randy notices that he has lost his watch, which is very precious to him.
어느 날 방과 후, 집으로 가는 길에 Randy는 자기 시계를 잃어버린 것을 알아차리는데, 그것은 그에게 매우 귀중한 것이다.
Emily asks Randy when he last had his watch.
Emily는 Randy에게 시계를 언제 마지막으로 지녔는지 묻는다.
Randy says it was during the last class.
Randy는 마지막 수업 시간 때였다고 말한다.
Emily remembers that she happened to see Randy come out from the bathroom shaking water off his hands.
Emily는 Randy가 손에서 물을 털며 화장실에서 나오는 모습을 우연히 봤던 것을 기억한다.
So, Emily thinks that Randy may have left his watch next to the bathroom sink.
그래서 Emily는 Randy가 화장실 세면대 옆에 시계를 놓고 나왔을지도 모른다고 생각한다.
Emily wants to ask Randy about this.
Emily는 Randy에게 이것에 관해 물어보고 싶다.
In this situation, what would Emily most likely say to Randy?
이 상황에서, Emily는 Randy에게 뭐라고 말할 것인가?

Emily : Didn't you take off your watch in the bathroom?
너 화장실에서 시계를 풀어놓지 않았어?

Why? 왜 정답일까?

상황에 따르면 Emily는 Randy가 화장실에서 손을 닦으며 세면대 옆에 시계를 놓고 나왔을지도 모른다고 생각해, Randy에게 이것에 관해 물어보려고 한다(**So, Emily thinks that Randy may have**

[문제편 p.014]

left his watch next to the bathroom sink. Emily wants to ask Randy about this.). 따라서 Emily가 Randy에게 할 말로 가장 적절한 것은 ③ '너 화장실에서 시계를 풀어놓지 않았어?'이다.

- precious ⓐ 귀중한
- sink ⓝ 세면대
- take off ~을 벗다
- shake ⓥ 털다
- lost and found 분실물 센터
- properly ad 제대로

16-17 스마트 도시 조성의 성공 사례

M : Hello, students.
안녕하세요, 학생 여러분.
Last class, we talked about IoT home devices.
지난 시간에, 우리는 사물 인터넷 가전에 관해 이야기했었죠.
「Today, let's expand the topic and learn about smart cities.
오늘은 주제를 확장해서 스마트 도시에 관해 배워봅시다.
Smart cities use technology to provide services and solve various problems.」 16번의 근거
스마트 도시는 기술을 이용해서 서비스를 제공하고 다양한 문제를 해결합니다.
「Singapore is one of the front-runners in the race to create fully smart cities, with IoT cameras monitoring the condition of the city, including the cleanliness of public spaces.」 17번 ①의 근거 일치
싱가포르는 완전한 스마트 도시를 조성하기 위한 경쟁에서 선두 주자 중 하나로, 사물 인터넷 카메라가 공공장소 청결을 포함해 도시 환경을 모니터링하고 있습니다.
It also has systems to monitor energy use, waste management, and water use in real time.
또한 에너지 사용, 쓰레기 처리, 물 사용을 실시간으로 감독하는 시스템도 있습니다.
「San Diego has installed 3,200 smart sensors to optimize traffic flow, and electric vehicles are supported by solar-to-electric charging stations.」 17번 ②의 근거 일치
샌 디에고는 교통 흐름을 최적화하기 위해 3,200개의 스마트 센서를 설치했고, 전기차는 태양열 전기 충전소의 지원을 받습니다.
「Traffic monitoring systems are also used in Dubai.」 17번 ④의 근거 일치
교통 감독 시스템은 두바이에서도 사용됩니다.
This city has telemedicine and smart healthcare solutions as well as smart tourism options.
이 도시는 스마트 관광 옵션 뿐 아니라 원격 의료와 스마트 보건 솔루션도 갖추고 있습니다.
「In New York, the police department has tested web-based software that uses historical crime data to predict and respond to crimes.」 17번 ⑤의 근거 일치
뉴욕에서는 경찰서에서 범죄를 예측하고 이에 대응하기 위해 과거 범죄 데이터를 활용하는 웹 기반 소프트웨어를 테스트했습니다.
The test has produced a marked decrease in violent crimes in the city.
이 테스트 결과 도시 내 강력 범죄가 눈에 띄게 감소했습니다.
Thanks to smart systems, many citizens around the world can improve their quality of life.
스마트 시스템 덕분에, 많은 세계 시민들은 삶의 질을 향상할 수 있게 됐습니다.

- IoT (Internet of Things) 사물 인터넷
- solve ⓥ 해결하다
- cleanliness ⓝ 청결
- optimize ⓥ 최적화하다
- support ⓥ 지원하다
- telemedicine ⓝ 원격 의료
- historical ⓐ 역사적인, 과거에 속한
- predict ⓥ 예측하다
- decrease ⓥ 줄다, 감소하다
- efficient ⓐ 효율적인
- expand ⓥ 확장하다
- front-runner ⓝ 선두 주자
- install ⓥ 설치하다
- flow ⓝ 흐름
- charging station 충전소
- police department (미국에서 특정 도시의) 경찰서
- crime ⓝ 범죄
- marked ⓐ 두드러지는
- violent crime 강력 범죄
- interconnectedness ⓝ 상호 연결성

16 주제 파악

정답률 68% | 정답 ④

남자가 하는 말의 주제로 가장 적절한 것은?

① steps in planning an efficient smart city - 효율적인 스마트 도시 계획의 단계
② pros and cons of developing smart cities - 스마트 도시 개발의 장단점
③ problems of smart cities and why they arise - 스마트 도시의 문제와 그 발생 이유
✔ successful smart cities and how they operate - 성공적인 스마트 도시와 그들의 기능 방식
⑤ interconnectedness of smart cities around the world - 전 세계 스마트 도시의 상호 연결성

Why? 왜 정답일까?

'Today, let's expand the topic and learn about smart cities. Smart cities use technology to provide services and solve various problems.'에서 담화의 주제가 스마트 도시의 서비스 제공과 문제 해결임을 알 수 있으므로, 남자가 하는 말의 주제로 가장 적절한 것은 ④ '성공적인 스마트 도시와 그들의 기능 방식'이다.

17 언급 유무 파악

정답률 91% | 정답 ③

언급된 도시가 아닌 것은?

① Singapore - 싱가포르　② San Diego - 샌 디에고　✔ London - 런던
④ Dubai - 두바이　⑤ New York - 뉴욕

Why? 왜 정답일까?

담화에서 남자는 스마트 도시를 구축한 장소의 예로 싱가포르, 샌 디에고, 두바이, 뉴욕을 언급하므로, 언급되지 않은 곳은 ③ '런던'이다.

Why? 왜 오답일까?

① 'Singapore is one of the front-runners ~'에서 '싱가포르'가 언급되었다.
② 'San Diego has installed 3,200 smart sensors ~'에서 '샌 디에고'가 언급되었다.
④ 'Traffic monitoring systems are also used in Dubai.'에서 '두바이'가 언급되었다.
⑤ 'In New York, the police department has tested web-based software ~'에서 '뉴욕'이 언급되었다.

Dictation 03

문제편 015쪽

01 inspect the school's electric facilities / electricity might temporarily go out / unexpected power cuts
02 send a link / get a large sample / increase the number of respondents
03 the characters from my comic book / make them super realistic / come to life
04 flattened backseats / make a romantic atmosphere / create my own cozy campsite
05 do the dishes / That bar of soap / the liquid detergent / send me the link
06 replaced some parts / changed both tires / cleaned the chain / $5 off the total
07 prefer to sit inside / a bit chilly / because of the fine dust / too noisy outside
08 ages 12 and over / have a workshop in English / get afternoon tea
09 all the lights will be turned off / memorable gallery experience / permanent collections and special exhibitions / limited capacity of 20
10 portable humidifiers / How about the capacity / with the mood light
11 I can't pick up the laundry
12 air purifier / the air quality is so bad
13 received the wrong size / in stock / all out of larges in yellow / a pink one
14 tap it / select the person / Type your message in it
15 he has lost his watch / shaking water off his hands / next to the bathroom sink
16-17 create fully smart cities / telemedicine and smart healthcare solutions / uses historical crime data / a marked decrease

04회 | 2021학년도 3월 학력평가 고3

| 정답과 해설 |

• 정답 •

01 ⑤ 02 ① 03 ① 04 ④ 05 ① 06 ④ 07 ② 08 ③ 09 ④ 10 ③ 11 ① 12 ③ 13 ① 14 ⑤ 15 ③ 16 ② 17 ⑤

01 공청회 참석 요청하기

정답률 81% | 정답 ⑤

다음을 듣고, 남자가 하는 말의 목적으로 가장 적절한 것을 고르시오.

① 재활용 쓰레기 분리 배출 방법을 안내하려고
② 재활용 쓰레기 배출 시간 준수를 당부하려고
③ 재활용 쓰레기 분리수거 요일 변경을 공지하려고
④ 재활용 쓰레기 관련 주민 회의 결과를 알려주려고
✔ 재활용 쓰레기 분리수거 관련 공청회 참석을 요청하려고

M : Hello, residents.
안녕하세요, 주민 여러분.
This is Andy from the management office.
저는 관리 사무실의 Andy입니다.
We're currently collecting recyclable garbage twice a week, on Wednesdays and Sundays, from 7 a.m. to 9 p.m.
우리는 현재 재활용 가능한 쓰레기를 일주일에 두 번씩, 수요일과 일요일마다 아침 7시부터 오후 9시까지 수거하고 있습니다.
But we've had a lot of complaints from residents concerning the time, location, and smell.
하지만 시간, 장소, 냄새와 관련하여 주민들로부터 많은 불만이 제기되어 왔습니다.
We're doing our best to address these complaints but it's been difficult to come up with satisfactory solutions.
저희는 이러한 불만을 처리하고자 최선을 다하고 있으나 만족스러운 해결책을 고안해내기 어렵습니다.
So, to deal with this matter effectively, we're going to hold a public hearing at the community hall on Friday, March 26, at 8 p.m.
그리하여, 이 문제를 효과적으로 다루기 위해, 저희는 3월 26일 금요일 오후 8시에 커뮤니티 홀에서 공청회를 열 것입니다.
We're asking everyone to attend the public hearing.
모두가 공청회에 참석해 주시기를 요청합니다.
Thank you in advance for your cooperation.
협조에 미리 감사합니다.

Why? 왜 정답일까?

'We're asking everyone to attend the public hearing.'에서 남자는 재활용 쓰레기 수거에 관련된 공청회에 모두가 참석해줄 것을 요구한다고 말하므로, 남자가 하는 말의 목적으로 가장 적절한 것은 ⑤ '재활용 쓰레기 분리수거 관련 공청회 참석을 요청하려고'이다.

- **recyclable** ⓐ 재활용 가능한
- **concerning** prep ~에 관하여
- **address** ⓥ 해결하다
- **come up with** ~을 고안하다, 생각해 내다
- **public hearing** 공청회

02 적절한 조리 도구의 중요성

정답률 93% | 정답 ①

대화를 듣고, 여자의 의견으로 가장 적절한 것을 고르시오.

✔ 적합한 조리 도구 사용은 요리를 쉽고 즐겁게 해 준다.
② 요리 동영상을 참고하면 누구나 요리를 할 수 있다.
③ 같은 재료라도 조리법에 따라 음식 맛이 달라진다.
④ 조리 도구는 훌륭한 인테리어 소품이 될 수 있다.
⑤ 조리 도구를 청결하게 관리하는 것이 중요하다.

W : Eric, I made this pizza myself. Try some.
Eric, 내가 이 피자 만들었어. 좀 먹어봐.
M : Thank you, Yujin. *[Pause]* Mmm.... It's delicious!
고마워, Yujin. *[잠시 멈춤]* 음... 맛있다!
W : Is it? I watched a cooking video and followed the recipe from it.
그래? 난 요리 영상을 보고 거기서 나오는 레시피를 따라했어.
M : You're a really good cook. Not everyone can just watch a video and make delicious food like you just did.
넌 요리를 참 잘해. 모두가 딱 너처럼 그냥 영상을 보고서 맛있는 음식을 만들지는 못하지.
W : Well, I think it's all thanks to the cooking tools I've recently bought.
음, 난 그게 다 내가 최근에 산 조리 도구 덕분인 것 같아.
M : Cooking tools? You mean utensils?
조리 도구라고? 부엌 용품을 말하는 거야?
W : Yes. Having the right utensils makes cooking much easier.
응. 적합한 조리 도구를 갖고 있는 것은 요리를 훨씬 쉽게 만들어줘.
M : You seem to be very happy with your utensils.
넌 네 조리 도구에 무척 만족하는 것 같네.
W : Yeah. They make cooking more enjoyable.
응. 그것들이 요리를 더 즐겁게 만들어줘.
M : Oh, that's why you're totally into cooking these days!
오, 그래서 네가 요새 요리에 푹 빠져 있구나!
W : Definitely.
바로 그거야.
M : Now I understand why chefs emphasize the importance of using the right utensils in cooking.
이제 왜 셰프들이 요리할 때 적합한 도구를 사용하는 것의 중요성을 강조하는지 알겠네.

Why? 왜 정답일까?

'Having the right utensils makes cooking much easier.'와 **'They make cooking more enjoyable.'**에서 여자는 적합한 조리 도구를 사용하면 요리가 쉽고 즐거워진다고 말하므로, 여자의 의견으로 가장 적절한 것은 ① '적합한 조리 도구 사용은 요리를 쉽고 즐겁게 해 준다.'이다.

- **utensil** ⓝ 가정 용품, 조리 도구
- **enjoyable** ⓐ 즐거운
- **emphasize** ⓥ 강조하다

03 꽃꽂이 수업 전 이야기 나누기

정답률 96% | 정답 ①

대화를 듣고, 두 사람의 관계를 가장 잘 나타낸 것을 고르시오.

✔ 꽃꽂이 강사 – 수강생
② 택배 기사 – 수령인
③ 웨딩 플래너 – 예비 신부
④ 꽃 판매 상인 – 사진작가
⑤ 인테리어 디자이너 – 건축가

M : Hi, Sofia. What did you do with the bouquet you made last Friday?
안녕하세요, Sofia. 지난 금요일에 만들어간 부케 어떻게 했어요?
W : Hi, Brandon. I had it delivered to my friend. She was really happy to get it.
안녕하세요, Brandon. 전 그걸 친구한테 보내줬어요. 그걸 받고 무척 기뻐하더라고요.
M : Did you tell her you made it yourself?
당신이 직접 만들었다고 말해줬어요?
W : Yes. I also told her that I made it in your class. She said she'd like to learn from you, too.
네. 전 친구에게 그걸 당신의 수업에서 만들었다고도 얘기했어요. 친구도 선생님께 배우고 싶대요.
M : I'm glad to hear that. Why don't you invite her to join my class sometime?
그 말을 들으니 기쁘네요. 언젠가 제 수업에 친구 분을 초대하면 어때요?
W : Yeah, I suggested signing up for the next one-day class together.
네, 다음 번 원데이 클래스에 같이 등록하자고 제안했어요.
M : Good. You will get to spend quality time together.
좋아요. 함께 좋은 시간을 보내겠군요.
W : I think so, too. I'll let her know how to register.
저도 그렇게 생각해요. 어떻게 신청하면 되는지 친구에게 알려줄게요.
M : Thank you. Today you'll learn how to arrange spring flowers in a vase. Look here. I've made this one in advance.
고마워요. 오늘은 당신은 꽃병에 봄꽃을 어떻게 꽂을지 배울 거예요. 여기 보세요. 제가 이걸 미리 만들어 놨어요.
W : Wow, it looks gorgeous. I can't wait to make one myself.
와, 근사해요. 제가 직접 하나 만들어볼 게 몹시 기대되네요.
M : Okay. Shall we get started?
그래요. 시작할까요?

Why? 왜 정답일까?

'What did you do with the bouquet you made last Friday?', 'I also told her that I made it in your class. She said she'd like to learn from you, too.', 'Why don't you invite her to join my class sometime?', 'Today you'll learn how to arrange spring flowers in a vase. Look here. I've made this one in advance.' 등을 통해 남자가 꽃꽂이 강사이고, 여자가 수강생임을 알 수 있다. 따라서 두 사람의 관계로 가장 적절한 것은 ① '꽃꽂이 강사 – 수강생'이다.

- **deliver** ⓥ 배달하다
- **sign up for** ~에 등록하다
- **arrange** ⓥ 정리하다, 배열하다
- **gorgeous** ⓐ 근사한

04 강아지를 위해 새로 꾸민 거실 사진 구경하기

정답률 94% | 정답 ④

대화를 듣고, 그림에서 대화의 내용과 일치하지 않는 것을 고르시오.

M : Rachel, I heard you adopted a puppy.
Rachel, 난 네가 강아지를 입양했다고 들었어.
W : Yes. His name is Coco. I've rearranged the living room for him. Take a look at this picture.
응. 그의 이름은 Coco야. 난 그를 위해 거실을 새로 꾸몄어. 이 사진을 봐.
M : Let's see. 『Oh, this must be Coco. He's playing with a ball.』 ①의 근거 일치
어디 보자. 오, 얘가 Coco구나. 공을 가지고 놀고 있네.
W : Yes. It's his favorite toy.
응. 그가 가장 좋아하는 장난감이야.
M : I see. 『Is this striped tent for Coco?』 ②의 근거 일치
그렇구나. 이 줄무늬 텐트도 Coco 거야?
W : Yeah. I bought it for him last week.
응. 난 지난주에 그에게 그것을 사줬어.
M : It looks cozy. 『You also put the steps in front of the sofa.』 What are they for? ③의 근거 일치
안락해 보이네. 소파 앞에 계단도 놔 두었구나. 왜 둔 거야?
W : They're pet steps to help Coco get on the sofa.
Coco가 소파 위에 올라갈 수 있게 도와주는 반려동물용 계단이야.
M : Ah, he can't jump onto it yet. 『Hey, Rachel, what's this elephant toy on the sofa?』 ④의 근거 불일치
아, 아직 뛰어서 올라갈 수 없구나. Rachel, 소파 위에 이 코끼리 장난감은 뭐야?
W : It's another toy for Coco.
그건 Coco를 위한 또 다른 장난감이야.
M : Well, is he being toilet trained?
음, 화장실 훈련은 하고 있어?
W : Yes, he is. 『Do you see the two pads near the potted plant?』 I'm using them for his toilet training. ⑤의 근거 일치
응. 화분 식물 옆에 패드 두 개 보여? 그것을 화장실 훈련에 쓰고 있어.
M : Good. Everything seems to be perfect for Coco.
좋네. 모든 게 Coco에게 딱 좋아 보여.

Why? 왜 정답일까?

대화에 따르면 소파 위에는 코끼리 장난감이 놓여 있는데(~ **what's this elephant toy on the** sofa?), 그림의 소파 위에는 오리 인형이 놓여 있다. 따라서 그림에서 대화의 내용과 일치하지 않는 것은 ④이다.

- rearrange ⓥ 재배열하다, 재조정하다
- jump onto ~에 뛰어오르다
- potted plant 화초

05 축구 결승전 준비하기

정답률 95% | 정답 ①

대화를 듣고, 여자가 남자를 위해 할 일로 가장 적절한 것을 고르시오.

① 물 가져가기 ② 안내 방송하기
③ 카메라 설치하기 ④ 배터리 충전하기
⑤ 구급상자 챙기기

[Cell phone rings.]
[휴대전화 벨이 울린다.]

M : Hi, Ms. Clark.
안녕하세요, Clark 선생님.

W : Mr. Dickson, where are you? The students' soccer final starts in 30 minutes.
Dickson 선생님, 어디 계세요? 학생 축구 결승전이 30분 뒤면 시작해요.

M : I'm on the playing field, checking the ground conditions.
전 경기장에 있어요, 그라운드 상태를 확인하느라요.

W : Well, I just made an announcement to the students about the match.
음, 제가 방금 학생들에게 시합에 관해 안내 방송을 했어요.

M : Thank you. I've already set up cameras to film the match.
고맙습니다. 전 경기를 촬영할 수 있도록 이미 카메라를 설치해 뒀어요.

W : Okay. How about extra batteries? Do you have them?
알겠어요. 여분의 배터리는요? 선생님이 갖고 계세요?

M : I checked. They're in the camera bag.
제가 확인했어요. 카메라 가방 안에 있어요.

W : What about the first-aid kit? We might need it during the game.
구급상자는요? 시합 중에 그게 필요할지도 몰라요.

M : The school nurse will bring it before the game.
보건 선생님이 그걸 시합 전에 갖고 오실 거예요.

W : I see. Did you bring the ice water for players to drink?
알겠어요. 선수들이 마시도록 얼음물은 갖다 두셨어요?

M : Oh, I forgot. Could you bring it for me? It's in the fridge.
오, 깜빡했어요. 그걸 좀 가져와 주실래요? 냉장고 안에 있어요.

W : Okay. I'll take it to the field right away.
알겠어요. 그걸 지금 경기장으로 가져갈게요.

M : Thanks.
고마워요.

Why? 왜 정답일까?

30분 뒤에 열릴 학생 축구 결승전을 위해 준비할 사항을 확인하던 여자는 남자가 잊은 얼음물을 가지고 경기장에 가기로 한다(**I'll take it to the field right away.**). 따라서 여자가 할 일로 가장 적절한 것은 ① '물 가져가기'이다.

- make an announcement 안내하다, 안내 방송을 하다
- first-aid kit 구급상자

06 여동생 생일 선물 사기

정답률 48% | 정답 ④

대화를 듣고, 남자가 지불할 금액을 고르시오. [3점]

① $117 ② $130 ③ $135 ④ $150 ⑤ $161

W : Welcome to Jo's Fragrance. How may I help you?
Jo's Fragrance에 오신 것을 환영합니다. 무엇을 도와드릴까요?

M : Hello. I want to buy a bottle of Wild Silverbell for my sister's birthday.
안녕하세요. 전 여동생 생일을 위해 Wild Silverbell 한 병을 사려고요.

W : I see. It's a very popular perfume these days.
알겠습니다. 요새 아주 인기 있는 향수죠.

M : My sister really loves its scent. How much is it?
제 여동생이 그 향을 무척 좋아해요. 얼마인가요?

W : This small bottle is $80, and that larger one is $100.
이 작은 병은 80달러이고, 더 큰 것은 100달러입니다.

M : I'll take the larger one.
더 큰 것을 사겠어요.

W : Okay. We also sell candles with the same scent for $50 each.
알겠습니다. 똑같은 향의 초도 하나에 50달러씩 판매하고 있어요.

M : Oh! My sister really likes scented candles. I'll take a candle, too.
오! 제 여동생은 향초를 무척 좋아해요. 초도 하나 사겠어요.

W : Great. Since you're buying two items, you also get a 10% discount voucher. You can use it for your next purchase.
좋습니다. 상품을 두 개 사시니까, 10퍼센트 할인 쿠폰을 드릴게요. 다음 구매에 사용하시면 됩니다.

M : I see. Could you wrap them up, please?
알겠습니다. 포장해주실 수 있나요?

W : Sure. Gift-wrapping is free, but we can tie a ribbon on it for an extra dollar.
물론이죠. 선물 포장은 무료인데, 1달러를 추가로 내시면 리본을 묶어드릴 수 있어요.

M : I don't need a ribbon. Just gift-wrap them, please. Here's my credit card.
리본은 필요 없어요. 그냥 포장만 해 주세요. 여기 제 신용카드요.

Why? 왜 정답일까?

대화에 따르면 남자는 100달러짜리 큰 향수와 50달러짜리 향초 하나를 사고, 무료로 선물 포장을 받았다. 10퍼센트짜리 할인 쿠폰은 다음 구매에 사용할 수 있는 것이므로 이번 구매에는 적용되지 않는다. 따라서 남자가 지불할 금액은 ④ '**$150**'이다.

- scent ⓝ 향기
- voucher ⓝ 쿠폰, 할인권, 상품권
- gift-wrapping ⓝ 선물 포장

07 배송이 더 빠른 온라인 매장 찾기

정답률 96% | 정답 ②

대화를 듣고, 여자가 다른 주문처를 찾고 있는 이유를 고르시오.

① 더 좋은 품질을 원해서
② 더 빠른 배송을 원해서
③ 더 싼 가격을 원해서
④ 무료 배송을 원해서
⑤ 대량 주문을 원해서

M : Ms. White, what are you doing on the Internet?
White 선생님, 인터넷으로 뭐 하고 계세요?

W : Oh, Mr. Brown. I'm looking for a store to order some file folders for my class.
오, Brown 선생님, 전 제 수업에 쓸 서류철을 좀 주문하려고 매장을 찾고 있어요.

M : Oh, I thought you already ordered them, didn't you?
오, 이미 주문하셨다고 생각했어요, 그렇지 않았나요?

W : Actually, I didn't. I thought I had found the right store, but now I changed my mind.
사실 안 했어요. 좋은 가게를 찾았다고 생각했는데, 이제 마음이 바뀌어서요.

M : Did you find a store that offers lower prices?
더 낮은 가격을 제시하는 곳을 찾은 거예요?

W : No. The store I found was the cheapest and even had free delivery.
아니요. 제가 찾았던 곳은 가장 싸고 심지어 무료 배송을 해줬어요.

M : Then, were the file folders sold out?
그럼, 서류철이 다 팔렸어요?

W : No. They have plenty in stock.
아니요. 재고는 많았어요.

M : If so, why are you still searching for another store?
그러면 왜 아직 다른 곳을 찾고 있는 거예요?

W : Because their scheduled delivery will take too long. I need the folders tomorrow.
거기 예정 배송 시간이 오래 걸려서요. 전 서류철이 내일 필요하거든요.

M : I see. So, you're looking for a store with faster delivery, right?
그렇군요. 그럼 배송이 더 빠른 매장을 찾고 있는 거군요, 그렇죠?

W : Yes. The sooner, the better!
맞아요. 빠를수록 더 좋아요!

Why? 왜 정답일까?

대화에 따르면 여자는 서류철이 내일 필요하기 때문에 원래 주문하려던 곳보다 배송이 더 빠른 곳을 찾고 있다(**So, you're looking for a store with faster delivery, right? / The sooner, the better!**). 따라서 여자가 다른 주문처를 찾고 있는 이유로 가장 적절한 것은 ② '더 빠른 배송을 원해서'이다.

- file folder 서류철
- delivery ⓝ 배송
- have in stock 재고가 있다

08 식당 매니저 인터뷰

정답률 95% | 정답 ③

대화를 듣고, Delizia에 관해 언급되지 않은 것을 고르시오.

① 창업 연도 ② 창업자 ③ 예약 방법
④ 장소 협찬 영화 ⑤ 야외 정원

M : Hello, viewers! I'm currently at one of the popular restaurants, Delizia. I'm here with the manager of Delizia.
안녕하세요, 시청자 여러분! 저는 지금 인기 있는 식당 중 한 곳인 Delizia에 나와 있습니다. Delizia의 매니저 분과 함께 있습니다.

W : Hi, viewers. I'm Laura, the manager of Delizia.
안녕하세요, 시청자 여러분. 저는 Delizia의 매니저인 Laura입니다.

M : Laura, Delizia is the oldest Italian restaurant in our city, isn't it?
Laura, Delizia는 우리 도시에서 가장 오래된 이탈리아 식당입니다, 그렇지 않나요?

W : Yes. 「It was founded in 1906.」 ①의 근거 일치
네. 1906년에 세워졌어요.

M : Wow! 「Could you tell us who founded it? ②의 근거 일치
와! 누가 이곳을 세웠는지 말해주실 수 있나요?

W : Fabio Cannavaro.」 Today, his granddaughter runs it.
Fabio Cannavaro입니다. 지금은 그분의 손녀가 운영하고 있죠.

M : Oh, it's a family business. Tell us more about Delizia.
오, 가업이군요. Delizia에 대해서 더 말해주세요.

W : Our restaurant is famous not only for its food, but also for its architectural value.
저희 식당은 음식뿐 아니라 건축적 가치로도 유명하죠.

M : I see. I know Delizia was used as a location for some famous movies.
그렇군요. Delizia는 몇몇 유명한 영화에 촬영 장소로 쓰였다고 알고 있어요.

W : Right. 「The movie, *From Rome with Love*, was recently filmed in our restaurant.」
네. *From Rome with Love*라는 영화가 최근에 저희 매장에서 촬영되었죠. ④의 근거 일치

M : Impressive! 「And Delizia has a very romantic outdoor garden, doesn't it?」 ⑤의 근거 일치
인상적이군요! 그리고 Delizia에는 아주 낭만적인 야외 정원이 있어요, 그렇지 않나요?

W : Yeah. It's often used for weddings.
네. 종종 결혼식에 쓰이곤 해요.

M : That's good. Now, could you show me around the garden?
좋네요. 이제, 저에게 정원을 구경시켜 주실 수 있나요?

W : Sure. Come this way, please.
물론이죠. 이쪽으로 와주세요.

Why? 왜 정답일까?

대화에서 남자와 여자는 **Delizia**의 창업 연도, 창업자, 장소 협찬 영화, 야외 정원에 관해 언급하였다. 따라서 언급되지 않은 것은 ③ '예약 방법'이다.

Why? 왜 오답일까?

① '**It was founded in 1906.**'에서 '창업 연도'가 언급되었다.
② '**Fabio Cannavaro.**'에서 '창업자'가 언급되었다.
④ '**The movie, *From Rome with Love*, was recently filmed in our restaurant.**'에서 '장소 협찬 영화'가 언급되었다.
⑤ '**And Delizia has a very romantic outdoor garden, doesn't it?**'에서 '야외 정원'이 언급되었다.

- found(-founded-founded) ⓥ 세우다, 설립하다
- currently [ad] 현재, 지금
- architectural ⓐ 건축적인
- impressive ⓐ 인상적인
- show A around (B) A에게 (B를) 구경시켜 주다

[문제편 p.019]

09 동굴 투어 소개

정답률 95% | 정답 ④

Nest Cave Boat Tour에 관한 다음 내용을 듣고, 일치하지 않는 것을 고르시오.

① 1시간 동안 진행된다.
② 보트당 최대 탑승 인원은 10명이다.
③ 동굴의 역사에 관해 들을 수 있다.
④ 동굴 내에서 사진 촬영을 할 수 있다.
⑤ 사전에 예약을 해야 한다.

W : Hello, listeners.
안녕하세요, 청취자 여러분.
Are you looking for a special activity for the upcoming holidays?
다가오는 휴일을 위해 특별한 활동을 찾고 계신가요?
Nest Cave Boat Tour is here for you.
Nest Cave Boat Tour가 여기 있습니다.
『You can explore the cave on a one-hour guided boat tour.』 ①의 근거 일치
여러분은 가이드가 있는 1시간짜리 보트 투어 동안 동굴을 탐험하실 수 있습니다.
『Up to ten people are allowed on each boat.』 ②의 근거 일치
보트당 최대 10명의 인원이 허용됩니다.
『Along the way, you can hear about the history and geological features of the cave.』
투어 동안, 여러분은 동굴의 역사와 지질학적 특징에 관해 들으실 수 있습니다. ③의 근거 일치
You can even see glowworms deep inside, but 『taking photos is not permitted inside the cave.』 ④의 근거 불일치
여러분은 안쪽 깊은 곳에서 심지어 반딧불이도 볼 수 있지만, 동굴 내에서 사진 촬영은 허용되지 않습니다.
With your cameras off, just enjoy the mysterious light from the glowworms.
카메라를 꺼 두신 상태로, 반딧불이의 신비로운 불빛을 그냥 즐겨주세요.
『For this wonderful cave tour, you need to make a reservation in advance.』 ⑤의 근거 일치
이 멋진 동굴 투어를 위해, 여러분은 사전에 예약하셔야 합니다.
For reservation, please visit our website. Thank you.
예약을 위해서는, 저희 웹 사이트를 방문해주세요. 고맙습니다.

Why? 왜 정답일까?

'~ **taking photos is not permitted inside the cave.**'에서 동굴 내 사진 촬영은 허용되지 않는다고 하므로, 내용과 일치하지 않는 것은 ④ '동굴 내에서 사진 촬영을 할 수 있다.'이다.

Why? 왜 오답일까?

① '**You can explore the cave on a one-hour guided boat tour.**'의 내용과 일치한다.
② '**Up to ten people are allowed on each boat.**'의 내용과 일치한다.
③ '**Along the way, you can hear about the history** ~'의 내용과 일치한다.
⑤ '~ **you need to make a reservation in advance.**'의 내용과 일치한다.

- **upcoming** ⓐ 다가오는
- **explore** ⓥ 탐험하다
- **geological** ⓐ 지질학적인
- **feature** ⓝ 특징, 특성
- **glowworm** ⓝ 반딧불이 (류의 곤충)
- **mysterious** ⓐ 신비로운
- **make a reservation** 예약하다

10 발판 사다리 사기

정답률 93% | 정답 ③

다음 표를 보면서 대화를 듣고, 두 사람이 주문할 사다리를 고르시오.

Stepladders

	Model	Price	Height (cm)	Load Capacity (kg)	Foldable
①	A	$55	90	80	○
②	B	$65	130	90	×
③	C	$75	150	110	○
④	D	$85	180	150	×
⑤	E	$105	210	200	○

W : Honey, what are you looking at on the computer?
여보, 컴퓨터로 뭘 보고 있어요?
M : I'm looking for a stepladder. We need one for when we do housework.
발판 사다리를 하나 찾고 있어요. 우리가 집안일 할 때 하나 필요해요.
W : Good idea. Let me see. All of these five ladders look good.
좋은 생각이에요. 어디 보죠. 이 다섯 개 사다리 다 괜찮아 보이네요.
M : Yes, but let's exclude this one. 『It's too much to spend over $100 for just a ladder.』
네, 그렇지만 이건 빼죠. 사다리 하나에 100달러 넘게 쓰는 것은 과해요. 근거1 Price 조건
W : I agree. 『What about the height? 근거2 Height 조건
동의해요. 높이는요?
M : Considering our house, it should be at least 120 cm.』
우리 집을 고려하면, 최소한 120센티미터는 되어야겠어요.
W : Okay. 『I think the weight a ladder can support is also important.
알겠어요. 사다리 하나가 지탱할 수 있는 무게도 중요하겠어요.
M : Oh, definitely. It should be able to hold more than 100 kg.』 근거3 Load Capacity 조건
오, 물론이죠. 100킬로그램 이상은 지탱할 수 있어야 해요.
W : Right. Then we only have two options now.
맞아요. 그럼 두 가지 선택권만 남죠.
M : Yes. 『Wouldn't it be better to buy a ladder that can fold? 근거4 Foldable 조건
네. 접히는 사다리를 사는 게 낫지 않겠어요?
W : Of course.』 It'll take up less storage space.
물론이죠. 보관하는 공간을 덜 차지할 거예요.
M : I agree. Let's order it now.
동의해요. 그것으로 지금 주문하죠.

Why? 왜 정답일까?

대화에 따르면 남자와 여자는 가격이 100달러를 넘지 않으면서, 높이는 120센티미터 이상이고, 100킬로그램 이상의 무게를 지탱할 수 있으며, 접어서 보관할 수 있는 사다리를 구매하려고 한다. 따라서 두 사람이 주문할 사다리는 ③ 'C'이다.

- **exclude** ⓥ 제외하다
- **height** ⓝ 높이
- **take up** (공간 등을) 차지하다

★★★ 등급을 가르는 문제!

11 백화점 가는 길 묻기

정답률 42% | 정답 ①

대화를 듣고, 여자의 마지막 말에 대한 남자의 응답으로 가장 적절한 것을 고르시오.

① Actually, it leads to the basement of the store. – 사실 거기가 매장 지하랑 이어져요.
② Please connect me with the marketing department. – 마케팅 부서로 연결해주세요.
③ No, the menswear is on the fifth floor of the store. – 아니요, 남성복은 매장 5층에 있어요.
④ Well, the department store opens at 10 in the morning. – 음, 백화점은 오전 10시에 개장합니다.
⑤ Not exactly. This is the direct number of the department. – 아니요, 이 번호는 부서 직통 전화입니다.

W : Excuse me. Can you tell me how I can get to Harriot Department Store?
실례합니다. Harriot 백화점으로 가는 길을 알려주실 수 있나요?
M : Sure. Go straight ahead until you find exit 5.
물론이죠. 5번 출구가 보일 때까지 앞으로 쭉 가세요.
W : Thank you. Is the department store close to exit 5?
고맙습니다. 백화점이 5번 출구랑 가까운가요?
M : Actually, it leads to the basement of the store.
사실 거기가 매장 지하랑 이어져요.

Why? 왜 정답일까?

직진해서 5번 출구를 찾으라는 남자의 말에 여자는 백화점이 5번 출구와 가까운지 묻는다(**Is the department store close to exit 5?**). 따라서 남자의 응답으로 가장 적절한 것은 ① '사실 거기가 매장 지하랑 이어져요.'이다.

- **department store** ⓝ 백화점
- **connect A with B** A를 B와 연결하다

★★ 문제 해결 꿀~팁 ★★

▶ 많이 틀린 이유는?
여자의 마지막 말은 백화점이 5번 출구와 가까운지를 묻는 말이므로, 남자의 응답으로는 가까운지 아닌지 직접 답해주는 말, 또는 백화점의 위치를 더 자세히 설명해주는 말이 적절하다. 최다 오답인 ③은 백화점 중 '남성복 매장(**menswear**)'의 위치만 알려주고 있으므로 답으로 부적절하다. ④는 백화점 '위치'가 아닌 '개장 시간'을 알려주는 말이므로 역시 답으로 부적절하다.
▶ 문제 해결 방법은?
정답인 ①의 **it**은 여자의 마지막 말에서 언급된 '5번 출구(**exit 5**)'를 가리키는 대명사이다. '5번 출구가 백화점 지하와 연결되기 때문에' 백화점으로 가려면 5번 출구를 찾아야 한다는 것이 대화의 주된 내용이다.

12 야구 연습에서 일찍 온 이유 말하기

정답률 89% | 정답 ③

대화를 듣고, 남자의 마지막 말에 대한 여자의 응답으로 가장 적절한 것을 고르시오.

① Of course. She'll be very happy to see you.
물론이지. 그녀는 너를 만나면 무척 기뻐할 거야.
② Thank you for the ride. Say hello to Daniel.
태워줘서 고마워. Daniel에게 안부 전해줘.
③ How nice! I'll call and thank her for the ride.
친절하셔라! 전화해서 태워주신 거 고맙다고 전화 드려야겠네.
④ Never mind. I'll take a bus to the baseball field.
신경 쓰지 마. 난 야구장까지 버스를 탈 거야.
⑤ Hurry up. You'll be late for baseball practice again.
서둘러. 너 또 야구 연습에 늦겠어.

M : Hi, Mom. I'm home.
엄마, 저 왔어요.
W : Oh, you're back from your baseball practice early today.
오, 오늘은 야구 연습에서 일찍 왔구나.
M : Yeah. While I was waiting at the bus stop, Daniel's mom drove by and gave me a ride.
네, 제가 버스를 기다리고 있는 동안, Daniel의 엄마가 차로 지나가시다가 저를 태워주셨어요.
W : How nice! I'll call and thank her for the ride.
친절하셔라! 전화해서 태워주신 거 고맙다고 전화 드려야겠네.

Why? 왜 정답일까?

평소보다 야구 연습에서 일찍 돌아온 남자는 **Daniel**의 어머니가 지나가다가 자신을 태워주었다고 여자에게 알리고 있다(**While I was waiting at the bus stop, Daniel's mom drove by and gave me a ride.**). 따라서 여자의 응답으로 가장 적절한 것은 ③ '친절하셔라! 전화해서 태워주신 거 고맙다고 전화 드려야겠네.'이다.

- **give a ride** 태워주다

13 합창단 활동

정답률 93% | 정답 ①

대화를 듣고, 여자의 마지막 말에 대한 남자의 응답으로 가장 적절한 것을 고르시오. [3점]

Man: ______

① Great. It'll be really nice if we sing together. – 좋아. 우리가 같이 노래한다면 정말 좋겠다.
② Thank you. I had a great time in your choir. – 고마워. 난 너의 합창단과 아주 좋은 시간을 보냈어.
③ Think twice. It's not easy to sing in a choir. – 잘 생각해. 합창단에서 노래하는 건 쉽지 않아.
④ Actually, I'm not a big fan of classical music. – 사실, 난 클래식을 그렇게 좋아하진 않아.
⑤ Never mind. The choir practice has been canceled. – 신경 쓰지 마. 합창단 연습은 취소되었어.

W : What's the tune you're humming, Kevin?
네가 흥얼거리는 노래 뭐야, Kevin?
M : Ah, it's a song I sang in choir last week.
아, 내가 지난주에 합창단에서 부른 노래야.
W : I didn't know you were in a choir!
난 네가 합창단을 하는지 몰랐어!
M : It's just a small choir. We meet every Wednesday night and sing together.
그냥 작은 합창단이야. 우린 매주 수요일 밤에 만나서 함께 노래를 불러.
W : What kind of songs does the choir sing?
합창단에서 어떤 종류의 노래를 불러?
M : A real mix, actually. We do classical, jazz, pretty much anything you can think of.
정말 다 부르지, 사실. 클래식도 하고, 재즈도 하고, 네가 생각할 수 있는 거 거의 다 해.

[문제편 p.019]

W : That sounds fun.
재미있겠다.
M : You seem interested. How about joining our choir?
너도 관심이 있는 것 같네. 우리 합창단에 드는 게 어때?
W : Well, I love music, but I'm not a good singer.
음, 난 음악을 좋아하긴 하는데, 노래를 잘하지는 못해.
M : It doesn't matter. What matters is that you enjoy what you're doing.
그건 상관 없어. 중요한 건 네가 하고 있는 걸 즐기는 거야.
W : Then I guess I'll give it a try.
그럼 시도해볼 수 있을 것 같아.
M : Great. It'll be really nice if we sing together.
좋아. 우리가 같이 노래한다면 정말 좋겠다.

Why? 왜 정답일까?

합창단 활동에 관심이 있지만 노래를 못한다며 주저하는 여자에게 남자는 즐기는 것이 가장 중요하다며 격려하고, 이에 여자는 시도해볼 수 있을 것 같다고 말한다(Then I guess I'll give it a try.). 따라서 남자의 응답으로 가장 적절한 것은 ① '좋아. 우리가 같이 노래한다면 정말 좋겠다.'이다.

- choir ⓝ 합창단
- give it a try 시도하다
- not a big fan of ~을 그다지 좋아하지 않는

14 주말 계획 이야기하기
정답률 88% | 정답 ⑤

대화를 듣고, 남자의 마지막 말에 대한 여자의 응답으로 가장 적절한 것을 고르시오. [3점]

Woman: ______________________

① I'm afraid I can't go with you this time. – 미안한데 이번에는 너랑 못 가겠어.
② I'm glad you've done the farm work in time. – 네가 마침 농장 일을 해냈다니 기쁘네.
③ Unfortunately, there are no more apples to pick. – 안타깝게도, 딸 사과가 더는 없어.
④ Thank you for the apples you sent me last week. – 네가 지난주에 보내준 사과 고마워.
✔⑤ You'll enjoy it. It's hard work but very rewarding. – 재미있을 거야. 힘든 일이지만 아주 보람차.

W : Hi, Lucas. How's it going?
안녕, Lucas. 요새 어때?
M : Not bad, Sarah. Do you have any special plans for this weekend?
괜찮아, Sarah. 너 이번 주말에 뭐 특별한 일정 있어?
W : Yes, I'm going to visit my grandparents' farm. They're short-handed, especially at harvest time.
응, 난 할머니 할아버지의 농장에 갈 거야. 특히 수확철에는 일손이 부족하거든.
M : You mean you're going to do some farm work?
네 말은 가서 농장 일을 할 거라는 거야?
W : That's right.
맞아.
M : What are you doing there?
거기서 뭐 해?
W : Well, I'm going to pick apples. If we don't pick them in time, we won't get a good price for them.
음, 난 사과를 딸 거야. 사과를 제때 따지 않으면, 좋은 가격을 받지 못하게 되거든.
M : I see. I want to have a chance to pick apples.
그렇구나. 나도 사과 딸 기회가 있었으면 좋겠어.
W : Really? Why don't you come along with me this weekend?
정말? 이번 주에 나랑 같이 가는 게 어때?
M : I've never done any farm work, but I'd love to.
난 한 번도 농장 일을 해본 적이 없지만, 해보고 싶어.
W : You'll enjoy it. It's hard work but very rewarding.
재미있을 거야. 힘든 일이지만 아주 보람차.

Why? 왜 정답일까?

사과 따는 일에 관심을 보이는 남자에게 여자는 농장에 함께 가자고 권하고, 남자는 경험이 없지만 해보고 싶다고 말한다(I've never done any farm work, but I'd love to.). 따라서 여자의 응답으로 가장 적절한 것은 ⑤ '재미있을 거야. 힘든 일이지만 아주 보람차.'이다.

- short-handed ⓐ 일손이 부족한
- in time 제때, 이윽고
- rewarding ⓐ 보람찬

15 자전거 탈 때 주의할 점
정답률 91% | 정답 ③

다음 상황 설명을 듣고, Katrina가 Simon에게 할 말로 가장 적절한 것을 고르시오.

Katrina: ______________________

① Let's go bicycle riding as often as possible. – 최대한 자주 자전거를 타러 가자.
② Go to the hospital before the pain gets worse. – 통증이 심해지기 전에 병원에 가봐.
✔③ You shouldn't do risky things while riding a bicycle. – 자전거 타는 동안에 위험한 짓을 해서는 안 돼.
④ I'll let you know the repair shop that I often go to. – 내가 자주 가는 수리점을 알려줄게.
⑤ You're brave to ride a bicycle with no hands. – 넌 손을 놓고 자전거를 타다니 용감하구나.

M : Katrina and Simon are close friends in the neighborhood.
Katrina와 Simon은 친한 이웃 친구이다.
Recently, they enjoy riding bicycles together.
최근에 이들은 함께 자전거 타는 것을 즐긴다.
But Katrina often notices Simon's careless behavior while riding a bicycle.
하지만 Katrina는 자전거를 타는 도중 Simon의 부주의한 행동을 종종 눈치챈다.
Although he is good at riding, there are some occasions where he almost falls over because he sometimes rides with his hands off the handlebars.
그는 자전거를 잘 타기는 하지만, 간혹 손잡이를 놓고 타느라 거의 떨어질 뻔했던 경우가 몇 번 있다.
Furthermore, he often uses his smartphone while riding.
더구나, 그는 타는 동안 종종 스마트폰을 사용한다.
Katrina is worried that such behavior may lead to a serious accident.
Katrina는 그런 행동이 심각한 사고로 이어질까봐 걱정이다.
So, Katrina wants to give Simon some safety advice.
그래서, Katrina는 Simon에게 안전에 관해 조언을 조금 해 주고 싶다.
In this situation, what would Katrina most likely say to Simon?
이 상황에서, Katrina는 Simon에게 뭐라고 말하겠는가?
Katrina : You shouldn't do risky things while riding a bicycle.
자전거 타는 동안에 위험한 짓을 해서는 안 돼.

Why? 왜 정답일까?

상황에 따르면 자전거를 타는 도중 손잡이를 잡지 않거나 스마트폰을 사용하는 Simon에게 Katrina는 안전에 관해 조언하려고 한다(So, Katrina wants to give Simon some safety advice.). 따라서 Katrina가 Simon에게 할 말로 가장 적절한 것은 ③ '자전거 타는 동안에 위험한 짓을 해서는 안 돼.'이다.

- close ⓐ 가까운, 친밀한
- careless ⓐ 부주의한
- occasion ⓝ 경우, 때
- risky ⓐ 위험한

16-17 동물이 포함된 관용 표현

W : Okay, students.
자, 학생 여러분.
We just talked about idiomatic expressions related to color.
우린 방금 색깔과 관련된 관용 표현에 관해 이야기했습니다.
As you know, idioms are creative descriptions.
여러분도 알다시피, 관용어구는 창의적인 표현입니다.
We use them to share an idea or feeling.
우리는 어떤 아이디어나 감정을 나누려고 이것들을 사용합니다.
「Now, let's learn some animal idioms in English.」 16번의 근거
이제, 영어에 있는 동물 관용어구를 몇 가지 배워봅시다.
「The first idiom is "at a snail's pace," which means moving very slowly.」 17번 ①의 근거 일치
첫 번째 관용어구는 'at a snail's pace(달팽이 같은 속도로, 느릿느릿)'인데, 이는 아주 느리게 움직인다는 뜻입니다.
This idiom is easy to understand because we all know how slowly snails move.
이 관용어는 우리 모두 달팽이가 얼마나 느리게 움직이는지를 알고 있기 때문에 이해하기 쉽습니다.
「The next one, "hold your horses," is a common way of telling someone to wait or slow down.」 17번 ②의 근거 일치
다음은 'hold your horses(흥분부터 하지 말라)'는 누군가에게 기다리거나 천천히 하라고 말하는 흔한 방법입니다.
If someone says "hold your horses," they're telling you to "wait a minute."
누군가 여러분에게 'hold your horses'라고 말하면, 그들은 여러분에게 '잠깐 기다려라'고 말하는 것입니다.
「And children often hear from their parents, "I'm watching you like a hawk."」 17번 ③의 근거 일치
그리고 아이들은 흔히 부모로부터 'I'm watching you like a hawk(나는 너를 엄중히 감시하고 있어)'라는 말을 듣습니다.
This expression is often used to make sure that someone doesn't misbehave or make a mistake.
이 표현은 흔히 누군가 나쁜 짓을 하거나 실수를 하지 않고 있음을 확실히 하기 위해 사용됩니다.
「The last idiom is "I'll be a monkey's uncle."」 17번 ④의 근거 일치
마지막 관용어는 'I'll be a monkey's uncle(깜짝 놀랐어)'입니다.
People use this expression when something unexpected or unlikely happens.
사람들은 예기치 못한 일이나 있을 법하지 않은 일이 일어날 때 이 표현을 씁니다.
It's used in a comical way.
이것은 우스꽝스럽게 사용됩니다.
These idioms may be confusing at first, but once you learn them, you'll have a fun new way of talking.
이 관용어들은 처음에는 헷갈리겠지만, 일단 익히고 나면 여러분은 새롭고 재미있는 표현법을 갖게 될 것입니다.

- idiomatic expression 관용 표현
- description ⓝ 설명, 묘사
- at a snail's pace 달팽이 같은 속도로, 느릿느릿
- hold your horses (주로 명령문으로) 흥분부터 하지 말라
- slow down 천천히 하다, 속도를 늦추다
- I'm watching you like a hawk. 나는 너를 엄중히 감시하고 있다.
- make sure 확실히 하다
- misbehave ⓥ 나쁜 짓을 하다
- unexpected ⓐ 예기치 못한
- unlikely ⓐ 일어날 법하지 않은
- comical ⓐ 우스꽝스러운
- confusing ⓐ 혼란스러운, 헷갈리는

16 주제 파악
정답률 89% | 정답 ②

여자가 하는 말의 주제로 가장 적절한 것은?

① colors to help animals protect themselves – 동물들이 자신을 보호하는 데 도움이 되는 색깔
✔② English animal expressions and their meanings – 영어 동물 표현과 그 의미
③ animal sounds expressed in different languages – 다양한 언어로 표현되는 동물 소리
④ classroom animal games and activities for children – 아이들을 위한 수업용 동물 게임 및 활동
⑤ animals that appear frequently in children's stories – 동화에 자주 나오는 동물들

Why? 왜 정답일까?

'Now, let's learn some animal idioms in English.'에서 여자는 영어 속 동물 관용 표현에 관해 배워보자고 하므로, 여자가 하는 말의 목적으로 가장 적절한 것은 ② '영어 동물 표현과 그 의미'이다.

17 언급 유무 파악
정답률 94% | 정답 ⑤

언급된 동물이 아닌 것은?

① snail – 달팽이
② horse – 말
③ hawk – 매
④ monkey – 원숭이
✔⑤ snake – 뱀

Why? 왜 정답일까?

담화에서 여자는 다양한 동물 관용 표현의 예를 들기 위해 달팽이, 말, 매, 원숭이를 언급하였다. 따라서 언급되지 않은 것은 ⑤ '뱀'이다.

Why? 왜 오답일까?

① 'The first idiom is "at a snail's pace," which means moving very slowly.'에서 '달팽이'가 언급되었다.
② 'The next one, "hold your horses," is a common way of telling someone to wait or slow down.'에서 '말'이 언급되었다.
③ 'And children often hear from their parents, "I'm watching you like a hawk."'에서 '매'가 언급되었다.
④ 'The last idiom is "I'll be a monkey's uncle."'에서 '원숭이'가 언급되었다.

[문제편 p.020]

Dictation 04

문제편 021쪽

01 collecting recyclable garbage / address these complaints / hold a public hearing

02 I've recently bought / Having the right utensils / why you're totally into cooking

03 you made it yourself / invite her to join my class / how to arrange spring flowers

04 put the steps in front of the sofa / is he being toilet trained / the two pads near the potted plant

05 I just made an announcement / What about the first-aid kit / the ice water for players to drink

06 take the larger one / candles with the same scent / You can use it for your next purchase

07 that offers lower prices / even had free delivery / their scheduled delivery will take too long

08 who founded it / for its architectural value / could you show me around the garden

09 Up to ten people / the history and geological features of the cave / taking photos is not permitted inside the cave

10 All of these five ladders / Considering our house / take up less storage space

11 Is the department store close to exit 5

12 drove by and gave me a ride

13 meet every Wednesday night / A real mix, actually / you enjoy what you're doing / give it a try

14 short-handed, especially at harvest time / I'm going to pick apples / Why don't you come along with me

15 with his hands off / often uses his smartphone / such behavior may lead to a serious accident

16-17 how slowly snails move / I'm watching you like a hawk / misbehave or make a mistake / something unexpected or unlikely happens

05회 | 2020학년도 3월 학력평가 고3

• 정답 •

01 ③ 02 ⑤ 03 ① 04 ⑤ 05 ② 06 ③ 07 ② 08 ⑤ 09 ③ 10 ② 11 ⑤ 12 ② 13 ③ 14 ② 15 ① 16 ② 17 ⑤

01 미세 먼지 대처 특강 안내

정답률 85% | 정답 ③

다음을 듣고, 여자가 하는 말의 목적으로 가장 적절한 것을 고르시오.

① 미세 먼지 차단용 마스크의 착용을 권장하려고
② 고농도 미세 먼지의 발생 원인에 대해 설명하려고
③ 미세 먼지에 대비한 건강 관리법 강연을 홍보하려고
④ 미세 먼지 절감을 위한 캠페인에 동참할 것을 호소하려고
⑤ 미세 먼지 경보 발령에 따른 실외 활동 자제를 당부하려고

W : Good morning, everybody.
안녕하세요, 여러분.
This is your principal Alexandra Hamilton.
저는 교장인 Alexandra Hamilton입니다.
Our field trip last week was canceled due to the fine dust alert.
지난주 우리 현장학습은 미세 먼지 경보로 인해 취소되었습니다.
Many students were disappointed and so was I.
많은 학생들이 실망했고 저 또한 그랬습니다.
Since there will be many days with high levels of fine dust this spring, we should learn how to take care of ourselves.
올봄에는 미세 먼지 농도가 높은 날이 많을 것이니 우리는 스스로 조심할 방법을 배워야 합니다.
So, our school is holding a special lecture on personal healthcare.
그래서, 우리 학교에서는 개인 건강관리에 대한 특강을 열 예정입니다.
Famous doctor and TV show host Dr. Linda Han will come and show you how to minimize the health risks of fine dust in everyday life.
유명 의사 겸 TV 프로그램 진행자인 Linda Han 박사가 와서 일상생활에서 미세 먼지의 건강상 위험을 최소화할 방법을 알려줄 것입니다.
It'll be held at 4 p.m., Wednesday.
이것은 수요일 오후 4시에 열립니다.
This lecture is open to all students and parents.
이 강의는 모든 학생과 학부모에게 열려 있습니다.
Every attendee will be given free dust masks.
모든 참석자들은 무료 먼지 차단 마스크를 받게 될 것입니다.
Don't miss out on this great opportunity!
이 좋은 기회를 놓치지 마세요!

Why? 왜 정답일까?

'Since there will be many days with high levels of fine dust this spring, we should learn how to take care of ourselves. So, our school is holding a special lecture on personal healthcare.'에서 여자는 미세 먼지가 많은 날들에 대비하기 위해 학교에서 개인 건강관리를 주제로 한 특강을 개최할 예정이라며 학생들의 참여를 독려하고 있다. 따라서 여자가 하는 말의 목적으로 가장 적절한 것은 ③ '미세 먼지에 대비한 건강 관리법 강연을 홍보하려고'이다.

- **fine dust** ⓝ 미세 먼지
- **healthcare** ⓝ 건강관리, 보건
- **attendee** ⓝ 참석자
- **opportunity** ⓝ 기회
- **alert** ⓝ 경보
- **minimize** ⓥ 최소화하다
- **miss out on** ⓥ ~을 놓치다

02 관광지 복장에 대한 조언

정답률 83% | 정답 ⑤

대화를 듣고, 남자의 의견으로 가장 적절한 것을 고르시오.

① 여행 중에는 비상 연락처를 항상 소지해야 한다.
② 여행 시 치안이 불안한 장소에는 가지 말아야 한다.
③ 현금이나 귀중품은 최소한만 가지고 여행해야 한다.
④ 여행지의 기후를 고려하여 여벌 옷을 가져가야 한다.
⑤ 여행지에서는 관광객처럼 보이는 복장을 피해야 한다.

M : Rebecca, I hear that you're planning a trip to France.
Rebecca, 네가 프랑스 여행을 계획하고 있다고 들었어.
W : Yeah. I'm very excited. It's my first trip abroad.
응. 매우 신나. 난 해외여행은 처음이야.
M : That's exciting. Where in France are you going?
신나는 일이네. 프랑스 어디로 갈 거야?
W : Paris. I'll visit many tourist spots there. I'm thinking of buying some clothes for the trip.
파리. 난 그곳의 많은 관광지를 방문할 거야. 난 여행을 위해 옷을 좀 살까 생각 중이야.
M : Well, speaking of clothes, can I give you some advice?
음, 옷 얘기가 나와서 말인데, 내가 조언을 좀 해도 될까?
W : Sure. What is it?
물론이지. 뭔데?
M : If you dress like a typical tourist there, you'll be an easy target for pickpockets.
거기서 전형적인 관광객처럼 옷을 입으면 넌 소매치기들의 손쉬운 표적이 될 거야.
W : Oh, I didn't know that. Then, what should I wear?
오, 그건 몰랐어. 그럼 나는 무엇을 입어야 할까?
M : If I were you, I'd avoid outfits that the locals would not wear.
내가 너라면, 나는 현지 주민들이 입지 않을 옷을 피하겠어.
W : I see. What clothes would make me look like a tourist in Paris?
알겠어. 어떤 옷을 입으면 파리의 관광객처럼 보일까?
M : As far as I know, the locals rarely wear hiking jackets or gym clothes on the street.
내가 아는 바로는, 현지인들은 길거리에서 등산복이나 체육복을 거의 입지 않는대.
W : Thanks. I'll keep that in mind.
고마워. 그 점을 명심할게.

Why? 왜 정답일까?

'If you dress like a typical tourist there, you'll be an easy target for pickpockets.'와 'If I were you, I'd avoid outfits that the locals would not wear.'에서 남자는 여행지에서 전형적인 관광객처럼 옷을 입고 다니면 소매치기의 표적이 되기 쉽다며 자신이라면 현지인들이 입지 않을 법한 옷을 피하겠다고 언급하고 있다. 따라서 남자의 의견으로 가장 적절한 것은 ⑤ '여행지에서는 관광객처럼 보이는 복장을 피해야 한다.'이다.

- speaking of ~에 관해 말하자면
- outfit ⓝ 옷, 복장
- hiking jacket ⓝ 등산복
- pickpocket ⓝ 소매치기
- as far as I know 내가 아는 바로는
- keep in mind ⓥ ~을 명심하다

03 무대 배치 상의하기

정답률 79% | 정답 ①

대화를 듣고, 두 사람의 관계를 가장 잘 나타낸 것을 고르시오.

✔ 안무가 – 무대 감독
② 무용 강사 – 수강생
③ 가구 제작자 – 의뢰인
④ 의상 디자이너 – 무용수
⑤ 카메라 감독 – 소품 담당자

M : Hey, Kimmy. Do you have a minute? I have something to say about the stage.
안녕하세요, Kimmy. 시간 좀 있으세요? 무대에 대해서 할 말이 있어요.

W : Okay. I'm listening.
네, 말씀하세요.

M : Last evening, I went on the stage and tried the dance moves myself.
어제 저녁에 무대에 올라가서 제가 직접 춤 동작을 해 봤어요.

W : Did everything go well?
모든 게 잘됐어요?

M : Pretty well, but we need to change some things.
꽤 괜찮았어요, 하지만 우린 몇 가지를 바꿔야겠어요.

W : Just a second. Let me pull out the stage layout sheet. *[Pause]* Go ahead.
잠시만요. 무대 배치도를 꺼내볼게요. *[잠시 멈춤]* 말씀하세요.

M : While I was doing the turns, I bumped into the bench. We need to move it.
전 회전을 하다가 벤치에 부딪쳤어요. 이걸 옮겨야 해요.

W : Well, I was told to place it in the center of the stage.
음, 전 그걸 무대 중앙에 놓으라고 들었어요.

M : True. But I changed some moves so that the dancers make bigger turns. That means we need more room.
맞아요. 하지만 나는 댄서들이 더 크게 돌 수 있도록 몇 가지 안무를 바꿨어요. 그건 우리에게 더 많은 공간이 필요하다는 것을 뜻하죠.

W : I see. I'll push the bench to the back.
그렇군요. 벤치를 뒤로 밀어둘게요.

M : Thanks. And please fix the bench to the floor. I created a move where the dancers jump from the bench.
고마워요. 그리고 벤치를 바닥에 고정해주세요. 전 댄서들이 벤치에서 뛰어내리는 안무를 만들었어요.

W : All right. I'll fix it nice and tight.
알겠어요. 제가 그걸 잘 단단하게 고정해 둘게요.

Why? 왜 정답일까?

'But I changed some moves so that the dancers make bigger turns.'와 'I created a move where the dancers jump from the bench.'에서 남자가 안무가임을, 'Let me pull out the stage layout sheet.', 'Well, I was told to place it in the center of the stage.', 'I'll push the bench to the back.' 등에서 여자가 무대 배치를 담당하는 무대 감독임을 알 수 있으므로, 두 사람의 관계로 가장 적절한 것은 ① '안무가 – 무대 감독'이다.

- pull out ⓥ ~을 꺼내다
- bump into ⓥ ~에 부딪히다
- layout sheet ⓝ 배치도

04 학교 도서관 공간 디자인 구경하기

정답률 88% | 정답 ⑤

대화를 듣고, 그림에서 대화의 내용과 일치하지 않는 것을 고르시오.

①
Read Aloud Space
②
③
④
⑤

W : Mr. Thompson. Can we talk about the design for the Read Aloud Space?
Thompson 씨, Read Aloud Space 디자인에 대해 이야기 좀 할 수 있나요?

M : Sure. Oh, is this a photo from another school?
물론이죠. 오, 이건 다른 학교에서 찍은 사진인가요?

W : Yes. I thought we could borrow some ideas.
네. 우리가 아이디어를 좀 얻어올 수 있을 거라고 생각했어요.

M : I'm sure we can. 「I can see the sign "Read Aloud Space" on the wall.」 ①의 근거 일치
분명 그럴 거예요. 벽에 'Read Aloud Space'라는 팻말이 보이네요.

W : Let's put up a sign like that, too. 「And they put a big round hole in the wall.」 ②의 근거 일치
우리도 저런 팻말을 붙이죠. 그리고 벽에 큰 둥근 구멍도 만들어 놨어요.

M : It's brilliant. Kids would enjoy going through the hole.
멋지네요. 아이들은 구멍을 통과해 다니는 걸 좋아할 거예요.

W : 「What do you think about this penguin between the hole and the bookcases?」 ③의 근거 일치
구멍과 책장 사이에 있는 이 펭귄은 어때요?

M : We should absolutely have something like that. Kids love stuffed animals.
우리도 꼭 저런 게 있어야 해요. 아이들은 동물 인형을 좋아해요.

W : 「The airplane hanging down from the ceiling looks pretty, doesn't it?」 ④의 근거 일치
천장에 매달려 있는 비행기가 예쁘네요, 그렇죠?

M : It looks lovely. Kids will like looking at it.
귀여워 보여요. 아이들은 저걸 보는 것을 좋아할 거예요.

W : Yeah. 「And I see a table on the floor.」 Maybe it's for the teacher. ⑤의 근거 불일치
맞아요. 그리고 바닥에 탁자가 보이네요. 아마 선생님이 쓰는 것인가봐요.

M : I guess so.
그런 것 같네요.

Why? 왜 정답일까?

대화에서 바닥에 탁자가 있다(And I see a table on the floor.)고 하는데, 그림에서는 바닥에 의자가 대신 놓여 있다. 따라서 그림에서 대화의 내용과 일치하지 않는 것은 ⑤이다.

- read aloud ⓥ 소리 내어 읽다
- brilliant ⓐ 멋진, 훌륭한
- stuffed animal ⓝ 동물 (봉제) 인형
- put up ⓥ (포스터 등을) 붙이다
- absolutely ad 꼭, 반드시

05 친구 초대 허락받기

정답률 90% | 정답 ②

대화를 듣고, 여자가 할 일로 가장 적절한 것을 고르시오.

① 침실 창문 닫기
✔ 식료품 사러 가기
③ 게임기 수리 맡기기
④ 영화 예매권 환불하기
⑤ 아들 친구 데려다주기

W : Sean, did you close your bedroom windows? The rain will start any minute.
Sean, 네 침실 창문을 닫았니? 비가 곧 올 거야.

M : Yes, Mom. I've already closed all the windows.
네, 엄마. 벌써 창문을 다 닫아놨어요.

W : Good. A storm is coming. So, let's keep them closed. Are you going out tonight?
잘했어. 폭풍이 오고 있어. 그러니 창문을 닫아두자. 오늘 밤에 외출하니?

M : No. I was planning to go to the movies, but I'm staying home.
아뇨. 영화 보러 갈 계획이었는데 집에 있을 거예요.

W : Good idea. What will you do?
좋은 생각이야. 뭐 할 거니?

M : Can I invite Eric to our house? I want to play video games with him.
Eric을 우리 집으로 초대해도 돼요? 전 그 애와 비디오 게임을 하고 싶어요.

W : Okay. Do you want me to cook for you two boys?
그래. 내가 너희 둘을 위해 요리해 줄까?

M : That'd be great. Eric loves your chicken stew.
그럼 아주 좋겠어요. Eric은 엄마의 치킨 스튜를 좋아해요.

W : All right. I'm going grocery shopping before it rains hard.
알겠어. 비가 심하게 오기 전에 난 식료품을 사러 갔다올게.

M : Do you want me to come with you?
같이 갈까요?

W : No, that's okay. I'll grab a few things and be right back.
아니, 괜찮아. 몇 가지만 사서 바로 돌아올 거야.

Why? 왜 정답일까?

폭풍 때문에 영화를 보러 가려던 계획을 취소한 남자는 대신에 친구를 초대해도 될지 엄마인 여자에게 묻고, 여자는 이를 허락하며 둘에게 요리를 해주겠다고 제안하고는 비가 심하게 오기 전에 장을 봐오겠다(I'm going grocery shopping before it rains hard.)고 이야기한다. 따라서 여자가 할 일로 가장 적절한 것은 ② '식료품 사러 가기'이다.

- go grocery shopping ⓥ 식료품을 사러 가다
- grab ⓥ 집어들다

06 한식 포장 주문하기

정답률 70% | 정답 ③

대화를 듣고, 여자가 지불할 금액을 고르시오. [3점]

① $44 ② $46 ✔ $48 ④ $50 ⑤ $52

M : Hi. Welcome to Korean Table. What would you like to order?
안녕하세요, Korean Table에 잘 오셨습니다. 무엇을 주문하시겠습니까?

W : I'd like to order a take-out meal. What would you recommend?
전 테이크아웃 식사를 주문하고 싶어요. 어떤 것을 추천해 주시겠어요?

M : What about the Korean BBQ Combo? It comes with *bulgogi*, rice and a soda.
한국 BBQ 콤보 어떠신가요? *불고기*와 밥과 탄산음료가 함께 나옵니다.

W : Sounds good. How much is it?
좋아요. 얼마인가요?

M : It's $18. And if you pay an extra $2, you can size up.
18달러입니다. 그리고 2달러를 더 내시면 사이즈업을 해드려요.

W : I want two combos but I don't want to size up.
전 콤보를 두 개 사고 싶지만 사이즈업은 원하지 않아요.

M : Sure. What do you want for your soda, Coke or lemonade?
알겠습니다. 탄산음료는 콜라와 레모네이드 중 무엇으로 하시겠습니까?

W : Lemonade for both combos, please. Do you also have dumplings?
두 콤보 다 레모네이드로 부탁드려요. 만두도 있나요?

M : Yes. We have fried dumplings and steamed dumplings. Fried are $14 for a plate, and steamed are $12.
네. 튀김만두와 찐만두가 있습니다. 튀긴 것은 한 접시에 14달러, 찐 것은 12달러입니다.

W : I'll have one plate of steamed dumplings. Here's my credit card.
찐만두 한 접시로 할게요. 여기 제 신용 카드요.

M : Okay. Your take-out will be ready in ten minutes.
알겠습니다. 포장은 10분 뒤에 준비될 겁니다.

Why? 왜 정답일까?

대화에 따르면 여자는 18달러짜리 BBQ 콤보를 2인분 사고, 사이즈업을 위한 추가 비용은 지불하지 않았으며, 추가로 12달러짜리 찐만두 한 접시를 주문했다. 이를 식으로 나타내면 '$18\times2+12=48$'이므로, 여자가 지불할 금액은 ③ '$48'이다.

- recommend ⓥ 추천하다
- steamed ⓐ (음식을) 찐
- dumpling ⓝ 만두

07 금요일에 동아리 모임에 참석하지 못하는 이유

정답률 88% | 정답 ②

대화를 듣고, 남자가 금요일에 Poetry Night에 가지 않는 이유를 고르시오.

① 병원에 가야 해서
✔ 침대를 조립해야 해서

[문제편 p.025]

③ 이삿짐을 포장해야 해서 ④ 동아리 모임에 가야 해서
⑤ 아파트 청소를 해야 해서

W : Hey, Neil. How's your new apartment?
안녕, Neil. 새 아파트는 어때?
M : It's fantastic. Thanks for helping me move in.
환상적이야. 내가 이사하는 것을 도와줘서 고마워.
W : No problem. You would've done the same for me.
천만에. 너도 나한테 똑같이 했을 걸.
M : Of course. By the way, I can't go to Poetry Night this Friday.
물론이지. 그나저나, 나 이번 주 금요일에는 Poetry Night에 못 가.
W : Really? All the club members will be expecting you.
정말? 모든 동아리 회원들이 네가 오길 기대할 텐데.
M : I know. But I need to take care of some other stuff.
나도 알지. 하지만 나는 다른 일을 좀 처리해야 해.
W : What do you need to do?
뭘 해야 하는데?
M : My new bed will be delivered this Friday. I have to assemble it myself.
내 새 침대가 이번 주 금요일에 배달될 거야. 난 그것을 직접 조립해야 해.
W : I see. But can't you assemble the bed on the weekend?
그렇구나. 하지만 침대를 주말에 조립할 수는 없니?
M : The thing is, I've been sleeping on the sofa for a week so my back hurts. I really want to sleep in a bed.
사실, 난 일주일째 소파에서 자고 있어서 허리가 아파. 난 정말 침대에서 자고 싶어.
W : Well, if you say so. See you later.
음, 하는 수 없네. 나중에 보자.

Why? 왜 정답일까?

남자는 금요일에 배달되는 침대를 조립해야 해서(My new bed will be delivered this Friday. I have to assemble it myself.) 그날 예정된 동아리 모임에 갈 수 없다고 하므로, 남자가 Poetry Night에 가지 못하는 이유로 가장 적절한 것은 ② '침대를 조립해야 해서'이다.

- deliver ⓥ 배달하다
- assemble ⓥ 조립하다
- the thing is 사실은, 문제는
- If you say so. 하는 수 없지.

08 도장 만들기 수업 정답률 88% | 정답 ⑤

대화를 듣고, 도장 만들기 수업에 관해 언급되지 않은 것을 고르시오.

① 사용 언어 ② 참가비 ③ 소요 시간
④ 장소 ⑤ 인원 제한

W : Hi, Rick. What are you doing tomorrow afternoon?
안녕, Rick. 내일 오후에 뭐 해?
M : I'm attending a one-day class for making hand-carved stamps. You can come along if you want.
나는 직접 새긴 도장을 만들기 위해 일일 수업을 들을 거야. 네가 좋다면 같이 가도 돼.
W : Sounds interesting. I'm in. 「Will the class be conducted in English?
재미있겠다. 나도 갈래. 수업은 영어로 진행되니?
M : The instructor will speak Korean, but there'll be an English translator.」 ①의 근거 일치
강사는 한국어를 할 텐데, 영어 통역사가 있을 거야.
W : Good. 「How much is the participation fee? ②의 근거 일치
좋아. 참가비는 얼마야?
M : It's 10,000 won per person.」 You can take your stamp home after class.
1인당 1만 원이야. 수업이 끝나면 네 도장을 집에 가져가도 돼.
W : That's reasonable. 「How long is the class? ③의 근거 일치
적당한데. 수업은 얼마나 오래 해?
M : It'll start at two and last about one hour.」 Let's have lunch together before the class.
두 시에 시작해서 한 시간 정도 해. 수업 전에 같이 점심 먹자.
W : Okay. 「Where's the class being held?
그래. 수업은 어디서 열려?
M : It's taking place at the City Art Center.」 ④의 근거 일치
City Art Center에서 열릴 거야.
W : Wonderful. I'll meet you in front of the Art Center at 1 p.m.
아주 좋아. 오후 1시에 Art Center 앞에서 만나자.
M : Cool. See you there.
좋아. 거기서 봐.

Why? 왜 정답일까?

대화에서 남자와 여자는 도장 만들기 수업의 사용 언어, 참가비, 소요 시간, 장소를 언급하였다. 따라서 언급되지 않은 것은 ⑤ '인원 제한'이다.

Why? 왜 오답일까?

① 'The instructor will speak Korean, but there'll be an English translator.'에서 '사용 언어'가 언급되었다.
② 'It's 10,000 won per person.'에서 '참가비'가 언급되었다.
③ 'It'll start at two and last about one hour.'에서 '소요 시간'이 언급되었다.
④ 'It's taking place at the City Art Center.'에서 '장소'가 언급되었다.

- hand-carved ⓐ 손으로 새긴
- stamp ⓝ 도장, 우표
- come along ⓥ 함께 가다
- conduct ⓥ 진행하다
- translator ⓝ 통역사
- participation fee ⓝ 참가비

09 연중 챌린지 프로그램 소개 정답률 84% | 정답 ③

Campbell Challenge Program에 관한 다음 내용을 듣고, 일치하지 않는 것을 고르시오.

① Challenge를 하나 이상 신청할 수 있다.
② Challenge의 목록은 학교 웹 사이트에 탑재되어 있다.
③ 한번 선택한 Challenge는 변경할 수 없다.
④ Challenge별 필수 요건을 충족하면 수료증을 받는다.
⑤ 등록은 3월 23일까지 온라인으로 가능하다.

M : Hello, students of Campbell High School.
안녕하세요, Campbell 고등학교 학생 여러분.
I'm happy to introduce our new program — the Campbell Challenge Program.
저희 새로운 프로그램인 Campbell Challenge Program을 소개하게 되어 기쁩니다.
It'll provide opportunities for students to take on challenges in diverse areas such as academics, sports, arts, and computers.
이것은 학생들이 학업, 스포츠, 예술, 컴퓨터 등 다양한 분야에서 도전을 해볼 기회를 제공할 것입니다.
「Following your interests, choose one or more Challenges every year and work on them throughout the year.」 ①의 근거 일치
여러분의 관심사에 따라 매년 하나 이상의 Challenge를 선택하고 일 년 동안 진행하세요.
「The list of Challenges you can choose from has been uploaded on our school website.」 ②의 근거 일치
여러분이 고를 수 있는 Challenge의 목록이 학교 웹 사이트에 탑재되어 있습니다.
「The Challenges you choose can be changed one time during the year.」 ③의 근거 불일치
여러분이 선택하는 Challenge는 한 해에 한 번 바꿀 수 있습니다.
「Students who satisfy the requirements of their selected Challenges will receive a certificate at the end of the year.」 ④의 근거 일치
자신이 선택한 Challenge의 필수 요건을 충족하는 학생들은 연말에 수료증을 받을 것입니다.
「You can sign up for the program online until March 23.」 ⑤의 근거 일치
3월 23일까지 온라인으로 프로그램 등록이 가능합니다.
Ask your teacher for more information.
더 많은 정보는 선생님께 문의하세요.

Why? 왜 정답일까?

'The Challenges you choose can be changed one time during the year.'에서 Challenge를 연중 한 번은 바꿀 수 있다고 하므로, 내용과 일치하지 않는 것은 ③ '한번 선택한 Challenge는 변경할 수 없다.'이다.

Why? 왜 오답일까?

① '~ choose one or more Challenges every year and work on them throughout the year.'의 내용과 일치한다.
② 'The list of Challenges you can choose from has been uploaded on our school website.'의 내용과 일치한다.
④ 'Students who satisfy the requirements of their selected Challenges will receive a certificate ~'의 내용과 일치한다.
⑤ 'You can sign up for the program online until March 23.'의 내용과 일치한다.

- take on ⓥ ~을 떠맡다, 착수하다
- satisfy ⓥ 충족하다
- requirement ⓝ 필수 요건
- certificate ⓝ 수료증
- sign up for ⓥ ~에 등록하다

10 비디오 스트리밍 서비스 구독하기 정답률 88% | 정답 ②

다음 표를 보면서 대화를 듣고, 두 사람이 선택한 비디오 스트리밍 상품을 고르시오.

Video Streaming Subscription Plans

		Number of Screens	Screen Quality	Monthly Fee
①	Basic	1 at once	SD (standard definition)	$10
②	Standard	2 at once	HD (high definition)	$14
③	Premium	3 at once	HD (high definition)	$15
④	VIP	3 at once	UHD (ultra-high definition)	$17
⑤	VVIP	4 at once	UHD (ultra-high definition)	$18

W : Kevin, have you heard of *The Two Suspects*? It's a really popular drama.
Kevin, 너 *The Two Suspects*라고 들어봤니? 정말 인기 있는 드라마야.
M : Yes, but I haven't had a chance to watch it yet.
들어봤어, 하지만 아직 볼 기회가 없었어.
W : Me, neither. Why don't we subscribe to a video streaming service? We can share an ID.
나도 그래. 우리 비디오 스트리밍 서비스를 구독하는 게 어때? 우린 ID를 공유할 수 있어.
M : Good idea. Let's find one online. *[Pause]* Here, we can choose from these five plans.
좋은 생각이야. 온라인으로 찾아보자. *[잠시 멈춤]* 이거 봐, 우린 이 다섯 가지 요금제 중에 선택하면 돼.
W : 「Since we'll be using one ID together, the number of screens allowed should be two or more at once.」 근거1 Number of Screens 조건
우린 ID 하나를 같이 사용할 테니까, 허용 (기기) 화면 수가 한 번에 2개 이상이어야 해.
M : Of course. What about screen quality?
물론이지. 화질은?
W : UHD is higher quality than HD. But is UHD available on your device?
UHD가 HD보다 화질이 더 좋지. 그런데 네 기기에서 UHD를 이용할 수 있어?
M : No, it's not. What about yours?
아니. 네 것은 어때?
W : Mine is compatible with UHD. But I'm fine with HD.
내 것은 UHD와 호환돼. 하지만 HD면 괜찮아.
M : Good. 「Then we'll go with HD.」 So we should choose between these two.
좋아. 그럼 HD로 하자. 그럼 우린 이 둘 중 하나를 선택해야 해. 근거2 Screen Quality 조건
W : 「If we choose this one, it'll be easier to split the price. Besides, it's cheaper.」
우리가 이걸 선택하면, 가격을 나누기가 더 쉬워질 거야. 게다가 이게 더 싸. 근거3 Monthly Fee 조건
M : Perfect. Let's subscribe to that one.
완벽해. 그걸로 한번 구독해 보자.

Why? 왜 정답일까?

대화에 따르면 여자와 남자는 동시 재생 기기 화면 수가 2개 이상이고, 화질은 HD이며, 월 구독료가 더 싼 요금제를 고르기로 한다. 따라서 두 사람이 선택한 비디오 스트리밍 상품은 ② 'Standard'이다.

- subscribe to ⓥ ~을 구독하다
- screen quality ⓝ 화질
- compatible with ~와 호환되는
- split ⓥ 나누다, 쪼개다
- besides ad 게다가

11 할아버지와 귀가하기 정답률 80% | 정답 ⑤

대화를 듣고, 여자의 마지막 말에 대한 남자의 응답으로 가장 적절한 것을 고르시오.

① Hurry up, or you'll be late for school.
서두르지 않으면 학교에 지각할 거야.
② Sure, why not? Let's go pick up your dad.
물론이지, 안 될 게 뭐니? 아빠 데리러 가자.
③ I'm sorry but the school bus has already left.
미안하지만 통학버스는 이미 출발했어.
④ Okay. I'll drive you to school tomorrow morning.
알겠어. 내일 아침에 차로 학교에 데려다 줄게.
⑤ Well, he's too busy working so he couldn't make it.
음, 네 아빠는 일을 하느라 너무 바빠서 올 수 없었어.

W : Grandpa! I didn't expect to see you here!
할아버지! 여기서 뵐 줄은 몰랐어요!

M : Hi, Molly. I came to pick you up. How was school?
안녕, Molly. 널 데리러 왔단다. 학교는 어땠어?

W : Great, but where's Dad? I thought he was picking me up today.
좋았어요. 그런데 아빠는 어디 계세요? 전 오늘 아빠가 절 데리러 올 줄 알았어요.

M : Well, he's too busy working so he couldn't make it.
음, 네 아빠는 일을 하느라 너무 바빠서 올 수 없었어.

Why? 왜 정답일까?

할아버지인 남자가 학교에 자신을 데리러 온 것을 보고 손녀인 여자는 할아버지가 아닌 아버지가 데리러 올 줄 알았다며 아버지의 행방을 묻고 있다. 따라서 남자의 응답으로 가장 적절한 것은 ⑤ '음, 네 아빠는 일을 하느라 너무 바빠서 올 수 없었어.'이다.

12 전화기 액정 수리하기

정답률 82% | 정답 ②

대화를 듣고, 남자의 마지막 말에 대한 여자의 응답으로 가장 적절한 것을 고르시오.

① Of course. This is the latest model. – 물론이지. 이것은 최신형이야.
② Really? Then, I need to get it fixed. – 정말? 그럼 이걸 고쳐야겠다.
③ Don't worry. Here's a bandage for you. – 걱정 마. 여기 네가 쓸 붕대가 있어.
④ Right. You should have been more careful. – 맞아. 넌 더 조심했어야 해.
⑤ Let me pay for the repair. It's all my fault. – 수리비는 내가 부담할게. 전부 내 잘못이야.

M : Jamie, the screen of your phone is cracked. You should get it fixed.
Jamie, 네 전화기 화면이 깨졌네. 그거 고쳐야겠다.

W : Well, the screen works just fine. I'll use it as is.
음, 화면은 잘 작동해. 난 그냥 그대로 쓸 거야.

M : But you may cut your finger on the sharp edge.
하지만 넌 날카로운 모서리에 손가락을 베일지도 몰라.

W : Really? Then, I need to get it fixed.
정말? 그럼 이걸 고쳐야겠다.

Why? 왜 정답일까?

남자는 전화 액정이 깨져도 그대로 쓰겠다는 여자에게 고치지 않고 쓰다가는 날카로운 부분에 손가락을 베일지도 모른다(**But you may cut your finger on the sharp edge.**)는 점을 상기시키고 있다. 따라서 여자의 응답으로 가장 적절한 것은 ② '정말? 그럼 이걸 고쳐야겠다.'이다.

- cracked ⓐ 깨진, 금이 간
- cut one's finger ⓥ 손을 베이다

13 팀 티칭 계획하기

정답률 84% | 정답 ③

대화를 듣고, 남자의 마지막 말에 대한 여자의 응답으로 가장 적절한 것을 고르시오. [3점]

Woman: ______________________________

① Sorry. I don't know much about biology.
죄송해요. 전 생물학을 잘 몰라요.
② I doubt I can come. Africa is too far away.
제가 갈 수 있을지 모르겠네요. 아프리카는 너무 멀어요.
③ Exactly. That's an advantage of team teaching.
바로 그거예요. 그것이 팀 티칭의 장점이죠.
④ That's true. Some students prefer to study alone.
맞아요. 일부 학생들은 혼자 공부하는 것을 선호하죠.
⑤ Not yet. I'm not ready to try the teaching model.
아직요. 전 아직 그 교수 모형을 시도할 준비가 되지 않았어요.

M : Ms. Smith. How was the teacher training course about team teaching?
Smith 선생님, 팀 티칭에 관한 교사 연수 과정은 어땠어요?

W : It was very helpful. Would you like to try team teaching with me?
아주 도움이 많이 됐어요. 저랑 팀 티칭 한번 해보실래요?

M : Sure. I've always wanted to try that. Do you have any topic in mind?
좋아요. 전 항상 그걸 해보고 싶었어요. 생각해 본 주제가 있으세요?

W : I'm planning to teach about the plants and animals in Africa in my biology class.
전 제 생물 시간에 아프리카의 동식물에 대해 가르칠 계획이에요.

M : Okay. In my social studies class, students can learn about the economies of African countries.
알겠어요. 제 사회 수업에서는 학생들이 아프리카 국가의 경제에 관해 배울 수 있어요.

W : Great. Afterwards we can give the students a chance to combine what they've learned.
훌륭해요. 나중에 우린 학생들에게 배운 것을 취합해볼 기회를 줄 수 있어요.

M : It could be in the form of a team project or a discussion.
그건 팀 프로젝트나 토론 형태로 될 수 있을 거고요.

W : From that point on, we can lead the class together.
그때부터, 우리는 함께 수업을 이끌 수 있어요.

M : Good idea. If we're both in the classroom, students will be able to approach their topic from more diverse perspectives.
좋은 생각이에요. 우리가 둘 다 교실에 있다면, 학생들은 더 다양한 관점에서 주제에 접근할 수 있을 거예요.

W : Exactly. That's an advantage of team teaching.
바로 그거예요. 그것이 팀 티칭의 장점이죠.

Why? 왜 정답일까?

여자와 함께 아프리카를 주제로 한 팀 티칭 계획을 짜던 남자는 대화 말미에서 둘 다 교실에 함께 있으면 학생들이 더 다양한 관점에서 주제에 접근하도록 수업을 이끌어나갈 수 있을 것이라고 말한다(**If we're both in the classroom, students will be able to approach their topic from more diverse perspectives.**). 따라서 여자의 응답으로 가장 적절한 것은 ③ '바로 그거예요. 그것이 팀 티칭의 장점이죠.'이다.

- have in mind ⓥ ~을 염두에 두다
- combine ⓥ 취합하다, 결합시키다
- approach ⓥ 접근하다
- perspective ⓝ 관점
- advantage ⓝ 장점, 이점

14 온라인 영상 채널을 인기 있게 만들 방법

정답률 73% | 정답 ②

대화를 듣고, 여자의 마지막 말에 대한 남자의 응답으로 가장 적절한 것을 고르시오. [3점]

Man: ______________________________

① Me, neither. I'm not into cooking videos.
나도. 난 요리 영상에 관심이 없어.
② Okay. I'll keep uploading videos on my channel.
알겠어. 난 계속해서 내 채널에 영상을 올릴게.
③ I'd rather not. It's too late to start a new project.
난 그렇게 안 하겠어. 새로운 프로젝트를 시작하기엔 너무 늦었어.
④ Thanks for your offer. I'm happy to work with you.
제안 고마워. 너와 함께 작업하게 되어서 행복해.
⑤ You've got a point. I'll try to reduce my screen time.
네 말은 일리가 있어. 난 내 화면 (사용) 시간을 줄여봐야겠어.

M : Kate, do you have a minute? I need your advice on something.
Kate, 시간 좀 있어? 난 조언이 필요한 게 있어.

W : Okay. What is it?
알았어. 뭐야?

M : I've recently started my online video channel.
난 최근에 온라인 영상 채널을 시작했어.

W : That's cool. What's it about?
멋지구나. 뭐에 관한 거야?

M : Mainly, it's about cooking. Since your video channel is so popular, I wanted to ask you how to attract more people to my channel.
주로 요리에 관한 거야. 네 영상 채널이 인기가 무척 많으니, 어떻게 하면 더 많은 사람들을 내 채널로 끌어들일 수 있는지 물어보고 싶었어.

W : Then you're asking the right person.
그럼 제대로 찾아왔네.

M : So tell me. What can I do to make my channel popular?
그럼 말해줘. 내 채널을 인기 있게 만들려면 어떻게 해야 할까?

W : First of all, upload as many videos as you can. You don't really know which video will attract people.
우선, 최대한 많은 영상을 올려. 어떤 동영상이 사람들을 끌어올릴지는 정말 모르는 거야.

M : I can do that. But I always feel disappointed when my videos get only a small number of views.
그렇게 할게. 그런데 난 내 영상이 조회수가 너무 적으면 항상 실망감을 느껴.

W : Well, if you put up a lot of videos, there's a better chance that some of them might catch people's attention.
음, 네가 영상을 많이 올리면, 그중 몇 개가 사람들의 관심을 끌 가능성이 더 높아져.

M : Okay. I'll keep uploading videos on my channel.
알겠어. 난 계속해서 내 채널에 영상을 올릴게.

Why? 왜 정답일까?

영상 업로드를 시작한지 얼마 안 된 남자가 어떻게 하면 채널을 인기 있게 만들 수 있는지 여자에게 묻자, 여자는 우선 최대한 업로드를 많이 하라면서 많이 올리다보면 그중 일부가 사람들을 끌어모을 가능성이 높아진다(**Well, if you put up a lot of videos, there's a better chance that some of them might catch people's attention.**)고 조언한다. 따라서 남자의 응답으로 가장 적절한 것은 ② '알겠어. 난 계속해서 내 채널에 영상을 올릴게.'이다.

- attract ⓥ (사람을) 끌어모으다
- disappointed ⓐ 실망한
- catch one's attention ⓥ ~의 관심을 끌다
- not into ~에 관심이 없는
- You've got a point. 네 말은 일리가 있어. 네 말이 맞아.
- screen time ⓝ (전자 기기) 화면 (사용) 시간

15 발표 두려움을 극복할 방법 조언하기

정답률 71% | 정답 ①

다음 상황 설명을 듣고, Scott이 Jane에게 할 말로 가장 적절한 것을 고르시오.

Scott: ______________________________

① Being well prepared will help you overcome your fear.
준비를 잘하는 것이 네가 두려움을 극복하는 데 도움이 될 거야.
② Come on. You can make up for the mistake next time.
괜찮아. 다음에 실수를 만회할 수 있어.
③ It was an excellent presentation. I'm quite impressed.
정말 뛰어난 발표였어. 난 매우 감명받았어.
④ Remember that a long speech can bore the audience.
긴 연설은 청중을 지루하게 할 수 있다는 걸 기억해.
⑤ You should take the psychology class this semester.
넌 이번 학기에 심리학 수업을 들어야 해.

M : Scott and Jane are college sophomores.
Scott와 Jane은 대학교 2학년이다.
This semester Jane is taking a psychology class.
이번 학기에 Jane은 심리학 수업을 듣고 있다.
The class requires an individual presentation.
그 수업에서는 개인 발표를 해야 한다.
The problem for Jane is that she is too afraid to speak in front of other students.
Jane에게 문제는 그녀가 두려움이 너무 많아 다른 학생들 앞에서 말을 못한다는 것이다.
She finds it hard to breathe just thinking about it.
그녀는 그것을 생각만 해도 숨도 쉬기 힘들다.
Jane asks Scott for help.
Jane은 Scott에게 도움을 요청한다.
Scott thinks that her lack of confidence is the problem.
Scott은 그녀의 자신감 부족이 문제라고 생각한다.
In his opinion, the best way to gain confidence is to be well prepared for the presentation.
그가 생각하기에, 자신감을 얻는 가장 좋은 방법은 발표를 잘 준비하는 것이다.
He wants to advise Jane to fully understand her topic and practice several times before the big day.
그는 Jane에게 주제를 완전히 숙지하고 발표날 전에 여러 번 연습을 하도록 충고하고 싶어 한다.
In this situation, what would Scott most likely say to Jane?
이 상황에서, Scott은 Jane에게 뭐라고 말할 것인가?

Scott : Being well prepared will help you overcome your fear.
준비를 잘하는 것이 네가 두려움을 극복하는 데 도움이 될 거야.

[문제편 p.026]

Why? 왜 정답일까?

상황에 따르면 Scott은 발표에 대한 두려움이 큰 Jane에게 주제를 숙지하고 발표 전까지 여러 번 연습해 보아서 자신감을 키우도록 권하고 싶어 한다(**He wants to advise Jane to fully understand her topic and practice several times before the big day.**). 따라서 Scott이 Jane에게 할 말로 가장 적절한 것은 ① '준비를 잘하는 것이 네가 두려움을 극복하는 데 도움이 될 거야.'이다.

- sophomore ⓝ 2학년생
- overcome ⓥ 극복하다
- impressed ⓐ 감명 깊은
- confidence ⓝ 자신감
- make up for ⓥ ~을 만회하다, 보상하다

16-17 실내 미세 플라스틱 농도를 줄이는 방법

W : Tiny pieces of plastic, or microplastics, are everywhere.
미세 플라스틱 조각들은 어디에나 있습니다.
According to recent findings, the concentration of microplastics in the air is higher indoors than outdoors.
최근 조사 결과에 따르면, 공기 중 미세 플라스틱의 농도는 실외보다 실내에서 더 높습니다.
Considering that we spend about 90 percent of our time indoors, this may pose significant health risks.
우리가 우리 시간의 약 90%를 실내에서 보낸다는 것을 고려하면, 이것은 상당한 건강상 해를 끼칠 수 있습니다.
「Here are some tips on how to reduce microplastics at your home.」 16번의 근거
여기 여러분의 집에 있는 미세 플라스틱을 줄일 방법에 관한 조언이 몇 가지 있습니다.
「First, remove carpets, which trap plastic fibers and particles.」 17번 ①의 근거 일치
우선, 카펫을 치워야 하는데, 이것은 플라스틱 섬유와 입자를 붙잡아둡니다.
「Also, do not buy toys made of plastic.」 17번 ②의 근거 일치
또한, 플라스틱으로 만들어진 장난감을 사지 마세요.
Rather, choose wood or natural rubber toys instead.
대신에 나무나 천연 고무 장난감을 선택하세요.
「There are many daily products that contain microplastics such as cosmetic products and toothpastes.」 17번 ③의 근거 일치
화장품과 치약 등 미세 플라스틱이 함유된 생활용품도 많이 있습니다.
If the label on the product says PP, PE, or PET, that means there are microplastics in it.
만약 제품 라벨에 PP, PE, PET이라고 쓰여 있다면, 이것은 그 안에 미세 플라스틱이 들어있음을 뜻합니다.
It's better to choose microplastic-free products.
미세 플라스틱이 없는 제품을 선택하는 것이 더 좋습니다.
「It's also a good idea to put an air purifier in your house.」 17번 ④의 근거 일치
집 안에 공기청정기를 놓는 것도 좋은 생각입니다.
Certain models are capable of filtering out microplastics.
어떤 제품들은 미세 플라스틱을 걸러낼 수 있습니다.
Scientists are still unsure what specific dangers microplastics may pose to our health.
과학자들은 미세 플라스틱이 우리 건강에 어떤 구체적인 위험을 가져오는지는 여전히 확신하지 못하고 있습니다.
Even so, we can never be too careful about our health.
그렇다고 해도, 건강에는 아무리 신경 쓰더라도 지나치지 않습니다.

- microplastic ⓝ 미세 플라스틱
- considering prep ~을 고려하면
- significant ⓐ 상당한
- air purifier ⓝ 공기청정기
- concentration ⓝ 농도
- pose a risk ⓥ 해를 끼치다
- toothpaste ⓝ 치약
- filter out ⓥ ~을 걸러내다

16 주제 파악

정답률 82% | 정답 ②

여자가 하는 말의 주제로 가장 적절한 것은?

① recycling household plastic items – 가정용 플라스틱 제품을 재활용하기
② reducing microplastics in the house – 가정 내 미세 플라스틱을 줄이기
③ extensive use of plastic in medicine – 의학에서 플라스틱의 광범위한 사용
④ technologies to remove plastic waste – 플라스틱 폐기물을 제거하기 위한 기술
⑤ environmental impact of microplastics – 미세 플라스틱의 환경적 영향

Why? 왜 정답일까?

담화에서 여자는 '**Here are some tips on how to reduce microplastics at your home.**'을 통해 집 안의 미세 플라스틱을 줄일 수 있는 방법에 관해 몇 가지 조언을 하겠다고 언급하므로, 여자가 하는 말의 주제로 가장 적절한 것은 ② '가정 내 미세 플라스틱을 줄이기'이다.

17 언급 유무 파악

정답률 88% | 정답 ⑤

언급된 물건이 아닌 것은?

① carpets – 카펫
② toys – 장난감
③ toothpastes – 치약
④ air purifier – 공기청정기
⑤ bottled water – 물병

Why? 왜 정답일까?

담화에서 여자는 미세 플라스틱을 포함하고 있는 물건으로 카펫, 장난감, 치약을 언급하고, 미세 플라스틱을 걸러내는 데 도움이 되는 물건으로 공기청정기를 언급하였다. 따라서 언급되지 않은 것은 ⑤ '물병'이다.

Why? 왜 오답일까?

① '**First, remove carpets, which trap plastic fibers and particles.**'에서 '카펫'이 언급되었다.
② '**Also, do not buy toys made of plastic.**'에서 '장난감'이 언급되었다.
③ '**There are many daily products that contain microplastics such as cosmetic products and toothpastes.**'에서 '치약'이 언급되었다.
④ '**It's also a good idea to put an air purifier in your house.**'에서 '공기청정기'가 언급되었다.

Dictation 05

문제편 027쪽

01 due to the fine dust alert / a special lecture on personal healthcare / how to minimize the health risks / Don't miss out on this great opportunity
02 speaking of clothes / dress like a typical tourist / I'd avoid outfits / rarely wear hiking jackets or gym clothes
03 pull out the stage layout sheet / I changed some moves / jump from the bench
04 Let's put up a sign / love stuffed animals / hanging down from the ceiling
05 let's keep them closed / Do you want me to cook / I'm going grocery shopping
06 order a take-out meal / don't want to size up / one plate of steamed dumplings
07 You would've done the same for me / My new bed will be delivered this Friday / my back hurts
08 attending a one-day class / making hand-carved stamps / take your stamp home / last about one hour
09 take on challenges in diverse areas / Following your interests / has been uploaded / satisfy the requirements
10 haven't had a chance / the number of screens allowed / Mine is compatible with UHD / split the price
11 he was picking me up
12 cut your finger on the sharp edge
13 try team teaching with me / a chance to combine / approach their topic from more diverse perspectives
14 you're asking the right person / upload as many videos as you can / get only a small number of views / might catch people's attention
15 requires an individual presentation / too afraid to speak / well prepared for the presentation
16-17 pose significant health risks / how to reduce microplastics / wood or natural rubber toys / capable of filtering out microplastics

06회 | 2024학년도 5월 학력평가

| 정답과 해설 | 고3

• 정답 •

01 ⑤ 02 ② 03 ① 04 ④ 05 ② 06 ④ 07 ② 08 ③ 09 ⑤ 10 ④ 11 ① 12 ③ 13 ④ 14 ① 15 ⑤ 16 ② 17 ③

01 학교 교육과정 엑스포 자원봉사자 모집

정답률 94% | 정답 ⑤

다음을 듣고, 남자가 하는 말의 목적으로 가장 적절한 것을 고르시오.

① 내년에 새로 개설되는 과목을 홍보하려고
② 영상 제작 시 유의해야 할 사항을 안내하려고
③ 교육 과정 박람회의 변경된 일정을 공지하려고
④ 학교 홍보 영상의 온라인 제출 방법을 설명하려고
✔ 교육 과정 박람회를 위한 자원봉사자를 모집하려고

[Chime bell rings.]
[종소리가 울린다.]

M : Hello, third graders. This is your school career counselor, Michael Cliff.
안녕하세요, 3학년 여러분. 저는 여러분의 진로 상담가인 Michael Cliff입니다.
As you know, the School Curriculum Expo will be held next month and many freshmen are excited to learn about the school curriculum and various subjects.
여러분도 알다시피, 학교 교육과정 엑스포가 다음 달에 열리고, 많은 신입생들이 학교 교육과정과 다양한 과목을 알아가기에 신나있어요.
So, we're looking for volunteers for the expo.
그래서, 우리는 엑스포를 위한 자원봉사자를 모집합니다.
Since third graders have already studied many subjects, I believe you can support the freshmen as mentors.
3학년들은 이미 많은 과목들을 공부했으므로, 신입생들을 멘토로서 지원해 줄 수 있을 거라고 믿어요.
Volunteers will create videos about different subjects, and these videos will be shown in the school lobby during the expo.
자원봉사자들은 다른 과목에 대한 영상을 제작할 것이고, 이 영상들은 엑스포 동안 학교 로비에서 상영될 거예요.
This will help the freshmen choose the subjects that are right for them.
신입생들이 그들에게 맞는 과목을 선택하는 데에 도움이 될 것입니다.
If you're interested, please visit the school website and apply for a volunteer position by this Friday. Thank you.
관심이 있다면, 학교 웹사이트를 방문하여 이번 금요일까지 자원봉사자 역할에 지원해 주세요. 감사합니다.

Why? 왜 정답일까?

신입생을 위한 학교 교육과정 박람회에 3학년 자원봉사자를 모집하는 글(**So, we're looking for volunteers for the expo.**)이므로, 담화의 목적은 ⑤ '교육 과정 박람회를 위한 자원봉사자를 모집하려고'이다.

- **career counselor** 진로 상담사
- **freshmen** ⓝ 신입생
- **volunteer** ⓝ 자원봉사자
- **mentor** ⓝ 멘토
- **different** ⓐ 다른
- **apply** ⓥ 신청하다, 지원하다
- **Curriculum Expo** 교육과정 박람회
- **subject** ⓝ 학과, 과목
- **support** ⓥ 지원하다
- **lobby** ⓝ 로비, 현관
- **interested** ⓐ (…에) 흥미를 가진, 관심이 있는
- **position** ⓝ 직책, 자리

02 유효기간 내에 화장품 사용하기

정답률 87% | 정답 ②

대화를 듣고, 여자의 의견으로 가장 적절한 것을 고르시오.

① 서늘한 곳에 화장품을 보관해야 한다.
✔ 유효 기간 내 화장품을 사용해야 한다.
③ 화장품 구매 시 성분을 확인해야 한다.
④ 화장 도구를 정기적으로 세척해야 한다.
⑤ 자외선 차단제를 사계절 내내 발라야 한다.

W : Honey, what are you doing?
여보, 뭐하고 있어?
M : I'm looking for the sunscreen before I go hiking.
등산 가기 전에 자외선 차단제를 찾고 있어.
W : Oh, here it is. *[Pause]* Wait, you'd better not use this.
아, 여기 있어. *[잠시 멈춤]* 잠깐, 이거 안 쓰는 게 좋겠어.
M : What's the matter?
뭐가 문제야?
W : The sunscreen is expired. I bought it a while ago. Cosmetics should be used before the expiration date.
이 자외선 차단제 유효 기간이 지났어. 내가 꽤 전에 샀었거든. 화장품은 유효 기간이 지나기 전에 사용되어야 해.
M : Why is that? They're not even food.
왜? 음식도 아니잖아.
W : It's not safe to keep using them after the date on the label. Bacteria can grow over time.
라벨에 표기된 날짜 지나서 화장품 쓰는 건 안전하지 않아. 박테리아가 시간이 지남에 따라 자랄 수 있어.
M : Oh, that could cause problems, I suppose.
오, 그건 문제가 되겠네, 아마도.
W : Exactly. It increases the risk of developing skin problems. Plus, when it comes to sunscreen, expired ones might not protect your skin.
정확해. 피부 문제를 일으킬 위험도 증가해. 게다가, 유효 기간이 지난 자외선 차단제는 피부를 보호하지 못할 수 있어.
M : I guess I should check on my cosmetic products.
내 화장품 제품들 확인해 봐야겠다.
W : Absolutely. It's important to use cosmetics before their expiration dates to maintain their freshness and effectiveness.
그럼. 화장품의 신선함과 효과를 유지하기 위해서는 유효 기간 전에 사용하는 것이 중요해.
M : Thanks for letting me know. I'll be more mindful of that now.
알려 줘서 고마워. 지금부터 주의 깊게 볼게.

Why? 왜 정답일까?

여자는 남자와의 대화에서 자외선 차단제를 비롯한 화장품들이 유효 기간이 지나면 효과가 떨어지고, 위생상 문제가 생길 수 있음을 언급한다. 따라서 여자의 의견으로 가장 적절한 것은 ② '유효 기간 내 화장품을 사용해야 한다.'이다.

- **expiration date** 유효 기간
- **develop** ⓥ 생기다
- **effectiveness** ⓝ 효과
- **cosmetic products** 화장품
- **hiking** ⓝ 하이킹, 등산
- **bacteria** ⓝ 박테리아, 세균
- **protect** ⓥ 보호하다
- **mindful** ⓐ 주의 깊은, 신경 쓰는
- **sunscreen** ⓝ 자외선 차단제
- **freshness** ⓝ 신선함

03 생산성을 향상시킬 팁

정답률 75% | 정답 ①

다음을 듣고, 남자가 하는 말의 요지로 가장 적절한 것을 고르시오.

✔ 어려운 일을 먼저 처리하면 생산성을 향상시킬 수 있다.
② 적절한 휴식은 업무 진행의 효율성을 증진시킬 수 있다.
③ 성공을 위해서는 과제를 완수하려는 태도가 필요하다.
④ 매일 실천하는 작은 일이 평생 지속되는 습관이 된다.
⑤ 할 일 목록 작성은 체계적인 일 처리에 도움이 된다.

M : Good afternoon, listeners! This is *Brian's Daily Management Tips*.
좋은 오후예요, 청취자 여러분! *Brian의 Daily Management Tips*입니다.
Many people these days feel overwhelmed by their to-do lists.
요즘 많은 사람들이 해야 할 일 리스트에 압도감을 느껴요.
They have many things to do every day and struggle with making progress.
매일 해야 할 일이 많고 진행하는 것에 어려움을 느끼죠.
If that's your case, doing the most difficult task first can help you improve productivity.
만약 당신도 이러하다면, 가장 어려운 일을 처음 하는 것이 효율성을 높이는 데에 도움이 될 수 있어요.
Have you ever heard of the saying "eat the frog first"?
"개구리를 먹는다"는 말을 들어본 적이 있으세요?
It means starting with the hardest task.
가장 어려운 일부터 시작한다는 뜻입니다.
Once that's out of the way, the rest of your work will feel like a piece of cake.
그 일을 다 하면, 나머지 일은 식은 죽 먹기처럼 느껴질 거예요.
Are you interested in boosting your productivity?
여러분의 생산성을 높이는 데에 관심이 있나요?
Dealing with the most challenging task first is a simple but powerful tool to help you get there.
가장 도전적인 일을 먼저 다루는 것이 생산성을 높일 간단하지만 강력한 도구입니다.
We'll catch up with you after this short break!
잠깐 쉬고 돌아올게요!

Why? 왜 정답일까?

남자는 할 일이 많을 때 생산성을 높이는 방법으로 '**eat the frog**'라는 격언을 언급하며 가장 어려운 일을 먼저 시작하라고 조언을 하고 있다. 따라서 남자가 하는 말의 요지로 가장 적절한 것은 ① '어려운 일을 먼저 처리하면 생산성을 향상시킬 수 있다.'이다.

- **overwhelmed** ⓐ 압도된
- **productivity** ⓝ 생산성
- **eat the frog first** 가장 어려운 일을 먼저 하다 (비유적 표현)
- **a piece of cake** 식은 죽 먹기 (아주 쉬운 일)
- **challenging** ⓐ 도전적인
- **efficiently** ad 효율적으로
- **start** ⓥ 시작하다
- **to-do list** 할 일 목록
- **boost** ⓥ 증가시키다, 향상시키다
- **manage** ⓥ 관리하다
- **forget** ⓥ 잊다

04 학교 도서관 사진

정답률 91% | 정답 ④

대화를 듣고, 그림에서 대화의 내용과 일치하지 않는 것을 고르시오.

M : Kate, I took a picture of the school library. My art club is drawing a wall painting there.
Kate야, 내가 학교 도서관 사진을 찍었어. 내 미술 동아리가 저기 벽화를 그리고 있어.
W : Let me have a look. *[Pause]* That's awesome. 「There's a book tree on the wall.」 ①의 근거 일치
내가 봐 볼게. *[잠시 멈춤]* 멋지다. 벽에 책나무가 있네.
M : All the club members worked together on it. 「Do you see the cloud-shaped sign above the door? I designed it.」 ②의 근거 일치
모든 동아리원들이 함께 작업했어. 문 위에 구름 모양 사인이 보여? 내가 디자인했어.
W : Superb! I love the slogan on the sign. 「Oh, I also like the flower-patterned rug.」 ③의 근거 일치
최고야! 사인에 있는 슬로건 마음에 든다. 아, 꽃 모양 러그도 마음에 들어.
M : I like it, too. It fits the setting well.
나도 마음에 들어. 설정에 잘 맞아.
W : 「Will the brush under the ladder be used to color the background?」 ④의 근거 불일치
사다리 밑 붓도 배경을 색칠하는 데에 쓰이니?
M : Yes. When the painting is complete, it'll come to life even more.
응. 그림이 완성되면 더 생기 있을 거야.
W : Absolutely! 「And those two light bulbs above the clock add to the atmosphere.」 ⑤의 근거 일치
완전! 시계 위에 전구 두 개도 분위기를 더하네.
M : Right. I hope you're looking forward to seeing the finished painting.
맞아. 네가 완성된 그림을 보기를 기대하면 좋겠다.

[문제편 p.031]

Why? 왜 정답일까?

대화에서 사다리 아래에 붓이 있다고 하였으나, 그림에서는 붓이 사다리 위에 놓여 있기 때문에 그림에서 대화의 내용과 일치하지 않는 것은 ④이다.

- wall painting 벽화
- patterned ⓐ 무늬가 있는
- come to life 생기를 띠다
- looking forward to ~을 기대하다
- slogan ⓝ 슬로건, 구호
- fit the setting 환경에 잘 어울리다
- atmosphere ⓝ 분위기

05 졸업 사진 찍기 준비

정답률 76% | 정답 ②

대화를 듣고, 여자가 할 일로 가장 적절한 것을 고르시오.

① 촬영 자세 검색하기 ✔② 문자 메시지 보내기
③ 조원들 분장시키기 ④ 의상 대여하기
⑤ 소품 주문하기

M : Molly, can you believe it's time for our graduation photo shoot? It's coming next week.
Molly야, 우리 졸업 사진 찍을 때라는 게 믿어져? 오는 다음 주야.

W : I know. Shall we check if everything's ready?
나도 알아. 다 준비 됐는지 확인할까?

M : Sure. Did you borrow the costumes?
그래. 의상 빌렸어?

W : Yes, I already did.
응, 이미 챙겼어.

M : Well done! I've searched for a few group poses to match those costumes.
아주 좋아! 나는 의상에 어울리는 단체 포즈를 몇 개 찾아봤어.

W : Cool. Did you remind our team members to bring some memorable items to pose with?
좋아. 우리 단체 멤버들에게 기억할 만한 물건들 가지고 오라고 다시 이야기했어?

M : Oh, I was supposed to send a text message to them. I completely forgot.
아, 내가 문자 메시지 보내기로 했어. 나 완전 까먹었다.

W : Don't worry. I'll do it. The items will help us recall our high school life.
걱정마. 내가 할게. 물건들이 우리 고등학교 시절을 상기시켜 줄거야.

M : Right. What do you think of the makeup style idea from the photos John sent?
응. John이 보낸 화장 아이디어에 대해서 어떻게 생각해?

W : I like it! It's a perfect match for our team's concept.
마음에 들어! 우리 팀의 컨셉에 딱 맞아.

M : I agree. I think we're all set now.
나도 동의해. 우리 준비 다 된 것 같다.

Why? 왜 정답일까?

단체 사진을 같이 찍을 조원들이 소품을 가지고 오는 것을 잊지 않도록 문자 메시지를 보내기로 했다. 따라서 여자가 할 일로 가장 적절한 것은 ② '문자 메시지 보내기'이다.

- graduation photo shoot 졸업 사진 촬영
- group poses 그룹 포즈
- recall ⓥ 기억하다
- concept ⓝ 개념
- remind ⓥ 상기시키다
- costume ⓝ 의상
- memorable items 기억에 남는 물건
- makeup style ⓝ 메이크업 스타일
- text message 문자 메시지
- all set 모든 준비가 완료된

06 건강 보조제 구매하기

정답률 83% | 정답 ④

대화를 듣고, 남자가 지불할 금액을 고르시오. [3점]

① $45 ② $50 ③ $55 ✔④ $60 ⑤ $65

W : Welcome to Darcy's Drug Store. How may I help you today?
Darcy의 드럭 스토어에 오신 것을 환영합니다. 오늘 어떻게 도와드릴까요?

M : Hello. I'm looking for a health supplement. I'm feeling a bit low on energy lately.
안녕하세요. 건강 보조제를 찾고 있어요. 요즘 기운이 없어서요.

W : I see. How about a multivitamin? It contains a combination of various vitamins in one pill.
그러시군요. 멀티비타민은 어때요? 한 알에 다양한 비타민의 조합이 포함되어 있어요.

M : That sounds convenient. How much does it cost?
편리할 것 같네요. 얼마에요?

W : It's $15 per bottle.
병 당 15 달러입니다.

M : Then I'll take one bottle.
그럼 한 병 주세요.

W : Okay. Anything else?
네. 다른 것도 필요하신가요?

M : I heard probiotics help support the immune system. Do you have any?
프로바이오틱스가 면역 체계 지원을 도와준다고 들었어요. 혹시 있나요?

W : Sure. I recommend this one. It's $25 per bottle.
네, 이것을 추천 드려요. 병 당 25 달러입니다.

M : Perfect. I'll take two bottles.
완벽해요. 두 병 주세요.

W : So, one multivitamin and two probiotics, correct?
그럼 멀티비타민 한 병과 프로바이오틱스 두 병 맞죠?

M : That's right. Will you check if I have a coupon? Here's my loyalty card.
네. 제게 쿠폰이 있는지 확인해 주시겠어요? 여기 제 적립 카드입니다.

W : Let me check. *[Beep sound]* You have a $5 discount coupon for the total purchase. Do you want to use it?
확인해 볼게요. *[삐 소리]* 총 구매 금액에서 5 달러 할인 쿠폰을 가지고 계시네요. 사용해 드릴까요?

M : Yes, please. And I'll pay in cash.
네, 부탁합니다. 현금으로 결제할게요.

Why? 왜 정답일까?

한 병에 15 달러인 멀티비타민과 한 병에 25 달러인 프로바이오틱스 두 병, 5 달러 할인 쿠폰을 사용했을 때 남자가 지불할 금액은 $(15\times1)+(25\times2)-5=60$ 달러이다. 따라서 답은 ④이다.

- loyalty card 적립 카드
- total purchase 총 구매 액
- check ⓥ 확인하다
- discount ⓝ 할인
- cash ⓝ 현금
- pay ⓥ 지불하다

[문제편 p.031]

07 프리 다이빙 체험에 참가할 수 없는 이유

정답률 96% | 정답 ②

대화를 듣고, 여자가 프리 다이빙 체험을 할 수 없는 이유를 고르시오.

① 물을 무서워해서 ✔② 가족여행을 가야 해서
③ 체육 보고서를 써야 해서 ④ 체험권에 당첨되지 않아서
⑤ 야구 경기를 관람해야 해서

M : Stella, have you heard about the new free-diving center in town?
Stella야, 동네에 새로 생긴 자유 다이빙 수업에 대해서 들었니?

W : Yeah, I went there for a P.E. report. Their training programs were really impressive.
응, 체육 보고서 때문에 갔었어. 훈련 프로그램이 굉장히 인상 깊었어.

M : You did! And you won't believe this. I got two one-day free-diving experience tickets!
갔었구나! 이건 못 믿을 거야. 나한테 원데이 프리 다이빙 체험 티켓 두 장 있어!

W : Congratulations! That's exciting news!
축하해! 신나는 소식인걸!

M : Thanks. It's next Saturday, and I can bring a friend. Would you like to join me?
고마워. 다음 주 토요일인데, 친구도 데려갈 수 있어. 나랑 같이 갈래?

W : I'd love to, but I don't think I can make it.
좋은데, 나 못갈 것 같아.

M : Why not? Are you afraid of water or something?
왜 안 돼? 혹시 물 무서워해?

W : Not at all. I'm practically a seal.
전혀. 나 사실상 물개야.

M : Oh, then are you going to go watch the Baseball All-Star Game?
아, 그럼 야구 올스타전 보러 가는 거야?

W : Yes, but that's next Sunday.
응, 근데 그건 다음 주 일요일이야.

M : So, can you tell me why?
그럼 왜 못가?

W : I'm taking a family trip that day to celebrate my parents' wedding anniversary.
부모님 결혼기념일 맞아서 가족 여행가.

M : How nice! Then, I'll find another friend to come with me.
좋다! 그럼 나 같이 갈 다른 친구 구해 볼게.

Why? 왜 정답일까?

대화에서 남자가 여자에게 프리 다이빙 수업에 같이 가자고 초대했지만 여자는 부모님 결혼기념일을 맞아 가족 여행을 떠나기 때문에(**I'm taking a family trip that day to celebrate my parents' wedding anniversary.**) 갈 수 없다. 따라서 여자가 프리 다이빙 체험을 할 수 없는 이유는 ② '가족 여행을 가야 해서'이다.

- report ⓝ 보고서
- impressive ⓐ 인상적인
- exciting ⓐ 신나는
- be afraid of ~을 무서워하다
- seal ⓝ 물개
- training ⓝ 훈련
- experience ⓝ 체험, 경험
- join ⓥ 참여하다
- practically ⓐⓓ 사실상
- celebrate ⓥ 축하하다

08 인공지능이 만든 예술

정답률 92% | 정답 ③

대화를 듣고, Fusion of Code and Canvas 전시회에 관해 언급되지 않은 것을 고르시오.

① 작품 수 ② 장소 ✔③ 휴관일
④ 전시 기간 ⑤ 입장료

M : Lily, what are you up to?
Lily야, 뭐하니?

W : Hi, Dad. I'm looking at art created by artificial intelligence! Isn't it amazing?
안녕하세요, 아빠. 전 인공 지능이 만든 예술을 보고 있어요! 대단하지 않아요?

M : Fascinating. You know what? The AI art exhibition, Fusion of Code and Canvas, will open soon.
멋지다. 그거 아니? 인공 지능 예술 전시회인 Fusion of Code and Canvas가 곧 열려.

W : Are the artists artificial intelligence?
예술가가 인공 지능인 거예요?

M : Exactly. 「They'll showcase 14 works.」 ①의 근거 일치
정확해. 14점을 선보일 거야.

W : Interesting. So, is the exhibition held online?
흥미로워요. 그럼, 전시회는 온라인으로 열리는 거예요?

M : 「No, it's at the Quantum Art Museum.」 ②의 근거 일치
아니, Quantum 미술 박물관에서 해.

W : Oh, I've been there before. The architecture of that museum is really impressive. When will the exhibition start?
오, 거기 가봤어요. 박물관의 건축이 아주 인상 깊었어요. 전시회가 언제 시작하나요?

M : 「The website says it starts on May 10th and runs for a month.」 ④의 근거 일치
웹사이트는 5월 10일에 시작해서 한 달 동안 운영한다고 하네.

W : It would be great to visit this weekend.
이번 주 주말에 가면 좋을 것 같아요.

M : Let's do that. There will be not just paintings but also photographs and media arts.
그러자. 그림뿐만 아니라 사진이랑 미디어 아트도 있을 거야.

W : That's really something! How much is the admission fee?
대단한 데요! 입장료는 얼마예요?

M : 「It's free.」 But, the earnings from the gift shop will be donated to charity. ⑤의 근거 일치
무료야. 하지만, 기념품 가게의 수익은 자선 단체에 기부될 거야.

W : Wow, AI is making a donation!
와, 인공 지능이 기부를 하네요!

Why? 왜 정답일까?

Fusion of Code and Canvas 전시회의 작품 수, 장소, 전시 기간, 입장료는 모두 언급되었지만 휴관일은 언급되지 않았기 때문에 ③ '휴관일'이 정답이다.

- create ⓥ 창작하다
- exhibition ⓝ 전시회
- hold ⓥ 개최하다
- photograph ⓝ 사진
- earning ⓝ 수익
- artificial ⓐ 인공적인
- intelligence ⓝ 지능
- impressive ⓐ 인상적인
- admission fee ⓝ 입장료
- donation 기부

09 2024 May Dog Festival 안내

정답률 93% | 정답 ⑤

2024 May Dog Festival에 관한 다음 내용을 듣고, 일치하지 않는 것을 고르시오.

① 2021년에 처음 개최되었다.
② 시청 앞 광장에서 열릴 것이다.
③ 놀이터 입장 시 주인이 반려견과 함께해야 한다.
④ 무료 셀프 사진 부스가 마련되어 있을 것이다.
⑤ 벼룩시장에서 수제 개 장난감을 구매할 수 없다.

W : Hello, dog lovers! This is Lisa from Pet Pals Podcast.
안녕하세요, 애견인 여러분! 전 Pet Pals 팟캐스트의 Lisa입니다.
If you're wondering where to go with your dogs on Merry Dog Day, how about going to the 2024 May Dog Festival?
만약 여러분이 즐거운 강아지의 날에 여러분의 강아지와 어디에 갈지 고민 중이라면, 2024 5월 강아지 축제에 오는 것은 어떤가요?
「It was first held in 2021 and continues to be loved by many dog lovers.」
2021년에 처음 열린 후 많은 애견인들에게서 꾸준히 사랑받고 있어요. ①의 근거 일치
Starting on May 17th, it'll run for three days.
5월 17일부터 삼일 동안 운영합니다.
「It'll take place at the square in front of City Hall.」 ②의 근거 일치
시청 앞의 광장에서 개최됩니다.
A dog playground will be divided into two areas for small and large dogs to ensure safe play.
강아지 놀이터는 안전한 놀이를 보장하기 위하여 소형견과 대형견을 위한 두 구역으로 나뉩니다.
「When entering the playground, owners must be with their dogs.」 ③의 근거 일치
놀이터에 입장할 때, 주인은 반려견과 함께여야 합니다.
「Also, to capture memorable moments with your companion animal, there will be a free self-service photo booth.」 ④의 근거 일치
또한, 여러분의 반려 동물과 기억할 만한 순간을 잡기 위해서, 무료 셀프 포토 부스가 있습니다.
「But that's not all. You can purchase handmade dog toys at the flea market.」
하지만 그게 다가 아닙니다. 여러분은 수제 강아지 장난감을 벼룩시장에서 구매할 수 있어요. ⑤의 근거 불일치
Come and make lasting memories with your furry friends!
와서 여러분의 털북숭이 친구들과 오래 남을 기억을 만드세요!

Why? 왜 정답일까?

2024 May Dog Festival의 벼룩시장에서 수제 개 장난감을 구매할 수 있으므로(You can purchase handmade dog toys at the flea market.), 일치하지 않는 것은 ⑤ '벼룩시장에서 수제 개 장난감을 구매할 수 없다.'이다.

- wonder ⓥ 고민하다
- run ⓥ 운영하다
- divide into ~로 나뉘다
- owner ⓝ 주인
- memorable ⓐ 기억할 만한
- purchase ⓥ 구매하다
- continue ⓥ 계속되다
- take place 개최되다
- area ⓝ 영역
- capture ⓥ 잡다
- companion ⓝ 동료

10 마사지 도구 고르기

정답률 78% | 정답 ④

다음 표를 보면서 대화를 듣고, 남자가 주문할 마사지 도구를 고르시오.

Massage Tools

	Product	Price	Target-Use Body Part	Material	Free Gift
①	A	$8	Head	Metal	Pouch
②	B	$10	Face	Ceramic	Aroma oil
③	C	$12	Feet	Rubber	Pouch
④	D	$16	Back	Wood	Aroma oil
⑤	E	$22	Whole body	Plastic	Massage cream

W : Shawn, what are you looking at on your phone?
Shawn, 휴대폰에서 뭐 찾고 있어?
M : Hi, Chloe. I'm buying a massage tool for my mom. Can you help me choose a good one?
안녕, Chloe. 나는 엄마를 위해 마사지 도구를 사고 있어. 좋은 거 고르는 거 도와줄래?
W : My pleasure. So, are these the top five best sellers?
기꺼이. 이게 제일 잘 팔리는 다섯 개 모델이야?
M : Yes. 「But I can't afford more than $20 because I'm on a tight budget.」 근거1 Price 조건
응, 하지만 나 예산이 빠듯해서 20 달러 이상으로는 쓸 수 없어.
W : All right. Options are narrowing down. Have you considered where your mom would want a massage?
그래. 옵션이 좁혀지고 있어. 너희 엄마가 어디를 마사지 하고 싶은지 생각해 봤어? 근거2 Target-Use Body Part 조건
M : 「Hmm, I think any product except the one for the face would be fine.」 She already has one.
음, 얼굴 마사지하는 제품 제외하고는 모두 괜찮을 것 같아. 이미 가지고 계시거든.
W : Okay. Does she have any preferences for materials?
그래. 좋아하는 재료가 있으셔?
M : 「I don't believe she likes the cold feeling of metal.」 근거3 Material 조건
금속의 차가운 느낌은 안 좋아하시는 것 같아.
W : That's not the right choice, then. Now, there are two options left.
그럼 그건 좋은 선택이 아니겠다. 이제, 두 가지 옵션만 남았네.
M : 「Oh, they come with a free gift. I think she'd prefer an aroma oil. I'll go with that one.」
아, 무료 선물도 같이 오네. 엄마가 아로마 오일을 좋아하실 것 같아. 이걸로 사야겠다. 근거4 Free Gift 조건
W : Great choice.
좋은 선택이야.
M : Thanks for helping me. I'll order it now.
도와줘서 고마워. 이제 주문할게.

Why? 왜 정답일까?

$20 이하이고, 사용 부위가 얼굴이 아니며 재료는 금속이 아니어야한다. 또한 무료 선물로 아로마 오일이 오는 상품은 D이므로, 남자가 주문할 마사지 도구는 ④이다.

- tool ⓝ 도구
- option ⓝ 옵션, 선택권
- afford ⓥ 여유가 되다
- narrow down 좁혀 내려가다
- consider ⓥ 생각하다
- preference ⓝ 선호
- choice ⓝ 선택
- except ⓟ 기대하다
- material ⓝ 재료
- order ⓥ 주문하다

11 회의실 사용 시간 연장하기

정답률 61% | 정답 ①

대화를 듣고, 여자의 마지막 말에 대한 남자의 응답으로 가장 적절한 것을 고르시오.

① No problem. You can leave it to me. – 걱정 마세요. 저한테 맡기세요.
② Too late. The meeting is already over. – 너무 늦었어요. 회의는 이미 끝났습니다.
③ Of course. You can use free wi-fi in the room. – 당연하죠. 무료 와이파이를 방에서 사용할 수 있습니다.
④ I'm sorry. We have no record of your reservation. – 미안해요. 당신의 예약 기록이 없네요.
⑤ Not really. It takes two hours for us to get there. – 아니요. 그곳에 가려면 두 시간이 걸려요.

W : Mr. Cooper, you said you booked the meeting room only for two hours. Now our time is almost up.
Cooper씨, 회의실을 두 시간만 예약했다고 하셨어요. 시간이 거의 다 됐습니다.
M : Oh, we still have some matters to discuss. I think we have to extend the time.
아, 우리 아직 회의할 것이 남았어요. 시간을 연장해야 할 것 같아요.
W : Agreed. Since you made the reservation, could you take care of that for us?
동의해요. 당신이 예약했으니, 우리를 위해서 연장해 줄 수 있어요?
M : No problem. You can leave it to me.
걱정 마세요. 저한테 맡기세요.

Why? 왜 정답일까?

회의실 사용 시간이 거의 다 되어 연장해야 하는 상황이다. 여자가 남자에게 회의실 사용 시간을 연장해 달라고 하였으므로, ① 'No problem. You can leave it to me.'가 가장 적절한 응답이다.

- book ⓥ 예약하다
- time is up 시간이 다 되다
- reservation ⓝ 예약
- meeting room 회의실
- extend ⓥ 연장하다
- take care sth ~을 처리하다

12 기차표 재구매하기

정답률 90% | 정답 ③

대화를 듣고, 남자의 마지막 말에 대한 여자의 응답으로 가장 적절한 것을 고르시오.

① Why not? The area is a popular tourist destination. – 왜 안 돼? 그 지역은 인기 있는 관광지야.
② Not yet. We haven't decided where to go on a trip. – 아직 안 돼. 여행에서 어디 갈지 결정 못했어.
③ My mistake. I'll change the tickets for the correct date. – 내가 실수했어. 맞는 날짜로 표 바꿀게.
④ That's okay. I can get to the train station by myself. – 괜찮아. 내가 스스로 기차역에 갈 수 있어.
⑤ I apologize. All the tickets for today are sold out. – 미안해. 오늘 표는 모두 팔렸어.

M : Honey, our trip is coming soon. Did you buy our train tickets?
여보, 우리 여행이 곧이야. 기차표 샀어?
W : Yes, I did. Here are our mobile tickets. Paris, Saturday the 11th, right?
응, 샀어. 모바일 티켓이야. 11일 토요일, 파리행 맞지?
M : Oh! The destination is correct, but they're for the wrong Saturday!
아! 목적지는 맞는데 다른 토요일이야!
W : My mistake. I'll change the tickets for the correct date.
내가 실수했어. 맞는 날짜로 표 바꿀게.

Why? 왜 정답일까?

여행을 위한 기차표를 잘못 구매한 상황이다. 따라서 남자의 마지막 말에 대한 여자의 응답으로 가장 적절한 것은 ③ 'My mistake. I'll change the tickets for the correct date.'이다.

- ticket ⓝ 표
- destination ⓝ 목적지
- mobile ⓝ 휴대폰
- wrong ⓐ 잘못된

13 자전거 루트 짜기

정답률 67% | 정답 ④

대화를 듣고, 여자의 마지막 말에 대한 남자의 응답으로 가장 적절한 것을 고르시오. [3점]

Man : ______

① I agree. I have to make a complaint.
동의해. 불만을 접수해야겠어.
② You're right. Let's learn to ride a bicycle.
네가 맞아. 자전거 타는 방법을 배우자.
③ That's true. I'm still waiting for it to be found.
맞아. 나는 그것이 발견될 때까지 기다리고 있어.
④ Good idea. I'll give it a shot and see if it helps.
좋은 생각이야. 시도해 보고 도움이 되는지 볼게.
⑤ Absolutely. That's why you should bike to work.
당연하지. 그게 일하러 갈 때 자전거를 타야할 이유야.

W : Ben, I heard you finally bought your dream bicycle. Congratulations!
Ben, 네가 드디어 꿈꾸던 자전거를 샀다고 들었어. 축하해!
M : Thanks, Amy. But I haven't received the bicycle yet.
고마워 Amy. 근데 나 자전거 아직 못 받았어.
W : How come? Are there any issues?
왜? 무슨 문제 있어?
M : Yes, there's an issue with the manufacturing process. It's going to take a few more weeks.
응, 제조 과정에서 문제가 있대. 몇 주는 더 걸릴 거래.
W : I'm sorry to hear that. You must be pretty frustrated.
유감이야. 너 꽤나 실망했겠다.
M : Yeah, it's disappointing. I'm trying to stay patient, but it's not easy.
응, 실망스러워. 침착하려고 노력하는데, 쉽지가 않네.
W : How about searching for some bicycle routes?
자전거를 탈 루트를 찾아보는 건 어때?
M : What do you mean?
무슨 말이야?
W : I mean you may turn this lemon of a situation into lemonade. You can find fantastic roads for cycling before the bicycle arrives.
내 말은 네가 이 레몬을 레몬에이드로 바꿀 수 있지 않을까 하는 말이야.(이 상황을 잘 이용해볼 수도 있지 않나는 말이야.) 자전거가 도착하기 전에 환상적인 사이클링 길을 찾을 수 있을 거야.
M : I hadn't thought of that, but I like the idea of turning this situation around.
그 생각은 못 해봤지만, 이 상황을 이용하자는 생각은 마음에 든다.

[문제편 p.031]

W : You could even create your own bicycle tour by using a route planner. I'm sure it'll be worth the wait.
루트 플래너를 이용해서 너만의 자전거 투어를 만들 수도 있어. 기다릴 만한 가치가 있을 거야.

M : Good idea. I'll give it a shot and see if it helps.
좋은 생각이야. 시도해 보고 도움이 되는지 볼게.

Why? 왜 정답일까?

남자는 원하는 자전거가 제조 과정 문제로 배송이 늦어져 실망한 상태이다. 이런 남자를 위로하기 위해서 여자는 자전거가 오기 전까지 자전거를 탈 루트를 생각해 보라고 제안했다. 남자는 이 아이디어를 마음에 들어 했기 때문에(but I like the idea of turning this situation around.), ④ 'Good idea. I'll give it a shot and see if it helps.'가 남자의 응답으로 가장 적절하다.

- receive ⓥ 받다
- manufacture ⓥ 제조하다
- frustrated ⓐ 실망한
- turn the lemon into lemonade 위기를 기회로 바꾸다
- worth ⓝ 가치
- issue ⓝ 문제
- process ⓝ 과정
- search ⓥ 찾다

14 한복 입어보기

정답률 87% | 정답 ①

대화를 듣고, 남자의 마지막 말에 대한 여자의 응답으로 가장 적절한 것을 고르시오.

Woman : ______________________

✔① Awesome. Let's go to the shop and get a hanbok.
멋지다. 가게로 가서 한복을 입어 보자.
② Look at me. It seems hanbok really suits me well.
나를 봐. 한복 나한테 잘 어울린다.
③ One moment. Let's find out how to download a travel app.
잠시만. 여행 앱을 어떻게 다운로드 받는지 알아보자.
④ No worries. I'll look for ways to get a discount for the class.
걱정 마. 내가 수업 할인 받는 방법을 찾아볼게.
⑤ Right. This is the clothing the royal family wore in the past.
맞아. 과거에 왕족 가족이 입었던 옷이야.

M : Claire, we've finally arrived.
Claire, 우리 드디어 도착했다.

W : It's my first time visiting a Korean royal palace. I'm really excited!
한국의 궁전에 방문하는 것은 이번이 처음이야. 나 진짜 신나!

M : Me, too. My friends in Korean class highly recommended this place. It has a lot of positive reviews on the travel app as well.
나도. 한국어 수업의 친구가 이 궁을 강력하게 추천했어. 여행 앱에도 긍정적인 리뷰들이 많더라.

W : Great. Let's quickly buy the tickets and go inside.
좋아. 빨리 표를 사고 안에 들어가자.

M : Wait! Normally, the entrance fee is $2, but if you wear a hanbok, it's free.
기다려! 보통 입장료는 2 달러지만, 한복을 입으면 공짜야.

W : Hanbok? What's that?
한복? 그게 뭐야?

M : Look at the clothes those people are wearing. It's the traditional Korean clothing.
저 사람들이 입고 있는 옷을 봐. 한국 전통 의복이야.

W : It's so beautiful. I want to wear it, too. Can we try it on?
진짜 예쁘다. 나도 입고 싶어. 입어볼 수 있어?

M : I think so. I saw some hanbok rental shops on the app.
그럴걸. 한복 렌탈 샵을 앱에서 봤어.

W : Really? Let's pick one with good reviews and head for the store right now.
진짜? 리뷰 좋은 데 고르고 가게로 당장 가자.

M : Hmm... How about this one? It has high ratings and it's just a short walk from here.
흠... 이거 어때? 별점도 높고 여기서 조금만 걸어가면 돼.

W : Awesome. Let's go to the shop and get a hanbok.
멋지다. 가게로 가서 한복을 입어 보자.

Why? 왜 정답일까?

한복을 입으면 궁의 입장료가 무료고, 한복이 예뻐서 여자가 입어 보고 싶어하는 상황이다. 남자가 앱에서 별점도 높고 거리도 가까운 한복 렌탈 샵을 찾았다. 따라서 여자의 응답으로 가장 적절한 것은 ① 'Awesome. Let's go to the shop and get a hanbok.'이다.

- arrive ⓥ 도착하다
- royal ⓐ 왕족
- recommend ⓥ 추천하다
- traditional ⓐ 전통적인
- rating ⓝ 평가, 별점
- visit ⓥ 방문하다
- palace ⓝ 궁전
- entrance ⓝ 입장
- try on 입어 보다

15 Taylor의 무대 불안에 대한 Ms.Kim의 조언

정답률 72% | 정답 ⑤

다음 상황 설명을 듣고, Ms. Kim이 Taylor에게 할 말로 가장 적절한 것을 고르시오. [3점]

Ms. Kim : ______________________

① You need to keep your audience focused during a show.
공연하는 동안 관객을 집중시켜야 해.
② You'd better practice harder to be on the school stage.
학교 무대에 오르기 위해 연습을 더 열심히 하는 것이 좋을 거야.
③ You should apply for an audition on a TV talent show.
넌 TV 탤런트쇼 오디션에 지원해야 해.
④ Why don't you memorize the song for the audition?
오디션을 위해 노래를 외우지 않을래?
✔⑤ How about singing in the upcoming school festival?
곧 오는 학교 축제에서 노래해 보는 건 어때?

M : Taylor is a high school student who wants to become a singer.
Taylor는 가수가 되고 싶어 하는 고등학교 학생입니다.
He spends a lot of time practicing to apply for an audition on a TV talent show.
그는 TV 탤런트 쇼의 오디션에 지원하기 위해서 많은 시간을 연습에 쏟고 있습니다.
However, whenever he thinks about being on stage, he still feels anxious.
그러나, 그가 무대에 오른다고 생각할 때마다, 그는 여전히 불안함을 느낍니다.
He asks his music teacher Ms. Kim for advice because she has a lot of stage experience.
그는 그의 음악 선생님인 Ms. Kim이 무대 경험이 많기 때문에 조언을 얻고자 물었습니다.
Ms. Kim believes Taylor is talented and can overcome his stage fright by singing in front of a smaller and more familiar audience.
Ms. Kim은 Taylor가 재능이 있고, 익숙하고 적은 대중 앞에서 노래하는 것으로 무대 공포를 극복할 수 있다고 믿습니다.
So Ms. Kim wants to suggest to Taylor that he give a performance in the school festival next month.
그래서 Ms. Kim은 Taylor가 다음 달 학교 축제에서 공연하는 것을 제안하고 싶어합니다.
In this situation, what would Ms. Kim most likely say to Taylor?
이러한 상황에서, Ms. Kim이 Taylor에게 할 말로 가장 적절한 것은?

Ms.Kim : How about singing in the upcoming school festival?
곧 오는 학교 축제에서 노래해 보는 건 어때?

Why? 왜 정답일까?

Ms.Kim은 적고 더 익숙한 대중 앞에서 노래를 부름으로써 Taylor가 무대에서 불안해 하는 것을 해결할 수 있다고 생각한다. 곧 오는 학교 축제에서 노래를 해 보라고 제안하고 싶어 하기 때문에, ⑤ 'How about singing in the upcoming school festival?'가 가장 적절한 대답이다.

- spend ⓥ 소비하다
- apply ⓥ 지원하다
- whenever conj 언제든
- believe ⓥ 믿다
- suggest ⓥ 제안하다
- likely to ~할 확률이 높다
- practice ⓥ 연습하다
- audition ⓝ 오디션
- experience ⓝ 경험
- audience ⓝ 관중
- situation ⓝ 상황

16-17 영웅들의 특징

W : Hello, future writers. In our last session, we learned about different epic heroes, from mythology to modern stories.
안녕하세요, 미래 작가 여러분들. 지난 수업에서, 우리는 신화에서부터 현대 이야기까지의 다른 서사 영웅들에 대해서 배웠죠.
「Today, we're going to focus on some traits that make such characters so attractive to readers of literature.」 16번의 근거
오늘, 우리는 그러한 등장인물을 문학의 독자들에게 아주 매력적으로 만드는 특징에 집중할 겁니다.
「First, one of the primary traits is courage.」 17번 ①의 근거 일치
첫째로, 주요한 특징들 중 하나는 용기이다.
These heroes fearlessly face challenges and their courage inspires others to overcome their own difficulties.
이러한 영웅들은 두려움 없이 도전을 마주하고, 그들의 용기는 타인들이 그들만의 어려움을 극복하도록 영감을 줍니다.
You can see it in Harry Potter.
Harry Potter에서 그것을 발견할 수 있습니다.
「Second, strength is an essential trait. Take Beowulf as an example.」 17번 ②의 근거 일치
두 번째, 힘은 필수적인 특징입니다. Beowulf를 예로 들어 볼게요.
He has the unbelievable strength of thirty men in his arm alone.
그는 그의 팔 하나에만 성인 서른 명의 믿을 수 없는 힘을 가지고 있어요.
「Next, let's take a look at the intelligence trait.」 17번 ④의 근거 일치
다음은, 지능의 특징을 살펴봅시다.
Epic heroes navigate tricky situations and solve mysteries.
서사 영웅들은 까다로운 상황들을 헤쳐 나가고 미스터리를 해결합니다.
Sherlock Holmes, for example, is a genius detective with extraordinary intelligence.
예를 들어서, Sherlock Holmes는 뛰어난 지능을 가진 천재 형사입니다.
「Lastly, selflessness is a key trait.」 17번 ⑤의 근거 일치
마지막으로, 이타적임은 핵심 특징입니다.
Heroes often sacrifice their well-being for the greater good.
영웅은 자주 대의를 위해 그들의 웰빙을 희생합니다.
This is evident in Prometheus, who stole fire for humans and was punished.
인간을 위해서 불을 훔치고 벌을 받은 프로메테우스에게서 두드러지게 나타납니다.
This selflessness makes readers love him.
이 이타적임은 독자들이 그를 사랑하게 만듭니다.
All of these traits make heroic characters stand out and turn them into captivating figures.
이 모든 특징들이 영웅적인 등장인물들을 돋보이게 하고 매혹적인 인물로 변화시킵니다.
Now, let's create your hero and craft a story.
이제, 여러분의 영웅을 만들고 이야기를 써 봅시다.

- epic hero 서사적 영웅
- trait ⓝ 특성
- inspire ⓥ 영감을 주다
- unbelievable ⓐ 믿기 어려운
- tricky ⓐ 까다로운
- selflessness ⓝ 이타심
- greater good ⓝ 더 큰 선
- mythology ⓝ 신화
- courage ⓝ 용기
- strength ⓝ 힘
- navigate ⓥ 헤쳐 나가다
- extraordinary ⓐ 비범한
- sacrifice ⓥ 희생하다

16 주제 파악

정답률 84% | 정답 ②

여자가 하는 말의 주제로 가장 적절한 것은?

① impacts of cultural traits on conflict situations
갈등 상황에서 문화적 특징의 영향
✔② traits that attract readers in heroic characters
독자의 관심을 이끄는 영웅적 등장인물의 특징들
③ strategies for teaching character traits in literature
문학에서 등장인물들의 특징을 가르치는 전략들
④ reasons why personality traits matter in writing an epic
서사를 쓸 때 성격적 특징이 중요한 이유들
⑤ changes to traits that have defined heroes through history
역사를 통해 영웅을 규정해 온 특징의 변화들

Why? 왜 정답일까?

여자는 작가 지망생들을 대상으로 영웅의 특징에 대한 수업을 진행했다. 따라서 여자가 하는 말의 주제로 가장 적절한 것은 ② 'traits that attract readers in heroic characters'이다.

17 언급 유무 파악

정답률 97% | 정답 ③

언급된 특성이 아닌 것은?

① courage – 용기
② strength – 힘
✔③ leadership – 리더십
④ intelligence – 지능
⑤ selflessness – 이타적임

Why? 왜 정답일까?

여자는 영웅의 특징으로 용기, 힘, 지능, 이타적임은 언급했지만 리더십은 언급하지 않았다. 따라서 정답은 ③ 'leadership'이다.

[문제편 p.032]

Dictation 06

문제편 033쪽

01 will be held / looking for volunteers / help the freshmen choose
02 a while ago / the date on the label / before their expiration dates
03 feel overwhelmed by / the most difficult task / eat the frog first
04 took a picture / cloud-shaped sign above / add to the atmosphere
05 borrow the costumes / bring some memorable items / makeup style idea / a perfect match
06 combination of various vitamins / support the immune system / discount coupon
07 free-diving experience tickets / I can make it / taking a family trip
08 artists artificial intelligence / architecture of that museum / the admission fee
09 run for three days / owners must be with / purchase handmade dog toys
10 buying a massage tool / are narrowing down / any preferences for materials
11 booked the meeting room / matters to discuss / take care of that
12 is coming soon / our mobile tickets / destination is correct
13 bought your dream bicycle / the manufacturing process / a situation into lemonade
14 travel app as well / the entrance fee / the traditional Korean clothing
15 apply for an audition / overcome his stage fright / school festival next month
16-17 different epic heroes / focus on some traits / fearlessly face challenges / navigate tricky situations

07 회 | 2023학년도 4월 학력평가

| 정답과 해설 |

고3

• 정답 •

01 ⑤ 02 ② 03 ② 04 ④ 05 ③ 06 ⑤ 07 ⑤ 08 ⑤ 09 ⑤ 10 ③ 11 ③ 12 ① 13 ① 14 ② 15 ① 16 ① 17 ④

01 취업 박람회 준비물 안내

정답률 88% | 정답 ⑤

다음을 듣고, 여자가 하는 말의 목적으로 가장 적절한 것을 고르시오.

① 행사에 참여하는 회사 명단을 공개하려고
② 참가자에게 박람회 장소 변경을 공지하려고
③ 자기소개서 작성 시 유의 사항을 전달하려고
④ 신입 사원 채용을 위한 면접 절차를 설명하려고
✔⑤ 취업 박람회에 가지고 가야 할 것을 안내하려고

W : Hello, students. I'm Olivia Watson, manager of the Yellowhill College Student Job Fair.
안녕하세요, 학생 여러분. 저는 Yellowhill College Student 직업 박람회, Olivia Watson관리자입니다.
This event is a great opportunity because more than 50 companies will visit in search of new qualified employees.
이 행사는 50군데가 넘는 회사가 자격 있는 신규 직원을 찾으러 온다는 점에서 대단한 기회입니다.
For participants to be fully prepared, I'd like to tell you what items you should bring.
만반의 준비가 된 참가자들을 위해, 저는 여러분에게 준비물에 관해 이야기해드리려 합니다.
First, you must show your student ID card since it'll be used as the entrance ticket.
먼저 여러분은 학생증을 가져오셔야 하는데, 이것이 입장권으로 쓰일 것이기 때문입니다.
Second, bring your résumé.
다음으로, 여러분의 이력서를 가져오세요.
Most interviewers will require it to get a deeper understanding of your experiences and skills.
면접관들 대부분은 여러분의 경력과 역량을 더 깊이 이해하기 위해 그것이 필요할 것입니다.
Finally, if you have any certificates for special skills, please print a few copies to share with companies.
마지막으로, 여러분의 특별한 능력을 보여줄 자격증이 있으시다면, 회사에 공유할 수 있도록 몇 부 출력해오세요.
Don't forget to bring the items that I mentioned and you'll have a better chance at success. Thank you.
제가 말씀드린 준비물을 잊지 말고 가져오시면, 성공할 확률이 더 높아질 겁니다. 고맙습니다.

Why? 왜 정답일까?

취업 박람회에 챙겨올 준비물을 안내하겠다(~ **I'd like to tell you what items you should bring.**)는 말로 보아, 여자가 하는 말의 목적으로 가장 적절한 것은 ⑤ '취업 박람회에 가지고 가야 할 것을 안내하려고'이다.

- **job fair** 취업 박람회
- **qualified** ⓐ 자격 있는
- **résumé** ⓝ 이력서
- **certificate** ⓝ 자격증

02 입지 않는 옷을 정리하라고 조언하기

정답률 73% | 정답 ②

대화를 듣고, 남자의 의견으로 가장 적절한 것을 고르시오.

① 자원 낭비를 줄이기 위해 옷을 재활용해야 한다.
✔② 옷장 정리 시 잘 입지 않는 옷을 처분해야 한다.
③ 유행을 덜 타는 디자인의 옷을 구매해야 한다.
④ 자주 입는 옷을 옷장 문 쪽에 배치해야 한다.
⑤ 비슷한 색깔끼리 옷을 정리해야 한다.

M : What are you doing, Jessie?
뭐 하고 있어, Jessie?
W : I'm cleaning out my closet. It's too small to hold all my clothes.
옷장 청소하고 있어. 이건 내 옷을 다 넣기에 너무 작아.
M : Well, the closet looks big enough. Did you sort your old clothes?
음, 옷장은 충분히 커 보이는데. 오래된 옷 좀 정리했어?
W : Not yet. I'm trying to arrange all of them by color now.
아직. 지금 다 색깔별로 정리하려고 하고 있어.
M : Oh, dear. You need to get rid of clothes you don't really wear.
오, 이런. 네가 실제 입지 않는 옷은 버려야 해.
W : But when it comes to fashion, trends come and go, and often come back again. I can wear them later.
그렇지만 패션에 관해서는, 유행은 생겼다가 없어지고, 또 자주 돌아오기도 하잖아. 나중에 입을 수 있어.
M : Well, nobody knows when a trend might come back.
흠, 유행이 돌아올지 말지는 아무도 모르는 거잖아.
W : I guess that makes sense.
그 말도 일리가 있는 것 같네.
M : And the colors will fade if you keep them for too long.
그리고 너무 오래 보관하면 색이 바랠 거야.
W : You're right. I have lots of old clothes whose colors are already gone.
맞는 말이네. 이미 색이 빠진 오래된 옷들이 많이 있어.
M : You see? When arranging your closet, you should dispose of clothes you don't usually wear.
그렇지? 네 옷장을 정리할 때는 평소 입지 않는 옷을 처분해야 해.
W : Okay. I think that's good advice.
알았어. 좋은 조언인 거 같아.

Why? 왜 정답일까?

옷장 정리를 할 때 평소 입지 않는 옷은 버릴 필요가 있다(**When arranging your closet, you should dispose of clothes you don't usually wear.**)고 조언하는 글이므로, 남자의 의견으로 가장 적절한 것은 ② '옷장 정리 시 잘 입지 않는 옷을 처분해야 한다.'이다.

- **sort** ⓥ 분류하다, 정리하다
- **get rid of** ~을 버리다
- **fade** ⓥ (색이) 옅어지다
- **dispose of** ~을 처분하다

[문제편 p.037]

03 이달의 집 사진 촬영
정답률 93% | 정답 ②

대화를 듣고, 두 사람의 관계를 가장 잘 나타낸 것을 고르시오.

① 건축가 – 의뢰인
② 집주인 – 사진사 ✔
③ 임대인 – 세입자
④ 기자 – 잡지사 편집장
⑤ 고객 – 이삿짐센터 직원

[Door bell rings.]
[초인종이 울린다.]

W : You must be Mr. Cooper. Nice to meet you. Come on in.
Mr. Cooper시겠군요. 만나서 반갑습니다. 들어오세요.

M : Hello, Ms. Wood. You have a really beautiful home.
안녕하세요, Ms. Wood. 집이 정말 아름답네요.

W : Thank you. Let me show you around.
고맙습니다. 보여드릴게요.

M : Okay. *[Pause]* Wow, I can see why your house was recommended for house of the month. Such elegant modern style!
알겠습니다. *[잠시 멈춤]* 와, 왜 당신의 집이 이달의 집으로 추천되었는지 알겠네요. 너무나 우아하고 모던한 스타일이에요!

W : I'm glad to hear that. My husband and I put lots of effort into decorating. Where do you want to start shooting?
그 말씀을 들으니 기뻐요. 우리 남편이랑 제가 장식에 많은 노력을 들였어요. 어디서 사진 촬영을 시작하고 싶으신가요?

M : I'd like to take pictures in the living room, and then move to the bedroom and bathroom.
거실에서 사진을 찍고, 그 뒤에 침실과 욕실로 이동하고 싶어요.

W : Sounds good.
좋네요.

M : As you know, the photos taken today will be published in *Family Home Magazine*.
아시다시피, 오늘 찍은 사진은 *Family Home Magazine*에 실릴 예정입니다.

W : Yes, in next month's issue, right?
네, 다음 달 호 맞죠?

M : Well, actually I'm not sure, but if you ask the editor, you'll get an answer.
음, 사실 그건 확실하지 않은데, 편집자분에게 물어보시면 답을 주실 겁니다.

W : I see. In case you need help, please give me a shout.
알겠습니다. 도움이 필요하시면, 저한테 말해주세요.

M : All right. I'll let you know when everything's done.
알겠습니다. 다 끝나면 알려드릴게요.

Why? 왜 정답일까?

'Wow, I can see why your house was recommended for house of the month.', 'My husband and I put lots of effort into decorating. Where do you want to start shooting?', 'I'd like to take pictures in the living room, and then move to the bedroom and bathroom.' 등에서 이달의 집에 뽑힌 집주인과 그 집을 촬영하러 온 사진사의 대화임을 알 수 있다. 따라서 두 사람의 관계로 가장 적절한 것은 ② '집주인 – 사진사'이다.

- **put effort into** ~에 노력을 들이다
- **give A a shout** A에게 말해주다

04 새로 이사한 화실 사진 구경하기
정답률 90% | 정답 ④

대화를 듣고, 그림에서 대화의 내용과 일치하지 않는 것을 고르시오.

M : Hi, Alice. Did you move to your new art studio?
안녕, Alice. 너 새로운 화실로 이사했어?

W : Yes, I did. Here's the picture of it. Take a look.
응, 이게 거기 사진이야. 한번 봐.

M : Okay. 「You set an easel near the window.」 ①의 근거 일치
그래. 너 창가에다 이젤을 뒀구나.

W : Yeah. I usually paint as I look out the window. 「And I put two paint brushes in the bucket.」 ②의 근거 일치
응. 난 보통 창밖을 내다보면서 그리거든. 그리고 물통에 붓 두 개를 넣어뒀어.

M : That'll make it easy to take them out and use them. 「And I like the sculpture of a head on the table.」 ③의 근거 일치 It adds to the atmosphere.
이렇게 하면 꺼내 쓰기 쉽겠네. 그리고 탁자에 두상 조각이 마음에 들어. 분위기를 더해주네.

W : Thanks. 「Look at the heart-shaped vase on the shelf.」 ④의 근거 불일치 It was a gift from my family to congratulate me on the new place.
고마워. 선반에 있는 하트 모양 꽃병 좀 봐. 우리 가족들이 내가 새로운 곳에 가서 축하한다고 준 선물이야.

M : They're so thoughtful. 「Did you paint the picture hanging on the wall?」 ⑤의 근거 일치
정말 사려 깊으시네. 벽에 걸어둔 그림은 네가 그렸어?

W : Yes, I did.
응.

M : Wow. You're so talented. Show me later what else you're working on.
와, 너 정말 재능 있다. 네가 작업하고 있는 다른 거 더 있으면 나중에 나도 보여줘.

W : Of course.
물론이지.

Why? 왜 정답일까?

대화에서 꽃병은 하트 모양이라고 했는데(**Look at the heart-shaped vase on the shelf.**), 그림의 꽃병은 기다란 모양이다. 따라서 그림에서 대화의 내용과 일치하지 않는 것은 ④이다.

- **easel** ⓝ 이젤
- **add to the atmosphere** 분위기를 더해주다
- **sculpture** ⓝ 조각
- **thoughtful** ⓐ 사려 깊은

05 동아리 부원 모집 준비하기
정답률 87% | 정답 ③

대화를 듣고, 여자가 할 일로 가장 적절한 것을 고르시오.

① 방송 부탁하기
② 간식 주문하기
③ 포스터 게시하기 ✔
④ 지원서 출력하기
⑤ QR 코드 제작하기

W : Oscar, the club recruitment period begins soon. Let's check how well we've prepared so far.
Oscar, 동아리 부원 모집 기간이 곧 시작돼. 우리가 지금까지 얼마나 잘 준비했는지 체크해보자.

M : Good idea. Did you ask Mr. Kim to inform students about the club recruitment?
좋은 생각이야. 너 Kim 선생님께 학생들한테 동아리 모집을 공지해 달라고 부탁 드렸어?

W : Of course. He'll broadcast the information to the students.
물론이지. 학생들한테 정보를 방송으로 말해주신대.

M : Good. By the way, how's it going with making our club poster?
좋네. 그나저나, 우리 동아리 포스터 만드는 건 어떻게 되어 가고 있어?

W : I finished it this morning. Do you want to take a look at it?
오늘 아침에 끝냈어. 너도 볼래?

M : Sure. *[Pause]* It's wonderful! I like the QR code in the corner.
물론이지. *[잠시 멈춤]* 근사하다! 귀퉁이에 있는 QR 코드가 마음에 들어.

W : Thanks. Students can scan this QR code and complete the application form online.
고마워. 학생들은 이 QR 코드를 찍어서 온라인으로 신청서를 작성하면 돼.

M : Awesome. That way we don't need to print out application forms.
근사해. 그러면 우리가 신청서를 뽑을 필요도 없고.

W : Yeah. Did you order snacks for the applicants?
맞아. 지원자들을 위한 간식은 주문했어?

M : Oh, I forgot. I'll do that right away.
오, 깜빡했다. 내가 지금 바로 할게.

W : Great. Then I'll put up the posters in the main hallway.
좋아. 그럼 난 중앙 복도에 포스터를 붙일게.

Why? 왜 정답일까?

남자가 동아리에 지원할 사람들을 위해 간식을 주문하기로 한 후, 여자는 복도에 포스터를 붙이기로 했으므로(**Then I'll put up the posters in the main hallway.**), 여자가 할 일로 가장 적절한 것은 ③ '포스터 게시하기'이다.

- **recruitment** ⓝ 모집
- **application form** 신청서, 지원서
- **scan** ⓥ 스캔하다, 찍다
- **put up** 게시하다, 붙이다

06 밴드 연습실 빌리기
정답률 68% | 정답 ⑤

대화를 듣고, 여자가 지불할 금액을 고르시오. [3점]

① \$30 ② \$36 ③ \$40 ④ \$45 ⑤ \$50 ✔

M : Stacey, we need to book a practice room for band rehearsal.
Stacey, 우리 밴드 리허설을 위해서 연습실을 예약해야 해.

W : Okay. Let's make a reservation online. *[Typing sound]* This rehearsal studio looks good.
그래. 온라인으로 예약하자. *[타자 치는 소리]* 이 리허설 스튜디오 괜찮아 보인다.

M : I think so, too. The studio has two kinds of rooms. The standard room costs \$15 per hour and the expert room costs \$20 per hour.
나도 그렇게 생각해. 이 스튜디오에는 방 종류가 두 개 있네. 일반실은 한 시간에 15달러이고, 전문가실은 한 시간에 20달러야.

W : They say that only one keyboard comes with the standard room. We'll definitely need the other room.
일반실에는 키보드가 하나만 있대. 우린 이거 말고 다른 방으로 꼭 해야겠네.

M : You're right. Let's reserve the expert room for two hours.
네 말이 맞아. 전문가실을 2시간 예약하자.

W : Good. Do they provide a recording service?
좋아. 녹음 서비스도 제공하나?

M : Of course, they do. It costs \$5 per song.
물론이지. 노래 하나에 5달러야.

W : That's a reasonable price. Let's record two songs.
적당한 가격이네. 두 곡 녹음하자.

M : Sounds good. Then we'll rent the expert room for two hours and use the recording service for two songs, right?
괜찮은 것 같네. 그럼 우린 전문가실을 2시간 빌리는 거고 녹음 서비스는 두 곡 이용하는 거, 맞지?

W : Yes. Look. They provide a 10% discount to students.
응. 이거 봐. 학생들한테는 10퍼센트 할인해 준대.

M : Oh, it doesn't apply to us. It's only for teenagers.
오, 우리한텐 적용이 안 되네. 십 대들만이야.

W : All right. I'll pay with my credit card.
알겠어. 내 신용 카드로 낼게.

Why? 왜 정답일까?

대화에 따르면 남자와 여자는 한 시간 대여에 20달러인 전문가 연습실을 두 시간 사용하고, 한 곡에 5달러인 녹음 서비스도 추가로 두 곡 이용하기로 했다. 학생 할인은 십 대에만 적용되어 받지 못했다. 이를 식으로 나타내면, '$20 \times 2 + 5 \times 2 = 50$'이므로, 여자가 지불할 금액은 ⑤ '\$50'이다.

- **expert** ⓝ 전문가
- **discount** ⓝ 할인
- **definitely** ad 꼭, 반드시

07 반려동물 박람회에 함께 갈지 묻기
정답률 94% | 정답 ⑤

대화를 듣고, 남자가 반려동물 박람회에 갈 수 없는 이유를 고르시오.

[문제편 p.037]

① 가족 여행을 떠나야 해서
② 반려동물을 입양해야 해서
③ 액세서리를 사러 가야 해서
④ 과학 프로젝트에 참여해야 해서
✔ 반려견에게 예방 접종을 해야 해서

W : Hi, Leon. I haven't seen you since you went on your family trip.
안녕, Leon. 네가 가족 여행 간 이후로 너를 보지 못했네.
M : Hi, Emilia. We just got back yesterday. What a lovely dog! Is this Lucy?
안녕, Emilia. 우린 어제 막 돌아왔어. 귀여운 개네! 얘가 Lucy야?
W : Yes. She's a bit shy.
응. 약간 수줍음을 타.
M : Oh. *[Pause]* Is she wearing a ribbon around her neck? It's so cute. I'd like to buy some unique fancy accessories like Lucy's.
오. *[잠시 멈춤]* 목에 리본을 두른 거야? 정말 귀엽다. 나도 Lucy 것처럼 특이하고 멋진 액세서리를 좀 사고 싶어.
W : So, you have a puppy, too?
너도 강아지 있지?
M : Yes. I recently adopted one. He's really adorable.
응. 난 최근에 한 마리 입양했어. 정말 사랑스러워.
W : Good for you. Then why don't we go to the Pet Expo together? It'll be held downtown this Saturday.
잘됐네. 그럼 반려동물 박람회에 같이 가면 어때? 이번 주 토요일에 시내에서 열려.
M : This Saturday? I'm sorry but I can't.
이번 주 토요일이라고? 미안한데 난 안 돼.
W : Are you still working on your science project?
너 아직 과학 프로젝트 작업 중인 거야?
M : No. I've already done it.
아니, 그건 이미 끝냈어.
W : Then why can't you come?
그럼 왜 못 가?
M : Actually, I'm going to vaccinate my puppy on that day.
사실, 나 그날 우리 강아지 예방 접종하러 가.
W : Okay. Nothing is more important than good health. Maybe next time.
그래. 건강보다 중요한 건 없지. 그럼 다음에 가자.

Why? 왜 정답일까?

남자는 반려동물 박람회에 같이 가자는 여자에게 강아지 예방 접종 일정이 있어(Actually, I'm going to vaccinate my puppy on that day.) 갈 수 없다고 답하므로, 남자가 반려동물 박람회에 갈 수 없는 이유로 가장 적절한 것은 ⑤ '반려견에게 예방 접종을 해야 해서'이다.

- shy ⓐ 수줍어하는
- adopt ⓥ 입양하다
- adorable ⓐ 사랑스러운
- vaccinate ⓥ 예방 접종하다

08 국제 게임 콘퍼런스

정답률 95% | 정답 ⑤

대화를 듣고, International Game Conference에 관해 언급되지 않은 것을 고르시오.

① 기간
② 장소
③ 강의 주제
④ 티켓 가격
✔ 기념품

[Cell phone rings.]
[휴대 전화 벨이 울린다.]
M : Hermia, what's up?
Hermia, 무슨 일이야?
W : Miles, did you hear that? The International Game Conference is going to take place soon.
Miles, 너 들었어? International Game Conference가 곧 열린대.
M : Oh, we've been waiting for so long! 「When is it held?
오, 우리가 엄청 기다렸던 거네! 언제 열린대?
W : It starts on May 4th, and lasts for 3 days.」 Do you want to join me?
5월 4일부터 시작해서 3일간 열린대. 나랑 같이 갈래? ①의 근거 일치
M : Are you kidding me? I'm already all set. 「Is it held at the same place as last year?
말이라고 해? 이미 준비 다 됐지. 작년하고 똑같은 데서 열려?
W : Yes. It's at the Central Convention Center.」 ②의 근거 일치
응. Central Convention Center에서 한대.
M : Good. It's definitely within walking distance. Could you text me the link to the website?
좋아. 확실히 걸어갈 거리네. 나한테 웹사이트 링크 좀 문자로 보내줄래?
W : Okay. *[Pause]* Check it out.
그래. *[잠시 멈춤]* 확인해봐.
M : Wow. The speakers are all well known in the game industry. 「Did you see the topics of their lectures?
와. 연사들이 다 게임 업계에서 유명한 사람들이네. 너 강의 주제 봤어?
W : Yeah. They'll talk about the metaverse, virtual reality, and mobile games.」 ③의 근거 일치
응. 메타버스, 가상 현실, 그리고 모바일 게임에 대해서 이야기한대.
M : Amazing! 「And a ticket only costs $30.」 It's quite reasonable.
멋지다! 그리고 티켓이 30달러밖에 안 해. 진짜 싸다. ④의 근거 일치
W : I agree. We can even freely attend any lectures we want during the conference.
그러게 말이야. 우린 심지어 콘퍼런스 동안 우리가 가고 싶은 강의는 아무거나 자유롭게 참석해도 돼.
M : Great. I can't wait.
근사하다. 몹시 기대돼.

Why? 왜 정답일까?

대화에서 남자와 여자는 International Game Conference의 기간, 장소, 강의 주제, 티켓 가격을 언급하므로, 언급되지 않은 것은 ⑤ '기념품'이다.

Why? 왜 오답일까?

① 'It starts on May 4th, and lasts for 3 days.'에서 '기간'이 언급되었다.
② 'It's at the Central Convention Center.'에서 '장소'가 언급되었다.
③ 'They'll talk about the metaverse, virtual reality, and mobile games.'에서 '강의 주제'가 언급되었다.
④ 'And a ticket only costs $30.'에서 '티켓 가격'이 언급되었다.

- Are you kidding me? 장난해? 말이라고 해?
- within walking distance 걸어서 갈 수 있는 거리인
- I can't wait. 몹시 기대돼.

09 슈퍼히어로 박물관 홍보

정답률 89% | 정답 ⑤

Superhero Museum에 관한 다음 내용을 듣고, 일치하지 않는 것을 고르시오.

① 7만 권이 넘는 만화책을 보유하고 있다.
② 시립 도서관 옆에 위치하고 있다.
③ 슈퍼히어로 의상을 대여해 준다.
④ 취학 연령 미만의 아동에게 무료 입장권을 준다.
✔ 생일에 방문한 고객에게 음료 쿠폰을 제공한다.

M : Hello, Animation World podcast listeners!
Animation World 팟캐스트 청취자 여러분, 안녕하세요!
Are you a huge fan of superhero comics and movies?
슈퍼히어로 만화와 영화의 열성 팬이신가요?
Then, why don't you visit our Superhero Museum and meet your favorite characters?
그럼, Superhero Museum을 방문하셔서 제일 좋아하는 캐릭터를 만나보시면 어떨까요?
「Our museum holds over 70,000 comic books and 40,000 films as well as over 10,000 toys.」 ①의 근거 일치
우리 박물관은 1만 여개의 장난감뿐 아니라, 7만 권이 넘는 만화책과 4만 편의 영화를 보유하고 있습니다.
「All of these fantastic pieces are on display in our museum located next to the city library.」 ②의 근거 일치
이 모든 판타지 작품이 시립 도서관 옆에 있는 우리 박물관에서 전시 중입니다.
「And we provide a superhero costume rental service for adults as well as kids.」
그리고 우리는 아동뿐만 아니라 성인에게도 슈퍼히어로 의상 대여 서비스를 제공합니다. ③의 근거 일치
To enjoy all the fun, the admission fee is only $8, and 「we offer free tickets to children under school age.」 ④의 근거 일치
이 모든 즐거움을 맛보시려면, 입장료는 8달러만 지불하시면 되고, 취학 연령 미만의 아동에게는 무료 입장권을 제공해 드립니다.
「Also, customers who visit our museum on their birthday will get a special piece of cake in our cafeteria.」 ⑤의 근거 불일치
또한, 생일에 우리 박물관을 찾아주시는 손님들께는 카페에서 특별히 케이크 한 조각을 드립니다.
For more information, please visit our website.
더 많은 정보를 얻으시려면, 우리 웹사이트를 방문해주세요.
Come and be a superhero with us!
오셔서 우리와 함께 슈퍼히어로가 되세요!

Why? 왜 정답일까?

'Also, customers who visit our museum on their birthday will get a special piece of cake in our cafeteria.'에서 생일에 박물관을 방문한 사람들에게는 박물관 카페 케이크가 제공된다고 하므로, 내용과 일치하지 않는 것은 ⑤ '생일에 방문한 고객에게 음료 쿠폰을 제공한다.'이다.

Why? 왜 오답일까?

① 'Our museum holds over 70,000 comic books and 40,000 films as well as over 10,000 toys.'의 내용과 일치한다.
② 'All of these fantastic pieces are on display in our museum located next to the city library.'의 내용과 일치한다.
③ 'And we provide a superhero costume rental service for adults as well as kids.'의 내용과 일치한다.
④ '~ we offer free tickets to children under school age.'의 내용과 일치한다.

- on display 전시 중인
- costume ⓝ 의상
- school age 취학 연령

10 손 세정제 구매하기

정답률 74% | 정답 ③

다음 표를 보면서 대화를 듣고, 두 사람이 주문할 손 세정제를 고르시오.

Hand Soap

	Product	Price	Form	Fragrance	Tested on Animals
①	A	$4	bar	lemon	×
②	B	$7	bar	lavender	○
✔	C	$10	bar	vanilla	×
④	D	$15	liquid	rosemary	○
⑤	E	$22	liquid	tea tree	×

M : Honey, we're almost out of hand soap.
여보, 우리 손 세정제가 거의 다 떨어졌어요.
W : Oh, I was just looking for some online. Will you choose with me?
오, 내가 방금 온라인에서 보고 있던 참이에요. 나랑 같이 고를래요?
M : Sure. Let's see. 「How about choosing one of these for less than $20? 근거1 Price 조건
그래요. 봅시다. 20달러 미만의 제품에서 하나 고르면 어때요?
W : I agree.」 I don't want to spend too much for hand soap, either. 「Which form of hand soap do you want?
같은 생각이에요. 나도 손 세정제에 너무 많은 돈을 쓰고 싶지 않아요. 어떤 형태의 손 세정제가 좋아요?
M : You know, liquid soap is easier to use but produces more plastic waste.
여보도 알다시피, 물비누가 쓰기는 더 편한데 플라스틱 쓰레기가 너무 많이 나와요.
W : Yeah. Then why don't we choose from among the bar soaps? 근거2 Form 조건
네. 그럼 고체 비누에서 고르면 어때요?
M : Good.」 「How about the fragrance? Do you have a preference?
좋아요. 향은 어떡하죠? 좋아하는 게 있어요? 근거3 Fragrance 조건
W : I'd like anything but lemon.」 We've used lemon for a long time. Let's make a change this time.
난 레몬만 아니면 돼요. 우린 레몬향을 오래 썼으니까요. 이번엔 바꿔봐요.
M : Okay. There are two options left, then.
그래요. 그럼 두 개 선택지가 남았네요.
W : 「Oh, this one is not tested on animals. I believe testing on living animals is not ethical.」 근거4 Tested on Animals 조건
오, 이건 동물 실험을 안 했대요. 난 살아 있는 동물을 대상으로 한 실험이 윤리적이지 않다고 생각해요.
M : I agree. Let's order it now.
동의해요. 이걸 지금 주문하죠.

[문제편 p.037]

Why? 왜 정답일까?

남자와 여자는 가격이 20달러 미만이고, 고체 제형이면서, 향은 레몬향이 아니고, 동물 실험을 거치지 않은 손 세정제를 사기로 했다. 따라서 두 사람이 주문할 손 세정제는 ③ 'C'이다.

- be[run] out of ~이 다 떨어지다
- waste ⓝ 쓰레기
- fragrance ⓝ 향기
- anything but ~만 제외하고

11 치킨 포장 주문하기

정답률 77% | 정답 ③

대화를 듣고, 여자의 마지막 말에 대한 남자의 응답으로 가장 적절한 것을 고르시오.

① The soccer match is going to start in 30 minutes.
축구 시합은 30분 뒤에 시작할 예정이에요.
② I'm disappointed that all the chicken was sold out.
치킨이 다 팔려서 실망이네요.
✔ No matter how much we hurry, it'll take about an hour.
저희가 아무리 서둘러도, 한 시간 정도는 걸릴 겁니다.
④ Seating is available on a first come, first served basis.
좌석은 선착순으로 이용 가능합니다.
⑤ Your order was cancelled due to a delivery problem.
배달 문제 때문에 귀하의 주문이 취소되었습니다.

W : Hello. Can I order a fried chicken to go please?
안녕하세요. 프라이드치킨 포장 주문되나요?
M : Yes, but the orders have piled up because of the big soccer match tonight. Is it okay for you to wait?
네, 그런데 오늘 밤 중요한 축구 경기 때문에 주문이 밀렸습니다. 기다리셔도 괜찮으세요?
W : Oh, I should have come much earlier. When do you think I'll receive my order?
오, 훨씬 더 일찍 왔어야 하나 봐요. 주문한 음식 언제쯤 받을 수 있을까요?
M : No matter how much we hurry, it'll take about an hour.
저희가 아무리 서둘러도, 한 시간 정도는 걸릴 겁니다.

Why? 왜 정답일까?

치킨 주문이 많아서 기다려야 한다는 남자의 말에 여자는 얼마나 걸릴 것인지 묻고 있으므로(**When do you think I'll receive my order?**), 남자의 응답으로 가장 적절한 것은 ③ '저희가 아무리 서둘러도, 한 시간 정도는 걸릴 겁니다.(**No matter how much we hurry, it'll take about an hour.**)'이다.

- pile up 쌓이다, 밀리다
- first come, first served 선착순(의)

12 동생을 대신 데려다주라고 부탁하기

정답률 68% | 정답 ①

대화를 듣고, 남자의 마지막 말에 대한 여자의 응답으로 가장 적절한 것을 고르시오.

✔ No problem. I can do that for you. – 문제 없어요. 제가 대신 할게요.
② Sorry. I'm not able to give you a ride. – 죄송해요. 전 아빠를 태워다 드릴 수가 없어요.
③ Definitely. He's already arrived there. – 물론이죠. 걘 이미 거기 도착했어요.
④ Sure. You can take him to the ice rink. – 그럼요. 아빠가 걔를 아이스링크에 데려다주시면 돼요.
⑤ Cheer up. Your presentation will be great. – 힘내세요. 발표를 훌륭하게 하실 거예요.

M : Sweetie, do you have any plans this Saturday?
얘야, 이번 토요일에 무슨 일정이라도 있니?
W : Nothing special. Why, Dad?
특별한 건 없어요. 왜요, 아빠?
M : Well, I have a business meeting that morning. So I need somebody to give your brother a ride to ice hockey practice.
음, 내가 그날 아침에 업무 미팅이 있어. 그래서 네 남동생을 아이스하키 연습에 태워다줄 사람이 필요하거든.
W : No problem. I can do that for you.
문제 없어요. 제가 대신 할게요.

Why? 왜 정답일까?

남자는 토요일 아침에 미팅이 있어 여자의 남동생을 아이스하키 연습에 데려다줄 수 없으니, 누군가 대신 그 일을 해주어야 한다고 말한다(**So I need somebody to give your brother a ride to ice hockey practice.**). 따라서 여자의 응답으로 가장 적절한 것은 ① '문제 없어요. 제가 대신 할게요.(**No problem. I can do that for you.**)'이다.

- business meeting 업무 미팅
- give a ride (차로) 태워다주다

13 코딩 수업 상담

정답률 91% | 정답 ①

대화를 듣고, 여자의 마지막 말에 대한 남자의 응답으로 가장 적절한 것을 고르시오. [3점]

Man: ______________________________

✔ All right. Then I'll wait for him to return.
알겠습니다. 그럼 그 선생님께서 돌아오시기를 기다릴게요.
② Stay calm. I know where he might be now.
침착하세요. 그분이 지금 어디 계실지 알아요.
③ Believe me. He'll come back before the deadline.
절 믿으세요. 그분은 마감 전에 돌아오실 거예요.
④ Never mind. He's already registered for the class.
신경 쓰지 마세요. 그는 이미 수업에 등록했어요.
⑤ No worries. The results of the consultation were fine.
걱정 마세요. 상담 결과는 괜찮았어요.

W : Hello, Kevin. What brings you to my office today?
안녕, Kevin. 오늘 무슨 일로 우리 교무실에 왔니?
M : Hello, Ms. Smith. I'd like to take the computer coding class, but I heard that it's already fully booked.
안녕하세요, Smith 선생님. 전 컴퓨터 코딩 수업을 듣고 싶은데, 벌써 예약이 다 찼다고 들었어요.
W : You're right. Far more students wanted to sign up for the class than we expected.
맞아. 우리가 예상한 것보다 훨씬 더 많은 학생들이 수업에 등록하고 싶어 했지.
M : Oh, no. I was really looking forward to it.
오, 이런. 전 그걸 정말 기대하고 있었거든요.
W : Then why don't you take it online? Our school also offers an online coding class.
그럼 온라인으로 수업을 들으면 어때? 우리 학교에서 온라인 코딩 수업도 제공하거든.
M : Lucky me. But I've never taken an online class.
잘됐네요. 그런데 전 온라인 수업을 한 번도 들어본 적이 없어요.
W : I'm sure Mr. Brown can give you more information. He's in charge of students taking online classes.
Brown 선생님이 정보를 분명 더 주실 거야. 그분이 온라인 수업을 듣는 학생들 담당이시거든.
M : Okay. Where's his office?
알겠습니다. 그 선생님 교무실은 어디인가요?
W : Well, he's on a business trip. You'll be able to see him this coming Thursday.
음, 지금 출장 가셨어. 돌아오는 화요일에 뵐 수 있을 거야.
M : Hmm. I'm afraid that'll be too late to register for the class.
흠. 그럼 수업 등록하기 너무 늦지 않을까 걱정이네요.
W : Don't worry. Registration is due next Friday. Before deciding whether to take the class, you should consult with Mr. Brown first.
걱정 마. 등록은 다음 주 금요일까지란다. 수업을 들을지 결정하기 전에, Brown 선생님과 먼저 상의해야 해.
M : All right. Then I'll wait for him to return.
알겠습니다. 그럼 그 선생님께서 돌아오시기를 기다릴게요.

Why? 왜 정답일까?

여자는 온라인 코딩 수업을 들을지 결정하려면 담당자인 Brown 선생님과의 사전 상담이 꼭 필요하다(**Before deciding whether to take the class, you should consult with Mr. Brown first.**)고 말하므로, 남자의 응답으로 가장 적절한 것은 ① '알겠습니다. 그럼 그 선생님께서 돌아오시기를 기다릴게요.(**All right. Then I'll wait for him to return.**)'이다.

- What brings you to ~? ~에는 무슨 일이니?
- Lucky me. 잘됐네요. 저는 운이 좋네요.
- due ⓐ 예정인, 마감이 다 된
- consult with ~와 상의하다

14 새로운 것을 배워 활력을 찾아보라고 조언하기

정답률 87% | 정답 ②

대화를 듣고, 남자의 마지막 말에 대한 여자의 응답으로 가장 적절한 것을 고르시오.

Woman: ______________________________

① I'm sorry. I'm tired of having music practice every day.
미안해. 난 매일 음악 연습하는 게 질렸어.
✔ Okay. I'll try to find something new to challenge myself.
알겠어. 내가 도전해볼 뭔가 새로운 걸 찾으려고 노력해볼게.
③ Absolutely. You'll be good at playing the ukulele one day.
당연하지. 너도 언젠가 우쿨렐레 연주를 잘하게 될 거야.
④ You're right. I'd better stay away from relationship stress.
네 말이 맞아. 나는 관계 스트레스에서 좀 멀어져 있어야겠어.
⑤ I agree. You should put more effort into the work you're doing.
같은 생각이야. 넌 네가 하고 있는 일에 노력을 더 들여야 해.

M : Molly, how have you been?
Molly, 어떻게 지냈어?
W : Hi, Ron. To tell you the truth, I've been feeling a little bit down lately. My life seems so repetitive.
안녕, Ron. 솔직히 말하면, 요새 마음이 좀 울적했어. 내 생활이 너무 반복되는 거 같아서.
M : I see. I've felt that way before, myself.
그렇구나. 나도 전에 그런 기분 느낀 적 있어.
W : Really? You've had this experience, too?
그래? 너도 이런 경험이 있어?
M : Of course. Last year, I felt like my life was so full of dull moments.
물론이지. 작년에 나도 내 인생이 너무 지루한 순간들로 가득한 거 같았어.
W : I didn't know that. How did you overcome?
난 몰랐네. 어떻게 극복했어?
M : For me, learning to play the ukulele helped a lot. Why don't you try learning a new hobby? That might help boost your spirits.
내 경우에는, 우쿨렐레 연주를 배운 게 큰 도움이 됐어. 새로운 취미를 배워보면 어때? 그게 활기를 높이는 데 도움이 될지도 몰라.
W : Interesting. But learning something new also causes stress, doesn't it?
흥미롭네. 그치만 뭔가 새로운 걸 배우는 건 스트레스도 될 수 있잖아, 그렇지 않아?
M : Yes, but in a positive way. I gained more energy in my life by pushing myself to try a new activity.
응, 하지만 좋은 쪽으로 그래. 내 자신을 몰아붙여서 새로운 활동을 해보니까 삶에 활력이 많이 생겼어.
W : That makes sense. Do you think it'll work for me, too?
일리가 있네. 나한테도 효과가 있을 거라고 보니?
M : Well, it did for me. I think it might do you good.
음, 나한테는 있었어. 너한테도 도움이 될지 모른다고 생각해.
W : Okay. I'll try to find something new to challenge myself.
알겠어. 내가 도전해볼 뭔가 새로운 걸 찾으려고 노력해볼게.

Why? 왜 정답일까?

새로운 무언가를 배우는 것이 자신에게도 효과가 있을 것 같냐는 여자의 물음에 남자는 그럴 거라고 생각한다(**I think it might do you good.**)고 말한다. 따라서 여자의 응답으로 가장 적절한 것은 ② '알겠어. 내가 도전해볼 뭔가 새로운 걸 찾으려고 노력해볼게.(**Okay. I'll try to find something new to challenge myself.**)'이다.

- How have you been? 어떻게 지냈어?
- to tell you the truth 솔직히 말하면
- dull ⓐ 지루한, 따분한
- do good (~에게) 도움이 되다

15 계산 확인 요청하기

정답률 75% | 정답 ①

다음 상황 설명을 듣고, Emma가 Tom에게 할 말로 가장 적절한 것을 고르시오. [3점]

Emma: ______________________________

✔ Could you check whether I got double charged? – 내가 돈을 두 번 낸 건지 확인해 줄래?
② Can I get a discount coupon via message again? – 할인 쿠폰을 메시지로 다시 받을 수 있을까?
③ Would it be okay for me to use your cell phone? – 내가 네 핸드폰을 써도 괜찮을까?
④ Did you insert your credit card to the card reader? – 카드 리더기에 네 카드를 넣었던 거야?
⑤ Is it possible to get a refund through a bank transfer? – 계좌 이체로 환불받는 게 가능하니?

M : Emma has lots of friends.
Emma는 친구가 많다.
One day, she plans to invite some close friends to her house and treat them to a home-cooked meal.
어느 날, 그녀는 친한 친구 몇 명을 집에 초대해서 집밥을 대접하려고 한다.
On the way home, she stops at the grocery store and puts foods and beverages in her cart.
집에 오는 길에, 그녀는 슈퍼에 들러서 음식과 음료를 카트에 담는다.
She stands at the counter and meets Tom, who works at the store as a cashier.

[문제편 p.038]

그녀는 카운터에 서 있다가 Tom을 만나는데, 그는 계산대 점원으로 가게에서 일한다.
Due to a temporary bank error, he has to swipe Emma's credit card two times.
일시적인 전산 오류 때문에, 그는 Emma의 신용 카드를 두 번 대야 한다.
After paying the bill, she checks the payment confirmation messages on her cell phone, and finds out she got two messages about the same amount of money.
돈을 지불하고 나서, 그녀는 지불 확인 메시지를 핸드폰으로 받는데, 똑같은 액수의 돈에 대해 메시지가 두 건 왔다는 것을 발견한다.
So she wants to ask Tom to see if the payment was made twice.
그래서 그녀는 Tom에게 두 번 지불된 것인지 확인해달라고 요청하려고 한다.
In this situation, what would Emma most likely say to Tom?
이 상황에서, Emma는 Tom에게 뭐라고 말할 것인가?

Emma : Could you check whether I got double charged?
내가 돈을 두 번 낸 건지 확인해 줄래?

Why? 왜 정답일까?

슈퍼마켓에서 지불 문자를 두 건 받은 Emma는 계산대 점원으로 마주쳤던 친구 Tom에게 확인을 요청하고 싶어 한다(**So she wants to ask Tom to see if the payment was made twice.**). 따라서 Emma가 Tom에게 할 말로 가장 적절한 것은 ① '내가 돈을 두 번 낸 건지 확인해 줄래?(**Could you check whether I got double charged?**)'이다.

- **temporary** ⓐ 일시적인
- **swipe** ⓥ (신용 카드 등을 단말기에) 대다, 읽히다
- **confirmation** ⓝ (사실이라는) 확인
- **charge** ⓥ (요금을) 청구하다
- **bank transfer** 계좌 이체

16-17 갈등 상황을 다스리는 유용한 전략

W : Good morning, students. It's good to see you again.
안녕하세요, 여러분. 다시 만나 반갑습니다.
Last time, we talked about how to express your anger in a healthy way.
저번 시간에, 우리는 화를 건강하게 표현하는 방법에 관해 이야기했죠.
「Today, I'm going to tell you some useful ways to manage conflict situations.」
오늘은 갈등 상황을 다스리는 몇 가지 유용한 방법들을 이야기하겠습니다. 16번의 근거
「First, try the accommodating strategy.」 17번 ①의 근거 일치
첫 번째로, 수용 전략을 사용하세요.
Simply accept the opponent's argument and you'll see that small disagreements can be handled quickly and easily with a minimum of effort.
그냥 상대방의 주장을 수용해주다 보면, 여러분은 작은 다툼을 최소의 노력으로 신속하고 쉽게 대처할 수 있다는 것을 알게 됩니다.
「Second, you can use compromising strategy.」 17번 ②의 근거 일치
둘째로, 타협 전략을 쓸 수 있습니다.
To reach agreement, each party sometimes needs to give up something that they want.
합의에 이르려면, 각 당사자는 자신이 원하는 무언가를 간혹 포기해야 하죠.
Through finding the middle ground, both parties can feel they've been listened to.
타협안을 찾아감으로써, 두 당사자는 서로 자기 의견이 받아들여졌다는 느낌을 갖게 됩니다.
「Next, competing strategy is helpful when you decide to hold to your principles.」
다음으로, 여러분이 원칙을 고수하기로 할 때에는, 경쟁 전략이 유용합니다. 17번 ③의 근거 일치
When it comes to moral judgment, you can reject compromise.
도덕적 판단에 관해서는 타협을 거부할 수 있죠.
Sometimes it's best to stick to what you believe is correct.
가끔은 여러분이 옳다고 믿는 것을 고수하는 게 최선입니다.
「Finally, avoiding strategy is another type of conflict management.」 17번 ⑤의 근거 일치
마지막으로, 회피 전략은 또 다른 갈등 통제 (전략)의 유형입니다.
This style aims to reduce conflict by ignoring it.
이 방식은 무시를 통해 갈등을 줄이려는 것을 목표로 합니다.
That can give you time to calm down and analyze the situation based on a more objective point of view.
이는 여러분에게 평정을 찾고 더 객관적인 시각에 근거해 상황을 분석할 시간을 줄 수 있습니다.
Now, let's watch a few videos and think about how to handle each situation.
이제, 영상 몇 편을 보고 각 상황에 어떻게 대처할지 생각해봅시다.

- **accommodate** ⓥ 수용하다, (필요에) 대응하다
- **opponent** ⓝ 상대방, 적수
- **disagreement** ⓝ 불일치, 다툼
- **compromise** ⓥ 타협하다
- **middle ground** 타협안, 절충안
- **hold to** ~을 고수하다
- **stick to** ~을 고수하다

16 주제 파악

정답률 78% | 정답 ①

여자가 하는 말의 주제로 가장 적절한 것은?

✔ practical methods of conflict management – 갈등 관리의 실용적 방안
② socially acceptable ways to express anger – 사회적으로 용인되는 분노 표현의 방법
③ various behaviors to trigger social conflict – 사회 갈등을 촉발하는 여러 가지 행동
④ communicative skills for customer satisfaction – 고객 만족을 위한 의사소통 기술
⑤ situations causing conflict between generations – 세대 갈등을 야기하는 상황

Why? 왜 정답일까?

갈등을 다스리는 방안에 관해 논해보자는(**Today, I'm going to tell you some useful ways to manage conflict situations.**) 내용으로 보아, 여자가 하는 말의 주제로 가장 적절한 것은 ① '갈등 관리의 실용적 방안(**practical methods of conflict management**)'이다.

17 언급 유무 파악

정답률 96% | 정답 ④

언급된 전략이 아닌 것은?

① accommodating – 수용
② compromising – 타협
③ competing – 경쟁
✔ assessing – 평가
⑤ avoiding – 회피

Why? 왜 정답일까?

담화에서 여자는 전략의 예시로 수용, 타협, 경쟁, 회피를 열거하고 있다. 언급되지 않은 것은 ④ '평가'이다.

Why? 왜 오답일까?

① '**First, try the accommodating strategy.**'에서 '수용'이 언급되었다.
② '**Second, you can use compromising strategy.**'에서 '타협'이 언급되었다.
③ '**Next, competing strategy is helpful when you decide to hold to your principles.**'에서 '경쟁'이 언급되었다.
⑤ '**Finally, avoiding strategy is another type of conflict management.**'에서 '회피'가 언급되었다.

Dictation 07

문제편 039쪽

01 what items you should bring / bring your résumé / any certificates for special skills
02 sort your old clothes / trends come and go / dispose of clothes you don't usually wear
03 why your house was recommended / put lots of effort into decorating / the photos taken today will be published
04 set an easel near the window / two paint brushes in the bucket / congratulate me on the new place
05 the club recruitment / making our club poster / put up the posters
06 book a practice room / Let's reserve the expert room for two hours / it doesn't apply to us
07 buy some unique fancy accessories / I recently adopted one / vaccinate my puppy
08 Are you kidding me / text me the link to the website / even freely attend any lectures
09 a huge fan of superhero comics and movies / located next to the city library / free tickets to children under school age
10 liquid soap is easier to use / How about the fragrance / not tested on animals
11 the orders have piled up / When do you think I'll receive my order
12 have a business meeting / give your brother a ride
13 it's already fully booked / why don't you take it online / Registration is due next Friday
14 My life seems so repetitive / so full of dull moments / help boost your spirits
15 stops at the grocery store / Due to a temporary bank error / if the payment was made twice
16-17 try the accommodating strategy / give up something that they want / stick to what you believe is correct

08 회 | 2022학년도 4월 학력평가 고3

| 정답과 해설 |

• 정답 •

01 ① 02 ④ 03 ② 04 ③ 05 ⑤ 06 ① 07 ④ 08 ④ 09 ⑤ 10 ③ 11 ② 12 ② 13 ⑤ 14 ③ 15 ①
16 ③ 17 ④

01 자선 경매 행사를 도와줄 자원봉사자 모집

정답률 81% | 정답 ①

다음을 듣고, 여자가 하는 말의 목적으로 가장 적절한 것을 고르시오.

✔ 자선 경매 행사를 위한 자원봉사자를 모집하려고
② 지역 아동을 위한 자선 물품 기부를 독려하려고
③ 봉사 활동 확인서 발급 절차를 안내하려고
④ 아동 병원 설립의 필요성을 강조하려고
⑤ 자원봉사 사전 교육 일정을 공지하려고

W : Hello, citizens of Grandsville. I'm your mayor, Clara Bennett.
안녕하세요, Grandsville의 시민 여러분. 저는 시장 Clara Bennett입니다.
As you know, our city is going to have a charity auction for the local children's hospital.
아시다시피, 우리 시에서 지역 아동 병원을 위한 자선 경매 행사를 열 예정입니다.
I'm sure that many citizens are paying attention to this special event, so we're looking for volunteers for the event.
분명 많은 시민 여러분들이 이 특별 행사에 관심을 갖고 계실 것이기에, 우리는 행사를 위한 자원봉사자를 찾고 있습니다.
The volunteers are going to take care of categorizing donated items and cleaning up the event hall.
자원봉사자는 기부된 물품을 분류하고 행사장을 치우는 일을 맡게 됩니다.
I hope you can make a truly memorable contribution to our community.
여러분이 우리 지역사회에 진정으로 기억에 남는 기여를 할 수 있다고 생각합니다.
If you're interested, please visit www.grandsville.gov and fill out the volunteer application.
관심이 있으시면, www.grandsville.gov를 방문하셔서 자원봉사 신청서를 작성해 주세요.
Thank you for your help in advance.
여러분의 도움에 미리 감사드립니다.

Why? 왜 정답일까?

'~ **we're looking for volunteers for the event.**'에서 여자는 자선 경매 행사를 도와줄 자원봉사자를 찾고 있다고 하므로, 여자가 하는 말의 목적으로 가장 적절한 것은 ① '자선 경매 행사를 위한 자원봉사자를 모집하려고'이다.

- **mayor** ⓝ 시장(市長)
- **auction** ⓝ 경매
- **volunteer** ⓝ 자원 봉사자
- **make a contribution** 기여하다, 이바지하다
- **charity** ⓝ 자선
- **pay attention to** ~에 관심을 갖다, 주의를 기울이다
- **categorize** ⓥ 분류하다
- **fill out** (양식을) 작성하다

02 노래를 통한 단어 학습의 유용성

정답률 96% | 정답 ④

대화를 듣고, 남자의 의견으로 가장 적절한 것을 고르시오.

① 교사의 칭찬은 학생의 불안감을 낮출 수 있다.
② 예술 교육은 학생의 사회성 발달을 촉진시킨다.
③ 어휘를 배우는 것은 독해력 향상에 필수적이다.
✔ 노래는 학생이 어휘를 쉽게 기억하도록 도와준다.
⑤ 음악 감상을 통해 학생의 창의력을 향상시킬 수 있다.

[Door knocks.]
[문을 노크하는 소리가 들린다.]
M : Come on in, Ms. Dale. Take a seat.
들어오세요, Dale 선생님. 앉으세요.
W : Good afternoon, Mr. Harrison. Thank you for your time.
안녕하세요, Harrison 선생님. 시간 내 주셔서 고맙습니다.
M : No problem. I'm happy to share my teaching experience with you. How can I help?
별 거 아니에요. 선생님과 제 수업 경험을 나누게 되어 기뻐요. 어떤 걸 도와드릴까요?
W : Well, students in my class are having a hard time memorizing vocabulary. Do you have any ideas on how to make it easier for them?
음, 저희 반 애들은 단어를 외우는 데 어려움을 겪고 있어요. 단어 학습을 더 쉽게 만들어줄 아이디어가 있으신가요?
M : Hmm, how about using songs? Songs are helpful for remembering vocabulary easily.
흠, 노래를 이용해 보시는 게 어때요? 노래는 어휘를 쉽게 기억하는 데 도움이 돼요.
W : Do you really think so?
정말로 그렇게 생각하세요?
M : Yes. The repetition of the melody and rhythm in a song can help them remember words for longer periods of time.
네, 노래 속 멜로디와 리듬의 반복은 아이들이 단어를 더 오랜 기간 기억하게 도와주죠.
W : That makes sense.
일리 있는 말씀이네요.
M : Also, you can see students enjoy learning vocabulary through songs. Learning is easier when it's fun.
게다가, 아이들이 노래로 단어 배우는 것을 즐거워한다는 걸 아실 수 있어요. 학습은 재미있을 때 더 쉬워지죠.
W : Sounds good. I should try that.
좋은 것 같네요. 시도해 봐야겠어요.
M : I'm sure songs will help your students to easily remember vocabulary.
분명 노래가 선생님네 학생들이 어휘를 쉽게 외우는 데 도움이 될 거예요.
W : Thank you for your advice.
조언 고맙습니다.

Why? 왜 정답일까?

'**Songs are helpful for remembering vocabulary easily.**'와 '**I'm sure songs will help your students to easily remember vocabulary.**'에서 남자는 학생들의 어휘 학습에 노래가 도움이 될 수 있다고 하므로, 남자의 의견으로 가장 적절한 것은 ④ '노래는 학생이 어휘를 쉽게 기억하도록 도와준다.'이다.

- **have a hard time ~ing** ~하는 데 어려움을 겪다
- **helpful** ⓐ 도움이 되는
- **period** ⓝ 기간, 시기(時期)
- **vocabulary** ⓝ 어휘(단어)
- **repetition** ⓝ 반복
- **make sense** 일리가 있다, 이해가 되다

03 동물 보호소 직원과 기부자의 대화

정답률 95% | 정답 ②

대화를 듣고, 두 사람의 관계를 가장 잘 나타낸 것을 고르시오.

① 운전자 – 주차 관리 요원
✔ 동물 보호소 직원 – 기부자
③ 인테리어 디자이너 – 의뢰인
④ 건물 관리인 – 청소업체 직원
⑤ 애견용품 판매점 주인 – 손님

W : Hello, Mr. Ryan. It's been a while.
안녕하세요, Ryan 씨. 오랜만이에요.
M : You're right, Ms. Brown. It's been a year since I visited here.
그러게요, Brown 씨. 여기 방문한 지 1년이 됐네요.
W : Did you notice some changes around the place?
주변이 좀 달라진 걸 아셨나요?
M : Yeah. The facilities look renovated and clean.
네, 시설이 보수된 것 같고 깨끗해 보이네요.
W : Due to the increasing concerns about abandoned animals, more donations were made, which allowed us to renovate.
유기 동물에 대한 우려가 높아지면서 기부가 더 많이 이루어졌고, 그래서 보수가 가능했어요.
M : That's good. It looks like the number of workers in this shelter has increased as well.
잘됐네요. 이 보호소에 있는 직원 분들 수도 늘어난 것 같아요.
W : That's true. There were only three people including me working here, but now there are five.
맞아요. 여기서 일하던 사람은 저를 포함해 세 명이었지만, 이제는 다섯 명이에요.
M : I see. Well, as I told you on the phone, I brought dog food to donate.
그렇군요. 음, 제가 전화로 말씀드렸던 것처럼, 전 강아지 음식을 기부하려고 갖고 왔어요.
W : Thank you so much. Your donations have always been a great help for our animals.
정말 감사합니다. 당신의 기부가 항상 저희 동물들에게 큰 도움이 돼요.
M : I'm glad to hear that. Then I'll bring the food from my car.
그 말씀을 들으니 기뻐요. 그럼 제가 차에서 음식을 갖고 올게요.
W : Can I help you?
도와드릴까요?
M : Thank you. Let's go to the parking lot together.
그럼 감사하죠. 같이 주차장으로 가시죠.

Why? 왜 정답일까?

'**There were only three people including me working here, but now there are five.**'를 통해 여자가 동물 보호소 직원임을 알 수 있고, '~ **I brought dog food to donate.**'에서 남자가 기부자임을 알 수 있다. 따라서 두 사람의 관계로 가장 적절한 것은 ② '동물 보호소 직원 – 기부자'이다.

- **facility** ⓝ (편의) 시설
- **concern** ⓝ 우려, 걱정
- **shelter** ⓝ 보호소, 쉼터
- **renovate** ⓥ 보수하다
- **abandoned animal** 유기 동물

04 음악 선생님 송별회 사진 보기

정답률 79% | 정답 ③

대화를 듣고, 그림에서 대화의 내용과 일치하지 않는 것을 고르시오.

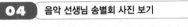

M : Mindy, you prepared a lot for your music teacher's farewell party. How did it go?
Mindy, 너네 음악 선생님 송별회를 위해 많은 걸 준비했지, 어떻게 됐니?
W : Dad, Mr. Peters loved it so much. Do you want to see a picture of it?
아빠, Peters 선생님이 무척 좋아하셨어요. 사진 한 번 보실래요?
M : Sure. *[Pause]* 『Oh, you drew a violin on the banner.』 ①의 근거 일치
그래. *[잠시 멈춤]* 오, 현수막에 바이올린을 그려놨구나.
W : Yeah. He used to play the violin in front of us. 『Look at the picture on the wall. It's a picture of the music club members.』 ②의 근거 일치
네, 선생님이 저희 앞에서 바이올린을 연주해주시곤 했거든요. 벽에 걸린 사진 좀 보세요. 저희 음악 동아리 회원들 사진이에요.
M : Looks lovely. 『By the way, what are those two boxes next to the plant for?』 ③의 근거 불일치
귀여워 보이네. 그나저나 화분 옆에 있는 상자 두 개는 뭐니?
W : Those are the gifts we prepared for Mr. Peters. 『And, do you see the cake on the table?』 ④의 근거 일치
Peters 선생님을 위해서 저희가 준비한 선물이에요. 그리고, 탁자 위에 케이크 보이세요?
M : Yes. Is that the cake you were baking last night? He must have loved it.
응. 네가 어젯밤 굽던 그 케이크니? 무척 좋아하셨겠구나.
W : He sure did. Also, we played the piano for Mr. Peters.
정말 그러셨어요. 그리고 저희는 Peters 선생님을 위해 피아노도 쳤어요.
M : 『Oh, I can see a piano under the clock.』 ⑤의 근거 일치
오, 시계 밑에 피아노가 보이는구나.
W : Right. I hope he had a great time with us.
맞아요. 선생님이 우리와 함께 즐거운 시간을 보내셨길 바라요.

Why? 왜 정답일까?

대화에서 화분 옆에 상자가 두 개 놓여있다(**By the way, what are those two boxes next to** the plant for?)고 하는데, 그림에서는 상자가 하나만 놓여 있다. 따라서 그림에서 대화의 내용과 일치하지 않는 것은 ③이다.

- prepare ⓥ 준비하다
- farewell ⓝ 작별

05 지구의 날 행사 준비 — 정답률 92% | 정답 ⑤

대화를 듣고, 남자가 할 일로 가장 적절한 것을 고르시오.

① 테이블 설치하기 ② 스피커 점검하기 ③ 포스터 제작하기
④ 배지 배송 확인하기 ⑤ 무선 마이크 가져오기

W : John, the Earth Day event is in an hour. Let's do a final check.
John, Earth Day 행사가 한 시간 뒤에 있어. 마지막으로 점검해 보자.
M : Okay, Kelly. The table for registration is nicely set in that booth.
그래, Kelly. 등록을 받을 테이블은 저 부스 안에 잘 설치돼 있어.
W : Wonderful. The earth-shaped badges we're going to give out to visitors were delivered in the morning.
좋네. 우리가 방문객들에게 나눠줄 지구 모양 배지는 아침에 배달됐어.
M : Perfect. I hope people will like them.
좋아. 사람들이 좋아하면 좋겠다.
W : I'm sure they will. And the materials for decorating reusable cups are in this box.
분명 그럴 거야. 그리고 재사용 가능한 컵을 꾸밀 재료는 이 상자에 있어.
M : Good. And I've already checked the speakers we're going to use for the broadcast. They work well.
좋아. 그리고 난 우리가 방송에 사용할 스피커를 이미 점검해 봤어. 작동 잘되더라.
W : Great. By the way, where's the wireless microphone?
훌륭해. 그나저나, 무선 마이크는 어디 있지?
M : Oh, I forgot to bring it from the school auditorium. I'll get it right away.
오, 학교 강당에서 가지고 오는 걸 잊었네. 내가 바로 갖고 올게.
W : Thanks. Then I'll put the Earth Day poster on the front of the table.
고마워. 그럼 난 테이블 앞쪽에 지구의 날 포스터를 붙여야겠어.

Why? 왜 정답일까?

행사 준비를 챙기던 여자가 무선 마이크를 찾자(**By the way, where's the wireless microphone?**) 남자는 강당에서 아직 안 가져왔다며 바로 가서 가져오겠다(**I'll get it right away.**)고 한다. 따라서 남자가 할 일로 가장 적절한 것은 ⑤ '무선 마이크 가져오기'이다.

- do a final check 마지막으로 점검하다
- nicely ad 잘, 좋게
- deliver ⓥ 배달하다
- reusable ⓐ 재사용 가능한
- wireless ⓐ 무선의
- registration ⓝ 등록
- give out 나눠주다
- decorate ⓥ 장식하다, 꾸미다
- broadcast ⓝ 방송
- right away 즉시, 곧, 바로

06 서핑 수업 등록하기 — 정답률 83% | 정답 ①

대화를 듣고, 여자가 지불할 금액을 고르시오.

① $108 ② $110 ③ $120 ④ $162 ⑤ $180

M : Welcome to King Wave Surfing.
King Wave Surfing에 잘 오셨습니다.
W : Hello. I'd like to sign up for a surfing lesson with my husband.
안녕하세요. 전 남편이랑 같이 서핑 수업에 등록하고 싶어요.
M : Sure. Which program do you want to register for?
알겠습니다. 어느 프로그램에 등록하고 싶으신가요?
W : Hmm, is there a beginners' lesson available this Friday for two people?
흠, 이번 주 금요일 초보자 수업에 두 사람 자리가 있나요?
M : Let me check. *[Typing sound]* Yes, we have a private lesson and a group lesson on that day. The private lesson costs $80 per person, and the group lesson costs $50 per person.
확인해 보겠습니다. *[타자 치는 소리]* 네, 그날 개인 수업과 단체 수업이 있습니다. 개인 수업은 1인당 80달러이고, 단체 수업은 1인당 50달러입니다.
W : I'd like to book a group lesson for two people.
단체 수업 2인 예약하고 싶어요.
M : All right. How about renting surfing suits? They're $10 per person.
알겠습니다. 서핑복 대여는 안 하시나요? 1인당 10달러입니다.
W : Yeah, I think we need to rent two of them.
네, 두 사람 것을 빌려야겠네요.
M : Okay. So that's two people for the group lesson and two suits, right?
알겠습니다. 그럼 2인 단체 레슨과 서핑복 두 벌, 맞으시죠?
W : Yes. Oh, can I use this coupon? I got it from the hotel where I'm staying.
네. 오, 이 쿠폰을 써도 될까요? 제가 묵고 있는 호텔에서 이걸 받았어요.
M : Let me see. Sure, you get 10% off the total.
확인해 보겠습니다. 물론이죠, 총 가격에서 10퍼센트 할인을 받으실 수 있어요.
W : Great. Here's my credit card.
좋네요. 여기 제 신용카드요.

Why? 왜 정답일까?

대화에 따르면 여자는 1인당 50달러인 서핑 단체 수업을 2인 예약하고, 서핑복도 한 벌에 10달러씩 두 벌 빌린 뒤, 총 가격에서 10퍼센트를 할인받았다. 이를 식으로 나타내면 '(50×2+10×2)×0.9=108'이므로, 여자가 지불할 총 금액은 ① '$108'이다.

- sign up for ~에 등록하다
- register ⓥ 등록하다
- available ⓐ 이용할 수 있는
- surfing suit 서핑복
- husband ⓝ 남편
- beginner ⓝ 초보자
- private ⓐ 개인의

07 건강 검진을 위해 영화 약속 취소하기 — 정답률 87% | 정답 ④

대화를 듣고, 남자가 영화를 보러 갈 수 없는 이유를 고르시오.

① 면접 준비를 해야 해서 ② 아르바이트를 해야 해서
③ 요가 수업을 들어야 해서 ④ 건강 검진을 받아야 해서
⑤ 동아리 모임에 참석해야 해서

[Cell phone rings.]
[휴대 전화 벨이 울린다.]
W : Hello, Ted.
여보세요, Ted.
M : Hi, Kristine. Have you finished your yoga class?
안녕, Kristine. 너 요가 수업 끝났어?
W : Yes, it has just finished. I'm on my way to a club meeting. What's up?
응, 방금 끝났어. 동아리 모임 가는 중이야. 무슨 일이야?
M : Guess what? I got accepted into the internship program.
있잖아, 나 인턴 프로그램에 합격했어.
W : Congratulations! You must have made a good impression during the interview.
축하해! 면접에서 분명 좋은 인상 남겼나보네.
M : Thanks. But that's not the only reason I called you.
고마워. 그런데 그것 때문에만 전화한 건 아냐.
W : Then why did you call me?
그럼 왜 전화했어?
M : Well, I have to tell you that I can't go to see the movie this Friday. I'm really sorry.
음, 나 이번 주 금요일에 영화 보러 못 갈 것 같아. 정말 미안해.
W : Didn't you say that you quit your part-time job?
아르바이트 그만뒀다고 하지 않았어?
M : Yes, I stopped working there last month.
맞아, 난 거기 일 지난달에 그만뒀어.
W : Then why can't you come?
그럼 왜 못 가?
M : Actually, I have a medical check-up for the internship on that day.
사실, 그날 인턴십 때문에 건강 검진 받으러 가.
W : I see. Maybe next time.
그렇구나. 그럼 다음에 보든가 하자.

Why? 왜 정답일까?

인턴 면접에 합격한 남자는 금요일에 건강 검진을 받아야 해서 영화 약속에 갈 수 없다(**Actually, I have a medical check-up for the internship on that day.**)고 하므로, 남자가 영화를 보러 갈 수 없는 이유로 가장 적절한 것은 ④ '건강 검진을 받아야 해서'이다.

- finish ⓥ 끝내다
- internship ⓝ 인턴사원 근무, 인턴직
- interview ⓝ 면접
- medical check-up 건강 검진
- get accepted into ~에 합격하다
- make a good impression 좋은 인상을 주다
- part-time job 시간제 근무, 아르바이트

08 주민 걷기 챌린지 — 정답률 93% | 정답 ④

대화를 듣고, Spring Walking Challenge에 관해 언급되지 않은 것을 고르시오.

① 운영 기간 ② 참가 대상 ③ 우승 상금
④ 주최 기관 ⑤ 신청 방법

M : Bella, did you see this leaflet about Spring Walking Challenge?
Bella, Spring Walking Challenge에 관한 이 전단지 봤어?
W : Walking Challenge? I've never heard of that.
Walking Challenge라고? 나 전혀 못 들어 봤어.
M : It's about tracking how many steps we walk and deciding who walks the longest distance with the Challenge Tracker app.
Challenge Tracker 앱으로 우리가 몇 걸음이나 걷는지 측정해서 제일 긴 거리를 걸은 사람을 가려내는 거야.
W : Interesting. 「When is it?
재미있겠다. 언제야?
M : It's held from April 17th to May 1st.」 ①의 근거 일치
4월 17일부터 5월 1일까지 열린대.
W : I see. 「Oh, the challenge is open to any community member.」 ②의 근거 일치
그렇구나. 오, 이 챌린지는 주민들 누구나 참여해도 된대.
M : Good. Then a lot of people can participate.
좋다. 그럼 많은 사람들이 참여할 수 있겠네.
W : I think it'll be a fun experience.
재미있는 경험이 될 것 같아.
M : Absolutely. 「And $500 will be given to the winner.」 ③의 근거 일치
그러게. 그리고 500달러가 우승자에게 수여될 거래.
W : Really? I want to participate in it. 「How can I sign up for the challenge?
정말? 나 참여하고 싶어. 챌린지에 어떻게 등록하지?
M : Just scan this QR code and fill in the application form on the website.」 ⑤의 근거 일치
이 QR코드를 찍어서 웹 사이트에서 신청서를 작성하기만 하면 돼.
W : Thanks. I'll do that now.
고마워. 지금 할래.

Why? 왜 정답일까?

대화에서 남자와 여자는 **Spring Walking Challenge**의 운영 기간, 참가 대상, 우승 상금, 신청 방법에 관해 언급하므로, 언급되지 않은 것은 ④ '주최 기관'이다.

Why? 왜 오답일까?

① '**It's held from April 17th to May 1st.**'에서 '운영 기간'이 언급되었다.
② '**Oh, the challenge is open to any community member.**'에서 '참가 대상'이 언급되었다.
③ '**And $500 will be given to the winner.**'에서 '우승 상금'이 언급되었다.
⑤ '**Just scan this QR code and fill in the application form on the website.**'에서 '신청 방법'이 언급되었다.

- leaflet ⓝ 전단
- decide ⓥ 결정하다, 결정을 내리다
- participate ⓥ 참여하다, 참가하다
- application form 신청서
- track ⓥ 추적하다
- distance ⓝ 거리
- fill in (서식을) 작성하다, 채우다

09 비트박스 경연 대회 안내 — 정답률 92% | 정답 ⑤

International Beatbox Championship에 관한 다음 내용을 듣고, 일치하지 않는 것을 고르시오.

① 5월 10일부터 시작한다.

[문제편 p.043]

② 단독 공연과 단체 공연이 있다.
③ 전년도 우승자들이 심사 위원으로 참여한다.
④ 결승전은 온라인으로 생중계된다.
✔ 표는 현장 구매가 가능하다.

M : Hello, listeners.
안녕하세요, 청취자 여러분.
I'm Jay Cloud, director of the International Beatbox Championship.
저는 International Beatbox Championship의 책임자인 Jay Cloud입니다.
I'm so thrilled to invite you to our upcoming championship.
저희 다가오는 챔피언십 행사에 여러분을 초대하게 되어 몹시 기쁩니다.
「It'll be a five-day event starting from May 10th in Miami.」 ①의 근거 일치
이것은 마이애미에서 5월 10일부터 시작되는 5일간의 행사입니다.
「There will be solo performances and group performances.」 ②의 근거 일치
단독 공연과 단체 공연이 있을 것입니다.
And guess what? 「The winners from last year will participate as judges.」 ③의 근거 일치
그리고 놀라지 마세요. 전년도 우승자들이 심사위원으로 참여할 것입니다.
「The finals will be broadcast live on our website.」 ④의 근거 일치
결승전은 우리 웹 사이트에서 생중계될 예정입니다.
「Tickets are only available to be purchased online,」 but seats will be assigned on a first come, first served basis. ⑤의 근거 불일치
표는 온라인에서만 구매하실 수 있지만, 좌석은 선착순으로 배정될 것입니다.
For more information, visit www.beatboxchamps.org.
더 많은 정보를 얻으시려면, www.beatboxchamps.org를 방문하세요.
Join us and feel the rhythm with your whole body.
저희와 함께하시고 리듬을 온몸으로 느껴보세요.

Why? 왜 정답일까?

'Tickets are only available to be purchased online, ~'에서 표는 온라인으로만 살 수 있다고 하므로, 내용과 일치하지 않는 것은 ⑤ '표는 현장 구매가 가능하다.'이다.

Why? 왜 오답일까?

① 'It'll be a five-day event starting from May 10th in Miami.'의 내용과 일치한다.
② 'There will be solo performances and group performances.'의 내용과 일치한다.
③ 'The winners from last year will participate as judges.'의 내용과 일치한다.
④ 'The finals will be broadcast live on our website.'의 내용과 일치한다.

- director ⓝ 책임자
- performance ⓝ 공연
- purchase ⓥ 구입하다, 구매하다
- upcoming ⓐ 다가오는, 곧 있을
- judge ⓝ 심사위원
- on a first come, first served basis 선착순으로

10 정수기 대여하기

정답률 91% | 정답 ③

다음 표를 보면서 대화를 듣고, 두 사람이 대여할 정수기를 고르시오.

Water Purifiers

	Product	Monthly Rental Fee	Hot Water	Filter Replacement	Color
①	A	$25	×	self	black
②	B	$30	○	self	black
✔	C	$35	○	self	white
④	D	$38	○	service visit	white
⑤	E	$42	×	service visit	gray

M : Honey, what are you doing?
여보, 뭐 해요?
W : I'm looking at this catalogue of water purifiers we can rent. Why don't we choose one together?
우리가 대여할 수 있는 정수기를 이 카탈로그에서 보고 있어요. 하나 골라보는 게 어때요?
M : Sure. 「How much can we spend on the monthly rental fee?
좋아요. 우리가 월 대여료로 얼마나 쓸 수 있죠?
W : We can't afford more than $40.」 근거1 Price 조건
40달러 이상은 쓸 수 없어요.
M : Then let's cross this out. 「Do you think we should get one with hot water?
그럼 이건 제외하죠. 뜨거운 물이 나오는 걸로 구해야 할까요? 근거2 Hot Water 조건
W : Yes.」 I drink a lot of hot tea, so a water purifier with hot water will be more convenient.
네, 난 뜨거운 차를 많이 마시니, 온수가 나오는 정수기가 더 편할 거예요.
M : All right. What about the filter replacement? We can ask service engineers to visit our home to change the filters or do that by ourselves.
알겠어요. 필터 교체는요? 서비스 기술자들에게 방문해서 필터를 교체해 달라고 요청할 수도 있고 우리가 직접 할 수도 있어요.
W : Well, which one is better?
흠, 어느 게 더 나을까요?
M : 「Hmm, replacing a filter by myself doesn't seem difficult. Let's choose the self replacement option.」 근거3 Filter Replacement 조건
흠, 필터를 직접 교체하는 것은 어렵지 않아 보여요. 직접 교체하는 것으로 고르죠.
W : Okay. Now, there are only two options left. 「Which color do you like?
알겠어요. 그럼, 선택권이 두 개밖에 안 남았어요. 어떤 색이 좋아요?
M : I prefer the white one since it'll match with our kitchen better.」 근거4 Color 조건
우리 부엌에 흰색이 더 잘 어울릴 것 같으니 그게 더 좋아요.
W : I agree. Then let's rent this.
동의해요. 그럼 이걸 대여하죠.

Why? 왜 정답일까?

대화에 따르면 두 사람은 월 대여료가 40달러를 넘지 않으면서, 온수가 나오고, 필터 교체를 직접 할 수 있으면서, 흰색인 정수기를 대여하려 한다. 따라서 두 사람이 대여할 정수기는 ③ 'C'이다.

- catalogue ⓝ (상품자료의) 목록, 카탈로그
- rental fee 대여료
- convenient ⓐ 편리한
- prefer ⓥ ~을 좋아하다
- water purifier 정수기
- afford ⓥ 여유가 있다
- replacement ⓝ 교체
- match with ~와 어울리다, 부합하다

11 드럼 실력 칭찬하기

정답률 89% | 정답 ②

대화를 듣고, 여자의 마지막 말에 대한 남자의 응답으로 가장 적절한 것을 고르시오.

① It wasn't easy to discover my new hobby. – 새로운 취미를 발견하기가 쉽지 않았어요.
✔ I began taking drum lessons in middle school. – 중학교 때 드럼 수업을 시작했어요.
③ It was very hard to practice drums every day. – 매일 드럼을 연습하는 건 아주 힘들었요.
④ I brought them from my home for this festival. – 이번 축제를 위해 그걸 저희 집에서 가져왔어요.
⑤ I used to enjoy listening to modern rock music. – 전 모던 록 음악을 즐겨듣곤 했었어요.

W : Jeremy, I was surprised to see you play the drums at the school festival. You were incredible.
Jeremy, 난 네가 학교 축제에서 드럼 치는 거 보고 놀랐어. 정말 대단하더라.
M : I'm flattered, Ms. Anderson. I play them as a hobby.
과찬이세요, Anderson 선생님. 취미로 하는 거예요.
W : Really? When did you start learning the drums?
정말? 드럼을 언제 배우기 시작했는데?
M : I began taking drum lessons in middle school.
중학교 때 드럼 수업을 시작했어요.

Why? 왜 정답일까?

남자의 드럼 실력에 놀라며 언제 드럼을 배우기 시작했냐(When did you start learning the drums?)는 여자의 말에 대한 남자의 응답으로 가장 적절한 것은 ② '중학교 때 드럼 수업을 시작했어요.'이다.

- incredible ⓐ 놀라운, 훌륭한, 대단한, 굉장한
- hobby ⓝ 취미
- practice ⓥ 연습하다
- I'm flattered. 과찬이에요.
- discover ⓥ 발견하다

12 부활절 행사 가정통신문 보여드리기

정답률 84% | 정답 ②

대화를 듣고, 남자의 마지막 말에 대한 여자의 응답으로 가장 적절한 것을 고르시오.

① No worries. His school grades will get better. – 걱정 마. 그의 학교 성적은 나아질 거야.
✔ Sure. I'll adjust my schedule to join the event. – 물론이지. 행사에 참석할 수 있도록 일정을 조정할게.
③ Wonderful. Your parents must be proud of you. – 훌륭해. 너희 부모님은 네가 자랑스러울 거야.
④ Hurry up. You're really late for the school event. – 서둘러. 넌 학교 행사에 정말 늦었어.
⑤ Absolutely. I'm happy to invite your teacher here. – 물론이지. 너희 선생님을 여기 초대해서 기뻐.

M : Mom, take a look at this school newsletter.
엄마, 이 가정통신문 좀 보세요.
W : Hmm, there's an Easter egg hunt. That looks like an exciting event.
흠, 부활절 달걀 찾기 행사가 있네. 신나는 행사 같아.
M : My teacher said parents are welcome to participate. And I really hope you come.
우리 선생님 말씀이 부모님 참여도 환영이래요. 그래서 전 엄마가 꼭 오시면 좋겠어요.
W : Sure. I'll adjust my schedule to join the event.
물론이지. 행사에 참석할 수 있도록 일정을 조정할게.

Why? 왜 정답일까?

부활절 달걀 행사에 꼭 와주었으면 좋겠다(And I really hope you come.)는 남자의 말에 대한 여자의 응답으로 가장 적절한 것은 ② '물론이지. 행사에 참석할 수 있도록 일정을 조정할게.'이다.

- Easter egg 부활절 달걀
- adjust ⓥ 조정하다

13 진로 상담 예약하기

정답률 83% | 정답 ⑤

대화를 듣고, 여자의 마지막 말에 대한 남자의 응답으로 가장 적절한 것을 고르시오. [3점]

Man: ____________

① No problem. I can help him find his future career.
문제 없어. 난 그가 미래 직업을 찾게 도와줄 수 있어.
② I got it. I'll send you the website about promising jobs.
알겠어. 유망 직업에 관한 웹 사이트를 너한테 보내줄게.
③ Don't worry. I won't be late for the counseling next time.
걱정 마. 다음 번 상담엔 안 늦을 테니까.
④ Of course. I'll keep the appointment with my homeroom teacher.
물론이지. 난 우리 담임 선생님과의 약속을 지킬 거야.
✔ Thanks. I'll check it out and book a meeting with the counselor.
고마워. 그걸 확인해 보고 나서 상담 선생님과의 만남을 예약해야지.

W : What are you doing, Jake?
뭐 하고 있어, Jake?
M : Hi, Diane. I'm reading a book about promising jobs in the future.
안녕, Diane. 난 미래에 유망한 직업에 관한 책을 읽는 중이야.
W : Great. What kind of future career are you interested in?
멋지네. 너는 어떤 미래 직업에 관심이 있는데?
M : Well, I don't have any specific career in mind.
음, 난 특별히 관심 있는 직업이 없어.
W : Oh, I see. So you're getting ideas from that book.
아, 그렇구나. 그럼 그 책에서 아이디어를 얻고 있는 거구나.
M : Yes. This book is really helpful, but I need more detailed information related to my preferences and interests.
응. 이 책은 무척 도움이 되는데, 내 선호와 관심에 관련된 더 구체적인 정보가 필요해.
W : Well, how about talking with our school career counselor?
음, 학교 진로 상담 선생님과 얘기해보는 게 어때?
M : I didn't think about that.
그건 생각 안 해 봤어.
W : He has given me lots of information in finding my future career through some counseling sessions.
그는 몇 번의 상담을 통해 내가 미래 직업을 찾는 데 많은 정보를 주셨어.
M : Sounds good. Then I should talk to him today.
좋을 것 같네. 그럼 오늘 이야기해 봐야겠다.
W : Hold on. You have to make an appointment first.
잠깐. 넌 예약부터 해야 해.
M : How can I do that?
그거 어떻게 해?

W : His schedule is posted on our school website. You should look at it and make an appointment online.
선생님 일정표가 우리 학교 웹 사이트에 게시돼 있어. 그걸 보고 온라인으로 약속을 잡는 거야.
M : Thanks. I'll check it out and book a meeting with the counselor.
고마워. 그걸 확인해 보고 상담 선생님과의 만남을 예약해야지.

Why? 왜 정답일까?

진로 상담 선생님과 만남 일정을 잡으려면 웹 사이트에서 일정을 확인하고 온라인으로 신청해야 한다 (**His schedule is posted on our school website. You should look at it and make an appointment online.**)는 여자의 말에 대한 남자의 응답으로 가장 적절한 것은 ⑤ '고마워. 그걸 확인해 보고 나서 상담 선생님과의 만남을 예약해야지.'이다.

- **promising** ⓐ 유망한
- **detailed** ⓐ 상세한, 자세한
- **interest** ⓝ 관심
- **keep an appointment** 약속을 지키다
- **career** ⓝ 직업
- **preference** ⓝ 선호
- **counseling session** 상담 시간
- **homeroom teacher** 담임 선생님

14 스마트폰을 쓰는 대신 그림 그리기

정답률 78% | 정답 ③

대화를 듣고, 남자의 마지막 말에 대한 여자의 응답으로 가장 적절한 것을 고르시오. [3점]

Woman: ______________________

① I'm sorry. I can't imagine living without new technology.
미안해요. 난 신기술 없이 사는 걸 상상할 수 없어요.
② Cheer up. You'll find more information from digital resources.
기운 내요. 디지털 자원으로부터 더 많은 정보를 찾게 될 거예요.
✔③ You get it. I'm sure it'll help reduce your digital device usage.
바로 그거예요. 분명 그게 당신의 디지털 기기 사용을 줄이는 데 도움이 될 거예요.
④ That makes sense. We're more productive using smartphones.
일리가 있어요. 우린 스마트폰을 쓰면 더 생산적이에요.
⑤ I agree. You can get more rest by giving up your painting time.
동의해요. 그림 그리는 시간을 포기하면 휴식을 더 취할 수 있어요.

M : Honey, what time is it now?
여보, 지금 몇 시예요?
W : It's already 2 o'clock. You've been looking at your smartphone for two hours.
거의 2시예요. 당신 두 시간 동안 스마트폰만 쳐다보고 있었어요.
M : Oh, I didn't realize that it was that long.
오, 그렇게 오래 됐는지 몰랐어요.
W : I'm worried that you've been spending too much time on your smartphone. Why don't you try a digital detox?
요새 당신 스마트폰에 너무 많은 시간을 쓰는 것 같아 걱정이에요. 디지털 디톡스를 시도해보면 어때요?
M : What's that?
그게 뭐예요?
W : It's voluntarily avoiding the use of digital devices like smartphones for a certain amount of time.
스마트폰 같은 디지털 기기 사용을 정해진 시간 동안 자발적으로 피하는 거예요.
M : But it'll be hard to just stop using them so suddenly.
하지만 너무 갑자기 그것들을 그냥 안 쓰기가 어려울 거예요.
W : Well, how about doing more productive activities instead? By focusing on other activities, you won't think of using digital devices.
음, 대신에 좀 더 생산적인 활동을 해보면 어때요? 다른 활동에 집중하면, 디지털 기기를 쓸 생각이 안 날 거예요.
M : Okay, you have a point. Once I get into a productive activity, I may not think about digital devices.
그래요, 일리가 있어요. 내가 생산적인 활동을 하면, 난 디지털 기기 생각을 안 할지도 몰라요.
W : Right. You can do anything you want during that time. Why don't you start painting again?
맞아요. 그 시간에 원하는 걸 뭐든 해 봐요. 그림 그리는 걸 다시 시작하면 어때요?
M : Good idea. It'll take my mind away from smart devices.
좋은 생각이에요. 그게 내 생각을 스마트 기기에서 멀어지게 해줄 거예요.
W : You get it. I'm sure it'll help reduce your digital device usage.
바로 그거예요. 분명 그게 당신의 디지털 기기 사용을 줄이는 데 도움이 될 거예요.

Why? 왜 정답일까?

그림을 다시 그리면 디지털 기기로부터 생각이 멀어질 것 같다(**Good idea. It'll take my mind away from smart devices.**)는 남자의 말에 대한 여자의 응답으로 가장 적절한 것은 ③ '바로 그거예요. 분명 그게 당신의 디지털 기기 사용을 줄이는 데 도움이 될 거예요.'이다.

- **realize** ⓥ 알아차리다
- **digital detox** 디지털 디톡스(전자기기를 일부러 잠시 꺼두는 시간)
- **voluntarily** ad 자발적으로
- **suddenly** ad 갑자기
- **You have a point.** 일리가 있어요.
- **reduce** ⓥ 줄이다
- **avoid** ⓥ 피하다
- **activity** ⓝ 활동
- **resource** ⓝ 자원
- **usage** ⓝ 사용

15 대회를 앞두고 긴장한 파트너 격려하기

정답률 66% | 정답 ①

다음 상황 설명을 듣고, Amy가 Terry에게 할 말로 가장 적절한 것을 고르시오. [3점]

Amy: ______________________

✔① We'll do great since we've worked so hard.
우린 아주 열심히 연습했으니 무척 잘할 거야.
② I signed up for the contest, so don't worry.
내가 대회에 신청했으니 걱정 마.
③ We need more practice to win the dance contest.
우린 댄스 경연 대회에서 우승하려면 연습이 더 필요해.
④ If you're nervous, I'll cancel the rehearsal for you.
네가 긴장되면, 내가 리허설을 취소해줄게.
⑤ You should follow my moves to correct your mistakes.
네 실수를 바로잡으려면 내 안무를 따라해야 해.

W : Amy and Terry are members in the same dance club.
Amy와 Terry는 같은 댄스 동아리 회원이다.
They come to know that there will be a dance contest for high school students.
그들은 고교생을 대상으로 한 댄스 경연 대회가 있을 것임을 알게 된다.
Amy asks Terry to apply for it as a pair, and he agrees.
Amy는 Terry에게 짝으로 대회를 신청하자고 하고, 그는 동의한다.
From that day, they have practiced really hard for the contest.
그날부터, 그들은 대회를 위해 정말로 열심히 연습했다.
Finally, the day of the contest comes, and they meet to rehearse one last time.
마침내, 대회 당일이 오고, 그들은 마지막으로 한 번 리허설을 하려고 만난다.
However, Terry keeps making mistakes, even for the dance moves that he used to do easily.
하지만, Terry는 전에 쉽게 해냈던 안무에서조차 계속 실수를 낸다.
Amy asks Terry what's going on with him, and he tells her that it's because he's really nervous about the competition.
Amy는 Terry에게 무슨 일이냐고 묻고, 그는 그녀에게 대회 때문에 너무 긴장이 되어서 그렇다고 말해준다.
Amy wants to assure him that since they have put a lot of effort in, they will do amazingly on the stage.
Amy는 그에게 그들이 아주 많이 노력했으니 무대에서 멋지게 잘해낼 거라고 확신을 주고 싶다.
In this situation, what would Amy most likely say to Terry?
이 상황에서, Amy는 Terry에게 뭐라고 말할 것인가?
Amy : We'll do great since we've worked so hard.
우린 아주 열심히 연습했으니 무척 잘할 거야.

Why? 왜 정답일까?

상황에 따르면 대회를 앞두고 긴장해서 실수하는 Terry에게 Amy는 여태까지 들인 노력이 있으니 잘해낼 것이라고 격려해주고 싶어 한다(**Amy wants to assure him that since they have put a lot of effort in, they will do amazingly on the stage.**). 따라서 Amy가 Terry에게 할 말로 가장 적절한 것은 ① '우린 아주 열심히 연습했으니 무척 잘할 거야.'이다.

- **apply** ⓥ 신청하다
- **nervous** ⓐ (…을 앞두고) 긴장한, 초조한
- **assure** ⓥ 장담하다
- **amazingly** ad 놀랄 만큼, 굉장하게
- **mistake** ⓝ 실수
- **competition** ⓝ 대회, 경쟁
- **put in effort** 노력을 기울이다
- **correct** ⓥ 바로잡다

16-17 바다 생물의 자기 보호

M : Good morning, students.
안녕하세요, 학생 여러분.
Last class, we talked about how animals in the ocean live together.
지난 시간에, 우리는 바다속 동물들이 어떻게 함께 살아가는지에 대해 이야기했죠.
「Today, I'm going to tell you how sea creatures defend themselves.」 16번의 근거
오늘은 바다 생물들이 어떻게 자신을 방어하는지를 말씀드릴게요.
First, many ocean inhabitants use large groups to protect themselves from predators.
먼저, 많은 해양 서식 동물들은 포식자로부터 자신을 보호하기 위해 큰 무리를 이용합니다.
「For example, penguins often enter the water in groups in an attempt to confuse predators.」 17번 ①의 근거 일치
예를 들어, 펭귄은 포식자에게 혼란을 주기 위해 종종 무리 지어 물속에 들어갑니다.
Second, one form of concealment animals use is disguising themselves to blend in with their surroundings.
두 번째로, 동물들이 사용하는 은폐의 한 가지 형태는 주변 환경에 섞이도록 위장하는 것입니다.
「Sea horses act like coral by clinging to it with their tails so a predator may not notice them.」 17번 ②의 근거 일치
해마들은 꼬리로 산호에 달라붙어서 산호처럼 구는데, 그래서 포식자들은 그들을 알아보지 못할 수도 있습니다.
Third, many forms of sea life use poisons to drive off predators.
셋째로, 많은 형태의 바다 생물들이 포식자를 물리치기 위해 독을 사용합니다.
「Jellyfish have stinging body parts, which not only paralyze their food but also provide protection from predators.」 17번 ③의 근거 일치
해파리는 침을 쏘는 신체 부위가 있는데, 이것은 먹이를 마비시킬 뿐 아니라 그들을 포식자로부터 보호해 줍니다.
Lastly, some marine creatures use protective shells that prevent predators from attacking them.
마지막으로, 몇몇 해양 생물은 포식자가 공격해오는 것을 막아주는 보호 덮개를 씁니다.
「Oysters have thick and hard covers that protect them.」 17번 ⑤의 근거 일치
굴은 자신을 보호해주는 두껍고 단단한 껍데기를 갖고 있습니다.
Isn't that interesting?
흥미롭지 않나요?
Now, let's watch a video to help you understand better.
이제, 이해가 더 잘되도록 도와줄 영상을 하나 봅시다.

- **sea creature** 해양 생물, 바다 생물
- **inhabitant** ⓝ 서식 동물, 거주민
- **predator** ⓝ 포식자
- **disguise** ⓥ 위장하다
- **surroundings** ⓝ 환경
- **cling** ⓥ 달라붙다, 매달리다
- **drive off** 물리치다
- **sting** ⓥ (침을) 쏘다, 따갑게 하다
- **protective** ⓐ 보호하는, 보호용의
- **oyster** ⓝ 굴
- **method** ⓝ 방법
- **pattern** ⓝ (정형화된) 양식, 패턴
- **adapt** ⓥ 적응하다
- **defend** ⓥ 방어하다
- **protect** ⓥ 보호하다, 지키다
- **concealment** ⓝ 은폐, 숨김
- **blend in** ~에 섞이다
- **coral** ⓝ 산호
- **poison** ⓝ 독, 독약
- **jellyfish** ⓝ 해파리
- **paralyze** ⓥ 마비시키다
- **prevent** ⓥ (…의 발생을) 막다
- **nutrition** ⓝ 영양
- **obtain** ⓥ 얻다
- **importance** ⓝ 중요성

16 주제 파악

정답률 87% | 정답 ③

남자가 하는 말의 주제로 가장 적절한 것은?

① methods of obtaining nutrition by marine creatures
해양 생물로 영양소를 얻는 방법
② causes of dramatic decrease in sea animal populations
바다 생물 개체 수의 극적인 감소의 원인
✔③ ways for creatures in the ocean to protect themselves
바다 속 생물들이 자기 자신을 지키는 방법
④ difficulties in observing ocean animals' hunting patterns
바다 동물의 사냥 패턴을 관찰할 때의 어려움
⑤ importance of adapting to new surroundings for sea creatures
바다 생물을 위한 새로운 환경에 적응하는 것의 중요성

Why? 왜 정답일까?

'**Today, I'm going to tell you how sea creatures defend themselves.**'에서 남자는 바다 생물이 자기 자신을 방어하는 법에 관해 설명하겠다고 하므로, 남자가 하는 말의 주제로 가장 적절한 것은 ③ '바다 속 생물들이 자기 자신을 지키는 방법'이다.

[문제편 p.044]

17 언급 유무 파악

정답률 96% | 정답 ④

언급된 해양 생물이 아닌 것은?

① penguins – 펭귄 ② sea horses – 해마 ③ jellyfish – 해파리
✔ whales – 고래 ⑤ oysters – 굴

Why? 왜 정답일까?

담화에서 남자는 해양 생물의 예로 펭귄, 해마, 해파리, 굴을 언급하므로, 언급되지 않은 것은 ④ '고래'이다.

Why? 왜 오답일까?

① 'For example, penguins often enter the water in groups ~'에서 '펭귄'이 언급되었다.
② 'Sea horses act like coral ~'에서 '해마'가 언급되었다.
③ 'Jellyfish have stinging body parts, ~'에서 '해파리'가 언급되었다.
⑤ 'Oysters have thick and hard covers ~'에서 '굴'이 언급되었다.

Dictation 08

문제편 045쪽

01 have a charity auction / looking for volunteers / categorizing donated items
02 how about using songs / melody and rhythm / learning vocabulary through songs / easily remember vocabulary
03 renovated and clean / abandoned animals / three people including me working here / brought dog food to donate
04 your music teacher's farewell party / drew a violin / must have loved it
05 final check / decorating reusable cups / forgot to bring it
06 group lesson / book a group lesson / renting surfing suits
07 I got accepted / a good impression / quit your part-time job / have a medical check-up
08 this leaflet / tracking how many steps we walk / scan this QR code
09 starting from May 10th / The winners from last year / available to be purchased online
10 water purifiers / monthly rental fee / replacing a filter by myself / the white one
11 I'm flattered / start learning the drums
12 school newsletter / parents are welcome to participate
13 promising jobs / our school career counselor / make an appointment first / His schedule is posted
14 try a digital detox / productive activities / get into a productive activity / take my mind away
15 as a pair / keeps making mistakes / nervous about the competition / put a lot of effort
16-17 sea creatures defend themselves / blend in with their surroundings / use protective shells

09회 | 2021학년도 4월 학력평가 고3

• 정답 •

01 ② 02 ⑤ 03 ① 04 ⑤ 05 ④ 06 ③ 07 ② 08 ③ 09 ④ 10 ④ 11 ① 12 ③ 13 ④ 14 ② 15 ⑤ 16 ① 17 ③

01 아파트 입주민용 앱 출시 안내

정답률 84% | 정답 ②

다음을 듣고, 남자가 하는 말의 목적으로 가장 적절한 것을 고르시오.

① 아파트 입주민 회의 참여를 독려하려고
✔ 아파트 입주민을 위한 앱을 소개하려고
③ 아파트 관리비 납부 방법 변경을 알리려고
④ 아파트 시설 보수 공사 계획을 안내하려고
⑤ 아파트 단지 내 승강기 점검 일정을 공지하려고

M : Hello, residents.
안녕하세요, 주민 여러분.
I'm Harry Robinson from the Sunnyville apartment management office.
Sunnyville 아파트 관리 사무실의 Harry Robinson입니다.
Our apartment staff has made a lot of effort to provide high-quality services for our residents.
저희 아파트 사무실 직원들은 주민 여러분들께 양질의 서비스를 제공해 드리기 위해 많은 노력을 기울였습니다.
One of the things we did was to create a mobile app for your convenience.
저희가 한 일 중 하나는 여러분들의 편의를 위해 모바일 앱을 개발한 것이었습니다.
With the app, you can easily check the monthly maintenance fee and important notices like elevator maintenance schedules or residents' meetings.
이 앱으로 여러분은 월별 관리비와, 엘리베이터 보수 일정 또는 주민 반상회 같은 중요 공지를 쉽게 확인하실 수 있습니다.
Also, when you have any requests about your apartment, you can quickly report the issue on the app.
또한, 아파트에 요구 사항이 있으시면 앱으로 그 문제를 빠르게 말씀하실 수 있습니다.
Please download the app and enjoy a more convenient life in Sunnyville apartment.
앱을 다운받아 주시고 Sunnyville 아파트에서 더 편리한 삶을 즐겨보세요.
Thank you.
고맙습니다.

Why? 왜 정답일까?

'One of the things we did was to create a mobile app for your convenience.' 이후로 남자는 아파트 주민들을 위한 앱이 개발되었으니 관리비나 공지사항을 확인할 때 편하게 이용하도록 안내하고 있다. 따라서 남자가 하는 말의 목적으로 가장 적절한 것은 ② '아파트 입주민을 위한 앱을 소개하려고'이다.

- make an effort 노력하다
- maintenance ⓝ 유지, 관리
- convenience ⓝ 편의

02 바른 자세로 운동하는 것의 중요성

정답률 90% | 정답 ⑤

대화를 듣고, 여자의 의견으로 가장 적절한 것을 고르시오.

① 근력 운동은 관절 강화에 효과적이다.
② 스트레칭을 통해 자세 교정이 가능하다.
③ 몸 상태에 따라 운동량을 조절할 필요가 있다.
④ 규칙적인 운동은 스트레스 완화에 도움이 된다.
✔ 바른 자세로 운동하는 것은 부상 위험을 줄인다.

W : Hello, Daniel. Did you finish the warm-up exercise?
안녕하세요, Daniel. 준비 운동 다 끝났어요?
M : Hi, Kelly. I did. I'm ready for today's workout.
안녕하세요, Kelly. 네. 오늘 운동을 위한 준비가 다 되었어요.
W : Great. Let's start with squats.
좋아요. 스쿼트부터 시작합시다.
M : Okay. I'll try.
네, 해볼게요.
W : Hmm, you're doing good, but your knees still extend over your toes.
흠, 잘하고 계시는데, 무릎이 아직 발가락 밖으로 나오네요.
M : Oh, I should be more careful.
오, 더 조심해야겠어요.
W : Yes. Working out with the correct posture is important because it can prevent you from getting injured.
네, 바른 자세로 운동하는 것은 당신이 다치지 않게 해주기 때문에 중요해요.
M : I'm aware of that, but it's hard.
알고 있는데 어렵네요.
W : But if you continue to exercise in the wrong position, you're more likely to get hurt by placing too much stress on your joints and muscles.
하지만 잘못된 자세로 계속 운동하면, 관절과 근육에 너무 많은 무리가 가기 때문에 다치기가 더 쉬워요.
M : Oh, that might cause an injury.
오, 그게 부상을 유발할 수 있군요.
W : That's right. That's why I always emphasize working out in the right way.
맞아요. 그래서 제가 항상 올바른 방법으로 운동하는 것을 강조하는 거예요.
M : Okay. I'll pay more attention to my workout posture.
그렇군요. 제 운동 자세에 더 주의해 볼게요.
W : Good. Let's try it again.
좋아요. 다시 해봅시다.

Why? 왜 정답일까?

'Working out with the correct posture is important because it can prevent you from getting injured.'에서 여자는 바른 자세로 운동을 해야 다치지 않을 수 있다고 말하므로, 여자의 의견으로 가장 적절한 것은 ⑤ '바른 자세로 운동하는 것은 부상 위험을 줄인다.'이다.

- extend ⓥ 뻗어나오다, 확장되다
- place stress on ~에 무리를 주다, ~을 강조하다
- emphasize ⓥ 강조하다
- injure ⓥ 다치게 하다, 부상 입히다
- joint ⓝ 관절
- pay attention to ~에 주의를 기울이다

03 드럼 연주자 진로 상담

정답률 94% | 정답 ①

대화를 듣고, 두 사람의 관계를 가장 잘 나타낸 것을 고르시오.

✔ 음악 교사 - 학생
② 학생회장 - 졸업생
③ 진로 상담사 - 학부모
④ 콘서트 진행자 - 관객
⑤ 드럼 연주자 - 악기점 주인

[Door knocks.]
[문 두드리는 소리가 난다.]

M : Come on in, Lily.
들어오렴, Lily.

W : Hello, Mr. Thompson. Thank you for seeing me.
안녕하세요, Thompson 선생님. 만나주셔서 고맙습니다.

M : No problem. You said you needed some advice, right?
천만에. 조언이 좀 필요하다고 했던 거 맞지?

W : Yes. I want to be a drummer, but these days I think I'm not that musically talented.
네. 저는 드럼 연주자가 되고 싶은데, 요새 전 제가 음악적으로 별로 재능이 없다는 생각이 들어요.

M : Oh, I disagree with that. You've been doing great in my music class.
오, 난 그 말에 동의하지 않아. 넌 내 음악 수업에서 무척 잘해오고 있잖아.

W : Even though I practice a lot, I feel my performance in the band isn't improving.
전 연습을 많이 하는데도 밴드에서의 연주 실력이 나아지고 있는 것 같지 않아요.

M : Lily, I can see your progress. You did a great job at the last school festival.
Lily, 난 네가 나아진 게 보여. 넌 지난 학교 축제에서 무척 잘해냈어.

W : But I don't know exactly what to do to improve my drumming skills.
하지만 전 제 드럼 실력을 높이기 위해 정확히 뭘 해야 할지 모르겠어요.

M : Hmm, what about meeting Elton, a drummer who graduated from our high school? He called me to say he would visit the school next Friday.
흠, 우리 고등학교를 졸업한 드럼 연주자인 Elton을 만나보면 어떨까? 그는 내게 다음 주 금요일에 학교로 오겠다고 전화했었어.

W : Really? That would be great.
정말요? 그럼 무척 좋겠어요.

M : He had similar concerns when I taught him. He can give you some advice.
내가 그를 지도할 때 그는 비슷한 걱정을 했었어. 그가 네게 조언을 좀 해줄 수 있을 거야.

W : Thank you, Mr. Thompson.
고맙습니다, Thompson 선생님.

Why? 왜 정답일까?

'**Yes. I want to be a drummer, but these days I think I'm not that musically talented.**', '**Oh, I disagree with that. You've been doing great in my music class.**'에서 남자가 음악 교사이고, 여자가 드럼 연주자를 준비하고 있는 학생임을 파악할 수 있으므로, 두 사람의 관계로 가장 적절한 것은 ① '음악 교사 - 학생'이다.

- talented ⓐ 재능 있는
- progress ⓝ 진전
- improve ⓥ 나아지다, 향상시키다
- concern ⓝ 걱정, 우려 ⓥ 걱정하다

04 동아리 방 사진 구경하기

정답률 96% | 정답 ⑤

대화를 듣고, 그림에서 대화의 내용과 일치하지 않는 것을 고르시오.

M : Jane, what are you looking at?
Jane, 뭘 보고 있어?

W : Hi, David. This is a picture of the film club room. We redecorated it last week.
안녕, David. 이건 영화 동아리 방 사진이야. 우리는 지난주에 여기를 다시 꾸몄어.

M : Let me see. *[Pause]* 「Oh, you put a slogan poster on the wall. I like that phrase 'LIFE IS LIKE A MOVIE.'」 ①의 근거 일치
어디 보자. *[잠시 멈춤]* 오, 벽에 표어 포스터를 걸었구나. '삶은 영화 같다'라는 구절이 마음에 들어.

W : Actually, it's a line from our first movie.
사실, 이건 우리 첫 영화에 나왔던 대사야.

M : Wonderful. 「And the computer under the clock must be for editing movies.」
멋지다. 그리고 시계 밑에 있는 컴퓨터는 영화를 편집하기 위해 놓은 거겠네. ②의 근거 일치

W : You're right. 「Look at the telephone on the round table in the middle of the room.」
맞아. 방 가운데 있는 원형 테이블에 놓인 전화 좀 봐. ③의 근거 일치

M : Is it the one you mentioned before? You said you bought it at the antique market.
이거 네가 전에 말했던 거야? 골동품 가게에서 샀다며.

W : Right. We're going to use it in our next movie.
맞아. 우린 다음 영화에 이걸 쓸 예정이야.

M : Good. 「By the way, what's the box next to the lockers for?」 ④의 근거 일치
좋네. 그나저나, 사물함 옆에 있는 상자는 뭐야?

W : We put the costumes for our next movie in that box.
우린 그 상자 안에 우리 다음 영화 의상을 넣어뒀어.

M : Cool. 「Oh, there are three trophies on the shelf.」 ⑤의 근거 불일치
멋지다. 오, 선반에 트로피가 세 개 있어.

W : Yeah. We won them at university film festivals.
응. 우린 그걸 대학 영화제에서 받았어.

M : Great. I hope your club continues making good movies.
근사하다. 너희 동아리가 계속해서 좋은 영화를 만들기를 바라.

W : Thanks.
고마워.

Why? 왜 정답일까?

대화에 따르면 선반에는 트로피가 세 개 있다고 하는데(**Oh, there are three trophies on the shelf.**), 그림에서는 트로피가 두 개 뿐이다. 따라서 그림에서 대화의 내용과 일치하지 않는 것은 ⑤이다.

- redecorate ⓥ 재단장하다
- antique ⓝ 골동품
- edit ⓥ 편집하다
- costume ⓝ 의상

05 축구 경기 보러 갈 준비하기

정답률 96% | 정답 ④

대화를 듣고, 남자가 여자에게 부탁한 일로 가장 적절한 것을 고르시오.

① 회의 참석하기
② 티켓 출력하기
③ 저녁 준비하기
✔ 유니폼 가져오기
⑤ 자동차 수리하기

[Cell phone rings.]
[휴대전화가 울린다.]

W : Hello, honey. What's up?
여보세요, 여보. 무슨 일이에요?

M : I'm sorry, honey. I think I'll be late for today's soccer match. The meeting just ended.
미안해요, 여보. 오늘 축구 시합에 늦을 거 같아요. 회의가 방금 끝났어요.

W : Really? Hmm, I also heard there was a car accident near the stadium.
정말요? 흠, 경기장 근처에서 차 사고도 났다고 들었어요.

M : Oh, I'll take the subway, then. By the way, did you download our mobile tickets?
오, 그럼 지하철을 탈게요. 그나저나, 우리 모바일 티켓은 다운받았어요?

W : Yeah. I did it this morning. What should we do about dinner?
네. 오늘 아침에 받아 놨어요. 저녁은 어떻게 하죠?

M : Hmm, let's buy some food at the snack bar in the stadium.
흠, 경기장 안 매점에서 음식을 좀 사죠.

W : Okay. Oh, the ticket says people who wear uniforms will get a free drink at the snack bar.
알겠어요. 오, 티켓에 쓰여있기로 유니폼을 입은 관객들은 매점에서 공짜 음료를 받을 수가 있대요.

M : Then, can you bring my uniform? I think it's in the bedroom closet.
그럼, 내 유니폼 좀 갖다 줄래요? 침실 옷장에 있을 거예요.

W : Sure. I'll do that.
물론이죠. 그렇게 할게요.

M : Thanks. See you soon.
고마워요. 곧 봐요.

Why? 왜 정답일까?

유니폼을 입은 관객은 무료 음료를 받을 수 있다는 말에 남자는 여자에게 자신의 유니폼을 챙겨 달라고 부탁하고 있다(**Then, can you bring my uniform?**). 따라서 남자가 여자에게 부탁한 일로 가장 적절한 것은 ④ '유니폼 가져오기'이다.

- car accident 교통사고
- snack bar 매점
- closet ⓝ 옷장
- stadium ⓝ 경기장
- by the way 그나저나, 그런데

06 아동용 캠핑 용품 사기

정답률 85% | 정답 ③

대화를 듣고, 여자가 지불할 금액을 고르시오. [3점]

① $90
② $99
✔ $108
④ $110
⑤ $120

M : Hello. Welcome to Adventure Camping Supplies. How can I help you?
안녕하세요. Adventure Camping Supplies에 잘 오셨습니다. 무엇을 도와드릴까요?

W : Hi. Can you recommend a children's tent?
안녕하세요. 아동용 텐트 좀 추천해 주실래요?

M : Okay. Could you follow me? *[Pause]* These two are the best selling models.
알겠습니다. 절 따라오시겠습니까? *[잠시 멈춤]* 이 두 개가 가장 잘 나가는 제품입니다.

W : They both look nice. How much are they?
둘 다 근사해 보이네요. 얼마예요?

M : The blue tent is $80, and the red tent is $70. The blue one is a bit bigger.
파란색 텐트는 80달러이고, 빨간색 텐트는 70달러입니다. 파란색이 조금 더 커요.

W : Well, I have two boys. So, the bigger one could be more comfortable. I'll take one blue tent.
음, 저는 아들이 둘이에요. 그러니 더 큰 것이 더 편하겠어요. 파란색 텐트로 하나 살게요.

M : Okay. Anything else?
알겠습니다. 더 필요하신 것은요?

W : How much is that children's camping chair?
저 아동용 캠핑 의자는 얼마나 해요?

M : It's $20. It's really popular because of the animal character on it.
20달러입니다. 동물 캐릭터가 있어서 무척 인기가 많죠.

W : That's my kids' favorite character. I'll buy two.
저건 우리 애들이 제일 좋아하는 캐릭터예요. 두 개 사겠어요.

M : I'm sure your kids will love them.
자녀분들이 무척 좋아하실 겁니다.

W : Oh, can I use this discount coupon?
오, 이 할인 쿠폰을 쓸 수 있나요?

M : Of course. You'll get 10% off the total price.
물론이죠. 총 가격에서 10퍼센트를 할인받으시게 됩니다.

W : Thank you. Here's my credit card.
고맙습니다. 여기 제 신용카드요.

Why? 왜 정답일까?

대화에 따르면 여자는 80달러짜리 파란색 텐트 1개와 20달러짜리 아동용 캠핑 의자를 2개 사고, 총 가격에서 10퍼센트를 할인받았다. 이를 식으로 나타내면 '(80+20×2)×0.9=108'이므로, 여자가 지불할 금액은 ③ '$108'이다.

[문제편 p.049]

- camping supplies 캠핑 용품
- a bit 조금, 다소
- recommend ⓥ 추천하다, 권하다

07 책 사인회에 갈 수 없는 이유 정답률 96% | 정답 ②

대화를 듣고, 여자가 Katie Wood의 책 사인회에 갈 수 없는 이유를 고르시오.

① 요리 수업을 들어야 해서
② 사촌 결혼식에 참석해야 해서
③ 중국어 시험공부를 해야 해서
④ 도서관 봉사 활동을 해야 해서
⑤ 에세이 쓰기 대회에 참가해야 해서

[Cell phone rings.]
[휴대전화가 울린다.]

W : Hello, Chris.
안녕, Chris.

M : Hi, Mindy. Is your cooking class over?
안녕, Mindy. 네 요리 수업 끝났어?

W : Yes, it's just finished. What's up?
응, 방금 끝났어. 무슨 일이야?

M : Have you heard about Katie Wood's book signing event?
너 Katie Wood의 책 사인회에 대해서 들었어?

W : No, I haven't. She's one of my favorite essay writers! When is it?
아니, 그녀는 내가 제일 좋아하는 에세이 작가 중 한 명이야! 그거 언제야?

M : It's next Saturday at 2 p.m. I saw a poster while volunteering at the library. Let's go together.
다음 주 토요일 오후 2시야. 난 도서관에서 자원봉사 하다가 포스터를 봤어. 같이 가자.

W : Next Saturday? Oh, no. I can't go then.
다음 주 토요일이라고? 오, 이런. 난 그때 못 가.

M : Oh, do you still have to prepare for the Chinese speaking test?
오, 아직 중국어 말하기 시험 준비해야 하는 거야?

W : No, I took the test last week.
아니, 시험은 지난주에 쳤어.

M : Okay. Then, why can't you go?
그렇구나. 그럼, 왜 갈 수 없는 거야?

W : I'm supposed to attend my cousin's wedding on that day.
난 그날 사촌 결혼식에 참석해야 해.

M : Oh, I see. If possible, I'll get her signature for you. Have a wonderful time at the wedding.
오, 그렇구나. 가능하다면 내가 너를 위해 사인을 받아다 줄게. 결혼식 잘 다녀와.

W : That would be great. Thanks.
그럼 좋겠다. 고마워.

Why? 왜 정답일까?

대화에 따르면 여자는 사촌 결혼식에 참석해야 해서(**I'm supposed to attend my cousin's wedding on that day.**) 다음 주 토요일에 열리는 책 사인회에 참석할 수 없다. 따라서 여자가 **Katie Wood**의 책 사인회에 갈 수 없는 이유로 가장 적절한 것은 ② '사촌 결혼식에 참석해야 해서'이다.

- book signing 책 사인회
- attend ⓥ 참석하다
- be supposed to ~하기로 되어 있다, ~해야 하다
- signature ⓝ 사인, 서명

08 컴퓨터 코딩 프로그램 참여 정답률 94% | 정답 ③

대화를 듣고, Summer Computer Coding Program에 관해 언급되지 않은 것을 고르시오.

① 장소 ② 운영 기간 ③ 수강료
④ 수업 시간 ⑤ 신청 마감일

M : Mom, what are you looking at?
엄마, 뭐 보고 계세요?

W : Look at this leaflet, Paul. It's for a Summer Computer Coding Program. Why don't you try this during summer vacation?
이 전단지를 좀 봐, Paul. Summer Computer Coding Program에 대한 거야. 여름 방학에 이거 좀 해보면 어떠니?

M : Sounds interesting. I've wanted to learn computer coding.
재미있겠네요. 전 컴퓨터 코딩을 배우고 싶었어요.

W : 『It'll be held at Greendale Community College.』 ①의 근거 일치 It's near our house.
Greendale Community College에서 열릴 거라네. 우리 집에서 가까워.

M : Oh, yeah! I know where that is. 『How long does the program last?
오, 그러네요! 거기 어딘지 알아요. 프로그램 기간은 얼마나 돼요?

W : It lasts for three weeks starting July 19th.』 ②의 근거 일치 Are you okay with that?
7월 19일부터 3주간이야. 괜찮니?

M : Yes. 『By the way, it says the class starts at 9 a.m. and finishes at 11 a.m.』 ④의 근거 일치 I think it starts too early.
네. 그나저나, 수업이 오전 9시에 시작해서 오전 11시에 끝난다고 쓰여 있네요. 너무 일찍 시작하는 것 같아요.

W : You might think so, but you're going to have so much fun.
그렇게 생각할 수 있지만, 아주 재미있을 거야.

M : Okay, Mom. I'll sign up for it.
알겠어요, 엄마. 신청할게요.

W : Good. 『By the way, the registration for the program must be done online by June 25th.』 ⑤의 근거 일치
좋아. 그런데 프로그램 신청은 6월 25일까지 온라인으로 해야 한대.

M : I'll do that now. Thanks, Mom.
지금 할게요. 고마워요, 엄마.

Why? 왜 정답일까?

대화에서 남자와 여자는 **Summer Computer Coding Program**의 장소, 운영 기간, 수업 시간, 신청 마감일에 관해 언급하였다. 따라서 언급되지 않은 것은 ③ '수강료'이다.

Why? 왜 오답일까?

① '**It'll be held at Greendale Community College.**'에서 '장소'가 언급되었다.
② '**It lasts for three weeks starting July 19th.**'에서 '운영 기간'이 언급되었다.
④ '**By the way, it says the class starts at 9 a.m. and finishes at 11 a.m.**'에서 '수업 시간'이 언급되었다.
⑤ '**By the way, the registration for the program must be done online by June 25th.**'에서 '신청 마감일'이 언급되었다.

- last ⓥ 지속되다
- registration ⓝ 등록
- sign up for ~에 등록하다, ~을 신청하다

09 동물 구조 기부 행사 안내 정답률 82% | 정답 ④

Rescue the Animals에 관한 다음 내용을 듣고, 일치하지 않는 것을 고르시오.

① 시청 광장에서 열릴 것이다.
② 20개가 넘는 부스가 있을 것이다.
③ 구조된 동물들의 사진들이 전시될 것이다.
④ 기부자들에게 동물 모양의 열쇠고리를 줄 것이다.
⑤ 시청 옆 공터는 주차장으로 사용될 것이다.

W : Hello, citizens!
안녕하세요, 시민 여러분!
I'm Rachel Hawkins, mayor of Campbell City.
저는 Campbell City의 시장인 Rachel Hawkins입니다.
This year, our city is going to hold a meaningful event called Rescue the Animals on May 15th.
올해 5월 15일 우리 시에서는 Rescue the Animals라고 불리는 유의미한 행사를 열 예정입니다.
『It'll be held at City Hall Square from 10 a.m. to 5 p.m.』 ①의 근거 일치
이것은 오전 10시부터 오후 5시까지 시청 광장에서 열릴 것입니다.
The aim of this event is to raise money for rescuing animals.
이 행사의 목적은 동물 구조를 위한 돈을 모금하는 것입니다.
『There will be more than twenty booths which will sell a wide range of products for animals.』 ②의 근거 일치
다양한 동물 용품을 파는 20개가 넘는 부스가 있을 것입니다.
『Also, a variety of photos of rescued animals will be on display.』 ③의 근거 일치
또한, 구조된 동물의 다양한 사진들이 전시될 것입니다.
For people who want to contribute, there will be a donation box, and 『an animal badge will be given to people who donate.』 ④의 근거 불일치
기부하고 싶은 분들을 위해 기부 상자가 있을 것이고, 기부자들에게는 동물 모양의 배지를 드릴 것입니다.
『For your convenience, the empty space next to City Hall will be used as a parking lot.』 ⑤의 근거 일치
여러분의 편의를 위해, 시청 옆 공터는 주차장으로 이용될 것입니다.
Please come and enjoy the event and contribute to rescuing animals.
오셔서 행사를 즐겨주시고 동물 구조에 기부해 주세요.
Thank you.
감사합니다.

Why? 왜 정답일까?

'~ **and an animal badge will be given to people who donate.**'에서 기부하는 사람들에게는 동물 모양의 열쇠고리가 아닌, 동물 모양의 배지가 주어질 것이라고 하므로, 내용과 일치하지 않는 것은 ④ '기부자들에게 동물 모양의 열쇠고리를 줄 것이다.'이다.

Why? 왜 오답일까?

① '**It'll be held at City Hall Square from 10 a.m. to 5 p.m.**'의 내용과 일치한다.
② '**There will be more than twenty booths** ~'의 내용과 일치한다.
③ '**Also, a variety of photos of rescued animals will be on display.**'의 내용과 일치한다.
⑤ '**For your convenience, the empty space next to City Hall will be used as a parking lot.**'의 내용과 일치한다.

- rescue ⓥ 구조하다
- a wide range of 매우 다양한
- contribute ⓥ 기부하다, 기여하다
- raise money 모금하다
- on display 전시 중인

10 음악 축제 선택하기 정답률 82% | 정답 ④

다음 표를 보면서 대화를 듣고, 두 사람이 선택할 음악 축제를 고르시오.

Music Festivals

	Festival	Date	Genre	Place	Pet-friendly
①	A	April 24	Rock	Union Square	○
②	B	May 8	Jazz	Limestone Island	○
③	C	May 22	Rock	Olympic Stadium	×
④	D	June 5	Jazz	Grand Park	○
⑤	E	June 12	Classical	Fitzroy Garden	×

W : Honey, did you see this brochure?
여보, 이 책자 봤어요?

M : What's this?
이게 뭐예요?

W : It's about music festivals. What about going to one of them?
음악 축제에 관한 거예요. 여기 중 한 군데 가보면 어때요?

M : That sounds fun. Oh, there are five different music festivals.
재미있겠네요. 오, 서로 다른 음악 축제가 다섯 개 있군요.

W : Yeah. Didn't you say your company's new project finishes at the end of April?
네. 당신 회사 새 프로젝트가 4월 말이면 끝난다고 하지 않았어요?

M : Right. 『So, I'd prefer a festival in May or June.』 근거1 Date 조건
맞아요. 그러니, 5월 또는 6월 축제가 좋겠어요.

W : Okay. 『We went to a classical concert last time, so I want to experience a different genre this time.』 근거2 Genre 조건
그래요. 우린 저번에 클래식 콘서트에 갔었으니까, 이번에 난 다른 장르를 경험해보고 싶어요.

M : Me, too. 『Hmm, isn't Limestone Island too far? It takes three hours by car.
나도 그래요. 흠, Limestone Island는 너무 멀지 않아요? 차로 세 시간이에요.

W : Yeah. I don't want to spend hours stuck in a car.』 근거3 Place 조건
맞아요. 난 차에 몇 시간을 갇혀 있고 싶지 않아요.

[문제편 p.049]

M : Then, we can choose between these two festivals.
그럼, 이 두 축제 중 하나를 고르죠.

W : Oh, why don't we go to this festival? 「Since it's pet-friendly, we can go there with our dog, Willy. 근거4 Pet-friendly 조건
오, 이 축제에 가는 게 어때요? 이건 반려동물 친화적이라고 하니까, 우리 개 Willy를 데리고 갈 수 있을 거예요.

M : Cool!」 We can make a special memory with Willy. Let's buy tickets for that festival.
좋아요! 우린 Willy에게 특별한 기억을 만들어줄 수 있네요. 그 축제 티켓을 사죠.

Why? 왜 정답일까?

대화에 따르면 남자와 여자는 5월 또는 6월에 열리면서, 클래식이 아닌 장르를 공연하고, Limestone Island에서 열리지 않으면서, 반려동물 친화적인 음악 축제에 가기로 한다. 따라서 두 사람이 선택할 음악 축제는 ④ 'D'이다.

- prefer ⓥ 선호하다
- stuck in ~에 갇힌
- pet-friendly ⓐ 반려동물에 친화적인

11 새로운 발령지에 언제 가는지 물어보기

정답률 84% | 정답 ①

대화를 듣고, 남자의 마지막 말에 대한 여자의 응답으로 가장 적절한 것을 고르시오.

✔ I should be there by the end of this month. – 이번 달 말까지는 거기 가 있어야 해요.
② Working on the marketing team isn't easy. – 마케팅 팀에서 일하는 건 쉽지 않아요.
③ I have to go to Canada for a job interview. – 전 캐나다에 일자리 면접을 보러 가야 해요.
④ They haven't hired a new manager yet. – 그들은 아직 새 매니저를 구하지 않았어요.
⑤ My family is going to travel with me. – 우리 가족이 나와 함께 여행할 거예요.

M : Jessica, I've just heard about your job promotion. Congratulations!
Jessica, 당신이 승진했다는 얘기 방금 들었어요. 축하해요!

W : Thanks, Sean. I'm going to be the manager of the international marketing team in Canada.
고마워요, Sean. 나는 캐나다에서 국제 마케팅 팀장을 맡을 거예요.

M : You've wanted that position for a long time. When do you have to be in Canada?
당신은 그 자리를 오랫동안 원했죠. 언제 캐나다로 가야 해요?

W : I should be there by the end of this month.
이번 달 말까지는 거기 가 있어야 해요.

Why? 왜 정답일까?

캐나다에서 국제 마케팅 팀장 자리를 맡게 되었다는 여자의 말에 남자는 언제 캐나다로 가야 하는지 묻고 있다(When do you have to be in Canada?). 따라서 여자의 응답으로 가장 적절한 것은 ① '이번 달 말까지는 거기 가 있어야 해요.'이다.

- promotion ⓝ 승진
- by the end of ~의 끝무렵에

12 항공편 티켓 사기

정답률 94% | 정답 ③

대화를 듣고, 여자의 마지막 말에 대한 남자의 응답으로 가장 적절한 것을 고르시오.

① Excuse me. I can't find where my baggage is.
실례합니다. 전 제 짐이 어디 있는지 못 찾겠어요.
② Hurry up. We might miss the train to the airport.
서둘러요. 우리는 공항으로 가는 기차를 놓칠지도 몰라요.
✔ Okay. I'd like to buy a ticket for the earlier flight.
그렇군요. 전 더 빠른 항공편 티켓을 사고 싶어요.
④ Really? I'm sorry that there are no seats available today.
정말요? 죄송하지만 오늘 이용 가능한 좌석이 없습니다.
⑤ I see. I'll let you know when we arrive at the destination.
그렇군요. 저희가 목적지에 도착하면 알려드릴게요.

W : Welcome to Blue Bird Airline. How may I help you, sir?
Blue Bird 항공사에 잘 오셨습니다. 무엇을 도와드릴까요?

M : I just missed my flight to Boston. Is there another flight I can take today?
전 방금 제 보스턴 행 비행기를 놓쳤어요. 제가 오늘 탈 수 있는 다른 비행기가 있을까요?

W : Let me check. *[Typing sound]* We have two flights available today. One departs at 5 p.m., and the other one at 8:30 p.m.
확인해 보겠습니다. *[타자 치는 소리]* 오늘 이용 가능한 항공편이 두 개 있습니다. 하나는 오후 5시에 출발하고, 다른 하나는 오후 8시 30분에 출발합니다.

M : Okay. I'd like to buy a ticket for the earlier flight.
그렇군요. 전 더 빠른 항공편 티켓을 사고 싶어요.

Why? 왜 정답일까?

보스턴으로 가는 비행기를 놓쳐서 다음 항공편 시간을 알아보고 있는 남자에게 여자는 오후 5시에 출발하는 것과 오후 8시 30분에 출발하는 것이 있다고 알려준다(One departs at 5 p.m., and the other one at 8:30 p.m.). 따라서 남자의 응답으로 가장 적절한 것은 ③ '그렇군요. 전 더 빠른 항공편 티켓을 사고 싶어요.'이다.

- available ⓐ 이용 가능한
- depart ⓥ 출발하다
- baggage ⓝ 짐, 수하물
- destination ⓝ 목적지

13 고객 후기를 참고하여 상품 고르기

정답률 81% | 정답 ④

대화를 듣고, 남자의 마지막 말에 대한 여자의 응답으로 가장 적절한 것을 고르시오.

Woman: ______________________________

① Right. That's why I always check customers' reviews.
맞아. 그래서 난 항상 고객 후기를 확인해 봐.
② I'd rather not. It's too late to get a refund for the laptop bag.
나라면 안할래. 그 노트북 가방을 환불받기에는 너무 늦었어.
③ Thanks for your tip. I can save money by using a rental service.
조언 고마워. 대여 서비스를 이용하면 돈을 아낄 수 있겠네.
✔ That makes sense. I should read the reviews to make a decision.
일리 있네. 결정을 내리려면 후기를 읽어봐야겠다.
⑤ Don't worry. The item I ordered online will be delivered soon.
걱정 마. 내가 온라인에서 주문한 상품이 곧 배달될 거야.

M : Anna, what are you doing?
Anna, 뭐 하고 있어?

W : Hi, Jeremy. I'm looking for a laptop bag online, but it's hard to decide which one to buy.
안녕, Jeremy. 난 온라인에서 노트북 가방을 찾고 있는데, 뭘 살지 결정하기 어려워.

M : Oh, do you need help?
오, 도와줄까?

W : Yes, please. Look at these models. I'm thinking of buying one of them.
응, 도와줘. 이 제품들 좀 봐. 난 이것들 중에서 하나를 사려고 하거든.

M : Wow, there are too many types of bags.
와, 가방 종류가 너무 많네.

W : Yeah, it's hard to pick one.
응, 하나 고르기가 어려워.

M : Hmm, what about reading other customers' reviews? When I shop online, I always read them.
흠, 다른 고객들의 후기를 읽어보는 게 어때? 난 온라인에서 쇼핑할 때 항상 읽어봐.

W : Really? I haven't done that before.
정말? 난 그래본 적이 없어.

M : It's helpful because some customers attach pictures and write detailed reviews.
몇몇 고객들은 사진도 첨부하고 자세한 후기를 써놓기 때문에 도움이 돼.

W : I see, but are those reviews reliable?
그렇구나, 그런데 그 후기가 믿을 만한 거야?

M : I believe so because those are the opinions of customers who actually used the items.
실제로 그 제품을 써본 고객들의 의견이니까 그렇다고 생각해.

W : That makes sense. I should read the reviews to make a decision.
일리 있네. 결정을 내리려면 후기를 읽어봐야겠다.

Why? 왜 정답일까?

노트북 가방을 하나 고르는 데 어려움을 겪고 있는 여자에게 남자는 고객 후기를 읽어볼 것을 추천하자, 여자는 그런 후기들이 믿을 만한 것인지 묻고, 남자는 이에 실제로 제품을 써본 사람들이 남기는 후기이니 믿을 만할 것이라고 설명해준다(I believe so because those are the opinions of customers who actually used the items.). 따라서 여자의 응답으로 가장 적절한 것은 ④ '일리 있네. 결정을 내리려면 후기를 읽어봐야겠다.'이다.

- attach ⓥ 첨부하다, 부착하다
- reliable ⓐ 믿을 만한
- get a refund 환불 받다

14 프랑스 해외 인턴십 지원 권유하기

정답률 72% | 정답 ②

대화를 듣고, 여자의 마지막 말에 대한 남자의 응답으로 가장 적절한 것을 고르시오. [3점]

Man: ______________________________

① That's true. I received an acceptance letter from the university.
맞아요. 전 그 대학에서 합격 통지서를 받았어요.
✔ You're right. I'll think about the internship in a more positive way.
맞는 말씀이에요. 그 인턴십을 더 긍정적으로 생각해 볼게요.
③ I agree. The experience helped me a lot in getting a job.
맞습니다. 그 경험은 제가 일자리를 구하는 데 큰 도움이 되었어요.
④ No problem. I can take the fashion class next semester.
물론입니다. 전 다음 학기에 패션 수업을 들을 수 있어요.
⑤ Thank you. I've dreamed of working in your company.
고맙습니다. 저는 귀사에서 일하기를 꿈꿔 왔어요.

W : Phillip, do you have a minute?
Phillip, 잠깐 시간 있니?

M : Yes, Professor Jones.
네, Jones 교수님.

W : Did you hear about the fashion internship program in France? How about applying for it?
프랑스에서 하는 패션 인턴십 프로그램 얘기 들었어? 지원해 보는 게 어떠니?

M : I heard. I know it's a great opportunity, but I have some concerns.
들었어요. 대단한 기회라는 걸 알고 있지만, 걱정거리가 좀 있어요.

W : Why? I know you really want to work in the fashion industry after graduating.
왜? 난 네가 졸업 후에 패션 업계에서 정말 일해보고 싶어 한다는 걸 알고 있어.

M : That's right, but I'm nervous about living alone in France.
맞는 말씀이지만, 프랑스에서 혼자 사는 게 걱정이에요.

W : I understand, but the company will provide dormitory rooms to international interns. So, you don't have to worry too much.
이해해, 하지만 회사에서 해외 인턴들에게 기숙사 방을 제공해줄 거야. 그러니, 너무 걱정하지 않아도 돼.

M : Oh, really? I didn't know that. That's good.
오, 정말요? 그건 몰랐어요. 좋네요.

W : Most of all, the experience you'll have there can't be acquired in a classroom.
무엇보다도, 거기서 네가 쌓을 경험은 교실에서는 얻을 수 없을 거야.

M : I understand what you mean.
무슨 말씀인지 알아요.

W : I'm sure that the experience there will be a stepping stone to achieving your dream.
그곳에서의 경험은 네 꿈을 이루는 데 발판이 되어줄 게 분명해.

M : You're right. I'll think about the internship in a more positive way.
맞는 말씀이에요. 그 인턴십을 더 긍정적으로 생각해 볼게요.

Why? 왜 정답일까?

여자는 프랑스에서의 인턴십 기회가 교실에서는 얻을 수 없는 경험을 선물해줄 것이며, 꿈을 이룰 발판 또한 되어줄 것이라는 말로 남자가 인턴십에 지원해 보도록 설득하고 있다(I'm sure that the experience there will be a stepping stone to achieving your dream.). 따라서 남자의 응답으로 가장 적절한 것은 ② '맞는 말씀이에요. 그 인턴십을 더 긍정적으로 생각해 볼게요.'이다.

- apply for ~에 지원하다
- concern ⓝ 걱정거리
- dormitory ⓝ 기숙사
- acquire ⓥ 얻다, 습득하다
- stepping stone 발판, 디딤돌
- acceptance ⓝ 수락, 합격

15 다양한 주제의 책을 읽도록 권하기

정답률 70% | 정답 ⑤

다음 상황 설명을 듣고, Ms. Brown이 Andrew에게 할 말로 가장 적절한 것을 고르시오. [3점]

Ms. Brown: ______________________________

① How about reading Spanish books on a regular basis?
스페인어 책을 꾸준히 읽는 게 어떠니?
② I recommend you read more science books for yourself.
난 네가 스스로를 위해 과학책을 더 많이 읽기를 추천해.
③ What do you think of taking an extra class to get a good score?
점수를 잘 받기 위해서 수업을 더 듣는 게 어때?
④ You'd better write book reports to improve your writing skills.
넌 글쓰기 실력을 키우기 위해서 서평을 써야겠어.

[문제편 p.050]

✔ Why not try books with different themes to grow your vocabulary?
어휘 실력을 키우도록 다양한 주제의 책을 읽어보는 게 어떠니?

M : Ms. Brown is a Spanish teacher and Andrew is one of her students.
Brown 선생님은 스페인어 교사이고 Andrew는 그녀의 학생 중 한 명이다.
Ms. Brown has given reading lessons in which students choose Spanish books and write book reports.
Brown 선생님은 학생들이 스페인어 책을 골라서 독후감을 쓰는 읽기 수업을 가르친다.
When Ms. Brown checks students' book reports, she finds out Andrew only reads science-related books.
Brown 선생님은 학생들의 서평을 검사하다가 Andrew가 과학에 관련된 책만 읽었다는 것을 발견한다.
She thinks if he reads books about other topics, he can learn various words and expressions.
그녀는 그가 다른 주제에 관한 책을 읽으면 다양한 단어와 표현을 익힐 수 있을 것이라고 생각한다.
So, Ms. Brown wants to suggest that Andrew read books dealing with other subjects to broaden his word knowledge.
그래서, Brown 선생님은 Andrew에게 단어 지식을 확장할 수 있도록 다른 주제를 다루는 책들도 읽어보라고 제안하고 싶다.
In this situation, what would Ms. Brown most likely say to Andrew?
이 상황에서, Brown 선생님은 Andrew에게 뭐라고 말할 것인가?
Ms. Brown : Why not try books with different themes to grow your vocabulary?
어휘 실력을 키우도록 다양한 주제의 책을 읽어보는 게 어떠니?

Why? 왜 정답일까?

상황에 따르면 Brown 선생님은 과학에 관련된 책만 읽는 Andrew에게 다른 주제를 다룬 책들도 읽어서 더 다양한 표현과 단어를 익혀보도록 제안하고 싶어 한다(So, Ms. Brown wants to suggest that Andrew read books dealing with other subjects to broaden his word knowledge.). 따라서 Ms. Brown이 Andrew에게 할 말로 가장 적절한 것은 ⑤ '어휘 실력을 키우도록 다양한 주제의 책을 읽어보는 게 어떠니?'이다.

- book report 독후감, 서평
- broaden ⓥ 확장하다
- improve ⓥ 향상시키다
- deal with ~을 다루다
- on a regular basis 꾸준히, 규칙적으로

16-17 종이 이전에 지면으로 활용된 다양한 소재들

W : Hello, students.
안녕하세요, 학생 여러분.
Last class, we learned about how writing first began in history.
지난 시간에 우리는 역사상 글쓰기가 어떻게 처음 시작되었는가에 대해 배웠습니다.
「Today, we'll discuss materials which were used for writing before paper was invented.」 16번의 근거
오늘, 우리는 종이가 발명되기 전에 글쓰기에 이용된 재료들에 대해 토의해 보겠습니다.
「First, in the river plains of Mesopotamia that are now part of Iraq, clay was an easily available material.」 17번 ①의 근거 일치
첫 번째로, 현재 이라크 지역의 일부인 Mesopotamia 평야에서, 점토는 쉽게 구할 수 있는 재료였습니다.
People dried clay in the sun and used it to write on.
사람들은 점토를 햇볕에 말려 글씨를 쓰기 위해 이용했습니다.
「Second, papyrus was the first paper-like medium in Egypt.」 17번 ②의 근거 일치
두 번째로, 파피루스는 이집트에서 최초의 종이 같은 수단이었습니다.
Since the papyrus plant was once abundant near the Nile River, people laid it out and pressed it together to create sheets.
파피루스는 한때 나일강에서 많이 났기 때문에, 사람들은 그것을 펼쳐서 함께 눌러서 종이를 만들었습니다.
「Third, people in ancient Greece used animal skins to write on.」 17번 ④의 근거 일치
세 번째로, 고대 그리스 사람들은 동물 가죽을 이용해 글씨를 썼습니다.
Animal skins had great advantages in that they were strong and flexible enough for making books.
동물 가죽은 책으로 만들 수 있을 만큼 충분히 튼튼하고 잘 구부러져서 많은 이점이 있었습니다.
「Lastly, silk was used as writing material in ancient China.」 17번 ⑤의 근거 일치
마지막으로, 고대 중국에서는 비단이 필기구로 이용되었습니다.
It was durable and more portable than wood.
그것은 내구성이 있었고 나무보다 더 들고 다니기 편했습니다.
So, people there used it to make a writing surface that could be used for scrolls.
그래서 그곳 사람들은 이것을 사용해 두루마리로 이용할 수 있는 지면을 만들었습니다.
Isn't it interesting?
흥미롭지 않나요?
Now, let's talk about the development of the printing technology.
이제 인쇄술의 발달에 관해 이야기해 봅시다.

- material ⓝ 소재, 재료
- river plain 평야
- abundant ⓐ 풍부한
- portable ⓐ 들고 다닐 수 있는, 휴대용의
- development ⓝ 발달, 전개
- invent ⓥ 발명하다
- medium ⓝ 매체, 수단
- lay out 펼치다
- scroll ⓝ 두루마리
- characteristic ⓝ 특징

16 주제 파악

정답률 93% | 정답 ①

여자가 하는 말의 주제로 가장 적절한 것은?

✔ materials used for writing before paper – 종이 이전에 글쓰기에 이용된 재료들
② difficulties of processing natural materials – 천연 재료를 가공하는 것의 어려움
③ ways raw materials were stored in the past – 원자재가 과거에 보관되었던 방식들
④ writing materials that affected printing techniques – 인쇄술에 영향을 미쳤던 필기구들
⑤ common characteristics of eco-friendly materials – 친환경 소재들의 공통적 특징

Why? 왜 정답일까?

'Today, we'll discuss materials which were used for writing before paper was invented.'에서 여자는 종이가 만들어지기 전에 글자를 쓸 지면으로 활용했던 재료들에 관해 언급하겠다고 하므로, 여자가 하는 말의 주제로 가장 적절한 것은 ① '종이 이전에 글쓰기에 이용된 재료들'이다.

17 언급 유무 파악

정답률 96% | 정답 ③

언급된 재료가 아닌 것은?

① clay – 점토
② papyrus – 파피루스
✔ stone – 돌
④ animal skins – 동물 가죽
⑤ silk – 비단

Why? 왜 정답일까?

담화에서 여자는 종이에 앞서 마치 종이처럼 활용되었던 재료들의 예로 점토, 파피루스, 동물 가죽, 비단을 언급하였다. 따라서 언급되지 않은 것은 ③ '돌'이다.

Why? 왜 오답일까?

① 'First, in the river plains of Mesopotamia that are now part of Iraq, clay was an easily available material.'에서 '점토'가 언급되었다.
② 'Second, papyrus was the first paper-like medium in Egypt.'에서 '파피루스'가 언급되었다.
④ 'Third, people in ancient Greece used animal skins to write on.'에서 '동물 가죽'이 언급되었다.
⑤ 'Lastly, silk was used as writing material in ancient China.'에서 '비단'이 언급되었다.

Dictation 09

문제편 051쪽

01 create a mobile app for your convenience / quickly report the issue on the app
02 your knees still extend over your toes / prevent you from getting injured / emphasize working out in the right way
03 I'm not that musically talented / improve my drumming skills / had similar concerns
04 put a slogan poster / on the round table / the box next to the lockers / three trophies on the shelf
05 did you download our mobile tickets / can you bring my uniform / it's in the bedroom closet
06 The blue one is a bit bigger / the bigger one could be more comfortable / the animal character on it
07 book signing event / supposed to attend my cousin's wedding / get her signature for you
08 How long does the program last / for three weeks starting July 19th / it starts too early / must be done online
09 raise money for rescuing animals / a wide range of products for animals / an animal badge will be given / contribute to rescuing animals
10 experience a different genre this time / stuck in a car / Since it's pet-friendly
11 the manager of the international marketing team / When do you have to be in Canada
12 Is there another flight I can take today / two flights available today
13 what about reading other customers' reviews / attach pictures and write detailed reviews / who actually used the items
14 work in the fashion industry after graduating / provide dormitory rooms to international interns / a stepping stone to achieving your dream
15 in which students choose Spanish books / learn various words and expressions / to broaden his word knowledge
16-17 materials which were used for writing / was once abundant / in that they were strong and flexible / more portable than wood

10회 | 2020학년도 4월 학력평가 고3

• 정답 •

01 ② 02 ② 03 ① 04 ④ 05 ⑤ 06 ② 07 ④ 08 ④ 09 ⑤ 10 ③ 11 ③ 12 ② 13 ② 14 ⑤ 15 ① 16 ① 17 ③

01 과학 보고서 작성 지침 안내

정답률 83% | 정답 ②

다음을 듣고, 남자가 하는 말의 목적으로 가장 적절한 것을 고르시오.

① 글쓰기 특강 참여를 독려하려고
✔ 보고서 작성 지침을 안내하려고
③ 발표 대회 유의 사항을 전달하려고
④ 모둠 프로젝트의 주제를 발표하려고
⑤ 학술 연구 공모전 일정을 공지하려고

M : Hello, students.
안녕하세요, 학생 여러분.
So far you've done a great job on your science project.
지금까지 여러분은 여러분의 과학 프로젝트를 잘해 왔습니다.
Now there's one last task to do.
이제 마지막으로 해야 할 과제 하나가 있습니다.
You must submit the report of your project by next Friday.
여러분은 다음 주 금요일까지 프로젝트 보고서를 제출해야 합니다.
Let me give you some guidelines to write a report.
보고서를 쓰기 위한 몇 가지 지침을 드리겠습니다.
First, you need to follow this basic structure: introduction, body, result, and discussion.
첫째, 서론, 본론, 결론, 논의의 기본 구조를 따라야 합니다.
Second, always stick to your data and evidence.
둘째, 항상 자료와 근거에 충실하세요.
You should make conclusions supported by them.
이것들로 뒷받침되는 결론을 내려야 합니다.
Third, give complete and correct references.
셋째, 참조 문헌을 완전하고 정확하게 달아주세요.
If not, you can be accused of stealing other people's ideas.
그렇게 하지 않으면, 당신은 다른 사람의 아이디어를 훔쳤다고 비난 받을 수 있습니다.
Lastly, the layout, tables, and graphs should be easy to understand.
마지막으로, 구성, 도표, 그래프가 이해하기 쉬워야 합니다.
It'll help you convey your ideas to the readers.
이것은 여러분이 독자들에게 여러분의 생각을 전달하는 데 도움을 줄 것입니다.
If you have any further questions about these guidelines, please ask me after class.
만일 이 지침들에 관한 추가 질문이 있다면, 방과 후에 제게 문의하세요.

Why? 왜 정답일까?

'Let me give you some guidelines to write a report.'에서 남자는 학생들이 제출해야 할 과학 보고서의 작성 지침을 안내하겠다고 하므로, 남자가 하는 말의 목적으로 가장 적절한 것은 ② '보고서 작성 지침을 안내하려고'이다.

- submit ⓥ 제출하다
- reference ⓝ 참조 (문헌)
- convey ⓥ 전달하다
- stick to ⓥ ~에 충실하다, ~을 고수하다
- be accused of ⓥ ~로 비난받다, 기소되다

02 반려동물 등록제의 장점

정답률 95% | 정답 ②

대화를 듣고, 두 사람이 하는 말의 주제로 가장 적절한 것을 고르시오.

① 개인 정보 자료 유출의 심각성
✔ 반려동물 등록제의 장점
③ 동물원 환경 개선의 필요성
④ 멸종 위기 동물 보호 방안
⑤ 생명 윤리 교육의 중요성

W : Hey, Simon. Did you see the news about pet registration?
안녕, Simon. 너 반려동물 등록제에 관한 뉴스 봤어?
M : I did. I think it's good that the government is beginning this pet registration system.
응. 난 정부가 이 반려동물 등록제를 시작하는 게 좋다고 생각해.
W : Right. After watching the news, I've been thinking it has a lot of benefits.
맞아. 뉴스를 보고 난 이후로, 난 그것이 많은 이점을 가지고 있다고 생각하고 있어.
M : Yes. It'll help pet owners find their lost pets more easily.
응. 그것은 반려동물 주인들이 잃어버린 반려동물을 더 쉽게 찾도록 도와줄 거야.
W : That's right. It's because the system records pet owners' information.
맞아. 이 시스템이 반려동물 주인의 정보를 기록하기 때문이지.
M : Also, I think the owners will have more responsibility thanks to this system.
또한, 나는 이 시스템 덕분에 주인들이 책임감을 더 가질 거라 생각해.
W : Yeah. People will think twice before abandoning their pets.
응. 사람들은 반려동물을 버리기 전에 다시 생각할 거야.
M : In addition, animal rescue workers can easily see who is responsible for the pet.
게다가, 동물 구조대원들은 누가 반려동물을 책임지는지 쉽게 알 수 있어.
W : It'll help them track down those bad people and make them pay fines.
그것은 이들이 나쁜 사람들을 추적하고 벌금을 물리는 데 도움이 될 거야.
M : By doing so, we'll have fewer abandoned pets.
그렇게 하면 유기 동물들이 줄어들 거야.
W : Yeah. The pet registration system seems good for both pets and pet owners!
맞아. 반려동물 등록제는 반려동물과 반려동물 주인 모두에게 좋은 것 같아!
M : You can say that again.
정말 그래.

Why? 왜 정답일까?

'I think it's good that the government is beginning this pet registration system. / After watching the news, I've been thinking it has a lot of benefits.'에서 남자와 여자는 반려동물 등록제에 많은 장점이 있는 것 같다고 이야기한 후, 장점의 구체적인 내용을 열거하고 있다. 따라서 두 사람이 하는 말의 주제로 가장 적절한 것은 ② '반려동물 등록제의 장점'이다.

- registration ⓝ 등록
- fine ⓝ 벌금
- You can say that again. 정말 그래. 전적으로 동의해.
- abandon ⓥ 버리다

03 공기 정화용 식물 구입하기

정답률 96% | 정답 ①

대화를 듣고, 두 사람의 관계를 가장 잘 나타낸 것을 고르시오.

✔ 꽃집 직원 – 고객
② 식물학자 – 기자
③ 숲 해설사 – 학생
④ 의사 – 환자
⑤ 전자 제품 판매원 – 택배원

W : Hi. What can I do for you?
안녕하세요. 무엇을 도와드릴까요?
M : Hi. I'm looking for something good for purifying the air in my house.
안녕하세요. 전 집안 공기를 정화하기에 좋은 것을 찾고 있어요.
W : You came to the right place. At our flower shop you can buy plants too.
잘 찾아 오셨습니다. 저희 꽃집에서는 식물도 사실 수 있어요.
M : Could you show me some popular ones?
인기 있는 것들을 좀 보여주실래요?
W : Of course. Here are the best-selling indoor plants that help remove pollutants from the air.
물론이죠. 여기 공기 중 오염원을 제거하는 데 도움을 주는 실내 식물 중 가장 잘 팔리는 것들이 있어요.
M : Hmm... I've never grown any plants before.
흠... 전 이전에 식물을 키워본 적이 없어요.
W : Okay. Then, this one might be perfect for you.
그러시군요. 그렇다면, 이것이 손님께 가장 적합할 겁니다.
M : It looks good. Is it easy to take care of?
좋아보이네요. 돌보기 쉬운 건가요?
W : Yes. All you have to do is water it twice a month.
네. 그저 두 달에 한 번 물만 주시면 돼요.
M : I like it. Is this the right price on this tag? It's cheaper than I thought.
좋네요. 이 가격표에 붙은 가격이 맞나요? 제가 생각한 것보다 싸네요.
W : That's right. It's on sale now.
맞습니다. 지금 세일 중이에요.
M : Great. I'll take it.
좋네요. 이걸 살게요.

Why? 왜 정답일까?

'At our flower shop you can buy plants too.'에서 여자가 꽃집 직원임을, 'I'm looking for something good for purifying the air in my house.'에서 남자가 공기 정화에 좋은 식물을 사러 온 손님임을 알 수 있으므로, 두 사람의 관계로 가장 적절한 것은 ① '꽃집 직원 – 고객'이다.

- purify ⓥ 정화하다
- take care of ⓥ ~을 돌보다
- pollutant ⓝ 오염원

04 어린이집 시설 구경하기

정답률 74% | 정답 ④

대화를 듣고, 그림에서 대화의 내용과 일치하지 않는 것을 고르시오.

M : Hi, Ms. Clark. I'm James Beck. I'm here to look around your day care center before I sign my son up.
안녕하세요, Clark 선생님. 전 James Beck입니다. 저희 아들을 등록시키기 전에 여기 어린이집을 둘러보러 왔어요.
W : Welcome, Mr. Beck. We talked on the phone yesterday, right? Let me show you this room first.
잘 오셨습니다, Beck 씨. 어제 전화로 말씀 나누었죠? 이 방부터 보여드릴게요.
M : That'll be great. 『I like the banner that says Happy Children's Day on the wall.』
그럼 좋겠네요. 벽에 Happy Children's Day라고 쓰여 있는 현수막이 마음에 드네요. ①의 근거 일치
W : Thanks. 『We also put the heart-shaped balloon under the banner for Children's Day next week.』 ②의 근거 일치
고맙습니다. 저희는 다음 주에 있을 어린이날을 위해 현수막 밑에 하트 모양 풍선도 놓아 두었어요.
M : The kids will love it. 『What's the picture next to the door?
아이들이 좋아하겠군요. 문 옆의 사진은 뭔가요?
W : It's a group picture of the kids.』 ③의 근거 일치
그것은 아이들의 단체 사진이에요.
M : Great. 『There are boxes on the table.』 ④의 근거 불일치 What are they for?
훌륭하군요. 탁자 위에 상자가 있네요. 무엇 때문에 있는 거죠?
W : We put toys in the boxes so the kids can play with them. Does your son like reading books?
저희는 아이들이 가지고 놀 수 있도록 장난감을 이 상자들에 넣어둡니다. 아드님이 책 읽는 것을 좋아하시나요?
M : Actually, he does. 『Oh, I see the bookshelf under the window.』 ⑤의 근거 일치
사실, 아이가 좋아해요. 오, 창문 밑에 책장이 보이는군요.
W : Yes. It has various kinds of books children would like.
네. 아이들이 좋아할 만한 여러 종류의 책들이 있어요.
M : How nice! My son would love this place.
근사하군요! 저희 아들이 이곳을 좋아하겠어요.
W : I bet he will.
분명 그럴 거예요.

[문제편 p.055]

Why? 왜 정답일까?

대화에서는 아이들이 가지고 놀 수 있는 장난감을 넣어둔 상자가 탁자 위에 있다(**There are boxes on the table.**)고 하는데, 그림에서 상자는 탁자 밑에 놓여있다. 따라서 그림에서 대화의 내용과 일치하지 않는 것은 ④이다.

- **day care center** ⓝ 어린이집, 탁아소
- **sign up** ⓥ 등록하다, 신청하다
- **bet** ⓥ 장담하다, 내기하다

05 실시간 라이브 토크 쇼 준비하기 정답률 96% | 정답 ⑤

대화를 듣고, 여자가 할 일로 가장 적절한 것을 고르시오.

① 의자 배열하기 ② 조명 확인하기 ③ 카메라 설치하기
④ 프로젝터 연결하기 ✔ 배터리 가져오기

W : Hey, Chris. I'm so excited for the student-teacher talk show today.
안녕, Chris. 난 오늘 있을 교사 – 학생 토크 쇼 때문에 몹시 들떴어!

M : Me, too. Since it's a live video streaming at the gym, we should be perfectly prepared.
나도 그래. 이건 체육관에서 실시간 영상으로 송출되는 거니까, 우리는 완벽하게 준비되어 있어야 해.

W : Absolutely. Let's mark off these items in the checklist one by one.
물론이지. 체크리스트에서 이 항목들을 하나씩 표시하면서 확인해보자.

M : Okay. First, we've already arranged the chairs for the audience, right?
좋아. 먼저, 우리는 관객들을 위한 의자들을 배열해두었지, 그렇지?

W : Yes, we have. Did you check the stage lights?
응. 너 무대 조명 확인했어?

M : They worked perfectly. I'll turn them on right before the show starts.
완벽하게 작동해. 쇼가 시작하기 바로 직전에 그것들을 켤 거야.

W : Next, cameras. Are the cameras set in the right places?
다음으로 카메라야. 카메라는 제 위치에 설치되어 있니?

M : Yeah. I've just set them up as you told me. How about the projector?
응. 네가 말해준대로 딱 설치해 두었어. 프로젝터는 어때?

W : Don't worry. I've connected it to the laptop.
걱정 마. 난 그걸 노트북에 연결해 두었어.

M : Good. Is there anything else left to do?
좋아. 남은 할 일이 있나?

W : You brought the wireless microphones, right?
너 무선 마이크 가져왔지, 그렇지?

M : Yes. *[Pause]* Oh, no! I forgot to bring the batteries for them.
응. *[잠시 멈춤]* 오, 이런! 마이크 배터리를 가져오는 걸 깜빡했어.

W : Really? Let me go get the batteries right away.
정말? 내가 지금 바로 가서 배터리를 가져올게.

M : Thanks a lot.
정말 고마워.

Why? 왜 정답일까?

대화에 따르면 남자는 무선 마이크는 잊지 않고 챙겼지만 마이크용 배터리를 가져오는 것을 잊었다. 이에 여자는 자신이 가서 배터리를 바로 가져오겠다(**Let me go get the batteries right away.**)고 하므로, 여자가 할 일로 가장 적절한 것은 ⑤ '배터리 가져오기'이다.

- **live video streaming** ⓝ 실시간 영상 송출
- **mark off** ⓥ (선을 그어) 표시하다
- **arrange** ⓥ 배열하다, 준비하다

06 조류 박물관 입장권 및 투어 구매하기 정답률 89% | 정답 ②

대화를 듣고, 남자가 지불할 금액을 고르시오. [3점]

① $40 ✔ $63 ③ $66 ④ $70 ⑤ $72

W : Welcome to Westlake Bird Museum. How may I help you?
Westlake Bird Museum에 오신 것을 환영합니다. 무엇을 도와드릴까요?

M : Hello, I'd like to buy admission tickets. My twin daughters are very interested in birds.
안녕하세요, 전 입장권을 사고 싶어요. 제 쌍둥이 딸들이 새에 몹시 관심이 많거든요.

W : Okay. Admission tickets are $20 for an adult and $10 for a child.
그러시군요. 입장권은 어른 1인에 20달러, 어린이 1인에 10달러입니다.

M : I'll take one adult ticket and two child tickets. What's this? A guided museum tour?
어른 한 장에 어린이 두 장을 살게요. 이건 뭐죠? 가이드가 있는 박물관 투어?

W : It's a tour where the guide gives excellent explanations about the exhibits of various birds and their habitats.
다양한 새와 서식지 전시물에 관해 가이드가 훌륭한 설명을 제공해주는 투어입니다.

M : Nice. How much is it?
근사하네요. 얼마인가요?

W : It's $10 per person. The tour starts soon. You can book it now.
1인당 10달러입니다. 투어가 곧 시작합니다. 지금 예약하실 수 있어요.

M : Okay. I'll do that for the three of us.
알겠습니다. 저희 세 명을 위해 예약할게요.

W : So, one adult and two child admission tickets and three guided tours.
그러면, 어른 1인과 어린이 2인 입장권과 가이드 투어 3인이군요.

M : Yes. Can I use this coupon?
네. 제가 이 쿠폰을 쓸 수 있나요?

W : Sure. You can get 10% off the total price with the coupon.
물론이죠. 쿠폰으로 전체 가격의 10퍼센트를 할인받으실 수 있습니다.

M : That's great. I'll pay by credit card.
좋군요. 신용 카드로 지불할게요.

Why? 왜 정답일까?

대화에 따르면 남자는 20달러짜리 어른 입장권 한 장, 10달러짜리 어린이 입장권을 두 장 사고, 1인당 10달러짜리 투어를 세 명 예약한 후, 전체 가격의 10퍼센트를 할인받았다. 이를 식으로 나타내면 '$\{20+(10\times2)+(10\times3)\}\times0.9=63$'이므로, 남자가 지불할 가격은 ② '$63'이다.

- **exhibit** ⓝ 전시물, 전시회
- **habitat** ⓝ 서식지

07 재즈 콘서트에 못 가는 이유 정답률 96% | 정답 ④

대화를 듣고, 여자가 재즈 콘서트에 갈 수 없는 이유를 고르시오.

① 피아노 레슨을 받아야 해서
② 취업 면접을 보러 가야 해서
③ 아르바이트를 해야 해서
✔ 남동생들을 돌봐야 해서
⑤ 결혼식에 참석해야 해서

M : Rachel. What are you doing?
Rachel, 뭐 하고 있어?

W : Hey, Jeremy. I'm watching a video clip of jazz pianists.
안녕, Jeremy. 난 재즈 피아니스트들의 영상을 보고 있어.

M : You like jazz! Do you go to jazz concerts often?
너 재즈를 좋아하는구나! 재즈 콘서트 자주 가?

W : No. I've never been to one.
아니, 한 번도 못 가봤어.

M : Well, my brother gave me two jazz concert tickets because he has a job interview that day. So, do you want to go with me?
음, 우리 형이 나한테 재즈 콘서트 티켓을 두 장 줬는데, 그는 그날 일자리 면접이 있거든. 그러니 나랑 같이 갈래?

W : That's amazing! When is the concert?
근사하다! 콘서트가 언제야?

M : It's next Saturday. Are you available?
다음 주 토요일이야. 너 시간 돼?

W : I'm afraid I'm not.
안 될 것 같아.

M : Oh, right! You said you started a part time job on weekends.
오, 맞다! 너 주말에 아르바이트를 시작했다고 했지.

W : No. It's only on Sundays. I have to take care of my younger brothers that day.
아니, 그건 일요일만 해. 난 그날은 내 남동생들을 돌봐야 해.

M : Why do you have to do that?
왜 그래야 해?

W : My parents asked me because they're celebrating their wedding anniversary.
우리 부모님이 그날 결혼기념일을 축하하기로 하셔서 내게 부탁하셨어.

M : I see. I hope we can go together next time.
그렇구나. 다음번에 같이 갈 수 있길 바라.

Why? 왜 정답일까?

대화에 따르면 여자는 다음 주 토요일 부모님의 부탁으로 남동생들을 돌봐야 해서(**I have to take care of my younger brothers that day.**) 남자와 함께 재즈 콘서트에 갈 수 없다. 따라서 여자가 재즈 콘서트에 갈 수 없는 이유로 가장 적절한 것은 ④ '남동생들을 돌봐야 해서'이다.

- **celebrate** ⓥ 축하하다, 기념하다
- **wedding anniversary** ⓝ 결혼기념일

08 아들을 위해 축구 교실 알아보기 정답률 95% | 정답 ④

대화를 듣고, Hampton Soccer Program에 관해 언급되지 않은 것을 고르시오.

① 장소 ② 기간 ③ 강사
✔ 모집 인원 ⑤ 참가 비용

M : Honey, we need to find a soccer program for Kevin.
여보, 우린 Kevin을 위해 축구 교실을 알아봐야 해요.

W : Right. I brought a brochure about Hampton Soccer Program from the community center.
맞아요. 난 주민 센터에서 Hampton Soccer Program에 관한 책자를 가져왔어요.

M : Good. Let me see. 「The program will be held in the soccer field in Riverside Park.」
좋아요. 나 좀 볼게요. 이 프로그램은 Riverside Park에 있는 축구장에서 열리는군요. ①의 근거 일치

W : Isn't that good? The park is near our house.
좋은 거 아니에요? 그 공원은 우리 집에서 가까워요.

M : Right. 「It says the program starts on May 2nd, and it goes every weekend for two months.」 ②의 근거 일치
맞아요. 여기 쓰여 있기로는 이 프로그램은 5월 2일에 시작하고, 두 달 동안 매주 주말에 진행된대요.

W : Yeah. He'll play and practice for three hours a day.
네, 아이는 하루에 세 시간 동안 경기하고 연습하고요.

M : Wow. It's a tough schedule.
와, 힘든 스케줄이군요.

W : Yes. But he'll improve his skills a lot. Look. 「The instructor is Aaron Smith.」 He's a well-known soccer coach in this town. ③의 근거 일치
네, 하지만 아이는 기술을 많이 향상시킬 수 있을 거예요. 봐요, 강사는 Aaron Smith예요. 그는 이 마을에서 유명한 축구 코치죠.

M : Really? He must be good at teaching. 「What about the participation fee for the program?」 ⑤의 근거 일치
그래요? 그는 틀림없이 잘 가르치겠군요. 프로그램 참가 비용은 어떤가요?

W : 「It's $400.」 Do you think it's expensive?
400달러예요. 비싸다고 생각하나요?

M : It's not bad considering the length of the program.
수업 기간을 생각하면 나쁘지 않아요.

W : Right. Kevin will be happy to hear about this.
맞아요. Kevin이 이걸 들으면 좋아할 거예요.

M : I'm sure he'll be.
당연히 그러겠죠.

Why? 왜 정답일까?

대화에서 남자와 여자는 **Hampton Soccer Program**의 장소, 기간, 강사, 참가 비용을 언급하였다. 따라서 언급되지 않은 것은 ④ '모집 인원'이다.

Why? 왜 오답일까?

① '**The program will be held in the soccer field in Riverside Park.**'에서 '장소'가 언급되었다.
② '**It says the program starts on May 2nd, and it goes every weekend for two months.**'에서 '기간'이 언급되었다.
③ '**The instructor is Aaron Smith.**'에서 '강사'가 언급되었다.
⑤ '**It's $400.**'에서 '참가 비용'이 언급되었다.

- **improve** ⓥ 향상시키다
- **instructor** ⓝ 강사
- **participation fee** ⓝ 참가비
- **considering** prep ~을 생각하면, 고려하면

[문제편 p.055]

09 재활용 축제 안내
정답률 94% | 정답 ⑤

Auburn Green City Festival에 관한 다음 내용을 듣고, 일치하지 않는 것을 고르시오.

① 5월 29일부터 6월 1일까지 열릴 것이다.
② 올해의 주제는 재활용이다.
③ 개막식에서 유명한 음악가들이 공연할 것이다.
④ 다양한 체험 활동이 준비되어 있다.
⑤ 야간에도 행사가 있을 것이다.

W : Hello, listeners.
안녕하세요, 청취자 여러분.
I'm Lily Johnson, festival manager.
저는 축제 관리자 Lily Johnson입니다.
I'm happy to announce the Auburn Green City Festival.
Auburn Green City Festival에 관해 알려드리게 되어 기쁩니다.
「It'll be held from May 29th to June 1st.」 ①의 근거 일치
이것은 5월 29일부터 6월 1일까지 열릴 예정입니다.
The location will be City Hall Square.
장소는 City Hall Square입니다.
「This year's theme is recycling.」 ②의 근거 일치
올해의 주제는 재활용입니다.
The festival provides various recycling events and activities.
축제에서는 다양한 재활용 행사와 활동을 제공할 예정입니다.
「At the opening ceremony, famous musicians will perform.」 ③의 근거 일치
개막식에서는 유명 음악가들이 공연합니다.
To spread the message of recycling, they'll play instruments made of recycled materials.
재활용이라는 주제를 널리 알리기 위해, 이들은 재활용된 재료로 만들어진 악기를 연주할 것입니다.
「Also, various hands-on activities are prepared.」 ④의 근거 일치
또한, 다양한 체험 활동이 준비되어 있습니다.
You can experience turning trash into treasure in activities like 'making a shopping bag out of old clothes' and 'creating a recycled art wall'.
여러분은 '오래된 옷으로 쇼핑백 만들기'와 '재활용 예술 벽 만들기'와 같은 활동에서 쓰레기를 보물로 바꾸는 것을 경험하시게 됩니다.
The festival runs from 9 a.m. to 5 p.m.
이 축제는 오전 9시부터 오후 5시까지 진행됩니다.
「There'll be no events at night.」 ⑤의 근거 불일치
야간에는 행사가 없습니다.
We're looking forward to seeing you.
여러분을 뵙기를 고대합니다.

Why? 왜 정답일까?

'There'll be no events at night.'에서 밤에는 행사가 없다고 하므로, 내용과 일치하지 않는 것은 ⑤ '야간에도 행사가 있을 것이다.'이다.

Why? 왜 오답일까?

① 'It'll be held from May 29th to June 1st.'의 내용과 일치한다.
② 'This year's theme is recycling.'의 내용과 일치한다.
③ 'At the opening ceremony, famous musicians will perform.'의 내용과 일치한다.
④ 'Also, various hands-on activities are prepared.'의 내용과 일치한다.

- recycling ⓝ 재활용
- made of ~로 만들어진
- hands-on ⓐ 체험의, 직접 해보는
- turn A into B ⓥ A를 B로 바꾸다

10 일일 서핑 강좌 고르기
정답률 82% | 정답 ③

다음 표를 보면서 대화를 듣고, 두 사람이 수강할 서핑 강좌를 고르시오.

One Day Surfing Lesson

	Lesson	Beach	Level	Group Size	Suit Rental
①	A	Sunrise	Beginner	5	○
②	B	Manson	Intermediate	2	×
③	C	Longport	Intermediate	2	○
④	D	Northwest	Advanced	5	○
⑤	E	Greenpoint	Advanced	2	×

M : Amelia, do you want to take a one day surfing lesson this weekend?
Amelia, 이번 주말에 일일 서핑 강좌를 들을래?
W : Sure. Let's look for the information online.
좋지. 온라인에서 정보를 찾아보자.
M : *[Typing sound]* Look. I found a popular surfing lesson website.
[타자 치는 소리] 이거 봐. 인기 있는 서핑 강좌 사이트를 찾았어.
W : Hmm... 「do you want to go to Manson beach again?
흠... Manson 해수욕장에 또 가고 싶어?
M : Manson beach is too far from here. Let's try another place.」 근거1 Beach 조건
Manson 해수욕장은 여기서 너무 멀어. 다른 곳을 가보자.
W : Okay. 「What about the level? I don't think we have to take the beginner level as we took lessons several times. 근거2 Level 조건
그래. 레벨은? 내 생각에 우리는 몇 번 수업을 받았기 때문에 초급 수준을 들을 필요는 없을 것 같아.
M : Right. Intermediate or advanced levels seem fine.」
맞아. 중급이나 고급이 괜찮아 보여.
W : Yes. 「And the group size. Should we take a lesson with others or only two of us?
그래. 그리고 수업 인원 말이야. 우린 다른 사람들과 함께 수업을 들어야 할까, 아니면 둘이서 들어야 할까?
M : We can each get more attention from the instructor if we choose the lesson for two.」 근거3 Group Size 조건
2인 수업을 선택하면 우리는 강사에게 각각 더 많은 관심을 받을 수 있어.
W : You're right. Then we have two options left.
네 말이 맞아. 그럼 두 가지 선택지가 남았어.
M : 「The suits are expensive to buy. Let's rent the suits.」 근거4 Suit Rental 조건
서핑 수트는 사기 비싸. 수트를 대여하자.
W : Okay. Good thinking.
알았어. 좋은 생각이야.
M : Great. Let's take this lesson.
좋아. 이 수업을 듣자.

Why? 왜 정답일까?

대화에 따르면 남자와 여자는 Manson 해수욕장이 아닌 다른 곳에서 진행되며, 난이도는 중급 또는 고급이고, 2인을 대상으로 하며, 서핑 수트 대여가 가능한 일일 서핑 강좌를 들으려고 한다. 따라서 두 사람이 수강할 서핑 강좌는 ③ 'C'이다.

- intermediate ⓐ 중급의
- suit ⓝ (특정한 활동을 위해 입는) 복장 ⓥ 어울리다
- Good thinking. 좋은 생각이야.

11 자선 행사 준비하기
정답률 95% | 정답 ③

대화를 듣고, 남자의 마지막 말에 대한 여자의 응답으로 가장 적절한 것을 고르시오.

① No. He won't be able to come. – 아니. 그는 올 수 없을 거야.
② Exactly. That's why I'm on a diet. – 바로 그거야. 그래서 내가 다이어트를 하는 거야.
③ Of course. That would be so great. – 물론이지. 그럼 정말 좋을 거야.
④ I agree. Baking is difficult to learn. – 동의해. 제빵은 배우기 어려워.
⑤ I'm sorry. The cookies are all sold out. – 미안해. 쿠키는 전부 팔렸어.

M : The cookies smell so good, mom. But why are you baking so many of them?
쿠키 냄새가 무척 좋아요, 엄마. 그런데 왜 그렇게 쿠키를 많이 구우시는 거예요?
W : These are the cookies to sell for Charity Night tomorrow.
이것들은 내일 Charity Night에서 팔 쿠키들이야.
M : I see. I have no plans tomorrow. Can I come and help you?
그렇군요. 전 내일 아무런 계획도 없어요. 저도 가서 도와드릴까요?
W : Of course. That would be so great.
물론이지. 그럼 정말 좋을 거야.

Why? 왜 정답일까?

여자가 다음날 자선 행사에서 팔기 위한 쿠키를 굽고 있다고 하자 아들인 남자는 자신도 함께 가서 돕겠다고 제안하고 있다(Can I come and help you?). 따라서 여자의 응답으로 가장 적절한 것은 ③ '물론이지. 그럼 정말 좋을 거야.'이다.

12 자동차 수리 요청하기
정답률 88% | 정답 ②

대화를 듣고, 여자의 마지막 말에 대한 남자의 응답으로 가장 적절한 것을 고르시오.

① It took me two months to learn to drive. – 제가 운전을 배우는 데 두 달이 걸렸어요.
② I'm at the parking lot of the city library. – 전 시립 도서관 주차장에 있어요.
③ I don't know how much fuel I need. – 전 연료가 얼마나 필요한지 모르겠어요.
④ You could rent this blue car. – 이 파란색 차를 대여하실 수 있을 겁니다.
⑤ I'll arrive there by 10 a.m. – 전 오전 10시까지는 거기 도착할 거예요.

[Phone rings.]
[전화벨이 울린다.]
W : Hello. This is Rodney's Car Repair Shop. How may I help you?
여보세요. Rodney's Car Repair Shop입니다. 무엇을 도와드릴까요?
M : My car has a problem. It doesn't start. Can you send someone to help me?
제 차에 문제가 있어요. 시동이 걸리지 않아요. 도와줄 사람을 보내주시겠어요?
W : No problem. Just tell me where you are now.
물론입니다. 지금 어디 계신지만 말씀해주세요.
M : I'm at the parking lot of the city library.
전 시립 도서관 주차장에 있어요.

Why? 왜 정답일까?

남자는 여자가 일하는 자동차 정비소에 전화를 걸어 자신의 차가 시동이 걸리지 않으니 사람을 보내달라고 청한다. 이에 여자는 남자의 위치를 알려달라(Just tell me where you are now.)고 하므로, 남자의 응답으로 가장 적절한 것은 ② '전 시립 도서관 주차장에 있어요.'이다.

- start ⓥ 시동이 걸리다, 시동을 걸다
- parking lot 주차장
- fuel ⓝ 연료
- rent ⓥ 대여하다, 빌리다

13 학교 신문 동아리 가입하기
정답률 93% | 정답 ②

대화를 듣고, 여자의 마지막 말에 대한 남자의 응답으로 가장 적절한 것을 고르시오.

Man: ______________________________

① Don't worry. I've already made some amazing friends here.
걱정 마. 난 이미 여기서 멋진 친구들을 몇몇 사귀었어.
② You're right. I think I should join the campus newspaper.
네 말이 맞아. 난 대학 신문 동아리에 들어야겠어.
③ Trust me. I can teach you how to write a good article.
날 믿어. 난 네게 좋은 기사를 쓰는 방법을 가르쳐줄 수 있어.
④ Correct. You shouldn't go to too many school events.
맞아. 넌 학교 행사에 너무 많이 가면 안 돼.
⑤ Sorry. Our school newspaper team is already full.
미안해. 우리 학교 신문 팀은 이미 인원이 다 찼어.

[Cell phone rings.]
[휴대 전화가 울린다.]
W : Hi, Noah. It's been a while. How's your first year of college going?
안녕, Noah. 오랜만이야. 대학 1학년은 어떻게 보내고 있어?
M : It's so nice to talk to you, Cathy. Making new friends here is very hard.
통화하게 돼서 좋다, Cathy. 여기서 새로운 친구를 사귀기는 너무 어려워.
W : I understand. It's not like high school.
이해해. 고등학교랑 다르지.
M : I don't know what to do.
어떻게 해야 할지 모르겠어.
W : Well, if you're looking for friends, joining a club might help.
글쎄, 친구를 찾는다면, 동아리에 드는 것이 도움이 될지도 몰라.
M : But I'm not sure about which one would be best.
하지만 어느 동아리가 가장 좋을지 모르겠어.
W : How about the campus newspaper? You wrote some newspaper articles in high school.
대학 신문 쪽은 어때? 넌 고등학교 때 신문 기사를 좀 썼잖아.

[문제편 p.055]

M : Yes. I enjoyed it even when I had to stay up all night.
그래. 심지어 밤을 새야 할 때도 즐거웠어.
W : See? You have a passion for writing.
그렇지? 넌 글쓰기에 열정이 있어.
M : I guess it would be fun to join a club I like.
내 마음에 드는 동아리에 가입하면 재미있을 것 같아.
W : And you can get involved in events with other reporters.
그리고 너는 다른 기자들이랑 행사에 참여할 수 있어.
M : True. I can have more chances to spend time with them regularly while covering stories.
맞아. 난 이야기도 다루면서 그들과 정기적으로 시간을 보낼 기회를 더 얻을 수 있어.
W : Yeah. It'll allow you to connect with people with the same interests at the campus newspaper.
응. 그것은 네가 대학 신문이라는 같은 관심사를 공유하는 사람들과 어울리게 해줄 거야.
M : You're right. I think I should join the campus newspaper.
네 말이 맞아. 난 대학 신문 동아리에 들어야겠어.

Why? 왜 정답일까?

대학 신입생이 되어 친구를 사귀는 데 어려움을 느끼고 있는 남자에게 여자는 대학 신문 동아리에 들어보라고 권하며 동아리에 드는 것이 같은 관심사를 지닌 친구들과 어울릴 기회를 줄 것이라고(**It'll allow you to connect with people with the same interests at the campus newspaper.**) 이야기하고 있다. 따라서 남자의 응답으로 가장 적절한 것은 ② '네 말이 맞아. 난 대학 신문 동아리에 들어야겠어.'이다.

- **article** ⓝ 기사
- **get involved in** ⓥ ~에 참여하다, 엮이다
- **connect with** ⓥ ~와 어울리다, 연결되다
- **stay up all night** ⓥ 밤을 새다
- **regularly** ad 정기적으로

14 사진 전공에 관해 조언해줄 사람 소개해주기

정답률 92% | 정답 ⑤

대화를 듣고, 남자의 마지막 말에 대한 여자의 응답으로 가장 적절한 것을 고르시오. [3점]

Woman: ______

① Exactly. It's important for you to take pictures more often.
바로 그거죠. 당신이 더 자주 사진을 찍어보는 게 중요해요.
② Yes. You'll get a college graduation photo album next week.
네. 다음 주면 당신은 대학 졸업 앨범을 받아볼 수 있습니다.
③ Sure. You'll be able to win an award for nature photography.
물론이죠. 당신은 자연 사진에 관한 상을 받을 수 있을 겁니다.
④ Right. I'll hire the same professional photographer as last year.
맞아요. 전 작년과 똑같은 전문 사진사를 고용하겠어요.
✔ Thanks. She can help me to learn about majoring in photography.
고맙습니다. 그분은 제가 사진 전공에 관해 알아가는 데 도움을 주실 수 있을 거예요.

M : Stephanie, I saw your photos of the school scenery in the lobby. They were amazing!
Stephanie, 네가 찍은 학교 풍경 사진을 로비에서 봤어. 멋지던걸!
W : Thanks, Mr. Brown. I'm really glad that people like my photos.
고맙습니다, Brown 선생님. 사람들이 제 사진을 좋아해서 정말 기뻐요.
M : Did you learn how to take photos professionally?
사진 찍는 법을 전문적으로 배웠니?
W : Not really. I learned it by myself, searching for information online.
아니요. 온라인에서 정보를 검색하면서 혼자 배웠어요.
M : How smart! Are you going to major in photography in college?
대단하구나! 넌 대학에서 사진학을 전공할 거니?
W : I think so. But I don't know much about how to prepare for all that.
그럴 것 같아요. 하지만 전 그 모든 걸 어떻게 준비해야 할지 잘 모르겠어요.
M : Do you know anyone who is majoring in that field?
그 분야를 전공하고 있는 사람을 좀 아니?
W : Not really. I wish I knew someone who could give me some advice on how to prepare.
아니요. 어떻게 준비해야 할지 조언을 좀 해줄 수 있는 사람을 알면 좋겠어요.
M : Hmm... oh! There's Julia Watson. She was one of my students, and she is now a famous photographer.
흠... 아! Julia Watson이 있구나. 그 애는 내 학생 중 한 명이었고, 지금은 유명한 사진 작가야.
W : Really? Do you keep in touch with her?
정말요? 그분과 계속 연락하시나요?
M : Yes. If you want, I'll set up a meeting for you.
그래. 원한다면 내가 만남을 잡아줄게.
W : Thanks. She can help me to learn about majoring in photography.
고맙습니다. 그분은 제가 사진 전공에 관해 알아가는 데 도움을 주실 수 있을 거예요.

Why? 왜 정답일까?

대화에서 남자는 사진 전공을 생각하지만 주변에 도움을 구할 사람이 없다는 여자에게 현직 사진 작가로 활동하고 있는 자신의 제자와 만남을 주선해주겠다(**If you want, I'll set up a meeting for you.**)고 제안한다. 따라서 여자의 응답으로 가장 적절한 것은 ⑤ '고맙습니다. 그분은 제가 사진 전공에 관해 알아가는 데 도움을 주실 수 있을 거예요.'이다.

- **scenery** ⓝ 풍경
- **major in** ⓥ ~을 전공하다
- **professionally** ad 전문적으로
- **keep in touch with** ⓥ ~와 연락하다

15 수업 참여도를 높일 방법 조언하기

정답률 83% | 정답 ①

다음 상황 설명을 듣고, David가 Jenny에게 할 말로 가장 적절한 것을 고르시오. [3점]

David: ______

✔ You should use fun activities to get the kids to participate in class.
넌 아이들을 수업에 참여시키기 위해서 재미있는 활동들을 이용해야 해.
② You don't have to do too many extracurricular activities in school.
넌 학교에서 과외 활동을 너무 많이 할 필요가 없어.
③ You need to know that playing games is not helpful for kids.
넌 게임을 하는 것이 아이들에게 도움이 되지 않는다는 것을 알아야 해.
④ Why don't you motivate the kids to study by themselves?
아이들이 스스로 공부하도록 동기 부여를 해주면 어때?
⑤ How about encouraging kids to respect each other more?
아이들에게 서로를 더 존중하도록 격려해주는 게 어때?

M : David has a lot of volunteering experience in teaching children, and Jenny has just started the same volunteering.
David는 아이들을 가르치는 자원봉사 경험이 많고, Jenny는 같은 자원봉사를 이제 막 시작했다.
Jenny imagines that kids will learn many things and focus on her class, but her first class doesn't go as well as she has expected.
Jenny는 아이들이 많은 것을 배우고 수업에 집중할 것이라고 상상하지만, 그녀의 첫 수업은 그녀가 기대했던 것만큼 잘 진행되지 않는다.
Jenny tries to teach what she knows as much as possible.
Jenny는 자신이 아는 것을 최대한 많이 가르치려고 노력한다.
However, the kids get bored easily and don't pay attention to her explanation.
하지만, 아이들은 쉽게 지루해하고 그녀의 설명에 주의를 기울이지 않는다.
Jenny feels frustrated and she asks David for advice.
Jenny는 좌절감을 느끼고 David에게 조언을 구한다.
After hearing Jenny's problem, David thinks she should include more interesting activities that would help children take part in her lesson.
Jenny의 문제를 들은 후에, David는 Jenny가 아이들이 수업에 참여하게 도움을 줄 보다 흥미로운 활동들을 포함시켜야 한다고 생각한다.
So, he wants to tell Jenny that she needs to provide children with enjoyable activities to engage them in learning.
그래서 그는 Jenny에게 아이들이 학습에 참여할 수 있도록 재미있는 활동을 제공할 필요가 있다고 말하고 싶어 한다.
In this situation, what would David most likely say to Jenny?
이 상황에서, David는 Jenny에게 뭐라고 말하겠는가?
David : You should use fun activities to get the kids to participate in class.
넌 아이들을 수업에 참여시키기 위해서 재미있는 활동들을 이용해야 해.

Why? 왜 정답일까?

상황에 따르면 David는 자원봉사 수업에서 만나는 학생들이 수업에 잘 집중하지 못해 고민하고 있는 Jenny에게 학생들의 참여를 독려할 재미있는 활동들을 고안해볼 것을 조언하고 싶어한다(**So, he wants to tell Jenny that she needs to provide children with enjoyable activities to engage them in learning.**). 따라서 David가 Jenny에게 할 말로 가장 적절한 것은 ① '넌 아이들을 수업에 참여시키기 위해서 재미있는 활동들을 이용해야 해.'이다.

- **pay attention to** ⓥ ~에 주의를 기울이다
- **take part in** ⓥ ~에 참여하다
- **extracurricular** ⓐ 교과 외의
- **frustrated** ⓐ 좌절한
- **engage A in B** ⓥ A를 B에 참여시키다

10회

16-17 세계 각지의 생일 음식

W : Hello, students. Last time we talked about traditional holiday foods.
안녕하세요, 학생 여러분. 지난번에 우리는 전통 명절 음식에 대해 이야기해 보았습니다.
「Today, let's talk about traditional birthday foods around the world.」 16번의 근거
오늘은 세계 각국의 전통 생일 음식에 대해 이야기해 봅시다.
Food is a big part of how birthdays are celebrated across the world.
음식은 전 세계에서 생일을 축하하는 방법에 있어 커다란 부분을 차지합니다.
「First, in Australia, Fairy Bread is a must-have birthday dessert.」 17번 ①의 근거 일치
첫째로, 호주에서 Fair Bread는 꼭 먹어야 하는 생일 디저트입니다.
It's a buttered piece of bread covered with sprinkles all over, and people cut the bread into triangles.
이것은 스프링클로 뒤덮인 버터 바른 빵인데, 사람들은 이 빵을 삼각형으로 자릅니다.
「Second, in Russia, people get a special message on their birthday, not from a card but from a personalized pie.」 17번 ②의 근거 일치
둘째로, 러시아에서 사람들은 생일날에 카드가 아닌, 그 사람만을 위한 파이를 통해 특별한 메시지를 받습니다.
The message is carved into the dough on top of the pie.
그 메시지는 파이 위 도우에 새겨집니다.
「Third, eating a bowl of noodles on one's birthday is a deeply rooted tradition in China.」 17번 ④의 근거 일치
셋째로, 생일날 국수 한 그릇을 먹는 것은 중국에서 뿌리 깊은 전통입니다.
It symbolizes the birthday person's long life.
그것은 생일인 사람의 장수를 상징합니다.
「Lastly, people in England bake fortune-telling cakes with certain symbolic small things inside on their birthday.」 17번 ⑤의 근거 일치
마지막으로, 영국 사람들은 생일날이면 안에 어떤 상징적인 작은 것들이 들어있는 포춘 케이크를 굽습니다.
For example, if someone bites a coin in their piece of cake, it means they'll be rich in the future.
예를 들어, 만약 누군가가 자기 케이크 조각 안에서 동전을 깨문다면, 그것은 그들이 앞으로 부자가 될 것임을 의미합니다.
Now let's watch a video about these foods.
이제 이 음식들에 대한 영상을 보도록 하죠.

- **celebrate** ⓥ 축하하다, 기념하다
- **carve** ⓥ 새기다, 조각하다
- **bite** ⓥ 깨물다
- **personalize** ⓥ 개인의 필요에 맞추다
- **symbolize** ⓥ 상징하다
- **trait** ⓝ 특성

16 주제 파악

정답률 94% | 정답 ①

여자가 하는 말의 주제로 가장 적절한 것은?

✔ foods to celebrate birthdays around the world – 세계 각지에서 생일을 기념하기 위한 음식
② mistaken ideas about global birthday traditions – 세계의 생일 전통에 대한 잘못된 생각
③ traditional dessert recipes around the globe – 세계 전역의 전통적인 디저트 요리법
④ common traits of holiday foods worldwide – 세계 휴일 음식의 공통된 특성
⑤ histories of world famous healthy dishes – 세계적으로 유명한 건강한 음식의 역사

Why? 왜 정답일까?

'**Today, let's talk about traditional birthday foods around the world.**'에서 여자는 세계 각지의 전통 생일 음식을 담화의 주제로 제시하고 있다. 따라서 여자가 하는 말의 주제로 가장 적절한 것은 ① '세계 각지에서 생일을 기념하기 위한 음식'이다.

17 언급 유무 파악

정답률 96% | 정답 ③

언급된 나라가 아닌 것은?

① Australia – 호주
② Russia – 러시아
✔ Sweden – 스웨덴
④ China – 중국
⑤ England – 영국

Why? 왜 정답일까?

담화에서 여자는 세계 각지에서 생일에 전통적으로 먹는 음식의 예를 제시하기 위해 호주, 러시아, 중국, 영국을 언급한다. 따라서 언급되지 않은 나라는 ③ '스웨덴'이다.

Why? 왜 오답일까?

① 'First, in Australia, Fairy Bread is a must-have birthday dessert.'에서 '호주'가 언급되었다.
② 'Second, in Russia, people get a special message on their birthday, not from a card but from a personalized pie.'에서 '러시아'가 언급되었다.
④ 'Third, eating a bowl of noodles on one's birthday is a deeply rooted tradition in China.'에서 '중국'이 언급되었다.
⑤ 'Lastly, people in England bake fortune-telling cakes with certain symbolic small things inside on their birthday.'에서 '영국'이 언급되었다.

Dictation 10

문제편 057쪽

01 some guidelines to write a report / complete and correct / accused of stealing other people's ideas
02 this pet registration system / the system records pet owners' information / make them pay fines
03 help remove pollutants from the air / water it twice a month / cheaper than I thought
04 before I sign my son up / put the heart-shaped balloon / a group picture of the kids / I bet he will
05 mark off these items / Are the cameras set in the right places / connected it to the laptop / forgot to bring the batteries
06 the exhibits of various birds and their habitats / three guided tours
07 he has a job interview / take care of my younger brothers / their wedding anniversary
08 in the soccer field / it goes every weekend for two months / considering the length of the program
09 play instruments made of recycled materials / various hands-on activities / no events at night
10 a popular surfing lesson website / take the beginner level / Intermediate or advanced levels / The suits are expensive to buy
11 why are you baking so many of them / the cookies to sell
12 Just tell me where you are now
13 joining a club might help / which one would be best / connect with people with the same interests
14 how to take photos professionally / major in photography in college / keep in touch with
15 don't pay attention to her explanation / take part in her lesson / enjoyable activities to engage them in learning
16-17 how birthdays are celebrated across the world / cut the bread into triangles / but from a personalized pie / they'll be rich in the future

11회 | 2025학년도 6월 모의평가 고3

• 정답 •

01③ 02⑤ 03③ 04④ 05④ 06③ 07② 08⑤ 09② 10② 11⑤ 12② 13② 14① 15③ 16① 17④

01 꽃 배송 서비스

정답률 93% | 정답 ③

다음을 듣고, 여자가 하는 말의 목적으로 가장 적절한 것을 고르시오.

① 계절별 꽃의 종류를 소개하려고
② 꽃꽂이 동호회 가입을 독려하려고
③ 정기적인 꽃 배송 서비스를 홍보하려고
④ 꽃을 신선하게 관리하는 법을 알리려고
⑤ 전문적으로 꽃을 가꾸는 사람을 모집하려고

W : Hello, viewers!
안녕하세요, 시청자 여러분!
Are you too busy to visit a flower shop but want to experience the happiness that comes from flowers?
너무 바빠서 꽃 가게를 방문하기는 어렵지만 꽃이 주는 행복을 경험하고 싶으신가요?
Happy Florette can save you time and energy while you enjoy the benefits of fresh flowers.
Happy Florette를 이용하면 시간과 에너지를 절약하면서 신선한 꽃의 혜택을 즐길 수 있습니다.
You can have them delivered weekly, every other week, or monthly at a reasonable price.
여러분은 매주, 격주 또는 매월 합리적인 가격으로 꽃을 배송 받을 수 있습니다.
The beautiful seasonal flowers are selected by our professional florists, and they are regularly delivered with advice to keep them fresh longer.
아름다운 제철 꽃이 전문 플로리스트에 의해 선별되며, 꽃을 더 오래 신선하게 유지할 수 있는 조언과 함께 정기적으로 배송됩니다.
Plus, for new customers, we send a special vase as a gift.
게다가, 신규 고객에게는 특별한 꽃병을 선물로 보내드립니다.
Don't miss out on our regular flower delivery service, and bring the beauty of the season into your house.
정기적인 꽃 배송 서비스를 놓치지 마시고, 계절의 아름다움을 여러분의 집 안으로 가져가세요.

Why? 왜 정답일까?

정기적인 꽃 배송 서비스를 놓치지 말라고 이야기하고 있으므로(**Don't miss out on our regular flower delivery service, and bring the beauty of the season into your house.**), 여자가 하는 말의 목적으로 가장 적절한 것은 ③ '정기적인 꽃 배송 서비스를 홍보하려고'이다.

- experience ⓝ 경험
- benefit ⓝ 혜택
- reasonable ⓐ 합리적인
- seasonal ⓐ 제철의
- regularly ad 정기적으로
- vase ⓝ 꽃병

02 소셜 미디어의 장점

정답률 92% | 정답 ⑤

대화를 듣고, 남자의 의견으로 가장 적절한 것을 고르시오.

① 자녀의 인터넷 사용 시간을 제한해야 한다.
② 소셜 미디어는 자녀의 학업에 도움이 된다.
③ 소셜 미디어를 통한 영화 홍보는 효과적이다.
④ 온라인에서 사생활을 공유하는 것은 위험하다.
⑤ 소셜 미디어를 통해 자녀를 더 잘 이해할 수 있다.

M : Honey, you look worried.
여보, 걱정이 있어 보여요.
W : Yeah. I don't know what's happening in our son Dave's life since we don't talk much these days.
맞아요. 요즘 대화를 많이 안 해서, 우리 아들 Dave의 생활에 무슨 일이 일어나고 있는지 모르겠어요.
M : I felt the same way. But using social media helps me understand him better.
나도 똑같이 느꼈어요. 하지만 소셜 미디어를 사용하는 것이 내가 그를 더 잘 이해하는 데 도움이 되고 있어요.
W : What do you mean?
무슨 뜻이에요?
M : I follow him on his favorite social media service, and it allows me to know him more deeply.
그가 가장 좋아하는 소셜 미디어 서비스를 팔로우하고 있는데, 이를 통해 그를 더 깊게 알게 돼요.
W : Honestly, I'm not a fan of social media.
솔직히, 저는 소셜 미디어를 별로 좋아하지 않아요.
M : I know. *[Tapping sound]* But look at this. Dave often posts his thoughts and feelings on it.
알아요. *[타자 치는 소리]* 하지만 이걸 봐요. Dave는 자주 자신의 생각과 감정을 거기에 올려요.
W : Wow, he posts so many things about himself.
와, 그는 자신에 대해 정말 많은 것을 올리네요.
M : Yes. You can see what music and movies he's interested in. I think if parents use social media like me, they will understand their children better.
네. 당신은 그가 어떤 음악과 어떤 영화에 관심이 있는지 알 수 있어요. 부모가 나처럼 소셜 미디어를 사용하면, 자녀를 더 잘 이해할 것이라고 생각해요.
W : Hmm. I guess I should start using it.
흠. 나도 그것을 사용하기 시작해야겠어요.

Why? 왜 정답일까?

소셜 미디어는 이용자가 자신에 대해 많은 것을 올리기 때문에 이를 통해서 자녀를 더 잘 이해할 수 있다고 이야기하고 있으므로(**I think if parents use social media like me, they will understand their children better.**), 남자의 의견으로 가장 적절한 것은 ⑤ '소셜 미디어를 통해 자녀를 더 잘 이해할 수 있다.'이다.

[문제편 p.061]

- allow ⓥ 허락하다
- be a fan of ~를 좋아하다
- thought ⓝ 생각
- deeply ad 깊게
- post ⓥ 올리다

03 동료 피드백의 효과 정답률 91% | 정답 ③

다음을 듣고, 여자가 하는 말의 요지로 가장 적절한 것을 고르시오.

① 적성에 맞는 업무를 맡으면 직장에 대한 만족도가 높아진다.
② 세미나에 참여하는 것은 팀워크 향상에 효과가 있다.
③ 동료의 피드백은 업무 능력 향상에 도움이 된다.
④ 동료와의 과도한 경쟁은 업무 효율성을 떨어뜨린다.
⑤ 프로젝트를 잘 수행하기 위해서는 사전 계획이 필수적이다.

W : Good morning, everyone.
안녕하세요, 여러분.
I'm Sharon Parker from the Lenyard Consulting Company.
저는 Lenyard 컨설팅 회사의 Sharon Parker입니다.
I'm honored to be here for the employee training seminar.
직원 교육 세미나를 위해 이 자리에 오게 되어 영광입니다.
I've heard many of you are struggling to get your projects done well.
저는 여러분 중 많은 분이 프로젝트를 잘 완수하기 위해 애쓰고 있다고 들었습니다.
However, there's one simple and effective way to improve your work performance.
하지만, 여러분의 업무 성과를 향상할 한 가지 간단하고 효과적인 방법이 있습니다.
Ask your co-workers to give you feedback on your work.
여러분의 동료에게 업무에 대한 피드백을 요청하세요.
They may have fresh perspectives and be able to find creative solutions that you haven't thought of.
그들은 새로운 관점을 가지고 여러분이 생각하지 못했던 창의적인 해결책을 찾아 줄 수도 있을 것입니다.
Furthermore, this feedback helps identify your strong and weak points at work.
그뿐만 아니라, 이러한 피드백은 업무에서 여러분의 강점과 약점을 파악하는 데 도움이 됩니다.
So, you should seek your colleagues' feedback, which will help you to perform better in the workplace.
따라서, 여러분은 동료의 피드백을 구해야 하며, 이는 여러분이 직장에서 더 나은 성과를 내는 데 도움을 줄 것입니다.
Give it a try and see the difference.
한번 시도해 보고 차이를 확인하세요.

Why? 왜 정답일까?

동료의 새로운 관점을 통해 창의적인 해결책을 찾거나 강점 및 약점을 파악할 수 있어 나은 성과를 낼 수 있다고 이야기 하므로(**So, you should seek your colleagues' feedback, which will help you to perform better in the workplace.**), 여자가 하는 말의 요지로 가장 적절한 것은 ③ '동료의 피드백은 업무 능력 향상에 도움이 된다.'이다.

- employee ⓝ 직원
- effective ⓐ 효과적인
- performance ⓝ 성과
- identify ⓥ 확인하다
- colleague ⓝ 동료
- struggle ⓥ 애쓰다
- improve ⓥ 향상하다
- perspective ⓝ 관점
- seek ⓥ 구하다

04 옥상 살펴보기 정답률 95% | 정답 ④

대화를 듣고, 그림에서 대화의 내용과 일치하지 않는 것을 고르시오.

M : Hey, Rachel. How was your weekend?
안녕하세요, Rachel. 주말은 어떻게 보내셨어요?
W : Hi, Liam. I had fun with my kids on my rooftop. Here's a picture.
안녕하세요, Liam. 옥상에서 제 아이들과 즐겁게 보냈어요. 여기 사진이 있답니다.
M : It looks nice. *[Pause]* 『Wow. I like the round pool.』 ①의 근거 일치
멋지네요. *[일시정지]* 와, 전 둥근 풀장이 마음에 드네요.
W : Yeah. It's perfect for my kids to play in. 『Do you see this stripe-patterned chair?』 ②의 근거 일치
네, 제 아이들이 안에서 놀기에 맞춤이죠. 이 줄무늬 의자 보이나요?
M : Yes. I love it. You can sit in the chair and watch your kids.
네, 마음에 들어요. 의자에 앉아서 아이들을 보실 수 있겠군요.
W : You're right. 『I just noticed my dog is under the table.』 Isn't she cute? ③의 근거 일치
맞아요. 강아지가 테이블 밑에 있는 걸 지금 봤네요. 귀엽지 않아요?
M : Oh, she's so lovely. 『I also see there are three beach balls on the bench.』 Your kids must love playing with them. ④의 근거 불일치
아, 정말 사랑스럽네요. 벤치에 비치볼이 세 개 있는 것도 보이네요. 아이들이 그걸 가지고 노는 걸 틀림없이 좋아하겠어요.
W : Yes, they do. They're gifts from their grandmother.
네, 그렇죠. 그건 애들 할머니가 주신 선물이에요. ⑤의 근거 일치
M : 『Look at the "NO RUNNING" sign on the wall.』 Does it make your kids more careful?
벽에 붙은 '뛰지 마세요'라는 표시 좀 봐요. 그걸 보면 아이들은 더 조심하게 되나요?
W : Yes, it does. I'm glad I put it up there. Why don't you bring your kids next weekend?
네, 그럼요. 저기에 그걸 게시하길 잘했어요. 다음 주말에 댁의 아이들을 데리고 오시면 어떨까요?
M : Sounds great!
좋아요!

Why? 왜 정답일까?

대화에서 벤치 위에 놓인 비치볼이 세 개 있다고 했는데(**I also see there are three beach balls on the bench.**), 그림 속에는 두 개가 있다. 따라서 그림에서 대화의 내용과 일치하지 않는 것은 ④이다.

- rooftop ⓝ 옥상
- careful ⓐ 조심하는
- stripe-patterned 줄무늬의
- put up ~를 게시하다

05 워크숍 준비 정답률 93% | 정답 ④

대화를 듣고, 남자가 할 일로 가장 적절한 것을 고르시오.

① 회의실 예약하기
② 참가 인원 확인하기
③ 유인물 복사하기
④ 음료 주문하기
⑤ 점심 메뉴 정하기

W : Steve, we've been working on the Greener Path Workshop for a few weeks. It's just around the corner.
Steve, 우리는 몇 주 동안 '더 친환경적인 길을 위한 워크숍'을 준비해 왔어요. 이제 얼마 남지 않았어요.
M : Right. I really want to make this workshop successful. We should go over the preparations.
맞아요. 전 이번 워크숍을 정말 성공적으로 이끌고 싶어요. 우리 준비 사항을 점검해 봐야겠어요.
W : Sure. Let's start with the conference room. I've got the confirmation that the room is for 100 people. Is that okay?
네, 회의실부터 시작하죠. 회의실이 100명을 수용할 수 있다는 확인을 받았어요. 괜찮을까요?
M : Of course. Around 80 people are expected to come, so it'll be large enough. How about the presentation handouts?
물론이죠. 80명 정도 오실 것으로 예상되니, 그 정도면 충분히 클 거예요. 발표용 유인물은 어때요?
W : I got them from Mr. Lee and made copies of them.
제가 Mr. Lee에게 받아서 복사해 놓았어요.
M : Great. I'm sure that they'll be helpful for the audience. Also, I've confirmed that lunch will be served right after the presentation.
좋아요. 틀림없이 청중들에게 도움이 될 거예요. 또 저는 발표 직후에 점심 식사가 제공되도록 확인해 두었어요.
W : Good. One last thing. Did you order drinks?
좋아요. 마지막으로 한 가지 더요. 음료는 주문하셨나요?
M : Not yet. Thanks for reminding me. I'll take care of it.
아직 안 했어요. 상기시켜 줘서 고마워요. 제가 그것을 맡아서 할게요.
W : Perfect! It seems like everything will be ready in time.
완벽해요! 모든 것이 제시간에 준비될 것 같네요.

Why? 왜 정답일까?

두 사람은 성공적인 워크숍을 위해 준비 사항을 점검하고 있는데 남자가 아직 음료를 주문하지 않아 자기가 맡아서 하겠다고(**Not yet. Thanks for reminding me. I'll take care of it.**) 말한다. 따라서 남자가 할 일로 가장 적절한 것은 ④ '음료 주문하기'이다.

- preparation ⓝ 준비
- confirmation ⓝ 확인
- remind ⓥ 상기시키다
- go over ~를 점검하다
- audience ⓝ 청중
- in time 제 시간에

06 촬영 현장 견학 정답률 91% | 정답 ③

대화를 듣고, 여자가 지불할 금액을 고르시오.

① $54 ② $60 ③ $72 ④ $80 ⑤ $90

M : Welcome to the filming site of *Secrets in Paris*. How may I help you?
Secrets in Paris 촬영 현장에 오신 것을 환영합니다. 무엇을 도와드릴까요?
W : Hi, I'd like to buy admission tickets.
안녕하세요, 입장권을 구매하고 싶습니다.
M : Certainly, admission tickets are $20 per adult and $10 per child.
네, 입장권은 성인 20달러, 어린이 10달러입니다.
W : I need two adult tickets and one child ticket.
성인 티켓 두 장과 어린이 티켓 한 장이 필요합니다.
M : All right. Do you want the family photo service?
알겠습니다. 가족사진 서비스를 원하시나요?
W : I'm not sure. What is it?
잘 모르겠어요. 그게 뭔가요?
M : We take family photos at each special filming location and provide you with a book of the photos.
각 특별 촬영 장소에서 가족사진을 찍어드리고 사진첩을 만들어 드립니다.
W : How interesting! How much is it?
아주 흥미롭네요! 얼마인가요?
M : It's $30.
30달러입니다.
W : Then, we'll get that as well.
그럼, 그것도 할게요.
M : Okay. So that's tickets for two adults and one child along with the family photo service, right?
좋습니다. 그럼 성인 두 명과 어린이 한 명의 티켓에 가족사진 서비스를 추가하시는 거죠?
W : Yes. Are there any discounts available?
네, 할인 혜택이 있나요?
M : Sure. You'll get a 10% discount off the total because today is a weekday.
물론이죠. 오늘은 평일이기 때문에 총액에서 10% 할인을 받으실 수 있습니다.
W : Great. Here is my credit card.
좋아요. 여기 제 신용 카드입니다.

Why? 왜 정답일까?

대화에 따르면 여자는 성인 티켓(**$20**) 두 장과 어린이 티켓(**$10**)을 구매하고, 가족 사진 서비스(**$30**)를 받기로 했다. 이어 **10%** 할인이 가능하다고 했으므로, 여자가 총 지불할 금액은 ③ '**$72**'이다.

- admission ⓝ 입장
- credit card 신용 카드
- weekday 평일

07 Prime Travel Writing Contest 불참 이유 정답률 96% | 정답 ②

대화를 듣고, 남자가 Prime Travel Writing Contest에 참가할 수 없는 이유를 고르시오.

① 여행이 계획되어 있어서
② 결혼식에 참석해야 해서

③ 글쓰기 수업을 들어야 해서
④ 다른 대회에 참가해야 해서
⑤ 대회를 준비할 시간이 없어서

[Cell phone rings.]
[휴대 전화가 울린다.]

W : Hello, Brian.
안녕, Brian.

M : Hello, Kate. What's up?
안녕, Kate. 무슨 일이야?

W : I heard about the Prime Travel Writing Contest, and I thought you might be interested.
Prime 여행 글쓰기 대회에 대해 들었는데, 네가 관심이 있을 거라고 생각했어.

M : Oh, I know about it. But I can't participate.
아, 나도 그것에 대해 알아. 하지만 나는 참가할 수 없어.

W : Really? You love writing. Are you planning to attend a different contest?
정말? 글 쓰는 거 좋아하잖아. 다른 대회에 참가할 계획이니?

M : Not at all. There aren't any other contests at that time.
전혀 아니야. 그때는 다른 어떤 대회도 없어.

W : Why not then? You have almost one month to prepare because the contest will be on July 13th.
그럼 왜 하지 않니? 대회가 7월 13일에 있기 때문에 거의 한 달이나 준비할 시간이 있잖아.

M : Well, I don't have a problem preparing by then.
음, 그때까지 준비하는 데는 문제가 없어.

W : That's good. Hmm. Is it because you have vacation plans?
그거 잘됐네. 음, 휴가 계획이 있어서 그런 거니?

M : No, I'm not traveling.
아니, 여행은 안 가.

W : Then, why can't you participate?
그럼, 왜 참가할 수 없니?

M : The simple truth is that I'm attending my sister's wedding that day.
간단한 사실은 내가 그날 여동생의 결혼식에 참석한다는 거야.

W : Oh, now I understand. Tell her congratulations for me.
아, 이제 알겠어. 그녀에게 축하한다고 전해 줘.

M : Of course, I'll let her know.
물론이지, 그녀에게 전할게.

Why? 왜 정답일까?

여자가 글쓰기를 좋아하지만 대회에 참석 할 수 없는 이유는 대회가 있는 날에 여동생의 결혼식에 참석해야 하기(**The simple truth is that I'm attending my sister's wedding that day.**) 때문이다. 따라서 답은 ② '결혼식에 참석해야 해서'이다.

- participate ⓥ 참석하다
- attend ⓥ 참가하다
- vacation ⓝ 휴가

08 Starry Family Reading Night 행사

정답률 97% | 정답 ⑤

대화를 듣고, Starry Family Reading Night 행사에 관해 언급되지 않은 것을 고르시오.

① 주제 ② 시작 시간 ③ 장소
④ 신청 방법 ⑤ 참가비 (✔)

M : Honey, Tony's school is going to have the Starry Family Reading Night.
여보, Tony 학교에서 '별이 빛나는 가족 독서의 밤'이 열린대요.

W : Oh, isn't it the event where we read and share about books?
아, 책을 읽고 책에 관해 (생각을) 나누는 행사 아닌가요?

M : Yes. 「The theme of this year's event is "Female Adventurers."」 ①의 근거 일치
맞아요. 올해 행사의 주제는 '여성 모험가'예요.

W : That sounds interesting. When is the event?
흥미롭네요. 행사는 언제인가요?

M : It'll be held next Friday night.
다음 주 금요일 밤에 열릴 거예요.

W : I see. I have an important meeting that afternoon. What time will it start?
그렇군요. 나는 그날 오후에 중요한 회의가 있어요. 그 행사는 몇 시에 시작하나요?

M : 「It starts at 8 p.m. Can you make it?」 ②의 근거 일치
저녁 8시에 시작해요. 시간에 맞춰 올 수 있겠어요?

W : Yes, I'm sure I can. Do you know where it will be? I heard the school library is being remodeled.
네, 분명히 갈 수 있을 거예요. 어디에서 열리는지 알아요? 학교 도서관이 리모델링 중이라고 들었어요.

M : Actually, it was finished last week. 「So the reading night is going to be in the library.」 ③의 근거 일치
사실, 그것(도서관 리모델링)은 지난주에 끝났어요. 그래서 독서의 밤은 도서관에서 열릴 거예요.

W : Oh, I didn't know that. How can we sign up?
아, 그걸 몰랐네요. 어떻게 신청할 수 있죠?

M : 「We can sign up on the school's website.」 I'll do it tomorrow. ④의 근거 일치
학교 웹사이트에서 신청할 수 있어요. 내가 내일 할게요.

W : Terrific! It's going to be a great night.
정말 좋네요! 멋진 밤이 될 거예요.

Why? 왜 정답일까?

대화에서 남자와 여자는 행사에 관해 주제, 시작 시간, 장소, 신청 방법을 언급하므로, 언급되지 않은 것은 ⑤ '참가비'이다.

- theme ⓝ 주제
- library ⓝ 도서관
- sign up 신청하다

09 Wondrous Tastes 행사 안내

정답률 88% | 정답 ②

Wondrous Tastes 행사에 관한 다음 내용을 듣고, 일치하지 않는 것을 고르시오.

① 3일 동안 진행된다.
② 한 개의 매장에서만 열린다. (✔)
③ 새로운 다섯 종류 도넛의 샘플이 제공된다.
④ 모든 방문객은 무료로 커피를 받는다.
⑤ 도넛 한 상자를 구매한 사람들은 할인 쿠폰을 받는다.

M : Hello, listeners.
안녕하세요, 청취자 여러분.
This is John Brady from Creamery Doughnut.
저는 Creamery Doughnut의 John Brady입니다.
I'm pleased to introduce the event, Wondrous Tastes, where you can taste our new doughnuts.
새로운 도넛을 맛볼 수 있는 '경이로운 맛'이라는 행사를 소개해 드리게 되어 기쁩니다.
「This event will be held for three days from June 21st to 23rd.」 ①의 근거 일치
이 행사는 6월 21일부터 23일까지 3일간 열릴 것입니다.
So make sure to mark your calendar. 「Wondrous Tastes will take place at all of our stores.」 ②의 근거 불일치
그러니 달력에 꼭 표시해 두세요. '경이로운 맛' 행사는 저희 모든 매장에서 열릴 것입니다.
You can find the closest store to you on our website.
여러분에게 가장 가까운 매장을 저희 웹사이트에서 찾을 수 있습니다.
「At the event, samples of five new kinds of doughnuts will be provided.」 ③의 근거 일치
행사에서는 다섯 종류의 새로운 도넛 샘플이 제공될 것입니다.
These doughnuts have special flavored creams and toppings.
이 도넛들은 특별한 맛의 크림과 토핑이 들어 있습니다.
「Also, all visitors to the event will receive a free coffee.」 ④의 근거 일치
또한, 행사에 오시는 모든 방문객에게는 무료 커피가 제공됩니다.
And you know, that's not the end of it.
그리고 그게 그것(행사)의 끝이 아닙니다.
「Those who buy a box of doughnuts will get a discount coupon.」 ⑤의 근거 일치
도넛 한 상자를 구매하시는 분들께는 할인 쿠폰이 제공됩니다.
Come and enjoy the wonderful tastes of our new doughnuts.
오셔서 저희 새 도넛의 훌륭한 맛을 즐겨 보세요.

Why? 왜 정답일까?

'경이로운 맛' 행사는 모든 매장에서 열릴 것이라고 이야기하고 있으므로, 내용과 일치하지 않는 것은 ② '한 개의 매장에서만 열린다.'이다.

- wondrous ⓐ 경이로운
- taste ⓥ 맛보다
- mark ⓥ 표시하다
- take place 열리다
- flavored 맛이 나는

10 연필꽂이 구매하기

정답률 89% | 정답 ②

다음 표를 보면서 대화를 듣고, 여자가 주문할 연필꽂이를 고르시오.

Pencil Holders

	Model	Price	Material	Shape	Phone Stand
①	A	$10	plastic	elephant	×
② (✔)	B	$10	metal	bear	○
③	C	$15	metal	elephant	○
④	D	$20	wood	bear	×
⑤	E	$25	wood	bear	○

W : Hi, Ben. Could you help me buy a pencil holder for my nephew?
안녕, Ben. 내 조카에게 줄 연필꽂이 구입을 도와줄 수 있니?

M : Sure, Jessie. Have you already found some online?
물론이지, Jessie. 온라인에서 벌써 몇 개 찾아봤어?

W : Yes, and I narrowed them down to these five models.
응, 그리고 그것들을 이 다섯 가지 모델로 범위를 좁혔어.

M : Let me see. 「I think a 25-dollar pencil holder is too expensive.」 근거1 Price 조건
어디 보자. 25달러짜리 연필꽂이는 너무 비싼 것 같아.

W : You're right. Hmm, they come in several materials. Which one would be good?
네 말이 맞아. 흠, 그것들이 여러 가지 재질로 되어 있네. 어떤 것이 좋을까?

M : 「I don't recommend plastic.」 근거2 Material 조건
플라스틱은 추천하지 않아.
Since it's light, it's too easily knocked over.
그건 가벼워서, 너무 쉽게 넘어지거든.

W : That's true. 「You know, the bear ones look cuter than the elephant ones. Plus, bears are my nephew's favorite.」 근거3 Shape 조건
맞아. 알다시피, 코끼리 모양 연필꽂이보다 곰 모양 연필꽂이가 더 귀엽게 보이잖아. 게다가 내 조카가 곰을 제일 좋아하거든.

M : Well, you have two options left. 「Do you think your nephew needs one with a phone stand?」 근거4 Phone Stand 조건
그럼, 두 가지 선택 사항이 남았어. 조카에게 휴대 전화 거치대가 있는 연필꽂이가 필요하다고 생각해?

W : Of course. It'll be convenient for him.
물론, 조카에게 편리할 거야.

M : Then you should go with this one.
그럼 이걸로 사야 할 거야.

W : Thanks for helping me. I'll order it now.
도와줘서 고마워. 지금 이걸로 주문할게.

Why? 왜 정답일까?

대화에 따르면 남자와 여자는 **25**달러 미만의, 플라스틱이 아니며, 곰 모양에 거치대가 있는 연필꽂이를 구매하고자 한다. 여자가 주문할 연필꽂이는 ② '**B**'이다.

- pencil holder 연필꽂이
- nephew ⓝ 조카
- narrow ⓥ 좁히다
- recommend ⓥ 추천하다
- light ⓐ 가벼운
- knock over 넘어지다
- convenient ⓐ 편리한

11 리조트 일정 변경 여부

정답률 63% | 정답 ⑤

대화를 듣고, 남자의 마지막 말에 대한 여자의 응답으로 가장 적절한 것을 고르시오. [3점]

① I agree. Let's look for another resort.
동의해요. 다른 리조트를 찾아봐요.
② How disappointing! The rooms are fully booked.
실망스럽네요! 방이 꽉 찼어요.
③ Congratulations! You did a good job at the conference.
축하해요! 회의에서 잘하셨어요.
④ That's okay. I'm sure we can reschedule the conference.
괜찮아요. 우리는 회의 일정을 다시 잡을 수 있다고 확신해요.

[문제편 p.061]

✔ What a relief! Now I don't need to change the reservation.
정말 다행이네요! 이제 예약을 변경할 필요가 없겠네요.

M : Honey, what are you doing?
여보, 뭐 하고 있어요?

W : I'm about to change the date for our booking at the resort. You told me you need to attend a conference on that day, right?
우리 리조트 예약 날짜를 변경하려고요. 그날 회의에 참석해야 한다고 했죠?

M : Oh, I forgot to tell you. The conference has been canceled, so I'll be completely free then.
아, 당신에게 말한다는 걸 깜빡했네요. 회의가 취소되어서 그때 나는 완전히 자유예요.

W : What a relief! Now I don't need to change the reservation.
정말 다행이네요! 이제 예약을 변경할 필요가 없겠네요.

Why? 왜 정답일까?

여자가 남자의 회의 때문에 리조트 일정을 변경하려고 했는데 회의가 취소된 상황이다(**The conference has been canceled, so I'll be completely free then.**). 따라서 여자의 응답으로 가장 적절한 것은 ⑤ '정말 다행이네요! 이제 예약을 변경할 필요가 없겠네요.'이다.

- **booking** ⓝ 예약
- **completely** ad 완전히
- **reservation** ⓝ 예약
- **conference** ⓝ 회의
- **relief** ⓐ 안도하는

12 콘서트 참석을 위한 교통수단 선택

정답률 87% | 정답 ②

대화를 듣고, 여자의 마지막 말에 대한 남자의 응답으로 가장 적절한 것을 고르시오.

① I'm sorry. You're on the wrong train.
죄송해요. 열차를 잘못 탔어요.
✔ Good point. I'll check the train schedule.
좋아요. 열차 시간표를 확인해 볼게요.
③ Don't worry. The concert lasts less than one hour.
걱정하지 마세요. 콘서트가 한 시간도 안 남았으니까요.
④ Hurry up! You'd better take a taxi rather than a train.
서둘러요! 열차보다는 택시를 타는 게 좋을 거예요.
⑤ No problem. I'm glad to give you a ride to the concert.
괜찮아요. 기꺼이 콘서트까지 태워다 드릴게요.

W : Hello, Andy. Do you have plans tonight?
안녕하세요, Andy. 오늘 밤에 계획이 있나요?

M : Hi, Lisa. I'm going to a jazz concert in Midtown City. How long does it take to get there by car? I need to be there by 7.
안녕하세요, Lisa. Midtown City에서 열리는 재즈 콘서트에 가려고요. 그곳까지 차로 가는 데 얼마나 걸리나요? 7시까지 그곳에 도착해야 해요.

W : Usually, one hour. But today's Friday, so the traffic will be horrible. Why don't you find a train that works for you?
보통, 한 시간 정도요. 하지만 오늘은 금요일이라 교통이 끔찍할 거예요. 당신에게 맞는 열차를 찾아보는 건 어때요?

M : Good point. I'll check the train schedule.
좋아요. 열차 시간표를 확인해 볼게요.

Why? 왜 정답일까?

여자는 남자에게 금요일이니 차가 막힐 수 있다고 말하며 다른 교통수단을 찾아볼 것을 제안하고 있다(**But today's Friday, so the traffic will be horrible. Why don't you find a train that works for you?**). 따라서 남자의 응답으로 가장 적절한 것은 ② '좋아요. 열차 시간표를 확인해 볼게요.'이다.

- **be going to** ~할 예정이다
- **horrible** ⓐ 끔찍한
- **usually** ad 보통

13 수학자 초청하기

정답률 79% | 정답 ②

대화를 듣고, 남자의 마지막 말에 대한 여자의 응답으로 가장 적절한 것을 고르시오.

Woman : ______

① Why not? You can take my math class.
물론이죠. 당신은 제 수학 수업을 들어도 됩니다.
✔ I hope so. I'll send him an email right away.
그러기를 바라요. 제가 그에게 바로 이메일을 보낼게요.
③ Probably not. He should've checked his message.
아마 아닐 거예요. 그는 메시지를 확인했어야 했어요.
④ Certainly. Thanks for choosing me to be your guest.
물론이죠. 저를 손님으로 선택해 주셔서 감사합니다.
⑤ That's right. We've already invited a mathematician.
맞아요. 우리는 이미 수학자를 한 명 초대했어요.

[Cell phone rings.]
[휴대 전화가 울린다.]

M : Hello, Ms. Miller. Did you see the message I sent this morning?
안녕하세요, Miller 씨. 오늘 아침에 제가 보낸 메시지 보셨나요?

W : Hi, Mr. Peterson. No, I didn't. I was busy all morning. What's it about?
안녕하세요, Peterson 씨. 아뇨, 보지 못했어요. 아침 내내 바빴거든요. 무슨 내용인가요?

M : It's about our math club activity on the last Friday of next month. I was thinking we could invite a mathematician as our special guest.
다음 달 마지막 금요일에 있을 우리 수학 동아리 활동에 관한 거예요. 저는 수학자 한 분을 특별 손님으로 초대할 수 있을지 생각 중이었어요.

W : Oh, I see. Can you tell me more?
오, 그렇군요. 좀 더 말씀해 주시겠어요?

M : Students would hear about a mathematician's life and work experiences. I think it would further inspire those who are interested in mathematics.
학생들은 수학자의 삶과 연구 경험에 대해 듣게 될 거예요. 수학에 관심이 있는 사람들에게 더 많은 영감을 줄 수 있을 것으로 생각해요.

W : Hmm, that makes sense. Actually, there are several students who want to be mathematicians in the future. So, let's do it.
흠, 일리가 있네요. 실은, 장래에 수학자가 되고 싶어 하는 학생들이 몇 명 있어요. 그럼, 해보죠.

M : Okay, but I can't think of any mathematicians to invite.
네, 하지만 초대할 수학자가 떠오르지 않아요.

W : I know someone I can contact. I met him at the math workshop I attended.
제가 연락할 만한 사람을 알고 있어요. 제가 참석했던 수학 워크숍에서 그를 만났어요.

M : Really? I wonder if he's available on that day.
정말요? 그날 그분이 시간이 있는지 궁금하네요.

W : I hope so. I'll send him an email right away.
그러기를 바라요. 제가 그에게 바로 이메일을 보낼게요.

Why? 왜 정답일까?

남자는 학생들을 위해 수학 동아리에 수학자를 초청하고 싶은데(**It's about our math club activity on the last Friday of next month. I was thinking we could invite a mathematician as our special guest.**) 마땅한 사람이 없어서 고민 중이었다. 이에 여자가 워크숍에서 만난 수학자를 초청하고자 한다. 따라서 여자의 응답으로 가장 적절한 것은 ② '그러기를 바라요. 제가 그에게 바로 이메일을 보낼게요.'이다.

- **mathematician** ⓝ 수학자
- **inspire** ⓥ 영감을 주다
- **make sense** 일리가 있다
- **contact** ⓥ 연락하다
- **further** ad 더
- **interested in** ~에 관심이 있다
- **invite** ⓥ 초대하다
- **wonder** ⓥ 궁금하다

14 안약 구매하기

정답률 86% | 정답 ①

대화를 듣고, 여자의 마지막 말에 대한 남자의 응답으로 가장 적절한 것을 고르시오. [3점]

Man : ______

✔ I see. Then I'll come back with it later.
알겠습니다. 그러면 나중에 그걸 가지고 다시 올게요.
② Oh, no. I can't find a pharmacy nearby.
오, 이런. 근처에 약국을 못 찾겠어요.
③ That's terrible. I hope you get well soon.
저런. 당신이 빨리 낫기를 바라요.
④ Of course. Relaxing is good for your eyes.
물론이죠. 쉬는 게 눈에 좋아요.
⑤ I'm not sure. You'd better try another medicine.
잘 모르겠어요. 당신은 다른 약을 시도해 보는 게 좋겠어요.

W : Good afternoon. May I help you?
안녕하세요. 도와드릴까요?

M : Yes. I'm looking for eye drops.
네. 안약을 찾고 있는데요.

W : We have various kinds. Do you have something in mind?
다양한 종류가 있습니다. 생각하고 계신 게 있나요?

M : Not really. What would you recommend?
그렇지는 않아요. 어떤 것을 추천해 주시겠어요?

W : It depends on your symptoms.
증상에 따라 다릅니다.

M : My eyes are dry and red.
제 눈이 건조하고 충혈됐어요.

W : Hmm. How long have you had those symptoms?
흠. 그런 증상이 나타난 지 얼마나 되었나요?

M : I've had them for around one week.
일주일 정도 됐어요.

W : Have you used these eye drops to relieve your symptoms?
증상 완화를 위해 이 안약을 사용해 보신 적이 있나요?

M : Yes, I'm using those eye drops now. They help but the problem isn't going away.
네, 지금 그 안약을 사용하고 있어요. 도움이 되긴 하지만 문제가 사라지지는 않아요.

W : In that case, people usually take stronger eye drops.
그런 경우 사람들은 보통 더 강한 안약을 사용해요.

M : Can I get those? I really want to get better as soon as possible.
그걸 살 수 있을까요? 가능한 한 정말 빨리 낫고 싶어요.

W : I'm sorry. But to get the stronger eye drops, you need a prescription from a doctor.
죄송합니다. 하지만 더 강한 안약을 받으시려면 의사의 처방전이 필요해요.

M : I see. Then I'll come back with it later.
알겠습니다. 그러면 나중에 그걸 가지고 다시 올게요.

Why? 왜 정답일까?

안약을 구매하려던 남자는 원래 사용하던 것 보다 더 강한 안약을 원하고 있다. 이에 여자는 의사의 처방전이 필요하다고 말한다. 이에 대한 남자의 응답으로 가장 적절한 것은 ① '알겠습니다. 그러면 나중에 그걸 가지고 다시 올게요.'이다.

- **eye drops** 안약
- **dry** ⓐ 건조한
- **relieve** ⓥ 완화하다
- **various** ⓐ 다양한
- **symptom** ⓝ 증상
- **prescription** ⓝ 처방전

15 Jason의 새 차

정답률 88% | 정답 ③

다음 상황 설명을 듣고, Jason이 Kathy에게 할 말로 가장 적절한 것을 고르시오. [3점]

Jason : ______

① Thanks for buying me a new pair of pants.
내게 새 바지를 사줘서 고마워.
② You need to wash your car as quickly as possible.
너는 가능한 한 빨리 세차해야 해.
✔ Get the dust off your clothes before getting in the car.
차에 타기 전에 네 옷의 먼지를 털어 내렴.
④ Can you first take off your jacket when we get home?
우리가 집에 도착하면 먼저 재킷을 벗을 수 있어?
⑤ Don't forget to put on warm clothes before you go hiking.
하이킹하러 가기 전에 따뜻한 옷 입는 것을 잊지 마.

W : Jason has a new car and tries to keep it from getting dirty.
Jason은 새 차가 있고, 이를 더럽히지 않으려고 애씁니다.
On one weekend, Jason and his daughter Kathy take a camping trip together.
어느 주말, Jason과 그의 딸 Kathy는 함께 캠핑 여행을 갑니다.
During the trip, they go fishing, hiking and rock climbing.
여행 중에 그들은 낚시, 하이킹, 그리고 암벽 등반을 합니다.
Due to the intense activities, their jackets and pants become covered with dust.
격렬한 활동으로 인해 재킷과 바지가 먼지로 뒤덮입니다.
Now it's time to go home.
이제 집에 갈 시간입니다.
Jason shakes the dust off from his clothes before he gets into the car because he wants to keep his car clean.
Jason은 차를 깨끗하게 유지하기를 원하기에 차에 타기 전에 자기 옷의 먼지를 털어 냅니다.
However, Kathy isn't concerned about the dust on her jacket and pants.
하지만, Kathy는 자신의 재킷과 바지에 묻은 먼지에 대해 신경 쓰지 않습니다.

[문제편 p.062]

So Jason wants to tell her to remove the dust from her clothes before she sits in the car.
그래서 Jason은 그녀가 차내에 앉기 전에 그녀의 옷에서 먼지를 제거하라고 말하고 싶습니다.
In this situation, what would Jason most likely say to Kathy?
이 상황에서 Jason은 Kathy에게 뭐라고 말하겠습니까?

Jason : Get the dust off your clothes before you go hiking.
차에 타기 전에 네 옷의 먼지를 털어 내렴.

Why? 왜 정답일까?

상황에 따르면 Jason은 새로운 차를 깨끗하게 쓰고 싶어 한다. 이에 야외 활동을 하느라 더러워진 옷을 털고 차에 타고 싶어 하는데 Kathy는 먼지에 대해 신경 쓰고 있지 않다. Jason이 차에 먼지를 털고 탈 것을 제안하고자 하므로(**So Jason wants to tell her to remove the dust from her clothes before she sits in the car.**), Jason이 Kathy에게 할 말로 가장 적절한 것은 ③ '차에 타기 전에 네 옷의 먼지를 털어 내렴.'이다.

- intense ⓐ 격렬한
- be concerned about ~에 신경 쓰다

16-17 사진의 실용적 활용

M : Hello, students.
안녕하세요, 학생 여러분.
Do you know how widespread photography is in our contemporary life?
여러분은 사진이 우리 현대 생활에서 얼마나 널리 퍼져 있는지 아시나요?
「Today, I'd like to talk about the practical applications of photography.」 16번의 근거
오늘은 사진의 실용적인 활용에 대해 말씀드리고자 합니다.
It's commonly used in several areas. Here are some examples.
그것은 여러 분야에서 흔하게 사용됩니다. 여기에 몇 가지 예가 있습니다.
「First, people use photography to look out into space.」 17번 ①의 근거 일치
첫째, 사람들은 우주를 내다보기 위해 사진을 사용합니다.
Photographs are used in space science to study other planets in our solar system and even distant stars.
사진은 우주 과학에서 우리 태양계의 다른 행성들과 심지어 멀리 떨어져 있는 별들을 연구하기 위해 사용됩니다.
「Second, photography is heavily used in biology to show what cannot be seen with the naked eye.」 17번 ②의 근거 일치
둘째, 사진은 생물학에서 맨눈으로 볼 수 없는 것을 보여 주기 위해 아주 많이 사용됩니다.
Biologists often use photographic images to study life forms that are extremely small.
생물학자들은 극도로 작은 생명체를 연구하기 위해 종종 사진 이미지를 사용합니다.
「Third, photography is used extensively in medicine.」 17번 ③의 근거 일치
셋째, 사진은 의학 분야에서 광범위하게 사용됩니다.
X-ray film reveals patients' inner structures, which helps doctors to choose the best treatment.
X선 필름은 환자의 내부 구조를 드러내어 의사가 최선의 치료법을 선택하도록 돕습니다.
「Lastly, photography provides a useful tool for education.」 17번 ⑤의 근거 일치
마지막으로 사진은 교육을 위한 유용한 도구를 제공합니다.
Photographs allow learners to visualize unfamiliar concepts and abstract ideas in clear and concrete ways.
사진은 학습자가 생소한 개념과 추상적인 관념을 명확하고 구체적인 방법으로 시각화할 수 있도록 해줍니다.
Various uses of photography are constantly being developed in the modern era.
사진의 다양한 활용법이 현대에 끊임없이 개발되고 있습니다.
Now let's watch a video about how photography is applied for practical purposes.
이제 사진이 실용적인 목적으로 어떻게 사용되는지에 대한 영상을 봅시다.

- widespread ⓐ 널리 퍼진
- contemporary ⓐ 현대의
- practical ⓐ 실용적인
- application ⓝ 이용
- look out into ~을 내다보다
- naked eye 맨눈
- extremely ad 극도의
- extensively ad 광범위하게
- reveal ⓥ 드러내다
- treatment ⓝ 치료
- visualize ⓥ 시각화하다
- unfamiliar ⓐ 생소한
- abstract ⓐ 추상적인
- concrete ⓐ 구체적인
- constantly ad 끊임없이

16 주제 파악

정답률 84% | 정답 ①

남자가 하는 말의 주제로 가장 적절한 것은?

✔ practical use of photography in various fields
다양한 분야에서의 사진의 실용적 사용
② importance of choosing a practical field for research
연구를 위해 실용적인 분야를 선택하는 것의 중요성
③ applications of high-speed cameras in academic fields
학문 분야에서의 고속 카메라의 이용
④ sudden decline of photography in the contemporary era
현시대에서의 사진의 급격한 쇠퇴
⑤ how to take photographs effectively in specialized fields
전문 분야에서 효과적으로 사진을 찍는 방법

Why? 왜 정답일까?

남자는 사진의 실용적인 활용에 대해 이야기(**Today, I'd like to talk about the practical applications of photography.**)하고자 하며 다양한 예시를 언급하고 있다. 따라서 남자가 하는 말의 주제로 가장 적절한 것은 ① '다양한 분야에서의 사진의 실용적 사용'이다.

17 언급 유무 파악

정답률 97% | 정답 ④

언급된 분야가 아닌 것은?

① space science - 우주 과학
② biology - 생물학
③ medicine - 의학
✔ psychology - 심리학
⑤ education - 교육

Why? 왜 정답일까?

담화에서 남자는 사진의 실용적 활용에 대한 예시로 우주 과학, 생물학, 의학, 교육을 언급하고 있으며, 언급되지 않은 것은 ④ '심리학'이다.

Why? 왜 오답일까?

① '**First, people use photography to look out into space.**'에서 '우주 과학'이 언급되었다.
② '**Second, photography is heavily used in biology to show what cannot be seen with the naked eye.**'에서 '생물학'이 언급되었다.
③ '**Third, photography is used extensively in medicine.**'에서 '의학'이 언급되었다.
⑤ '**Lastly, photography provides a useful tool for education.**'에서 '교육'이 언급되었다.

Dictation 11

문제편 063쪽

01 at a reasonable price / with advice to keep them fresh longer / a special vase as a gift
02 I don't know what's happening / helps me understand him better /what music and movies he's interested in
03 I'm honored to be here / to give you feedback on your work / that you haven't thought of
04 noticed my dog is under the table / Does it make your kids more careful / I put it up there
05 we've been working / go over the preparations / lunch will be served right after the presentation
06 the filming site of / we'll get that as well / because today is a weekday
07 you might be interested / aren't any other contests / can't you participate
08 theme of this year's event / What time will it start / where it will be
09 make sure to mark / that's not the end of it / will get a discount coupon
10 Have you already found / narrowed them down to / it's too easily knocked over
11 I'm about to change / has been canceled
12 How long does it take to / Why don't you find a train
13 was busy all morning / mathematician as our special guest / think of any mathematicians to invite
14 have various kinds / How long have you had / to get better as soon as possible
15 become covered with dust / isn't concerned about / she sits in the car
16-17 how widespread photography is in our contemporary life / is heavily used in biology / reveals patients' inner structures

[문제편 p.062]

12회 | 2024학년도 6월 모의평가 고3

• 정답 •

01 ⑤ 02 ② 03 ① 04 ⑤ 05 ① 06 ③ 07 ① 08 ④ 09 ② 10 ③ 11 ⑤ 12 ② 13 ③ 14 ① 15 ⑤ 16 ④ 17 ②

01 수조 유리벽을 두드리지 말아 달라고 요청하기

정답률 95% | 정답 ⑤

다음을 듣고, 남자가 하는 말의 목적으로 가장 적절한 것을 고르시오.

① 수족관 직원 채용 광고를 하려고
② 수족관 내 기념품 상점을 홍보하려고
③ 수족관 내부 사진 촬영 금지를 안내하려고
④ 수족관 물고기에게 먹이를 주지 말 것을 당부하려고
✔ 수족관 수조의 유리벽을 두드리지 말 것을 요청하려고

M : Visitors, may I have your attention please?
방문객 여러분, 주목해 주시겠습니까?
This is Anderson Thompson, manager of Benjiville Aquarium.
저는 Benjiville 수족관 관장 Anderson Thompson입니다.
While enjoying your time at our aquarium, we kindly request that you not hit the glass walls of the aquarium tanks.
저희 수족관에서 즐거운 시간을 보내시는 동안, 여러분께서 수족관 수조의 유리벽을 두드리지 말아 주시기를 정중히 요청합니다.
Even light knocking can be quite loud for the fish in the water.
가볍게 치는 소리조차도 물속에 있는 물고기에게는 상당히 클 수 있습니다.
The vibrations from the knocking can make the fish stressed, and they might become sick.
두드려서 생기는 진동은 물고기에게 스트레스를 줄 수 있고, 물고기가 병이 날 수도 있습니다.
So, to keep our fish healthy, we ask you not to hit the glass walls of the aquarium tanks.
그래서, 저희 물고기들이 계속 건강할 수 있도록 여러분께 수족관 수조의 유리벽을 두드리지 말 것을 요청드립니다.
Thank you for your cooperation.
협조 감사합니다.

Why? 왜 정답일까?

물고기에게 스트레스가 되지 않도록 수조를 두드리지 말아 달라고 요청하는 내용이다(**we kindly request that you not hit the glass walls of the aquarium tanks / So, to keep our fish healthy, we ask you not to hit the glass walls of the aquarium tanks.**). 따라서 남자가 하는 말의 목적으로 가장 적절한 것은 ⑤ '수족관 수조의 유리벽을 두드리지 말 것을 요청하려고'이다.

- **aquarium** ⓝ 수족관
- **request** ⓥ 요청하다
- **vibration** ⓝ 진동
- **cooperation** ⓝ 협조, 협력

02 새로 태어난 사촌에게 모자 선물하기

정답률 95% | 정답 ②

대화를 듣고, 여자의 의견으로 가장 적절한 것을 고르시오.

① 아기용 선물은 깨끗이 소독해야 한다.
✔ 아기의 체온 유지에 모자가 도움이 된다.
③ 실내에서는 모자를 벗는 것이 바람직하다.
④ 아기의 방은 적절한 온도 유지가 중요하다.
⑤ 에어컨 사용 시 주기적인 환기가 필요하다.

M : Hey, Laura. Mom asked me what we're going to buy for our newborn baby cousin.
안녕, Laura. 엄마가 우리 새로 태어난 아기 사촌한테 뭘 사줄 건지 나한테 물어보셨어.
W : Oh, yeah. What should we get? Did Mom suggest anything?
오, 맞아. 뭘 사야 하지? 엄마가 뭔가 추천해 주셨니?
M : She said a hat might be a good choice.
엄마는 모자가 좋은 선택일 수도 있다셔.
W : That sounds good. As far as I know, wearing a hat helps maintain babies' body temperature.
그거 좋네. 내가 알기로는, 모자를 쓰는 것이 아기의 체온을 유지하는 데 도움이 된대.
M : It's the beginning of summer, though. Do you think the baby will really need one?
하지만 지금은 초여름인걸. 아기한테 정말로 모자가 필요할 거라고 생각해?
W : Yes. Without a hat on, the baby might get cold when the air conditioning is on.
응. 모자를 쓰지 않으면, 에어컨을 틀었을 때 아기가 추울 수도 있어.
M : I didn't consider that. Now I understand why I've seen so many babies wearing hats indoors in the summer.
그건 생각지 못했네. 이제 왜 여름에 실내에서 모자를 쓴 아기들이 그렇게 많이 보였던 건지 이해가 돼.
W : Right. Hats help to keep babies' body temperature steady.
맞아. 모자는 아기의 체온을 일정하게 유지하는 데 도움이 돼.
M : Okay. Let's find the cutest hat in the world for our baby cousin!
좋아. 우리의 아기 사촌을 위해 세상에서 가장 귀여운 모자를 찾아보자!
W : Absolutely.
그래.

Why? 왜 정답일까?

여자는 어머니의 추천대로 신생아 사촌에게 모자를 사주자며, 모자가 아기의 체온 유지에 도움이 된다(**~ wearing a hat helps maintain babies' body temperature. / Hats help to keep babies' body temperature steady.**)고 말한다. 따라서 여자의 의견으로 가장 적절한 것은 ② '아기의 체온 유지에 모자가 도움이 된다.'이다.

- **as far as I know** 내가 알기로는
- **maintain** ⓥ 유지하다
- **temperature** ⓝ 온도, 체온
- **indoors** ad 실내에서
- **steady** ⓐ 일정한, 꾸준한

03 생각을 비울 수 있게 해주는 취미 만들기

정답률 96% | 정답 ①

다음을 듣고, 남자가 하는 말의 요지로 가장 적절한 것을 고르시오.

✔ 생각을 비울 수 있는 취미가 필요하다.
② 악기 연주는 감수성 발달에 도움이 된다.
③ 작문 능력 향상에는 생각의 정리가 중요하다.
④ 올바른 자세를 위해 운동을 꾸준히 해야 한다.
⑤ 메시지를 명확하게 전달하는 습관을 길러야 한다.

M : Hello, listeners. This is *Claude's Radio Advice Show*.
안녕하세요, 청취자 여러분. *Claude's Radio Advice Show*입니다.
One of our listeners sent me a message.
저희 청취자 중 한 분이 저에게 메시지를 보내셨습니다.
It says that she's having a hard time these days because she has a lot on her mind.
청취자분은 요즘 생각이 많아서 힘들다고 하시는데요.
I think many of you may be having a similar problem.
제 생각에 여러분 중 많은 분이 비슷한 문제를 겪고 계실 것 같아요.
If this is true for you, you need a hobby that can help clear your mind.
이것이 여러분에게도 해당한다면, 마음을 비우는 데 도움이 될 수 있는 취미가 필요하신 겁니다.
For example, you can try going camping, gardening, or playing a musical instrument.
예를 들면, 여러분은 캠핑, 정원 가꾸기, 혹은 악기 연주를 시도해보실 수 있죠.
And any kind of exercise, such as hiking, can also be good.
그리고 하이킹처럼 어떤 운동이든 또한 좋을 수 있습니다.
How about clearing your mind with one of these hobbies?
이런 취미 중 하나로 여러분의 마음을 비우는 것이 어떨까요?
We'll be right back after the break with more tips. Stay tuned!
잠시 쉬었다가 더 많은 조언으로 돌아오겠습니다. 채널 고정해 주세요!

Why? 왜 정답일까?

생각이 많을 때는 취미를 가져보는 것이 도움이 된다는 내용이므로(**~ you need a hobby that can help clear your mind. / How about clearing your mind with one of these hobbies?**), 남자가 하는 말의 요지로 가장 적절한 것은 ① '생각을 비울 수 있는 취미가 필요하다.'이다.

- **true for** ~에 해당하는
- **clear one's mind** 마음을 비우다

04 연극 리허설 사진 구경

정답률 95% | 정답 ⑤

대화를 듣고, 그림에서 대화의 내용과 일치하지 않는 것을 고르시오.

W : Arthur, how did the rehearsal for your drama club go?
Arthur, 연극 동아리 리허설은 어땠어?
M : It went well. Oh, I have a picture of it on my smartphone. Do you want to see it?
잘 끝났어. 오, 내 스마트폰에 사진이 있어. 볼래?
W : Sure. Let me have a look. *[Pause]*『You must be the knight in front of the window.』
물론이지. 보자. *[잠시 멈춤]* 창문 앞에 있는 기사가 너구나. ①의 근거 일치
M : Yeah. That's me.
응, 그거 나야.
W : You look so cool in the costume.
의상을 입은 모습이 정말 근사하네.
M : Thanks.『Do you see the two paintings on the wall?』I painted them myself. ②의 근거 일치
고마워. 벽에 걸린 그림 두 점 보여? 내가 직접 그렸어.
W : Wow, they look great.『I also like the tea pot on the table.』Where did you get that? ③의 근거 일치
와, 멋져. 테이블 위에 있는 찻주전자도 마음에 들어. 그걸 어디서 구했어?
M : I bought it at a flea market.『I also got the flower-patterned rug at the market.』
벼룩시장에서 샀어. 꽃무늬 깔개도 그 시장에서 산 거야. ④의 근거 일치
W : They all fit the setting well.『Oh, there's a cat under the chair.』I think it's so cute.
모두 세트랑 잘 어울린다. 오, 의자 밑에 고양이가 있네. 너무 귀여운 것 같아. ⑤의 근거 불일치
M : I agree. By the way, you're going to come and see my play, right?
동감이야. 그건 그렇고, 내 연극 보러 올 거지?
W : Of course! I'm looking forward to seeing you perform.
당연하지! 네가 공연하는 걸 보는 게 기대돼.

Why? 왜 정답일까?

대화에서 고양이는 의자 밑에 있다(**Oh, there's a cat under the chair.**)고 하는데, 그림에서 고양이는 의자에 앉아 있는 인물의 무릎 위에 있으므로, 그림에서 대화의 내용과 일치하지 않는 것은 ⑤이다.

- **knight** ⓝ 기사
- **costume** ⓝ 의상
- **flea market** 벼룩시장

05 이사 준비 점검하기

정답률 94% | 정답 ①

대화를 듣고, 여자가 할 일로 가장 적절한 것을 고르시오.

✔ 청소 업체 예약하기
② 인터넷 설치 신청하기
③ 아들의 새 학교에 연락하기
④ 버릴 의자에 스티커 붙이기
⑤ 이사 업체에 이사 날짜 확인하기

W : Honey, our moving day is coming up in two weeks.
여보, 우리 이삿날이 2주 앞으로 다가왔어요.
M : Yeah. I think we need to check our to-do list again.
네, 우리는 해야 할 일 목록을 다시 확인해야 할 것 같아요.
W : Okay. We got the confirmation from the moving company for the date, right?
알겠어요. 우리 이삿짐 회사에서 날짜를 확인 받았어요, 그렇죠?
M : Yes, we did. Did you sign up for the Internet at our new place?
네, 우리 새집 인터넷 가입은 했어요?

[문제편 p.067]

W : Uh-huh, I did. It should be connected by the move-in date. And I already put stickers on the chairs we will throw away.
그럼요, 했죠. 입주일까지는 인터넷이 연결될 거예요. 그리고 우리가 버릴 의자들에 스티커는 내가 벌써 붙여놨어요.
M : Great. Oh, I still have to wrap the crystal vases.
좋군요. 아, 난 아직 크리스털 꽃병들을 포장해야 해요.
W : That's okay. You have time. Did you call our son's new school? Did they tell you what he needs to take with him on his first day?
괜찮아요. 시간 있어요. 아들네 새 학교엔 전화했어요? 학교에서 애가 첫날에 뭘 가져가야 할지 말해줬어요?
M : Yes, he has to bring the uniform for his gym class. Oh, we forgot to make a reservation with the cleaning company.
네, 체육 수업이 있으니 체육복을 가져오래요. 아, 우린 청소 회사에 예약해놓는 걸 잊어버렸어요.
W : No worries. I'll do it right now.
걱정 마요. 그거 내가 바로 할게요.
M : Thanks.
고마워요.

Why? 왜 정답일까?

남자가 청소 회사에 예약해두는 걸 잊었다(**Oh, we forgot to make a reservation with the cleaning company.**)고 하자 여자는 자신이 바로 하겠다(**No worries. I'll do it right now.**)고 말한다. 따라서 여자가 할 일로 가장 적절한 것은 ① '청소 업체 예약하기'이다.

- **confirmation** ⓝ (맞다는) 확인
- **date** ⓝ 날짜
- **throw away** 버리다
- **wrap** ⓥ 싸다, 포장하다
- **vase** ⓝ 꽃병

06 샐러드 주문하기

정답률 87% | 정답 ③

대화를 듣고, 남자가 지불할 금액을 고르시오. [3점]

① $36 ② $40 ③ $45 ④ $50 ⑤ $54

W : Welcome to the Fresh Salad Store. What would you like to have?
Fresh Salad Store에 오신 것을 환영합니다. 뭘 드실 건가요?
M : Hi. I'm not sure. What do you recommend?
안녕하세요. 잘 모르겠네요. 뭘 추천해 주실래요?
W : The beef salad is pretty popular. And some people like the chicken salad too.
쇠고기 샐러드가 꽤 인기가 많아요. 치킨 샐러드를 좋아하시는 분들도 있고요.
M : Okay. How much are they?
네. 얼마죠?
W : It's $20 for the beef salad and $15 for the chicken salad.
쇠고기 샐러드는 20달러이고 치킨 샐러드는 15달러입니다.
M : Then, I'll take one beef salad and two chicken salads.
그럼 쇠고기 샐러드 한 개와 치킨 샐러드 두 개를 살게요.
W : Good choice.
잘 고르셨습니다.
M : Is dressing included with the salads?
샐러드에 드레싱이 포함되어 있나요?
W : Yes. All salads come with lemon dressing for free. But if you want a different kind of dressing, you need to pay $5 extra for each.
네. 모든 샐러드는 레몬 드레싱이 무료로 따라 나옵니다. 하지만 다른 종류의 드레싱을 원하시면 각각 5달러를 추가로 내셔야 해요.
M : I'll just take the lemon dressing. Can I use this 10% discount coupon?
레몬 드레싱만 할게요. 이 10% 할인 쿠폰을 써도 되나요?
W : Yes, you can. So, that's one beef salad and two chicken salads. Will that be all?
네. 그러면 쇠고기 샐러드 한 개와 치킨 샐러드 두 개입니다. 다 되셨나요?
M : Yes. Here's my coupon and credit card.
네. 여기 제 쿠폰과 신용 카드요.

Why? 왜 정답일까?

남자는 20달러짜리 쇠고기 샐러드 하나와 15달러짜리 치킨 샐러드를 두 개 사고, 추가금이 붙는 드레싱은 따로 주문하지 않았으며, 총 금액에서 10퍼센트를 할인받았다. 이를 식으로 나타내면 '$(20+15\times2)\times0.9=45$'이므로, 남자가 지불할 금액은 ③ '$45'이다.

- **for free** 무료로
- **Will that be all?** 다 되셨나요?

07 독서 모임에 불참한 이유

정답률 95% | 정답 ①

대화를 듣고, 여자가 독서 모임에 참석하지 못한 이유를 고르시오.

① 고객과의 대화가 계획보다 오래 걸려서 ② 아이를 돌봐 줄 사람을 찾지 못해서
③ 공상 과학 장르를 이해하지 못해서 ④ 신제품을 온라인에 출시해야 해서
⑤ 모임 날짜를 전달받지 못해서

M : Sandra, I didn't see you at the company book club meeting yesterday.
Sandra, 어제 회사 독서 모임에서 당신을 못 봤네요.
W : Yeah, I really wanted to go, but I couldn't make it.
네, 정말 가고 싶었지만 갈 수가 없었어요.
M : You missed a really interesting discussion about our science fiction novel. That's your favorite genre.
공상 과학 소설에 관한 정말 흥미로운 토론을 놓쳤군요. 당신이 제일 좋아하는 장르죠.
W : It is. But I had to take care of something.
그래요. 하지만 나는 뭔가 처리해야 했어요.
M : What was that? You couldn't find a babysitter for your son like last time?
뭐였는데요? 지난번처럼 아들을 돌봐줄 베이비시터를 못 구했어요?
W : No. My husband was with him.
아니요. 남편이 아들과 같이 있었어요.
M : Well, then was it because your department launched a new product online yesterday?
음, 그러면 당신 부서에서 어제 온라인으로 신제품을 출시해서였나요?
W : No, I wasn't involved with that.
아니요, 난 거기 관여 안 했어요.
M : Then, why couldn't you come to the meeting?
그렇다면 왜 모임에 못 왔던 거죠?
W : A conversation with a client took longer than I had planned.
고객과의 대화가 내가 계획했던 것보다 더 오래 걸렸어요.
M : Oh, I see. I was worried about you. I hope everything went well.
아, 그렇군요. 걱정했어요. 모든 일이 잘되었기를 바라요.
W : Yes, it did. Thanks for asking.
네, 잘됐어요. 물어봐줘서 고마워요.

Why? 왜 정답일까?

여자는 고객과의 대화가 길어져서(**A conversation with a client took longer than I had planned.**) 회사 독서 모임에 참석하지 못했다고 하므로, 여자가 참석하지 못한 이유로 가장 적절한 것은 ① '고객과의 대화가 계획보다 오래 걸려서'이다.

- **science fiction** 공상 과학
- **novel** ⓝ 소설
- **department** ⓝ 부서
- **launch** ⓥ 출시하다

08 소설 로봇 기술 쇼케이스

정답률 96% | 정답 ④

대화를 듣고, Now-and-Then Tech Showcase에 관해 언급되지 않은 것을 고르시오.

① 목적 ② 시작일 ③ 장소 ④ 관람 시간 ⑤ 입장료

M : Hannah, I saw a poster at the library that you might be interested in.
Hannah, 도서관에서 네가 관심 있을지도 모르는 포스터를 봤어.
W : What's it about, Dad?
뭐에 관한 건데요, 아빠?
M : It says the Now-and-Then Tech Showcase is coming to our city soon. 「The purpose of the showcase is to introduce social robot technologies that local companies have developed.」 ①의 근거 일치
Now-and-Then Tech Showcase가 곧 우리 도시에 온대. 그 쇼케이스의 목적은 지역 기업들이 개발해온 소셜 로봇 기술을 소개하는 거야.
W : Great! 「When does it start?
잘됐네요! 언제 시작한대요?
M : It'll open from Saturday, June 24th.」 ②의 근거 일치
6월 24일 토요일부터 열린대.
W : Good! I think I can go then. 「Do you remember where it's going to be held?
좋아요! 그때 갈 수 있을 것 같아요. 어디서 열리는지 기억나세요?
M : Yes, at Golden Maples Field Stadium.」 ③의 근거 일치
응, Golden Maples Field Stadium에서 한대.
W : That's awesome! I can walk there. Is there an admission fee?
멋져요! 거긴 걸어서 갈 수 있어요. 입장료가 있나요?
M : Um... I don't remember. Maybe you can check that online.
음… 기억이 안 나네. 아마 온라인에서 확인할 수 있을 거야.
W : Yeah. Just a second. *[Tapping sounds]* 「Oh, the admission fee is $12 per person.」 ⑤의 근거 일치
네. 잠시만요. *[가볍게 치는 소리]* 오, 입장료가 1인당 12달러네요.
M : Sounds good. You should go.
괜찮은 것 같네. 가보렴.
W : Definitely. Thanks for telling me about it.
그래야겠어요. 알려주셔서 고마워요.

Why? 왜 정답일까?

대화에서 남자와 여자는 **Now-and-Then Tech Showcase**의 목적, 시작일, 장소, 입장료에 관해 언급하므로, 언급되지 않은 것은 ④ '관람 시간'이다.

Why? 왜 오답일까?

① '**The purpose of the showcase is to introduce social robot technologies that local companies have developed.**'에서 '목적'이 언급되었다.
② '**It'll open from Saturday, June 24th.**'에서 '시작일'이 언급되었다.
③ '**Yes, at Golden Maples Field Stadium.**'에서 '장소'가 언급되었다.
⑤ '**Oh, the admission fee is $12 per person.**'에서 '입장료'가 언급되었다.

- **awesome** ⓐ 멋진
- **tap** ⓥ 가볍게 두드리다

09 분실물 추적 서비스 소개

정답률 88% | 정답 ②

Found 211에 관한 다음 내용을 듣고, 일치하지 않는 것을 고르시오.

① H-rail 기차에서 분실한 물건에 대한 정보를 제공한다.
② 웹사이트 회원이 아니어도 사용할 수 있다.
③ 분실한 물건 발견 시 문자 메시지로 통지한다.
④ 다양한 언어로 외국어 서비스가 제공된다.
⑤ 모바일 앱에서도 사용할 수 있다.

W : Attention, H-rail train passengers.
H-rail 기차 승객 여러분, 주목해 주세요.
We would like to introduce a new website called Found 211 to help you find your lost items.
분실물 찾기를 도와 드릴 Found 211이라는 새 웹사이트를 소개하고자 합니다.
「Found 211 provides information about items you've lost on H-rail trains.」 ①의 근거 일치
Found 211은 여러분이 H-rail 기차에서 분실하신 물건에 관한 정보를 제공합니다.
「To use Found 211, you first have to be a member of the website.」 ②의 근거 불일치
Found 211을 이용하려면 먼저 웹사이트 회원이 되셔야 합니다.
Then, you need to post the details of your lost items to the website.
그런 다음, 여러분은 분실물 세부사항을 웹사이트에 게재해 주셔야 합니다.
「If your lost items are found, Found 211 will inform you by a text message.」
분실물이 발견되면, Found 211은 여러분께 문자 메시지로 통지할 것입니다. ③의 근거 일치
「In addition, foreign language services are provided in various languages, including French, Spanish and Chinese.」 ④의 근거 일치
나아가, 프랑스어, 스페인어, 중국어를 포함한 다양한 언어로 외국어 서비스를 제공합니다.
「You can also use Found 211 through our mobile application.」 ⑤의 근거 일치
저희 모바일 앱에서도 Found 211을 사용하실 수 있습니다.
We hope you have a pleasant trip to your destination. Thank you.
목적지까지 즐거운 여행 하시기 바랍니다. 감사합니다.

Why? 왜 정답일까?

'**To use Found 211, you first have to be a member of the website.**'에서 **Found 211**의 분실물 추적 서비스를 이용하려면 먼저 웹사이트에 회원으로 가입해야 한다고 하므로, 내용과 일치하지 않는 것은 ② '웹사이트 회원이 아니어도 사용할 수 있다.'이다.

[문제편 p.067]

Why? 왜 오답일까?

① 'Found 211 provides information about items you've lost on H-rail trains.'의 내용과 일치한다.
③ 'If your lost items are found, Found 211 will inform you by a text message.'의 내용과 일치한다.
④ 'In addition, foreign language services are provided in various languages, ~'의 내용과 일치한다.
⑤ 'You can also use Found 211 through our mobile application.'의 내용과 일치한다.

- lost item 분실물
- destination ⓝ 목적지

10 쿠키 커터 세트 사기

정답률 89% | 정답 ③

다음 표를 보면서 대화를 듣고, 여자가 구매할 쿠키 커터 세트를 고르시오.

Cookie Cutter Sets

	Type	Shape	Price	Material	Color
①	A	Heart	$11	Metal	Yellow
②	B	Circle	$11	Plastic	Red
✔	C	Heart	$14	Silicone	Yellow
④	D	Star	$14	Metal	Red
⑤	E	Circle	$20	Silicone	Yellow

M : Ellie, what are you looking at on your tablet PC?
Ellie, 태블릿 PC로 뭘 보고 있어?
W : I'm looking for a set of new cookie cutters. Can you help me pick a new set out from among these five?
새 쿠키 커터 세트를 찾고 있어. 이 다섯 가지 중에서 새 쿠키 커터 세트를 고르는 걸 도와줄래?
M : Sure. There are many shapes to choose from. Do you have one in mind?
물론이지. 선택할 수 있는 모양이 많네. 마음에 드는 게 있어?
W : The star-shaped cutters look cool.
별 모양의 커터가 멋져 보여.
M : They do, but I've heard it's difficult to take the dough out of them.
그렇긴 한데, 반죽을 꺼내기 어렵다고 들었어.
W : Really? 『Then, I don't want to get the star-shaped ones.』 근거1 Shape 조건
진짜? 그럼 별 모양 커터는 안 사야겠다.
M : That makes sense. 『How much do you want to spend?
그게 좋겠어. 얼마를 쓰고 싶어?
W : I'd like to spend less than $20.』 근거2 Price 조건
20달러 밑으로 쓰고 싶어.
M : I see. 『Which material do you prefer?
그렇구나. 어떤 소재를 더 좋아해?
W : I've been using metal cutters. But I want to use a different kind this time.』
나는 금속 커터를 쓰고 있었어. 하지만 이번에는 다른 종류를 사용하고 싶어. 근거3 Material 조건
M : Okay, then you have two options left.
좋아, 그럼 두 가지 선택지가 남았어.
W : 『Yellow is my favorite color, so I'll buy the yellow set.』 근거4 Color 조건
노란색이 제가 제일 좋아하는 색이니, 노란색 세트를 사야겠어.

Why? 왜 정답일까?

대화에 따르면 여자는 별 모양이 아니면서, 가격은 20달러를 넘지 않고, 소재는 금속이 아니며, 색상이 노란색인 쿠키 커터를 사기로 한다. 따라서 여자가 구매할 쿠키 커터 세트는 ③ 'C'이다.

- pick out ~을 고르다
- have in mind 마음에 두다
- take out of ~에서 꺼내다
- make sense 말이 되다, 이해가 되다

11 사진 나눠주기

정답률 70% | 정답 ⑤

대화를 듣고, 여자의 마지막 말에 대한 남자의 응답으로 가장 적절한 것을 고르시오.

① Sorry. I forgot to invite him to my birthday party last week.
미안하다. 내가 그를 지난주 내 생일 파티에 초대하는 걸 깜빡했구나.
② That's too bad. I'll let him know the meeting is cancelled.
참 안됐네. 내가 그에게 만남이 취소되었다고 알려주마.
③ That's weird. He took all the pictures away with him.
이상하다. 그가 사진을 다 가져갔구나.
④ Alright. Please say thanks to Mr. Williams for them.
알았다. Williams 씨한테 고맙다고 해주렴.
✔ I'd be happy to. He'll love to have the pictures.
기꺼이 가져다주지. 그 사진을 받으면 매우 좋아할 거야.

W : Grandpa, I took some pictures at your birthday party last week. And your best friend Mr. Williams was in a few of them.
할아버지, 제가 지난주에 할아버지 생신 파티에서 사진을 몇 장 찍었어요. 그리고 그중 몇 장에 할아버지의 가장 친한 친구이신 Williams 씨가 나왔어요.
M : Oh, really? That's great. I'm meeting him today, and he might want those pictures.
오, 그래? 잘됐구나. 오늘 내가 그 친구를 만나는데, 사진을 좀 갖고 싶어할 수도 있겠어.
W : Well, I can print out the pictures now. Would you like to take them to him?
그럼, 제가 지금 그 사진을 뽑을 수 있어요. 그분께 그 사진을 가져다주실래요?
M : I'd be happy to. He'll love to have the pictures.
기꺼이 가져다주지. 그 사진을 받으면 매우 좋아할 거야.

Why? 왜 정답일까?

여자는 할아버지인 남자의 생일파티에 왔다가 사진에 찍힌 남자의 친구에게 사진을 갖다줄 것을 부탁하고 있다(Would you like to take them to him?). 따라서 남자의 응답으로 가장 적절한 것은 ⑤ '기꺼이 가져다주지. 그 사진을 받으면 매우 좋아할 거야.'이다.

- take away 가지고 가다, 제거하다, 치우다
- say thanks to ~에게 고맙다고 하다

12 아이의 결석 통지

정답률 86% | 정답 ②

대화를 듣고, 남자의 마지막 말에 대한 여자의 응답으로 가장 적절한 것을 고르시오.

① What do you mean? The trip was last week.
무슨 말씀이시죠? 여행은 지난주였어요.
✔ I'm sorry to hear that. I hope he'll get better soon.
유감이네요. 아이가 빨리 낫길 바라겠습니다.
③ That's a relief. I'm glad that he's doing well in school.
다행이네요. 아이가 학교에서 잘하고 있어서 다행이에요.
④ Pardon me? I completely forgot the festival tomorrow.
네? 전 내일 축제를 완전히 잊고 있었어요.
⑤ It's no big deal. I'll check the opening day for the festival.
별거 아니에요. 제가 축제 개막일을 확인해 볼게요.

[Cell phone rings.]
[휴대 전화가 울린다.]
M : Hello, Ms. Davis. This is Kevin's father. His class is visiting the Pop Art Culture Festival tomorrow, right?
안녕하세요, Davis 선생님. 저는 Kevin 아빠입니다. 아이네 반에서 내일 Pop Art Culture Festival을 방문하죠, 그렇죠?
W : Yes. We're going to go as scheduled. Is there anything wrong?
네. 예정대로 가려고 합니다. 무슨 문제라도 있으세요?
M : Actually, Kevin has a fever, so I don't think he can go tomorrow.
실은 Kevin이 열이 나서 내일 못 갈 것 같아요.
W : I'm sorry to hear that. I hope he'll get better soon.
유감이네요. 아이가 빨리 낫길 바라겠습니다.

Why? 왜 정답일까?

Kevin의 아빠인 남자는 Kevin의 선생님인 여자에게 아이가 아파서 내일 축제에 갈 수 없을 것 같다고 말하므로(Actually, Kevin has a fever, so I don't think he can go tomorrow.), 여자의 응답으로 가장 적절한 것은 ② '유감이네요. 아이가 빨리 낫길 바라겠습니다.'이다.

- as scheduled 예정대로
- have a fever 열이 나다
- no big deal 대단한 일이 아니다

12회

13 대학 전공 결정하기

정답률 89% | 정답 ③

대화를 듣고, 여자의 마지막 말에 대한 남자의 응답으로 가장 적절한 것을 고르시오. [3점]

Man: ______________________

① Of course. He'll be grateful for my valuable tips.
물론이죠. 제 귀중한 조언에 그는 고마워할 거예요.
② I hope not. You don't have enough time to study psychology.
안 그러길 바라요. 엄마는 심리학을 공부할 시간이 없을 거예요.
✔ Good idea. I can definitely get information on that from him.
좋은 생각이에요. 분명 선생님께 관련 정보를 얻을 수 있을 거예요.
④ What a shame! I should've invited the former graduates.
안타까워요! 내가 이전 졸업생을 초대했어야 했는데.
⑤ No wonder. They didn't show up yesterday.
당연하죠. 그들은 어제 나타나지 않았어요.

W : Liam, have you decided what you want to study at college?
Liam, 대학에서 하고 싶은 공부 결정했니?
M : Not yet, Mom. Yesterday, some former graduates came to our school and gave us some tips on choosing a major.
아직요, 엄마. 어제 옛날 졸업생 몇 명이 학교에 와서 전공 선택에 대한 몇 가지 조언을 해줬어요.
W : Great. What did they say?
잘됐네. 그들이 뭐라고 했니?
M : They told us that we should first think about what we are most interested in.
먼저 우리가 가장 관심 있는 게 뭔지 생각해보라고 했어요.
W : That's good advice. Are there any particular subjects that you like?
좋은 조언이네. 네가 좋아하는 특정 과목이 있어?
M : I like children very much, so I'd like to study something related to children.
전 아이들을 되게 좋아해서, 아이들과 관련된 뭔가를 공부하고 싶어요.
W : How about studying early childhood education?
유아교육을 공부하는 건 어떠니?
M : That sounds interesting, but I'm also interested in psychology.
재미있을 것 같은데, 전 심리학에도 관심이 있어요.
W : Then, you might want to major in psychology and become a counselor for children.
그럼, 심리학을 전공해서 아이들을 위한 상담사가 돼볼 수도 있겠네.
M : I've never thought of that. But I'm not sure about which colleges have a psychology major.
그건 생각해본 적이 없네요. 하지만 어느 대학에 심리학 전공이 있는지 잘 모르겠어요.
W : Me, neither. But your teacher, Mr. Scott, might be able to help you find out more about that.
나도 잘 몰라. 하지만 너의 선생님이신 Scott 선생님은 네가 그걸 좀 더 많이 알아보도록 도움을 주실 수도 있어.
M : Good idea. I can definitely get information on that from him.
좋은 생각이에요. 분명 선생님께 관련 정보를 얻을 수 있을 거예요.

Why? 왜 정답일까?

대학 전공을 정하려는 남자가 어느 대학에 심리학과가 있는지 잘 모르겠다고 말하자, 엄마인 여자는 선생님께 도움을 청해볼 것을 제안하고 있다(But your teacher, Mr. Scott, might be able to help you find out more about that.). 따라서 남자의 응답으로 가장 적절한 것은 ③ '좋은 생각이에요. 분명 선생님께 관련 정보를 얻을 수 있을 거예요.'이다.

- graduate ⓝ 졸업생 ⓥ 졸업하다
- early childhood education 유아교육
- major in ~을 전공하다
- grateful for ~을 고마워하는
- What a shame! 유감이네요! 안타깝네요!
- No wonder. 당연하죠.

14 개를 돌봐달라고 부탁하기

정답률 93% | 정답 ①

대화를 듣고, 남자의 마지막 말에 대한 여자의 응답으로 가장 적절한 것을 고르시오.

Woman: ______________________

✔ No problem. I can walk him and get some exercise too.
문제 없어요. 제가 산책 시키고 운동도 좀 시킬 수 있어요.
② Certainly. He can help me with my assignment this weekend.
물론이죠. 그가 이번 주말에 내 과제를 도와줄 수 있어요.
③ Absolutely! You can join me on my business trip tomorrow.
그럼요! 내일 제 출장에 함께 가셔도 돼요.
④ Keep it up! You can take care of yourself by working out.
계속 그렇게 하세요! 운동하면 스스로를 챙길 수 있어요.
⑤ Not at all. I don't mind walking you to your house.
아주 괜찮죠. 전 집까지 걸어서 바래다 드려도 좋아요.

[Cell phone rings.]
[휴대 전화벨이 울린다.]

M : Hello, Claire.
안녕, Claire.

W : Hi, Uncle Louis. How are you doing?
안녕하세요, Louis 삼촌. 잘 지내세요?

M : I'm good. Are you busy this weekend?
잘 있지. 너 이번 주말에 바쁘니?

W : Not really. I'll be home doing my assignment. Do you need anything?
별로 안 바빠요. 집에서 숙제할 거예요. 뭐 필요한 거 있으세요?

M : Yeah, I was wondering if you could take care of my dog for the weekend.
응, 네가 주말 동안 내 개를 돌봐줄 수 있을지 궁금하구나.

W : Sure. He's such a good dog. Are you going somewhere?
물론이죠. 삼촌네 개 너무 착하잖아요. 삼촌 어디 가세요?

M : Yes. I have an unexpected business trip.
그래. 예상치 못한 출장이 있어.

W : I see. Are you going to drop him off at my house tomorrow?
알겠어요. 내일 개를 저희 집에 태워다주고 가실 거예요?

M : Sorry, I can't. I have a few things to do before the trip. Could you come and get him this evening?
미안, 그럴 수가 없구나. 출장 전에 해야 할 게 좀 있어서. 네가 오늘 저녁에 와서 애 좀 데려갈래?

W : Yes, I can. Is there anything I need to know to take care of him?
네, 그럴게요. 개를 챙기는 데 알아둬야 할 게 있을까요?

M : Actually, he's on a diet. Do you think you can take him for a walk once a day?
사실, 얘가 다이어트를 하고 있어. 하루에 한 번씩 산책을 시켜줄 수 있니?

W : No problem. I can walk him and get some exercise too.
문제 없어요. 제가 산책 시키고 운동도 좀 시킬 수 있어요.

Why? 왜 정답일까?

남자는 출장 가 있는 동안 개를 돌봐달라고 여자에게 부탁하며, 개가 다이어트 중이니 하루에 한 번씩 산책시켜줄 것을 당부하고 있다(**Do you think you can take him for a walk once a day?**). 따라서 여자의 응답으로 가장 적절한 것은 ① '문제 없어요. 제가 산책 시키고 운동도 좀 시킬 수 있어요.'이다.

- **business trip** 출장
- **on a diet** 다이어트 중인
- **work out** 운동하다
- **drop off** (차로) 내려주다
- **Keep it up!** 계속 그렇게 하세요!

15 발표 날짜를 미룰 수 있는지 확인하기

정답률 87% | 정답 ⑤

다음 상황 설명을 듣고, Kate가 Professor Lee에게 할 말로 가장 적절한 것을 고르시오. [3점]

Kate: ______________________________

① Do you mind if I change my topic for the writing contest?
에세이 대회에 낼 제 주제를 바꿔도 될까요?
② I was wondering why my presentation was postponed.
왜 제 발표가 미뤄졌는지 궁금합니다.
③ I'm looking forward to awarding you the first prize.
당신에게 1등 상을 드리게 될 걸 기대하고 있어요.
④ I'm afraid you're not allowed to attend the ceremony.
유감이지만 당신은 그 시상식에 참석할 수 없습니다.
✔⑤ Could I switch my presentation date with another student's?
제 발표 날짜를 다른 학생과 바꿀 수 있을까요?

M : Kate is taking Professor Lee's East Asian history class.
Kate는 Lee 교수님의 동아시아사 수업을 듣고 있다.
She is given an assignment to make an individual presentation on Monday of the following week.
그녀는 다음 주 월요일에 개인 발표를 해야 한다는 과제를 받는다.
However, she finds out that she won the first prize in a national essay writing contest, and she is asked to attend the awards ceremony.
하지만 그녀는 전국 에세이 쓰기 대회에서 1등을 했다는 것을 알게 되고, 시상식에 참석하라는 요청을 받는다.
She's happy to hear the good news and really wants to go to the ceremony to receive her award.
그녀는 그 좋은 소식을 들어서 기쁘고, 시상식에 상을 받으러 정말 가고 싶다.
But she's not sure about whether she can go because the awards ceremony and the presentation are both scheduled for the same time.
하지만 시상식과 발표가 똑같은 시간에 예정되어 있어서 그녀는 갈 수 있을지 확신이 없다.
So, she wants to ask Professor Lee if it is possible for her to change the date of the presentation with another student in the class.
그래서 그녀는 Lee 교수님께 다른 수강생과 발표 날짜를 바꿔도 될지 여쭤보려고 한다.
In this situation, what would Kate most likely say to Professor Lee?
이런 상황에서, Kate는 Lee 교수님께 뭐라고 말하겠는가?

Kate : Could I switch my presentation date with another student's?
제 발표 날짜를 다른 학생과 바꿀 수 있을까요?

Why? 왜 정답일까?

상황에 따르면 에세이 대회 상을 받게 된 Kate는 시상식과 같은 시간에 예정된 발표 일정을 다른 학생과 바꿀 수 있는지 수업 담당 교수에게 물으려고 한다(**So, she wants to ask Professor Lee if it is possible for her to change the date of the presentation with another student in the class.**). 따라서 Kate가 Lee 교수에게 할 말로 가장 적절한 것은 ⑤ '제 발표 날짜를 다른 학생과 바꿀 수 있을까요?'이다.

- **East Asian history** 동아시아사
- **make a presentation** 발표하다
- **win the first prize** 1등상을 타다
- **switch** ⓥ 바꾸다
- **assignment** ⓝ 과제
- **individual** ⓐ 개인의 ⓝ 개인, 개체
- **awards ceremony** 시상식

16-17 비가 올 때 곤충들이 하는 일

W : Hello, students.
안녕하세요, 학생 여러분.
Have you ever thought about what's happening in the insect world when it's raining?
비가 오고 있을 때 곤충 세계에서 무슨 일이 일어나고 있을지 생각해 본 적이 있나요?
「Today, we're going to talk about what insects do on a rainy day.」 16번의 근거
오늘 우리는 곤충들이 비 오는 날 뭘 하는지 이야기해 볼게요.
Some insects come outside from their home.
어떤 곤충들은 집에서 밖으로 나옵니다.
「For example, cockroaches living in drains have to escape from there to survive when it rains.」 17번 ①의 근거 일치
예를 들어, 하수구에 사는 바퀴벌레는 비가 올 때 생존하려면 거기서 탈출해야 합니다.
It's because their homes get flooded easily.
그들의 집이 쉽게 침수되기 때문이죠.
They leave, so they will not drown.
그들은 떠나야 익사하지 않습니다.
「To give another example, mosquitos come out in the rain to lay eggs.」 17번 ③의 근거 일치
다른 예로, 모기는 비가 오면 밖으로 나와 알을 낳습니다.
Rainy days are the best time since newborn mosquitos need water to grow.
갓 태어난 모기가 자라려면 물이 필요하기 때문에 비 오는 날이 (알 낳기에) 가장 좋은 때입니다.
However, other insects have to hide to stay alive.
하지만 다른 곤충들은 생존을 위해 숨어야 합니다.
「For instance, some types of ants hide themselves to get away from the rain because their body temperature drops when it rains.」 17번 ④의 근거 일치
예를 들어, 어떤 종류의 개미는 비를 피하려고 몸을 숨기는데, 비가 오면 그들의 체온이 떨어지기 때문입니다.
If they get cold during a rainy day, their bodies can freeze and they could die.
비 오는 날에 추워지면 그들은 몸이 얼어 죽을 수도 있습니다.
「Also, some kinds of flies go underground to avoid the rain.」 17번 ⑤의 근거 일치
또한 어떤 종류의 파리는 비를 피하려고 지하로 내려갑니다.
When their wings get wet, they can't fly, so they have to find some place to stay dry.
이들은 날개가 젖으면 날 수 없어서, 마른 상태로 있을 수 있는 어떤 장소를 찾아야 합니다.
As we can see, the rain affects various insects' behavior in different ways.
이렇듯 비는 다양한 방식으로 다양한 곤충들의 행동에 영향을 줍니다.
Now, let's watch a video.
이제 동영상을 보시죠.

- **insect** ⓝ 곤충
- **drain** ⓝ 하수구 ⓥ 배수시키다
- **drown** ⓥ 익사하다
- **lay an egg** 알을 낳다
- **cockroach** ⓝ 바퀴벌레
- **flood** ⓥ 넘치다, 범람하다
- **mosquito** ⓝ 모기
- **significance** ⓝ 중요성, 의의

16 주제 파악

정답률 93% | 정답 ④

여자가 하는 말의 주제로 가장 적절한 것은?

① the communication patterns of insects – 곤충들의 의사소통 패턴
② the reasons why insects dry their wings – 곤충들이 날개를 말리는 이유
③ the ways insects protect their eggs in the rain – 곤충들이 비가 올 때 알을 지키는 방식
✔④ the behavior of various insects on a rainy day – 비 오는 날 다양한 곤충의 행동
⑤ the significance of insects' role in the food chain – 먹이 사슬에서 곤충이 하는 역할의 중요성

Why? 왜 정답일까?

곤충이 비 오는 날 무엇을 하는지(**Today, we're going to talk about what insects do on a rainy day.**)에 관한 내용이므로, 여자가 하는 말의 주제로 가장 적절한 것은 ④ '비 오는 날 다양한 곤충의 행동'이다.

17 언급 유무 파악

정답률 93% | 정답 ②

언급된 곤충이 아닌 것은?

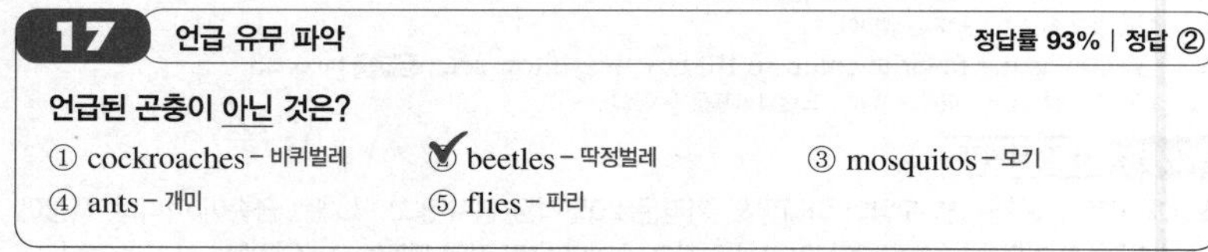

① cockroaches – 바퀴벌레
✔② beetles – 딱정벌레
③ mosquitos – 모기
④ ants – 개미
⑤ flies – 파리

Why? 왜 정답일까?

담화에서 여자는 곤충의 예로 바퀴벌레, 모기, 개미, 파리를 언급하므로, 언급되지 않은 것은 ② '딱정벌레'이다.

Why? 왜 오답일까?

① '**For example, cockroaches living in drains have to escape from there to survive when it rains.**'에서 '바퀴벌레'가 언급되었다.
③ '**To give another example, mosquitos come out in the rain to lay eggs.**'에서 '모기'가 언급되었다.
④ '**For instance, some types of ants hide themselves to get away from the rain because their body temperature drops when it rains.**'에서 '개미'가 언급되었다.
⑤ '**Also, some kinds of flies go underground to avoid the rain.**'에서 '파리'가 언급되었다.

[문제편 p.068]

Dictation 12

문제편 069쪽

01 you not hit the glass walls / Even light knocking / keep our fish healthy
02 As far as I know / wearing hats indoors / keep babies' body temperature steady
03 has a lot on her mind / need a hobby / clearing your mind
04 You must be the knight / the tea pot on the table / fit the setting
05 got the confirmation / wrap the crystal vases / bring the uniform
06 one beef salad and two chicken salads / Is dressing included / Will that be all
07 couldn't make it / your favorite genre / your department launched a new product
08 introduce social robot technologies / That's awesome / Is there an admission fee
09 help you find your lost items / have to be a member / through our mobile application
10 new cookie cutters / take the dough out of them / Which material do you prefer
11 print out the pictures / take them to him
12 go as scheduled / has a fever
13 some former graduates / any particular subjects / major in psychology
14 doing my assignment / an unexpected business trip / drop him off
15 attend the awards ceremony / both scheduled for the same time / change the date
16-17 escape from there to survive / will not drown / get away from the rain

13회 | 2023학년도 6월 모의평가 고3

• 정답 •

01④ 02⑤ 03③ 04⑤ 05③ 06② 07① 08② 09④ 10④ 11① 12⑤ 13① 14② 15① 16② 17④

01 웹사이트 제작 프로그램 소개

정답률 95% | 정답 ④

다음을 듣고, 남자가 하는 말의 목적으로 가장 적절한 것을 고르시오.

① 저작권 위반 사례를 소개하려고
② 홈페이지 점검 시간을 공지하려고
③ 보안 시스템 업그레이드를 권장하려고
④ 웹사이트 제작 프로그램을 홍보하려고
⑤ 조립식 컴퓨터 구매 방법을 설명하려고

M : Hello, everyone.
안녕하세요, 여러분.
Are you looking for an easier way to create your own website?
여러분만의 웹사이트를 만드는 더 쉬운 방법을 찾고 계신가요?
Then use Dream Website Wizard, an easy-to-use program for building websites.
그렇다면 쓰기 편한 웹사이트 구축 프로그램인 Dream Website Wizard를 사용하세요.
With Dream Website Wizard, no technical skills are needed to build a well-designed website that fits your needs.
Dream Website Wizard가 있으면, 여러분의 필요에 맞는 잘 설계된 웹사이트를 구축하기 위해 전문 기술이 필요하지 않습니다.
This program has a variety of designer templates for you to choose from.
이 프로그램에는 여러분이 선택할 수 있는 다양한 설계자 견본이 있습니다.
You'll also find hundreds of images and video backgrounds at your fingertips.
또한 여러분이 즉시 이용할 수 있는 수백 개의 이미지와 비디오 배경을 찾을 수 있을 겁니다.
You can use them for your own website without worrying about copyright issues.
여러분은 이것을 저작권 걱정 없이 여러분의 웹사이트에 이용할 수 있습니다.
Download the program for a 30-day free trial and start making your own website today.
30일 무료 체험판을 받아 오늘 여러분의 웹사이트를 만들기 시작하세요.

Why? 왜 정답일까?

'Then use Dream Website Wizard, ~ building websites.' 이후로 쓰기 편한 웹 사이트 제작 프로그램을 소개하는 내용이 이어지므로, 남자가 하는 말의 목적으로 가장 적절한 것은 ④ '웹사이트 제작 프로그램을 홍보하려고'이다.

- **create** ⓥ 창조하다, 만들어 내다
- **well-designed** ⓐ 잘 설계된
- **template** ⓝ 견본, 본보기
- **copyright** ⓝ 저작권
- **easy-to-use** ⓐ 사용하기 편한
- **fit one's needs** 필요에 맞추다
- **at one's fingertips** 즉시 이용할 수 있는
- **trial** ⓝ 체험, 시험

02 익혀 먹어야 좋은 채소

정답률 93% | 정답 ⑤

대화를 듣고, 여자의 의견으로 가장 적절한 것을 고르시오.

① 매일 다양한 색의 채소를 섭취해야 한다.
② 채소의 종류에 따라 세척 방법이 달라야 한다.
③ 채소는 수확 시기에 따라 맛이 달라질 수 있다.
④ 채소는 냉장 보관하면 비타민 파괴를 늦출 수 있다.
⑤ 익혀서 조리하는 것이 건강에 더 좋은 채소가 있다.

M : Hi, honey. I bought these carrots on my way home.
안녕, 여보. 나는 집에 오는 길에 이 당근들을 샀어요.
W : Great. We can add roasted carrots to our dinner.
좋아요. 우리는 구운 당근을 저녁 식사에 추가할 수 있네요.
M : Well, isn't it healthier to eat vegetables raw rather than cooked?
글쎄요, 채소를 조리해서 먹는 것보다 생으로 먹는 것이 더 건강에 좋지 않나요?
W : Not necessarily. Some vegetables are healthier for us when cooked.
꼭 그렇지는 않아요. 어떤 채소들은 조리되었을 때 건강에 더 좋아요.
M : What do you mean?
무슨 뜻이죠?
W : For example, by roasting carrots and tomatoes, it helps us to receive more substances that are good for our health.
예를 들어, 당근과 토마토를 구우면 우리가 건강에 좋은 물질을 더 많이 받아들이는 데 도움이 돼요.
M : Oh, really? What other vegetables are better when cooked?
오, 정말요? 또 어떤 채소들이 조리되었을 때 더 좋나요?
W : When we steam broccoli and cabbage, they release a compound that helps to prevent certain types of cancer.
브로콜리와 양배추를 찌면, 그것들은 특정 종류의 암을 예방하는 데 도움이 되는 화합물을 방출해요.
M : I see. That's why you always put steamed broccoli in our salad.
그렇군요. 그래서 당신이 항상 우리의 샐러드에 찐 브로콜리를 넣는 거군요.
W : Exactly. Cooking can be a good way to increase some vegetables' health benefits.
바로 그거예요. 조리는 몇몇 채소의 건강상 이점을 증가시키는 좋은 방법이 될 수 있어요.
M : Okay. Then I'll prepare the roasted carrots.
알았어요. 그러면 내가 구운 당근을 준비할게요.

Why? 왜 정답일까?

'Some vegetables are healthier for us when cooked.'와 'Cooking can be a good way to increase some vegetables' health benefits.'에서 여자는 조리해서 먹어야 건강에 더 좋은 채소가 있다고 언급하므로, 여자의 의견으로 가장 적절한 것은 ⑤ '익혀서 조리하는 것이 건강에 더 좋은 채소가 있다.'이다.

- **roast** ⓥ 굽다
- **vegetable** ⓝ 채소, 야채

- raw ⓐ 익히지 않은, 날것의
- not necessarily 반드시[꼭] ~은 아닌
- substance ⓝ 물질
- compound ⓝ 화합물
- cancer ⓝ 암
- increase ⓥ 증가하다
- rather than ~보다는
- receive ⓥ 받다, 받아들이다
- release ⓥ 방출하다, 배출하다
- certain ⓐ 특정한, 일정한
- steam ⓥ (음식을) 찌다

03 미술 전시회 관람

정답률 95% | 정답 ③

대화를 듣고, 두 사람의 관계를 가장 잘 나타낸 것을 고르시오.

① 공연 기획자 – 연극배우
② 패션 디자이너 – 사진작가
✔ 예술가 – 전시회 관람객
④ 건축가 – 인테리어 업체 직원
⑤ 보안 요원 – 기념품 판매원

W : Hi, are you enjoying the exhibition?
안녕하세요, 전시회를 즐겁게 보고 계신가요?

M : Yes. It's the most unique art exhibition that I've ever been to.
네, 제가 가본 곳 중에서 가장 독특한 미술 전시회네요.

W : Thanks. I'm glad that you like my paper sculpture exhibition.
감사합니다. 저의 종이 조각 전시회가 마음에 드신다니 기쁩니다.

M : Oh, you must be Karen Edwards. I can't believe I'm getting the chance to meet you in front of your artwork.
오, 선생님이 Karen Edwards이시군요. 선생님이 만드신 예술 작품 앞에서 선생님을 만나뵐 기회를 갖다니 믿어지지 않습니다.

W : Well, I'll be here for the first three days of my exhibition. Is this your first time visiting this gallery?
음, 저는 전시회 첫 사흘 동안 여기 있을 겁니다. 이 갤러리를 이번에 처음 방문하신 건가요?

M : Yeah. I'm especially impressed with this paper sculpture. What does it symbolize, though?
네. 저는 특히 이 종이 조각에 감명을 받았습니다. 그런데, 이것은 무엇을 나타내는 건가요?

W : I intended to represent family love when I created it.
저는 이걸 만들 때 가족의 사랑을 표현하려고 의도했어요.

M : How's that?
어떻게 그런 의미가 되나요?

W : By putting different pieces of paper together, it becomes complete just like a family.
서로 다른 종이 조각들을 한데 붙여 그것은 바로 가족처럼 완전해지죠.

M : Wow, I can appreciate your artwork even more after your explanation. I'm so lucky that I visited this gallery today.
와, 선생님의 설명을 듣고 나니 작품이 훨씬 잘 이해됩니다. 제가 오늘 이 갤러리를 방문해서 정말 운이 좋았네요.

W : Good to hear that. Thanks for coming.
그런 말씀을 들으니 기쁘네요. 와 주셔서 고맙습니다.

Why? 왜 정답일까?

'It's the most unique art exhibition that I've ever been to.', 'I'm glad that you like my paper sculpture exhibition.', 'I can't believe I'm getting the chance to meet you in front of your artwork.', 'Is this your first time visiting this gallery?'에서 여자가 예술가, 남자가 전시회 관람객임을 알 수 있으므로, 두 사람의 관계로 가장 적절한 것은 ③ '예술가 – 전시회 관람객'이다.

- exhibition ⓝ 전시회
- sculpture ⓝ 조각
- especially [ad] 특히
- symbolize ⓥ (상징으로) 나타내다
- represent ⓥ 표현하다, 나타내다
- explanation ⓝ 설명
- unique ⓐ 독특한
- artwork ⓝ 미술품, 공예품
- impressed ⓐ 감명 받은
- intend ⓥ 의도하다
- appreciate ⓥ 이해하다, 감상하다

04 리모델링한 학교 방송실 사진 보기

정답률 96% | 정답 ⑤

대화를 듣고, 그림에서 대화의 내용과 일치하지 않는 것을 고르시오.

M : Kate, I heard the school broadcasting studio has been remodeled. How did it turn out?
Kate, 학교 방송실을 리모델링했다고 들었어. 어떻게 됐니?

W : It's great. All our club members are excited about it. Here, check out this picture.
잘됐어. 우리 동아리 부원들 모두 그것 때문에 신이 났어. 여기, 이 사진을 살펴봐.

M : Wow, it's much better than I imagined. 『There's even an ON AIR sign above the clock.』
와, 내가 상상했던 것보다 훨씬 좋아. 심지어 시계 위에 '방송 중' 표시등도 있네. ①의 근거 일치

W : Isn't it cool? That's my favorite part of this studio.
멋지지 않아? 그게 내가 이 방송실에서 제일 좋아하는 부분이야.

M : Awesome. 『Oh, there's a bookshelf in the corner.』 ②의 근거 일치
멋지다. 아, 구석에 책장이 있네.

W : We're going to keep our scripts in it. 『What do you think of the world map on the wall?』
거기에 우리 대본을 보관할 거야. 벽에 있는 세계 지도는 어떻게 생각해? ③의 근거 일치

M : That's perfect for the background. 『I also like this stripe-patterned rug on the floor.』
배경으로 딱 맞네. 바닥의 이 줄무늬 양탄자도 마음에 들어. ④의 근거 일치

W : Yeah, it makes the place feel so cozy.
응, 그것 덕분에 방송실이 정말 아늑하게 느껴져. ⑤의 근거 불일치

M : I agree. 『Oh, there are three cameras.』 They give the studio a professional look.
동의해. 아, 카메라가 세 대 있구나. 그게 있어서 방송실이 전문적으로 보이네.

W : I know. I can't wait to start broadcasting the school news.
그러게. 어서 학교 소식을 방송하기 시작하면 좋겠어.

Why? 왜 정답일까?

대화에서 카메라는 세 대라고 하는데(Oh, there are three cameras.), 그림 속에는 카메라가 두 대만 있으므로, 그림에서 대화의 내용과 일치하지 않는 것은 ⑤이다.

- broadcasting studio 방송실
- imagine ⓥ 상상하다
- favorite ⓐ 아주 좋아하는, 마음에 드는
- script ⓝ 대본
- rug ⓝ 양탄자
- remodel ⓥ 개조하다, 리모델링하다
- turn out (~라고) 판명되다
- bookshelf ⓝ 책장
- stripe-patterned ⓐ 줄무늬의
- cozy ⓐ 아늑한

05 동아리 홍보 포스터 제작하기

정답률 93% | 정답 ③

대화를 듣고, 남자가 할 일로 가장 적절한 것을 고르시오.

① 배드민턴 레슨 등록하기
② 신입 회원에게 행사 공지하기
✔ 홍보 포스터 제작하기
④ 소셜 미디어 계정 만들기
⑤ 안내문 게시하기

W : Jason, you look worried. Is something wrong?
Jason, 걱정이 있어 보여. 무슨 일 있어?

M : Well, you know our badminton club has been losing members recently.
음, 알다시피, 최근에 우리 배드민턴 동아리 회원이 줄고 있어.

W : That's right. We may need something to promote our club.
맞아. 우리 클럽을 홍보할 무언가가 필요할 것 같아.

M : How about a special event like offering one-on-one beginner lessons?
일대일 초급 수업 제공 같은 특별 행사는 어때?

W : I don't think we have enough members for that. Hmm, how about promotional posters instead?
우린 그 행사를 위한 대상 회원이 충분하지 않은 것 같아. 음, 대신 홍보 포스터는 어때?

M : Good idea. Do you want to try creating the poster?
좋은 생각이야. 포스터 만드는 걸 해 보고 싶어?

W : Well, I'm not sure. I'm not good at design.
글쎄, 잘 모르겠어. 난 디자인을 잘하지 못해.

M : Then I'll make the poster. I'll try my best to make it eye-catching.
그럼 내가 포스터를 만들게. 시선을 끌 수 있게 최선을 다해볼게.

W : Thanks. Once you're done, I'll put the posters up around the school and on social media as well.
고마워. 네가 그걸 다 하면, 내가 학교 주변과 소셜 미디어에도 포스터를 게시할게.

M : Good. I hope this will get many students to join our club.
좋아. 이걸로 많은 학생이 우리 동아리에 가입하면 좋겠어.

Why? 왜 정답일까?

대화에 따르면 남자와 여자는 동아리를 홍보하기 위해 포스터를 만들어 배포하기로 하는데, 남자가 포스터 제작을(Then I'll make the poster.), 여자가 게시를 각각 맡는다. 따라서 남자가 할 일로 가장 적절한 것은 ③ '홍보 포스터 제작하기'이다.

- promote ⓥ 홍보하다
- promotional ⓐ 홍보의
- put up ~을 게시하다
- one-on-one ⓐ 일대일의
- eye-catching ⓐ (단번에) 시선을 끄는

06 집에 둘 화분 사기

정답률 84% | 정답 ②

대화를 듣고, 여자가 지불할 금액을 고르시오. [3점]

① $40 ✔ $45 ③ $50 ④ $55 ⑤ $65

M : Welcome to Spring Road Garden. May I help you?
Spring Road Garden에 오신 것을 환영합니다. 도와드릴까요?

W : Hi. I'm thinking of putting some flowers in the living room. What would you recommend?
안녕하세요. 저는 거실에 꽃을 좀 둘까 생각하고 있어요. 무엇을 추천해 주시겠어요?

M : How about carnations or tulips in flowerpots? They're popular for home decoration.
화분에 심은 카네이션이나 튤립은 어떠세요? 집안 장식용으로 인기가 있어요.

W : I like them. How much are they?
마음에 드네요. 얼마죠?

M : A pot of carnations is $20, and a pot of tulips is $30.
카네이션 화분은 20달러이고, 튤립 화분은 30달러입니다.

W : I'll take two pots of carnations.
카네이션 화분 두 개를 살게요.

M : Good choice. I also recommend getting a spray bottle to water your flowers.
잘 선택하셨습니다. 꽃에 물을 줄 분무기도 구매하시길 권해드립니다.

W : Oh, I was thinking of buying one. How much is it?
오, 하나 살까 생각하고 있었어요. 얼마죠?

M : It's normally $10, but I'll give you a $5 discount on it.
보통은 10달러이지만 5달러 할인해드릴게요.

W : Thanks. I'll buy one.
고맙습니다. 하나 살게요.

M : So, two pots of carnations and one spray bottle. Would you like them delivered? It's only $5.
그럼 카네이션 화분 두 개와 분무기 한 개네요. 배달해 드릴까요? 5달러만 내시면 됩니다.

W : No, thanks. I brought my car.
아니요, 괜찮습니다. 차를 가져왔어요.

M : Okay. How would you like to pay?
알겠습니다. 어떻게 지불하시겠습니까?

W : I'll pay with cash.
현금 결제할게요.

Why? 왜 정답일까?

대화에 따르면 여자는 하나에 20달러짜리 카네이션 화분을 두 개 사고, 추가로 10달러짜리 분무기를

[문제편 p.073]

5달러 할인받아 산 뒤, 배송 서비스는 이용하지 않기로 한다. 이를 식으로 나타내면 '$20\times2+(10-5)=45$'이므로, 여자가 지불할 금액은 ② '$45'이다.

- **recommend** ⓥ 추천하다
- **decoration** ⓝ 장식품, 장식
- **deliver** ⓥ 배달하다
- **flowerpot** ⓝ 화분
- **spray bottle** 분무기

07 과학 보고서 대회에 관해 피드백 받기 정답률 94% | 정답 ①

대화를 듣고, 남자가 과학 보고서 대회에서 상을 받지 못한 이유를 고르시오.

① 실험 사진을 포함시키지 않아서
② 마감 기한을 지키지 못해서
③ 주제가 창의적이지 않아서
④ 부정확한 정보를 사용해서
⑤ 제시된 분량을 초과해서

W : Hi, Dave. Come in.
안녕, Dave. 들어와.
M : You wanted to see me, Ms. Adams?
저를 보자고 하셨다고요, Adams 선생님?
W : Yes. It's about the science report competition. You must be disappointed that you didn't get a prize.
그래. 과학 보고서 대회 때문이란다. 네가 상을 타지 못해서 실망했겠구나.
M : Well, I tried my best until the last minute, so I was wondering why.
음, 저는 마지막 순간까지 최선을 다했고, 그래서 이유가 궁금했어요.
W : Actually, your topic was creative and interesting.
사실 네 주제는 창의적이고 흥미로웠단다.
M : How about the length? Was my report too long?
길이는요? 제 보고서가 너무 길었나요?
W : No, the length was not the issue.
아니, 길이는 문제가 아니었어.
M : Then, did I use any incorrect information?
그럼, 제가 부정확한 정보를 사용했나요?
W : Not at all. It seemed that you researched the topic thoroughly.
전혀 아니야. 너는 그 주제를 철저히 조사한 것처럼 보였어.
M : Yes. I tried to use reliable sources from the Internet and books.
맞아요. 저는 인터넷과 책에서 믿을 만한 자료를 사용하려고 노력했어요.
W : Good. However, you didn't include the experiment pictures in your report.
잘했어. 그런데 보고서에 실험 사진을 포함하지 않았더구나.
M : Really? I thought I put them in my report.
정말요? 전 제가 사진을 보고서에 넣은 줄 알았어요.
W : Unfortunately, you didn't. That's the reason why you didn't get a prize.
안타깝게도 아니었어. 그래서 네가 상을 타지 못했지.
M : Oh, I see. I won't make the same mistake next time.
오, 알겠습니다. 다음번에는 같은 실수를 하지 않겠어요.

Why? 왜 정답일까?

대화에 따르면 남자는 과학 보고서에 실험 사진을 포함시키지 않아(**However, you didn't include the experiment pictures in your report.**) 입상하지 못했다고 한다. 따라서 남자가 과학 보고서 대회에서 상을 받지 못한 이유로 가장 적절한 것은 ① '실험 사진을 포함시키지 않아서'이다.

- **competition** ⓝ 대회, 경쟁
- **prize** ⓝ 상, 상품
- **actually** ad 사실은
- **incorrect** ⓐ 부정확한
- **reliable** ⓐ 믿을 만한
- **experiment** ⓝ 실험
- **disappoint** ⓥ 실망하다
- **wonder** ⓥ 궁금해 하다
- **length** ⓝ 길이
- **thoroughly** ad 철저하게
- **include** ⓥ 포함시키다
- **unfortunately** ad 불행하게도, 유감스럽게도

08 과학 박람회 알아보기 정답률 92% | 정답 ②

대화를 듣고, 2022 Technology Fair에 관해 언급되지 않은 것을 고르시오.

① 주제 ② 참여 업체 ③ 장소
④ 입장료 ⑤ 종료일

M : Rosa, did you find anything interesting on the community board?
Rosa, 지역사회 게시판에 재밌는 것 좀 있어?
W : Hey, James. Look. The 2022 Technology Fair is going on right now.
안녕, James. 이것 좀 봐. 2022 Technology Fair가 바로 지금 진행 중이야.
M : Let me see. 「It says the theme of this fair is "AI and the Fourth Industrial Revolution."」
어디 보자. 이 박람회의 주제가 '인공 지능과 4차 산업 혁명'이라고 쓰여 있네. ①의 근거 일치
W : Yeah, AI technology is the topic for our group presentation.
그래. 인공 지능 기술은 우리 모둠의 발표 주제잖아.
M : Right. I bet we could get a lot of useful information there. 「Hmm, do you see where it's taking place?
맞아. 분명 우리가 거기에서 많은 유용한 정보를 얻을 수 있을 것 같아. 음, 어디서 열리는지 봤어?
W : Yes, look here. It's being held at the civic center downtown.」 It's within walking distance from here.
③의 근거 일치
응, 여기를 봐. 도심에 있는 시민 센터에서 열리는 중이래. 여기에서 걸어갈 수 있는 거리 안에 있어.
M : Perfect. 「And the admission fee is $10 for students.」 Should we go?
아주 좋아. 그리고 입장료는 학생은 10달러야. 우리 갈래? ④의 근거 일치
W : Definitely. How about going next weekend?
물론이야. 다음 주말에 가는 게 어떨까?
M : No, we have to go this weekend. 「The fair ends on June 15th.」 ⑤의 근거 일치
안 돼, 우리는 이번 주말에 가야 해. 박람회가 6월 15일에 끝나.
W : Okay. Let's look into getting tickets.
그래. 표 사는 걸 알아보자.

Why? 왜 정답일까?

대화에서 남자와 여자는 **2022 Technology Fair**의 주제, 장소, 입장료, 종료일에 관해 이야기하므로, 언급되지 않은 것은 ② '참여 업체'이다.

Why? 왜 오답일까?

① '**It says the theme of this fair is "AI and the Fourth Industrial Revolution."**'에서 '주제'가 언급되었다.
③ '**It's being held at the civic center downtown.**'에서 '장소'가 언급되었다.
④ '**And the admission fee is $10 for students.**'에서 '입장료'가 언급되었다.
⑤ '**The fair ends on June 15th.**'에서 '종료일'이 언급되었다.

- **AI** 인공 지능(= artificial intelligence)
- **useful** ⓐ 유용한, 도움이 되는, 쓸모 있는
- **within walking distance** 걸어갈 수 있는 거리에 있는
- **admission fee** 입장료
- **look into** ~을 살펴보다, 조사하다
- **industrial revolution** 산업 혁명
- **civic** ⓐ 시민의
- **definitely** ad 확실히, 분명히

09 고등학생 대상 경제 강좌 소개 정답률 95% | 정답 ④

Junior Money Smart Course에 관한 다음 내용을 듣고, 일치하지 않는 것을 고르시오.

① 강사는 경제학 교수이다.
② 고등학생만을 대상으로 한다.
③ 월요일부터 금요일까지 진행될 것이다.
④ 7월에 등록이 시작된다.
⑤ 등록자 전원에게 선물을 제공할 것이다.

W : Hello, parents.
안녕하십니까, 학부모님.
Do you want your children to learn how to be smart with their money?
여러분의 자녀가 돈을 잘 관리하는 법을 배우기를 원하십니까?
Then, sign them up for the Junior Money Smart Course.
그럼 아이들을 Junior Money Smart Course에 등록해 주세요.
「The instructor of this course is an economics professor, who will teach your children basic accounting principles and money management skills.」 ①의 근거 일치
강사는 경제학 교수로, 여러분 자녀에게 기본적인 회계 원칙과 돈 관리 기술을 가르쳐줄 것입니다.
「This course is only for high school students.」 ②의 근거 일치
이 강좌는 고등학생만을 대상으로 합니다.
「It'll be held at the Shellburne Community Center from Monday to Friday in the afternoon.」 ③의 근거 일치
강좌는 Shellburne Community Center에서 월요일부터 금요일 오후에 진행될 것입니다.
「Registration can be done on our website starting from August 1st.」 ④의 근거 불일치
등록은 저희 웹사이트에서 8월 1일부터 할 수 있습니다.
Please note that on-site registration is not available.
현장 등록은 불가하다는 점 주의해 주세요.
「Everyone who signs up will receive a planner as a gift.」 ⑤의 근거 일치
등록자 전원은 플래너를 선물로 받을 것입니다.
Set your children on the right path for their financial security.
자녀를 재정적 안정으로 향하는 올바른 길로 인도해 주세요.
For more information, visit our website, www.juniormoneysmart.com.
더 많은 정보를 보시려면 저희 웹사이트인 www.juniormoneysmart.com을 방문하세요.

Why? 왜 정답일까?

'**Registration can be done on our website starting from August 1st.**'에서 강좌 등록은 8월 1일부터 시작된다고 하므로, 내용과 일치하지 않는 것은 ④ '7월에 등록이 시작된다.'이다.

Why? 왜 오답일까?

① '**The instructor of this course is an economics professor, ~**'의 내용과 일치한다.
② '**This course is only for high school students.**'의 내용과 일치한다.
③ '**It'll be held at the Shellburne Community Center from Monday to Friday in the afternoon.**'의 내용과 일치한다.
⑤ '**Everyone who signs up will receive a planner as a gift.**'의 내용과 일치한다.

- **smart with money** 돈 관리를 잘하는
- **instructor** ⓝ 강사
- **accounting** ⓝ 회계
- **registration** ⓝ 등록
- **financial security** 재정적인 안정
- **sign up for** ~에 등록하다
- **economics** ⓝ 경제학
- **management skill** 관리기술
- **on-site** ⓐ 현장의

10 태블릿 거치대 고르기 정답률 80% | 정답 ④

다음 표를 보면서 대화를 듣고, 여자가 구입할 책상용 태블릿 거치대를 고르시오.

Tablet Stands for Desks

	Model	Price	Material	Foldable	Color
①	A	$11	Plastic	×	White
②	B	$12	Plastic	○	Silver
③	C	$14	Wood	○	Black
④	D	$16	Aluminum	×	Silver
⑤	E	$21	Aluminum	○	Black

M : Emily, what are you shopping for on your computer?
Emily, 컴퓨터로 뭘 쇼핑해요?
W : I'm looking at these tablet stands for desks. Can you help me choose one?
책상용 태블릿 거치대를 보고 있어요. 하나 고르는 걸 도와줄래요?
M : Sure. Let me take a look. *[Pause]* Hmm, these five models all look pretty good. 「How much do you want to spend?
물론이죠. 어디 한 번 봐요. *[잠시 멈춤]* 음, 이 다섯 가지 모델은 모두 꽤 괜찮아 보여요. 얼마를 쓰고 싶어요?
W : I'd like to keep it under $20.」 근거1 Price 조건
20달러 미만으로 하고 싶어요.
M : Okay. Oh, it seems they come in three different materials. Do you have any preference?
알겠어요. 오, 그것들은 세 가지 다른 재료로 나온 것 같네요. 선호하는 것이 있나요?
W : 「Well, I don't like the texture of wood. The other materials are fine, though.」
음, 저는 나무의 질감을 좋아하지 않아요. 하지만 다른 소재는 괜찮아요. 근거2 Material 조건
M : I see. 「And I think you should consider a foldable model because it's easier to carry around.
알겠어요. 그리고 접을 수 있는 제품을 생각해봐야 할 것 같아요. 들고 더 다니기 쉬우니까요.

[문제편 p.073]

W : But I'll mainly use it at home, so I don't need a foldable one.」 근거3 Foldable 조건
하지만 저는 그걸 주로 집에서 쓸 거라서 접히는 제품은 필요하지 않아요.
Plus, it seems less stable.
게다가 그건 덜 안정적으로 보여요.

M : Then there are two options left. Which one do you like?
그러면 두 가지 선택이 남았네요. 어느 게 더 마음에 들어요?

W : 「This silver one looks fancier.」 근거4 Color 조건
이 은색 것이 더 근사해 보여요.

M : I agree.
나도 동의해요.

W : Okay. I'll buy this one then. Thanks for your help.
좋아요. 그럼 이걸 살게요. 도와줘서 고마워요.

Why? 왜 정답일까?

대화에 따르면 여자는 비용이 20달러 미만이면서, 나무 소재가 아니고, 접히는 제품이 아니며, 색상이 은색인 태블릿 거치대를 구매하려고 한다. 따라서 여자가 구매할 책상용 태블릿 거치대는 ④ 'D'이다.

- preference ⓝ 선호
- consider ⓥ 잘 생각해 보다, 고려하다
- carry around 운반하다
- texture ⓝ 질감
- foldable ⓐ 접을 수 있는
- stable ⓐ 안정적인

11 생선을 냉장고에 넣어 달라고 부탁하기

정답률 74% | 정답 ①

대화를 듣고, 여자의 마지막 말에 대한 남자의 응답으로 가장 적절한 것을 고르시오.

✔ No problem. I'll put it in the refrigerator. – 문제없어요. 냉장고에 넣어 둘게요.
② Of course. I'll check tomorrow's weather. – 물론이죠. 내가 내일 날씨를 확인할게요.
③ Okay. We can buy it at the store after work. – 알겠어요. 우리는 퇴근 후에 상점에서 그것을 살 수 있어요.
④ Great. Let's order from a seafood restaurant. – 좋아요. 해산물 식당에서 주문해요.
⑤ Never mind. I don't care if it's delivered late. – 상관없어요. 그것이 늦게 배달되어도 괜찮아요.

[Cell phone rings.]
[휴대 전화가 울린다.]

W : Honey, did you get home from work yet? The fish I ordered yesterday has just arrived, but I'll be home late today.
여보, 아직 퇴근 안 했어요? 어제 주문한 생선이 방금 도착했는데 나는 오늘 늦게 집에 갈 거예요.

M : Oh, I'll be home in two hours. Won't it go bad because the weather is so hot?
오, 나는 두 시간 뒤면 집에 도착할 거예요. 날이 너무 더워서 그게 상하지 않을까요?

W : I hope not. Can you store the fish as soon as you get home?
그러지 않길 바라요. 집에 가자마자 생선을 보관해 줄 수 있나요?

M : No problem. I'll put it in the refrigerator.
문제없어요. 냉장고에 넣어 둘게요.

Why? 왜 정답일까?

여자는 어제 주문한 생선이 집에 도착했으니 남자에게 집에 도착하는 대로 생선을 냉장고에 넣어달라고(**Can you store the fish as soon as you get home?**) 부탁하고 있다. 따라서 여자의 말에 대한 남자의 응답으로 가장 적절한 것은 ① '문제없어요. 냉장고에 넣어 둘게요.'이다.

- order ⓥ 주문하다, 시키다
- deliver ⓥ 배달하다
- store ⓥ 보관하다

12 롤러코스터 탑승이 가능한지 확인하기

정답률 75% | 정답 ⑤

대화를 듣고, 남자의 마지막 말에 대한 여자의 응답으로 가장 적절한 것을 고르시오.

① Absolutely. I'm proud of my son. – 물론입니다. 저는 제 아들이 자랑스럽습니다.
② Fantastic. He'll really enjoy the ride. – 멋지네요. 그는 정말로 즐겁게 탈 거예요.
③ Too bad. He should have come earlier. – 참 아쉽네요. 그가 더 일찍 왔어야 했어요.
④ It's all right. The line is getting shorter. – 괜찮습니다. 줄이 점점 더 짧아지고 있어요.
✔ I'm sorry. Then he's not allowed to ride. – 죄송합니다. 그렇다면 아드님은 탈 수 없습니다.

M : Hello, my son would love to ride on this roller coaster. Can he?
안녕하세요, 우리 아들이 이 롤러코스터를 몹시 타고 싶어 해요. 탈 수 있을까요?

W : Well, he must be at least 130 cm tall to ride it. How tall is he?
음, 탑승하려면 적어도 키가 130센티미터는 되어야 합니다. 아드님 키가 얼마죠?

M : Oh, my son is much shorter than that.
오, 우리 아들은 그것보다 훨씬 작아요.

W : I'm sorry. Then he's not allowed to ride.
죄송합니다. 그렇다면 아드님은 탈 수 없습니다.

Why? 왜 정답일까?

롤러코스터에 타려면 키가 130센티미터는 되어야 한다는 여자의 말에 남자는 아들이 그것보다 훨씬 작다고 말한다(**Oh, my son is much shorter than that.**). 따라서 남자의 말에 대한 여자의 응답으로 가장 적절한 것은 ⑤ '죄송합니다. 그렇다면 아드님은 탈 수 없습니다.'이다.

- ride on ~에 타다
- at least 적어도, 최소한

13 버터 유효 기간 확인하기

정답률 71% | 정답 ①

대화를 듣고, 여자의 마지막 말에 대한 남자의 응답으로 가장 적절한 것을 고르시오. [3점]

Man: ____________________

✔ Don't worry. I'll check the date for you. – 걱정 마세요. 제가 날짜를 확인해 드릴게요.
② Oh, no. We don't have time to print it out. – 오, 이런. 그것을 프린터로 출력할 시간이 없네요.
③ I see. I'll put the bread back in the package. – 알겠어요. 그 빵을 꾸러미에 다시 담을게요.
④ I agree. We need to buy more cream cheese. – 동의해요. 우리는 크림치즈를 더 사야 해요.
⑤ Good. I'll bring some bread to the neighbors. – 좋아요. 제가 이웃들에게 빵을 좀 가져다드릴게요.

M : Grandma, I'm home. What are you making?
할머니, 저 집에 왔어요. 뭘 요리하세요?

W : Hi, Kevin. I'm about to bake some cream cheese bread. I know how much you love it.
안녕, Kevin. 크림치즈 빵을 좀 구우려던 참이야. 네가 그걸 얼마나 좋아하는지 알지.

M : Of course, I do. It's really soft and delicious.
물론이죠, 전 좋아해요. 정말로 부드럽고 맛있잖아요.

W : Oh, sweetheart, you're too kind.
오, 얘야, 다정하기도 해라.

M : No, really. It's the best. Is there anything I can help you with?
아뇨, 정말로요. 그 빵이 최고예요. 제가 할머니를 도울 수 있는 일이 있을까요?

W : That'd be lovely. Can you get the butter from the refrigerator?
그럼 좋지. 냉장고에서 버터를 갖다줄 수 있니?

M : Sure. *[Pause]* Here it is. What should I do next?
물론이죠. *[잠시 멈춤]* 여기 있어요. 또 뭘 할까요?

W : Wait. The butter looks slightly old. Do you remember when we bought it?
잠깐. 그 버터가 약간 오래돼 보인다. 우리가 그것을 언제 샀는지 기억하니?

M : Probably a few months ago. But usually butter lasts a long time, so it should be okay.
아마 몇 달 전에요. 하지만 버터는 보통 오래 가니 괜찮을걸요.

W : Yeah, but it's important to always check the expiration dates before cooking.
그래, 하지만 요리하기 전에 늘 유효 기간을 확인하는 게 중요하지.

M : I guess you're right. It's better to be safe.
할머니 말씀이 맞는 것 같아요. 안전한 것이 더 나아요.

W : Let me take a look. *[Pause]* Oh, dear. The print on the package is too small for me to read.
어디 한번 보마. *[잠시 멈춤]* 오, 이런. 포장지 글자가 너무 작아서 내가 읽을 수가 없구나.

M : Don't worry. I'll check the date for you.
걱정 마세요. 제가 날짜를 확인해 드릴게요.

Why? 왜 정답일까?

요리에 쓸 버터의 유효 기간을 확인하려는 여자는 포장지에 인쇄된 글자가 너무 작아서 읽을 수가 없다(**Oh, dear. The print on the package is too small for me to read.**)고 말하므로, 남자의 응답으로 가장 적절한 것은 ① '걱정 마세요. 제가 날짜를 확인해 드릴게요.'이다.

- be about to ~하려던 참이다
- refrigerator ⓝ 냉장고
- last ⓥ 지속되다
- package ⓝ 포장지
- delicious ⓐ 맛있는
- slightly ad 약간
- expiration date 유효 기간
- neighbour ⓝ 이웃

14 환경 축제 준비하기

정답률 81% | 정답 ②

대화를 듣고, 남자의 마지막 말에 대한 여자의 응답으로 가장 적절한 것을 고르시오.

Woman: ____________________

① No, thanks. We already have enough eco-bags.
아니요, 괜찮습니다. 이미 에코백이 충분해요.
✔ That's a relief. Then we can prepare more presents.
다행이네요. 그러면 저희는 선물을 더 준비할 수 있겠어요.
③ That's true. Last year's festival was a great success.
맞아요. 작년 축제는 대성공이었죠.
④ I appreciate that. That's why I've won the quiz event.
고맙습니다. 그 이유로 제가 퀴즈 이벤트에서 우승했어요.
⑤ Right. The book you recommended was so interesting.
맞아요. 선생님께서 추천해 주신 책은 정말 재미있었어요.

W : Hi, Mr. Taylor.
안녕하세요, Taylor 선생님.

M : Hi, Christie. How is the preparation for the school's Eco-Festival going?
안녕, Christie. 학교 환경 축제 준비는 잘 되고 있니?

W : Well, our club is planning to hold a quiz event during the festival.
음, 저희 동아리는 축제 중에 퀴즈 이벤트를 열 계획이에요.

M : Sounds interesting. What is the quiz about?
재미있겠구나. 퀴즈는 뭐에 관한 거니?

W : It'll be on the best-selling book, *An Eco-Friendly Way of Life*.
베스트셀러인 *친환경 생활 방식*이란 책에 관한 거예요.

M : I've read that book. It's educational and fascinating.
그 책 읽어봤어. 교육적이고 대단히 흥미롭지.

W : Yeah. I think the students will be really into it. Plus, as a present, each participant will receive an eco-bag made from recycled materials.
네. 학생들이 정말로 그 책에 푹 빠질 거라고 생각해요. 게다가, 모든 참가자는 재활용 재료로 만든 에코백을 선물로 받게 될 거예요.

M : Oh, that's why you asked me to order the eco-bags. How many students have signed up for the quiz event so far?
오, 그래서 내게 에코백을 주문해달라고 요청했던 거구나. 지금까지 몇 명이 퀴즈 이벤트에 신청했니?

W : Far more than we expected.
저희가 예상했던 것보다 훨씬 더 많아요.

M : That's great news!
정말 좋은 소식이네!

W : Yeah, but I'm really concerned because we didn't prepare enough eco-bags.
네, 하지만 에코백을 충분히 준비하지 못해서 정말 걱정이에요.

M : Don't worry. I'll order more if you need. We still have funds that can be used for the festival.
걱정 마. 필요하면 내가 더 주문해 줄게. 아직 축제에 사용할 수 있는 돈이 남았단다.

W : That's a relief. Then we can prepare more presents.
다행이네요. 그러면 저희는 선물을 더 준비할 수 있겠어요.

Why? 왜 정답일까?

축제 때 선물로 나눠줄 에코백이 모자랄까봐 걱정하는 여자에게 남자는 돈이 아직 남았다며 더 주문할 수 있다(**I'll order more if you need. We still have funds that can be used for the festival.**)고 말하므로, 여자의 응답으로 가장 적절한 것은 ② '다행이네요. 그러면 저희는 선물을 더 준비할 수 있겠어요.'이다.

- preparation ⓝ 준비
- eco-friendly ⓐ 친환경적인, 환경 친화적인
- fascinating ⓐ 대단히 흥미로운
- participant ⓝ 참가자
- expect ⓥ 예상하다
- fund ⓝ 자금, 기금
- hold ⓥ 열다, 개최하다
- educational ⓐ 교육적인
- be into ~에 푹 빠지다
- recycle ⓥ 재활용하다
- prepare ⓥ 준비하다
- relief ⓝ 안도, 안심

15 부정적인 리뷰 활용에 관한 조언

정답률 74% | 정답 ①

다음 상황 설명을 듣고, Tom이 Alice에게 할 말로 가장 적절한 것을 고르시오. [3점]

[문제편 p.074]

Tom: ____________________

✓ You should take advantage of negative reviews for your business.
사업을 위해 부정적인 평가를 잘 이용해야 해.
② You'd better take an online class to get a degree in marketing.
마케팅 학위를 받기 위해 온라인 수업을 듣는 게 좋을 거야.
③ Don't forget the negative effects of enlarging your business.
사업 확장의 부정적인 영향을 잊지 마.
④ Why don't you put up an advertisement for your products?
네 제품에 대한 광고를 올리는 게 어때?
⑤ How about starting a new online business together?
같이 새로운 온라인 사업을 시작하는 건 어때?

M : Alice runs an online shopping mall.
Alice는 온라인 쇼핑몰을 운영한다.
Recently, some of her customers left negative reviews about her products.
최근, 고객 중 몇 명이 그녀의 제품에 대해 부정적인 평가를 남겼다.
She's worried that these comments will cause customers to turn away from her business.
그녀는 이런 평가로 인해 고객이 자기 회사를 외면하게 될까 봐 걱정하고 있다.
She visits her friend Tom, who also runs an online shopping mall, and asks for his advice.
그녀는 마찬가지로 온라인 쇼핑몰을 운영하는 친구 Tom을 찾아가 그의 조언을 구한다.
Tom thinks that those negative comments can be useful, as they can help owners to better understand consumers' needs and to improve the quality of the products.
Tom은 이러한 부정적인 평가는 사업 소유주가 소비자의 요구를 더 잘 이해하고 제품의 품질을 향상하는 데 도움이 될 수 있기 때문에 유용할 수 있다고 생각한다.
He believes this can contribute to a sales increase in the end.
그는 이것이 결국 매출 증가에 이바지할 수 있다고 믿는다.
So, Tom wants to tell Alice that she needs to make use of negative reviews to improve her business.
그래서 Tom은 Alice에게 사업을 개선하려면 부정적인 평가를 이용할 필요가 있다고 말해주고 싶다.
In this situation, what would Tom most likely say to Alice?
이런 상황에서, Tom은 Alice에게 뭐라고 말할 것인가?
Tom : You should take advantage of negative reviews for your business.
사업을 위해 부정적인 평가를 잘 이용해야 해.

Why? 왜 정답일까?

대화에 따르면 Tom은 쇼핑몰에 대한 부정적인 평가 때문에 걱정하는 Alice에게 오히려 그것을 잘 활용해 보라고(So, Tom wants to tell Alice ~ to improve her business.) 조언하려 한다. 따라서 Tom이 Alice에게 할 말로 가장 적절한 것은 ① '사업을 위해 부정적인 평가를 잘 이용해야 해.'이다.

- recently ad 최근에
- negative ⓐ 부정적인
- product ⓝ 제품
- turn away from ~을 외면하다, ~로부터 돌아서다
- ask for ~을 구하다
- contribute to ~에 이바지하다
- make use of ~을 이용하다, 활용하다
- degree ⓝ 학위
- customer ⓝ 고객
- review ⓝ 비평
- comment ⓝ 언급, 논평
- improve ⓥ 개선하다, 향상하다
- in the end 결국
- take advantage of ~을 이용하다
- enlarge ⓥ 확장하다, 확대하다

16-17 새 둥지에 사용되는 재료

W : Hello, students.
안녕하세요, 학생 여러분.
We all know birds are expert nest builders.
우리는 모두 새들이 둥지 짓기의 전문가라는 것을 알고 있습니다.
「So today, we'll learn about the reasons that some materials are used in bird nests.」
그래서 오늘 우리는 어떤 재료들이 새 둥지에 사용되는 이유에 대해 배울 것입니다. 16번의 근거
Firstly, many types of birds incorporate different kinds of materials to keep their nests warm.
우선, 많은 종류의 새가 자기 둥지를 따뜻하게 유지하기 위해 다양한 종류의 재료들을 포함합니다.
「Particularly, feathers are commonly used for this purpose.」 17번 ①의 근거 일치
특히 이러한 목적으로 깃털이 흔히 사용됩니다.
Secondly, some bird species build their nests along the side of cliffs or buildings, which requires sticky substances.
둘째로, 일부 새의 종들은 절벽이나 건물의 측면을 따라 둥지를 짓는데 그러려면 접착 물질이 필요합니다.
「These birds use mud because it attaches well to vertical surfaces.」 17번 ②의 근거 일치
이러한 새들은 진흙이 수직 표면에 잘 붙기 때문에 진흙을 사용합니다.
Next, some tiny birds normally build small cup-like nests with light materials, so they need an additional material to bind them.
다음으로, 일부 매우 작은 새들은 보통 가벼운 재료로 작은 컵 모양의 둥지를 짓기 때문에, 그것들을 묶을 수 있는 추가적인 재료가 필요합니다.
「They often use spiderwebs to fasten these nesting materials together.」 17번 ③의 근거 일치
그들은 이런 둥지를 짓는 물질들을 한데 고정하기 위해 흔히 거미줄을 사용합니다.
Lastly, some species of birds that live in cold environments use certain objects to protect their eggs.
마지막으로, 추운 환경에서 사는 일부 새의 종들은 자기 알을 보호하기 위해 특정한 물체를 사용합니다.
「These birds gather stones for their nests to place their eggs on.」 17번 ⑤의 근거 일치
이러한 새들은 알을 올려놓기 위해 자기 둥지에 돌을 모읍니다.
This keeps their eggs above ground level, which reduces the danger of flooding from melting ice.
이것은 알을 지표면보다 높게 두어, 녹는 얼음 때문에 물에 잠길 위험을 줄여줍니다.
Now, let's watch a short video clip about these fascinating bird nests.
이제, 이 매혹적인 새 둥지에 대한 짧은 비디오 영상을 시청합시다.

- expert ⓐ 전문적인
- incorporate ⓥ (~의 일부로) 포함하다
- feather ⓝ 깃털
- purpose ⓝ 목적
- require ⓥ 필요하다, 필요로 하다
- attach ⓥ 붙다, 부착하다
- tiny ⓐ 매우 작은
- bind ⓥ 묶다
- fasten ⓥ 고정하다, (단단히) 잠그다
- gather ⓥ 모으다
- reduce ⓥ 줄이다, 감소시키다
- nest ⓝ 둥지
- particularly ad 특히
- commonly ad 흔히, 보통
- species ⓝ 종(種)
- sticky ⓐ 끈적거리는
- vertical ⓐ 수직의
- normally ad 보통
- spiderweb ⓥ 거미줄로 덮다
- environment ⓝ 환경
- ground level 지표면
- fascinating ⓐ 매혹적인
- cooperate ⓥ 협력하다
- harmful ⓐ 해로운
- inspire ⓥ 영감을 주다
- collect ⓥ 모으다
- shortage ⓝ 부족, 결핍

16 주제 파악

정답률 74% | 정답 ②

여자가 하는 말의 주제로 가장 적절한 것은?

① how birds cooperate to collect nesting materials
새들이 둥지를 지을 재료를 모으기 위해 협력하는 방법
✓ why birds use certain materials in nest building
왜 새들은 둥지를 지을 때 특정 재료를 쓰는가
③ natural substances that are harmful to bird nests
새 둥지에 해로운 천연 물질들
④ shortage of birds' nesting materials in urban areas
도시에서 새들이 둥지 짓는 데 쓸 재료의 부족
⑤ industrial building materials inspired by bird nests
새 둥지에서 영감을 얻은 산업용 건축 재료들

Why? 왜 정답일까?

'So today, we'll learn ~ used in bird nests.'에서 여자는 새가 둥지를 지을 때 왜 특정 재료가 사용되는지 그 이유를 알아보자고 하므로, 여자가 하는 말의 주제로 가장 적절한 것은 ② '왜 새들은 둥지를 지을 때 특정 재료를 쓰는가'이다.

17 언급 유무 파악

정답률 90% | 정답 ④

언급된 재료가 아닌 것은?

① feathers – 깃털 ② mud – 진흙 ③ spiderwebs – 거미줄
✓ leaves – 나뭇잎 ⑤ stones – 돌

Why? 왜 정답일까?

담화에서 여자는 새가 둥지 짓기에 활용하는 재료의 예로 깃털, 진흙, 거미줄, 돌을 언급하므로, 언급되지 않은 것은 ④ '나뭇잎'이다.

Why? 왜 오답일까?

① 'Particularly, feathers are commonly used for this purpose.'에서 '깃털'이 언급되었다.
② 'These birds use mud because it attaches well to vertical surfaces.'에서 '진흙'이 언급되었다.
③ 'They often use spiderwebs to fasten these nesting materials together.'에서 '거미줄'이 언급되었다.
⑤ 'These birds gather stones for their nests to place their eggs on.'에서 '돌'이 언급되었다.

Dictation 13

문제편 075쪽

01 an easy-to-use program for building websites / at your fingertips / copyright issues
02 Some vegetables are healthier / roasting carrots and tomatoes / release a compound
03 paper sculpture exhibition / What does it symbolize / represent family love / appreciate your artwork
04 the school broadcasting studio / there's a bookshelf / keep our scripts / a professional look
05 beginner lessons / how about promotional posters / make it eye-catching
06 getting a spray bottle / $5 discount on it / Would you like them delivered
07 science report competition / was not the issue / researched the topic thoroughly / didn't include the experiment pictures
08 get a lot of useful information / within walking distance / going next weekend
09 money management skills / starting from August 1st / on-site registration is not available / receive a planner / financial security
10 come in three different materials / the texture of wood / foldable model / need a foldable one / This silver one looks fancier
11 Won't it go bad / as soon as you get home
12 this roller coaster / much shorter than that
13 looks slightly old / the expiration dates /too small for me to read
14 educational and fascinating / Far more than we expected / order more if you need
15 left negative reviews / turn away from her business / a sales increase / make use of negative reviews
16-17 expert nest builders / cliffs or buildings / attaches well to vertical surfaces / place their eggs on

14회 | 2022학년도 6월 모의평가 고3

• 정답 •

01 ⑤ 02 ① 03 ① 04 ③ 05 ② 06 ④ 07 ② 08 ③ 09 ④ 10 ③ 11 ① 12 ④ 13 ⑤ 14 ① 15 ②
16 ⑤ 17 ③

01 댄스 동아리 인원 추가 모집 안내

정답률 96% | 정답 ⑤

다음을 듣고, 남자가 하는 말의 목적으로 가장 적절한 것을 고르시오.

① 댄스 동아리 가입 조건을 안내하려고
② 동아리 개설 신청 기간을 홍보하려고
③ 동아리 만족도 설문 조사 참여를 당부하려고
④ 댄스 동아리 활동 장소 폐쇄 이유를 설명하려고
✔ 댄스 동아리 회원 모집 인원 증원을 공지하려고

M : Good afternoon, students of Robinson High School.
안녕하세요, Robinson 고등학교 학생 여러분.
This is Mr. Anderson, coach of the school dance club.
저는 교내 댄스 동아리 코치인 Anderson 선생입니다.
I'd like to announce that we'll be recruiting additional new members for our school dance club.
우리 교내 댄스 동아리의 신입 회원을 추가로 모집할 것임을 알려드리려고 합니다.
Previously we were looking for 10 new club members, and many students showed interest in joining.
이전에 10명의 동아리 신입 회원을 모집했는데, 많은 학생들이 가입에 관심을 보여 주었습니다.
Luckily, we've been assigned to a bigger room than expected.
다행스럽게도, 우리는 예상보다 더 큰 동아리방을 배정받았습니다.
Now we're allowed to accept five additional new members to make a total of 15 students.
이제 우리는 5명의 신입 회원을 추가로 받아서 총 15명의 학생을 받을 수 있게 되었습니다.
Once again, I'm happy to inform you that our school dance club has increased the number of new members to recruit.
다시 한 번, 우리 교내 댄스 동아리가 모집할 신입 회원의 수를 증원하게 되었다는 것을 알리게 되어 기쁘다는 말씀 드립니다.
Thank you for your interest.
관심을 보여 주셔서 감사합니다.

Why? 왜 정답일까?

'I'd like to announce that we'll be recruiting additional new members for our school dance club.'과 '~ I'm happy to inform you that our school dance club has increased the number of new members to recruit.'에서 남자는 교내 댄스 동아리의 모집 인원이 늘어났다는 사실을 알리고 있다. 따라서 남자가 하는 말의 목적으로 가장 적절한 것은 ⑤ '댄스 동아리 회원 모집 인원 증원을 공지하려고'이다.

- announce ⓥ 알리다, 발표하다
- additional ⓐ 추가적인
- expect ⓥ 기대하다, 예상하다
- recruit ⓥ 모집하다
- assign ⓥ 배정하다, 할당하다

02 과대 포장 지양하기

정답률 93% | 정답 ①

대화를 듣고, 여자의 의견으로 가장 적절한 것을 고르시오.

✔ 불필요한 쓰레기를 줄이기 위해 과도한 포장을 지양해야 한다.
② 환경 보호를 위해 쓰레기 분리배출을 철저히 해야 한다.
③ 선물을 고를 때는 받는 사람의 취향을 고려해야 한다.
④ 사용 빈도가 높지 않은 물건은 상자에 보관해야 한다.
⑤ 선물 종류에 따라 포장 방법을 달리해야 한다.

W : Hey, Connor. What are you doing with all of these gift boxes?
Connor야, 이 모든 선물 상자를 가지고 뭘 하고 있니?
M : Mom, I'm wrapping a scarf for Grandma. You know, her birthday is in a week.
엄마, 할머니께 드릴 스카프를 포장하고 있어요. 아시다시피, 할머니 생신이 일주일 후잖아요.
W : Great. But do you really need these three boxes for just one scarf?
훌륭하구나. 그런데 단 한 개의 스카프에 상자 세 개가 꼭 필요하니?
M : Yes. The boxes are all different sizes, and I'll put each one inside the other.
네. 상자 크기가 모두 다르고, 각 상자를 다른 상자 속에 넣을 거예요.
W : Well, don't you feel bad about wasting all of those boxes?
음, 그 상자들을 모두 낭비하는 것에 대해 마음이 안 좋지 않니?
M : What do you mean? I just wanted the gift to look fancy and interesting.
무슨 말이세요? 저는 단지 선물이 멋지고 재미있어 보이기를 원했을 뿐이에요.
W : I understand. However, the boxes will end up being thrown away, right?
이해해. 하지만 그 상자들은 결국 버려질 거잖아, 그렇지?
M : So, you mean it's overpackaging? Oh, I didn't know I was wasting boxes.
그럼, 이게 과대 포장이라는 말인가요? 제가 상자들을 낭비하는 줄은 몰랐어요.
W : Yeah. I think we should avoid overpackaging to reduce unnecessary waste.
그래. 불필요한 쓰레기를 줄이기 위해 우리는 과대 포장을 피해야 한다고 생각해.
M : You're right. I'll use one box for now and save the others for later.
엄마 말이 맞아요. 지금은 상자 한 개를 사용하고 나머지는 나중을 위해 보관할게요.
W : Good idea. No matter how it looks, Grandma will love your gift.
좋은 생각이야. 그것의 겉모습이 어떻든 간에, 할머니는 네 선물을 좋아하실 거야.

Why? 왜 정답일까?

'I think we should avoid overpackaging to reduce unnecessary waste.'에서 여자는 불필요한 쓰레기를 줄이기 위해서 과대 포장을 피해야 한다고 생각한다는 의견을 제시한다. 따라서 여자의 의견으로 가장 적절한 것은 ① '불필요한 쓰레기를 줄이기 위해 과도한 포장을 지양해야 한다.'이다.

- end up ~ing 결국 ~하게 되다
- unnecessary ⓐ 불필요한
- overpackaging ⓝ 과대 포장

03 시나리오 작가 인터뷰

정답률 95% | 정답 ①

대화를 듣고, 두 사람의 관계를 가장 잘 나타낸 것을 고르시오.

✔ 잡지 기자 – 시나리오 작가
② 아나운서 – 작사가
③ 라디오 진행자 – 음악 평론가
④ 영화감독 – 배우
⑤ 신문 기자 – 모델

M : Hello, Ms. Lee. It's an honor to meet you in person.
Lee 선생님, 안녕하세요. 직접 만나 뵙게 되어 영광입니다.
W : Oh, thank you for interviewing me, Mr. Wilson. I'm a big fan of your magazine.
오, Wilson 선생님, 인터뷰해 주셔서 고맙습니다. 저는 선생님 잡지의 열렬한 팬입니다.
M : Thanks. People love your movie *Short Days*. I was wondering who picked out the title.
고맙습니다. 사람들은 선생님의 영화 *Short Days*를 매우 좋아합니다. 제목은 누가 선택했는지 궁금했습니다.
W : Well, it was basically my idea and the movie director agreed.
음, 그것은 기본적으로 제 생각이었고, 영화감독님이 동의해 주었어요.
M : It really catches the theme of the movie. Why do you think people love your stories?
그것이 정말 영화의 주제를 잘 포착하고 있어요. 사람들이 왜 선생님의 이야기를 매우 좋아한다고 생각하나요?
W : When writing film scripts, I always try to make the characters as realistic as possible.
영화 대본을 쓸 때, 저는 늘 등장인물들을 최대한 현실감 있게 만들려고 해요.
M : Maybe that's why people feel stronger connections to them. What inspires you when you write your scripts?
어쩌면 그래서 사람들은 그들과 더 잘 교감하겠군요. 대본을 쓸 때 무엇이 선생님께 영감을 주나요?
W : Often, my own life experiences help create many of the scenes in my scripts.
흔히, 제 인생 경험이 제 대본 속의 많은 장면들을 창작하는 데 도움이 돼요.
M : I see. Thank you. The readers of our magazine will appreciate you sharing your time with us.
그렇군요. 고맙습니다. 우리 잡지 독자들이 선생님이 저희와 시간을 함께해 준 것에 대해 고마워할 겁니다.
W : My pleasure. Could you please email me the article?
저도 기쁩니다. 제게 기사를 이메일로 보내주실 수 있나요?
M : No problem.
그러겠습니다.

Why? 왜 정답일까?

'I'm a big fan of your magazine.', 'When writing film scripts, I always try to make the characters as realistic as possible.', 'What inspires you when you write your scripts?', 'Often, my own life experiences help create many of the scenes in my scripts.', 'The readers of our magazine will appreciate you sharing your time with us.' 등에서 남자가 잡지 기자이고, 여자가 영화 시나리오 작가임을 알 수 있으므로, 두 사람의 관계로 가장 적절한 것은 ① '잡지 기자 – 시나리오 작가'이다.

- be a big fan of ~의 열렬한 팬이다
- realistic ⓐ 현실적인
- appreciate ⓥ 고마워하다
- pick out 선택하다
- inspire ⓥ 영감을 주다

04 수리된 욕실 사진 구경하기

정답률 90% | 정답 ③

대화를 듣고, 그림에서 대화의 내용과 일치하지 않는 것을 고르시오.

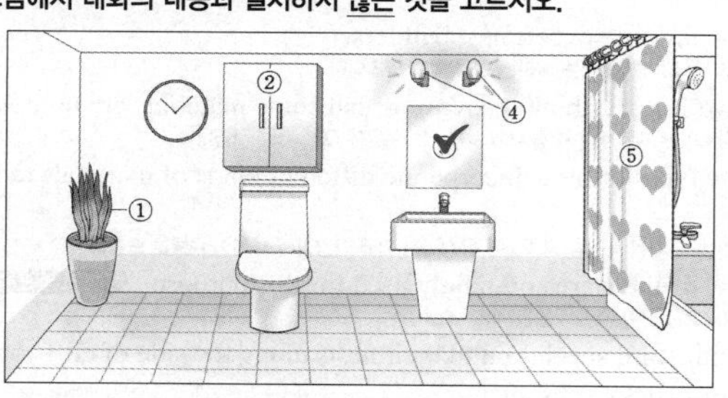

W : Honey, today I went to the house we'll be moving in to. I really liked the bathroom renovations.
여보, 오늘 난 우리가 이사 갈 집에 갔었어요. 욕실 수리한 게 정말 맘에 들었어요.
M : Oh, really? Did you take a picture of the bathroom?
오, 정말요? 욕실 사진을 찍었나요?
W : Of course. Here it is. 『How's the plant in the corner?』 I bought it on the way to the house. ①의 근거 일치
물론이죠. 여기 있어요. 구석에 있는 식물은 어때요? 그 집에 가는 길에 그걸 샀어요.
M : Excellent choice. 『The cabinet next to the clock is perfect for our family.』 ②의 근거 일치
탁월한 선택이에요. 벽시계 옆의 수납장은 우리 가족에게 안성맞춤이네요.
W : Yeah, it'll be useful for storing all of our towels.
그래요, 우리 수건을 전부 수납하는 데 유용할 거예요.
M : You're right. 『And look at this round mirror over the bathroom sink.』 It's very modern. ③의 근거 불일치
당신 말이 맞아요. 그리고 욕실 싱크대 위에 있는 이 원형 거울을 보세요. 매우 현대적이에요.
W : Yes. That's my favorite part. 『And I also like the two lights on the wall.』 ④의 근거 일치
그래요, 내가 제일 좋아하는 부분이에요. 그리고 벽에 있는 두 개의 조명도 마음에 들어요.
M : Me, too. Aren't they unique?
나도 그래요. 독특하지 않나요?
W : Absolutely. 『What do you think about the shower curtain with the heart pattern?』 ⑤의 근거 일치
물론이죠. 하트 무늬가 있는 샤워 커튼은 어떻게 생각하나요?
M : The kids will definitely love it.
아이들이 분명히 아주 좋아할 거예요.
W : I agree. I'm excited to move in to our new house this weekend.
동의해요. 이번 주말에 우리 새집으로 이사하게 돼서 설레네요.

Why? 왜 정답일까?

대화에서 욕실 싱크대 위의 거울은 원형이라고 하는데(And look at this round mirror over the bathroom sink.), 그림의 거울은 사각형이다. 따라서 그림에서 대화의 내용과 일치하지 않는 것은 ③이다.

[문제편 p.079]

- renovation ⓝ 수리
- unique ⓐ 독특한
- definitely ad 분명히, 확실히

05 자원봉사 신청 도와주기
정답률 95% | 정답 ②

대화를 듣고, 여자가 남자를 위해 할 일로 가장 적절한 것을 고르시오.

① 경제학 과제 자료 조사하기
✔ 자원봉사 신청서 제출하기
③ 환경 캠페인 포스터 만들기
④ 학생회관 가는 길 알려 주기
⑤ 마라톤 코스 답사하기

W : Hey, Brandon. Have you seen this poster?
안녕, Brandon. 이 포스터 본 적 있어?
M : What's this? Oh, it's the Earth Hour Marathon.
이게 뭐야? 아, Earth Hour Marathon이네.
W : Yeah, it's to raise students' awareness about protecting the environment.
응, 그건 환경 보호에 관한 학생들의 인식을 높이기 위해서 하는 거야.
M : That sounds like a great campaign. Are you participating in it?
멋진 캠페인처럼 들리네. 넌 거기에 참여할 거야?
W : Actually, I'm a staff member of the event and I'm looking for volunteers.
사실, 난 행사 요원인데 자원봉사자를 찾고 있어.
M : Oh, is that so? Then, what's the role of a volunteer?
아, 그래? 그러면 자원봉사자의 역할은 뭐야?
W : A volunteer hands out water to the runners during the race.
자원봉사자는 경기 중에 선수들에게 물을 나눠 주지.
M : That sounds good. When does it take place?
좋은 것 같아. 언제 열려?
W : It's next Saturday at City Hall. Are you interested?
시청에서 다음 주 토요일에 열려. 관심 있어?
M : Sure. How do I apply to be a volunteer?
물론이지. 자원봉사자가 되려면 어떻게 신청해?
W : Here. You must submit this application form to the student center by 5 o'clock today.
여기 있어. 이 신청서를 오늘 5시까지 학생회관에 제출해야 해.
M : Oh! I have economics class in 10 minutes, and it finishes at 6 o'clock.
아! 난 10분 후에 경제학 수업이 있는데, 그게 6시에 끝나.
W : Just write your name and phone number. I'll submit your application form for you.
네 이름과 전화번호만 적어. 내가 널 위해 신청서를 제출할게.
M : Thanks. *[Writing sound]* Here you go.
고마워. *[적는 소리]* 여기 있어.

Why? 왜 정답일까?

여자는 환경 보호 행사에 자원봉사로 참여하고 싶어 하는 남자를 대신해서 남자의 참가 신청서를 제출해 주겠다고 한다(**I'll submit your application form for you.**). 따라서 여자가 남자를 위해 할 일로 가장 적절한 것은 ② '자원봉사 신청서 제출하기'이다.

- **raise awareness** 인식을 높이다
- **hand out** 나눠주다
- **application form** 신청서, 지원서

06 반려견 용품 구입하기
정답률 89% | 정답 ④

대화를 듣고, 여자가 지불할 금액을 고르시오. [3점]

① $30 ② $36 ③ $40 ✔ $45 ⑤ $50

M : Welcome to Family Pet Shop. May I help you?
Family Pet Shop에 오신 걸 환영합니다. 무엇을 도와드릴까요?
W : Hi, I'm looking for dog food.
안녕하세요. 개 사료를 찾고 있습니다.
M : Let me show you.
제가 보여드리겠습니다.
W : Thanks. How much is it for a bag of dog food?
고맙습니다. 개 사료 한 봉지에 얼마인가요?
M : That depends on your dog's age.
그건 손님 개의 나이에 따라 다릅니다.
W : Oh, does it make a difference?
아, 그것 때문에 차이가 나나요?
M : Yes. It costs $15 per bag for little puppies and $20 per bag for adult dogs.
네. 작은 강아지용은 한 봉지에 15달러이고, 성견용은 한 봉지에 20달러입니다.
W : My dogs are all grown up. So, I'll get two bags of dog food for adult dogs.
우리 집 개들은 다 컸습니다. 그래서 성견용 사료 두 봉지를 사겠습니다.
M : All right. Do you need anything else?
알겠습니다. 그 밖에 또 필요한 게 있으신가요?
W : Well, can you recommend a good brush?
저, 좋은 솔을 추천해 줄 수 있나요?
M : Oh, how about this one? It's very popular among our customers and only costs $10.
아, 이건 어떠세요? 우리 고객들 사이에서 매우 인기가 있는 건데요, 가격은 10달러밖에 안 합니다.
W : Perfect. I'll take one.
완벽해요. 하나 사겠습니다.
M : Good. So you want two bags of dog food for adult dogs and one brush, right?
좋습니다. 그러면 성견용 사료 두 봉지와 솔 하나를 원하시는 것 맞습니까?
W : Yes. Can I use this discount coupon?
네. 이 할인 쿠폰을 사용할 수 있나요?
M : Let me see. *[Pause]* Yes, you can get 10% off the total with this coupon.
어디 볼까요. *[잠시 멈춤]* 네, 이 쿠폰으로 전체 금액의 10%를 할인받을 수 있습니다.
W : Great. I'll pay in cash.
아주 좋네요. 현금으로 계산할게요.

Why? 왜 정답일까?

대화에 따르면 여자는 20달러짜리 성견용 사료 두 봉지와 10달러짜리 솔 하나를 사고, 총 가격의 10퍼센트를 할인받기로 했다. 이를 식으로 나타내면 '$(20\times2+10)\times0.9=45$'이므로, 여자가 지불할 금액은 ④ '$45'이다.

- **make a difference** 차이가 나다, 변화가 생기다
- **pay in cash** 현금 계산하다

07 프로그래밍 수업을 듣지 못하는 이유
정답률 95% | 정답 ②

대화를 듣고, 남자가 컴퓨터 프로그래밍 강좌를 신청하지 않은 이유를 고르시오.

① 수업이 30분 일찍 시작되어서
✔ 다른 도시로 이사를 가게 되어서
③ 컴퓨터 프로그래밍에 흥미를 잃어서
④ 퇴근 후에 수업 듣는 것이 너무 피곤해서
⑤ 컴퓨터 프로그래밍이 자신의 경력과 무관해서

W : Hey, Blake. It's the last day of the class. Did you sign up for the next computer programming class?
안녕, Blake. 오늘이 수업 마지막 날이네요. 다음 컴퓨터 프로그래밍 수업 등록했어요?
M : No, Angela. I cannot take the class anymore.
아니요, Angela. 저는 더 이상 그 수업을 들을 수 없어요.
W : Oh, I thought you enjoyed the programming class.
아, 프로그래밍 수업을 즐거워한다고 생각했는데요.
M : Yeah. I found it really helpful for my career, too.
네. 수업이 제 경력에도 정말 도움이 된다는 것을 알았어요.
W : Then, what's the reason? Are you too tired to attend the class after work?
그럼, 이유가 뭔가요? 퇴근 후에 수업에 참석하기가 너무 피곤한가요?
M : Not at all. The class is quite exciting.
전혀 그렇지 않아요. 수업이 꽤 재미있어요.
W : Is it because the new class starts 30 minutes earlier?
새로운 수업이 30분 일찍 시작하기 때문인가요?
M : No. That's actually better for my schedule. The problem is that I have to move to another city.
아니요. 사실 그게 제 일정에는 더 좋아요. 문제는 제가 다른 도시로 이사를 해야 한다는 겁니다.
W : Oh, you're moving?
아, 이사하세요?
M : Yes. So, I don't think I can make it.
네. 그래서 수업에 참석을 못 할 것 같아요.
W : I'm sorry to hear that. It was nice taking the class with you.
그 말 들으니 아쉽네요. 수업을 함께 들어서 좋았어요.
M : Same here. Let's keep in touch.
저도 그랬어요. 우리 연락하고 지내요.

Why? 왜 정답일까?

대화에 따르면 남자는 다른 도시로 이사를 가야 해서 프로그래밍 수업을 더 이상 들을 수 없게 되었다(**The problem is that I have to move to another city.**). 따라서 남자가 컴퓨터 프로그래밍 강좌를 신청하지 않은 이유로 가장 적절한 것은 ② '다른 도시로 이사를 가게 되어서'이다.

- **sign up for** ~에 등록하다
- **make it** 참석하다, 성공하다, 해내다
- **keep in touch** 연락하고 지내다, 소식을 계속 접하다

08 목공 수업 등록하기
정답률 96% | 정답 ③

대화를 듣고, Samuel's Woodworking Class에 관해 언급되지 않은 것을 고르시오.

① 장소 ② 시간 ✔ 복장
④ 등록비 ⑤ 모집 인원

M : Gina, come check out this flyer.
Gina, 와서 이 전단 확인해 봐.
W : What's this, Ted? *[Pause]* Oh, Samuel's Woodworking Class. Looks interesting.
이게 뭐야, Ted? *[잠시 후]* 오, Samuel's Woodworking Class네. 재밌어 보인다.
M : 『It's a one-time class in the art studio of the community center.』 ①의 근거 일치 I think you'd like it, too.
주민센터에 있는 미술 스튜디오에서 한 번 하는 수업이야. 너도 좋아할 것 같아.
W : Absolutely! Look, we can get some hands-on practice making a pencil case or a wooden plate.
당연하지! 이봐, 우리는 필통이나 나무 접시를 만드는 실습을 할 수 있어.
M : Yes! 『The class will be held from 7 p.m. to 9 p.m. next Friday.』 ②의 근거 일치
그래! 수업은 다음 주 금요일 저녁 7시부터 9시까지 진행될 거야.
W : I'll be available then. Do you want to take the class together?
난 그때 시간이 될 거야. 함께 수업을 듣고 싶어?
M : Sure. I think I'm going to make a pencil case. What about you?
물론이지. 난 필통을 만들 것 같아. 넌?
W : I'd like to make a wooden plate. 『How much is the registration fee?
난 나무 접시를 만들고 싶어. 등록비는 얼마야?
M : It's only $40 per person.』 ④의 근거 일치
1인당 40달러밖에 안 해.
W : That's a good price. Does it say how we can register?
적절한 가격이네. 등록 방법은 적혀 있어?
M : Here. We can register on the community center website.
여기. 주민센터 웹 사이트에서 등록할 수 있어.
W : Yes, and look. 『Only 12 people can register.』 We'd better hurry.
그러네. 그리고 봐. 12명만 등록할 수 있어. 서둘러야겠다. ⑤의 근거 일치
M : Let's sign up now.
지금 등록하자.

Why? 왜 정답일까?

대화에서 남자와 여자는 Samuel's Woodworking Class의 장소, 시간, 등록비, 모집 인원을 언급하였다. 따라서 언급되지 않은 것은 ③ '복장'이다.

Why? 왜 오답일까?

① 'It's a one-time class in the art studio of the community center.'에서 '장소'가 언급되었다.
② 'The class will be held from 7 p.m. to 9 p.m. next Friday.'에서 '시간'이 언급되었다.
④ 'It's only $40 per person.'에서 '등록비'가 언급되었다.
⑤ 'Only 12 people can register.'에서 '모집 인원'이 언급되었다.

- **woodworking** ⓝ 목공
- **hands-on** ⓐ 직접 해보는
- **registration fee** 등록비, 참가비

09 에세이 대회 안내
정답률 96% | 정답 ④

2021 Lakeside Essay Contest에 관한 다음 내용을 듣고, 일치하지 않는 것을 고르시오.

① 주제는 여름으로부터의 메시지이다.
② Lakeside High School 전교생이 참가할 수 있다.
③ 에세이 분량은 3페이지를 넘으면 안 된다.
✔ 제출 마감은 다음 주 금요일이다.
⑤ 상위 10편의 에세이는 학교 웹 사이트에 게시될 예정이다.

W : Okay, class.
자, 여러분.
Before I let you go, I'd like to remind you about the 2021 Lakeside Essay Contest.
보내드리기 전에, 여러분께 2021 Lakeside Essay Contest에 대해 상기시켜 드리려고 합니다.
「As you know, the theme of this year is "messages from summer."」 ①의 근거 일치
여러분이 알다시피, 올해의 주제는 '여름으로부터의 메시지'입니다.
Last year, the contest was only open to freshmen.
작년에, 그 대회는 1학년만 참가할 수 있었습니다.
「But this year, all students at Lakeside High School can participate.」 ②의 근거 일치
하지만 올해에는 Lakeside 고등학교의 전교생이 참가할 수 있습니다.
You can submit your essay to me by email.
여러분의 에세이를 제게 이메일로 제출해 주시면 됩니다.
「Don't forget your essay should be no longer than three pages.」 ③의 근거 일치
에세이는 3페이지를 넘으면 안 된다는 것을 잊지 마십시오.
「Please start writing your essay today because the deadline is next Wednesday.」
마감일이 다음 주 수요일이기 때문에 오늘 에세이를 쓰기 시작하세요. ④의 근거 불일치
You can check the results of the contest on July 3rd.
여러분은 7월 3일에 대회 결과를 확인할 수 있습니다.
「The top 10 essays will be posted on our school website.」 ⑤의 근거 일치
상위 10편의 에세이는 학교 웹 사이트에 게시될 예정입니다.
I hope many of you participate in this contest!
저는 여러분 중 많은 학생이 이 대회에 참가하기를 바랍니다!
All right, everyone. See you next time.
자, 여러분. 다음 시간에 만납시다.

Why? 왜 정답일까?

'~ the deadline is next Wednesday.'에서 에세이 제출 마감은 다음 주 수요일이라고 하므로, 내용과 일치하지 않는 것은 ④ '제출 마감은 다음 주 금요일이다.'이다.

Why? 왜 오답일까?

① '~ the theme of this year is "messages from summer."'의 내용과 일치한다.
② '~ all students at Lakeside High School can participate.'의 내용과 일치한다.
③ 'Don't forget your essay should be no longer than three pages.'의 내용과 일치한다.
⑤ 'The top 10 essays will be posted on our school website.'의 내용과 일치한다.

- remind ⓥ 상기시키다
- be open to ~을 대상으로 하다, ~에 개방되다
- freshman ⓝ 1학년, 신입생
- submit ⓥ 제출하다

10 자전거 고르기
정답률 87% | 정답 ③

다음 표를 보면서 대화를 듣고, 남자가 주문할 자전거를 고르시오.

Bicycles for Commuters

	Model	Color	Price	Frame Size	Foldable
①	A	Black	$190	Small	×
②	B	Yellow	$210	Medium	×
✔	C	Silver	$270	Large	×
④	D	White	$290	Large	○
⑤	E	Blue	$320	Medium	○

M : Hey, Olivia. You know a lot about bicycles. Would you help me choose one from this list?
안녕하세요, Olivia. 당신은 자전거에 대해 많이 알죠. 제가 이 목록 중에서 하나 고르는 것 좀 도와주실래요?
W : Sure. Let me see. *[Pause]* Oh, you're looking at bicycles for commuters. 「Well, I don't recommend the black one for your safety at night.」 근거1 Color 조건
물론이죠. 어디 봐요. *[잠시 멈춤]* 아, 통근자들을 위한 자전거를 보고 있군요. 그렇다면, 밤에 안전을 위해 검은색 자전거는 추천하지 않아요.
M : You're right. It won't be safe when it's dark. Then I'll go for the other colors.
맞아요. 검은색은 어두울 때는 안전하지 않겠네요. 그럼 다른 색으로 할게요.
W : Good idea. 「What's your budget?
좋은 생각이에요. 예산이 어떻게 되죠?
M : I can spend up to $300.」 근거2 Price 조건
300달러까지는 쓸 수 있어요.
W : Okay. Now you need to choose a frame size.
알겠어요. 이제 프레임 크기를 선택해야 해요.
M : 「Should I choose a medium-sized frame?
중간 크기의 프레임을 골라야 할까요?
W : No. Because you're tall, you'll need a bigger one.」 근거3 Frame Size 조건
아니요. 키가 크시니까 더 큰 것이 필요할 거예요.
M : Okay. I'll get one of these then. Do you think I need a foldable bicycle?
알겠어요. 그럼 이것들 중 하나로 해야겠군요. 접이식 자전거가 필요할까요?
W : Hmm, it depends on how often you use public transportation.
음, 그것은 대중교통을 얼마나 자주 이용하느냐에 달렸어요.
M : I rarely use public transportation, so 「I guess I don't need a foldable one.」
저는 대중교통을 거의 이용하지 않아서, 접이식 자전거는 필요 없을 것 같아요. 근거4 Foldable 조건
W : Then, this model is the best choice for you.
그렇다면, 이 제품이 당신을 위한 최선의 선택이에요.
M : Great. I'll order it now. Thanks.
훌륭해요. 지금 그것을 주문할게요. 고마워요.

Why? 왜 정답일까?

대화에 따르면 남자는 검은색이 아니면서, 가격은 300달러를 넘지 않고, 프레임은 중간보다 큰 크기에, 접이식이 아닌 자전거를 구매하려고 한다. 따라서 남자가 주문할 자전거는 ③ 'C'이다.

- commuter ⓝ 통근하는 사람
- go for ~을 선택하다
- foldable ⓐ 접을 수 있는, 접이식의
- public transportation 대중교통

11 미용실 예약 권하기
정답률 83% | 정답 ①

대화를 듣고, 여자의 마지막 말에 대한 남자의 응답으로 가장 적절한 것을 고르시오.

✔ Sure. Let me call him now.
물론이죠. 지금 그에게 전화할게요.
② Not at all. My hair is really long.
전혀 아니죠. 제 머리가 정말 길어요.
③ Yes. I really like my new hairstyle.
네. 저는 제 새 머리 모양이 정말 마음에 들어요.
④ Why not? I'll text the number to you.
왜 안 되겠어요? 제가 당신에게 문자로 번호를 알려드릴게요.
⑤ Not really. I don't need to check your schedule.
그렇지는 않아요. 제가 당신의 일정을 확인할 필요는 없어요.

W : Honey, your hair's getting pretty long.
여보, 당신 머리가 꽤 길어지고 있어요.
M : Yeah. I was thinking about getting a haircut today. What about the hairstylist you talked about?
그래요. 오늘 이발을 할까 생각 중이었어요. 당신이 말했던 미용사는 어떤가요?
W : He's good, but you should call him first and check if he's available. Do you want the phone number?
잘하지만, 당신은 먼저 그에게 전화해서 시간이 되는지 확인해 봐야 해요. 전화번호를 알려줄까요?
M : Sure. Let me call him now.
물론이죠. 지금 그에게 전화할게요.

Why? 왜 정답일까?

여자는 남자에게 이발을 권하며 전에 자신이 추천했던 미용사의 전화번호를 알려줄지 남자에게 물어보고 있다(Do you want the phone number?). 따라서 남자의 응답으로 가장 적절한 것은 ① '물론이죠. 지금 그에게 전화할게요.'이다.

- get a haircut 이발하다, 머리를 자르다
- available ⓐ (사람이) 시간이 있는
- text ⓥ 문자 메시지를 보내다

12 드럼 연주자 자리 제안하기
정답률 80% | 정답 ④

대화를 듣고, 남자의 마지막 말에 대한 여자의 응답으로 가장 적절한 것을 고르시오.

① Fine. I'll look for another band. – 좋아. 다른 밴드를 찾아볼게.
② Great! You can be our drummer. – 멋지다! 너는 우리의 드럼 연주자가 될 수 있어.
③ Sorry. I can't offer you the position. – 미안해. 나는 네게 그 자리를 줄 수 없어.
✔ Really? It'll be great to play in your band. – 정말이야? 너희 밴드에서 연주하면 아주 멋질 거야.
⑤ What a surprise! I didn't know you play drums. – 놀라운데! 네가 드럼을 연주하는 줄 몰랐어.

M : Hey, Lauren. Are you still looking for a band to play drums in?
안녕, Lauren. 아직도 드럼 연주할 밴드를 찾고 있니?
W : Yes, but I haven't found one yet. Your band is still my first choice, but I know you already have a drummer.
응, 하지만 아직 찾지 못했어. 여전히 난 너희 밴드가 제일 좋은데, 너희한테는 이미 드럼 연주자가 있는 걸 알지.
M : Actually, our drummer had to quit for personal reasons. We want you to play drums in our band.
사실, 우리 드럼 연주자는 개인적인 사정으로 그만두게 되었어. 우리는 네가 우리 밴드에서 연주해주면 좋겠어.
W : Really? It'll be great to play in your band.
정말이야? 너희 밴드에서 연주하면 아주 멋질 거야.

Why? 왜 정답일까?

남자는 자신이 속한 밴드의 드럼 연주자가 개인 사정으로 그만두었음을 여자에게 알려주며, 여자가 드럼 연주자가 되어 주면 좋겠다고 말한다(We want you to play drums in our band.). 따라서 여자의 응답으로 가장 적절한 것은 ④ '정말이야? 너희 밴드에서 연주하면 아주 멋질 거야.'이다.

- quit ⓥ 그만두다
- personal ⓐ 개인적인, 사적인

13 스커트를 다른 색으로 보내주겠다고 제안하기
정답률 91% | 정답 ⑤

대화를 듣고, 여자의 마지막 말에 대한 남자의 응답으로 가장 적절한 것을 고르시오. [3점]

Man: ____________

① No problem. You'll get your refund. – 문제 없습니다. 고객님은 환불받으실 겁니다.
② Of course. That's why I canceled my order. – 물론입니다. 그것이 제가 주문을 취소한 이유입니다.
③ Excellent. I'll exchange it with a bigger size. – 아주 좋습니다. 저는 그것을 더 큰 치수로 교환하겠습니다.
④ Good. I'm glad to hear you received the package. – 잘됐군요. 소포를 받으셨다는 말을 들으니 기쁩니다.
✔ Okay. We'll send the gray skirt to you right away. – 알겠습니다. 바로 회색 스커트를 보내드리겠습니다.

[Cell phone rings.]
[휴대 전화가 울린다.]
W : Hello.
여보세요.
M : Good afternoon. This is S&G Clothing Company. Can I speak to Ms. Thompson, please?
안녕하세요. 여기는 S&G Clothing Company입니다. Thompson 씨와 통화할 수 있을까요?
W : Yes, speaking.
네, 말씀하세요.
M : I'm calling to tell you about the order you placed.
고객님께서 하신 주문에 관해 말씀드리려고 전화 드렸습니다.
W : Oh, is there a problem?
오, 문제가 있나요?
M : Yes. Unfortunately, the black skirt you ordered is out of stock at the moment.
네. 유감스럽게도, 고객님이 주문하신 검은색 스커트가 지금 재고가 없습니다.
W : Oh, no. I need it for my graduation ceremony this weekend.
오, 안 돼요. 저는 이번 주말 제 졸업식에 그게 필요해요.
M : We're very sorry for the inconvenience.

[문제편 p.079]

불편을 끼쳐 정말 죄송합니다.

W : Okay. Then, what are my options?
알겠어요. 그럼, 제가 선택할 수 있는 게 뭐죠?

M : You may cancel your order and get a full refund. Or we could send you the same skirt, but in a different color.
주문을 취소하시고 전액 환불받으실 수 있습니다. 또는 고객님께 똑같은 스커트를 다른 색깔로 보내드릴 수 있습니다.

W : Hmm... What colors do you have?
흠... 어떤 색깔이 있나요?

M : We currently have only gray in stock. If we send it out today, it'll arrive by Thursday.
저희는 현재 회색만 재고가 있습니다. 저희가 오늘 그것을 보내면 목요일까지 도착할 겁니다.

W : Well, I like the design of the skirt, so gray's fine.
음, 저는 그 스커트 디자인이 마음에 들어서 회색도 좋아요.

M : Okay. We'll send the gray skirt to you right away.
알겠습니다. 바로 회색 스커트를 보내드리겠습니다.

Why? 왜 정답일까?

남자는 여자가 주문한 스커트 재고가 없는 상태여서 디자인은 같되 색깔이 다른 스커트를 보내주겠다고 제안하고, 이를 여자는 승낙한다(**Well, I like the design of the skirt, so gray's fine.**). 따라서 남자의 응답으로 가장 적절한 것은 ⑤ '알겠습니다. 바로 회색 스커트를 보내드리겠습니다.'이다.

- **place an order** 주문하다
- **out of stock** 재고가 없는
- **graduation ceremony** 졸업식
- **inconvenience** ⓝ 불편

14 신용카드가 옷에 있는지 확인 부탁하기

정답률 88% | 정답 ①

대화를 듣고, 남자의 마지막 말에 대한 여자의 응답으로 가장 적절한 것을 고르시오.

Woman: ______________________

✔ All right. I'll check if it's in the jacket and call you back.
알겠어요. 그게 그 재킷에 있는지 확인해보고 다시 전화할게요.
② Don't worry. I'll visit the lost and found for you.
걱정하지 말아요. 당신 대신 분실물 보관소에 가볼게요.
③ Too bad. Let me have my credit card replaced.
너무 안됐어요. 제 신용카드를 교체할게요.
④ I see. I'll buy a new jacket if you can't find it.
알겠어요. 그걸 못 찾으면 새 재킷을 사 줄게요.
⑤ Thank you. Pick me up at the grocery store.
고마워요. 슈퍼로 나를 태우러 와요.

[Cell phone rings.]
[휴대 전화가 울린다.]

W : Hi, honey. What's up?
안녕, 여보. 무슨 일이에요?

M : Where are you right now?
당신 지금 어디예요?

W : I just parked my car. I'll be home in a minute. How about you?
방금 주차했어요. 곧 집에 갈 거예요. 당신은요?

M : I'm at the grocery store, but I've just realized one of my credit cards is missing.
난 지금 슈퍼에 있는데, 내 신용카드 중 하나가 없어진 걸 방금 알았어요.

W : Really? You should call the credit card company and cancel your card right away.
정말요? 당장 신용카드 회사에 전화해서 당신 카드를 취소해야 해요.

M : I will. But before I do that, can you check the pockets of my jacket, please?
그럴게요. 그런데 그러기 전에 당신이 내 재킷 주머니를 좀 확인해 줄 수 있어요?

W : Okay. Which jacket do you want me to check?
알았어요. 어느 재킷을 확인해 줄까요?

M : It's the brown one. I wore it yesterday.
갈색 재킷이요. 어제 그걸 입었어요.

W : You mean the one I bought for you last spring?
내가 지난봄에 당신한테 사 준 거 말이에요?

M : That's right. It's in the living room. Meanwhile, I'll look around the grocery store just in case I dropped the card.
맞아요. 그게 거실에 있어요. 그동안 나는 혹시 카드를 떨어뜨렸는지 슈퍼를 둘러볼게요.

W : All right. I'll check if it's in the jacket and call you back.
알겠어요. 그게 그 재킷에 있는지 확인해보고 다시 전화할게요.

Why? 왜 정답일까?

남자는 아내인 여자에게 자신이 신용카드를 잃어버린 것 같으니 분실신고를 하기 전에 어제 입었던 재킷을 확인해달라고 부탁한다. 그러자 여자는 작년 봄에 샀던 자켓이 맞는지 남자에게 다시 묻고 남자는 맞다는 말과 함께 자신은 슈퍼에 혹시 카드를 흘리지 않았는지 살펴보겠다고 한다(**Meanwhile, I'll look around the grocery store just in case I dropped the card.**). 따라서 여자의 응답으로 가장 적절한 것은 ① '알겠어요. 그게 그 재킷에 있는지 확인해보고 다시 전화할게요.'이다.

- **grocery store** 슈퍼, 식료품 가게
- **meanwhile** ⓐⓓ 그동안, 한편
- **just in case** ~한 경우에 대비하여
- **lost and found** 분실물 보관소

15 운동할 장소 선택하기

정답률 78% | 정답 ②

다음 상황 설명을 듣고, Rachel이 Kevin에게 할 말로 가장 적절한 것을 고르시오. [3점]

Rachel: ______________________

① Is it necessary to exercise every day? – 매일 운동하는 게 필요하니?
✔ Why don't you work out at the closer one? – 더 가까운 데서 운동하는 게 어때?
③ I recommend the one with good facilities. – 나는 시설이 좋은 곳을 추천해.
④ You should choose the one within your budget. – 너는 네 예산 안에 있는 것을 골라야 해.
⑤ What about looking for a better place to work at? – 더 나은 직장을 찾아보는 것은 어때?

M : Kevin is looking for a place to work out every day.
Kevin은 매일 운동할 장소를 찾고 있다.
He has found two fitness centers with good facilities.
그는 좋은 시설을 갖춘 헬스클럽 두 곳을 찾았다.
The first one is a 5-minute walk from home, and the second one is a 30-minute walk.
첫 번째 헬스클럽은 집에서 걸어서 5분 거리에 있고, 두 번째 헬스클럽은 걸어서 30분 거리에 있다.
Kevin likes the first fitness center because it's closer to home.
Kevin은 집에서 가까워서 첫 번째 헬스클럽이 마음에 든다.
However, he also thinks that the second fitness center can be a good choice because it offers a great discount for new members.
그런데 그는 또한 두 번째 헬스클럽에서 신입 회원에게 큰 할인을 제공하기 때문에 좋은 선택일 수 있다고 생각한다.
Kevin cannot decide which one to choose and asks his sister, Rachel, for advice.
Kevin은 어느 헬스클럽을 선택할지 결정할 수 없어서 누나인 Rachel에게 조언을 구한다.
Rachel remembers that he quit exercising in the past because the fitness centers were far from home.
Rachel은 이전에 그가 헬스클럽이 집에서 멀다는 이유로 운동을 그만두었던 일을 기억하고 있다.
She thinks that Kevin should choose a fitness center based on distance, not cost.
그녀는 Kevin이 비용이 아니라 거리에 근거해서 헬스클럽을 선택해야 한다고 생각한다.
So, Rachel wants to suggest to Kevin that he should choose the fitness center near home.
그래서, Rachel은 Kevin에게 집 근처에 있는 헬스클럽을 선택해야 한다고 제안하고 싶다.
In this situation, what would Rachel most likely say to Kevin?
이런 상황에서 Rachel은 Kevin에게 뭐라고 말하겠는가?

Rachel : Why don't you work out at the closer one?
더 가까운 데서 운동하는 게 어때?

Why? 왜 정답일까?

대화에 따르면 Rachel은 헬스클럽 두 곳을 두고 고민 중인 동생인 Kevin에게 비용이 싼 곳보다는 거리가 가까운 곳을 선택해 다니는 것이 좋겠다고 조언하고 싶어 한다(**So, Rachel wants to suggest to Kevin that he should choose the fitness center near home.**). 따라서 Rachel이 Kevin에게 할 말로 가장 적절한 것은 ② '더 가까운 데서 운동하는 게 어때?'이다.

- **work out** 운동하다
- **fitness center** 헬스클럽, 체력 단련실
- **facility** ⓝ 시설

16-17 다양한 직군에서의 드론 사용

W : Hello, students.
안녕하세요, 학생 여러분.
Last time, you learned about the people who invented drones.
지난 시간에 여러분은 드론을 발명한 사람들에 관해 배웠습니다.
「As technology develops, drones are being used more frequently around the world.
기술이 발달하면서 드론은 전 세계적으로 더 자주 사용되고 있습니다.
So, today, we'll talk about how they're used in different jobs.」 16번의 근거
그래서 오늘 우리는 갖가지 직업에서 그것이 어떻게 사용되고 있는지 이야기할 겁니다.
「First, drones help farmers grow crops more efficiently.」 17번 ①의 근거 일치
첫째로, 드론은 농부가 더 효율적으로 작물을 키우는 것을 돕습니다.
For example, drones are used to spread seeds that may be difficult to plant.
예를 들어, 드론은 심기 어려울 수 있는 씨앗을 뿌리는 데 사용됩니다.
They also spray chemicals to protect plants from harmful insects.
그것은 또한 해로운 벌레들로부터 식물을 보호하기 위해 농약을 뿌립니다.
「Second, photographers use drones to easily access areas that are hard to reach.」
둘째로, 사진 작가는 도달하기 어려운 지역에 쉽게 접근하기 위해 드론을 사용합니다. 17번 ②의 근거 일치
Specifically, nature and wildlife photographers no longer need to go through dangerous jungles and rainforests.
구체적으로 말하자면, 자연과 야생동물을 찍는 사진작가는 이제는 위험한 정글과 열대 우림을 통과할 필요가 없습니다.
「Next, drones are useful for police officers when they control traffic.」
그다음으로, 드론은 경찰관이 교통을 통제할 때 유용합니다. 17번 ④의 근거 일치
Drones could provide updates on traffic flow and accidents, and even help identify anyone driving dangerously.
드론은 교통의 흐름과 사고에 관한 최신 정보를 제공할 수 있고, 누구든 위험하게 운전하는 사람의 신원을 밝히는 데 도움이 되기까지 합니다.
「Last, drones aid firefighters.」 17번 ⑤의 근거 일치
마지막으로, 드론은 소방관을 돕습니다.
Firefighters use drones that drop tanks of special chemicals to prevent the spread of fire.
소방관은 화재 확산을 막기 위해 특수한 화학물질 탱크를 떨어뜨리는 드론을 사용합니다.
Now, let's watch an incredible video of drones in action.
이제, 활약 중인 드론의 놀라운 동영상을 함께 봅시다.

- **frequently** ⓐⓓ 흔히, 자주
- **efficiently** ⓐⓓ 효율적으로
- **spread** ⓥ 퍼뜨리다 ⓝ 확산
- **harmful** ⓐ 해로운
- **wildlife** ⓝ 야생동물
- **identify** ⓥ 신원을 밝히다
- **incredible** ⓐ 놀라운, 믿을 수 없는
- **decline** ⓝ 감소
- **regulation** ⓝ 규제

16 주제 파악

정답률 92% | 정답 ⑤

여자가 하는 말의 주제로 가장 적절한 것은?

① decline in employment opportunities due to drones – 드론으로 인한 고용 기회 감소
② regulations for using drones in various fields – 다양한 분야의 드론 사용 관련 규제
③ job skills necessary for drone development – 드론 개발에 필요한 직무 능력
④ workplace accidents caused by drone use – 드론 사용으로 인해 생기는 직장 내 사고
✔ various uses of drones in different jobs – 갖가지 직군에서의 다양한 드론 이용

Why? 왜 정답일까?

'**As technology develops, drones are being used more frequently around the world. So, today, we'll talk about how they're used in different jobs.**'에서 여자는 전 세계적으로 사용 빈도가 높아지고 있는 드론이 특히 다양한 직업군에서 어떻게 쓰이는지 알아보겠다고 말한다. 따라서 여자가 하는 말의 주제로 가장 적절한 것은 ⑤ '갖가지 직군에서의 다양한 드론 이용'이다.

17 언급 유무 파악

정답률 91% | 정답 ③

언급된 직업이 아닌 것은?

① farmers – 농부
② photographers – 사진 작가
✔ soldiers – 군인
④ police officers – 경찰관
⑤ firefighters – 소방관

Why? 왜 정답일까?

담화에서 여자는 드론을 업무에 활용하고 있는 직업의 예로 농부, 사진 작가, 경찰관, 소방관을 언급하였다. 따라서 언급되지 않은 것은 ③ '군인'이다.

[문제편 p.080]

Why? 왜 오답일까?

① 'First, drones help farmers grow crops more efficiently.'에서 '농부'가 언급되었다.
② 'Second, photographers use drones to easily access areas that are hard to reach.'에서 '사진 작가'가 언급되었다.
④ 'Next, drones are useful for police officers when they control traffic.'에서 '경찰관'이 언급되었다.
⑤ 'Last, drones aid firefighters.'에서 '소방관'이 언급되었다.

Dictation 14

문제편 081쪽

01 recruiting additional new members / we've been assigned to a bigger room / make a total of 15 students
02 end up being thrown away / we should avoid overpackaging to reduce unnecessary waste
03 a big fan of your magazine / catches the theme of the movie / make the characters as realistic as possible
04 storing all of our towels / Aren't they unique / the shower curtain with the heart pattern
05 to raise students' awareness / How do I apply to be a volunteer / I'll submit your application form
06 does it make a difference / can you recommend a good brush
07 really helpful for my career / too tired to attend the class / move to another city
08 in the art studio of the community center / get some hands-on practice / Only 12 people can register
09 only open to freshmen / should be no longer than three pages / the deadline is next Wednesday
10 go for the other colors / how often you use public / rarely use public transportation
11 What about the hairstylist you talked about / check if he's available
12 a band to play drums in / to play drums in our band
13 out of stock at the moment / in a different color / it'll arrive by Thursday
14 one of my credit cards is missing / can you check the pockets of my jacket / look around the grocery store
15 offers a great discount / quit exercising in the past / based on distance
16-17 drones are being used more frequently / grow crops more efficiently / hard to reach

15회 | 2021학년도 6월 모의평가 고3

• 정답 •
01 ① 02 ② 03 ③ 04 ③ 05 ② 06 ④ 07 ① 08 ④ 09 ④ 10 ② 11 ④ 12 ① 13 ⑤ 14 ⑤ 15 ①
16 ② 17 ③

01 발명 대회 신청 마감일 변경 공지

정답률 93% | 정답 ①

다음을 듣고, 남자가 하는 말의 목적으로 가장 적절한 것을 고르시오.

✔ 발명 대회 참가 신청 마감일 변경을 안내하려고
② 수업 과제의 온라인 제출 방법을 설명하려고
③ 학교 홈페이지 운영 도우미를 모집하려고
④ 발명 아이디어 우수 사례를 소개하려고
⑤ 발명가 초청 특별 강연을 홍보하려고

M : Good morning, Hotwells High School students.
안녕하세요, Hotwells 고등학교 학생 여러분.
This is your science teacher, Mr. Moore, with an announcement about our invention contest.
저는 여러분의 과학 교사인 Mr. Moore이며 우리의 발명 대회에 관해 알려드리고자 합니다.
I know you all have creative invention ideas, and I'm excited to see them.
저는 여러분 모두에게 창의적인 발명 아이디어가 있다는 것을 알고 있으며 그것을 보게 되어 신이 납니다.
As you know, we were accepting applications until July 8th through the school website.
아시다시피 학교 웹 사이트를 통해 7월 8일까지 신청서를 접수하고 있었습니다.
However, the deadline has been changed due to website maintenance on July 7th and 8th.
그런데 7월 7일과 8일의 웹 사이트 보수로 인해 마감일이 변경되었습니다.
So, I'd like to inform you that we've moved the deadline to July 10th.
따라서 마감일이 7월 10일로 옮겨졌다는 것을 알려드리고자 합니다.
Thank you for understanding, and please don't forget the changed deadline.
이해 감사드리고 변경된 마감일을 잊지 마시기 바랍니다.
If you have questions, please visit me in my office.
문의 사항이 있으시면 제 사무실로 저를 찾아와 주시기 바랍니다.
Thank you.
감사합니다.

Why? 왜 정답일까?

'However, ~ please don't forget the changed deadline.'에서 웹 사이트 보수로 인해 마감일이 변경되었으니 이를 잊지 말라고 당부하고 있다. 따라서 남자가 하는 말의 목적으로 가장 적절한 것은 ① '발명 대회 참가 신청 마감일 변경을 안내하려고'이다.

• invention ⓝ 발명
• application ⓝ 신청서
• maintenance ⓝ (유지) 보수

02 도표를 활용하여 수치를 효과적으로 제시하기

정답률 82% | 정답 ②

대화를 듣고, 여자의 의견으로 가장 적절한 것을 고르시오.

① 보고서 주제는 구체적이어야 한다.
✔ 도표 활용은 자료 제시에 효과적이다.
③ 설문 대상에 따라 질문을 달리해야 한다.
④ 설문 조사자를 위한 사전 교육이 필요하다.
⑤ 보고서 작성 시 도표 제시 순서에 유의해야 한다.

M : Ms. Lee. Can you help me with my sociology report?
Lee 선생님, 제 사회학 보고서를 도와주실 수 있나요?
W : Sure, Alex. You surveyed teens about their travel preferences, right?
물론이지, Alex. 십 대들에게 여행 선호도에 관해 설문 조사한 것 맞지?
M : Yes, I did. I've collected data, but I'm not sure how to present the numbers effectively.
네, 맞아요. 자료를 수집했지만, 어떻게 하면 숫자를 효과적으로 제시할 수 있을지 확신이 서지 않아요.
W : Let's see. Oh, you just listed all the numbers. Why don't you use charts or graphs, instead? They help present data effectively.
어디 보자. 오, 모든 숫자를 그냥 나열만 했구나. 대신에 차트나 그래프를 사용해 보는 게 어떠니? 그것들이 자료를 효과적으로 제시하는 데 도움이 될 거야.
M : Okay. What kind can I use?
그렇군요. 어떤 종류를 사용할 수 있을까요?
W : For example, you can use pie charts or bar graphs.
예를 들면, 원형 차트나 막대그래프를 사용할 수 있지.
M : Oh, I didn't think about that.
아, 그건 생각해보지 않았어요.
W : Yeah. Charts and graphs can be helpful. They can represent numbers in a simple image.
그래, 차트와 그래프가 도움이 될 수 있어. 그것들은 숫자를 간단한 이미지로 나타내줄 수 있어.
M : That's good.
좋네요.
W : Also, they can help people see the relationship between numbers quickly.
또한, 그것들은 사람들이 숫자 사이의 관계를 빠르게 볼 수 있도록 도와줄 수 있어.
M : So, charts and graphs can make data easy to understand.
그러니까 차트와 그래프는 자료를 이해하기 쉽게 해 줄 수 있는 거네요.
W : Right. Using those can be effective in presenting data.
맞아. 그것들을 사용하면 자료를 제시하는 데 효과적일 수 있어.
M : I got it. Thanks for your help.
알겠어요. 도움을 주셔서 감사합니다.

Why? 왜 정답일까?

'Why don't you use charts or graphs, instead? They help present data effectively.'

[문제편 p.085]

에서 여자는 숫자를 단순히 나열만 하지 말고 차트나 그래프를 써서 나타내면 데이터를 효과적으로 보여줄 수 있다고 이야기한다. 따라서 여자의 의견으로 가장 적절한 것은 ② '도표 활용은 자료 제시에 효과적이다.'이다.

- sociology ⓝ 사회학
- present ⓥ 제시하다
- represent ⓥ 나타내다
- preference ⓝ 선호
- effectively [ad] 효과적으로

03 시인 초청 특강 정답률 96% | 정답 ③

대화를 듣고, 두 사람의 관계를 가장 잘 나타낸 것을 고르시오.

① 화가 – 기자 ② 작곡가 – 가수 ③ 시인 – 교사
④ 영화감독 – 배우 ⑤ 무용가 – 사진작가

[Cell phone rings.]

W : Hi, Mr. Parker.
안녕하세요, Parker 선생님.

M : Hi, Ms. Jones. I'm so glad you agreed to give a special lesson to my literature class.
안녕하세요, Jones 선생님. 제 문학반 학생들에게 특강을 하는 것에 동의해 주셔서 매우 기쁩니다.

W : My pleasure. You said you have 20 students. Is there anything special you'd like me to do?
천만에요. 20명의 학생이 있다고 하셨지요. 제가 특별히 하기를 바라는 어떤 것이 있습니까?

M : Well, they've read your poems in my class. Could you read some aloud and explain their meaning?
음, 학생들이 제 수업에서 선생님의 시를 읽었습니다. 몇 편 낭독하신 후 그것의 의미를 설명해 주실 수 있을까요?

W : Sure thing. I could explain my writing process, too.
그럼요. 제 글쓰기 과정도 또한 설명할 수 있습니다.

M : Great. Also, my students wrote poems. Maybe you could hear some of them.
좋습니다. 또한, 제 학생들이 시를 썼습니다. 어쩌면 그중 몇 편을 들어보실 수 있겠어요.

W : Absolutely. And I'd like to give a signed copy of my latest poetry book to each of your students.
물론이지요. 그리고 제 사인이 있는 최신 시집을 선생님의 학생들 모두에게 주고 싶습니다.

M : Oh, thank you. That would be such a meaningful gift.
오, 감사합니다. 그것은 매우 의미 있는 선물이 될 겁니다.

W : So, when should I arrive at your high school?
그러면, 제가 선생님의 고등학교에 언제 도착해야 하나요?

M : Could you come by 3 p.m.? I'll meet you in the lobby.
오후 3시까지 와주실 수 있나요? 로비에서 만나 뵙겠습니다.

W : Okay. I'll be there.
좋습니다. 그리로 가겠습니다.

Why? 왜 정답일까?

'I'm so glad you agreed to give a special lesson to my literature class.', 'Well, they've read your poems in my class.', 'And I'd like to give a signed copy of my latest poetry book to each of your students.' 등에서 여자는 시인이고 남자는 여자를 자신이 운영하는 학교 문학반 특강 연사로 초대하려는 교사임을 알 수 있다. 따라서 두 사람의 관계로 가장 적절한 것은 ③ '시인 – 교사'이다.

- literature ⓝ 문학
- read aloud ⓥ 낭독하다, 소리 내어 읽다
- poem ⓝ 시
- meaningful ⓐ 의미 있는

04 애완동물 카페 사진 구경하기 정답률 83% | 정답 ③

대화를 듣고, 그림에서 대화의 내용과 일치하지 않는 것을 고르시오.

M : Hello, Susan. How was the pet cafe you visited yesterday?
안녕하세요, Susan. 어제 방문하신 애완동물 카페는 어땠나요?

W : Hi, Sam. It was wonderful. Look at this picture I took there.
안녕하세요, Sam. 매우 좋았어요. 거기서 제가 찍은 이 사진을 보세요.

M : Okay. 「Oh, the dog next to the counter looks sweet.」 Is it yours? ①의 근거 일치
알겠습니다. 아, 계산대 옆에 있는 개가 귀엽네요. 당신 개인가요?

W : No. He's the cafe owner's.
아닙니다. 카페 주인의 개입니다.

M : I'd love to play with the dog.
그 개와 놀고 싶네요.

W : Yeah, we should go together. 「Check out the flowerbed between the trees.」 ②의 근거 일치 Isn't it beautiful?
네, 함께 가시지요. 나무 사이에 있는 화단을 보세요. 아름답지 않나요?

M : It really is. And I see many good photo spots here.
정말 아름답습니다. 그리고 여기에 사진 찍기에 좋은 장소가 많이 보이네요.

W : You know my favorite spot? 「It's the mug sculpture that has a star pattern on it.」 ③의 근거 불일치
제가 제일 좋아하는 장소 아세요? 별 모양이 하나 있는 머그잔 조각이에요.

M : I like it. It makes the cafe unique. 「Hmm, what are these balls in the basket?」 ④의 근거 일치
그것 맘에 드네요. 그것이 카페를 독특하게 해주고 있어요. 흠, 바구니에 있는 이 공들은 뭔가요?

W : People can use them to play catch with their dogs.
사람들이 그것들을 사용해 자신의 개들과 잡기 놀이를 할 수 있어요.

M : Sounds fun. 「By the way, there are only two tables.」 ⑤의 근거 일치 Don't they need more?
재밌을 것 같습니다. 그런데, 테이블이 2개밖에 없네요. 더 필요하지 않나요?

W : Well, they need space so pets can run around.
음, 애완동물들이 뛰어다닐 수 있도록 공간이 필요하거든요.

M : I see. It looks like a great place to visit.
알겠습니다. 방문하기에 좋은 장소인 것 같네요.

Why? 왜 정답일까?

대화에서는 머그잔 조각에 별 모양이 있다고 하는데(**It's the mug sculpture that has a star pattern on it.**), 그림의 머그잔 조각에는 동그라미 무늬가 있다. 따라서 그림에서 대화의 내용과 일치하지 않는 것은 ③이다.

- flowerbed ⓝ 화단
- unique ⓐ 독특한
- sculpture ⓝ 조각상

05 포스터 인쇄 대신해주기 정답률 91% | 정답 ②

대화를 듣고, 여자가 남자를 위해 할 일로 가장 적절한 것을 고르시오.

① 저작권 확인하기 ② 포스터 인쇄하기 ③ 프린터 구매하기
④ 파일 전송하기 ⑤ 만화 그리기

W : Hi, Ted. How are you doing with the poster for the Student Dance Festival?
안녕, Ted. Student Dance Festival는 어떻게 되어 가고 있니?

M : Hello, Ms. Wood. Here, take a look at my monitor. It's the final draft of the poster.
안녕하세요, Wood 선생님. 여기, 제 모니터를 보세요. 포스터 최종안이에요.

W : Let's see. Wow, you did a great job. It looks like you're all done.
어디 보자. 와, 너 정말 잘했다. 다 끝난 것 같구나.

M : Thank you, Ms. Wood.
감사합니다, Wood 선생님.

W : Oh, I like the cartoon at the bottom. Did you draw it yourself?
오, 나는 아래쪽에 있는 만화가 마음에 들어. 네가 그것을 직접 그렸니?

M : No, I downloaded the image. I checked the copyright and it's free to use.
아뇨, 그 이미지를 내려받았어요. 저작권을 확인했는데 무료로 사용할 수 있어요.

W : That's great. Are you ready to print the poster, then?
그거 잘됐구나. 그러면 포스터를 인쇄할 준비가 되었니?

M : Yes, but our printer isn't working, so I can't print it now.
네, 하지만 저희 프린터가 작동되지 않아서, 그것을 지금 인쇄할 수가 없어요.

W : Don't worry. I can do it for you in the teachers' lounge.
걱정하지 마라. 내가 교사 휴게실에서 네 대신 해줄 수 있어.

M : That'd be great.
그렇게 해주시면 아주 좋겠어요.

W : How many copies of the poster do you need?
포스터는 몇 장 필요하니?

M : Ten copies will be enough.
열 장이면 충분할 거예요.

W : No problem. Just send me the file.
문제없어. 파일만 나에게 보내줘.

M : Thank you so much.
대단히 감사합니다.

Why? 왜 정답일까?

남자는 댄스 축제 포스터를 다 만들었지만 프린터가 제대로 작동하지 않아 인쇄하지 못하고 있고, 이를 들은 여자는 자신이 교사 휴게실에서 대신 해주겠다고 말한다(**I can do it for you in the teachers' lounge.**). 따라서 여자가 할 일로 가장 적절한 것은 ② '포스터 인쇄하기'이다.

- final draft ⓝ 최종안
- copyright ⓝ 저작권

15회

06 비누 구입하기 정답률 86% | 정답 ④

대화를 듣고, 남자가 지불할 금액을 고르시오. [3점]

① $54 ② $55 ③ $60 ④ $63 ⑤ $70

M : Good afternoon.
안녕하세요.

W : Hi, welcome to the gift shop. How was the soap art exhibition?
안녕하세요, 선물 가게에 오신 걸 환영합니다. 비누 예술 전시는 어땠나요?

M : It was amazing. I never imagined such impressive artwork made of soap.
놀라웠어요. 저는 비누로 만들어진 그렇게 인상적인 예술작품을 전혀 상상하지 못했어요.

W : Many visitors say that. And you know what? We're having a promotion this week. All items are 10% off.
많은 방문객이 그렇게 말씀하십니다. 그리고 그거 아세요? 저희는 이번 주에 판촉 행사를 하고 있습니다. 모든 품목이 10% 할인됩니다.

M : That's great. I like this handmade soap. How much is it?
그거, 잘됐네요. 저는 이 수제 비누가 마음에 듭니다. 얼마입니까?

W : It's $20 for one set.
한 세트에 20달러입니다.

M : Good. I'll buy two sets. Oh, is this a soap flower?
좋네요. 두 세트를 사겠어요. 오, 이건 비누 꽃인가요?

W : Uh-huh. You can use it as an air freshener. The large one is $10, and the small one is $5.
네, 그것을 방향제로 사용하실 수 있습니다. 큰 것은 10달러이고 작은 것은 5달러입니다.

M : It smells really nice. I'll take three large ones, please.
냄새가 정말 좋네요. 큰 것으로 세 개 사겠습니다.

W : Okay. Anything else?
좋습니다. 다른 건 없으세요?

M : No, thanks. That's it.
아뇨, 됐습니다. 그거면 됐어요.

W : So, here are two sets of handmade soap, and three large soap flowers. And like I said, you get a discount.
자, 여기 수제 비누 두 세트와 큰 비누 꽃 세 개입니다. 그리고 제가 말씀드렸듯이 할인을 받으시게 됩니다.

M : Thanks. Here's my credit card.
고맙습니다. 여기 제 신용 카드요.

Why? 왜 정답일까?

대화에 따르면 남자는 20달러짜리 수제 비누 세트를 두 세트 구입하고, 10달러짜리 큰 비누 꽃을 세 개 구입한 뒤, 판촉 행사로 인해 총 금액의 10퍼센트를 할인받았다. 이를 식으로 나타내면 '$(20\times2+10\times3)\times0.9=63$'이므로, 남자가 지불할 금액은 ④ '$63'이다.

● exhibition ⓝ 전시
● promotion ⓝ 판촉
● impressive ⓐ 인상적인
● air freshener ⓝ 방향제

07 노숙자 보호소 자원봉사 활동이 연기된 이유

정답률 81% | 정답 ①

대화를 듣고, 동아리 봉사 활동이 연기된 이유를 고르시오.

✔ 기부받은 옷 정리 시간이 더 필요해서
② 동아리 홍보 동영상을 제작해야 해서
③ 중간고사 기간이 얼마 남지 않아서
④ 동아리 정기 회의를 개최해야 해서
⑤ 기부 행사 참가자가 부족해서

W : Hi, John. We just finished the volunteer club meeting.
안녕, John. 우리는 방금 자원봉사 동아리 모임을 끝냈어.
M : Hi, Alice. Sorry, I'm late. Did I miss anything important?
안녕, Alice. 미안해, 늦었어. 내가 중요한 걸 놓쳤니?
W : Well, we postponed our volunteer work at the homeless shelter until next week.
음, 우리는 노숙자 보호소에서의 자원봉사 활동을 다음 주로 연기했어.
M : Why? Is it because midterm exams are coming up?
왜? 중간고사가 다가와서 그런 거니?
W : No. That's not a problem. All of our members still want to participate.
아니야. 그건 문제가 아니야. 우리 회원들 모두 그래도 참여하기를 원해.
M : Then, why did we postpone?
그렇다면 왜 미뤘니?
W : You know we posted a video online about our club last week, right?
너 우리가 지난주에 우리 동아리에 관한 동영상을 인터넷에 올린 거 알지?
M : Sure. I helped make the video. It was a big hit.
물론이지. 내가 그 동영상 제작을 도왔잖아. 그것은 큰 성공이었지.
W : Well, since then, we've received more clothes donations than ever.
음, 그때 이후로 우리는 그 어느 때보다도 더 많은 의류 기부를 받았어.
M : Oh, that's great news. But it sounds like a lot of work.
오, 그거 좋은 소식이구나. 하지만 그것은 많은 일거리처럼 들리네.
W : Yes. We need more time to organize the clothes by size and season. That's why we postponed.
맞아. 옷을 크기와 계절별로 정리하려면 우리는 더 많은 시간이 필요해. 그래서 연기한 거야.
M : I get it. When will we start?
알겠어. 언제 시작할 거니?
W : We're going to start organizing them tomorrow morning.
우리는 내일 아침에 그것들을 정리하기 시작할 거야.
M : Okay. I'll see you then.
알았어. 그때 보자.

Why? 왜 정답일까?

대화에 따르면 동아리에 관한 영상이 인터넷에 업로드되면서 의류 기부량이 늘었기에 동아리에서는 옷을 정리할 시간을 더 갖기 위해 자원봉사를 연기하였다(**We need more time to organize the clothes by size and season. That's why we postponed.**). 따라서 동아리 봉사활동이 연기된 이유로 가장 적절한 것은 ① '기부받은 옷 정리 시간이 더 필요해서'이다.

● postpone ⓥ 연기하다
● organize ⓥ 정리하다
● homeless ⓝ 노숙자

08 연례 자선 야구 경기

정답률 89% | 정답 ④

대화를 듣고, Annual Charity Baseball Game에 관해 언급되지 않은 것을 고르시오.

① 참가 선수 ② 일시 ③ 입장료 ✔ 기념품 ⑤ 장소

M : Hey, Clara. What are you looking at on your phone?
안녕, Clara. 핸드폰으로 무엇을 보고 있니?
W : Hi, Harry. I'm looking at information about the Annual Charity Baseball Game.
안녕, Harry. 나는 Annual Charity Baseball Game에 관한 정보를 보고 있어.
M : Oh, I went to see the game last year. It was so fun. 「Who are the players this year?
아, 나 작년에 그 경기를 보러 갔었어. 그것은 아주 재미있었어. 올해는 선수들이 누구니?
W : The actors from the movie *Heroes from Mercury* are playing.」 Let's go together. ①의 근거 일치
영화 *Heroes from Mercury*의 배우들이 경기를 해. 같이 가자.
M : Great idea. 「When is it?
좋은 생각이야. 언제니?
W : It's at 3 p.m. on June 27th.」 ②의 근거 일치
6월 27일 오후 3시야.
M : Okay. Then, we'd better hurry to buy tickets.
좋아. 그렇다면, 우리 서둘러 입장권을 사는 것이 좋겠어.
W : You're right. 「Tickets are $30 each.」 Isn't it a little expensive? ③의 근거 일치
네 말이 맞아. 입장권은 한 장에 30달러야. 조금 비싸지 않니?
M : Maybe. But all ticket sales will be donated to local charities.
그렇지도. 하지만 모든 입장권 판매액은 지역 자선 단체에 기부될 거야.
W : Yeah, that's true. And the game is going to be held here in town.
응, 맞아. 그리고 그 경기는 여기 시내에서 열릴 거야.
M : 「Oh, is it at Clifton Baseball Stadium again? ⑤의 근거 일치
아, 또 Clifton 야구장에서 열리니?
W : That's right.」 I'll book the tickets now.
맞아. 내가 지금 입장권을 예매할게.

Why? 왜 정답일까?

대화에서 남자와 여자는 **Annual Charity Baseball Game**의 참가 선수, 일시, 입장료, 장소에 관해 언급하였다. 따라서 언급되지 않은 것은 ④ '기념품'이다.

Why? 왜 오답일까?

① '**The actors from the movie *Heroes from Mercury* are playing.**'에서 '참가 선수'가 언급되었다.
② '**It's at 3 p.m. on June 27th.**'에서 '일시'가 언급되었다.
③ '**Tickets are $30 each.**'에서 '입장료'가 언급되었다.
⑤ '**is it at Clifton Baseball Stadium again? / That's right.**'에서 '장소'가 언급되었다.

● annual ⓐ 연례의, 매년의
● donate ⓥ 기부하다
● charity ⓝ 자선 (단체)
● in town 시내에서

09 Kaufman 특별전 안내

정답률 94% | 정답 ④

Kaufman Special Exhibition에 관한 다음 내용을 듣고, 일치하지 않는 것을 고르시오.

① 1995년에 처음 개최되었다.
② 월요일에는 열리지 않는다.
③ 올해의 주제는 예술과 기술의 결합이다.
✔ 일일 관람객 수를 100명으로 제한한다.
⑤ 예매를 통해 할인을 받을 수 있다.

W : Hi, DSNB listeners!
안녕하세요, DSNB 청취자 여러분!
This is Olivia Wilson with One Minute Culture News.
저는 '1분 문화 뉴스'의 Olivia Wilson입니다.
I'd like to introduce the upcoming Kaufman Special Exhibition.
저는 곧 있을 Kaufman 특별전을 소개해드리고 싶습니다.
「This event was first held in 1995 and continues to be loved by the art community.」 ①의 근거 일치
이 행사는 1995년에 처음 개최되어 예술계의 사랑을 계속 받고 있습니다.
「Starting August 1st, the exhibition is open for a month, every day except Mondays.」 ②의 근거 일치
8월 1일부터 월요일을 제외한 매일 한 달 동안 전시회가 열립니다.
You can experience the exhibition in the West Hall of Timothy Kaufman Gallery.
여러분은 Timothy Kaufman 미술관의 West Hall에서 전시회를 경험할 수 있습니다.
「This year's theme is the combination of art and technology.」 ③의 근거 일치
올해의 주제는 예술과 기술의 결합입니다.
You can see unique artwork created with the help of modern technology.
여러분은 현대 기술의 도움으로 만들어진 독특한 예술작품을 볼 수 있습니다.
「The number of daily visitors is limited to 300 to avoid crowding.」 ④의 근거 불일치
혼잡을 피하기 위해 일일 관람객 수를 300명으로 제한합니다.
「You can buy tickets on site, but booking in advance gets you a 20% discount.」 ⑤의 근거 일치
현장에서 입장권을 구입할 수 있지만, 사전에 예매하면 20% 할인을 받습니다.
To learn more, please visit their website.
더 알고 싶으시면, 전시회 웹 사이트를 방문하세요.
Next is weather with Sean.
다음은 Sean이 전해드리는 날씨입니다.
Stay tuned.
채널 고정해 주세요.

Why? 왜 정답일까?

'**The number of daily visitors is limited to 300 to avoid crowding.**'에서 혼잡을 피할 목적으로 일일 관람객 수는 **300**명으로 제한된다고 하였다. 따라서 내용과 일치하지 않는 것은 ④ '일일 관람객 수를 **100**명으로 제한한다.'이다.

Why? 왜 오답일까?

① '**This event was first held in 1995 ~**'의 내용과 일치한다.
② '**Starting August 1st, the exhibition is open for a month, every day except Mondays.**'의 내용과 일치한다.
③ '**This year's theme is the combination of art and technology.**'의 내용과 일치한다.
⑤ '**~ booking in advance gets you a 20% discount.**'의 내용과 일치한다.

● upcoming ⓐ 곧 있을, 다가오는
● with the help of ~의 도움으로
● in advance 사전에, 미리
● combination ⓝ 결합
● crowding ⓝ 혼잡

10 주민 센터 강좌 등록하기

정답률 90% | 정답 ②

다음 표를 보면서 대화를 듣고, 여자가 등록할 강좌를 고르시오.

Community Center Classes in July

	Class	Fee	Location	Start Time
①	Graphic Design	$50	Greenville	5 p.m.
✔	Coding	$70	Greenville	7 p.m.
③	Photography	$80	Westside	7 p.m.
④	Flower Art	$90	Westside	5 p.m.
⑤	Coffee Brewing	$110	Greenville	8 p.m.

M : Hi, can I help you?
안녕하세요, 도와드릴까요?
W : Hi. I'd like to see which classes your community center is offering in July.
안녕하세요. 7월에 주민 센터에서 어떤 강좌를 제공하는지 알고 싶습니다.
M : Here. Take a look at this flyer.
여기 있습니다. 이 전단지를 보세요.
W : Hmm... 「I'm interested in all five classes, but I shouldn't take this one. I'm allergic to certain flowers.」 근거1 Class 조건
음... 저는 다섯 강좌에 모두 관심이 있는데, 이 강좌는 들을 수가 없네요. 저는 특정한 꽃에 알레르기가 있거든요.
M : Oh, that's too bad. Well, now you've got four options.
아, 안됐네요. 음, 이제 네 개의 선택권이 있군요.
W : I see there's a wide range of fees. 「I don't want to spend more than $100, though.」 근거2 Fee 조건
수업료 차이가 크네요. 그런데 저는 100달러가 넘는 돈을 쓰고 싶지 않아요.
M : All right. 「And how about the location? Do you care which location you go to?
알겠습니다. 그리고 장소는 어떠세요? 어디로 가는지를 신경 쓰시나요?
W : Yeah. Greenville is closer to my home, so I'd prefer my class to be there.」 근거3 Location 조건
네. Greenville이 저희 집에 더 가까워서 저는 제 강좌가 그곳에 있는 걸 더 선호해요.
M : Okay. 「What time is good for you?
좋습니다. 어느 시간이 좋으신가요?
W : Well, I'm busy until 6 p.m., so I'll take a class after that.」 근거4 Start Time 조건
음, 제가 오후 6시까지는 바빠서 그 이후에 있는 강좌를 수강할 거예요.
M : I see. There's just one left then. It's a really popular class.
알겠습니다. 그러면 딱 한 개가 남는군요. 그건 정말 인기 있는 강좌입니다.

[문제편 p.085]

W : Great. Sign me up.
잘됐네요. 등록해 주세요.

Why? 왜 정답일까?

대화에 따르면 여자는 꽃 수업이 아니면서, 수업료가 100달러를 넘지 않고, Greenville에서 열리면서, 오후 6시 이후로 열리는 강좌를 들으려고 한다. 따라서 여자가 등록할 강좌는 ② 'Coding'이다.

- community center ⓝ 주민 센터
- allergic to ~에 알레르기가 있는
- close to ~에 가까운

11 저녁 약속 상기시키기
정답률 79% | 정답 ④

대화를 듣고, 남자의 마지막 말에 대한 여자의 응답으로 가장 적절한 것을 고르시오.

① I'll be back tomorrow. – 나는 내일 돌아올 거예요.
② You liked the food there. – 당신은 거기 음식을 좋아했잖아요.
③ I go to the gym every day. – 나는 매일 체육관에 가요.
✔ You should be here by six. – 여섯 시까지 집에 와야 해요
⑤ We finished dinner already. – 우리는 이미 저녁을 다 먹었어요.

M : Honey, I'm going to the gym now.
여보, 나는 지금 체육관에 갈 거예요.
W : Don't forget our neighbors are coming to have dinner with us. Make sure to be back before then.
우리 이웃들이 저녁을 먹으러 올 거라는 것을 잊지 말아요. 그전에 꼭 돌아와요.
M : I know. What time do you want me back home?
알아요. 내가 몇 시에 집에 다시 돌아오면 좋겠어요?
W : You should be here by six.
여섯 시까지 집에 와야 해요.

Why? 왜 정답일까?

체육관에 가겠다는 남자에게 여자는 오늘 이웃들과의 저녁 약속이 있음을 상기시키고, 남자는 알고 있다고 답하며 몇 시까지 돌아오면 될지 묻는다(What time do you want me back home?). 따라서 여자의 응답으로 가장 적절한 것은 ④ '여섯 시까지 집에 와야 해요.'이다.

- gym ⓝ 체육관
- make sure ⓥ 반드시 ~하다

12 학교 버스를 타고 등교하기
정답률 90% | 정답 ①

대화를 듣고, 여자의 마지막 말에 대한 남자의 응답으로 가장 적절한 것을 고르시오.

✔ All right. I'll take the bus then. – 좋아요. 그럼 버스를 탈게요.
② No. My bicycle is broken again. – 아니요. 제 자전거는 또 고장 났어요.
③ No problem. I'll give you a ride. – 문제 없어요. 태워드릴게요.
④ Don't worry. I'm already at school. – 걱정하지 마세요. 이미 학교에 도착했어요.
⑤ Indeed. I'm glad it's getting warmer. – 맞아요. 날씨가 더 따뜻해지고 있어서 기뻐요.

W : Michael, you're going to take the school bus today, right?
Michael, 오늘 학교 버스 타는 거지, 그렇지?
M : If it's warmer than yesterday, I'm going to take my bicycle, Mom. Why?
날이 어제보다 더 따뜻하면 자전거를 탈 거예요, 엄마. 왜요?
W : It's much colder and windier today. You'd better not ride your bicycle.
오늘이 훨씬 더 춥고 바람도 더 많이 불어. 자전거를 타지 않는 게 좋겠어.
M : All right. I'll take the bus then.
좋아요. 그럼 버스를 탈게요.

Why? 왜 정답일까?

엄마인 여자는 날씨가 어제보다 더 춥고 바람도 많이 불기 때문에 아들인 남자에게 자전거를 타고 등교하지 말 것을 권하고 있다(You'd better not ride your bicycle.). 따라서 남자의 응답으로 가장 적절한 것은 ① '좋아요. 그럼 버스를 탈게요.'이다.

- give a ride ⓥ 태워주다

13 새 영화 출연 부탁하기
정답률 80% | 정답 ⑤

대화를 듣고, 남자의 마지막 말에 대한 여자의 응답으로 가장 적절한 것을 고르시오. [3점]

Woman: ______________________

① Absolutely. I was impressed after reading this script.
그럼요. 이 대본을 읽은 후에 감명을 받았어요.
② No doubt. I think I acted well in the last comedy.
당연하죠. 지난번 코미디 영화에서 제가 연기를 잘했던 것 같아요.
③ Great. I'll write the script for your new drama.
멋져요. 제가 당신의 새로운 드라마를 위한 대본을 쓸게요.
④ I'm sorry. I'm not able to direct the movie.
미안해요. 저는 그 영화를 감독할 수 없어요.
✔ Okay. I'll let you know my decision soon.
네. 곧 제 결정을 알려 드릴게요.

M : Hey, Sylvia. I saw your new movie a few days ago. You played the character beautifully.
안녕하세요, Sylvia. 며칠 전에 당신의 새 영화를 봤어요. 등장인물을 멋지게 연기했더군요.
W : Thanks, Jack. I had so much fun acting in that movie.
고마워요, Jack. 그 영화에서 연기하면서 아주 재미있었어요.
M : I'm sure you did. Sylvia, I'm going to be directing a new movie. You'd be perfect for the lead role.
분명히 그랬을 거예요. Sylvia, 제가 새 영화를 감독할 거예요. 당신이 주연으로 적격일 거예요.
W : Oh, really? What's the movie about?
오, 정말요? 무엇에 관한 영화죠?
M : It's a comedy about a dreamer who just moved to a new town.
새로운 마을로 갓 이주한 몽상가에 관한 코미디 영화예요.
W : That sounds interesting, and I'd like to be in your movie. But I'm not sure I'm the right person for the role.
흥미롭게 들리고, 당신 영화에 참여하고 싶어요. 하지만 제가 그 역에 적절한 사람이라는 확신이 들지 않네요.
M : Why do you say that?
왜 그렇게 말하세요?
W : Well, I haven't acted in a comedy before.
음, 전에 코미디 영화에서 연기해본 적이 없어요.
M : Don't worry. You're a natural actor.
걱정하지 말아요. 당신은 타고난 배우니까요.
W : That's kind of you. Can I read the script and then decide?
친절하시네요. 대본을 읽고 난 다음 결정해도 되죠?
M : Sure. I'll send you a copy of the script. I'll be waiting to hear from you.
물론이죠. 대본 한 부를 보내드릴게요. 당신의 연락을 기다리고 있겠어요.
W : Okay. I'll let you know my decision soon.
네. 곧 제 결정을 알려 드릴게요.

Why? 왜 정답일까?

남자는 여자에게 자신의 새 코미디 영화에서 주연으로 연기해줄 것을 청하지만 여자는 전에 코미디 영화에 나온 적이 없다면서 대본을 읽고 결정해도 되는지 묻고 있다(Can I read the script and then decide?). 이에 남자는 대본을 한 부 보내주겠다면서 연락을 기다리겠다고 하므로(Sure. I'll send you a copy of the script. I'll be waiting to hear from you.), 여자의 응답으로 가장 적절한 것은 ⑤ '네. 곧 제 결정을 알려 드릴게요.'이다.

- lead role ⓝ 주연
- impressed ⓐ 감명을 받은
- No doubt. 당연하죠.

14 회사 운동회 장소 알아보기
정답률 78% | 정답 ⑤

대화를 듣고, 여자의 마지막 말에 대한 남자의 응답으로 가장 적절한 것을 고르시오. [3점]

Man: ______________________

① That's okay. You can reserve another place.
괜찮아요. 당신은 다른 장소를 예약할 수 있어요.
② I see. I should hurry to join your company event.
알겠어요. 당신 회사 행사에 참여하려면 전 서둘러야 해요.
③ Why not? My company has its own sports facilities.
왜 아니겠어요? 우리 회사에는 자체 체육 시설이 있답니다.
④ I agree. We should wait until the remodeling is done.
동의해요. 개조 공사가 끝날 때까지 우리는 기다려야 해요.
✔ Thanks. I'll call now to see if they're available that day.
고마워요. 그날 사용할 수 있는지 알아보기 위해 지금 전화할게요.

W : Jason, I heard you're planning a sports day for your company.
Jason, 당신이 당신 회사를 위해 운동회 날을 계획하고 있다는 말을 들었어요.
M : Yeah, it's next Saturday. But the problem is that I haven't been able to reserve a place yet.
네, 다음 주 토요일이에요. 하지만 문제는 제가 아직도 장소를 예약하지 못했다는 거예요.
W : Oh, really? Have you looked into Portman Sports Center?
오, 정말요? Portman Sports Center는 살펴봤나요?
M : I have. Unfortunately, they're remodeling now.
그랬죠. 유감스럽게도, 지금 개조 공사 중이에요.
W : That's too bad. It's perfect for sports events.
그거 참 아쉽네요. 체육 행사를 위해서 완벽한 곳인데요.
M : I know. Well, I've been looking everywhere, but every place I've called is booked.
알고 있어요. 흠, 여기저기 살펴보고 있지만, 전화한 곳은 모두 예약이 되어 있더군요.
W : Oh, no. Can you postpone the event until they finish remodeling?
오, 저런. 개조 공사가 끝날 때까지 그 행사를 연기할 수 있나요?
M : No, we can't. The company has a busy schedule after that day.
아니요, 그럴 수 없어요. 그날 이후에는 회사 일정이 바빠요.
W : Hmm... How about Whelford High School? They have great sports facilities.
흠... Whelford 고등학교는요? 훌륭한 체육 시설이 있는 곳이죠.
M : Really? Are they open to the public?
정말요? 일반인에게 개방을 하나요?
W : Sure, they are. We rented them for a company event last month.
물론이죠. 개방해요. 저희는 지난달에 회사 행사를 위해 그것을 빌렸었죠.
M : Sounds like a good place to reserve.
예약하기에 좋은 장소 같군요.
W : Yes, it is. But the facilities are popular, so you'd better hurry up.
네, 맞아요. 하지만 시설이 인기가 있어서 서두르는 것이 좋겠어요.
M : Thanks. I'll call now to see if they're available that day.
고마워요. 그날 사용할 수 있는지 알아보기 위해 지금 전화할게요.

Why? 왜 정답일까?

회사 운동회를 위해 장소를 알아보고 있는 남자에게 여자는 지난달 자신의 회사에서 행사를 진행하느라 빌렸던 곳을 추천해주고, 시설이 인기가 있으니 서둘러 예약하는 것이 좋겠다(But the facilities are popular, so you'd better hurry up.)고 조언한다. 따라서 남자의 응답으로 가장 적절한 것은 ⑤ '고마워요. 그날 사용할 수 있는지 알아보기 위해 지금 전화할게요.'이다.

- reserve ⓥ 예약하다
- facility ⓝ 시설
- open to the public 대중에 개방된

15 아픈 직원에게 휴가를 쓰고 쉬라고 권하기
정답률 78% | 정답 ①

다음 상황 설명을 듣고, Mary가 Steve에게 할 말로 가장 적절한 것을 고르시오.

Mary: ______________________

✔ Why don't you take leave today and look after yourself?
오늘 휴가를 쓰고 스스로를 좀 돌보면 어때요?
② Your interests should be the priority in your job search.
당신의 관심사가 구직에서 우선 사항이 되어야 해요.
③ You'd better actively support your teammates' ideas.
팀원의 생각을 적극적으로 지지하는 게 좋겠어요.
④ Let's find a way to increase sales of health products.
건강 제품 판매를 늘릴 방법을 찾아봅시다.
⑤ How about changing the details of the contract?
그 계약의 세부사항을 바꾸는 게 어떨겠어요?

M : Mary is leading a sales team at a company.
Mary는 한 회사에서 영업팀을 이끌고 있다.
Her team is working hard on a proposal for a very important contract.
그녀의 팀은 매우 중요한 계약의 제안서 작업을 열심히 하고 있다.
In the morning, Mary notices that Steve, one of her team members, is frequently massaging his shoulder while frowning.
오전에 Mary는 팀원 중 한 명인 Steve가 얼굴을 찡그리며 수시로 어깨를 마사지하고 있는 것을 알게 된다.

15회

Mary asks Steve if he is feeling okay.
Mary는 Steve에게 괜찮은지 묻는다.
Steve says that he has been feeling pain in his shoulder for the last few days, but he also says that he is okay to continue working.
Steve는 지난 며칠 동안 어깨에 통증이 느껴진다고 말하지만, 계속 일을 해도 괜찮다고도 말한다.
Mary is concerned that if Steve continues to work despite his pain, his health could become worse.
Mary는 Steve가 아픈데도 계속 일하면 건강이 악화될까봐 걱정이다.
She believes that his health should be the first priority.
그녀는 그의 건강이 최우선 사항이 되어야 한다고 믿는다.
So, she wants to suggest to Steve that he take the day off and take care of himself.
그래서 그녀는 Steve에게 하루 휴가를 내고 스스로를 챙겨야 한다고 제안하고 싶어 한다.
In this situation, what would Mary most likely say to Steve?
이 상황에서, Mary는 Steve에게 뭐라고 말하겠는가?

Mary : Why don't you take leave today and look after yourself?
오늘 휴가를 쓰고 스스로를 좀 돌보면 어때요?

Why? 왜 정답일까?

상황에 따르면 영업팀장 **Mary**는 팀원인 **Steve**가 아파 하는 것을 보고 하루 휴가를 내어 스스로를 돌볼 시간을 가지라고(**So, she wants to suggest to Steve that he take the day off and take care of himself.**) 권하고 싶어 한다. 따라서 **Mary**가 **Steve**에게 할 말로 가장 적절한 것은 ① '오늘 휴가를 쓰고 스스로를 좀 돌보면 어때요?'이다.

- contract ⓝ 계약
- concerned ⓐ 걱정하는
- take a day off ⓥ 하루 휴가를 내다
- frequently ad 수시로, 자주
- priority ⓝ 우선 사항

16-17 위험에 대한 식물의 자기 방어책

W : Good morning, students.
안녕하세요, 학생 여러분.
Previously, we learned about various environments in which plants grow.
지난 시간에 우리는 식물이 자라는 다양한 환경에 관해 배웠습니다.
「Today, we'll discuss how plants defend themselves from threat.」 16번의 근거
오늘 우리는 식물이 위협으로부터 어떻게 자신을 방어하는지에 관해 토론할 것입니다.
Even though plants cannot run away from danger, they know how to keep themselves safe.
식물은 위험으로부터 도망칠 수는 없지만, 자신을 안전하게 지키는 방법은 알고 있습니다.
「First, many plants, like roses, have sharp thorns.」 17번 ①의 근거 일치
첫째, 장미와 같은 많은 식물에는 날카로운 가시가 있습니다.
When animals get too close, these thorns cut them, warning them to stay away.
동물이 너무 가까이 오면, 이 가시가 그 동물을 베어 가까이 오지 말라고 경고합니다.
Also, plants can create substances that cause a bad taste.
또한, 식물은 불쾌한 맛이 나는 물질을 만들 수 있습니다.
「When insects attack, for example, tomato plants release chemicals, making their leaves taste bad.」 17번 ②의 근거 일치
예를 들어, 곤충들이 공격할 때, 토마토 식물은 화학 물질을 방출하여 잎이 불쾌한 맛이 나게 합니다.
Next, some plants form partnerships with insects.
그다음으로, 어떤 식물은 곤충과 동반자 관계를 형성합니다.
「For instance, some cherry trees attract ants by making a sweet liquid.」 17번 ④의 근거 일치
예를 들어, 어떤 벚나무는 달달한 액체를 만들어 개미를 유혹합니다.
The ants guard the tree from enemies to keep this food source safe.
개미는 이 식량원을 안전하게 지키기 위해 적으로부터 나무를 보호합니다.
Finally, there are plants that generate a poison to protect themselves.
마지막으로, 자신을 보호하기 위해 독을 생성하는 식물이 있습니다.
「For example, certain walnut trees see other nearby trees as a danger, so they produce a poison to prevent the other trees from growing.」 17번 ⑤의 근거 일치
예를 들어, 어떤 호두나무는 주변의 다른 나무를 위험으로 여겨서, 그 다른 나무가 자라는 것을 막기 위해 독을 만들어 냅니다.
Now, let's watch a video about these incredible plants.
이제, 이 놀라운 식물들에 관한 비디오를 봅시다.

- previously ad 먼젓번에, 지난 시간에
- thorn ⓝ 가시
- generate ⓥ 만들어 내다
- overgrow ⓥ (식물 등이) 무성하게 자라다
- run away from ⓥ ~에게서 도망치다
- substance ⓝ 물질
- incredible ⓐ 놀라운, 믿기 힘든

16 주제 파악 정답률 86% | 정답 ②

여자가 하는 말의 주제로 가장 적절한 것은?

① reasons why chemicals are harmful to plants
화학 물질이 식물에게 해로운 이유
✔ ways that plants protect themselves from danger
식물이 위험으로부터 자신을 보호하는 방법
③ difficulties in preventing plants from overgrowing
식물이 무성하게 자라는 것을 막는 것의 어려움
④ tips for keeping dangerous insects away from plants
위험한 곤충을 식물에게서 떨어뜨려 놓기 위한 방법
⑤ importance of recognizing poisonous plants in the wild
야생에서 독성이 있는 식물을 알아보는 것의 중요성

Why? 왜 정답일까?

'**Today, we'll discuss how plants defend themselves from threat.**'에서 여자는 식물이 위협에서 스스로를 방어하는 방법을 토론 주제로 제시하고 있다. 따라서 여자가 하는 말의 주제로 가장 적절한 것은 ② '식물이 위험으로부터 자신을 보호하는 방법'이다.

17 언급 유무 파악 정답률 89% | 정답 ③

언급된 식물이 아닌 것은?

① roses - 장미 ② tomato plants - 토마토 식물 ✔ clovers - 벚나무
④ cherry trees - 호두나무 ⑤ walnut trees - 클로버

Why? 왜 정답일까?

담화에서 여자는 식물의 방어책을 언급하기 위한 예시로 장미, 토마토 식물, 벚나무, 호두나무를 언급한다. 따라서 언급되지 않은 것은 ③ '클로버'이다.

Why? 왜 오답일까?

① '**First, many plants, like roses, have sharp thorns.**'에서 '장미'가 언급되었다.
② '**When insects attack, for example, tomato plants release chemicals,** ~'에서 '토마토 식물'이 언급되었다.
④ '**For instance, some cherry trees attract ants by making a sweet liquid.**'에서 '벚나무'가 언급되었다.
⑤ '**For example, certain walnut trees see other nearby trees as a danger,** ~'에서 '호두나무'가 언급되었다.

Dictation 15

문제편 087쪽

01 due to website maintenance / we've moved the deadline to July 10th
02 about their travel preferences / help present data effectively / represent numbers in a simple image
03 you agreed to give a special lesson / read some aloud / a signed copy of my latest poetry book
04 Check out the flowerbed between the trees / that has a star pattern / use them to play catch
05 draw it yourself / our printer isn't working / Ten copies will be enough
06 such impressive artwork made of soap / as an air freshener / like I said, you get a discount
07 Did I miss anything important / postponed our volunteer work / more clothes donations than ever / organize the clothes by size and season
08 Who are the players this year / on June 27th / we'd better hurry to buy tickets / donated to local charities
09 the exhibition is open for a month / the combination of art and technology / with the help of modern technology / booking in advance
10 allergic to certain flowers / there's a wide range of fees / closer to my home
11 Make sure to be back before then / want me back home
12 If it's warmer / You'd better not ride your bicycle
13 had so much fun acting / a comedy about a dreamer / I'm the right person for the role / You're a natural actor
14 Unfortunately, they're remodeling now / Are they open to the public / Sounds like a good place to reserve / the facilities are popular
15 frequently massaging his shoulder while frowning / his health could become worse / he take the day off
16-17 have sharp thorns / substances that cause a bad taste / form partnerships with insects

16회 | 2023학년도 7월 학력평가

| 정답과 해설 | 고3

• 정답 •

01 ① 02 ② 03 ⑤ 04 ④ 05 ③ 06 ④ 07 ⑤ 08 ④ 09 ⑤ 10 ② 11 ② 12 ① 13 ⑤ 14 ④ 15 ④ 16 ① 17 ③

01 발코니 사용 수칙 공지

정답률 95% | 정답 ①

다음을 듣고, 남자가 하는 말의 목적으로 가장 적절한 것을 고르시오.

✔ 발코니 사용 수칙을 안내하려고
② 화재 시 대피 방법을 설명하려고
③ 발코니 보수공사 동의를 요청하려고
④ 아파트 안전 점검 계획을 공지하려고
⑤ 아파트 주민 친목 행사를 홍보하려고

M : Hello, residents. This is an announcement from the maintenance office.
안녕하세요, 주민 여러분. 관리 사무소에서 드리는 공지 사항입니다.
Last week, we conducted a safety inspection of the apartments and found some inappropriate uses of the balconies.
지난주 우리는 아파트 안전 점검을 실시했고, 몇몇 발코니가 부적절하게 이용되는 것을 발견했습니다.
Please be aware of the rules for using balconies as follows.
다음과 같은 발코니 사용 수칙을 인지해 주십시오.
First, balconies should not be used for the storage of goods, such as barbecue fuel materials which can cause a fire.
첫째로, 발코니는 화재를 일으킬 수 있는 바비큐 연료 재료 등의 물건 보관을 위해 이용되어선 안 됩니다.
Second, lightweight outdoor furniture should be removed when winds are strong because the objects can be blown off of the balcony.
둘째로, 바람이 셀 때는 경량의 실외 가구를 치워주셔야 하는데, 발코니로부터 물건들이 바람에 날아가버릴 수 있기 때문입니다.
Lastly, please avoid watering plants too much to prevent flooding.
마지막으로, 침수 방지를 위해 식물에 물을 너무 많이 주는 것을 삼가주세요.
Thank you for your cooperation for your safe and pleasant residence.
안전하고 쾌적한 주거를 위한 여러분의 협조에 감사합니다.

Why? 왜 정답일까?

발코니 사용 수칙을 공지하는(Please be aware of the rules for using balconies as follows.) 내용이므로, 남자가 하는 말의 목적으로 가장 적절한 것은 ① '발코니 사용 수칙을 안내하려고'이다.

• maintenance office 관리 사무소
• inspection ⓝ 점검, 조사
• be aware of ~을 인지하다, 알다
• storage ⓝ 보관
• blow off (바람에) 불어 날리다

02 외국어 학습에 관한 조언

정답률 89% | 정답 ②

대화를 듣고, 여자의 의견으로 가장 적절한 것을 고르시오.

① 언어 교육은 일찍 시작할수록 효과적이다.
✔ 외국어 학습 시 구체적인 목표를 설정해야 한다.
③ 외국어 교육을 위한 다양한 학습 방법 개발이 필요하다.
④ 외국어 말하기 연습 시 실수를 두려워하지 않아야 한다.
⑤ 언어를 통해 그 언어 사용자들의 문화를 이해할 수 있다.

M : Grace, I'm thinking about learning Korean. But I don't know where to start.
Grace, 나 한국어 배우려고 생각 중이야. 그런데 어디서부터 시작할지 모르겠어.
W : Why do you want to learn it?
왜 배우고 싶은데?
M : I'm interested in Korean culture, so I'm curious about the language.
난 한국 문화에 관심이 있어서, 언어에도 호기심이 들어.
W : Well, if you've decided to learn a foreign language, you need to set a specific goal.
음, 네가 외국어로 배우기로 마음 먹었다면, 넌 구체적인 목표를 설정해야 해.
M : A specific goal? What's that?
구체적인 목표라고? 그게 뭐야?
W : It's something that you hope to achieve by learning a foreign language. For example, watching dramas without subtitles.
네가 외국어를 배워서 성취하길 바라는 뭔가이지. 예컨대, 자막 없이 드라마를 본다든가.
M : That sounds interesting.
재미있겠다.
W : The more detailed your goal, the better you can choose your learning methods.
네 목표가 더 구체적일수록, 학습 방법을 선택하기 더 좋아지지.
M : I see. Now I have a better idea of what I have to do.
알겠어. 이제 내가 뭘 해야 할지 더 잘 알겠어.
W : Yeah. Also, a specific goal will keep you motivated and focused.
그래. 게다가, 구체적인 목표는 네가 계속 의욕을 갖고 집중하게 해줄 거야.
M : All right! I'll clarify what I want to achieve.
알겠어! 내가 이루고 싶은 게 뭔지 분명히 해볼게.
W : Good luck!
행운을 빌어!

Why? 왜 정답일까?

외국어 학습의 구체적인 목표를 세워볼 것을 조언하는 내용이므로(Well, if you've decided to learn a foreign language, you need to set a specific goal.), 여자의 의견으로 가장 적절한 것은 ② '외국어 학습 시 구체적인 목표를 설정해야 한다.'이다.

• curious ⓐ 호기심 많은
• set a goal 목표를 설정하다
• achieve ⓥ 성취하다
• subtitle ⓝ 자막 ⓥ 자막 처리하다
• clarify ⓥ 분명히 하다, 명확히 하다

03 유기견 달력 제작을 위한 사진 의뢰하기

정답률 93% | 정답 ⑤

대화를 듣고, 두 사람의 관계를 가장 잘 나타낸 것을 고르시오.

① 방송 작가 – 애견 훈련사
② 고객 – 애견 미용사
③ 달력 디자이너 – 인쇄소 직원
④ 자원봉사자 – 수의사
✔ 사진작가 – 유기견보호소 직원

[Cell phone rings.]
[휴대 전화가 울린다.]
M : Ms. Evans! Hi, how are you?
Evans 씨! 안녕하세요, 잘 지내세요?
W : I'm good, Mr. Johnson. Actually, our shelter's dog calendar sold really well. The photos you took for it were great.
잘 있어요, Johnson 씨. 사실, 우리 보호소 강아지 달력이 정말 많이 팔렸어요. 달력용으로 찍어주신 사진이 훌륭했어요.
M : Thanks. I hope it helped your shelter and the care of abandoned dogs.
고맙습니다. 당신의 보호소와 유기견 케어에 도움이 되었길 바라요.
W : It definitely did. Thanks to the calendar, we had more visitors interested in adopting a dog.
물론 그랬고말고요. 달력 덕분에 강아지 입양에 관심 있는 방문자들이 늘어났어요.
M : I'm glad to hear that.
그 말씀을 들으니 기쁘네요.
W : So we've decided to make a calendar for next year, too. Would you take pictures for us again?
그래서 내년에도 달력을 만들기로 했어요. 저희를 위해 또 사진을 찍어주실래요?
M : I'd love to! I'm happy to help those homeless dogs to find a home!
좋죠! 유기견들이 가정을 찾도록 도울 수 있어 기뻐요!
W : Thanks so much! When do you think you'll be available?
정말 감사합니다! 언제 시간이 되실까요?
M : I'm taking pictures for another client this week. I'll be available right after it's done.
이번 주에는 다른 고객분을 위해 사진을 찍고 있어요. 그거 끝나면 바로 시간이 될 거예요.
W : Great. So is there something we should prepare differently this time?
아주 좋아요. 그럼 이번에 저희가 뭐 다르게 준비해야 할 게 있을까요?
M : Could you just get the dogs bathed like last year?
작년처럼 강아지들 목욕만 시켜주실 수 있을까요?
W : Sure, I'll wash and brush them.
물론이죠. 씻기고 빗질도 해놓을게요.
M : Perfect! I'll visit your shelter soon to get ready.
완벽합니다! 곧 준비를 위해 보호소로 찾아뵐게요.
W : Great, thanks! I look forward to more of your amazing pictures!
아주 좋아요. 감사합니다! 당신의 멋진 사진을 더 기대하고 있을게요!

Why? 왜 정답일까?

'Actually, our shelter's dog calendar sold really well. The photos you took for it were great.', 'Would you take pictures for us again?', 'Perfect! I'll visit your shelter soon to get ready.' 등에서 사진작가인 남자에게 유기견보호소 직원인 여자가 달력용 촬영을 의뢰하는 상황임을 알 수 있다. 따라서 두 사람의 관계로 가장 적절한 것은 ⑤ '사진작가 – 유기견보호소 직원'이다.

• shelter ⓝ 보호소
• abandon ⓥ 버리다, 유기하다
• adopt ⓥ 입양하다
• homeless ⓐ 집 잃은

04 베이비 샤워 사진 구경하기

정답률 94% | 정답 ④

대화를 듣고, 그림에서 대화의 내용과 일치하지 않는 것을 고르시오.

W : Honey, look at this! I've found one of our baby shower photos!
여보, 이것 좀 봐요! 우리 베이비 샤워 사진 중 하나를 찾았어요!
M : Oh, it's been a long time since I saw this! It was just a month before Amy was born!
오, 엄청 오랜만에 이걸 보네요! Amy가 태어나기 딱 한달 전쯤이에요!
W : 「You remember the heart balloon under the banner?」 You really struggled to blow it up. ①의 근거 일치
현수막 밑에 하트 풍선 기억나요? 당신이 저걸 부느라 정말 고생했잖아요.
M : Right, I was so dizzy after doing it.
맞아요, 저거 하고 나서 몹시 어지러웠어요.
W : 「I loved those three notes on the message board.」 ②의 근거 일치 But your note was the sweetest.
메시지 보드에 있는 쪽지 세 개도 너무 마음에 좋았어요. 하지만 당신 쪽지가 제일 사랑스러웠죠.
M : Thank you, dear. Oh! 「Is that Kiki the rabbit on the sofa?」 ③의 근거 일치
고마워요, 여보. 오! 소파에 있는 저거 토끼 인형 Kiki인가요?
W : Yes! It's amazing that rabbit doll has been Amy's best friend for years.
네! 저 토끼 인형이 몇 년 동안 Amy의 가장 친한 친구라는 게 놀랍네요.
M : 「But, most of all, you were so beautiful in your striped dress.」 ④의 근거 불일치
하지만 무엇보다도, 당신이 줄무늬 원피스를 입고 있는 게 몹시 아름다워요.
W : That dress was one of my favorites. I was grateful that I received so many presents that day.
저 원피스 내가 가장 좋아하던 것 중 하나죠. 저날 너무도 많은 선물을 받아 고마웠어요.
M : I was happy, too. 「Just look at the gift boxes beside you.」 ⑤의 근거 일치
나도 기뻤어요. 당신 옆에 있는 선물 상자들 좀 봐요.
W : It was really a great celebration for our whole family!
우리 가족 모두에게 몹시 근사했던 축하 행사였어요!

Why? 왜 정답일까?

대화에서 여자는 줄무늬 원피스를 입고 있다(~ you were so beautiful in your striped dress.)고 하는데, 그림 속 여자는 도트 무늬 원피스를 입고 있다. 따라서 그림에서 대화의 내용과 일치하지 않는 것은 ④이다.

• baby shower 베이비 샤워(출산을 앞둔 임신부에게 아기용 선물을 주는 파티)
• dizzy ⓐ 어지러운

05 방문학생 맞이 준비

정답률 93% | 정답 ③

대화를 듣고, 남자가 할 일로 가장 적절한 것을 고르시오.

① 공항에 마중 나가기
② 안내 학생 선정하기
③ 안내 학생 이름표 만들기
④ 학교 방문단 사진 찍기
⑤ 학교 방문단 점심 준비하기

M : Ms. Valentine, is everything ready for the students from Thailand to visit?
Valentine 선생님, 태국에서 오는 방문 학생들을 위한 준비가 다 되었나요?

W : Almost. Our students are all excited about our first international visitors.
거의 다 됐습니다. 우리 학생들은 모두 처음 맞는 국제 방문객을 기대하고 있어요.

M : Are you picking them up at the airport? Shall I go with you?
선생님이 공항에서 픽업하실 거예요? 저도 같이 갈까요?

W : Thanks, but I'll greet them with Mr. Howard.
감사하지만 Howard 선생님과 맞이하기로 했어요.

M : All right! What time will you get back?
알겠습니다! 언제 돌아오시죠?

W : Probably at about 1 o'clock. We're all having lunch together in the school cafeteria.
아마 1시쯤일 거예요. 우리 학교 구내식당에서 다같이 점심을 먹을 예정이에요.

M : That'll be lovely. Who will guide the Thai students on the campus tours?
그거 좋겠어요. 캠퍼스 투어에서는 누가 태국 학생들을 안내하나요?

W : Some students already volunteered for that. I have a list of their names.
학생들 몇 명이 이미 그 일에 자원했어요. 그들의 이름 목록이 저한테 있어요.

M : Good! Would it be helpful if the guides wear name tags?
좋아요! 가이드들이 이름표를 다는 게 도움이 될까요?

W : That's a great idea. But I'm leaving soon, so could you make the tags?
좋은 생각이네요. 하지만 전 곧 출발해서, 이름표를 만들어주실 수 있어요?

M : Absolutely! And how about taking photos of the campus tours?
물론이죠! 그리고 캠퍼스 투어 때 사진을 찍으면 어때요?

W : I already asked some students from the photography club to do that.
이미 사진 동아리 애들 몇 명한테 그걸 해달라고 부탁해 놨어요.

M : Perfect. I can't wait to meet our international guests!
아주 좋아요. 외국 방문객을 맞이할 게 몹시 기대되네요!

Why? 왜 정답일까?

여자는 캠퍼스 투어 가이드들에게 나눠줄 이름표를 남자에게 만들어달라고 부탁하므로(**But I'm leaving soon, so could you make the tags?** / **Absolutely!**), 남자가 할 일로 가장 적절한 것은 ③ '안내 학생 이름표 만들기'이다.

• international ⓐ 국제의, 외국의
• pick up 데리러 가다
• greet ⓥ 맞이하다, 인사하다
• volunteer ⓥ 자원(봉사)하다

06 샌드위치와 음료 주문하기

정답률 72% | 정답 ④

대화를 듣고, 여자가 지불할 금액을 고르시오. [3점]

① $68 ② $75 ③ $81 ④ $86 ⑤ $95

M : Ms. Anderson, for our staff meeting today, how about we order some sandwiches?
Anderson 씨, 우리 오늘 직원 회의를 위해서 샌드위치를 좀 주문하면 어때요?

W : Good idea! I'll order them from Jolly Sandwiches right now.
좋은 생각이에요! 제가 지금 바로 Jolly Sandwiches에서 시킬게요.

M : We can use a delivery app.
배달 앱을 쓰면 돼요.

W : Sounds good. *[Pause]* How about tuna sandwiches or chicken sandwiches?
좋네요. 참치 샌드위치나 치킨 샌드위치 어때요?

M : How much are they?
얼마인가요?

W : Tuna sandwiches are $8 each and chicken sandwiches are $6 each.
참치 샌드위치는 하나에 8달러이고, 치킨 샌드위치는 하나에 6달러예요.

M : Let's have just tuna sandwiches.
그럼 참치 샌드위치만 하죠.

W : Okay, I'll add ten of them to our order. We also need beverages.
알겠어요. 우리 주문에 그거 10개 추가할게요. 그리고 우리 음료수도 필요해요.

M : Sure. I think bottled water would be good for everyone.
물론이죠. 물이 모두에게 좋을 거 같아요.

W : They're $1 each. I'll add ten bottles.
그건 하나에 1달러예요. 10병 추가할게요.

M : Please check if they have a delivery fee.
배달료가 있나 확인해 주세요.

W : It says it's $5. Oh, we can use a 10% off coupon for our order, but not for the delivery fee.
5달러래요. 오, 우리 주문에는 10퍼센트 할인 쿠폰을 쓸 수 있는데, 배달료에는 해당 없대요.

M : All right, so the discount is only for the food and drinks.
알겠어요, 그럼 할인은 음식과 음료에만 적용되는군요.

W : Correct. I'll place the order and pay.
맞아요. 제가 주문하고 지불할게요.

Why? 왜 정답일까?

대화에 따르면 두 사람은 직원 회의 때 먹을 점심을 위해 8달러짜리 참치 샌드위치를 10개 시키고, 1달러짜리 물도 10개 주문하기로 한 후, 주문 가격에서 10퍼센트를 할인받았다. 배달료 5달러는 할인 없이 추가 지불해야 한다. 이를 식으로 나타내면, '$(8\times10+1\times10)\times0.9+5=86$'이므로, 여자가 지불할 금액은 ④ '$86'이다.

• staff meeting 직원 회의
• delivery ⓝ 배달
• tuna ⓝ 참치

07 스쿨버스를 못 탄 이유

정답률 95% | 정답 ⑤

대화를 듣고, 남자가 스쿨버스를 놓친 이유를 고르시오.

① 늦잠을 자서
② 병원에 다녀와서
③ 아침 운동을 오래 해서
④ 수업 발표 자료를 두고 와서
⑤ 아파트 엘리베이터가 고장 나서

W : Hi, Steve. I didn't see you on the school bus today.
안녕, Steve. 오늘 너 스쿨버스에서 못 봤네.

M : Yes, I missed it.
응, 그거 놓쳤어.

W : I saw you running in the park early this morning. So you didn't wake up late.
너 매일 아침 일찍 공원에서 달리기 하는 거 봤어. 그러니 너 늦잠은 안 잤을 텐데.

M : Not at all. I'm working out to improve my health after I caught a cold.
절대 안 잤지. 감기 걸리고 나서는 내 건강을 증진하기 위해서 운동하고 있어.

W : But you're still coughing. Did you see a doctor this morning?
그런데 여전히 기침을 하는구나. 오늘 아침 병원에 간 거야?

M : Not yet.
아직.

W : Then why did you miss the bus?
그럼 왜 버스를 놓친 거야?

M : Actually, I left home as usual, but my apartment elevator was out of order.
사실, 평소대로 집은 나왔는데, 우리 아파트 엘리베이터가 고장났더라고.

W : Wait... Don't you live on a pretty high floor?
잠깐··· 너 꽤 높은 층 살지 않아?

M : Yeah. I ran down the stairs as quickly as I could, but the bus drove away right before my eyes.
응. 최대한 빨리 계단을 뛰어내려 왔는데, 눈앞에서 버스가 가더라.

W : I'm sorry that you had a tough morning. How did you get to school?
힘든 아침을 보냈다니 안쓰럽네. 학교 어떻게 왔어?

M : The subway. Fortunately, it was quite empty, so I could read the presentation material for history class.
지하철. 다행히 꽤 비어서, (타 있는 동안) 역사 수업을 위한 발표 자료를 읽을 수 있었어.

Why? 왜 정답일까?

남자는 아파트 엘리베이터가 고장 나는 바람에(~ **my apartment elevator was out of order.**) 최대한 빨리 계단을 뛰어내려 왔지만 눈앞에서 스쿨버스를 놓쳤다고 한다. 따라서 남자가 스쿨버스를 놓친 이유로 가장 적절한 것은 ⑤ '아파트 엘리베이터가 고장 나서'이다.

• see a doctor 진찰을 받다, 병원에 가다
• out of order 고장 난

08 언어 전공 대학생 인턴십 프로그램

정답률 96% | 정답 ④

대화를 듣고, Translators For All에 관해 언급되지 않은 것을 고르시오.

① 지원 자격
② 근무 장소
③ 급여
④ 채용 인원
⑤ 지원 방법

W : David, what are you doing on your smartphone?
David, 스마트폰으로 뭐 하고 있어?

M : I'm researching internship programs to join. This one looks quite interesting.
참여할 인턴십 프로그램을 조사하고 있어. 이게 꽤 흥미로워 보여.

W : What is it?
뭐야?

M : It's called Translators For All. The interns participate in various language service projects.
Translators For All이라는 거야. 인턴들이 다양한 언어 서비스 프로젝트에 참여한대.

W : That is pretty cool. Could I apply, too?
꽤 근사하다. 나도 지원할 수 있나?

M : Definitely. 『It says here they want college students majoring in languages.』
물론이지. 여기 언어 전공 대학생들을 원한다고 써 있어. ①의 근거 일치

W : Sounds like a good fit for both of us!
우리 둘 다한테 딱인 것 같다!

M : Absolutely. 『And what I like most about it is we can work from home.』 ②의 근거 일치
그러게. 게다가 내가 제일 마음에 드는 건 우리가 집에서 일할 수 있다는 거야.

W : That's fantastic! 『But how much does the job pay?
그거 환상적이다! 그런데 이 일 급여는 얼마나 돼?

M : Usually $500 a month.』 ③의 근거 일치
보통 한 달에 500달러야.

W : Wow! 『Okay, so how do I apply?
와! 그래, 내가 어떻게 지원하면 되지?

M : We just have to fill out this online application form.』 ⑤의 근거 일치
우린 그냥 이 온라인 신청서만 작성하면 돼.

W : I'll get my smartphone and apply as well. It'll be a great experience.
나도 스마트폰을 가져와서 지원할래. 훌륭한 경험이 되겠어.

Why? 왜 정답일까?

대화에서 남자와 여자는 **Translators For All**의 지원 자격, 근무 장소, 급여, 지원 방법을 언급하므로, 언급되지 않은 것은 ④ '채용 인원'이다.

Why? 왜 오답일까?

① '~ **they want college students majoring in languages.**'에서 '지원 자격'이 언급되었다.
② '~ **we can work from home.**'에서 '근무 장소'가 언급되었다.
③ '**Usually $500 a month.**'에서 '급여'가 언급되었다.
⑤ '**We just have to fill out this online application form.**'에서 '지원 방법'이 언급되었다.

• translator ⓝ 번역가
• work from home 재택 근무하다

09 반딧불이를 볼 수 있는 산책 행사 안내

정답률 82% | 정답 ⑤

Firefly Walk에 관한 다음 내용을 듣고, 일치하지 않는 것을 고르시오.

① 곤충 전문가가 안내한다.
② 일일 최대 참여 인원은 12명이다.
③ 사전에 예약을 해야 한다.
④ 기부금만으로 운영된다.
⑤ 비가 오면 다른 행사로 대체된다.

[문제편 p.091]

W : Hello, listeners!
안녕하세요, 청취자 여러분!

Lakeside Park invites you to the Firefly Walk this summer.
Lakeside Park에서 이번 여름 Firefly Walk로 여러분을 초대합니다.

「You'll see the magical world of fireflies on a two-hour walk guided by insect experts.」 ①의 근거 일치
곤충 전문가가 안내하는 2시간짜리 산책에서 마법 같은 반딧불이의 세계를 만나보시게 될 겁니다.

「This event will be held from August 19th to 27th, open to a maximum of 12 participants per day.」 ②의 근거 일치
이 행사는 8월 19일부터 27일까지 열리며, 일일 최대 12명의 참여 인원을 대상으로 합니다.

「To join this event, you should make reservations in advance on our website.」 ③의 근거 일치
이 행사에 참여하시려면, 저희 웹사이트에서 사전에 예약을 하셔야 합니다.

We're happy to offer this wonderful experience at no cost to participants.
이 멋진 경험을 참가자분들께 무료로 제공하게 되어 기쁩니다.

「However, we operate the Firefly Walk based only on donations, so we would greatly appreciate your generous contributions.」 ④의 근거 일치
하지만, 저희는 Firefly Walk를 기부금으로만 운영하기 때문에, 여러분의 관대한 기부금을 매우 감사히 받겠습니다.

「We'll hold the event even if it rains because it does not affect the firefly viewing.」 ⑤의 근거 불일치
이 행사는 비가 와도 열릴 예정인데, 비가 반딧불이를 구경하는 데 영향을 주지 않기 때문입니다.

So join us for this unforgettable adventure at Lakeside Park!
그러니 Lakeside Park에서 열리는 이 잊지 못할 모험에 함께해주세요!

Why? 왜 정답일까?

'We'll hold the event even if it rains because it does not affect the firefly viewing.'에서 행사는 우천 시에도 진행된다고 하므로, 내용과 일치하지 않는 것은 ⑤ '비가 오면 다른 행사로 대체된다.'이다.

Why? 왜 오답일까?

① '~ guided by insect experts.'의 내용과 일치한다.
② 'This event ~ open to a maximum of 12 participants per day.'의 내용과 일치한다.
③ 'To join this event, you should make reservations in advance on our website.'의 내용과 일치한다.
④ 'However, we operate the Firefly Walk based only on donations, ~'의 내용과 일치한다.

- firefly ⓝ 반딧불이
- at no cost 무료로
- donation ⓝ 기부(금)

10 베개 사기

정답률 86% | 정답 ②

다음 표를 보면서 대화를 듣고, 두 사람이 주문할 베개를 고르시오.

Pillows

	Model	Price	Thickness(inches)	Filling Material	Machine Wash
①	A	$60	4	Goose Down	×
✓②	B	$62	5	Cotton	○
③	C	$80	6	Goose Down	○
④	D	$85	6	Cotton	×
⑤	E	$110	7	Cotton	○

W : Honey, it looks like our pillows are pretty old. Why don't we buy new ones online?
여보, 우리 베개가 너무 낡아 보여요. 온라인에서 새것을 사면 어때요?

M : All right. *[Typing sound]* I found the top five pillow recommendations on the online store.
그래요. *[타자 치는 소리]* 온라인 매장에서 가장 인기 많은 베개 추천 제품 다섯 개를 찾았어요.

W : Great! Let's see.... 「I don't think I want to pay more than $100 for just one pillow.」 근거1 Price 조건
좋아요! 어디 봐요… 난 베개 하나에 100달러 이상을 쓰고 싶지 않아요.

M : I agree. 「So how thick would you like the pillows?
같은 생각이에요. 그럼 베개는 얼마나 두꺼우면 좋겠어요?

W : I guess four inches would be too thin for our necks, right?
우리 목에 4인치는 너무 얇은 거 같죠, 그렇죠?

M : Probably. Something thicker than that would be better.」 근거2 Thickness 조건 「Now, let's choose a filling material.
그럴 거 같아요. 그거보다 좀 두꺼운 게 더 낫겠어요. 이제, 속재료를 골라보죠.

W : We've always used goose down. But how about picking another material instead of goose down this time?」 근거3 Filling Material 조건
항상 우린 구스다운을 썼지요. 하지만 이번에는 구스다운 말고 다른 재료를 골라보면 어때요?

M : Good point. 「Shall we get washable pillows again?
좋은 지적이에요. 또 세탁 가능한 걸로 사야겠죠?

W : Yes, but this time I want to get ones with a machine-wash option.」 근거4 Machine Wash 조건
네, 그렇지만 이번엔 기계 세탁 옵션이 있는 것으로 사요.

M : Definitely! Let's order them now!
그래요! 이제 이걸 주문하죠!

Why? 왜 정답일까?

대화에 따르면 두 사람은 가격이 100달러를 넘지 않으면서, 두께는 4인치 이상이고, 속재료는 구스다운이 아니면서, 기계 세탁이 가능한 베개를 구매하기로 한다. 따라서 두 사람이 주문할 베개는 ② 'B'이다.

- pillow ⓝ 베개
- thick ⓐ 두꺼운
- machine-wash ⓥ 세탁기로 빨다

11 전시회 준비 상황 물어보기

정답률 74% | 정답 ②

대화를 듣고, 여자의 마지막 말에 대한 남자의 응답으로 가장 적절한 것을 고르시오.

① That painting won't be displayed in this exhibition. – 그 그림은 이번 전시회에 전시되지 않을 거야.
✓② I'll pack all my paintings for delivery to the gallery. – 갤러리에 배송하기 위해 내 모든 그림을 싸야 해.
③ I should start learning to paint like you. – 나도 너처럼 그림 그리기를 배우기 시작해야겠어.
④ I've already met some of the other painters. – 난 이미 다른 화가들 몇 명을 만나봤어.
⑤ It was sold on the first day of the gallery exhibition. – 그건 전시회 첫날에 팔렸어.

W : Andy, your exhibition is coming up soon. Are the preparations going well?
Andy, 네 전시회가 곧 열리겠네. 준비 잘 돼 가?

M : Yeah, almost done. I finally finished my last painting for the exhibition yesterday.
응, 거의 다 됐어. 난 어제 마침내 전시회에 낼 마지막 작품을 다 그렸어.

W : Great! I can't wait to see your work. What do you have to do next for the exhibition?
잘됐다! 네 작품 몹시 보고 싶어. 전시회를 위해서 이다음엔 뭐 해야 해?

M : I'll pack all my paintings for delivery to the gallery.
갤러리에 배송하기 위해 내 모든 그림을 싸야 해.

Why? 왜 정답일까?

여자는 남자에게 전시회 준비를 위해 또 무엇을 해야 할지 묻고 있으므로(What do you have to do next for the exhibition?), 남자의 응답으로 가장 적절한 것은 ② '갤러리에 배송하기 위해 내 모든 그림을 싸야 해.'이다.

- exhibition ⓝ 전시(회)
- pack ⓥ (짐을) 싸다

12 여행 패키지 취소 문의

정답률 75% | 정답 ①

대화를 듣고, 남자의 마지막 말에 대한 여자의 응답으로 가장 적절한 것을 고르시오.

✓① Of course. When are you available?
물론이죠. 언제 시간이 되시나요?
② No worries. Your package is the cheapest one.
걱정 마세요. 귀하의 패키지가 가장 가격이 쌉니다.
③ Sure. The package is refundable if you don't open it.
물론이죠. 열지 않으셨다면 소포는 환불 가능해요.
④ Absolutely. I'm happy to contact you before you leave.
그럼요. 떠나시기 전에 연락드리게 되어 기쁘네요.
⑤ Be careful. You should get enough information on the trip.
조심하세요. 여행에 대해 충분한 정보를 구하셔야 합니다.

M : Hi. I'd like to cancel the trip package I booked. Here's my reservation number.
안녕하세요. 제가 예약한 여행 패키지를 취소하고 싶어요. 여기 제 예약 번호요.

W : Sure. *[Typing sound]* I'm sorry but we cannot give you a refund because you bought the special discounted package.
물론이죠. *[타자 치는 소리]* 죄송하지만 특별 할인 패키지를 구매하셨기 때문에 환불은 어렵습니다.

M : Oh, in that case, I wonder if I can change the dates of the trip.
오, 그렇다면, 여행 날짜를 바꿀 수 있는지 알고 싶네요.

W : Of course. When are you available?
물론이죠. 언제 시간이 되시나요?

Why? 왜 정답일까?

남자는 여행 패키지 예약을 취소하려 했다가 환불이 불가능하다는 말에 날짜를 바꿀 수 있는지(Oh, in that case, I wonder if I can change the dates of the trip.) 알고 싶다고 한다. 따라서 여자의 응답으로 가장 적절한 것은 ① '물론이죠. 언제 시간이 되시나요?'이다.

- cancel ⓥ 취소하다
- give a refund 환불해주다
- refundable ⓐ 환불 가능한

16회

13 테니스 라켓에 관한 조언 받기

정답률 79% | 정답 ⑤

대화를 듣고, 여자의 마지막 말에 대한 남자의 응답으로 가장 적절한 것을 고르시오. [3점]

Man: ____________________

① Great. A powerful stroke is my strongest point in tennis.
훌륭합니다. 힘 있는 스트로크가 테니스를 칠 때 저의 제일 큰 강점이죠.
② I see. Is there any lighter racket I can borrow from you?
알겠습니다. 제가 선생님께 빌릴 만한 더 가벼운 라켓이 있을까요?
③ I agree. Try to practice your stroke more with this racket.
맞는 말씀입니다. 이 라켓으로 귀하의 스트로크를 더 연습해 보세요.
④ That's true. I'll be a respectful tennis player from now on.
맞아요. 지금부터 공손한 테니스 선수가 되겠어요.
✓⑤ Okay. I should drop by a shop to see which racket suits me.
알겠습니다. 상점에 들러서 어느 라켓이 저한테 맞는지 봐야겠어요.

M : Thanks for today's tennis lesson, Ms. Rossini.
오늘 테니스 수업 고맙습니다, Rossini 선생님.

W : Oh, Mr. Chen, you did great with your backhand stroke today.
오, Chen 님, 오늘 백핸드 스트로크 아주 잘하셨어요.

M : It's all thanks to you. I couldn't even hit the ball at first!
다 선생님 덕분이죠. 처음에는 공을 치지도 못했는걸요!

W : Just remember to increase your power and stability when you strike.
단지 칠 때 힘과 안정성을 더하는 것 잊지 마세요.

M : I try to, but it's not easy.
그러려고 하는데, 쉽지 않아요.

W : Really? Can I see your racket?
그러세요? 제가 라켓 좀 봐도 될까요?

M : Sure, here it is.
물론이죠. 여기 있습니다.

W : The head size is good for you, but this is too light.
헤드 크기가 알맞긴 한데, 이건 너무 가볍군요.

M : Well... it's what my older sister used.
음… 이건 제 누나가 쓰던 거예요.

W : Light rackets make it challenging to put force on the ball when striking. I think an around 300-gram racket is fit for you.
가벼운 라켓을 쓰면 공을 칠 때 공에 힘을 가하기가 어려워요. 대략 300그램 무게의 라켓이 적합해 보여요.

M : Oh, so a heavier racket makes it easier for me to control the ball?
오, 그럼 더 무거운 라켓을 쓰면 제가 공을 다루기가 더 쉬워지는 건가요?

W : That's right. Choosing the right racket for you is essential.
맞아요. 적합한 라켓을 고르는 것이 필수입니다.

M : Okay. I should drop by a shop to see which racket suits me.
알겠습니다. 상점에 들러서 어느 라켓이 저한테 맞는지 봐야겠어요.

Why? 왜 정답일까?

테니스 선생님인 여자는 남자가 사용 중인 라켓이 너무 가볍다면서, 적당한 무게의 라켓을 고르는 것이 아주 중요하다고 말한다(Choosing the right racket for you is essential.). 따라서 남자의 응답으로 가장 적절한 것은 ⑤ '알겠습니다. 상점에 들러서 어느 라켓이 저한테 맞는지 봐야겠어요.'이다.

- stability ⓝ 안정성
- strike ⓥ 치다, 타격하다

[문제편 p.092]

- challenging ⓐ 어려운, 까다로운
- respectful ⓐ 공손한
- essential ⓐ 필수적인
- drop by ~에 들르다

14 배달 음식 쓰레기 줄이기

정답률 79% | 정답 ④

대화를 듣고, 남자의 마지막 말에 대한 여자의 응답으로 가장 적절한 것을 고르시오.

Woman: ______________________________

① That's why I changed all of my glass cups to plastic.
그래서 난 내 모든 유리컵을 플라스틱으로 바꾼 거야.
② I'll try to look for a delivery restaurant to save time.
시간을 아끼기 위해 배달 음식점을 찾아보겠어.
③ There's a reason that restaurant is popular with people.
그 식당이 사람들한테 인기가 많은 이유가 있네.
✔ You really made me think again about using food delivery.
네 덕분에 음식 배달을 이용하는 걸 정말로 다시 생각해보게 됐어.
⑤ I hope people know how important it is to eat fresh food.
사람들이 신선한 음식을 먹는 게 얼마나 중요한지 알면 좋겠어.

W : Jason, do you know any good Indian restaurants that deliver?
Jason, 배달해주는 인도 음식 식당 좋은 데 좀 알아?

M : Oh, I don't use food delivery, so I'm not sure.
오, 난 음식 배달을 안 써서, 잘 모르겠어.

W : Really? I can get food delivered right to my front door with my smartphone.
정말? 난 스마트폰으로 우리 현관 바로 앞까지 배달 음식을 받아볼 수 있어.

M : Sure, it's convenient, but delivery food makes a lot of waste from all its packaging.
맞아, 그게 편하지. 그런데 배달 음식은 그 모든 포장 때문에 쓰레기가 많이 나와.

W : Well, unless we cook at home all the time, delivery is easier.
음, 우리가 항상 집에서 음식을 해먹는 게 아니면, 배달이 더 편하지.

M : Have you thought about how many plastic containers are used in just one order?
주문 단 한 번에 얼마나 많은 플라스틱 용기가 쓰이는지 생각해 봤어?

W : Oh, that's true... I always put them in the recycling after, though.
오, 그건 그래… 하지만 난 항상 나중에 그걸 재활용하는 데 넣어두는 걸.

M : That's not always enough. When I don't cook, I go to the restaurant and get the food served in my own personal container.
그거로 항상 충분한 게 아냐. 내가 요리를 안 할 때면 나는 식당에 가서 내 개인 그릇에 음식을 받아.

W : I've never thought about that. What a responsible way to reduce plastic use!
그건 생각 못해 봤어. 플라스틱 사용을 줄일 책임감 있는 방법이구나!

M : People need to be aware of what the consequences of their actions will be in the future.
사람들은 자기 행동이 미래에 초래할 결과가 뭘지 인식할 필요가 있어.

W : You really made me think again about using food delivery.
네 덕분에 음식 배달을 이용하는 걸 정말로 다시 생각해보게 됐어.

Why? 왜 정답일까?

남자는 음식 배달 한 번에 플라스틱 쓰레기가 너무 많이 나온다면서, 사람들 모두 자신의 행동이 (환경에) 끼칠 영향을 유념하고 행동할 필요가 있다고 말한다(**People need to be aware of what the consequences of their actions will be in the future.**). 따라서 여자의 응답으로 가장 적절한 것은 ④ '네 덕분에 음식 배달을 이용하는 걸 정말로 다시 생각해보게 됐어.'이다.

- convenient 편리한
- recycling ⓝ 재활용
- container ⓝ 용기, 그릇

15 합주 제안 수락하기

정답률 75% | 정답 ④

다음 상황 설명을 듣고, Nicky가 Chris에게 할 말로 가장 적절한 것을 고르시오. [3점]

Nicky: ______________________________

① You need to stick to your musical identity.
네 음악적 정체성을 고수할 필요가 있어.
② Can you invite me to your band's performance?
너희 밴드 연주에 나 초대해 줄래?
③ Think about becoming a professional musician later.
나중에 전문 뮤지션이 되는 걸 고려해봐.
✔ Why don't we accept the proposal to try something new?
뭔가 새로운 걸 시도해보게 제안을 받아들이는 게 어때?
⑤ Let's keep practicing so we win instead of that other team.
상대 팀 말고 우리가 이길 수 있게 계속 연습하자.

W : Chris is the passionate leader of an electronic music band at his university.
Chris는 자기 대학교 전자 음악 밴드의 열정 넘치는 리더이다.
His band is pretty good, close to professional level when it comes to electronic music.
그의 밴드는 아주 잘해서, 전자 음악에 관해서는 전문가 수준에 가깝다.
Then one day, another band on his campus, which plays classical music, offers his band the chance to perform together at the upcoming campus festival.
그러던 어느 날, 그의 캠퍼스에 있는 다른 클래식 연주 밴드가 다가올 캠퍼스 축제에서 함께 연주할 기회를 그의 밴드 쪽에 제안한다.
Chris hesitates to respond because classical music feels quite unfamiliar to him.
Chris는 클래식 음악이 그에게 꽤 생소하기 때문에 답하기를 망설인다.
But Nicky, another member of his band, thinks if they work with musicians of the seemingly distant genre, they'd be able to present a different side of their music.
하지만 그의 밴드에 있는 다른 멤버 Nicky는 그들이 겉보기에 동떨어진 장르의 뮤지션들과 함께 작업해보면 그들 음악의 다른 면을 보여줄 수 있을 것이라 생각한다.
So, Nicky wants to suggest to Chris that their team take the offer to collaborate in an attempt to play music they've never done before.
그래서, Nicky는 Chris에게 그들의 팀이 전에 한 번도 해보지 않은 음악을 연주해보기 위해서 합주 제안을 받아들이자고 제안하려 한다.
In this situation, what would Nicky most likely say to Chris?
이 상황에서, Nicky는 Chris에게 뭐라고 말할 것인가?

Nicky : Why don't we accept the proposal to try something new?
뭔가 새로운 걸 시도해보게 제안을 받아들이는 게 어때?

Why? 왜 정답일까?

상황에 따르면 Nicky는 클래식 음악을 연주하는 밴드 쪽에서 온 합주 제안을 받아들이자고 제안하고 싶어 하므로(**So, Nicky wants to suggest to Chris that their team take the offer to collaborate in an attempt to play music they've never done before.**), Nicky가 Chris에게 할 말로 가장 적절한 것은 ④ '뭔가 새로운 걸 시도해보게 제안을 받아들이는 게 어때?'이다.

- passionate ⓐ 열정 넘치는
- hesitate ⓥ 망설이다
- seemingly ad 겉보기에
- stick to ~을 고수하다
- upcoming ⓐ 다가오는
- unfamiliar ⓐ 생소한, 낯선
- in an attempt to ~하기 위해서
- identity ⓝ 정체성

16-17 금융 시장에서 동물이 상징하는 바

M : Hello, students.
안녕하세요, 학생 여러분.
Have you ever heard a market analyst or an investment banker use animal references?
시장 분석가 또는 증권 인수업자들이 동물을 언급하는 걸 들어봤나요?
It's because such expressions give you some insight into the financial industry.
그런 표현이 여러분에게 금융업계에 대한 통찰력을 주기 때문입니다.
「I'll introduce some examples of what animals represent in the market.」 16번의 근거
동물이 시장에서 어떤 것을 나타내는지에 관한 예를 몇 가지 소개할게요.
「Let's start with bulls.」 17번 ①의 근거 일치
황소부터 시작해보죠.
You've probably seen them raising their horns when they attack.
여러분은 이들이 공격할 때 뿔을 치켜세우는 것을 봤을 겁니다.
So a 'bull market' represents a period when prices are generally rising.
그래서 '황소 시장'은 가격이 대체로 오르고 있는 기간을 나타내지요.
「The next one is sheep.」 17번 ②의 근거 일치
다음으로 양입니다.
As they move in a herd, the 'sheep-flock effect' means a bias that influences the decisions of investors, often causing irrational reactions.
이들은 무리 지어 움직이기 때문에, '양떼 효과'란 투자자들의 결정에 영향을 미쳐 흔히 불합리한 반응을 야기하는 편견을 의미합니다.
「Pigs are also fairly common in finance-speak.」 17번 ④의 근거 일치
돼지들 또한 금융 담화에서 꽤 흔합니다.
They are used to define investors who are greedy and take high risks in anticipation of making huge profits.
이들은 탐욕 넘치고 엄청난 수익을 낼 것을 기대하며 큰 위험을 감수하는 투자자들을 정의하고자 사용됩니다.
「Finally, chicken indicates investors who are reluctant to take risks and prefer a safer approach.」 17번 ⑤의 근거 일치
마지막으로, 닭은 위험을 감수하기를 꺼리고 더 안전한 접근법을 선호하는 투자자들을 가리킵니다.
From these few examples, you can get an idea of the variety of financial vocabulary.
이 몇 가지 예를 통해, 여러분은 금융 쪽 어휘의 종류를 파악할 수 있을 것입니다.
Why don't you look for other examples and find your favorite one?
다른 예시를 살펴보고, 가장 여러분 마음에 드는 것을 찾아볼까요?

- analyst ⓝ 분석가
- bull ⓝ 황소
- herd ⓝ 무리, 떼
- bias ⓝ 편견
- greedy ⓐ 탐욕스러운
- reluctant ⓐ 꺼리는, 마지못해 하는
- symbolize ⓥ 상징하다
- investment banker 증권 인수업자
- horn ⓝ 뿔
- flock ⓝ 무리, 떼 ⓥ 모이다
- irrational ⓐ 불합리한
- anticipation ⓝ 기대
- sector ⓝ 부문
- domesticate ⓥ 길들이다, 사육하다

16 주제 파악

정답률 67% | 정답 ①

남자가 하는 말의 주제로 가장 적절한 것은?

✔ animal-related terms in the financial sector – 금융 부문의 동물 관련 용어
② what animals symbolize by country – 나라별로 동물이 상징하는 바
③ aggressive tendencies of animals – 동물의 공격적 성향
④ how humans have domesticated animals – 사람들이 동물을 사육해온 방식
⑤ risks and benefits of livestock industry investment – 축산업 투자의 위험과 이익

Why? 왜 정답일까?

'**I'll introduce some examples of what animals represent in the market.**' 이하로 남자는 동물이 시장에서 어떤 것을 상징하는지 예시와 함께 설명하고 있다. 따라서 남자가 하는 말의 주제로 가장 적절한 것은 ① '금융 부문의 동물 관련 용어'이다.

17 언급 유무 파악

정답률 97% | 정답 ③

언급된 동물이 아닌 것은?

① bulls – 황소 ② sheep – 양 ✔ cats – 고양이
④ pigs – 돼지 ⑤ chicken – 닭

Why? 왜 정답일까?

담화에서 남자는 동물의 예로 황소, 양, 돼지, 닭을 언급하므로, 언급되지 않은 것은 ③ '고양이'이다.

Why? 왜 오답일까?

① '**Let's start with bulls.**'에서 '황소'가 언급되었다.
② '**The next one is sheep.**'에서 '양'이 언급되었다.
④ '**Pigs are also fairly common in finance-speak.**'에서 '돼지'가 언급되었다.
⑤ '**Finally, chicken indicates investors who are reluctant to take risks and prefer a safer approach.**'에서 '닭'이 언급되었다.

[문제편 p.092]

Dictation 16

문제편 093쪽

01 conducted a safety inspection / the rules for using balconies / to prevent flooding
02 set a specific goal / The more detailed your goal / motivated and focused
03 the care of abandoned dogs / interested in adopting a dog / get the dogs bathed
04 struggled to blow it up / I was so dizzy / your striped dress
05 first international visitors / wear name tags / taking photos of the campus tours
06 just tuna sandwiches / bottled water would be good / not for the delivery fee
07 you're still coughing / my apartment elevator was out of order / read the presentation material
08 various language service projects / majoring in languages / work from home
09 guided by insect experts / at no cost to participants / your generous contributions
10 too thin for our necks / a filling material / get washable pillows
11 finished my last painting / can't wait to see
12 cannot give you a refund / change the dates
13 all thanks to you / increase your power and stability / Light rackets make it challenging
14 my own personal container / reduce plastic use / the consequences of their actions
15 the passionate leader / the chance to perform together / take the offer to collaborate
16-17 insight into the financial industry / prices are generally rising / investors who are greedy

17회 | 2022학년도 7월 학력평가 고3

• 정답 •

01 ② 02 ① 03 ③ 04 ⑤ 05 ④ 06 ① 07 ① 08 ⑤ 09 ② 10 ② 11 ② 12 ③ 13 ③ 14 ② 15 ⑤ 16 ① 17 ③

01 생태정원 이름짓기 공모 안내

정답률 97% | 정답 ②

다음을 듣고, 여자가 하는 말의 목적으로 가장 적절한 것을 고르시오.

① 환경보호 표어 대회 참여를 독려하려고
② 학교 생태정원 이름짓기 공모를 안내하려고
③ 학교 시설 보수공사 기간 연장을 공지하려고
④ 학생회장 선출을 위한 온라인 투표 방법을 알리려고
⑤ 생태정원 가꾸기 활동을 위한 자원봉사자를 모집하려고

W : Good afternoon, students. This is Vice Principal Webster.
안녕하세요, 여러분. 교감인 Webster입니다.
As you know, our school's new eco garden will open next month.
알다시피, 우리 학교의 새로운 생태정원이 다음 달 오픈합니다.
I'm very happy to have a new school garden.
새 학교 정원을 갖게 되어 몹시 기쁘네요.
Completing construction is thanks to your help.
공사를 마무리하게 된 것은 여러분의 도움 덕분입니다.
However, our new eco garden doesn't have a proper name yet.
하지만, 우리 새로운 생태정원에 아직 적당한 이름이 없습니다.
So, we're holding a school garden naming contest.
그래서, 학교 정원 이름짓기 대회를 열려고 합니다.
I'm sure you'll be proud of yourself if you suggest the winning name.
여러분이 제안한 이름이 공모에 당선되면 매우 뿌듯할 거라 확신합니다.
You can participate in this naming contest by clicking the banner on our school website.
우리 학교 웹 사이트에 있는 배너를 눌러서 이 이름짓기 대회에 참가할 수 있습니다.
The deadline is next Tuesday.
마감은 다음 주 화요일입니다.
We'll select the top three submissions and hold an online vote next Friday.
우리는 최고의 제출작 세 가지를 뽑아서 다음 주 금요일에 온라인 투표에 부칠 것입니다.
The name with the most votes wins.
가장 많은 표를 얻은 이름이 우승합니다.
We're looking forward to seeing your brilliant and witty ideas for the garden name!
생태정원 이름을 위한 여러분의 훌륭하고 재기 넘기는 아이디어를 보기를 고대합니다!

Why? 왜 정답일까?

새로 개장하는 학교 생태정원에 붙일 이름 공모전이 열린다는 것을 공지하는 담화이다. 따라서 여자가 하는 말의 목적으로 가장 적절한 것은 ② '학교 생태정원 이름짓기 공모를 안내하려고'이다.

- **construction** ⓝ 건설, 공사
- **proud** ⓐ 자랑스러워하는, 자랑스러운
- **participate** ⓥ 참가하다
- **submission** ⓝ 제출물
- **brilliant** ⓐ 훌륭한, 멋진
- **proper** ⓐ 적당한
- **suggest** ⓥ 제안하다
- **deadline** ⓝ 기한, 마감 시간
- **vote** ⓝ 투표

02 온라인 수업에서 동료 피드백 활용하기

정답률 93% | 정답 ①

대화를 듣고, 남자의 의견으로 가장 적절한 것을 고르시오.

① 학생 간 동료 피드백은 온라인 수업에 효과적이다.
② 수업 전 학생들과의 대화로 친밀감을 형성할 수 있다.
③ 온라인 자료를 수업에 활용할 때 저작권에 유의해야 한다.
④ 긍정적인 격려로 학생들에게 자신감을 심어 주는 것이 좋다.
⑤ 학생의 다양한 수준을 고려하여 온라인 수업을 계획해야 한다.

M : Have you finished class for today?
오늘 수업 끝나셨어요?
W : Yeah. But it's really hard for me to manage my online classes.
네. 그런데 온라인 수업 관리하는 게 너무 어렵네요.
M : Why? I thought you were accustomed to it.
왜요? 전 선생님이 적응하신 줄 알았어요.
W : I'm comfortable with teaching. The problem is that students have a hard time interacting with one another.
가르치는 건 편해요. 문제는 학생들이 서로 소통하는 데 어려움이 있다는 점이에요.
M : I see. *[Pause]* In my case, I encourage students to give peer reviews. It's very effective during online class.
그렇군요. *[잠시 멈춤]* 제 경우에는, 학생들보고 동료 피드백을 주도록 격려하는 편이에요. 이건 온라인 수업 중에 아주 효과가 좋아요.
W : What do you mean by "peer review"?
'동료 피드백'이 무슨 뜻이죠?
M : During class, I get students to review each other's work and to provide meaningful feedback. It helps encourage students to interact.
수업 중에 저는 아이들이 서로 학습한 걸 검토하고 유의미한 피드백을 주게 하고 있어요. 학생들의 소통을 장려하는 데 도움이 되죠.
W : How do they give each other feedback?
아이들이 서로 피드백을 어떻게 주나요?
M : I usually use chatrooms. It allows students to talk with one another.
전 채팅방을 이용해요. 그럼 학생들이 서로 이야기를 나눌 수 있죠.
W : Hmm.... That makes sense. Plus, that can help them achieve higher understanding.
흠... 일리가 있네요. 더구나, 그것은 아이들이 이해도 더 잘하는 데 도움이 될 수 있고요.
M : Exactly. Having students give peer feedback makes my online classes much more effective.

바로 그거예요. 아이들이 동료 피드백을 주게 하는 것이 제 온라인 수업을 훨씬 효과적으로 만들어 줘요.

W : Okay. I'll give it a try for my online classes.
알겠어요. 제 온라인 수업에 시도해 볼게요.

Why? 왜 정답일까?

온라인 수업 중에 학생들끼리 소통하게 할 방법을 고민하던 여자에게 남자는 동료 피드백이 효과적이라고 조언하고 있으므로(Having students give ~ much more effective.), 남자의 의견으로 가장 적절한 것은 ① '학생 간 동료 피드백은 온라인 수업에 효과적이다.'이다.

- manage ⓥ 관리하다
- comfortable ⓐ 편한, 편안한
- encourage ⓥ 격려하다
- effective ⓐ 효과적인
- meaningful ⓐ 의미 있는
- achieve ⓥ 해내다, 잘 해내다
- be accustomed to ~에 적응하다
- have a hard time ~ing ~하기 어려워하다
- peer review 동료 심사(평가)
- provide ⓥ 제공하다
- feedback ⓝ 피드백, 반응, 의견, 감상
- give it a try 시도해 보다

03 학생 미술 전시회 관람

정답률 94% | 정답 ③

대화를 듣고, 두 사람의 관계를 가장 잘 나타낸 것을 고르시오.

① 사진작가 – 학생　② 화가 – 잡지사 기자
③ 미술 교사 – 학부모　④ 전시회 기획자 – 의뢰인
⑤ 큐레이터 – 인쇄물 제작업자

M : Welcome to the exhibition!
전시회에 오신 것을 환영합니다!

W : Thank you for putting together such an amazing show. The paintings are so impressive.
이렇게 멋진 쇼를 준비해 주셔서 고마워요. 그림이 무척 인상적이에요.

M : All the works here are watercolor paintings, so you can clearly feel the painters' moods.
여기 있는 모든 작품은 수채화라서, 작가들의 기분을 명확하게 느끼실 수 있어요.

W : I can't believe they were made by students. The canvases featuring flowers are especially colorful and detailed.
이걸 학생들이 그린 거라니 믿을 수 없네요. 꽃이 그려진 캔버스가 특히 다채롭고 세밀하네요.

M : They practiced color mixing with different brush sizes to develop their skills. That's the most important part of teaching my art class.
아이들은 다양한 크기의 붓으로 색상 혼합을 연습해 그림 기술을 익혔어요. 그게 제 미술 수업에서 가장 중요한 부분이고요.

W : It was really helpful. How my daughter uses color is better than before. She enjoys your class a lot.
무척 도움이 됐어요. 우리 딸아이가 색을 쓰는 방식이 전보다 좋아졌어요. 우리 애는 선생님 수업을 많이 좋아해요.

M : Oh, really? It's a great pleasure to see our high school's students improve.
오, 정말요? 우리 고등학교 학생들이 실력이 느는 것을 보게 되어 기뻐요.

W : Can I take some pictures of the works?
작품 사진을 좀 찍어도 될까요?

M : Absolutely. There's also more information about the artworks in the leaflets at the entrance.
물론입니다. 그리고 입구에 있는 안내 책자에 미술 작품에 관한 정보가 더 있어요.

W : I'll be sure to pick up a leaflet before I go.
가기 전에 책자를 하나 꼭 챙겨갈게요.

Why? 왜 정답일까?

'That's the most important part of teaching my art class.', 'How my daughter uses color is better than before. She enjoys your class a lot.', 'It's a great pleasure to see our high school's students improve.'에서 남자가 미술 교사, 여자가 학부모임을 알 수 있으므로, 두 사람의 관계로 가장 적절한 것은 ③ '미술 교사 – 학부모'이다.

- exhibition ⓝ 전시회
- watercolor painting 수채화
- especially [ad] 특히
- detailed ⓐ 상세한
- helpful ⓐ 도움이 되는
- improve ⓥ 나아지다, 개선되다
- put together 준비하다, 모으다
- clearly [ad] 명확히, 확실히
- colorful ⓐ 다채로운
- practice ⓥ 연습하다
- daughter ⓝ 딸, 여식
- leaflet ⓝ (안내) 책자, 전단

04 새로 개원한 어린이 병원 둘러보기

정답률 96% | 정답 ⑤

대화를 듣고, 그림에서 대화의 내용과 일치하지 않는 것을 고르시오.

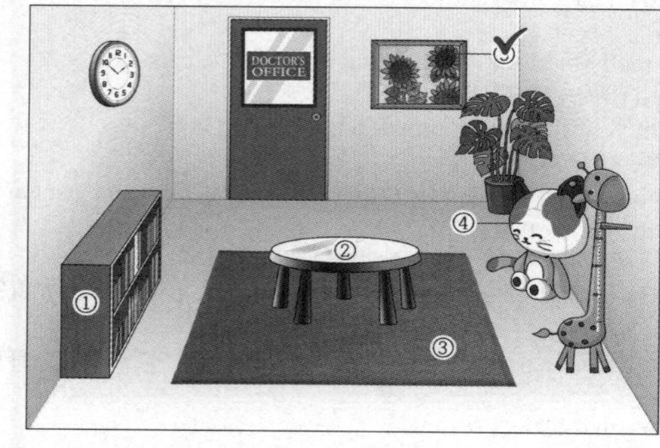

M : Hi, Grace. Congratulations on opening your hospital. It looks amazing.
안녕, Grace. 병원 개원 축하해. 멋져 보이네.

W : Thanks for coming. Feel free to look around.
와줘서 고마워. 편하게 둘러봐.

M : You prepared children's books. 「The bookcase with two shelves displays them perfectly.」 ①의 근거 일치
어린이용 책을 준비했구나. 2단 선반 책장에 책이 멋지게 진열돼있네.

W : Right. The children can reach the books easily.
맞아. 아이들이 책을 쉽게 집을 수 있어.

M : 「Oh, they can read books at the table in the middle of the room.
오, 그들이 방 가운데 있는 탁자에서 책을 읽을 수 있구나.

W : I chose the round one for their safety.」 ②의 근거 일치
아이들의 안전을 위해 원탁으로 골랐어.

M : Good thinking. 「I love the rug under the table.」 It looks very cozy.
좋은 생각이야. 탁자 아래 깐 러그 마음에 드네. 무척 아늑해 보여.

W : Sure. Children can sit on it comfortably.
맞아. 아이들이 편하게 그 위에 앉을 수 있지.

M : 「Wow, look at the big cat doll between the giraffe measuring stick and the plant.」 ③의 근거 일치 It's so cute!
와, 키 재는 기린이랑 식물 사이에 있는 큰 고양이 인형 좀 봐. 너무 귀여워!

W : Children really love it because it's so soft. 「What do you think about the painting on the wall?」 ④의 근거 일치
그게 엄청 부드러워서 아이들이 무척 좋아해. 벽에 있는 그림은 어때 보여?

M : I like it. The picture of the rainbow is very bright and cheerful.」 ⑤의 근거 불일치
마음에 들어. 무지개 그림이 무척 밝고 활기차 보여.

W : My daughter drew it. She's excited that all our visitors get to see her art.
우리 딸아이가 그렸어. 모든 우리 병원 손님들이 자기 그림을 보게 되어서 아이는 신이 났어.

M : It goes well with your children's hospital.
네 어린이 병원과 잘 어울리네.

Why? 왜 정답일까?

대화에서 여자의 딸이 그린 그림(The picture of the rainbow is very bright and cheerful.)은 무지개 그림이라고 하는데, 그림 속 벽에는 해바라기 그림이 걸려 있다. 따라서 그림에서 대화의 내용과 일치하지 않는 것은 ⑤이다.

- feel free to 편하게 ~하다
- prepare ⓥ 준비하다
- reach ⓥ (손을) 뻗다, ~에 이르다
- cozy ⓐ 포근한, 아늑한
- giraffe ⓝ 기린
- look around 둘러보다
- perfectly [ad] 완벽하게, 멋지게
- safety ⓝ 안전
- comfortably [ad] 편안하게
- measuring stick 키 재는 막대

05 영화의 밤 준비하기

정답률 88% | 정답 ④

대화를 듣고, 남자가 할 일로 가장 적절한 것을 고르시오.

① 영화 고르기　② 스피커 설치하기　③ 간식 만들기
④ 담요 가지고 오기　⑤ 쿠션 빌려오기

M : Honey, the backyard looks fantastic. You did a great job.
여보, 뒷마당이 근사해 보이네요. 정말 잘 꾸몄어요.

W : Thanks! I tried to decorate it like a little theater.
고마워요! 난 그곳을 작은 극장처럼 꾸며보려고 했어요.

M : I'm very excited to host a movie night, especially for Lauren and her friends.
영화의 밤을 여는 게 기대되네요, 특히 Lauren과 친구들을 위해서요.

W : Did you pick out a movie for the kids?
애들을 위한 영화는 골랐어요?

M : I chose *My Little Dragon*, Lauren's favorite musical.
*My Little Dragon*을 골랐어요. Lauren이 제일 좋아하는 뮤지컬이죠.

W : Perfect. I just set up the speakers, and they sound amazing.
완벽해요. 방금 스피커를 설치했는데, 소리가 근사해요.

M : Good quality sound is essential, especially for a musical film!
좋은 음질은 필수죠, 특히 뮤지컬 영화를 위해서는요!

W : Totally! I prepared some popcorn, drinks, and candy for the kids as well. Do we need anything else?
그러니까요! 애들을 위해 팝콘이랑 음료수, 그리고 캔디도 좀 준비했어요. 다른 게 더 필요할까요?

M : Oh, I forgot to check the weather for tonight.
오, 오늘 밤 날씨를 확인하는 걸 깜빡했어요.

W : Let's check it now. *[Pause]* Well, they say it might be a little bit chilly tonight.
지금 확인해보죠. *[잠시 멈춤]* 음, 오늘 밤 약간 쌀쌀할지도 모른다고 하네요.

M : I'll bring some blankets for the kids then.
그럼 애들을 위해 담요를 좀 갖다 놓을게요.

W : That's very thoughtful. I'll prepare some comfortable cushions.
아주 사려 깊네요. 난 편한 쿠션을 준비할게요.

M : Great. This movie night is going to be terrific.
좋아요. 오늘 영화의 밤은 아주 멋질 거예요.

Why? 왜 정답일까?

딸과 친구들을 위한 영화의 밤을 준비 중인 남자는 밤 날씨가 쌀쌀할 것이라는 예보에 담요를 가져다 놓겠다고 하므로, 남자가 할 일로 가장 적절한 것은 ④ '담요 가지고 오기'이다.

- backyard ⓝ 뒷마당
- theater ⓝ 극장
- musical film 뮤지컬 영화
- blanket ⓝ 담요
- terrific ⓐ 아주 좋은, 멋진, 훌륭한
- decorate ⓥ 꾸미다, 장식하다
- pick out 고르다, 선택하다
- chilly ⓐ 쌀쌀한
- thoughtful ⓐ 사려 깊은

06 조명 및 전구 구입하기

정답률 81% | 정답 ①

대화를 듣고, 여자가 지불할 금액을 고르시오. [3점]

① $225　② $250　③ $255　④ $280　⑤ $315

M : Lamps Plus Lighting! How may I help you?
Lamps Plus Lighting입니다! 무엇을 도와드릴까요?

W : Hi, I'm looking for pendant lights for my kitchen. How much are the ones displayed in the window?
안녕하세요, 전 부엌에 달 펜던트 조명을 찾고 있어요. 창문에 전시된 건 얼마인가요?

M : The pendant light with the metal shade is 100 dollars and the one with the glass shade is 150 dollars.
금속 갓이 달린 펜던트 조명은 100달러이고 유리 갓이 달린 건 150달러입니다.

W : Hmm.... Both look great, but the metal one will go better with my kitchen. I'll take two with metal shades.
흠…. 둘 다 멋져 보이는데, 금속 갓 조명이 저희 집 부엌에 더 잘 맞겠어요. 금속 갓이 달린 걸 두 개 살게요.

M : All right. Can I help you with anything else?
알겠습니다. 다른 거 도와드릴 게 있을까요?

W : I need some lightbulbs for the pendant lights. What is the best kind for these lights?
펜던트 조명을 위해 전구도 좀 필요해요. 이런 조명에 가장 좋은 종류는 뭘까요?

[문제편 p.097]

M : We have many options, but I recommend LED lightbulbs for energy efficiency. They're 10 dollars each.
선택권이 많지만, 에너지 효율을 위해 LED 전구를 추천합니다. 하나에 10달러예요.

W : Okay. I'll take five LED lightbulbs.
알겠습니다. LED 전구를 다섯 개 살게요.

M : So, that's two pendant lights and five lightbulbs. By the way, for our store's 10th anniversary, you'll receive a 10% discount from the total price.
그럼, 펜던트 조명 두 개와 전구 다섯 개요. 그런데 저희 가게 10주년 기념일을 맞아, 총 가격에서 10퍼센트 할인을 받으실 수 있어요.

W : Sounds great.
좋네요.

M : Do you need help installing the lights? We offer an installation service for 30 dollars.
조명 설치에 도움이 필요하신가요? 30달러에 설치 서비스를 제공하고 있습니다.

W : No, thanks. I can install them myself. Here's my credit card.
아뇨, 괜찮아요. 제가 직접 설치할 수 있어요. 여기 제 신용 카드요.

Why? 왜 정답일까?

대화에 따르면 여자는 금속 갓이 달린 100달러짜리 펜던트 조명을 두 개, 10달러짜리 LED 조명을 다섯 개 산 후, 총 가격에서 10퍼센트를 할인 받았고, 30달러짜리 설치 서비스는 신청하지 않았다. 이를 식으로 나타내면 '$(100\times2+10\times5)\times0.9=225$'이므로, 여자가 지불할 금액은 ① '$225'이다.

- shade ⓝ (전등의) 갓, 그늘, 그림자
- option ⓝ 선택권
- efficiency ⓝ 효율
- install ⓥ 설치하다
- lightbulb ⓝ 전구
- recommend ⓥ 추천하다
- anniversary ⓝ 기념일

07 벼룩시장을 미룬 이유 묻기

정답률 50% | 정답 ①

대화를 듣고, 여자가 벼룩시장 운영을 연기한 이유를 고르시오.

① 공원 긴급 보수 작업이 계획되어서
② 행사 당일 폭우가 예상되어서
③ 행사 물품 배송이 지연되어서
④ 다른 행사와 시간이 겹쳐서
⑤ 참가 인원이 적어서

M : Rosie, how's organizing the flea market going?
Rosie, 벼룩시장 준비는 어떻게 돼 가?

W : Good, I'm pretty busy sorting event supplies that were delivered today.
잘되고 있어, 난 오늘 배달된 이벤트 용품을 분류하느라 꽤 바빠.

M : I heard a lot of people have signed up for the market.
많은 사람들이 벼룩시장에 신청했다고 들었어.

W : Yes. Thirty-six people so far.
응, 지금까지 36명이야.

M : That's amazing! It'll be held at Sunkist Park this Saturday afternoon, right?
대단하다! 이번 주 토요일 오후에 Sunkist Park에서 열리지, 그렇지?

W : Unfortunately, the market is being delayed one week. But it'll be held at the same place.
안타깝게도, 벼룩시장은 한 주 연기될 예정이야. 하지만 장소는 같은 데서 열려.

M : Why? Is there another event scheduled at the park?
왜? 공원에 예정된 다른 행사가 있는 거야?

W : No. Only our market was supposed to be held during that time.
아니, 그 기간엔 우리 벼룩시장만 열릴 예정이야.

M : Is it due to bad weather? I've heard that it's supposed to rain.
날씨가 안 좋아서 그래? 내가 듣기로 비가 올 거랬어.

W : It'll only rain a little, so I'm not worried about that. Actually, the park scheduled urgent repair work for Saturday. So, we put off the flea market.
비는 조금밖에 안 올 거라서, 그건 걱정 안 해. 실은, 공원에서 토요일에 긴급 보수 작업을 잡았대. 그래서 벼룩시장을 연기했어.

M : I'm sorry to hear that. Well, I'm still planning to go.
그 말을 들으니 유감이네. 뭐, 난 그래도 갈 예정이야.

W : Thanks. I'll see you at the market!
고마워. 벼룩시장에서 보자!

Why? 왜 정답일까?

대화에서 여자가 준비 중인 벼룩시장은 행사날 잡힌 긴급 보수 작업 때문에 한 주 미뤄졌다고 하므로, 여자가 벼룩시장 운영을 연기한 이유로 가장 적절한 것은 ① '공원 긴급 보수 작업이 계획되어서'이다.

- organize ⓥ 준비하다
- sort ⓥ 분류하다
- unfortunately ad 불행하게도, 유감스럽게도
- urgent ⓐ 긴급한, 다급한
- put off 미루다, 연기하다
- flea market 벼룩시장
- supply ⓝ 용품, 비품
- delay ⓥ 연기하다
- repair ⓝ 수리, 보수, 수선

08 동아리 현장 학습에 적합한 과학 프로그램

정답률 92% | 정답 ⑤

대화를 듣고, Young Edison Science Program에 관해 언급되지 않은 것을 고르시오.

① 장소
② 주제
③ 참여 가능 인원
④ 운영 시간
⑤ 준비물

W : Adam, I can't find an exciting place for my club's field trip.
Adam, 난 우리 동아리 현장 학습을 갈 만한 멋진 장소를 못 찾겠어.

M : 「I'm reading about the Young Edison Science Program at the Discovery Science Museum.」 ①의 근거 일치 I think that would be a great field trip.
난 Discovery Science 박물관에서 열리는 Young Edison Science Program에 대해 읽어보는 중이야. 근사한 현장 학습이 될 거 같아.

W : Oh, I've heard about that program. 「What's the theme of it?
오, 나도 그 프로그램 들어봤어. 주제가 뭐래?

M : It's a group experience program about the intersection of art and technology.」 ②의 근거 일치
예술과 기술의 교차 지점에 관한 단체 체험 프로그램이야.

W : Sounds cool. When we built robots that could paint in science class, everyone was really into it.
멋진 것 같네. 우리가 과학 수업에서 그림을 그릴 수 있는 로봇을 만들었을 때, 모두가 푹 빠졌잖아.

M : 「It says the maximum number of daily participants is 60.」 ③의 근거 일치 How about both our clubs go together?
하루 최대 참가 인원이 60명이래. 우리 두 동아리가 같이 가면 어때?

W : Really? That would be wonderful!
진짜? 아주 멋지겠다!

M : Okay, let's make a reservation. 「It says the program only takes place in the morning from 9 to 12.」 ④의 근거 일치 Does that work for you?
그래, 예약을 해보자. 프로그램은 아침 9시부터 12시까지만 열린다고 쓰여 있어. 너네 괜찮아?

W : That's fine. The other club members are usually busy in the afternoon, so going in the morning is better.
괜찮아. 다른 회원들도 오후에는 보통 바쁘니까, 아침에 가는 게 더 나아.

M : All right. Is August 3rd at 9 a.m. okay?
알겠어. 8월 3일 오전 9시, 괜찮지?

W : Perfect. My club members will love it.
딱이야. 우리 동아리 회원들도 좋아할 거야.

Why? 왜 정답일까?

대화에서 남자와 여자는 Young Edison Science Program의 장소, 주제, 참여 가능 인원, 운영 시간에 관해 이야기하므로, 언급되지 않은 것은 ⑤ '준비물'이다.

Why? 왜 오답일까?

① 'I'm reading about the Young Edison Science Program at the Discovery Science Museum.'에서 '장소'가 언급되었다.
② 'It's a group experience program about the intersection of art and technology.'에서 '주제'가 언급되었다.
③ 'It says the maximum number of daily participants is 60.'에서 '참여 가능 인원'이 언급되었다.
④ 'It says the program only takes place in the morning from 9 to 12.'에서 '운영 시간'이 언급되었다.

- field trip 현장 학습
- intersection ⓝ 교차로
- participant ⓝ 참가자
- experience ⓝ 체험, 경험
- be into ~에 빠지다, ~에 관심이 있다
- reservation ⓝ 예약

09 영어 단편 소설 쓰기 대회 안내

정답률 89% | 정답 ②

Flash Fiction Contest에 관한 다음 내용을 듣고, 일치하지 않는 것을 고르시오.

① 출품작의 단어 수에 제한이 있다.
② 참가자는 다수의 작품을 제출할 수 있다.
③ 제출 마감일은 7월 15일이다.
④ 심사는 학년별로 이루어진다.
⑤ 입상작은 학교 신문에 게재된다.

M : Good morning. I'm Mr. Thomas from the English department.
안녕하세요. 저는 영어과의 Thomas 선생입니다.

I'm excited to be hosting our Flash Fiction Contest.
저는 Flash Fiction Contest를 주최하게 되어 설렙니다.

Writing a very short story can be a great way to push your creativity to new boundaries.
아주 짧은 단편을 써보는 것은 여러분의 창의력을 새로운 범위까지 끌어올려줄 훌륭한 방법이 될 수 있습니다.

You can write on any topic.
여러분은 어떤 주제에 대해서든 써도 됩니다.

「Entries must be no more than 600 words in length.」 ①의 근거 일치
출품작은 길이가 600단어 이내여야 합니다.

All stories must be in English and be your original work.
모든 단편은 영어로 쓰여야 하고 여러분의 창작물이어야 합니다.

Entries must be written by only one writer.
출품작은 작가가 단독 집필해야 합니다.

「Each participant is allowed to submit only one story.」 ②의 근거 불일치
각 참가자는 딱 한 작품만을 제출할 수 있습니다.

「Entries will be accepted July 11th through July 15th.」 ③의 근거 일치
출품작은 7월 11일부터 7월 15일까지 접수됩니다.

「The flash fiction stories will be judged in three different grade groups: first, second, and third grades.」 ④의 근거 일치
이 짧은 단편 소설들은 학년별로 세 집단, 즉 1학년, 2학년, 3학년으로 나누어 심사됩니다.

「The winning stories from each grade will be published in the school newspaper.」 ⑤의 근거 일치
학년별 입상작은 학교 신문에 게재될 예정입니다.

For more information, visit our school website.
더 많은 정보가 필요하면, 학교 웹 사이트를 방문하세요.

Don't miss this fun event!
이 재미있는 행사를 놓치지 마세요!

Why? 왜 정답일까?

'Each participant is allowed to submit only one story.'에서 각 참가자는 작품을 하나씩만 출품할 수 있다고 하므로, 내용과 일치하지 않는 것은 ② '참가자는 다수의 작품을 제출할 수 있다.'이다.

Why? 왜 오답일까?

① 'Entries must be no more than 600 words in length.'의 내용과 일치한다.
③ 'Entries will be accepted July 11th through July 15th.'의 내용과 일치한다.
④ 'The flash fiction stories will be judged in three different grade groups: first, second, and third grades.'의 내용과 일치한다.
⑤ 'The winning stories from each grade will be published in the school newspaper.'의 내용과 일치한다.

- department ⓝ 과, 부서
- topic ⓝ 화제, 주제
- length ⓝ 길이
- allow ⓥ 인정하다, 허용하다
- accept ⓥ 받아 주다
- judge ⓥ 심사하다
- host ⓥ 주최하다
- entry ⓝ 출품작
- original work 창작물, 원저작물
- submit ⓥ 제출하다
- flash fiction 짧은 단편
- publish ⓥ 게재하다, 싣다

10 아웃도어용 시계 고르기

정답률 88% | 정답 ②

다음 표를 보면서 대화를 듣고, 남자가 주문할 아웃도어용 시계를 고르시오.

17회

Outdoor Watches

	Model	Price	GPS tracking	Material	Feature
①	A	$200	×	Plastic	Waterproof
②	B	$240	○	Plastic	Waterproof
③	C	$260	○	Plastic	Solar charging
④	D	$290	○	Metal	Waterproof
⑤	E	$320	○	Metal	Solar charging

W : Hey, Simon. What are you doing?
안녕, Simon. 뭐 하고 있어?

M : I'm looking at a brochure for outdoor watches. I need one for when I go hiking.
난 아웃도어용 시계 책자를 보고 있어. 하이킹 갈 때 필요해서.

W : Great idea. You can use it when you go to Halla Mountain this summer.
좋은 생각이야. 너 여름에 한라산 갈 때 쓰면 되겠어.

M : Exactly. Can you help me choose one?
바로 그거야. 내가 하나 고르게 도와줄래?

W : Sure. 『How much do you want to spend on it?
물론이지. 돈은 얼마나 쓰고 싶은데?

M : I think paying more than $300 for a watch isn't reasonable.』 근거1 Price 조건
시계 하나에 300달러 넘게 지출하는 것은 합리적이지 않은 것 같아.

W : All right. *[Pause]* 『Oh! GPS tracking is an important function. You should get an outdoor watch that has it.』 근거2 GPS tracking 조건
알겠어. *[잠시 멈춤]* 오! GPS 추적은 중요한 기능이지. 이 기능이 있는 시계로 사야 해.

M : You're right. I think it'll be very useful. 『What about the material?
네 말이 맞아. 매우 유용한 것 같아. 소재는?

W : A lighter material would be better for hiking. You should go with the plastic one.』 근거3 Material 조건
가벼운 소재가 하이킹에 더 낫지. 플라스틱으로 사.

M : I agree. 『Hmm, I think the waterproof feature is more practical than solar charging.』 근거4 Feature 조건
네 말이 맞아. 흠, 태양 충전보다 방수 기능이 더 실용적인 것 같아.

W : Good point. You never know when it'll rain while you're on a mountain.
좋은 지적이야. 산에 있을 땐 언제 비가 올지 절대 모르거든.

M : Okay. This watch is perfect. I'll order it.
알겠어. 이 시계가 딱 좋겠다. 주문하겠어.

Why? 왜 정답일까?

대화에 따르면 남자는 가격이 300달러를 넘지 않으면서, GPS 추적 기능이 있고, 플라스틱 소재로 되어 있으며, 방수 기능이 있는 아웃도어용 시계를 사려고 한다. 따라서 남자가 주문할 아웃도어용 시계는 ② 'B'이다.

- **brochure** ⓝ (안내·광고용) 책자
- **reasonable** ⓐ 합리적인
- **function** ⓝ 기능
- **material** ⓝ 소재
- **solar** ⓐ 태양의
- **pay** ⓥ 지출하다
- **track** ⓥ 추적하다 ⓝ 추적
- **useful** ⓐ 유용한, 도움이 되는
- **waterproof** ⓐ 방수의
- **practical** ⓐ 실용적인

11 딸을 어린이집에 데려다달라고 부탁하기

정답률 74% | 정답 ②

대화를 듣고, 여자의 마지막 말에 대한 남자의 응답으로 가장 적절한 것을 고르시오.

① Let's ask where Monica's classroom is. – Monica네 교실이 어디인지 물어보죠.
② I'll take her a bit earlier than usual then. – 그럼 내가 평소보다 좀 빨리 아이를 데려다줄게요.
③ Okay. I'll ask her teacher when they close. – 알겠어요. 내가 아이 선생님께 언제 닫는지 물어볼게요.
④ No problem. My meeting ended successfully. – 문제 없어요. 내 미팅은 성공적으로 끝났어요.
⑤ Thank you. I'll take care of the client instead. – 고마워요. 내가 대신 고객을 맡을게요.

W : Honey, can you take Monica to daycare tomorrow morning?
여보, 내일 아침에 Monica 좀 어린이집에 데려다줄 수 있어요?

M : I have a client meeting at 10 a.m. What time should I drop her off?
내일 나 오전 10시에 고객 미팅이 있어요. 아이를 언제 내려줘야 해요?

W : She usually goes to daycare around 10, but it opens at 8.
아이는 보통 10시쯤 어린이집에 가는데, 어린이집은 8시에 열어요.

M : I'll take her a bit earlier than usual then.
그럼 내가 평소보다 좀 빨리 아이를 데려다줄게요.

Why? 왜 정답일까?

여자는 남자에게 내일 딸을 어린이집까지 태워다 줄 것을 부탁하며, 보통 딸은 10시쯤 어린이집에 가지만 8시에 어린이집이 연다고 말해준다. 따라서 남자의 응답으로 가장 적절한 것은 ② '그럼 내가 평소보다 좀 빨리 아이를 데려다줄게요.'이다.

- **take A to B** A를 B에 데려다주다
- **client** ⓝ 고객
- **drop off** ~을 (차에서) 내려주다
- **successfully** ad 성공적으로
- **daycare** ⓥ 탁아소에 맡기다
- **meeting** ⓝ 회의
- **bit** ⓝ 조금, 약간
- **instead** ad 대신에

12 고장난 복사기 때문에 도움 요청하기

정답률 66% | 정답 ③

대화를 듣고, 남자의 마지막 말에 대한 여자의 응답으로 가장 적절한 것을 고르시오.

① Sorry. I can't remember my script at all. – 미안해. 난 내 대본이 전혀 기억이 안 나.
② With your help, the repairman fixed the copier. – 네 도움으로 수리기사가 복사기를 고쳤어.
③ Let's try a different copier on the second floor. – 2층에 있는 다른 복사기로 해 보자.
④ I was impressed by your presentation last time. – 난 지난번 네 발표에 감명받았어.
⑤ Don't panic. You can finish your script next week. – 당황하지 마. 넌 다음 주에 대본을 완성할 수 있어.

M : Emma! Can you help me out? This copier isn't working.
Emma! 나 좀 도와줄 수 있어? 이 복사기 작동이 안 돼.

W : Ryan, your presentation starts in 5 minutes. Why are you making copies now?
Ryan, 너 5분 있으면 발표 시작이야. 왜 지금 복사를 하고 있어?

M : I changed something, so I need to print out the final script. What should I do?
내가 뭔가 좀 바꿔서, 최종 대본을 출력해야 해. 나 어떻게 하지?

W : Let's try a different copier on the second floor.
2층에 있는 다른 복사기로 해 보자.

Why? 왜 정답일까?

발표를 5분 앞두고 왜 복사기와 씨름 중인지 묻는 여자에게 남자는 최종 대본을 수정해서 다시 뽑아야 하는데 복사기가 제대로 작동하지 않아 어떻게 해야 할지 모르겠다고 말한다. 따라서 여자의 응답으로 가장 적절한 것은 ③ '2층에 있는 다른 복사기로 해 보자.'이다.

- **copier** ⓝ 복사기
- **script** ⓝ 대본
- **repairman** ⓝ 수리공, 수리기사
- **impress** ⓥ 감명을 주다
- **print out** 출력하다
- **different** ⓐ 다른
- **fix** ⓥ 수리하다

13 춤 동아리 회원 추가 모집

정답률 91% | 정답 ③

대화를 듣고, 여자의 마지막 말에 대한 남자의 응답으로 가장 적절한 것을 고르시오. [3점]

Man: ______________________________

① It's better to get dance training this time. – 이번엔 춤 강습을 받는 게 좋겠어.
② Why don't you try auditioning to join our team? – 너 우리 팀에 들어오게 오디션을 봐 보면 어때?
③ Okay. I'll be sure to make the post by tomorrow. – 알겠어. 내가 내일까지 꼭 포스팅을 해 볼게.
④ Good job! The audition was tough, but we made it! – 잘했어! 오디션은 어려웠지만 우린 해냈어!
⑤ Offline performances are more fun than online ones. – 오프라인 공연이 온라인 공연보다 더 재밌어.

W : Erik, did you enjoy the Seoul Dance Festival yesterday?
Erik, 어제 Seoul Dance Festival은 잘 즐겼어?

M : I did. Phantom Dance Group's performance was the best.
응. Phantom Dance Group의 공연이 최고였어.

W : I agree. I was so excited to see their new hip hop performance.
나도 같은 생각이야. 그들의 새로운 힙합 공연을 보게 되어 몹시 신났어.

M : I found a video of their performance online today. Why don't we learn their dance for our school's dance festival?
오늘 온라인에서 그들의 공연 영상을 찾았어. 우리 학교 축제를 위해 그들의 춤을 배워보면 어때?

W : Sounds great. I think it'll be good for the festival.
좋을 거 같아. 축제에 좋겠네.

M : But their dance is for five people. Our club has only four members.
그런데 그 춤은 다섯 명이 춰야 해. 우리 동아리는 네 명 뿐이고.

W : We should look for another member. Do you have any ideas for how we can find one?
또 다른 회원을 구해야겠네. 어떻게 찾을지 아이디어 좀 있어?

M : Well, how about posting on the school website? And we can hold an audition next week.
음, 학교 웹 사이트에 올려보면 어때? 그리고 다음 주에 오디션을 열면 돼.

W : That's a good idea. I'll prepare the audition if you take care of the rest.
좋은 생각이네. 내가 오디션을 준비할게, 네가 나머지를 맡아줘.

M : Okay. I'll be sure to make the post by tomorrow.
알겠어. 내가 내일까지 꼭 포스팅을 해 볼게.

Why? 왜 정답일까?

춤 동아리의 새로운 회원을 찾기 위해 웹 사이트에 게시물을 올리고 오디션을 열자는 남자의 제안에 여자는 본인이 오디션을 맡을 테니 남자에게 나머지 일을 처리해달라고 한다. 따라서 남자의 응답으로 가장 적절한 것은 ③ '알겠어. 내가 내일까지 꼭 포스팅을 해 볼게.'이다.

- **festival** ⓝ 축제
- **another** ⓐ 다른, 별개의
- **make the post** 포스팅을 하다, 게시물을 올리다
- **performance** ⓝ 공연
- **hold an audition** 오디션을 열다

14 조리 기능 시험에 관한 조언 구하기

정답률 86% | 정답 ②

대화를 듣고, 남자의 마지막 말에 대한 여자의 응답으로 가장 적절한 것을 고르시오. [3점]

Woman: ______________________________

① Of course. I'll practice making Japanese dishes with you.
물론이죠. 내가 일식 만드는 것을 같이 연습해 줄게요.
② Right. You'll build confidence through continual practice.
맞아요. 지속적인 연습으로 자신감이 쌓일 거예요.
③ Great! I'm so proud of you for passing the test.
훌륭해요! 당신이 시험을 통과하다니 아주 자랑스러워요.
④ Well, you need to be careful while cooking.
음, 요리 중에는 주의를 해야 해요.
⑤ I agree. Empathy is the key to success.
동의해요. 공감이 성공의 핵심이죠.

M : Hi, Chef. Can I get some advice?
안녕하세요, 셰프님. 제가 조언을 좀 구해도 될까요?

W : Sure. Is it about your performance test for Western food next month?
물론이죠. 다음 달 있을 양식 기능 시험에 관한 건가요?

M : Yeah. Actually, I'm afraid I won't pass.
네. 실은, 전 제가 통과하지 못할까봐 두려워요.

W : What's the issue?
문제가 뭐죠?

M : I'm supposed to make two dishes in an hour, but I'm not sure if I can do it.
한 시간 안에 요리 두 개를 해야 하는데, 제가 할 수 있을지 모르겠어요.

W : I think you're good enough to pass the test.
제 생각에 당신은 테스트를 통과할 만큼 충분히 잘해요.

M : But when it comes to making both dishes within the time limit, I've succeeded only twice. I'm losing confidence.
하지만 시간 제한 내에 두 가지 음식을 다 만드는 것은 전 두 번밖에 성공하지 못했어요. 전 자신감을 잃어가고 있어요.

W : Don't worry. Everybody fails at first and needs practice to get better.
걱정 마요. 모두가 처음에는 실패하고 나아지려면 연습이 필요하죠.

M : Did you ever have a difficult time like I'm having?
셰프님도 저 같은 어려운 시기를 겪으셨나요?

W : Of course. It was pretty tough for me to get my license for Japanese food. But the more I practiced, the more confident I felt.
물론이죠. 난 일식 자격증을 따는 게 몹시 어려웠어요. 하지만 더 많이 연습할수록 더 자신감이 붙었죠.

M : I see. So you mean I just need more practice?
그렇군요. 그럼 셰프님 말씀은 제가 그저 연습이 더 필요하다는 것이죠?

[문제편 p.098]

W : Right. You'll build confidence through continual practice.
맞아요. 지속적인 연습으로 자신감이 쌓일 거예요.

Why? 왜 정답일까?

양식 조리 기능 시험을 통과하지 못할까봐 걱정하는 남자에게 여자는 연습을 통해 자신감을 얻을 수 있다고 조언해주고, 남자는 그럼 자신도 연습을 더 하면 되냐며 여자가 한 말의 의미를 확인하고 있다. 따라서 여자의 응답으로 가장 적절한 것은 ② '맞아요. 지속적인 연습으로 자신감이 쌓일 거예요.'이다.

- **performance test** 기능 시험, 직능 검사
- **dish** ⓝ 요리
- **license** ⓝ 면허증, 허가증, 자격증
- **continual** ⓐ 지속적인, 계속되는
- **afraid** ⓐ 두려워하는
- **time limit** 제한 시간
- **lose confidence** 자신감을 잃다
- **empathy** ⓝ 공감, 감정 이입

15 소셜 미디어 알림을 꺼두라고 말하기

정답률 89% | 정답 ⑤

다음 상황 설명을 듣고, Clara가 Jacob에게 할 말로 가장 적절한 것을 고르시오.

Clara: ______________________

① You'll have more followers soon, so don't worry.
넌 곧 팔로워가 더 많이 생길 테니까 걱정 마.
② Be more responsible when posting to social media.
소셜 미디어에 글을 쓸 때는 더 책임감을 가지렴.
③ It's essential to actively interact with your followers.
네 팔로워들과 적극적으로 소통하는 건 필수야.
④ How about putting away your smartphone at bedtime?
잠잘 때는 스마트폰을 치워두는 게 어떠니?
✔ You should disable social media notifications during dinner.
저녁 식사 중에는 알림을 꺼둬야 해.

W : Clara has noticed that her son, Jacob, spends all his time checking his social media accounts.
Clara는 아들 Jacob이 소셜 미디어 계정을 확인 하느라 온 시간을 다 쓴다는 것을 알았다.
Recently, Jacob started to actively post pictures and videos for his followers to see, so he thinks it's important to read and respond to comments right away.
최근에 Jacob은 적극적으로 사진과 영상을 올려 팔로워들이 볼 수 있게 하기 시작했고, 그래서 댓글을 바로 읽고 답해주는 것이 중요하다고 생각한다.
With every sound, buzz, or flash from the notification light, he immediately checks his phone, even while having dinner with the family.
모든 소리, 진동, 또는 알림 불빛의 번쩍이는 신호가 있을 때마다 그는 즉시 자기 전화를 확인하고, 심지어 가족들과 식사 중에도 그렇게 한다.
Although Clara knows interacting with his followers is important to him, she thinks spending time with the family is more important than checking social media and that it's not appropriate to pay no attention to the family.
Clara도 팔로워와 소통하는 것이 그에게 중요하다는 것을 알고 있지만, 그녀는 가족과 시간을 보내는 것이 소셜 미디어를 확인하는 것보다 중요하며, 가족에게 주의를 기울이지 않는 것은 적절하지 않다고 생각한다.
So, Clara wants to tell Jacob that he needs to turn off notifications while the family is eating dinner.
그래서 Clara는 Jacob에게 가족들이 저녁 먹는 동안에는 알림을 꺼 둘 필요가 있다고 이야기하고 싶다.
In this situation, what would Clara most likely say to Jacob?
이 상황에서, Clara는 Jacob에게 뭐라고 말할 것인가?

Clara : You should disable social media notifications during dinner.
저녁 식사 중에는 알림을 꺼둬야 해.

Why? 왜 정답일까?

상황에 따르면 Clara는 가족과의 식사 시간 중에도 소셜 미디어 계정을 확인하느라 바쁜 아들 Jacob에게 식사 중에는 알림을 꺼두라고 이야기하고 싶어 한다. 따라서 Clara가 Jacob에게 할 말로 가장 적절한 것은 ⑤ '저녁 식사 중에는 알림을 꺼둬야 해.'이다.

- **account** ⓝ 계정, 계좌
- **right away** 즉시, 곧
- **immediately** ad 즉시, 즉각
- **appropriate** ⓐ 적절한
- **disable** ⓥ (기기나 소프트웨어의 기능을) 억제하다
- **respond** ⓥ 대답하다
- **notification** ⓝ 알림
- **interact** ⓥ 소통하다
- **attention** ⓝ 관심

16-17 현악기의 종류와 소리

M : Hello, class.
안녕하세요, 여러분.
We discussed the four main instrument sections of an orchestra last week.
지난 주 우리는 오케스트라의 네 가지 주요 악기 섹션에 관해 논의했죠.
「Today, I'll tell you about how string instruments sound and what they play in an orchestra.」 16번의 근거
오늘은 현악기가 어떻게 소리 나고 그것들이 오케스트라에서 무엇을 연주하는지 알려 드리겠습니다.
「The first is the violin.」 17번 ①의 근거 일치
첫 번째로 바이올린입니다.
The violin is the baby of the string family, and like babies, it makes the highest sounds.
바이올린은 현악기의 아기인데, 이것은 아기들처럼 가장 높은 소리를 냅니다.
Violins often play the melody in an orchestra.
바이올린은 흔히 오케스트라에서 멜로디를 연주합니다.
「Next is the viola.」 17번 ②의 근거 일치
그다음은 비올라입니다.
Violas produce a richer, warmer sound than the violin, and they almost always play the harmony in an orchestra.
비올라는 바이올린보다 더 풍부하고 따뜻한 소리를 내고, 거의 항상 오케스트라의 화음을 연주합니다.
「The third is the cello.」 17번 ④의 근거 일치
세 번째로 첼로입니다.
Of all the string instruments, cellos sound the most like a human voice, and they can make a wide variety of tones, from warm, low pitches to bright, higher notes.
모든 현악기 중에서, 첼로는 인간의 목소리와 가장 비슷하게 들리며, 따뜻하고 낮은 음역부터 밝고 높은 음까지 폭넓은 음조를 낼 수 있습니다.
They play both harmony and melody.
이것은 화음과 멜로디를 모두 연주합니다.
「Lastly, the harp is different from the other string instruments.」 17번 ⑤의 근거 일치
마지막으로, 하프는 나머지 현악기들과 다릅니다.
The sound of the harp is often dreamlike, almost like a fairy tale.
하프의 소리는 흔히 꿈결 같고, 거의 동화 같습니다.
It plays both melody and harmony.
이것은 멜로디와 화음을 모두 연주합니다.
Now, shall we listen to the sound of each instrument to learn the differences?
이제, 각 악기 소리를 들어보면서 차이를 알아볼까요?

- **discuss** ⓥ 논의하다, 상의하다
- **a wide variety of** 폭넓은
- **dreamlike** ⓐ 꿈같은
- **instrument** ⓝ 악기, 기구
- **pitch** ⓝ 음높이
- **fairy tale** 동화

16 주제 파악

정답률 86% | 정답 ①

남자가 하는 말의 주제로 가장 적절한 것은?

✔ sounds and roles of string instruments in an orchestra
오케스트라 안에서 현악기의 소리와 역할
② ways to tune different types of string instruments
다양한 종류의 현악기를 조율하는 방법
③ importance of playing in harmony in an orchestra
오케스트라에서 화음을 이루며 연주하는 것의 중요성
④ stage positions of various orchestral instruments
다양한 오케스트라 악기의 무대 자리 배치
⑤ origins of the names of musical instruments
악기 이름의 유래

Why? 왜 정답일까?

'Today, I'll tell you about how string instruments sound and what they play in an orchestra.'에서 남자는 오케스트라에서 현악기가 어떤 소리를 내고 각각 어떤 파트를 연주하는지 알아보자고 하므로, 남자가 하는 말의 주제로 가장 적절한 것은 ① '오케스트라 안에서 현악기의 소리와 역할'이다.

17 언급 유무 파악

정답률 98% | 정답 ③

언급된 악기가 아닌 것은?

① violin - 바이올린 ② viola - 비올라 ✔ double bass - 더블베이스
④ cello - 첼로 ⑤ harp - 하프

Why? 왜 정답일까?

담화에서 남자는 현악기의 예시로 바이올린, 비올라, 첼로, 하프를 언급하므로, 언급되지 않은 것은 ③ '더블베이스'이다.

Why? 왜 오답일까?

① 'The first is the violin.'에서 '바이올린'이 언급되었다.
② 'Next is the viola.'에서 '비올라'가 언급되었다.
④ 'The third is the cello.'에서 '첼로'가 언급되었다.
⑤ 'Lastly, the harp is different from the other string instruments.'에서 '하프'가 언급되었다.

Dictation 17

문제편 099쪽

01 doesn't have a proper name / hold an online vote / your brilliant and witty ideas
02 you were accustomed to it / interacting with one another / give peer reviews / achieve higher understanding
03 The paintings are so impressive / practiced color mixing / teaching my art class
04 the rug under the table / the giraffe measuring stick / bright and cheerful / My daughter drew it
05 host a movie night / set up the speakers / a little bit chilly / bring some blankets
06 displayed in the window / two with metal shades / installing the lights
07 busy sorting event supplies / is being delayed / due to bad weather / put off the flea market
08 the theme of it / robots that could paint / going in the morning is better
09 push your creativity to new boundaries / All stories must be in English / The flash fiction
10 an important function / A lighter material / more practical than solar charging
11 to daycare / drop her off
12 print out the final script
13 look for another member / can hold an audition / if you take care of the rest
14 good enough to pass the test / needs practice to get better / pretty tough / the more confident I felt
15 actively post pictures and videos / respond to comments / pay no attention to the family
16-17 how string instruments sound / a richer, warmer sound / is often dreamlike / fairy tale

17회

18회 | 2021학년도 7월 학력평가 고3

• 정답 •

01 ① 02 ① 03 ④ 04 ⑤ 05 ④ 06 ③ 07 ① 08 ③ 09 ③ 10 ③ 11 ② 12 ④ 13 ② 14 ② 15 ⑤
16 ① 17 ③

01 학교 정원 관리를 담당할 자원봉사자 모집 안내

정답률 96% | 정답 ①

다음을 듣고, 남자가 하는 말의 목적으로 가장 적절한 것을 고르시오.

✔ 학교 정원 관리 봉사자를 모집하려고
② 식물원 체험 학습 일정을 공지하려고
③ 봉사 활동 확인서 신청 방법을 안내하려고
④ 학교 정원에 심을 모종 기부를 부탁하려고
⑤ 정원의 잡초를 제거하는 요령을 설명하려고

M : Hello, students.
안녕하세요, 학생 여러분.
This is the president of the student council, Jason Miller, with an announcement about our school garden.
저는 학생회장인 Jason Miller이고, 학교 정원에 관해 안내 말씀 드리려고 합니다.
The school garden is very special to us because we ourselves maintain and enjoy it.
학교 정원은 우리가 직접 관리하고 즐기고 있기 때문에 우리에게 매우 특별합니다.
So, we're recruiting students who can do volunteer work for our school garden.
그래서, 우리는 학교 정원을 위해 자원봉사를 해줄 수 있는 학생들을 모집하고 있습니다.
Volunteering is done twice a week, mainly by watering plants and removing weeds.
자원봉사는 일주일에 두 번 이루어지고, 주로 식물에 물을 주고 잡초를 제거하게 됩니다.
If you're interested, please stop by the student council room by next Friday.
관심이 있으시면, 다음 주 금요일까지 학생회실에 들러주세요.
We're looking for at least ten students to volunteer to maintain our school garden.
우리 학교 정원 관리 봉사를 해줄 최소 10명의 학생을 모집하고 있습니다.
Please participate in this wonderful opportunity to contribute to our school.
우리 학교에 기여할 수 있는 이 멋진 기회에 참여해 주세요.

Why? 왜 정답일까?

'So, we're recruiting students who can do volunteer work for our school garden.'에서 남자는 학교 정원 관리 자원봉사를 해줄 사람을 모집하고 있다고 말하므로, 남자가 하는 말의 목적으로 가장 적절한 것은 ① '학교 정원 관리 봉사자를 모집하려고'이다.

- student council 학생회
- recruit ⓥ 모집하다
- weed ⓝ 잡초
- contribute to ~에 기여하다, 이바지하다

02 체력 수준을 고려해 운동 강도 설정하기

정답률 96% | 정답 ①

대화를 듣고, 여자의 의견으로 가장 적절한 것을 고르시오.

✔ 자신의 체력 수준에 맞게 운동 계획을 세우는 것이 좋다.
② 과도한 운동은 심리적 불안정을 초래할 수 있다.
③ 운동 일지 작성이 체력 관리에 도움이 된다.
④ 근력 운동과 유산소 운동을 병행하는 것이 유익하다.
⑤ 운동 중 부상 예방을 위해 적절한 장비를 착용해야 한다.

W : Justin, you look tired. What happened?
Justin, 너 피곤해 보여. 무슨 일이야?
M : I made a plan to run five miles a day. I went running this morning, so I'm exhausted.
난 하루에 5마일씩 달리는 계획을 세웠어. 오늘 아침에 뛰고 왔더니 몹시 피곤해.
W : Isn't that too much to run in one day?
하루에 달리기에는 과하지 않아?
M : It's challenging, but I believe the harder I work out, the better result I'll get.
어렵긴 한데, 더 열심히 운동할수록 더 좋은 결과를 얻을 거라 생각해.
W : Not always. What's important is to plan your exercise routine to match your physical fitness level.
항상 그런 건 아냐. 중요한 건 네 운동 루틴을 네 체력 수준에 맞추는 거야.
M : Why is that?
왜?
W : Exercising beyond your fitness level could cause injury, or even sickness.
체력 이상의 수준으로 운동하는 건 부상이나 심지어 병으로 이어질 수 있어.
M : That makes sense. How can I know my fitness level?
일리가 있네. 내가 내 체력 수준을 어떻게 알 수 있지?
W : Well, you could measure how long it takes for you to run one mile and compare it to a fitness scale on the Internet.
음, 1마일을 달리는 데 얼마나 오래 걸리는지 재보고 그것을 인터넷에 있는 체력 척도와 비교해보는 거야.
M : Oh, that sounds simple.
오, 간단해 보인다.
W : I'm sure that planning your exercise routine based on your physical fitness level will definitely be beneficial.
네 체력 수준에 바탕을 둔 운동 루틴을 설계하는 게 확실히 도움이 될 거라고 장담해.
M : I agree. Thanks for your advice.
동의해. 조언 고마워.

Why? 왜 정답일까?

'What's important is to plan your exercise routine to match your physical fitness level.'와 'I'm sure that planning your exercise routine based on your physical fitness level will definitely be beneficial.'에서 여자는 체력 수준에 맞는 운동 루틴 설계가 중요하다고 언급하므로, 여자의 의견으로 가장 적절한 것은 ① '자신의 체력 수준에 맞게 운동 계획을 세우는 것이 좋다.'이다.

- challenging ⓐ 어려운, 도전적인
- work out 운동하다
- important ⓐ 중요한
- exercise ⓝ 운동
- physical fitness 체력
- injury ⓝ 부상
- scale ⓝ 척도
- definitely ad 확실히, 분명히
- beneficial ⓐ 이로운

03 홈 쇼핑 감자 판매 방송

정답률 95% | 정답 ④

대화를 듣고, 두 사람의 관계를 가장 잘 나타낸 것을 고르시오.

① 기자 – 농업 연구원
② 콜센터 직원 – 고객
③ 방송 연출가 – 작가
✔ 홈 쇼핑 쇼 호스트 – 농부
⑤ 식료품 가게 직원 – 조리사

W : Michael, look! They're almost sold out! Everybody who ordered, thank you so much!
Michael, 이것 보세요! 거의 매진입니다! 주문해주신 모든 분들, 정말 감사합니다!
M : Wow! Thank you Lisa, for the great explanations and comments on my potatoes!
와! 제 감자에 대해 훌륭하게 설명해주시고 코멘트 해주셔서 고마워요, Lisa!
W : The calls for orders flooded in when we showed how to cook them.
우리가 감자를 요리하는 모습을 보여줄 때 주문 전화가 쇄도했어요.
M : Right, I wanted to show the viewers all the delicious ways to enjoy my potatoes.
맞아요, 전 시청자 분들에게 제 감자를 맛있게 즐길 수 있는 모든 방법을 알려드리고 싶었어요.
W : Also, our viewers loved hearing from you since you actually grew the product.
게다가, 우리 시청자 분들은 당신이 직접 감자를 키웠기 때문에 당신에게 설명 듣는 것을 좋아했어요.
M : I'm just happy to appear on your home-shopping channel. I put so much devotion into this harvest. I'm so proud of these premium organic potatoes.
당신의 홈쇼핑 채널에 출연하다니 그야말로 기쁘네요. 이 작물에 공을 아주 많이 들였어요. 이 프리미엄 유기농 감자가 몹시 자랑스러워요.
W : You should be! Everyone at home, you don't want to miss this. Great potatoes at a great price.
그러실 만도 하죠! 댁에 계신 모든 분들, 이걸 놓치고 싶지 않으시겠죠. 훌륭한 감자가 아주 좋은 가격에 나와 있어요.
M : I guarantee these are the best potatoes you'll ever eat.
여러분들이 드셔본 감자 중 최고일 거라고 자부합니다.
W : There aren't many left in stock! So order right now, and get a free recipe book.
재고가 얼마 남지 않았습니다! 그러니 지금 주문하시고, 무료 레시피 책을 받아가세요!
M : I know you'll enjoy the potatoes. Please leave a lot of good reviews!
모두들 감자를 맛있게 드실 거예요. 좋은 리뷰 많이 남겨주세요!

Why? 왜 정답일까?

'They're almost sold out! Everybody who ordered, thank you so much!', 'I'm just happy to appear on your home-shopping channel.'을 통해 여자가 홈 쇼핑 쇼 호스트임을, 'Also, our viewers loved hearing from you since you actually grew the product.', 'I put so much devotion into this harvest. I'm so proud of these premium organic potatoes.'을 통해 남자가 감자를 직접 키운 농부임을 알 수 있으므로, 두 사람의 관계로 가장 적절한 것은 ④ '홈 쇼핑 쇼 호스트 – 농부'이다.

- flood in 쇄도하다
- put devotion into ~에 공을 들이다, 헌신하다
- in stock 재고로, 비축되어

04 새로 꾸민 운동 공간 구경하기

정답률 90% | 정답 ⑤

대화를 듣고, 그림에서 대화의 내용과 일치하지 않는 것을 고르시오.

W : Honey, look. I changed this room into a workout space while you were on a business trip, like we talked about before.
여보, 이거 봐요. 우리가 전에 말했던 대로 당신이 출장 가 있는 동안 내가 이 방을 운동 공간으로 바꿨어요.
M : Wow, it's fantastic! We can work out at home now.
와, 환상적이네요! 이제 우린 집에서 운동할 수 있겠어요.
W : Right. 『Did you notice the two exercise balls under the clock?』 I bought them for us.
맞아요. 시계 밑에 있는 짐볼 두 개 봤어요? 우리가 쓰려고 그걸 샀어요. ①의 근거 일치
M : Great. I heard exercise balls are good for stretching. 『I see a pair of shoes on the shelf.』
좋아요. 짐볼이 스트레칭에 좋다고 들었어요. 선반에는 신발 한 켤레가 있네요. ②의 근거 일치
W : Yeah. It's important to wear shoes to prevent injury when exercising indoors.
네. 실내에서 운동할 때에는 부상을 막기 위해 신발을 신는 게 중요해요.
M : Good point. 『And you put a fan in the corner.』 ③의 근거 일치
좋은 지적이에요. 그리고 구석에 선풍기를 놔뒀네요.
W : It'll help us cool down after exercising hard.
우리가 열심히 운동하고 나서 몸을 식히는 데 도움이 될 거예요.
M : Okay. 『What's the laptop on the table for?』 ④의 근거 일치
그래요. 테이블에 노트북은 왜 있는 거예요?
W : We can play exercise videos and follow along. 『And check out the star-patterned exercise mat on the floor.』 Doesn't it look nice? ⑤의 근거 불일치
운동 영상을 틀어서 따라할 수 있게요. 그리고 바닥에 별 무늬 운동 매트도 봐요. 근사하지 않아요?
M : It sure does. Thank you for doing all this while I was away.
정말 그래요. 내가 없는 동안 이걸 다 해줘서 고마워요.

Why? 왜 정답일까?

대화에서 여자는 바닥에 별 무늬 매트가 있다고 했는데(And check out the star-patterned exercise mat on the floor.), 그림에 그려진 매트 무늬는 원 무늬이다. 따라서 그림에서 대화의 내용과 일치하지 않는 것은 ⑤이다.

- business trip 출장
- injury ⓝ 부상
- follow along 따라가다

[문제편 p.103]

05 구직 면접 준비하기

정답률 93% | 정답 ④

대화를 듣고, 남자가 여자를 위해 할 일로 가장 적절한 것을 고르시오.

① 이미지 검색하기
② 발표 대본 검토하기
③ 면접 예상 질문 만들기
④ 포트폴리오 우편 발송하기
⑤ 발표 연습 영상 촬영하기

W : Bob, I got a call from the company I applied to last week. I'm one of the final candidate for the assistant manager position.
Bob, 나 내가 지난 주 지원했던 회사에서 연락 받았어. 내가 부팀장 최종 후보 중 한 명이래.
M : Great! What do you have to do next?
잘됐다! 다음에 뭘 해야 해?
W : I have to do a presentation based on a set of questions.
질문 몇 개에 기반해서 발표를 해야 해.
M : It'd be helpful to record a video of yourself to practice.
네가 연습하는 걸 영상으로 녹화하는 게 도움이 될 거야.
W : Okay, I'll try it. I'm going to write a script first, and then make the presentation slides.
그래, 해 볼게. 난 먼저 대본을 쓰고, 그러고 나서 발표 슬라이드를 만들 거야.
M : You should add appropriate images to the slides to show your message clearly.
네 메시지를 분명하게 보여줄 수 있도록 슬라이드에 적절한 그림을 넣어줘야 해.
W : Yes. But it takes quite long to search for such images.
응. 그런데 그런 이미지를 찾는 데 시간이 너무 오래 걸려.
M : Definitely. You must be very busy.
정말 그렇지. 너 많이 바쁠 텐데.
W : Yeah. Actually, I still need to mail in one more portfolio for another company, but I don't have time to go to the post office.
응. 사실, 난 다른 회사에 포트폴리오를 아직 하나 더 우편 발송해야 하는데, 우체국에 갈 시간이 없어.
M : Oh, let me do it for you.
오, 내가 그걸 해줄게.
W : Really? Then I'll bring it to you. Thank you so much.
정말? 그럼 내가 너한테 가져다줄게. 정말 고마워.
M : It's my pleasure.
천만에.

Why? 왜 정답일까?

면접 준비로 바쁜 여자가 다른 회사에 포트폴리오를 우편으로 보내야 하지만 시간이 없다고 하자(**Actually, I still need to mail in one more portfolio for another company, but I don't have time to go to the post office.**) 남자는 자신이 대신 발송해주겠다고 제안한다(**Oh, let me do it for you.**). 따라서 남자가 할 일로 가장 적절한 것은 ④ '포트폴리오 우편 발송하기'이다.

- **candidate** ⓝ 후보자
- **assistant manager** 부팀장, 대리
- **appropriate** ⓐ 적절한

06 공룡 박람회 표 사기

정답률 85% | 정답 ③

대화를 듣고, 여자가 지불할 금액을 고르시오.

① $30 ② $32 ③ $35 ④ $39 ⑤ $40

M : Welcome to the Jurassic Adventure Fair. How can I help you?
Jurassic Adventure Fair에 오신 것을 환영합니다. 무엇을 도와드릴까요?
W : I'd like to buy tickets for the event. How much are they?
행사 티켓을 사고 싶어요. 얼마죠?
M : It's 15 dollars for adults and ten dollars for children under ten.
어른은 15달러이고 10살 미만 어린이는 10달러입니다.
W : Then one ticket for me and one for my son, please. He's eight years old.
그럼 저 한 장, 제 아들 한 장 주세요. 아들은 여덟 살이에요.
M : Okay. Would you like to rent a VR headset to enjoy the fair even more?
알겠습니다. 박람회를 훨씬 더 즐기실 수 있도록 VR 헤드셋을 대여하시겠어요?
W : A VR headset? What can I do with that?
VR 헤드셋이요? 그걸로 뭘 하나요?
M : You can see the dinosaurs move and hear them roar in virtual reality while you walk around the fair.
박람회장을 돌아다니는 동안 가상현실로 공룡이 움직여 다니는 걸 볼 수 있고 공룡 울음 소리도 들을 수 있어요.
W : Wow, my son would love that. How much is the rental fee?
와, 우리 애가 좋아할 것 같네요. 대여료가 얼마인가요?
M : It's seven dollars for one headset, but if you rent two or more, it's five dollars each.
헤드셋 하나 대여에 7달러입니다만, 2개 이상을 빌리시면 각각 5달러예요.
W : That's great. I'll rent two VR headsets.
아주 좋네요. VR 헤드셋 두 개를 빌릴게요.
M : You won't regret it. How would you like to pay?
후회 안 하실 겁니다. 어떻게 결제하시겠어요?
W : I'll pay in cash.
현금 결제할게요.

Why? 왜 정답일까?

대화에 따르면 여자는 15달러짜리 어른 표 한 장, 10달러짜리 어린이 표 한 장을 사고, 두 개 이상 빌리면 한 개당 5달러에 빌릴 수 있는 헤드셋을 두 개 빌렸다. 이를 식으로 나타내면 '15+10+(5×2)=35'이므로, 여자가 지불할 금액은 ③ '$35'이다.

- **dinosaur** ⓝ 공룡
- **virtual reality** 가상현실
- **regret** ⓝ 후회
- **pay in cash** 현금 결제하다

07 연구 주제를 바꾼 이유

정답률 87% | 정답 ①

대화를 듣고, 남자가 연구 주제를 변경한 이유를 고르시오.

① 관련 데이터를 찾기 어려워서
② 지도 교수를 구하지 못해서
③ 희망하는 진로가 바뀌어서
④ 연구 지원금을 확보하지 못해서
⑤ 다른 학생과 연구 주제가 겹쳐서

W : Hey, how's the science research going? I like your idea about dream recording technology.
야, 과학 연구 어떻게 돼 가? 꿈을 기록하는 기술에 관한 네 아이디어 마음에 들어.
M : Well, I changed my topic, so I'm pretty busy preparing new research.
음, 난 주제를 바꿔서 새 연구 준비하느라 무척 바빠.
W : Really? Aren't you interested in that field anymore?
진짜? 너 그 분야에 더 이상 관심 없는 거야?
M : I am. I still want to become a neuroscientist.
관심은 있지. 난 아직도 신경 과학자가 되고 싶은 걸.
W : Then why did you change it? Did your professor ask you to?
그럼 왜 그걸 바꿨어? 너희 교수님이 바꾸라고 했어?
M : No. Actually, she said it could be an interesting topic because many people are curious about this new technology.
아니, 사실 교수님은 사람들이 이 신기술에 호기심이 많기 때문에 그게 흥미로운 주제라고 하셨어.
W : It is very new, so I was wondering how you would find related data.
아주 새롭지. 그래서 난 네가 관련 데이터를 어떻게 찾을지 궁금했었어.
M : That's the problem. The topic was so new that it was hard to find relevant data. So, I decided to do research on brain scanning technology instead.
그게 문제야. 주제가 너무 새로워서 관련 데이터를 찾기가 어렵더라고. 그래서 대신 뇌 스캔 기술에 관해 연구하기로 마음 먹었어.
W : Oh, I see. What are you going to do for that?
오, 그렇구나. 그걸 위해 뭘 할 건데?
M : I'm thinking of applying for research funding.
연구 펀딩을 신청할까 생각 중이야.
W : I hope you'll get it. Good luck.
네가 받으면 좋겠다. 행운을 빌어.

Why? 왜 정답일까?

대화에 따르면 남자는 기존에 잡았던 연구 주제가 너무 참신했던 나머지 관련 데이터를 찾는 데 어려움을 겪어서(**The topic was so new that it was hard to find relevant data.**) 연구 주제를 바꾸게 되었다고 한다. 따라서 남자가 연구 주제를 변경한 이유로 가장 적절한 것은 ① '관련 데이터를 찾기 어려워서'이다.

- **be busy ~ing** ~하느라 바쁘다
- **neuroscientist** ⓝ 신경 과학자
- **curious** ⓐ 호기심이 많은
- **relevant** ⓐ 관련된, 적절한
- **apply for** ~에 지원하다, ~을 신청하다

18회

08 핸드폰 던지기 대회 참가하기

정답률 84% | 정답 ③

대화를 듣고, Mobile Throwing Championship에 관해 언급되지 않은 것을 고르시오.

① 최초 개최 연도 ② 개최 목적 ③ 참가비
④ 우승 상품 ⑤ 심사 기준

M : Rachael, there'll be a competition called the Mobile Throwing Championship next month. Why don't we join it?
Rachael, 다음 달에 Mobile Throwing Championship이라는 대회가 열릴 거야. 우리 참가해 볼래?
W : Mobile Throwing Championship? I've never heard of it.
Mobile Throwing Championship이라고? 한 번도 못 들어봤어.
M : It's been around quite long. 「It was first held in 2000 in Finland, and is now held around the world.」 ①의 근거 일치
열린 지 꽤 됐어. 2000년에 핀란드에서 처음 열렸고, 지금은 전 세계에서 열려.
W : 「What's the purpose of holding the contest?
그 대회를 여는 목적이 뭐야?
M : It's to give people a chance to feel free from their mobile phones even for a moment.」 ②의 근거 일치
사람들이 잠깐이라도 핸드폰에서 해방된 기분을 느낄 기회를 주는 거야.
W : Oh, I see. Sometimes I just want to throw my phone away, too! So, do I have to bring a phone to participate in the contest?
오, 그렇구나. 가끔 나도 그냥 내 핸드폰을 던져버리고 싶을 때가 있어! 그럼, 대회에 참가하려면 핸드폰을 들고 가야 해?
M : No. The organizers will provide one to each participant. 「If you win, you get a fancy new phone as a prize.」 ④의 근거 일치
아니, 대회 운영자들이 참가자들에게 핸드폰을 하나씩 제공할 거야. 우승하면, 상품으로 근사한 새 전화를 받게 될 거야.
W : Really? 「What are the judging criteria?
정말? 심사 기준이 뭐야?
M : Participants are judged for the distance and technique of their throw.」 ⑤의 근거 일치
참가자들은 던진 거리와 기술로 평가받게 돼.
W : Sounds fun! Let's sign up for the competition.
재미있겠다! 대회에 등록하자.
M : Okay, I'll do it now online.
그래, 내가 지금 온라인에서 할게.

Why? 왜 정답일까?

대화에서 남자와 여자는 Mobile Throwing Championship의 최초 개최 연도, 개최 목적, 우승 상품, 심사 기준에 관해 언급하였다. 따라서 언급되지 않은 것은 ③ '참가비'이다.

Why? 왜 오답일까?

① 'It was first held in 2000 in Finland, ~'에서 '최초 개최 연도'가 언급되었다.
② 'It's to give people a chance to feel free from their mobile phones even for a moment.'에서 '개최 목적'이 언급되었다.
④ 'If you win, you get a fancy new phone as a prize.'에서 '우승 상품'이 언급되었다.
⑤ 'Participants are judged for the distance and technique of their throw.'에서 '심사 기준'이 언급되었다.

- **purpose** ⓝ 목적
- **feel free from** ~로부터 해방감을 느끼다
- **criterion** 기준 (*pl.* criteria)
- **sign up for** ~에 등록하다, 신청하다

09 휴대용 사진 인화기 구입하기

정답률 94% | 정답 ③

다음 표를 보면서 대화를 듣고, 두 사람이 주문할 휴대용 사진인화기를 고르시오.

[문제편 p.103]

Portable Photo Printers

	Model	Price	Power	Bluetooth Connection	Free Photo Paper (sheets)
①	A	$139	plug-in	×	20
②	B	$149	built-in battery	○	20
✔	C	$169	built-in battery	○	40
④	D	$189	built-in battery	×	40
⑤	E	$219	plug-in	○	30

M : Honey, what are you doing on your computer?
여보, 컴퓨터로 뭐 하고 있어요?
W : I'm looking for a portable photo printer. If we buy one, we can easily print pictures that are on our phones.
휴대용 사진 인화기를 찾고 있어요. 하나 사면 우리 핸드폰에 있는 사진을 쉽게 뽑을 수 있어요.
M : Great idea. Let's order one together.
좋은 생각이에요. 하나 주문하죠.
W : Sure. These five models look good, but『I don't want to spend more than 200 dollars.』
그래요. 여기 다섯 개 제품이 좋아 보이는데, 난 200달러 이상 쓰고 싶지는 않아요. 근거1 Price 조건
M : Me, neither.『And I think the ones that use plug-in power would be inconvenient. What do you think?
나도 그래요. 그리고 내 생각에 플러그인 전원을 쓰는 것은 불편할 것 같아요. 어떻게 생각해요?
W : I agree. I'd like one with a built-in battery.』 근거2 Power 조건
동의해요. 내장 배터리가 있는 게 좋겠어요.
M : Great.『Do you think we need a Bluetooth connection? 근거3 Bluetooth Connection 조건
좋아요. 블루투스 연결이 필요할까요?
W : Yeah.』 With that function, we can print pictures directly from our phones without cables.
네. 그 기능이 있으면 우리 케이블 없이 핸드폰에서 바로 사진을 뽑을 수 있어요.
M : You're right. Then we have these two options left.
당신 말이 맞아요. 그럼 두 가지 선택권이 있네요.
W : Hmm... they both look good, so『the one that comes with more free photo paper is better.』 근거4 Free Photo Paper 조건
흠... 둘 다 좋아 보이니, 무료 사진 인화지가 더 많이 딸려오는 게 더 좋겠어요.
M : I think so, too. Let's order this one then.
나도 그렇게 생각해요. 그럼 이것으로 주문하죠.

Why? 왜 정답일까?

대화에 따르면 남자와 여자는 가격이 200달러를 넘지 않으면서, 내장 배터리가 있고, 블루투스 연결 기능이 있으며, 무료 사진 인화지가 더 많이 제공되는 휴대용 사진 인화기를 사기로 한다. 따라서 두 사람이 주문할 휴대용 사진 인화기는 ③ 'C'이다.

- portable ⓐ 휴대용의
- inconvenient ⓐ 불편한
- built-in ⓐ 내장된

10 바이올린 제작 경연대회 정답률 65% | 정답 ③

2021 International Violin Making Competition에 관한 다음 내용을 듣고, 일치하지 않는 것을 고르시오.

① 참가 신청서에 바이올린 사진을 첨부하여 제출해야 한다.
② 5월 1일까지 등록하면 등록비가 할인된다.
✔ 바이올린을 우편으로 제출할 수 있다.
④ 유명 바이올린 연주자가 심사 위원에 포함된다.
⑤ 우승자는 10,000유로를 받는다.

W : Are you interested in showing the world your own original violin?
여러분만의 독창적인 바이올린을 세상에 보여주고 싶으신가요?
Then enter the 2021 International Violin Making Competition.
그렇다면 2021 International Violin Making Competition에 참가하세요.
This year, it will be held in Vienna, Austria, from July 13th to 16th.
올해 이 대회는 오스트리아 빈에서 7월 13일부터 16일까지 열립니다.
『To enter, submit an application form with two photos of your violin attached by June 1st.』 ①의 근거 일치
참가하시려면 6월 1일까지 여러분의 바이올린 사진 두 장이 부착된 참가 신청서를 제출하세요.
『The enrollment fee is 90 euros, but you can get a 30% discount if you register by May 1st.』 ②의 근거 일치
등록비는 90유로이지만, 5월 1일까지 등록하시면 30퍼센트를 할인해 드립니다.
『We will not accept any violins sent by post, so you must be present in Vienna with your instruments during the competition.』 ③의 근거 불일치
우편으로는 바이올린을 접수하지 않으므로, 대회 기간 중 악기를 가지고 빈에 오셔야 합니다.
『A number of famous violinists as well as professional violin makers will serve as judges for the competition.』 ④의 근거 일치
전문 바이올린 제작자뿐 아니라 다수의 유명 바이올린 연주자들이 대회 심사 위원 역할을 해주실 겁니다.
『The winner will receive 10,000 euros.』 ⑤의 근거 일치
우승자는 1만 유로를 받게 됩니다.
For more details, visit www.2021VMC.org.
더 많은 세부 사항을 보시려면, www.2021VMC.org을 방문해 주세요.

Why? 왜 정답일까?

'We will not accept any violins sent by post, ~'에서 우편으로는 바이올린을 받지 않는다고 하므로, 내용과 일치하지 않는 것은 ③ '바이올린을 우편으로 제출할 수 있다.'이다.

Why? 왜 오답일까?

① 'To enter, submit an application form with two photos of your violin attached by June 1st.'의 내용과 일치한다.
② 'The enrollment fee is 90 euros, but you can get a 30% discount if you register by May 1st.'의 내용과 일치한다.
④ 'A number of famous violinists ~ will serve as judges for the competition.'의 내용과 일치한다.
⑤ 'The winner will receive 10,000 euros.'의 내용과 일치한다.

- application form 참가 신청서
- attach ⓥ 부착하다
- enrollment fee 등록비
- serve as ~의 역할을 하다

11 독서 모임 일정 바꾸기 정답률 77% | 정답 ②

대화를 듣고, 남자의 마지막 말에 대한 여자의 응답으로 가장 적절한 것을 고르시오.

① Why don't you put off visiting the doctor? – 병원 가는 걸 미루면 어때?
✔ Let's ask David if we can reschedule. – 일정을 다시 잡을 수 있는지 David에게 물어보자.
③ How about inviting David to our club? – David를 우리 모임에 초대하면 어때?
④ I'll go to the bookstore without you both. – 너네 둘 없이 내가 서점에 갈게.
⑤ We should find a place for today's meeting. – 오늘 모임 장소를 찾아야 해.

M : Jenny, I'm afraid I cannot make it to our book club today. So, will you and David meet without me?
Jenny, 나 오늘 우리 독서 모임에 못 갈 것 같아. 그러니 나 없이 너랑 David랑 만날래?
W : Well... I have to miss it, too. I have an upset stomach.
음... 나도 빠져야 해. 배탈이 났어.
M : That means only David will be there. It seems we cannot meet today. What should we do?
그럼 David만 있겠네. 우리 오늘 못 만날 것 같다. 어떡하지?
W : Let's ask David if we can reschedule.
일정을 다시 잡을 수 있는지 David에게 물어보자.

Why? 왜 정답일까?

남자는 자신뿐 아니라 여자 또한 독서 모임에 못 갈 것임을 알고 모임을 그대로 진행하기 어려워 보이는데 어떻게 해야 할지 여자에게 묻고 있다(**It seems we cannot meet today. What should we do?**). 따라서 여자의 응답으로 가장 적절한 것은 ② '일정을 다시 잡을 수 있는지 David에게 물어보자.'이다.

- make it (약속에) 가다, (일을) 성공하다, 해내다
- put off 미루다
- reschedule ⓥ 일정을 조정하다

12 과제 제출 방법 문의 정답률 70% | 정답 ④

대화를 듣고, 여자의 마지막 말에 대한 남자의 응답으로 가장 적절한 것을 고르시오.

① No worries. I've already got your file. – 걱정할 거 없어. 난 이미 네 파일을 받았어.
② Right. There's no assignment today. – 그래. 오늘은 과제가 없어.
③ Sorry. Your file has been deleted. – 미안해. 네 파일이 삭제되었어.
✔ Yes. You can send it to me by email. – 있지. 내게 이메일로 과제를 보내주면 된단다.
⑤ Sure. Try downloading it from our website. – 물론이지. 그것을 우리 웹 사이트에서 다운받아 보렴.

W : Professor Smith, I'm having trouble with uploading my assignment file to our online course website.
Smith 교수님, 저희 온라인 강좌 웹 사이트에 제 과제 파일을 올리는 데 문제가 있어요.
M : Maybe it's because your file is too big. It has to be less than ten megabytes.
아마 네 파일이 너무 커서 그런 것 같구나. 용량이 10메가보다 작아야 하거든.
W : Oh, mine is bigger than that. I wonder if there's another way to submit my assignment.
오, 제 것은 그거보다 커요. 제 과제를 제출할 다른 방법이 없는지 궁금합니다.
M : Yes. You can send it to me by email.
있지. 내게 이메일로 과제를 보내주면 된단다.

Why? 왜 정답일까?

과제 파일이 너무 커서 사이트에 올리는 데 애를 먹고 있는 여자는 교수인 남자에게 파일을 다른 방법으로 제출할 수 있는지 묻고 있다(**I wonder if there's another way to submit my assignment.**). 따라서 남자의 응답으로 가장 적절한 것은 ④ '있지. 내게 이메일로 과제를 보내주면 된단다.'이다.

- have trouble -ing ~하는 데 문제가 있다, 애를 먹다
- assignment ⓝ 과제, 숙제
- submit ⓥ 제출하다

13 영화 추천하기 정답률 76% | 정답 ②

대화를 듣고, 남자의 마지막 말에 대한 여자의 응답으로 가장 적절한 것을 고르시오. [3점]

Woman: ____________________

① I'll find out who directed them for you. – 누가 그것들을 감독했는지 내가 찾아봐 줄게.
✔ I'll give you a list of his best films then. – 그럼 내가 그 감독이 찍은 최고의 영화 목록을 줄게.
③ That's why I prefer watching popular movies. – 그래서 난 대중 영화 보는 걸 선호해.
④ They didn't leave a lasting impression on me. – 그것들은 나한테 오랜 인상을 남기지 못했어.
⑤ You shouldn't worry about getting bad reviews. – 악평을 받을까 봐 걱정하지 마.

W : How did you like the film I recommended?
내가 추천해준 영화 어땠어?
M : I really enjoyed it! The story was so refreshing. I've never seen anything like it before.
정말 재밌었어! 이야기가 참 신선하더라. 그런 거 한 번도 본 적 없었어.
W : It's an independent film, so it was possible for the director to try new and creative things.
독립 영화라서 감독이 새롭고 창의적인 걸 시도하는 게 가능했어.
M : Yeah. And he created remarkable scenes using impressive color and sound effects.
그러게. 그리고 그는 인상적인 색채와 음향 효과 사용으로 놀랄 만한 장면을 만들어냈어.
W : I agree. What did you think of the characters?
같은 생각이야. 인물들은 어땠어?
M : They were really different compared to what we see in popular movies.
우리가 대중 영화에서 보는 거랑 비교했을 때 정말 색달랐어.
W : Yes. The director is famous for creating unique characters. And the film received enthusiastic reviews from movie critics.
응. 감독이 독특한 인물 설정으로 유명해. 그리고 그 영화는 영화 평론가들에게서 열광적인 평을 받았어.
M : I can see why! People should be more interested in his films.
그 이유를 알겠어! 사람들은 이 감독의 영화에 더 관심을 가져야 해.
W : Absolutely. I really enjoy his other works as well.

[문제편 p.104]

정말 그래. 난 이 감독의 다른 작품도 좋아해.
M : Oh, I'd really like to watch them, too!
오, 나도 그것들을 정말 보고 싶어!
W : I'll give you a list of his best films then.
그럼 내가 그 감독이 찍은 최고의 영화 목록을 줄게.

Why? 왜 정답일까?

남자는 여자가 추천했던 영화를 재미있게 봤다면서 같은 감독이 찍은 다른 영화도 보고 싶다고 말한다(Oh, I'd really like to watch them, too!). 따라서 여자의 응답으로 가장 적절한 것은 ② '그럼 내가 그 감독이 찍은 최고의 영화 목록을 줄게.'이다.

- How do you like~? ~은 어때?
- remarkable ⓐ 놀랄 만한, 주목할 만한
- enthusiastic ⓐ 열렬한, 열광적인
- refreshing ⓐ 신선한
- impressive ⓐ 인상적인
- lasting ⓐ 오래가는, 지속적인

14 휴식에 큰 도움이 되지 않는 게임

정답률 90% | 정답 ②

대화를 듣고, 여자의 마지막 말에 대한 남자의 응답으로 가장 적절한 것을 고르시오. [3점]

Man: ______

① I see. I'll take a break more often to increase concentration.
그렇구나. 집중력을 높이기 위해 더 자주 쉬어야겠어.
② Okay. I should avoid playing games during study breaks.
알겠어. 휴식 시간에 게임하는 것을 피해야겠어.
③ Certainly. You'll enjoy playing mobile games, too.
물론이지. 너도 핸드폰 게임을 재미있어 할 거야.
④ All right. I'd rather study alone to prepare for my exam.
알겠어. 시험 준비를 위해 혼자서 공부할래.
⑤ Interesting. I thought mobile games do more harm than good.
흥미롭네. 난 핸드폰 게임이 백해무익하다고 생각했어.

W : Hi, John. Oh, you're playing a mobile game.
안녕, John. 오, 너 핸드폰 게임 하고 있구나.
M : Yes, it's so fun. Do you want to join me?
응, 너무 재미있어. 너도 같이 할래?
W : Not right now. I have to prepare for the math exam. Did you finish studying?
지금은 말고. 난 수학 시험을 준비해야 해. 넌 공부 다 했어?
M : Not yet. I'm taking a break now after two hours of studying. I play games during study breaks to relax.
아직. 2시간 동안 공부하고서 지금은 쉬는 중이야. 난 휴식 시간에 쉬려고 게임을 해.
W : Playing games to relax? That's not a good idea.
쉬려고 게임을 한다고? 그건 좋은 생각이 아냐.
M : How come? It's important to rest in between studying sessions.
어째서? 공부 시간 사이사이에 쉬어주는 건 중요해.
W : That's true. But while playing games, your brain cannot rest enough. I read that in an article.
그건 맞아. 그런데 게임을 하는 도중에는 뇌가 충분히 쉬지 못해. 난 그걸 기사에서 읽었어.
M : Really? I thought I'd be able to get refreshed when playing games.
정말? 난 게임하는 동안 뇌가 회복될 수 있다고 생각했어.
W : Actually, your brain is still working while you're playing.
사실, 네 뇌는 네가 게임하는 동안 계속 활동하고 있어.
M : Maybe that's why I couldn't focus after I came back from my breaks.
아마 그래서 난 쉬는 시간이 끝나고 와서 집중을 할 수 없었나 보다.
W : Exactly. Playing games may not have allowed you to rest fully.
바로 그거야. 게임하는 것은 네가 온전히 쉬지 못하게 했을지도 몰라.
M : Okay. I should avoid playing games during study breaks.
알겠어. 휴식 시간에 게임하는 것을 피해야겠어.

Why? 왜 정답일까?

공부하다가 쉴 때 게임을 한다는 남자의 말에 여자는 게임하는 동안 뇌가 온전히 쉬지 못한다고 이야기하고 있으므로(Playing games may not have allowed you to rest fully.), 남자의 응답으로 가장 적절한 것은 ② '알겠어. 휴식 시간에 게임하는 것을 피해야겠어.'이다.

- in between 중간에, 사이사이에
- concentration ⓝ 집중(력)
- fully ad 온전히, 완전히, 충분히
- article ⓝ 기사
- do more harm than good 백해무익하다

15 사진을 포스터 디자인에 써도 될지 허락 구하기

정답률 81% | 정답 ⑤

다음 상황 설명을 듣고, Nancy가 Jake에게 할 말로 가장 적절한 것을 고르시오. [3점]

Nancy: ______

① We'd rather stay with our original design.
우리 원래 디자인대로 가는 게 낫겠어.
② Why don't we design the poster by ourselves?
우리가 직접 포스터를 디자인하면 어때?
③ Don't forget to apply for the contest this time.
이번엔 대회 신청하는 걸 까먹지 마.
④ How about going outdoors to take photos for a change?
기분 전환으로 야외 나가서 사진 찍는 게 어때?
⑤ We should ask your friends if it's okay to use their photo.
먼저 네 친구들에게 사진을 써도 괜찮은지 물어봐야 해.

M : Nancy and Jake are students at an arts high school.
Nancy와 Jake는 예술고등학교 학생들이다.
They plan to participate in a graphic design poster contest.
그들은 그래픽 디자인 포스터 대회에 참가할 계획이다.
They want to include images of their fellow students on their poster.
그들은 포스터에 자기 친구들 이미지를 넣고 싶어 한다.
Jake shows Nancy a photo of his classmates taken during an outdoor field trip.
Jake는 Nancy에게 야외 현장 학습 때 찍은 반 친구들 사진을 보여준다.
Jake says the photo would look good with their design, so he wants to include it on their poster.
Jake는 그 사진이 디자인과 잘 어울려 보여서, 그것을 포스터에 넣고 싶다고 말한다.
Nancy agrees, but she thinks Jake's classmates should first agree to their photo being used.
Nancy는 같은 생각이지만, Jake의 반 친구들이 먼저 그들 사진을 쓰는 데 동의해 주어야 한다고 생각한다.
So, Nancy decides to tell Jake that they should get his friends' permission to use the photo for the poster.
그래서 Nancy는 친구들에게 포스터에 사진을 쓰겠다는 허락을 구해야 한다고 Jake에게 말하려고 한다.
In this situation, what would Nancy most likely say to Jake?
이 상황에서, Nancy는 Jake에게 뭐라고 말할 것인가?
Nancy : We should ask your friends if it's okay to use their photo.
먼저 네 친구들에게 사진을 써도 괜찮은지 물어봐야 해.

Why? 왜 정답일까?

상황에 따르면 친구들 사진을 포스터 디자인에 쓰려는 Jake에게 Nancy는 먼저 사진을 써도 되는지 허락부터 구하자고 말하려 한다(So, Nancy decides to tell Jake that they should get his friends' permission to use the photo for the poster.). 따라서 Nancy가 할 말로 가장 적절한 것은 ⑤ '먼저 네 친구들에게 사진을 써도 괜찮은지 물어봐야 해.'이다.

- participate in ~에 참여하다
- agree to ~에 동의하다
- for a change 기분 전환으로
- apply for ~에 지원하다
- outdoor field trip 야외 현장 학습
- permission ⓝ 허락, 허가
- by oneself 혼자서, 직접

16-17 피부 관리 목적에 이용되어 온 천연 재료

W : Hello, students.
안녕하세요, 여러분.
Last time, we learned about various natural substances used by our ancestors in medicine.
지난 시간에 우리는 우리 조상들이 약에 썼던 다양한 천연 물질들을 배웠습니다.
『Today, we'll discuss some natural ingredients that have been used for skincare purposes throughout history.』 16번의 근거
오늘 우리는 역사를 통틀어 피부 관리 목적으로 이용되어 왔던 천연 재료들 몇 가지에 관해 논의해 보겠습니다.
『First, coconut oil has been loved as a moisturizer for a very long time in India.』
첫째, 코코넛 오일은 인도에서 아주 오랫동안 보습제로 사랑받아 왔습니다. 17번 ①의 근거 일치
It has a high moisture retaining capacity, so it acts as an excellent moisturizer for our skin.
이것은 보습력이 좋아서 우리 피부에 탁월한 보습제 역할을 해줍니다.
Secondly, rose water has been in use for thousands of years and is still easily found in the market today.
둘째, 장미 향수는 수천 년 간 사용되어 왔고 오늘날도 여전히 시장에서 쉽게 찾을 수 있습니다.
『It's thought to have originated in Iran, and is known to prevent the aging of the skin.』
이것은 이란에서 유래한 것으로 여겨지고, 피부 노화를 막아준다고 알려져 있습니다. 17번 ②의 근거 일치
『Next, pearl powder has long been used in China to brighten skin.』 17번 ④의 근거 일치
다음으로, 진주 분말은 오랫동안 중국에서 피부 미백을 위해 사용되어 왔습니다.
It helps to remove dead skin naturally and promotes restoration of the skin.
이것은 죽은 피부를 자연스럽게 제거하도록 도와주고 피부 회복을 촉진합니다.
『Finally, in Greece, people have used yogurt as a facial mask for centuries.』
마지막으로 그리스에서, 사람들은 수 세기 동안 요거트를 얼굴 마스크팩으로 이용해 왔습니다. 17번 ⑤의 근거 일치
Greeks even used yogurt on their skin to calm burns from the sun.
그리스인들은 심지어 햇볕 화상을 진정시키기 위해 피부에 요거트를 사용하기도 했습니다.
Now, I'll show you a video about how these natural ingredients are used.
이제, 이 천연 재료들이 어떻게 이용되는지에 관한 영상을 보여주겠습니다.

- substance ⓝ 물질
- retain ⓥ 보유하다
- originate ⓥ 기원하다
- restoration ⓝ 회복, 복구
- properly ad 적절히
- property ⓝ 특성, 속성
- ingredient ⓝ 재료
- capacity ⓝ 능력, 용량
- promote ⓥ 촉진하다
- traditionally ad 전통적으로
- harmful ⓐ 해로운

16 주제 파악

정답률 86% | 정답 ①

여자가 하는 말의 주제로 가장 적절한 것은?

① natural materials traditionally used for skincare
피부 관리를 위해 전통적으로 이용된 천연 재료
② how to store natural skincare products properly
천연 피부 관리 제품을 적절히 보관하는 방법
③ differences in the cultural perception of skincare
피부 관리에 대한 문화적 인식의 차이
④ ways to prevent skin troubles caused by facial masks
얼굴 마스크 팩으로 생기는 피부 트러블을 예방하는 방법
⑤ examples of natural substances with harmful properties
해로운 속성을 가진 천연 물질의 예

Why? 왜 정답일까?

'Today, we'll discuss some natural ingredients that have been used for skincare purposes throughout history.'에서 여자는 역사를 통틀어 피부 관리에 이용되어 온 천연 물질을 소개하겠다고 하므로, 여자가 하는 말의 주제로 가장 적절한 것은 ① '피부 관리를 위해 전통적으로 이용된 천연 재료'이다.

17 언급 유무 파악

정답률 96% | 정답 ③

언급된 나라가 아닌 것은?

① India - 인도 ② Iran - 이란 ③ Poland - 폴란드
④ China - 중국 ⑤ Greece - 그리스

Why? 왜 정답일까?

담화에서 여자는 피부 관리에 이용되는 천연 재료의 예를 들기 위해 인도, 이란, 중국, 그리스를 언급하였다. 따라서 언급되지 않은 나라는 ③ '폴란드'이다.

Why? 왜 오답일까?

① 'First, coconut oil has been loved as a moisturizer for a very long time in India.'에서 '인도'가 언급되었다.
② 'It's thought to have originated in Iran, ~'에서 '이란'이 언급되었다.
④ 'Next, pearl powder has long been used in China ~'에서 '중국'이 언급되었다.
⑤ 'Finally, in Greece, people have used yogurt as a facial mask for centuries.'에서 '그리스'가 언급되었다.

Dictation 18

문제편 105쪽

01 because we ourselves maintain and enjoy it / watering plants and removing weeds / looking for at least ten students to volunteer

02 match your physical fitness level / could cause injury / compare it to a fitness scale

03 The calls for orders flooded in / put so much devotion into this harvest / There aren't many left in stock

04 wear shoes to prevent injury / help us cool down / check out the star-patterned exercise mat

05 add appropriate images to the slides / to search for such images / mail in one more portfolio

06 rent a VR headset / hear them roar in virtual reality / You won't regret it

07 busy preparing new research / how you would find related data / hard to find relevant data

08 feel free from their mobile phones / What are the judging criteria / the distance and technique of their throw

09 a portable photo printer / the ones that use plug-in power / comes with more free photo paper

10 with two photos of your violin attached / as well as professional violin makers

11 have an upset stomach / It seems we cannot meet today

12 having trouble with uploading my assignment file / to submit my assignment

13 How did you like the film / What did you think of the characters / creating unique characters / enthusiastic reviews from movie critics

14 in between studying sessions / your brain cannot rest enough / why I couldn't focus

15 include images of their fellow students / during an outdoor field trip / agree to their photo being used

16-17 prevent the aging of the skin / promotes restoration of the skin / calm burns from the sun

19 회 | 2020학년도 7월 학력평가 고3

• 정답 •

01 ① 02 ② 03 ① 04 ④ 05 ② 06 ④ 07 ④ 08 ④ 09 ⑤ 10 ③ 11 ④ 12 ③ 13 ⑤ 14 ① 15 ⑤ 16 ② 17 ④

01 개조 공사 중 박물관 이용에 관한 안내

정답률 87% | 정답 ①

다음을 듣고, 남자가 하는 말의 목적으로 가장 적절한 것을 고르시오.

✓ 개조 공사 중 박물관 운영에 대해 안내하려고
② 박물관 시설 안전 점검 계획을 공지하려고
③ 박물관 개관식 참석을 요청하려고
④ 전시관 관람 시 안전 질서 유지를 당부하려고
⑤ 시설 파손에 따른 불편에 대해 양해를 구하려고

M : Can I have your attention, please?
잠시 주목해 주시겠습니까?
This is an announcement for visitors of our museum.
저희 박물관을 방문하신 분들께 드리는 안내 말씀입니다.
There will be renovations to the Dumbarton Museum from November 23rd through the end of 2020.
11월 23일부터 2020년 연말까지 Dumbarton 박물관 개조 공사가 있을 예정입니다.
During this period, the entire facilities on the third floor will be closed.
이 기간 중에는 3층의 전체 시설이 폐쇄됩니다.
So, we won't be able to accommodate scheduled tours of the museum.
그래서, 저희는 예정된 박물관 투어를 소화할 수 없습니다.
However, the special art exhibition for children will continue on the first floor.
하지만 어린이들을 위한 특별 미술 전시는 1층에서 계속 진행됩니다.
The gardens will be open, and the Museum Shop will move to the greenhouse in the gardens.
정원은 개방될 예정이고, Museum Shop은 정원의 온실로 이동될 것입니다.
More information can be found on our website.
더 많은 정보는 저희 웹 사이트에서 찾으실 수 있습니다.
We're sorry for the inconvenience caused by the renovations, and we look forward to seeing you at the newly renovated museum.
개조 공사로 초래되는 불편에 죄송한 말씀 드리며, 새로 개조된 박물관에서 여러분을 만나뵙기를 고대하겠습니다.

Why? 왜 정답일까?

'**There will be renovations to the Dumbarton Museum from November 23rd through the end of 2020.**' 이후로 연말까지 진행되는 개조 공사 기간에 박물관 운영이 어떻게 이루어지는지가 공지되고 있다. 따라서 남자가 하는 말의 목적으로 가장 적절한 것은 ① '개조 공사 중 박물관 운영에 대해 안내하려고'이다.

- **renovation** ⓝ 개조 공사
- **exhibition** ⓝ 전시
- **accommodate** ⓥ (시설 등에) 수용하다

02 환경 보호를 위해 플라스틱 사용을 줄이기

정답률 94% | 정답 ②

대화를 듣고, 여자의 의견으로 가장 적절한 것을 고르시오.

① 자원 재활용 교육을 강화해야 한다.
✓ 일상생활에서 플라스틱 소비를 줄여야 한다.
③ 친환경 플라스틱 제품 개발을 확대해야 한다.
④ 해양 생태계 보존을 위한 기금 마련이 필요하다.
⑤ 일회용품 사용 규제를 위한 법률 제정이 시급하다.

W : Honey, look at these horrific photographs!
여보, 이 끔찍한 사진들 좀 봐요!
M : It looks like these animals are suffering a lot.
이 동물들은 많이 고통받고 있는 것처럼 보이네요.
W : Yes, it's our fault! Many marine animals are dying from plastic products that we throw away.
네, 이건 우리 잘못이에요! 우리가 버리는 플라스틱 제품 때문에 많은 해양 동물들이 죽어가고 있어요.
M : I didn't know it was that serious. But isn't it impossible to live entirely without plastic?
이렇게 심각한 줄 몰랐어요. 하지만 아예 플라스틱 없이 사는 건 불가능하지 않나요?
W : True, but as a result of our current plastic use, millions of tons of plastics have ended up in the sea, damaging the environment. We should reduce the consumption of plastic products in our daily routine.
맞아요, 하지만 현재의 플라스틱 사용의 결과로 수백 만 톤의 플라스틱이 바다로 가게 되었고, 환경을 파괴시키고 있어요. 우리는 일상에서 플라스틱 제품의 소비를 줄여야 해요.
M : But plastics are very useful and convenient. How can we live with less plastic in our lives?
하지만 플라스틱은 매우 유용하고 편한 걸요. 일상에서 플라스틱을 어떻게 줄이며 살지요?
W : We can start by minimizing the use of disposable plastic. Instead, we can use things like refillable water bottles and reuseable shopping bags.
우리는 일회용 플라스틱의 사용을 최소화하는 것으로 시작할 수 있어요. 그 대신에 우리는 리필이 가능한 물병과 재사용 가능한 쇼핑백 같은 것들을 쓸 수 있어요.
M : You mean that we should accept a little inconvenience for our environment?
당신 말은 우리가 환경을 위해 조금의 불편함을 받아들여야 한다는 거예요?
W : Exactly!
바로 그거죠!

Why? 왜 정답일까?

'**We should reduce the consumption of plastic products in our daily routine.**'에서 여자는 환경 보호를 위해 일상에서 플라스틱 소비를 줄여야 한다고 말하므로, 여자의 의견으로 가장 적절한 것은 ② '일상생활에서 플라스틱 소비를 줄여야 한다.'이다.

[문제편 p.109]

- entirely ad 전적으로
- consumption ⓝ 소비
- disposable ⓐ 일회용의, 사용 후 버릴 수 있는
- reuseable ⓐ 재사용 가능한
- end up ⓥ 결국 ~하게 되다
- minimize ⓥ 최소화하다
- refillable ⓐ 리필 가능한, 다시 채울 수 있는
- inconvenience ⓝ 불편

03 체험 농장 활동 마무리 인사 정답률 94% | 정답 ①

대화를 듣고, 두 사람의 관계를 가장 잘 나타낸 것을 고르시오.

✔ 교사 – 체험농장 운영자 ② 관광객 – 버스 운전기사
③ 수강생 – 요리학원 강사 ④ 학생 – 동물원 사육사
⑤ 고객 – 키즈 카페 직원

W : Mr. Johns, we had such a wonderful time here today. Thank you so much.
Johns 씨, 저희는 오늘 여기서 아주 멋진 시간을 보냈어요. 정말 감사합니다.
M : It's been my pleasure, Ms. Parker.
천만에요, Parker 선생님.
W : I think my students had a lot of fun doing all the hands-on activities you had planned.
제 학생들은 당신이 계획한 그 모든 체험 활동들을 해보며 재미있는 시간을 보낸 것 같아요.
M : I'm glad they enjoyed them.
아이들이 즐거워했다니 기뻐요.
W : They were especially excited about feeding the sheep and milking the cows.
그들은 특히 양들에게 먹이를 주고 젖소의 우유를 짜며 신나 했어요.
M : I could tell that from their faces. They also worked hard to harvest the potatoes and onions.
그들의 얼굴을 보고 알겠더군요. 또한 그들은 감자와 양파를 수확하느라 열심히 일했어요.
W : Yeah. When we go back to school, we'll do some cooking activities with the vegetables they collected today.
네, 저희가 학교로 돌아가면, 그들이 오늘 수확한 야채들을 가지고 요리 활동을 좀 해볼 거예요.
M : That's a great idea. I hope they'll have good memories of my farm.
좋은 생각이네요. 그들이 저희 농장에 대해 좋은 기억을 갖길 바라요.
W : I'm sure they will. Before we get on the bus, can you take a picture of us in front of the farmhouse?
분명 그럴 거예요. 저희가 차에 타기 전에, 농가 앞에서 저희 사진을 찍어주실래요?
M : Of course. Please tell me when you're ready.
물론이죠. 준비 되시면 말해주세요.
W : Okay. Thanks.
네, 고맙습니다.

Why? 왜 정답일까?

'I think my students had a lot of fun ~'와 'When we go back to school, we'll do some cooking activities with the vegetables they collected today.' 등에서 여자가 교사임을, '~ doing all the hands-on activities you had planned.'와 'I hope they'll have good memories of my farm.' 등에서 남자가 체험 농장을 운영하는 사람임을 알 수 있다. 따라서 두 사람의 관계로 가장 적절한 것은 ① '교사 – 체험농장 운영자'이다.

- feed ⓥ 먹이를 주다
- harvest ⓥ 수확하다

04 아들의 기숙사 방 사진 구경하기 정답률 95% | 정답 ④

대화를 듣고, 그림에서 대화의 내용과 일치하지 않는 것을 고르시오.

[Telephone rings.]
[전화벨이 울린다.]
M : Hello, Mom!
여보세요, 엄마!
W : Oh, Peter! Dad and I are just looking at the picture you sent.
오, Peter! 아빠랑 난 네가 보내준 사진을 보고 있는 참이야.
M : The picture I took of my dormitory room?
제가 제 기숙사 방을 찍은 사진이요? ①의 근거 일치
W : Yeah. 「I see two beds in there.」 Is the room for two people?
응, 여기 침대가 두 개 보이네. 2인실인 거야?
M : Yes. 「Do you see the boy lying on the bed wearing glasses?」 That's my roommate, Jack.
네, 침대에 누운 안경 낀 남자애 보이세요? 제 룸메이트인 Jack이에요. ②의 근거 일치
W : I see. 「The room looks cozy because of the striped rug on the floor.」 ③의 근거 일치
그렇구나. 바닥에 있는 줄무늬 깔개 때문에 방이 아늑해 보여.
M : Jack brought it. He's willing to share his stuff.
Jack이 그것을 가져왔어요. 그는 자기 물건을 기꺼이 공유해요.
W : How kind of him! 「Did he also bring the shelf under the clock?
친절하기도 하지! 그 애가 시계 밑에 있는 책장도 가져왔니?
M : Yes. It's full of our books.」 I didn't realize we would need that many books for our classes. ④의 근거 불일치
네, 그것은 저희 책들로 꽉 차 있어요. 우리가 수업에 그렇게 많은 책이 필요할 줄은 몰랐어요.
W : It seems you've got a lot of work to do.
공부할 게 많아 보이는구나.
M : Right. 「And I hung a flower painting on the wall over my bed.」 It's a good decoration.
맞아요. 그리고 전 제 침대 위쪽 벽에 꽃 그림도 걸어두었어요. 좋은 장식품이죠. ⑤의 근거 일치
W : Great. I'm glad you're doing well there.
근사하구나. 네가 거기서 잘 지내길 바란다.

Why? 왜 정답일까?

대화에 따르면 시계 밑에 책장이 있는데(Did he also bring the shelf under the clock? / Yes. It's full of our books.), 그림 속 시계 밑에는 로봇이 있다. 따라서 그림에서 대화의 내용과 일치하지 않는 것은 ④이다.

- dormitory ⓝ 기숙사
- be willing to ⓥ 기꺼이 ~하다
- cozy ⓐ 아늑한

05 아버지의 생신 파티 준비하기 정답률 95% | 정답 ②

대화를 듣고, 남자가 할 일로 가장 적절한 것을 고르시오.

① 선물 포장하기 ✔ 파티 의상 찾아오기 ③ 축하 영상 편집하기
④ 생일 케이크 주문하기 ⑤ 카메라 배터리 충전하기

W : Jason, let's check everything that we need for Dad's 70th birthday party.
Jason, 아빠의 70번째 생신 파티를 위해 필요한 모든 것들을 점검해 보자.
M : Okay. I've packed the camera and lenses for taking pictures.
알겠어. 난 사진을 찍기 위해 카메라와 렌즈를 챙겼어.
W : Good. How about the battery?
좋아. 배터리는?
M : I've fully charged it and also prepared an extra one.
그것을 완전 충전해 두었고 여분도 하나 챙겼어.
W : All right. Did you finish editing the celebration video?
알겠어. 축하 영상 편집은 끝냈어?
M : Yes, I did. I'm sure Dad will be touched when he sees it.
응, 난 아버지가 그것을 보면 감동하실 거라고 생각해.
W : I'm looking forward to watching it.
나도 그것을 보는 것이 기대돼.
M : Oh, wait! Did you order a birthday cake?
오, 잠깐! 너 생일 케이크 주문했어?
W : Yes, I placed a special order for one.
응, 하나 특별 주문해 뒀어.
M : Great. Then what else do we have to do?
좋아. 그럼 우리가 뭘 더 해야 하지?
W : Hmm.... We should pick up our party costumes from the rental shop and wrap the gifts for the guests.
흠... 우리는 대여점에서 우리 파티 의상을 찾아오고 손님들을 위한 선물을 포장해야 해.
M : I think we should divide the work.
내 생각에 우린 일을 나눠야 할 것 같아.
W : Okay. I'll do the wrapping.
알겠어. 내가 포장을 할게.
M : In that case, I'll go to the rental shop.
그렇다면, 내가 대여점으로 갈게.

Why? 왜 정답일까?

아버지의 생신 파티를 준비 중인 남자와 여자는 의상 대여점에 가서 파티 의상을 챙겨오는 일과 손님들의 선물을 포장하는 일이 남았음을 알고 일을 나누기로 한다. 여자가 포장을 하겠다고 자원하자, 남자는 자신이 대여점에 가겠다(In that case, I'll go to the rental shop.)고 하므로, 남자가 할 일로 가장 적절한 것은 ② '파티 의상 찾아오기'이다.

- pack ⓥ 챙기다, (짐을) 싸다
- costume ⓝ 의상
- celebration ⓝ 축하, 기념

06 밴드 굿즈 구매하기 정답률 81% | 정답 ④

대화를 듣고, 남자가 지불할 금액을 고르시오. [3점]

① $60 ② $63 ③ $70 ✔ $72 ⑤ $80

W : Welcome to the Band Teen Spirit's Goods House. May I help you?
Band Teen Spirit's Goods House에 잘 오셨습니다. 도와드릴까요?
M : Thanks. I've come here all the way from America to watch the band's concert and visit this store. What are the most popular items here?
고맙습니다. 전 이 밴드 콘서트를 보고 여기 매장을 방문하러 미국에서부터 여기까지 왔어요. 여기서 가장 인기 있는 상품이 뭔가요?
W : This poster set and that T-shirt. The poster set is 14 dollars and the T-shirt is 24 dollars.
이 포스터 세트와 저 티셔츠입니다. 포스터 세트는 14달러이고 티셔츠는 24달러입니다.
M : I already have the poster set. I love that T-shirt! I'll take one.
저는 이미 포스터 세트는 가지고 있어요. 저 티셔츠 정말 마음에 들어요! 하나 살래요.
W : All right. Do you want anything else?
알겠습니다. 다른 필요하신 게 있으신가요?
M : Yes, the key rings with each member's figure.
네, 각 멤버들 피규어가 달린 열쇠고리요.
W : Here they are. They cost eight dollars each.
여기 있습니다. 하나에 8달러입니다.
M : There are seven members, so I'll take one for each of them.
멤버가 일곱 명이니까, 한 명당 하나씩 사겠어요.
W : Okay, one T-shirt and seven key rings. Do you need anything else?
알겠습니다, 티셔츠 한 장과 열쇠고리 일곱 개요. 다른 필요하신 게 있나요?
M : No, but can I use the coupon from the band's official app?
아니요, 그런데 제가 밴드 공식 앱에서 받은 쿠폰을 써도 되나요?
W : Of course. You can get a 10% discount.
물론이죠. 10퍼센트 할인을 받으실 수 있어요.
M : Great. I'll use my smart pay.
아주 좋아요. 전 스마트 페이를 쓰겠어요.

Why? 왜 정답일까?

대화에 따르면 남자는 24달러짜리 티셔츠 한 장과 8달러짜리 열쇠고리를 일곱 개 사고, 총 가격에서 10퍼센트를 할인받았다. 이를 식으로 나타내면 '{24 + (8 × 7)} × 0.9 = 72'이므로, 남자가 지불할 가격은 ④ '$72'이다.

- key ring ⓝ 열쇠고리
- official ⓐ 공식적인

07 스페인어 구술시험이 연기된 이유 정답률 89% | 정답 ④

대화를 듣고, 여자가 응시할 스페인어 시험이 연기된 이유를 고르시오.

① 졸업 시험과 날짜가 겹쳐서　　② 수업 진도를 다 마치지 못해서
③ 수강생들이 시험 연기를 요청해서　　✔ 강사가 해외 세미나에 참석해야 해서
⑤ 수강생 중 다수가 구직 면접을 보러 가서

M : Natalie, you seem to be working hard for your Spanish exam.
Natalie, 넌 네 스페인어 시험을 위해 열심히 공부하고 있는 것 같구나.
W : Yes, it's a one-on-one oral interview with my class instructor.
응, 그것은 내 수업 강사님과의 일대일 구술시험이야.
M : Haven't you just finished taking your graduation exam? With all of these exams, you must feel quite stressed.
너 막 졸업시험이 끝나지 않았어? 너 그 모든 시험들 때문에 꽤나 스트레스를 받겠구나.
W : In a way, but I'm thinking of it as an opportunity to prepare for my job interviews after graduation.
조금은, 하지만 난 이것이 졸업 후 취업 면접을 준비할 수 있는 기회라고 생각하고 있어.
M : Good. Then, when is the Spanish exam?
좋아. 그럼, 스페인어 시험이 언제야?
W : It's on June 24th.
6월 24일이야.
M : Really? Aren't most exams scheduled between June 15th and 19th?
그래? 대부분 시험은 6월 15일에서 19일 사이에 있지 않아?
W : Yes, my speaking exam was supposed to take place on June 17th, but it was postponed to a week later.
응, 구술시험은 6월 17일에 있을 예정이었는데, 한 주 연기되었어.
M : Did your class ask for a delay?
수강생들이 연기를 요청한 거야?
W : No, we didn't. Our instructor has to attend an overseas seminar on the original test day.
아니, 우리 강사님이 원래 시험 날에 해외 세미나에 참석해야 해.
M : I think this could work out better for you. You have one extra week to prepare.
이건 네게 더 잘될 수도 있을 것 같아. 한 주 더 준비할 시간이 있는 거잖아.
W : Yeah. I'll try my best.
응, 난 최선을 다할 거야.

Why? 왜 정답일까?

대화에 따르면 여자가 듣고 있는 스페인어 수업을 지도하는 강사가 원래 예정되었던 구술시험일에 해외 세미나에 참석해야 해서 시험이 한 주 뒤로 연기되었다(**Our instructor has to attend an overseas seminar on the original test day.**). 따라서 여자가 응시할 스페인어 시험이 연기된 이유로 가장 적절한 것은 ④ '강사가 해외 세미나에 참석해야 해서'이다.

- **oral interview** ⓝ 구술시험
- **graduation** ⓝ 졸업
- **postpone** ⓥ 연기하다
- **overseas** ⓐ 해외의 ad 해외로

08 미얀마 여행 상품 추천하기

정답률 94% | 정답 ④

대화를 듣고, Classic Myanmar Tour에 관해 언급되지 않은 것을 고르시오.

① 기간　　② 방문 도시　　③ 이동 수단
✔ 비용　　⑤ 최대 참가 인원

W : David, I heard you're traveling to Myanmar this summer.
David, 난 네가 이번 여름에 미얀마로 여행을 간다고 들었어.
M : Right. I'm going with a tour program named the Classic Myanmar Tour.
맞아. 난 Classic Myanmar Tour라는 이름의 투어 프로그램을 이용할 거야.
W : Actually, I'm planning to travel around Myanmar this summer, too.
사실, 나도 이번 여름에 미얀마로 여행을 가려고 계획 중이야.
M : Really? Then, you might be interested in this tour I'm taking.
정말? 그럼, 넌 내가 가는 투어에 관심이 생길지도 몰라.
W : Sure. 『How long is the tour?』 ①의 근거 일치
물론이지. 투어 기간이 얼마나 돼?
M : 『It's seven days, from July 10th to 16th.』
7월 10일부터 16일까지 7일이야.
W : Good. 『Does the tour visit Yangon? I'd really like to go there.
좋네. 투어가 Yangon을 방문하는 거야? 난 거기 정말 가보고 싶어.
M : Yes. The tour also includes visiting other major cities, such as Mandalay.』 ②의 근거 일치
응. 이 투어에는 Mandalay와 같은 다른 주요 도시 방문도 포함되어 있어.
W : Great. 『What kind of transportation do you use during the tour? ③의 근거 일치
잘됐다. 투어 동안에는 어느 교통수단을 이용해?
M : We'll take trains between cities and use buses in cities.』 We'll also travel on a river cruise through the jungle.
도시들 간에 이동할 때에는 기차를 타고 도시 안에서는 버스를 이용해. 우린 또한 강 유람선을 타고 정글을 지나갈 거야.
W : That sounds fun. Can I still sign up for the tour?
그거 재미있겠다. 내가 아직 투어에 등록할 수 있을까?
M : If you want to, you have to hurry! 『The tour has a limit of ten people.』 ⑤의 근거 일치
하고 싶다면 서둘러야 해! 투어 인원은 10명으로 제한돼 있어.
W : I'll contact the travel agency. Thank you for the information.
여행사에 연락해 봐야겠다. 정보 고마워.

Why? 왜 정답일까?

대화에서 남자와 여자는 **Classic Myanmar Tour**의 기간, 방문 도시, 이동 수단, 최대 참가 인원에 관해 언급하였다. 따라서 언급되지 않은 것은 ④ '비용'이다.

Why? 왜 오답일까?

① '**It's seven days, from July 10th to 16th.**'에서 '기간'이 언급되었다.
② '**The tour also includes visiting other major cities, such as Mandalay.**'에서 '방문 도시'가 언급되었다.
③ '**We'll take trains between cities and use buses in cities.**'에서 '이동 수단'이 언급되었다.
⑤ '**The tour has a limit of ten people.**'에서 '최대 참가 인원'이 언급되었다.

- **transportation** ⓝ 교통 수단
- **sign up for** ⓥ ~에 등록하다

09 교내 인포그래픽 대회 안내

정답률 89% | 정답 ⑤

2020 Student Infographic Contest에 관한 다음 내용을 듣고, 일치하지 않는 것을 고르시오.

① 모든 학년의 학생이 참여할 수 있다.
② 주제는 자유롭게 선택 가능하다.
③ 출품작을 이미지 파일로 제출해야 한다.
④ 수상자는 상품으로 영화 관람권을 받을 것이다.
✔ 수상작은 한 달 동안 전시될 것이다.

W : Hello, everyone. This is Ms. Harris, your social studies teacher.
안녕하세요, 여러분. 저는 사회 교사인 Harris 선생입니다.
I'm glad to announce the 2020 Student Infographic Contest.
2020 Student Infographic Contest에 관해 알려드리게 되어 기쁩니다.
As you know, an infographic is a visual way to present data or information that makes it easier to understand.
여러분도 알다시피, 인포그래픽은 데이터나 정보를 이해하기 더 쉽게 제시해주는 시각적 방법입니다.
『The contest is open to students of all grades.』 ①의 근거 일치
이 대회는 모든 학년의 학생들이 참여할 수 있습니다.
『To enter the contest, create an infographic on the topic of your choice and turn it in by November 15th.』 ②의 근거 일치
대회에 참여하려면, 여러분이 선정한 주제로 인포그래픽을 만들어서 그것을 11월 15일까지 제출하세요.
『Please be sure to submit your entry as an image file.』 ③의 근거 일치
반드시 출품작을 이미지 파일로 제출해 주세요.
『There will be three winners and they'll each receive two movie tickets as a prize.』
세 명의 우승자가 있을 것이며 그들 각각은 상품으로 영화 관람권 두 장을 받게 됩니다. ④의 근거 일치
『Winning entries will be on display in the library for the first week of December.』
수상작은 12월 첫 주 동안 도서관에 전시될 것입니다. ⑤의 근거 불일치
For questions or more information, please come to my office. Thank you.
질문이 있거나 더 많은 정보가 필요하다면, 제 사무실로 와 주세요. 고맙습니다.

Why? 왜 정답일까?

'**Winning entries will be on display in the library for the first week of December.**'에서 수상작은 12월 첫 주에 한 주 동안 전시될 예정이라고 하므로, 내용과 일치하지 않는 것은 ⑤ '수상작은 한 달 동안 전시될 것이다.'이다.

Why? 왜 오답일까?

① '**The contest is open to students of all grades.**'의 내용과 일치한다.
② '**~ create an infographic on the topic of your choice ~**'의 내용과 일치한다.
③ '**Please be sure to submit your entry as an image file.**'의 내용과 일치한다.
④ '**~ they'll each receive two movie tickets as a prize.**'의 내용과 일치한다.

- **present** ⓥ 제시하다
- **turn in** ⓥ ~을 제출하다
- **entry** ⓝ 출품작
- **on display** 전시 중인

10 눈 마사지기 구매하기

정답률 90% | 정답 ③

다음 표를 보면서 대화를 듣고, 남자가 구매할 눈 마사지기를 고르시오.

Eye Massagers

	Model	Price	Heat Setting	Number of Massage Modes	Music Function
①	A	$90	×	2	×
②	B	$120	×	3	×
✔	C	$150	○	5	×
④	D	$190	○	3	○
⑤	E	$210	○	6	○

M : Jessica, I'm thinking of buying one of these eye massagers. Can you help me choose one?
Jessica, 난 이 눈 마사지기들 중 하나를 구매하려고 생각 중이야. 내가 하나 고르는 걸 도와줄래?
W : Sure. 『The cheapest one here is the one I have. It's not bad, but I don't think it's comfortable to wear.
물론이지. 여기 제일 싼 게 내가 가지고 있는 거야. 나쁘지 않은데, 쓰기 편한 것 같지는 않아.
M : Okay. I won't buy it then.』 근거1 Price 조건
알겠어. 그럼 그건 안 살래.
W : 『Do you need a heat setting? 근거2 Heat Setting 조건
온열 설정이 필요해?
M : Yes.』 It probably relaxes the muscles and improves blood circulation around the eyes.
응. 그게 어쩌면 근육을 풀어주고 눈 주위 혈액 순환을 개선시켜 줄 거야.
W : All right. Then, you may also want different massage modes. They help to ease eye fatigue with their different vibration functions.
그래. 그럼 넌 다양한 마사지 모드를 같이 원할 수도 있겠구나. 다양한 진동 기능이 있으면 눈 피로를 푸는 데 도움이 돼.
M : 『Great. I'll get one that has at least five modes.』 Hmm, what's a music function?
아주 좋아. 난 최소한 모드가 다섯 개 있는 것으로 사겠어. 흠, 음악 기능은 뭐야? 근거3 Number of Massage Modes 조건
W : With that function, you can listen to calming music through built-in speakers.
그 기능이 있으면, 넌 내장된 스피커를 통해 마음을 편하게 해주는 음악을 들을 수 있어.
M : That sounds interesting, but 『I don't think it's necessary.』 근거4 Music Function 조건
그거 관심은 가는데, 필요할 것 같지는 않아.
W : Then, this one is perfect for you.
그럼, 이게 너한테 딱이겠다.
M : Okay, I'll buy it.
그래, 그걸 사겠어.

Why? 왜 정답일까?

대화에 따르면 남자는 가격이 제일 싼 것을 제외하고, 온열 기능이 있으며, 최소 다섯 개의 마사지 모드를 제공하고, 음악 기능은 없는 눈 마사지기를 구매하려고 한다. 따라서 남자가 구매할 눈 마사지기는 ③ 'C'이다.

- **blood circulation** ⓝ 혈액순환
- **fatigue** ⓝ 피로
- **vibration** ⓝ 진동
- **calming** ⓐ 마음을 편안하게 해주는, 진정시키는

11 깁스를 한 친구에게 상황 물어보기

정답률 72% | 정답 ④

대화를 듣고, 남자의 마지막 말에 대한 여자의 응답으로 가장 적절한 것을 고르시오.

[문제편 p.109]

① In fact, I'm not sure what the problem is. – 사실, 난 문제가 뭔지 잘 모르겠어.
② Well, you'd better ice your sprained ankle. – 음, 넌 삔 발목에 얼음찜질을 해야 해.
③ You're right. I'd rather stay at home and rest. – 네 말이 맞아. 난 집에 있으면서 쉬어야겠어.
✔ One week or so, but I have to see how it heals. – 한 주 정도인데, 잘 낫는지 지켜봐야 해.
⑤ Terrible. I should have worn a cast for two weeks. – 끔찍하다. 난 2주 동안 깁스를 했어야 했어.

M : Hey, Sally, why are you wearing a cast on your foot?
안녕, Sally, 왜 발에 깁스를 하고 있어?
W : I tripped over a rock yesterday and sprained my ankle.
어제 바위에 걸려 넘어져서 발목을 삐었어.
M : That sounds bad. How long do you have to wear your cast?
그거 안됐다. 깁스를 얼마나 해야 해?
W : One week or so, but I have to see how it heals.
한 주 정도인데, 잘 낫는지 지켜봐야 해.

Why? 왜 정답일까?

발목을 삐어 깁스를 했다는 여자에게 남자는 얼마나 깁스를 해야 하는지 묻고 있다(**How long do you have to wear your cast?**). 따라서 여자의 응답으로 가장 적절한 것은 ④ '한 주 정도인데, 잘 낫는지 지켜봐야 해.'이다.

12 설문조사 참여 부탁하기

정답률 89% | 정답 ③

대화를 듣고, 여자의 마지막 말에 대한 남자의 응답으로 가장 적절한 것을 고르시오.

① Great. Let's go shopping together. – 좋아. 같이 쇼핑 가자.
② No. I haven't decided on my survey topic. – 아니. 난 아직 설문조사 주제를 정하지 못했어.
✔ Okay. Please send me the link to the survey. – 알겠어. 설문조사로 연결되는 링크를 내게 보내줘.
④ Yes. I've finished writing the survey questions. – 응. 난 설문조사 문항을 작성하는 것을 마쳤어.
⑤ I see. I'll take the marketing class online today. – 알겠어. 난 오늘 온라인으로 마케팅 수업을 들을게.

[Phone rings.]
[전화벨이 울린다.]
W : Steve, I'm conducting a survey for my marketing class. I wonder if you can take it.
Steve, 난 내 마케팅 수업을 위한 설문조사를 하고 있어. 네가 그것을 해줄 수 있는지 궁금해.
M : Sure, I'd be happy to help. What's the survey about?
물론이지, 기꺼이 도와줄게. 뭐에 관한 설문인데?
W : It's about college students' shopping habits. You can do it online by visiting the survey website.
대학생들의 쇼핑 습관에 관한 거야. 넌 설문조사 웹 사이트를 방문해서 그것을 온라인으로 할 수 있어.
M : Okay. Please send me the link to the survey.
알겠어. 설문조사로 연결되는 링크를 내게 보내줘.

Why? 왜 정답일까?

여자는 마케팅 수업 때문에 대학생들의 소비 습관에 관한 설문조사를 하고 있다면서 남자에게 웹 사이트를 통해 조사에 참여해 줄 것을 부탁하고 있다(**You can do it online by visiting the survey website.**). 따라서 남자의 응답으로 가장 적절한 것은 ③ '알겠어. 설문조사로 연결되는 링크를 내게 보내줘.'이다.

- **conduct** ⓥ 실시하다
- **wonder** ⓥ 궁금해 하다
- **survey** ⓝ 설문조사
- **decide on** ⓥ ~에 대해 결정하다

13 자녀들의 스마트폰 이용 시간 제한하기

정답률 79% | 정답 ⑤

대화를 듣고, 여자의 마지막 말에 대한 남자의 응답으로 가장 적절한 것을 고르시오. [3점]

Man: ______

① Sure, you can take the boxes home if you want.
물론이죠, 원한다면 그 상자들을 집에 가져가셔도 돼요.
② Well, my children have lost interest in smartphones.
음, 제 아이들은 스마트폰에 흥미를 잃었어요.
③ I agree. Storing the phones in a box isn't the answer.
동의해요. 전화기를 상자 안에 넣어두는 것은 답이 아니에요.
④ Actually, we need to update our phones on a regular basis.
사실, 우리는 주기적으로 우리 전화기를 업데이트할 필요가 있어요.
✔ Definitely. I'll get a box and see if it works for my family.
물론이에요. 난 상자를 구해와서 이게 우리 가족에게 효과가 있는지 보겠어요.

W : Stanley, you look very concerned.
Stanley, 당신 무척 걱정스러워 보여요.
M : Well, I'm worried about my children's smartphone use. They won't put their phones down, even at the family dinner table.
음, 난 우리 아이들의 스마트폰 사용에 대해 염려하고 있어요. 그들은 심지어 가족 저녁 식사 자리에서도 스마트폰을 내려놓지 않아요.
W : I can imagine. Smartphones are useful, but they often distract us and take away precious family time.
상상이 가네요. 스마트폰은 유용하지만 종종 우리를 산만하게 하고 소중한 가족 시간을 빼앗아 가지요.
M : I totally agree. How can I make my children spend less time on their phones?
전적으로 동의해요. 어떻게 하면 우리 아이들이 스마트폰에 시간을 덜 쓰게 할 수 있을까요?
W : You can do that by first setting a good example. Your children will change if you start limiting your own phone time.
좋은 본보기를 설정하여 그렇게 할 수 있죠. 당신이 당신 자신의 전화기 사용 시간을 제한하기 시작하면 아이들도 변할 거예요.
M : Good point. But isn't it too tempting to be on your phone when you have it nearby?
좋은 지적이에요. 하지만 전화기가 주변에 있으면 그것을 몹시 쓰고 싶지 않나요?
W : Of course. For that reason, many parents have started to put their cellphones away in a storage box at home and have asked their children to do the same.
물론이죠. 그 이유로, 많은 부모들이 집에서는 보관 상자 안에 핸드폰을 넣어서 치우고 아이들에게 똑같이 하도록 요청하고 있어요.
M : Great idea. If we don't see our phones, we'll feel less tempted.
좋은 생각이네요. 우리가 우리 전화기를 안 보면 덜 유혹되겠죠.
W : Yes, maybe you should consider trying this at home.
네, 어쩌면 당신도 집에서 이걸 해보는 걸 고려해 봐야겠네요.
M : Definitely. I'll get a box and see if it works for my family.
물론이에요. 난 상자를 구해와서 이게 우리 가족에게 효과가 있는지 보겠어요.

Why? 왜 정답일까?

자녀들이 가족 시간에 스마트폰을 너무 많이 써서 걱정이라는 남자에게 여자는 요새 부모들이 집에서 자신의 전화를 보관 상자에 넣어 치워버리고 자녀들에게 똑같이 하도록 지도하고 있다(**For that reason, many parents have started to put their cellphones away in a storage box at home and have asked their children to do the same.**)는 것을 알려준다. 대화 마지막에서 여자는 남자 또한 집에서 이대로 해보면 좋겠다(**Yes, maybe you should consider trying this at home.**)고 언급하므로, 남자의 응답으로 가장 적절한 것은 ⑤ '물론이에요. 난 상자를 구해와서 이게 우리 가족에게 효과가 있는지 보겠어요.'이다.

- **concerned** ⓐ 걱정하는
- **precious** ⓐ 소중한, 귀중한
- **on a regular basis** 주기적으로
- **distract** ⓥ 산만하게 하다, 주의를 흩뜨리다
- **tempting** ⓐ 유혹적인, 솔깃한

14 외국인 사업가와의 인터뷰 준비

정답률 79% | 정답 ①

대화를 듣고, 남자의 마지막 말에 대한 여자의 응답으로 가장 적절한 것을 고르시오. [3점]

Woman: ______

✔ Great. Let's ask her if she can help us with the interview.
아주 좋아. 그녀에게 우리 인터뷰를 도와줄 수 있는지 물어보자.
② Sure. I'll look at the questions and tell you what I think.
물론이지. 내가 질문들을 살펴보고 나서 내 생각을 말해줄게.
③ Don't worry. I'll recommend a good translator for her.
걱정 마. 내가 그녀를 위해 좋은 통역가를 추천하겠어.
④ Wow! I didn't know you are that good at Chinese.
와! 난 네가 중국어를 그렇게 잘하는지 몰랐어.
⑤ Right. Mr. Chen is fluent in both languages.
맞아. Chen 씨는 두 언어에 모두 능해.

W : Andrew, guess what? I've just got an email saying that Mr. Chen agreed to give an interview for our student magazine.
있잖아, Andrew, 나 방금 Chen 씨가 우리 학생 잡지에 인터뷰를 해주는 데 동의한다고 쓰여 있는 이메일을 받았어.
M : The Chinese CEO? That's such good news.
그 중국인 CEO? 엄청 좋은 소식이네.
W : The email says he hopes his business success will help inspire young business majors like us.
그 이메일에는 그가 자신의 사업 성공이 우리처럼 젊은 경영 전공자들에게 영감을 주는 데 도움이 되기를 바란다고 쓰여 있어.
M : How nice of him! So when is he available for the interview?
친절하시네! 그래서 그가 언제 시간이 되신대?
W : Next Friday afternoon.
다음주 금요일 오후야.
M : Okay. We'll have to talk about possible questions we could ask. Is there anything else we should prepare?
알겠어. 우린 물어볼 수 있는 가능한 질문들에 대해 이야기를 해봐야 해. 우리가 준비해야 하는 다른 게 있나?
W : There's one important thing that should be taken care of.
처리되어야 할 한 가지 중요한 게 있어.
M : What is it?
그게 뭐야?
W : While doing research for the interview, I found out that Mr. Chen doesn't speak English that well. So I think we should find someone who can interpret for us.
인터뷰를 위해 조사하다가, 나는 Chen 씨가 영어를 그렇게 잘하지 못한다는 것을 알아냈어. 그러니 내 생각에 우리를 위해 통역해줄 사람을 찾아야 할 것 같아.
M : Hmm.... Doesn't Julia speak Chinese fluently? I think she can translate our questions into Chinese and tell us Mr. Chen's responses in English.
흠... Julia가 중국어를 유창하게 하지 않아? 내 생각에 그녀가 우리 질문을 중국어로 번역해 주고 Chen 씨의 답변을 우리에게 영어로 말해줄 수 있을 것 같아.
W : Great. Let's ask her if she can help us with the interview.
아주 좋아. 그녀에게 우리 인터뷰를 도와줄 수 있는지 물어보자.

Why? 왜 정답일까?

대화에서 여자는 영어가 유창하지 않은 중국어 사업가와 인터뷰를 하기 위해서 통역을 해줄 사람이 필요하다고 말하고, 이에 남자는 Julia가 중국어를 유창하게 하므로 통역을 도와줄 수 있을 것이라고 언급하고 있다(**Doesn't Julia speak Chinese fluently? I think she can translate our questions into Chinese and tell us Mr. Chen's responses in English.**). 따라서 여자의 응답으로 가장 적절한 것은 ① '아주 좋아. 그녀에게 우리 인터뷰를 도와줄 수 있는지 물어보자.'이다.

- **inspire** ⓥ 영감을 주다
- **do research** ⓥ 조사하다
- **fluently** ad 유창하게
- **take care of** ⓥ ~을 처리하다
- **interpret** ⓥ 통역하다, 해석하다, 이해하다
- **translate** ⓥ 번역하다, 통역하다

15 발표 준비로 스트레스를 받는 친구에게 조언하기

정답률 65% | 정답 ⑤

다음 상황 설명을 듣고, Alex가 Carol에게 할 말로 가장 적절한 것을 고르시오.

Alex: ______

① I think you need to take a break right now.
난 네가 당장 쉬어야 할 것 같아.
② Why not sign up for the presentation contest?
발표 대회에 등록하는 게 어때?
③ Don't be afraid if you're selected as a representative.
네가 대표로 뽑히더라도 두려워하지 마.
④ You'd better set aside your routine activities for a while.
넌 당분간 일상의 활동을 고려하지 않는 게 낫겠어.
✔ How about setting a daily plan to prepare for the contest?
대회를 준비하기 위한 일일 계획을 짜는 게 어때?

M : Carol is going to enter a presentation contest in a month as the school representative.
Carol은 한 달 뒤 학교 대표로 발표 대회에 나갈 예정이다.
She feels anxious even when going about her daily life because she doesn't think she can manage all of her routine activities and still have time to prepare for the contest.
그녀는 일상을 살아가는 도중에도 불안감을 느끼는데 왜냐하면 그녀는 자신이 모든 일상의 활동을 처리하면서도 대회를 준비할 시간이 있다고 생각하지 않기 때문이다.
But her classmate Alex thinks Carol doesn't have to feel so stressed, because a month is actually plenty of time to prepare for it.
하지만 그녀의 반 친구인 Alex는 Carol이 그렇게 스트레스를 받지 않아도 된다고 생각하는데, 왜냐하면 한 달은 사실 대회 준비에 넉넉한 시간이기 때문이다.
Alex thinks that if she breaks down the preparation process into what she can do each day, she'll be better able to prepare while still having time for her other activities.
Alex는 그녀가 자기가 매일 할 수 있는 일로 준비 과정을 쪼갠다면 다른 활동을 할 시간을 두면서도 준비를 더 잘할 수 있을 것이라 생각한다.

19회

[문제편 p.110]

So Alex wants to suggest to Carol that she plan out specific goals to accomplish each day for her preparation.
그래서 Alex는 Carol에게 준비를 위해 매일 달성해야 하는 구체적인 목표를 계획하도록 제안하고 싶어 한다.
In this situation, what would Alex most likely say to Carol?
이런 상황에서, Alex는 Carol에게 뭐라고 말할 것인가?
Alex : How about setting a daily plan to prepare for the contest?
대회를 준비하기 위한 일일 계획을 짜는 게 어때?

Why? 왜 정답일까?

상황에 따르면 발표 대회를 한 달 앞두고 스트레스를 받고 있는 Carol에게 Alex는 일일 계획을 세워본다면 다른 일을 병행하면서도 효과적으로 준비를 마칠 수 있을 것이라고 제안하려 한다(So Alex wants to suggest to Carol that she plan out specific goals to accomplish each day for her preparation.). 따라서 Alex가 Carol에게 할 말로 가장 적절한 것은 ⑤ '대회를 준비하기 위한 일일 계획을 짜는 게 어때?'이다.

- representative ⓝ 대표 ⓐ (특정 단체를) 대표하는
- anxious ⓐ 불안해하는, 걱정하는
- routine ⓐ 일상적인
- plenty of 많은
- specific ⓐ 구체적인
- accomplish ⓥ 달성하다
- set aside ⓥ (다른 더 중요한 일들 때문에) ~을 고려하지 않다

16-17 운동 기구로 활용할 수 있는 집안 사물 소개하기

W : Hello, listeners. Welcome to Fitness Expert Radio Broadcast!
안녕하세요, 청취자 여러분. Fitness Expert Radio Broadcast에 잘 오셨습니다!
Is a gym membership or fancy equipment necessary to get in shape?
몸매를 가꾸기 위해 체육관 회원권 또는 근사한 기구가 필수일까요?
No. 「Luckily, there are some objects around your home that are perfect for helping you get fit.」 16번의 근거
아닙니다. 다행히도 여러분이 건강해지도록 도움을 주는 데 적격인 몇 가지 물건들이 여러분 집 도처에 있습니다.
「First, a chair is a good tool for your at-home workouts.」 17번 ①의 근거 일치
첫째로, 의자는 집안에서 운동하는 데 좋은 도구입니다.
Consider using one to do your aerobics, leg raises and incline push-ups.
에어로빅, 레그 레이즈(다리 올리기), 경사 팔굽혀펴기를 하기 위해 의자를 이용하는 것을 고려해 보세요.
「Next, one person's towel is another person's resistance band!」 17번 ②의 근거 일치
다음으로, 어떤 사람의 수건이 다른 사람에게는 탄력 밴드입니다!
Try stretching with one.
수건을 하나 가지고 스트레칭을 해보세요.
「You can also do shoulder stretches with a broomstick.」 17번 ③의 근거 일치
여러분은 또한 빗자루로 어깨 스트레칭을 할 수 있습니다.
A broomstick can help increase flexibility and improve your posture by keeping your spine in line.
빗자루는 유연성을 높이는 데 도움이 되고 척추를 일렬로 잡아주어서 자세를 개선시켜 줍니다.
「Lastly, use filled water bottles.」 17번 ⑤의 근거 일치
마지막으로, 가득 채워진 물병을 이용하세요.
One in each hand can be used for aerobic exercises.
한 손에 하나씩 잡아 유산소 운동을 위해 사용할 수 있습니다.
Most water bottles are designed to be gripped, making them the ideal dumbbell substitute.
대부분의 물병은 잡기 위해 만들어졌고, 이로 인해 이상적인 덤벨 대체품이 됩니다.
Now, are you ready to try these at home?
이제, 이것들을 집에서 시도해볼 준비가 되셨나요?
For more fitness tips, please visit our website www.fitnessexpert.com.
더 많은 운동 조언을 얻으시려면, 저희 웹 사이트인 www.fitnessexpert.com을 방문해 주세요.
We can't wait to help you feel the burn!
여러분이 이 열기를 느끼도록 어서 도와드리고 싶네요!

- get in shape ⓥ 몸매를 가꾸다, 건강해지다
- incline ⓝ 경사(면), 비탈
- broomstick ⓝ 빗자루
- grip ⓥ 잡다, 쥐다
- substitute ⓝ 대체품
- properly ad 적절히
- home appliance ⓝ 가전제품

16 주제 파악

정답률 91% | 정답 ②

여자가 하는 말의 주제로 가장 적절한 것은?

① positive effects of regular exercise on flexibility - 정기적인 유연성 운동의 긍정적 효과
✔ using ordinary household items for home exercise - 일상의 생활용품을 집안 운동 기구로 활용하기
③ physical benefits of doing household chores - 집안일을 하는 것의 신체적 이점
④ maintaining workout equipment properly - 운동 기구를 적절히 관리하기
⑤ useful tips on buying home appliances - 가전제품 구매에 관한 유용한 조언

Why? 왜 정답일까?

'Luckily, there are some objects around your home that are perfect for helping you get fit.'에서 여자는 집에서 운동을 하는 데 도움이 될 일상의 사물들이 있다고 언급한 후, 이어서 의자, 수건 등 사물의 예시를 열거하고 있다. 따라서 여자가 하는 말의 주제로 가장 적절한 것은 ② '일상의 생활용품을 집안 운동 기구로 활용하기'이다.

17 언급 유무 파악

정답률 95% | 정답 ④

언급된 물건이 아닌 것은?

① chair - 의자 ② towel - 수건 ③ broomstick - 빗자루
✔ basket - 바구니 ⑤ water bottle - 물병

Why? 왜 정답일까?

담화에서 여자는 집안에서 운동 기구를 대체하여 활용할 수 있는 물건으로 의자, 수건, 빗자루, 물병을 언급하였다. 따라서 언급되지 않은 것은 ④ '바구니'이다.

Why? 왜 오답일까?

① 'First, a chair is a good tool for your at-home workouts.'에서 '의자'가 언급되었다.
② 'Next, one person's towel is another person's resistance band!'에서 '수건'이 언급되었다.
③ 'You can also do shoulder stretches with a broomstick.'에서 '빗자루'가 언급되었다.
⑤ 'Lastly, use filled water bottles.'에서 '물병'이 언급되었다.

Dictation 19

문제편 111쪽

01 the entire facilities on the third floor / won't be able to accommodate scheduled tours
02 dying from plastic products / reduce the consumption of plastic products / accept a little inconvenience
03 feeding the sheep / milking the cows / harvest the potatoes and onions / have good memories of my farm
04 the boy lying on the bed wearing glasses / willing to share his stuff / hung a flower painting on the wall
05 editing the celebration video / pick up our party costumes / do the wrapping
06 What are the most popular items here / the key rings with each member's figure / from the band's official app
07 a one-on-one oral interview / postponed to a week later / attend an overseas seminar
08 How long is the tour / includes visiting other major cities / travel on a river cruise through the jungle
09 visual way to present data or information / create an infographic / submit your entry as an image file
10 comfortable to wear / improves blood circulation around the eyes / has at least five modes
11 wearing a cast / sprained my ankle
12 I wonder if you can take it / college students' shopping habits
13 spend less time on their phones / put their cellphones away in a storage box / feel less tempted
14 help inspire young business majors like us / possible questions we could ask / who can interpret for us
15 manage all of her routine activities / breaks down the preparation process / plan out specific goals
16-17 helping you get fit / increase flexibility and improve your posture / making them the ideal dumbbell substitute

20회 | 2025학년도 9월 모의평가 고3

| 정답과 해설 |

• 정답 •

01 ④ 02 ① 03 ⑤ 04 ⑤ 05 ① 06 ① 07 ⑤ 08 ③ 09 ⑤ 10 ③ 11 ② 12 ① 13 ④ 14 ② 15 ③ 16 ① 17 ③

01 엘리베이터 공사 안내 정답률 99% | 정답 ④

다음을 듣고, 여자가 하는 말의 목적으로 가장 적절한 것을 고르시오.

① 새로 부임한 교직원을 소개하려고
② 시설 안전 포스터 공모전을 홍보하려고
③ 학교 복도에서 뛰지 말 것을 당부하려고
✔ 학교 엘리베이터 수리 일정을 공지하려고
⑤ 엘리베이터 사용 실태 조사를 안내하려고

W : Hello, everyone at Philston High School.
안녕하세요, Philston 고등학교에 계신 여러분.
This is Principal Jackson.
저는 Jackson 교장입니다.
This announcement is to inform students and staff of the school elevator repair schedule.
이 공지는 학생과 교직원께 학교 엘리베이터 수리 일정을 알려 드리기 위함입니다.
As you know, the school elevator stopped working yesterday.
아시다시피, 학교 엘리베이터가 어제 작동을 멈췄습니다.
It's scheduled to be repaired starting at 1 p.m. this afternoon.
그것은 오늘 오후 1시에 시작하여 수리될 예정입니다.
The repair is expected to take about 3 hours.
수리는 3시간 정도 소요될 것으로 예상됩니다.
In the meantime, you'll have to continue using the stairs.
그동안은, 계속 계단을 이용하셔야 합니다.
Once again, please be aware that the school elevator will be undergoing repairs from 1 p.m. to about 4 p.m. today.
다시 한번, 오늘 오후 1시부터 약 4시까지 학교 엘리베이터 수리가 실시될 예정임을 유의해 주시기를 부탁드립니다.
We'll announce when the elevator is running again. Sorry for the inconvenience.
엘리베이터가 다시 운행되면 방송으로 알려 드리겠습니다. 불편을 드려 죄송합니다.

Why? 왜 정답일까?

학교 엘리베이터 수리 일정을 공지(This announcement is to inform students and staff of the school elevator repair schedule.)하고 있으므로, 여자의 의견으로 가장 적절한 것은 ④ '학교 엘리베이터 수리 일정을 공지하려고'이다.

- vice principal 교감
- undergo ⓥ 실시하다
- hallway ⓝ 복도
- inform ⓥ 알리다
- upcoming ⓐ 다가오는

02 단백질 과잉 섭취 정답률 99% | 정답 ①

대화를 듣고, 남자의 의견으로 가장 적절한 것을 고르시오.

✔ 과도한 양의 단백질 섭취는 건강에 좋지 않다.
② 칼슘 보충을 위해 채소를 많이 섭취해야 한다.
③ 회사 구내식당에서 식사하는 것이 경제적이다.
④ 갑작스러운 운동량 변화는 신체에 부담이 된다.
⑤ 도시락을 싸 오면 음식물 쓰레기를 줄일 수 있다.

M : Oh, Susan. You're eating lunch here in the office.
오, Susan, 여기 사무실에서 점심을 먹고 있군요.
W : Hi, Aaron. I've been bringing my own lunch.
안녕하세요, Aaron. 점심을 싸 오고 있어요.
M : That's why I haven't seen you in the company cafeteria recently. Wait. That's a lot of chicken breast for one meal!
그래서 최근에 회사 구내식당에서 당신을 못 봤던 거군요. 잠시만요. 한 끼치고는 닭 가슴살이 많은데요!
W : Yeah. I've been eating a lot of protein for each meal these days because I want to build bigger muscles.
네. 근육을 더 크게 키우고 싶어서 요즘 매 끼니마다 단백질을 많이 먹고 있어요.
M : Well, it seems that you're eating too much protein. Overconsuming protein is unhealthy.
글쎄요, 단백질을 너무 많이 드시는 것 같아요. 단백질을 과잉 섭취하는 것은 건강에 안 좋아요.
W : Don't we need a lot of protein to build bigger muscles?
근육을 더 크게 키우려면 많은 단백질이 필요하지 않아요?
M : Yes, but too much protein can cause stomachaches.
네, 하지만 단백질을 너무 많이 먹으면 복통이 생길 수 있어요.
W : Oh, that's probably why I've felt uncomfortable after each meal lately.
오, 아마 그래서 최근에 매번 식사하고 나면 불편하다고 느꼈나 봐요.
M : Besides, eating too much protein may cause calcium loss. It can lead to poor bone health.
게다가, 단백질을 너무 많이 먹으면 칼슘 손실이 생길 수 있어요. 그건 뼈 건강 악화로 이어질 수 있고요.
W : Really? I didn't know that.
정말요? 몰랐어요.
M : So, taking in too much protein is harmful for your health.
그러니까, 단백질을 너무 많이 섭취하는 건 당신의 건강에 해로워요.
W : I see. Then I'll cut down on the amount of protein I eat.
알겠어요. 이제 제 단백질 섭취량을 줄일게요.

Why? 왜 정답일까?

단백질을 많이 먹으면 복통이 생기고, 칼슘 손실이 생길 수 있음을 예시로 들며 건강에 안 좋다(So, taking in too much protein is harmful for your health.)고 이야기하고 있다. 따라서, 남자의 의견으로 가장 적절한 것은 ① '과도한 양의 단백질 섭취는 건강에 좋지 않다.'이다.

- breast ⓝ 가슴
- overconsume ⓥ 과잉 섭취하다
- protein ⓝ 단백질

03 학생들과 좋은 관계 형성하기 정답률 97% | 정답 ⑤

다음을 듣고, 여자가 하는 말의 요지로 가장 적절한 것을 고르시오.

① 학생에게 실생활에 필요한 역량을 키워 줄 필요가 있다.
② 학생 인성 교육을 위해 충분한 상담 지식을 갖추어야 한다.
③ 학생을 잘 이해하려면 그 학생의 관심사를 파악해야 한다.
④ 효과적인 수업을 하려면 교사 간의 많은 대화가 필수적이다.
✔ 학생 이름을 부르는 것은 그 학생과의 좋은 관계 형성에 기여한다.

W : Hello, fellow teachers.
안녕하세요, 동료 교사 여러분.
Welcome back to my video channel, *Ms. Freeman's Teaching Tips*. Do you have difficulty developing good relationships with your students?
제 비디오 채널 *Ms. Freeman's Teaching Tips*에 다시 오신 것을 환영합니다. 여러분은 학생들과 좋은 관계를 형성하는 데 어려움이 있으신가요?
I understand how that can be frustrating. Here's a tip.
저는 그것이 얼마나 좌절감을 주는 일인지 이해합니다. 여기 조언이 있습니다.
Calling your students by their names can help you develop a good relationship with them.
학생을 그들의 이름으로 부르는 것이 여러분이 그들과 좋은 관계를 형성하는 데 도움이 될 수 있습니다.
It'll show the students that you're interested in them, and they'll feel more comfortable with you.
그것은 여러분이 학생들에게 관심이 있다는 것을 그들에게 보여 줄 것이고, 그들은 여러분을 더 편안하게 느낄 것입니다.
Then, the students will be more likely to open up to you. So, call your students by their names, and it'll contribute to building a good relationship with them.
그러면 학생들이 여러분에게 마음을 열 가능성은 더 커집니다. 그러니까, 학생의 이름으로 그들을 부르면 그들과 좋은 관계를 형성하는 데 도움이 될 것입니다.
Thanks for watching and don't forget to subscribe.
시청해 주셔서 감사드리고 구독하는 것을 잊지 마십시오.

Why? 왜 정답일까?

학생을 이름으로 부르면 좋은 관계를 형성하는 데 도움이 된다(So, call your students by their names, and it'll contribute to building a good relationship with them.)고 이야기하므로, 여자가 하는 말의 요지로 가장 적절한 것은 ⑤ '학생 이름을 부르는 것은 그 학생과의 좋은 관계 형성에 기여한다.'이다.

- frustrating ⓐ 좌절감을 주는
- subscribe ⓥ 구독하다
- contribute to ~에 도움이 되다, 기여하다

04 카페 인테리어 소개 정답률 94% | 정답 ⑤

대화를 듣고, 그림에서 대화의 내용과 일치하지 않는 것을 고르시오.

M : Ellen, yesterday I visited the new café we talked about last week.
Ellen, 어제 우리가 지난주에 얘기했던 그 카페를 갔어.
W : Really? Is it nice?
정말? 좋았어?
M : Yes, it is. Look. Here's a picture of the café.
응. 봐. 여기 카페 사진이야.
W : It seems lovely. 『There's a leaf-shaped mirror on the wall!』 ①의 근거 일치
예쁘다. 벽에 나뭇잎 모양의 거울이 있어!
M : Right, it's so unique. 『What do you think about the painting between the windows?』 ②의 근거 일치
응, 독특해. 창문 사이에 있는 그림은 어때?
W : Whoever painted it is really talented. 『I also like the two flowerpots on the shelf.』 ③의 근거 일치 They're so pretty.
누가 그렸든 정말 재능이 있네. 선반 위에 있는 두 개의 화분도 마음에 들어. 정말 예쁘다.
M : They really brighten up the room. 『And do you see the star-patterned table cloth?』 ④의 근거 일치
그것들은 정말 방을 밝게 해 줘. 그리고 별무늬 테이블 보여?
W : 『Yes, it's eye-catching. Oh, the round rug is really neat.』 ⑤의 근거 불일치
응, 시선을 사로잡네. 오, 둥근 양탄자가 정말 깔끔하다.
M : It creates a comfortable mood.
그게 편안한 분위기를 만들어 줘.
W : Yeah, I feel the same way. I'll definitely visit the café when I have the chance.
응, 나도 같은 느낌이야. 기회가 되면 꼭 그 카페에 가 볼게.

Why? 왜 정답일까?

대화에서 둥근 양탄자가 깔끔하다(Yes, it's eye-catching. Oh, the round rug is really neat.)고 했는데, 그림 속에는 사각형의 양탄자가 있다. 따라서 그림에서 대화의 내용과 일치하지 않는 것은 ⑤이다.

- flowerpot ⓝ 화분
- neat ⓐ 깔끔한
- eye-catching 시선을 사로잡는

05 전시회 견학 준비 정답률 83% | 정답 ①

대화를 듣고, 남자가 할 일로 가장 적절한 것을 고르시오.

✔ 유인물 만들기
② 점심 주문하기

[문제편 p.115]

③ 버스 대절하기 ④ 입장권 예약하기
⑤ 문자 메시지 보내기

W : Andy, our art club's visit to the Waneville Art Museum is just a week away.
Andy, 우리 미술 동아리의 Waneville 미술관 방문이 딱 일주일 남았어.

M : Right, Ms. Peterson. Our club members are really excited to see the Jonathan Vinston exhibit. He's so popular on social media nowadays.
네, Peterson 선생님, 우리 동아리 회원들은 Jonathan Vinston 전시회를 보게 되어 정말 신나요. 그는 요즘 소셜 미디어에서 매우 인기가 많거든요.

W : Great. For transportation, I arranged for a bus to take us there. Have you and the other students decided what we'll eat for lunch?
잘됐네. 교통편으로는 우리를 그곳에 데려다 줄 버스를 준비했어. 너와 다른 학생들은 점심으로 뭘 먹을지 정했니?

M : Yes. Yesterday, I ordered 25 sandwiches.
네, 어제 샌드위치 25개를 주문했어요.

W : Excellent. Do our members know about the meeting time and place?
잘했네. 우리 회원들이 모임과 시간 장소를 알고 있니?

M : Not yet. Do you want me to text them the details?
아직이요. 자세한 내용을 문자로 보낼까요?

W : No, I'll do that.
아니, 그건 내가 할게.

M : Thank you. Have you booked the admission tickets?
감사합니다. 입장권은 예약하셨나요?

W : Of course. I've received the online confirmation. Oh, it might be good to provide the members with information about the artist beforehand.
물론이야. 온라인 확인을 받았어. 아, 회원들에게 미술가에 대한 정보를 미리 알려 주면 좋을 것 같아.

M : Okay. I'll make a handout about him right away.
네, 제가 그에 관한 유인물을 바로 만들게요.

W : Thanks. I'm sure everyone will enjoy the visit.
고마워. 틀림없이 모두가 그 방문을 즐길 거야.

Why? 왜 정답일까?

두 사람은 전시회 견학을 준비 중인데 남자가 회원들에게 줄 유인물을 만들겠다(**Okay. I'll make a handout about him right away.**)고 대답한다. 따라서 남자가 할 일로 가장 적절한 것은 ① '유인물 만들기'이다.

- arrange ⓥ 준비하다
- confirmation ⓝ 확인
- admission ⓝ 입장
- beforehand [ad] 미리

06 하이킹 여행 준비

정답률 94% | 정답 ①

대화를 듣고, 여자가 지불할 금액을 고르시오.

✔ $45 ② $50 ③ $54 ④ $63 ⑤ $70

M : Welcome to Winsley's Drugstore. How may I help you?
Winsley의 약국에 오신 걸 환영합니다. 어떻게 도와드릴까요?

W : Hi. I need some foot cream for my hiking trip.
안녕하세요. 하이킹 여행을 위해 발 크림이 좀 필요합니다.

M : What size are you looking for? The small size is $10 and the regular size is $20.
어떤 사이즈를 찾고 있나요? 작은 사이즈는 10달러이고, 보통 사이즈는 20달러입니다.

W : That small size would be handy. I'll take two.
작은 사이즈가 편리할 것 같네요. 두 개 주세요.

M : Good. Anything else?
좋습니다. 더 필요한 건 없으신가요?

W : I also need lip balm.
립밤도 필요합니다.

M : Is there any particular brand you have in mind?
마음에 두고 있는 특정 브랜드가 있으신가요?

W : Not really.
딱히 없습니다.

M : Then, this one is quite popular. It's only $5.
그럼, 이 제품이 꽤 인기 있어요. 5달러밖에 안 해요.

W : All right. I'll take six. I'll give them out to my fellow hikers. And, that's all.
좋아요. 여섯 개 주세요. 다른 하이킹 동료들에게 나눠 줄 거예요. 그리고 그게 다입니다.

M : Okay. So, two small size foot creams and six lip balms, right?
알겠습니다. 그러면 작은 사이즈의 발 크림 두 개와 립밤 여섯 개 맞으신가요?

W : Yes. And I heard there's a sales event this week.
네, 그리고 이번 주에 할인 행사가 있다고 들었어요.

M : Right. You'll get a 10% discount off the total.
맞아요. 총 금액에서 10% 할인을 받으실 겁니다.

W : Great. Here's my credit card.
네, 여기 제 신용카드입니다.

Why? 왜 정답일까?

대화에 따르면 여자는 하이킹 여행을 위해 **10**달러인 작은 사이즈 발 크림 두 개와 **5**달러인 립밤 여섯 개를 구입하기로 했다. 이때 총 금액에서 **10%** 할인을 받는다 하였으므로, 여자가 지불할 금액은 ① '**45**달러'이다.

- handy ⓐ 편리한
- quite ⓐ 꽤
- have ~ in mind ~을 마음에 두다
- fellow ⓝ 동료

07 직업 박람회 불참 이유

정답률 98% | 정답 ⑤

대화를 듣고, 여자가 Kenton Biotech Career Fair에 갈 수 없는 이유를 고르시오.

① 마케팅 특강을 들어야 해서
② 생명과학 실험을 해야 해서
③ 요양원 자원봉사를 해야 해서
④ 역사 시험 공부를 해야 해서
✔ 뮤지컬 오디션에 가야 해서

M : Jane, have you heard about the Kenton Biotech Career Fair this Saturday?
Jane, 이번 토요일에 있을 Kenton Biotech Career Fair에 대해 들어본 적 있어?

W : Yes, Daniel. It's a one-day event that covers biotechnology, health care, and marketing, right?
응, Daniel. 그건 생명공학, 의료, 마케팅을 다루는 하루 동안의 행사지, 맞지?

M : Yeah. There'll even be special lectures on the subjects. Would you like to go?
맞아. 그 주제에 관한 특별 강연도 있을 거야. 가고 싶어?

W : I'd like to, but I'm afraid I can't.
가고 싶지만, 그럴 수 없어서 유감이야.

M : Oh, are Saturdays when you're volunteering at the nursing home?
아, 토요일은 네가 양로원에서 자원봉사를 하는 날이지?

W : No, that's on Sundays.
아니, 그건 일요일이야.

M : Then, do you have to study for your history exam?
그러면, 역사 시험공부를 해야 하는 거야?

W : I took it last week. Actually, on that day I have to go to an audition for a musical.
그건 지난주에 봤어. 사실, 그날 나는 뮤지컬 오디션에 가야 해.

M : Really? That's awesome! I bet you'll do great.
정말? 멋지다! 분명 잘 해낼 거야.

W : Thanks. I hope I get the part.
고마워. 배역을 맡으면 좋겠어.

Why? 왜 정답일까?

여자가 직업 박람회에 갈 수 없는 이유는 뮤지컬 오디션에 가야 하기(**Actually, on that day I have to go to an audition for a musical.**) 때문이다. 따라서 답은 ⑤ '뮤지컬 오디션에 가야 해서'이다.

- cover ⓥ 다루다
- volunteer ⓥ 자원봉사를 하다
- subject ⓝ 주제
- awesome ⓐ 멋진

08 우승 축하 행사

정답률 93% | 정답 ③

대화를 듣고, Dallers City Sharks의 우승 축하 행사에 관해 급되지 않은 것을 고르시오.

① 날짜 ② 장소 ✔ 경품
④ 입장료 ⑤ 반입 금지 물품

W : Dad, I can't believe our Dallers City Sharks won the National Baseball League Championship.
아빠, Dallers City Sharks가 내셔널리그 베이스볼 챔피언십에서 우승했다니 믿기지 않아요.

M : Yeah. This is the first championship in their 27-year history. The city's going wild.
그래. 이번에 27년 역사상 첫 우승이야. 도시가 열광하고 있어.

W : There'll be a big celebration to honor this historic victory.
이 역사적인 승리를 기념하기 위해 큰 축하 행사가 열릴 거예요.

M : Right. Look. There's an announcement about it on the team's website. 『It'll be held on Friday, November 1st.』 ①의 근거 일치
맞아. 봐봐. 팀 웹사이트에 그에 대한 소식이 있어. 11월 1일 금요일에 열릴 거야.

W : There's no way I'm going to miss it. 『It says the celebration will take place at Dallers City Sharks Stadium.』 ②의 근거 일치
저는 그것을 절대 놓치지 않을 거예요. 축하 행사는 Dallers City Sharks 경기장에서 열린대요.

M : I'm sure it'll be crowded. Oh, there's an admission fee.
틀림없이 붐비겠구나. 아, 입장료가 있네.

W : 『Yeah, it's $20 per person.』 Do you want to go with me, Dad? ④의 근거 일치
네, 인당 20달러예요. 저랑 같이 가실래요, 아빠?

M : Sure. Oh, look. 『There's a list of items that are banned. We're not allowed to bring fireworks or drones.』 ⑤의 근거 일치
물론이지. 오, 여길 봐, 반입 금지 물품 목록이 있네. 불꽃놀이나 드론은 가져갈 수 없어.

W : That makes sense. They can be dangerous in a stadium. Anyway, I can't wait to take part in the celebration!
일리가 있어요. 그건 경기장에서 위험할 수 있으니까요. 아무튼, 저는 축하 행사에 참여하는 게 너무 기대돼요!

Why? 왜 정답일까?

대화에서 **Dallers City Sharks**에 관해 '날짜, 장소, 입장료, 반입 금지 물품'을 언급하므로, 언급되지 않은 것은 ③ '경품'이다.

- historic ⓐ 역사적인
- ban ⓥ 금지하다
- admission fee 입장료
- stadium ⓝ 경기장

09 호텔 인턴십

정답률 95% | 정답 ⑤

Williamton Hotel Internship에 관한 다음 내용을 듣고, 일치하지 않는 것을 고르시오.

① 8주간 이어질 것이다.
② 근무 시간 동안 유니폼을 입고 있어야 한다.
③ 회의가 월요일 아침마다 있을 것이다.
④ 업무에는 음식 서비스와 테이블 세팅이 포함될 것이다.
✔ 종료 후 참가 인턴 중 절반이 호텔에 고용될 것이다.

M : Welcome to the Williamton Hotel Internship.
Williamton 호텔 인턴십에 오신 것을 환영합니다.
I'm Matthew Collins, the hotel manager.
저는 호텔 매니저 Matthew Collins입니다.
Let me provide some general guidelines for your internship.
인턴십에 대한 몇 가지 일반적인 지침을 알려 드리겠습니다.
『This internship will last for eight weeks starting today.』 You'll be working weekdays from 9 a.m. to 6 p.m. ①의 근거 일치
이번 인턴십은 오늘부터 시작하여 8주 동안 진행됩니다. 여러분은 평일 오전 9시부터 오후 6시까지 근무하게 됩니다.
『You must be dressed in your uniform during working hours.』 ②의 근거 일치
근무 시간 중에는 반드시 유니폼을 착용해야 합니다.
『Also, you should remember that there'll be a meeting each Monday morning at 9 in this seminar room, where you'll receive your tasks for the week.』 ③의 근거 일치
또한, 매주 월요일 오전 9시에 이 세미나실에서 회의가 있을 것이며, 회의에서 그 주에 있을 업무를 받게 된다는 것을 기억하세요.
『Your duties will involve food service and table setting.』 ④의 근거 일치
여러분의 업무는 음식 서비스와 테이블 세팅을 포함할 것입니다.
Our staff will be sharing all the details with you about how to perform your tasks and how you'll be evaluated.
저희 직원이 업무 수행 방법과 평가 방법에 대한 세부 사항을 여러분에게 이야기해 드릴 것입니다.
『After this internship, the top 10% of the interns will be employed by the hotel. Thank you.』 ⑤의 근거 불일치
이번 인턴십 종료 후, 인턴 중 상위 10%가 호텔에 고용될 것입니다. 감사합니다.

[문제편 p.115]

Why? 왜 정답일까?

인턴십 종료 후 참가 인원 중 상위 10%가 호텔에 고용된다(**After this internship, the top 10% of the interns will be employed by the hotel.**)고 이야기하고 있으므로, 내용과 일치하지 않는 것은 ⑤ '종료 후 참가 인턴 중 절반이 호텔에 고용될 것이다.'이다.

- **guideline** ⓝ 지침
- **perform** ⓥ 수행하다
- **evaluate** ⓥ 평가하다
- **duty** ⓝ 업무
- **task** ⓝ 업무
- **employ** ⓥ 고용하다

10 전자 도어 록 구매하기

정답률 87% | 정답 ③

다음 표를 보면서 대화를 듣고, 남자가 주문할 전자 도어 록을 고르시오.

Electronic Door Locks

	Model	Price	Case Material	Color	Fingerprint Recognition
①	A	$100	Plastic	Red	×
②	B	$120	Steel	Gold	×
✓	C	$170	Aluminum	Black	×
④	D	$190	Plastic	Blue	○
⑤	E	$220	Aluminum	Silver	○

W : Honey, we need to change the electronic door lock on the front door.
자기야, 우리 현관문의 전자 도어 록을 바꿔야 해.

M : Yeah. So I've been looking online to find a replacement.
응. 그래서 대체할 제품을 찾기 위해 내가 온라인으로 찾아보고 있어.

W : Have you found any good options?
좋은 선택지를 찾았어?

M : These five look promising. Take a look. What do you think?
이 다섯 가지가 좋은 것 같아. 한번 봐봐. 어떻게 생각해?

W : 「Well, I don't want to spend more than $200.」 근거1 Price 조건
음, 난 200달러보다 더 많이 쓰고 싶진 않은데.

M : 「Okay. How about the case material?」 근거2 Case Material 조건
알겠어. 덮개 재질은 어때?

W : Definitely not the steel one. It looks old-fashioned.
철제는 절대 안 돼. 너무 구식 같이 보여.

M : 「I agree. And, I don't like the red one.」 근거3 Color 조건
나도 동의해. 그리고 빨간 건 마음에 안 들어.

W : Yeah, it wouldn't go well with our door.
응, 우리 문과 잘 안 어울릴 거야.

M : Now, we're down to these two. Do you think we need the fingerprint recognition feature?
이제 이 두 개로 좁혀졌네. 지문 인식 기능이 필요할 것 같아?

W : 「I don't think we'll use it much. Let's choose the one without it.」
별로 많이 쓸 것 같진 않아. 그 기능이 없는 걸 고르자. 근거4 Fingerprint Recognition 조건

M : Sounds like a good choice. I'll order this one.
좋은 선택인 것 같아. 이걸로 주문할게.

Why? 왜 정답일까?

대화에 따르면 남자와 여자는 200달러 미만의, 철제가 아니고, 빨간색이 아닌, 지문 인식 기능이 없는 제품을 골랐다. 따라서 그들이 주문할 전자 도어 록은 ③ 'C'이다.

- **electronic** ⓐ 전자의
- **promising** ⓐ 좋을 것 같은
- **recognition** ⓝ 인식
- **replacement** ⓝ 대체품
- **go well with** ~와 잘 어울리다

11 치과 예약

정답률 94% | 정답 ②

대화를 듣고, 여자의 마지막 말에 대한 남자의 응답으로 가장 적절한 것을 고르시오.

① No problem. The dentist recommended this toothbrush.
문제없어요. 치과 의사가 이 칫솔을 추천해 줬어요.
✓ Thanks. I'll be able to get to my appointment on time.
고마워요. 예약 시간에 맞게 도착할 수 있어요.
③ Sounds great. I'll make an appointment for 3 o'clock.
좋아요. 3시로 예약할게요.
④ How unfortunate. The clinic is closed for lunch.
아쉽네요. 병원이 점심시간이라 문을 닫았어요.
⑤ Never mind. You can pay the parking fee later.
신경 쓰지 마세요. 주차 요금은 나중에 내시면 돼요.

W : Josh, it's already 3 o'clock! Isn't your dentist appointment at 3:30 today?
Josh, 벌써 3시야! 너 치과 예약이 오늘 3시 반에 있지 않아?

M : Oh, no. Mom, we've been chatting for so long! I think I'm going to be late. Can you give me a ride?
오, 이런. 엄마, 우리가 너무 오래 이야기했어요! 저 늦을 것 같아요. 차로 저를 태워다 주실 수 있나요?

W : Sure, I can do that. I'm free this afternoon.
물론이지, 그렇게 할 수 있어. 오늘 오후에 시간이 있단다.

M : Thanks. I'll be able to get to my appointment on time.
고마워요. 예약 시간에 맞게 도착할 수 있어요.

Why? 왜 정답일까?

남자는 치과에 늦을까 봐 차를 태워 달라고 한 상황(**Can you give me a ride?**)이다. 엄마가 흔쾌히 차로 데려다준다고 대답하였으므로 이에 대한 남자의 응답으로 가장 적절한 것은 ② '고마워요. 예약 시간에 맞게 도착할 수 있어요.'이다.

- **dentist** ⓝ 치과 의사
- **give ~ a ride** 차로 ~를 태워다 주다
- **appointment** ⓝ 예약

12 장바구니 목록 정하기

정답률 92% | 정답 ①

대화를 듣고, 남자의 마지막 말에 대한 여자의 응답으로 가장 적절한 것을 고르시오. [3점]

✓ Good idea. That way, we won't forget to buy what we need.
좋은 생각이야. 그렇게 하면 우리가 필요한 걸 사는 걸 잊지 않겠네.
② All right. Keep a daily record of how many calories you eat.
좋아. 당신이 얼마나 많은 칼로리를 섭취하는지 매일 기록해.
③ Too bad. Next time, bring a bag when you buy groceries.
안됐다. 다음에는 장 볼 때 바구니를 가져가.
④ Sorry. I should've checked where the onions were from.
미안해. 내가 양파의 원산지를 확인해야 했어.
⑤ That's true. We need to clean out the refrigerator often.
맞아. 우리 냉장고를 자주 청소할 필요가 있어.

M : Honey, I don't see any onions in the shopping bags.
자기야, 장바구니에 양파가 한 개도 안 보여.

W : Let me check. *[Pause]* Oh, we forgot to buy them again. And we also didn't remember to buy milk.
확인해 볼게. *[일시 정지]* 오, 우리 그것을 사는 걸 또 잊었네. 그리고 우유도 기억하지 못했어.

M : Well, how about making a grocery list before we go shopping next time?
음, 다음에 우리가 장보러 가기 전엔 구매할 식료품의 목록을 만들어 보는 건 어때?

W : Good idea. That way, we won't forget to buy what we need.
좋은 생각이야. 그렇게 하면 우리가 필요한 걸 사는 걸 잊지 않겠네.

Why? 왜 정답일까?

남자는 장바구니를 보며 사야할 제품이 몇 개 빠졌다고 이야기 하고 있다. 다음에는 목록을 만들자고(**Well, how about making a grocery list before we go shopping next time?**) 하였으므로, 여자의 응답으로 가장 적절한 것은 ① '좋은 생각이야. 그렇게 하면 우리가 필요한 걸 사는 걸 잊지 않겠네.'이다.

- **grocery** ⓝ 식료품

13 요리 수업 등록하기

정답률 98% | 정답 ④

대화를 듣고, 여자의 마지막 말에 대한 남자의 응답으로 가장 적절한 것을 고르시오.

Man: ______________________________

① Excuse me. You're not allowed to cook here.
실례합니다. 이곳에서는 취사 금지입니다.
② Thanks for refunding my class registration fee.
수업 등록비를 환급해 주셔서 감사합니다.
③ Excellent. Everyone's going to like your videos.
멋져요. 모두가 당신의 동영상을 좋아할 거예요.
✓ Okay. I'll wait until then to sign up for that class.
네. 그때까지 기다렸다가 그 수업에 등록할게요.
⑤ I prepared some Italian food for my students last week.
저는 지난주에 학생들을 위해 이탈리아 음식을 좀 준비했어요.

[Telephone rings.]
[전화기가 울린다.]

W : Hello, Benjamin Cooking Academy. How can I help you?
안녕하세요, Benjamin 요리 아카데미입니다. 무엇을 도와드릴까요?

M : Hi, I'd like to register for Chef Antonio's Italian cooking class for beginners.
Antonio 셰프의 초보자를 위한 이탈리아 요리 수업에 등록하고 싶어요.

W : All right. Chef Antonio teaches that class on two different days.
알겠습니다. Antonio 셰프가 다른 요일에 이틀에 걸쳐 그 수업을 가르칩니다.

M : When are they?
언제인가요?

W : He has a weekday class on Tuesdays and a weekend class on Saturdays.
화요일에는 평일 수업이 있고 토요일에는 주말 수업이 있습니다.

M : I'll take the weekend class because I can't do weekdays.
평일 수업은 수강을 못 하니 주말 수업을 들을게요.

W : *[Mouse clicking sound]* Oh, I'm sorry. That class is full this month.
[마우스 클릭 소리] 아, 죄송해요. 그 수업은 이번 달에 정원이 꽉 찼습니다.

M : Oh, no. I really want to learn from Chef Antonio. I'm a big fan of his online cooking videos. Will he teach the same class next month?
오, 안 돼요. Antonio 셰프님께 정말 배우고 싶어요. 저는 그의 온라인 요리 동영상을 매우 좋아해요. 그가 다음 달에도 같은 수업을 가르치시나요?

W : Yes, that's correct.
네, 맞습니다.

M : Can I register for that class now?
지금 그 수업에 등록할 수 있나요?

W : Sorry. Registration starts next Monday.
죄송합니다. 다음 주 월요일에 등록이 시작됩니다.

M : Okay. I'll wait until then to sign up for that class.
네. 그때까지 기다렸다가 그 수업에 등록할게요.

Why? 왜 정답일까?

남자는 정원이 꽉 찬 요리 수업을 수강하고 싶어(**Oh, no. I really want to learn from Chef Antonio.**) 한다. 따라서 남자의 응답으로 가장 적절한 것은 ④ '네. 그때까지 기다렸다가 그 수업에 등록할게요.'이다.

- **register** ⓥ 등록하다
- **weekday** ⓝ 평일
- **beginner** ⓝ 초보

14 자전거 타기로 인한 자신감 상승

정답률 92% | 정답 ②

대화를 듣고, 남자의 마지막 말에 대한 여자의 응답으로 가장 적절한 것을 고르시오. [3점]

Woman: ______________________________

① Don't worry. You'll learn to ride a bike quickly.
걱정하지 마세요. 자전거 타는 법을 빨리 배우실 거예요.
✓ That'll be nice. I hope that'll enhance my confidence.
그거 좋겠어요. 그것으로 제 자신감이 올라가길 바라요.
③ Yes. You haven't been physically active at all these days.
네. 요즘 신체 활동을 전혀 하지 않으셨잖아요.
④ Terrific. I'm glad you got a good score on the presentation.
멋져요. 당신이 발표에서 좋은 점수를 받아서 기뻐요.
⑤ Not really. I prefer watching team sports to individual sports.
사실 그렇지는 않아요. 저는 개인 스포츠보다 팀 스포츠 관람을 좋아해요.

M : Kristen, you seem worried. What's wrong?
Kristen, 걱정이 있어 보이는구나. 무슨 일이니?

W : Well, Grandpa. I'm feeling down these days. I did horribly in the coding competition last week even though I'd prepared really hard.
네, 할아버지. 요즘 기분이 안 좋아요. 매우 열심히 준비했는데도 지난주 코딩 대회에서 형편없었거든요.

M : It's all right. It happens to everyone.

괜찮아. 누구에게나 일어날 수 있는 일이란다.

W : It's not only that. I have a chemistry presentation coming up, and I'm afraid I'm going to mess that up, too.
그것뿐만이 아니에요. 곧 화학 발표가 있는데 그것도 망칠 것 같아 걱정돼요.

M : You've been working so hard on it that I'm sure you'll do great. Maybe you just need to boost your confidence.
그것을 매우 열심히 준비해 왔으니 너는 분명 잘할 수 있을 거야. 어쩌면 너는 단지 자신감을 높여야 할 것 같구나.

W : But I don't know how.
하지만 어떻게 해야 할지 모르겠어요.

M : How about getting involved in physical activities? You can go for a bike ride.
신체 활동에 참여하는 건 어때? 자전거를 타러 갈 수 있어.

W : How does riding a bike help boost my confidence?
자전거 타기가 자신감을 높이는 데 어떻게 도움이 되나요?

M : It causes the release of endorphins, which can lead to a boost in confidence.
자전거를 타면 엔도르핀이 분비되어 자신감이 상승할 수 있어.

W : Okay, I'll give it a try. But I don't want to ride alone.
알겠어요, 한번 해 볼게요. 하지만 혼자 타고 싶지는 않아요.

M : Why don't you join me? You know I ride a bike every evening.
나와 같이 타는 건 어떠니? 너는 내가 매일 저녁 자전거 타는 거 알잖아.

W : That'll be nice. I hope that'll enhance my confidence.
그거 좋겠어요. 그것으로 제 자신감이 올라가길 바라요.

Why? 왜 정답일까?

할아버지가 자신감이 부족한 손녀에게 같이 자전거를 타면서 자신감을 높여보자고 제안한다(Why don't you join me? You know I ride a bike every evening.). 따라서 여자의 응답으로 가장 적절한 것은 ② '그거 좋겠어요. 그것으로 제 자신감이 올라가길 바라요.'이다.

- competition ⓝ 대회
- boost ⓥ 높이다 ⓝ 상승
- ride ⓥ 타다
- mess up ~을 망치다
- give ~ a try ~을 해보다
- enhance ⓥ 올라가다, 강화하다

15 강아지 입양 허락 구하기

정답률 72% | 정답 ③

다음 상황 설명을 듣고, Roger가 Monica에게 할 말로 가장 적절한 것을 고르시오. [3점]

Roger: ______

① We'd better take our dogs for a check-up on a regular basis.
우리 개를 정기적으로 검진 받도록 하는 게 낫겠어.
② You'll have to spend a lot of money on feeding the puppies.
너는 강아지를 먹이는 데 많은 돈을 써야 할 거야.
✔③ I must ask my roommate if it's okay for me to adopt a puppy.
내가 강아지를 입양해도 괜찮은지 내 룸메이트에게 물어봐야겠어.
④ I'll gladly look after your pets while you're on your trip.
네가 여행 가 있는 동안 내가 기꺼이 네 반려동물을 돌봐 줄게.
⑤ You should get to know the dogs before adopting them.
너는 강아지들을 입양하기 전에 그들에 대해 잘 알아봐야 해.

W : Roger and Monica are close friends.
Roger와 Monica는 절친한 친구 사이입니다.
Monica has two dogs, and one of them gave birth to four puppies recently.
Monica는 두 마리의 개를 키우고 있는데, 그중 한 마리가 최근에 네 마리의 강아지를 낳았습니다.
Now, she's looking for someone to adopt one of the puppies because she cannot raise all of them by herself.
지금 그녀는 혼자서 그들 모두를 키울 수 없어 강아지 중 한 마리를 입양할 사람을 찾고 있습니다.
She asks Roger if he can adopt one.
그녀는 Roger에게 한 마리를 입양할 수 있는지 물어봅니다.
Roger's been thinking about raising a dog himself.
Roger는 개를 직접 키울 생각을 하고 있었습니다.
He knows how to take care of dogs since he's spent a lot of time with Monica's dogs.
그는 Monica의 개들과 많은 시간을 보냈기 때문에 개를 돌보는 방법을 알고 있습니다.
However, he's currently living with one of his co-workers.
하지만 현재 그는 동료 중 한 명과 함께 살고 있습니다.
So, Roger wants to tell Monica that he needs to first make sure that his roommate agrees with him adopting a puppy.
그래서 Roger는 강아지를 입양하는 것에 대해 먼저 자신의 룸메이트가 동의하는지를 확인해야 한다고 Monica에게 말하고 싶습니다.
In this situation, what would Roger most likely say to Monica?
이 상황에서 Roger는 Monica에게 뭐라고 말하겠습니까?

Roger : I must ask my roommate if it's okay for me to adopt a puppy.
내가 강아지를 입양해도 괜찮은지 내 룸메이트에게 물어봐야겠어.

Why? 왜 정답일까?

Roger는 강아지를 입양 받고 싶은데 동거인이 있어 허락을 구해야 하는 상황(So, Roger wants to tell Monica that he needs to first make sure that his roommate agrees with him adopting a puppy.)이다. 따라서 Roger가 할 말로 가장 적절한 것은 ③ '내가 강아지를 입양해도 괜찮은지 내 룸메이트에게 물어봐야겠어.'이다.

- give birth to ~을 낳다
- adopt ⓥ 입양하다
- currently ⓐⓓ 현재

16-17 빠른 동물들

M : Good morning, students.
안녕하세요, 학생 여러분.
「Today, we're going to learn about the key characteristics that enable some animals to reach high speeds.」 16번의 근거
오늘 우리는 몇몇 동물이 빠른 속도에 도달할 수 있도록 해 주는 주요 특징에 대해 알아볼 것입니다.
「First, there's no animal faster on land than the cheetah.」 17번 ①의 근거 일치
첫째, 육상에서 치타보다 더 빠른 동물은 없습니다.
Its flexible backbone and joints allow for extreme extension, enabling it to stretch its legs very far and push off its back legs with great force like a spring.
치타의 유연한 척추와 관절은 극도로 늘어날 수 있어서, 치타는 다리를 아주 멀리 뻗고 스프링처럼 큰 힘으로 뒷다리를 밀어낼 수 있습니다.
「Second, the falcon is one of the fastest birds.」 17번 ②의 근거 일치 Its large breastbone allows more muscle to be attached to it, so it can beat its wings with greater power.
두 번째로, 매는 가장 빠른 새 중 하나입니다. 매의 거대한 가슴뼈에는 더 많은 근육이 붙어 있어 매가 날개를 더 큰 힘으로 퍼덕일 수 있게 합니다.
「Third, the swordfish is among the fastest fish in the sea.」 17번 ④의 근거 일치 It releases a special, slippery oil from its head that coats the front of its body, enabling it to swim with less resistance.
세 번째로, 황새치는 바다에서 가장 빠른 물고기 중 하나입니다. 그것은 머리에서 특수한, 미끄러운 기름을 분비하여 몸 앞부분을 덮어서 저항을 덜 받고 헤엄칠 수 있습니다.
「Lastly, the dragonfly is considered the world's fastest flying insect.」 17번 ⑤의 근거 일치 It has the unique ability to slightly twist its wings as they swing down, causing a small tornado-like wind that gives it a boost of speed.
마지막으로, 잠자리는 세계에서 가장 빨리 나는 곤충으로 꼽힙니다. 잠자리는 아래로 방향을 바꿀 때 날개를 살짝 비틀 수 있는 독특한 능력이 있는데, 이것이 작은 회오리바람과 같은 바람을 일으켜 잠자리에게 속도의 증가를 가져다줍니다.
Now, let's watch a video of nature's speedsters.
이제 자연의 속도광들 영상을 함께 봅시다.

- loyalty ⓝ 충실
- depart ⓥ 출발하다
- abroad ⓐⓓ 승선하여, 해외로
- exclusive ⓐ 독점의
- specialty ⓝ 특별
- journey ⓝ 여행

16 주제 파악

정답률 86% | 정답 ①

남자가 하는 말의 주제로 가장 적절한 것은?

✔① features that allow certain animals to achieve high speeds
특정 동물이 빠른 속도를 낼 수 있게 해주는 특징
② effects of environmental changes on animal behaviors
환경 변화가 동물의 행동에 미치는 영향
③ difficulties that the fastest animals have in common
가장 빠른 동물들이 공통으로 겪는 어려움
④ reasons for certain species' faster growth over others
특정 종의 성장 속도가 다른 종보다 더 빠른 이유
⑤ hunting patterns of animals genetically close to humans
인간과 유전적으로 가까운 동물들의 사냥 양식

Why? 왜 정답일까?

남자는 특정 동물이 왜 빠른 속도를 가질 수 있는지 (Today, we're going to learn about the key characteristics that enable some animals to reach high speeds.)에 대해 이야기하고 있다. 따라서 남자가 하는 말의 주제로 가장 적절한 것은 ① '특정 동물이 빠른 속도를 낼 수 있게 해주는 특징'이다.

17 언급 유무 파악

정답률 98% | 정답 ③

언급된 동물이 아닌 것은?

① cheetah – 치타
② falcon – 매
✔③ iguana – 이구아나
④ swordfish – 황새치
⑤ dragonfly – 잠자리

Why? 왜 정답일까?

담화에서 남자는 빠른 동물들에 대한 예시로 '치타, 매, 황새치, 잠자리'를 언급하고 있으며, 언급되지 않은 것은 ③ '이구아나'이다.

Why? 왜 오답일까?

① 'First, there's no animal faster on land than the cheetah.'에서 '치타'가 언급되었다.
② 'Second, the falcon is one of the fastest birds.'에서 '매'가 언급되었다.
④ 'Third, the swordfish is among the fastest fish in the sea.'에서 '황새치'가 언급되었다.
⑤ 'Lastly, the dragonfly is considered the world's fastest flying insect.'에서 '잠자리'가 언급되었다.

Dictation 20

문제편 117쪽

01 to inform students and staff / scheduled to be repaired starting / be aware that
02 I've been bringing / a lot of protein to build / may cause calcium loss
03 difficulty developing good relationships with / how that can be frustrating / it'll contribute to building
04 new café we talked about last week / Whoever painted it is / brighten up the room
05 arranged for a bus to take / want me to text them the details / information about the artist beforehand
06 are you looking for / particular brand you have in mind / You'll get a 10% discount off
07 even be special lectures on / on that day I have to go to / bet you'll do great
08 an announcement about it on / it'll be crowded / items that are banned
09 will last for eight weeks / must be dressed in / how to perform your tasks
10 I've been looking / Definitely not the steel one / it wouldn't go well
11 Isn't your dentist appointment / give me a ride
12 forgot to buy them / making a grocery list
13 I'd like to register / a weekday class / I'm a big fan of
14 did horribly in the coding competition / to mess that up / don't want to ride alone
15 one of them gave birth to / raise all of them by herself / wants to tell Monica
16-17 enabling it to stretch / allows more muscle to be attached / the unique ability to slightly twist

[문제편 p.116]

21회 | 2024학년도 9월 모의평가 고3

| 정답과 해설 |

• 정답 •

01 ③ 02 ① 03 ② 04 ③ 05 ④ 06 ③ 07 ② 08 ④ 09 ⑤ 10 ⑤ 11 ④ 12 ① 13 ② 14 ③ 15 ① 16 ⑤ 17 ④

01 어린이 동물 캠프 안내

정답률 96% | 정답 ③

다음을 듣고, 여자가 하는 말의 목적으로 가장 적절한 것을 고르시오.

① 멸종 위기 동물을 소개하려고
② 동물원 관람 예절을 안내하려고
✔ 어린이 동물 캠프를 홍보하려고
④ 신입 동물 훈련사를 모집하려고
⑤ 야생 동물 보호를 독려하려고

W : Hello, viewers!
안녕하세요, 시청자 여러분!
Are you looking for a fun activity for your kids to enjoy on the weekend?
주말에 아이들이 즐길 수 있는 재미있는 활동을 찾고 계신가요?
Then, come and join our animal camp for kids.
그럼 아이들을 위한 저희 동물 캠프에 와서 함께하세요.
Happy Animal Friends Camp will be held every weekend in September.
Happy Animal Friends Camp가 9월 매주 주말 열립니다.
We'll provide hands-on activities with a wide variety of animals such as rabbits, turtles, and parrots.
저희는 토끼와 거북이, 앵무새 등 매우 다양한 동물과 함께하는 체험 활동을 제공합니다.
Your kids will learn how to care for and interact with the animals under the guidance of experienced trainers.
아이들은 경험이 풍부한 훈련사의 지도하에 동물을 돌보고 교감하는 방법을 배울 것입니다.
If your children like spending time with animals, sign them up for the Happy Animal Friends Camp!
자녀가 동물과 함께 시간을 보내는 것을 좋아한다면 Happy Animal Friends Camp에 등록시켜 주세요!
You can find more information on our website.
웹사이트에서 더 많은 정보를 얻을 수 있습니다.
Don't miss this great opportunity!
이 좋은 기회를 놓치지 마세요!

Why? 왜 정답일까?

아이들과 함께 즐길 수 있는 동물 캠프를 홍보하는(**If your children like spending time with animals, sign them up for the Happy Animal Friends Camp!**) 내용이므로, 여자가 하는 말의 목적으로 가장 적절한 것은 ③ '어린이 동물 캠프를 홍보하려고'이다.

- hands-on ⓐ 직접 하는
- parrot ⓝ 앵무새
- experienced ⓐ 숙련된

02 점심시간에 운동하는 것의 장점

정답률 95% | 정답 ①

대화를 듣고, 남자의 의견으로 가장 적절한 것을 고르시오.

✔ 점심시간에 운동하는 것은 활력과 집중력을 높인다.
② 개인의 건강 상태에 따라 운동 강도를 조절해야 한다.
③ 부상 방지를 위해 올바른 자세로 운동하는 것이 중요하다.
④ 규칙적인 운동은 정서 안정에 도움을 줄 수 있다.
⑤ 과도한 아침 운동은 업무에 방해가 될 수 있다.

W : Hey, Kevin! Where are you going?
안녕, Kevin! 어디 가요?
M : I'm going to take the staff fitness program.
직원 피트니스 프로그램을 하러 가고 있어요.
W : Oh, is it the 25-minute lunch break workout that the company is offering?
아, 회사에서 제공하는 25분짜리 점심시간 운동 말이에요?
M : That's right. I find that exercising at lunch time boosts my energy and helps me focus on my work.
맞아요. 점심시간에 운동하면 활력을 높이고 일에 집중하는 데 도움이 되더라구요.
W : Really? I think it would make me more tired. I usually just want to take a rest.
정말요? 그것 때문에 더 피곤해질 것 같아요. 전 보통 그냥 휴식을 취하고 싶어요.
M : I did, too. But I actually feel more energized after the lunch break workout. It even improves my concentration.
저도 그랬어요. 하지만 점심시간 운동 뒤에 전 실제로 활력이 더 넘치는 걸 느껴요. 집중력까지 좋아지고요.
W : You mean you have more energy and can focus better when you get back to your desk?
다시 자리에 왔을 때 힘이 더 나고 더 잘 집중할 수 있다는 말이에요?
M : Exactly. It's been very helpful for me.
맞아요. 저한테는 매우 도움이 됐어요.
W : Okay. Maybe I'll join. Thanks for the information.
알았어요. 저도 참여해야 할 것 같네요. 알려줘서 고마워요.
M : My pleasure.
천만에요.

Why? 왜 정답일까?

점심 시간 운동이 활력을 증진하고 집중력을 향상시키는 데 도움이 된다(**~ exercising at lunch time boosts my energy and helps me focus on my work.**)는 남자의 말로 보아, 남자의 의견으로 가장 적절한 것은 ① '점심시간에 운동하는 것은 활력과 집중력을 높인다.'이다.

- fitness ⓝ 건강, 적합성
- workout ⓝ 운동
- energized ⓐ 활력이 넘치는
- concentration ⓝ 집중

[문제편 p.121]

03 메모로 과제 관리하기

정답률 93% | 정답 ②

다음을 듣고, 여자가 하는 말의 요지로 가장 적절한 것을 고르시오.

① 정기적인 학습 상담은 학습 능률을 높여 줄 수 있다.
✔ 메모하는 것은 과제를 관리하는 데 효율적인 방법이다.
③ 자신만의 암기법을 활용하면 성적을 향상시킬 수 있다.
④ 두뇌의 균형적인 발달은 메모하는 습관으로 촉진된다.
⑤ 실천 가능한 계획 수립이 과제 해결의 출발점이다.

W : Good morning, students.
좋은 아침입니다, 학생 여러분.
I'm Ms. Thompson, your learning consultant for today's workshop.
저는 오늘 워크숍의 학습 컨설턴트인 Ms. Thompson입니다.
Many of you have expressed concerns that you're having difficulty submitting your homework on time.
여러분 중 많은 사람이 과제를 제때 제출하는 데 어려움을 겪는다는 걱정을 토로합니다.
But you know what? Making a memo is an efficient way to manage your assignments.
하지만 알고 있나요? 메모를 하는 것은 과제를 관리하는 효율적인 방법입니다.
You can't only rely on your memory.
기억력에만 의존할 수는 없습니다.
You need to make a note about what to do and when to do it so that you don't forget.
여러분이 뭘 해야 하고 언제 할지를 메모해서 잊지 않도록 해야 합니다.
Writing a memo might be annoying at first, but you'll get used to it in no time.
처음에는 메모를 쓰는 것이 성가실 수 있지만, 금방 익숙해질 겁니다.
With a memo, you can organize your assignments better.
메모를 하면 과제를 더 잘 정리할 수 있어요.
Now, we're going to see some good examples of students' memos. Let's look at the screen.
이제 학생들이 한 메모의 몇 가지 좋은 사례를 살펴보겠습니다. 화면을 보시죠.

Why? 왜 정답일까?

메모를 하면 과제를 관리하는 데 도움이 된다(**Making a memo is an efficient way to manage your assignments.**)는 내용이므로, 여자가 하는 말의 요지로 가장 적절한 것은 ② '메모하는 것은 과제를 관리하는 데 효율적인 방법이다.'이다.

- consultant ⓝ 컨설턴트, 자문 위원
- have difficulty ~ing ~하는 데 어려움이 있다
- efficient ⓐ 효율적인
- assignment ⓝ 숙제

04 새로 생긴 열람실 사진 구경하기

정답률 92% | 정답 ③

대화를 듣고, 그림에서 대화의 내용과 일치하지 않는 것을 고르시오.

M : Clara, I took a picture of the new reading room at our community center. Come and take a look!
Clara, 우리 주민센터에 새로 생긴 열람실 사진을 찍었어. 와서 봐!
W : Okay, Dad. Let me see. *[Pause]* Oh, look at the table in front of the window! 『There are three chairs at the table.』 ①의 근거 일치
네, 아빠. 보여주세요. *[잠시 후]* 오, 창문 앞에 있는 책상 좀 보세요! 책상 앞에 의자가 세 개 있네요.
M : You're right. So we can enjoy reading books together. 『How about the lamp standing in the left corner?』 ②의 근거 일치
맞아. 그래서 우리는 함께 독서를 즐길 수 있어. 왼쪽 구석에 세워진 램프는 어떻니?
W : Cool! It looks much taller than me. 『Wow, I love the star-patterned rug under the bookshelf.』 ③의 근거 불일치
멋지네요! 제 키보다 훨씬 큰 거 같아요. 와, 책장 밑에 있는 별무늬 깔개가 마음에 들어요.
M : It's nice, isn't it?
근사하다, 그렇지?
W : Yeah, we can also read books sitting on the rug.
네, 깔개 위에 앉아서 책을 읽을 수도 있어요.
M : And look! 『There's a heart-shaped cushion on the sofa.』 ④의 근거 일치
게다가 봐봐! 소파에 하트 모양의 쿠션이 있어.
W : It's so cute. Hmm... 『Dad, what's the board under the clock for?』 ⑤의 근거 일치
정말 귀여워요. 흠... 아빠, 시계 밑에 게시판은 왜 있을까요?
M : That's for introducing new events at the community center.
그것은 주민센터에서 하는 새로운 행사를 소개하려고 둔 거야.
W : I see. I want to go soon.
그렇군요. 빨리 가보고 싶어요.

Why? 왜 정답일까?

대화에서 책장 밑에는 별무늬 깔개가 있다(**Wow, I love the star-patterned rug under the bookshelf.**)고 하는데, 그림 속 깔개는 체크무늬이다. 따라서 그림에서 대화의 내용과 일치하지 않는 것은 ③이다.

- community center 주민센터

05 교통안전 교육 준비사항 점검하기

정답률 82% | 정답 ④

대화를 듣고, 여자가 할 일로 가장 적절한 것을 고르시오.

① 간식 준비하기
② 유인물 출력하기

③ 학교 체육관 예약하기 ✔강사에게 연락하기
⑤ 배너 배송 일정 확인하기

M : Ms. Jackson, the traffic safety education is just one week away.
Jackson 선생님, 교통안전 교육까지 겨우 일주일 남았네요.
W : You're right, Mr. Kim. I think it'll be helpful for our 1st graders since many of them are starting to walk to school.
맞아요, Kim 선생님. 그건 우리 1학년들한테 도움이 될 거 같아요, 많은 애들이 걸어서 등교하기 시작할 거니까요.
M : Shall we check if everything's ready?
다 준비됐는지 확인해 볼까요?
W : Sure. Let's see... Did you reserve the school gym?
물론이죠. 어디 볼까요… 학교 체육관은 예약하셨어요?
M : Yes, I did it yesterday.
네, 어제 했어요.
W : How about the traffic safety handouts?
교통안전 배부 자료는요?
M : I've already printed them out. Ah, do you know when the banner will be delivered?
이미 다 출력했지요. 아, 현수막은 언제 배달되는지 아세요?
W : Yeah, I checked it already. It'll arrive tomorrow.
네, 벌써 확인했어요. 내일 온대요.
M : Okay. Did you call the instructor?
좋아요. 강사님께는 전화하셨나요?
W : That's right! I almost forgot. I'll contact him this afternoon.
맞네요! 거의 잊고 있었어요. 오늘 오후에 연락할게요.
M : Great. And I'm going to prepare some snacks for the students.
좋아요. 그리고 전 학생들이 먹을 간식을 좀 준비할게요.
W : Good idea! The kids will love it.
좋은 생각이에요! 아이들이 좋아할 거예요.

Why? 왜 정답일까?

안전 교육 준비 상황을 점검하던 남자가 강사에게 연락을 해뒀는지 묻자 여자는 오늘 오후에 하겠다(**I'll contact him this afternoon.**)고 답한다. 따라서 여자가 할 일로 가장 적절한 것은 ④ '강사에게 연락하기'이다.

- **traffic** ⓝ 교통
- **safety** ⓝ 안전
- **reserve** ⓥ 예약하다
- **handout** ⓝ 배부 자료, 유인물
- **instructor** ⓝ 강사

06 미술관 티켓 사기

정답률 86% | 정답 ③

대화를 듣고, 남자가 지불할 금액을 고르시오. [3점]

① $60 ② $63 ✔$70 ④ $75 ⑤ $80

W : Hello, welcome to the Monet Art Museum. What can I do for you?
안녕하세요, Monet 미술관에 오신 것을 환영합니다. 무엇을 도와드릴까요?
M : Hi, I'd like to purchase admission tickets.
안녕하세요, 입장권을 구매하고 싶어요.
W : Sure. Tickets are $30 for adults, and $15 for children under 12.
그러시군요. 입장권은 어른은 30달러이고, 12세 미만 어린이는 15달러입니다.
M : My sons are both under 12. So, I'll get one adult and two child tickets.
제 아들들은 둘 다 12세가 안 됐어요. 그러니 어른 1장, 어린이 2장을 살게요.
W : Okay.
알겠습니다.
M : We're also interested in the kids' oil painting program. How much is it?
저희는 어린이 유화 프로그램에도 관심이 있어요. 얼마인가요?
W : It's $5 per child, and parents are welcome to join for free.
어린이 한 명당 5달러이고, 부모님은 무료로 참여하실 수 있습니다.
M : That's great. Then, two tickets for the program as well.
참 좋군요. 그럼 그 프로그램 티켓도 2장 살게요.
W : Okay. Do you want to join our annual membership? It's only $10, and you'll receive our monthly art magazine.
알겠습니다. 저희 연간 회원에 가입하시겠어요? 단돈 10달러이고, 저희 월간 미술 잡지를 받아보실 수 있어요.
M : No, thank you. Just the tickets, please.
괜찮습니다. 표만 살게요.
W : Alright. So, that's admission tickets for one adult and two children. And, two oil painting program tickets, right?
알겠습니다. 그럼, 어른 1명과 어린이 2명 입장권이요. 그리고, 유화 프로그램 티켓 2장요. 맞으신가요?
M : Perfect. Here's my credit card.
그렇습니다. 여기 제 신용카드요.

Why? 왜 정답일까?

대화에 따르면 남자는 어른 1인, 어린이 2인의 미술관 입장권을 샀고, 어린이 유화 프로그램 표도 2장 추가로 구입했다. 어른 입장권은 한 장에 30달러, 어린이 입장권은 15달러이며, 유화 프로그램 표는 5달러이므로, 식을 세워보면 '30+15×2+5×2=70'이다. 따라서 남자가 지불할 금액은 ③ '$70'이다.

- **art museum** 미술관
- **admission** ⓝ 입장
- **oil painting** 유화

07 컴백 콘서트에 가지 못하는 이유

정답률 97% | 정답 ②

대화를 듣고, 여자가 콘서트에 갈 수 없는 이유를 고르시오.

① 콘서트 티켓을 예매하지 못해서 ✔과학 토론 대회에 참가해야 해서
③ 아르바이트 대체 근무자를 찾지 못해서 ④ 부모님과 함께 여행을 가야 해서
⑤ 축구 경기에 출전해야 해서

M : Hey, Stella. Aren't you a fan of Miracle Girls?
안녕, Stella. 너 Miracle Girls 팬 아냐?
W : I sure am. Any good news?
그렇고말고. 좋은 소식이라도 있어?
M : They're going to have a comeback concert in our city next month.
다음 달에 그들이 우리 도시에서 컴백 콘서트를 할 예정이야.
W : Nice. I've been waiting so long to see them perform. When is the concert?
잘됐네. 난 오랫동안 그들의 공연을 보길 기다렸어. 콘서트는 언제야?
M : It's on October 6th.
10월 6일이래.
W : Oh, no! I can't make it.
오, 이런! 나 못 가.
M : Why not? Is it because you have to work at your part-time job?
왜? 아르바이트 해야 해서 그래?
W : No, it's not that. I could easily change my schedule with another person.
아니, 그게 아냐. 다른 사람하고 일정 바꾸는 건 쉬워.
M : What is it then? Don't tell me you have to play soccer.
그럼 뭔데? 설마 축구해야 해서는 아니겠지.
W : No. Actually, I have to join a science debate competition that day.
아냐. 사실, 나 그날 과학 토론 대회에 나가야 해.
M : Science debate competition? That's amazing! I'll keep my fingers crossed.
과학 토론 대회라고? 굉장하다! 행운을 빌어줄게.
W : Thanks. I hope I can make it next time.
고마워. 다음에는 갈 수 있음 좋겠다.

Why? 왜 정답일까?

여자는 가고 싶었던 가수 공연 날짜와 과학 토론 대회 날짜가 겹쳐 공연에 갈 수 없다고 하므로(**Actually, I have to join a science debate competition that day.**), 여자가 콘서트에 갈 수 없는 이유로 가장 적절한 것은 ② '과학 토론 대회에 참가해야 해서'이다.

- **debate** ⓝ 토론
- **competition** ⓝ 대회, 경쟁
- **I'll keep my fingers crossed.** 행운을 빌어줄게.

08 책 사인회 신청

정답률 92% | 정답 ④

대화를 듣고, Raven Elliott의 책 사인회에 관해 언급되지 않은 것을 고르시오.

① 날짜 ② 장소 ③ 시작 시간 ✔기념품 ⑤ 신청 방법

[Cell phone rings.]
[휴대 전화가 울린다.]
W : What's up, James?
잘 지냈어, James?
M : Hey, Amanda. What are you doing this Friday?
안녕, Amanda, 이번 주 금요일에 뭐해?
W : Not much. Why?
별일 없어. 왜?
M : Raven Elliott's book signing event is on Friday.
Raven Elliott의 책 사인회가 금요일에 있어.
W : Really? 「That's November 3rd, right?」 ①의 근거 일치
그래? 11월 3일이네, 맞지?
M : That's right. 「The event will be held at Pineway bookstore.」 You know, she released her new novel. ②의 근거 일치
맞아. 사인회는 Pineway 서점에서 열린대. 알다시피, 그분이 새 소설을 발표했잖아.
W : Yes, I know. I heard it's really good. 「What time does the event start? ③의 근거 일치
그래, 알고 있어. 책이 정말 좋다고 들었어. 행사는 몇 시에 시작해?
M : It starts at 7 p.m.」 Do you want to go?
저녁 7시에 시작해. 갈래?
W : Definitely! Do we need to sign up?
물론이지! 신청해야 하는 거야?
M : Yeah, I just did it. 「I'll send you the link to the form. You should fill it out and submit it soon.」 ⑤의 근거 일치
어, 난 방금 했어. 양식 링크 보내줄게. 빨리 그것을 작성해서 제출해야 해.
W : Thanks. I'll do it today.
고마워. 오늘 할게.
M : You'd better hurry! It's limited to only 100 people.
서둘러야 해! 100명 한정이야.
W : Got it.
알겠어.

Why? 왜 정답일까?

대화에서 남자와 여자는 Raven Elliott의 책 사인회에 관해 날짜, 장소, 시작 시간, 신청 방법을 언급하고 있다. 따라서 언급되지 않은 것은 ④ '기념품'이다.

Why? 왜 오답일까?

① '**That's November 3rd, right?**'에서 '날짜'가 언급되었다.
② '**The event will be held at Pineway bookstore.**'에서 '장소'가 언급되었다.
③ '**It starts at 7 p.m.**'에서 '시작 시간'이 언급되었다.
⑤ '**I'll send you the link to the form. You should fill it out and submit it soon.**'에서 '신청 방법'이 언급되었다.

- **signing event** 사인회
- **novel** ⓝ 소설
- **fill out** (서류를) 작성하다
- **limited to** ~에 한정된, 제한된

09 공원 청소 행사 홍보

정답률 87% | 정답 ⑤

Grandhill Park Cleanup 행사에 관한 다음 내용을 듣고, 일치하지 않는 것을 고르시오.

① 9월 30일에 열릴 것이다.
② 참가자들은 둘이서 짝을 이루어 쓰레기를 주울 것이다.
③ 유명 인사들이 참가할 것이다.
④ 모든 참가자들은 에코백을 받을 것이다.
✔참가자들은 쓰레기봉투와 장갑을 가져와야 한다.

M : Hello, listeners. I'm John Anderson, president of Greenism, an environmental volunteering group.
안녕하세요, 청취자 여러분. 저는 환경 봉사 단체인 Greenism의 회장인 John Anderson입니다.
「We'll be holding the Grandhill Park Cleanup event on September 30th.」 ①의 근거 일치
우리는 9월 30일에 Grandhill Park Cleanup 행사를 개최할 예정입니다.
Come and help clean up the local park!
오셔서 지역 공원의 청소를 도와주세요!

[문제편 p.121]

『In this event, participants will pick up trash in pairs.』 ②의 근거 일치
이 행사에서, 참가자들은 둘씩 짝을 이루어 쓰레기를 줍게 될 것입니다.
It'll be good for the environment and our community.
이것은 환경과 우리 지역사회에 도움이 될 것입니다.
『Over 20 celebrities will join in our event, including local influencers and entertainers.』
지역 인플루언서와 연예인을 포함하여, 20명이 넘는 유명 인사들이 우리 행사에 참여할 것입니다. ③의 근거 일치
I'm sure you'll have a meaningful time enjoying the beautiful scenery.
분명 아름다운 경치를 즐기며 의미 있는 시간을 보내시게 될 겁니다.
『At the end of the event, all participants will be given an eco bag made from recycled materials.』 ④의 근거 일치
행사가 끝나면 참가자 전원에게 재활용 소재로 만든 에코백을 드릴 겁니다.
『You don't need to bring trash bags and gloves. We'll provide them!』 ⑤의 근거 불일치
쓰레기봉투와 장갑은 가져오실 필요가 없습니다. 저희가 제공해 드립니다!
I look forward to seeing you all there!
여러분 모두를 만나 뵙기를 고대합니다!

Why? 왜 정답일까?

'**You don't need to bring trash bags and gloves. We'll provide them!**'에서 쓰레기봉투와 장갑은 제공되므로 가져올 필요가 없다고 한다. 따라서 내용과 일치하지 않는 것은 ⑤ '참가자들은 쓰레기봉투와 장갑을 가져와야 한다.'이다.

Why? 왜 오답일까?

① '**We'll be holding the Grandhill Park Cleanup event on September 30th.**'의 내용과 일치한다.
② '**In this event, participants will pick up trash in pairs.**'의 내용과 일치한다.
③ '**Over 20 celebrities will join in our event, including local influencers and entertainers.**'의 내용과 일치한다.
④ '**~ all participants will be given an eco bag made from recycled materials.**'의 내용과 일치한다.

- **trash** ⓝ 쓰레기
- **in pairs** 짝지어서
- **celebrity** ⓝ 유명 인사
- **scenery** ⓝ 경치

10 방과 후 운동 수업 고르기
정답률 84% | 정답 ⑤

다음 표를 보면서 대화를 듣고, 여자가 수강할 스포츠 프로그램을 고르시오.

After-school Sports Programs

	Program	Sport	Grade	Day	Equipment provided
①	A	Volleyball	All	Monday	○
②	B	Baseball	All	Tuesday	○
③	C	Soccer	3rd	Wednesday	×
④	D	Badminton	1st & 2nd	Thursday	×
✓	E	Table tennis	2nd & 3rd	Friday	○

M : Anna, what are you doing on your tablet?
Anna, 태블릿으로 뭐 하고 있어?
W : I'm checking out the list of after-school sports programs. Did you pick one?
방과 후 스포츠 프로그램 목록을 확인하고 있어. 너도 골랐어?
M : No, I'm learning computer programming this time. Do you want some help?
아니, 이번엔 컴퓨터 프로그래밍을 배울 거야. 내가 도와줄까?
W : Sure.
그래.
M : 『Which sports do you like?
넌 어떤 스포츠를 좋아해? 근거1 Sport 조건
W : Anything but baseball.』 I don't like baseball that much.
야구 빼고 다. 난 야구를 별로 안 좋아해.
M : Okay. This one is out. 『Some programs are limited to certain grades.
알았어. 이건 안 되겠네. 몇몇 프로그램은 특정 학년에만 한정돼 있네.
W : Yeah. We're in 2nd grade, so I cannot take this one.』 근거2 Grade 조건
맞아. 우린 2학년이라서, 나는 이건 못 들어.
M : 『What about the day?
요일은 어때?
W : Hmm... I have a piano lesson on Mondays, so that day doesn't work for me.』
음... 월요일마다 피아노 레슨이 있어서 그때는 나랑 안 맞아. 근거3 Day 조건
M : Now you have two options.
이제 두 가지 선택지가 있네.
W : Well, the school provides equipment for this program but not for the other one.
그런데, 학교에서 이 프로그램에는 장비를 제공해주는데, 다른 프로그램에는 제공하지 않네.
M : Which one do you like more?
어느 쪽이 더 좋아? 근거4 Equipment provided 조건
W : 『I like this program better, and the school provides equipment for it.』 So I'll take this one.
난 이 프로그램이 더 마음에 들어, 게다가 학교에서 장비도 주고. 그러니 난 이걸로 할래.

Why? 왜 정답일까?

대화에 따르면 여자는 야구가 아니면서, 2학년생이 들을 수 있고, 월요일에 열리지 않으면서, 장비가 제공되는 프로그램을 고르기로 했다. 따라서 여자가 수강할 스포츠 프로그램은 ⑤ '**E**'이다.

- **anything but** ~만 빼고 전부
- **equipment** ⓝ 장비

11 저녁식사로 피자 주문하기
정답률 95% | 정답 ④

대화를 듣고, 남자의 마지막 말에 대한 여자의 응답으로 가장 적절한 것을 고르시오.

① Why don't you download the app first? – 먼저 앱을 다운받는 게 어때요?
② I agree! We can open a new pizza place. – 맞는 말이에요! 우리는 새로운 피자 가게를 열 수 있어요.
③ Really? I wonder why they don't deliver. – 정말요? 거기서 왜 배달을 안 하는지 궁금하네요.
✓ That's great! Can you order the pizza now? – 잘됐네요! 지금 그 피자를 주문해줄래요?
⑤ Okay. I'll attend the meeting in person then. – 알겠어요. 그럼 내가 직접 회의에 참석할게요.

M : Honey, shall we go to the new pizza place that you keep talking about?
여보, 당신이 계속 얘기하는 새로 연 피자집에 갈까요?
W : I'd really love to. But I have to stay home to attend an online meeting soon. Do they deliver?
그럼 좋죠. 그런데 곧 온라인 회의에 참석해야 해서 집에 있어야 해요. 거기 배달돼요?
M : Let me check the delivery app. *[Tapping sound]* Yep, they have delivery service. Oh, they have shrimp pizza, your favorite.
배달 앱을 확인해 볼게요. *[톡톡 누르는 소리]* 네, 배달 서비스가 있네요. 오, 당신이 제일 좋아하는 새우 피자가 있어요.
W : That's great! Can you order the pizza now?
잘됐네요! 지금 그 피자를 주문해줄래요?

Why? 왜 정답일까?

여자가 온라인 회의 때문에 집에 있어야 하니 피자를 배달시켜 먹자고 하자, 남자는 여자가 좋아하는 새우 피자가 배달 메뉴에 있다고 알려준다(**Yep, they have delivery service. Oh, they have shrimp pizza, your favorite.**). 따라서 여자의 응답으로 가장 적절한 것은 ④ '잘됐네요! 지금 그 피자를 주문해줄래요?'이다.

- **delivery** ⓝ 배달, 배송
- **shrimp** ⓝ 새우

12 수학여행 중 추운 밤 날씨에 대비하도록 조언하기
정답률 88% | 정답 ①

대화를 듣고, 여자의 마지막 말에 대한 남자의 응답으로 가장 적절한 것을 고르시오.

✓ That's a good idea. You'd better take it. – 좋은 생각이네. 그걸 가져가는 게 좋을 거야.
② Sorry, but you're not allowed to go outside. – 미안하지만 넌 밖에 나가면 안 돼.
③ Cheer up. We'll take a trip to the mountains. – 기운 내. 우리는 산으로 여행을 갈 거야.
④ That's true. We saw a shooting star last night. – 맞아. 우리는 어젯밤에 별똥별을 봤어.
⑤ Don't worry. I can give you a ride to your school. – 걱정하지 마. 내가 너를 학교까지 태워다줄 수 있어.

W : Dad, I'm so excited. It's my first time to go on a school trip to the mountains in the fall.
아빠, 저 너무 신나요. 가을에 산으로 수학여행 가는 건 처음이에요.
M : Right. It'll be especially great to look at the stars outside. Maybe you'll need something to keep yourself warm because it's getting colder at night.
그래. 밖에서 별을 보면 특히 좋을 거야. 아마 넌 몸을 따뜻하게 해줄 게 필요할 거야, 밤에는 더 추워지니까.
W : So, do you think I should bring my little blanket?
그러면, 작은 담요를 가져갈까요?
M : That's a good idea. You'd better take it.
좋은 생각이네. 그걸 가져가는 게 좋을 거야.

Why? 왜 정답일까?

밤에는 쌀쌀하니 보온용 물품을 챙겨가라는 남자에게 여자는 작은 담요를 가져가면 될지 물어보고 있다(**So, do you think I should bring my little blanket?**). 따라서 남자의 응답으로 가장 적절한 것은 ① '좋은 생각이네. 그걸 가져가는 게 좋을 거야.'이다.

- **school trip** 수학여행, 소풍
- **shooting star** 별똥별

13 수선된 의류를 찾으러 갈 시간 정하기
정답률 78% | 정답 ②

대화를 듣고, 남자의 마지막 말에 대한 여자의 응답으로 가장 적절한 것을 고르시오.

Woman: ____________

① Excellent! I'll see you at 7 p.m. on Sunday. – 좋습니다! 일요일 저녁 7시에 뵙겠어요.
✓ I'd appreciate it if you could do that for me. – 그래주시면 고맙겠습니다.
③ Why not? I want to pick them up right now. – 물론이죠. 바로 지금 그걸 가지러 가고 싶네요.
④ Please remember to fix the zipper on time. – 반드시 지퍼를 제때 고쳐주시길 바랍니다.
⑤ Well done! The repaired pants fit me well. – 잘됐네요! 수선된 바지는 저한테 잘 맞아요.

[Cell phone rings.]
[휴대 전화벨이 울린다.]
W : Hello?
여보세요?
M : Good afternoon, Ms. Ford. This is Fine Line clothing repair shop.
안녕하세요, Ford 씨. Fine Line 의류 수선점입니다.
W : Oh, hi.
오, 안녕하세요.
M : I'm calling to let you know that your pants are ready to be picked up.
바지를 찾아가실 준비가 다 되어서 알려드리려고 전화했어요.
W : The pants with the broken zipper? Wow! You fixed them earlier than expected.
지퍼 고장 났던 바지요? 와! 예상보다 빨리 고치셨네요.
M : Yes. Do you want to stop by and pick them up sometime today?
네. 오늘 언제 들러서 가져가실래요?
W : Actually, I'm out of town on a business trip, but I'll be back on Sunday. I can come in then.
실은 제가 출장으로 타지에 와 있는데, 일요일에는 복귀할 거예요. 그때 갈 수 있어요.
M : I'm sorry, but we're closed on Sundays.
죄송하지만, 저희가 일요일에는 닫습니다.
W : I see. Then, how late are you open this coming Monday?
그렇군요. 그럼 돌아오는 월요일 언제까지 오픈하세요?
M : We're open until 7 p.m.
오후 7시까지 영업합니다.
W : Hmm, I finish work at 6:30 p.m. I'm afraid I might be a little bit late.
음, 저는 오후 6시 30분에 퇴근해요. 죄송한데 제가 좀 늦을 수도 있겠어요.
M : It's alright. I can wait until you arrive.
괜찮습니다. 도착하실 때까지 기다릴 수 있어요.
W : I'd appreciate it if you could do that for me.
그래주시면 고맙겠습니다.

Why? 왜 정답일까?

수선을 맡겼던 의류를 수거해가기 위해 영업시간을 묻던 여자가 조금 늦게 도착할 것 같다고 하자, 남자는 여자가 올 때까지 기다릴 수 있다고 한다(**It's alright. I can wait until you arrive.**). 따라서 여자의 응답으로 가장 적절한 것은 ② '그래주시면 고맙겠습니다.'이다.

- **stop by** ~에 들르다
- **out of town** 타지에 있는
- **business trip** 출장

[문제편 p.122]

14 맨발 걷기 제안하기
정답률 94% | 정답 ③

대화를 듣고, 여자의 마지막 말에 대한 남자의 응답으로 가장 적절한 것을 고르시오.

Man: ______________________

① I know what you mean. You can stay home.
무슨 말인지 알아요. 당신은 집에 있어도 돼요.
② Absolutely. I would never go barefoot walking.
물론이죠. 난 절대 맨발 걷기 하러 안 가요.
✔ Sounds good to me. Let's try it this weekend!
좋은 것 같아요. 이번 주말에 해보죠!
④ It's my fault. I should've booked the event earlier.
내 잘못이에요. 내가 그 행사를 더 일찍 예약했어야 하는데.
⑤ I had a nice time there. You should do it.
난 거기서 즐거운 시간을 보냈어요. 당신도 해봐요.

W : Honey, do we have any plans this weekend?
여보, 우리 이번 주말에 뭐 계획 있어요?
M : Nothing special. Why?
특별한 건 없어요. 왜요?
W : I saw an interesting event in a brochure.
나 홍보 책자에서 흥미로운 행사를 봤어요.
M : Oh, yeah? What's that?
오, 그래요? 그게 뭔가요?
W : Barefoot walking in the woods. Have you heard of it?
숲속에서 맨발로 걷기예요. 들어봤어요?
M : You mean walking without shoes? That doesn't sound comfortable. Why would people want to do that?
신발 없이 걷는 거 말이죠? 별로 편할 거 같지 않아요. 사람들은 왜 그걸 하고 싶어 한대요?
W : According to the brochure, it's effective for relieving foot pain.
홍보 책자에 따르면, 이게 발 통증을 완화하는 데 효과가 있대요.
M : Really? My feet have been a little bit sore these days. How does it work?
정말요? 요즘 난 발이 좀 아팠어요. 어떻게 효과가 있는 거래요?
W : It works like a foot massage.
발 마사지 같은 역할을 한대요.
M : Aha! Walking in bare feet probably improves blood circulation.
아하! 맨발로 걷는 건 어쩌면 혈액순환을 좋아지게 해주겠군요.
W : Yes. Plus, it can help you reduce stress.
그래요. 게다가 그건 스트레스 해소에도 도움이 될 수 있어요.
M : It seems like barefoot walking will be good for both body and mind.
맨발 걷기가 심신에 다 좋은 것 같군요.
W : Exactly. I think we should do it.
맞아요. 우리도 해봐야겠어요.
M : Sounds good to me. Let's try it this weekend!
좋은 것 같아요. 이번 주말에 해보죠!

Why? 왜 정답일까?

여자는 맨발 걷기의 이점을 말하며 직접 해보자고 제안하고 있으므로(**Exactly. I think we should do it.**), 남자의 응답으로 가장 적절한 것은 ③ '좋은 것 같아요. 이번 주말에 해보죠!'이다.

- **brochure** ⓝ 홍보 책자
- **barefoot** ⓐ 맨발의 ad 맨발로
- **sore** ⓐ 아픈, 따가운
- **blood circulation** 혈액순환

15 영상 리뷰 날짜 조정하기
정답률 81% | 정답 ①

다음 상황 설명을 듣고, Jack이 Amy에게 할 말로 가장 적절한 것을 고르시오. [3점]

Jack: ______________________

✔ No problem. We can reschedule our meeting.
괜찮아. 우리 회의 일정을 변경하면 돼.
② Don't be upset. I'll record the interview for you.
속상해하지 마. 내가 너를 위해 인터뷰를 녹화할게.
③ Calm down. Did you call the computer service center?
진정해. 컴퓨터 서비스 센터에 전화했니?
④ I see. We can exchange your laptop for a new one.
알겠습니다. 우리는 고객님의 노트북을 새것으로 교환해 드릴 수 있습니다.
⑤ No way. Are you done editing the video clips?
말도 안 돼. 영상 편집을 끝냈니?

M : Jack and Amy are members of their high school orchestra club.
Jack과 Amy는 고등학교 오케스트라 부원이다.
They're creating a video to introduce their club at the freshmen orientation next month.
그들은 다음 달 있을 신입생 오리엔테이션에서 동아리를 소개할 영상을 제작하고 있다.
Jack records the orchestra during practice and interviews some members.
Jack은 연습 도중에 오케스트라를 녹음하고 몇몇 부원을 인터뷰한다.
Amy says she'll edit the video clips so they can review them in their meeting tomorrow.
Amy는 그들이 내일 모임에서 검토할 수 있도록 영상을 편집하겠다고 한다.
However, she cannot finish the work because her laptop suddenly stops working.
하지만 그녀는 노트북이 갑자기 멎어서 작업을 끝마칠 수 없다.
She takes her laptop to the computer service center, but it'll take two days to fix.
그녀는 노트북을 컴퓨터 서비스 센터에 가져가지만, 고치는 데 이틀이 걸릴 예정이다.
Amy feels bad that she cannot complete the work by tomorrow and calls Jack to explain.
Amy는 내일까지 작업을 못 마치게 되어 속이 상하고, Jack에게 전화해 설명한다.
Jack thinks that they have enough time to finish the video.
Jack은 그들이 영상을 마무리할 시간이 충분하다고 생각한다.
So Jack wants to let Amy know that it's okay and offer to change their meeting date.
그래서 Jack은 Amy에게 괜찮다고 알려주고 미팅 날짜를 조정하자고 제안하고 싶다.
In this situation, what would Jack most likely say to Amy?
이 상황에서, Jack은 Amy에게 뭐라고 말하겠는가?
Jack : No problem. We can reschedule our meeting.
괜찮아. 우리 회의 일정을 변경하면 돼.

Why? 왜 정답일까?

상황에 따르면 영상을 내일까지 못 끝내게 되어 속상해하는 Amy에게 Jack은 시간상 여유가 있으니 회의 날짜를 조정해보자고 제안하려 한다(**So Jack wants to let Amy know that it's okay and offer to change their meeting date.**). 따라서 Jack이 Amy에게 할 말로 가장 적절한 것은 ① '괜찮아. 우리 회의 일정을 변경하면 돼.'이다.

- **freshman** ⓝ 신입생
- **laptop** ⓝ 노트북

16-17 동물의 수면 패턴에 영향을 주는 요인

W : Hello, students.
안녕하세요, 학생 여러분.
As you know, sleep is common to all animals, but their sleep patterns vary in many ways.
여러분도 알다시피, 수면은 모든 동물에게 공통적이지만, 수면 패턴은 여러 면에서 다릅니다.
「Today, we'll learn what makes animals sleep differently.」 16번의 근거
오늘 우리는 무엇 때문에 동물이 다르게 자는지 배울 것입니다.
First, what animals eat can impact their sleep patterns.
첫째, 동물이 무엇을 먹는가가 수면 패턴에 영향을 줄 수 있습니다.
As grass has much fewer calories than meat, large grass-eating animals sleep only a few hours and spend the majority of their time eating.
풀이 고기보다 칼로리가 훨씬 적기 때문에, 덩치 큰 초식 동물은 단 몇 시간만 자고, 대부분 시간을 먹는 데 씁니다.
「Elephants sleep only three to four hours a day.」 17번 ①의 근거 일치
코끼리는 하루에 서너 시간만 자죠.
Second, temperature affects animals' sleep patterns.
둘째, 기온이 동물의 수면 패턴에 영향을 줍니다.
High temperatures can cause some animals to overheat.
고온은 몇몇 동물이 과열되게 할 수 있습니다.
「Thus, bats sleep during the day to avoid overheating.」 17번 ②의 근거 일치
따라서 박쥐는 과열되지 않으려고 낮 동안에 잡니다.
Next, another factor is the fear of dangerous meat-eating animals.
다음으로, 또 다른 요인은 위험한 육식 동물에 대한 두려움입니다.
「For protection against these hunters, sheep generally sleep closely together.」
양들은 이 사냥꾼들로부터 (자신들을) 보호하기 위해 일반적으로 가까이 붙어 잡니다. 17번 ③의 근거 일치
Finally, the living environment.
마지막으로, 생활 환경입니다.
「Flamingos live in shallow waters that contain high amounts of salt.」 17번 ⑤의 근거 일치
홍학은 많은 양의 염분을 함유한 얕은 물에 삽니다.
In such a harmful environment, there's no place for them to lie down.
이런 해로운 환경에는 누울 장소가 없죠.
This is a reason why flamingos sleep standing up.
그래서 홍학은 서서 잠을 자는 것입니다.
Now, let's watch a video clip.
이제 영상을 보도록 하죠.

- **grass-eating** ⓐ 초식의, 풀을 먹는
- **majority** ⓝ 대다수
- **temperature** ⓝ 온도
- **overheat** ⓥ 과열되다
- **meat-eating** ⓐ 육식의
- **closely** ad 가까이
- **shallow** ⓐ 얕은
- **endangered** ⓐ 멸종 위기에 처한
- **make up for** ~을 보상하다
- **factor** ⓝ 요인

16 주제 파악
정답률 91% | 정답 ⑤

여자가 하는 말의 주제로 가장 적절한 것은? [3점]

① survival strategies of endangered animals
멸종 위기 동물들의 생존 전략
② impacts of environmental changes on animals' diet
환경 변화가 동물의 식단에 끼치는 영향
③ methods animals adopt to make up for lack of sleep
동물들이 수면 부족을 보상하기 위해 취하는 방법
④ hunting patterns used by animals in the wild
야생에 사는 동물들이 사용하는 사냥 전략
✔ factors that affect animals' sleep patterns
동물들의 수면 패턴에 영향을 주는 요인

Why? 왜 정답일까?

동물의 수면 패턴이 각자 달라지게 만드는 요소를 알아보는 내용이므로(**Today, we'll learn what makes animals sleep differently.**), 여자가 하는 말의 주제로 가장 적절한 것은 ⑤ '동물들의 수면 패턴에 영향을 주는 요인'이다.

17 언급 유무 파악
정답률 97% | 정답 ④

언급된 동물이 아닌 것은?

① elephants – 코끼리
② bats – 박쥐
③ sheep – 양
✔ lions – 사자
⑤ flamingos – 홍학

Why? 왜 정답일까?

담화에서 여자는 수면 패턴에 영향을 끼치는 요인을 설명하기 위해 코끼리, 박쥐, 양, 홍학을 언급하므로, 언급되지 않은 동물은 ④ '사자'이다.

Why? 왜 오답일까?

① '**Elephants sleep only three to four hours a day.**'에서 '코끼리'가 언급되었다.
② '**Thus, bats sleep during the day to avoid overheating.**'에서 '박쥐'가 언급되었다.
③ '**For protection against these hunters, sheep generally sleep closely together.**'에서 '양'이 언급되었다.
⑤ '**Flamingos live in shallow waters that contain high amounts of salt.**'에서 '홍학'이 언급되었다.

[문제편 p.122]

Dictation 21

문제편 123쪽

01 our animal camp for kids / provide hands-on activities / spending time with animals
02 the staff fitness program / make me more tired / improves my concentration
03 difficulty submitting your homework on time / manage your assignments / annoying at first
04 standing in the left corner / the star-patterned rug / introducing new events
05 reserve the school gym / Did you call the instructor / I almost forgot
06 welcome to join for free / our annual membership / Just the tickets
07 have a comeback concert / a science debate competition / keep my fingers crossed
08 she released her new novel / fill it out / You'd better hurry
09 clean up the local park / Over 20 celebrities / will be given an eco bag
10 after-school sports programs / Anything but baseball / What about the day
11 attend an online meeting / they have shrimp pizza
12 keep yourself warm / bring my little blanket
13 clothing repair shop / out of town / I might be a little bit late
14 walking without shoes / relieving foot pain / improves blood circulation
15 at the freshmen orientation / take two days to fix / change their meeting date
16-17 animals sleep differently / some animals to overheat / for them to lie down

22회 | 2023학년도 9월 모의평가 고3

• 정답 •

01 ④ 02 ① 03 ⑤ 04 ④ 05 ③ 06 ③ 07 ④ 08 ⑤ 09 ⑤ 10 ② 11 ② 12 ④ 13 ② 14 ① 15 ① 16 ② 17 ③

01 버스 내 전화 통화 자제 요청

정답률 98% | 정답 ④

다음을 듣고, 남자가 하는 말의 목적으로 가장 적절한 것을 고르시오.

① 비상 시 대피 장소를 안내하려고
② 버스 출발 시간 변경을 공지하려고
③ 차량 운행 중 안전벨트 착용을 당부하려고
✔ 버스 내 휴대 전화 통화 자제를 요청하려고
⑤ 차량 내 무선 인터넷 연결 방법을 설명하려고

M : Good afternoon, Bolden Express Bus passengers.
안녕하세요, Bolden 고속버스 승객 여러분.
My name is Logan Campbell, and I'll be your bus driver today.
저는 Logan Campbell이며, 오늘 여러분의 버스 운전기사가 되어 드리겠습니다.
Before departing, I'd like to ask you to avoid talking on your cell phone on the bus.
출발하기 전에, 여러분께 버스에서 휴대 전화로 통화하는 것을 피해 주시기를 부탁드리려 합니다.
Loud conversations on the phone may bother the other passengers.
큰 소리로 통화하는 것은 다른 승객들을 방해할 수도 있습니다.
We kindly ask you to wait until you've reached your destination to talk on the phone.
목적지에 도착할 때까지 기다리셨다가 통화해 주시기를 간곡히 부탁드립니다.
If you must answer a call, please keep it short and lower your voice while speaking on the phone.
꼭 전화를 받으셔야 한다면, 통화는 짧게 해주시고 통화하는 동안 목소리를 낮춰 주십시오.
Thank you for your cooperation.
협조에 감사합니다.

Why? 왜 정답일까?

'Before departing, I'd like to ask you to avoid talking on your cell phone on the bus.'에서 남자는 버스 안에서 휴대 전화로 통화하는 것을 피해달라고 말하므로, 남자가 하는 말의 목적으로 가장 적절한 것은 ④ '버스 내 휴대 전화 통화 자제를 요청하려고'이다.

- **passenger** ⓝ 승객
- **depart** ⓥ 출발하다, 떠나다
- **avoid** ⓥ 피하다
- **loud** ⓐ 큰, 시끄러운
- **conversation** ⓝ 대화
- **bother** ⓥ 귀찮게 하다, 성가시게 하다
- **destination** ⓝ 목적지
- **answer a call** 전화를 받다
- **lower** ⓥ 낮추다

02 라디오 청취와 행복감 증진

정답률 99% | 정답 ①

대화를 듣고, 여자의 의견으로 가장 적절한 것을 고르시오.

✔ 라디오를 듣는 것은 행복감을 높여 준다.
② 인터넷 발달은 라디오의 대중화에 기여한다.
③ 노년층을 위한 멀티미디어 교육이 필요하다.
④ 대화할 때는 상대방의 말을 경청하는 것이 중요하다.
⑤ 라디오 프로그램 편성 시 청취 연령을 고려해야 한다.

M : Hi, Grandma. What are you doing?
안녕하세요, 할머니. 뭐 하고 계세요?
W : I'm listening to the radio. I really like it.
라디오를 듣고 있단다. 나는 라디오를 아주 좋아해.
M : I wonder why some people love the radio. It seems boring.
어떤 사람들이 왜 라디오를 좋아하는지 궁금해요. 지루할 것 같아요.
W : You may think so. But listening to the radio can increase your sense of happiness.
그렇게 생각할 수도 있지. 하지만 라디오를 듣는 것이 행복감을 높여 줄 수 있단다.
M : I don't understand.
이해가 안 돼요.
W : Well, by listening to a radio talk show, for example, you often feel like you're part of the conversation.
음, 예를 들어 라디오 토크 쇼를 들으면 종종 그 대화의 일부가 된 것 같은 기분이 들지.
M : Hmm... That makes sense.
흠... 일리 있는 말씀이에요.
W : Then, you feel emotionally connected and less lonely.
그러면 감정적으로 연결되어 있다고 느껴서 외로움을 덜 느낀단다.
M : And that can eventually make you happy, right?
그리고 그게 결국 할머니를 행복하게 만들 수 있군요, 그렇죠?
W : That's correct. Also, when you feel down, listening to the radio brings you joy and good laughs.
맞아. 게다가 우울할 때 라디오를 들으면 즐겁고 실컷 웃을 수 있게 되지.
M : Wow. I never thought that the radio has this much power.
우와, 라디오에 이렇게 큰 힘이 있다고 전혀 생각하지 못했어요.
W : See? Listening to the radio can boost happiness.
이제 알겠니? 라디오 청취는 행복감을 높여 줄 수 있어.
M : Now I understand why you love the radio so much.
이제 할머니가 왜 라디오를 그렇게 좋아하시는지 이해가 돼요.

Why? 왜 정답일까?

'But listening to the radio can increase your sense of happiness.'와 'Listening to the radio can boost happiness.'에서 여자는 라디오를 들으면 행복감이 증진된다고 언급하므로, 여자의 의견으로 가장 적절한 것은 ① '라디오를 듣는 것은 행복감을 높여 준다.'이다.

- **boring** ⓐ 지루한
- **sense of happiness** 행복감

- feel like ~처럼 느끼다
- emotionally ad 감정적으로, 정서적으로
- boost ⓥ 증진하다, 높이다
- make sense 일리가 있다
- lonely ⓐ 외로운

03 과일 농장 홍보 의뢰

정답률 97% | 정답 ⑤

대화를 듣고, 두 사람의 관계를 가장 잘 나타낸 것을 고르시오.

① 건축가 – 건물 주인
② 코딩 강사 – 수강생
③ 영양사 – 과일 도매상
④ 음식 평론가 – 요리사
✔ 홍보 회사 직원– 과일 농장 주인

[Telephone rings.]
[전화벨이 울린다.]

W : Good morning. Cathy Sullivan speaking.
여보세요. Cathy Sullivan입니다.

M : Hello, Ms. Sullivan. This is Josh Gordon from Gordon's Fresh Fruits.
안녕하세요, Sullivan 씨. Gordon's Fresh Fruits의 Josh Gordon입니다.

W : Hi, Mr. Gordon! How's this year's fruit harvest?
안녕하세요, Gordon 씨! 올해 과일 수확은 어떤가요?

M : This has been the best year since I started my farm. I've already begun packaging the summer fruits for sale.
제가 농장을 시작한 이후로 올해가 최고예요. 전 이미 판매용 여름 과일을 포장하기 시작했어요.

W : That's good to hear. How may I help you today?
좋은 소식이네요. 오늘은 뭘 도와드릴까요?

M : Well, I'd like to promote my fruit farm more actively on the Internet.
음, 저는 제 과일 농장을 인터넷에 더 적극적으로 홍보하고 싶어요.

W : In that case, we can make a digital banner and display it on personal blogs and social networking sites.
그런 경우라면, 디지털 배너를 만들어 개인 블로그와 소셜 네트워킹 사이트에 게시할 수 있어요.

M : That sounds like a good idea.
좋은 생각인 듯하네요.

W : Our advertisements will definitely help you attract new customers and increase your fruit sales.
저희 광고가 고객님이 새로운 손님을 유치하고 과일 판매를 늘리는 데 틀림없이 도움이 될 거예요.

M : Sounds wonderful. When can you start promoting my farm?
근사할 것 같네요. 언제 저희 농장 홍보를 시작할 수 있나요?

W : I'll ask my boss and call you back.
저희 사장님께 물어보고 다시 전화 드릴게요.

M : Great. Thank you.
좋아요. 감사합니다.

Why? 왜 정답일까?

'How's this year's fruit harvest?', '~ we can make a digital banner and display it on personal blogs and social networking sites.', 'Our advertisements will definitely help you attract new customers and increase your fruit sales.' 등에서 과일 농장주가 광고를 의뢰하는 상황임을 알 수 있으므로, 두 사람의 관계로 가장 적절한 것은 ⑤ '홍보 회사 직원 – 과일 농장 주인'이다.

- harvest ⓝ 수확 ⓥ 수확하다
- display ⓥ 보여주다, 전시하다
- attract ⓥ (고객을) 유치하다, 매혹시키다
- promote ⓥ 홍보하다
- advertisement ⓝ 광고
- call back (전화를) 회신하다

04 야외 수영장 사진 구경하기

정답률 93% | 정답 ④

대화를 듣고, 그림에서 대화의 내용과 일치하지 않는 것을 고르시오.

한 줄 해석

M : Honey, let's take Jack to the outdoor pool at the park across the road.
여보, Jack을 데리고 도로 건너편 공원에 있는 야외 수영장에 가죠.

W : Does the park have a pool?
공원에 수영장이 있어요?

M : Yes. Check out this picture I found on the Internet. 「Look! There's a see-saw in the pool.」
네. 내가 인터넷에서 찾은 이 사진을 확인해 봐요. 이것 봐요! 수영장에 시소가 있어요. ①의 근거 일치

W : I'm sure he'd want to go on it with you. 「And I see a painting of a dolphin on the slide.」
아이는 분명 당신하고 같이 그걸 타고 싶어 할 거예요. 그리고 미끄럼틀에 돌고래 그림이 있네요. ②의 근거 일치

M : Jack loves dolphins. I bet he'll go up and down the slide all day.
Jack은 돌고래를 좋아해요. 아이는 온종일 미끄럼틀을 오르내릴 게 분명해요. ③의 근거 일치

W : I think so, too. 「There's a striped bucket at the top of the slide.」 What's that for?
나도 그렇게 생각해요. 미끄럼틀 위에는 줄무늬 양동이가 하나 있네요. 무슨 용도죠?

M : Hmm... I think it pours out water every few minutes. 「Look at the two tents near the shower.」 ④의 근거 불일치
음, 몇 분 간격으로 물을 부어주는 거 같아요. 샤워기 근처에 있는 텐트 두 개를 보세요.

W : Those must be for changing clothes.
옷을 갈아입으라고 있는 것 같네요.

M : That's convenient. 「Oh, I see a bench between the trees.」 ⑤의 근거 일치
편리하네요. 오, 나무들 사이에 벤치가 하나 있어요.

W : We could sit there while Jack plays in the pool.
Jack이 수영장에서 노는 동안 우린 거기 앉아 있을 수 있겠어요.

M : Yeah. That'll be nice. Let's get ready to go.
네, 좋을 것 같네요. 갈 준비를 해봐요.

Why? 왜 정답일까?

대화에서 옷을 갈아입을 수 있는 텐트가 2개 있다고 하는데(Look at the two tents near the shower.), 그림에는 텐트가 1개 뿐이다. 따라서 그림에서 대화의 내용과 일치하지 않는 것은 ④이다.

- dolphin ⓝ 돌고래
- bucket ⓝ 양동이
- pour ⓥ 붓다
- change clothes 옷을 갈아입다
- get ready to ~할 준비를 하다
- slide ⓝ 미끄럼틀 ⓥ 미끄러지다
- at the top of ~의 위에
- every few minutes 몇 분마다
- convenient ⓐ 편리한

05 야외 음악회 준비하기

정답률 97% | 정답 ③

대화를 듣고, 여자가 할 일로 가장 적절한 것을 고르시오.

① 현수막 걸기
② 의자 배치하기
✔ 카메라 설치하기
④ 디제이 일정 조율하기
⑤ 마이크 상태 확인하기

W : Hi, Mr. Kane. How's the preparation going for tomorrow's outdoor school concert?
안녕하세요, Kane 선생님. 내일 학교 야외 음악회 준비는 어떻게 되어가고 있나요?

M : Hi, Ms. Anderson. I've been working on it all morning, and I just finished confirming the schedule with the DJ.
안녕하세요, Anderson 선생님. 아침 내내 준비 중이고, 방금 DJ와의 일정을 확인했어요.

W : Would you like me to help you with anything?
제가 뭐 도와드릴 거라도 있나요?

M : That would be great. There are still a few more things that need to be done.
그래 주시면 좋지요. 해야 할 일들이 아직 몇 가지 남았어요.

W : Okay. Do you want me to place the chairs for the audience?
좋아요. 제가 관객들을 위한 의자를 배치할까요?

M : No. That's not necessary. I have volunteers to do that this afternoon.
아니요, 그건 안 하셔도 돼요. 오늘 오후에 그 일을 할 자원봉사자들이 있어요.

W : I see. How about hanging up the banners? I don't see them anywhere.
그렇군요. 현수막을 거는 건요? 현수막이 보이질 않네요.

M : I'll take care of it when they arrive. Actually, it would be helpful if you set up the camera on the stage.
그게 오면 제가 할게요. 사실, 카메라를 무대에 설치해주시면 도움이 될 거예요.

W : Sure. I'll do that.
그래요, 제가 그걸 할게요.

M : Great! The camera is on that table. Thank you.
좋아요! 카메라는 저 탁자 위에 있어요. 고맙습니다.

Why? 왜 정답일까?

'Actually, it would be helpful if you set up the camera on the stage. / Sure. I'll do that.'에서 남자가 카메라 설치를 부탁하고, 여자가 응한 상황임을 알 수 있다. 따라서 여자가 할 일로 가장 적절한 것은 ③ '카메라 설치하기'이다.

- preparation ⓝ 준비, 대비
- place ⓥ 배치하다, 놓다
- necessary ⓐ 필요한
- hang up 걸다
- confirm ⓥ (맞음을) 확인하다
- audience ⓝ 관객, 청중
- volunteer ⓝ 자원봉사자

06 종이 예술 갤러리 입장권 사기

정답률 87% | 정답 ③

대화를 듣고, 남자가 지불할 금액을 고르시오. [3점]

① $45 ② $54 ✔ $63 ④ $65 ⑤ $70

W : Welcome to the Mentonberg Paper Art Gallery. How may I help you?
Mentonberg Paper Art Gallery에 오신 것을 환영합니다. 무엇을 도와드릴까요?

M : Hi. I need four admission tickets. How much do they cost?
안녕하세요. 입장권을 네 장 사려고요. 얼마인가요?

W : It's $15 per adult and $10 per child under the age of 13.
어른은 1인에 15달러이고 13세 미만 어린이는 1인에 10달러입니다.

M : My twin daughters are only 10 years old, so I'll get two adult tickets and two child tickets.
제 쌍둥이 딸들은 10살밖에 안 돼서, 어른 표 두 장과 어린이 표 두 장을 살게요.

W : Okay. So, you want four tickets.
알겠습니다. 그럼 네 장을 원하시는군요.

M : Yes. We're also interested in your special program. How much is it?
맞아요. 저희는 특별 프로그램에도 관심 있는데요. 얼마인가요?

W : You mean the "Traditional Paper-Making" program? It's $5 per person.
'전통 종이 만들기' 프로그램 말씀이신가요? 1인에 5달러입니다.

M : Good. All four of us would love to participate in the program.
좋아요. 저희 네 명 다 그 프로그램에 참여하고 싶어요.

W : All right. So, let me confirm. Admission tickets for two adults and two children. Plus, four special program tickets, right?
알겠습니다. 그럼, 확인해 드리겠습니다. 입장권 어른 2인, 어린이 2인. 추가로, 특별 프로그램 표 네 장, 맞으시죠?

M : That's right. Can I get the 10% resident discount off the total price?
맞아요. 총 금액에서 주민 할인 10퍼센트를 받을 수 있나요?

W : Sure. Do you have your IDs with you?
물론입니다. 신분증 갖고 계신가요?

M : Yeah. Here are our IDs and my credit card.
네, 여기 저희 신분증이랑 제 신용 카드요.

Why? 왜 정답일까?

대화에 따르면 남자는 가족과 함께 종이 예술 갤러리에 입장하기 위해 15달러짜리 어른 표 2장, 10달러짜리 어린이 표 2장을 구매하고, 추가로 5달러짜리 특별 프로그램 표도 4장 구매한 후, 총 금액에서 주민 할인 10%를 적용받았다. 이를 식으로 나타내면 '$\{(15\times2)+(10\times2)+(5\times4)\}\times0.9=63$'이므로, 남자가 지불할 금액은 ③ '$63'이다.

- admission ticket 입장권
- adult ⓝ 성인, 어른
- resident ⓝ 주민, 거주자
- cost ⓥ ~의 비용이 들다
- interested in ~에 관심이 있는

[문제편 p.127]

07 밴드 오디션에 가지 못한 이유

정답률 97% | 정답 ④

대화를 듣고, 여자가 밴드 오디션에 참가하지 않은 이유를 고르시오.

① 기타에 문제가 생겨서
② 몸 상태가 좋지 않아서
③ 졸업 시험을 치러야 해서
✔ 취업 면접 일정과 겹쳐서
⑤ 가족 행사에 참여해야 해서

M : Hi, Nancy. How are you today? I heard you were sick last week.
안녕, Nancy. 오늘 어때? 지난주에 아팠다고 들었어.
W : Hello, Scott. Yes. I had a stomachache but I'm all right now.
안녕, Scott. 맞아. 배가 아팠는데 지금은 괜찮아.
M : I'm glad to hear that. So, how was the band audition yesterday?
그 말을 들으니 기쁘네. 어제 밴드 오디션은 어땠어?
W : Actually, I didn't go to the audition.
사실, 나는 오디션에 가지 않았어.
M : Really? Why not? Did you have to do something with your family?
정말? 왜 안 갔어? 가족하고 일이 있었어?
W : Not at all. It had nothing to do with my family.
전혀 아니야. 가족하고는 아무 상관 없었어.
M : Was there a problem with your guitar again?
기타에 또 문제가 있었던 거야?
W : No. My guitar works just fine.
아니, 내 기타는 멀쩡해.
M : Then, why didn't you go to the audition?
그럼, 왜 오디션에 가지 않았어?
W : I had a job interview with a company I want to work for. Unfortunately, it was at the same time as the audition.
난 내가 가고 싶었던 회사에서 취업 면접을 봤어. 안타깝게도 오디션하고 같은 시간이었지.
M : Well, you were worried about what you should do after you graduate. How did the interview go?
음, 너는 졸업 후에 무엇을 해야 할지 걱정했잖아. 면접은 어땠어?
W : It went well. Thanks for asking.
괜찮았어. 물어봐줘서 고마워.

Why? 왜 정답일까?

대화에 따르면 여자는 밴드 오디션 시간과 취업 면접 시간이 겹치는 바람에(**I had a job interview with a company I want to work for. Unfortunately, it was at the same time as the audition.**) 오디션을 포기하고 면접을 봤다고 한다. 따라서 여자가 밴드 오디션에 참가하지 않은 이유로 가장 적절한 것은 ④ '취업 면접 일정과 겹쳐서'이다.

- **have a stomachache** 배가 아프다
- **work fine** 잘 작동하다
- **worried** ⓐ 걱정하는
- **go well** 잘 진행되다
- **have nothing to do with** ~와 관련이 없다
- **work for** ~에서 일하다
- **graduate** ⓥ 졸업하다

08 초콜릿 박물관 견학 계획

정답률 97% | 정답 ⑤

대화를 듣고, Kint Chocolate Museum에 관해 언급되지 않은 것을 고르시오.

① 위치 ② 개관 시간 ③ 입장료
④ 선물 가게 ✔ 휴관일

M : Ms. Brown. Have you decided where you're taking the students on the school trip next month?
Brown 선생님, 다음 달 학교 여행 때 학생들을 어디로 데려갈지 결정했어요?
W : Yes, Principal Thompson. We're going to the Kint Chocolate Museum.
네, Thompson 교장 선생님. Kint 초콜릿 박물관에 가려고요.
M : Oh, I've heard about that museum. 『It's located in the center of Queen's City, right?』 ①의 근거 일치
오, 그 박물관 들어봤어요. Queen's City의 중심부에 있죠, 그렇죠?
W : That's right. 『We're going to leave at 9 a.m. from the school because the museum opens at 10 a.m.』 ②의 근거 일치
맞아요. 박물관이 오전 10시에 문을 열기 때문에, 학교에서 오전 9시에 출발할 예정이에요.
M : I didn't know it takes an hour to get there.
거기 가는 데 한 시간이 걸리는 걸 몰랐네요.
W : It doesn't. But we wanted to make sure that we arrive early.
그렇게 걸리지 않아요. 그런데 일찍 도착하고 싶어서요.
M : Well planned! 『How about the admission fee?
잘 계획했네요! 입장료는 어떻지요?
W : Each entry ticket costs $12 and includes a chocolate-tasting event.』 ③의 근거 일치
입장권은 한 장에 12달러이고, 초콜릿 맛보기 행사가 포함돼 있어요.
M : The students will love it. I'm sure they'll want to buy some chocolates.
학생들이 무척 좋아하겠네요. 분명 아이들은 초콜릿을 좀 사고 싶어하겠어요.
W : Absolutely. 『The museum is famous for its gift shop, and it has various chocolate-related items.』 ④의 근거 일치
물론이죠. 그 박물관은 선물 가게로 유명하고, 다양한 초콜릿 관련 상품이 있어요.
M : Sounds great!
아주 좋네요!

Why? 왜 정답일까?

대화에서 남자와 여자는 **Kint Chocolate Museum**의 위치, 개관 시간, 입장료, 선물 가게에 관해 언급하므로, 언급되지 않은 것은 ⑤ '휴관일'이다.

Why? 왜 오답일까?

① '**It's located in the center of Queen's City, right?**'에서 '위치'가 언급되었다.
② '**~ the museum opens at 10 a.m.**'에서 '개관 시간'이 언급되었다.
③ '**Each entry ticket costs $12 ~**'에서 '입장료'가 언급되었다.
④ '**The museum is famous for its gift shop, and it has various chocolate-related items.**'에서 '선물 가게'가 언급되었다.

- **decided** ⓐ 결정한
- **museum** ⓝ 박물관
- **trip** ⓝ 여행
- **be located in** ~에 위치하다
- **in the center of** ~의 중심부에
- **admission fee** 입장료
- **famous for** ~로 유명한
- **make sure** 확실히 ~하다
- **entry** ⓝ 입장
- **various** ⓐ 다양한

09 야생 동물 사진전 안내

정답률 97% | 정답 ⑤

Endangered Animals Photo Exhibition에 관한 다음 내용을 듣고, 일치하지 않는 것을 고르시오.

① 3주 동안 지속된다.
② 멸종 위기 동물들의 사진 100장이 전시된다.
③ 사진 속 동물들이 멸종 위기에 처한 이유가 설명되어 있다.
④ 수익금 전액은 동물 보호 센터에 기부될 것이다.
✔ 멸종 위기 동물 포스터를 무료로 제공할 것이다.

W : Hello, listeners. If you're interested in wildlife photography, don't miss the Endangered Animals Photo Exhibition at the Kenton Cultural Center.
안녕하세요, 청취자 여러분. 만약 야생 동물 사진에 관심이 있으시다면, Kenton 문화 센터에서 하는 멸종 위기 동물 사진전을 놓치지 마세요.
『It starts on December 2nd, and continues for three weeks.』 ①의 근거 일치
이것은 12월 2일에 시작해서 3주 동안 계속됩니다.
Wildlife photographer, Richard Burrow, has taken pictures of many endangered species around the world.
야생 동물 사진작가 Richard Burrow가 전 세계의 많은 멸종 위기종 사진을 찍어 왔습니다.
『The exhibition displays 100 pictures of endangered animals, including birds and fish.』 ②의 근거 일치
전시회에는 새와 물고기를 포함한 멸종 위기 동물들의 사진 100장이 전시됩니다.
『Under the photographs, there are explanations for why the animals in the photos are in danger of extinction.』 ③의 근거 일치
사진 하단에는 사진 속 동물들이 멸종 위기에 처한 이유에 대한 설명이 있습니다.
Admission will be $20, and 『all the profits from the exhibition will be donated to an animal-protection center.』 ④의 근거 일치
입장료는 20달러이고, 전시회의 수익금 전액은 동물 보호 센터에 기부될 것입니다.
『At the end of the exhibition hall, posters of the endangered animals will be for sale at $5 each.』 ⑤의 근거 불일치
전시장의 끝에서 멸종 위기 동물의 포스터가 장당 5달러에 판매될 것입니다.
For more information, please visit the website, www.kentonculturalcenter.com.
더 많은 정보를 원하시면, 웹 사이트 www.kentonculturalcenter.com을 방문하세요.

Why? 왜 정답일까?

'**At the end of the exhibition hall, posters of the endangered animals will be for sale at $5 each.**'에서 멸종 위기 동물 포스터는 장당 5달러에 판매될 예정이라고 하므로, 내용과 일치하지 않는 것은 ⑤ '멸종 위기 동물 포스터를 무료로 제공할 것이다.'이다.

Why? 왜 오답일까?

① '**It starts on December 2nd, and continues for three weeks.**'의 내용과 일치한다.
② '**The exhibition displays 100 pictures of endangered animals, including birds and fish.**'의 내용과 일치한다.
③ '**Under the photographs, there are explanations for why the animals in the photos are in danger of extinction.**'의 내용과 일치한다.
④ '**~ all the profits from the exhibition will be donated to an animal-protection center.**'의 내용과 일치한다.

- **wildlife** ⓝ 야생 동물
- **explanation** ⓝ 설명
- **extinction** ⓝ 멸종
- **donate** ⓥ 기부하다
- **at the end of** ~의 끝에
- **endangered** ⓐ 멸종 위기에 처한
- **in danger of** ~의 위험에 처한
- **profit** ⓝ 수익(금)
- **protection** ⓝ 보호
- **for sale** 팔려고 내놓은

10 딸이 쓸 기내 휴대용 가방 사기

정답률 85% | 정답 ②

다음 표를 보면서 대화를 듣고, 두 사람이 주문할 기내 휴대용 가방을 고르시오.

Carry-On Bags for Kids

	Model	Price	Height(inches)	Color	Material
①	A	$35	14	Red	Plastic
✔	B	$50	16	Blue	Plastic
③	C	$70	16	Pink	Fabric
④	D	$95	18	Black	Fabric
⑤	E	$110	18	Purple	Aluminum

W : Honey. Could you come here and help me buy a carry-on bag for Sarah?
여보, 이리 와서 Sarah가 쓸 기내 가방 사는 걸 도와줄래요?
M : Of course. She's old enough to have her own carry-on bag for our family trip next month.
물론이죠. 아이는 다음 달 우리 가족 여행에 따로 기내용 가방을 가져가도 될 만큼 컸어요.
W : Right. Look at this website. There are five models to choose from.
맞아요. 이 웹 사이트를 봐요. 선택할 수 있는 제품이 다섯 개 있어요.
M : Hmm... 『How much should we spend?
흠... 얼마를 써야 할까요?
W : Let's not spend more than $100.』 근거1 Price 조건
100달러 이상은 쓰지 말죠.
M : That sounds reasonable. 『What about the size? How tall should it be?
그게 적당하겠네요. 크기는요? 높이가 얼마나 되어야 할까요?
W : The one that's 14 inches in height isn't big enough.』 근거2 Height 조건 She always likes to bring lots of toys and books with her.
높이가 14인치인 것은 충분히 크지 않아요. 아이는 항상 많은 장난감과 책을 가지고 다니고 싶어 하잖아요.
M : Okay. 『Do you think she'd like the black one?
그래요. 아이가 검은색 가방을 좋아할까요? 근거3 Color 조건
W : No. She doesn't like the color black.』 So, there are only two options left.
아니요. 그녀는 검은색을 좋아하지 않아요. 그러니 단 두 가지 선택권이 남네요.

[문제편 p.127]

M : 「I don't think the fabric one is practical. It'll easily get dirty. 근거4 Material 조건
천 가방은 실용적이지 않은 것 같아요. 쉽게 더러워지잖아요.
W : I agree.」 Let's order the other one.
동의해요. 다른 것으로 주문합시다.

Why? 왜 정답일까?

대화에 따르면 남자와 여자는 가격이 100달러를 넘지 않으면서, 높이는 14인치 이상 되고, 색상은 검은색이 아니면서, 소재는 천이 아닌 기내 휴대용 가방을 구입하려고 한다. 따라서 두 사람이 주문할 기내 휴대용 가방은 ② 'B'이다.

- carry-on bag 기내용 휴대 가방
- reasonable ⓐ 적당한, 합리적인
- fabric ⓝ 천, 직물
- easily ad 쉽게
- spend ⓥ 소비하다, 쓰다
- height ⓝ 높이
- practical ⓐ 실용적인
- get dirty 더러워지다

11 라벨을 함께 제거하자고 요청하기
정답률 90% | 정답 ②

대화를 듣고, 남자의 마지막 말에 대한 여자의 응답으로 가장 적절한 것을 고르시오.

① Sorry. I broke the bottles by accident. - 죄송해요, 제가 실수로 병을 깨뜨렸어요.
✔② Sure. Let's remove the labels together. - 물론이죠, 라벨을 함께 제거해요.
③ You shouldn't. Your hands are still dirty. - 하시면 안 돼요, 아빠 손이 여전히 더러워요.
④ I agree. Recycled paper bags are cheaper. - 동의해요, 재활용 종이가방이 더 저렴해요.
⑤ No problem. I'm going to order some bottles. - 문제 없어요, 제가 병을 좀 주문할게요.

M : Rachel, we have too many plastic bottles to throw away. Let's take them to the recycling area.
Rachel, 버릴 플라스틱 병이 너무 많구나. 이걸 재활용 구역에 갖다 놓자.
W : Okay, Dad. But wait. There are still labels on the bottles. They need to be removed first.
좋아요, 아빠. 그런데 잠시만요. 병에 아직 라벨이 있어요. 그걸 먼저 제거해야 해요.
M : Oh, you're right! Then, could you give me a hand?
오, 그러네! 그럼 나 좀 도와줄래?
W : Sure. Let's remove the labels together.
물론이죠, 라벨을 함께 제거해요.

Why? 왜 정답일까?

재활용 플라스틱 병을 내다버리기 전에 라벨을 제거해야 한다는 여자의 말에 남자는 동의하며 자신을 도와달라고 요청한다(Then, could you give me a hand?). 따라서 여자의 응답으로 가장 적절한 것은 ② '물론이죠, 라벨을 함께 제거해요.'이다.

- bottle ⓝ 병
- remove ⓥ 제거하다
- break ⓥ 깨다, 부수다
- cheap ⓐ 값싼
- recycling ⓝ 재활용
- give a hand 도와주다
- by accident 실수로, 우연히
- No problem. 문제 없어요.

12 회의 일정 조정 요청하기
정답률 94% | 정답 ④

대화를 듣고, 여자의 마지막 말에 대한 남자의 응답으로 가장 적절한 것을 고르시오.

① Sounds wonderful! That fits our budget.
멋지네요! 그건 우리 예산에 맞아요.
② Terrific! I'm glad we're done with the project.
아주 좋아요! 우리가 프로젝트를 끝내서 기뻐요.
③ Too bad. There's no ticket available for your trip.
안됐네요. 당신의 여행에 맞는 표가 없어요.
✔④ Okay. I'll reschedule the meeting and let you know.
알겠습니다. 회의 일정을 다시 잡아 알려드리겠습니다.
⑤ Thanks for offering. I'll be happy to join your team.
제안 고맙습니다. 당신 팀에 함께하게 되어 기쁩니다.

W : Daniel, I'm sorry but can we reschedule our project meeting? I cannot attend it tomorrow.
Daniel, 미안하지만 우리 프로젝트 회의 일정을 다시 잡을 수 있을까요? 제가 내일 모임에 갈 수가 없네요.
M : Oh. It's impossible to have this meeting without your presentation, Ms. Robinson. May I ask what the problem is?
저런, 당신의 프레젠테이션이 없으면 이 회의를 할 수 없어요, Robinson 씨. 무슨 문제인지 여쭤봐도 될까요?
W : Well, there was a last minute change to my business trip schedule. I'll be available any day after next Monday.
음, 제 출장 일정이 막바지에 변경되었어요. 다음 월요일 이후로는 언제든 가능해요.
M : Okay. I'll reschedule the meeting and let you know.
알겠습니다. 회의 일정을 다시 잡아 알려드리겠습니다.

Why? 왜 정답일까?

출장 일정이 바뀌어서 다음 주 월요일 이후로 회의에 참석할 시간이 난다는(I'll be available any day after next Monday.)는 여자의 말에 대한 남자의 응답으로 가장 적절한 것은 ④ '알겠습니다. 회의 일정을 다시 잡아 알려드리겠습니다.'이다.

- reschedule ⓥ (일정을) 재조정하다
- impossible ⓐ 불가능한
- last minute change 막바지 변경 사항
- available ⓐ (사람에게) 시간이 있는
- budget ⓝ 예산
- be done with ~을 끝내다
- attend ⓥ 참석하다
- presentation ⓝ 발표
- business trip 출장
- fit ⓥ 맞다, 적합하다
- terrific ⓐ 멋진, 대단한

13 고급 발레 수업 등록하기
정답률 97% | 정답 ②

대화를 듣고, 남자의 마지막 말에 대한 여자의 응답으로 가장 적절한 것을 고르시오.

Woman: ______

① Of course. I accept the instructor position. - 물론이에요, 저는 그 강사 자리를 수락할게요.
✔② Great. Let me sign up for the 8 p.m. class, then. - 좋아요, 그럼 오후 8시 수업 신청할게요.
③ Please write your name down on the waiting list. - 대기자 명단에 귀하의 이름을 적어주세요.
④ Thanks for the refund of my class registration fee. - 강좌 등록비를 환급해 주셔서 감사합니다.
⑤ Sounds exciting. Good luck on your ballet performance. - 신나겠네요, 발레 공연에 행운을 빌어요.

M : Good afternoon. Welcome to Swan Palace Ballet Studio.
안녕하세요. Swan Palace Ballet Studio에 잘 오셨습니다.
W : Hello. I'm here to register for one of your classes.
안녕하세요. 여기 수업 중 하나에 등록하려고 왔어요.
M : Great. We offer three levels of classes from beginner to advanced. Which class do you want to take?
좋습니다. 초급부터 고급까지 세 가지 수준의 강좌가 있습니다. 어느 수업을 원하시나요?
W : I'd like to take the advanced class.
고급 강좌를 수강하려고요.
M : Okay. Do you have any particular instructor in mind?
좋습니다. 마음에 둔 특정 강사가 있으신가요?
W : Actually, I do. I heard Gina Miller has a really good reputation.
사실 있어요. Gina Miller가 정말 평판이 좋다고 들었어요.
M : Indeed. She's a popular instructor. She has two advanced classes on Wednesdays, one at 7 p.m. and one at 8 p.m.
맞습니다. 그분은 인기 있는 선생님이죠. 그분은 매주 수요일 고급 강좌 두 반을 운영하세요. 오후 7시와 8시에요.
W : I think the 7 p.m. class would be good.
7시 수업이 좋을 것 같네요.
M : Sure. Let me check if there are any spots left. *[Typing sound]* Oh, her 7 p.m. class is full. Sorry.
알겠습니다. 남은 자리가 있는지 확인해 볼게요. *[타자 치는 소리]* 오, 7시 강좌는 꽉 찼네요. 죄송해요.
W : Hmm... Then, what about the 8 p.m. class? I really want to take her class.
음... 그러면 오후 8시 강좌는 어떤가요? 전 그 선생님 수업을 꼭 듣고 싶어요.
M : One moment, please. *[Pause]* Yes, there's one spot left.
잠시만요. *[잠시 멈춤]* 네, 한 자리 남았습니다.
W : Great. Let me sign up for the 8 p.m. class, then.
좋아요, 그럼 오후 8시 수업 신청할게요.

Why? 왜 정답일까?

여자는 인기 있는 강사의 고급 발레 수업에 등록하려고 하는데, 희망했던 7시 수업은 자리가 다 차서 8시 수업에 남아 있는 한 자리를 신청해야 하는 상황이다(Yes, there's one spot left.). 따라서 여자의 응답으로 가장 적절한 것은 ② '좋아요, 그럼 오후 8시 수업 신청할게요.'이다.

- register for ~에 등록하다
- advanced ⓐ 고급의
- instructor ⓝ 강사
- spot ⓝ (특정한) 장소, 자리
- beginner ⓝ 초급자 ⓐ 초급의
- have in mind ~을 염두에 두다
- popular ⓐ 인기 있는
- sign up for ~에 등록하다

14 친구의 테니스 경기에 오지 못한 이유 묻기
정답률 92% | 정답 ①

대화를 듣고, 여자의 마지막 말에 대한 남자의 응답으로 가장 적절한 것을 고르시오. [3점]

Man: ______

✔① Thanks for telling me. I'll call her and apologize.
얘기해줘서 고마워. 그녀에게 전화해서 사과할게.
② Good idea. Don't forget to bring your tennis shoes.
좋은 생각이야. 네 테니스화를 잊지 말고 가져와.
③ Not really. The match wasn't as good as I expected.
별로 안 그랬어. 경기는 내가 예상했던 것만큼 좋지 않았어.
④ Fine. Promise me you'll do your best to win the match.
좋아. 네가 그 경기에서 이기기 위해 최선을 다하겠다고 약속해줘.
⑤ I understand. I'll give you more time to finish the series.
이해해. 네가 그 시리즈를 다 볼 수 있도록 시간을 더 줄게.

[Cell phone rings.]
[휴대 전화가 울린다.]
M : Hello, Clara. What's up?
여보세요, Clara. 잘 지냈어?
W : Hi, Brian. I've been trying to reach you all morning. Why didn't you answer your phone?
안녕, Brian. 아침 내내 네게 연락하고 있었어. 왜 전화를 받지 않았어?
M : Sorry. I just woke up. What's the matter?
미안. 지금 일어났어. 무슨 일이야?
W : Jane had her tennis match early this morning. We promised her that we would come and cheer for her.
오늘 아침 일찍 Jane이 테니스 경기를 치렀잖아. 우린 그 애한테 가서 응원하겠다고 약속했었고.
M : Oh, right! That was this morning! I forgot.
아, 맞다! 그게 오늘 아침이었구나! 잊어버렸어.
W : Oh, no. How could you forget?
오, 이런. 어떻게 잊을 수가 있어?
M : I stayed up all night watching a fascinating TV series. I guess Jane's tennis match completely slipped my mind.
난 대단히 재미있는 TV 시리즈물을 보느라 밤을 꼬박 새웠어. Jane의 테니스 경기를 완전히 깜빡 잊었던 것 같아.
W : Well, after the match, Jane told me that she was disappointed because you didn't come.
음, 경기 후에 Jane은 네가 오지 않아서 실망했다고 내게 말했어.
M : Oh, I feel awful to have disappointed her.
오, 그녀를 실망시켰다니 마음이 안 좋네.
W : I think it would be good if you told her that you didn't mean to miss it.
경기를 놓칠 생각은 없었다고 그녀한테 말해주면 좋을 것 같아.
M : Thanks for telling me. I'll call her and apologize.
얘기해줘서 고마워. 그녀에게 전화해서 사과할게.

Why? 왜 정답일까?

친구의 테니스 경기가 있다는 사실을 깜빡 잊고 밤새 TV 시리즈물을 본 뒤 늦잠을 자 버린 남자에게 여자는 전화해서 일부러 안 간 것이 아니었음을 설명하라고 조언해준다(I think it would be good if you told her that you didn't mean to miss it.). 따라서 남자의 응답으로 가장 적절한 것은 ① '얘기해줘서 고마워. 그녀에게 전화해서 사과할게.'이다.

- reach ⓥ ~에게 연락하다
- stay up all night 밤을 새다
- slip one's mind 잊어버리다
- awful ⓐ 끔찍한, 지독한
- match ⓝ 시합
- fascinating ⓐ 대단히 흥미로운, 매력적인
- disappointed ⓐ 실망한
- apologize ⓥ 사과하다

15 드론 동아리 창설 권하기
정답률 87% | 정답 ①

다음 상황 설명을 듣고, Randy가 Angela에게 할 말로 가장 적절한 것을 고르시오. [3점]

[문제편 p.128]

Randy: ______________________

✔ Why don't you find members to form a drone racing club?
드론 경주 동아리를 만들 회원을 찾아보면 어때?
② I think you should become friends with the transfer student.
넌 전학 온 애랑 친구가 돼야 할 것 같아.
③ Practice more if you want to participate in the next race.
다음 경주에 참여하려면 더 많이 연습해.
④ Safety comes first when it comes to flying drones.
드론 날리기에서는 안전이 최우선이야.
⑤ How about buying a drone of your own?
네 드론을 사면 어때?

M : Angela transferred to a new school a few months ago.
Angela는 몇 달 전에 새 학교로 전학 왔다.
She has adjusted to life at the new school and has made many new friends.
그녀는 새 학교에서의 생활에 적응했고 새로운 친구를 많이 사귀었다.
However, there's one thing that she isn't happy about.
하지만 그녀가 아쉬워하는 것이 한 가지 있다.
Her previous school had a drone racing club, but her new school doesn't.
그녀의 예전 학교에는 드론 경주 동아리가 있었지만, 새 학교에는 없다.
One day, she meets Randy, one of her old club members, and talks about how much she misses flying drones together.
어느 날, 그녀는 예전 동아리 회원 중 한 명인 Randy를 만나서 함께 드론 날리던 것이 얼마나 그리운지 이야기한다.
Randy thinks that there could be some students in Angela's new school who would love racing drones.
Randy는 Angela의 새 학교에 드론 경주를 매우 좋아할 학생들이 있을 수 있다고 생각한다.
So, Randy wants to suggest to Angela that she look for members to start a drone racing club.
그래서 Randy는 Angela에게 드론 경주 동아리를 시작해볼 회원을 찾아보라고 제안하고 싶다.
In this situation, what would Randy most likely say to Angela?
이 상황에서, Randy는 Angela에게 뭐라고 말하겠는가?
Randy : Why don't you find members to form a drone racing club?
드론 경주 동아리를 만들 회원을 찾아보면 어때?

Why? 왜 정답일까?

상황에 따르면 새로 전학 간 학교에 드론 경주 동아리가 없어 아쉬워하는 Angela에게 Randy는 드론 경주 동아리 회원을 직접 찾아보라고 제안하려 한다(So, Randy wants to suggest to Angela that she look for members to start a drone racing club.). 따라서 Randy가 Angela에게 할 말로 가장 적절한 것은 ① '드론 경주 동아리를 만들 회원을 찾아보면 어때?'이다.

- transfer to ~로 옮기다
- previous ⓐ 이전의
- situation ⓝ 상황, 처지, 환경
- safety ⓝ 안전
- How about ~ing ~? ~하는 게 어때?
- adjust ⓥ 적응하다
- drone ⓝ 드론, 무인 항공기
- form ⓥ 만들다, 형성하다
- when it comes to ~에 관해서는

16-17 식물이 소통하는 이유

W : Good morning, students. Did you know that plants can send out messages?
안녕하세요, 학생 여러분. 식물이 메시지를 보낼 수 있다는 것을 알고 있었나요?
「Today, we're going to learn about the various reasons that plants communicate.」 16번의 근거
오늘 우리는 식물이 의사소통하는 다양한 이유에 관해 배우겠습니다.
First, plants communicate to call for help.
첫째, 식물은 도움을 요청하기 위해 의사소통합니다.
「When cotton plants are attacked by bugs, these plants send out a chemical signal to attract the bugs' natural enemy that eats them.」 17번 ①의 근거 일치
목화는 곤충에게 공격받을 때 화학적인 신호를 내보내서 그 곤충을 먹는 천적을 끌어들이려고 합니다.
Second, plants communicate to recognize their relatives.
둘째, 식물은 자기 친척을 알아보기 위해 의사소통합니다.
「When mustard plants recognize their family members by exchanging chemical signals, they grow shorter roots to avoid competing with one another.」 17번 ②의 근거 일치
겨자는 화학적인 신호를 교환하여 동종의 구성원을 알아보면, 서로 경쟁하는 것을 피하려고 뿌리를 더 짧게 기릅니다.
Third, some plants communicate with other plant species to scare insects away.
셋째, 몇몇 식물은 곤충을 겁주어 쫓아내기 위해 다른 식물 종과 의사소통합니다.
「For example, tomato plants use low vibrating sounds to attract other plants that produce a smell, which is unpleasant to insects.」 17번 ④의 근거 일치
예를 들어, 토마토는 낮은 진동음을 사용해 냄새를 뿜어내는 다른 식물을 끌어들이는데, 그 냄새는 곤충들에게 불쾌합니다.
Last, plants communicate to warn other plants and defend their territory.
마지막으로, 식물은 다른 식물에 경고하고 자신의 영역을 지키기 위해 의사소통합니다.
「Walnut trees spread toxic chemicals to hurt or kill plants nearby.」 17번 ⑤의 근거 일치
호두나무는 주위의 식물을 상하게 하거나 죽이기 위해 유독한 화학물질을 퍼뜨립니다.
It's their way of saying, "Stay away from me."
이것은 그들이 '내게서 떨어져'라고 말하는 방식입니다.
Now, let's watch some related videos.
이제, 관련된 영상을 몇 편 봅시다.

- send out 내보내다
- attack ⓥ 공격하다 ⓝ 공격
- recognize ⓥ 인식하다, 알아보다
- exchange ⓥ 교환하다
- scare away ~을 겁주어 쫓아버리다
- defend ⓥ 지키다, 방어하다
- non-verbal ⓐ 비언어적인
- call for help 도움을 청하다
- natural enemy 천적
- relative ⓝ 친척
- compete with ~와 경쟁하다
- unpleasant ⓐ 불쾌한
- stay away from ~에게서 떨어지다

16 주제 파악 정답률 91% | 정답 ②

여자가 하는 말의 주제로 가장 적절한 것은?

① positive effects of plants on insects
식물이 곤충에 미치는 긍정적인 영향
✔ diverse purposes of plant communication
식물 의사소통의 다양한 목적
③ different methods for controlling toxic chemicals
유독한 화학물질을 통제하는 다양한 방법
④ key aspects of non-verbal human communication
인간의 비언어적인 의사소통에 있어 핵심적인 측면
⑤ important roles of plants in balancing the food chain
먹이 사슬의 균형을 이루는 데 있어 식물의 중요한 역할

Why? 왜 정답일까?

'Today, we're going to learn about the various reasons that plants communicate.'에서 식물이 메시지를 내보내 의사소통하는 다양한 이유에 관해 알아보자고 하므로, 여자가 하는 말의 주제로 가장 적절한 것은 ② '식물 의사소통의 다양한 목적'이다.

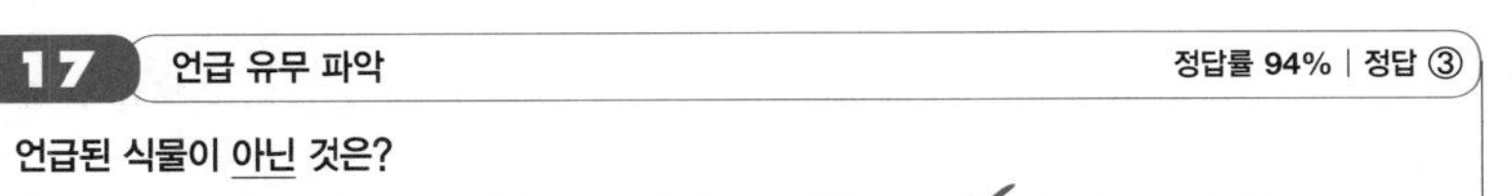

17 언급 유무 파악 정답률 94% | 정답 ③

언급된 식물이 아닌 것은?

① cotton plants – 목화 ② mustard plants – 겨자 ✔ pine trees – 소나무
④ tomato plants – 토마토 ⑤ walnut trees – 호두나무

Why? 왜 정답일까?

담화에서 여자는 식물의 의사소통을 설명하기 위해 목화, 겨자, 토마토, 호두나무를 언급하므로, 언급되지 않은 것은 ③ '소나무'이다.

Why? 왜 오답일까?

① 'When cotton plants are attacked by bugs, ~'에서 '목화'가 언급되었다.
② 'When mustard plants recognize their family members ~'에서 '겨자'가 언급되었다.
④ 'For example, tomato plants use low vibrating sounds ~'에서 '토마토'가 언급되었다.
⑤ 'Walnut trees spread toxic chemicals to hurt or kill plants nearby.'에서 '호두나무'가 언급되었다.

Dictation 22

문제편 129쪽

01 Before departing / avoid talking on your cell phone / lower your voice
02 It seems boring / emotionally connected and less lonely / can boost happiness
03 make a digital banner / attract new customers / promoting my farm
04 painting of a dolphin / go up and down the slide / striped bucket / for changing clothes
05 place the chairs / hanging up the banners / set up the camera
06 two adult tickets and two child tickets / would love to participate / let me confirm
07 how was the band audition / had a job interview / after you graduate / It went well
08 we arrive early / Well planned / famous for its gift shop
09 interested in wildlife photography / in danger of extinction / posters of the endangered animals
10 buy a carry-on bag / bring lots of toys and books / the fabric one is practical
11 still labels on the bottles
12 reschedule our project meeting / a last minute change
13 has a really good reputation / two advanced classes / any spots left / one spot left
14 stayed up all night / slipped my mind / awful to have disappointed her
15 a drone racing club / misses flying drones together / look for members
16-17 call for help / recognize their relatives / scare insects away

23회 | 2022학년도 9월 모의평가 고3

| 정답과 해설 |

• 정답 •

01 ⑤ 02 ① 03 ② 04 ③ 05 ① 06 ④ 07 ③ 08 ⑤ 09 ④ 10 ④ 11 ⑤ 12 ① 13 ② 14 ① 15 ⑤ 16 ③ 17 ④

01 문자 투표 독려하기

정답률 91% | 정답 ⑤

다음을 듣고, 남자가 하는 말의 목적으로 가장 적절한 것을 고르시오.

① 학생회장 선거 투표 결과를 공지하려고
② 음악 경연 대회 참가 신청을 권장하려고
③ 홈 쇼핑 가전제품 구매 방법을 설명하려고
④ 새로운 음악 프로그램 방송 일정을 안내하려고
⑤ 노래 경연 우승자 선정을 위한 투표를 독려하려고

M : Welcome back to the final episode of *Tomorrow's Singer*.
*Tomorrow's Singer*의 마지막 회에 다시 오신 것을 환영합니다.
We hope you enjoyed the performances of our two finalists.
저희 결승 진출자 두 명의 공연을 즐기셨기를 바랍니다.
Now, it's time to pick the winner of our singing competition.
이제, 저희 노래 경연 우승자를 뽑을 시간입니다.
Vote now by texting the name of your favorite contestant to the number at the bottom of your TV screen.
이제 TV 화면 하단에 있는 번호로 여러분이 좋아하는 출전자의 이름을 문자메시지로 보내서 투표하세요.
This is your last chance to help your favorite contestant become a super star.
이것이 여러분이 좋아하는 출전자가 슈퍼스타가 되도록 도울 수 있는 마지막 기회입니다.
You can also win exciting prizes just by voting.
여러분은 또한 투표를 하는 것만으로 멋진 상을 받을 수도 있습니다.
Remember voting closes in only five minutes.
투표가 5분 만에 종료된다는 데 유념하세요.
So, cast your vote now and decide who'll be tomorrow's singer.
그러니 지금 여러분의 표를 던져 누가 내일의 가수가 될지 결정하세요.
We'll be right back after a short commercial break.
짧은 광고 시간 후에 바로 다시 돌아오겠습니다.

Why? 왜 정답일까?

'Vote now by texting the name of your favorite contestant to the number at the bottom of your TV screen.'과 'So, cast your vote now and decide who'll be tomorrow's singer.'에서 좋아하는 참가자 이름을 문자메시지로 보내 투표해달라고 권하는 것으로 보아, 남자가 하는 말의 목적으로 가장 적절한 것은 ⑤ '노래 경연 우승자 선정을 위한 투표를 독려하려고'이다.

- finalist ⓝ 결승 진출자
- contestant ⓝ 출전자
- cast ⓥ 던지다
- commercial break (중간) 광고 시간

02 아이들이 집안일을 하는 것의 이점

정답률 91% | 정답 ①

대화를 듣고, 여자의 의견으로 가장 적절한 것을 고르시오.

① 아이들은 집안일을 함으로써 자존감을 높일 수 있다.
② 아이들의 나이에 맞는 균형 잡힌 식단 관리가 필요하다.
③ 집안일을 통해 아이들에게 경제관념을 심어 줄 수 있다.
④ 적절한 보상은 아이들의 독서 습관 형성에 도움이 된다.
⑤ 여행을 통해 아이들에게 가족의 중요성을 일깨워 줄 수 있다.

M : Honey, I just saw Amy folding laundry in the living room. Did you ask her to do it?
여보, 방금 거실에서 Amy가 빨래를 개고 있는 것을 봤어요. 당신이 걔한테 그 일을 하라고 시켰나요?
W : Well, she said she wanted to help with the housework.
음, 걔가 집안일을 돕고 싶다고 말했어요.
M : That's fine. But don't you think she's too young to do housework? She's just six years old.
잘됐네요. 그런데 집안일을 하기에는 너무 어린 것 같지 않아요? 걔는 고작 여섯 살이잖아요.
W : Maybe. But I think doing housework helps children improve their self-esteem.
그럴 수도요. 그런데 집안일을 하는 것이 아이가 자신의 자존감을 높이는 데 도움이 된다고 생각해요.
M : Why do you think so?
왜 그렇게 생각하나요?
W : I read in a book that when kids participate in housework, they feel like they're more important to the family.
아이가 집안일에 참여할 때 아이는 자기가 가족에게 더 중요해진 것처럼 느낀다고 책에서 읽었어요.
M : Hmm, that makes sense.
음, 일리가 있네요.
W : Besides, children often gain a sense of achievement from completing household tasks.
게다가, 아이는 흔히 집안일을 완수하는 데서 성취감을 얻어요.
M : Oh, and maybe it could help Amy to feel proud of herself, too.
오, 그리고 아마 그게 Amy가 또한 자신을 자랑스럽게 여기는 데 도움이 될 수도 있겠군요.
W : Exactly. That's why children who do housework often have higher self-esteem.
맞아요. 그래서 집안일을 하는 아이가 흔히 더 높은 자존감을 갖죠.
M : You're right. Then let's think about other kinds of housework Amy would enjoy.
맞는 말이에요. 그럼 Amy가 즐겁게 할 것 같은 다른 집안일에 관해 생각해 봅시다.
W : Sounds good.
좋은 생각이에요.

Why? 왜 정답일까?

'But I think doing housework helps children improve their self-esteem.'에서 여자는 아이들이 집안일을 하면서 자존감을 높일 수 있다고 언급한 후, 왜 그렇게 생각하는지 근거를 들고 있다. 따라서 여자의 의견으로 가장 적절한 것은 ① '아이들은 집안일을 함으로써 자존감을 높일 수 있다.'이다.

- improve ⓥ 높이다, 향상시키다
- self-esteem ⓝ 자존감
- participate in ~에 참여하다
- achievement ⓝ 성취

03 식당 장식을 위한 꽃 사기

정답률 96% | 정답 ②

대화를 듣고, 두 사람의 관계를 가장 잘 나타낸 것을 고르시오.

① 정원사 – 파티 플래너
② 꽃집 점원 – 식당 주인
③ 꽃꽂이 강사 – 수강생
④ 식물학 교수 – 행정실 직원
⑤ 잡지 편집장 – 음식 칼럼니스트

W : Hello, Mr. Miller. It's been a while. How's your business?
안녕하세요, Miller 씨. 오랜만이에요. 사업은 잘 되나요?
M : The restaurant is doing pretty good. Jessica, I'd like to buy some purple flowers.
식당이 꽤 잘 되고 있어요. Jessica, 자주색 꽃을 좀 사고 싶어요.
W : I'm sorry. We don't have any purple flowers right now. Why are you looking for that specific color?
죄송합니다. 지금 당장은 자주색 꽃이 없어요. 왜 딱 그 색깔을 찾고 계신가요?
M : I need that color to decorate my restaurant. My customer is having a company anniversary party, and its logo is purple.
제 식당을 장식하는 데 그 색깔이 필요해요. 저희 고객이 회사 기념일 파티를 열 예정이고 그 회사의 로고가 자주색이에요.
W : I see. When do you need the flowers?
알겠습니다. 그 꽃이 언제 필요하세요?
M : This Friday.
이번 주 금요일이요.
W : Okay. Shall I ask my boss to order purple lilies?
알겠습니다. 저희 사장님께 자주색 백합을 주문하라고 부탁할까요?
M : That'd be perfect. I didn't know there were purple lilies.
그러면 딱 좋겠어요. 자주색 백합이 있는 줄 몰랐어요.
W : They're rare and stand for pride and success. They'd be a great fit for this event in your restaurant.
그 꽃은 희귀하고 자부심과 성공을 나타냅니다. 그 꽃이 손님의 식당에서 있을 이번 행사에 딱 맞을 거예요.
M : Great to know. And I could put notes about the flower's meaning on the tables.
아주 좋네요. 그리고 꽃의 의미에 관한 메모를 테이블에 두면 되겠네요.
W : Good idea. My boss will call you with the details.
좋은 생각입니다. 저희 사장님이 세부 사항 관련해서 전화 드릴 겁니다.
M : Thanks for all your help.
도와주셔서 고맙습니다.

Why? 왜 정답일까?

'I'd like to buy some purple flowers.', 'I'm sorry. We don't have any purple flowers right now.', 'Shall I ask my boss to order purple lilies?' 등에서 여자가 꽃집에서 일하는 점원임을 알 수 있고, 'The restaurant is doing pretty good.', 'I need that color to decorate my restaurant.' 'They'd be a great fit for this event in your restaurant.' 등에서 남자가 식당 주인임을 알 수 있다. 따라서 두 사람의 관계로 가장 적절한 것은 ② '꽃집 점원 – 식당 주인'이다.

- specific ⓐ 특정한
- anniversary ⓝ 기념일
- stand for ~을 의미하다, 상징하다

04 리모델링한 북카페 사진 구경하기

정답률 95% | 정답 ③

대화를 듣고, 그림에서 대화의 내용과 일치하지 않는 것을 고르시오.

M : Hi, Jane. What are you doing?
안녕, Jane. 뭐 하고 있어?
W : Hi, Sam. I'm reading a blog about that book cafe we used to visit.
안녕, Sam. 우리가 가곤 했던 그 북카페에 관한 블로그를 읽고 있어.
M : Oh, I heard that it was recently remodeled.
오, 그곳이 최근에 리모델링했다고 들었어.
W : Right. Take a look at this picture of the first floor. 『I love the stairs next to the windows.』 ①의 근거 일치
맞아. 1층을 찍은 이 사진을 봐. 나는 창문 옆에 있는 계단이 마음에 들어.
M : Yeah, the view from the stairs is amazing.
그래, 계단에서 보이는 전망이 근사하네.
W : For sure. 『Do you remember the square clock on the wall?』 ②의 근거 일치
맞아. 벽에 걸린 정사각형 모양의 시계 기억나니?
M : Of course. It's been there since we first visited. 『Oh, there are two speakers beside the bookcase now.』 ③의 근거 불일치
물론이지. 그건 우리가 처음 갔을 때부터 거기 있었잖아. 오, 이제 책장 옆에 스피커가 두 개 있구나.
W : Fantastic. I love to listen to music while I read.
환상적이야. 나는 책 읽는 동안 음악 듣는 것을 아주 좋아해.
M : That's the best. 『And look at the stripe-patterned cushion on the chair.』 I love it. ④의 근거 일치
그게 최고지. 그리고 의자 위에 있는 줄무늬 쿠션을 봐. 나는 그게 마음에 들어.
W : So do I. I actually have the same one at home.
나도 그래. 나는 사실 집에 똑같은 게 있어.
M : Cool. 『Hey, check out the lamp on the table.』 ⑤의 근거 일치
근사하다. 이봐, 테이블 위에 있는 램프를 봐.
W : Yeah, it'll be easier to read now. I really like how the book cafe has been remodeled.
그래, 이제 책 읽기가 더 쉬울 거야. 나는 그 북카페가 리모델링된 모습이 정말 마음에 들어.

Why? 왜 정답일까?

대화에서 책장 옆에 스피커가 두 개 있다고 말하는데(Oh, there are two speakers beside the

[문제편 p.133]

bookcase now.), 그림에서는 스피커가 한 개 있다. 따라서 그림에서 대화의 내용과 일치하지 않는 것은 ③이다.

- take a look at ~을 보다
- bookcase ⓝ 책장
- stripe-patterned ⓐ 줄무늬의

05 어항 필터 주문하기 정답률 94% | 정답 ①

대화를 듣고, 남자가 할 일로 가장 적절한 것을 고르시오.

✔ 필터 주문하기
② 어항 물 갈기
③ 체리 주스 만들기
④ 세탁물 맡기기
⑤ 히터 온도 조절하기

W : Hi, honey. How was school today?
안녕, 얘야. 오늘 학교는 어땠니?
M : Fine, Mom. But I spilled some cherry juice on my shirt.
괜찮았어요, 엄마. 근데 체리 주스를 셔츠에 쏟았어요.
W : Don't worry. I'll take it to the dry cleaner's later.
걱정하지 마. 나중에 내가 그것을 세탁소에 맡길게.
M : Thanks. By the way, what are you doing?
고마워요. 그런데 뭐 하고 계세요?
W : I was just about to change the water in the fish tank.
어항의 물을 갈아주려던 참이었어.
M : Do you need some help?
좀 도와드려요?
W : No, it's okay. But thanks for asking.
아니, 괜찮아. 하지만 물어봐 줘서 고마워.
M : Okay. Be careful with the water heater. You almost broke it last time.
네, 온수기 조심하세요. 저번에 하마터면 부술 뻔하셨잖아요.
W : I'm not going to make the same mistake twice. Oh, we need to replace the filter in the tank with a new one.
같은 실수를 두 번 반복하진 않을 거야. 아, 어항 안에 있는 필터를 새것으로 교체해야 해.
M : Really? But we're out of filters. Should I order some online right now?
정말요? 근데 필터가 다 떨어졌어요. 지금 온라인으로 좀 주문할까요?
W : Great.
좋아.
M : Okay, I'll do it. I think they'll arrive in about two days.
네, 제가 할게요. 이틀 정도 후에 도착할 것 같아요.

Why? 왜 정답일까?

어항 속 필터를 교체해야 한다는 여자의 말에 남자는 필터가 다 떨어졌으니 자신이 온라인에서 주문하겠다고 말한다(Should I order some online right now?). 따라서 남자가 할 일로 가장 적절한 것은 ① '필터 주문하기'이다.

- spill ⓥ 쏟다
- be about to ~할 참이다
- fish tank 어항
- replace A with B A를 B로 교체하다

06 배드민턴 용품 사기 정답률 58% | 정답 ④

대화를 듣고, 여자가 지불할 금액을 고르시오.

① $50 ② $60 ③ $65 ✔ $75 ⑤ $85

M : Hello. May I help you?
안녕하세요. 도와드릴까요?
W : Yes. I need a badminton racket for my son. He's starting lessons next week.
네, 제 아들을 위한 배드민턴 라켓이 필요해요. 아이가 다음주에 레슨을 시작해서요.
M : How old is your son?
아드님이 몇 살이죠?
W : Seven. What's a good one?
일곱 살이에요. 어떤 게 좋나요?
M : How about this one? It's only $20 and perfect for children that age.
이건 어떠세요? 20달러밖에 안 하고 그 나이 아이들에게는 안성맞춤입니다.
W : Okay. I'll take it.
알겠습니다. 그걸로 할게요.
M : What about rackets for adults in case you want to play with your son?
아드님과 경기하고 싶을 때를 대비해서 성인용 라켓은 어떠십니까?
W : Oh, that's a great idea.
오, 그거 좋은 생각이네요.
M : I recommend these two. This is $30 and the other is $55. But the $55 racket is much lighter.
이 두 가지를 추천합니다. 이것은 30달러이고 다른 것은 55달러입니다. 하지만 55달러짜리 라켓이 훨씬 더 가볍습니다.
W : I really like the lighter one, but it's a bit expensive.
더 가벼운 것이 정말 마음에 드는데, 좀 비싸네요.
M : Well, if you buy the lighter one, I can give you a dozen shuttlecocks worth $10 for free. You'll need shuttlecocks anyway.
음, 만약 더 가벼운 것을 사시면, 10달러 상당의 셔틀콕 12개를 공짜로 드릴 수 있습니다. 어차피 셔틀콕은 필요하실 거예요.
W : That's a good deal. Then I'll get the lighter one.
좋은 거래네요. 그럼 더 가벼운 것으로 할게요.
M : Okay. So, the rackets for you and your son. And of course, the free shuttlecocks.
네, 그럼, 손님과 아드님을 위한 라켓이요. 그리고 물론 무료 셔틀콕도요.
W : Thank you. Here's my credit card.
고맙습니다. 여기 제 신용 카드요.

Why? 왜 정답일까?

대화에 따르면 여자는 20달러짜리 아동용 라켓과 55달러짜리 어른용 라켓을 하나씩 사고, 10달러 상당의 셔틀콕을 무료로 제공받았다. 이를 식으로 나타내면 '20 + 55 = 75'이므로, 여자가 지불할 금액은 ④ '$75'이다.

- in case ~의 경우를 대비하여
- light ⓐ 가벼운

07 행사 장소를 바꾸어야 하는 이유 정답률 95% | 정답 ③

대화를 듣고, 남자가 Career Day 행사 장소를 변경하려는 이유를 고르시오.

① 초청 강사의 요청이 있어서
② 다른 행사와 장소가 겹쳐서
✔ 신청 학생이 예상보다 많아서
④ 보수 공사 소음이 시끄러워서
⑤ 세미나실 프로젝터가 고장 나서

W : Mr. Bresnan, how's the preparation for this month's Career Day going?
Bresnan 선생님, 이번 달 Career Day 준비는 어떻게 되어가나요?
M : Pretty well, Ms. Potter. This time, a local baker is visiting our school to speak with our students.
잘하고 있어요, Potter 선생님. 이번에는 동네 제빵사가 학생들과 이야기하기 위해 우리 학교를 방문해요.
W : It'll be good for our students to learn about what bakers do. The event will be held in the seminar room tomorrow, right?
학생들이 제빵사가 하는 일에 대해 배운다면 좋을 것 같네요. 행사는 내일 세미나실에서 열리죠, 그렇죠?
M : Well, I think I have to change the place of the event.
음, 제 생각에 행사 장소를 바꿔야 할 것 같아요.
W : Why? Is there another event scheduled in that room?
왜요? 그 방에서 다른 행사가 예정되어 있나요?
M : No, I already checked.
아뇨, 이미 확인했어요.
W : Then is it because of the repair work going on next door?
그럼 옆에서 진행 중인 보수 작업 때문인가요?
M : That's not an issue. It starts after school.
그건 문제가 안 돼요. 방과 후에 시작하니까요.
W : So, why do you want to change the place?
그럼 왜 장소를 바꾸려고 하죠?
M : Actually, more students signed up than I expected.
사실, 예상보다 많은 학생이 신청했어요.
W : Oh, I see. How about using the conference room, then? It has more space.
아, 그렇군요. 그럼 회의실을 이용하는 건 어때요? 공간이 더 커요.
M : Great idea. I'll go check if it's available and let the students know.
좋은 생각이네요. 제가 가서 가능한지 알아보고 학생들에게 알릴게요.

Why? 왜 정답일까?

대화에 따르면 Career Day는 본래 세미나실에서 열릴 예정이었지만 예상보다 많은 학생이 신청하였기에 (Actually, more students signed up than I expected.) 더 넓은 곳으로 장소를 바꾸어야 한다고 하였다. 따라서 남자가 Career Day 행사 장소를 변경하려는 이유로 가장 적절한 것은 ③ '신청 학생이 예상보다 많아서'이다.

- sign up 신청하다, 등록하다
- conference room 회의실
- available ⓐ 이용 가능한

08 디지털 출판 박람회 정답률 92% | 정답 ⑤

대화를 듣고, Digital Publishing Workshop에 관해 언급되지 않은 것을 고르시오.

① 목적 ② 대상 ③ 날짜 ④ 등록 방법 ✔ 준비물

[Cell phone rings.]
[휴대 전화가 울린다.]
M : Hey, Charlotte. What's up?
안녕, Charlotte. 무슨 일이야?
W : Hi, Chris. I'm looking at information about an online course called Digital Publishing Workshop. How about taking it with me?
안녕, Chris. 난 Digital Publishing Workshop이라는 온라인 강좌에 관한 정보를 보고 있어. 나랑 같이 수강하는 게 어때?
M : Sounds interesting. Tell me more.
재미있을 것 같네. 좀 더 알려줘.
W : 『The purpose of the workshop is to provide guidelines for publishing digital magazines and e-books.』 What do you think? ①의 근거 일치
이 워크숍의 목적은 디지털 잡지 및 전자책 출판에 대한 가이드라인을 제공하는 거야. 어때?
M : Actually, I've been dreaming about publishing my own e-books. But, is it okay if I don't have any experience?
사실, 나는 내 전자책을 출판하는 것을 꿈꿔 왔어. 그런데 경험이 없어도 괜찮을까?
W : Of course. 『It's targeted at college students who're just starting out.』 ②의 근거 일치
물론이지. 그것은 이제 막 시작하는 대학생들을 대상으로 해.
M : Great. 『Then when is the workshop?
좋아. 그럼 워크숍은 언제야?
W : It's held for three days from October 27th to 29th.』 ③의 근거 일치
10월 27일부터 29일까지 3일간 열려.
M : Excellent. Midterm exams will be over by then. 『Do we need to register?
잘됐다. 그때쯤이면 중간고사가 끝날 거야. 등록해야 해?
W : Yes. We can do it online.』 There's a link to the registration page on our library's website. ④의 근거 일치
응, 온라인으로 하면 돼. 우리 도서관 웹 사이트에 등록 페이지 링크가 있어.
M : Okay. Let's sign up.
좋아. 등록하자.

Why? 왜 정답일까?

대화에서 남자와 여자는 Digital Publishing Workshop의 목적, 대상, 날짜, 등록 방법에 관해 언급하였다. 따라서 언급되지 않은 것은 ⑤ '준비물'이다.

Why? 왜 오답일까?

① 'The purpose of the workshop is to provide guidelines for publishing digital magazines and e-books.'에서 '목적'이 언급되었다.
② 'It's targeted at college students who're just starting out.'에서 '대상'이 언급되었다.
③ 'It's held for three days from October 27th to 29th.'에서 '날짜'가 언급되었다.
④ 'We can do it online.'에서 '등록 방법'이 언급되었다.

- publishing ⓝ 출판 (사업)
- be targeted at ~을 대상으로 하다
- midterm exam 중간고사

[문제편 p.133]

09 어린이 대상의 실외 행사 안내

정답률 95% | 정답 ④

2021 Playground in the Park에 관한 다음 내용을 듣고, 일치하지 않는 것을 고르시오.

① 라디오 방송국이 주최한다.
② 다섯 개의 놀이 구역이 있다.
③ 최대 60명의 아이들이 참여할 수 있다.
✔ 행사장에서 음식을 구입할 수 없다.
⑤ 비가 오면 일정이 조정된다.

W : Hello, listeners.
안녕하세요, 청취자 여러분.
Would you like your kids to have a good time in a park away from smartphones and video games?
자녀가 스마트폰과 비디오 게임에서 벗어나서 공원에서 즐거운 시간을 보내길 원하십니까?
Then there's an exciting event for all of you.
그렇다면 여러분 모두를 위한 신나는 행사가 있습니다.
「Our radio station is hosting the 2021 Playground in the Park.」 ①의 근거 일치
우리 라디오 방송국은 2021 Playground in the Park를 주최할 것입니다.
This event will be on Saturday, September 25th from 10 a.m. to 3 p.m. at the Queens Quarter Park.
이 행사는 9월 25일 토요일에 오전 10시부터 오후 3시까지 Queens Quarter 공원에서 열릴 것입니다.
「There are five play zones, including giant seesaws, tree houses, and elephant-shaped slides.」 ②의 근거 일치
거대한 시소, 나무 위의 집, 코끼리 모양의 미끄럼틀을 포함해서 다섯 개의 놀이 구역이 있습니다.
「Hurry and sign up now because only up to 60 kids can participate in this event.」
최대 60명의 아이들만 행사에 참여할 수 있으니 서둘러서 지금 등록하세요. ③의 근거 일치
「There'll be food trucks, so you can buy a variety of foods at the event site.」
푸드 트럭이 있을 것이므로 다양한 음식을 행사장에서 구입하실 수 있습니다. ④의 근거 불일치
「This is an outdoor event, so the event will be rescheduled if it rains.」 ⑤의 근거 일치
이것은 야외 행사이므로 비가 오면 행사의 일정이 조정될 것입니다.
Visit our website for more information.
자세한 내용을 원하신다면 저희 웹 사이트를 방문하세요.

Why? 왜 정답일까?

'~ you can buy a variety of foods at the event site.'에서 푸드 트럭이 있어 현장에서 음식 구매가 가능하다고 하므로, 내용과 일치하지 않는 것은 ④ '행사장에서 음식을 구입할 수 없다.'이다.

Why? 왜 오답일까?

① 'Our radio station is hosting the 2021 Playground in the Park.'의 내용과 일치한다.
② 'There are five play zones, ~'의 내용과 일치한다.
③ '~ only up to 60 kids can participate in this event.'의 내용과 일치한다.
⑤ '~ the event will be rescheduled if it rains.'의 내용과 일치한다.

- host ⓥ 주최하다
- a variety of 다양한
- reschedule ⓥ 일정을 조정하다

10 블루투스 이어폰 사기

정답률 93% | 정답 ④

다음 표를 보면서 대화를 듣고, 여자가 구매할 블루투스 이어폰을 고르시오.

Bluetooth Earphones

	Model	Battery Life	Wireless Charging	Price	Case Cover Material
①	A	2 hours	×	$49.99	Silicone
②	B	3 hours	○	$69.99	Silicone
③	C	3 hours	×	$79.99	Leather
✔	D	4 hours	○	$89.99	Leather
⑤	E	5 hours	○	$109.99	Leather

M : Welcome to Aiden's Electronics. What can I do for you?
Aiden's Electronics에 잘 오셨습니다. 무엇을 도와 드릴까요?
W : Hi. I'm looking for bluetooth earphones.
안녕하세요. 블루투스 이어폰을 찾고 있어요.
M : Okay. These are the five models we carry. Do you have any particular brand in mind?
알겠습니다. 이게 저희한테 있는 다섯 가지 제품입니다. 생각하고 있는 특정 브랜드가 있나요?
W : 「No, but I want earphones with a battery that lasts at least three hours.」 It takes me more than two hours to go to work. 근거1 Battery Life 조건
아니요. 하지만 배터리가 적어도 3시간 지속되는 이어폰을 원해요. 출근하는 데 두 시간 넘게 걸리거든요.
M : All right. 「Are you interested in wireless charging?
알겠습니다. 무선 충전에 관심이 있나요?
W : Yes. It'd be nice to charge my earphones without connecting to a charging cable.」
네. 충전 케이블에 연결하지 않고 이어폰을 충전하면 좋을 것 같아요. 근거2 Wireless Charging 조건
M : Got it. 「What about the price?
알겠습니다. 가격은요?
W : I definitely don't want to spend more than $100.」 근거3 Price조건
절대로 100달러 이상은 쓰고 싶지 않아요.
M : No problem. Then you are down to these two. 「This model comes with a silicone case cover, and that one comes with a leather case cover.
문제없어요. 그러면 결국 이 두 개네요. 이 제품은 실리콘 케이스 커버가 딸려 있고, 저 제품은 가죽 케이스 커버가 딸려 있어요.
W : Well, I don't like the feel of the silicone. It feels weird.」 근거4 Case Cover Material 조건
음, 실리콘의 감촉이 마음에 들지 않네요. 느낌이 이상해요.
M : Then, this is the model for you.
그럼, 이게 손님을 위한 제품이네요.
W : Perfect. I'll take it.
완벽해요. 이걸로 살게요.

Why? 왜 정답일까?

대화에 따르면 여자는 배터리가 3시간 이상 지속되고, 무선 충전이 가능하면서, 가격은 100달러를 넘지 않고, 실리콘 커버가 딸려오지 않는 블루투스 이어폰을 구매하려고 한다. 따라서 여자가 구매할 블루투스 이어폰은 ④ 'D'이다.

- last ⓥ 지속되다
- connect to ~에 연결하다
- charging cable 충전 케이블
- definitely ad 절대로, 분명히
- weird ⓐ 이상한

11 조별 모임 방법 제안

정답률 92% | 정답 ⑤

대화를 듣고, 여자의 마지막 말에 대한 남자의 응답으로 가장 적절한 것을 고르시오.

① Yes. I only communicate face-to-face. – 응, 난 면대면 소통만 해.
② Me, too. Don't put me in the chat room. – 나도 그래. 날 그 대화방에 넣지 마.
③ Right. We don't have biology class today. – 맞아. 우린 오늘 생물학 수업이 없어.
④ No. We've already finished our group project. – 아니. 우린 이미 조별 과제를 끝냈어.
✔ Sure. I'll open a chat room and invite everyone. – 물론이지. 내가 대화방을 열어서 모두를 초대할게.

W : Andy, it's hard to get together for our biology group project. All our group members seem busy.
Andy, 우리 생물학 조별 과제를 하러 모이기가 힘들어. 우리 조원들 모두 바쁜 것 같아.
M : I know. Why don't we make an online group chat room? Then, we can communicate easily without face-to-face meetings.
그러게. 온라인 단체 채팅방을 만드는 게 어때? 그러면 면대면 회의 없이도 쉽게 의사소통할 수 있잖아.
W : That's a wonderful idea. Could you do it for us?
멋진 생각이네. 우리를 위해 그거 좀 해줄 수 있어?
M : Sure. I'll open a chat room and invite everyone.
물론이지. 내가 대화방을 열어서 모두를 초대할게.

Why? 왜 정답일까?

조별 과제를 하러 모이기 힘들다는 여자에게 남자는 온라인 채팅방을 열어서 소통하자고 제안하고(Why don't we make an online group chat room?), 이에 여자는 남자에게 방을 열어달라고 부탁한다(Could you do it for us?). 따라서 남자의 응답으로 가장 적절한 것은 ⑤ '물론이지. 내가 대화방을 열어서 모두를 초대할게.'이다.

- get together 모이다
- biology ⓝ 생물학
- face-to-face ⓐ 면대면의

12 여행 떠나기 전 전등 확인하기

정답률 90% | 정답 ①

대화를 듣고, 남자의 마지막 말에 대한 여자의 응답으로 가장 적절한 것을 고르시오.

✔ Thank you. I'm relieved to hear that. – 고마워요. 그 말을 들으니 안심이 되네요.
② It's terrible. I'll go check if it's ready. – 끔찍하네요. 내가 가서 준비되었나 볼게요.
③ That's great. It's good to be back home. – 훌륭해요. 집에 오니까 좋네요.
④ Okay. You're free to read in the living room. – 알겠어요. 거실에서 편하게 책을 읽어요.
⑤ No way. Turn off the lights when you go to bed. – 절대 안 돼요. 잠자리에 들 때 불을 꺼요.

M : I'm excited to go on this trip. Honey, did you fasten your seatbelt?
이번 여행을 떠나게 되어 신나요. 여보, 안전벨트 맸어요?
W : Yes. *[Pause]* Oh, wait. I'm not sure if I turned off the lights in the living room when I left the house.
네. *[잠시 멈춤]* 아, 잠깐만요. 집을 나올 때 거실 불을 껐나 모르겠어요.
M : Don't worry. I turned them off. And I checked all the other rooms, too.
걱정하지 말아요. 내가 껐어요. 그리고 내가 다른 방도 다 확인했어요.
W : Thank you. I'm relieved to hear that.
고마워요. 그 말을 들으니 안심이 되네요.

Why? 왜 정답일까?

여행을 떠나기 직전 여자가 집을 나오면서 거실 불을 껐는지 모르겠다고 말하자 남자는 자신이 껐고 다른 방 불도 모두 확인했다는 사실을 말해준다(Don't worry. I turned them off. And I checked all the other rooms, too.). 따라서 여자의 응답으로 가장 적절한 것은 ① '고마워요. 그 말을 들으니 안심이 되네요.'이다.

- go on a trip 여행을 떠나다
- relieved ⓐ 안심한
- be free to 자유롭게 ~하다

13 사이클링 대회 출전

정답률 90% | 정답 ②

대화를 듣고, 여자의 마지막 말에 대한 남자의 응답으로 가장 적절한 것을 고르시오. [3점]

Man: ______________________________

① Too bad. I hope you'll feel better soon. – 안됐네. 금방 낫기를 바랄게.
✔ Of course. I'm sure you'll win the race. – 물론이지. 난 네가 경주에서 우승할 거라고 확신해.
③ I see. I've never been a cycling champion. – 그렇구나. 난 사이클링 대회 우승자가 되어본 적이 없어.
④ All right. I'll be just fine at the competition. – 알겠어. 난 대회에서 잘할 거야.
⑤ Terrific. I'm also looking forward to the camp. – 아주 멋져. 나도 캠프가 기대돼.

W : Hi, Uncle James. I'm back from the cycling camp.
안녕하세요, James 삼촌. 사이클링 캠프에서 돌아왔어요.
M : Hey, Clara. How was it?
안녕, Clara. 사이클링 캠프는 어땠니?
W : It was great. My cycling improved a lot. I want to be a national cycling champion just like you.
아주 좋았어요. 제 사이클링 실력이 많이 향상됐어요. 저도 삼촌처럼 전국 사이클링 대회 우승자가 되고 싶어요.
M : I know you will. You're participating in the national youth cycling competition next month, right?
나는 네가 그렇게 될 거라고 생각해. 다음 달에 전국 청소년 사이클링 대회에 참가하는 거 맞지?
W : Yeah, but I'm a little bit nervous because it's my first national competition.
네, 하지만 첫 전국 대회라 조금 긴장돼요.
M : I felt the same way. But once you start racing, you'll forget about being nervous.
나도 같은 기분이었어. 하지만 일단 경주가 시작되면, 긴장한 것을 잊게 될 거야.
W : I hope so. I really want to get first place.
그랬으면 좋겠어요. 전 정말 1등 하고 싶어요.
M : Well, you did set the record at the city competition this year.
그래, 넌 올해 시 대회에서 정말로 기록을 세웠잖아.

[문제편 p.133]

W : That's true. And I've trained really hard all year.
맞아요. 그리고 저는 1년 내내 정말 열심히 훈련했어요.
M : See, I know you're ready.
거봐, 난 네가 준비된 걸 알아.
W : Thank you. I hope all my hard work pays off. Wish me luck.
감사해요. 제 모든 노력이 결실을 보기를 바라요. 행운을 빌어주세요.
M : Of course. I'm sure you'll win the race.
물론이지. 난 네가 경주에서 우승할 거라고 확신해.

Why? 왜 정답일까?

청소년 사이클링 대회에 참가하는 여자는 그간 열심히 해온 노력에 꼭 결실을 맺고 싶다면서 남자에게 행운을 빌어달라고 말한다(I hope all my hard work pays off. Wish me luck.). 따라서 남자의 응답으로 가장 적절한 것은 ② '물론이지. 난 네가 경주에서 우승할 거라고 확신해.'이다.

- improve ⓥ 향상되다
- pay off 성과를 올리다, 성공하다
- look forward to ~을 고대하다
- set a record 기록을 세우다
- terrific ⓐ 아주 멋진, 훌륭한

14 과학 박물관 프로그램 문의

정답률 83% | 정답 ①

대화를 듣고, 남자의 마지막 말에 대한 여자의 응답으로 가장 적절한 것을 고르시오.

Woman: ____________________

✔ No problem. I can email you the details of our program.
그럼요. 제가 우리 프로그램 세부사항을 메일로 보내드리겠습니다.
② No worries. I'll let you know what day is available.
걱정 마세요. 어느 날이 가능한지 알려드릴게요.
③ That's right. I need to get more students.
맞습니다. 학생들을 더 모아야 합니다.
④ That's true. It's difficult to explain scientific principles.
맞아요. 과학 원리를 설명하는 건 어렵습니다.
⑤ Brilliant. I can recommend a good science fiction movie.
멋지네요. 제가 괜찮은 공상 과학 영화를 추천해 드릴 수 있어요.

[Phone rings.]
[전화가 울린다.]
W : Ashton Science Museum. How can I help you?
Ashton 과학 박물관입니다. 무엇을 도와드릴까요?
M : Hi. I'm planning a field trip for my students, and I was wondering if your museum had any programs for high school students.
안녕하세요. 저는 학생들을 위한 현장 학습을 계획하고 있는데요, 박물관에 고등학생들을 위한 프로그램이 있는지 궁금해요.
W : Yes, we have one. It's named Teen Science Adventure. When is the field trip?
네, 하나 있습니다. Teen Science Adventure라는 겁니다. 현장 학습이 언제인가요?
M : It's October 14th. I'm bringing about 50 students. Is it available that day?
10월 14일이에요. 약 50명의 학생들을 데려가려고 합니다. 그날 이용 가능한가요?
W : Let me check. *[Mouse clicking sound]* It's available in the afternoon.
확인해 보겠습니다. *[마우스 클릭하는 소리]* 오후에 이용 가능합니다.
M : Perfect. Can you briefly explain the program?
딱 좋네요. 프로그램에 대해 간단히 설명해주실 수 있을까요?
W : Sure. It includes workshops, hands-on activities, and AI robot demonstrations.
그럼요. 프로그램에는 워크숍, 체험 활동, 인공지능 로봇 시연이 포함됩니다.
M : Amazing.
근사하네요.
W : And the highlight of this program is the VR Escape Room where students get to solve virtual challenges using scientific knowledge.
그리고 이 프로그램의 하이라이트는 학생들이 과학 지식을 이용해 가상의 과제를 해결해보는 VR Escape Room입니다.
M : It sounds fun and educational. My students would love that.
재미있고 교육적일 것 같네요. 학생들이 좋아할 거예요.
W : Would you like to make a reservation then?
그럼 예약하시겠습니까?
M : It'd be nice if you could send me more information today, so I can discuss it with my principal.
교장 선생님과 상의할 수 있도록 오늘 제게 더 많은 정보를 보내주시면 좋겠습니다.
W : No problem. I can email you the details of our program.
그럼요. 제가 우리 프로그램 세부사항을 메일로 보내드리겠습니다.

Why? 왜 정답일까?

남자는 여자의 박물관에서 운영하는 과학 체험 프로그램에 관심을 보이며, 교장 선생님과 검토할 수 있도록 더 많은 자료를 보내달라고 말한다(It'd be nice if you could send me more information today, so I can discuss it with my principal.). 따라서 여자의 응답으로 가장 적절한 것은 ① '그럼요. 제가 우리 프로그램 세부사항을 메일로 보내드리겠습니다.'이다.

- field trip 현장 학습
- hands-on ⓐ 직접 해보는
- principle ⓝ 원리
- briefly ad 간단하게, 짧게
- demonstration ⓝ 시연
- brilliant ⓐ 멋진, 눈부신

15 서점 회원 할인

정답률 68% | 정답 ⑤

다음 상황 설명을 듣고, Megan이 Philip에게 할 말로 가장 적절한 것을 고르시오. [3점]

Megan: ____________________

① You can sign up for our membership and get a discount.
저희 회원을 신청하시고 할인을 받으실 수 있어요.
② I regret to say that I can't find your membership number.
유감이지만 손님의 회원 번호를 찾을 수가 없어요.
③ Unfortunately, the poster you're looking for is not for sale.
안타깝지만 손님이 찾고 계신 포스터는 판매용이 아닙니다.
④ Congratulations on the successful release of your new book.
성공적인 신간 출간 축하드려요.
✔ I'm afraid the members' discount doesn't apply to this book.
죄송하지만 이 책에는 회원 할인이 적용되지 않습니다.

M : Philip goes to a bookstore to buy a recently published book titled *The Psychology of Everyday Affairs*.
Philip은 최근 출간된 *The Psychology of Everyday Affairs*라는 제목의 책을 사기 위해 서점에 간다.
While Philip is looking for the book, he happens to see an advertisement poster on the wall.
그 책을 찾다가, Philip은 우연히 벽에 붙어 있는 광고 포스터를 본다.
It says that if people sign up for a membership, they can get a 10% discount on books.
거기에는 회원에 등록하면 책을 10% 할인받을 수 있다고 적혀 있다.
At the counter, he meets Megan, who works at the bookstore.
계산대에서 그는 서점에서 일하는 Megan을 만난다.
He tells her that he wants to become a bookstore member to get a discount on the book.
그는 그녀에게 책 할인을 받기 위해 서점 회원이 되고 싶다고 말한다.
However, Megan knows that the membership discount is only for books that were published more than a year ago.
그러나 Megan은 회원 할인은 출간된 지 1년 이상 된 책에만 적용된다는 것을 알고 있다.
Even though Megan doesn't want to disappoint Philip, she has to tell him that he cannot get the discount on the book he wants to buy.
Megan은 Philip을 실망시키고 싶지 않지만, 그녀는 그가 사고 싶은 책은 할인을 받을 수 없다는 것을 그에게 말해주어야 한다.
In this situation, what would Megan most likely say to Philip?
이런 상황에서, Megan은 Philip에게 뭐라고 말하겠는가?
Megan : I'm afraid the members' discount doesn't apply to this book.
죄송하지만 이 책에는 회원 할인이 적용되지 않습니다.

Why? 왜 정답일까?

상황에 따르면 Philip은 서점 회원이 되면 책 할인을 받을 수 있다는 포스터를 보고 회원 가입을 문의하지만, 할인은 출간된 지 1년 이상 된 책에만 적용되기에 할인을 받을 수 없다. 서점 직원인 Megan은 그에게 이 사실을 말해주려 하므로(~ she has to tell him that he cannot get the discount on the book he wants to buy.), Megan이 Philip에게 할 말로 가장 적절한 것은 ⑤ '죄송하지만 이 책에는 회원 할인이 적용되지 않습니다.'이다.

- publish ⓥ 출간하다
- get a discount on ~을 할인 받다
- release ⓝ 출간, 출시
- advertisement ⓝ 광고
- disappoint ⓥ 실망시키다

16-17 도시에서 야생동물이 번성한 이유

W : Hello, students.
안녕하세요, 학생 여러분.
I'm sure you've encountered some wild animals in cities.
저는 여러분이 도시에서 몇몇 야생동물을 마주쳐 봤다고 확신합니다.
「Let's look at some reasons that wild animals have done well and their populations have grown in cities.」 16번의 근거
야생동물이 도시에서 잘 살고 그들의 개체 수가 증가한 몇 가지 이유를 살펴봅시다.
「First, pigeons were rare in cities like Paris, but now you can easily find them.」
첫째, 비둘기는 파리 같은 도시에는 드물었지만, 지금은 쉽게 발견할 수가 있습니다. 17번 ①의 근거 일치
Urban expansion reduced the number of animals hunting them, and food waste in cities has been a great food source for them.
도시 확장으로 인해 비둘기를 사냥하는 동물의 수가 줄어들었고, 도시의 음식물 쓰레기는 비둘기에게 훌륭한 식량원이 되었습니다.
「And, while London is not by the sea, it has many seagulls.」 17번 ②의 근거 일치
그리고 런던은 바다 인근에 있지 않은데도 갈매기가 많습니다.
This is because nesting on the roofs of buildings protects their chicks from danger.
이는 건물의 옥상에 둥지를 틀면 갈매기 새끼들이 위험으로부터 보호되기 때문입니다.
「Next, Delhi is home to about 30,000 monkeys.」 17번 ③의 근거 일치
다음으로, 델리는 30,000마리 원숭이들의 서식지입니다.
Experts say that monkeys' high intelligence and comfort with humans let them flourish in the city.
전문가들은 원숭이의 높은 지능과 인간에 대한 친숙함이 그들로 하여금 도시에서 번성하게 한다고 합니다.
「Lastly, in the 19th century, there was a small population of squirrels in New York City.」 17번 ⑤의 근거 일치
마지막으로, 19세기에는 뉴욕시에 다람쥐 개체 수가 적었습니다.
Squirrels were seen as public pets, so the city planted nut-bearing trees as their food source.
다람쥐는 공공 애완동물로 여겨졌고, 그래서 뉴욕시는 그것의 식량원으로 견과류가 열리는 나무를 심었습니다.
This increased their population in the city.
이 때문에 뉴욕시에서 그것들의 개체 수가 증가했습니다.
Let's watch a video about these animals' city lives.
이 동물들의 도시 생활에 관한 영상을 봅시다.

- encounter ⓥ 마주치다
- expansion ⓝ 확장, 팽창
- protect A from B A를 B로부터 보호하다
- flourish ⓥ 번성하다
- rare ⓐ 드문
- seagull ⓝ 갈매기
- intelligence ⓝ 지능
- arise ⓥ 발생하다

16 주제 파악

정답률 79% | 정답 ③

여자가 하는 말의 주제로 가장 적절한 것은? [3점]

① what issues arise from abandoned pets – 유기 동물로부터 어떤 문제가 발생하는가
② how city growth affected wildlife diversity – 도시 성장이 야생동물의 다양성에 어떤 영향을 미쳤는가
✔ why wild animals came to flourish in cities – 왜 야생동물들이 도시에서 번성하게 되었는가
④ ways to make cities environmentally friendly – 도시를 친환경적으로 만드는 방법
⑤ problems between humans and animals in cities – 도시에서 인간과 동물 사이의 문제

Why? 왜 정답일까?

'Let's look at some reasons that wild animals have done well and their populations have grown in cities.'에서 여자는 야생동물이 도시에서 어떻게 잘 사는 것이며 왜 이들의 개체수가 증가하게 된 것인지 살펴보자고 하므로, 여자가 하는 말의 주제로 가장 적절한 것은 ③ '왜 야생동물들이 도시에서 번성하게 되었는가'이다.

17 언급 유무 파악

정답률 96% | 정답 ④

언급된 도시가 아닌 것은?

① Paris – 파리
② London – 런던
③ Delhi – 델리
✔ Bangkok – 방콕
⑤ New York City – 뉴욕시

[문제편 p.134]

Why? 왜 정답일까?

담화에서 여자는 야생동물이 번성한 도시의 예로 파리, 런던, 델리, 뉴욕시를 언급하였다. 따라서 언급되지 않은 것은 ④ '방콕'이다.

Why? 왜 오답일까?

① 'First, pigeons were rare in cities like Paris, but now you can easily find them.'에서 '파리'가 언급되었다.
② 'And, while London is not by the sea, it has many seagulls.'에서 '런던'이 언급되었다.
③ 'Next, Delhi is home to about 30,000 monkeys.'에서 '델리'가 언급되었다.
⑤ 'Lastly, in the 19th century, there was a small population of squirrels in New York City.'에서 '뉴욕시'가 언급되었다.

Dictation 23

문제편 135쪽

01 pick the winner of our singing competition / texting the name of your favorite contestant / cast your vote
02 helps children improve their self-esteem / when kids participate in housework / gain a sense of achievement
03 It's been a while / having a company anniversary party / order purple lilies / stand for pride and success
04 it was recently remodeled / two speakers beside the bookcase / check out the lamp
05 change the water / replace the filter / out of filters
06 rackets for adults / it's a bit expensive / give you a dozen shuttlecocks
07 change the place of the event / because of the repair work / more students signed up
08 publishing digital magazines and e-books / don't have any experience / targeted at college students
09 away from smartphones and video games / only up to 60 kids / buy a variety of foods
10 lasts at least three hours / without connecting to a charging cable / It feels weird
11 make an online group chat room
12 if I turned off the lights / checked all the other rooms
13 My cycling improved a lot / get first place / all my hard work pays off
14 a field trip / briefly explain the program / where students get to solve virtual challenges / send me more information
15 sign up for a membership / that were published more than a year ago / cannot get the discount
16-17 their populations have grown / protects their chicks from danger / let them flourish / planted nut-bearing trees

24회 | 2021학년도 9월 모의평가 고3

• 정답 •

01 ② 02 ② 03 ① 04 ⑤ 05 ③ 06 ② 07 ⑤ 08 ③ 09 ④ 10 ④ 11 ① 12 ④ 13 ① 14 ③ 15 ④ 16 ② 17 ⑤

01 학교 매점 운영 재개 안내 — 정답률 96% | 정답 ②

다음을 듣고, 여자가 하는 말의 목적으로 가장 적절한 것을 고르시오.

① 등교 시간 변경을 알리려고
✔ 학교 매점의 영업 재개를 안내하려고
③ 체육관 신축 공사 일정을 예고하려고
④ 교실 의자와 책상 교체 계획을 공지하려고
⑤ 학교 급식 만족도 조사 참여를 독려하려고

W : Hello, students.
안녕하세요, 학생 여러분.
This is your principal, Ms. Carson.
교장인 Carson 선생입니다.
I'm sure you've all been looking forward to the reopening of our school store.
여러분 모두가 학교 매점 영업 재개를 고대하고 있다는 것을 잘 알고 있습니다.
I'm very happy to announce that after some improvements the store will finally open again tomorrow.
몇 가지 개선을 마치고 매점이 마침내 내일 다시 열릴 예정임을 알리게 되어 몹시 기쁩니다.
Based on your comments and requests, we have expanded the space of the store and replaced the chairs and tables.
여러분의 의견과 요청에 따라, 매점 공간을 넓혔고 의자와 테이블도 교체했습니다.
So now, the school store has become a better place for you to relax and enjoy your snacks.
그러니 이제 학교 매점은 여러분들이 쉬고 간식을 먹기에 더 좋은 곳이 되었습니다.
The store's operating hours will remain the same as before.
매점 운영 시간은 전과 동일할 것입니다.
Once again, our school store is reopening tomorrow.
다시 한번 말씀드리면, 우리 학교 매점은 내일 영업을 재개합니다.
I hope you will all enjoy it.
여러분 모두가 즐기기를 바랍니다.

Why? 왜 정답일까?

'**I'm very happy to announce that after some improvements the store will finally open again tomorrow.**'에서 교장인 여자는 몇 가지 개선 작업 끝에 학교 매점이 내일부터 다시 운영될 예정임을 공지하고 있다. 따라서 여자가 하는 말의 목적으로 가장 적절한 것은 ② '학교 매점의 영업 재개를 안내하려고'이다.

- improvement ⓝ 개선
- expand ⓥ 확장하다
- replace ⓥ 교체하다

02 야생동물들에게 먹이를 주지 말아야 하는 이유 — 정답률 96% | 정답 ②

대화를 듣고, 남자의 의견으로 가장 적절한 것을 고르시오.

① 등산 전에는 과식을 삼가는 것이 좋다.
✔ 야생동물에게 먹이를 주지 말아야 한다.
③ 야외 활동은 가족 간의 유대를 돈독히 한다.
④ 산에서 야생동물을 만났을 때는 침착해야 된다.
⑤ 반려동물을 키우는 것은 정서 안정에 도움이 된다.

M : Cathy, it feels so great to be out in the mountains, doesn't it?
Cathy, 산에 나오니 기분 너무 좋지, 그렇지 않아?
W : Yes, Dad. Look at that tree. There's a squirrel.
네, 아빠. 저 나무 좀 보세요. 다람쥐가 있어요.
M : Oh, there's also a bird on the branch.
오, 나뭇가지 위에 새도 한 마리 있어.
W : I want to feed them. Is it okay if I share my sandwich with them?
그들에게 먹이를 주고 싶어요. 제 샌드위치를 나누어줘도 괜찮을까요?
M : Hmm... I don't think feeding wildlife is a good idea.
흠... 나는 야생동물에게 먹이를 주는 것이 좋은 생각 같지 않구나.
W : Why do you think so, Dad? Isn't giving food to them helpful?
왜 그렇게 생각하세요, 아빠? 그들에게 먹이를 주는 게 도움이 되지 않나요?
M : No. If people feed wild animals, they'll stop looking for wild food and they could lose their survival abilities in nature.
아니. 만일 사람들이 야생동물들에게 먹이를 주면, 그들은 야생의 먹을거리를 찾아 나서는 것을 그만두게 되고 자연 속에서의 생존 능력을 잃어버릴 수 있어.
W : I didn't know that.
그건 몰랐어요.
M : Also, certain nutrients in human foods are harmful to some animals. This is another reason why we shouldn't feed wild animals.
더구나, 사람이 먹는 음식에 들어있는 특정 영양소들은 일부 동물들에게 해롭단다. 우리가 야생동물들에게 먹이를 주지 말아야 하는 또 한 가지 이유지.
W : I guess giving food to wildlife is not as helpful as I thought.
야생동물들에게 먹이를 주는 것이 제가 생각했던 것만큼 도움이 되지 않는 것 같군요.
M : That's right.
맞아.
W : I'll keep that in mind.
그걸 명심할게요.

Why? 왜 정답일까?

남자는 야생동물들에게 먹이를 주는 것이 좋은 생각 같지 않다(**I don't think feeding wildlife is a**

[문제편 p.139]

good idea.)고 말하며 먹이를 주어서는 안 되는 이유를 여자에게 설명하고 있다. 따라서 남자의 의견으로 가장 적절한 것은 ② '야생동물에게 먹이를 주지 말아야 한다.'이다.

- branch ⓝ 나뭇가지
- wildlife ⓝ 야생 생물
- nutrient ⓝ 영양소

03 일기 예보 방송 준비하기
정답률 95% | 정답 ①

대화를 듣고, 두 사람의 관계를 가장 잘 나타낸 것을 고르시오.

① 스타일리스트 – 기상 캐스터
② 연출가 – 극작가
③ 매니저 – 뮤지컬 배우
④ 해군 장교 – 항해사
⑤ 디자이너 – 신문 기자

W : Jack, I've been waiting with these clothes for you. You're going on air in 30 minutes.
Jack, 이 옷을 가지고 기다리고 있었어요. 당신은 30분 뒤에 생방송을 하게 돼요.
M : Sorry, Amy. It took longer than usual to organize the weather data and write my script for the weather broadcast.
미안해요, Amy. 날씨 자료를 정리하고 기상 예보 대본을 쓰는 것이 평소보다 오래 걸렸어요.
W : I was worried you might be late for the live weather report.
당신이 생방송 일기 예보에 늦을까 봐 걱정했어요.
M : I'm ready. What am I wearing today?
전 준비됐어요. 제가 오늘 무엇을 입나요?
W : I suggest this gray suit with a navy tie.
남색 타이에 이 회색 양복을 입어보세요.
M : Okay. I'll go get dressed.
알겠어요. 가서 옷을 입을게요.
W : Wait. Put on these glasses, too. They'll give you a more professional look.
잠깐만요. 이 안경도 쓰세요. 당신에게 더 전문적인 인상을 줄 거예요.
M : Whatever you say. I can always count on you when it comes to clothing and style.
말씀대로 다 하죠. 전 의상과 스타일에 관해서는 항상 당신을 믿어요.
W : That's what I'm here for. By the way, thanks to your weather forecast yesterday, I was prepared for the sudden showers this morning.
그게 제가 여기 있는 이유죠. 그나저나, 어제 당신의 일기 예보 덕분에 저는 오늘 아침 갑작스러운 소나기를 대비했어요.
M : I did say there was an 80% chance of rain in the morning.
아침에 비가 올 확률이 80%였다고 제가 그랬었죠.
W : Yes, you did. Now, go get changed.
맞아요. 이제 가서 갈아입으세요.

Why? 왜 정답일까?

'~ **I've been waiting with these clothes for you.**', '**I suggest this gray suit with a navy tie.**', '**I can always count on you when it comes to clothing and style. / That's what I'm here for.**' 등에서 여자가 스타일리스트임을, '**It took longer than usual to organize the weather data and write my script for the weather broadcast.**', '~ **thanks to your weather forecast yesterday, I was prepared for the sudden showers this morning.**' 등에서 남자가 기상 캐스터임을 알 수 있다. 따라서 두 사람의 관계로 가장 적절한 것은 ① '스타일리스트 – 기상 캐스터'이다.

- count on ⓥ ~을 믿다, ~에 의지하다
- when it comes to ~에 관해서
- shower ⓝ 소나기

04 가족 소풍 사진 구경하기
정답률 94% | 정답 ⑤

대화를 듣고, 그림에서 대화의 내용과 일치하지 않는 것을 고르시오.

W : Hi, David. How was your picnic with your family on the weekend?
안녕, David. 주말에 가족들과 갔던 소풍 어땠어요?
M : It was good. Do you want to see a picture I took?
좋았어요. 제가 찍은 사진 좀 보실래요?
W : Sure. *[Pause]* Wow, your son has grown a lot.
그래요. *[잠시 멈춤]* 와, 당신 아들 많이 컸네요.
M : He sure has. He just turned 11 years old.
많이 컸죠. 막 11살이 되었어요.
W : Time flies. 『The drone on top of the box must be his.』 ①의 근거 일치
시간 참 빠르네요. 상자 위 드론은 아들 것이겠군요.
M : Yeah. He brings it with him everywhere.
네. 그는 그것을 어디든 가지고 다녀요.
W : I see. 『Oh, there are three bicycles.』 ②의 근거 일치
그렇군요. 오, 자전거가 세 대 있어요.
M : Yes. We love riding bicycles these days.
네. 우린 요새 자전거 타는 것을 몹시 즐기고 있어요.
W : That's good. 『I like that checkered-patterned mat.』 ③의 근거 일치
좋네요. 전 저 체크 무늬 돗자리가 마음에 들어요.
M : That's my wife's favorite pattern. 『Do you recognize that heart-shaped cushion?』 ④의 근거 일치
제 아내가 제일 좋아하는 무늬예요. 저 하트 모양 쿠션 알아보시겠어요?
W : Of course. We each got that cushion from our company last year.
그럼요. 우린 그걸 작년에 회사에서 하나씩 받았잖아요.
M : Right. My wife loves it.
맞아요. 제 아내가 그것을 좋아해요.
W : Me, too. 『Oh, I guess your wife did the bird painting on the canvas.』 ⑤의 근거 불일치
저도 그래요. 오, 아내 분이 캔버스에 새 그림을 그리셨나 봐요.
M : Uh-huh. We all had a great time.
맞아요. 우리는 모두 멋진 시간을 보냈어요.

Why? 왜 정답일까?

대화에서 여자는 캔버스에 새 그림이 그려져 있다고 하는데(**Oh, I guess your wife did the bird painting on the canvas.**), 그림의 캔버스 위에는 꽃 그림이 그려져 있다. 따라서 그림에서 대화의 내용과 일치하지 않는 것은 ⑤이다.

- drone ⓝ 드론, 무인 항공기
- checkered-patterned ⓐ 체크 무늬의

05 캠핑 준비하기
정답률 80% | 정답 ③

대화를 듣고, 여자가 할 일로 가장 적절한 것을 고르시오.

① 프로젝터와 스크린 챙기기
② 담요 가져오기
③ 영화 선택하기
④ 접이식 의자 구매하기
⑤ 짐을 차에 싣기

M : Honey, I'm so excited about going camping tomorrow.
여보, 내일 캠핑 가는 것이 몹시 신나요.
W : Me, too. I especially like our plan of watching a movie outdoors by the campfire.
나도 그래요. 특히 야외 캠프파이어 옆에서 영화를 볼 계획이 마음에 들어요.
M : Absolutely! I think it's a great idea.
그러니까요! 아주 근사한 생각인 것 같아요.
W : It's going to be so romantic. Did you pack the projector and screen?
아주 낭만적일 거예요. 프로젝터랑 스크린 챙겼어요?
M : Of course. I've put them in the car.
물론이죠. 그것들을 차에 실어놨어요.
W : Great. Thanks.
좋아요. 고마워요.
M : Shall we take some blankets just in case it gets cold in the evening?
저녁에 추워질 때를 대비해서 담요를 좀 가져가야 할까요?
W : I've already packed them in our luggage.
내가 그것들을 이미 짐으로 챙겨놨어요.
M : Good. Oh, we haven't decided which movie we're going to watch tomorrow. Could you pick one?
좋아요. 오, 우린 내일 무슨 영화를 볼지 정하지 않았어요. 하나 골라줄래요?
W : Sure. I'll choose a movie.
그래요. 내가 영화를 고를게요.
M : Thanks. Do you know where the folding chairs are?
고마워요. 접이식 의자가 어디 있는지 알아요?
W : I think I last saw them in the trunk.
내 생각에 그것들을 트렁크에서 마지막으로 봤던 것 같아요.
M : Alright. I'll check when I'm putting the luggage in the car.
알겠어요. 내가 짐을 차에 실을 때 확인해 볼게요.
W : Great. I cannot wait for tomorrow!
아주 좋아요. 내일이 몹시 기다려져요!

Why? 왜 정답일까?

남자와 여자는 다음날 캠핑을 하며 야외에서 영화를 볼 계획인데, 아직 어느 영화를 볼지 정하지 않았기에 여자는 자신이 영화를 고르겠다(**I'll choose a movie.**)고 말한다. 따라서 여자가 할 일로 가장 적절한 것은 ③ '영화 선택하기'이다.

- luggage ⓝ 짐, 수하물
- folding chair ⓝ 접이식 의자

06 온라인 수업을 위한 전자제품 사기
정답률 66% | 정답 ②

대화를 듣고, 남자가 지불할 금액을 고르시오. [3점]

① $126 ② $130 ③ $140 ④ $144 ⑤ $150

W : Welcome to Vestian Electronics. How can I help you?
Vestian Electronics에 잘 오셨습니다. 무엇을 도와드릴까요?
M : Hi. I need webcams for my son and daughter for their online classes. Which one would you recommend?
안녕하세요. 저는 우리 아들과 딸이 온라인 수업에 쓸 웹캠이 필요해요. 어떤 것을 추천해 주시겠어요?
W : This one is really popular among youngsters. It has a great design and picture quality.
이것이 청소년들 사이에서 정말 인기가 많습니다. 디자인과 화질이 훌륭하죠.
M : That model seems good. How much is it?
그 제품이 좋아 보이네요. 얼마죠?
W : The original price was $70, but it's on sale. It's $60 now.
원래는 70달러이지만, 할인 중입니다. 지금은 60달러예요.
M : Nice! I'll take two.
좋아요! 두 개 사겠어요.
W : Anything else?
더 필요한 건 없으신가요?
M : I also need a wireless speaker.
전 무선 스피커도 필요해요.
W : I recommend this one. The sound quality is good and it's only $20.
이걸 추천해 드리죠. 음질이 좋고 20달러밖에 안 합니다.
M : Perfect. Then I'll take that as well.
좋아요. 그럼 그것도 사겠어요.
W : Do you also need two of these?
이것도 두 개 필요하신가요?
M : No. Just one is enough. I already have one speaker at home.
아니요. 하나면 충분해요. 이미 집에 스피커가 하나 있어요.
W : Okay. Also, this week, we're having an autumn sales event. With any purchase of $100 or more, we're giving a $10 discount to customers.
알겠습니다. 그리고 이번 주에 저희는 가을 할인 행사를 진행 중입니다. 100달러 이상의 어느 구매에든 저희는 고객 분들께 10달러 할인을 해 드려요.

[문제편 p.139]

M : Great! Here's my credit card.
아주 좋아요! 여기 제 신용 카드요.

Why? 왜 정답일까?

대화에 따르면 남자는 할인 행사 중이어서 하나에 60달러인 웹캠을 두 개 사고, 20달러짜리 무선 스피커도 하나 산 뒤, 총 가격에서 10달러를 할인받았다. 이를 식으로 나타내면 '60×2+20−10=130'이므로, 남자가 지불할 금액은 ② '$130'이다.

- youngster ⓝ 청소년, 젊은이
- picture quality ⓝ 화질
- wireless ⓐ 무선의

07 송별회 장소 변경 알려주기

정답률 96% | 정답 ⑤

대화를 듣고, 여자가 송별회 장소를 변경한 이유를 고르시오.

① 참석 인원에 변경 사항이 생겨서
② 예약한 레스토랑의 평이 안 좋아서
③ 모임 장소로 가는 교통편이 불편해서
④ 송별회 주인공이 다른 메뉴를 원해서
✔⑤ 해산물 알레르기가 있는 동료들이 있어서

M : Hey, Laura. What's up?
안녕하세요, Laura. 무슨 일이에요?
W : You know we're having a farewell party for our boss, Miranda, next Friday, right?
다음 주 금요일에 우리 상사이신 Miranda를 위한 송별회가 있는 것 알고 계시죠?
M : Yes. The party is at 7 p.m. at the seafood restaurant downtown, isn't it?
네. 송별회는 저녁 7시에 해산물 식당에서 하죠, 그렇지 않나요?
W : That was the original plan. But I changed the place.
그게 원래 계획이었어요. 그런데 제가 장소를 변경했어요.
M : Oh, really? Didn't you say that restaurant is known for their great service and reasonable price?
오, 정말요? 그 식당이 훌륭한 서비스와 적당한 가격으로 유명하다고 하지 않았어요?
W : Yeah. That's why I booked a table there. But I changed the place to the Italian restaurant near the seafood restaurant.
네. 그래서 제가 거기 자리를 예약했던 거예요. 하지만 전 해산물 식당 근처의 이탈리아 음식점으로 장소를 변경했어요.
M : I guess you did that because Miranda loves Italian food.
Miranda가 이탈리아 음식을 좋아해서 그렇게 하셨나 보군요.
W : She does, but she also really likes seafood.
그녀가 이탈리아 음식을 좋아하기는 하는데, 해산물도 무척 좋아해요.
M : Then, why did you change the place?
그럼, 왜 장소를 바꾸신 건가요?
W : I found out that some of our coworkers have seafood allergies.
우리 동료 중 몇 명이 해산물 알레르기가 있다는 것을 알게 되었어요.
M : Oh, that's why. By the way, Janet from the sales department said she wanted to come.
오, 그래서였군요. 그나저나, 영업부의 Janet이 오고 싶다고 했어요.
W : Great! I'm sure Miranda will be happy to see her.
좋아요! Miranda가 그녀를 보면 분명 좋아할 거예요.

Why? 왜 정답일까?

대화에 따르면 여자는 본래 상사의 송별회 장소로 해산물 식당을 알아봤었지만 몇몇 동료에게 해산물 알레르기가 있다는 사실을 알고(**I found out that some of our coworkers have seafood allergies.**) 이탈리아 음식점으로 장소를 변경했다고 한다. 따라서 여자가 송별회 장소를 변경한 이유로 가장 적절한 것은 ⑤ '해산물 알레르기가 있는 동료들이 있어서'이다.

- farewell ⓝ 작별
- reasonable ⓐ (가격이) 적당한

08 동물 보호소를 위한 자선 행사 알아보기

정답률 96% | 정답 ③

대화를 듣고, Run with Your Dog 행사에 관해 언급되지 않은 것을 고르시오.

① 목적 ② 날짜 ✔③ 복장
④ 장소 ⑤ 참가비

W : Hey, Lucas. What are you doing?
안녕, Lucas. 뭐 하고 있어?
M : Hi, Erica. I'm reading an email about a charity event called Run with Your Dog.
안녕, Erica. 난 Run with Your Dog라는 자선 행사에 관한 이메일을 읽고 있어.
W : I've never heard about that before. 『What is it for?
난 그거 들어본 적이 없어. 왜 열리는 거야?
M : This event is to raise money for animal shelters in the neighborhood.』 ①의 근거 일치
이 행사는 근처 동물 보호소를 위한 기금을 모으기 위한 거야.
W : That sounds like a really good cause. Are you going to sign up?
아주 좋은 명분인 것 같네. 너 등록할 거야?
M : Yes. Are you interested?
응. 너 관심 있어?
W : Maybe. 『When is it?
아마도. 언제야?
②의 근거 일치
M : It's on Saturday, September 19th.』 The event will run from 7 a.m. to 10 a.m.
9월 19일 토요일이야. 행사는 오전 7시부터 10시까지 진행돼.
W : That's good. I'm free, then. 『Where will it be held?
좋다. 난 그때 시간이 있어. 어디서 열릴 거래?
M : It'll take place at Magic River Park.』 ④의 근거 일치
Magic River Park에서 열려.
W : Oh, I often walk my dog there. 『Is there a participation fee? ⑤의 근거 일치
오, 난 내 개를 거기서 종종 산책시켜. 참가비가 있니?
M : Yes. It's $5.』 If you would like to join, I'll send you the link to the website, which provides more detailed information.
응. 5달러야. 네가 참가하고 싶다면, 내가 네게 웹 사이트 링크를 보내줄게, 거기서 더 자세한 정보를 제공해.
W : Yes, please. I want to participate in the event, too.
응, 그렇게 해줘. 나도 그 행사에 참여하고 싶어.
M : Good. I expect to see you there.
좋아. 거기서 만나길 기대할게.

Why? 왜 정답일까?

대화에서 남자와 여자는 Run with Your Dog 행사의 목적, 날짜, 장소, 참가비를 언급하였다. 따라서 언급되지 않은 것은 ③ '복장'이다.

Why? 왜 오답일까?

① 'This event is to raise money for animal shelters in the neighborhood.'에서 '목적'이 언급되었다.
② 'It's on Saturday, September 19th.'에서 '날짜'가 언급되었다.
④ 'It'll take place at Magic River Park.'에서 '장소'가 언급되었다.
⑤ 'It's $5.'에서 '참가비'가 언급되었다.

- raise ⓥ (기금을) 모으다
- shelter ⓝ (학대 받는 동물들의) 보호소
- cause ⓝ 대의명분
- sign up ⓥ 등록하다

09 소금 광산 개장 500주년 기념행사

정답률 94% | 정답 ④

Bluemont Salt Mine의 특별 행사에 관한 다음 내용을 듣고, 일치하지 않는 것을 고르시오.

① 10월 10일부터 10월 16일까지 진행된다.
② 가장 깊은 구역에 입장이 허용된다.
③ 사진 촬영이 가능하다.
✔④ 입장료는 무료이다.
⑤ 방문객들에게 선물을 준다.

M : Hello, listeners.
안녕하세요, 청취자 여러분.
I'm Bernard Reed from Bluemont Salt Mine.
저는 Bluemont Salt Mine 소속의 Bernard Reed입니다.
『I'm pleased to announce that we're having a special event from October 10th to October 16th.』 ①의 근거 일치
10월 10일부터 10월 16일까지 저희가 특별 행사를 열 예정임을 알려드리게 되어 기쁩니다.
It's to celebrate the 500th anniversary of the salt mine's opening.
이것은 저희 소금 광산 개장의 500번째 기념일을 축하하기 위한 것입니다.
『During this event, visitors will be allowed to enter the deepest part of our mine.』
이 행사 동안, 방문객들은 우리 광산의 가장 깊은 곳에 입장하는 것이 허용됩니다. ②의 근거 일치
Also, you'll have the chance to dress up in our traditional miner's clothes.
또한, 여러분들은 전통 광부 옷을 입어볼 기회도 얻게 될 것입니다.
『Feel free to take pictures to remember your visit.』 ③의 근거 일치
여러분들의 방문을 기억하기 위해 편하게 사진을 찍으세요.
But that's not all.
하지만 이게 전부가 아닙니다.
『There will be a 50% discount on the admission fee for all visitors.』 ④의 근거 불일치
모든 방문객에게 입장료 50% 할인이 제공될 것입니다.
『Last but not least, we're giving away a gift to all visitors.』 ⑤의 근거 일치
마지막으로, 모든 방문객에게 선물을 드립니다.
It's a badge with the Bluemont logo on it.
그것은 Bluemont 로고가 있는 배지입니다.
For more information, please visit our website.
더 많은 정보를 보시려면 저희 웹 사이트를 방문하세요.

Why? 왜 정답일까?

'There will be a 50% discount on the admission fee for all visitors.'에서 모든 방문객에게는 입장료 50% 할인이 제공될 것이라고 하므로, 내용과 일치하지 않는 것은 ④ '입장료는 무료이다.'이다.

Why? 왜 오답일까?

① '~ we're having a special event from October 10th to October 16th.'의 내용과 일치한다.
② 'During this event, visitors will be allowed to enter the deepest part of our mine.'의 내용과 일치한다.
③ 'Feel free to take pictures to remember your visit.'의 내용과 일치한다.
⑤ 'Last but not least, we're giving away a gift to all visitors.'의 내용과 일치한다.

- mine ⓝ 광산
- anniversary ⓝ 기념일
- give away ⓥ (공짜로) 주다

10 손녀 생일 선물 사기

정답률 94% | 정답 ④

다음 표를 보면서 대화를 듣고, 두 사람이 주문할 크레용 세트를 고르시오.

Crayon Sets

	Set	Number of Crayons	Price	Washable	Free Gift
①	A	24	$9	×	coloring book
②	B	24	$11	○	sharpener
✔③	C	36	$15	×	sharpener
④	D	36	$17	○	coloring book
⑤	E	48	$21	○	coloring book

W : Honey, what should we get for our granddaughter, Emily, for her birthday?
여보, 우리 손녀 Emily에게 생일 선물로 뭘 사줘야 할까요?
M : Well, I've been looking up crayon sets on the Internet. Do you want to see?
음, 난 인터넷에서 크레용 세트를 보고 있었어요. 당신도 볼래요?
W : Sure. *[Pause]* 『How many crayons do you think are enough? 근거1 Number of Crayons 조건
좋아요. *[잠시 멈춤]* 크레용이 몇 개면 충분하다고 생각하나요?
M : I think 48 crayons are too many for a six year old.』
여섯 살짜리에게 48색 크레용은 너무 많지 싶어요.
W : I agree. 『But I also want to spend more than $10 on our granddaughter's present.』
동의해요. 하지만 우리 손녀 선물에 10달러 이상은 쓰고 싶어요. 근거2 Price 조건
M : Definitely. 『Do you think she needs washable ones? 근거3 Washable 조건

[문제편 p.139]

물론이죠. 아이한테 물에 지워지는 크레용이 필요할까요?

W : Yes.」 That way Emily can wash off crayon marks if she gets them on her hands.
네. 그렇게 하면 Emily가 손에 크레용이 묻어도 크레용 자국을 씻어낼 수 있을 거예요.

M : I see. Look. Each set comes with a free gift.
알겠어요. 봐요. 세트마다 무료 상품이 와요.

W : Oh, that's right. 「Which one is better for her, a sharpener or a coloring book?
오, 그러네요. 크레용깎이랑 색칠놀이 책 중 어느 것이 아이에게 더 좋을까요?

M : I think the coloring book is better because she likes to collect all kinds of coloring books.」 근거4 Free Gift 조건
아이가 온갖 종류의 색칠놀이 책을 모으는 것을 좋아하니 색칠놀이 책이 더 좋겠어요.

W : Right. I really think she's going to love our present.
네. 아이가 우리 선물을 마음에 들어 할 거라고 생각해요.

M : Then, it's settled. Let's order this one.
그럼, 정했어요. 이것으로 주문합시다.

Why? 왜 정답일까?

대화에 따르면 남자와 여자는 손녀의 생일 선물로 색깔 개수가 48색보다 적으면서, 가격이 10달러 이상이고, 물에 씻어 지울 수 있고, 색칠놀이 책을 선물로 주는 크레용 세트를 사주려고 한다. 따라서 두 사람이 주문할 크레용 세트는 ④ 'D'이다.

- washable ⓐ 물에 씻기는
- sharpener ⓝ (연필, 크레용 등을) 깎는 기구
- coloring book ⓝ 색칠놀이 책

11 다리를 다친 친구의 안부 묻기

정답률 68% | 정답 ①

대화를 듣고, 남자의 마지막 말에 대한 여자의 응답으로 가장 적절한 것을 고르시오.

✔ I think so. I should be fine by then.
그럴 거 같아. 그때까지면 다 나을 거야.
② I'm sorry. I forgot to bring my racket.
미안해. 난 내 라켓을 들고 오는 것을 잊어버렸어.
③ Of course. Keep me posted on his recovery.
당연하지. 그의 회복에 관한 소식 계속 알려줘.
④ I'm afraid not. The doctor's schedule is full today.
미안하지만 안 되겠어. 의사 선생님 일정이 오늘 꽉 찼어.
⑤ Good idea. Let's watch the tennis match at my house.
좋은 생각이야. 내 집에서 테니스 경기를 보자.

[Cell phone rings.]
[전화벨이 울린다.]

M : Hello, Chloe. How's your leg?
안녕, Chloe. 네 다리 어때?

W : Hey, Sean. It still hurts, but the doctor said I'll be fully recovered in a few days.
안녕, Sean. 아직 아픈데, 의사 선생님이 며칠이면 다 나을 거라고 하셨어.

M : I'm glad to hear that. Then, will you be able to play in the tennis match next weekend as scheduled?
그 말을 들으니 기쁘네. 그럼, 예정대로 다음 주말에 테니스 시합을 할 수 있는 거야?

W : I think so. I should be fine by then.
그럴 거 같아. 그때까지면 다 나을 거야.

Why? 왜 정답일까?

다리를 다쳤지만 곧 회복될 것 같다는 여자의 말에 남자는 예정대로 다음 주에 테니스 시합을 할 수 있겠는지 묻고 있다(**Then, will you be able to play in the tennis match next weekend as scheduled?**). 따라서 여자의 응답으로 가장 적절한 것은 ① '그럴 거 같아. 그때까지면 다 나을 거야.'이다.

- recover ⓥ 회복하다
- as scheduled 예정대로
- Keep me posted. 계속 소식 들려줘.

12 분실된 체육복 신고하기

정답률 58% | 정답 ④

대화를 듣고, 여자의 마지막 말에 대한 남자의 응답으로 가장 적절한 것을 고르시오.

① I remember where I left my uniform. – 난 내 체육복을 어디에 뒀는지 기억나.
② We can't participate in P.E. class now. – 우린 지금 체육 수업에 참여할 수 없어.
③ You should hurry before the cafeteria closes. – 넌 학교 식당이 닫기 전에 서둘러야 해.
✔ You can leave it with me and I'll find the owner. – 그걸 나한테 주고 가면 내가 주인을 찾아보마.
⑤ I hope someone will bring it with your belongings. – 누군가 네 소지품을 가지고 오길 바랄게.

W : Mr. Brown, I brought this P.E. uniform that somebody left in the cafeteria.
Brown 선생님, 누가 학교 식당에 두고 간 이 체육복을 가져왔어요.

M : That's very considerate of you. Is the student's name on the uniform?
아주 사려 깊구나. 체육복에 학생 이름이 있니?

W : Yes, but the student is not from our homeroom class. The uniform must belong to a student in another class.
있어요, 하지만 저희 반 애는 아니에요. 이 체육복은 다른 반 애 것이 분명해요.

M : You can leave it with me and I'll find the owner.
그걸 나한테 주고 가면 내가 주인을 찾아보마.

Why? 왜 정답일까?

학생인 여자는 식당에 놓고 간 체육복을 선생님인 남자에게 가져와 자신의 반 친구가 아닌 다른 반 학생이 체육복 주인일 것 같다고 말하고 있다(**~ the student is not from our homeroom class. The uniform must belong to a student in another class.**). 따라서 남자의 응답으로 가장 적절한 것은 ④ '그걸 나한테 주고 가면 내가 주인을 찾아보마.'이다.

- P.E. uniform ⓝ 체육복
- considerate ⓐ 사려 깊은
- belonging ⓝ 소지품

13 요리 수업에 같이 가자고 제안하기

정답률 90% | 정답 ①

대화를 듣고, 남자의 마지막 말에 대한 여자의 응답으로 가장 적절한 것을 고르시오. [3점]

Woman: ______________________

✔ I'll give it a try. What time shall we meet? – 나도 시도해 볼래. 우리 몇 시에 만날까?
② Not yet. We need to wait for the food to be ready. – 아직 아냐. 우린 음식이 준비되는 것을 기다려야 해.
③ I don't know. Do you want me to send the recipe? – 나도 몰라. 내가 레시피를 보내줄까?
④ Absolutely. I'll stress the importance of education. – 물론이지. 난 교육의 중요성을 강조할 거야.
⑤ Cheer up. We can relax after our homework is done. – 기운 내. 우리는 숙제가 끝나면 쉴 수 있어.

[Cell phone rings.]
[전화벨이 울린다.]

M : Hi, Stacy. What are you doing this afternoon?
안녕, Stacy. 오늘 오후에 뭐해?

W : Hi, Ben. I hope to finish my math homework around noon, and after that I don't have any plans. Why?
안녕, Ben. 난 정오쯤에 내 수학 숙제를 끝내고 싶고, 그러고 나서는 아무 계획 없어. 왜?

M : I was thinking about going to a cooking class at 5 p.m. Do you want to come?
난 오후 5시에 요리 수업에 갈까 생각 중이었어. 너도 갈래?

W : A cooking class? Isn't cooking difficult? I'm already stressed out from doing my homework.
요리 수업이라고? 요리는 어렵지 않아? 난 숙제하는 것으로 이미 스트레스를 받았어.

M : Well, actually, I recently read an article that said cooking is very effective in relieving stress.
음, 사실, 난 최근에 요리가 스트레스 해소에 무척 효과가 좋다는 내용의 기사를 읽었어.

W : What do you mean?
무슨 말이야?

M : When you cook, the smell from the food you're making can help you feel relaxed.
네가 요리할 때, 네가 만드는 음식 냄새는 네가 편안한 기분을 느끼게 하는 데 도움이 된대.

W : I can see that. The smell of a freshly-cooked meal calms me down.
알 것 같아. 갓 요리한 음식 냄새는 나를 편안하게 만들어줘.

M : That's what I mean. Also, when you eat the delicious food you make, you'll feel happy.
내 말이 그 말이야. 게다가, 네가 만든 맛있는 음식을 먹을 때면 넌 행복할 거야.

W : That does sound appealing. Perhaps it'll help me take my mind off schoolwork.
그거 정말 매력적으로 들리네. 아마 그건 내가 학교 공부로부터 머리를 식히는 데 도움이 될 거야.

M : Exactly. You should definitely come with me.
바로 그거야. 너도 나랑 같이 가야 해.

W : I'll give it a try. What time shall we meet?
나도 시도해 볼래. 우리 몇 시에 만날까?

Why? 왜 정답일까?

남자는 요리 수업이 스트레스를 완화하는 데 도움이 될 수 있다고 설명하며 여자에게 함께 요리 수업에 가자고 제안하고 있다(**Exactly. You should definitely come with me.**). 따라서 여자의 응답으로 가장 적절한 것은 ① '나도 시도해 볼래. 우리 몇 시에 만날까?'이다.

- stressed out ⓐ 스트레스가 쌓인, 스트레스를 받는
- freshly-cooked ⓐ 갓 요리한
- appealing ⓐ 매력적인
- take one's mind off ⓥ ~에서 관심을 돌리다, 머리를 식히다
- stress ⓥ 강조하다

14 주차 공간을 검색하는 앱 알려주기

정답률 91% | 정답 ③

대화를 듣고, 여자의 마지막 말에 대한 남자의 응답으로 가장 적절한 것을 고르시오.

Man: ______________________

① Not now. It'll be easier to park there late at night.
지금은 말고요. 거기는 밤늦게 주차하는 게 더 쉬워요.
② Sounds good. I'm glad to hear that you'll arrive soon.
좋네요. 당신이 곧 도착한다는 말을 들으니 기뻐요.
✔ Sure. I'll check the app for a spot and make a reservation.
물론이죠. 내가 앱에서 자리를 찾아서 예약해 둘게요.
④ One moment. The kids should be back from the museum.
잠깐만요. 아이들이 박물관에서 돌아와야 해요.
⑤ No problem. I'll remove the app for the children's safety.
문제없어요. 내가 아이들의 안전을 위해서 그 앱을 지울게요.

M : Honey, what time are we visiting the museum?
여보, 우리 몇 시에 박물관을 방문하는 거죠?

W : We should be able to get to the museum at around 2 p.m. after having lunch at Nanco's Restaurant.
Nanco's Restaurant에서 점심을 먹고 오후 2시쯤이면 박물관에 도착할 수 있을 거예요.

M : Okay. Are we taking the bus?
알겠어요. 버스를 타나요?

W : We have two kids with us and the museum is pretty far from the restaurant. Let's drive.
우리가 아이 둘을 데리고 있고 박물관은 식당에서 꽤 멀어요. 운전해서 가죠.

M : But it'll be hard to find a parking space at the museum today. There are so many visitors on the weekend.
하지만 오늘 박물관에 주차할 공간을 찾기가 어려울 거예요. 주말에는 방문객이 몹시 많잖아요.

W : How about using an app to search for parking lots near the museum?
앱을 사용해서 박물관 근처 주차장을 찾으면 어때요?

M : Is there an app for that?
그걸 위한 앱이 있어요?

W : Yes. The app is called Parking Paradise. It helps you find and reserve a parking spot.
네. 그 앱은 Parking Paradise라는 거예요. 그것은 당신이 주차 공간을 찾아서 예약할 수 있게 도와줘요.

M : That's cool! Have you tried it?
멋지네요! 그걸 써봤어요?

W : No. But I heard that it's user-friendly and convenient.
아니요. 하지만 그것은 사용자 친화적이고 편하다고 들었어요.

M : It sounds handy. Let me find the app and download it.
편할 것 같네요. 앱을 찾아서 다운로드할게요.

W : Okay. Can you find a parking space while I get the kids ready?
알겠어요. 내가 아이들을 준비시키는 동안 주차 공간을 찾아볼래요?

M : Sure. I'll check the app for a spot and make a reservation.
물론이죠. 내가 앱에서 자리를 찾아서 예약해 둘게요.

Why? 왜 정답일까?

여자는 주차 공간을 찾아 예약할 수 있는 앱이 있음을 남자에게 알려주며 자신이 아이들의 외출 준비를 돕는 동안 남자에게 앱에서 박물관 근처 주차 공간이 있는지 알아봐 달라고 요청하고 있다(**Can you find a parking space while I get the kids ready?**). 따라서 남자의 응답으로 가장 적절한 것은 ③ '물론이죠. 내가 앱에서 자리를 찾아서 예약해 둘게요.'이다.

- reserve ⓥ 예약하다
- user-friendly ⓐ 사용자 친화적인
- convenient ⓐ 편리한
- handy ⓐ 편리한, 유용한

[문제편 p.140]

15 중고 물품 판매에 관한 조언 정답률 72% | 정답 ④

다음 상황 설명을 듣고, Jane이 Andrew에게 할 말로 가장 적절한 것을 고르시오. [3점]

Jane: ________________

① Make sure everybody is prepared for next week.
모든 사람이 다음 주에 준비될 수 있도록 하렴.
② I think you should wear this jacket for the festival.
난 네가 축제에 이 재킷을 입고 가야 한다고 생각해.
③ Thank you for keeping all your things in perfect shape.
네 모든 물건을 완벽한 상태로 유지해 줘서 고마워.
✔ How about choosing just the items that are in a good state?
상태가 좋은 물건만 골라내는 것은 어떠니?
⑤ Why don't you buy secondhand items instead of new ones?
새 물건 대신 중고품을 사는 게 어떠니?

W : Andrew is preparing to sell his used things at his school festival next week.
Andrew는 다음 주 학교 축제에서 그의 중고 물건들을 팔려고 준비하고 있다.
Andrew gathers all the stuff that he wants to sell and asks his mother, Jane, what she thinks of his selections.
Andrew는 자신이 팔고 싶어 하는 모든 물건을 모으고는 어머니인 Jane에게 자신이 고른 물건들을 어떻게 생각하는지 묻는다.
Jane looks through the items and notices that some of them are old and in poor condition.
Jane은 물품들을 살펴보는 몇 가지가 낡고 상태가 좋지 못함을 알아차린다.
She thinks that Andrew shouldn't take such worn-out things to the festival because people won't be interested in buying them.
그녀는 사람들이 그렇게 낡은 물건을 사는 데 관심 있어 하지 않을 것이므로 Andrew가 그런 물건들을 가져가지 말아야 한다고 생각한다.
So, Jane wants to suggest that Andrew should only pick out the ones that are in fine condition.
그래서 Jane은 Andrew에게 상태가 좋은 물건만 골라낼 것을 제안하고 싶어 한다.
In this situation, what would Jane most likely say to Andrew?
이 상황에서, Jane은 Andrew에게 뭐라고 말하겠는가?

Jane : How about choosing just the items that are in a good state?
상태가 좋은 물건만 골라내는 것은 어떠니?

Why? 왜 정답일까?

상황에 따르면 아들인 Andrew가 팔려고 모아둔 중고품 중 상태가 좋지 않은 것들이 섞여 있는 것을 발견한 어머니 Jane은 상태가 좋은 것만 골라내 판매하라고 제안하고 싶어 한다(**So, Jane wants to suggest that Andrew should only pick out the ones that are in fine condition.**). 따라서 Jane이 Andrew에게 할 말로 가장 적절한 것은 ④ '상태가 좋은 물건만 골라내는 것은 어떠니?'이다.

- **gather** ⓥ 모으다
- **pick out** ⓥ 골라내다
- **worn-out** ⓐ 낡은, 닳은
- **secondhand** ⓐ 중고의

16-17 곤충이 인간에게 주는 이로움

M : Hello, students.
안녕하세요, 학생 여러분.
Last class, we discussed the harm caused by insects.
지난 시간에 우리는 곤충에 의해 초래되는 해로움을 논의했습니다.
「Today, we're going to learn about the advantages that insects can bring us.」 16번의 근거
오늘 우리는 곤충이 우리에게 가져다줄 수 있는 이점에 관해 배울 것입니다.
「First, honeybees play a crucial role in the reproductive process of plants by helping them to produce seeds.」 17번 ①의 근거 일치
첫째, 꿀벌은 식물이 씨앗을 만들어내게 도와서 식물들의 번식 과정에 중대한 역할을 합니다.
In the U.S., the honeybees' assistance in this process accounts for about $20 billion in crops per year, including fruits and vegetables.
미국에서, 이 과정에서의 꿀벌의 도움은 과일과 채소를 포함해서 약 200억 달러어치의 농작물에 이릅니다.
「Second, insects like grasshoppers are a major food source in the world because they're high in protein and low in cholesterol.」 17번 ②의 근거 일치
둘째, 메뚜기 같은 곤충들은 세계의 주요 식량 자원인데 왜냐하면 이들은 단백질이 많고 콜레스테롤은 낮기 때문입니다.
In Mexico, for example, you can easily find fried grasshoppers sold in village markets.
예컨대 멕시코에서는 마을 시장에서 메뚜기 튀김을 파는 것을 쉽게 찾아볼 수 있습니다.
「Next, silkworms are responsible for producing most of the world's silk, which is recognized as a valuable product.」 17번 ③의 근거 일치
다음으로, 누에는 세계 대부분의 실크를 생산하는 역할을 하는데, 이것은 귀한 물건으로 여겨집니다.
In China, silkworms produce approximately 30,000 tons of raw silk annually.
중국에서, 누에가 연간 대략 3만 톤의 실크 원사를 생산해 냅니다.
「Finally, fruit flies have been used by many researchers in genetic studies.」 17번 ④의 근거 일치
마지막으로, 초파리는 유전자 연구에서 많은 연구자에 의해 이용되어 왔습니다.
Fruit flies are practical test subjects for such studies due to their short lifespan.
초파리는 짧은 수명 때문에 그러한 연구들에 적합한 실험 대상입니다.
Now, let's watch some video clips to help you understand better.
이제, 여러분이 더 잘 이해하게 도와줄 영상을 몇 개 봅시다.

- **play a role in** ⓥ ~에 역할을 하다
- **reproductive** ⓐ 번식의, 재생의
- **grasshopper** ⓝ 메뚜기
- **annually** ad 연간, 매년
- **lifespan** ⓝ 수명
- **crucial** ⓐ 중대한
- **account for** ⓥ ~을 차지하다
- **approximately** ad 대략
- **genetic** ⓐ 유전의
- **prevent A from B** ⓥ A가 B하지 못하게 하다

16 주제 파악 정답률 82% | 정답 ②

남자가 하는 말의 주제로 가장 적절한 것은?

① positive effects of plants on insects – 식물이 곤충에게 끼치는 긍정적 영향
✔ benefits of insects to human beings – 곤충이 인간에게 미치는 이로움
③ various methods of insect reproduction – 곤충 번식의 다양한 방법
④ relationship between diseases and insects – 질병과 곤충의 관계
⑤ ways to prevent insects from damaging crops – 곤충이 농작물에 피해를 주는 것을 막을 방법

Why? 왜 정답일까?

'Today, we're going to learn about the advantages that insects can bring us.'에서 남자는 곤충이 인간에게 주는 이점에 관해 배워보겠다고 하므로, 남자가 하는 말의 주제로 가장 적절한 것은 ② '곤충이 인간에게 미치는 이로움'이다.

17 언급 유무 파악 정답률 96% | 정답 ⑤

언급된 곤충이 아닌 것은?

① honeybees – 꿀벌
② grasshoppers – 메뚜기
③ silkworms – 누에
④ fruit flies – 초파리
✔ ladybugs – 무당벌레

Why? 왜 정답일까?

담화에서 남자는 인간에게 이로움을 주는 곤충의 예로 꿀벌, 메뚜기, 누에, 초파리를 언급하였다. 따라서 언급되지 않은 것은 ⑤ '무당벌레'이다.

Why? 왜 오답일까?

① 'First, honeybees play a crucial role in the reproductive process of plants by helping them to produce seeds.'에서 '꿀벌'이 언급되었다.
② 'Second, insects like grasshoppers are a major food source in the world because they're high in protein and low in cholesterol.'에서 '메뚜기'가 언급되었다.
③ 'Next, silkworms are responsible for producing most of the world's silk, which is recognized as a valuable product.'에서 '누에'가 언급되었다.
④ 'Finally, fruit flies have been used by many researchers in genetic studies.'에서 '초파리'가 언급되었다.

Dictation 24

문제편 141쪽

01 reopening of our school store / have expanded the space of the store / is reopening tomorrow
02 feeding wildlife is a good idea / lose their survival abilities / certain nutrients in human foods are harmful
03 organize the weather data and write my script / when it comes to clothing and style / prepared for the sudden showers
04 your son has grown a lot / The drone on top of the box / did the bird painting
05 watching a movie outdoors by the campfire / where the folding chairs are / putting the luggage
06 popular among youngsters / I already have one speaker at home / having an autumn sales event
07 I changed the place / their great service and reasonable price / some of our coworkers have seafood allergies
08 raise money for animal shelters / Where will it be held / provides more detailed information
09 enter the deepest part of our mine / Feel free to take pictures / we're giving away a gift
10 48 crayons are too many / she needs washable ones / a sharpener or a coloring book
11 play in the tennis match
12 not from our homeroom class
13 stressed out from doing my homework / calms me down / take my mind off schoolwork
14 find and reserve a parking spot / user-friendly and convenient / get the kids ready
15 what she thinks of his selections / looks through / old and in poor condition
16-17 play a crucial role in the reproductive process / high in protein and low in cholesterol / due to their short lifespan

[문제편 p.140]

25회 | 2023학년도 10월 학력평가 고3

• 정답 •

01 ⑤ 02 ① 03 ① 04 ⑤ 05 ⑤ 06 ④ 07 ⑤ 08 ④ 09 ④ 10 ③ 11 ③ 12 ③ 13 ⑤ 14 ② 15 ② 16 ③ 17 ③

01 야외 놀이 기구 운행 중단 안내 정답률 93% | 정답 ⑤

다음을 듣고, 여자가 하는 말의 목적으로 가장 적절한 것을 고르시오.

① 놀이공원 운영 시간 연장을 공지하려고
② 새로 생긴 실내 놀이 기구를 홍보하려고
③ 놀이공원 내 공연 장소의 변경을 알리려고
④ 놀이 기구 탑승 시 안전 수칙 준수를 당부하려고
⑤ 야외 놀이 기구의 일시적 운행 중단을 안내하려고

W : Attention, please.
주목해 주시기 바랍니다.
Welcome to the Wonderland Amusement Park.
Wonderland 놀이공원에 오신 것을 환영합니다.
We take great pride in providing you with thrilling rides, shows, and attractions.
짜릿한 놀이기구, 쇼, 그리고 어트랙션을 여러분들께 자랑스럽게 제공합니다.
However, we regret to inform you that due to the bad weather, outdoor rides will be temporarily closed.
하지만, 유감스럽게도 악천후로 인해 야외 놀이 기구는 임시로 중단할 예정입니다.
We'll monitor the weather and reopen outdoor rides as soon as conditions permit.
저희는 날씨를 관찰하고 상황이 허락하는 대로 야외 놀이 기구를 재개장할 것입니다.
In the meantime, please enjoy our exciting indoor rides, shows, and interactive exhibits.
그동안 신나는 실내 놀이 기구와 쇼, 그리고 인터랙티브 전시를 즐겨주세요.
We kindly request that you cooperate, as your safety is our top priority.
여러분의 안전이 최우선이기 때문에, 여러분의 협조를 정중히 부탁드립니다.
We apologize for any inconvenience. Thank you.
불편을 끼쳐 사과드립니다. 감사합니다.

Why? 왜 정답일까?

야외 놀이 기구의 운행 중단을 공지하는 내용이므로(**However, we regret to inform you that due to the bad weather, outdoor rides will be temporarily closed.**), 여자가 하는 말의 목적으로 가장 적절한 것은 ⑤ '야외 놀이 기구의 일시적 운행 중단을 안내하려고'이다.

- take great pride in ~에 자부심을 갖다
- regret to ~하게 되어 유감이다
- permit ⓥ 허락하다
- temporarily ad 임시로
- inconvenience ⓝ 불편

02 온라인 계정 비밀번호 관리하기 정답률 98% | 정답 ①

대화를 듣고, 남자의 의견으로 가장 적절한 것을 고르시오.

① 온라인 계정 비밀번호는 주기적으로 바꿔야 한다.
② 중요한 비밀번호는 메모해 두어야 한다.
③ 소셜 미디어 사용 시간을 줄여야 한다.
④ 보안 프로그램은 수시로 업데이트해야 한다.
⑤ 소셜 미디어에서 개인 정보 노출에 유의해야 한다.

M : Jennifer, what are you doing?
Jennifer, 뭐 하고 있어?
W : I'm checking an email. It says that I should change my password on my social media account.
이메일 확인하고 있어. 내 소셜미디어 계정 비밀번호를 바꿔야 한다고 하네.
M : When was the last time you changed your password?
마지막으로 비밀번호를 바꾼 게 언제야?
W : Actually I've never changed it since I created my account.
사실 난 계정을 만든 이후로 한 번도 비밀번호를 바꾸지 않았어.
M : You mean you've been using the same password all this time?
그럼 내내 똑같은 비밀번호를 쓰고 있었다는 얘기야?
W : Yes. I haven't changed any of my passwords on my online accounts. I forget my passwords easily.
응. 난 내 온라인 계정 비밀번호를 아무것도 바꾸지 않았어. 난 내 비밀번호를 잘 잊어버리거든.
M : That's too risky! It's important to change your passwords regularly to prevent potential hacking attempts.
그건 너무 위험해! 잠재적 해킹 시도를 예방하려면 네 비밀번호를 주기적으로 바꾸는 게 중요해.
W : That makes sense. How often should I change my passwords?
일리가 있네. 내가 얼마나 자주 비밀번호를 바꿔야 하지?
M : Experts recommend changing passwords every three to six months.
전문가들이 추천하기로는 3~6개월마다 한 번씩 바꾸래.
W : I'll keep that in mind. Thanks.
그걸 명심할게. 고마워.

Why? 왜 정답일까?

해킹을 막기 위해서는 온라인 계정의 비밀번호를 주기적으로 바꿔야 한다(**It's important to change your passwords regularly to prevent potential hacking attempts.**)는 말로 보아, 남자의 의견으로 가장 적절한 것은 ① '온라인 계정 비밀번호는 주기적으로 바꿔야 한다.'이다.

- risky ⓐ 위험한
- regularly ad 주기적으로
- potential ⓐ 잠재적인
- keep in mind 염두에 두다, 명심하다

03 우아하게 거절하는 기술 정답률 57% | 정답 ①

다음을 듣고, 여자가 하는 말의 요지로 가장 적절한 것을 고르시오.

① 상대방의 부탁을 거절할 때는 이유를 제시해야 한다.
② 무리한 부탁은 처음부터 거절하는 것이 바람직하다.
③ 부탁을 들어 준 상대방에게 감사 인사를 해야 한다.
④ 친한 사이일수록 예의를 지켜서 부탁하는 것이 좋다.
⑤ 부탁을 하기 전에 상대방의 상황을 확인하는 것이 필요하다.

W : Hello, listeners! I'm Jessica, your host from Happy Days.
안녕하세요, 청취자 여러분! 저는 Happy Days 진행자인 Jessica입니다.
Today, we're going to explore the art of gracefully declining someone's request.
오늘 우리는 누군가의 부탁을 우아하게 거절하는 기술을 탐색해볼 겁니다.
The key to this is offering a reason when saying no.
이것의 핵심은 거절할 때 이유를 제시하는 것입니다.
By doing so, we create understanding, prevent any potential misunderstandings, and strengthen our connections with others.
그렇게 하면, 우리는 이해를 형성할 수 있고, 그 어떤 잠재적 오해도 방지할 수 있으며, 타인과의 유대를 강화할 수 있습니다.
Of course, there may be exceptions, but in general, giving an explanation can truly make a big difference.
물론 예외가 있긴 하지만, 일반적으로 설명을 해주는 것은 진정 큰 차이를 만들 수 있습니다.
It shows that we care about the other person's feelings while still being honest about our own limitations.
그것은 우리가 우리 자신의 한계에 관해 솔직하면서도 다른 사람의 기분을 신경 쓴다는 것을 보여줍니다.
We'll be back with more tips after the break. Stay tuned.
잠시 쉬고 더 많은 조언과 함께 돌아오겠습니다. 채널 고정해 주세요.

Why? 왜 정답일까?

상대방의 부탁을 거절할 때 이유를 제시하는 것이 좋다(**The key to this is offering a reason when saying no.**)고 조언하는 글이므로, 여자가 하는 말의 요지로 가장 적절한 것은 ① '상대방의 부탁을 거절할 때는 이유를 제시해야 한다.'이다.

- host ⓝ 진행자
- misunderstanding ⓝ 오해
- strengthen ⓥ 강화하다
- exception ⓝ 예외

04 푸드 트럭 사진 보기 정답률 94% | 정답 ⑤

대화를 듣고, 그림에서 대화의 내용과 일치하지 않는 것을 고르시오.

W : Ted, what are you looking at on your smartphone?
Ted, 스마트폰으로 뭐 보고 있어?
M : Hi, Nancy, it's a photo of the food truck that my brother Tom recently opened. Take a look.
안녕, Nancy, 우리 형 Tom이 최근에 연 푸드 트럭 사진이야. 한번 봐.
W : Okay. 「Oh, I love this teddy bear on top of the truck.」 It's very cute.
알겠어. 오, 나 트럭 맨 위에 있는 이 테디베어가 마음에 들어. 정말 귀엽다. ①의 근거 일치
M : Right. 「Do you see the sign on the truck?
맞아. 트럭에 있는 표지판 봤어? ②의 근거 일치
W : Yes, it says Tom's Organic Food.」 Your brother is selling organic food. Nice!
응, Tom's Organic Food라고 쓰여 있네. 형이 유기농 음식을 팔고 계시구나. 멋지다!
M : Yeah. 「This man inside the truck is my brother.
응, 트럭 안에 있는 이 남자가 우리 형이야.
W : He looks cool wearing his chef's hat!」 ③의 근거 일치
셰프 모자 쓰고 계시니까 근사하다!
M : 「Look at this standing signboard for the menu. Isn't it pretty?
이 세워져 있는 메뉴판 좀 봐! 예쁘지 않아?
W : Absolutely. I like that it's decorated with flowers.」 ④의 근거 일치
그러게, 꽃으로 장식돼 있어서 좋네.
M : 「And my brother set up this table with a parasol for the customers.
그리고 우리 형이 손님들을 위해서 파라솔이랑 이 탁자를 설치했어.
W : Yeah, the stripe-patterned parasol looks good.」 ⑤의 근거 불일치
응, 줄무늬 파라솔이 근사해 보여.
I'd like to visit the food truck someday.
나도 언젠가 이 푸드 트럭을 방문하고 싶어.
M : Sure. Let's go there together.
물론이지. 같이 가자.

Why? 왜 정답일까?

대화에서 파라솔은 줄무늬라고 하는데(**Yeah, the stripe-patterned parasol looks good.**), 그림 속 파라솔에는 무늬가 없다. 따라서 그림에서 대화의 내용과 일치하지 않는 것은 ⑤이다.

- food truck 푸드 트럭
- organic ⓐ 유기농의
- signboard ⓝ 간판

05 미술 및 공예품 마켓 준비하기 정답률 95% | 정답 ⑤

대화를 듣고, 남자가 할 일로 가장 적절한 것을 고르시오.

① 후원 업체 구하기
② 행사장 예약하기
③ 등록 현황 파악하기
④ 지역 예술가 섭외하기
⑤ 자원봉사자 모집하기

M : Hey, Stella! How's everything going with the arts and crafts market preparations?
안녕, Stella! 미술 및 공예품 마켓 준비는 어떻게 되어 가?
W : Hi, Anthony! It's going well. Many local artists are excited to join.

안녕, Anthony! 잘돼 가고 있어. 많은 지역 예술가들이 합류하기를 기대하고 있어.
M : That's fantastic news! Have you secured any sponsors for the event?
멋진 소식이네! 행사 후원 업체는 좀 확보했어?
W : Yes, two local businesses have agreed to sponsor the market.
응, 지역 업체 두 곳에서 마켓 후원에 동의해줬어.
M : Wonderful! Have you found a suitable location?
근사하다! 알맞은 위치는 찾았어?
W : Sure, I've already reserved the town square.
물론이지, 난 이미 마을 광장을 예약해 뒀어.
M : You're doing an amazing job! Is there anything I can do to help?
멋지게 처리하고 있구나! 내가 뭐 도와줄 거 없어?
W : On the market day, we'll need some volunteers to help with setup and registration. Do you think you could find some?
마켓 행사 날에, 우리는 설치와 등록을 도와줄 자원봉사자가 좀 필요해. 구하는 걸 도와줄 수 있어?
M : Of course! I'll recruit volunteers through a promotional message on my social media.
물론이지! 내 소셜 미디어에 홍보 메시지를 올려서 자원봉사자를 모집해볼게.
W : That'd be great. Thank you so much!
그럼 좋겠어. 정말 고마워!

Why? 왜 정답일까?

여자가 미술 및 공예품 마켓이 열리는 날 행사를 보조해줄 자원봉사자를 구해줄 수 있는지(**On the market day, we'll need some volunteers to help with setup and registration. Do you think you could find some?**) 물어보자 남자는 수락한다(**Of course! I'll recruit volunteers through a promotional message on my social media.**). 따라서 남자가 할 일로 가장 적절한 것은 ⑤ '자원봉사자 모집하기'이다.

- **craft** ⓝ 공예
- **suitable** ⓐ 적절한, 알맞은
- **square** ⓝ 광장
- **promotional** ⓐ 홍보의

06 솜사탕 준비물 사기 정답률 81% | 정답 ④

대화를 듣고, 여자가 지불할 금액을 고르시오. [3점]

① $62 ② $65 ③ $70 ✔$82 ⑤ $85

M : Honey, what are you doing on the Internet?
여보, 인터넷으로 뭐 하고 있어요?
W : I'm shopping for a cotton candy machine for Jason's birthday party.
Jason의 생일 파티를 위해서 솜사탕 기계를 사고 있어요.
M : That's a good idea. Jason will love it.
좋은 생각이에요. Jason이 좋아할 거예요.
W : Sure. I'm having difficulty choosing between these two options, though. One is $50, and the other is $70.
그럼요. 그런데 이거 두 개 중 고르는 데 애를 먹고 있어요. 하나는 50달러이고, 다른 건 70달러예요.
M : I think the $70 one will be better. Look, it has better reviews.
70달러짜리가 더 좋을 것 같아요. 봐요, 평이 더 좋아요.
W : I agree. I'll go for it.
동의해요. 그거로 할래요.
M : Don't we need packs of sugar powder for the cotton candy, too?
솜사탕을 만들 슈가 파우더 묶음도 사야 하지 않아요?
W : You're right. Let's buy some. *[Clicking sound]* How about these? They're $5 per pack.
맞아요. 좀 사보죠. *[클릭하는 소리]* 이건 어때요? 한 팩에 5달러밖에 안 한대요.
M : Good. Hang on. If we buy three packs, we can get $3 off the total price.
좋네요. 잠깐만요. 우리가 세 팩을 사면, 총 가격에서 3달러가 할인돼요.
W : Great, let's get three packs then. I'll place the order now.
아주 좋네요. 그럼 세 팩을 사죠. 지금 주문할게요.
M : Go ahead.
그렇게 해요.

Why? 왜 정답일까?

대화에 따르면 여자는 70달러짜리 솜사탕 기계 한 대와 한 팩에 5달러인 슈가 파우더를 세 팩 사고, 총 가격에서 3달러를 할인받았다. 이를 식으로 나타내면 '70+5×3−3=82'이므로, 여자가 지불할 금액은 ④ '$82'이다.

- **cotton candy** 솜사탕
- **have difficulty ~ing** ~하는 데 애를 먹다
- **Hang on.** 잠깐만, 가만 있어봐.
- **Go ahead.** 그렇게 하세요, 먼저 하세요.

07 학교 정원 음악회에 나갈 수 없는 이유 정답률 97% | 정답 ⑤

대화를 듣고, 남자가 학교 정원 음악회에 참가할 수 없는 이유를 고르시오.

① 아직 손목이 낫지 않아서
② 첼로 대회에 참가해야 해서
③ 첼로 연습을 오랫동안 쉬어서
④ 함께 연주할 사람을 찾지 못해서
✔대학 입학 면접 준비를 해야 해서

W : Hi, Brenden. Long time no see! How have you been?
안녕, Brenden. 오랜만이다! 어떻게 지냈어?
M : Hi, Laura. I had some trouble with my wrist, but now I'm feeling much better.
안녕, Laura. 난 손목에 좀 문제가 있었는데, 이제 훨씬 나아.
W : I didn't know that. So you're back in the music room today to practice the cello?
그건 몰랐네. 그래서 오늘 첼로 연습하러 음악실 다시 온 거야?
M : Yeah, I missed being here a lot.
응, 여기 엄청 오고 싶었어.
W : I was wondering if you'd like to join me for the school garden music concert.
네가 학교 정원 음악회에 나랑 같이 나가고 싶은지 궁금했어.
M : I'd love to. When is it?
나가고 싶어. 언제야?
W : It's on Friday, November 24th. We'll have plenty of time to practice.
11월 24일 금요일이야. 연습할 시간이 많이 있어.
M : Well, I'm afraid I won't be able to make it then.
음, 그때라면 못 나갈 것 같아.
W : Ah, you're entering the cello contest around that time, right?
아, 그때쯤 첼로 대회 나가는구나, 그렇지?
M : I decided not to. I have to focus on preparing for a college entrance interview.
안 가기로 했어. 대학 입학 면접 준비에 집중해야 해.
W : Oh, when is it?
오, 그건 언제야?
M : It's the day after the garden concert. That's why I can't participate in the concert.
정원 음악회 바로 다음 날이야. 그래서 내가 음악회에 나갈 수 없는 거야.
W : I understand. Good luck with your interview!
이해해. 면접에 행운을 빌어!

Why? 왜 정답일까?

남자는 대학 입학 면접 준비(**I have to focus on preparing for a college entrance interview.**) 때문에 여자와 함께 음악회에 나갈 수 없다고 하므로, 남자가 학교 정원 음악회에 참가할 수 없는 이유로 가장 적절한 것은 ⑤ '대학 입학 면접 준비를 해야 해서'이다.

- **wrist** ⓝ 손목
- **college entrance** 대학 입학

08 어르신들을 위한 컴퓨터 수업 정답률 97% | 정답 ④

대화를 듣고, 컴퓨터 수업에 관해 언급되지 않은 것을 고르시오.

① 장소 ② 내용 ③ 기간
✔준비물 ⑤ 신청 방법

M : Grandma, look at this leaflet. It was in your postbox.
할머니, 이 전단지 좀 보세요. 이거 할머니 우편함에 있었어요.
W : What is it, sweetheart?
그게 뭔데, 얘야?
M : It's about free computer classes specifically designed for the elderly. Are you interested?
어르신들을 위해 특별히 만들어진 무료 컴퓨터 강좌에 관한 거예요. 관심 있으세요?
W : Sure. Let me have a look. 「Oh, they take place in the Cromby community center.」 ①의 근거 일치 That's quite convenient.
물론이지. 어디 보자꾸나. 오, Cromby 주민센터에서 하는구나. 꽤 편하네.
M : Right. Volunteers from the college will come to teach older people like you.
네. 대학 자원봉사자들이 할머니 같은 어르신 분들을 가르쳐 드리러 온대요.
W : Cool. 「What kind of things will they teach us?
멋지네. 그들이 우리한테 뭘 가르쳐주는 거니?
M : Many things, including sending emails and surfing the web.」 ②의 근거 일치
이메일 보내기나 웹 서핑 등등 여러 가지요.
W : Perfect. 「And the classes will run for three months, starting on October 16th.」 ③의 근거 일치
아주 잘됐네. 그리고 수업은 10월 16일부터 시작해서 세 달 동안 열리는구나.
M : Yeah, they'll be held every Monday and Wednesday.
네, 매주 월요일과 수요일에 열릴 거래요.
W : That's great timing. 「How do I sign up for them?
좋은 시간대네. 어떻게 신청한다니?
M : You can simply call the community center and register.」 ⑤의 근거 일치
주민센터에 전화하셔서 등록하시기만 하면 된대요.
W : I see.
알겠어.

Why? 왜 정답일까?

대화에서 남자와 여자는 어르신들을 위한 컴퓨터 수업의 장소, 내용, 기간, 신청 방법을 언급하고 있다. 따라서 언급되지 않은 것은 ④ '준비물'이다.

Why? 왜 오답일까?

① '**Oh, they take place in the Cromby community center.**'에서 '장소'가 언급되었다.
② '**Many things, including sending emails and surfing the web.**'에서 '내용'이 언급되었다.
③ '**And the classes will run for three months, starting on October 16th.**'에서 '기간'이 언급되었다.
⑤ '**You can simply call the community center and register.**'에서 '신청 방법'이 언급되었다.

- **the elderly** 어르신
- **surf the web** 웹 서핑하다
- **sign up for** ~에 등록하다

09 커피 엑스포 홍보 정답률 97% | 정답 ④

Sunnyville Coffee Expo에 관한 다음 내용을 듣고, 일치하지 않는 것을 고르시오.

① 11월 18일과 19일에 개최될 것이다.
② 티켓당 무료 머그잔을 하나씩 받게 된다.
③ 올해의 주제는 'From Bean to Brew'이다.
✔커피를 생산하는 10개국의 커피를 맛볼 수 있다.
⑤ 일찍 예매하면 할인을 받을 수 있다.

M : Coffee lovers, listen up! The Sunnyville Coffee Expo is back.
커피를 사랑하시는 분들, 잘 들어주세요! Sunnyville Coffee Expo가 돌아왔습니다.
「It'll be held on November 18th and 19th at the Jefferson Convention Center.」
11월 18일과 19일에 Jefferson Convention Center에서 열리는데요. ①의 근거 일치
For just $20 per day, you can be part of this fantastic event with famous coffee experts.
하루 단 20달러에, 여러분은 유명 커피 전문가와 함께 이 환상적인 행사의 일원이 되실 수 있습니다.
「And here's the best part — you get a free mug with each ticket.」 ②의 근거 일치
그리고 여기 제일 좋은 점이 있는데요, 티켓당 무료 머그잔을 하나씩 받으시게 됩니다.
「This year's theme is "From Bean to Brew," which means you'll learn everything about coffee, from the cultivation of the beans to the art of brewing.」 ③의 근거 일치
올해의 주제는 "From Bean to Brew"로, 커피 재배부터 커피를 내리는 기술까지 커피에 관한 모든 것을 배우시게 된다는 의미입니다.
「Plus, you'll be able to taste coffee from six coffee-producing countries, including Brazil and Vietnam.」 ④의 근거 불일치
추가로, 브라질과 베트남을 포함해 커피를 생산하는 6개국의 커피를 맛보실 수 있습니다.
「You can get a discount if you book early.」 ⑤의 근거 일치
일찍 예매하시면 할인을 받으실 수 있어요.
Visit our website for more information. See you there!
저희 웹 사이트를 방문해 추가 정보를 얻으세요. 거기서 뵙겠습니다!

Why? 왜 정답일까?

'**Plus, you'll be able to taste coffee from six coffee-producing countries, including**

[문제편 p.145]

Brazil and Vietnam.'에 따르면, 커피를 생산하는 **6**개국의 커피를 맛볼 수 있다고 하므로, 내용과 일치하지 않는 것은 ④ '커피를 생산하는 **10**개국의 커피를 맛볼 수 있다.'이다.

Why? 왜 오답일까?

① '**It'll be held on November 18th and 19th at the Jefferson Convention Center.**'의 내용과 일치한다.
② '**And here's the best part — you get a free mug with each ticket.**'의 내용과 일치한다.
③ '**This year's theme is "From Bean to Brew,"** ~'의 내용과 일치한다.
⑤ '**You can get a discount if you book early.**'의 내용과 일치한다.

- **Listen up!** 잘 들어주세요!
- **cultivation** ⓝ 재배
- **brew** ⓥ 끓이다, (커피를) 내리다

10 SIM 카드 구매하기

정답률 92% | 정답 ③

다음 표를 보면서 대화를 듣고, 여자가 구매할 SIM 카드를 고르시오.

SIM Cards for Australia

	Plan	Days	Data (GB)	Free International Calls	Price
①	A	5	10	○	$20
②	B	10	15	×	$25
③✔	C	15	20	○	$30
④	D	20	30	×	$35
⑤	E	30	50	○	$50

W : Paul, I need to buy a SIM card for my upcoming trip to Australia. Do you know any good website?
Paul, 나 곧 있을 호주 여행을 위해서 SIM 카드를 사야 해. 웹 사이트 좋은 데 알아?

M : Yes. I'll show you one on my smartphone. *[Pause]* Here it is. Have a look.
응, 내가 스마트폰으로 한 군데 보여줄게. *[잠시 멈춤]* 여기 있어. 한번 봐봐.

W : Okay. 「Hmm, I don't think this plan will work for me since I'll be traveling for more than a week.」 근거1 Days 조건
응, 흠, 내가 일주일 넘게 여행을 할 거라서 이 요금제는 나한테 괜찮지 않을 거 같아.

M : Then you can choose one from these four. How about this one?
그럼 이 네 개 중에 골라봐. 이거 어때?

W : I'm afraid the data is not enough for me. 「I need at least 20GB.」 근거2 Data 조건 I'm a heavy Internet user.
데이터가 나한테 충분하지 않을 거 같아. 난 최소한 20GB는 필요해. 난 인터넷을 정말 많이 쓰거든.

M : I see. That eliminates this option. 「I recommend one with free international calls.
그렇구나. 그럼 이 선택지는 제외되네. 무료 인터넷 전화가 되는 걸로 추천하겠어. 근거3 Free International Calls 조건

W : Right.」 I'll make a lot of calls to my family and friends.
맞아. 난 가족과 친구들한테 전화를 많이 할 거야.

M : Now you have two options left. 「Which one do you prefer?
그럼 두 가지 선택지가 남았어. 어느 걸 선호해?

W : This one seems expensive to me. I'll go for the other one.」 근거4 Price 조건
이건 나한테 비싼 거 같아. 다른 거로 할래.

M : Good choice.
좋은 생각이야.

Why? 왜 정답일까?

대화에 따르면 여자는 기간이 **7**일 이상이면서, 데이터는 **20GB** 이상이고, 무료 인터넷 전화가 되면서, 가격은 더 싼 **SIM** 카드를 고르려고 한다. 따라서 여자가 구매할 **SIM** 카드는 ③ '**C**'이다.

- **upcoming** ⓐ 다가오는
- **eliminate** ⓥ 제외하다, 없애다

11 출산한 이모 찾아가기

정답률 79% | 정답 ③

대화를 듣고, 남자의 마지막 말에 대한 여자의 응답으로 가장 적절한 것을 고르시오.

① I'm not sure where they are now.
그들이 지금 어디 있는지는 모르겠어.
② My aunt is expecting her baby soon.
우리 이모는 곧 아기를 낳을 거야.
✔③ My aunt and the baby are both in good health.
우리 이모와 아기 둘 다 건강하대.
④ I'm on my way to the hospital for a health checkup.
나는 건강 검진을 받으러 가는 길이야.
⑤ I don't know whether they'll like the gift and flowers.
그들이 선물과 꽃을 마음에 들어할지 모르겠어.

M : Hey, Sonia, where are you going with that gift box and flowers?
안녕, Sonia, 그 선물 상자랑 꽃 들고 어디 가?

W : Hi, Ethan! I'm heading to the hospital to visit my aunt Lisa. She had a baby yesterday.
안녕, Ethan! 난 우리 Lisa 이모를 만나러 병원에 가고 있어. 어제 아기를 낳으셨거든.

M : What amazing news! Congratulations! How are they doing?
놀라운 소식이네! 축하해! 그들은 어떻대?

W : My aunt and the baby are both in good health.
우리 이모와 아기 둘 다 건강하대.

Why? 왜 정답일까?

여자의 이모가 아기를 낳았다는 말에 남자는 축하한다고 전하며 두 사람의 안부를 묻고 있다(**How are they doing?**). 따라서 여자의 응답으로 가장 적절한 것은 ③ '우리 이모와 아기 둘 다 건강하대.'이다.

- **have a baby** 아기를 낳다
- **health checkup** 건강 검진

12 수영장 온도가 괜찮은지 묻기

정답률 90% | 정답 ③

대화를 듣고, 여자의 마지막 말에 대한 남자의 응답으로 가장 적절한 것을 고르시오.

① Exactly. That's why I gave up swimming.
바로 그거야. 그래서 내가 수영을 관뒀어.
② Right. It's cheaper to buy a monthly pass.
맞아. 한 달짜리 정기권을 사는 게 더 싸.
✔③ Not at all. The pool is warm enough to swim in.
전혀. 수영장은 수영하기 알맞게 따뜻해.
④ I don't think so. We're not allowed to dive into the pool.
난 그렇게 생각지 않아. 우린 수영장에 뛰어들면 안 돼.
⑤ Good point. Swimming is an exercise for the whole body.
좋은 지적이야. 수영은 전신 운동이지.

W : Mark, I remember that you learned how to swim last year. Do you still go swimming?
Mark, 나 네가 작년에 수영하는 법 배운 거 기억나는데. 너 아직 수영 다녀?

M : Of course. I make sure to visit the swimming pool at least three times a week.
물론이지. 난 최소한 일주일에 세 번은 수영장에 꼭 가고 있어.

W : Good for you. But isn't it too cold to swim these days?
잘하고 있네. 그런데 요새 수영하기에 너무 춥지 않아?

M : Not at all. The pool is warm enough to swim in.
전혀. 수영장은 수영하기 알맞게 따뜻해.

Why? 왜 정답일까?

일주일에 적어도 세 번씩 꾸준히 수영을 다니고 있다는 남자에게 여자는 수영하기에 너무 춥지 않은지 묻고 있다(**But isn't it too cold to swim these days?**). 따라서 남자의 응답으로 가장 적절한 것은 ③ '전혀. 수영장은 수영하기 알맞게 따뜻해.'이다.

- **go swimming** 수영하러 가다
- **make sure to** 반드시 ~하다
- **give up** 포기하다
- **cheap** ⓐ 값싼
- **monthly pass** 한 달 정기권
- **dive into** ~에 뛰어들다
- **whole body** 전신

13 생물 시간에 할 실험 이야기하기

정답률 67% | 정답 ⑤

대화를 듣고, 남자의 마지막 말에 대한 여자의 응답으로 가장 적절한 것을 고르시오. [3점]

Woman: ______

① I'm sorry. I can't go to the lab with you now.
미안해. 난 지금 너랑 실험실에 갈 수 없어.
② I totally agree. We should wash vegetables thoroughly.
전적으로 동의해. 우린 채소를 꼼꼼히 씻어야 해.
③ Sure. It'll be nice to study for the biology exam together.
좋아. 생물 시험을 같이 공부하는 건 좋을 거야.
④ Yeah. Vegetables like broccoli are good for our health.
그래. 브로콜리 같은 채소는 우리 건강에 좋아.
✔⑤ Indeed. I can't wait to do the broccoli cell experiment.
그러게. 브로콜리 세포 실험을 하는 게 몹시 기대돼.

M : Gina, do you know what experiment we're doing in biology class today?
Gina, 너 오늘 생물학 시간에 무슨 실험을 하는지 알고 있어?

W : Sure. We're going to use a microscope to observe broccoli cells.
물론이지. 우린 현미경을 사용해서 브로콜리 세포를 관찰할 거야.

M : That's pretty cool. Have you ever had a chance to do this kind of experiment before?
꽤 근사한걸. 우리가 전에 이런 실험을 해볼 기회가 있었나?

W : No, it's my first time getting a close look at plant cells.
아니, 이번에 난 처음으로 식물 세포를 자세히 살펴보는 거야.

M : Same here. I've only seen illustrations of them in the textbook.
나도 그래. 난 교과서에서 삽화만 봤었어.

W : Me too! I wonder what real plant cells look like.
나도 그래! 진짜 식물 세포는 어떻게 생겼나 궁금해.

M : I guess we'll find out soon.
곧 알 수 있을 거야.

W : Yeah. Oh, the class is about to start. Let's head to the lab quickly.
그러게. 오, 수업 시작할 때야. 빨리 실험실로 가자.

M : Okay. We'll have a lot of fun in the lab, exploring a hidden world within a vegetable.
응, 실험실에서 엄청 재미있을 거야, 채소 안의 숨겨진 세계를 탐구하면서 말이야.

W : Indeed. I can't wait to do the broccoli cell experiment.
그러게. 브로콜리 세포 실험을 하는 게 몹시 기대돼.

Why? 왜 정답일까?

브로콜리 세포 관찰 실험에 관해 이야기하던 남자가 실험이 몹시 재미있을 것이라고 하므로(**We'll have a lot of fun in the lab, exploring a hidden world within a vegetable.**), 여자의 응답으로 가장 적절한 것은 ⑤ '그러게. 브로콜리 세포 실험을 하는 게 몹시 기대돼.'이다.

- **microscope** ⓝ 현미경
- **have a chance to** ~할 기회를 갖다
- **illustration** ⓝ 삽화, 예시
- **lab (laboratory)** ⓝ 실험실
- **thoroughly** ad 꼼꼼히, 철저히

14 서점에 헌책 팔기

정답률 82% | 정답 ②

대화를 듣고, 여자의 마지막 말에 대한 남자의 응답으로 가장 적절한 것을 고르시오.

Man: ______

① Thanks. Donating books is a way to help those in need.
감사합니다. 책 기부는 어려운 분들을 돕는 방법이죠.
✔② My pleasure. My customers will love your books.
제가 감사하죠. 고객분들이 귀하의 책을 좋아할 거예요.
③ Me too. Joining the book club is worth it.
저도 그래요. 독서 동아리에 드는 건 그럴 가치가 있어요.
④ I'd love to. But we don't buy old books anymore.
저도 그러고 싶어요. 하지만 저희는 더 이상 헌책을 사지 않는답니다.
⑤ That's right. So I've ordered those novels for you.
맞아요. 그래서 귀하를 위해 그 소설들을 주문했습니다.

M : Good afternoon. How may I help you?
안녕하세요. 무엇을 도와드릴까요?

W : Hi. I heard that your bookstore buys old books from customers. Is that true?
안녕하세요. 여기 서점은 고객들한테서 헌책을 사신다고 들었는데요. 맞나요?

M : Yes. We buy and sell old books here.
네. 저희 여기서 헌책을 사고팝니다.

W : That's great. Actually, I have a bag of classic novels that you might be interested in.
아주 잘됐네요. 사실 저는 여기서 관심 있을 수도 있는 고전 소설을 좀 가져왔어요.

M : Good! Show me what you have.
좋습니다! 가지고 오신 걸 보여주세요.

W : Here they are.
여기 있습니다.

M : *[Pause]* Wow, these are all remarkable books. I'd love to purchase them. How about $50 for the whole lot?

[문제편 p.146]

[잠시 멈춤] 와, 이것들 모두 드문 책들이네요. 구매하고 싶습니다. 전체 다 해서 50달러 어떠세요?

W : Okay. I'm happy with that.
네, 좋아요.

M : Perfect. Your books contribute to the quality collection in our store. Thank you for bringing them in.
아주 좋습니다. 귀하의 책은 우리 서점의 양질의 소장에 기여하겠네요. 가져와주셔서 감사합니다.

W : You're welcome. It feels great to sell my old books to someone who appreciates them.
별 말씀을요. 제 헌책의 진가를 아시는 분께 책을 팔게 되어서 아주 기뻐요.

M : My pleasure. My customers will love your books.
제가 감사하죠. 고객분들이 귀하의 책을 좋아할 거예요.

Why? 왜 정답일까?

남자의 서점에 중고 책을 팔러 온 여자는 소장품의 질을 높여주어 고맙다는 남자에게 진가를 인정해주는 곳에 책을 팔고 가서 기쁘다고 답한다(**You're welcome. It feels great to sell my old books to someone who appreciates them.**). 따라서 남자의 응답으로 가장 적절한 것은 ② '제가 감사하죠. 고객분들이 귀하의 책을 좋아할 거예요.'이다.

- **remarkable** ⓐ 드문, 놀라운, 주목할 만한
- **appreciate** ⓥ 진가를 알다, 인정하다
- **lot** ⓝ 전부, 많음, 다수
- **those in need** 어려운[도움이 필요한] 사람들

15 홍보 책자에 이름 넣어달라고 요청하기

정답률 76% | 정답 ②

다음 상황 설명을 듣고, Lydia가 Mr. Robinson에게 할 말로 가장 적절한 것을 고르시오. [3점]

Lydia: ______________________

① I'd like to enter the brochure competition next time.
전 다음에 홍보 책자 대회에 참가하고 싶어요.
✔ I'm afraid you forgot to put my name on the brochure.
죄송한데 제 이름을 홍보 책자에 넣는 걸 잊으신 것 같아요.
③ I'm deeply disappointed that I didn't win the competition.
제가 대회에 우승하지 못해 깊이 실망했어요.
④ You haven't shown me the first draft of the brochure.
제게 홍보 책자 초안을 안 보여주셨어요.
⑤ You should've informed me about the competition.
제게 대회에 관해서 알려주셨어야죠.

W : Lydia is a talented high school student who dreams of attending an art college.
Lydia는 미대에 가기를 꿈꾸는 재능 있는 고등학생이다.
This year, she decides to enter the school festival brochure competition.
올해 그녀는 학교 축제 홍보 책자 대회에 나가기로 결심한다.
She is eager to win because the winning artist's name will be included on the brochure.
우승한 아티스트의 이름이 홍보 책자에 포함될 것이기 때문에 그녀는 몹시 우승하고 싶다.
Lydia works hard to create a beautiful design and submits it to Mr. Robinson, the person responsible for the brochure.
Lydia는 아름다운 디자인을 만들려고 열심히 노력하고, 그것을 홍보 책자 담당자인 Robinson 선생님에게 제출한다.
Her hard work pays off when she wins the competition.
그녀의 노력은 그녀가 대회에 우승했을 때 빛을 발한다.
She excitedly looks forward to seeing her name alongside her artwork on the brochure.
그녀는 설레는 마음으로 홍보 책자에 자기 이름이 작품과 함께 실린 걸 보기를 고대한다.
However, when Mr. Robinson shows her the first draft of the brochure, Lydia notices that her name is missing.
하지만, Robinson 선생님이 그녀에게 홍보 책자 초안을 주었을 때, Lydia는 자기 이름이 빠져 있는 것을 발견한다.
She wants to point out the problem to Mr. Robinson.
그녀는 이 문제를 Robinson 선생님에게 지적하고 싶다.
In this situation, what would Lydia most likely say to Mr. Robinson?
이 상황에서, Lydia는 Robinson 선생님에게 뭐라고 말하겠는가?

Lydia : I'm afraid you forgot to put my name on the brochure.
죄송한데 제 이름을 홍보 책자에 넣는 걸 잊으신 것 같아요.

Why? 왜 정답일까?

상황에 따르면 홍보 책자 대회 우승 부상으로 자신의 작품과 이름이 홍보 책자에 함께 실리길 기대했던 Lydia는 이름이 빠진 것을 알고 담당 선생님께 문제를 제기하려 한다(**However, when Mr. Robinson shows her the first draft of the brochure, Lydia notices that her name is missing. She wants to point out the problem to Mr. Robinson.**). 따라서 Lydia가 Robinson 선생님에게 할 말로 가장 적절한 것은 ② '죄송한데 제 이름을 홍보 책자에 넣는 걸 잊으신 것 같아요.'이다.

- **talented** ⓐ 재능 있는
- **be eager to** 몹시 ~하고 싶어하다
- **disappointed** ⓐ 실망한
- **art college** 미술 대학
- **first draft** 초안

16-17 어미와 더 오랜 시간을 보내는 동물들

M : Hello, class! Let's continue talking about animals today.
안녕하세요, 여러분! 동물 이야기를 오늘도 계속해 보죠.
Most animals become independent quite early, some even shortly after they're born.
대부분의 동물들은 꽤 일찍부터 독립하는데, 몇몇은 출생 바로 직후에 그렇게 됩니다.
「However, some animals really enjoy staying with their mothers for a long time.」
하지만, 어떤 동물들은 오래도록 어미와 머물기를 정말 좋아하지요. 16번의 근거
「Chimpanzees live with their mothers for an extended period of time.」 17번 ①의 근거 일치
침팬지는 장기간에 걸쳐 어미와 함께 삽니다.
They are reported to stay with their mothers until they are teenagers.
그들은 10대가 될 때까지 어미 곁에 머무는 것으로 보고됩니다.
「Elephants are also known to live with their mothers for up to 16 years, and sometimes even a lifetime.」 17번 ②의 근거 일치
코끼리도 어미와 최장 16년 같이 사는 것으로 알려져 있고, 때로는 심지어 평생 같이 살기도 합니다.
「Giraffes typically enjoy the company of their mothers for up to two years.」
기린은 보통 생후 2년까지 어미와 함께 있기를 좋아합니다. 17번 ④의 근거 일치
Occasionally female giraffes travel with their mothers until the parent dies.
때때로, 암컷 기린은 어미가 죽을 때까지 자기 어미와 다닙니다.
「Lastly, polar bears remain with their mothers until they are two and a half years old.」
마지막으로, 북극곰은 2살 반이 될 때까지 어미와 함께 지냅니다. 17번 ⑤의 근거 일치
During this period, they learn important survival skills necessary for living in the Arctic environment.
이 기간 동안, 그들은 북극 환경에서 살아가는 데 필요한 중요한 생존 기술을 배웁니다.
Now, let's watch a video clip about these animals.
이제, 이 동물들에 관한 영상을 보시죠.

- **extended** ⓐ 장기간의
- **video clip** 영상
- **similarity** ⓝ 유사점, 공통점
- **Arctic** ⓐ 북극의
- **life expectancy** 기대 수명
- **parenting** ⓝ 양육

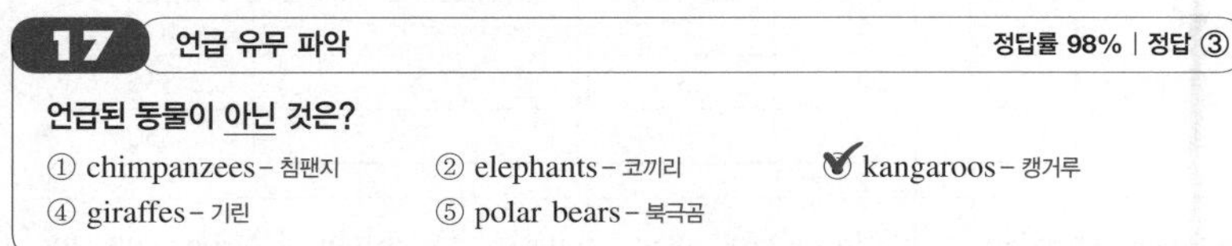

16 주제 파악

정답률 95% | 정답 ③

남자가 하는 말의 주제로 가장 적절한 것은?

① the average life expectancy of animals – 동물들의 평균 기대 수명
② similarities between humans and animals – 동물과 인간의 공통점
✔ animals that stay longer with their mothers – 어미와 더 오래 머무는 동물들
④ independent animals that travel and live alone – 혼자 다니고 살아가는 독립적인 동물들
⑤ different roles of mothers and fathers in parenting – 양육에 있어 엄마와 아빠의 서로 다른 역할

Why? 왜 정답일까?

동물들은 대부분 일찍 독립하지만, 부모와 더 오래 붙어 사는 동물들도 있다(**However, some animals really enjoy staying with their mothers for a long time.**)는 내용이므로, 여자가 하는 말의 주제로 가장 적절한 것은 ③ '어미와 더 오래 머무는 동물들'이다.

17 언급 유무 파악

정답률 98% | 정답 ③

언급된 동물이 아닌 것은?

① chimpanzees – 침팬지 ② elephants – 코끼리 ✔ kangaroos – 캥거루
④ giraffes – 기린 ⑤ polar bears – 북극곰

Why? 왜 정답일까?

담화에서 여자는 어미와 더 오래 머무는 동물들의 예로 침팬지, 코끼리, 기린, 북극곰을 언급하므로, 언급되지 않은 동물은 ③ '캥거루'이다.

Why? 왜 오답일까?

① '**Chimpanzees live with their mothers for an extended period of time.**'에서 '침팬지'가 언급되었다.
② '**Elephants are also known to live with their mothers for up to 16 years, and sometimes even a lifetime.**'에서 '코끼리'가 언급되었다.
④ '**Giraffes typically enjoy the company of their mothers for up to two years.**'에서 '기린'이 언급되었다.
⑤ '**Lastly, polar bears remain with their mothers until they are two and a half years old.**'에서 '북극곰'이 언급되었다.

Dictation 25

문제편 147쪽

01 take great pride in / outdoor rides will be temporarily closed / our top priority
02 using the same password / prevent potential hacking attempts / every three to six months
03 gracefully declining someone's request / offering a reason when saying no / honest about our own limitations
04 selling organic food / wearing his chef's hat / the stripe-patterned parasol
05 the arts and crafts market preparations / secured any sponsors / through a promotional message
06 a cotton candy machine / it has better reviews / let's get three packs then
07 plenty of time to practice / I decided not to / a college entrance interview
08 specifically designed for the elderly / surfing the web / run for three months
09 a free mug with each ticket / the art of brewing / if you book early
10 more than a week / a heavy Internet user / That eliminates this option
11 heading to the hospital / What amazing news
12 make sure to visit / isn't it too cold to swim
13 use a microscope / illustrations of them / the class is about to start
14 all remarkable books / contribute to the quality collection / someone who appreciates them
15 attending an art college / Her hard work pays off / her name is missing
16-17 for an extended period of time / enjoy the company of their mothers / learn important survival skills

[문제편 p.146]

26회 | 2022학년도 10월 학력평가 고3

| 정답과 해설 |

• 정답 •

01 ② 02 ② 03 ④ 04 ⑤ 05 ① 06 ③ 07 ① 08 ③ 09 ⑤ 10 ② 11 ② 12 ⑤ 13 ② 14 ③ 15 ③ 16 ② 17 ②

01 홍보 영상 참가 지원자 댄스 오디션 공지

정답률 82% | 정답 ②

다음을 듣고, 남자가 하는 말의 목적으로 가장 적절한 것을 고르시오.

① 동영상 편집 강좌를 홍보하려고
✔ 학교 홍보 영상 출연자를 모집하려고
③ 교내 댄스 동아리 가입을 권유하려고
④ 웹 사이트 제작 경연 대회를 안내하려고
⑤ 신입생 환영 행사 아이디어를 공모하려고

M : Hello, students. This is your vice principal, Mr. Smith.
안녕하세요, 학생 여러분. 교감인 Smith 선생입니다.
Our school is going to make a promotional video for future freshmen.
우리 학교에서 미래 신입생을 위한 홍보 영상을 제작하려고 합니다.
It'll be a music video with students doing dances.
학생들이 춤을 추는 뮤직비디오가 될 것입니다.
The famous dance director, Kiera Turner, will help us.
유명한 댄스 감독인 Kiera Turner가 우리를 도와줄 것입니다.
She'll be auditioning the applicants in the auditorium on Tuesday, October 25th.
그녀는 10월 25일 화요일 강당에서 지원자 오디션을 볼 예정입니다.
If you want to participate and show off your talents, just sign up using the QR code posted on the school bulletin board by this Friday.
참가해서 여러분의 끼를 선보이고 싶다면, 학교 게시판에 올라온 QR코드를 이용해 이번 주 금요일까지 등록하기만 하면 됩니다.
We'll upload the video on our school website after it's been completed, so please don't miss out on this wonderful opportunity to contribute to our school.
영상이 완성되고 나면 학교 웹 사이트에 올릴 예정이니, 우리 학교를 위해 기여할 수 있는 이 멋진 기회를 놓치지 마세요.

Why? 왜 정답일까?

'Our school is going to make a promotional video for future freshmen.'과 'If you want to participate and show off your talents, just sign up using the QR code posted on the school bulletin board by this Friday.'에서 학교 홍보 영상에서 춤추기를 희망하는 지원자는 QR코드로 오디션에 등록해 참가하라고 하므로, 남자가 하는 말의 목적으로 가장 적절한 것은 ② '학교 홍보 영상 출연자를 모집하려고'이다.

- vice principal 교감
- promotional ⓐ 홍보의
- freshman ⓝ 신입생
- applicant ⓝ 지원자
- auditorium ⓝ 강당
- show off ~을 선보이다, 자랑하다
- miss out on ~을 놓치다

02 목 통증을 야기할 수 있는 수면 자세

정답률 97% | 정답 ②

대화를 듣고, 여자의 의견으로 가장 적절한 것을 고르시오.

① 장시간의 컴퓨터 작업은 위장 활동을 저해한다.
✔ 엎드려 자는 자세는 목에 통증을 유발할 수 있다.
③ 잠자기 전 가벼운 스트레칭은 숙면에 도움을 준다.
④ 올바른 자세를 위해 모니터 높이를 조절해야 한다.
⑤ 잠자는 자세를 보면 그 사람의 성격을 알 수 있다.

W : Owen, why are you massaging your neck?
Owen, 왜 목을 마사지하고 있어?
M : Hey, Karen. My neck feels stiff.
안녕, Karen. 목이 좀 뻣뻣한 것 같아서.
W : That's too bad. When did it start?
안됐네. 언제부터 그랬어?
M : It's been stiff for a while, but it's gotten worse lately. I think it might be because my monitor is too low.
뻣뻣한 지 좀 됐는데, 최근에 심해졌어. 아마 내 모니터가 너무 낮게 있어서 그런가봐.
W : The height seems fine. Umm... Do you sleep on your stomach, by any chance?
높이는 괜찮아 보이는데. 음… 혹시 너 엎드려서 자?
M : How did you know that? Yes, I'm a stomach sleeper.
어떻게 알았어? 맞아, 나 엎드려서 자.
W : Well... Sleeping on your stomach may lead to some pretty bad pain in your neck.
음… 엎드려서 자는 건 네 목에 꽤 심한 통증을 야기할 수 있어.
M : Are you saying that my neck pain came from my sleeping position?
내 목 통증이 내 잠자는 자세 때문이란 말야?
W : Right. Your neck gets twisted to one side when you sleep on your stomach. It can cause neck pain.
맞아. 네 목은 네가 잠자는 동안 한쪽으로 꺾이게 돼. 그게 목 통증을 일으킬 수 있지.
M : That makes sense. I'll try changing my sleeping position, then.
일리가 있네. 그럼, 내 잠자는 자세를 바꿔봐야겠다.
W : Yeah. I'm sure it'll help.
응. 분명 그건 도움이 될 거야.

Why? 왜 정답일까?

'Sleeping on your stomach may lead to some pretty bad pain in your neck.'에서 여자는 엎드려 자는 자세가 목 통증을 일으킬 수 있다고 말한 뒤 근거를 들고 있으므로, 여자의 의견으로 가장 적절한 것은 ② '엎드려 자는 자세는 목에 통증을 유발할 수 있다.'이다.

- stiff ⓐ 뻣뻣한
- get worse 나빠지다, 심해지다
- lately ad 최근에, 얼마 전에
- sleep on one's stomach 엎드려 자다
- by any chance (의문문에서) 혹시
- twist ⓥ 구부리다, 비틀다
- make sense 일리가 있다

03 환경 운동가 취재

정답률 92% | 정답 ④

대화를 듣고, 두 사람의 관계를 가장 잘 나타낸 것을 고르시오.

① 소설가 – 편집자
② 환경미화원 – 관광객
③ 기자 – 프로듀서
✔ 방송 작가 – 환경 운동가
⑤ 사진작가 – 낚시꾼

M : Ms. Lopez, I'm pleased to meet you.
Lopez 씨, 만나서 반갑습니다.
W : Hello, Mr. Stewart. You are preparing scripts for a documentary TV show, right?
안녕하세요, Stewart 씨. 다큐멘터리 TV 프로그램 대본을 준비하고 계신다고요, 맞죠?
M : Yes, so I need your story. You've been fighting to save the environment for 20 years?
네, 그래서 당신의 이야기가 필요해요. 당신은 20년 동안 환경 보호를 위해 분투 중이시죠?
W : Yes. I can't believe it's been that long.
네, 그게 그렇게 오래 됐다니 믿을 수 없군요.
M : What made you start your journey as an activist in the first place?
맨 처음에 무엇 때문에 환경 운동가로서의 여정을 시작하시게 됐나요?
W : Actually, it started from a simple accident.
사실, 그건 간단한 사고로 시작됐어요.
M : Really? What happened?
정말요? 무슨 일이 있었죠?
W : A friend of mine cut his foot on a fishhook while walking barefoot on the beach with me.
제 친구 중 한 명이 저랑 맨발로 바닷가를 걷다가 낚시바늘에 발을 베였죠.
M : Ouch! A careless fisherman must have left it after fishing.
저런! 조심성 없는 낚시꾼이 낚시를 하고 나서 두고 갔나 보군요.
W : Right. I saw all kinds of waste materials around me and organized my first beach clean-up. That was the beginning of my career.
맞아요. 주위에 있는 온갖 쓰레기를 보고서 제 최초의 해변 청소를 기획했죠. 그게 제 경력의 시작이었어요.
M : I see. I'd like to use your story when I write the introductory scene for the show.
그렇군요. 제가 프로그램의 도입부 장면을 쓸 때 당신의 이야기를 쓰고 싶어요.

Why? 왜 정답일까?

'You are preparing scripts for a documentary TV show, right?'와 'You've been fighting to save the environment for 20 years?'을 통해 TV 다큐멘터리 프로그램을 준비하는 방송 작가가 20년 경력의 환경 운동가를 인터뷰하는 상황임을 알 수 있으므로, 두 사람의 관계로 가장 적절한 것은 ④ '방송 작가 – 환경 운동가'이다.

- prepare ⓥ 준비하다
- fight ⓥ 싸우다, 분투하다
- save the environment 환경을 보호하다
- activist ⓝ 운동가, 활동가
- in the first place 처음에, 애초에
- fishhook ⓝ 낚시바늘
- barefoot ad 맨발로
- careless ⓐ 조심성 없는
- introductory ⓐ 도입의, 서두의

04 촬영 세트장 점검하기

정답률 91% | 정답 ⑤

대화를 듣고, 그림에서 대화의 내용과 일치하지 않는 것을 고르시오.

W : The shooting starts soon. Are you ready, Jackson?
촬영이 곧 시작될 거예요. 준비됐어요, Jackson?
M : Yes. I'm adjusting the camera angles for the set.
네, 전 카메라 각도를 세트 쪽으로 맞추고 있어요.
W : 『I like the floor lamp on the left.』 It goes well with the set. ①의 근거 일치
왼쪽에 있는 플로어 스탠드 마음에 드네요. 세트랑 잘 어울려요.
M : Yeah. 『There are three different chairs around the table.』 Are they for our guests?
네, 테이블 주위에 의자가 세 개 있네요. 우리 게스트를 위한 건가요? ②의 근거 일치
W : Yes. 『Look at the star-shaped cushion on one of the chairs.』 The star represents our program's title, StarMaking. ③의 근거 일치
네, 의자 중 하나에 놓인 별 모양 쿠션 좀 봐요. 별은 우리 프로그램 제목인 StarMaking을 상징해요.
M : Good. 『I see the piano next to the plant.』 ④의 근거 일치
좋아요. 화분 옆에 피아노가 있네요.
Is someone going to play the piano?
누가 피아노를 치나요?
W : Of course, our guests are all musicians. I want to film them singing along to the piano.
물론이죠, 우리 게스트는 다 뮤지션인걸요. 그들이 피아노에 맞춰 노래하는 모습을 찍고 싶어요.
M : Great. The audience will enjoy their performance. 『There are bottles of water on the table.』 Are they from our program's sponsor? ⑤의 근거 불일치
좋아요. 관객들이 그들의 공연을 즐기겠군요. 테이블 위에 물병이 있어요. 우리 프로그램 스폰서로부터 온 건가요?
W : Yes. The brand name should be visible when the guests drink them.
네, 게스트들이 그걸 마실 때 브랜드가 눈에 보여야 해요.
M : Okay. I'll take care of it.
알겠습니다. 그렇게 할게요.

Why? 왜 정답일까?

대화에서는 테이블 위에 물병이 있다고 하는데(There are bottles of water on the table.), 그림 속 물병은 테이블 밑에 놓여 있다. 따라서 그림에서 대화의 내용과 일치하지 않는 것은 ⑤이다.

[문제편 p.151]

- shooting ⓝ 촬영
- go well with ~와 잘 어울리다
- take care of ~을 처리하다
- adjust ⓥ 조정하다, 맞추다
- sing along to ~에 맞추어 노래하다

05 리조트 퇴실 준비하기

정답률 84% | 정답 ①

대화를 듣고, 남자가 할 일로 가장 적절한 것을 고르시오.

✔ 튜브에서 바람 빼기
② 수영복 챙기기
③ 숙박 시설 검색하기
④ 식당 예약하기
⑤ 퇴실 시간 문의하기

W : Honey, I can't believe it's our last day at this resort.
여보, 이 리조트에서의 마지막 밤이라니 믿을 수 없어요.
M : Yeah, but it was nice to relax throughout our stay here.
네, 하지만 여기 머무는 내내 휴식을 취해서 좋았어요.
W : Right. I liked the swimming pool the most.
맞아요. 난 수영장이 제일 마음에 들었어요.
M : So did I. It was great to swim every day. Anyway, what's the checkout time?
나도 그랬어요. 매일 수영해서 아주 좋았어요. 그나저나, 퇴실 시간이 몇 시죠?
W : By 11 a.m. Why don't we have lunch at Del Casa after checkout?
아침 11시까지예요. 퇴실하고 나서 Del Casa에서 점심을 먹으면 어때요?
M : Good. Should I make a reservation?
좋아요. 내가 예약을 해야 할까요?
W : Actually, they don't accept reservations.
사실, 거긴 예약을 받지 않아요.
M : Don't they? Let's finish packing first. Did you put our swimsuits in the bag?
그래요? 짐 싸는 것부터 먼저 끝내죠. 가방에 우리 수영복 챙겨 넣었어요?
W : Yes, I already did. We also need to let the air out of the pool tube.
네, 이미 넣었죠. 우린 튜브 공기도 빼야 해요.
M : Okay. I'll do it right away.
알겠어요. 내가 그걸 바로 할게요.
W : Thanks. In the meantime, I'll do a final check.
고마워요. 그동안 나는 최종 점검을 할게요.

Why? 왜 정답일까?

여자가 수영할 때 썼던 튜브 공기를 빼야 한다고 말하자(We also need to let the air out of the pool tube.) 남자는 자신이 바로 빼겠다고 하므로(Okay. I'll do it right away.), 남자가 할 일로 가장 적절한 것은 ① '튜브에서 바람 빼기'이다.

- relax ⓥ 휴식을 취하다
- make a reservation 예약하다
- pack ⓥ 짐을 싸다
- in the meantime 그동안, 한편
- checkout ⓝ 체크아웃, 퇴실, 반납
- accept ⓥ 접수하다, 받다
- let out ~을 빼다
- do a final check 최종 점검을 하다

06 자전거 대여하기

정답률 90% | 정답 ③

대화를 듣고, 여자가 지불할 금액을 고르시오. [3점]

① $54 ② $60 ✔ $63 ④ $70 ⑤ $75

M : Welcome to Purple Bike Rental Shop. How may I help you?
Purple Bike Rental Shop에 잘 오셨습니다. 무엇을 도와드릴까요?
W : Hi. I want to rent some bikes.
안녕하세요. 전 자전거를 좀 빌리고 싶어요.
M : We have regular bikes and electric bikes.
일반 자전거와 전기 자전거가 있습니다.
W : Okay. How much do they cost to rent for a day?
그렇군요. 하루 빌리는 데 얼마죠?
M : Regular bikes are $25 each, and electric bikes are $30 each.
일반 자전거는 한 대에 25달러이고, 전기 자전거는 한 대에 30달러입니다.
W : Then, I'll rent two electric bikes. Does the rental include a helmet?
그럼, 전기 자전거 두 대를 빌릴게요. 대여에 헬멧도 포함인가요?
M : It sure does.
물론입니다.
W : Very good. Do you offer a bike collection service?
아주 좋네요. 자전거 수거 서비스는요?
M : Yes, but there's an additional charge. It costs $5 for one bike.
있습니다. 하지만 추가 비용이 듭니다. 자전거 한 대당 5달러입니다.
W : I'll use the collection service for the two bikes. Can I use this discount coupon?
수거 서비스 두 대 이용할게요. 이 할인 쿠폰을 쓸 수 있나요?
M : Sure. You'll get a 10% discount off the total.
네. 총 금액에서 10퍼센트 할인을 받으시게 됩니다.
W : Good. Here's my credit card.
좋아요. 여기 제 신용카드요.

Why? 왜 정답일까?

대화에 따르면 여자는 한 대당 30달러에 전기 자전거 두 대를 빌리기로 하고(~ electric bikes are $30 each. / Then, I'll rent two electric bikes.), 한 대에 5달러씩인 수거 서비스도 이용하기로 했으며(It costs $5 for one bike. / I'll use the collection service for the two bikes.), 총 금액에서 10퍼센트를 할인받았다. 이를 식으로 나타내면 '$(30\times2+5\times2)\times0.9=63$'이므로, 여자가 지불할 금액은 ③ '$63'이다.

- rent ⓥ 빌리다, 대여하다
- cost ⓥ (비용이) ~이다
- additional ⓐ 추가적인
- electric ⓐ 전기의
- collection ⓝ 수거, 모음
- charge ⓝ 비용 ⓥ 부과하다

07 학생회 자선 행사에 갈 수 없는 이유

정답률 97% | 정답 ①

대화를 듣고, 남자가 학생회 자선 행사에 갈 수 없는 이유를 고르시오.

✔ 뮤지컬을 보러 가야 해서
② 병원 진료를 받아야 해서
③ 농구 시합에 출전해야 해서
④ 기말고사 준비를 해야 해서
⑤ 자원봉사를 하러 가야 해서

W : Scott, the Student Council Charity Event is this Saturday at the gym, right?
Scott, 학생회 자선 행사가 이번 주 토요일 체육관에서 열리지, 맞아?
M : No. It's next Saturday.
아니, 다음 주 토요일이야.
W : Really? I thought it's this Saturday.
정말? 난 그게 이번 주인줄 알았어.
M : You must be mistaken. There's a basketball match scheduled this Saturday.
착각했나보네. 이번 주에는 농구 경기가 예정돼 있어.
W : I see. Then, why don't we go to the charity event together next Saturday?
그렇구나. 그럼, 다음 주 토요일에 자선 행사 같이 가면 어때?
M : I'm afraid I can't.
미안한데 못 갈 것 같아.
W : Oh, I forgot you sometimes do volunteer work at the hospital on Saturday.
오, 나 네가 토요일에 병원에서 가끔 자원봉사 하는 걸 잊고 있었네.
M : Yes, but I'm not doing it next Saturday.
맞아, 그런데 다음 주 토요일에는 하지 않아.
W : Then why can't you go to the charity event?
그럼 왜 자선 행사에 못 가?
M : I promised to see a musical with my younger brother. I couldn't spend much time with him recently because of the final exams.
난 내 남동생하고 뮤지컬 보기로 약속했어. 요새 기말고사 때문에 동생이랑 시간을 많이 못 보냈거든.
W : No problem. I hope you have a good time with your brother.
괜찮아. 남동생하고 즐거운 시간 보내길 바랄게.

Why? 왜 정답일까?

대화에 따르면 남자는 기말고사 기간에 시간을 함께 보내지 못한 남동생과 뮤지컬을 보러 가기로 해서(I promised to see a musical with my younger brother.) 학생회 자선 행사에 갈 수 없다고 하므로, 남자가 자선 행사에 갈 수 없는 이유로 가장 적절한 것은 ① '뮤지컬을 보러 가야 해서'이다.

- charity event 자선행사
- You must be mistaken. 너 오해했나보다. 착각했나 보다.
- match ⓝ 시합, 경기
- final exam 기말고사
- do volunteer work 자원봉사를 하다

08 김치 요리 대회

정답률 93% | 정답 ③

대화를 듣고, Kimchi Dish Contest에 관해 언급되지 않은 것을 고르시오.

① 경연 과제
② 주최 기관
✔ 우승 상금
④ 시작 연도
⑤ 참가 자격

M : Hey, Clara. Guess what I did last weekend.
안녕, Clara. 내가 지난 주말에 뭐했는지 맞춰 봐.
W : I heard you won the Kimchi Dish Contest. Congratulations!
네가 Kimchi Dish Contest에서 우승했다고 들었어. 축하해!
M : Thank you. I'm happy to be this year's winner.
고마워. 난 올해의 우승자가 되어서 기뻐.
W : I didn't know that there's a kimchi-themed cooking contest. Is it an annual event, then?
난 김치를 주제로 한 요리 대회가 있다는 걸 몰랐어. 그거 그럼 해마다 하는 행사야?
M : Yes. 『Every year, all participants are required to make a fusion dish using kimchi.』 I made kimchi pizza. ①의 근거 일치
응. 매년 모든 참가자가 김치를 사용해서 퓨전 요리를 만들어야 해. 난 김치 피자를 만들었어.
W : Sounds good. 『Who organizes the contest?
괜찮았을 거 같다. 누가 대회를 주최해?
M : It's the Institute of Korean Food and Culture.』 ②의 근거 일치
Institute of Korean Food and Culture야.
W : I see. 『How long has it been running?
그렇구나. 열린 지 얼마나 됐어?
M : The first contest was held in 2015.』 ④의 근거 일치
첫 대회가 2015년에 열렸어.
W : That's quite some time ago. I want to participate myself next year. 『Are there any special requirements for me to participate?
꽤 오래 전이구나. 나도 내년엔 직접 참가해보고 싶어. 내가 참가하기 위한 뭐 특별한 자격요건이 있니?
M : Any foreigners residing in Korea can compete.』 ⑤의 근거 일치
한국에 거주 중인 외국인이면 누구나 참가할 수 있어.
W : Great. I'll give it a try.
좋네. 나도 시도해봐야지.

Why? 왜 정답일까?

대화에서 남자와 여자는 Kimchi Dish Contest의 경연 과제, 주최 기관, 시작 연도, 참가 자격을 언급하고 있으므로, 언급되지 않은 것은 ③ '우승 상금'이다.

Why? 왜 오답일까?

① 'Every year, all participants are required to make a fusion dish using kimchi.'에서 '경연 과제'가 언급되었다.
② 'It's the Institute of Korean Food and Culture.'에서 '주최 기관'이 언급되었다.
④ 'The first contest was held in 2015.'에서 '시작 연도'가 언급되었다.
⑤ 'Any foreigners residing in Korea can compete.'에서 '참가 자격'이 언급되었다.

- annual ⓐ 연마다 하는
- fusion dish 퓨전 요리
- requirement ⓝ 요구사항
- be required to ~해야 하다
- institute ⓝ (교육) 기관

09 도시 투어 버스 특가 행사 안내

정답률 95% | 정답 ⑤

Full Day City Tour에 관한 다음 내용을 듣고, 일치하지 않는 것을 고르시오.

① 호텔 투숙객에게 특가로 제공한다.
② 매일 오전 10시에 버스가 출발한다.
③ 여섯 곳의 주요 관광 명소에 들른다.

[문제편 p.151]

④ 전문 여행 가이드가 동행한다.
✓⑤ 점심 식사를 무료로 제공한다.

W : Good evening, Central Hotel guests.
안녕하세요, Central Hotel 투숙객 여러분.
We are happy to inform you about a special promotion for the Full Day City Tour.
여러분들께 Full Day City Tour의 특별 프로모션을 알려드릴 수 있어 기쁩니다.
「This tour normally costs $90 but is offered to our hotel guests at a special price of just $55.」①의 근거 일치
이 투어는 원래 90달러인데, 우리 호텔 투숙객 분들께는 단돈 55달러라는 특가에 제공됩니다.
「Leaving at 10 a.m. every morning, a luxury coach bus takes you around the city.」②의 근거 일치
매일 오전 10시에 출발하는 호화 대형 버스가 여러분을 태우고 도시를 돕니다.
「It stops at six major tourist attractions, including the waterfront and the Museum of Art History.」③의 근거 일치
이것은 여섯 곳의 주요 관광 명소에 들르는데, 해안가와 Museum of Art History가 여기 포함됩니다.
「Professional tour guides are with you every step of the way, answering questions and providing fascinating information.」④의 근거 일치
가는 내내 전문 여행 가이드가 여러분과 동행하며, 질문에 답하고 아주 흥미로운 정보를 제공해 드립니다.
「There is also a stop so that you can buy lunch.」⑤의 근거 불일치
여러분이 점심을 살 수 있는 정거장도 있습니다.
Please come to the reception desk if you're interested in signing up. Thank you.
등록에 관심이 있으시면 안내 데스크로 와주시기 바랍니다. 감사합니다.

Why? 왜 정답일까?

'There is also a stop so that you can bVuy lunch.'에서 관광객들이 점심을 사 먹을 수 있는 정거장도 있다고 하므로, 내용과 일치하지 않는 것은 ⑤ '점심 식사를 무료로 제공한다.'이다.

Why? 왜 오답일까?

① 'This tour normally costs $90 but is offered to our hotel guests at a special price of just $55.'의 내용과 일치한다.
② 'Leaving at 10 a.m. every morning, a luxury coach bus takes you around the city.'의 내용과 일치한다.
③ 'It stops at six major tourist attractions, including the waterfront and the Museum of Art History.'의 내용과 일치한다.
④ 'Professional tour guides are with you every step of the way, ~'의 내용과 일치한다.

- coach bus 대형 버스
- tourist attraction 관광 명소
- waterfront ⓝ 해안가
- fascinating ⓐ 대단히 흥미로운

10 캔들 워머 램프 고르기

정답률 80% | 정답 ②

다음 표를 보면서 대화를 듣고, 남자가 구입할 캔들 워머 램프를 고르시오.

Candle Warmer Lamp

	Model	Price	Shade Color	Base Material	Timer
①	A	$65	gold	metal	○
✓②	B	$52	white	marble stone	○
③	C	$45	black	marble stone	×
④	D	$40	pink	marble stone	○
⑤	E	$37	white	metal	×

M : Hey, Emily. Would you help me choose a candle warmer lamp for my sister's birthday gift?
안녕, Emily. 내 여동생 생일 선물로 캔들 워머 램프 좀 고르는 걸 도와줄래?
W : Sure. *[Pause]* These five models look pretty good. 「What's your budget?
그래. *[잠시 멈춤]* 이 다섯 개 제품이 꽤 괜찮아 보이네. 예산이 얼마야?
M : I can spend up to $60.」근거1 Price 조건
60달러까지는 쓸 수 있어.
W : Okay. The lamp shades come in different colors. 「Does your sister have any color preferences?
알겠어. 램프 갓이 각기 다른 색깔로 나오네. 네 여동생이 좋아하는 색이 있어?
M : She doesn't like pink. I think the other colors will be okay.」근거2 Shade Color 조건
걔는 분홍색을 안 좋아해. 나머지 색은 괜찮을 것 같아.
W : Got it. 「I recommend the ones with a marble stone base.」 They're strong and beautiful.
알겠어. 대리석 받침이 있는 것을 추천할게. 그게 튼튼하고 예뻐. 근거3 Base material 조건
M : Great. They can also be used as a beautiful home decoration.
좋았어. 그게 또 아름다운 집 장식품으로 사용될 수도 있고.
W : Then these two are the best options.
그럼 이거 두 개가 제일 낫겠네.
M : Right. 「Do you think the candle warmer lamp with a timer is better?
맞아. 타이머가 있는 캔들 워머 등이 더 나을까?
W : With that function, your sister doesn't need to worry about the warmer getting overheated.」근거4 Timer 조건
그 기능이 있으면, 네 여동생은 워머가 과열될까봐 걱정할 필요가 없어.
M : Then, I'll buy the one with a timer. Thanks.
그럼, 타이머가 있는 것으로 사야겠다. 고마워.

Why? 왜 정답일까?

대화에 따르면 남자는 가격이 60달러를 넘지 않으면서, 램프 갓의 색상은 분홍색이 아니고, 대리석 받침과 타이머 기능이 있는 캔들 워머 램프를 사려고 한다. 따라서 남자가 구입할 캔들 워머 램프는 ② 'B'이다.

- candle warmer lamp 캔들 워머 램프
- budget ⓝ 예산
- marble ⓝ 대리석
- overheat ⓥ 과열하다

11 메뉴 주문 받기

정답률 84% | 정답 ②

대화를 듣고, 여자의 마지막 말에 대한 남자의 응답으로 가장 적절한 것을 고르시오.

① I'm glad to hear you enjoyed your food today.
오늘 음식을 맛있게 드셨다니 기쁩니다.
✓② We've run out of ingredients to make the dish.
그 요리 재료가 다 떨어졌습니다.
③ Thank you for bringing your home-cooked food.
당신이 집에서 만든 음식을 가져와 주셔서 고맙습니다.
④ I'll let you know when your seats are available.
고객님의 좌석이 생기면 알려드리겠습니다.
⑤ I'll recommend the special creamy salmon pasta.
스페셜 연어 크림 파스타를 추천하겠습니다.

W : Excuse me. I'd like to order the special creamy salmon pasta.
실례합니다. 스페셜 연어 크림 파스타 주문하고 싶어요.
M : We're very sorry. We can't take any orders for that dish right now.
대단히 죄송합니다. 지금 그 파스타 주문은 받을 수가 없어요.
W : Why not? I've come here especially to eat that pasta.
왜요? 전 특별히 그걸 먹으려고 여기 왔는데요.
M : We've run out of ingredients to make the dish.
그 요리 재료가 다 떨어졌습니다.

Why? 왜 정답일까?

여자는 특별히 먹고 싶었던 파스타 주문이 불가하다는 말에 이유를 묻고 있으므로(Why not? I've come here especially to eat that pasta.), 남자의 응답으로 가장 적절한 것은 ② 'We've run out of ingredients to make the dish.(그 요리 재료가 다 떨어졌습니다.)'이다.

- salmon ⓝ 연어
- take an order 주문을 받다
- run out of ~이 다 떨어지다
- home-cooked ⓐ 집에서 요리한

12 발표에 입고 갈 정장 찾기

정답률 78% | 정답 ⑤

대화를 듣고, 남자의 마지막 말에 대한 여자의 응답으로 가장 적절한 것을 고르시오.

① I'm afraid that I can't get this stain out. – 미안하지만 이 얼룩은 못 뺄 것 같구나.
② Sorry. I'll take it to the dry cleaner's now. – 미안해. 지금 그걸 드라이클리닝 맡겨줄게.
③ No way. You should organize the closet today. – 절대 안 돼. 넌 오늘 옷장 정리를 해야 한다.
④ You should have worn the suit at the presentation. – 그 정장을 발표에 입고 갔어야지.
✓⑤ Don't worry. I'm going to pick it up this afternoon. – 걱정 마. 오늘 오후에 찾으러 갈게.

M : Have you seen my gray suit, Mom? It was in the closet a week ago, but I can't find it now.
제 회색 정장 보셨어요, 엄마? 일주일 전에 옷장에 있었는데 지금 못 찾겠어요.
W : I took it to the dry cleaner's because it had a big stain.
큰 얼룩이 있길래 드라이클리닝 맡겼지.
M : Oh, my! I need to wear it to an important presentation tomorrow.
오, 이런! 저 내일 중요한 발표에 그걸 입고 가야 해요.
W : Don't worry. I'm going to pick it up this afternoon.
걱정 마. 오늘 오후에 찾으러 갈게.

Why? 왜 정답일까?

자신이 찾던 회색 정장을 세탁소에 맡겼다는 여자에게 남자는 내일 중요한 발표가 있어 그 옷을 입어야 한다(I need to wear it to an important presentation tomorrow.)고 하므로, 여자의 응답으로 가장 적절한 것은 ⑤ 'Don't worry. I'm going to pick it up this afternoon.(걱정 마. 오늘 오후에 찾으러 갈게.)'이다.

- suit ⓝ 정장
- closet ⓝ 옷장
- stain ⓝ 얼룩

13 늦은 생일 선물 챙기기

정답률 90% | 정답 ②

대화를 듣고, 여자의 마지막 말에 대한 남자의 응답으로 가장 적절한 것을 고르시오. [3점]

Man: ______

① Hurry up. Her birthday is coming soon.
서둘러. 그녀의 생일이 곧 다가오고 있어.
✓② Sounds great. I'm sure it'll make her feel better.
좋을 것 같네. 그게 분명 친구 기분을 나아지게 해줄 거야.
③ Sure. You should have bought her another model.
물론이지. 넌 그녀에게 다른 제품을 사줬어야 했어.
④ No worries. This keyboard is what I want to have.
걱정 마. 이 키보드는 내가 갖고 싶은 거야.
⑤ A belated happy birthday to you. This gift is for you.
늦었지만 생일 축하해. 이 선물 네 거야.

M : You look down. What's wrong, Jennifer?
우울해 보이네. 무슨 일이야, Jennifer?
W : Dad, you know my best friend Betty? Her birthday was the day before yesterday, but I totally forgot about it.
아빠, 제 제일 친한 친구 Betty 아시죠? 걔 생일이 그저께였는데, 제가 완전히 잊어버렸어요.
M : Oh dear. She must have been very disappointed.
오, 저런. 그 친구가 매우 실망했겠구나.
W : Absolutely. Now I understand why she has been so cold to me since yesterday.
맞아요. 왜 어제부터 걔가 저한테 그렇게 차가웠는지 이제 이해가 가요.
M : It would have been nice if she had told you in advance that her birthday was coming.
친구가 자기 생일이 다가오고 있다고 미리 너한테 말해주면 좋았을 텐데.
W : Well... I think so too.
음… 저도 그렇게 생각해요.
M : Why don't you give her a birthday gift even though it's late?
늦었지만 친구한테 생일 선물을 주는 게 어떨까?
W : That's exactly what I'm thinking.
제가 딱 그렇게 생각하고 있었어요.
M : Do you have anything good in mind?
뭐 좋은 걸 생각한 게 있니?
W : I'm going to buy her a bluetooth keyboard. She has always wanted to get one.
블루투스 키보드를 사주려고요. 항상 갖고 싶어 했거든요.
M : Sounds great. I'm sure it'll make her feel better.
좋을 것 같네. 그게 분명 친구 기분을 나아지게 해줄 거야.

Why? 왜 정답일까?

친구의 생일을 잊고 못 챙긴 여자에게 남자는 비록 늦었지만 생일 선물을 챙겨주는 것이 어떤지 제안하고, 여자는 마침 친구가 갖고 싶어하던 블루투스 키보드를 사줄 예정이라고 말한다(I'm going to buy her a bluetooth keyboard. She has always wanted to get one.). 따라서 남자의 응답으로 가장

적절한 것은 ② 'Sounds great. I'm sure it'll make her feel better.(좋을 것 같네. 그게 분명 친구 기분을 나아지게 해줄 거야.)'이다.

- You look down. 우울해 보이네.
- birthday gift 생일 선물
- disappointed ⓐ 실망한
- belated ⓐ 뒤늦은

14 인터넷 수리 일정 변경하기 정답률 93% | 정답 ③

대화를 듣고, 남자의 마지막 말에 대한 여자의 응답으로 가장 적절한 것을 고르시오. [3점]

Woman: ______

① Right. He's been away from work for five days.
맞습니다. 그는 5일간 부재중이세요.
② No problem. I'll send you an engineer right away.
알겠습니다. 지금 바로 기사님을 보내겠습니다.
③ Okay. He'll call you before he makes the visit tomorrow.
알겠습니다. 내일 기사님이 방문하시기 전에 전화 드릴 거예요.
④ Sure. You can use the Internet service anywhere at home.
물론입니다. 집안 어디서든 인터넷을 사용하실 수 있어요.
⑤ Sorry. You need to change your Internet service provider.
죄송합니다. 인터넷 서비스 제공사를 바꾸셔야 합니다.

[Telephone rings.]
[전화벨이 울린다.]

W : Gladmax Broadband. How may I help you?
Gladmax Broadband입니다. 무엇을 도와드릴까요?

M : Hello, my name is Morris Davis. I called yesterday.
안녕하세요, 제 이름은 Morris Davis입니다. 어제 전화드렸었어요.

W : Hold on, please. *[Typing sound]* Yes, you called us because of a bad Internet connection.
잠시 기다려주세요. *[타자 치는 소리]* 네, 어제 인터넷 연결 불량으로 전화 주셨었군요.

M : Yes. An engineer is supposed to come to my house at 3 p.m. today.
네. 기사님이 오늘 오후 3시에 저희 집에 방문하시기로 했어요.

W : Right. Is there any problem?
맞습니다. 문제가 있으신가요?

M : Can you reschedule the visit? I won't be home at that time.
방문 일정을 조정할 수 있을까요? 제가 그때 집에 없을 것 같아요.

W : Okay. What time would be better for you?
알겠습니다. 언제가 더 좋으실까요?

M : Can you schedule it for around 1 p.m. tomorrow?
내일 오후 1시쯤으로 잡을 수 있나요?

W : Let me check. *[Pause]* I'm afraid that the engineer has already been scheduled for that time. But he's available after 4 p.m.
확인해 보겠습니다. *[잠시 멈춤]* 죄송하지만 기사님이 그때는 이미 일정이 잡혀 계시네요. 하지만 오후 4시 이후로는 기사님 시간이 비어 있습니다.

M : Good. I'll be home around that time.
좋네요. 그때쯤엔 제가 집에 있을 것 같아요.

W : Okay. He'll call you before he makes the visit tomorrow.
알겠습니다. 내일 기사님이 방문하시기 전에 전화 드릴 거예요.

Why? 왜 정답일까?

인터넷 수리 기사의 방문 일정을 조정하려는 남자에게 여자는 내일 오후 4시 이후로 가능하다고 말하고, 남자는 괜찮다고 답한다(Good. I'll be home around that time.). 따라서 여자의 응답으로 가장 적절한 것은 ③ 'Okay. He'll call you before he makes the visit tomorrow.(알겠습니다. 내일 기사님이 방문하시기 전에 전화 드릴 거예요.)'이다.

- connection ⓝ 연결
- reschedule ⓥ 일정을 조정하다
- engineer ⓝ 기사, 수리공
- make a visit 방문하다

15 주연 배우 의상 색상 정하기 정답률 89% | 정답 ③

다음 상황 설명을 듣고, Sofia가 Hannah에게 할 말로 가장 적절한 것을 고르시오.

Sofia: ______

① I think our costume preparation is way behind schedule.
내 생각에 우리 의상 준비가 일정보다 너무 뒤쳐진 것 같아.
② Please put the leading actor in the middle of the poster.
주연 캐릭터를 포스터 중간에 배치해 줘.
③ Let's pick a color that makes the main character noticeable.
주연 캐릭터를 돋보이게 하는 색상을 골라보자.
④ I'll recommend someone to take over my position next year.
내년에 내 자리를 맡아줄 사람을 추천할게.
⑤ More comfortable clothing will be better for the character.
더 편한 의상이 캐릭터한테 더 나을 것 같아.

M : Sofia and Hannah are members of the school drama club.
Sofia와 Hannah는 학교 연극 동아리 부원이다.
They are in charge of stage costumes for this year's play.
그들은 올해 연극의 무대 의상을 담당하고 있다.
Sofia is the head, and Hannah is quite new on the costume team.
Sofia는 의상 팀장이고, Hannah는 의상 팀 일에 꽤 초보이다.
They have sketched some costume ideas and now it's time to choose colors for the costumes.
그들은 의상 아이디어를 스케치했고, 이제 의상 색상을 고를 시간이다.
Hannah suggests yellow for their leading role's costume.
Hannah는 주연 의상 색상으로 노란색을 제안한다.
However, Sofia thinks that yellow is not a good idea because the stage background will also be mostly yellow.
하지만 Sofia는 노란색이 좋은 아이디어라고 생각지 않는데, 무대 배경 또한 거의 노랗기 때문이다.
She wants to tell Hannah to choose a color different from that of the set to make the main character stand out.
그녀는 Hannah에게 주연 캐릭터가 돋보일 수 있도록 세트 색깔과 다른 색상을 고르자고 제안하고 싶다.
In this situation, what would Sofia most likely say to Hannah?
이 상황에서, Sofia는 Hannah에게 뭐라고 말할 것인가?

Sofia : Let's pick a color that makes the main character noticeable.
주연 캐릭터를 돋보이게 하는 색상을 골라보자.

Why? 왜 정답일까?

상황에 따르면 Sofia는 무대 세트와 비슷한 색상의 의상을 주연에게 입히자고 제안하는 Hannah에게 다른 색상을 골라보자고 말해주려 한다(She wants to tell Hannah to choose a color different from that of the set to make the main character stand out.). 따라서 Sofia가 Hannah에게 할 말로 가장 적절한 것은 ③ 'Let's pick a color that makes the main character noticeable.(주연 캐릭터를 돋보이게 하는 색상을 골라보자.)'이다.

- drama club 연극부
- stand out 돋보이다, 두드러지다
- take over ~을 이어받다, 대체하다
- in charge of ~을 담당하는
- noticeable ⓐ 눈에 띄는

16-17 도구를 사용하는 동물

W : Hello, students.
안녕하세요, 여러분.
Do you think only humans are smart enough to use tools? Absolutely not.
여러분은 사람만이 도구를 사용할 만큼 똑똑하다고 생각하나요? 절대 아닙니다.
「Today, we'll learn about animals using tools available to them.」 16번의 근거
오늘, 우리는 자신들이 이용할 수 있는 도구를 사용하는 동물들에 관해 배워볼 겁니다.
「It's no secret that crows have been observed using tools.」 17번 ①의 근거 일치
까마귀가 도구를 사용하는 것이 관찰됐다는 점은 비밀이 아닙니다.
Their clever tricks include manipulating sticks to extract insects from logs and dropping walnuts in front of moving cars to crack them.
그들의 똑똑한 수법에는 곤충을 통나무에서 꺼내기 위해 막대기를 이용하거나, 호두를 까기 위해 움직이는 차 앞에 호두를 떨어뜨려 놓는 것이 포함됩니다.
「Elephants also have problem solving abilities.」 17번 ③의 근거 일치
코끼리도 문제 해결력을 지니고 있습니다.
They use branches for scratching parts of their body that their tail and trunk cannot reach.
이들은 나뭇가지를 이용해 꼬리와 코로 닿지 않는 신체 부위를 긁습니다.
They also chew on bark and use it as a sponge to absorb scarce drinking water.
그들은 또한 나무껍질을 씹어서 부족한 식수를 빨아들이기 위한 스폰지로 씁니다.
Clever animals are observed in water, too.
똑똑한 동물은 물속에서도 관찰되지요.
「Beavers construct dams to protect themselves from predators.」 17번 ④의 근거 일치
비버는 자기 자신을 포식자로부터 보호하기 위해 댐을 짓습니다.
They build these by cutting down trees and packing them with mud and stones.
그들은 나무를 잘라서 그것을 진흙과 돌로 채워 댐을 건설합니다.
「Some octopuses have been observed carrying two halves of a shell.」 17번 ⑤의 근거 일치
몇몇 문어는 둘로 갈라진 껍질을 가지고 다니는 모습이 관찰됩니다.
Threatened by predators, they close the shells over themselves to hide.
포식자에게 위협을 당하면 이들은 자기 몸을 껍질 속에 닫아넣어 몸을 숨깁니다.
Now, let's watch a video clip about these intelligent animals.
이제, 이 똑똑한 동물들에 관한 영상을 봅시다.

- clever ⓐ 똑똑한
- crack ⓥ 깨다
- scratch ⓥ 긁다
- disadvantage ⓝ 불리한 점, 난점
- extract ⓥ 꺼내다, 추출하다
- branch ⓝ 나뭇가지
- absorb ⓥ 흡수하다

16 주제 파악 정답률 89% | 정답 ②

여자가 하는 말의 주제로 가장 적절한 것은?

① tools used to study animal behaviors – 동물 행동을 연구하기 위해 사용되는 도구들
② animals that make clever use of tools – 도구를 똑똑하게 이용하는 동물들
③ cooperation between humans and animals – 인간과 동물의 협력
④ types of communication between animals – 동물 간 의사소통의 유형
⑤ disadvantages of animals living in the wild – 야생에서 사는 동물들의 난점

Why? 왜 정답일까?

'Today, we'll learn about animals using tools available to them.'에서 여자는 인간과 마찬가지로 도구를 사용하는 동물들에 관해 배워보자고 하므로, 여자가 하는 말의 주제로 가장 적절한 것은 ② 'animals that make clever use of tools(도구를 똑똑하게 이용하는 동물들)'이다.

17 언급 유무 파악 정답률 96% | 정답 ②

언급된 동물이 아닌 것은?

① crows – 까마귀 ② monkeys – 원숭이 ③ elephants – 코끼리
④ beavers – 비버 ⑤ octopuses – 문어

Why? 왜 정답일까?

담화에서 여자는 도구를 이용하는 동물의 예시로 까마귀, 코끼리, 비버, 문어를 언급하므로, 언급되지 않은 것은 ② '원숭이'이다.

Why? 왜 오답일까?

① 'It's no secret that crows have been observed using tools.'에서 '까마귀'가 언급되었다.
③ 'Elephants also have problem solving abilities.'에서 '코끼리'가 언급되었다.
④ 'Beavers construct dams to protect themselves from predators.'에서 '비버'가 언급되었다.
⑤ 'Some octopuses have been observed carrying two halves of a shell.'에서 '문어'가 언급되었다.

[문제편 p.152]

Dictation 26

문제편 153쪽

01 make a promotional video / auditioning the applicants / show off your talents
02 It's been stiff / sleep on your stomach / Your neck gets twisted
03 save the environment / your journey as an activist / cut his foot on a fishhook
04 star-shaped cushion / film them singing along / on the table / The brand name should be visible
05 throughout our stay / Let's finish packing first / let the air out of the pool tube
06 include a helmet / a bike collection service / there's an additional charge
07 You must be mistaken / do volunteer work / see a musical
08 an annual event / Who organizes the contest / quite some time ago / Any foreigners residing in Korea
09 a special promotion / takes you around the city / every step of the way / providing fascinating information
10 any color preferences / a marble stone base / the warmer getting overheated
11 creamy salmon pasta / can't take any orders for that dish
12 it had a big stain
13 very disappointed / she has been so cold to me / give her a birthday gift
14 because of a bad Internet connection / reschedule the visit / Can you schedule it
15 in charge of stage costumes / stage background / make the main character stand out
16-17 smart enough to use tools / crows have been observed / absorb scarce drinking water / protect themselves from predators

27회 | 2021학년도 10월 학력평가 고3

• 정답 •
01③ 02④ 03⑤ 04③ 05④ 06③ 07① 08⑤ 09④ 10② 11① 12② 13② 14② 15① 16③ 17④

01 동물 사진을 잘 찍는 요령

정답률 96% | 정답 ③

다음을 듣고, 남자가 하는 말의 목적으로 가장 적절한 것을 고르시오.
① 사진 동아리 부원을 모집하려고
② 동물원 견학 프로그램을 홍보하려고
✔ 동물 사진을 찍는 요령을 알려 주려고
④ 동물원 관람 시 유의 사항을 안내하려고
⑤ 새로 출시된 카메라의 사용법을 설명하려고

M : Hello, students of the Live Photography Club.
안녕하세요, Live Photography Club 학생 여러분.
I'm glad to see you at East Hills Zoo today.
오늘 여러분을 East Hills Zoo에서 만나게 되어 기쁩니다.
Before we start, I want to share some tips for taking good photos of animals.
시작하기 전에, 동물 사진을 잘 찍을 수 있는 요령을 몇 가지 공유하려고 합니다.
First, be patient.
첫째, 인내심을 가지세요.
Take your time until the animal is positioned for a good shot.
동물이 찍기 좋은 위치에 자리잡을 때까지 기다리세요.
Second, try to avoid using the flash on your camera.
둘째, 카메라 플래시를 사용하는 것을 피하세요.
The flash impacts some of the shadows that natural light creates, making the picture look "flat" and less interesting.
플래시는 자연광이 만들어내는 그림자에 영향을 끼쳐서 사진이 '평평해' 보이거나 덜 흥미로워 보이게 만들 수 있습니다.
Lastly, I also recommend you try using burst mode.
마지막으로, 또한 연속 촬영 모드를 쓰기를 권합니다.
Burst mode allows you to rapidly take a sequence of photos and capture action shots of animals.
연속 촬영은 여러분이 사진을 연속해서 재빨리 찍고 동물의 움직임을 포착할 수 있게 해줍니다.
Now, let's split up and try to get the best animal pictures.
이제 흩어져서 최고의 동물 사진을 찍어봅시다.

Why? 왜 정답일까?

'Before we start, I want to share some tips for taking good photos of animals.'에서 남자는 동물 사진을 잘 찍는 요령을 알려주겠다고 하므로, 남자가 하는 말의 목적으로 가장 적절한 것은 ③ '동물 사진을 찍는 요령을 알려 주려고'이다.

- **patient** ⓐ 인내심 있는
- **burst mode** 연속 촬영
- **capture** ⓥ 포착하다
- **impact** ⓥ 영향을 끼치다 ⓝ 영향
- **sequence** ⓝ 연속, 차례

02 불필요한 이메일을 지워 탄소 배출량 낮추기

정답률 91% | 정답 ④

대화를 듣고, 여자의 의견으로 가장 적절한 것을 고르시오.
① 개인 이메일 계정을 업무용으로 사용하지 말아야 한다.
② 환경을 보호하기 위해 종이 우편물을 줄일 필요가 있다.
③ 출처가 불분명한 이메일의 첨부 파일을 열어서는 안 된다.
✔ 탄소 배출량 감소를 위해 불필요한 이메일을 삭제해야 한다.
⑤ 개인 정보 유출을 방지하기 위해 휴면 계정을 정리해야 한다.

M : Olivia, what are you doing on your computer?
Olivia, 컴퓨터로 뭐 하고 있어?
W : Hi, Jason. I'm clearing out old emails from my inbox.
안녕, Jason. 난 내 받은편지함의 오래된 이메일을 지우고 있어.
M : Why are you deleting them?
왜 그걸 지우는 거야?
W : Because deleting old, unnecessary emails can be a step to saving the planet by reducing our carbon footprint.
오래되고 불필요한 이메일을 지우는 것은 우리의 탄소 발자국을 줄여서 지구를 지키는 조치가 될 수 있거든.
M : What do you mean by that?
그게 무슨 말이야?
W : You know emails you never deleted are stored in data centers, right?
너 네가 절대 지우지 않은 이메일이 데이터 센터에 보관되는 거 알지, 그렇지?
M : Yeah, I know that.
응, 알고 있어.
W : The data centers consume quite a lot of electricity. A lot of electricity is still generated by burning fossil fuels.
데이터 센터는 꽤 많은 전기를 소비해. 많은 전기가 아직도 화석 연료를 태워서 만들어지고.
M : You mean using less data storage helps save electricity?
네 말은 데이터 저장량을 더 적게 쓰는 것이 전기를 아끼는 데 도움이 된다는 거야?
W : Right. We need to delete unneeded emails to reduce carbon emissions.
맞아. 우린 탄소 배출량을 줄이기 위해서 불필요한 이메일을 지워야 해.
M : Now I understand the environmental impact of undeleted emails. I'll check my own inbox now.
이제 지우지 않은 이메일의 환경적 영향을 알겠어. 지금 내 받은편지함을 확인해 볼래.

Why? 왜 정답일까?

'Because deleting old, unnecessary emails can be a step to saving the planet by reducing our carbon footprint.'와 'We need to delete unneeded emails to reduce carbon emissions.'에서 여자는 불필요한 이메일을 지워서 탄소 배출량을 줄여야 한다고 언급하고

있다. 따라서 여자의 의견으로 가장 적절한 것은 ④ '탄소 배출량 감소를 위해 불필요한 이메일을 삭제해야 한다.'이다.

- clear out (~을 없애고) 청소하다
- inbox ⓝ 받은편지함
- carbon footprint 탄소 발자국
- consume ⓥ 소비하다
- unneeded ⓐ 불필요한

03 건설 현장의 먼지 발생에 관한 건의

정답률 80% | 정답 ⑤

대화를 듣고, 두 사람의 관계를 가장 잘 나타낸 것을 고르시오.

① 환경 운동가 – 기자
② 고객 – 청소업체 직원
③ 집주인 – 실내 디자이너
④ 건축가 – 건축 자재 판매자
⑤ 지역 주민 – 건설 현장 직원

W : Excuse me.
실례합니다.

M : Hello. How may I help you?
안녕하세요. 무엇을 도와드릴까요?

W : Hi. I'm here to talk about your building construction. Who should I talk to about it?
안녕하세요. 전 당신의 건설 현장에 관해 이야기 하려고 왔어요. 제가 그것에 관해 어떤 분께 말씀드려야 하나요?

M : I'm in charge. You can talk to me.
제가 책임자입니다. 저한테 말씀하시죠.

W : Okay. Your construction site is producing a lot of dust.
알겠습니다. 당신의 건설 현장에서 먼지가 많이 나고 있어요.

M : Oh, really? We've already set up a dust screen.
오, 그런가요? 저희는 먼지 여과기를 이미 설치했는데요.

W : I know, but I live right across the street from here, and I still can't open the windows in my house.
저도 알지만, 저는 여기서 바로 길 건너편에 사는데 아직도 제 집 창문을 열지 못하고 있어요.

M : Oh, we're very sorry for your inconvenience.
오, 불편을 드려 정말 죄송합니다.

W : I'd like you to take additional measures to solve this problem.
이 문제를 해결하기 위해 추가 조치를 취해 주셨으면 합니다.

M : All right. We'll have a meeting and try to find a better solution as soon as possible.
알겠습니다. 저희가 회의를 열어서 가급적 빨리 더 나은 해결책을 찾겠습니다.

W : Okay. Thank you.
알겠습니다. 고맙습니다.

Why? 왜 정답일까?

'Hi. I'm here to talk about your building construction. Who should I talk to about it? / I'm in charge.', 'Your construction site is producing a lot of dust.', '~ I live right across the street from here, and I still can't open the windows in my house.' 등을 통해 여자가 지역 주민이고, 남자가 건설 현장 직원임을 알 수 있다. 따라서 두 사람의 관계로 가장 적절한 것은 ⑤ '지역 주민 – 건설 현장 직원'이다.

- building construction 건설 현장
- be in charge 책임지다, 담당하다
- inconvenience ⓝ 불편, 폐
- take measures 조치를 취하다

04 가족 소풍 사진 구경하기

정답률 61% | 정답 ③

대화를 듣고, 그림에서 대화의 내용과 일치하지 않는 것을 고르시오.

M : Silvia, guess what I did last weekend.
Silvia, 내가 지난 주말에 뭐 했나 맞춰봐.

W : Sounds like you did something special.
뭔가 특별한 걸 하고 온 것 같네.

M : Yes, I went on a family picnic. Look at this picture.
응, 나 가족 소풍 갔다 왔어. 이 사진 좀 봐.

W : It looks great! 「Who is this girl in the boat? She's wearing a striped hat.」 ①의 근거 일치
근사해 보인다! 보트에 타고 있는 이 여자애 누구야? 줄무늬 모자를 쓰고 있어.

M : She's my younger sister, Jenny. She likes to wear that hat outside.
내 여동생 Jenny야. 그녀는 밖에서 모자 쓰는 것을 좋아해.

W : 「Oh, you're rowing the boat.」 Wasn't it hard work?
오, 넌 노를 젓고 있구나. 힘들지 않았어? ②의 근거 일치

M : Yeah, it was a little hard, but my sister really enjoyed the boat ride.
응, 약간 힘들었는데, 내 여동생이 보트 타는 걸 무척 즐기더라고.

W : You're such a good brother. 「And what is this in front of your boat?
착한 오빠네. 그리고 보트 앞에 이건 뭐야?

M : It's a duck. Its head is under the surface of the water.」 ③의 근거 불일치
오리야. 오리 머리는 물 밑에 있어.

W : I guess it's trying to get some food in the water.
물속에서 먹이를 찾으려고 하나 보다.

M : 「The man sitting under the triangular sun shade is my father.」 He's relaxing.
삼각 차양 밑에 앉아 계신 남자분은 우리 아빠야. 그는 쉬고 계셔. ④의 근거 일치

W : I see. 「The two hot air balloons in the sky look awesome.」 ⑤의 근거 일치
그렇구나. 하늘에 있는 열기구 두 개가 멋져 보여.

M : Yeah, it was my first time seeing real hot air balloons.
응, 진짜 열기구를 본 건 처음이었어.

W : Cool! You must have had a really great weekend.
멋지다! 넌 정말 멋진 주말을 보냈겠구나.

Why? 왜 정답일까?

대화에서 오리는 머리를 물속에 넣고 있다고 하므로(**Its head is under the surface of the water.**), 그림에서 대화의 내용과 일치하지 않는 것은 ③이다.

- family picnic 가족 소풍
- row ⓥ 노를 젓다
- surface ⓝ 표면, 수면
- hot air balloon 열기구

05 학교 음악회 준비하기

정답률 90% | 정답 ④

대화를 듣고, 남자가 할 일로 가장 적절한 것을 고르시오.

① 무대 조명 점검하기
② 사회자에게 연락하기
③ 피아노 위치 조정하기
④ 무선 마이크 가져가기
⑤ 참가자에게 공연 순서 알리기

W : Hi, Mr. White. The school concert starts in the afternoon.
안녕하세요, White 선생님. 학교 음악회가 오후에 시작되네요.

M : Yeah, I know. I think we need to check if everything is well prepared.
그래, 알고 있어. 모든 게 잘 준비되었는지 확인해봐야 할 것 같구나.

W : Good idea.
좋은 생각이에요.

M : Did you call Henry this morning? He's the student MC for the concert.
오늘 아침에 Henry에게 전화했니? 그는 음악회의 학생 MC잖아.

W : I told him to come to the auditorium by 10 a.m. for the rehearsal.
그 애보고 아침 10시까지 리허설을 위해 강당에 오라고 했어요.

M : Good. The participants know the order of their performances, right?
잘했어. 참가자들은 공연 순서를 알고 있지, 그렇지?

W : I told them all about it. Ah, we should also adjust the position of the piano on the stage.
애들에게 다 말해줬어요. 아, 무대 위 피아노 위치도 조정해야 해요.

M : Don't worry. I already did it yesterday afternoon.
걱정 마라. 그건 내가 어제 오후에 이미 했어.

W : Thank you, Mr. White. Then now I think all we have to do is check the stage lighting and get some wireless microphones ready.
고맙습니다, White 선생님. 그럼 제 생각에 이제 해야 할 일은 무대 조명을 점검하고 무선 마이크 몇 개를 준비하는 일뿐이에요.

M : The wireless microphones are in the broadcasting room. I'll go and take them to the auditorium.
무선 마이크는 방송실에 있어. 내가 가서 그것을 강당에 갖다 놓으마.

W : Okay. Then, I'll go to the auditorium and check the lighting.
알겠습니다. 그럼, 저는 강당에 가서 조명을 점검할게요.

M : All right. See you there in a minute.
알겠어. 이따 거기서 보자.

Why? 왜 정답일까?

대화 마지막 부분에서 남자는 무선 마이크 준비를(**The wireless microphones are in the broadcasting room. I'll go and take them to the auditorium.**), 여자는 강당 조명 점검을 맡기로 한다. 따라서 남자가 할 일로 가장 적절한 것은 ④ '무선 마이크 가져가기'이다.

- adjust ⓥ 조정하다
- broadcasting room 방송실

06 원예 도구 사기

정답률 91% | 정답 ③

대화를 듣고, 여자가 지불할 금액을 고르시오. [3점]

① $26 ② $28 ③ $30 ④ $34 ⑤ $36

M : Welcome to Lynn's Garden Center. How may I help you?
Lynn's Garden Center에 오신 것을 환영합니다. 무엇을 도와드릴까요?

W : Hi, I'm looking for some gardening tools. Do you have any shovels?
안녕하세요. 저는 원예 도구를 좀 찾고 있어요. 삽 있나요?

M : Of course. We have two types of shovel.
물론입니다. 삽은 두 종류가 있습니다.

W : What's the difference between the two types?
두 종류의 차이점이 뭔가요?

M : One has a plastic handle, and the other has a wooden handle.
하나는 플라스틱 손잡이가 있고, 다른 하나는 나무 손잡이가 있습니다.

W : Well, wooden handles are stronger than plastic ones. I'll buy a shovel with a wooden handle. How much is it?
음, 나무 손잡이가 플라스틱 손잡이보다 더 튼튼하죠. 전 나무 손잡이가 있는 것으로 사겠어요. 얼마죠?

M : Originally they cost $20 each, but all shovels are 10% off this week.
원래 그것은 하나에 20달러이지만, 모든 삽이 이번 주에는 10퍼센트 할인됩니다.

W : Great! I also need some gardening gloves.
좋네요! 그리고 전 원예용 장갑도 필요해요.

M : Okay. I recommend these rubber-coated gloves. A pair of them cost $8, but two pairs cost only $12.
알겠습니다. 이 고무로 도포된 장갑을 추천합니다. 한 켤레에 8달러인데, 두 켤레는 12달러밖에 안 합니다.

W : Oh, I'll buy two pairs.
오, 두 켤레를 사겠어요.

M : Good. So you want one shovel with a wooden handle and two pairs of gardening gloves, right?
좋습니다. 그러면 나무 손잡이 삽 한 자루와 원예용 장갑 두 켤레, 맞으시죠?

W : Yes, that's all. Here's my credit card.
네, 그거면 됐어요. 여기 제 신용 카드요.

Why? 왜 정답일까?

대화에 따르면 여자는 나무 손잡이가 달린 20달러짜리 삽 한 자루를 10퍼센트 할인가에 구입하였고, 두 켤레에 12달러인 원예용 장갑 또한 구입하였다. 이를 식으로 나타내면 '$(20\times0.9)+12=30$'이므로, 여자가 지불할 금액은 ③ '$30'이다.

[문제편 p.157]

- gardening tool 원예 도구
- shovel ⓝ 삽
- rubber-coated ⓐ 고무로 도포된

07 전자책을 사려는 이유

정답률 95% | 정답 ①

대화를 듣고, 남자가 전자책을 사려는 이유를 고르시오.

✔글자 크기를 조절할 수 있어서　② 종이책 재고가 부족해서
③ 휴대하기가 편리해서　④ 종이책보다 가격이 저렴해서
⑤ 서점에 가지 않고 구매할 수 있어서

M : Hi, Nicole. What are you reading?
안녕, Nicole. 뭐 읽고 있어?

W : Hi, Danny. I'm reading the newly released book, *London Ever After*.
안녕, Danny. 난 새로 출시된 책 *London Ever After*를 읽고 있어.

M : Oh, I want to buy that book, too.
오, 나도 그 책을 사고 싶어.

W : You can get a copy of its limited hardcover edition at Jackson's bookstore.
Jackson 서점에 가면 한정판 양장본을 구입할 수 있어.

M : I know, but I'm going to buy its eBook version, instead.
나도 알아. 그런데 난 그것보다도 전자책 버전을 사려고.

W : Is there any reason you prefer eBooks? Are they cheaper?
전자책을 선호하는 이유가 있어? 더 싼가?

M : Well, there isn't much difference in the price.
음, 가격에는 큰 차이가 없어.

W : Is that so? Then, is it because eBooks are more convenient to carry around?
그래? 그럼, 전자책이 들고 다니기 더 편해서 그래?

M : Well, that's not the reason, either. Actually, you can change the text size while reading eBooks.
음, 그것도 이유가 아니야. 사실, 전자책을 읽을 때 글자 크기를 변경할 수 있어.

W : You mean you're able to adjust the font size?
네 말은 네가 글자 크기를 조절할 수 있다는 거야?

M : Exactly. That's why I want to buy the eBook version.
바로 그거야. 그래서 난 전자책 버전을 사려는 거야.

W : I see.
그렇구나.

Why? 왜 정답일까?

대화에 따르면 남자는 전자책의 경우 글자 크기를 조절할 수 있기에(**Actually, you can change the text size while reading eBooks.**) 신간을 전자책으로 구입하고자 한다. 따라서 남자가 전자책을 사려는 이유로 가장 적절한 것은 ① '글자 크기를 조절할 수 있어서'이다.

- release ⓥ 출시하다
- convenient ⓐ 편리한

08 꽃 도매 시장 가보기

정답률 96% | 정답 ⑤

대화를 듣고, Central Flower Market에 관해 언급되지 않은 것을 고르시오.

① 운영 시간　② 위치　③ 휴무 요일
④ 주차 요금　✔입점 매장 수

M : Lauren, what are all these flowers?
Lauren, 이 꽃은 다 뭐야?

W : Hi, Brian. I bought them at Central Flower Market this morning.
안녕, Brian. 난 이것들을 오늘 아침에 Central Flower Market에서 샀어.

M : Is that the wholesale flower market?
거긴 꽃 도매 시장이야?

W : Yes. I often buy flowers there. I have to go there very early in the morning, though.
응. 난 종종 거기서 꽃을 사. 그런데 거긴 아침에 아주 일찍 가야 해.

M : 「When does the flower market open?
꽃 시장이 언제 열리는데?

W : It opens as early as 4 a.m. and closes around 10 a.m.」 ①의 근거 일치
오전 4시에 열어서 오전 10시쯤에 닫아.

M : They start quite early. 「Where is the market located?
아주 일찍 여네. 시장 위치는 어디야?

W : Near Central Station on 6th Street.」 ②의 근거 일치
6번 가 Central Station 근처야.

M : It's not that far from here. 「Is it open on weekends?
여기서 그렇게 멀지 않구나. 주말에 열어?

W : Yes, but it's closed on Mondays.」 ③의 근거 일치
응, 그런데 월요일에는 휴무야.

M : Okay. Does it have a lot of parking spaces?
그렇구나. 주차 공간이 많아?

W : Of course. The parking lot is large and 「the parking fee is only two dollars per hour.」 ④의 근거 일치
물론이지. 주차장이 크고 주차비가 한 시간에 2달러밖에 안 해.

M : Sounds good. I'll take some time to go there next week.
괜찮네. 다음 주에 시간 좀 내서 거기 가 봐야겠다.

Why? 왜 정답일까?

대화에서 남자와 여자는 **Central Flower Market**의 운영 시간, 위치, 휴무 요일, 주차 요금을 언급하였다. 따라서 언급되지 않은 것은 ⑤ '입점 매장 수'이다.

Why? 왜 오답일까?

① '**It opens as early as 4 a.m. and closes around 10 a.m.**'에서 '운영 시간'이 언급되었다.
② '**Near Central Station on 6th Street.**'에서 '위치'가 언급되었다.
③ '~ **it's closed on Mondays.**'에서 '휴무 요일'이 언급되었다.
④ '~ **the parking fee is only two dollars per hour.**'에서 '주차 요금'이 언급되었다.

- wholesale ⓝ 도매 ⓐ 도매의
- quite ad 아주
- parking lot 주차장

09 낚시 대회 안내

정답률 85% | 정답 ④

2021 Robinson Fishing Contest에 관한 다음 내용을 듣고, 일치하지 않는 것을 고르시오.

① 10월 22일부터 23일까지 개최된다.　② 대회 장소는 Silver Cloud 호수이다.
③ 1등 상품은 고급 낚싯대 한 세트이다.　✔잡은 물고기의 수를 기준으로 심사한다.
⑤ 대회가 끝난 후에 호수를 청소하는 행사가 있다.

M : Hello, fishermen. I'm Bruce Miller, the president of Robinson Fishing Association.
안녕하세요, 어부 여러분. 저는 Robinson Fishing Association 협회장 Bruce Miller입니다.
You've been waiting for a long time, but now I'm happy to announce that we're hosting the '2021 Robinson Fishing Contest.'
오래 기다리셨죠, 이제 저희가 2021 Robinson Fishing Contest를 열 예정임을 알려드리게 되어 기쁩니다.
「It'll be held from the 22nd to the 23rd of October.」 ①의 근거 일치
이것은 10월 22일부터 23일까지 개최됩니다.
「The contest is taking place at Lake Silver Cloud this year.」 ②의 근거 일치
올해 이 대회는 Silver Cloud 호수에서 열립니다.
「The first place winner will be awarded a set of premium fishing rods」 and the second place winner will receive a multi-purpose fishing chair. ③의 근거 일치
1등 입상자는 고급 낚싯대 한 세트를 받게 될 것이고 2등 입상자는 다목적 낚시 의자를 받게 될 것입니다.
「Judges will not count the number of fish you catch.
심사 위원들은 여러분들이 잡는 물고기 수를 세지 않을 것입니다.
Only the length of the fish matters!」 ④의 근거 불일치
오로지 물고기의 길이가 중요합니다!
「After the contest, we're also having a lake cleaning event.」 ⑤의 근거 일치
대회가 끝난 후에, 호수를 청소하는 행사도 있을 것입니다.
We strongly encourage you to join the event.
여러분이 이 대회에 참여하시기를 강력히 권합니다.
You can sign up for the contest on our website.
저희 웹 사이트에서 대회에 등록하실 수 있습니다.
Thank you very much.
대단히 감사합니다.

Why? 왜 정답일까?

'**Judges will not count the number of fish you catch. Only the length of the fish matters!**'에서 잡은 물고기의 수가 아닌 물고기 길이가 중요하다고 하므로, 내용과 일치하지 않는 것은 ④ '잡은 물고기의 수를 기준으로 심사한다.'이다.

Why? 왜 오답일까?

① '**It'll be held from the 22nd to the 23rd of October.**'의 내용과 일치한다.
② '**The contest is taking place at Lake Silver Cloud this year.**'의 내용과 일치한다.
③ '**The first place winner will be awarded a set of premium fishing rods** ~'의 내용과 일치한다.
⑤ '**After the contest, we're also having a lake cleaning event.**'의 내용과 일치한다.

- association ⓝ 협회
- announce ⓥ 발표하다, 알리다
- fishing rod 낚싯대
- sign up for ~에 등록하다

10 와플 메이커 사기

정답률 81% | 정답 ②

다음 표를 보면서 대화를 듣고, 두 사람이 주문할 와플 메이커를 고르시오.

Waffle Makers

	Model	Price	Plates	Waffle Shape	Audible Alert
①	A	$20	Fixed	Square	×
✔	B	$33	Removable	Round	×
③	C	$48	Fixed	Round	×
④	D	$52	Removable	Round	○
⑤	E	$70	Removable	Square	○

M : Honey, look at this website. There are five waffle maker models on sale now.
여보, 이 웹 사이트 좀 봐요. 와플 메이커 다섯 개 제품이 지금 세일 중이에요.

W : Oh, I was thinking of buying one.
오, 나도 하나 사려고 했어요.

M : 「Should we buy the cheapest one?
가장 싼 것을 살까요?

W : No. I've heard of this model, and its reviews aren't that good. 근거1 Price 조건
아니요. 이 제품에 대해서 들어봤는데, 평이 그다지 좋지 않았어요.

M : Then, we won't buy it.」 「Hmm..., some of the waffle makers come with removable plates, but the others don't.
그럼 이건 사지 말죠. 흠… 어떤 와플 메이커는 분리 가능한 접시가 딸려 오고 다른 것은 그렇지 않네요.

W : The ones with fixed plates are hard to clean.
고정된 접시가 있는 것은 닦기 어려울 거예요.

M : Then the ones with fixed plates are out.」 「What about the waffle shape?
그럼 접시가 고정된 것들은 빼죠. 와플 모양은요? 근거2 Plates 조건

W : I like round waffles better than square ones.
난 사각 와플보다 둥근 와플이 좋아요.

M : All right. Let's choose from the ones that make round waffles.」 근거3 Waffle Shape 조건
알겠어요. 둥근 와플을 만드는 것들 중 골라보죠.

W : Great. 「Do you think we need an audible alert? It goes off when the waffles are done.
좋아요. 알람음이 필요하다고 생각해요? 와플이 다 되면 이게 울려요.

M : Well, I'm afraid the sound might wake up our baby while he's sleeping.
음, 우리 아이가 자고 있을 때 알람이 아이를 깨울까봐 걱정이에요.

W : Good point. Let's order the one without it.」 근거4 Audible Alert 조건
좋은 지적이에요. 그게 없는 것으로 주문합시다.

M : Perfect!
완벽해요!

Why? 왜 정답일까?

대화에 따르면 남자와 여자는 가격이 가장 싼 와플 메이커는 평이 좋지 않아 제외하고, 분리 가능한 접시가 딸려 오면서, 둥근 와플을 만들 수 있고, 알람음이 없는 제품을 고르려고 한다. 따라서 두 사람이 주문할 와플 메이커는 ② 'B'이다.

- removable ⓐ 분리 가능한, 떼어낼 수 있는
- fixed ⓐ 고정된
- audible ⓐ 들을 수 있는, 가청의
- go off (알람 등이) 울리다

[문제편 p.157]

11 야구 모자 찾기

정답률 84% | 정답 ①

대화를 듣고, 여자의 마지막 말에 대한 남자의 응답으로 가장 적절한 것을 고르시오.

✔ Thank you. Please let me know if you find it. – 고마워. 그걸 찾으면 내게 알려줘.
② Don't worry. I can find your house by myself. – 걱정 마. 난 혼자서 너희 집을 찾아갈 수 있어.
③ Why don't you try it on? It'll look nice on you. – 써 보는 게 어때? 너한테 잘 어울릴 거야.
④ I'm sorry. I don't think I can make it to your party. – 미안해. 난 네 파티에 못 갈 것 같아.
⑤ I think you're right. The baseball cap doesn't fit me. – 네 말이 맞아. 야구 모자는 내게 어울리지 않아.

[Cell phone rings.]
[휴대 전화 벨이 울린다.]

W : Hello, Jake. What's up?
여보세요, Jake. 무슨 일이야?

M : Hi, Kate. I had a great time at your party last night, but I think I left my baseball cap at your house. Have you seen it?
안녕, Kate. 지난밤 네 파티에서 근사한 시간 보냈는데, 내 생각에 내 야구 모자를 너희 집에 두고 온 것 같아. 본 적 있어?

W : Oh, I'm afraid not. I'll search for it while tidying up my house.
오, 유감스럽지만 못 봤어. 집을 치우면서 그걸 찾아볼게.

M : Thank you. Please let me know if you find it.
고마워. 그걸 찾으면 내게 알려줘.

Why? 왜 정답일까?

남자가 지난밤 여자네 집에서 열린 파티 때 야구 모자를 놓고 온 것 같다고 하자, 여자는 집을 치우면서 모자를 찾아봐 주겠다(**I'll search for it while tidying up my house.**)고 한다. 따라서 남자의 응답으로 가장 적절한 것은 ① '고마워. 그걸 찾으면 내게 알려줘.'이다.

- **baseball cap** 야구 모자
- **tidy up** ~을 치우다, 정리하다
- **make it** (시간 맞춰) 가다, 해내다, 성공하다

12 화장실 전구 바꾸기

정답률 81% | 정답 ②

대화를 듣고, 남자의 마지막 말에 대한 여자의 응답으로 가장 적절한 것을 고르시오.

① Be careful. You might get an electric shock.
조심해요. 감전될지도 몰라요.
✔ Oh, I see. Then I'll go get some new ones now.
오, 알겠어요. 그럼 지금 가서 새것을 사 올게요.
③ Great. The bathroom is much brighter than before.
좋아요. 화장실이 전보다 훨씬 밝아졌어요.
④ All right. I'll replace the garage light bulb right now.
알겠어요. 내가 차고 전등을 지금 교체할게요.
⑤ Never mind. I'll come back when the items are in stock.
신경 쓰지 마요. 재고가 있을 때 다시 올게요.

M : Honey, the bathroom light is blinking now. I guess it's time to change the light bulb.
여보, 화장실 불이 깜박거려요. 전구를 바꿀 때가 된 것 같아요.

W : You're right. Don't we have an extra light bulb?
당신 말이 맞아요. 우리한테 여분의 전구가 있나요?

M : Well, I used it when I replaced the light bulb in the garage. We don't have any at home.
음, 전에 내가 차고 전등을 바꿀 때 썼어요. 집에 여분의 전구가 없어요.

W : Oh, I see. Then I'll go get some new ones now.
오, 알겠어요. 그럼 지금 가서 새것을 사 올게요.

Why? 왜 정답일까?

화장실 전구를 갈아야 해서 여분의 전구가 있는지 확인하는 여자에게 남자는 다 쓰고 없다(**We don't have any at home.**)고 말해준다. 따라서 여자의 응답으로 가장 적절한 것은 ② '오, 알겠어요. 그럼 지금 가서 새것을 사 올게요.'이다.

- **blink** ⓥ 깜박이다
- **get an electric shock** 감전되다
- **in stock** 재고가 있는

13 전통 문화에서 영감을 얻어 새것 디자인하기

정답률 93% | 정답 ②

대화를 듣고, 여자의 마지막 말에 대한 남자의 응답으로 가장 적절한 것을 고르시오. [3점]

Man: ______________________________

① I'm sorry I can't join the design project this time.
내가 이번에 디자인 프로젝트에 참여하지 못해서 유감이야.
✔ Traditional culture can be a great source of creativity.
전통 문화는 창의성의 훌륭한 원천이 될 수 있지.
③ Our preference should be quality over brand and price.
우리는 브랜드와 가격보다도 품질을 우선시해야 해.
④ I'll change the pattern of the dress as you suggested.
네가 제안한 대로 드레스 무늬를 바꿔볼게.
⑤ We should have handed in the assignment on time.
우리는 과제를 제때 제출했어야 했어.

W : Hi, Minsu. How's it going with the clothing design assignment?
안녕, Minsu. 의상 디자인 과제는 어떻게 되어 가?

M : Hey, Jessica. I'm almost done with it. How about you?
안녕, Jessica. 거의 다 끝났어. 넌 어때?

W : I'm not doing well. As you know, our professor always emphasizes the importance of originality, but I can't come up with any ideas.
난 잘 안 되어가. 너도 알다시피, 우리 교수님이 항상 독창성의 중요성을 강조하시는데, 나는 아무 아이디어도 생각나지 않아.

M : I know what you mean. It wasn't easy for me, either.
네 말이 무슨 말인지 알아. 나도 쉽지 않았어.

W : Minsu, if you don't mind, can I see what you've designed?
Minsu, 혹시 괜찮다면 네가 디자인한 것을 나한테 보여 줄 수 있어?

M : Sure. Look at my sketch.
물론이지. 내 스케치를 봐.

W : Wow, it's an evening dress. Its pattern looks very unique.
와, 이브닝 드레스네. 무늬가 무척 독특해 보인다.

M : Thanks. I got the idea from *hanbok*.
고마워. 난 *한복*에서 아이디어를 얻었어.

W : You mean traditional Korean clothes, right?
한국 전통 의상 말하는 거 맞지?

M : That's right. I designed this dress using the traditional patterns of *hanbok*.
맞아. 난 *한복*의 전통 무늬를 이용해서 이 드레스를 디자인했어.

W : Awesome! I've never thought I could create something new from something old.
근사하다! 난 오래된 것에서 새로운 것을 만들어낼 수 있다고 생각하지 못했어.

M : Traditional culture can be a great source of creativity.
전통 문화는 창의성의 훌륭한 원천이 될 수 있지.

Why? 왜 정답일까?

남자가 한국 전통 의상인 한복에서 영감을 받아 새로운 의상을 디자인했다(**I designed this dress using the traditional patterns of *hanbok*.**)고 이야기하자 여자는 오래된 것에서 새로운 것을 만들어낼 수 있다고 생각해보지 않았다(**I've never thought I could create something new from something old.**)며 감탄한다. 따라서 남자의 응답으로 가장 적절한 것은 ② '전통 문화는 창의성의 훌륭한 원천이 될 수 있지.'이다.

- **emphasize** ⓥ 강조하다
- **originality** ⓝ 독창성
- **come up with** ~을 떠올리다
- **hand in** ~을 제출하다

14 비상구에 놓아둔 상자를 치워달라고 요청하기

정답률 69% | 정답 ②

대화를 듣고, 남자의 마지막 말에 대한 여자의 응답으로 가장 적절한 것을 고르시오. [3점]

Woman: ______________________________

① Great. I can't wait to open the boxes myself.
좋습니다. 직접 상자를 열어볼 것이 기대되네요.
✔ Right. I'll ask about replacing it with a new one.
맞습니다. 그것을 새것으로 바꾸는 것에 관해 문의해 보겠어요.
③ Yes. You should return the product within a week.
네. 상품은 일주일 안에 반송하셔야 합니다.
④ Sorry. The delivery will be a little later than usual.
죄송합니다. 배달이 평소보다 약간 늦을 것입니다.
⑤ No problem. I've already moved all the boxes for you.
문제 없어요. 제가 이미 당신을 위해 상자를 모두 옮겨뒀어요.

W : Excuse me, sir.
실례합니다.

M : Yes, ma'am.
네.

W : What are those boxes?
저 상자들은 뭐죠?

M : These are the goods to be delivered to offices on the 7th floor.
7층 사무실로 배달될 물품입니다.

W : Well, I'm afraid you can't stack those boxes there.
음, 말씀드리기 곤란하지만 저 상자를 저기 쌓아두시면 안 될 것 같아요.

M : I'll deliver them to each office soon.
각 사무실로 곧 배달할 겁니다.

W : I'm sorry, but all the emergency doorways must be cleared and accessible at all times.
죄송하지만 모든 비상 출입구는 항상 치워져 있어야 하고 접근 가능해야 합니다.

M : Oh, is this an emergency exit?
오, 이곳이 비상구인가요?

W : Actually, there is a sign here saying "Emergency Exit."
사실, 여기 '비상 출입구'라는 표시가 있어요.

M : I didn't notice it. I'll move the boxes right away.
못 봤습니다. 제가 바로 상자들을 옮기겠습니다.

W : Thanks. It's not surprising you didn't notice the sign. It's very old.
감사합니다. 표시를 못 보신 것도 당연하지요. 너무 낡았어요.

M : It'd be better if the sign were bigger and more noticeable.
표시가 더 크고 더 눈에 띄면 더 좋을 것 같네요.

W : Right. I'll ask about replacing it with a new one.
맞습니다. 그것을 새것으로 바꾸는 것에 관해 문의해 보겠어요.

Why? 왜 정답일까?

비상구에 상자를 쌓아두었던 남자가 비상구 표시를 미처 못 봤었다고 말하자 여자는 표시가 너무 낡아서 못 본 것도 당연하다고 답한다. 이에 남자는 표시가 더 크고 눈에 띈다면 좋을 것 같다는 의견을 덧붙이고 있으므로(**It'd be better if the sign were bigger and more noticeable.**), 여자의 응답으로 가장 적절한 것은 ② '맞습니다. 그것을 새것으로 바꾸는 것에 관해 문의해 보겠어요.'이다.

- **stack** ⓥ 쌓다
- **accessible** ⓐ 접근 가능한
- **noticeable** ⓐ 눈에 띄는
- **replace A with B** A를 B로 교체하다

15 재활용 시 주의할 점 일러주기

정답률 86% | 정답 ①

다음 상황 설명을 듣고, Sarah가 Emily에게 할 말로 가장 적 절한 것을 고르시오.

Sarah: Emily, ______________________________

✔ you should rinse plastic containers before recycling them.
플라스틱 용기를 재활용하기 전에 헹구어야 해.
② I want you to do your laundry by yourself more often.
난 네가 네 빨래를 더 자주 직접 하면 좋겠어.
③ our recycling center requires us to remove the labels.
우리 재활용 센터에서는 라벨을 제거하라고 해.
④ we need to refill these containers with some fruits.
우리는 이 용기에 과일을 다시 채워놔야 해.
⑤ you have to wipe the table right after you eat.
식사한 다음 바로 식탁을 닦아야 해.

W : Sarah has lived by herself since last year, when she started working at a company.
Sarah는 작년에 회사에서 일하기 시작한 이후로 혼자 살고 있다.
This year, her sister Emily moved in because she entered a college near Sarah's house.
올해 그녀의 동생 Emily가 이사를 왔는데, Sarah의 집 근처 대학에 입학했기 때문이다.
Now they share the housework.
이제 그들은 집안일을 나눠서 한다.
Emily usually prepares breakfast, and Sarah cooks dinner after work.
Emily는 보통 아침을 준비하고, Sarah는 퇴근 후 저녁을 요리한다.
Emily does the laundry, and Sarah takes out the recycling.
Emily는 세탁을 하고, Sarah는 재활용품을 내다 놓는다.
One day Sarah finds Emily puts plastic food containers which are still dirty into their recycling bin.
어느 날 Sarah는 Emily가 아직 더러운 플라스틱 음식 용기를 재활용 쓰레기통에 넣는 것을 발견한다.
Sarah knows that the local recycling center does not accept contaminated items.
Sarah는 지역 재활용 센터에서 오염된 물품을 받지 않는다는 것을 알고 있다.

[문제편 p.158]

She wants to tell Emily to clean out the containers with water before putting them into the bin.
그녀는 Emily에게 용기를 쓰레기통에 버리기 전에 물로 씻으라고 말해주고 싶다.

In this situation, what would Sarah most likely say to Emily?
이 상황에서, Sarah는 Emily에게 뭐라고 말할 것인가?

Sarah : Emily, you should rinse plastic containers before recycling them.
Emily, 플라스틱 용기를 재활용하기 전에 헹구어야 해.

Why? 왜 정답일까?

상황에 따르면 Emily가 더러운 플라스틱 용기를 재활용 통에 넣는 모습을 목격한 Sarah는 재활용 전에 용기를 물로 씻어내야 한다고 말해주고 싶어 한다(**She wants to tell Emily to clean out the containers with water before putting them into the bin.**). 따라서 Sarah가 Emily에게 할 말로 가장 적절한 것은 ① '플라스틱 용기를 재활용하기 전에 헹구어야 해.'이다.

- **do the laundry** 세탁하다
- **recycling bin** 재활용 쓰레기통
- **wipe** ⓥ (먼지나 물기를 없애려고) 닦다
- **container** ⓝ 그릇, 용기
- **contaminate** ⓥ 오염시키다

16-17 도시의 별명과 그 근원

W : Okay, students.
자, 학생 여러분.

We just learned about the ten most popular visitor destinations in the world.
우리는 방금 세계에서 가장 인기 있는 관광지 열 곳에 관해 배웠습니다.

「Did you know that many cities have an alternative way of referring to them?
많은 도시에서 이런 곳들을 다르게 일컫는 방법을 갖고 있다는 것을 알았나요?

You may have heard of some of these famous nicknames, but you might not know how they originated.」 16번의 근거
몇 가지 유명한 별명은 들어보았을 것이지만, 그것들이 어떻게 기원했는지는 모를 겁니다.

「Rome's nickname, "The Eternal City" can be traced far back to Ancient Rome!」
로마의 별명인 '영원의 도시'는 고대 로마까지 거슬러 올라갈 수 있습니다! 17번 ①의 근거 일치

Citizens of this original settlement believed the city would never fall and would thrive forever.
이 독특한 정착지에 살던 시민들은 이 도시가 절대 무너지지 않고 영원히 번성할 것으로 믿었습니다.

「Paris came to be called "The City of Light."」 17번 ②의 근거 일치
파리는 '빛의 도시'라고 불리게 되었죠.

One origin of this nickname is that by the 19th century Paris used gas street lighting and Europeans who passed through Paris spread the reputation of Paris as "The City of Light."
이 별명의 한 가지 기원은 19세기 무렵 파리에서 가스 가로등을 이용했고 파리를 지나던 유럽 사람들이 파리가 '빛의 도시'라는 명성을 퍼뜨렸다는 것입니다.

「As for Singapore, it's known as "The Lion City."」 17번 ③의 근거 일치
싱가포르로 말하자면, 이곳은 '사자 도시'로 알려져 있습니다.

The city earned this name when an ancient prince spotted a lion while out hunting for deer.
이 도시는 고대 왕자가 사슴 사냥을 나갔다가 사자를 발견했을 때 이 이름을 얻었습니다.

「Lastly, Seattle is surrounded by greenery year-round.」 17번 ⑤의 근거 일치
마지막으로, 시애틀은 1년 내내 녹색 잎으로 둘러싸여 있죠.

With all of its forestry, it's no surprise that Seattle is known as "The Emerald City."
그 모든 숲 때문에 시애틀이 '에메랄드 도시'로 알려진 것은 놀랄 일도 아닙니다.

Interesting, isn't it?
흥미롭죠, 그렇지 않나요?

You can find more city nicknames and their origins in the following video clip.
다음 영상에서 더 많은 도시의 별명과 그 기원을 알 수 있습니다.

Now, let's watch it together.
지금 함께 보죠.

- **visitor destination** 관광지
- **originate** ⓥ 기원하다
- **settlement** ⓝ 정착지
- **reputation** ⓝ 명성, 평판
- **alternative** ⓐ 대안의
- **trace back to** ~의 기원이 …까지 거슬러 올라가다
- **thrive** ⓥ 번성하다

16 주제 파악

정답률 92% | 정답 ③

여자가 하는 말의 주제로 가장 적절한 것은?

① the origins of national sports teams' nicknames – 국가대표 팀 별명의 유래
② the ways countries choose their capital cities – 국가에서 수도를 선택하는 방법
✔ city nicknames and how they came to be – 도시의 별명과 그 근원
④ commonly confused capital cities in the world – 세계에서 흔히 혼동되는 수도
⑤ famous tourist attractions and their economic value – 유명한 관광지와 그 경제적 가치

Why? 왜 정답일까?

'**Did you know that many cities have an alternative way of referring to them? You may have heard of some of these famous nicknames, but you might not know how they originated.**'에서 여자는 많은 도시가 별명을 갖고 있다고 언급하며 그 기원을 설명하려 함을 시사한다. 따라서 여자가 하는 말의 주제로 가장 적절한 것은 ③ '도시의 별명과 그 근원'이다.

17 언급 유무 파악

정답률 93% | 정답 ④

언급된 도시가 아닌 것은?

① Rome – 로마 ② Paris – 파리 ③ Singapore – 싱가포르
✔ Sydney – 시드니 ⑤ Seattle – 시애틀

Why? 왜 정답일까?

담화에서 여자는 별명을 지닌 도시의 예로 로마, 파리, 싱가포르, 시애틀을 언급하였다. 따라서 언급되지 않은 것은 ④ '시드니'이다.

Why? 왜 오답일까?

① '**Rome's nickname, "The Eternal City" can be traced far back to Ancient Rome!**'에서 '로마'가 언급되었다.
② '**Paris came to be called "The City of Light."**'에서 '파리'가 언급되었다.
③ '**As for Singapore, it's known as "The Lion City."**'에서 '싱가포르'가 언급되었다.
⑤ '**Lastly, Seattle is surrounded by greenery year-round.**'에서 '시애틀'이 언급되었다.

Dictation 27

문제편 159쪽

01 positioned for a good shot / avoid using the flash / rapidly take a sequence of photos
02 reducing our carbon footprint / using less data storage / the environmental impact of undeleted emails
03 to talk about your building construction / producing a lot of dust / take additional measures
04 wearing a striped hat / rowing the boat / sitting under the triangular sun shade
05 if everything is well prepared / adjust the position / check the lighting
06 stronger than plastic ones / some gardening gloves / one shovel with a wooden handle
07 there isn't much difference / change the text size / adjust the font size
08 the wholesale flower market / Where is the market located / closed on Mondays
09 premium fishing rods / receive a multi-purpose fishing chair / a lake cleaning event
10 come with removable plates / hard to clean / an audible alert / wake up our baby
11 tidying up my house
12 the bathroom light is blinking / replaced the light bulb in the garage
13 emphasizes the importance of originality / what you've designed / using the traditional patterns
14 to be delivered to offices / cleared and accessible / bigger and more noticeable
15 share the housework / accept contaminated items / clean out the containers
16-17 how they originated / would thrive forever / while out hunting for deer / surrounded by greenery year-round

28 회 | 2020학년도 10월 학력평가

고3

• 정답 •

01 ② 02 ② 03 ① 04 ④ 05 ② 06 ③ 07 ② 08 ② 09 ③ 10 ③ 11 ① 12 ① 13 ① 14 ⑤ 15 ⑤ 16 ② 17 ③

01 반려견 산책 시 유의 사항

정답률 96% | 정답 ②

다음을 듣고, 남자가 하는 말의 목적으로 가장 적절한 것을 고르시오.

① 반려견을 위한 공원 시설 개선 아이디어를 공모하려고
② 반려견과의 공원 산책 시 준수 사항을 안내하려고
③ 반려견의 감염병 발병 시 대처법을 소개하려고
④ 반려견을 동반한 공원 출입 자제를 요청하려고
⑤ 공원 시설 수리를 위한 휴관을 공지하려고

M : Hello, visitors!
안녕하세요, 방문객 여러분!
I'm Henry Stratton, Manager of Wellington Park.
저는 Wellington Park의 관리인인 Henry Stratton입니다.
I'd like to ask you to keep in mind a few things when you're walking your dog in the park.
여러분들이 공원에서 개를 산책시키실 때 몇 가지 명심해 주시기를 요청드리려고 합니다.
First of all, please pick up after your dog.
먼저, 개의 뒤처리를 해주세요.
No one likes to step on dog waste, and it can transfer infectious particles to other dogs or even to people.
누구도 개똥을 밟고 싶어 하지 않으며, 그것은 다른 개 또는 심지어 사람에게 전염성 입자를 옮길 수 있습니다.
Cleaning up after your dog is the price of walking your dog in this beautiful park.
개의 뒤처리를 하는 것은 여러분의 개를 아름다운 공원에서 산책시키는 것의 대가입니다.
There is one more thing.
한 가지 더 있습니다.
Always make sure to keep your dog on a leash.
항상 개에게 목줄을 꼭 묶어주세요.
We're getting more complaints about unleashed dogs these days.
요새 저희는 목줄에 묶지 않은 개들에 대해 항의를 더 많이 받고 있습니다.
Please watch your dog and keep it under control at all times.
항상 개를 살펴봐 주시고 통제해 주세요.
Your neighbors will appreciate your thoughtfulness.
여러분의 이웃들이 여러분의 배려를 고마워할 것입니다.
Thank you.
고맙습니다.

Why? 왜 정답일까?

'I'd like to ask you to keep in mind a few things when you're walking your dog in the park.'에서 남자는 개를 공원에서 산책시킬 때 주의할 점 몇 가지를 언급하겠다고 하므로, 남자가 하는 말의 목적으로 가장 적절한 것은 ② '반려견과의 공원 산책 시 준수 사항을 안내하려고'이다.

- **pick up after** ~의 뒤처리를 하다
- **transfer** ⓥ (병을) 옮기다, 전염시키다
- **infectious** ⓐ 감염성의
- **leash** ⓝ (개 등을 매어두는) 줄
- **thoughtfulness** ⓝ 배려, 사려 깊음

02 인테리어 계획하기

정답률 92% | 정답 ②

대화를 듣고, 여자의 의견으로 가장 적절한 것을 고르시오.

① 의뢰인의 취향을 존중하여 인테리어를 디자인해야 한다.
② 인테리어 작업은 전문가에게 맡기는 것이 좋다.
③ 인테리어 공사는 예산 안에서 진행해야 한다.
④ 집안의 색이 가족의 기분에 영향을 미친다.
⑤ 주기적으로 가구를 재배치하는 것이 좋다.

W : Honey, are you reading that magazine on interior design?
여보, 인테리어 디자인에 관한 그 잡지를 읽고 있어요?
M : Yes. We talked about making some changes around the house. Remember?
네. 우린 집에 좀 변화를 주기로 얘기했었잖아요. 기억나요?
W : Of course. I can't wait to give our house a new look.
물론이죠. 어서 우리 집을 단장하고 싶어요.
M : I'm thinking of changing the color of the walls and replacing the old tiles and doors.
난 벽 색깔을 바꾸고 낡은 타일과 문을 교체할까 생각하고 있어요.
W : Good idea. Do you know any good interior designers?
좋은 생각이에요. 근사한 인테리어 디자이너들 좀 알고 있어요?
M : Well, I thought we could save money if we did it ourselves.
음, 우리가 직접 한다면 돈을 아낄 수 있을 것 같아요.
W : I disagree. If we're not happy with the work we've done, we'll eventually have to hire someone to fix it.
난 뜻이 달라요. 만일 우리가 한 작업에 만족하지 못하면, 우리는 결국 그걸 바로잡아줄 사람을 고용해야 할 거예요.
M : Hmm.... In that case, we could end up spending more money.
흠... 그런 경우라면, 우리는 결국 돈을 더 많이 쓸 수도 있겠군요.
W : Also, think of all the time and energy we'll have to put in. Let's get the professionals to do it for us.
더구나, 우리가 들여야 할 그 모든 시간과 에너지를 생각해봐요. 우리를 위해 그 일을 해줄 전문가를 찾아보죠.
M : You're right. We can discuss what we want with them.
당신 말이 맞아요. 우리가 뭘 원하는지 그들과 논의할 수 있겠죠.
W : There's a reason people hire professionals to renovate their house.
사람들이 집을 개조할 때 전문가를 고용하는 이유가 있어요.
M : Okay. I'll ask around and find someone.
알겠어요. 내가 주변에 물어보고 사람을 찾아볼게요.

Why? 왜 정답일까?

집 인테리어 작업을 직접 해보자는 남자에게 여자는 전문가를 고용하자고 설득하고 있다(**Let's get the professionals to do it for us.**). 따라서 여자의 의견으로 가장 적절한 것은 ② '인테리어 작업은 전문가에게 맡기는 것이 좋다.'이다.

- **replace** ⓥ (낡은 것·손상된 것 등을) 바꾸다, 교체하다
- **eventually** ad 결국
- **end up ~ing** 결국 ~하다
- **professional** ⓝ 전문가
- **renovate** ⓥ 개조하다

03 자전거 수리 맡기기

정답률 90% | 정답 ①

대화를 듣고, 두 사람의 관계를 가장 잘 나타낸 것을 고르시오.

① 자전거 수리공 – 고객
② 스포츠 기자 – 사이클 선수
③ 건물 청소부 – 입주민
④ 골동품 감정사 – 의뢰인
⑤ 농기구 판매상 – 농장주

M : Hello, Ms. Sandburg. I'm glad you made it here. Please come on in.
안녕하세요, Sandburg 씨. 여기 와주셔서 기뻐요. 들어오세요.
W : Good morning. Thanks for meeting me so early in the morning.
안녕하세요. 저를 이렇게 이른 아침부터 만나주셔서 감사해요.
M : No problem. Is this the bike you mentioned on the phone?
천만에요. 이게 당신이 전화로 말씀하셨던 자전거인가요?
W : Yes. This is my mom's old bike.
네. 저희 엄마의 오래된 자전거예요.
M : It's a beautiful classic road bicycle. Let me take a look. *[Pause]* It looks like it hasn't been used for a long time.
아름답고 고전적인 도로용 자전거로군요. 제가 살펴볼게요. *[잠시 멈춤]* 이건 오랫동안 사용되지 않은 것 같군요.
W : Right. It's been kept in the garage at my parents' farmhouse for years.
맞아요. 몇 년 동안 저희 부모님 농가 차고에 보관돼 있었어요.
M : Still it's in pretty good shape, but some parts need to be replaced.
그래도 아직 꽤 상태가 좋지만, 부품 몇 개는 교체해야겠어요.
W : I figured. Can you still get original parts for this model?
그렇게 생각했어요. 이 제품의 원래 부품을 아직 구할 수 있나요?
M : I'll try. But if I can't, I'll be able to find other ones that could work.
구해 보겠습니다. 하지만 만일 불가능하면, 괜찮을 것 같은 다른 부품을 찾아볼 수 있을 거예요.
W : Okay. It also needs a thorough cleaning. Do you do that, too?
알겠습니다. 또한 이것은 꼼꼼한 청소가 필요해요. 그것도 해주시나요?
M : Of course. The cleaning will take another day or two.
물론입니다. 청소 작업은 추가로 하루 이틀 정도가 걸릴 거예요.
W : Thanks. Give me a call when you're finished.
고맙습니다. 다 되시면 전화해 주세요.

Why? 왜 정답일까?

'Is this the bike you mentioned on the phone?', 'Still it's in pretty good shape, but some parts need to be replaced. / I figured. Can you still get original parts for this model? / ~ if I can't, I'll be able to find other ones that could work.' 등에서 남자가 자전거 수리공임을, 여자가 자전거를 맡기러 온 고객임을 알 수 있다. 따라서 두 사람의 관계로 가장 적절한 것은 ① '자전거 수리공 – 고객'이다.

- **make it** 도착하다
- **in good shape** 상태가 좋은
- **thorough** ⓐ 꼼꼼한, 철저한

04 서핑 학교 로비 사진 구경하기

정답률 86% | 정답 ④

대화를 듣고, 그림에서 대화의 내용과 일치하지 않는 것을 고르시오.

W : Hey, Ben. I hear you're back from Surf School. How was it?
안녕, Ben. 난 네가 Surf School에서 돌아왔다고 들었어. 어땠어?
M : It was tough, but I had so much fun. This is a photo of the school's main lobby.
어려웠지만, 몹시 즐거웠어. 이건 학교 메인 로비 사진이야.
W : Let me see. *[Pause]* 「Oh, there are surfboards leaning on the back wall.
좀 보자. *[잠시 멈춤]* 오, 뒤쪽 벽에 서핑 보드가 기대어 세워져 있네.
M : The bigger ones are for beginners, and the smaller ones are for more skilled surfers.」 ①의 근거 일치
큰 것이 초보자용이고, 작은 것이 더 숙련된 서퍼들용이야.
W : Interesting. 「The wetsuits are hanging under the sign that says SURF SCHOOL.」 ②의 근거 일치 Are those for rent?
재밌네. SURF SCHOOL이라고 쓰인 표지 밑에 잠수복이 걸려있구나. 저것들은 대여용이야?
M : Yes. People can put on their wetsuits in the changing room. 「See the door next to the wetsuits?」 ③의 근거 일치
응. 사람들은 탈의실에서 잠수복을 입을 수 있어. 잠수복 옆에 문이 보여?
W : Yeah. 「What's that big round basket on the floor for?」 ④의 근거 불일치
응. 바닥에 있는 저 큰 원형 바구니는 뭐야?
M : It's for people to return their used wetsuits.
사람들이 입고 난 잠수복을 반납하라고 있는 거야.
W : 「Who is the surfer in the poster on the left wall?
왼쪽 벽에 있는 포스터 속 서퍼는 누구야?
M : He's a legendary surfing champion.」 ⑤의 근거 일치
그는 전설적인 서핑 챔피언이야.
W : Wow. I would love to go to Surf School someday.
와, 나도 언젠가 Surf School에 가보고 싶다.

[문제편 p.163]

Why? 왜 정답일까?

대화에서 여자는 바닥에 큰 원형 바구니가 놓여있다(What's that big round basket on the floor for?)고 말하는데, 그림 속 바구니는 사각형이다. 따라서 그림에서 대화의 내용과 일치하지 않는 것은 ④이다.

- lean on ~에 기대다
- wetsuit ⓝ 잠수복
- skilled ⓐ 숙련된
- legendary ⓐ 전설적인

05 채식주의자를 위한 김치 조리법 보내주기

정답률 96% | 정답 ②

대화를 듣고, 여자가 남자를 위해 할 일로 가장 적절한 것을 고르시오.

① 요리 강습 신청하기
✓② 김치 조리법 전송하기
③ 김치 시식 후기 쓰기
④ 채식 도시락 주문하기
⑤ 요리 재료 구매하기

W : Hi, Eric. I didn't expect to see you here at the bookstore.
안녕하세요, Eric. 당신을 이곳 서점에서 볼 거라고 예상 못 했어요.

M : Hi, Kimmy. I'm browsing books to get inspiration. I need some fresh ideas for my writing.
안녕하세요, Kimmy. 전 영감을 좀 받으려고 책을 둘러보고 있어요. 제 글을 위해 새로운 아이디어가 좀 필요해요.

W : What are you writing?
뭘 쓰고 계신데요?

M : It's a book based on my life as a vegan.
제 채식주의자 생활을 기반으로 한 책이에요.

W : That's great. When you finish writing, I'd love to read it. I'm a vegan, too.
근사하네요. 글을 다 끝내시면 저도 읽고 싶어요. 저도 채식주의자거든요.

M : Okay, I'll send you a copy. I think you'll like the special section that introduces easy-to-cook vegan recipes.
좋아요, 제가 한 부를 보내드릴게요. 당신은 쉽게 요리할 수 있는 채식주의 조리법을 소개하는 특별 섹션을 좋아하실 것 같네요.

W : That'd be useful. It's not easy to find those.
유용하겠군요. 그런 걸 찾기는 쉽지 않은데 말이에요.

M : That's what I mean. I'm looking for some good vegan kimchi recipes.
제 말이 그 말이에요. 전 괜찮은 채식주의의 김치 조리법을 좀 찾고 있어요.

W : Oh, I happen to have a vegan kimchi recipe. It uses soy sauce instead of fermented fish.
오, 저한테 마침 채식주의의 김치 조리법이 있어요. 그것은 젓갈 대신 간장을 이용해요.

M : Sounds interesting. Could you send me the recipe? Maybe I can add it to my book.
흥미롭군요. 저한테 조리법을 보내주실 수 있나요? 어쩌면 그걸 제 책에 추가할 수 있을 것 같아요.

W : Sure. I'll email it to you.
물론이죠. 제가 이메일로 보내드릴게요.

Why? 왜 정답일까?

채식주의에 관한 책을 쓰고 있는 남자는 여자가 채식주의 김치 조리법을 가지고 있다는 말에 자신에게도 보내달라고 부탁하고(Could you send me the recipe?), 여자는 이에 알겠다고 답한다(Sure. I'll email it to you.). 따라서 여자가 할 일로 가장 적절한 것은 ② '김치 조리법 전송하기'이다.

- expect ⓥ 예상하다, 기대하다
- inspiration ⓝ 영감
- soy sauce 간장
- add A to B A를 B에 추가하다
- browse ⓥ 둘러보다, 훑어보다
- vegan ⓝ (완전) 채식주의자
- ferment ⓥ 발효시키다

06 아이스링크 입장권 사기

정답률 86% | 정답 ③

대화를 듣고, 남자가 지불할 금액을 고르시오. [3점]

① $25 ② $30 ✓③ $35 ④ $40 ⑤ $45

M : Good morning. I'd like to buy tickets to the ice rink.
안녕하세요. 전 아이스링크 티켓을 사고 싶어요.

W : Okay. Tickets are $10 per adult, and $5 per child under 12.
네, 티켓은 어른 한 장에 10달러, 12세 미만 어린이는 한 장에 5달러입니다.

M : I need tickets for one adult and two children. Both kids are under 12.
어른 한 장과 어린이 두 장이 필요해요. 아이들은 둘 다 12세 미만이에요.

W : Sure. Do you want to rent some skates as well?
알겠습니다. 스케이트도 빌리실 건가요?

M : No, thanks. We brought our own skates.
아니요, 괜찮습니다. 저희는 스케이트를 가져왔어요.

W : Good. Do your children need a private skating lesson?
알겠습니다. 자녀분들에게 스케이팅 개인 강습이 필요한가요?

M : Oh, I didn't know you had private lessons.
오, 개인 강습이 있는지 몰랐어요.

W : We do, actually. It's a one-hour session for children.
정말로 있습니다. 어린이들을 위한 한 시간짜리 강습이에요.

M : I think my younger one needs a lesson. He is not very confident on the ice yet.
동생인 아이가 강습을 받아야 할 것 같네요. 아직 얼음 위에서 별로 자신 있어 하지 않거든요.

W : Good choice. So you're signing up for a private lesson for just one of your children.
좋은 선택입니다. 그럼 자녀들 중 한 분만 개인 강습에 등록하시는 거고요.

M : That's right. How much is the lesson fee?
맞아요. 강습료는 얼마지요?

W : It's $15. How would you like to pay?
15달러입니다. 어떻게 지불하시겠습니까?

M : I'll pay with my credit card.
신용카드로 지불하겠습니다.

Why? 왜 정답일까?

대화에 따르면 자녀들을 데리고 아이스링크에 온 남자는 10달러짜리 어른용 입장권 한 장과 5달러짜리 어린이용 입장권을 두 장 산 후, 자녀 중 한 명을 15달러짜리 개인 강습에 등록시켰다. 이를 식으로 나타내면 '$10+5\times2+15=35$'이므로, 남자가 지불할 금액은 ③ '$35'이다.

- as well (문미에서) 또한
- session ⓝ (강의, 회의 등의) 시간
- sign up for ~에 등록하다
- private ⓐ 사적인
- confident ⓐ 자신 있는

[문제편 p.163]

07 화상 회의에 불참한 이유

정답률 96% | 정답 ②

대화를 듣고, 남자가 화상 회의에 참석하지 못한 이유를 고르시오.

① 회의 시간을 착각해서
✓② 휴대 전화가 고장 나서
③ 접속 비밀번호를 잊어서
④ 인터넷 접속이 불안정해서
⑤ 다른 회의에 참석해야 해서

M : Hey, Diane. I'm sorry I couldn't attend the video conference this morning.
안녕하세요, Diane. 오늘 아침 화상 회의에 참석하지 못해 미안해요.

W : That's okay. I just assumed you were occupied with something important.
괜찮아요. 그냥 뭔가 중요한 일로 바쁘신가 했어요.

M : Not exactly. I was on the train coming back from my business trip.
꼭 그런 건 아니었어요. 전 출장에서 돌아오는 기차에 있었어요.

W : Oh, I guess you had a problem accessing the Internet on the train.
오, 기차에서 인터넷에 접속하는 데 문제가 있었나 봐요.

M : No, the Internet was fine and the train had wifi.
아니요, 인터넷은 괜찮았고 기차에는 와이파이가 있었어요.

W : Then, were you too busy and lost track of time?
그럼, 너무 바빠서 시간 가는 줄 모르셨던 거예요?

M : No. When I took out my phone to join, the person next to me hit my hand with his bag.
아뇨, 제가 참여하려고 휴대 전화를 꺼냈을 때, 제 옆자리 사람이 가방으로 제 손을 쳤어요.

W : Oh, no! Did you drop your phone?
오, 이런! 전화를 떨어뜨리셨나요?

M : Yes. The screen totally cracked, and my phone wasn't working anymore.
네, 액정이 완전히 깨지고, 제 휴대 전화는 더 이상 작동하지 않았어요.

W : I'm so sorry to hear that.
그 말씀을 들으니 몹시 유감이네요.

M : So, there was no way I could join the conference.
그래서, 도저히 제가 회의에 참여할 수가 없었어요.

W : I understand. I'll share the details of the morning conference later.
이해해요. 나중에 자세한 아침 회의 내용을 공유해 드릴게요.

Why? 왜 정답일까?

'When I took out my phone to join, the person next to me hit my hand with his bag.' 와 'The screen totally cracked, and my phone wasn't working anymore.'에 따르면 남자는 화상 회의에 참여하려고 휴대 전화를 꺼낸 순간 옆 사람이 가방으로 손을 치는 바람에 전화를 떨어뜨렸고, 전화가 고장 나 버려서 회의에 참여할 수 없게 되었다. 따라서 남자가 화상 회의에 참석하지 못한 이유로 가장 적절한 것은 ② '휴대 전화가 고장 나서'이다.

- video conference 화상 회의
- business trip 출장
- crack ⓥ 깨지다, 부서지다
- be occupied with ~로 바쁘다, ~에 열중하다
- lose track of time 시간 가는 줄 모르다

08 재즈 기타 대회

정답률 75% | 정답 ②

대화를 듣고, Jazz Guitar Contest에 관해 언급되지 않은 것을 고르시오.

① 주최 단체 ✓② 개최 장소 ③ 개최 시기
④ 우승 상금 ⑤ 참가비

W : Hey, Tim. What are you doing on your phone?
안녕, Tim. 핸드폰으로 뭐 하고 있어?

M : Oh, Cathy. I'm applying for the Jazz Guitar Contest.
오, Cathy. 난 Jazz Guitar Contest에 신청하고 있어.

W : 「You mean the contest hosted by the World Guitarist Association?」 ①의 근거 일치
World Guitarist Association에서 주최하는 그 대회 말야?

M : Yes. It's a huge event that has tons of participants every year. I'm signing up early so I can focus on my practice.
응, 매년 엄청 많은 참가자들이 몰리는 큰 행사야. 난 연습에 집중할 수 있도록 일찍 신청하고 있어.

W : Great. I hope you'll have enough time to practice.
좋다. 네가 연습할 시간이 충분하길 바랄게.

M : 「It's held during the first week of December.」 So I have two months.
대회는 12월 첫 주에 열려. 그러니 나한테 두 달이 있어. ③의 근거 일치

W : 「What are the prizes for the winners?
우승 상품이 뭐야?

M : The first place winner will receive $10,000, and the top three winners will be awarded a trip to New Orleans.」 ④의 근거 일치
1등은 1만 달러를 받게 되고, 상위 3명은 New Orleans 여행을 부상으로 받게 돼.

W : It'd be great if you won the contest. 「Is there an entry fee?
네가 대회에서 우승하면 정말 멋지겠다. 참가비가 있어?

M : Yes, it's $50.」 ⑤의 근거 일치
응, 50달러야.

W : You're an excellent guitarist. I'm sure you have a strong chance of winning.
넌 뛰어난 기타리스트야. 난 네가 우승할 가능성이 크다고 믿어.

M : Thanks for saying so.
그렇게 말해줘서 고마워.

Why? 왜 정답일까?

대화에서 남자와 여자는 Jazz Guitar Contest의 주최 단체, 개최 시기, 우승 상금, 참가비에 관해 언급하였다. 따라서 언급되지 않은 것은 ② '개최 장소'이다.

Why? 왜 오답일까?

① 'You mean the contest hosted by the World Guitarist Association?'에서 '주최 단체'가 언급되었다.
③ 'It's held during the first week of December.'에서 '개최 시기'가 언급되었다.
④ 'The first place winner will receive $10,000, ~'에서 '우승 상금'이 언급되었다.
⑤ 'Yes, it's $50.'에서 '참가비'가 언급되었다.

- apply for ~에 신청하다
- huge ⓐ 거대한
- have a strong chace of ~할 가능성이 크다
- host ⓥ (행사를) 주최하다
- entry fee 참가비

09 열기구 축제 개최 안내

정답률 93% | 정답 ③

The 10th International Hot Air Balloon Fiesta에 관한 다음 내용을 듣고, 일치하지 않는 것을 고르시오.

① 다음 주 월요일부터 2주간 개최된다.
② 열기구 탑승 시각은 매일 오전 10시와 오후 5시이다.
✔ 첫날 열기구 탑승권은 20% 할인된다.
④ 열기구는 다양한 국기로 장식된다.
⑤ 웹 사이트에서 실시간으로 스트리밍된다.

W : Hello, ballooning fans!
안녕하세요, 열기구 여행을 좋아하시는 분들!
The 10th International Hot Air Balloon Fiesta is coming!
제10회 International Hot Air Balloon Fiesta가 다가오고 있습니다!
This Fiesta has been bringing ballooning fans together from around the world since 2011.
이 축제는 2011년부터 전 세계 열기구 여행 팬들을 한데 모으고 있습니다.
『Starting next Monday, the Fiesta will be presenting a magical world of balloons for two weeks at Titan National Park.』 ①의 근거 일치
다음 주 월요일부터 2주간 이 축제는 Titan National Park에서 마법 같은 열기구의 세계를 선보일 예정입니다.
Anybody can enjoy a hot air balloon ride.
누구든 열기구 탑승을 즐길 수 있습니다.
『Boarding times are 10 a.m. and 5 p.m. every day.』 ②의 근거 일치
탑승 시각은 매일 오전 10시와 오후 5시입니다.
『Ticket prices for the ride are 50% off on the first day of the Fiesta.』 ③의 근거 불일치
축제 첫날에는 열기구 탑승권이 50퍼센트 할인됩니다.
『This year's theme is "National Flags," so the balloons will be decorated with various national flags.』 ④의 근거 일치
올해의 주제는 '국기'이므로, 열기구 풍선들은 다양한 국기로 장식될 것입니다.
『This event will be streamed live on the Fiesta website.』 ⑤의 근거 일치
이 행사는 축제 웹 사이트에서 실시간으로 스트리밍될 예정입니다.
If you cannot make it to Titan National Park, you can enjoy the vibrant balloons floating in the sky on your screen!
만일 Titan National Park에 오실 수 없다면, 화면을 통해 색색의 풍선들이 하늘에 떠오르는 모습을 즐기실 수 있습니다!

Why? 왜 정답일까?

'Ticket prices for the ride are 50% off on the first day of the Fiesta.'에서 축제 첫날 열기구 탑승권은 50% 할인된다고 하므로, 내용과 일치하지 않는 것은 ③ '첫날 열기구 탑승권은 20% 할인된다.'이다.

Why? 왜 오답일까?

① 'Starting next Monday, the Fiesta will be presenting a magical world of balloons for two weeks at Titan National Park.'의 내용과 일치한다.
② 'Boarding times are 10 a.m. and 5 p.m. every day.'의 내용과 일치한다.
④ '~ the balloons will be decorated with various national flags.'의 내용과 일치한다.
⑤ 'This event will be streamed live on the Fiesta website.'의 내용과 일치한다.

- ballooning ⓝ 열기구 여행
- make it to ~에 오다
- vibrant ⓐ (색깔이) 강렬한, 선명한

10 캣 트리 사기

정답률 94% | 정답 ③

다음 표를 보면서 대화를 듣고, 여자가 구매할 캣 트리를 고르시오.

Multi-Level Cat Trees

	Model	Price	No. of Levels	Size	Assembly Required
①	A	$65	5	Medium	○
②	B	$85	4	Medium	×
✔	C	$75	5	Large	○
④	D	$95	5	Large	×
⑤	E	$105	4	X-Large	○

W : Neil, I'm looking for a cat tree for my cats. Would you help me choose a good one?
Neil, 난 내 고양이들을 위한 캣 트리를 찾고 있어. 내가 하나 좋은 걸 고르게 도와줄래?
M : Okay. Hmm.... You're going to choose one of these five models, right?
알겠어. 흠... 넌 이 다섯 개 제품 중 하나를 고르겠구나, 맞지?
W : Yes, but I don't want to buy this one. 『I'd like to stay under $100.』 근거1 Price 조건
응, 그런데 난 이것은 사고 싶지 않아. 난 100달러 이하로 맞추고 싶어.
M : I see. How about we take a look at these four?
알겠어. 이 네 개 중 살펴보면 어떨까?
W : Yeah. 『How many levels would you recommend?
그래. 넌 몇 층짜리를 추천하니?
M : Usually, the more levels the better.
보통은 층이 많을수록 더 좋아.
W : Then I'll go with something that has five levels.』 근거2 No. of Levels 조건
그럼 난 5층짜리로 골라야겠다.
M : Now, you should choose the size. 『How big are your cats?
이제 크기를 골라야 해. 네 고양이들은 얼마나 크니?
W : My cats are young and small now, but they'll grow bigger soon. I'd rather buy a large one.』 근거3 Size 조건
내 고양이들은 지금은 어리고 작은데, 금방 클 거야. 큰 것을 사야겠어.
M : Good choice. You'll be able to use it longer.
좋은 선택이야. 넌 그것을 더 오래 쓸 수 있을 거야.
W : Now I have two options left. 『Is it okay to get something that requires assembly?
이제 두 가지 선택권이 남았어. 조립해야 되는 것을 사도 괜찮을까?
M : It's not difficult to assemble. Why don't you get the cheaper one?
조립하는 건 어렵지 않아. 더 싼 것을 고르면 어때? 근거4 Assembly Required 조건
W : Okay.』 I'll take your advice and order this one.
알겠어. 네 조언을 받아들여서 이걸 사겠어.

Why? 왜 정답일까?

대화에 따르면 여자는 가격이 100달러를 넘지 않으면서, 5층짜리이고, 크기가 크면서, 조립이 필요하지만 보다 싼 캣 트리를 구매하려고 한다. 따라서 여자가 주문할 캣 트리는 ③ 'C'이다.

- take a look at ~을 살펴보다
- level ⓝ (건물의) 층
- recommend ⓥ 추천하다
- assembly ⓝ 조립

11 깁스한 친구에게 식당에 함께 가자고 제안하기

정답률 91% | 정답 ①

대화를 듣고, 여자의 마지막 말에 대한 남자의 응답으로 가장 적절한 것을 고르시오.

✔ Thanks. That would be a great help. – 고마워. 큰 도움이 될 거야.
② Really? You'd better leave school early. – 정말? 넌 오늘 학교에서 일찍 가야겠네.
③ Okay. Then, let me call my doctor later. – 그래. 그럼 내가 의사 선생님께 나중에 전화할게.
④ I know how you feel. It must hurt a lot. – 네 기분 어떤지 알아. 그거 무척 아프겠다.
⑤ Oh, no. You should have been more careful. – 오, 이런. 더 조심했어야지.

W : Jake, you have a cast on your leg. What happened?
Jake, 너 다리에 깁스했네. 무슨 일이야?
M : I fell down the stairs. I'm having trouble walking around.
계단에서 넘어졌어. 걸어 다니기가 불편해.
W : Do you want me to go to the cafeteria with you at lunch? I can help you with your food tray.
점심 때 식당에 같이 가줄까? 내가 네 식판을 들어줄 수 있어.
M : Thanks. That would be a great help.
고마워. 큰 도움이 될 거야.

Why? 왜 정답일까?

다리를 다쳐 깁스를 한 남자에게 여자는 점심 때 식판을 들고 오가는 것을 도와주겠다(Do you want me to go to the cafeteria with you at lunch? I can help you with your food tray.)고 제안하고 있다. 따라서 남자의 응답으로 가장 적절한 것은 ① '고마워. 큰 도움이 될 거야.'이다.

- have a cast 깁스하다
- fall down 넘어지다
- have trouble ~ing ~하기가 어렵다
- food tray 식판

12 유통기한이 지난 케첩 버리기

정답률 74% | 정답 ①

대화를 듣고, 남자의 마지막 말에 대한 여자의 응답으로 가장 적절한 것을 고르시오.

✔ Definitely. Don't forget to wash it after emptying it.
물론이죠. 그걸 비우고 나서 닦는 것도 잊지 마세요.
② Look at the expiration date! We shouldn't buy this.
유통기한 좀 봐요! 우린 이걸 사지 말아야 해요.
③ Yes. It's cheaper to buy it from an online store.
네. 이건 온라인 매장에서 사는 게 더 싸요.
④ No. We shouldn't put too much ketchup on the food.
아니요. 우린 음식에 너무 많은 케첩을 뿌리면 안 돼요.
⑤ Sure. We can keep the ketchup at room temperature.
물론이죠. 우린 케첩을 상온에 둘 수 있어요.

M : Honey, this ketchup is way past the expiration date. But there's still some left in the bottle.
여보, 이 케첩은 유통기한을 훨씬 넘겼어요. 하지만 병 안에 아직 조금 남아있어요.
W : Oh, what a waste! We'd better throw it away.
오, 정말 낭비네요! 그걸 버리는 게 낫겠어요.
M : Okay. Do I have to empty the bottle before putting it into the recycling bin?
알겠어요. 이걸 재활용품 통 안에 넣기 전에 병을 비워야 할까요?
W : Definitely. Don't forget to wash it after emptying it.
물론이죠. 그걸 비우고 나서 닦는 것도 잊지 마세요.

Why? 왜 정답일까?

유통기한이 한참 지난 케첩을 버리려는 남자는 병을 재활용하기 전에 내용물을 비워야할지(Do I have to empty the bottle before putting it into the recycling bin?) 여자에게 묻고 있다. 따라서 여자의 응답으로 가장 적절한 것은 ① '물론이죠. 그걸 비우고 나서 닦는 것도 잊지 마세요.'이다.

- expiration date 유통기한
- recycling bin 재활용품 통
- room temperature 상온

13 캠핑 장비 처분하기

정답률 89% | 정답 ①

대화를 듣고, 여자의 마지막 말에 대한 남자의 응답으로 가장 적절한 것을 고르시오.

Man: ________

✔ That's a good idea. I'll sign up for a booth.
좋은 생각이다. 부스를 신청해야겠어.
② I disagree. Camping equipment is overpriced.
난 동의하지 않아. 캠핑 장비는 값이 너무 비싸게 매겨져 있어.
③ Yes. I'm looking for a two-bedroom apartment.
응. 난 침실이 2개인 아파트를 찾고 있어.
④ I see it differently. Selling offline is much easier.
난 다르게 생각해. 오프라인에서 파는 게 훨씬 더 쉬워.
⑤ Thanks. But I can manage the packing on my own.
고마워. 하지만 난 짐 싸는 것을 혼자 처리할 수 있어.

W : Liam, you're moving in a month. How's everything going?
Liam, 너 한 달 뒤에 이사 가네. 어떻게 되어 가고 있어?
M : Pretty well, but I find packing very time-consuming.
잘 돼 가고 있어. 하지만 짐 싸는 데 무척 시간이 많이 걸리네.
W : You have a lot of camping equipment. It must be hard to pack it all.
넌 캠핑 용품이 많잖아. 그걸 다 싸려면 힘들겠다.
M : It is. I'm trying to get rid of some items.
맞아. 난 몇 가지 물품을 치우려고 해.
W : Are you trying to sell them online?
그걸 온라인에 팔려는 거야?
M : Yeah. Since I'm moving to a smaller apartment, I need to downsize.
어. 난 더 작은 아파트로 이사 가니까 짐을 줄여야 해.
W : You know you can sell them offline, too.
그걸 오프라인에서도 팔 수 있는 거 알지.

[문제편 p.163]

M : Do you know a good place to sell?
팔기 좋은 장소를 알아?
W : The community flea market is being held next weekend. You can get a booth there.
지역 벼룩시장이 다음 주말에 열릴 예정이야. 거기서 부스를 잡으면 돼.
M : Cool! Do you have any ideas on how I can attract people to my booth?
좋다! 사람들을 내 부스로 끌어모을 수 있는 방법이 있을까?
W : Set up a camping tent and display your equipment nicely. It'll surely draw attention.
캠핑 텐트를 세워놓고 네 장비들을 근사하게 진열해 봐. 분명 이목을 끌 거야.
M : That's a good idea. I'll sign up for a booth.
좋은 생각이다. 부스를 신청해야겠어.

Why? 왜 정답일까?

남자가 캠핑 장비를 팔 계획이라고 말하자 여자는 오프라인 벼룩시장에서 팔아볼 것을 권하며 부스 앞에 텐트를 세워놓고 장비를 근사하게 진열해 두면 사람들의 이목을 끌 수 있을 것(**Set up a camping tent and display your equipment nicely. It'll surely draw attention.**)이라고 조언한다. 따라서 남자의 응답으로 가장 적절한 것은 ① '좋은 생각이다. 부스를 신청해야겠어.'이다.

- **time-consuming** ⓐ 시간이 많이 걸리는
- **get rid of** ~을 치우다, 없애다
- **flea market** 벼룩시장
- **overprice** ⓥ 값을 비싸게 매기다
- **equipment** ⓝ 장비
- **downsize** ⓥ (규모를) 줄이다, 축소하다
- **draw attention** 이목을 끌다

14 책 읽는 자리 만들어주기

정답률 92% | 정답 ⑤

대화를 듣고, 남자의 마지막 말에 대한 여자의 응답으로 가장 적절한 것을 고르시오. [3점]

Woman: ____________________

① Oh, really? Good luck with your book search.
오, 그래요? 책 검색에 행운을 빌게요.
② I don't think so. Reading is not for everybody.
전 그렇게 생각하지 않아요. 독서가 모두에게 통하지는 않아요.
③ Hold on. Let me bring the books you requested.
잠시만요. 당신이 요청한 책을 제가 가져갈게요.
④ Not at all. You should respect his taste in books.
전혀 아니에요. 당신은 그의 책 취향을 존중해야 해요.
✔⑤ Okay. I hope my son enjoys reading books there.
알겠어요. 제 아들이 거기서 즐겁게 책을 읽기를 바라요.

W : Nate, my son doesn't seem to enjoy reading. How can I get him to read more?
Nate, 제 아들이 독서를 좋아하는 것 같지 않아요. 어떻게 하면 아이가 책을 더 많이 읽게 할 수 있을까요?
M : When I think about my children, they love to take their books to their reading nook.
우리 애들을 생각해보면, 아이들은 책 읽는 자리로 책을 가져가는 것을 좋아해요.
W : What's a reading nook?
책 읽는 자리가 뭐예요?
M : It's a cozy place for reading. It's also called a reading corner.
독서를 위한 안락한 장소 말이에요. 책 읽는 구석이라고 부르기도 해요.
W : Oh, I thought that children should always read at a desk.
오, 전 아이들이 항상 책상에서 독서해야 한다고 생각했어요.
M : Let me put it this way. When you're in a relaxing environment, you can concentrate better.
이렇게 말해 보죠. 당신은 편안한 환경에 있을 때 더 잘 집중할 수 있죠.
W : My mom likes to read in her armchair. Is that her reading nook?
우리 어머니는 안락의자에서 읽기를 좋아하세요. 그게 어머니의 책 읽는 자리인 건가요?
M : Maybe. And it'd be even better if there is good lighting.
그럴지도 몰라요. 만일 조명이 좋다면 훨씬 더 좋아요.
W : I see. I'll set up a reading corner for my son. Is there anything else I should consider?
그렇군요. 전 아들을 위해 책 읽는 구석을 마련할게요. 제가 또 고려해야 할 게 있을까요?
M : Yes. The place should be quiet and free from distractions.
네. 그 장소는 조용해야 하고 정신을 산만하게 하는 것으로부터 벗어나 있어야 해요.
W : Okay. I hope my son enjoys reading books there.
알겠어요. 제 아들이 거기서 즐겁게 책을 읽기를 바라요.

Why? 왜 정답일까?

아이에게 책 읽을 자리를 만들어줄 것을 권하는 남자에게 여자가 자리를 만들 때 주의해야 할 점이 있는지 묻자 남자는 조용하고 정신을 분산시키는 것이 없는 장소여야 한다(**The place should be quiet and free from distractions.**)고 설명해 준다. 따라서 여자의 응답으로 가장 적절한 것은 ⑤ '알겠어요. 제 아들이 거기서 즐겁게 책을 읽기를 바라요.'이다.

- **nook** ⓝ 자리, 장소, 구석
- **Let me put it this way.** 이렇게 말해 보죠.
- **distraction** ⓝ 주의를 산만하게 하는 것
- **cozy** ⓐ 안락한
- **free from** ~로부터 벗어난

15 피처폰 사용 권하기

정답률 79% | 정답 ⑤

다음 상황 설명을 듣고, Josh가 Lily에게 할 말로 가장 적절한 것을 고르시오. [3점]

Josh: ____________________

① It's too bad that your phone is not working.
네 전화기가 제대로 작동하지 않는다니 참 안됐다.
② Just turn off your phone when you go to bed.
잠자리에 들 때 전화기를 그냥 꺼 버려.
③ Did you check out the latest model at the shop?
너 매장에서 최신 모델 살펴봤니?
④ You're not allowed to use your phone during class.
넌 수업 시간에 전화기를 쓰면 안 돼.
✔⑤ Why don't you switch your phone to one like mine?
네 전화기를 내 전화기 같은 것으로 바꾸면 어때?

M : Josh and Lily are friends.
Josh와 Lily는 친구이다.
Josh notices that Lily looks tired at school these days.
Josh는 Lily가 요새 학교에서 피곤해 보인다는 것을 알아차린다.
Josh is worried about Lily and asks her if she's okay.
Josh는 Lily를 걱정하며 그녀에게 괜찮은지 물어본다.
Lily says she's using her phone too much.
Lily는 자신이 핸드폰을 너무 많이 사용하고 있다고 말한다.
She finds it hard to put her smartphone down late at night, watching videos and playing games.
그녀는 영상을 보고 게임을 하느라 밤늦게까지 스마트폰을 내려놓기가 어렵다고 생각한다.
Josh wants to offer her a solution to break her bad habit.
Josh는 그녀에게 나쁜 습관을 버릴 수 있는 해결책을 주고 싶어 한다.
That is, changing her phone to a feature phone.
그것은 전화기를 피처폰으로 바꾸는 것이다.
He's using one himself, and he's happy with it.
그는 직접 피처폰을 쓰고 있고, 그것에 만족해 한다.
It has limited functions, so he uses his phone only for phone calls and text messages.
그것은 기능이 제한되어 있어서, 그는 전화 통화나 문자 메시지를 위해서만 핸드폰을 쓴다.
Using a feature phone helps him avoid wasting time on his phone.
피처폰을 쓰는 것은 그가 전화기에 시간을 낭비하는 것을 피하는 데 도움이 된다.
Josh wants to recommend that Lily use the same kind of phone as his.
Josh는 Lily에게 자신과 같은 종류의 핸드폰을 쓰라고 권하고 싶어 한다.
In this situation, what would Josh most likely say to Lily?
이런 상황에서, Josh는 Lily에게 뭐라고 말할 것인가?
Josh : Why don't you switch your phone to one like mine?
네 전화기를 내 전화기 같은 것으로 바꾸면 어때?

Why? 왜 정답일까?

상황에 따르면 스마트폰을 너무 많이 사용하는 Lily에게 Josh는 자신과 마찬가지로 피처폰을 써보도록 권유하려고 한다(**Josh wants to recommend that Lily use the same kind of phone as his.**). 따라서 Josh가 Lily에게 할 말로 가장 적절한 것은 ⑤ '네 전화기를 내 전화기 같은 것으로 바꾸면 어때?'이다.

- **break a habit** 습관을 버리다
- **be allowed to** ~하도록 허용되다
- **limited** ⓐ 제한된
- **switch A to B** A를 B로 바꾸다

16-17 식물성 기름과 그 이점

W : Last class we learned about the origins of different cooking oils.
지난 시간에 우리는 다양한 식용유의 기원에 대해 배웠습니다.
「Today, I'd like to focus on vegetable oils and what good characteristics they have.」 16번의 근거
오늘은 식물성 기름, 그리고 그것들이 어떤 유익한 특성을 지니고 있는지에 집중해 보려고 합니다.
「First, coconut oil.」 17번 ①의 근거 일치
첫 번째로, 코코넛 오일입니다.
Fats from coconut oil easily convert to energy.
코코넛 오일 속 지방은 쉽게 에너지로 전환됩니다.
They help boost metabolism and aid in weight loss.
이것은 신진대사 증진과 체중 감량을 도와줍니다.
「Second, olive oil.」 17번 ②의 근거 일치
두 번째로, 올리브 오일입니다.
It contains natural vitamins and minerals and of course, it's a nutritious staple of the Mediterranean diet.
이것은 천연 비타민과 무기질을 함유하고 있으며, 당연하게도 지중해식 식단의 영양가 풍부한 주식입니다.
Next, sesame oil.
다음으로, 참기름입니다.
It's loaded with antioxidants that slow down cell aging.
이것은 세포 노화 속도를 늦춰주는 항산화 물질로 가득 차 있습니다.
It's also known to lower blood pressure and reduce wrinkles.
이것은 또한 혈압을 낮춰주고 주름을 줄여주는 것으로 알려져 있습니다.
「If you find these three oils rather expensive, there's a reasonable alternative, which is grapeseed oil.」 17번 ④의 근거 일치
만일 여러분들이 이 기름들은 다소 비싸다고 생각하고 있다면, 적당한 가격의 대체재가 있는데, 그것은 포도씨 기름입니다.
This is a great source of essential fatty acids and vitamin E.
이것은 필수 지방산과 비타민 E의 훌륭한 원천입니다.
Its high smoking point works well for any cooking method such as roasting and frying.
이것의 높은 발연점은 굽기와 튀기기 등 어느 요리법에든 적합합니다.
Before we move on, I'd like to mention one more oil.
넘어가기 전에, 한 가지 기름을 더 언급하려 합니다.
「Walnut oil contains omega-3 fatty acids and minerals like iron and zinc.」
호두 기름은 오메가3 지방산과 철분 및 아연 같은 무기질을 포함하고 있습니다. 17번 ⑤의 근거 일치
Its rich flavor can add a kick to your salad.
이것의 진한 풍미는 여러분의 샐러드에 짜릿함을 더해줍니다.
Now, let's look into each of these oils in detail.
이제, 각각의 기름들을 자세히 살펴보겠습니다.

- **convert** ⓥ 전환하다
- **nutritious** ⓐ 영양가 풍부한
- **antioxidant** ⓝ 항산화 물질
- **essential** ⓐ 필수적인
- **composition** ⓝ 구성 (요소)
- **metabolism** ⓝ 신진대사
- **staple** ⓝ 주식
- **be loaded with** ~로 가득 차다
- **add a kick to** ~에 짜릿함을 더하다
- **flavor enhancer** 화학 조미료

16 주제 파악

정답률 88% | 정답 ②

여자가 하는 말의 주제로 가장 적절한 것은?

① chemical compositions of fatty acids – 지방산의 화학적 구성
✔② benefits of various vegetable cooking oils – 다양한 식물성 식용유의 이점
③ tips for choosing fresh vegetable cooking oils – 신선한 식용유를 고르는 법에 관한 조언
④ roles of fatty acids in delaying the aging process – 노화 과정을 늦추는 데 있어 지방산의 역할
⑤ advantages of vegetable oils as a flavor enhancer – 화학 조미료로서의 식물성 기름의 이점

Why? 왜 정답일까?

'**Today, I'd like to focus on vegetable oils and what good characteristics they have.**'에서 여자는 식물성 기름과 그 유익한 특성에 주목해 보겠다고 하므로, 여자가 하는 말의 주제로 가장 적절한 것은 ② '다양한 식물성 식용유의 이점'이다.

17 언급 유무 파악

정답률 96% | 정답 ③

언급된 기름이 아닌 것은?

① coconut oil – 코코넛 오일　② olive oil – 올리브 오일
✔ avocado oil – 아보카도 오일　④ grapeseed oil – 포도씨 기름
⑤ walnut oil – 호두 기름

Why? 왜 정답일까?

담화에서 여자는 유익한 성분을 지닌 식물성 기름의 예로 코코넛 오일, 올리브 오일, 참기름, 포도씨 기름, 호두 기름을 언급하였다. 따라서 언급되지 않은 것은 ③ '아보카도 오일'이다.

Why? 왜 오답일까?

① '**First, coconut oil.**'에서 '코코넛 오일'이 언급되었다.
② '**Second, olive oil.**'에서 '올리브 오일'이 언급되었다.
④ '**~ there's a reasonable alternative, which is grapeseed oil.**'에서 '포도씨 기름'이 언급되었다.
⑤ '**Walnut oil contains omega-3 fatty acids and minerals like iron and zinc.**'에서 '호두 기름'이 언급되었다.

Dictation 28

문제편 165쪽

01 pick up after your dog / transfer infectious particles / keep your dog on a leash
02 give our house a new look / with the work we've done / Let's get the professionals to do it
03 in pretty good shape / still get original parts / also needs a thorough cleaning
04 surfboards leaning on the back wall / for more skilled surfers / that big round basket / a legendary surfing champion
05 browsing books to get inspiration / introduces easy-to-cook vegan recipes / instead of fermented fish
06 We brought our own skates / not very confident on the ice / signing up for a private lesson
07 occupied with something important / lost track of time / The screen totally cracked
08 has tons of participants / will be awarded a trip / have a strong chance of winning
09 has been bringing ballooning fans together / be presenting / decorated with various national flags / will be streamed live
10 one of these five models / the more levels the better / not difficult to assemble
11 having trouble walking around / help you with your food tray
12 way past the expiration date / We'd better throw it away
13 find packing very time-consuming / get rid of some items / attract people to my booth / equipment nicely
14 a cozy place for reading / there is good lighting / free from distractions
15 break her bad habit / changing her phone to a feature phone / avoid wasting time on his phone
16-17 easily convert to energy / slow down cell aging / there's a reasonable alternative / add a kick to your salad

29회 | 2025학년도 대학수학능력시험　고3

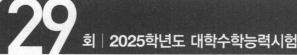

• 정답 •
01 ② 02 ⑤ 03 ① 04 ③ 05 ① 06 ④ 07 ③ 08 ④ 09 ⑤ 10 ② 11 ② 12 ① 13 ⑤ 14 ① 15 ② 16 ③ 17 ④

01 일정 변경 안내　정답률 94% | 정답 ②

다음을 듣고, 여자가 하는 말의 목적으로 가장 적절한 것을 고르시오.
① 학교 종소리 교체 계획을 알리려고
✔ 학교 수업 시간 단축을 공지하려고
③ 등교 시간 변경을 안내하려고
④ 학부모 상담 신청서 제출을 독려하려고
⑤ 학교 행사 후 교실 정리 정돈을 당부하려고

W : Good morning, students.
좋은 아침입니다, 학생들.
This is your vice principal, Ms. Morris.
전 교감인 Ms. Morris입니다.
I want to inform you that each class period will be reduced from 50 minutes to 40 minutes next Tuesday.
다음주 화요일에 수업 시간이 50분에서 40분으로 줄어든다고 알려드리고 싶습니다.
Due to the parent-teacher conferences that will beheld on that day, school will end one hour earlier than usual.
화요일에 개최될 학부모–교사 회의로 인해, 학교는 평소보다 1시간 일찍 끝날 예정입니다.
You'll still take the same classes that you normally would on that day.
화요일에 같은 수업을 들을 것입니다.
The starting and ending bells will ring according to the reduced class time schedule.
시작종과 끝나는 종이 줄어든 수업 시간에 따라 울릴 것입니다.
Once again, please keep in mind that next Tuesday's class periods will be shortened by 10 minutes each.
다시 한번, 다음 주 화요일 수업이 10분씩 단축될 예정이라는 점을 기억해 주세요.
Thank you.
감사합니다.

Why? 왜 정답일까?

교감 선생님인 여자는 학생들에게 다음 주 화요일 학교 수업 시간이 단축된다는 것(**Due to the parent-teacher conferences that will beheld on that day, school will end one hour earlier than usual.**)을 알리고 있으므로, 여자가 하는 말의 목적으로 가장 적절한 것은 ② '학교 수업 시간 단축을 공지하려고'이다.

- inform ⓥ 알리다
- conference ⓝ 협의회, 회의
- ring ⓥ 울리다
- reduce ⓥ 줄이다
- normally ad 평소에
- shorten ⓥ 단축하다

02 드라마 캠프 설득하기　정답률 91% | 정답 ⑤

대화를 듣고, 남자의 의견으로 가장 적절한 것을 고르시오.
① 드라마 캠프는 효율적인 여가 시간 활용 수단이다.
② 좋은 연기를 하려면 다른 사람과의 협력이 중요하다.
③ 드라마에는 독특한 개성을 가진 등장인물이 필요하다.
④ 원만한 교우 관계를 위해 친구의 말에 귀 기울여야 한다.
✔ 드라마 캠프 참여는 다양한 시각을 갖는 데 도움이 된다.

M : Honey, I was thinking about asking our daughter to sign up for drama camp this winter. What do you think?
여보, 우리 딸이 이번 겨울에 드라마 캠프에 신청하는 거 어떤지 생각해봤어요. 어때요?
W : Hmm. Why do you want her to participate in drama camp?
흠, 왜 딸이 드라마 캠프에 참가했으면 하나요?
M : I think drama camp is helpful for gaining diverse perspectives.
드라마 캠프가 다양한 시각을 얻는 데에 도움이 될 것 같아요.
W : How will the camp help her with that?
캠프가 어떻게 도움이 돼요?
M : In the camp, she'll play different types of characters. This can help her see things from others' perspectives.
캠프에서, 딸은 다른 종류의 역할을 맡을 거예요. 이렇게 하면 다른 사람의 시각으로 볼 수 있게 도울 거예요.
W : That makes sense.
말이 되네요.
M : Also, she'll be expected to listen to other kids while collaborating with them.
또한, 딸은 다른 아이들과 협동하며 그들의 말을 들을 거예요.
W : Oh, that could help her broaden her views.
아, 그러면 그것이 그녀의 시각을 넓히는 데 도움이 되겠어요.
M : Right. So, participating in drama camp is helpful for obtaining various perspectives.
맞아요. 그래서 드라마 캠프에 참여하는 것이 다양한 시각을 얻는 데 도움이 돼요.
W : Okay. Then let's suggest it to her.
좋아요. 그러면 그녀에게 제안해 봐요.

Why? 왜 정답일까?

남자는 여자에게 딸이 드라마 캠프에 등록하면 여러 등장인물을 연기하고 다른 사람의 말에 귀 기울이면서 다양한 시각을 얻는 데 도움이 될 것(**This can help her see things from others' perspectives. / she'll be expected to listen to other kids while collaborating with them. / So, participating in drama camp is helpful for obtaining various perspectives.**)이라고 말하고 있다. 따라서 남자의 의견으로 가장 적절한 것은 ⑤ '드라마 캠프 참여는 다양한 시각을 갖는 데 도움이 된다.'이다.

[문제편 p.169]

- sign up ~에 등록하다
- perspective ⓝ 시각
- collaborate ⓥ 협력하다
- diverse ⓐ 다양한
- character ⓝ 등장인물
- broaden ⓥ 넓히다

03 예술 작품 잘 이해하기
정답률 92% | 정답 ①

다음을 듣고, 여자가 하는 말의 요지로 가장 적절한 것을 고르시오.

✔ 예술가에 관해 알면 작품을 더 잘 이해할 수 있다.
② 지역 사회는 예술가에 대한 지원을 확대해야 한다.
③ 예술 작품을 전시할 때 조명 효과를 고려해야 한다.
④ 정기적인 미술관 방문은 작품 감상 능력을 높여 준다.
⑤ 예술 작품은 보는 사람에 따라 다양한 해석이 가능하다.

W : Hello, viewers!
시청자 여러분, 안녕하세요.
I'm Kate and welcome back to my channel, Art Pier 25.
저는 Kate이고 제 채널 Art Pier 25에 다시 오신 것을 환영합니다.
Have you ever felt like you couldn't understand the artwork in a museum?
여러분은 미술관에서 작품을 이해하기 어렵다고 느낀 적이 있으신가요?
If so, here's a simple tip for understanding artists' work better.
만약 그렇다면, 예술가들의 작품을 더 잘 이해하기 위한 간단한 팁을 알려 드리겠습니다.
Knowing about the artists can deepen your appreciation of their work.
예술가에 대해 알면 여러분이 그들의 작품을 더 깊이 이해할 수 있습니다.
Art is often a reflection of their feelings and thoughts.
예술은 흔히 그들의 감정과 생각을 반영한 것입니다.
Therefore, by exploring their lives and experiences, you can see what influenced their work.
따라서 그들의 삶과 경험을 탐구함으로써 여러분은 그들의 작품에 영향을 준 것이 무엇인지 알 수 있습니다.
So, the next time you go to an art museum, why not explore the artists' backgrounds first?
그러니 다음에 미술관에 가실 때는 먼저 예술가들의 배경을 탐구해보는 게 어떨까요?
Once you know about the artists, you'll be able to have a better understanding of their work. I hope this helps.
예술가들에 대해 알게 되면, 여러분은 그들의 작품을 더 잘 이해할 수 있을 것입니다. 도움이 되셨기를 바랍니다.

Why? 왜 정답일까?

여자는 미술관에서 작품을 이해할 때 예술가의 배경을 아는 것이 작품 이해에 도움이 된다(**Knowing about the artists can deepen your appreciation of their work. / Therefore, by exploring their lives and experiences, you can see what influenced their work.**)고 말하고 있다. 따라서 여자가 하는 말의 요지로 가장 적절한 것은 ① '예술가에 관해 알면 작품을 더 잘 이해할 수 있다.'이다.

- deepen ⓥ 깊게 하다
- reflection ⓝ 반영한 것
- explore ⓥ 탐구하다
- appreciation ⓝ 이해
- influence ⓥ 영향을 주다
- background ⓝ 배경

04 벼룩시장 사진 비교하기
정답률 98% | 정답 ③

대화를 듣고, 그림에서 대화의 내용과 일치하지 않는 것을 고르시오.

M : Hi, Sarah. What are you doing?
Sarah, 안녕. 뭐 하고 있어?
W : I'm looking at a picture that I took last weekend. Do you want to take a look?
지난 주말에 찍은 사진을 보고 있어. 한번 볼래?
M : Sure. 『I see a flea market sign hanging from the tree.』 ①의 근거 일치
응. 나무에 매달린 벼룩시장 표지판이 보이네.
W : I was selling some of my old stuff at the flea market.
내가 벼룩시장에서 내 오래된 물건 몇 개를 팔고 있었어.
M : 『Oh, I like the crown-shaped balloon the girl is holding.』 ②의 근거 일치
오, 여자아이가 잡고 있는 왕관 모양의 풍선이 마음에 들어.
W : She's my daughter. 『Hey, do you remember that stripe-patterned tent?』 ③의 근거 불일치
내 딸이야. 야, 저 줄무늬 텐트 기억해?
M : Of course. That's the one I gave you. 『Oh, there are three vases on the table.』 ④의 근거 일치
물론이지. 내가 네게 준 거잖아. 오, 테이블 위에 꽃병이 세 개 있네.
W : Unfortunately, I wasn't able to sell them.
안타깝게도, 그것들을 팔지 못했어.
M : I guess people weren't interested in them.
사람들이 그것들에 관심이 없었나 보구나.
W : Yeah. 『People were more interested in the speaker on the chair even though it wasn't for sale.』 ⑤의 근거 일치 I turned on music to attract customers.
응. 판매하려던 것이 아니었는데도 사람들은 의자 위에 있는 스피커에 더 관심이 많았어. 손님을 끌기 위해 음악을 틀어놓았어.
M : I see. Looks like you had a busy weekend.
그렇군. 네가 바쁜 주말을 보낸 것 같네.

Why? 왜 정답일까?

대화에서는 텐트가 줄무늬(**Hey, do you remember that stripe-patterned tent?**)라고 언급되었는데 그림에서는 텐트가 꽃무늬이므로, 그림에서 대화의 내용과 일치하지 않는 것은 ③이다.

- flea market ⓝ 벼룩시장
- hang ⓥ 매달다
- crown-shaped ⓐ 왕관 모양의
- attract ⓥ 끌다
- stripe-patterned ⓐ 줄무늬의

05 대회 준비
정답률 91% | 정답 ①

대화를 듣고, 남자가 할 일로 가장 적절한 것을 고르시오.

✔ 트로피 가져오기
② 사진 출력하기
③ 이메일 확인하기
④ 스티커 주문하기
⑤ 게시판 사용 허락받기

W : Hey, Brian. The Playful Cat Photo Contest is only two days away.
야, Brian. '장난기 많은 고양이 사진 대회'가 이제 이틀밖에 남지 않았어.
M : That's right, Lisa. Many students are excited about our club's contest.
맞아, Lisa. 많은 학생이 우리 동아리의 대회에 대해 신이 나 있어.
W : Yeah. Let's check the preparations we've done so far.
그래. 우리가 지금까지 준비해 놓은 것들을 확인해 보자.
M : Alright. I checked our email and confirmed that all the participants had submitted their photos.
좋아. 나는 우리 이메일을 확인했고 모든 참가자가 자신의 사진을 제출한 것을 확인했어.
W : Great. I'll print them out tomorrow.
정말 잘했어. 내가 내일 그것들을 출력할게.
M : Okay. What about the bulletin board in the school lobby? We'll need it to post the photos on.
알았어. 학교 로비에 있는 게시판은 어떡하지? 우리는 사진들을 게시하기 위해 그것이 필요할 거야.
W : Don't worry. I already got permission to use it. Have you ordered stickers yet?
걱정하지 마. 내가 그것을 써도 된다는 허락을 이미 받았어. 스티커는 주문했니?
M : Yes, I ordered enough for everyone to use when voting for their favorite photos.
응, 모두가 각자 마음에 드는 사진에 투표할 때 쓰기에 충분히 주문했어.
W : Good. What about the trophy for the winner?
잘했어. 우승자를 위한 트로피는 어떻게 됐어?
M : It's at my house. I'll bring it tomorrow.
그건 우리 집에 있어. 내가 내일 그것을 가져올게.
W : Thanks, I think we're all set.
고마워. 우리는 모든 준비가 된 것 같아.

Why? 왜 정답일까?

두 사람은 사진 대회를 위해 준비한 것들을 확인하고 있는데, 여자가 우승자를 위한 트로피는 어떻게 됐는지(**What about the trophy for the winner?**) 묻자, 남자가 그것이 자신의 집에 있으며 내일 그것을 가져오겠다(**It's at my house. I'll bring it tomorrow.**)고 말했으므로, 남자가 할 일로 가장 적절한 것은 ① '트로피 가져오기'이다.

- preparation ⓝ 준비 사항, 준비
- submit ⓥ 제출하다
- permission ⓝ 허락, 허가
- participant ⓝ 참가자
- bulletin board ⓝ 게시판
- vote ⓥ 투표하다

06 민속 마을 입장하기
정답률 90% | 정답 ④

대화를 듣고, 여자가 지불할 금액을 고르시오.

① $100 ② $150 ③ $180 ✔ $200 ⑤ $220

M : Welcome to Camoo Traditional Village. How can I help you?
Camoo Traditional Village에 오신 것을 환영합니다. 무엇을 도와드릴까요?
W : Hi. I'd like to buy admission tickets for my family. Is there a discount for senior citizens?
안녕하세요. 제 가족을 위한 입장권을 사고 싶어요. 고령자를 위한 할인이 있나요?
M : Yes. Regular tickets are $30 each, and senior tickets are $20 each for people over 65 years old.
네. 일반 입장권은 각 30달러이고, 65세가 넘는 분들께는 고령자 입장권이 각 20달러입니다.
W : Good. My parents are in their 70s. So I'll take two regular tickets and two senior tickets.
좋네요. 제 부모님은 70대세요. 그래서 일반 입장권 두 장과 고령자 입장권 두 장을 살게요.
M : Great. Would you also like lunch tickets? We serve traditional local food. It's $25 per person.
좋습니다. 점심 식사권도 함께 구매하시겠어요? 저희는 전통 현지 음식을 제공합니다. 한 사람당 25달러입니다.
W : I'd love that. Is the lunch ticket cheaper for senior citizens?
그러고 싶어요. 점심 식사권은 고령자에게 더 저렴한가요?
M : No. I'm sorry. It's the same price.
아니요. 죄송합니다. 같은 가격입니다.
W : Ah, okay. I'll buy four lunch tickets as well.
아, 알겠어요. 점심 식사권도 네 장 살게요.
M : Alright. So you want two regular tickets and two senior tickets with four lunch tickets, right?
알겠습니다. 그러면 일반 입장권 두 장, 고령자 입장권 두 장과 점심 식사권 네 장이 필요하시군요, 그렇죠?
W : That's right. Here's my credit card.
맞아요. 여기 제 신용카드예요.

Why? 왜 정답일까?

여자는 한 장에 30달러인 일반 입장권 두 장과 한 장에 20달러인 고령자 입장권 두 장, 그리고 한 장에 25달러인 점심 식사권 네 장을 샀으므로, 여자가 지불할 금액은 ④ '200달러'이다.

- admission ticket ⓝ 입장권
- local ⓐ 현지의
- credit ⓐ 신용의
- senior citizen ⓝ 고령자, 어르신
- cheap ⓐ 싸다

07 학생 워크숍 포스터
정답률 98% | 정답 ③

대화를 듣고, 남자가 Streamline Broadcasting Workshop에 갈 수 없는 이유를 고르시오.

① 동아리 공연에 참여해야 해서
② 교내 방송 준비를 해야 해서
✔ 야구 경기를 보러 가야 해서
④ 생일 파티에 참석해야 해서
⑤ 선물을 사러 가야 해서

[문제편 p.169]

W : Hey, John. Come and look at this poster.
이봐, John. 와서 이 포스터 좀 봐.
M : Hi, Sharon. The Streamline Broadcasting Workshop? What's that?
안녕, Sharon. Streamline Broadcasting Workshop? 그게 뭐야?
W : It's a student workshop that offers an opportunity to connect with experts in broadcasting. How about going together?
방송 전문가들과 관계를 맺을 기회를 제공하는 학생 워크숍이야. 같이 가는 거 어때?
M : Oh, it's on Friday. I wish I could, but I can't.
아, 금요일에 하는구나. 갈 수 있다면 좋겠지만, 난 못 가.
W : Why not? Is your dance club's performance on that day?
왜 못 가니? 너희 춤 동아리 공연이 그날이야?
M : No, the performance is next month.
아니, 공연은 다음 달이야.
W : Then, is your little brother's birthday party on Friday?
그럼, 네 남동생 생일 파티가 금요일에 있니?
M : No, it was last week. I got him a hat as a present.
아니, 그건 지난주였어. 내가 선물로 모자를 사줬어.
W : So why can't you go to the workshop?
그러면 왜 워크숍에 못 가는 건데?
M : Actually, I'm going to see a baseball game on that day. I have tickets for that game.
실은 그날 야구 경기를 보러 갈 거야. 그 경기 표가 있어.
W : Oh, I see. I hope your team wins.
아, 그렇구나. 너희 팀이 이기길 바랄게.

Why? 왜 정답일까?

남자는 금요일에 야구 경기를 보러 가야 해서 Streamline Broadcasting Workshop에 갈 수 없다(I'm going to see a baseball game on that day.)고 말한다. 따라서 남자가 Streamline Broadcasting Workshop에 갈 수 없는 이유는 ③ '야구 경기를 보러 가야 해서'이다.

- expert ⓝ 전문가
- broadcasting ⓝ 방송
- performance ⓝ 공연
- ticket ⓝ 표
- hope ⓥ 희망하다

08 문어 알리기 행사 정답률 98% | 정답 ④

대화를 듣고, Outstanding Octopuses 행사에 관해 언급되지 않은 것을 고르시오.

① 목적 ② 프로그램 ③ 후원 기관
✔ 입장료 ⑤ 기간

M : Honey, did you hear that the local aquarium is holding an event called Outstanding Octopuses?
여보, 지역 수족관에서 Outstanding Octopuses라는 행사를 개최하고 있는 것을 들었어요?
W : Outstanding Octopuses? What's it for?
Outstanding Octopuses라고요? 그건 무엇을 위한 것인가요?
M : The purpose of the event is 「to promote World Octopus Day.」 ①의 근거 일치
그 행사의 목적은 세계 문어의 날을 홍보하는 거예요.
W : Sounds interesting. What programs does the event have?
흥미롭군요. 그 행사에는 어떤 프로그램이 있나요?
M : There are several programs. They include 「exhibiting various octopuses from the Pacific Ocean and showing a documentary about how to protect them.」 ②의 근거 일치
여러 가지 프로그램이 있어요. 태평양의 다양한 문어를 전시하는 것과 그것을 보호하는 방법에 대한 다큐멘터리를 상영하는 것을 포함해서요.
W : Really? Let me search for more information on my phone. *[Pause]* 「Oh, it's sponsored by the Aqua Life Council.」 ③의 근거 일치
정말요? 내 전화기로 더 많은 정보를 검색해 볼게요. *[잠시 후]* 오, 그것은 Aqua Life Council의 후원을 받는군요.
M : I'm glad that they're helping people realize how remarkable these creatures are.
이 생명체가 얼마나 놀라운지를 사람들이 깨닫게 하는데 그들이 도움을 주고 있다니 기쁘네요.
W : I agree. 「The event started on October 4th and will end on December 8th.」 ⑤의 근거 일치
동감이에요. 그 행사는 10월 4일에 시작했고 12월 8일에 끝날 거예요.
M : Good. We still have a lot of time to visit.
좋아요. 우리에게는 아직 방문할 시간이 많아요.
W : You're right. Let's make plans to go soon.
맞아요. 조만간 가볼 계획을 세워 보아요.

Why? 왜 정답일까?

Outstanding Octopuses 행사에 관해 목적, 프로그램, 후원 기관, 기간은 언급되었지만, ④ '입장료'는 언급되지 않았다.

Why? 왜 오답일까?

① 'The purpose of the event is to promote World Octopus Day'에서 목적이 언급되었다.
② 'They include exhibiting various octopuses from the Pacific Ocean and showing a documentary about how to protect them.'에서 프로그램이 언급되었다.
③ 'Oh, it's sponsored by the Aqua Life Council.'에서 후원 기관이 언급되었다.
⑤ 'The event started on October 4th and will end on December 8th.'에서 기간이 언급되었다.

- aquarium ⓝ 수족관
- octopus ⓝ 문어
- sponsor ⓥ 후원하다
- realize ⓥ 깨닫다
- remarkable ⓐ 눈에 띄는

09 나비 서커스 안내 정답률 97% | 정답 ⑤

2024 Grand Butterfly Circus에 관한 다음 내용을 듣고, 일치 하지 않는 것을 고르시오.

① 5일 동안 진행될 것이다.
② 마술 쇼를 포함한다.
③ 2세 미만의 아이는 무료로 입장한다.
④ 할인 쿠폰을 웹사이트에서 다운로드할 수 있다.
✔ 지정석이 있다.

M : Hello, listeners. Are you looking for something fun to do with your family?
안녕하세요, 청취자 여러분. 가족과 함께 즐길 거리를 찾고 계시나요?
Well, we're pleased to announce that the 2024 Grand Butterfly Circus is coming to town.
자, 저는 2024 Grand Butterfly Circus가 시내에 온다는 것을 알려드리게 되어 기쁩니다.
「It'll run for five days from November 15th to 19th.」 ①의 근거 일치
그것은 11월 15일부터 19일까지 5일간 진행될 것입니다.
The circus starts at 8 p.m. each night at City Square.
서커스는 매일 밤 8시에 City 광장에서 시작됩니다.
「It includes a spectacular magic show, high-rope walking, and juggling.」 ②의 근거 일치
그것에는 화려한 마술쇼, 고공 줄타기, 저글링이 포함되어 있습니다.
「Admission tickets are $35 per person, and children under 2 years old are admitted for free.」 ③의 근거 일치
입장권은 1인당 35달러이며, 2세 미만 어린이는 무료로 입장합니다.
Tickets are available online as well as on site.
입장권은 현장에서뿐만 아니라 온라인에서도 구입 가능합니다.
「You can download a discount coupon on the circus website.」 ④의 근거 일치
서커스 웹사이트에서 할인 쿠폰을 다운로드 하실 수 있습니다.
「If you want the best seats, please come early because there are no assigned seats.」
가장 좋은 자리를 원하시면 지정석이 없으니 일찍 오세요. ⑤의 근거 불일치
Join us for a breathtaking night of excitement for you and your family!
여러분과 여러분의 가족을 위한 숨 막히는 짜릿한 밤을 저희와 함께 하세요!

Why? 왜 정답일까?

남자는 가장 좋은 자리를 원하면 지정석이 없으니 일찍 오라(If you want the best seats, please come early because there are no assigned seats.)고 했으므로, 담화의 내용과 일치하지 않는 것은 ⑤ '지정석이 있다.'이다.

Why? 왜 오답일까?

① 'It'll run for five days from November 15th to 19th.'의 내용과 일치한다.
② 'It includes a spectacular magic show, high-rope walking, and juggling.'의 내용과 일치한다.
③ 'Admission tickets are $35 per person, and children under 2 years old are admitted for free.'의 내용과 일치한다.
④ 'You can download a discount coupon on the circus website.'의 내용과 일치한다.

- spectacular ⓐ 화려한, 볼 만한
- juggling ⓝ 저글링, 곡예
- admission ⓝ 입장
- assigned ⓐ 지정된, 할당된
- breathtaking ⓐ 숨 막히는

10 식물 키우기 세트 고르기 정답률 91% | 정답 ②

다음 표를 보면서 대화를 듣고, 여자가 구입할 식물 씨앗 키트를 고르시오.

Plant Seed Kits

	Kit	Price	Plant Varieties	Pot Material	Plant Growing Guide
①	A	$40	3	Plastic	×
✔	B	$45	4	Wood	○
③	C	$45	5	Metal	×
④	D	$50	5	Ceramic	○
⑤	E	$60	6	Glass	○

W : Jason, what's that in your hand?
Jason, 손에 든 게 뭐니?
M : It's a flyer from the neighborhood flower shop, Mom.
동네 꽃집에서 온 전단이에요, 엄마.
W : Oh, they're selling plant seed kits! I want one. Can you help me choose?
오, 식물 씨앗 키트를 팔고 있구나! 나도 하나 사고 싶어. 고르는 거 도와줄래?
M : Sure. 「I don't think you need the most expensive kit since it's your first try.」
물론이에요. 처음 시도하시는 거니까 가장 비싼 키트는 필요하지 않을 것 같아요. 근거1 Price 조건
W : Right. But I'd like some variety. 「So, at least four kinds of plants would be nice.」
맞아. 하지만 좀 다양하면 좋겠어. 그러니 최소한 네 종류의 식물이 있으면 좋을 것 같아. 근거2 Plant Varieties 조건
M : Okay. What about the pots? They come in different materials.
좋아요. 화분은 어때요? 그것들은 다양한 소재로 나와요.
W : 「I don't want the ceramic one.」 It'll be too heavy for me. 근거3 Pot Material 조건
도자기 화분은 싫어. 그건 내게 너무 무거울 것 같아.
M : Good point. 「I think the one that comes with a plant growing guide would be helpful for you.」 근거4 Plant Growing Guide 조건
맞는 말씀이에요. 식물 재배 가이드가 함께 제공되는 것이 엄마에게 도움이 될 것 같아요.
W : Yes, I can easily find out how to grow plants.
그래, 식물 키우는 방법을 쉽게 찾을 수 있겠네.
M : Then this seed kit is perfect for you.
그럼 이 씨앗 키트가 엄마에게 딱 맞네요.
W : Thanks for helping me. I'll buy that one.
도와줘서 고마워. 그것을 살게.

Why? 왜 정답일까?

여자는 전단에 있는 것 중 가장 비싼 것을 제외하고, 식물의 종류가 적어도 네 종류 이상이면서, 도자기 화분이 아니면서, 식물 재배 가이드가 함께 제공되는 식물 씨앗 키트를 구입하기로 결정했다. 따라서 여자가 구입할 식물 씨앗 키트는 ②이다.

- flyer ⓝ 전단
- variety ⓝ 다양성
- ceramic ⓐ 도자기의
- easily ad 쉽게
- guide ⓥ 이끌다

11 테니스 코치 송별 파티 케이크 준비 정답률 89% | 정답 ②

대화를 듣고, 남자의 마지막 말에 대한 여자의 응답으로 가장 적절한 것을 고르시오. [3점]

① Great idea! Let's ask him to come to the party.
좋은 생각이야! 그에게 파티에 와달라고 부탁할게.
✔ That's okay. I'll check if I can change the order.
괜찮아. 주문을 변경할 수 있는지 확인할게
③ I can't believe it! We finally won a tennis match.
그것을 믿을 수가 없어! 우리가 드디어 테니스 시합에서 이겼어.

[문제편 p.169]

④ No thanks. I don't really like cakes with nuts on them.
고맙지만 괜찮아. 견과류가 들어간 케이크는 정말 좋아하지 않아.
⑤ No problem. I won't eat foods that cause allergic reactions.
괜찮아. 나는 알레르기 반응을 일으키는 음식은 먹지 않을 거야.

M : Jane, have you ordered a cake for our tennis coach's farewell party next week?
Jane, 다음 주에 있을 우리 테니스 코치 송별 파티를 위해 케이크를 주문했니?
W : Yes, I ordered a walnut cake with pistachio nuts on top. I'll pick it up next Wednesday afternoon from the bakery.
응, 피스타치오 견과류를 올린 호두 케이크를 주문했어. 다음 주 수요일 오후에 제과점에서 가져올 거야.
M : Oh, no. I should have told you that he's allergic to all kinds of nuts.
오, 안돼. 코치님이 모든 종류의 견과류에 알레르기가 있다고 네게 말했어야 했는데.
W : That's okay. I'll check if I can change the order.
괜찮아. 주문을 변경할 수 있는지 확인할게.

Why? 왜 정답일까?

여자가 다음 주에 있을 테니스 코치 송별 파티를 위해 견과류를 올린 호두 케이크를 주문했다고 하자 남자는 코치님이 모든 종류의 견과류에 알레르기가 있다(**I should have told you that he's allergic to all kinds of nuts.**)고 말했으므로, 이에 대한 여자의 응답으로 가장 적절한 것은 ② '**That's okay. I'll check if I can change the order.**'이다.

- **farewell party** ⓝ 송별 파티
- **walnut** ⓝ 호두
- **pistachio** ⓝ 피스타치오
- **order** ⓥ 주문하다
- **allergic** ⓐ 알레르기가 있는

12 요가 수업 듣기

정답률 73% | 정답 ①

대화를 듣고, 여자의 마지막 말에 대한 남자의 응답으로 가장 적절한 것을 고르시오.

✔ In that case, let's give it a try. – 그렇다면, 한번 해보도록 해요.
② I don't know. It's a bit expensive. – 모르겠어요. 좀 비싸네요.
③ That's the best class we've ever taken. – 그것은 우리가 지금까지 들어본 수업 중 최고였어요.
④ I'd be happy to teach yoga to beginners. – 초보자에게 기꺼이 요가를 가르칠게요.
⑤ You're right. The hotel's view is amazing. – 맞아요. 호텔 경치가 정말 멋져요.

W : Honey, the hotel offers a free yoga class on the beach to the guests. Do you want to go with me tomorrow morning?
여보, 호텔에서 투숙객에게 해변에서 하는 무료 요가 수업을 제공한대요. 내일 아침에 나랑 같이 갈래요?
M : Oh, really? I definitely want to try yoga, but I'm afraid we might be the only beginners.
아, 정말요? 요가를 꼭 해보고 싶은데 우리만 초보자일까 봐 걱정돼요.
W : Don't worry. This class is for true beginners who have never done yoga before. So why don't we take it?
걱정하지 말아요. 이 수업은 요가를 한 번도 해본 적이 없는 진정한 초보자를 위한 수업이에요. 그럼 함께 해 보는 게 어때요?
M : In that case, let's give it a try.
그렇다면, 한번 해 보도록 해요.

Why? 왜 정답일까?

호텔에서 투숙객에게 제공하는 무료 요가 수업에 대해 남자는 자신들만 초보자일까 봐 걱정(**I definitely want to try yoga, but I'm afraid we might be the only beginners.**)이라고 하자 여자는 이 수업은 진정한 초보자를 위한 수업이니 함께 해 보자(**This class is for true beginners who have never done yoga before. So why don't we take it?**)고 한다. 따라서 이에 대한 남자의 응답으로 가장 적절한 것은 ① '**In that case, let's give it a try.**'이다.

- **definitely** ad 꼭, 반드시
- **tomorrow** ⓝ 내일
- **morning** ⓝ 아침
- **free** ⓐ 공짜의
- **offer** ⓥ 제공하다

13 시 교통국 자전거 경매

정답률 70% | 정답 ⑤

대화를 듣고, 남자의 마지막 말에 대한 여자의 응답으로 가장 적절한 것을 고르시오.

Woman: ____________________

① Too bad. I hope you can find your lost bike.
안됐네. 네가 잃어버린 자전거를 찾길 바라.
② Good job. You'll get used to riding a bike soon.
잘했어. 곧 자전거 타는 데 익숙해질 거야.
③ Awesome! Thank you for lending me your new bike.
멋지다! 네 새 자전거를 내게 빌려줘서 고마워.
④ I'm sorry. I'm afraid our auction has already finished.
미안해. 우리 경매가 이미 끝난 것 같아.
✔ Excellent! I'm sure your donation will be appreciated.
훌륭하네! 네 기부에 대해 고마워할 거라고 확신해.

[Cell phone rings.]
[휴대 전화가 울린다.]
M : Hi, Rachel. What's up?
안녕, Rachel. 무슨 일이야?
W : Hi, Kevin. Do you have any plans for next weekend?
안녕, Kevin. 다음 주말에 계획 있어?
M : No, I'm free. Why do you ask?
아니, 시간은 비어. 왜 물어보니?
W : The City Transportation Office is hosting a bike auction at their parking lot. Do you want to check it out together?
시 교통국에서 그들의 주차장에서 자전거 경매를 연대. 함께 살펴보러 가볼래?
M : Sounds like fun. Are they selling new bicycles?
재밌겠네. 새 자전거를 파는 거야?
W : No, they're selling used bikes. People have donated them for a good cause.
아니, 중고 자전거를 팔아. 사람들이 좋은 목적에 쓰라고 기증한 거래.
M : What's the cause?
무슨 목적에 쓰이는데?
W : I heard all the money they raise will be used to support youth sports clubs.
내가 듣기로는 모금된 모든 돈이 청소년 스포츠 클럽을 지원하는 데 쓰인대.
M : Oh, really? Then, I'd like to contribute to the auction. Actually, I have a bike that I don't ride anymore.
오, 정말? 그럼 나도 경매에 기증하고 싶어. 사실, 내가 더 이상 타지 않는 자전거가 있거든.
W : That's great. Just make sure it's in a good enough condition to be sold.
잘됐네. 판매될 수 있을 만큼 상태가 충분히 좋은지만 확인해 줘.
M : Not to worry. It's only been used two or three times.
걱정하지 마. 두세 번밖에 안 탔어.
W : Excellent! I'm sure your donation will be appreciated.
훌륭하네! 네 기부에 대해 고마워할 거라고 확신해.

Why? 왜 정답일까?

시 교통국에서 여는 자전거 경매를 함께 가고자 제안하기 위해 전화를 건 여자는 남자가 자신도 경매에 내놓을 자전거가 있다고 말하자, 자전거의 상태가 좋은지 확인하라(**Just make sure it's in a good enough condition to be sold.**)고 말했고, 이에 남자는 자전거를 두세 번밖에 안 탔다(**It's only been used two or three times.**)고 말했으므로, 이에 대한 여자의 응답으로 가장 적절한 것은 ⑤ '**Excellent! I'm sure your donation will be appreciated.**'이다.

- **transportation** ⓝ 교통
- **auction** ⓝ 경매
- **donate** ⓥ 기증하다
- **cause** ⓝ 목적, 대의
- **contribute** ⓥ 기증하다

14 심사위원 참여 부탁하기

정답률 70% | 정답 ①

대화를 듣고, 여자의 마지막 말에 대한 남자의 응답으로 가장 적절한 것을 고르시오. [3점]

Man: ____________________

✔ Sure. I hope you'll be able to judge the competition.
네. 박사님이 대회에서 심사할 수 있기를 바랍니다.
② Well done. You've advanced to the final round.
잘했어요. 결승 라운드에 진출하셨습니다.
③ Great. Text me the dates of the competition.
좋아요. 대회 날짜를 문자로 보내 주세요.
④ Don't worry. We'll announce the winners shortly.
걱정하지 마세요. 저희는 곧 우승자를 발표할 겁니다.
⑤ I understand. It's hard to be fair when judging others.
이해합니다. 다른 사람들을 심사할 때 공정하기가 어렵죠.

[Telephone rings.]
[전화벨이 울린다.]
W : Hello, Dr. Wilson speaking.
여보세요, Wilson 박사입니다.
M : Hello, this is Glenn Scott from the organizing committee of the National Science Talent Competition.
안녕하세요, National Science Talent Competition 조직 위원회의 Glenn Scott입니다.
W : Hi, Mr. Scott. How can I help you?
안녕하세요, Scott 씨. 무엇을 도와드릴까요?
M : I'm calling to see if you would be a judge for this year's competition.
올해 대회의 심사위원이 되어 주실 수 있는지 여쭤 보려고 전화 드렸습니다.
W : Thanks. I'd be happy to take part in it again. When is the competition?
감사합니다. 이번에도 기꺼이 참여하고 싶네요. 대회가 언제 열리나요?
M : It starts on December 9th and continues for three days.
12월 9일에 시작하여 3일간 계속됩니다.
W : Oh, no. I have a meeting to attend on December 9th.
어쩌죠, 저는 12월 9일에 참석할 회의가 있어요.
M : Is there any chance that you can change the date of your meeting? I really want to have you as a judge.
혹시 회의 날짜를 변경할 수 있는 가능성이 있을까요? 꼭 심사위원으로 모시고 싶습니다.
W : I'm afraid I can't answer that right now.
지금 당장은 답변 드리지 못할 것 같네요.
M : When can you let me know? I can wait a couple of days.
언제쯤 알려주실 수 있나요? 며칠은 기다릴 수 있습니다.
W : I'll let you know by the end of the day.
오늘 중으로 알려드리겠습니다.
M : Sure. I hope you'll be able to judge the competition.
네. 박사님이 대회에서 심사할 수 있기를 바랍니다.

Why? 왜 정답일까?

National Science Talent Competition의 심사를 맡아줄 것을 제안한 남자에게 여자가 이미 그때 다른 일정이 있다고 하자, 남자는 일정을 바꿀 수 있는지 물었고, 여자는 오늘 중으로 알려주겠다(**I'll let you know by the end of the day.**)고 말했으므로, 이에 대한 남자의 응답으로 가장 적절한 것은 ① '네. 박사님이 대회에서 심사할 수 있기를 바랍니다.'이다.

- **organizing committee** ⓝ 조직 위원회
- **competition** ⓝ 대회
- **judge** ⓝ 심사위원
- **afraid** ⓥ 두려워하다
- **meeting** ⓝ 회의

15 콘서트 갈 시간 정하기

정답률 45% | 정답 ②

다음 상황 설명을 듣고, Sophia가 Jack에게 할 말로 가장 적절한 것을 고르시오. [3점]

Sophia: ____________________

① I think it'll be better to stick to your plan.
내 생각엔 네 계획을 고수하는 게 더 나을 것 같아.
✔ Let's head out for the concert far in advance.
훨씬 더 일찍 콘서트에 가자.
③ We can ask for a seat change so we can sit together.
우리가 같이 앉을 수 있도록 좌석을 바꿔 달라고 요청할 수 있어.
④ Don't you think we need to rehearse one more time?
우리가 한 번 더 예행연습을 할 필요가 있다고 생각하진 않아?
⑤ How about leaving the concert early to avoid traffic?
교통 체증을 피하기 위해 일찍 콘서트를 떠나는 건 어때?

M : Sophia and Jack are sister and brother.
Sophia와 Jack은 남매입니다.
They're going to their favorite singer's concert tonight.
그들은 오늘 밤 자신들이 가장 좋아하는 가수의 콘서트에 갈 예정입니다.
The concert starts at 7 p.m., and since it takes an hour to get to the concert, Jack proposes that they leave their house at 6 p.m.
그 콘서트는 오후 7시에 시작하며, 콘서트까지 가는 데 한 시간이 걸리기 때문에 Jack은 오후 6시에 집을 나서자고 제안합니다.
While this is Jack's first time going to a concert, Sophia has been to several concerts.
Jack은 이번이 콘서트에 처음 가는 것이지만, Sophia는 여러 콘서트에 가본 적이 있습니다.
She knows that even after they arrive at the concert site, it takes a long time to go through the security line and get to their seats.

29회

그녀는 콘서트장에 도착한 후에도 보안 대기 줄을 통과하고 자신의 자리에 앉는 데 오랜 시간이 걸린다는 것을 알고 있습니다.
Also, she wants to take pictures and stop by the gift shops before the concert.
또한 그녀는 콘서트 전에 사진을 찍고 기념품 가게에 들르고 싶어 합니다.
So, Sophia wants to suggest to Jack that they should leave for the concert much earlier than he proposed.
그래서 Sophia는 Jack이 제안한 것보다 훨씬 더 일찍 콘서트에 가야 한다고 제안하고 싶어 합니다.
In this situation, what would Sophia most likely say to Jack?
이런 상황에서, Sophia는 Jack에게 뭐라고 말하겠습니까?
Sophia : Let's head out for the concert far in advance.
훨씬 더 일찍 콘서트에 가자.

Why? 왜 정답일까?

Sophia는 여러 콘서트에 가본 경험을 바탕으로 콘서트장에 도착한 후에도 오랜 시간이 걸린다(**it takes a long time to go through the security line and get to their seats.**)는 것을 알고, 콘서트 전에 사진을 찍고 기념품 가게에 들르고 싶어(**she wants to take pictures and stop by the gift shops before the concert.**)서 Jack이 제안한 것보다 훨씬 더 일찍 콘서트에 가자고 제안하고 싶어 하는 상황(**Sophia wants to suggest to Jack that they should leave for the concert much earlier than he proposed.**)이다. 이런 상황에서 Sophia가 Jack에게 할 말로 가장 적절한 것은 ② '훨씬 더 일찍 콘서트에 가자.'이다.

- **propose** ⓥ 제안하다
- **gift shop** ⓝ 기념품 가게
- **security** ⓝ 보안
- **stop by** ~에 들르다
- **arrive** ⓥ 도착하다

16-17 식량 부족 상황의 식량

W : Hello, students. As you know, we may be facing serious food shortages down the road.
안녕하세요, 학생 여러분. 여러분도 아시다시피, 우리는 장래에 심각한 식량 부족에 직면할 수도 있습니다.
「So, today let's talk about foods that are appropriate for dealing with food shortages in the future.」 16번의 근거
그래서 오늘은 미래에 식량 부족을 해결하기에 적합한 음식에 관해 이야기해 봅시다.
「First, seaweed is cost-efficient because it doesn't take up land or need to be watered.」
첫째, 해조류는 땅을 차지하지 않거나 물을 줄 필요가 없기 때문에 비용 효율적입니다. 17번 ①의 근거 일치
It not only contains lots of minerals and vitamins but also can be used to make diverse types of dishes.
그것은 많은 미네랄과 비타민을 포함할 뿐만 아니라 다양한 종류의 요리를 만드는 데 사용될 수도 있습니다.
「Second, beans are adapted to growing in a wide range of environments from ocean shores to mountain slopes.」 17번 ②의 근거 일치
둘째, 콩은 해안가부터 산비탈까지 다양한 환경에서 자라는 데 적응되어 있습니다.
Plus, they offer us a rich source of fiber and protein.
게다가 섬유질과 단백질의 풍부한 공급원을 제공합니다.
「Third, pumpkins grow large and their leaves and flowers can be consumed as well.」
셋째, 호박은 크게 자라고 그 잎과 꽃도 섭취할 수 있습니다. 17번 ③의 근거 일치
These precious parts are often thrown away, but they are a good source of nutrients and flavor.
이러한 소중한 부분이 버려지는 경우가 많지만, 그것은영양소와 맛의 좋은 원천입니다.
「Finally, mushrooms grow all year round and where many other foods would not.」
마지막으로, 버섯은 일 년 내내 자라고 다른 많은 식량이 자랄 수 없을 곳에서 자랍니다. 17번 ⑤의 근거 일치
They are very affordable and rich in various nutrients.
그것은 (가격이) 매우 적정하고 다양한 영양소가 풍부합니다.
Now let's watch a video demonstrating the value of these foods.
이제 이러한 음식의 가치를 보여 주는 영상을 봅시다.

- **seaweed** 해초
- **pumpkins** 호박
- **potatoes** 감자
- **food shortage** ⓝ 식량 부족
- **appropriate** ⓐ 적합한
- **water** ⓥ 물을 주다
- **fiber** ⓝ 섬유질
- **nutrient** ⓝ 영양소
- **rich** ⓐ 풍부한
- **beans** 콩
- **mushrooms** 버섯
- **face** ⓥ 직면하다
- **down the road** 장래에
- **cost-efficient** ⓐ 비용 효율적인
- **slope** ⓝ (산)비탈
- **precious** ⓐ 소중한, 가치가 있는
- **affordable** ⓐ (가격이) 적정한
- **demonstrate** ⓥ 보여 주다

16 주제 파악

정답률 90% | 정답 ③

여자가 하는 말의 주제로 가장 적절한 것은?

① desirable conditions to store food – 음식을 저장하기 위한 바람직한 조건
② importance of having a nutritious diet – 영양가 있는 식단을 갖는 것의 중요성
③ suitable foods to solve future food shortages – 미래의 식량 부족을 해결할 적합한 음식
④ popular dishes made from unusual ingredients – 흔하지 않은 재료로 만든 인기 있는 요리
⑤ future technologies to cope with food shortages – 식량 부족에 대처하기 위한 미래의 기술

Why? 왜 정답일까?

여자는 미래에 심각한 식량 부족을 해결하기에 적합한 네 가지 음식을 소개(**As you know, we may be facing serious food shortages down the road. So, today let's talk about foods that are appropriate for dealing with food shortages in the future.**)하고 있다. 따라서 여자가 하는 말의 주제로 가장 적절한 것은 ③ '미래의 식량 부족을 해결할 적합한 음식'이다.

17 언급 유무 파악

정답률 98% | 정답 ④

언급된 음식이 아닌 것은?

① seaweed – 해초
② beans – 콩
③ pumpkins – 호박
④ potatoes – 감자
⑤ mushrooms – 버섯

Why? 왜 정답일까?

seaweed, beans, pumpkins, mushrooms는 언급되었지만, ④ '**potatoes**'는 언급되지 않았다.

Dictation 29

문제편 171쪽

01 Due to the parent-teacher / reduced class time schedule / please keep in mind
02 participate in drama camp / things from others' perspectives / while collaborating with them
03 understand the artwork / Knowing about the artists / explore the artists' backgrounds
04 that stripe-patterned tent / were more interested in / turned on music to attract
05 participants had submitted / bulletin board in / permission to use it
06 buy admission tickets for / serve traditional local food / lunch ticket cheaper
07 opportunity to connect with / hat as a present / see a baseball game
08 local aquarium is holding / promote World Octopus Day / include exhibiting various octopuses
09 a spectacular magic show / Tickets are available online / breathtaking night of excitement
10 come in different materials / a plant growing guide / easily find out
11 have you ordered / pistachio nuts on top / allergic to all kinds
12 offers a free yoga / definitely want to try / true beginners who
13 hosting a bike auction / have donated them / be used to support
14 from the organizing committee / a meeting to attend / afraid I can't answer
15 been to several concerts / take pictures and stop by / they should leave for
16-17 appropriate for dealing with / environments from ocean shores / all year round

30회 | 2024학년도 대학수학능력시험 고3

• 정답 •

01 ⑤ 02 ① 03 ④ 04 ③ 05 ② 06 ③ 07 ④ 08 ③ 09 ④ 10 ② 11 ⑤ 12 ① 13 ⑤ 14 ① 15 ① 16 ② 17 ③

01 자선 축구 경기를 도와줄 봉사자 모집

정답률 95% | 정답 ⑤

다음을 듣고, 여자가 하는 말의 목적으로 가장 적절한 것을 고르시오.

① 축구 경기장 사용 수칙을 설명하려고
② 지역 아동 병원의 개원을 홍보하려고
③ 자선 축구 경기의 변경된 일정을 공지하려고
④ 축구 경기 티켓의 구매 사이트를 소개하려고
✔ 자선 축구 경기 자원봉사자 모집을 안내하려고

W : Hello, Timberglade High School students.
안녕하세요, Timberglade 고등학교 학생 여러분.
This is your P.E. teacher, Ms. Larsen.
저는 체육 교사인 Larsen 선생입니다.
I'd like to announce that we're looking for volunteers to help with the charity soccer match next month.
우리가 다음 달에 있을 자선 축구 경기를 도울 자원봉사자를 찾고 있다는 것을 알려드리고자 합니다.
As you know, our best players will compete against our graduates at Ebanwood Stadium.
여러분도 알고 있듯이, 우리 최고의 선수들이 Ebanwood 경기장에서 우리 졸업생들과 겨룰 것입니다.
Volunteers will show the audience to their seats and tidy up after the match.
자원봉사자들은 관중들을 자리로 안내하고, 경기 후에 정리 정돈을 할 것입니다.
All the money from the ticket sales will get donated to the local children's hospital.
티켓 판매로 얻은 모든 돈은 지역 어린이 병원에 기부될 것입니다.
This will be a great opportunity to get involved in helping children.
이것은 어린이들을 돕는 일에 참여할 좋은 기회가 되어줄 겁니다.
Please don't hesitate to apply for this volunteer work at our charity soccer match.
우리 자선 축구 경기에서 하는 이 자원봉사 활동에 망설이지 말고 신청하세요.
For more information, you can check the school website. Thank you.
더 많은 정보를 원하시면, 학교 웹사이트에서 확인할 수 있습니다. 고맙습니다.

Why? 왜 정답일까?

자선 축구 경기 진행을 도와줄 자원봉사자를 모집한다는 안내이므로(**I'd like to announce that we're looking for volunteers to help with the charity soccer match next month.**), 여자가 하는 말의 목적으로 가장 적절한 것은 ⑤ '자선 축구 경기 자원봉사자 모집을 안내하려고'이다.

- **P.E. (physical education)** ⓝ 체육
- **volunteer** ⓝ 자원봉사자
- **compete against** ~와 겨루다
- **audience** ⓝ 관중
- **donate** ⓥ 기부하다
- **Don't hesitate to ~** 망설이지 말고 ~하세요
- **announce** ⓥ 발표하다, 알리다
- **charity** ⓝ 자선
- **graduate** ⓝ 졸업생
- **tidy up** ~을 깔끔하게 정리하다
- **apply** ⓥ 신청하다

02 상대방의 말을 중간에 끊지 않기

정답률 84% | 정답 ①

대화를 듣고, 남자의 의견으로 가장 적절한 것을 고르시오.

✔ 상대방이 말할 때는 말을 끊지 말아야 한다.
② 회의 발언은 주제에서 벗어나지 않아야 한다.
③ 적절한 제스처는 대화의 전달력을 높일 수 있다.
④ 회의를 진행할 때는 개인적인 감정을 배제해야 한다.
⑤ 자신의 의견을 주장할 때는 충분한 근거를 들어야 한다.

M : Ellie, you seem down. What's on your mind?
Ellie, 기분이 안 좋아 보이는구나. 무슨 일이야?
W : Well, Dad, Tiffany and I got into an argument at school.
저, 아빠, Tiffany와 제가 학교에서 말다툼을 했어요.
M : You two are so close. What happened?
너희 둘 아주 친하잖아. 무슨 일이 있었던 거니?
W : During our student council meeting, she was taking too long to make her point, so I had to jump in to finish her sentence.
우리 학생회 회의 중에, 그 애가 너무 오랫동안 자기 요점을 말하고 있어서, 제가 끼어들어서 그 애 말을 끊어야 했어요.
M : Oh, no. You shouldn't interrupt someone when they're in the middle of speaking.
오, 이런. 누군가가 한창 말하고 있을 때 가로막으면 안 돼.
W : I know. But she kept talking about so many details.
알고 있어요. 하지만 걔는 계속 세부 사항을 너무 많이 얘기했어요.
M : Still, that's not polite. How would you feel if you were her?
그래도 그건 예의가 아니야. 네가 그 애라면 기분이 어떨 것 같니?
W : I'd probably be upset.
아마 화가 날 거예요.
M : Exactly. That's why when somebody's talking, you shouldn't cut them off.
맞아. 그래서 누군가가 말을 하고 있을 때 말을 끊으면 안 돼.
W : You're right. I guess I didn't see things from her point of view.
아빠 말씀이 맞아요. 제가 그 애 입장에서 생각하지 못했던 것 같아요.
M : So, how about letting others finish what they're saying next time?
그럼, 다음에는 다른 사람들이 말을 끝마치도록 하는 게 어떨까?
W : Okay. Thanks, Dad. I'll apologize to her tomorrow.
알겠어요. 고마워요, 아빠. 내일 그 애한테 사과할게요.

Why? 왜 정답일까?

남자는 딸인 여자에게 상대방이 말하는 도중에 말을 끊어서는 안 된다(**You shouldn't interrupt someone when they're in the middle of speaking.** / ~ **when somebody's talking, you shouldn't cut them off.**)고 조언하고 있다. 따라서 남자의 의견으로 가장 적절한 것은 ① '상대방이 말할 때는 말을 끊지 말아야 한다.'이다.

- **get into an argument** 논쟁하다
- **student council** 학생회
- **interrupt** ⓥ 가로막다, 방해하다
- **cut off** ~을 끊다
- **apologize** ⓥ 사과하다
- **close** ⓐ 가까운, 친밀한
- **jump in** (대화에) 불쑥 끼어들다
- **polite** ⓐ 공손한, 예의 바른
- **point of view** 관점, 시각

03 잠잘 때 수면 안대 끼기

정답률 85% | 정답 ④

다음을 듣고, 여자가 하는 말의 요지로 가장 적절한 것을 고르시오.

① 일정한 실내 온도 유지는 건강에 중요한 역할을 한다.
② 충분한 햇빛 노출은 수면 호르몬 분비를 촉진한다.
③ 정서 안정을 위해서는 양질의 수면이 필요하다.
✔ 수면 안대를 착용하면 잠드는 데 도움이 될 수 있다.
⑤ 적당한 밝기의 조명은 일의 능률을 향상시킬 수 있다.

W : Hello, listeners. This is *Dr. Graham's One-minute Health Tips*.
안녕하세요, 청취자 여러분. *Graham 박사의 1분 건강 조언*입니다.
Getting a good night's sleep is important for your health.
숙면을 취하는 것은 여러분의 건강에 중요합니다.
But recently, more and more people are experiencing trouble falling asleep.
하지만 최근, 점점 더 많은 사람이 잠드는 데 어려움을 겪고 있습니다.
If that's your case, wearing an eye mask for sleeping can help you fall asleep.
만약 여러분도 그렇다면, 수면 안대를 착용하면 잠드는 데 도움이 될 수 있습니다.
If your room doesn't get dark enough, it'll be difficult to fall asleep.
여러분의 방이 충분히 어두워지지 않으면, 잠들기 어려울 것입니다.
This is because light interferes with the release of the hormone that makes you sleepy.
이것은 빛이 여러분을 졸리게 만드는 호르몬의 분비를 방해하기 때문입니다.
An eye mask can block the light, which makes it easier for you to fall asleep.
수면 안대는 빛을 차단해줄 수 있고, 이것이 여러분이 잠들기 더 쉽게 합니다.
Why not try one tonight? I'll be back with more tips next time!
오늘 밤 시도해보면 어떠세요? 다음에 또 더 많은 조언으로 돌아오겠습니다!

Why? 왜 정답일까?

수면 안대 착용이 더 쉽게 잠드는 데 도움이 될 수 있다(~ **wearing an eye mask for sleeping can help you fall asleep.**)는 내용이므로, 여자가 하는 말의 요지로 가장 적절한 것은 ④ '수면 안대를 착용하면 잠드는 데 도움이 될 수 있다.'이다.

- **get a good night's sleep** 숙면을 취하다
- **eye mask** 안대
- **release** ⓝ 분비 ⓥ 내보내다, 방출하다
- **fall asleep** 잠들다
- **interfere with** ~을 방해하다
- **block** ⓥ 차단하다

04 캠핑 장비 코너 점검하기

정답률 97% | 정답 ③

대화를 듣고, 그림에서 대화의 내용과 일치하지 않는 것을 고르시오.

M : Ms. Blake, I've finished decorating the camping gear section to look like a campsite.
Blake 씨, 캠핑 장비 코너를 캠핑장처럼 꾸미는 걸 다 했어요.
W : Thanks, Chris. It's much nicer than what's represented in our sales plan. 『I like that banner on the wall.』 ①의 근거 일치
고마워요, Chris. 우리 영업 계획서에 제시된 것보다 훨씬 좋군요. 벽에 있는 현수막이 마음에 들어요.
M : I think it'll attract our customers' attention. 『And I set up the cone-shaped tent as you suggested before.』 ②의 근거 일치
그것이 고객의 관심을 끌 것이라고 생각해요. 그리고 전에 제안하신 대로 원뿔 모양의 텐트를 설치했어요.
W : Good. That Native American-style tent is quite popular these days.
좋아요. 저 북미 원주민 스타일 텐트가 요즘 꽤 인기예요.
M : Yes, it is. 『Also, the backpack next to the box is currently our best-selling item.』 ③의 근거 불일치
네, 그렇죠. 그리고 상자 옆에 있는 배낭이 현재 가장 잘 팔리는 상품이에요.
W : That's true. I love its design. 『Oh, those two chairs look comfortable.』 ④의 근거 일치 I'd like to sit on one of them and make myself some coffee.
여: 맞아요. 디자인이 마음에 들어요. 아, 저 두 의자는 편해 보이네요. 저 중 하나에 앉아서 커피 좀 타 먹고 싶어요.
M : Me, too. 『And isn't that striped tablecloth really eye-catching?』 ⑤의 근거 일치
저도요. 그리고 저 줄무늬 식탁보는 정말 눈길을 끌지 않나요?
W : It certainly is. Everything looks really good. You did an excellent job!
확실히 그래요. 모든 게 정말 좋아 보이네요. 정말 잘하셨어요!

Why? 왜 정답일까?

대화에서 배낭은 상자 옆에 있다(**Also, the backpack next to the box is currently our best-selling item.**)고 하는데, 그림에서는 배낭이 상자 위에 있다. 따라서 그림에서 대화의 내용과 일치하지 않는 것은 ③이다.

- **decorate** ⓥ 꾸미다, 장식하다
- **campsite** ⓝ 캠핑장
- **banner** ⓝ 현수막
- **set up** 설치하다
- **Native American** 북미 원주민(의)
- **comfortable** ⓐ 편안한
- **eye-catching** ⓐ 눈길을 끄는
- **excellent** ⓐ 탁월한
- **gear** ⓝ 장비
- **represent** ⓥ 나타내다, 제시하다
- **attract** ⓥ (관심을) 끌다, 매혹하다
- **cone** ⓝ 원뿔
- **currently** ad 현재
- **tablecloth** ⓝ 식탁보
- **certainly** ad 확실히

05 테니스부 신입 회원 파티 준비

정답률 93% | 정답 ②

대화를 듣고, 여자가 할 일로 가장 적절한 것을 고르시오.

① 신입 회원 선물 준비하기
✔ 대회 일정 인쇄하기
③ 음악 재생 목록 만들기
④ 식당 예약하기
⑤ 문자 메시지 보내기

W : Oliver, I'm so excited about the party for the new members of our tennis club this Friday.
Oliver, 이번 주 금요일 우리 테니스부 신입 회원 파티 무척 기대돼.
M : Me, too. Let's go through the to-do list. I want it to be perfect.
나도 그래. 할 일 목록을 살펴보자. 완벽하면 좋겠어.
W : Agreed. Did you reserve the Mexican restaurant downtown for the party?
맞는 말이야. 파티를 위해 시내에 있는 멕시코 식당 예약했어?
M : Yes, I did. The restaurant is spacious, so it's perfect for a party like ours.
응, 했어. 식당이 넓어서 우리 같은 파티에 안성맞춤이야.
W : Plus, the food there is terrific. And you prepared gifts for the new members, right?
게다가 거기 음식도 훌륭해. 그리고 신입 회원을 위한 선물도 준비했지, 그렇지?
M : Yeah, they're in my car. Did you remind the members about the party?
응, 내 차에 있어. 회원들에게 파티에 대해 다시 한번 알려줬어?
W : I've just sent a text message to everyone.
방금 모두에게 문자 메시지를 보냈어.
M : Great. What about the tennis competition schedule? Have you printed it out?
좋아. 테니스 대회 일정은? 인쇄해 놨어?
W : Oh, I almost forgot. I'll do it tonight. Um, is the music ready?
아, 잊을 뻔했어. 내가 오늘 밤에 할게. 음, 음악은 준비됐어?
M : Uh-huh. I made a playlist last night.
응, 어젯밤에 재생 목록을 만들었어.
W : That's great. I think we're good to go!
좋네. 우리 준비 잘한 것 같아!

Why? 왜 정답일까?

테니스 대회 일정을 인쇄해 두었냐는 남자의 물음(**What about the tennis competition schedule? Have you printed it out?**)에 여자는 오늘 밤에 해주겠다(**I'll do it tonight.**)고 답하므로, 여자가 할 일로 가장 적절한 것은 ② '대회 일정 인쇄하기'이다.

- **go through** 검토하다
- **to-do list** 할 일 목록
- **reserve** ⓥ 예약하다
- **spacious** ⓐ (공간이) 넓은
- **terrific** ⓐ 훌륭한
- **remind** ⓥ 상기시키다
- **print out** 출력하다

06 친구들을 위한 크리스마스 선물 사기

정답률 94% | 정답 ③

대화를 듣고, 남자가 지불할 금액을 고르시오. [3점]

① $63 ② $70 ✔ $72
④ $78 ⑤ $80

W : Welcome to Jamie's Gift Shop! What can I do for you?
Jamie의 선물 가게에 오신 것을 환영합니다! 무엇을 도와드릴까요?
M : Hi. I need to get Christmas gifts for my friends. Is there anything you can recommend?
안녕하세요. 친구들에게 줄 크리스마스 선물을 사야 해요. 추천해주실 게 있나요?
W : Sure. How about this photo tumbler? You can insert a picture of your friends into the tumbler to decorate it.
물론입니다. 이 사진 텀블러는 어떠세요? 텀블러에 친구들의 사진을 넣어 장식할 수 있어요.
M : Ooh, my friends will love it. How much is it?
오, 제 친구들이 매우 좋아하겠어요. 얼마죠?
W : It's $30.
30달러입니다.
M : It seems a bit pricey, but I like it. I'll take two of them.
약간 비싼 것 같지만 마음에 드네요. 두 개 살게요.
W : Okay. Anything else?
알겠습니다. 다른 거 더 필요하신 건요?
M : These Christmas key chains look cute. Oh, they're $5 each.
이 크리스마스 열쇠고리 귀여워 보이네요. 오, 하나에 5달러군요.
W : Yes. They're only available this month.
네. 그것들은 이번 달에만 사실 수 있어요.
M : Are they? I'll take four then. I think that's all.
그래요? 그러면 네 개 사겠습니다. 이제 된 것 같아요.
W : So, that's two tumblers and four key chains.
그럼, 텀블러 두 개와 열쇠고리 네 개요.
M : That's right.
네, 맞아요.
W : And you get 10% off the total cost for our Christmas promotion.
그리고 크리스마스 판촉으로 총 가격의 10%를 할인해 드려요.
M : Great. Here's my credit card.
아주 좋아요. 여기 제 신용 카드요.

Why? 왜 정답일까?

대화에 따르면 남자는 하나에 30달러인 텀블러 2개와, 하나에 5달러인 열쇠고리를 4개 사고, 총 가격에서 10퍼센트를 할인받았다. 이를 식으로 나타내면 '(30×2+5×4)×0.9=72'이므로, 남자가 지불할 금액은 ③ '$72'이다.

- **gift shop** 선물 가게
- **recommend** ⓥ 추천하다
- **insert** ⓥ 넣다, 삽입하다
- **pricey** ⓐ 비싼
- **key chain** 열쇠고리
- **available** ⓐ 이용할 수 있는
- **promotion** ⓝ 판촉, 홍보

07 산책을 함께하지 못하는 이유

정답률 97% | 정답 ④

대화를 듣고, 여자가 산책을 할 수 없는 이유를 고르시오.

① 얇은 재킷을 입어서
② 회의 준비를 해야 해서
③ 알레르기 증상이 심해서
✔ 경찰서에 방문해야 해서
⑤ 병원 진료를 받아야 해서

W : It was nice having lunch outside the office.
사무실 밖에서 점심을 먹으니 좋았어요.
M : Yes. It feels so good now that fall is in the air. Shall we take a walk as usual before going back to the office?
네. 가을 공기가 느껴지니 기분이 아주 좋아요. 사무실로 돌아가기 전에 평소처럼 산책할까요?
W : I'd love to, but I can't today.
그러고 싶은데 오늘은 안 되겠어요.
M : Is it too cold? Your jacket does look thin.
너무 춥나요? 재킷이 얇아 보이긴 하네요.
W : No, I'm okay. This jacket is warmer than it looks.
아뇨, 전 괜찮아요. 이 재킷은 보기보다 더 따뜻해요.
M : Then, are your allergy symptoms bothering you again?
그럼 알레르기 증상 때문에 또 고생인 거예요?
W : Not really. I had a runny nose, but I've already seen a doctor. It's okay now.
그런 건 아니에요. 콧물이 나긴 했었는데, 벌써 병원에 갔다 왔어요. 지금은 괜찮아요.
M : So, why not today?
그럼 오늘 왜 안 돼요?
W : Actually, I need to visit the police station. I got a text message saying that my new driver's license is ready.
사실 저 경찰서에 가야 해요. 제 새 운전 면허증이 준비되었다는 문자 메시지를 받았어요.
M : I see. Then I'll just go back to prepare for the afternoon meeting.
그렇군요. 그럼 저는 그냥 들어가서 오후 회의를 준비해야겠어요.
W : Okay. See you at the office.
알겠어요. 사무실에서 봐요.

Why? 왜 정답일까?

여자는 새 운전 면허증을 받으러 경찰서에 가야 하기 때문에(**Actually, I need to visit the police station.**) 산책을 하러 갈 수 없다고 말한다. 따라서 여자가 산책을 할 수 없는 이유로 가장 적절한 것은 ④ '경찰서에 방문해야 해서'이다.

- **take a walk** 산책하다
- **thin** ⓐ 얇은
- **symptom** ⓝ 증상
- **bother** ⓥ 괴롭히다
- **have a runny nose** 콧물이 흐르다
- **driver's license** 운전 면허증

08 연극 단체 관람 예약하기

정답률 90% | 정답 ③

대화를 듣고, 남자가 예약할 연극 공연에 관해 언급되지 않은 것을 고르시오.

① 제목 ② 날짜 ✔ 출연자
④ 입장료 ⑤ 시작 시각

[Telephone rings.]
[전화벨이 울린다.]
W : Jason Theater. How may I help you?
Jason 극단입니다. 무엇을 도와드릴까요?
M : Hi, this is William Parker from Breezeville Senior Center.
안녕하세요, Breezeville Senior Center의 William Parker라고 합니다.
W : Oh, Mr. Parker. You called yesterday about bringing your seniors to see the play.
아, Parker 씨. 어제 센터 어르신들 모시고 연극 보러 오시는 건으로 전화 주셨죠.
M : Yes. Before I book, I'd like to double check the title. 「It's *The Shiny Moments*, right?」
네. 예약하기 전에 제목을 다시 한번 확인하려고요. 제목이 *The Shiny Moments* 맞죠? ①의 근거 일치
W : That's right. Have you decided on the date?
맞습니다. 날짜는 정하셨나요?
M : Yes. 「Could I reserve seats for 25 people on December 27th?」 ②의 근거 일치
네. 12월 27일에 25명 자리 예약할 수 있을까요?
W : Absolutely. But in that case, you'll need to pay today.
물론이죠. 하지만 그러면 오늘 결제하셔야 합니다.
M : Okay. 「You said admission tickets for seniors are $30 each.」 ④의 근거 일치
좋습니다. 노인 입장권은 장당 30달러라고 하셨죠.
W : That's correct. I'll send you the link for the payment.
맞습니다. 결제 링크를 보내드리겠습니다.
M : Thank you. I'll pay tonight.
고맙습니다. 오늘 밤에 결제할게요.
W : That'll be fine. 「The play starts at 3 p.m., but please come 30 minutes early.」
그래주시면 됩니다. 연극 시작은 오후 3시인데, 30분 먼저 도착해 주세요. ⑤의 근거 일치
M : No problem. See you then.
그럼요. 그때 뵐게요.

Why? 왜 정답일까?

대화에서 남자가 예약할 연극 공연의 제목, 날짜, 입장료, 시작 시각이 언급되므로, 언급되지 않은 것은 ③ '출연자'이다.

Why? 왜 오답일까?

① 'It's *The Shiny Moments*, right?'에서 '제목'이 언급되었다.
② 'Could I reserve seats for 25 people on December 27th?'에서 '날짜'가 언급되었다.
④ 'You said admission tickets for seniors are $30 each.'에서 '입장료'가 언급되었다.
⑤ 'The play starts at 3 p.m., ~'에서 '시작 시각'이 언급되었다.

- **senior** ⓝ 노인, 어르신
- **book** ⓥ 예약하다
- **double check** 재확인하다
- **decide on** ~을 정하다
- **admission** ⓝ 입장
- **payment** ⓝ 지불

09 영화 촬영지 걷기 투어

정답률 83% | 정답 ④

Golden Palette Walking Tour에 관한 다음 내용을 듣고, 일치하지 않는 것을 고르시오.

① 11월에 매일 진행된다.
② 안내 책자가 무료로 제공된다.

[문제편 p.175]

③ 오전 10시 30분에 시작한다.
✓ 출발 지점은 Central Studio의 남쪽 문이다.
⑤ 참가자 전원은 선물을 받을 것이다.

M : Hello, viewers.
안녕하세요, 시청자 여러분.
Are you looking for an interesting experience?
흥미로운 경험을 찾고 계신가요?
How about joining the *Golden Palette* Walking Tour?
Golden Palette 걷기 투어에 참여해 보시면 어떠세요?
You'll get the chance to see some of the famous filming sites from the movie *Golden Palette*.
영화 *Golden Palette*의 유명한 촬영지 일부를 둘러볼 기회가 있을 것입니다.
『This tour runs every day in November.』 ①의 근거 일치
이 투어는 11월에 매일 운영됩니다.
It's a three-hour walking tour with one of our professional guides.
저희의 전문 안내인 중 한 명과 함께하는 3시간 동안의 걷기 투어입니다.
『Also, brochures are provided for free, and you can find additional information about the filming sites there.』 ②의 근거 일치
또한 안내 책자가 무료로 제공되고, 거기서 촬영지에 대한 추가 정보를 찾을 수 있습니다.
『The tour begins at 10:30 a.m. and takes you to six locations from the movie.』 ③의 근거 일치
투어는 오전 10시 30분에 시작되고, 영화에 나오는 장소 여섯 곳으로 여러분을 안내합니다.
『The starting point is at the north gate of Central Studio.』 ④의 근거 불일치
출발 지점은 Central Studio의 북쪽 문입니다.
The price for this tour is $40 per person.
이 투어의 참가비는 1인당 40달러입니다.
『All participants will receive a postcard as a gift.』 ⑤의 근거 일치
참가자 전원은 선물로 엽서를 받을 것입니다.
Book it now on our website!
지금 저희 웹사이트에서 예약하세요!

Why? 왜 정답일까?

'The starting point is at the north gate of Central Studio.'에서 출발 지점은 북쪽 문이라고 하므로, 내용과 일치하지 않는 것은 ④ '출발 지점은 Central Studio의 남쪽 문이다.'이다.

Why? 왜 오답일까?

① 'This tour runs every day in November.'의 내용과 일치한다.
② 'Also, brochures are provided for free, ~'의 내용과 일치한다.
③ 'The tour begins at 10:30 a.m. ~'의 내용과 일치한다.
⑤ 'All participants will receive a postcard as a gift.'의 내용과 일치한다.

- filming site 영화 현장
- brochure ⓝ 안내 책자
- location ⓝ 위치
- postcard ⓝ 엽서
- run ⓥ 운영되다, (위험 등을) 감수하다, 무릅쓰다
- additional ⓐ 추가적인
- starting point 출발점

10 카트 고르기

정답률 90% | 정답 ②

다음 표를 보면서 대화를 듣고, 남자가 주문할 접이식 카트를 고르시오.

Foldable Carts

	Model	Price	Weight Limit	Color	Handle Material
①	A	$38	30kg	Black	Silicone
✓②	B	$42	40kg	Green	Silicone
③	C	$44	45kg	Blue	Metal
④	D	$48	50kg	White	Metal
⑤	E	$53	45kg	Red	Rubber

W : Honey, what are you doing on your laptop?
여보, 노트북으로 뭐 해요?
M : I'm trying to choose one of these foldable carts. You know our cart broke yesterday.
이 접이식 카트 중 하나를 사려고요. 알다시피 어제 우리 카트 고장 났잖아요?
W : Oh, that's right. Let me see the ones you're looking at.
오, 맞아요. 당신이 보고 있는 것 좀 보여줘요.
M : Sure. There are these five. 『They all look good, but let's not spend more than $50.』 근거1 Price 조건
그럼요. 이 다섯 가지가 있어요. 모두 좋아 보이지만, 50달러 넘게는 쓰지 않도록 하죠.
W : All right. 『How about the weight limit? Our last one was 30 kilograms.
좋아요. 무게 한도는 어떻게 되나요? 우리 저번 건 30킬로그램이었어요.
M : Hmm, that wasn't strong enough.』 근거2 Weight Limit 조건
흠, 그건 충분히 튼튼하지 않았어요.
W : Okay. Then, this one won't be any good.
알았어요. 그럼 이건 안 되겠네요.
M : Yeah. 『Do you have any color preference?
네. 선호하는 색이 있나요?
W : The old one was blue. Why don't we get a different color this time?』 근거3 Color 조건
예전 것은 파란색이었어요. 이번엔 다른 색으로 사면 어떨까요?
M : Good idea. Now, there are two options left. 『Which handle material do you like better?
좋은 생각이에요. 이제 두 가지 선택안이 남았네요. 손잡이 소재로 어떤 게 더 좋아요?
W : Well, metal gets too cold in winter.』 근거4 Handle Material 조건
음, 금속은 겨울에 너무 차가워져요.
M : Good point. Then, let's get the other model. I'll order it now.
좋은 지적이네요. 그럼 다른 제품을 사죠. 내가 지금 주문할게요.

Why? 왜 정답일까?

대화에 따르면 남자는 가격대가 50달러 미만이면서, 무게 한도는 30킬로그램을 넘고, 색상은 파란색이 아니면서, 손잡이 소재는 금속이 아닌 카트를 사려고 한다. 따라서 남자가 주문할 접이식 카트는 ② 'B'이다.

- foldable ⓐ 접이식의
- limit ⓝ 한도
- preference ⓝ 선호, 호불호
- Good point. 좋은 지적이네요.
- weight ⓝ 무게
- strong ⓐ 튼튼한
- metal ⓝ 금속

[문제편 p.176]

11 불꽃놀이 보러 나갈 준비하기

정답률 62% | 정답 ⑤

대화를 듣고, 여자의 마지막 말에 대한 남자의 응답으로 가장 적절한 것을 고르시오.

① Right. We should've watched them. – 맞아. 우린 그걸 봤어야 했어.
② Why not? Just put the mat on the shelf. – 안 될 게 뭐니? 매트 그냥 선반 위에 둬.
③ Great. We can store some snacks at home. – 아주 좋아. 우린 집에다 간식을 좀 보관할 수 있을 거야.
④ I'm sorry. I can't find the parking lot. – 미안해. 주차장을 못 찾겠어.
✓⑤ No problem. I'll take care of it. – 물론이지. 내가 맡을게.

W : Dad, we should leave soon to watch the fireworks in the park. Shall we bring something to eat?
아빠, 공원에서 열리는 불꽃놀이를 보러 우리 곧 출발해야 해요. 먹을 것 좀 가져갈까요?
M : Yeah, we might get hungry. Oh, we also need the picnic mat to sit on. I think I put it on one of the shelves in the storage room, but I'm not sure.
그래, 배고파질 수 있지. 오, 앉을 야외용 돗자리도 필요해. 창고 선반 중 하나에 올려놨던 것 같은데, 잘 모르겠네.
W : Then, could you find the mat while I pack some snacks and soft drinks?
그럼, 제가 간식과 음료수 좀 챙기는 동안 돗자리를 찾아 주실래요?
M : No problem. I'll take care of it.
물론이지. 내가 맡을게.

Why? 왜 정답일까?

여자는 자신이 불꽃놀이 행사를 보러 가서 먹을 간식을 준비하는 동안 아버지인 남자에게 돗자리를 찾아봐 달라고 요청하고 있다(Then, could you find the mat while I pack some snacks and soft drinks?). 따라서 남자의 응답으로 가장 적절한 것은 ⑤ '물론이지. 내가 맡을게.'이다.

- firework ⓝ 불꽃놀이, 폭죽
- shelf ⓝ 선반
- pack ⓥ 챙기다, 싸다
- take care of ~을 처리하다
- picnic mat 야외용 돗자리
- storage ⓝ 보관
- soft drink 청량음료

12 생일 파티에 못 간다고 말하기

정답률 80% | 정답 ①

대화를 듣고, 남자의 마지막 말에 대한 여자의 응답으로 가장 적절한 것을 고르시오.

✓① That's too bad. I was looking forward to seeing you there.
아쉽네. 널 만나길 고대하고 있었는데.
② Thank you. I'm so glad you could make it to the party.
고마워. 네가 파티에 올 수 있다니 정말 기뻐.
③ That's okay. The birthday party has already finished.
괜찮아. 생일 파티는 이미 끝났어.
④ Sure. I'll arrange the business trip for you and your team.
물론이지. 너와 너의 팀의 출장을 준비할게.
⑤ Don't worry. My boss will return from the trip this Monday.
걱정하지 마. 이번 주 월요일에 내 상사가 여행에서 돌아올 거야.

M : Hey, Tina. I have something to tell you about your birthday party this Saturday.
안녕, Tina. 이번 주 토요일에 있을 네 생일 파티에 관해 할 말이 있어.
W : Oh, Clark. You're coming, right? I'd really love it if you could come. All our friends will be there.
오, Clark. 너 오지, 그렇지? 네가 와 주면 정말 좋겠어. 우리 친구들이 다 올 거야.
M : I'm afraid I can't make it this time. I have to go on a business trip with my boss this weekend.
미안한데 이번엔 못 갈 거 같아. 이번 주말에 상사와 출장을 가야 해.
W : That's too bad. I was looking forward to seeing you there.
아쉽네. 널 만나길 고대하고 있었는데.

Why? 왜 정답일까?

출장 때문에 여자의 생일 파티에 못 갈 것 같다는 남자의 말(I'm afraid I can't make it this time. I have to go on a business trip with my boss this weekend.)에 대한 여자의 응답으로 가장 적절한 것은 ① '아쉽네. 널 만나길 고대하고 있었는데.'이다.

- make it (시간 맞춰) 가다, 해내다
- That's too bad. 안됐네, 아쉽네.
- arrange ⓥ 정리하다, 배치하다, 배열하다
- go on a business trip 출장 가다
- look forward to ~을 고대하다
- return ⓥ 돌아오다, 반품하다

13 꿈을 추구하기 좋은 타이밍

정답률 83% | 정답 ⑤

대화를 듣고, 여자의 마지막 말에 대한 남자의 응답으로 가장 적절한 것을 고르시오. [3점]

Man: ______

① Don't give up! You've inspired me to be a painter.
포기하지 마세요! 당신은 내가 화가가 되도록 자극을 줬어요.
② Cheer up! The fashion market is open to everybody.
힘내요! 패션 시장은 모두에게 열려 있어요.
③ You have a point. I don't have any fashion sense at all.
당신 말씀이 일리가 있네요. 저는 패션 감각이 전혀 없어요.
④ I agree. You should make a balance between work and life.
동의해요. 당신은 일과 삶 사이에 균형을 맞춰야 해요.
✓⑤ Be positive. You can start pursuing your dream at any time.
긍정적으로 봐요. 언제든 꿈을 좇기 시작할 수 있어요.

W : Shaun, you really rocked the runway as a senior fashion model yesterday!
Shaun, 어제 당신은 시니어 패션모델로서 무대를 흔들어 놓았어요!
M : Thanks for coming to my first show, Grace.
제 첫 쇼에 와줘서 고마워요, Grace.
W : My pleasure. You'll be an inspiration to many people our age.
천만에요. 당신은 우리 또래의 많은 사람에게 영감이 되어줄 거예요.
M : I'm so flattered.
과찬이에요.
W : It's amazing that you successfully switched careers.
성공적으로 전업하셨다니 놀라워요.
M : Thank you. My dream has finally come true.
고마워요. 제 꿈이 마침내 이뤄졌어요.
W : It couldn't have been easy to realize your dream in your 60s.
60대에 꿈을 실현하는 게 쉽지 않았을 것 같은데요.
M : It wasn't. But I've always believed in myself, and age was never an issue for me.
쉽지 않았죠. 하지만 저는 항상 제 자신을 믿어 왔어서, 나이는 저한테 전혀 문제가 되지 않았어요.
W : You make me think of my old passion to be a painter, but I put it off for too long.

당신을 보니 저도 화가가 되고 싶었던 옛 열정이 생각나지만, 너무 오래 미뤘네요.

M : Now is the time to give it a try.
지금이 바로 그것을 시도해 볼 때예요.

W : I think it's too late for that.
그러기엔 너무 늦은 거 같은걸요.

M : Be positive. You can start pursuing your dream at any time.
긍정적으로 봐요. 언제든 꿈을 좇기 시작할 수 있어요.

Why? 왜 정답일까?

옛날에 화가가 될 꿈을 갖고 있었지만 다시 해보기에 너무 늦은 것 같다는 여자의 말(**I think it's too late for that.**)에 대한 남자의 응답으로 가장 적절한 것은 ⑤ '긍정적으로 봐요. 언제든 꿈을 좇기 시작할 수 있어요.'이다.

- **rock** ⓥ 뒤흔들다
- **inspiration** ⓝ 영감, 자극
- **realize** ⓥ (꿈을) 실현하다
- **put off** ~을 미루다
- **You have a point.** 당신 말이 일리가 있네요.
- **pursue** ⓥ 추구하다
- **My pleasure.** 천만에요.
- **switch careers** 전업하다
- **passion** ⓝ 열정
- **give it a try** 시도하다
- **make a balance** 균형을 맞추다

14 서점에서 책 찾기

정답률 81% | 정답 ①

대화를 듣고, 남자의 마지막 말에 대한 여자의 응답으로 가장 적절한 것을 고르시오.

Woman: ______________________

✔ No worries. I can go pick it up now. – 괜찮아요. 지금 가서 살 수 있어요.
② All right. Just be sure to return it tomorrow. – 좋아요. 그걸 내일까지 반납만 꼭 해 주세요.
③ That's okay. We can fix the system next week. – 괜찮습니다. 저흰 다음 주에 그 시스템을 고칠 수 있어요.
④ Sorry to hear that. You can buy it next time. – 말씀 유감이네요. 다음 번에 사시면 됩니다.
⑤ Never mind. I'll bring a new copy for you. – 신경 쓰지 마세요. 새 책 한 부를 가져다 드리겠습니다.

W : Excuse me. Can you tell me where the non-fiction books are?
실례합니다. 논픽션 책이 어디 있는지 알려주실 수 있나요?

M : Sure. They're right over here. Are you looking for anything in particular?
물론입니다. 바로 이쪽입니다. 특별히 찾는 게 있으신가요?

W : I want to buy the latest book by Harriot Braun.
Harriot Braun의 최신 책을 사고 싶어요.

M : You mean *Follow Your Own Trail*?
Follow Your Own Trail 말씀이신가요?

W : Yes, that's the book.
네, 그 책이요.

M : Sorry. We don't have any copies left at the moment.
죄송합니다. 현재 저희 서점에는 남아 있는 책이 없네요.

W : I can't believe it. It just came out three weeks ago.
믿을 수가 없네요. 겨우 3주 전에 나온 책인걸요.

M : The book is so popular that it sold out very quickly. Do you want me to find out if any of our other stores has a copy?
그 책은 인기가 너무 많아서 아주 빨리 매진됐어요. 저희 다른 매장에 책이 있는지 알아볼까요?

W : Yes, please. I really need to buy one for my book club meeting tomorrow. Could you check the store downtown? It's on my way home.
네, 부탁드립니다. 내일 독서부 모임이 있어서 한 권 꼭 사야 해요. 시내 매장을 확인해 주실래요? 저희 집 가는 길에 있거든요.

M : Certainly. Let me look it up in our system. *[Typing sound]* Oh, there's one copy left there, but unfortunately we can't hold it for you.
물론입니다. 우리 시스템에서 찾아볼게요. *[타자 치는 소리]* 아, 그쪽에 한 권 남아 있는데, 안타깝게도 저희가 그 책을 맡아둘 수는 없습니다.

W : No worries. I can go pick it up now.
괜찮아요. 지금 가서 살 수 있어요.

Why? 왜 정답일까?

남자는 여자가 집에 가는 길에 있는 시내 쪽의 매장에 여자가 찾는 책이 있지만 그 책을 다른 사람들이 사 가지 못하도록 할 수는 없다(~ **unfortunately we can't hold it for you.**)고 말한다. 따라서 여자의 응답으로 가장 적절한 것은 ① '괜찮아요. 지금 가서 살 수 있어요.'이다.

- **non-fiction** ⓝ 논픽션, 실화
- **trail** ⓝ 길, 자국, 자취
- **come out** 나오다, 출간되다
- **look up** 찾아보다
- **be sure to** 꼭 ~하다
- **in particular** 특히
- **at the moment** 지금
- **on one's way home** 집에 가는 길에
- **unfortunately** ad 안타깝게도
- **Never mind.** 신경 쓰지 마세요.

15 사진 다시 찍어달라고 부탁하기

정답률 83% | 정답 ①

다음 상황 설명을 듣고, Jake가 Yuna에게 할 말로 가장 적절한 것을 고르시오. [3점]

Jake: ______________________

✔ Could you please take my picture again with the rock in it?
바위가 나오게 사진 다시 찍어줄 수 있어?
② I'd appreciate it if you could come to the mountain with me.
네가 나랑 그 산에 가줄 수 있으면 고맙겠어.
③ You shouldn't take any photos while climbing the rock.
그 바위를 오르는 동안에는 사진 절대 찍으면 안 돼.
④ I'm wondering if you can pose in front of the rock.
너 그 바위 앞에서 포즈 취해줄 수 있는지 궁금해.
⑤ Why don't you take a selfie in the national park?
그 국립공원에서 셀피를 찍지 않을래?

M : Jake and Yuna are members of a climbing club.
Jake와 Yuna는 등산 동아리의 회원이다.
Today, they're visiting a national park with other club members.
오늘 그들은 동아리의 다른 회원들과 함께 한 국립공원을 찾았다.
At the top of the mountain, Jake sees a beautiful rock.
그 산의 정상에서 Jake는 아름다운 바위를 발견한다.
He starts taking selfies with it.
그는 그것과 함께 셀피를 찍기 시작한다.
When Yuna sees Jake, she offers to take photos for him.
Yuna가 Jake를 보자, 그녀는 그에게 사진을 찍어 주겠다고 제안한다.
Jake finds a great spot to take a photo with the rock and gives Yuna his smartphone.
Jake는 그 바위를 사진에 담을 근사한 장소를 발견하고 Yuna에게 자기 스마트폰을 준다.
After Yuna takes some photos of him, Jake looks at the photos and notices that the rock is not in them.
Yuna가 그의 사진을 몇 장 찍고 나서, Jake는 사진들을 살펴보고, 바위가 사진에 나오지 않았음을 알아차린다.
So Jake wants to ask Yuna to get another shot of him and this time include the rock.
그래서 Jake는 Yuna에게 사진을 한 장 더 찍어주되, 이번에는 바위가 나오게 해달라고 부탁하고 싶다.
In this situation, what would Jake most likely say to Yuna?
이 상황에서, Jake는 Yuna에게 뭐라고 말하겠는가?

Jake: Could you please take my picture again with the rock in it?
바위가 나오게 사진 다시 찍어줄 수 있어?

Why? 왜 정답일까?

상황에 따르면 Jake는 자기 사진 안에 바위가 나오게 해달라고 부탁하려 하므로(**So Jake wants to ask Yuna to get another shot of him and this time include the rock.**), Jake가 Yuna에게 할 말로 가장 적절한 것은 ① '바위가 나오게 사진 다시 찍어줄 수 있어?'이다.

- **climbing** ⓝ 등산
- **at the top of** ~의 꼭대기에
- **spot** ⓝ 장소 ⓥ 찾아내다
- **national park** 국립공원
- **selfie** ⓝ 셀피
- **appreciate** ⓥ 고마워하다

16-17 업사이클링을 볼 수 있는 세계의 건축물

W : Hello, students.
안녕하세요, 학생 여러분.
Last week, we learned about upcycling, the process of reusing old materials to make a new object more valuable than the original pieces.
지난주에는 업사이클링, 즉 오래된 재료를 재사용하여 원래의 물품보다 더 가치 있는 새로운 물건을 만드는 과정에 대해 배웠습니다.
「Today, I'll focus on how this eco-friendly practice is employed in architecture around the world.」 16번의 근거
오늘은 이 친환경적 관행이 세계 전역의 건축에 어떻게 이용되는지에 중점을 둬 볼게요.
「Our first example is a community center in Singapore, called Enabling Village.」
우리의 첫 번째 사례는 Enabling Village라 불리는 싱가포르의 커뮤니티 센터입니다. 17번 ①의 근거 일치
Its buildings are famous for being made from old shipping containers.
그곳의 건물들은 오래된 선적 컨테이너로 만들어진 것으로 유명하죠.
「Second, we have a hotel in Mexico, called Tubohotel.」 17번 ②의 근거 일치
두 번째는 Tubohotel이라 불리는 멕시코의 호텔입니다.
The capsule-style rooms of this hotel were built using huge upcycled concrete pipes.
이 호텔의 캡슐형 객실들은 업사이클된 대형 콘크리트 관을 이용해 지어졌습니다.
「Next, Microlibrary Bima is a small local library located in Indonesia.」
다음으로, Microlibrary Bima는 인도네시아에 위치한 작은 지역 도서관입니다. 17번 ④의 근거 일치
The building was constructed by arranging 2,000 plastic ice cream buckets.
이 건물은 2,000개의 플라스틱 아이스크림 통을 배열해서 지었습니다.
「Finally, there's the Circular Pavilion in France.」 17번 ⑤의 근거 일치
마지막으로, 프랑스의 Circular Pavilion이 있습니다.
It is known for its exterior design which consists of 180 reused wooden doors.
그것은 재사용 목재 문 180개로 구성된 외관 디자인으로 유명합니다.
「Each of these examples shows how upcycling is applied in architecture globally to minimize our environmental footprint.」 16번의 근거
이 각각의 예시는 우리의 환경 발자국을 최소화할 수 있도록 업사이클링이 세계 건축에 어떻게 응용되고 있는지 보여줍니다.
Now, let's watch a video showing how these buildings were made.
이제, 이 건물들이 어떻게 만들어졌는지 보여주는 동영상을 보죠.

- **upcycling** ⓝ 업사이클링
- **valuable** ⓐ 가치 있는
- **eco-friendly** ⓐ 친환경적인
- **employ** ⓥ 사용하다
- **famous for** ~로 유명한
- **huge** ⓐ 거대한
- **bucket** ⓝ 통, 양동이
- **wooden** ⓐ 나무로 만든
- **environmental footprint** 환경 발자국, 환경에 악영향을 미친 범위
- **supplies** ⓝ 용품, 자재
- **reuse** ⓥ 재사용하다
- **original** ⓐ 원래의
- **practice** ⓝ 관행
- **architecture** ⓝ 건축
- **shipping** ⓝ 선적, 해운
- **construct** ⓥ 짓다, 건축하다
- **exterior** ⓐ 외부의
- **minimize** ⓥ 최소화하다
- **strategic** ⓐ 전략적인

16 주제 파악

정답률 86% | 정답 ②

여자가 하는 말의 주제로 가장 적절한 것은?

① various natural materials as a source of building supplies
건축 자재 공급원으로서의 다양한 천연 재료
✔ how upcycling is used in architecture across the globe
세계적으로 건축에서 업사이클링이 활용되는 방법
③ strategic use of upcycled plastics in different countries
여러 국가에서 업사이클된 플라스틱의 전략적 활용
④ impact of architectural waste on the global environment
건축 폐기물이 지구 환경에 미치는 영향
⑤ why nations should employ eco-friendly shipping methods
국가들이 친환경 운송 방법을 이용해야 하는 이유

Why? 왜 정답일까?

여자는 세계 각국 건축물의 예시로 업사이클링이 어떻게 건축에 활용되는지(**how upcycling is applied in architecture globally**) 설명하고 있다. 따라서 여자가 하는 말의 주제로 가장 적절한 것은 ② '세계적으로 건축에서 업사이클링이 활용되는 방법'이다.

17 언급 유무 파악

정답률 98% | 정답 ③

언급된 나라가 아닌 것은?

① Singapore – 싱가포르 ② Mexico – 멕시코 ✔ Australia – 호주
④ Indonesia – 인도네시아 ⑤ France – 프랑스

Why? 왜 정답일까?

담화에서 여자는 업사이클링을 볼 수 있는 건축의 예시를 들기 위해 싱가포르, 멕시코, 인도네시아, 프랑스를 언급하므로, 언급되지 않은 것은 ③ '호주'이다.

[문제편 p.176]

Why? 왜 오답일까?

① 'Our first example is a community center in Singapore, called Enabling Village.'에서 '싱가포르'가 언급되었다.
② 'Second, we have a hotel in Mexico, called Tubohotel.'에서 '멕시코'가 언급되었다.
④ 'Next, Microlibrary Bima is a small local library located in Indonesia.'에서 '인도네시아'가 언급되었다.
⑤ 'Finally, there's the Circular Pavilion in France.'에서 '프랑스'가 언급되었다.

Dictation 30

문제편 177쪽

01 looking for volunteers / compete against our graduates / tidy up after the match
02 too long to make her point / shouldn't interrupt someone / letting others finish
03 trouble falling asleep / wearing an eye mask / interferes with the release of the hormone
04 next to the box / make myself some coffee / that striped tablecloth
05 The restaurant is spacious / Have you printed it out / I almost forgot
06 insert a picture of your friends / only available this month / two tumblers and four key chains
07 fall is in the air / had a runny nose / visit the police station
08 bringing your seniors / double check the title / please come 30 minutes early
09 the famous filming sites / a three-hour walking tour / receive a postcard as a gift
10 that wasn't strong enough / get a different color / Which handle material
11 watch the fireworks / put it on one of the shelves
12 your birthday party / I'm afraid I can't make it
13 rocked the runway / successfully switched careers / put it off for too long
14 don't have any copies left / it sold out very quickly / we can't hold it for you
15 starts taking selfies / the rock is not in them / get another shot of him
16-17 make a new object more valuable / employed in architecture / minimize our environmental footprint

31회 | 2023학년도 대학수학능력시험 고3

| 정답과 해설 |

• 정답 •

01③ 02② 03③ 04④ 05② 06③ 07⑤ 08③ 09② 10① 11② 12① 13④ 14④ 15③ 16① 17⑤

01 책갈피 디자인 대회 참여 독려 정답률 97% | 정답 ③

다음을 듣고, 남자가 하는 말의 목적으로 가장 적절한 것을 고르시오.

① 도서관의 변경된 운영 시간을 안내하려고
② 독후감 쓰기 대회의 일정을 공지하려고
③ 책갈피 디자인 대회 참가를 독려하려고
④ 기한 내 도서 반납을 촉구하려고
⑤ 전자책 이용 방법을 설명하려고

M : Hello, Lockwood High School students.
안녕하세요, Lockwood 고등학교 학생 여러분.
This is your school librarian, Mr. Wilkins.
저는 여러분의 학교 사서인 Mr. Wilkins입니다.
I'm sure you're aware that our school library is hosting a bookmark design competition.
여러분은 분명 우리 학교 도서관에서 책갈피 디자인 경연 대회를 개최한다는 것을 알고 있을 겁니다.
I encourage students of all grades to participate in the competition.
모든 학년의 학생들이 경연 대회에 참가하기를 권장합니다.
The winning designs will be made into bookmarks, which will be distributed to library visitors.
수상한 디자인은 책갈피로 만들어져 도서관 방문자들에게 배부될 것입니다.
We're also giving out a variety of other prizes.
우리는 또한 다양한 다른 상들을 줄 겁니다.
So don't let this great opportunity slip away.
그러니 이런 좋은 기회를 놓치지 마세요.
Since the registration period for the bookmark design competition ends this Friday, make sure you visit our school library to submit your application.
책갈피 디자인 경연 대회 등록 기간이 이번 주 금요일에 끝나니, 꼭 학교 도서관을 방문해서 지원서를 내세요.
Come and participate to display your creativity and talents.
오셔서 참가하시고, 여러분의 창의력과 재능을 보여주세요.

Why? 왜 정답일까?

'I encourage students of all grades to participate in the competition.'에서 남자는 모든 학년 학생들이 교내에서 열리는 책갈피 디자인 대회에 참가하기를 권하고 있다. 따라서 남자가 하는 말의 목적으로 가장 적절한 것은 ③ '책갈피 디자인 대회 참가를 독려하려고'이다.

- librarian ⓝ (도서관의) 사서
- aware ⓐ 알고 있는
- competition ⓝ 대회, 경연, 경쟁
- grade ⓝ 학년
- distribute ⓥ 배부하다
- prize ⓝ 상, 상품
- registration ⓝ 등록
- creativity ⓝ 창의성
- host ⓥ 개최하다 ⓝ 진행자
- bookmark ⓝ 책갈피
- encourage ⓥ 권장하다
- participate ⓥ 참여하다, 참가하다
- a variety of 다양한
- slip away 사라지다, 훌쩍 지나가 버리다
- submit ⓥ 제출하다

02 사과 껍질의 피부 개선 효능 정답률 99% | 정답 ②

대화를 듣고, 여자의 의견으로 가장 적절한 것을 고르시오.

① 사과를 먹으면 장운동이 원활해진다.
② 사과 껍질은 피부 상태 개선에 도움이 된다.
③ 충분한 수면은 건강한 피부 유지에 필수적이다.
④ 사과를 먹기 전에 껍질을 깨끗이 씻어야 한다.
⑤ 주기적인 수분 섭취는 피부 노화를 늦춘다.

M : Honey, do you want some apples with breakfast?
여보, 아침 식사 때 사과를 좀 먹을래요?
W : Sounds great. Can you save the apple peels for me?
괜찮은 것 같네요. 사과 껍질은 내가 쓰게 챙겨줄래요?
M : Why? What do you want them for?
왜요? 왜 그걸 원하나요?
W : I'm going to use them to make a face pack. Apple peels are effective for improving skin condition.
얼굴 팩을 만드는 데 쓰려고요. 사과 껍질은 피부 상태를 개선하는 데 효과적이에요.
M : Where did you hear about that?
그걸 어디에서 들었나요?
W : I recently read an article about their benefits for our skin.
최근에 우리 피부에 대한 그것의 이점에 관한 기사를 읽었어요.
M : Interesting. What's in them?
흥미롭군요. 그 속에 무엇이 들었죠?
W : It said apple peels are rich in vitamins and minerals, so they moisturize our skin and enhance skin glow.
기사에 따르면 사과 껍질은 비타민과 미네랄이 풍부해서 우리 피부에 수분을 공급하고 피부 윤기를 개선해 준대요.
M : That's good to know.
잘 알아둘 점이군요.
W : Also, they remove oil from our skin and have a cooling effect.
또한, 그것은 우리 피부에서 기름을 제거하고 피부를 식혀주는 효과가 있어요.
M : Wow! Then I shouldn't throw them away.
와! 그러면 껍질을 버리지 말아야겠어요.
W : Right. Apple peels can help improve our skin condition.
맞아요. 사과 껍질은 우리 피부 상태를 개선하는 데 도움이 될 수 있어요.

M : I see. I'll save them for you.
알겠어요. 당신을 위해 그것을 챙겨둘게요.

Why? 왜 정답일까?

여자는 사과 껍질이 피부 상태를 나아지게 하는 데 도움이 된다(Apple peels are effective for improving skin condition. / Apple peels can help improve our skin condition.)고 말하므로, 여자의 의견으로 가장 적절한 것은 ② '사과 껍질은 피부 상태 개선에 도움이 된다.'이다.

- **peel** ⓝ (과일 등의) 껍질 ⓥ 껍질을 벗기다
- **improve** ⓥ 개선하다, 향상시키다
- **recently** ad 최근에
- **benefit** ⓝ 이점
- **enhance** ⓥ 개선하다
- **throw away** ~을 버리다
- **effective** ⓐ 효과적인
- **condition** ⓝ 상태
- **article** ⓝ 기사
- **moisturize** ⓥ 수분을 공급하다
- **glow** ⓝ 윤기, 빛

03 수영 코치 취재하기

정답률 97% | 정답 ③

대화를 듣고, 두 사람의 관계를 가장 잘 나타낸 것을 고르시오.

① 평론가 – 영화감독
② 심판 – 수영 선수
③ 작가 – 수영 코치
④ 서점 주인 – 유치원 교사
⑤ 잡지사 편집장 – 광고주

W : Hello, Mr. Roberts. I appreciate you taking the time to share your experience and knowledge.
안녕하세요, Mr. Roberts. 당신의 경험과 지식을 공유하기 위해 시간을 내주셔서 고맙습니다.

M : My pleasure, Ms. Lee. I've enjoyed all your bestselling books. So, I'm excited to help you.
저도 기쁩니다, Ms. Lee. 저는 당신의 모든 베스트셀러를 잘 읽었어요. 그래서 당신을 돕게 되어 마음이 설레네요.

W : Thanks. Since I'm writing about world-class athletes, I wanted to hear how you've trained children who became Olympic swimming champions.
감사합니다. 저는 세계적인 선수들에 관한 글을 쓰고 있어서, 당신이 올림픽 수영 챔피언이 된 아이들을 어떻게 훈련시켰는지 듣고 싶었어요.

M : Then we should start with what I observe on the first day of my swimming classes.
그렇다면 제가 수영 수업 첫날에 무엇을 관찰하는지로 시작해야겠네요.

W : Do some children stand out right away?
어떤 아이들은 눈에 바로 띄나요?

M : Yes. Some kids are able to pick up my instructions quickly and easily.
예. 일부 아이들은 제가 가르치는 것을 빠르고 쉽게 익힐 수 있어요.

W : I see. So did many of those kids go on to become Olympic champions?
그렇군요. 그러면 그런 아이들 중 많은 수가 나중에 올림픽 챔피언이 되었나요?

M : Well, practicing is much more important. Those who consistently practiced made great improvements and ultimately became champions.
음, 연습이 훨씬 더 중요합니다. 꾸준히 연습한 아이들이 큰 발전을 이뤘고, 결국 챔피언이 되었습니다.

W : This is good insight I can use in my book.
이건 제 책에 쓸 수 있는 좋은 통찰이네요.

M : I hope it helps.
도움이 되면 좋겠습니다.

Why? 왜 정답일까?

'I've enjoyed all your bestselling books.', 'I wanted to hear how you've trained children who became Olympic swimming champions.' 'Then we should start with what I observe on the first day of my swimming classes.', 'This is good insight I can use in my book.' 등에서 작가가 글 쓰는 데 참고하기 위해 올림픽 챔피언들을 지도했던 수영 코치를 취재하는 상황임을 알 수 있으므로, 두 사람의 관계로 가장 적절한 것은 ③ '작가 – 수영 코치'이다.

- **appreciate** ⓥ 감사하다
- **excited** ⓐ 신나는, 설레는
- **observe** ⓥ 관찰하다
- **instruction** ⓝ 지시, 가르침
- **make an improvement** 개선되다
- **knowledge** ⓝ 지식
- **athlete** ⓝ 운동선수
- **stand out** 두드러지다, 눈에 띄다
- **consistently** ad 일관되게, 계속해서, 꾸준히

04 공원 사진 구경하기

정답률 97% | 정답 ④

대화를 듣고, 그림에서 대화의 내용과 일치하지 않는 것을 고르시오.

M : Hi, Jane. What are you looking at on your phone?
안녕, Jane. 핸드폰으로 뭘 보고 있어?

W : Hi, Brian. It's a picture I took at Grand Boulder National Park. I went hiking there last weekend.
안녕, Brian. Grand Boulder 국립공원에서 내가 찍은 사진이야. 지난 주말에 거기로 하이킹을 갔어.

M : Let me see. 「I like the bear statue wearing the check pattern jacket.」 ①의 근거 일치
어디 보자. 체크무늬 재킷을 입은 곰 조각상이 마음에 들어.

W : It's cute, right?
귀엽지, 그렇지?

M : Yeah. 「There's a park map between the lights.」 ②의 근거 일치 It seems to include useful information.
응. 등 사이에 공원 지도가 있구나. 유용한 정보를 담고 있는 것 같아.

W : It helps me pick a different trail each time I go hiking. 「Do you see the two flowerpots in front of the cabin?」 ③의 근거 일치
그것은 내가 하이킹할 때마다 다른 길을 선택하는 데 도움이 돼. 오두막집 앞에 화분 두 개 보이지?

M : Yes. They look beautiful. 「Oh, there's a round table by the path.」 ④의 근거 불일치
응. 아름다워 보여. 오, 길 옆에 둥근 테이블이 있어.

W : I had lunch there.
나는 거기서 점심을 먹었어.

M : What a nice place to enjoy lunch! 「Look at the bird on the tree branch.」 ⑤의 근거 일치
점심을 즐기기에 정말 좋은 곳이구나! 나뭇가지 위에 있는 새 좀 봐.

W : Isn't it lovely? I love going there and being close to nature.
귀엽지 않아? 나는 거기 가서 자연과 가까워지는 것을 좋아해.

Why? 왜 정답일까?

대화에 따르면 길 옆에 둥근 테이블이 있다(Oh, there's a round table by the path.)고 하는데, 그림 속 테이블은 사각형이다. 따라서 그림에서 대화의 내용과 일치하지 않는 것은 ④이다.

- **go hiking** 하이킹을 가다
- **trail** ⓝ (작은) 길
- **cabin** ⓝ 오두막
- **statue** ⓝ 조각상
- **flowerpot** ⓝ 화분
- **branch** ⓝ 나뭇가지

05 식당 재개업 행사 준비하기

정답률 85% | 정답 ②

대화를 듣고, 남자가 할 일로 가장 적절한 것을 고르시오.

① 음식 재료 주문하기
② 와인 잔 포장하기
③ 추가 메뉴 선정하기
④ 초대 문자 메시지 보내기
⑤ 노래 목록 확인하기

W : Honey, I'm so excited for our restaurant's reopening event tomorrow.
여보, 내일 우리 식당 재개업 행사가 있어서 너무 신이 나요.

M : So am I. Let's see. We've ordered enough ingredients, right?
나도 그래요. 어디 봐요. 우리는 재료를 충분히 주문했죠, 그렇죠?

W : I think so. We need to remind our loyal customers of the event.
그런 것 같아요. 단골 고객들에게 행사를 상기시킬 필요가 있어요.

M : I already sent text messages.
내가 이미 문자 메시지를 보냈어요.

W : Good. I hope people like the new menu items that we added.
좋아요. 사람들이 우리가 추가한 신메뉴를 좋아하면 좋겠어요.

M : Don't worry. We have a great chef. So I'm sure the new dishes will be a hit.
걱정 마요. 우리에게는 훌륭한 요리사가 있는 걸요. 그러니 새로운 요리는 분명 인기를 끌 거예요.

W : What about the live music? Did you confirm the song list with the band?
라이브 음악은 어때요? 밴드랑 곡 목록은 확인했어요?

M : Not yet. And we also need to wrap wine glasses to give as gifts for the customers.
아직이요. 그리고 우린 손님들에게 선물로 줄 와인 잔도 포장해야 해요.

W : Okay. Could you wrap them?
알겠어요. 그것 좀 포장해 줄래요?

M : Sure. I'll do it now.
물론이죠. 지금 할게요.

W : Great! Then I'll contact the band.
좋아요! 그럼 내가 밴드와 연락해 볼게요.

Why? 왜 정답일까?

여자와 함께 식당 재개업 행사를 준비하던 남자가 손님들에게 선물로 줄 와인 잔을 포장해야 한다고 말하자, 여자는 남자에게 포장을 해 달라고 부탁하고(Could you wrap them?), 남자는 이를 수락한다(Sure. I'll do it now.). 따라서 남자가 할 일로 가장 적절한 것은 ② '와인 잔 포장하기'이다.

- **reopening** ⓝ 재개업
- **ingredient** ⓝ 재료
- **wrap** ⓥ 포장하다
- **order** ⓥ 주문하다
- **live music** 라이브 음악
- **customer** ⓝ 고객

06 어린이 농장에서 동물 먹이와 승마 체험 표 사기

정답률 92% | 정답 ③

대화를 듣고, 여자가 지불할 금액을 고르시오.

① $55　② $63　③ $70　④ $81　⑤ $90

M : Hello, are you enjoying your time here at Magic Unicorn Children's Farm?
안녕하세요, 저희 Magic Unicorn 어린이 농장에서 즐거운 시간을 보내고 계신가요?

W : Yes, thank you. I'd like to buy some snacks to feed the animals.
네, 고맙습니다. 전 동물들에게 먹일 간식을 좀 사고 싶어요.

M : Sure. We sell two kinds of food for the animals, vegetable sticks and sliced fruits.
네. 저희는 동물을 위한 두 종류의 먹이를 팔고 있어요, 야채 스틱과 얇게 썬 과일이죠.

W : How much do they cost?
가격이 얼마인가요?

M : It's $5 for a pack of vegetable sticks and $10 for a pack of sliced fruits.
야채 스틱은 한 팩에 5달러, 얇게 썬 과일은 한 팩에 10달러입니다.

W : I'll take four packs of vegetable sticks. Are there any other activities?
야채 스틱 네 팩을 사겠어요. 다른 활동 거리는 없나요?

M : We offer horseback riding. A ticket for a ride around the farm is $25.
승마 체험이 있습니다. 말을 타고 농장을 한 바퀴 도는 표가 25달러입니다.

W : Oh, my son and daughter will love it. Two tickets, please.
오, 제 아들과 딸이 좋아할 거예요. 표 두 장 주세요.

M : So, four packs of vegetable sticks and two horseback riding tickets, correct?
그러면 야채 스틱 네 팩과 승마 표 두 장, 맞지요?

W : Right. And I heard you're offering a 10% discount as an autumn promotional event.
맞아요. 그리고 가을 홍보 행사로 10% 할인해 주신다고 들었어요.

M : I'm sorry. That event ended last week.
죄송합니다. 그 행사는 지난주에 끝났어요.

W : I see. Here's my credit card.
알겠습니다. 여기 제 신용 카드요.

Why? 왜 정답일까?

대화에 따르면 여자는 동물 먹이로 한 팩에 5달러인 야채 스틱을 네 팩 사고, 한 장에 25달러인 승마 체험 표를 두 장 사기로 했다. 10% 할인은 행사 기간이 끝나 받지 못했다. 이를 식으로 나타내면 '$5\times4+25\times2=70$'이므로, 여자가 지불할 금액은 ③ '$70'이다.

[문제편 p.181]

- **feed** ⓥ 먹이를 주다, 먹이다
- **cost** ⓥ ~의 비용이 들다, 희생시키다
- **promotional** ⓐ 홍보의, 판촉의
- **slice** ⓥ 자르다, 쪼개다
- **horseback riding** 승마
- **credit card** 신용 카드

07 토요일에 축제에 못 가는 이유

정답률 99% | 정답 ⑤

대화를 듣고, 남자가 K-Trend Festival에 갈 수 없는 이유를 고르시오.

① 영화관에서 일해야 해서
② 유학 설명회에 참석해야 해서
③ 경제학 시험공부를 해야 해서
④ 태권도 시합에 출전해야 해서
✔ 동생을 공항에 데려다줘야 해서

W : Sam, do you want to go to the K-Trend Festival with me this Saturday?
Sam, 이번 토요일에 나랑 K-Trend Festival에 가지 않을래?

M : Hi, Olivia. Is that the festival held at Central Square?
안녕, Olivia. 그거 Central Square에서 열리는 축제야?

W : Yeah, that's it. There'll be many attractions including Taekwondo performances that incorporate K-pop dance moves.
응, 그거. 케이팝 댄스 동작을 결합한 태권도 공연을 포함해서 볼거리가 많을 거야.

M : Really? Sounds cool! What time does it start?
정말? 근사하겠네! 몇 시에 시작해?

W : It starts at 5 p.m. Will you be working at the movie theater at that time?
오후 5시에 시작해. 너 그 시간에 영화관에서 일하니?

M : No, I'm not working this Saturday. But I can't come to the festival.
아니, 이번 주 토요일에는 근무 안 해. 그런데 나 그 축제 못 가.

W : Too bad. Do you have to study for your economics exam?
아쉽네. 경제학 시험 공부를 해야 하는 거야?

M : Actually, I already took the exam yesterday.
사실, 그 시험은 어제 이미 봤어.

W : Then, what's the matter?
그럼, 무슨 일이야?

M : I have to take my younger sister to the airport on Saturday evening.
토요일 저녁에 여동생을 공항에 데려다줘야 해.

W : Where's she going?
여동생이 어디 가는데?

M : She's going to Canada to study abroad.
캐나다로 유학 갈 거야.

W : That's awesome. I hope she has a good experience there.
그거 굉장한데. 동생이 거기서 좋은 경험 하길 바라.

Why? 왜 정답일까?

남자는 토요일 저녁에 유학 가는 여동생을 공항에 데려다 줘야 해서(**I have to take my younger sister to the airport on Saturday evening.**) 여자와 함께 축제에 갈 수 없다고 말한다. 따라서 남자가 **K-Trend Festival**에 갈 수 없는 이유로 가장 적절한 것은 ⑤ '동생을 공항에 데려다줘야 해서'이다.

- **attraction** ⓝ 볼거리, 명물
- **dance move** 안무
- **take an exam** 시험을 치다
- **study abroad** 유학하다
- **incorporate** ⓥ 결합하다, 통합하다
- **economics** ⓝ 경제학
- **take A to B** A를 B에 데려다 주다
- **awesome** ⓐ 멋진, 근사한, 기막히게 좋은

08 졸업 사진 촬영 일정 확인

정답률 97% | 정답 ③

대화를 듣고, 졸업 사진 촬영에 관해 언급되지 않은 것을 고르시오.

① 날짜
② 장소
✔ 복장
④ 참여 학생 수
⑤ 소요 시간

[Telephone rings.]
[전화벨이 울린다.]

W : Hello, Jennifer Porter speaking.
여보세요, Jennifer Porter입니다.

M : Hi, Ms. Porter. This is Steve Jackson from Lifetime Photo Studio.
안녕하세요, Ms. Porter. 저는 Lifetime Photo Studio의 Steve Jackson입니다.

W : Oh, how are you?
오, 잘 지내셨어요?

M : Good. 『I'm scheduled to shoot your school's graduation photos on Wednesday, November 23rd.』 ①의 근거 일치 So, I'm calling to confirm the details.
네, 전 11월 23일 수요일에 선생님 학교의 졸업 사진을 찍을 예정입니다. 그래서 세부 사항을 확인하려고 전화 드렸어요.

W : Sure. 『As we previously discussed, the place will be Lily Pond Park.』 ②의 근거 일치
네. 이전에 논의한 것처럼 장소는 Lily 호수 공원이 될 거예요.

M : Okay. 『Could you tell me the exact number of students taking part in the photo session?
그렇군요. 사진 촬영 시간에 참가하는 정확한 학생 수를 알려 주실 수 있나요?

W : Let me check. *[Pause]* Well, it'll be 180 students.』 ④의 근거 일치
확인해 볼게요. *[잠시 후]* 음, 180명일 거예요.

M : I see. The same as you said before.
그렇군요. 전에 말씀하신 것과 같네요.

W : That's right. 『How long will it take to shoot the photos?
맞습니다. 사진을 찍는 데 얼마나 걸릴까요?

M : It'll take almost three hours.』 ⑤의 근거 일치 We should finish by noon.
거의 세 시간 걸릴 겁니다. 정오까지는 끝날 거예요.

W : Great. Is there any other information you need?
좋군요. 필요하신 정보 또 있으세요?

M : No, I'm all set. Bye.
아닙니다, 충분합니다. 안녕히 계세요.

Why? 왜 정답일까?

대화에서 남자와 여자는 졸업 사진 촬영에 관해 날짜, 장소, 참여 학생 수, 소요 시간을 언급하므로, 언급되지 않은 것은 ③ '복장'이다.

Why? 왜 오답일까?

① '**I'm scheduled to shoot your school's graduation photos on Wednesday, November 23rd.**'에서 '날짜'가 언급되었다.
② '**As we previously discussed, the place will be Lily Pond Park.**'에서 '장소'가 언급되었다.
④ '**Well, it'll be 180 students.**'에서 '참여 학생 수'가 언급되었다.
⑤ '**It'll take almost three hours.**'에서 '소요 시간'이 언급되었다.

- **be scheduled to** ~할 예정이다
- **graduation** ⓝ 졸업
- **previously** ad 이전에
- **be all set** 다 준비되다
- **shoot** ⓥ 촬영하다
- **confirm** ⓥ (맞는지) 확인하다
- **exact** ⓐ 정확한

09 화초 박람회 행사 안내

정답률 74% | 정답 ②

Greenville Houseplant Expo에 관한 다음 내용을 듣고, 일치하지 않는 것을 고르시오.

① 3일 동안 진행될 것이다.
✔ 식물 관리 방법에 관한 강의가 매일 있을 것이다.
③ 희귀종을 포함한 다양한 식물을 구입할 수 있다.
④ 티켓 구입은 온라인으로만 가능하다.
⑤ 에메랄드 컨벤션 센터에서 열릴 것이다.

W : Hello, listeners. I'm Melinda Jones from the organizing committee of the Greenville Houseplant Expo.
안녕하세요, 청취자 여러분. 저는 Greenville 화초 박람회 조직위원회의 Melinda Jones입니다. ①의 근거 일치
『I'm here to announce that the expo will run for three days starting on March 17th, 2023.』 저는 박람회가 2023년 3월 17일부터 3일간 개최된다는 것을 알려드리려고 이 자리에 왔습니다.』
『Just on the opening day, there'll be a lecture on plant care methods.』 ②의 근거 불일치
개막날에 한해, 식물 관리 방법에 관한 강의가 있을 것입니다.
This lecture will be given by Dr. Evans, host of the TV show *Plants Love You*.
이 강의는 TV 프로그램 *Plants Love You*의 진행자인 Evans 박사님이 하실 것입니다.
『Most importantly, you can buy a variety of plants, including rare species, exhibited in the expo.』 ③의 근거 일치
가장 중요한 것은, 희귀종을 포함해 박람회에 전시된 다양한 식물들을 구매하실 수 있다는 겁니다.
Due to its popularity, you'd better get your tickets early.
인기 때문에 티켓은 빨리 구매하시는 편이 좋습니다.
『Tickets are available through online purchase only.』 ④의 근거 일치
티켓은 온라인 구매를 통해서만 구할 수 있습니다.
『If you're a plant lover, come to the expo, which will take place at the Emerald Convention Center, and refresh your houseplant collection.』 ⑤의 근거 일치
식물 애호가라면 에메랄드 컨벤션 센터에서 열리는 박람회에 오셔서 여러분의 화초 콜렉션을 새로이 채워보세요.

Why? 왜 정답일까?

'**Just on the opening day, there'll be a lecture on plant care methods.**'에서 식물 관리법에 대한 강좌는 개막날에만 열릴 것이라고 하므로, 내용과 일치하지 않는 것은 ② '식물 관리 방법에 관한 강의가 매일 있을 것이다.'이다.

Why? 왜 오답일까?

① '**I'm here to announce that the expo will run for three days starting on March 17th, 2023.**'의 내용과 일치한다.
③ '**Most importantly, you can buy a variety of plants, including rare species, exhibited in the expo.**'의 내용과 일치한다.
④ '**Tickets are available through online purchase only.**'의 내용과 일치한다.
⑤ '**If you're a plant lover, come to the expo, which will take place at the Emerald Convention Center,** ~'의 내용과 일치한다.

- **committee** ⓝ 위원회
- **method** ⓝ 방법
- **rare** ⓐ 희귀한
- **popularity** ⓝ 인기
- **lecture** ⓝ 강의
- **importantly** ad 중요하게
- **exhibit** ⓥ 전시하다

10 첼로 케이스 고르기

정답률 80% | 정답 ①

다음 표를 보면서 대화를 듣고, 여자가 구매할 첼로 케이스를 고르시오.

Hard Cello Cases

	Model	Price	Interior Material	Length(inches)	Wheels
✔	A	$140	Nylon	51	×
②	B	$160	Cotton	49	○
③	C	$175	Velvet	53	×
④	D	$190	Cotton	52	○
⑤	E	$215	Cotton	55	×

M : Welcome to Uptown Music Shop. How can I help you?
Uptown Music Shop에 잘 오셨습니다. 무엇을 도와드릴까요?

W : Hi, I'm looking for a hard cello case.
안녕하세요, 저는 단단한 첼로 케이스를 찾고 있어요.

M : All right. Here's our catalog. These are the ones we have in stock. 『How much are you willing to spend?
알겠습니다. 여기 저희 카탈로그가 있습니다. 이게 저희 재고에 있는 거고요. 비용은 얼마나 생각하세요?

W : I can spend up to $200.』 근거1 Price 조건
저는 200달러까지 쓸 수 있어요.

M : Okay. 『How about the interior material? Do you have a preference?
알겠습니다. 안감은 어떤가요? 선호하시는 것이 있나요? 근거2 Interior Material 조건

W : Well, I don't want the velvet one.』 It seems difficult to take care of.
음, 벨벳은 원하지 않아요. 관리하기가 힘든 것 같아요.

M : Right. 『Then how about the length?
알겠습니다. 그럼 길이는요?

W : I have a full-size cello, so I want a case that's at least 50 inches long.』 근거3 Length 조건
저는 풀사이즈(4/4) 첼로를 갖고 있어서, 길이가 최소한 50인치는 되는 케이스를 원해요.

M : Now you have two options left. 『Do you need wheels on your case?
이제 고르실 수 있는 것이 두 개 남았습니다. 케이스에 바퀴가 달려 있어야 하나요?

[문제편 p.181]

W : No, I don't need them.」 I won't carry it around a lot. 근거4 Wheels 조건
아니요, 없어도 됩니다. 많이 가지고 다니지 않을 거라서요.

M : Then this is the one for you.
그럼 이것이 손님께 맞겠네요.

W : Thank you. I'll take it.
고맙습니다. 그걸로 살게요.

Why? 왜 정답일까?

대화에 따르면 여자는 가격이 200달러를 넘지 않으면서, 안감은 벨벳이 아니고, 길이가 50인치 이상이면서, 바퀴는 달려 있지 않은 첼로 케이스를 구매하기로 한다. 따라서 여자가 구매할 케이스는 ① 'A'이다.

- have in stock 재고가 있다
- interior ⓐ 내부의
- wheel ⓝ 바퀴
- be willing to 기꺼이 ~하다
- preference ⓝ 선호
- carry around 들고 다니다, 휴대하다

11 새 자전거 헬멧이 필요한 이유 정답률 97% | 정답 ②

대화를 듣고, 남자의 마지막 말에 대한 여자의 응답으로 가장 적절한 것을 고르시오.

① Never mind. I'm selling my old helmet.
걱정하지 마. 내가 썼던 헬멧을 팔게.
② All right. I'll buy a bigger one that fits you.
알았어. 네게 맞는 더 큰 것을 사 줄게.
③ No way. You should not ride a bicycle at night.
절대 안 돼. 밤에는 자전거를 타면 안 돼.
④ Great. I think it matches your bicycle perfectly.
좋아. 그게 네 자전거와 완벽하게 어울리는 것 같아.
⑤ No. We don't have to worry about the tight schedule.
아니. 우리는 빡빡한 일정 때문에 걱정할 필요가 없어.

M : Mom, I'd like to get a new bicycle helmet. Can you buy me one?
엄마, 자전거 헬멧을 새로 사고 싶어요. 사 주실 수 있어요?

W : I'll buy you a new helmet if you need it. But what's the problem with the one you have now?
필요하면 새 헬멧을 하나 사 줄게. 그런데 지금 있는 것에 무슨 문제라도 있니?

M : My helmet feels too tight. It hurts my head.
헬멧이 너무 꽉 끼는 것 같아요. 머리가 아파요.

W : All right. I'll buy a bigger one that fits you.
알았어. 네게 맞는 더 큰 것을 사 줄게.

Why? 왜 정답일까?

지금 가지고 있는 헬멧에 문제가 있는지 묻는 여자의 말에 남자는 헬멧이 꽉 끼어 아프다고 한다(**My helmet feels too tight. It hurts my head.**). 따라서 여자의 응답으로 가장 적절한 것은 ② '알았어. 네게 맞는 더 큰 것을 사 줄게.(**All right. I'll buy a bigger one that fits you.**)'이다.

- helmet ⓝ 헬멧
- hurt ⓥ 아프게 하다, 아프다
- match ⓥ ~와 맞다, 어울리다
- tight ⓐ 꽉 끼는, 조이는
- Never mind. 신경 쓰지 마.

12 아들과 함께 직업 박람회에 가기로 하기 정답률 84% | 정답 ①

대화를 듣고, 여자의 마지막 말에 대한 남자의 응답으로 가장 적절한 것을 고르시오.

① Okay. Let's go and look at his career options together.
좋아요. 가서 아이가 직업으로 선택할 수 있는 것들을 함께 살펴보죠.
② Don't worry. There's no admission fee for the fair.
걱정 마요. 그 박람회는 입장료가 없어요.
③ Too bad. The career fair doesn't suit my purpose.
너무 안됐네요. 그 직업 박람회는 내 목적에 맞지 않아요.
④ Why not? He can join the firm as a freelancer.
왜 아니겠어요? 그는 프리랜서로 그 회사에 들어갈 수 있어요.
⑤ Awesome! Good luck with your new career.
굉장해요! 당신의 새로운 직업에 행운을 빌어요.

W : Honey, are you free on Saturday afternoon? Our son said he's going to a career fair and asked if we can come along.
여보, 토요일 오후에 시간 있어요? 우리 아들이 직업 박람회에 갈 거라면서, 우리가 함께 갈 수 있는지 물어봤어요.

M : Great, I'm free. I've been wondering what kinds of emerging careers might suit him.
좋아요, 난 시간이 있어요. 어느 새로 생긴 직업이 아이한테 잘 맞을지 궁금했어요.

W : Me, too. Then why don't we join him?
나도 그래요. 그럼 아이랑 같이 가는 게 어때요?

M : Okay. Let's go and look at his career options together.
좋아요. 가서 아이가 직업으로 선택할 수 있는 것들을 함께 살펴보죠.

Why? 왜 정답일까?

아들과 함께 직업 박람회에 가자고 제안하는(**Then why don't we join him?**) 여자의 말에 대한 남자의 응답으로 가장 적절한 것은 ① 좋아요. 가서 아이가 직업으로 선택할 수 있는 것들을 함께 살펴보죠.(**Okay. Let's go and look at his career options together.**)이다.

- career fair 직업 박람회
- emerging ⓐ 떠오르는, 생겨나는, 신흥의
- admission fee 참가비
- come along 함께 가다
- suit ⓥ ~에 적합하다
- freelancer ⓝ 프리랜서

13 단어 공부 조언 구하기 정답률 75% | 정답 ④

대화를 듣고, 남자의 마지막 말에 대한 여자의 응답으로 가장 적절한 것을 고르시오. [3점]

Woman: ______________________

① Not really. It's better to speak in simple sentences.
그렇지 않아. 간단한 문장으로 말하는 것이 더 나아.
② Yes. Try to memorize words by learning the root words.
그래. 어근 단어를 익히면서 단어를 암기하려고 노력해 봐.
③ That's right. I'm glad you've studied the proper examples.
그게 맞아. 네가 적절한 예를 공부했다니 기쁘구나.
④ Exactly. That way you can use the proper words in context.
바로 그거야. 그렇게 하면 문맥에 맞는 적절한 단어를 사용할 수 있어.
⑤ I don't think so. Always use an Italian-to-Italian dictionary.
난 그렇게 생각하지 않아. 항상 이탈리아 단어를 이탈리아어로 설명하는 사전을 써보렴.

M : Can I come in, Professor Rossini?
Rossini 교수님, 들어가도 될까요?

W : Of course. Come on in, Ben. What brings you here?
물론이지. 들어와, Ben. 어쩐 일이니?

M : I came to ask for advice on studying Italian.
이탈리아어 공부에 대한 조언을 구하러 왔어요.

W : Is there anything specific you're having trouble with?
네가 어려움을 겪는 뭔가 구체적인 부분이 있니?

M : Yes. I'm experiencing difficulty using words properly. Could I get some tips?
네. 단어를 제대로 사용하는 데 어려움을 겪고 있어요. 조언을 좀 받을 수 있을까요?

W : Sure. First, let me ask how you use your dictionary.
물론이지. 먼저, 네가 사전을 어떻게 사용하는지 좀 묻자.

M : Well, I use it to look up words that I don't know the meanings of.
음, 저는 사전을 이용해서 제가 의미를 모르는 단어를 찾아봐요.

W : Dictionaries provide example sentences for most words. Do you read them, too?
사전은 단어 대부분에 예문을 제공하지. 그것도 읽니?

M : No, I don't pay attention to the example sentences.
아니요, 전 예문에는 별로 주목하지 않아요.

W : Knowing the meaning of words is important, but you should also understand the context in which the words are properly used.
단어의 의미를 아는 게 중요하지만, 단어들이 적절하게 사용되는 맥락도 이해해야 해.

M : I see. So you're suggesting that I study the example sentences as well, right?
그렇군요. 그러니까 제가 예문도 공부해야 한다고 제안하시는 거죠?

W : Exactly. That way you can use the proper words in context.
바로 그거야. 그렇게 하면 문맥에 맞는 적절한 단어를 사용할 수 있어.

Why? 왜 정답일까?

사전을 찾아볼 때 예문은 주의 깊게 보지 않았다는 남자에게 여자는 문맥의 중요성을 설명해 주고, 이에 남자는 예문이 중요하다는 뜻인지 다시 한 번 확인하고 있다(**So you're suggesting that I study the example sentences as well, right?**). 따라서 여자의 응답으로 가장 적절한 것은 ④ '바로 그거야. 그렇게 하면 문맥에 맞는 적절한 단어를 사용할 수 있어.(**Exactly. That way you can use the proper words in context.**)'이다.

- What brings you here? 어쩐 일이니?
- have trouble with ~에 문제가 있다
- dictionary ⓝ 사전
- context ⓝ 맥락
- ask for ~을 요청하다
- properly ad 적절히, 알맞게
- look up (사전이나 책 등에서) ~을 찾아보다
- memorize ⓥ 암기하다, 외우다

14 아이를 캠핑에 초대해달라고 청하기 정답률 91% | 정답 ④

대화를 듣고, 여자의 마지막 말에 대한 남자의 응답으로 가장 적절한 것을 고르시오. [3점]

Man: ______________________

① I had the photos from our trip printed out yesterday.
우리 여행에서 찍은 사진을 어제 인화했어.
② The problem is that I already put out the campfire.
문제는 내가 모닥불을 이미 껐다는 거야.
③ I gladly accept his invitation to the fishing camp.
나는 그의 낚시 캠프 초대를 기꺼이 받아들일 거야.
④ Then I'll ask him to come with me on this trip.
그럼 내가 아이한테 이번 여행에 같이 가자고 해야겠구나.
⑤ Remember not to set up your tent near a river.
강 가까이에 텐트를 치지 말아야 한다는 것을 명심해.

W : Dad, I found these old photos of our camping trip from 25 years ago.
아빠, 전 25년 전 우리 캠핑 여행을 찍은 이 오래된 사진들을 찾았어요.

M : Oh, I remember this trip. You were about the same age as your son, Peter.
아, 이 여행 기억난다. 네가 네 아들인 Peter 또래였지.

W : Right. It was a really fun trip.
맞아요. 그것은 정말 재미있는 여행이었어요.

M : Yeah. I still go camping often, but that's the most memorable one.
그래. 나는 아직도 캠핑을 자주 가지만, 그것이 가장 기억에 남는 여행이야.

W : I agree. I want Peter to have that experience, too. But he always refuses to go.
동의해요. 저는 Peter도 그런 경험을 하면 좋겠어요. 하지만 그는 항상 안 가려고 해요.

M : Why doesn't he want to go camping?
아이가 왜 캠핑을 가고 싶어 하지 않지?

W : He just wants to stay home and spend all his time on his smartphone.
아이는 그저 집에 있으면서 내내 스마트폰을 하고 싶어 해요.

M : Don't worry. I'm sure Peter will like camping once he experiences how fun it is.
걱정 마라. Peter가 캠핑이 얼마나 재미있는지 일단 경험하면 분명 캠핑을 좋아할 거야.

W : You're probably right. Dad, when is the next time you're going camping?
그 말씀이 맞을 거예요. 아빠, 다음에 언제 캠핑을 가실 건가요?

M : This weekend. We should all go together.
이번 주말이란다. 우리 다 같이 가야지.

W : That'd be great. Peter might come as well if his favorite grandpa invites him.
그러면 좋죠. Peter도 자기가 가장 좋아하는 할아버지가 초대해주시면 올지도 몰라요.

M : Then I'll ask him to come with me on this trip.
그럼 내가 아이한테 이번 여행에 같이 가자고 해야겠구나.

Why? 왜 정답일까?

여자는 아버지인 남자와 함께 어린 시절 찍었던 캠핑 사진을 보며 추억을 되새기다가, 자신의 아들인 Peter는 캠핑에 잘 동행하려 하지 않는다며 아쉬움을 표현하고 있다. 대화 마지막에서, 여자는 남자에게 할아버지가 초대하면 아이가 캠핑에 따라나설지도 모른다고 말하고 있다(**Peter might come as well if his favorite grandpa invites him.**). 따라서 남자의 응답으로 가장 적절한 것은 ④ '그럼 내가 아이한테 이번 여행에 같이 가자고 해야겠구나.(**Then I'll ask him to come with me on this trip.**)'이다.

- about ad 약, 대략
- refuse ⓥ 거부하다
- put out (불을) 끄다
- set up a tent 텐트를 치다
- memorable ⓐ 기억에 남는
- print out 인쇄하다
- gladly ad 기쁘게

15 요양원에서 할 활동 계획하기 정답률 80% | 정답 ③

다음 상황 설명을 듣고, Katie가 Jacob에게 할 말로 가장 적절한 것을 고르시오. [3점]

Katie: ______________________

① You should check how many nursing homes there are.
넌 얼마나 많은 요양원이 있는지 확인해야 해.
② Why don't you reuse the activity you prepared last time?
네가 지난번에 준비했던 활동을 다시 사용해 보는 건 어떨까?
③ How about preparing multiple activities for your next visit?
다음 방문 때는 여러 활동을 준비하면 어때?

[문제편 p.182]

④ You need to gain more practical knowledge about nursing.
넌 간호 업무에 대해서 더 실용적인 지식을 얻어야 해.
⑤ You'd better speak to the residents of the neighborhood.
네가 이웃 주민들에게 말을 하는 것이 좋겠어.

M : Jacob just started volunteering at a nursing home and is planning his next visit.
Jacob은 요양원에서 자원봉사를 막 시작했고 다음 방문을 계획하고 있다.
He recalls that not every resident in the nursing home enjoyed the activity he had prepared last time.
그는 요양원의 모든 거주자가 자신이 지난번에 준비한 활동을 즐긴 것은 아니었다는 것을 기억한다.
To avoid this situation, he tries to find an activity that all residents in the nursing home can enjoy.
이러한 상황을 피하고자, 그는 요양원의 모든 거주자가 즐길 수 있는 활동을 찾으려 한다.
But he can't come up with one that everyone would like.
그러나 그는 모든 사람이 좋아할 만한 활동을 생각해 내지 못한다.
He asks his friend Katie for advice because she has lots of experience volunteering at a nursing home.
그는 친구 Katie가 요양원에서 자원봉사를 한 경험이 많기 때문에 그녀에게 조언을 구한다.
Katie thinks there's no single activity that can interest all the residents.
Katie는 모든 거주자들의 흥미를 끌 수 있는 딱 한 가지 활동은 없다고 생각한다.
So Katie wants to suggest to Jacob that next time he should plan more than one activity.
그래서 Katie는 Jacob에게 다음번에는 한 가지 이상의 활동을 계획해 보라고 제안하고 싶다.
In this situation, what would Katie most likely say to Jacob?
이런 상황에서, Katie는 Jacob에게 뭐라고 말하겠는가?

Katie : How about preparing multiple activities for your next visit?
다음 방문에는 여러 활동을 준비하면 어때?

Why? 왜 정답일까?

상황에 따르면 요양원 자원봉사 때 진행할 단체 활동을 생각 중인 Jacob은 봉사 경험이 많은 Katie에게 조언을 구하려 한다. Katie는 한 가지 활동으로 모두를 만족시키기는 어렵다고 생각하기 때문에, Jacob에게 여러 가지 활동을 계획해보면 어떨지 제안하려 한다(**So Katie wants to suggest to Jacob that next time he should plan more than one activity.**). 따라서 Katie가 Jacob에게 할 말로 가장 적절한 것은 ③ '다음 방문 때는 여러 활동을 준비하면 어때?(**How about preparing multiple activities for your next visit?**)'이다.

- **nursing home** 요양원
- **resident** ⓝ 거주민
- **multiple** ⓐ 여럿의, 다수의
- **recall** ⓥ 회상하다
- **reuse** ⓥ 다시 사용하다
- **practical** ⓐ 실용적인

16-17 인간 문명 발전에 기여한 금속

W : Hello, students.
안녕하세요, 학생 여러분.
Perhaps no material on earth has been more important in human history than metal.
아마도 지구상의 어떤 물질도 인류 역사에서 금속보다 더 중요하지 않았을 것입니다.
「Today, we're going to discuss the contribution of metals to the development of civilization.」 16번의 근거
오늘 우리는 금속이 문명 발전에 기여한 바에 관해 논하겠습니다.
「First, gold was considered the most valuable metal due to its beauty and scarcity.」
첫째, 금은 그 아름다움과 희소성 때문에 가장 가치 있는 금속으로 여겨졌습니다. 17번 ①의 근거 일치
Because of its visual appeal and ability to be easily shaped, it's been used to decorate religious places and objects.
시각적 매력과 쉽게 모양을 만들 수 있는 특성 때문에, 그것은 종교적인 장소와 사물을 장식하는 데 사용되었죠.
「Second, silver was mainly prized for being the shiniest of all metals.」 17번 ②의 근거 일치
둘째, 은은 주로 모든 금속 중 가장 빛나는 금속으로 귀하게 여겨졌습니다.
It's been one of the main forms of currency since it was the chief metal used for making coins.
그것은 동전을 만드는 데 사용된 주요 금속이었기 때문에 화폐의 주요한 형태 중 하나였습니다.
「Next, iron became widely used once humans discovered techniques to strengthen it.」
다음으로, 철은 인간이 그것을 강화하는 기술을 발견하자마자 널리 사용되었습니다. 17번 ③의 근거 일치
This metal was fashioned into tools that revolutionized farming, and later, machines that industrialized the world.
이 금속은 농업에 혁명을 일으킨 도구로, 나중에는 세계를 산업화시킨 기계로 만들어졌습니다.
「Finally, aluminum is the most abundant metal in the world and is also lightweight.」
마지막으로, 알루미늄은 세계에서 가장 풍부한 금속이며 또한 가볍습니다. 17번 ④의 근거 일치
That's why it's been essential to countless industries in modern society from automotive to aerospace to household products.
이런 이유로 그것은 자동차 부품에서 항공 우주 제품, 가정용품에 이르기까지 현대 사회의 수많은 산업에 필수적이었습니다.
Now, let's watch a short related video.
자, 그럼 관련된 짧은 영상을 보죠.

- **contribution** ⓝ 기여, 이바지
- **valuable** ⓐ 가치 있는
- **appeal** ⓝ 매력
- **religious** ⓐ 종교적인
- **currency** ⓝ 화폐
- **fashion** ⓥ (~로) 만들다
- **industrialize** ⓥ 산업화하다
- **countless** ⓐ 수많은
- **civilization** ⓝ 문명
- **scarcity** ⓝ 희소성
- **decorate** ⓥ 꾸미다, 장식하다
- **be prized for** ~로 귀하게 여겨지다
- **strengthen** ⓥ 강화하다
- **revolutionize** ⓥ ~에 혁명을 일으키다
- **abundant** ⓐ 풍부한, 많은
- **automotive** ⓝ 자동차 부품 ⓐ 자동차의

16 주제 파악 정답률 87% | 정답 ①

여자가 하는 말의 주제로 가장 적절한 것은?

✔ how metals advanced human civilization – 금속이 인간 문명을 진보시킨 방식
② how techniques applied to metals improved – 금속에 적용되는 기술이 향상된 방식
③ where most precious metals originated from – 대부분의 귀금속이 기원한 곳
④ why metals were used in the fashion industry – 금속이 패션 산업에 사용된 이유
⑤ why ancient civilizations competed for metals – 고대 문명이 금속을 얻기 위해 경쟁한 이유

Why? 왜 정답일까?

'**Today, we're going to discuss the contribution of metals to the development of civilization.**'에서 여자는 금속이 문명 발전에 기여한 바에 관해 살펴보겠다고 하므로, 여자가 하는 말의 주제로 가장 적절한 것은 ① '금속이 인간 문명을 진보시킨 방식(**how metals advanced human civilization**)'이다.

17 언급 유무 파악 정답률 98% | 정답 ⑤

언급된 금속이 아닌 것은?

① gold – 금 ② silver – 은 ③ iron – 철
④ aluminum – 알루미늄 ✔ nickel – 니켈

Why? 왜 정답일까?

담화에서 여자는 문명 발전에 기여한 금속의 예를 들기 위해 금, 은, 철, 알루미늄을 사례로 든다. 따라서 언급되지 않은 것은 ⑤ '니켈'이다.

Why? 왜 오답일까?

① '**First, gold was considered the most valuable metal due to its beauty and scarcity.**'에서 '금'이 언급되었다.
② '**Second, silver was mainly prized for being the shiniest of all metals.**'에서 '은'이 언급되었다.
③ '**Next, iron became widely used once humans discovered techniques to strengthen it.**'에서 '철'이 언급되었다.
④ '**Finally, aluminum is the most abundant metal in the world and is also lightweight.**'에서 '알루미늄'이 언급되었다.

31회

Dictation 31

문제편 183쪽

01 all grades to participate in the competition / slip away / participate to display your creativity
02 save the apple peels for me / effective for improving skin condition / moisturize our skin and enhance
03 world-class athletes / my instructions quickly and easily / consistently practiced made great improvements and ultimately
04 bear statue wearing the check pattern / two flowerpots in front of the cabin / on the tree branch
05 ordered enough ingredients / confirm the song list with / wrap wine glasses
06 vegetable sticks and sliced fruits / son and daughter will love it / two horseback riding tickets
07 attractions including Taekwondo performances that incorporate / study for your economics exam / to the airport
08 scheduled to shoot your school's graduation / calling to confirm the details / take to shoot the photos
09 a lecture on plant care methods / available through online purchase only / houseplant collection
10 looking for a hard cello case / ones we have in stock / interior material / seems difficult to take care of
11 My helmet feels too tight
12 wondering what kinds of emerging careers
13 experiencing difficulty using words properly / provide example sentences for most words / the context
14 same age as your son / memorable one / like camping once he experiences / might come as well if his favorite
15 enjoyed the activity he had prepared / can't come up with / experience volunteering at a nursing home
16-17 its beauty and scarcity / decorate religious places and objects / discovered techniques to strengthen it / automotive to aerospace to household products

[문제편 p.182]

32회 | 2022학년도 대학수학능력시험 고3

• 정답 •

01 ⑤ 02 ② 03 ① 04 ④ 05 ② 06 ④ 07 ① 08 ④ 09 ③ 10 ④ 11 ① 12 ② 13 ③ 14 ⑤ 15 ⑤ 16 ③ 17 ⑤

01 개 행동 훈련 센터 소개 정답률 96% | 정답 ⑤

다음을 듣고, 여자가 하는 말의 목적으로 가장 적절한 것을 고르시오.

① 조련사 자격증 취득 방법을 설명하려고
② 동물 병원 확장 이전을 공지하려고
③ 새로 출시된 개 사료를 소개하려고
④ 반려동물 입양 절차를 안내하려고
⑤ 개 훈련 센터를 홍보하려고

W : Hello, dog lovers.
안녕하세요, 애견가 여러분.
Does your dog chew up your shoes or bark for no reason at times?
가끔 여러분의 개가 신발을 씹거나 아무 이유 없이 짖나요?
Is it hard to control your dog during walks?
산책하는 동안 개를 통제하기가 어려운가요?
You no longer have to worry.
더 이상 걱정하실 필요 없습니다.
We'll help you solve these problems.
저희가 이 문제를 해결하도록 도와드릴게요.
At the Chester Dog Training Center, we have five professional certified trainers who will improve your dog's behavior.
Chester Dog Training Center에 개의 행동을 개선해줄 전문 자격증을 갖춘 트레이너 다섯 명이 있습니다.
We also teach you how to understand your dog and what to do when it misbehaves.
저희는 또한 여러분이 개를 이해하고 개가 잘못 행동할 때 어떻게 해야 하는지 알려드립니다.
Leave it to the Chester Dog Training Center.
Chester Dog Training Center에 맡겨 주세요.
We'll train your dog to become a well-behaved pet.
여러분의 개를 얌전한 반려동물로 훈련시켜 드립니다.
Call us at 234-555-3647 or visit our website at www.chesterdogs.com.
234-555-3647로 저희에게 전화 주시거나 저희 웹 사이트인 www.chesterdogs.com을 찾아주세요.

Why? 왜 정답일까?

'At the Chester Dog Training Center, ~' 이후로 여자는 개의 행동 개선에 도움을 줄 훈련 센터를 소개하고 있다. 따라서 여자가 하는 말의 목적으로 가장 적절한 것은 ⑤ '개 훈련 센터를 홍보하려고'이다.

- chew up 씹다, 엉망으로 부수다
- bark ⓥ (개가) 짖다
- certified ⓐ 자격증을 갖춘
- behavior ⓝ 행동, 태도
- misbehave ⓥ 못된 짓을 하다
- train ⓥ (사람·짐승을) 훈련하다, 몸을 단련하다
- well-behaved ⓐ 얌전한, 예의 바른

02 여행 때 할 일을 너무 많이 계획하지 말기 정답률 96% | 정답 ②

대화를 듣고, 남자의 의견으로 가장 적절한 것을 고르시오.

① 여행 전에 합리적으로 예산을 계획해야 한다.
② 여행 가서 할 것을 너무 많이 계획하면 안 된다.
③ 인생에서 자신의 원칙을 고수하는 것이 중요하다.
④ 여행은 사고의 폭을 확장시켜 사람을 성장하게 한다.
⑤ 보호자 없이 학생끼리 여행하는 것은 안전하지 않다.

M : Monica. Have you made plans for your trip to Busan?
Monica, 부산 여행 계획은 세웠어?
W : Yes, Dad. I'm going to the beach and visiting an aquarium in the morning. Then I'll eat lunch at a fish market and go hiking.
네, 아빠. 저는 아침에 해변에 갔다가 수족관을 방문할 거예요. 그러고 나서 수산시장에서 점심을 먹고 하이킹을 할 거예요.
M : Hold on! That sounds quite demanding.
잠깐만! 너무 부담스러울 것 같구나.
W : You know, it's my first trip after starting college.
아시다시피, 이건 대학에 들어가고 첫 여행이잖아요.
M : I understand, but I think you shouldn't plan too many things to do for a trip.
나도 알지만, 여행 가서 할 것을 너무 많이 계획해선 안 된다고 생각해.
W : Well, I only have one day, and I want to experience as much as possible.
음, 전 하루밖에 없으니 최대한 많이 경험하고 싶어요.
M : You'll be worn out if you stick to your plan. Also, consider the time it takes to move to each place.
그 계획을 따르면 완전히 지쳐버릴 거야. 추가로, 장소마다 이동하는 데 걸리는 시간도 고려하렴.
W : I guess you're right. And there could be a long waiting line at some places.
아빠 말씀이 맞는 것 같아요. 그리고 몇몇 장소에는 대기자가 많을 수도 있어요.
M : Right. That's why you shouldn't fill your trip plan with too many things.
맞아. 그래서 네 여행 계획을 너무 많은 것들로 채우면 안 되는 거란다.
W : Okay. I'll revise my plan.
알겠어요. 제 계획을 수정할게요.

Why? 왜 정답일까?

여자의 부산 여행 계획을 들은 남자는 한 번의 여행에 너무 많은 것을 계획하면 안 된다고(~ I think you shouldn't plan too many things to do for a trip.) 조언하고 있다. 따라서 남자의 의견으로 가장 적절한 것은 ② '여행 가서 할 것을 너무 많이 계획하면 안 된다.'이다.

- demanding ⓐ 부담스러운
- stick to ~을 고수하다, 지키다
- revise ⓥ 수정하다

03 제빵사와의 라디오 인터뷰 정답률 95% | 정답 ①

대화를 듣고, 두 사람의 관계를 가장 잘 나타낸 것을 고르시오.

① 라디오 쇼 진행자 – 제빵사
② 리포터 – 과수원 주인
③ 광고주 – 요리사
④ 방송 작가 – 경제학자
⑤ 유통업자 – 농부

W : Hello, Mr. Newton. Welcome to the *Delicacies Show*.
안녕하세요, Newton 씨. *Delicacies Show*에 오신 것을 환영합니다.
M : Thanks for inviting me.
초대해 주셔서 고마워요.
W : I want to first start talking about your famous apple bread. Can you briefly introduce it to our radio show listeners?
당신의 유명한 사과 빵에 관해서 먼저 이야기를 시작하고 싶어요. 우리 라디오 청취자 분들에게 간단히 소개해 주실래요?
M : Sure. Instead of sugar, I use home-made apple sauce when I bake bread.
네, 전 빵을 구울 때 설탕 대신 직접 만든 사과 소스를 씁니다.
W : That's interesting. What inspired the recipe?
흥미롭네요. 레시피 영감을 어떻게 받으셨나요?
M : Well, one day, I saw a news report about local apple farmers. They were experiencing difficulty due to decreasing apple consumption.
음, 어느 날 전 지역 사과 농부들에 대한 뉴스를 보았어요. 그들은 사과 소비가 줄어서 어려움을 겪고 있었죠.
W : So you created this new recipe to help the local economy.
그래서 지역 경제를 돕기 위해 이 새로운 레시피를 만드신 거군요.
M : Yes. I also thought that the apple's sweetness could add a special flavor.
네. 그리고 전 사과의 단맛이 특별한 풍미를 더해줄 수 있다고 생각했어요.
W : Sounds delicious. I'll definitely go to your bakery and try some of your bread.
맛있을 것 같네요. 당신의 빵집에 꼭 가서 맛을 좀 보고 싶어요.
M : Actually, I brought some for you and your radio show staff.
사실, 당신과 라디오 스태프분들을 위해 좀 가져왔어요.
W : Oh, thank you. We'll be back after a commercial break.
오, 고맙습니다. 광고 듣고 다시 올게요.

Why? 왜 정답일까?

'Can you briefly introduce it to our radio show listeners?', 'Actually, I brought some for you and your radio show staff.'에서 여자가 라디오 쇼 진행자임을, 'Instead of sugar, I use home-made apple sauce when I bake bread.', 'I'll definitely go to your bakery and try some of your bread.'에서 남자가 제빵사임을 알 수 있다. 따라서 두 사람의 관계로 가장 적절한 것은 ① '라디오 쇼 진행자 – 제빵사'이다.

- delicacy ⓝ 맛있는 것, 별미
- briefly ⓐⓓ 간단하게
- consumption ⓝ 소비
- flavor ⓝ 풍미
- definitely ⓐⓓ 반드시, 꼭

04 교환 학생 환영 행사 준비하기 정답률 96% | 정답 ④

대화를 듣고, 그림에서 대화의 내용과 일치하지 않는 것을 고르시오.

M : Wow, Ms. Peters! It looks like everything is ready for the exchange student welcoming ceremony.
와, Peters 선생님! 교환 학생 환영 행사를 위해 모든 게 준비된 것 같네요.
W : Almost, Mr. Smith. What do you think?
거의 다 되었어요, Smith 선생님. 어때요?
M : It looks great. 「There's a basket beside the stairs.」 ①의 근거 일치 What is it for?
근사해 보이네요. 계단 옆에 바구니가 있군요. 왜 있는 건가요?
W : We're going to put flowers in it for the exchange students.
교환 학생들을 위해 꽃을 넣어둘 거예요.
M : That'll be nice. 「I like the striped tablecloth on the table.」 ②의 근거 일치 It makes the table look fancy.
멋지겠네요. 탁자 위의 줄무늬 식탁보가 마음에 들어요. 탁자가 세련돼 보이게 하네요.
W : Yeah, I'm going to put water bottles there. 「What do you think about the balloons next to the welcome banner?」 ③의 근거 일치
그렇죠, 저기에 물병을 놔두려고요. 환영 현수막 옆에 있는 풍선은 어때요?
M : They really brighten up the stage. 「Oh, look at the bear on the flag.」 ④의 근거 불일치 It's cute.
무대를 정말 환하게 해주네요. 오, 깃발에 있는 곰 좀 보세요. 귀엽네요.
W : Yes. It's the symbol of the exchange students' school.
네, 교환 학생들의 학교 상징이에요.
M : I see. 「And you set up two microphones.」 ⑤의 근거 일치
그렇군요. 그리고 마이크도 두 대 설치했네요.
W : It's because there'll be two MCs.
MC가 두 명일 거라서 그래요.
M : Good idea. Everything looks perfect.
좋아요. 모든 것이 완벽해 보이네요.

Why? 왜 정답일까?

대화에서 깃발에 곰이 그려져 있다(Oh, look at the bear on the flag.)고 하는데, 그림 속 깃발에는 돌고래가 그려져 있다. 따라서 그림에서 대화의 내용과 일치하지 않는 것은 ④이다.

- exchange student 교환 학생
- brighten up 환하게 하다, 밝히다

[문제편 p.187]

05 동아리 사진 촬영 준비하기

정답률 96% | 정답 ②

대화를 듣고, 남자가 할 일로 가장 적절한 것을 고르시오.

① 리본 가져오기
② 선글라스 주문하기
③ 사진사 섭외하기
④ 설문 조사 실시하기
⑤ 졸업 연설문 작성하기

W : Brian. I'm so excited about our school club photo this Friday.
Brian, 난 이번 주 금요일 우리 학교 동아리 사진이 몹시 기대돼.
M : Me, too. The photo will be included in our graduation album. Let's check our preparations for it.
나도야. 그 사진은 우리 졸업앨범에 실릴 거야. 우리가 준비한 걸 살펴보자.
W : All right. I'm going to decorate our club's room with ribbons.
알겠어. 난 우리 동아리 방을 리본으로 꾸밀 거야.
M : You said you'll bring some from home, right?
집에서 좀 가져올 거라고 했었지, 그렇지?
W : Yes. When is the photographer coming?
응. 사진사가 언제 오지?
M : The photographer is coming after lunch.
사진사는 점심 시간 후에 올 거야.
W : Great. That gives us time to get ready. You know I surveyed our club members about what to wear for the photo.
좋아. 그럼 준비할 시간이 있겠네. 너도 알다시피 난 동아리 회원들한테 사진을 위해 어떤 복장을 할지 조사했어.
M : Right. What were the results?
그렇지. 결과가 어땠어?
W : Most of our members wanted to wear heart-shaped sunglasses. Now all that's left is to buy them for our members.
회원 대부분이 하트 모양 선글라스를 쓰고 싶어 했어. 이제 남은 것은 우리 회원들을 위해 그걸 사는 것뿐이야.
M : I know a good online store. I can order the sunglasses.
내가 괜찮은 온라인 매장을 알아. 내가 선글라스를 주문할 수 있어.
W : Could you? That'll be great.
그래줄래? 그럼 좋지.
M : No problem. I'll take care of that.
문제 없어. 내가 처리할게.

Why? 왜 정답일까?

남자와 함께 동아리 사진 촬영을 준비 중이던 여자는 회원들이 쓸 하트 모양 선글라스만 주문하면 준비가 끝난다고 말하고, 남자는 이에 자신이 주문하겠다고 말한다(**I can order the sunglasses.**). 따라서 남자가 할 일로 가장 적절한 것은 ② '선글라스 주문하기'이다.

- preparation ⓝ 준비
- survey ⓥ 조사하다

06 포장 음식 주문하기

정답률 94% | 정답 ④

대화를 듣고, 여자가 지불할 금액을 고르시오. [3점]

① $36 ② $45 ③ $50 ④ $54 ⑤ $60

M : Welcome to Daisy Valley Restaurant.
Daisy Valley 식당에 오신 것을 환영합니다.
W : Hi. I'd like to order some food to go. How much is the shrimp pasta and the chicken salad?
안녕하세요. 포장 음식 좀 주문하려고요. 새우 파스타랑 치킨 샐러드가 얼마인가요?
M : The shrimp pasta is $20, and the chicken salad is $10.
새우 파스타는 20달러이고, 치킨 샐러드는 10달러입니다.
W : I'll take two shrimp pastas and one chicken salad, please.
새우 파스타 둘이랑 치킨 샐러드 하나 주세요.
M : Sure. Would you like some dessert, too?
알겠습니다. 디저트도 주문하시겠어요?
W : Yes. What do you recommend?
네. 뭘 추천해 주시겠어요?
M : The mini cheese cake is one of the best sellers in our restaurant. It's $5 each.
미니 치즈 케이크가 저희 식당에서 가장 잘 나가는 메뉴 중 하나입니다. 하나에 5달러입니다.
W : Great! I'll order two of them.
좋아요! 두 개 주문할게요.
M : Okay. Let me confirm your order. Two shrimp pastas, one chicken salad, and two mini cheese cakes. Is that correct?
알겠습니다. 주문 확인해드리겠습니다. 새우 파스타 둘, 치킨 샐러드 하나, 그리고 미니 치즈 케이크 두 개, 맞으시죠?
W : Yes. And I have a birthday coupon here. Can I use it?
네. 그리고 전 생일 쿠폰이 있어요. 사용할 수 있나요?
M : Let me see. *[Pause]* Yes. You can get a 10% discount off the total.
확인해보겠습니다. *[잠시 멈춤]* 네. 총 가격에서 10퍼센트를 할인받으시게 됩니다.
W : Terrific. I'll use this coupon. Here's my credit card.
아주 좋아요. 이 쿠폰 쓸게요. 여기 제 신용 카드요.

Why? 왜 정답일까?

대화에 따르면 여자는 20달러짜리 새우 파스타 2인분, 10달러짜리 치킨 샐러드 1인분, 5달러짜리 미니 치즈 케이크를 두 개 주문한 후, 총 가격에서 10퍼센트를 할인받았다. 이를 식으로 나타내면 '$(20\times2+10+5\times2)\times0.9=54$'이므로, 여자가 지불할 금액은 ④ '$54'이다.

- food to go 포장 음식
- shrimp ⓝ 새우
- confirm ⓥ (맞다는 것을) 확인하다

07 탁구 연습을 갈 수 없는 이유

정답률 96% | 정답 ①

대화를 듣고, 남자가 탁구 연습을 할 수 없는 이유를 고르시오.

① 학교 도서관에 자원봉사를 하러 가야 해서
② 과학 퀴즈를 위한 공부를 해야 해서
③ 연극부 모임에 참가해야 해서
④ 역사 숙제를 제출해야 해서
⑤ 어깨에 통증이 있어서

W : Hey, Mike. How's your shoulder? Are you still in pain?
안녕, Mike. 어깨는 어때? 여전히 아파?
M : No, I feel totally fine, Emily. I should be ready for the table tennis tournament.
아니, 이제 완전히 괜찮아, Emily. 탁구 시합을 준비해야지.
W : That's good to hear. Then do you want to practice with me now?
그렇다니 다행이네. 그럼 나랑 지금 연습할래?
M : I'm sorry but I can't right now.
미안한데 지금은 안 돼.
W : Why not? Do you have to work on your history homework?
왜? 역사 숙제 해야 해?
M : No, I already submitted it to Mr. Jackson.
아니, 그건 이미 Jackson 선생님께 제출했어.
W : Oh, then I guess you have to study for the science quiz, right?
오, 그럼 과학 퀴즈 공부해야 하나 보구나, 그렇지?
M : I think I'm ready for it. Actually, I'm on my way to volunteer at the school library.
그건 준비가 다 된 것 같아. 사실, 난 학교 도서관에 자원봉사를 하러 가는 길이야.
W : I see. Then, don't forget about our drama club meeting tomorrow.
그렇구나. 그럼, 내일 우리 연극 동아리 모임 잊지 마.
M : Of course not. See you there.
당연하지. 거기서 봐.

Why? 왜 정답일까?

남자는 학교 도서관에 자원봉사를 하러 가는 길이어서(**Actually, I'm on my way to volunteer at the school library.**) 여자와 함께 탁구 연습을 하러 갈 수 없다고 한다. 따라서 남자가 탁구 연습을 할 수 없는 이유로 가장 적절한 것은 ① '학교 도서관에 자원봉사를 하러 가야 해서'이다.

- table tennis 탁구
- submit ⓥ 제출하다
- on one's way to ~하러 가는 길이다

32회

08 어린이 독서 강좌 알려주기

정답률 96% | 정답 ④

대화를 듣고, Little Readers' Class에 관해 언급되지 않은 것을 고르시오.

① 장소 ② 시간 ③ 대상 연령
④ 모집 인원 ⑤ 등록 방법

M : Christine, I heard your daughter Jennifer loves reading. Unfortunately, my daughter doesn't.
Christine, 당신의 딸 Jennifer는 독서를 좋아한다고 들었어요. 안타깝게도 우리 딸은 안 그래요.
W : Actually, Jennifer didn't enjoy reading until she took the Little Readers' Class. It provides various fun reading activities.
사실, Jennifer는 Little Readers' Class를 수강하기 전까지 독서를 즐기지 않았었어요. 여기서 여러 가지 재미있는 독서 활동을 제공해요.
M : Really? It might be good for my daughter, too. Where's it held?
정말요? 우리 딸한테도 괜찮을지도 모르겠네요. 어디서 열리나요?
W : 「It's held at the Stonefield Library.」 ①의 근거 일치 I have a picture of the flyer somewhere in my phone. *[Pause]* Here.
Stonefield 도서관에서 열려요. 제 전화 어딘가에 전단지 사진이 있어요. *[잠시 멈춤]* 여기요.
M : Oh. 「The class is from 4 p.m. to 5 p.m. every Monday.」 ②의 근거 일치
오. 매주 월요일 오후 4시부터 5시까지군요.
W : Is that time okay for her?
딸아이한테 괜찮은 시간인가요?
M : Yeah, she's free on Monday afternoons.
네, 아이는 월요일 오후에는 시간이 있어요.
W : Great. 「The class is for children ages seven to nine.」 ③의 근거 일치 Your daughter is eight years old, right?
좋네요. 이 수업은 7세부터 9세까지의 아이들 대상이에요. 당신의 딸은 여덟 살이죠, 그렇죠?
M : Yes, she can take it. 「So, to register, I should send an email to the address on the flyer.」 ⑤의 근거 일치
네, 들을 수 있겠어요. 그럼, 등록하려면 전단지에 있는 주소로 이메일을 보내야 하는군요.
W : That's right. I hope the class gets your daughter into reading.
맞아요. 이 수업으로 당신의 딸이 독서에 흥미를 가지길 바라요.

Why? 왜 정답일까?

대화에서 남자와 여자는 **Little Readers' Class**의 장소, 시간, 대상 연령, 등록 방법을 언급하였다. 따라서 언급되지 않은 것은 ④ '모집 인원'이다.

Why? 왜 오답일까?

① '**It's held at the Stonefield Library.**'에서 '장소'가 언급되었다.
② '**The class is from 4 p.m. to 5 p.m. every Monday.**'에서 '시간'이 언급되었다.
③ '**The class is for children ages seven to nine.**'에서 '대상 연령'이 언급되었다.
⑤ '**So, to register, I should send an email to the address on the flyer.**'에서 '등록 방법'이 언급되었다.

- flyer ⓝ 전단지
- get A into B A가 B에 흥미를 갖게 하다

09 가족이 참여할 수 있는 과학 축제 소개

정답률 90% | 정답 ③

2021 Family Science Festival에 관한 다음 내용을 듣고, 일치하지 않는 것을 고르시오.

① 12월 7일부터 일주일 동안 진행된다.
② 8개의 프로그램이 제공될 것이다.
③ 어린이 과학 잡지를 판매할 것이다.
④ 11세 미만의 어린이들은 성인을 동반해야 한다.
⑤ 참가를 위해 미리 등록해야 한다.

M : Hello, WBPR listeners.
안녕하세요, WBPR 청취자 여러분.
Are you looking for a chance to enjoy quality family time?
양질의 가족 시간을 보낼 기회를 찾고 계신가요?
Then, we invite you to the 2021 Family Science Festival.
그럼, 여러분을 2021 Family Science Festival에 초대합니다.
「It starts on December 7th and runs for one week at the Bermont Science Museum located near City Hall.」 ①의 근거 일치

[문제편 p.187]

이것은 시청 근처에 위치한 Bermont Science Museum에서 12월 7일부터 1주일 동안 진행됩니다.
「Eight programs will be offered for parents and children to enjoy together, including robot building and VR simulations.」 ②의 근거 일치
로봇 만들기와 VR 시뮬레이션을 포함해서, 부모와 아이가 함께 즐길 수 있는 8개의 프로그램이 제공될 것입니다.
「We'll also give out a children's science magazine for free.」 ③의 근거 불일치
또한 어린이 과학 잡지도 무료 배포할 것입니다.
This event is open to anyone, but remember that 「all children under age 11 must be accompanied by an adult.」 ④의 근거 일치
이 행사는 누구나 대상으로 하지만, 11세 미만의 모든 어린이는 성인을 동반해야 합니다.
There's no admission fee, but 「to participate, you must register in advance.」 ⑤의 근거 일치
입장료는 없지만, 참가하려면 미리 등록해 주세요.
Come and learn about the exciting world of science with your family.
오셔서 가족들과 함께 신나는 과학의 세계를 배워 보세요.
For more information, visit our website, www.wbpr.com.
더 많은 정보를 얻으시려면, 저희 웹 사이트인 www.wbpr.com을 방문하세요.

Why? 왜 정답일까?

'We'll also give out a children's science magazine for free.'에서 어린이 과학 잡지는 무료 배포된다고 하므로, 2021 Family Science Festival에 관한 내용과 일치하지 않는 것은 ③ '어린이 과학 잡지를 판매할 것이다.'이다.

Why? 왜 오답일까?

① 'It starts on December 7th and runs for one week ~'의 내용과 일치한다.
② 'Eight programs will be offered ~'의 내용과 일치한다.
④ '~ children under age 11 must be accompanied by an adult.'의 내용과 일치한다.
⑤ '~ to participate, you must register in advance.'의 내용과 일치한다.

- give out 나눠주다, 배포하다
- accompany ⓥ 동반하다

10 스터디룸 예약하기

정답률 94% | 정답 ④

다음 표를 보면서 대화를 듣고, 두 사람이 예약할 스터디룸을 고르시오.

Study Rooms

	Room	Capacity (persons)	Available Times	Price (per hour)	Projector
①	A	2-3	9 a.m. – 11 a.m.	$10	×
②	B	4-6	9 a.m. – 11 a.m.	$16	○
③	C	4-6	2 p.m. – 4 p.m.	$14	×
✔	D	6-8	2 p.m. – 4 p.m.	$19	○
⑤	E	6-9	4 p.m. – 6 p.m.	$21	×

M : Megan, did you reserve a study room for our group project meeting tomorrow?
Megan, 너 내일 우리 모둠 프로젝트 모임을 위한 스터디룸을 예약했어?
W : I'm looking at a website to book a room. Let's book it together.
웹 사이트에서 방을 예약하려고 보고 있어. 같이 예약하자.
M : Sure. *[Pause]* Oh, only these rooms are available.
그래. *[잠시 멈춤]* 오, 이 방들만 이용 가능하구나.
W : Yeah. Hmm, this one is too small for us.
응. 흠, 이 방은 우리한테 너무 작네.
M : Right. 「We need a room big enough to accommodate six of us.」 근거1 Capacity 조건
맞아. 우리 여섯 명을 충분히 수용할 만한 크기의 방이 필요해.
W : Okay. 「Now, let's look at the times. We all agreed to meet after 1 p.m., right?」
그래. 이제 시간을 보자. 우리 모두 오후 1시 이후에 만나는 데 동의했어, 그렇지? 근거2 Available Times 조건
M : Yes. Then let's skip this one.
응. 그러니 이건 건너뛰자.
W : 「How much can we spend on the study room?
우리가 스터디룸에 돈을 얼마나 쓸 수 있지?
M : Since we're meeting for two hours, I don't think we can spend more than $20 per hour.」 It's beyond our budget. 근거3 Price 조건
우린 두 시간 동안 만나니까, 시간당 20달러 이상은 쓸 수 없을 것 같아. 우리 예산을 넘어.
W : Then, there are two options left. 「Should we choose a study room with a projector?
그럼, 두 가지 선택권이 남네. 프로젝터가 있는 스터디룸을 골라야 할까? 근거4 Projector 조건
M : Absolutely.」 We'll need it to practice for our presentation.
물론이지. 발표를 연습하려면 필요할 거야.
W : Then let's reserve this one.
그럼 여기로 예약하자.

Why? 왜 정답일까?

대화에 따르면 남자와 여자는 6인을 수용 가능하면서, 오후 1시 이후에 이용할 수 있고, 시간당 가격이 20달러를 넘지 않으며, 프로젝터가 있는 스터디룸을 잡으려고 한다. 따라서 두 사람이 예약할 스터디룸은 ④ 'D'이다.

- reserve ⓥ 예약하다
- accommodate ⓥ (공간에 인원을) 수용하다
- beyond one's budget 예산을 초과하는

11 산책 나가자고 제안하기

정답률 92% | 정답 ①

대화를 듣고, 여자의 마지막 말에 대한 남자의 응답으로 가장 적절한 것을 고르시오.

✔ Just give me about ten minutes. – 10분 정도만 줘요.
② It took an hour for us to get back home. – 우리가 집으로 돌아오는 데 한 시간이 걸렸어요.
③ I think you need to focus on your work. – 당신은 일에 집중해야 할 것 같아요.
④ It was nice of you to invite my co-workers. – 내 동료들을 초대해주다니 당신은 친절했어요.
⑤ Call me when you finish sending the email. – 이메일을 다 보내면 전화해 줘요.

W : Honey, I'm going out for a walk. Do you want to join me?
여보, 나 산책 나가요. 당신도 같이 갈래요?
M : Sure. But can you wait for a moment? I have to send an email to one of my co-workers right now.
물론이죠. 그런데 잠깐 기다려 줄래요? 지금 동료 중 한 명한테 이메일을 보내야 해요.
W : No problem. How long do you think it'll take?
문제 없어요. 얼마나 걸릴 것 같아요?
M : Just give me about ten minutes.
10분 정도만 줘요.

Why? 왜 정답일까?

산책을 나가기 전 동료에게 이메일만 보내겠다는 남자에게 여자는 시간이 얼마나 소요될 것 같은지 물어보고 있다(How long do you think it'll take?)이다. 따라서 남자의 응답으로 가장 적절한 것은 ① '10분 정도만 줘요.'이다.

- go out for a walk 산책 가다
- co-worker ⓝ 동료

12 카메라 찾으러 가기 전 확인 전화하기

정답률 83% | 정답 ②

대화를 듣고, 남자의 마지막 말에 대한 여자의 응답으로 가장 적절한 것을 고르시오.

① Excellent. I like the camera you bought for me. – 아주 좋아요. 당신이 제게 사준 카메라가 마음에 들어요.
✔ Good. I'll stop by and get it on my way home. – 알겠습니다. 집에 가는 길에 들러서 가져갈게요.
③ Never mind. I'll drop off the camera tomorrow. – 신경 쓰지 마세요. 내일 카메라를 맡길게요.
④ I see. Thanks for taking those pictures of me. – 그렇군요. 제 사진을 찍어주셔서 고맙습니다.
⑤ No way. That's too expensive for the repair. – 그럴 리 없어요. 수리비로 너무 비싸요.

[Telephone rings.]
[전화벨이 울린다.]
M : Hello, this is Bob's Camera Shop.
여보세요, Bob's Camera Shop입니다.
W : Hi, this is Clara Patterson. I'm calling to see if I can pick up my camera today.
안녕하세요, 저는 Clara Patterson입니다. 오늘 제 카메라를 찾으러 가도 되는지 알아보려고 연락드렸어요.
M : Let me check. *[Clicking sound]* Yes. I've finished repairing your camera. It's ready to go.
확인해 보겠습니다. *[클릭하는 소리]* 네, 고객님의 카메라 수리가 끝났습니다. 가져가셔도 됩니다.
W : Good. I'll stop by and get it on my way home.
알겠습니다. 집에 가는 길에 들러서 가져갈게요.

Why? 왜 정답일까?

카메라를 찾아갈 수 있는지 확인하려 전화했다는 여자의 말에 남자는 카메라 수리가 끝나서 찾아가도 된다(I've finished repairing your camera. It's ready to go.)고 답변한다. 따라서 여자의 응답으로 가장 적절한 것은 ② '알겠습니다. 집에 가는 길에 들러서 가져갈게요.'이다.

- pick up (맡겼던 물건을) 찾아오다, (사람을 차로) 태워오다
- stop by ~에 들르다
- drop off (수선 등을 위해 물건을) 맡기다
- repair ⓝ 수리, 보수

13 혼자만의 시간 갖도록 조언하기

정답률 88% | 정답 ③

대화를 듣고, 여자의 마지막 말에 대한 남자의 응답으로 가장 적절한 것을 고르시오. [3점]

Man: ______________________

① No worries. Stress is not always as bad as you think.
걱정 마요. 스트레스는 당신이 생각하는 것만큼 늘 나쁜 것은 아니에요.
② Don't forget to bring a charger whenever you go out.
외출할 때면 늘 충전기를 챙기는 것을 잊지 마요.
✔ Great. That'll be a good way to take time for yourself.
좋네요. 그게 당신이 혼자 시간을 보낼 수 있는 좋은 방법이 될 거예요.
④ I think working out too much will burn all your energy.
운동을 너무 많이 하면 에너지가 전부 소모되는 것 같아요.
⑤ Fantastic. Let's enjoy ourselves at the exhibition with the kids.
환상적이에요. 아이들과 함께 즐겁게 전시회를 보죠.

W : Honey, I'm home.
여보, 나 왔어요.
M : Is everything all right? You seem low on energy.
괜찮은 거예요? 힘이 없어 보여요.
W : I am. I'm pretty burnt out.
맞아요. 난 너무 지쳤어요.
M : It's no wonder. You've been so stressed out from work these days.
그런 것도 당연해요. 요새 직장에서 스트레스 너무 많이 받았잖아요.
W : Yeah, I can't remember the last time that I really got to enjoy myself.
네, 내가 언제 마지막으로 정말 즐겁게 보냈는지 기억도 나지 않아요.
M : You need to recharge your batteries. Why don't you spend some time alone this weekend?
배터리를 충전해야겠군요. 이번 주말에 혼자 시간을 좀 보내는 게 어때요?
W : Maybe you're right. I might need my own personal time.
당신 말이 맞아요. 난 나만의 개인적인 시간이 필요한지도 몰라요.
M : Yes. And don't worry about the kids. I'll take care of them.
그래요. 그리고 아이들은 걱정하지 말아요. 내가 챙길게요.
W : Sounds good. Then let me think about what I can do.
좋네요. 그럼 내가 뭘할 수 있는지 생각해 볼게요.
M : You can go to the theater, ride your bike along the river, or do whatever makes you feel happy.
영화를 보러 가도 되고, 강변에서 자전거를 타도 되고, 뭐든 당신이 행복해지는 걸 하면 돼요.
W : Well, there's an exhibition that I've been interested in.
음, 내가 관심 있었던 전시가 있어요.
M : Great. That'll be a good way to take time for yourself.
좋네요. 그게 당신이 혼자 시간을 보낼 수 있는 좋은 방법이 될 거예요.

Why? 왜 정답일까?

일 때문에 지친 여자에게 남자는 혼자만의 시간을 보내볼 것을 권하며, 무엇이든 하면 행복해지는 일을 해보라고 조언한다. 이에 여자는 자신이 관심을 가졌던 전시가 있다(Well, there's an exhibition that I've been interested in.)고 이야기하므로, 남자의 응답으로 가장 적절한 것은 ③ '좋네요. 그게 당신이 혼자 시간을 보낼 수 있는 좋은 방법이 될 거예요.'이다.

- low on energy 힘이 없는, 에너지가 부족한
- burnt out 극도로 피로한
- stressed out 스트레스를 받는
- enjoy oneself 즐기다, 즐겁게 보내다
- exhibition ⓝ 전시
- work out 운동하다

[문제편 p.188]

14 방을 바꿔달라고 요청하기
정답률 91% | 정답 ⑤

대화를 듣고, 남자의 마지막 말에 대한 여자의 응답으로 가장 적절한 것을 고르시오.

Woman: ______________________

① Please check it again. The hotel can't be fully booked.
다시 확인해 주세요. 호텔 예약이 다 찼을 리 없어요.
② Too bad. I should've checked out as early as possible.
안됐네요. 제가 최대한 일찍 확인했어야 했어요.
③ Sure. I'm very satisfied with your cleaning service.
물론이죠. 청소 서비스에 굉장히 만족해요.
④ I'm sorry. You can't switch your room with mine.
죄송합니다. 제 방과 당신의 방을 바꿀 수는 없어요.
✔ Perfect. That's high enough to avoid the smell.
아주 좋아요. 냄새를 피할 수 있을 만큼 높네요.

[Telephone rings.]
[전화벨이 울린다.]

M : Front desk. How may I help you?
프런트입니다. 무엇을 도와드릴까요?

W : I'm in Room 201. I specifically booked a non-smoking room, but I smell cigarette smoke in my room.
전 201호 객실에 있는데요. 특별히 금연실을 예약했었는데, 제 방에서 담배 냄새가 나요.

M : We're sorry about that. Let me check that for you. *[Typing sound]* You're Wendy Parker, right?
죄송합니다. 제가 확인해 드리겠습니다. *[타이핑하는 소리]* Wendy Parker 님, 맞으시죠?

W : Yes, that's correct.
네, 맞아요.

M : Hmm, the record says we assigned you a non-smoking room.
흠, 기록으로 보면 저희는 고객님께 금연실을 배정해 드렸습니다.

W : Then why do I smell cigarette smoke here?
그럼 왜 여기서 담배 냄새가 나는 거죠?

M : Well, since your room is close to the ground level, cigarette smoke must have come in from outside. Sorry for the inconvenience. Would you like to switch rooms?
음, 고객님의 객실이 지면과 가까워서, 밖으로부터 담배 연기가 들어온 것 같습니다. 불편을 끼쳐 죄송합니다. 방을 바꾸시겠어요?

W : Yes, please. The smell is really bothering me.
네. 냄새가 정말 거슬리네요.

M : Let me first check if there are any rooms available.
이용 가능한 방이 있는지 먼저 확인해 드리겠습니다.

W : If it's possible, I'd like to move to a higher floor. Maybe higher than the 5th floor?
만일 그게 가능하면, 전 더 높은 층으로 옮기고 싶어요. 혹시 5층 이상으로요?

M : Okay. *[Typing sound]* Oh, we have one. Room 908 on the 9th floor is available.
네. *[타이핑하는 소리]* 오, 하나 있습니다. 9층에 있는 908호 객실이 비었습니다.

W : Perfect. That's high enough to avoid the smell.
아주 좋아요. 냄새를 피할 수 있을 만큼 높네요.

Why? 왜 정답일까?

금연실을 요청했지만 방에서 담배 냄새가 나 프런트에 전화한 여자는 층이 낮아서 바깥의 담배 연기가 들어온 것 같다는 남자의 설명에 5층 이상의 방으로 옮기고 싶다고 말한다. 이에 방을 조회해 본 남자는 9층 객실이 이용 가능한 상태임을 말해준다(**Room 908 on the 9th floor is available.**). 따라서 여자의 응답으로 가장 적절한 것은 ⑤ '아주 좋아요. 냄새를 피할 수 있을 만큼 높네요.'이다.

- specifically ad 특별히, 분명히
- inconvenience ⓝ 불편, 폐
- fully booked 예약이 다 찬
- assign ⓥ 배정하다
- switch ⓥ 바꾸다
- avoid ⓥ 피하다

15 조각상 작업을 제때 끝낼 수 있는지 확인하기
정답률 70% | 정답 ⑤

다음 상황 설명을 듣고, Jason이 Sarah에게 할 말로 가장 적절한 것을 고르시오. [3점]

Jason: ______________________

① Good luck. I hope you finish your work in time.
행운을 빌어요. 작업을 제때 끝내기를 바랍니다.
② Okay. Let's meet to discuss the changes to the sculpture.
알겠습니다. 만나서 조각상 수정에 대해 논의해 보죠.
③ That's terrible. I'm sorry that the reopening was postponed.
안됐네요. 재개장이 미뤄져서 유감입니다.
④ Hurry up. You have to send the final design immediately.
서둘러 주세요. 즉시 최종 디자인을 보내주셔야 합니다.
✔ Don't worry. I can get the job done before the deadline.
걱정 마세요. 기한 전에 작업을 끝낼 수 있습니다.

W : Jason is a sculptor and Sarah is the head of a local library.
Jason은 조각가이고 Sarah는 지역 도서관장이다.
A few days ago, Sarah hired Jason to create a sculpture for the library's reopening by the end of next month.
며칠 전, Sarah는 다음 달 말까지 도서관 재개장을 위해 조각상을 만들고자 Jason을 고용했다.
This morning, Sarah received the final design of the sculpture from Jason.
오늘 아침, Sarah는 Jason으로부터 조각상의 최종 디자인을 받았다.
She likes his design, but it looks quite complicated to her.
그녀는 그의 디자인이 마음에 들었지만, 그녀에게 그것은 몹시 복잡해 보였다.
She's worried whether he can finish in time, so she calls him to express her concern.
그녀는 그가 제 시간에 끝낼 수 있을 것인지 걱정되어, 전화를 해서 우려를 표한다.
However, Jason thinks that he has enough time to make it since he has worked on these types of sculptures before.
하지만, Jason은 전에도 이러한 유형의 조각상을 작업해 보았기 때문에 완성할 시간이 충분하다고 생각한다.
So Jason wants to tell Sarah that he can finish it in time and that she doesn't have to be concerned.
그래서 Jason은 Sarah에게 제때 끝낼 수 있으니 걱정할 필요가 없다고 말해주고 싶다.
In this situation, what would Jason most likely say to Sarah?
이 상황에서, Jason은 Sarah에게 뭐라고 말할 것인가?

Jason : Don't worry. I can get the job done before the deadline.
걱정 마세요. 기한 전에 작업을 끝낼 수 있습니다.

Why? 왜 정답일까?

상황에 따르면 Jason은 도서관 재개장 전에 조각상 작업을 끝낼 수 있을지 걱정하는 Sarah에게 시간이 충분하니 걱정하지 말라고 말해주고 싶어 한다(**So Jason wants to tell Sarah that he can finish it in time and that she doesn't have to be concerned.**). 따라서 Jason이 Sarah에게 할 말로 가장 적절한 것은 ⑤ '걱정 마세요. 기한 전에 작업을 끝낼 수 있습니다.'이다.

- sculptor ⓝ 조각가
- in time 제 시간에, 때맞춰
- immediately ad 즉시
- complicated ⓐ 복잡한
- postpone ⓥ 미루다, 연기하다

16-17 다양한 예술에 응용되는 수학

M : Good morning, students.
안녕하세요, 학생 여러분.
You might think that math is all about boring formulas, but actually it involves much more.
여러분은 수학은 지겨운 공식이 전부라고 생각할지도 모르겠지만, 사실은 훨씬 더 많은 것들이 포함됩니다.
「Today, we'll learn how mathematics is used in the arts.」 16번의 근거
오늘, 우리는 예술에서 수학이 어떻게 쓰이는지 배워볼 것입니다.
「First, let's take music.」 17번 ①의 근거 일치
첫째로, 음악을 예로 들어봅시다.
Early mathematicians found that dividing or multiplying sound frequencies created different musical notes.
초기 수학자들은 주파수를 나누거나 곱하는 것이 각기 다른 음을 만들어낸다는 것을 발견했습니다.
Many musicians started applying this mathematical concept to make harmonized sounds.
많은 음악가들이 이 수학적 개념을 적용하여 화음을 만들어내기 시작했지요.
「Second, painting frequently uses math concepts, particularly the "Golden Ratio."」
둘째로, 회화는 종종 수학적 개념, 특히 '황금률'을 이용합니다. 17번 ②의 근거 일치
Using this, great painters created masterpieces that display accurate proportions.
이것을 사용하여, 위대한 화가들은 정확한 비례를 나타내는 걸작들을 만들어냈습니다.
The *Mona Lisa* is well-known for its accurate proportionality.
*모나리자*는 그 정밀한 비례로 잘 알려져 있죠.
「Photography is another example of using mathematical ideas.」 17번 ③의 근거 일치
사진은 수학적 개념을 이용하는 또 다른 예시입니다.
Photographers divide their frames into 3 by 3 sections and place their subjects along the lines.
사진가들은 프레임을 3×3으로 나눠서 선을 따라 대상을 배치합니다.
By doing so, the photo becomes balanced, thus more pleasing.
그렇게 해서 사진은 균형이 잡히게 되고, 그래서 더 보기 좋아지지요.
「Lastly, dance applies mathematics to position dancers on the stage.」 17번 ④의 근거 일치
마지막으로, 무용은 수학을 이용하여 무대 위에 무용수들을 배치합니다.
In ballet, dancers calculate distances between themselves and other dancers, and adjust to the size of the stage.
발레에서, 무용수들은 자기 자신과 다른 무용수 사이의 거리를 계산하여 무대 크기 따라 맞춥니다.
This gives the impression of harmonious movement.
이것은 조화로운 움직임이라는 인상을 주지요.
I hope you've gained a new perspective on mathematics.
여러분이 수학에 대해 새로운 관점을 얻었기를 바랍니다.

- formula ⓝ 공식
- frequency ⓝ 주파수
- accurate ⓐ 정확한
- pleasing ⓐ 즐거운, 만족스러운
- impression ⓝ 인상
- incorporate A into B A를 B에 통합시키다
- multiply ⓥ 곱하다
- masterpiece ⓝ 걸작
- proportion ⓝ 비례, 비율
- calculate ⓥ 계산하다
- perspective ⓝ 관점
- analysis ⓝ 분석

16 주제 파악
정답률 85% | 정답 ③

남자가 하는 말의 주제로 가장 적절한 것은?

① effects of incorporating painting into math education – 그림을 수학 교육에 통합시키는 것의 효과
② mathematical analysis of the art industry's growth – 예술 산업 성장의 수학적 분석
✔ application of mathematics in different types of art – 다양한 유형의 예술에서 수학의 적용
④ historical review of important concepts in the arts – 예술에서 중요한 개념에 대한 역사적 검토
⑤ challenges of harmonizing mathematics and art – 수학과 예술을 조화시키는 것의 어려움

Why? 왜 정답일까?

'**Today, we'll learn how mathematics is used in the arts.**'에서 남자는 예술에서 수학이 어떻게 응용되는지에 관해 배워볼 것이라고 하므로, 남자가 하는 말의 주제로 가장 적절한 것은 ③ '다양한 유형의 예술에서 수학의 적용'이다.

17 언급 유무 파악
정답률 96% | 정답 ⑤

언급된 예술 분야가 아닌 것은?

① music – 음악 ② painting – 회화 ③ photography – 사진
④ dance – 무용 ✔ cinema – 영화

Why? 왜 정답일까?

담화에서 남자는 수학 개념을 적용하는 예술 형태의 예시로 음악, 회화, 사진, 무용을 언급한다. 따라서 언급되지 않은 것은 ⑤ '영화'이다.

Why? 왜 오답일까?

① '**First, let's take music.**'에서 '음악'이 언급되었다.
② '**Second, painting frequently uses math concepts, ~**'에서 '회화'가 언급되었다.
③ '**Photography is another example of using mathematical ideas.**'에서 '사진'이 언급되었다.
④ '**Lastly, dance applies mathematics to position dancers on the stage.**'에서 '무용'이 언급되었다.

32회

Dictation 32

문제편 189쪽

01 bark for no reason / professional certified trainers / improve your dog's behavior
02 That sounds quite demanding / plan too many things to do / be worn out
03 home-made apple sauce / decreasing apple consumption / the apple's sweetness
04 the striped tablecloth on the table / brighten up the stage / set up two microphones
05 decorate our club's room with ribbons / what to wear for the photo / buy them for our members
06 Would you like some dessert / one of the best sellers / confirm your order / a birthday coupon
07 Are you still in pain / already submitted it / on my way to volunteer
08 provides various fun reading activities / free on Monday afternoons / ages seven to nine / gets your daughter into reading
09 runs for one week / including robot building and VR simulations / accompanied by an adult
10 reserve a study room / accommodate six of us / How much can we spend
11 send an email
12 if I can pick up my camera / I've finished repairing
13 pretty burnt out / do whatever makes you feel happy
14 we assigned you a non-smoking room / close to the ground level / move to a higher floor
15 to create a sculpture for the library's reopening / looks quite complicated / enough time to make it
16-17 dividing or multiplying sound frequencies / display accurate proportions / the impression of harmonious movement

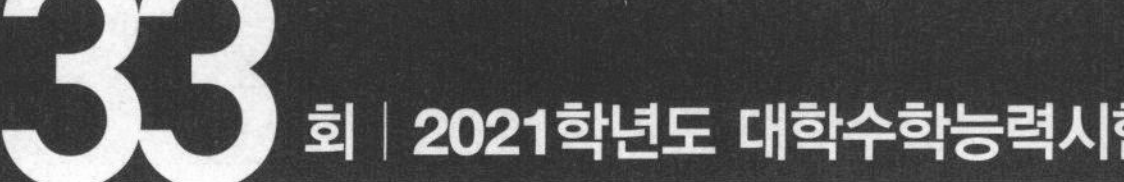

33회 | 2021학년도 대학수학능력시험 고3

• 정답 •

01 ⑤ 02 ① 03 ① 04 ⑤ 05 ① 06 ② 07 ③ 08 ④ 09 ③ 10 ④ 11 ③ 12 ① 13 ② 14 ④ 15 ① 16 ⑤ 17 ⑤

01 운동 채널 홍보하기

정답률 96% | 정답 ⑤

다음을 듣고, 남자가 하는 말의 목적으로 가장 적절한 것을 고르시오.

① 헬스클럽 할인 행사를 안내하려고
② 동영상 업로드 방법을 설명하려고
③ 스포츠 중계방송 중단을 예고하려고
④ 체육관 보수 공사 일정 변경을 공지하려고
✔ 운동 방법에 관한 동영상 채널을 홍보하려고

M : Hello, viewers. Thank you for clicking on this video.
안녕하세요, 시청자 여러분. 이 영상을 클릭해주셔서 감사합니다.
I'm Ronnie Drain, and I've been a personal fitness trainer for over 15 years.
저는 Ronnie Drain이고, 15년 이상 개인 헬스 트레이너였습니다.
Today, I'd like to tell you about my channel, *Build Your Body*.
오늘 저는 제 채널인 *Build Your Body*에 관해 말씀드리려 합니다.
On my channel, you can watch videos showing you how to do a variety of exercises that you can do at home or at your office.
제 채널에서 여러분은 집이나 사무실에서 할 수 있는 다양한 운동을 어떻게 하는지 보여드리는 영상들을 보실 수 있어요.
If you've experienced difficulty exercising regularly, my videos can provide easy guidelines and useful resources on exercise routines.
여러분이 규칙적으로 운동하는 데 어려움을 겪으셨다면, 제 영상들이 운동 루틴에 대한 쉬운 가이드라인과 유용한 자료를 제공해드릴 수 있습니다.
New videos will be uploaded every Friday.
새로운 영상은 매주 금요일마다 올라갑니다.
Visit my channel and build a stronger, healthier body.
제 채널을 방문해주시고 더 튼튼하고 건강한 신체를 만드세요.

Why? 왜 정답일까?

'Today, I'd like to tell you about my channel, *Build Your Body*.' 이후로 남자는 자신의 채널에서 다양한 실내 운동 방법을 알려주는 영상을 볼 수 있다고 언급하며 자신의 채널을 홍보하고 있다. 따라서 남자가 하는 말의 목적으로 가장 적절한 것은 ⑤ '운동 방법에 관한 동영상 채널을 홍보하려고'이다.

- **personal fitness trainer** 개인 헬스 트레이너
- **a variety of** 다양한
- **regularly** ad 규칙적으로
- **routine** ⓝ (늘 하도록 정해진) 루틴, 습관
- **build a body** 신체를 단련하다, 몸을 만들다
- **exercise** ⓝ 운동
- **resource** ⓝ 자원, 재료

02 별 보기 활동의 효과

정답률 95% | 정답 ①

대화를 듣고, 여자의 의견으로 가장 적절한 것을 고르시오.

✔ 별 관찰은 아이들이 수학 개념에 친숙해지도록 도와준다.
② 아이들은 별 관찰을 통해 예술적 영감을 얻는다.
③ 야외 활동이 아이들의 신체 발달에 필수적이다.
④ 아이들은 자연을 경험함으로써 인격적으로 성장한다.
⑤ 수학 문제 풀이는 아이들의 논리적 사고력을 증진시킨다.

W : Good morning, Chris.
안녕하세요, Chris.
M : Good morning, Julie. How was your weekend?
안녕하세요, Julie. 주말 어땠어요?
W : It was wonderful. I went to an event called Stargazing Night with my 7-year-old son.
멋졌어요. 전 저희 7살짜리 아들과 Stargazing Night라는 행사에 다녀왔어요.
M : Oh, so you went outdoors to look up at stars. Your son must have had a great time.
오, 그럼 별을 보러 밖에 나가셨군요. 아드님이 무척 좋은 시간을 보냈겠어요.
W : Yes. And I think it helped my son become familiar with mathematical concepts.
네. 그리고 그것 덕분에 제 아들이 수학 개념에 친숙해졌다고 생각해요.
M : Interesting! How does it do that?
흥미롭네요! 어떻게 그렇게 된 건가요?
W : By counting the stars together, my son had a chance to practice counting to high numbers.
함께 별을 세면서 제 아들은 큰 숫자까지 세는 연습을 해볼 기회가 있었어요.
M : Ah, that makes sense.
아, 일리가 있네요.
W : Also, he enjoyed identifying shapes and tracing patterns that stars form together.
게다가, 아들은 모양을 알아보고 별자리를 찾아내는 것을 재미있어했어요.
M : Sounds like you had a magical and mathematical night!
아드님하고 마법 같고도 수학적인 밤을 보내신 것 같네요!
W : Absolutely. I think looking at stars is a good way for kids to get used to mathematical concepts.
바로 그래요. 별을 보는 것은 아이들이 수학 개념에 친숙해질 좋은 방법인 것 같아요.
M : Maybe I should take my daughter to the event next time.
어쩌면 저도 다음번에 저희 딸을 데리고 그 행사에 가봐야겠어요.

Why? 왜 정답일까?

'I think it helped my son become familiar with mathematical concepts.'와 'I think looking at stars is a good way for kids to get used to mathematical concepts.'에서 여자는 별 관찰이 아이들로 하여금 수학 개념에 친숙해지도록 도와준다는 의견을 말하고 있으므로, 여자의 의견으로 가장 적절한 것은 ① '별 관찰은 아이들이 수학 개념에 친숙해지도록 도와준다.'이다.

[문제편 p.193]

- stargazing ⓝ 별 보기, 천문학
- mathematical ⓐ 수학적인
- trace ⓥ (추적하여) 찾아내다, 밝혀내다
- familiar with ~에 친숙한
- identify ⓥ 알아보다, 확인하다
- get used to ~에 익숙해지다

03 건축가 인터뷰하기

정답률 94% | 정답 ①

대화를 듣고, 두 사람의 관계를 가장 잘 나타낸 것을 고르시오.

✔ 학생 – 건축가　② 신문 기자 – 화가
③ 탐험가 – 환경 운동가　④ 건물 관리인 – 정원사
⑤ 교사 – 여행사 직원

M : Hello, Ms. Watson. Thank you for accepting my interview request.
안녕하세요, Watson 씨. 제 인터뷰 요청을 받아주셔서 감사합니다.

W : My pleasure. You must be Michael from Windmore High School.
천만에요. Windmore 고등학교의 Michael이겠군요.

M : Yes. I'm honored to interview the person who designed the school I'm attending.
네, 제가 다니고 있는 학교를 설계하신 분을 인터뷰하게 되어 영광입니다.

W : Thank you. I'm very proud of that design.
고맙습니다. 나도 그 설계가 무척 자랑스러워요.

M : What was the concept behind it?
설계 컨셉이 무엇이었나요?

W : When planning the design of the school building, I wanted to incorporate elements of nature into it.
학교 건물 설계를 계획할 때, 설계에 자연 요소를 포함시키고 싶었어요.

M : I see. Did you apply this concept in any other building designs?
그렇군요. 이 컨셉을 다른 건물 설계에도 적용해보셨나요?

W : Yes. Skyforest Tower. My design included mini gardens for each floor and a roof-top garden, making the building look like a rising forest.
네, Skyforest Tower에요. 제 설계에는 층마다 소형 정원이 포함되어 있고 옥상 정원도 있어서, 건물이 점점 자라나는 숲처럼 보이게 해요.

M : That's impressive. Actually, my art teacher is taking us on a field trip there next week.
인상적이군요. 사실, 저희 미술 선생님이 다음 주에 그곳에 저희를 현장학습 차 데려가세요.

W : Really? Make sure to visit the observation deck on the 32nd floor. The view is spectacular.
정말요? 32층 전망대를 꼭 방문하시길 바랍니다. 경치가 장관이에요.

M : Thanks. I'll check it out with my classmates.
고맙습니다. 저희 반 친구들과 확인해 볼게요.

Why? 왜 정답일까?

'I'm honored to interview the person who designed the school I'm attending.'에서 남자는 학생이고, 여자는 남자가 다니는 학교 건물을 설계한 건축가임을 알 수 있다. 추가로 'My design included mini gardens for each floor and a roof-top garden, making the building look like a rising forest.', 'Actually, my art teacher is taking us on a field trip there next week.' 등을 근거로 참고할 수 있다. 따라서 두 사람의 관계로 가장 적절한 것은 ① '학생 – 건축가'이다.

- incorporate A into B A를 B에 포함시키다, 통합하다
- impressive ⓐ 인상적인
- spectacular ⓐ 장관인, (경치가) 멋진
- observation deck 전망대

04 새로 꾸민 핫초코 부스 구경하기

정답률 96% | 정답 ⑤

대화를 듣고, 그림에서 대화의 내용과 일치하지 않는 것을 고르시오.

HOT CHOCOLATE

W : Wow, Sam. You turned the student council room into a hot chocolate booth.
와, Sam. 너 학생회실을 핫초코 부스로 바꿨구나.

M : Yes, Ms. Thompson. We're ready to sell hot chocolate to raise money for children in need.
네, Thompson 선생님. 저희는 불우아동을 위한 모금을 하기 위해 핫초코를 팔 준비가 다 되었어요.

W : Excellent. 『What are you going to put on the bulletin board under the clock?』 ①의 근거 일치
훌륭해. 시계 밑에 있는 게시판에는 뭘 붙일 예정이니?

M : I'll post information letting people know where the profits will go.
수익이 어디로 갈지 사람들에게 알려주는 정보를 붙이려고 해요.

W : Good. 『I like the banner on the wall.』 ②의 근거 일치
좋네. 벽에 걸린 현수막이 마음에 들어.

M : Thanks. I designed it myself.
고맙습니다. 제가 직접 디자인했어요.

W : Awesome. 『Oh, I'm glad you put my stripe-patterned tablecloth on the table.』 ③의 근거 일치
근사해. 오, 내 줄무늬 식탁보를 탁자에 깔았다니 기쁘구나.

M : Thanks for letting us use it. 『Did you notice the snowman drawing that's hanging on the tree?』 ④의 근거 일치
저희보고 쓰게 해주셔서 감사합니다. 트리에 걸려 있는 눈사람 그림도 보셨어요?

W : Yeah. I remember it was drawn by the child you helped last year. 『By the way, there are three boxes on the floor.』 ⑤의 근거 불일치 What are they for?
응. 네가 작년에 도와준 아이가 그린 그림인 걸 기억해. 그나저나, 바닥에 상자가 세 개 있네. 무엇을 위한 것이니?

M : We're going to fill those up with donations of toys and books.
그 상자들을 기부된 장난감과 책으로 채울 거예요.

W : Sounds great. Good luck.
멋지다. 행운을 빌게.

[문제편 p.193]

Why? 왜 정답일까?

대화에서 여자는 바닥에 상자가 세 개 있다(By the way, there are three boxes on the floor.)고 말하는데, 그림에서 상자는 두 개뿐이다. 따라서 그림에서 대화의 내용과 일치하지 않는 것은 ⑤이다.

- student council 학생회
- in need 불우한, 도움이 필요한
- profit ⓝ 수익
- raise money 모금하다
- bulletin board 게시판
- fill up 채우다

05 야생화 사진 보내주기

정답률 96% | 정답 ①

대화를 듣고, 남자가 여자를 위해 할 일로 가장 적절한 것을 고르시오.

✔ 사진 전송하기
② 그림 그리기
③ 휴대 전화 찾기
④ 생물 보고서 제출하기
⑤ 야생화 개화 시기 검색하기

M : Hi, Mary. You look worried. What's the matter?
안녕, Mary. 걱정스러워 보이는구나. 무슨 일 있어?

W : Hi, Steve. Remember the report about wildflowers I've been working on?
안녕, Steve. 내가 작업하고 있던 야생화 보고서 기억나?

M : Of course. That's for your biology class, right?
물론이지. 네 생물학 보고서잖아, 그렇지?

W : Yeah. I was able to get pictures of all the wildflowers in my report except for daisies.
맞아. 난 내 보고서에 들어갈 야생화 사진을 다 구할 수 있었어, 데이지만 빼고.

M : I see. Can't you submit your report without pictures of daisies?
그렇구나. 데이지 사진 없이 보고서를 제출할 수는 없는 거야?

W : No. I really need them. I even tried to take pictures of daisies myself, but I found out that they usually bloom from spring to fall.
안 돼. 정말로 필요해. 난 심지어 직접 데이지 사진을 찍으려고 해봤는데, 알아보니까 데이지는 보통 봄에서 가을까지밖에 안 피더라고.

M : You know what? This spring, I went hiking with my dad and took some pictures of wildflowers.
있지, 이번 봄에 난 아빠랑 하이킹을 나갔다가 야생화 사진을 몇 장 찍었어.

W : Do you have them on your phone? Can I see them?
그거 네 핸드폰에 있어? 내가 봐도 돼?

M : Sure. Have a look.
물론이지. 봐봐.

W : Oh, the flowers in the pictures are daisies! These will be great for my report.
오, 사진 속 꽃은 데이지야! 내 보고서에 딱 좋겠어.

M : Really? Then I'll send them to you.
정말? 그럼 내가 이것들을 너한테 보내줄게.

W : Thanks. That would be very helpful.
고마워. 몹시 도움이 될 거야.

Why? 왜 정답일까?

데이지 사진을 구하지 못해 야생화 보고서를 완성하지 못하고 있는 여자에게 남자는 자신이 지난봄에 우연히 찍은 데이지 사진을 보내주기로 한다(Then I'll send them to you.). 따라서 남자가 할 일로 가장 적절한 것은 ① '사진 전송하기'이다.

- work on ~을 작업하다
- submit ⓥ 제출하다
- wildflower ⓝ 야생화
- bloom ⓥ (꽃이) 피다, 개화하다

06 호텔 예약 확인

정답률 93% | 정답 ②

대화를 듣고, 여자가 지불할 금액을 고르시오.

① $180　✔ $190　③ $200　④ $210　⑤ $230

M : Welcome to the Chestfield Hotel. How may I help you?
Chestfield 호텔에 잘 오셨습니다. 무엇을 도와드릴까요?

W : Hi, I'm Alice Milford. I made a reservation for me and my husband.
안녕하세요, 저는 Alice Milford입니다. 저와 제 남편을 위해 예약했어요.

M : *[Typing sound]* Here it is. You reserved one room for one night at the regular rate of $100.
[타자 치는 소리] 여기 있군요. 정가 100달러에 1박으로 방 하나를 예약하셨네요.

W : Can I use this 10% discount coupon?
이 10퍼센트 할인 쿠폰을 쓸 수 있나요?

M : Sure, you can.
물론이죠, 쓰실 수 있습니다.

W : Fantastic. And is it possible to stay one more night?
환상적이네요. 그리고 1박 더 투숙할 수 있을까요?

M : Let me check. *[Mouse clicking sound]* Yes, the same room is available for tomorrow.
확인해 보겠습니다. *[마우스 클릭하는 소리]* 네, 같은 방을 내일도 이용 가능하세요.

W : Good. Do I get a discount for the second night, too?
좋아요. 2일차 밤에도 할인을 받을 수 있나요?

M : Sorry. The coupon doesn't apply to the second night. It'll be $100. Do you still want to stay an extra night?
죄송합니다. 쿠폰이 2일차 밤에는 적용되지 않습니다. 가격은 100달러가 될 겁니다. 그래도 추가로 숙박하시겠어요?

W : Yes, I do.
네, 그렇게 할게요.

M : Great. Will you and your husband have breakfast? It's $10 per person for each day.
좋습니다. 고객님과 남편분께서 조식을 드시나요? 하루마다 1인당 10달러입니다.

W : No thanks. We'll be going out early to go shopping. Here's my credit card.
괜찮아요. 저희는 쇼핑하러 일찍 나가요. 여기 제 신용카드요.

Why? 왜 정답일까?

대화에 따르면 여자는 원래 예약했던 1박에서 정가(100달러)의 10퍼센트를 할인받고, 더 할인을 받지 못한 채 2일차 밤을 추가로 예약했다. 조식은 먹지 않기로 하였다. 이를 식으로 나타내면 '100×0.9+100=190'이므로, 여자가 지불할 금액은 ② '$190'이다.

- make a reservation 예약하다
- apply to ~에 적용되다
- rate ⓝ 요금

07 텐트를 반품하는 이유 정답률 96% | 정답 ③

대화를 듣고, 남자가 텐트를 반품하려는 이유를 고르시오.

① 크기가 작아서
② 캠핑이 취소되어서
③ 운반하기 무거워서
④ 설치 방법이 어려워서
⑤ 더 저렴한 제품을 찾아서

W : Honey, I'm home.
여보, 나 왔어요.
M : How was your day?
오늘 하루 어땠어요?
W : Alright. Hey, did you order something? There's a large box outside the door.
괜찮았어요. 여보, 뭐 시켰어요? 문 밖에 큰 상자가 하나 있어요.
M : It's the tent we bought online for our camping trip. I'm returning it.
우리가 캠핑 여행을 위해 온라인에서 샀던 텐트예요. 그거 반품하려고요.
W : Is it because of the size? I remember you said it might be a little small to fit all of us.
사이즈 때문에 그래요? 우리 모두가 들어가기에 좀 작을 수도 있겠다고 당신이 얘기한 게 기억나요.
M : Actually, when I set up the tent, it seemed big enough to hold us all.
사실, 내가 텐트를 설치해보니까, 우리 모두가 들어가기에 충분하게 큰 것 같았어요.
W : Then, did you find a cheaper one on another website?
그럼, 다른 웹 사이트에서 더 싼 것을 찾은 거예요?
M : No, price is not the issue.
아니요, 가격은 문제가 아녜요.
W : Then, why are you returning the tent?
그럼 왜 텐트를 반품하는 거예요?
M : It's too heavy to carry around. We usually have to walk a bit to get to the campsite.
들고 다니기 너무 무거워요. 우린 보통 캠핑장까지 가려면 좀 걸어야 되잖아요.
W : I see. Is someone coming to pick up the box?
그렇군요. 누가 와서 상자를 가져가는 거예요?
M : Yes. I already scheduled a pickup.
네. 수거를 벌써 예약해 뒀어요.

Why? 왜 정답일까?

대화에 따르면 남자는 온라인에서 샀던 텐트가 들고 다니기에 너무 무거워서(**It's too heavy to carry around.**) 반품하려고 하므로, 남자가 텐트를 반품하려는 이유로 가장 적절한 것은 ③ '운반하기 무거워서' 이다.

- **fit** ⓥ ~에 맞다, 적합하다
- **set up** 설치하다

08 실패작을 전시하는 박물관 알려주기 정답률 95% | 정답 ④

대화를 듣고, Bradford Museum of Failure에 관해 언급되지 않은 것을 고르시오.

① 전시품 ② 설립 목적 ③ 개관 연도 ④ 입장료 ⑤ 위치

M : Hey, Kelly. Have you been to the Bradford Museum of Failure?
안녕, Kelly. 너 Bradford Museum of Failure에 가본 적 있어?
W : I've never even heard of it.
그런 곳 들어보지도 못했어.
M : Well, I went there yesterday and it was amazing.
음, 난 어제 거기 가봤는데 근사하더라.
W : 「What does the museum exhibit?
그 박물관에서 뭘 전시해?
M : It exhibits numerous failed products from the world's best-known companies.」
세계 가장 유명한 회사들에서 실패했던 수많은 제품을 전시하는 거야. ①의 근거 일치
W : Interesting. 「That makes me curious about the purpose of founding the museum.
재밌겠다. 그렇다고 하니 박물관을 설립한 목적이 궁금해지네.
M : It was founded to deliver the message that we need to admit our failures to truly succeed.」 ②의 근거 일치
우리가 진정 성공하기 위해서는 우리의 실패를 받아들일 필요가 있다는 메시지를 전달하려고 설립되었어.
W : That's quite a message, and it makes a lot of sense. 「Did it just open?
의미 있는 메시지네, 게다가 무척 일리도 있어. 개관한 지 얼마 안 된 거야?
M : No, it opened in 2001.」 ③의 근거 일치
아니, 2001년에 개관했어.
W : How come I've never heard of it?
내가 어떻게 못 들어봤을 수가 있지?
M : I guess many people don't know about it. But visiting the museum was an eye-opening experience.
많은 사람들이 모르는 것 같아. 하지만 그 박물관에 가보는 건 정말 경이로운 경험이었어.
W : 「Where is it?
어디에 있어?
M : It's located in Greenfalls, Hillside.」 ⑤의 근거 일치
Hillside의 Greenfalls에 있어.
W : That's not too far from here. I'll be sure to visit it.
여기서 멀지도 않네. 나도 꼭 가봐야겠어.

Why? 왜 정답일까?

대화에서 남자와 여자는 Bradford Museum of Failure의 전시품, 설립 목적, 개관 연도, 위치에 관해 언급하므로, 언급되지 않은 것은 ④ '입장료'이다.

Why? 왜 오답일까?

① 'It exhibits numerous failed products from the world's best-known companies.'에서 '전시품'이 언급되었다.
② 'It was founded to deliver the message that we need to admit our failures to truly succeed.'에서 '설립 목적'이 언급되었다.
③ 'No, it opened in 2001.'에서 '개관 연도'가 언급되었다.
⑤ 'It's located in Greenfalls, Hillside.'에서 '위치'가 언급되었다.

- **amazing** ⓐ 멋진, 놀라운
- **exhibit** ⓥ 전시하다
- **numerous** ⓐ 수많은
- **found** ⓥ 설립하다
- **eye-opening** ⓐ 경이로운, 놀랄 만한

09 제빵 대회 안내 정답률 96% | 정답 ③

National Baking Competition에 관한 다음 내용을 듣고, 일치하지 않는 것을 고르시오.

① 해마다 열리는 행사이다.
② 올해의 주제는 건강한 디저트이다.
③ 20명이 결선에 진출할 것이다.
④ 수상자들의 조리법이 잡지에 실릴 것이다.
⑤ 웹 사이트에서 생중계될 것이다.

W : Hello, listeners. I'm Carla Jones from the National Baking Association.
안녕하세요, 청취자 여러분. 저는 National Baking Association에서 나온 Carla Jones입니다.
I'm glad to announce that we're hosting the National Baking Competition on December 20th.
저희가 12월 20일에 National Baking Competition을 주최할 것임을 알려드리게 되어 기쁩니다.
「It's an annual event aimed to discover people with a talent and passion for baking.」
이것은 제빵에 재능과 열정이 있는 사람들을 발굴할 목적으로 해마다 열리는 행사입니다. ①의 근거 일치
「This year, the theme of the competition is "healthy desserts."」 ②의 근거 일치
올해 대회의 주제는 '건강한 디저트'입니다.
We had the most applicants in the history of this competition, and 「only 10 participants will advance to the final round.」 ③의 근거 불일치
이 대회 역사상 가장 많은 지원자들이 모였고, 오직 10명의 참가자만이 결선에 진출할 것입니다.
The top three will win the grand prize of $10,000 each, and 「the recipes of the winners will appear in our magazine.」 ④의 근거 일치
상위 3명은 각각 10,000달러의 상금을 수여받으며, 수상자들의 조리법은 우리 잡지에 실릴 것입니다.
You can enjoy watching the entire competition from home.
집에서 대회 전체를 즐겁게 시청하실 수 있습니다.
「It'll be broadcast live on our website starting from 9 a.m.」 ⑤의 근거 일치
저희 웹 사이트에서 아침 9시부터 생중계될 예정입니다.
If you're a food lover, you won't want to miss watching this event.
음식 애호가라면, 이 행사 시청을 결코 놓치고 싶지 않을 것입니다.

Why? 왜 정답일까?

'~ only 10 participants will advance to the final round.'에서 많은 지원자 중 오직 10명만이 결선에 진출할 것이라고 하므로, 내용과 일치하지 않는 것은 ③ '20명이 결선에 진출할 것이다.'이다.

Why? 왜 오답일까?

① 'It's an annual event ~'의 내용과 일치한다.
② 'This year, the theme of the competition is "healthy desserts."'의 내용과 일치한다.
④ '~ the recipes of the winners will appear in our magazine.'의 내용과 일치한다.
⑤ 'It'll be broadcast live on our website starting from 9 a.m.'의 내용과 일치한다.

- **association** ⓝ 협회, 조합
- **passion** ⓝ 열정
- **applicant** ⓝ 지원자
- **advance** ⓥ 진출하다, 나아가다
- **entire** ⓐ 전체의

10 재사용 빨대 세트 구매하기 정답률 95% | 정답 ④

다음 표를 보면서 대화를 듣고, 여자가 주문할 재사용 빨대 세트를 고르시오.

Reusable Straw Sets (3 pieces)

	Set	Material	Price	Length (inches)	Carrying Case
①	A	Bamboo	$5.99	7	×
②	B	Glass	$6.99	7	○
③	C	Glass	$7.99	8	×
④	D	Silicone	$8.99	8	○
⑤	E	Stainless Steel	$11.99	9	○

M : Hi, Nicole. What are you doing?
안녕, Nicole. 뭐 하고 있어?
W : Hi, Jack. I'm trying to buy a reusable straw set on the Internet. Do you want to see?
안녕, Jack. 난 재사용 빨대 세트를 인터넷에서 구매하려는 중이야. 너도 볼래?
M : Sure. *[Pause]* 「These bamboo ones seem good. They're made from natural materials.
물론이지. *[잠시 멈춤]* 이 대나무 빨대 괜찮아 보이네. 천연 재료로 만들어졌어.
W : That's true, but I'm worried they may not dry quickly.
맞아, 하지만 난 그것들이 빨리 건조되지 않을까봐 걱정돼.
M : Okay. Then let's look at straws made from other materials.」 「How much are you willing to spend on a set of straws? 근거1 Material 조건
알겠어. 그럼 다른 재료로 만들어진 빨대를 살펴보자. 빨대 세트 하나에 얼마 정도 쓸 생각이야?
W : I don't want to spend more than $10.」 근거2 Price 조건
10달러 넘게 쓰고 싶지는 않아.
M : That's reasonable. 「How about length?
적당하네. 길이는?
W : To use with my tumbler, eight or nine inches should be perfect.」 근거3 Length 조건
내 텀블러와 함께 쓰려면 8인치나 9인치가 딱 좋겠어.
M : Then you're down to these two. 「A carrying case would be very useful when going out.」
그럼 이거 두 개로 좁혀지네. 휴대용 케이스는 외출할 때 몹시 유용할 거야. 근거4 Carrying Case 조건
W : Good point. I'll take your recommendation and order this set now.
좋은 지적이야. 네 추천을 받아들여서 이 세트로 지금 주문할래.

Why? 왜 정답일까?

대화에 따르면 여자는 대나무로 만들어지지 않았으면서, 가격은 10달러를 넘지 않고, 길이는 8～9인치 정도 되면서, 휴대용 케이스가 딸린 재사용 빨대 세트를 사려고 한다. 따라서 여자가 주문할 빨대 세트는 ④ 'D'이다.

- **reusable** ⓐ 재사용 가능한
- **bamboo** ⓝ 대나무
- **be made from** ~로 만들어지다
- **be willing to** ~할 의향이 있다
- **recommendation** ⓝ 추천

11 관광 중 뭔가 마시며 쉴 곳 찾기 정답률 91% | 정답 ③

대화를 듣고, 남자의 마지막 말에 대한 여자의 응답으로 가장 적절한 것을 고르시오.

[문제편 p.193]

① I don't feel like going out today. – 전 오늘 나가고 싶지 않아요.
② You must get to the airport quickly. – 아빠는 빨리 공항에 가셔야 해요.
③ How about going to the cafe over there? – 저쪽 카페에 가면 어때요?
④ I didn't know you wanted to go sightseeing. – 아빠가 관광을 다니고 싶어 하셨는지 몰랐어요.
⑤ Why didn't you wear more comfortable shoes? – 왜 더 편한 신발을 신지 않으신 거예요?

M : Lisa, are you okay from all the walking we did today?
Lisa, 우리 오늘 그렇게 많이 걸었는데 괜찮아?

W : Actually, Dad, my feet are tired from all the sightseeing. Also, I'm thirsty because the weather is so hot out here.
사실 아빠, 그 관광을 다 하고 나니 발이 몹시 피로해요. 게다가 여기 밖에 날씨가 너무 더워서 목이 말라요.

M : Oh, then let's go somewhere inside and get something to drink. Where should we go?
오, 그럼 어디 안에 들어가서 뭘 좀 마시자. 어디로 가야 할까?

W : How about going to the cafe over there?
저쪽 카페에 가면 어때요?

Why? 왜 정답일까?

딸인 여자가 관광 중 날이 더워 목이 마르다고 하자, 남자는 뭔가 마실 수 있는 곳을 찾자며 어디로 갈지 묻고 있다(**Where should we go?**). 따라서 여자의 응답으로 가장 적절한 것은 ③ '저쪽 카페에 가면 어때요?'이다.

- **be tired from** ~로 피곤하다
- **feel like ~ing** ~하고 싶지 않다
- **sightseeing** ⓝ 관광
- **comfortable** ⓐ 편한, 편안한

12 주차를 다른 곳에 해야 한다고 알려주기

정답률 84% | 정답 ①

대화를 듣고, 여자의 마지막 말에 대한 남자의 응답으로 가장 적절한 것을 고르시오.

① I see. Then I'll park somewhere else. – 그렇군요. 그럼 어디 다른 곳에 주차할게요.
② It's all right. I'll bring your car over here. – 괜찮아요. 제가 당신 차를 여기로 가져올게요.
③ No thanks. I don't want my car to be painted. – 사양하겠습니다. 제 차를 칠하고 싶지 않아요.
④ Never mind. I'll pay the parking fee later. – 신경 쓰지 마세요. 제가 나중에 주차비를 지불하겠습니다.
⑤ Okay. I'll choose another car instead. – 알겠습니다. 대신 다른 차를 고를게요.

W : Excuse me, sir. I'm from the management office. You cannot park here because we're about to close off this section of the parking lot.
실례합니다. 관리사무소에서 나왔습니다. 이 주차 구역을 지금 폐쇄할 거라서 이곳에 주차하시면 안 됩니다.

M : Why? What's going on here?
왜요? 여기 무슨 일이 있나요?

W : We're going to paint the walls in this section. If there are cars parked here, we cannot start our work.
이 구역 벽을 페인트칠할 겁니다. 여기 차가 주차되어 있으면 저희가 작업을 시작할 수 없습니다.

M : I see. Then I'll park somewhere else.
그렇군요. 그럼 어디 다른 곳에 주차할게요.

Why? 왜 정답일까?

관리사무소 직원인 여자는 남자가 차를 대려는 주차 구역이 곧 페인트칠 작업으로 인해 폐쇄되므로 차를 대지 말아야 한다고 알려주고 있다. 따라서 남자의 응답으로 가장 적절한 것은 ① '그렇군요. 그럼 어디 다른 곳에 주차할게요.'이다.

- **management office** 관리사무소
- **close off** 폐쇄하다

13 진열된 세탁기 구매하기

정답률 81% | 정답 ②

대화를 듣고, 남자의 마지막 말에 대한 여자의 응답으로 가장 적절한 것을 고르시오. [3점]

Woman: ______________

① Sorry. I don't think I can wait until tomorrow for this one.
죄송해요. 내일까지 이것을 기다릴 수 없을 것 같아요.
② I agree. The displayed one may be the best option for me.
동의해요. 진열된 것이 제게 최선의 선택일 것 같아요.
③ Oh, no. It's too bad you don't sell the displayed model.
이런. 진열된 제품을 판매하지 않는다니 너무 유감이네요.
④ Good. Call me when my washing machine is repaired.
좋아요. 제 세탁기가 수리되면 전화해 주세요.
⑤ Exactly. I'm glad that you bought the displayed one.
맞아요. 진열된 것을 구매해주셔서 기쁩니다.

W : Hi. Can I get some help over here?
안녕하세요. 여기 좀 도와주실래요?

M : Sure. What can I help you with?
물론입니다. 무엇을 도와드릴까요?

W : I'm thinking of buying this washing machine.
전 이 세탁기를 살까 해요.

M : Good choice. It's our best-selling model.
좋은 선택입니다. 저희 제품 중 가장 잘 팔리는 것이죠.

W : I really like its design and it has a lot of useful features. I'll take it.
전 이 세탁기 디자인이 몹시 마음에 들고 이 세탁기는 유용한 기능도 많아요. 사겠어요.

M : Great. However, you'll have to wait for two weeks. We're out of this model right now.
좋습니다. 하지만, 2주 동안 기다려 주셔야 할 겁니다. 지금 이 제품 재고가 없습니다.

W : Oh, no. I need it today. My washing machine broke down yesterday.
오, 이런. 오늘 필요해요. 제 세탁기가 어제 고장 났어요.

M : Then how about buying the one on display?
그럼 진열되어 있는 제품을 사시면 어떨까요?

W : Oh, I didn't know I could buy the displayed one.
오, 진열된 것을 살 수 있는지 몰랐어요.

M : Sure, you can. We can deliver and install it today.
사실 수 있죠. 오늘 배송해서 설치해 드릴 수 있습니다.

W : That's just what I need, but it's not a new one.
그게 딱 제가 원하는 건데, 이건 새것이 아니잖아요.

M : Not to worry. It's never been used. Also, like with the new ones, you can get it repaired for free for up to three years.
걱정하지 않으셔도 됩니다. 한 번도 사용된 적이 없습니다. 또한, 새것과 마찬가지로 3년까지는 무상 수리를 받으실 수 있습니다.

W : That's good.
좋네요.

[문제편 p.194]

M : We can also give you a 20% discount on it. It's a pretty good deal.
또한 20퍼센트 할인도 해 드립니다. 아주 잘 사시는 거지요.

W : I agree. The displayed one may be the best option for me.
동의해요. 진열된 것이 제게 최선의 선택일 것 같아요.

Why? 왜 정답일까?

세탁기가 고장 나 당장 새 제품을 사야 하는 여자는 남자의 권유에 따라 진열된 상품을 살까 하지만 새것이 아니라는 생각에 망설이고 있다. 이에 남자는 진열된 상품이 한 번도 실제 사용된 적이 없으며, 새것과 마찬가지로 3년간 무상 수리가 제공되고, 20퍼센트 할인도 추가로 제공되기 때문에 훌륭한 선택이라고 말하며(**It's a pretty good deal.**) 여자에게 구매하도록 설득하고 있다. 따라서 여자의 응답으로 가장 적절한 것은 ② '동의해요. 진열된 것이 제게 최선의 선택일 것 같아요.'이다.

- **feature** ⓝ 기능, 특징
- **on display** 진열 중인, 전시 중인
- **repair** ⓥ 수리하다
- **break down** 고장 나다
- **install** ⓥ 설치하다

14 시상식에 올 의사가 있는지 묻기

정답률 71% | 정답 ④

대화를 듣고, 여자의 마지막 말에 대한 남자의 응답으로 가장 적절한 것을 고르시오. [3점]

Man: ______________

① Don't worry. I already found his briefcase.
걱정하지 마세요. 제가 이미 그의 서류 가방을 찾았어요.
② Of course. You deserve to receive the award.
물론이에요. 당신은 그 상을 받을 자격이 있어요.
③ Don't mention it. I just did my duty as a citizen.
별말씀을요. 저는 단지 시민의 의무를 다했을 뿐이에요.
④ Definitely. I want to go to congratulate him myself.
물론이에요. 제가 가서 직접 그 아이를 축하해 주고 싶어요.
⑤ Wonderful. It was the best ceremony I've ever been to.
멋지네요. 제가 가 본 최고의 시상식이었어요.

33회

[Cell phone rings.]

M : Hello, Joe Burrow speaking.
여보세요, Joe Burrow입니다.

W : Hello. This is Officer Blake from the Roselyn Police Station.
여보세요, Roselyn 경찰서의 Blake 경관입니다.

M : Oh, it's good to speak to you again.
아, 다시 통화하게 되어 반갑습니다.

W : Nice to speak to you, too. Do you remember the boy who found your briefcase and brought it here?
저도 통화하게 되어 반갑습니다. 귀하의 서류 가방을 발견해서 여기로 가져온 소년을 기억하시나요?

M : Sure. I wanted to give him a reward. But he wouldn't accept it.
물론이죠. 저는 그 아이에게 사례를 하고 싶었어요. 하지만 그 아이가 그것을 받으려 하지 않았어요.

W : I remember you saying that before.
전에 그렇게 말씀하신 것이 저도 생각나네요.

M : Yeah. I'd still like to somehow express my thanks in person.
네. 저는 아직도 어떻게든 제 고마운 마음을 직접 표현하고 싶어요.

W : Good. That's why I'm calling you. Are you available next Friday at 10 a.m.?
좋네요. 그래서 제가 전화를 드리는 겁니다. 다음 주 금요일 오전 10시에 시간 되시나요?

M : Yes. I'm free at that time. Why?
네, 그때 한가합니다. 왜죠?

W : The boy will receive the Junior Citizen Award for what he's done for you.
아이가 귀하를 위해 한 일로 Junior Citizen Award를 수상할 거예요.

M : That's great news!
정말 좋은 소식이네요!

W : There'll be a ceremony for him at the police station, and he invited you as his guest. I was wondering if you can make it.
경찰서에서 아이를 위한 시상식이 열릴 것이고, 아이가 귀하를 내빈으로 초대했습니다. 오실 수 있는지 궁금해서요.

M : Definitely. I want to go to congratulate him myself.
물론이에요. 제가 가서 직접 그 아이를 축하해 주고 싶어요.

Why? 왜 정답일까?

대화에서 여자는 남자가 분실한 서류 가방을 찾아주어 상을 받게 된 소년이 남자를 시상식에 초대했다고 알려주며 올 의향이 있는지 물어보고 있다(**There'll be a ceremony for him at the police station, and he invited you as his guest. I was wondering if you can make it.**). 따라서 남자의 응답으로 가장 적절한 것은 ④ '물론이에요. 제가 가서 직접 그 아이를 축하해 주고 싶어요.'이다.

- **briefcase** ⓝ 서류 가방
- **in person** 직접
- **reward** ⓝ 보상, 사례
- **make it** 참석하다, 해내다

15 토마토를 언제든 따 가도 된다고 허락하기

정답률 73% | 정답 ①

다음 상황 설명을 듣고, Ben이 Stacy에게 할 말로 가장 적절한 것을 고르시오. [3점]

Ben: ______________

① Feel free to take the tomatoes from my backyard.
내 뒤뜰에서 토마토를 마음껏 따 가세요.
② Tell me if you need help when planting tomatoes.
토마토 심을 때 도움이 필요하면 제게 말씀하세요.
③ Do you want the ripe tomatoes I picked yesterday?
내가 어제 딴 익은 토마토를 원하세요?
④ Why don't we grow tomatoes in some other places?
어딘가 다른 곳에서 토마토를 재배하는 게 어떻겠어요?
⑤ Let me take care of your tomatoes while you're away.
안 계시는 동안 제가 댁의 토마토를 돌볼게요.

W : Ben and Stacy are neighbors.
Ben과 Stacy는 이웃이다.
Ben has been growing tomatoes in his backyard for several years.
Ben은 몇 년 동안 뒤뜰에서 토마토를 기르고 있다.
Ben shares his tomatoes with Stacy every year because she loves his fresh tomatoes.
Ben은 자신의 토마토를 Stacy와 매년 나누어 먹는데, 그녀가 그의 신선한 토마토를 매우 좋아하기 때문이다.
Today, Ben notices that his tomatoes will be ready to be picked in about a week.
오늘 Ben은 자신의 토마토가 약 1주일 뒤면 딸 준비가 되리라는 것을 알아차린다.
However, he leaves for a month-long business trip tomorrow.
하지만 그는 내일부로 한 달 동안 출장을 떠난다.
He's worried that there'll be no fresh tomatoes left in his backyard by the time he comes back.

그는 자신이 돌아올 때쯤에는 뒤뜰에 신선한 토마토가 하나도 남아 있지 않을까봐 걱정한다.
He'd like Stacy to have them while they are fresh and ripe.
그는 토마토가 신선하고 다 익었을 때 Stacy가 먹기를 바란다.
So, Ben wants to tell Stacy that she can come and get the tomatoes from his backyard whenever she wants.
그래서 Ben은 Stacy가 원할 때 언제든지 와서 자신의 뒤뜰에서 토마토를 가져가도 된다고 말하고 싶어 한다.
In this situation, what would Ben most likely say to Stacy?
이 상황에서, Ben은 Stacy에게 뭐라고 말하겠는가?

Ben : Feel free to take the tomatoes from my backyard.
내 뒤뜰에서 토마토를 마음껏 따 가세요.

Why? 왜 정답일까?

상황에 따르면 앞으로 한 달간 출장을 떠나는 Ben은 이웃인 Stacy에게 먹을 수 있도록 자신이 없는 동안에도 언제든 와서 토마토를 가져가도 된다(So, Ben wants to tell Stacy that she can come and get the tomatoes from his backyard whenever she wants.)고 이야기해주려 한다. 따라서 Ben이 Stacy에게 할 말로 가장 적절한 것은 ① '내 뒤뜰에서 토마토를 마음껏 따 가세요.'이다.

- ripe ⓐ 다 익은
- take care of ~을 돌보다, 처리하다
- Feel free to ~. 마음껏 ~하세요, 편하게 ~하세요.

16-17 색깔과 관련된 영어 표현 알려주기

M : Hello, students.
안녕하세요, 학생 여러분.
「Last time, I gave you a list of English expressions containing color terms.
지난 시간에 여러분에게 색깔 용어가 포함된 영어 표현 목록을 주었죠.
Today, we'll learn how these expressions got their meanings.」 16번의 근거
오늘은 이 표현들이 어떻게 그 의미를 갖게 되었는지 배워볼 것입니다.
「The first expression is "out of the blue," meaning something happens unexpectedly.」 17번 ①의 근거 일치
첫 번째 표현은 어떤 일이 예기치 않게 발생한다는 의미의 'out of the blue(난데없이, 갑자기)'입니다.
It came from the phrase "a lightning bolt out of the blue," which expresses the idea that it's unlikely to see lightning when there's a clear blue sky.
그것은 'a lightning bolt out of the blue(청천벽력)'라는 구절에서 유래했는데, 그것은 하늘이 맑고 푸를 때는 번개를 볼 가능성이 없다는 생각을 나타냅니다.
「The next expression, "white lie," means a harmless lie to protect someone from a harsh truth.」 17번 ②의 근거 일치
그다음 표현인 'white lie(선의의 거짓말)'는 가혹한 진실로부터 누군가를 보호하려는 악의 없는 거짓말을 의미합니다.
This is because the color white traditionally symbolizes innocence.
이는 흰색이 전통적으로 결백을 상징하기 때문입니다.
「Another expression, "green thumb," refers to a great ability to cultivate plants.」
또 다른 표현인 'green thumb(원예의 재능)'은 식물을 재배하는 뛰어난 능력을 가리킵니다. 17번 ③의 근거 일치
Planting pots were often covered with tiny green plants, so those who worked in gardens had green-stained hands.
화분은 흔히 작은 녹색 식물들로 뒤덮여 있어서, 정원에서 일하는 사람들은 양손에 녹색 얼룩이 져 있었습니다.
「The last expression, "to see red," means to suddenly get very angry.」 17번 ④의 근거 일치
마지막 표현인 'to see red(붉으락푸르락하다, 화를 벌컥 내다)'라는 말은 갑자기 크게 화를 낸다는 의미입니다.
Its origin possibly comes from the belief that bulls get angry and attack when a bullfighter waves a red cape.
이것의 기원은 아마도 투우사가 붉은 망토를 흔들면 황소가 화가 나서 공격한다는 믿음에서 나왔을 것입니다.
I hope this lesson helps you remember these phrases better.
여러분이 이 구절들을 더 잘 기억하는 데 이 수업이 도움이 되기를 바랍니다.

- out of the blue 난데없이, 갑자기
- white lie 선의의 거짓말
- harmless ⓐ 무해한
- innocence ⓝ 결백
- cultivate ⓥ 재배하다, 기르다
- see red 붉으락푸르락하다, 화를 벌컥 내다
- unexpectedly ad 예기치 않게
- harsh ⓐ 가혹한
- symbolize ⓥ 상징하다
- green thumb 원예의 재능
- stained ⓐ 얼룩진
- bullfighter ⓝ 투우사

16 주제 파악 정답률 89% | 정답 ⑤

남자가 하는 말의 주제로 가장 적절한 것은?

① color change in nature throughout seasons
계절 내내 있는 자연의 색채 변화
② various colors used in traditional English customs
영국의 전통 풍습에 쓰이는 다양한 색깔
③ differences in color perceptions according to culture
문화에 따른 색채 지각의 차이
④ why expressions related to colors are common in English
왜 색깔과 관련된 표현이 영어에 흔한가
⑤ how color-related English expressions gained their meanings
색깔과 관련된 영어 표현이 어떻게 그 의미를 갖게 되었나

Why? 왜 정답일까?

'Last time, I gave you a list of English expressions containing color terms. Today, we'll learn how these expressions got their meanings.'에서 남자는 지난 시간에 나눠준 색깔 관련 영어 표현이 어떻게 해서 그런 의미를 갖게 된 것인지 알아보겠다고 말하므로, 남자가 하는 말의 주제로 가장 적절한 것은 ⑤ '색깔과 관련된 영어 표현이 어떻게 그 의미를 갖게 되었나'이다.

17 언급 유무 파악 정답률 96% | 정답 ⑤

언급된 색깔이 아닌 것은?

① blue – 파란색 ② white – 하얀색 ③ green – 초록색 ④ red – 빨간색 ⑤ yellow – 노란색

Why? 왜 정답일까?

담화에서 남자는 색깔과 연관된 영어 표현의 예를 들며 파란색, 하얀색, 초록색, 빨간색을 언급하였다. 따라서 언급되지 않은 것은 ⑤ '노란색'이다.

Why? 왜 오답일까?

① 'The first expression is "out of the blue," meaning something happens unexpectedly.'에서 '파란색'이 언급되었다.
② 'The next expression, "white lie," means a harmless lie to protect someone from a harsh truth.'에서 '하얀색'이 언급되었다.
③ 'Another expression, "green thumb," refers to a great ability to cultivate plants.'에서 '초록색'이 언급되었다.
④ 'The last expression, "to see red," means to suddenly get very angry.'에서 '빨간색'이 언급되었다.

Dictation 33

문제편 195쪽

01 a personal fitness trainer / how to do a variety of exercises / you've experienced difficulty exercising regularly
02 look up at stars / By counting the stars together / identifying shapes and tracing patterns
03 designed the school I'm attending / incorporate elements of nature into it / visit the observation deck
04 raise money for children in need / my stripe-patterned tablecloth / drawn by the child you helped
05 except for daisies / they usually bloom from spring to fall / send them to you
06 get a discount for the second night / doesn't apply to the second night / Will you and your husband have breakfast
07 Is it because of the size / too heavy to carry around / scheduled a pickup
08 numerous failed products / admit our failures to truly succeed / an eye-opening experience
09 aimed to discover people with / only 10 participants will advance / won't want to miss watching
10 buy a reusable straw set / How much are you willing to spend / To use with my tumbler
11 tired from all the sightseeing / get something to drink
12 about to close off / paint the walls in this section
13 out of this model / buying the one on display / buy the displayed one / get it repaired for free
14 who found your briefcase / somehow express my thanks in person / invited you as his guest
15 has been growing tomatoes / ready to be picked / no fresh tomatoes left
16-17 out of the blue / unlikely to see lightning / traditionally symbolizes innocence / a great ability to cultivate plants

34회 | 2020학년도 대학수학능력시험 고3

| 정답과 해설 |

• 정답 •

01 ① 02 ③ 03 ③ 04 ④ 05 ④ 06 ② 07 ⑤ 08 ③ 09 ④ 10 ④ 11 ① 12 ② 13 ② 14 ② 15 ⑤ 16 ① 17 ③

01 백화점 주말 행사 안내

정답률 96% | 정답 ①

다음을 듣고, 남자가 하는 말의 목적으로 가장 적절한 것을 고르시오.

✔ 백화점 주말 특별 행사를 안내하려고
② 백화점 층별 신규 매장을 소개하려고
③ 주차장 이용 요금 변경을 공지하려고
④ 고객 만족도 조사 참여를 요청하려고
⑤ 백화점 회원 가입 방법을 설명하려고

M : Shoppers, may I have your attention please?
고객 여러분, 잠시 주목해 주시겠습니까?
Thank you for visiting Miracle Department Store.
Miracle 백화점을 방문해주셔서 감사합니다.
We'd like to inform you of the special events going on through this weekend.
저희는 주말 동안 계속되는 특별 행사에 대해 여러분께 알려드리려고 합니다.
First, we're offering a 50 percent discount on certain electronics and sporting goods on the seventh floor.
첫째로, 7층의 특정 전자제품과 운동 용품들에 대해 50퍼센트 할인을 제공합니다.
Second, we're providing a free beverage at our coffee shop on the first floor to shoppers who spend over $50.
둘째로, 50달러 이상을 쓰시는 고객님들께는 1층 커피숍에서 무료 음료를 제공해 드립니다.
Third, we're also giving away $10 gift certificates to all shoppers who spend over $100.
셋째로, 100달러 이상을 쓰시는 모든 고객님들께 10달러짜리 상품권도 증정합니다.
Last but not least, you don't have to worry about parking fees this weekend.
마지막으로, 이번 주말에는 주차비를 걱정하실 필요가 없습니다.
Parking is free.
주차는 무료입니다.
We hope you enjoy this weekend's special events at our department store.
저희 백화점의 이번 주말 특별 행사를 여러분들이 즐기시기를 바랍니다.

Why? 왜 정답일까?

'We'd like to inform you of the special events going on through this weekend.'에서 남자는 주말 동안 개최되는 백화점 특별 행사를 안내하겠다고 하므로, 남자가 하는 말의 목적으로 가장 적절한 것은 ① '백화점 주말 특별 행사를 안내하려고'이다.

• inform ⓥ 알리다 • certain ⓐ 특정한

02 왼쪽으로 누워 자는 것의 이점

정답률 96% | 정답 ③

대화를 듣고, 여자의 의견으로 가장 적절한 것을 고르시오.

① 왼쪽 신체의 잦은 사용은 두뇌 활동을 촉진한다.
② 수면 시간과 심장 기능은 밀접한 관련이 있다.
✔ 왼쪽으로 누워 자는 것은 건강에 도움이 된다.
④ 규칙적인 운동은 소화 불량 개선에 필수적이다.
⑤ 숙면은 정신 건강을 유지하는 데 중요한 요인이다.

W : Hi, Sam. How are you?
안녕, Sam. 잘 지내?
M : Fine. How about you, Christine?
응. 넌 어때, Christine?
W : I feel really good.
난 아주 좋아.
M : Wow! What happened to you? You usually say you're tired.
와! 무슨 일이야? 넌 보통 피곤하다고 말하잖아.
W : Well, I changed how I sleep. I started sleeping on my left side, and it has improved my health.
음, 난 잠자는 방식을 바꿨어. 난 왼쪽으로 누워 자기 시작했고, 그것이 내 건강을 개선시켜 주었어.
M : Really?
정말로?
W : Yeah. I've done it for a week, and my digestion has got better.
응. 난 한 주 동안 그렇게 했는데, 소화력이 더 나아졌어.
M : I didn't know how we sleep has something to do with digestion.
난 우리가 어떻게 자는지가 소화랑 관련되어 있다는 걸 몰랐어.
W : It does. Sleeping on your left side helps the digestive process because your stomach is on the left.
관련이 있어. 왼쪽으로 누워 자는 것은 소화 과정에 도움이 되는데 위가 왼쪽에 있기 때문이야.
M : I can see that. But does improving digestion make you that much healthier?
그렇구나. 하지만 소화 능력을 높이는 게 너를 그렇게 훨씬 더 건강해지게 해?
W : Sleeping on the left side does more than that. I think it's good for health because it also helps blood circulation to the heart.
왼쪽으로 누워 자는 건 그 이상을 하지. 내 생각에 이것은 심장으로 향하는 혈액 순환에도 도움이 돼서 건강에 좋은 것 같아.
M : That makes sense. I guess I should try it.
일리가 있네. 나도 시도해 봐야겠다.

Why? 왜 정답일까?

'I started sleeping on my left side, and it has improved my health.'에서 여자는 왼쪽으로 누워 자기 시작하여 건강을 개선했다고 언급한 후, 'Sleeping on your left side helps the digestive process ~'와 '~ it's good for health because it also helps blood circulation to the heart.'을 통해 왼쪽으로 누워 자는 것이 소화나 심장 혈액 순환에 도움이 된다고 덧붙이고 있다. 따라서 여자의 의견으로 가장 적절한 것은 ③ '왼쪽으로 누워 자는 것은 건강에 도움이 된다.'이다.

• improve ⓥ 향상시키다 • digestion ⓝ 소화
• stomach ⓝ 위(소화 기관) • circulation ⓝ 순환

03 유기농으로 쌀을 재배하는 농부와의 잡지 인터뷰

정답률 95% | 정답 ③

대화를 듣고, 두 사람의 관계를 가장 잘 나타낸 것을 고르시오.

① 곤충학자 – 학생
② 동물 조련사 – 사진작가
✔ 농부 – 잡지기자
④ 요리사 – 음식 평론가
⑤ 독자 – 소설가

M : Hello, I'm Ted Benson. You must be Ms. Brown.
안녕하세요, Ted Benson입니다. Brown 씨이시겠군요.
W : Hi, Mr. Benson. Thank you for sparing time for this interview. I've wanted to meet you since you won the "Best Rice Award."
안녕하세요, Benson 씨. 이 인터뷰를 위해 시간을 내주셔서 감사합니다. 당신이 Best Rice Award를 수상한 이후 만나 뵙기를 바라 왔어요.
M : I'm honored. I'm a regular reader of your magazine. The articles are very informative.
영광이군요. 전 당신 잡지의 정기 구독자입니다. 기사들이 매우 유익하더군요.
W : Thank you. Can you tell me the secret to your success?
고맙습니다. 당신의 성공 비결을 알려주실 수 있나요?
M : I grow rice without using any chemicals to kill harmful insects. It's organic.
전 해로운 곤충들을 죽이기 위한 어떤 화학물질도 쓰지 않은 채 쌀을 재배합니다. 유기농이죠.
W : How do you do that?
어떻게 그렇게 하시나요?
M : I put ducks into my fields, and they eat the insects.
전 제 땅에 오리를 풀어놓고, 그들이 곤충을 먹어요.
W : So that's how you grew the best rice in the country. What a great idea!
그것이 당신이 이 나라 최고의 쌀을 재배하신 비결이군요. 훌륭한 아이디어네요!
M : Yeah, that's the know-how I've got from my 30 years of farming life.
네, 그것은 제가 30년 간의 농사 생활을 통해 얻은 노하우예요.
W : Well, it's amazing. May I take a picture of you in front of your rice fields for my magazine article?
놀랍습니다. 저희 잡지 기사를 위해 당신의 논 앞에서 당신의 사진을 찍어도 될까요?
M : Go ahead.
물론입니다.

Why? 왜 정답일까?

'I grow rice without using any chemicals to kill harmful insects. It's organic.'과 '~ that's the know-how I've got from my 30 years of farming life.'에서 남자가 농부임을, 'I'm a regular reader of your magazine.'과 'May I take a picture of you in front of your rice fields for my magazine article?'에서 여자가 잡지 기자임을 알 수 있으므로, 두 사람의 관계로 가장 적절한 것은 ③ '농부 – 잡지기자'이다.

• informative ⓐ 유익한 • harmful ⓐ 해로운

04 Peter를 위한 방 사진 구경하기

정답률 96% | 정답 ④

대화를 듣고, 그림에서 대화의 내용과 일치하지 않는 것을 고르시오.

W : What are you looking at, honey?
뭘 보고 있어요, 여보?
M : Aunt Mary sent me a picture. She's already set up a room for Peter.
Mary 이모가 내게 사진 한 장을 보내줬어요. 그녀는 벌써 Peter를 위한 방을 꾸몄대요.
W : Wow! She's excited for him to stay during the winter vacation, isn't she?
와! 그가 겨울 방학 동안 머물게 되어 신나시나 봐요, 그렇죠?
M : Yes, she is. 『I like the blanket with the checkered pattern on the bed.』 ①의 근거 일치
그러게요. 난 침대 위의 체크 무늬 담요가 마음에 들어요.
W : I'm sure it must be very warm. 『Look at the chair below the window.』 ②의 근거 일치
분명 그건 무척 따뜻할 거예요. 창문 밑에 있는 의자를 봐요.
M : It looks comfortable. He could sit there and read.
편안해 보이네요. 그는 저기 앉아서 책을 읽을 수 있을 거예요.
W : Right. 『I guess that's why Aunt Mary put the bookcase next to it.』 ③의 근거 일치
맞아요. 그래서 Mary 이모가 옆에 책장을 놔둔 것 같네요.
M : That makes sense. 『Oh, there's a toy horse in the corner.』 ④의 근거 불일치
일리가 있어요. 오, 구석에 장난감 말이 있어요.
W : It looks real. I think it's a gift for Peter.
진짜 같아 보이네요. 내 생각에 그건 Peter를 위한 선물 같아요.
M : Yeah, I remember she mentioned it. 『And do you see the round mirror on the wall?』 ⑤의 근거 일치
네, 이모가 그 말씀을 하셨던 게 기억나요. 그리고 벽에 둥근 거울 보여요?
W : It's nice. It looks like the one Peter has here at home.
근사하네요. Peter가 여기 집에 가지고 있는 것과 비슷해 보여요.
M : It does. Let's show him this picture.
그러네요. 그에게 이 사진을 보여줍시다.

Why? 왜 정답일까?

대화에서 구석에는 장난감 말이 있다(Oh, there's a toy horse in the corner.)고 하는데, 그림에서는 구석 자리에 큰 곰 인형이 놓여 있다. 따라서 그림에서 대화의 내용과 일치하지 않는 것은 ④이다.

• stay ⓥ 머무르다 • mention ⓥ 말하다

05 노인정에서 자원봉사하기

정답률 91% | 정답 ④

대화를 듣고, 여자가 할 일로 가장 적절한 것을 고르시오.

① 간식 가져오기 ② 책 기부하기 ③ 점심 준비하기
④ 설거지하기 ⑤ 세탁실 청소하기

M : Good morning, Jane.
안녕, Jane.

W : Good morning, Mr. Smith.
안녕하세요, Mr. Smith.

M : Thanks for volunteering to work at our senior citizen's center again.
우리 노인정에서 다시 자원봉사로 일해 줘서 고마워.

W : I'm happy to help. And I brought some snacks for the elderly.
도움이 되어 기뻐요. 그리고 전 어르신들을 위한 간식을 좀 가져왔어요.

M : How considerate of you! Last time you donated some books. Everyone really enjoyed reading them.
참 사려 깊구나! 저번에는 책을 좀 기부했었지. 모든 분들이 그 책들을 정말 재미있게 읽으셨어.

W : It was my pleasure. So, what am I supposed to do today? Should I prepare lunch like I did before?
별 말씀을요. 그럼, 오늘은 뭘 하면 되나요? 저번에 했던 것처럼 점심을 준비해야 하나요?

M : There are some other volunteers today, and they'll do that work.
오늘 다른 자원봉사자가 몇 사람 있어서, 그들이 그 일을 할 거야.

W : Good. Then what would you like me to do?
잘됐네요. 그럼 전 뭘 할까요?

M : Well, you could do the dishes or clean the laundry room.
음, 넌 설거지를 하거나 세탁실을 치우면 될 거야.

W : I'm good at washing dishes. So I'll do that.
전 설거지를 잘해요. 그러니 그걸 할게요.

M : Great. We'll have someone else clean the laundry room.
잘됐구나. 다른 사람에게 세탁실 청소를 시킬게.

Why? 왜 정답일까?

노인정에 봉사하러 온 여자에게 남자가 설거지를 하거나 세탁실을 치우면 된다고 하자, 여자는 설거지를 하겠다(**I'm good at washing dishes. So I'll do that.**)고 자원한다. 따라서 여자가 할 일로 가장 적절한 것은 ④ '설거지하기'이다.

• volunteer ⓥ 자원봉사하다 • bring ⓥ 가져오다
• considerate ⓐ 사려 깊은 • prepare ⓥ 준비하다

06 과학기술 박물관 입장권 구매

정답률 85% | 정답 ②

대화를 듣고, 여자가 지불할 금액을 고르시오. [3점]

① $72 ② $74 ③ $76 ④ $78 ⑤ $80

M : Welcome to the Science and Technology Museum. How can I help you?
Science and Technology Museum에 오신 것을 환영합니다. 무엇을 도와드릴까요?

W : Hi. I want to buy admission tickets.
안녕하세요. 전 입장권을 사고 싶어요.

M : Okay. They're $20 for adults and $10 for children.
알겠습니다. 성인은 20달러이고 어린이는 10달러입니다.

W : Good. Two adult tickets and two child tickets, please. And I'm a member of the National Robot Club. Do I get a discount?
좋아요. 성인 두 장과 어린이 두 장 주세요. 그리고 전 National Robot Club의 회원이에요. 제가 할인을 받나요?

M : Yes. You get 10 percent off all of those admission tickets with your membership.
네. 회원이시면 이 모든 입장권을 10퍼센트 할인받으시게 됩니다.

W : Excellent.
훌륭해요.

M : We also have the AI Robot program. You can play games with the robots and take pictures with them.
저희는 인공지능 로봇 프로그램도 있습니다. 로봇하고 게임도 하고 사진도 찍을 수 있어요.

W : That sounds interesting. How much is it?
재미있겠네요. 얼마인가요?

M : It's just $5 per person. But the membership discount does not apply to this program.
1인당 단돈 5달러랍니다. 하지만 회원 할인은 이 프로그램에 적용되지 않아요.

W : Okay. I'll take four tickets.
알겠어요. 티켓 네 장을 사겠어요.

M : So two adult and two child admission tickets, and four AI Robot program tickets, right?
그럼 성인 입장권 두 장과 어린이 입장권 두 장, 그리고 인공지능 로봇 프로그램 티켓 네 장, 맞으시죠?

W : Yes. Here are my credit card and membership card.
네. 여기 제 신용카드와 회원 카드요.

Why? 왜 정답일까?

대화에 따르면 여자는 20달러짜리 성인 입장권 두 장, 10달러짜리 어린이 입장권 두 장을 사고 전체 입장권 가격에서 10퍼센트를 할인받았으며, 할인이 적용되지 않는 5달러짜리 인공지능 로봇 프로그램 티켓을 네 장 샀다. 이를 식으로 나타내면 '$(20\times2+10\times2)\times0.9+(5\times4)=74$'이므로, 여자가 지불할 금액은 ② '$74'이다.

• admission ⓝ 입장 • apply ⓥ 적용되다

07 해외 유학 때문에 요리 대회를 포기한 남자

정답률 83% | 정답 ⑤

대화를 듣고, 남자가 요리 대회 참가를 포기한 이유를 고르시오.

① 다친 팔이 낫지 않아서
② 조리법을 완성하지 못해서
③ 다른 대회와 일정이 겹쳐서
④ 입학시험 공부를 해야 해서
⑤ 대회 전에 유학을 떠나야 해서

W : Hi, Michael.
안녕, Michael.

M : Hi, Sarah. Did you apply for the cooking contest?
안녕, Sarah. 너 요리 대회에 신청했니?

W : I did. I've already finished developing a recipe.
했어. 난 이미 레시피 개발도 끝냈어.

M : That's great. Actually, I gave up participating in it.
멋지다. 사실, 난 거기 참가하는 걸 포기했어.

W : Why? Is your arm still hurt?
왜? 네 팔이 아직 아픈 거야?

M : No, it's fully healed.
아니, 그건 다 나았어.

W : Is your recipe not ready yet?
네 레시피가 아직 준비되지 않은 거야?

M : I already created a unique recipe for the contest.
난 이미 대회를 위해 독특한 레시피를 만들어 뒀어.

W : Then, what made you give up the contest?
그럼 무엇 때문에 대회를 포기한 거야?

M : You know I've planned to study abroad. The cooking school in Italy just informed me that I've been accepted. The problem is I have to leave before the contest begins.
너도 내가 해외 유학할 계획이었던 거 알잖아. 이탈리아에 있는 요리학교에서 날 받아준다고 막 알려줬어. 문제는 내가 대회가 시작되기 전에 떠나야 한다는 거야.

W : I'm sorry you'll miss the contest. But it's good for you since you've always wanted to study in Italy.
네가 대회를 놓치게 되어 유감이네. 그렇지만 넌 항상 이탈리아에서 공부하고 싶어했으니 너한테 잘됐다.

M : I think so, too. I wish you luck in the contest.
나도 그렇게 생각해. 대회에서 행운을 빌게.

W : Thanks. I'll do my best.
고마워. 최선을 다할게.

Why? 왜 정답일까?

대화에 따르면 남자는 평소 바라던 대로 이탈리아 유학을 가게 되었는데 이로 인해 요리 대회 이전에 출국해야 해서(**The problem is I have to leave before the contest begins.**) 대회에 참가할 수 없다. 따라서 남자가 요리 대회 참가를 포기한 이유로 가장 적절한 것은 ⑤ '대회 전에 유학을 떠나야 해서'이다.

• develop ⓥ 개발하다 • participate ⓥ 참가하다
• unique ⓐ 독특한 • abroad ad 해외에서

08 동창회 준비에 관해 이야기하기

정답률 90% | 정답 ③

대화를 듣고, Ten Year Class Reunion Party에 관해 언급되지 않은 것을 고르시오.

① 장소 ② 날짜 ③ 회비 ④ 음식 ⑤ 기념품

W : Hi, Ross. How's everything going for our Ten Year Class Reunion Party?
안녕, Ross. 우리 Ten Year Class Reunion Party를 위한 모든 준비가 잘 되어 가?

M : I think we're done, Jennifer.
다 된 것 같아, Jennifer.

W : Then let's go over what we've prepared.
그럼 우리가 준비한 것을 점검해 보자.

M : 「I already booked the Silver Corral Restaurant for the party.」 ①의 근거 일치
난 이미 파티를 위해 Silver Corral Restaurant을 예약해 두었어.

W : Good. 「It must have been very difficult to get a reservation because our party is on December 24th.」 ②의 근거 일치
좋아. 우리 파티가 12월 24일이니까 예약하기가 분명 무척 어려웠을 텐데.

M : Yeah, we were lucky.
응, 우린 운이 좋았어.

W : 「What food will they serve?
어떤 음식이 나온대?

M : Their steak, spaghetti, and pizza are famous, so that's what I ordered.」 ④의 근거 일치
거기 스테이크와 스파게티와 피자가 유명해서, 그걸 내가 주문했어.

W : Sounds delicious. 「And the souvenirs for the party are ready, too. ⑤의 근거 일치
맛있겠다. 그리고 파티 기념품도 준비가 되었어.

M : You ordered mugs for souvenirs, right?」
넌 기념품으로 머그잔을 주문했지, 그렇지?

W : Yes, I did. I'll bring them that day.
응, 그날 내가 그걸 가져갈 거야.

M : Perfect. It's going to be a great party.
딱이네. 근사한 파티가 되겠어.

Why? 왜 정답일까?

대화에서 남자와 여자는 Ten Year Class Reunion Party에 관해 장소, 날짜, 음식, 기념품을 언급하였다. 따라서 언급되지 않은 것은 ③ '회비'이다.

Why? 왜 오답일까?

① 'I already booked the Silver Corral Restaurant for the party.'에서 '장소'가 언급되었다.
② '~ our party is on December 24th.'에서 '날짜'가 언급되었다.
④ 'Their steak, spaghetti, and pizza are famous, so that's what I ordered'에서 '음식'이 언급되었다.
⑤ 'You ordered mugs for souvenirs, right?'에서 '기념품'이 언급되었다.

• book ⓥ 예약하다 • reservation ⓝ 예약
• souvenir ⓝ 기념품 • mug ⓝ 머그잔

09 영화 시사회 안내

정답률 95% | 정답 ④

***Green Ocean* 영화 시사회에 관한 다음 내용을 듣고, 일치하지 않는 것을 고르시오.**

① 100명을 초대할 예정이다.
② 다음 주 토요일 오후 4시에 시작할 것이다.
③ 영화 출연 배우와 사진을 찍을 수 있다.
④ 입장권을 우편으로 보낼 예정이다.
⑤ 초대받은 사람은 극장에서 포스터를 받을 것이다.

[문제편 p.199]

W : Hello, listeners.
안녕하세요, 청취자 여러분.
Welcome to *Good Day Movie*.
*Good Day Movie*에 오신 것을 환영합니다.
We'd like to let you know about a great chance to see the preview of the movie *Green Ocean* by Feather Pictures.
저희는 여러분께 Feather Pictures의 영화 *Green Ocean*의 시사회를 볼 수 있는 멋진 기회에 관해 알려드리려고 합니다.
「One hundred people will be invited to the event.」 ①의 근거 일치
100명이 행사에 초대될 것입니다.
「It'll begin at the Glory Theater at 4 p.m. next Saturday.」 ②의 근거 일치
이것은 다음 주 토요일 오후 4시에 Glory Theater에서 시작할 예정입니다.
「After watching the movie, you can meet and take pictures with the actors of the movie.」 ③의 근거 일치
영화를 보고 난 후 여러분은 영화 출연 배우들과 만나 사진을 찍을 수 있습니다.
If you're interested, apply for admission tickets on the *Green Ocean* homepage, and 「the tickets will be sent by text message to the first 100 people who apply.」 ④의 근거 불일치
관심이 있으시다면, *Green Ocean* 홈페이지에서 입장권을 신청하시고, 티켓은 가장 먼저 신청해주신 100명에게 문자 메시지로 발송됩니다.
「Those who are invited will be given a poster at the theater.」 ⑤의 근거 일치
초대받은 분들은 영화관 앞에서 포스터를 받으시게 됩니다.
Hurry up and don't miss this chance to watch *Green Ocean* in advance.
서둘러 주시고 *Green Ocean*을 미리 볼 수 있는 이 기회를 놓치지 마세요.
Now we'll be back after the commercial break.
이제 저희는 광고 뒤에 돌아오겠습니다.
So stay tuned.
채널 고정해 주세요.

Why? 왜 정답일까?

'~ **the tickets will be sent by text message to the first 100 people who apply.**'에서 입장권은 선착순 **100**명에게 문자 메시지로 발송된다고 하므로, 내용과 일치하지 않는 것은 ④ '입장권을 우편으로 보낼 예정이다.'이다.

Why? 왜 오답일까?

① '**One hundred people will be invited to the event.**'의 내용과 일치한다.
② '**It'll begin at the Glory Theater at 4 p.m. next Saturday.**'의 내용과 일치한다.
③ '**After watching the movie, you can meet and take pictures with the actors of the movie.**'의 내용과 일치한다.
⑤ '**Those who are invited will be given a poster at the theater.**'의 내용과 일치한다.

- **preview** ⓝ 시사회
- **admission ticket** ⓝ 입장권
- **apply** ⓥ 신청하다
- **in advance** 미리, 사전에
- **commercial** ⓝ 광고

10 출장을 위한 항공편 예약

정답률 94% | 정답 ④

다음 표를 보면서 대화를 듣고, 두 사람이 예약할 항공편을 고르시오.

Flight Schedule to New York City Area

	Flight	Ticket Price	Departure Time	Arrival Airport	Stops
①	A	$600	6:00 a.m.	JFK	1 stop
②	B	$625	10:00 a.m.	Newark	Nonstop
③	C	$700	11:30 a.m.	JFK	1 stop
✔	D	$785	2:30 p.m.	JFK	Nonstop
⑤	E	$810	6:30 p.m.	Newark	1 stop

M : Ms. Roberts, we're going on a business trip to New York City next week. Why don't we book the flight on this website?
Ms. Roberts, 우린 다음 주에 뉴욕시로 출장을 갈 예정이에요. 이 웹 사이트에서 항공편을 예약하는 게 어때요?
W : Okay, Mr. White. Let's take a look at the flight schedule.
좋아요, Mr. White. 비행 스케줄을 보죠.
M : Sure. 「How much can we spend on the flight?
그래요. 우리가 항공편에 얼마나 쓸 수 있죠?
W : Our company policy doesn't allow us to spend more than $800 per ticket.」
우리 회사 정책상 우리는 티켓당 800달러 이상을 쓰도록 허용되지 않아요. 근거1 Ticket Price 조건
M : I see. 「And what about the departure time? I have to take my daughter to daycare early in the morning that day.
알겠어요. 그럼 출발 시간은요? 전 그날 제 딸을 아침 일찍 어린이집에 데려다줘야 해요.
W : Then how about choosing a flight after 9 a.m.?」 근거2 Departure Time 조건
그럼 오전 9시 이후 항공편을 고르는 게 어때요?
M : That'll be great. 「Which airport should we arrive at?
그게 좋겠네요. 우리 어느 공항에 내려야 하나요?
W : JFK is closer to the company we're visiting.」 근거3 Arrival Airport 조건
JFK가 우리가 방문할 회사와 더 가까워요.
M : Oh, you're right. Let's go there.
오, 맞아요. 그리로 가죠.
W : Then we have two options left, nonstop or one stop.
그럼 우린 직행 아니면 1회 경유, 이렇게 두 가지 선택권이 남아요.
M : 「I don't want to spend hours waiting for a connecting flight.
전 연결 항공편을 기다리며 몇 시간씩 쓰고 싶지 않아요.
W : Me, neither. We should choose the nonstop flight.」 근거4 Stops 조건
저도 그래요. 우린 직행 항공편을 골라야겠네요.
M : Okay. Let's book the flight now.
알겠어요. 지금 비행기를 예약하죠.

Why? 왜 정답일까?

대화에 따르면 남자와 여자는 티켓값이 **800**달러를 넘지 않으면서, 오전 **9**시 이후에 출발하고, **JFK** 공항에 도착하며, 목적지까지 직행하는 항공편을 예약하려 한다. 따라서 두 사람이 예약할 항공편은 ④ '**D**'이다.

- **policy** ⓝ 정책
- **allow** ⓥ 허락하다
- **daycare** ⓝ 어린이집
- **connecting flight** 연결 항공편

[문제편 p.200]

11 세탁물 수거 부탁하기

정답률 95% | 정답 ①

대화를 듣고, 남자의 마지막 말에 대한 여자의 응답으로 가장 적절한 것을 고르시오.

✔ Okay. I'll send the address to your phone. – 알겠어요. 당신 전화로 주소를 보내줄게요.
② Yes. I'll have your dress cleaned by noon. – 네. 제가 당신 옷을 정오까지 세탁해 둘게요.
③ Of course. I'll open the shop tomorrow. – 물론이죠. 전 내일 가게를 열어요.
④ No. I'm not moving to a new place. – 아니요. 전 새로운 곳으로 이사를 가지 않아요.
⑤ Too late. I'm already back at home. – 너무 늦었어요. 전 이미 집에 왔어요.

[Cell phone rings.]
[휴대전화가 울린다.]
M : Honey, I've just left work. I'll be home in half an hour.
여보, 나 방금 퇴근했어요. 집에 30분이면 도착해요.
W : Good. Is it possible for you to stop by the dry cleaner's shop and pick up my dress?
좋아요. 당신 세탁소에 들러서 내 옷을 찾아올 수 있겠어요?
M : Sure. Can you tell me where the shop is located?
물론이죠. 가게 위치가 어디인지 내게 말해줄래요?
W : Okay. I'll send the address to your phone.
알겠어요. 당신 전화로 주소를 보내줄게요.

Why? 왜 정답일까?

여자가 남자에게 퇴근길에 세탁소에 들러 옷을 찾아와달라고 부탁하자 남자는 가게가 어디 있는지 말해달라고 요청하고 있다(**Can you tell me where the shop is located?**). 여자의 응답으로 가장 적절한 것은 ① '알겠어요. 당신 전화로 주소를 보내줄게요.'이다.

- **stop by** ~에 잠시 들르다
- **pick up** (어디에서) ~을 찾다[찾아오다]
- **address** ⓝ 주소

34회

12 좋아하는 가수의 공연 일정 알려주기

정답률 85% | 정답 ②

대화를 듣고, 여자의 마지막 말에 대한 남자의 응답으로 가장 적절한 것을 고르시오.

① Unbelievable. I'm really going to be on stage today.
믿기지 않네요. 전 오늘 정말로 무대에 서게 돼요.
✔ Absolutely. I'm so eager to see him sing in person.
당연하죠. 전 그를 실제로 몹시 보고 싶어요.
③ Not really. He wasn't as amazing as I expected.
아니요. 그는 제가 기대한 만큼 대단하지 않았어요.
④ Sure. I'll find someone else to perform instead.
물론이죠. 대신 공연할 다른 사람을 찾아볼게요.
⑤ Oh, no. You shouldn't have missed his performance.
오, 이런. 그의 공연을 놓치지 말았어야 했어요.

W : David, look at this advertisement! Jason Stevens is going to sing at the opening of City Concert Hall next Saturday.
David, 이 광고 좀 봐! Jason Stevens가 다음 주 토요일 시청 콘서트홀 개관식에서 노래할 거래.
M : Wow! You know I'm a big fan of him, Mom. Luckily, I don't have anything scheduled that day.
와! 아시다시피 전 그의 열렬한 팬이에요, 엄마. 다행히 전 그날 아무 일정도 없어요.
W : Great. Mark the date on your calendar, so you don't miss his performance.
잘됐다. 그의 공연을 놓치지 않게 날짜를 네 달력에 표시해 두렴.
M : Absolutely. I'm so eager to see him sing in person.
당연하죠. 전 그를 실제로 몹시 보고 싶어요.

Why? 왜 정답일까?

여자는 남자가 좋아하는 가수가 시청 콘서트홀 개관식에서 노래를 부를 예정임을 알려주며 공연을 놓치지 않도록 달력에 날짜를 표시해두라고 말하고 있다. 따라서 남자의 응답으로 가장 적절한 것은 ② '당연하죠. 전 그를 실제로 몹시 보고 싶어요.'이다.

- **advertisement** ⓝ 광고
- **mark** ⓥ 표시하다

13 축제 때 입을 정장 마련하기

정답률 94% | 정답 ②

대화를 듣고, 여자의 마지막 말에 대한 남자의 응답으로 가장 적절한 것을 고르시오.

Man: ______

① It's worthwhile to spend money on my suit.
내 정장에 돈을 쓰는 것은 가치 있어.
✔ It would be awesome to borrow your brother's.
네 오빠 것을 빌리면 무척 좋겠다.
③ Your brother will have a fun time at the festival.
네 오빠는 축제에서 재밌는 시간을 보내실 거야.
④ I'm looking forward to seeing you in a new suit.
난 네가 새로운 정장을 입은 모습을 보기를 고대하고 있어.
⑤ You're going to build a great reputation as an MC.
넌 사회자로서 대단한 명성을 쌓게 될 거야.

W : Hi, Justin. I heard you're going to be the MC at the school festival.
안녕, Justin. 난 네가 학교 축제에서 사회를 볼 거라고 들었어.
M : Yes, I am, Cindy.
응, Cindy.
W : Do you have everything ready?
모든 게 다 준비되었니?
M : Mostly. I have all the introductions ready and I've practiced a lot.
거의. 난 모든 소개 멘트를 준비해 두었고 연습을 많이 했어.
W : I'm sure you'll do a great job.
넌 분명 훌륭하게 해낼 거야.
M : I hope so, too. But there's one thing I'm worried about.
나도 그러길 바라. 그런데 걱정되는 게 한 가지 있어.
W : What is it?
그게 뭔데?
M : I need a suit, so I'm thinking of buying one. But it's expensive, and I don't think I'll wear it after the festival.
난 정장이 필요해서 하나 살 생각이야. 그런데 그건 비싸고, 축제가 끝난 뒤에 내가 그걸 입을 것 같지도 않아.
W : Well, if you want, I can ask my older brother to lend you one of his suits. He has a lot of them.
음, 원한다면 내가 우리 오빠한테 네게 정장 중 하나를 빌려주라고 부탁할 수 있어. 오빠한텐 정장이 많거든.

M : Could you please?
그래줄 수 있어?
W : I'd be happy to.
기꺼이 그럴게.
M : Thanks. But will his suit be my size?
고마워. 그런데 오빠 정장이 내 사이즈일까?
W : It will. You and my brother pretty much have the same build.
그럴 거야. 너와 우리 오빠는 체구가 꽤 비슷해.
M : It would be awesome to borrow your brother's.
네 오빠 것을 빌리면 무척 좋겠다.

Why? 왜 정답일까?

대화에 따르면 학교 축제에서 사회를 볼 예정인 남자는 정장을 사야 하지만 너무 비싸고 축제 이후에 입을 것 같지도 않아 망설이고 있다. 이에 여자는 자신의 오빠에게 정장을 빌려달라고 부탁해 보겠다며, 남자와 오빠가 서로 체구가 비슷하다(**You and my brother pretty much have the same build.**)고 말해준다. 따라서 남자의 응답으로 가장 적절한 것은 ② '네 오빠 것을 빌리면 무척 좋겠다.'이다.

- **introduction** ⓝ 도입
- **lend** ⓥ 빌려주다
- **awesome** ⓐ 좋은, 엄청난

14 철학 서적을 더 잘 이해하기 위해 토론 모임 들기 정답률 82% | 정답 ②

대화를 듣고, 남자의 마지막 말에 대한 여자의 응답으로 가장 적절한 것을 고르시오. [3점]

Woman: ________________

① Definitely! This book isn't as interesting as yours.
당연하죠! 이건 당신의 책만큼 재미있지 않아요.
✔ Terrific! I'll check right away if there are any nearby.
멋져요! 근처에 좀 있는지 바로 찾아볼래요.
③ Never mind. I won't take that course next semester.
걱정 마세요. 전 그 수업을 다음 학기엔 듣지 않을 거예요.
④ Really? I didn't know you have a degree in philosophy.
정말요? 전 당신이 철학에 학위가 있는지 몰랐어요.
⑤ Why not? You can join my philosophy discussion group.
안 될 게 뭐예요? 제 철학 토론 모임에 들어도 돼요.

M : Amy, what are you reading?
Amy, 무엇을 읽고 있니?
W : Dad, it's a book for my philosophy course.
아빠, 이건 제 철학 수업을 위한 책이에요.
M : Let me take a look. Wow! It's a book by Kant.
어디 보자. 와! 이건 칸트가 쓴 책이구나.
W : Yeah. It's very difficult to understand.
네. 이해하기 몹시 어려워요.
M : You're right. His books take a lot of effort to read since they include his deep knowledge and thoughts.
네 말이 맞아. 그의 책들은 그의 깊은 지식과 사상을 담고 있어서 읽는 데 많은 노력이 들지.
W : I think so, too. Do you have any ideas for me to understand the book better, Dad?
저도 그렇게 생각해요. 제가 이 책을 더 잘 이해할 수 있기 위한 아이디어가 있으세요, 아빠?
M : Well, why don't you join a philosophy discussion group? You can find one in our area.
음, 철학 토론 모임에 들어보는 건 어떠니? 우리 지역에서 하나 찾을 수 있을 거야.
W : Are there discussion groups for philosophy? That sounds interesting.
철학을 위한 토론 모임도 있어요? 재미있을 것 같아요.
M : Yeah. You can share ideas with others in the group about the book you're reading.
응. 넌 모임의 다른 사람들과 네가 읽고 있는 책에 관한 생각들을 공유할 수 있어.
W : You mean I can understand Kant's book more clearly by discussing it?
아빠 말씀은 제가 칸트의 책에 관해 토론해 봄으로써 책을 더 잘 이해할 수 있다는 뜻이죠?
M : Absolutely. Plus, you can develop critical thinking skills in the group as well.
바로 그거야. 게다가, 넌 모임에서 비판적 사고력도 기를 수 있지.
W : Terrific! I'll check right away if there are any nearby.
멋져요! 근처에 좀 있는지 바로 찾아볼래요.

Why? 왜 정답일까?

여자가 어려운 철학 서적을 더 쉽게 이해할 수 있는 방법에 대해 조언을 구하자, 남자는 철학 토론 모임에 들어볼 것을 권하며(~ **why don't you join a philosophy discussion group?**) 모임에 들었을 때의 장점을 열거하고 있다(**You can share ideas with others ~. / Plus, you can develop critical thinking skills ~.**). 따라서 여자의 응답으로 가장 적절한 것은 ② '멋져요! 근처에 좀 있는지 바로 찾아볼래요.'이다.

- **philosophy** ⓝ 철학
- **include** ⓥ 포함하다
- **discussion** ⓝ 토론
- **share** ⓥ 공유하다

15 수학여행 짐 싸기 정답률 80% | 정답 ⑤

다음 상황 설명을 듣고, Brian의 어머니가 Brian에게 할 말로 가장 적절한 것을 고르시오. [3점]

Brian's mother: ________________

① Make sure to call me whenever you go somewhere new.
새로운 곳에 갈 때마다 내게 꼭 전화해 주렴.
② School trips are good opportunities to make friends.
수학여행은 친구를 사귈 수 있는 좋은 기회야.
③ I believe traveling broadens your perspective.
난 여행이 네 시각을 넓혀준다고 믿어.
④ How about carrying the luggage on your own?
네가 짐을 직접 들고 가는 게 어떠니?
✔ Why don't you pack your bag by yourself for the trip?
여행 짐을 네가 혼자서 챙겨보는 게 어떠니?

W : Brian is a high school student.
Brian은 고등학생이다.
He has only traveled with his family before.
그는 전에 자기 가족과만 여행을 해 보았다.
Until now his mother has always taken care of his travel bag, so he doesn't have any experience preparing it himself.
지금까지 그의 어머니는 늘 그의 여행 가방을 챙겨주었고, 그래서 그는 스스로 가방을 준비해본 경험이 없다.
This weekend, Brian is supposed to go on a school trip with his friends.
이번 주말에 Brian은 친구들과 수학여행을 갈 예정이다.
He asks his mother to get his stuff ready for his trip this time, too.
그는 어머니에게 이번에도 자기 여행을 위한 짐을 챙겨달라고 부탁한다.
However, she believes Brian is old enough to prepare what he needs, and she thinks this time is a great opportunity for him to learn to be more independent.
하지만 어머니는 Brian이 자기가 필요한 것을 준비할 만큼 컸다고 생각하고, 이번이 그가 보다 자립하는 법을 배울 기회라고 생각한다.
So, she wants to tell Brian that he should get his things ready and put them in his bag without her help.
그래서, 그녀는 Brian에게 그녀의 도움 없이 자기 짐을 직접 준비하고 그것들을 자기 가방에 넣을 기회라고 말해주고 싶다.
In this situation, what would Brian's mother most likely say to Brian?
이 상황에서, Brian의 어머니는 Brian에게 뭐라고 말하겠는가?
Brian's mother : Why don't you pack your bag by yourself for the trip?
여행 짐을 네가 혼자서 챙겨보는 게 어떠니?

Why? 왜 정답일까?

상황에 따르면 Brian의 어머니는 여태까지 늘 Brian의 여행가방을 챙겨주었지만 이번에는 혼자 짐을 준비하고 싸 보게 하려고 한다(**So, she wants to tell Brian that he should get his things ready and put them in his bag without her help.**). 따라서 Brian의 어머니가 Brian에게 할 말로 가장 적절한 것은 ⑤ '여행 짐을 네가 혼자서 챙겨보는 게 어떠니?'이다.

- **experience** ⓝ 경험
- **stuff** ⓝ 물건
- **opportunity** ⓝ 기회
- **independent** ⓐ 독립적인

16-17 동물을 이용한 우편 배달 체계

M : 「How did people send mail before they had access to cars and trains?
사람들이 차와 기차를 이용하기 전에는 어떻게 우편을 보냈을까요?
There were simple options out there, like delivery by animal.」 16번의 근거
간단한 선택권들이 있었는데, 동물에 의한 배달 같은 것입니다.
「Horses were frequently utilized in delivery of letters and messages.」 17번 ①의 근거 일치
말은 편지와 메시지를 전달하는 데 자주 이용되었습니다.
In the 19th century, a mail express system that used horses serviced a large area of the United States.
19세기에, 말을 이용한 속달 우편 시스템이 미국의 넓은 지역에 서비스를 제공했습니다.
「Pigeons may be seen as a problem by many people today. 17번 ②의 근거 일치
비둘기는 오늘날 많은 사람들에게 문제로 여겨질지도 모릅니다.
However, in ancient Greece, they were used to mail people the results of the Olympics between cities.」
하지만 고대 그리스에서는 그들이 도시들 간에 사람들에게 올림픽의 결과를 전달해 주는 데 이용되었습니다.
Alaska and Canada are known for their cold winters.
알래스카와 캐나다는 추운 겨울로 유명합니다.
「In their early days, dogs were utilized to deliver mail because they've adapted to run over ice and snow.」 17번 ④의 근거 일치
초기에는, 개들이 우편 배달에 이용되었는데 이들이 눈과 얼음 위를 달리는 데 적응했기 때문입니다.
「Maybe the most fascinating of all delivery animals is the camel.」 17번 ⑤의 근거 일치
아마도 모든 배달 동물들 중 가장 매력적인 것은 낙타입니다.
Australia imported camels from the Middle East and utilized them to transfer mail across vast deserts.
호주는 중동에서 낙타를 수입하여 광활한 사막을 건너 우편을 전달하기 위해 이용했습니다.
They were ideally suited to this job because they can go without water for quite a while.
그들은 이 일에 이상적으로 잘 맞았는데 왜냐하면 꽤 오랫동안 물 없이 이동할 수 있기 때문이었습니다.
Fortunately, we've developed faster and more reliable delivery systems, but we should not ignore the important roles these animals played in the past.
다행히도, 우리는 더 빠르고 믿을만한 배달 체계를 발전시켜 왔지만, 우리는 이 동물들이 과거에 수행한 중요한 역할을 무시해서는 안 될 것입니다.

- **access** ⓝ 이용
- **delivery** ⓝ 배달
- **frequently** ad 자주
- **utilize** ⓥ 활용하다
- **pigeon** ⓝ 비둘기
- **adapt** ⓥ 적응하다
- **fascinating** ⓐ 매력적인
- **transfer** ⓥ 옮기다
- **ideally** ad 이상적으로
- **reliable** ⓐ 믿을 만한

16 주제 파악 정답률 91% | 정답 ①

남자가 하는 말의 주제로 가장 적절한 것은?

✔ animals used in delivering mail in history – 역사상 우편을 배달하는 데 이용된 동물들
② difficulty of training animals from the wild – 야생에서 온 동물들을 훈련시키는 것의 어려움
③ animals' adaptation to environmental changes – 환경 변화에 대한 동물들의 적응
④ endangered animals in different countries – 다양한 국가에 있는 멸종 위기의 동물들
⑤ ways animals sent each other messages – 동물들이 서로에게 메시지를 보냈던 방법

Why? 왜 정답일까?

'**How did people send mail before they had access to cars and trains? There were simple options out there, like delivery by animal.**'에서 남자는 차와 기차 이전에는 동물을 이용한 우편 배달이 있었다고 언급한 후, 어떤 동물들이 배달에 이용되었는지 열거하고 있다. 따라서 남자가 하는 말의 주제로 가장 적절한 것은 ① '역사상 우편을 배달하는 데 이용된 동물들'이다.

17 언급 유무 파악 정답률 93% | 정답 ③

언급된 동물이 아닌 것은?

① horses – 말 ② pigeons – 비둘기 ✔ eagles – 독수리
④ dogs – 개 ⑤ camels – 낙타

Why? 왜 정답일까?

담화에서 남자는 우편 배달에 이용된 동물의 예로 말, 비둘기, 개, 낙타를 언급하였다. 따라서 언급되지 않은 것은 ③ '독수리'이다.

Why? 왜 오답일까?

① '**Horses were frequently utilized in delivery of letters and messages.**'에서 '말'이 언급되었다.
② '**Pigeons may be seen as a problem by many people today. However, in ancient**

[문제편 p.200]

Greece, they were used to mail people the results of the Olympics between cities.'에서 '비둘기'가 언급되었다.
④ 'In their early days, dogs were utilized to deliver mail because they've adapted to run over ice and snow.'에서 '개'가 언급되었다.
⑤ 'Maybe the most fascinating of all delivery animals is the camel.'에서 '낙타'가 언급되었다.

Dictation 34

문제편 201쪽

01 inform you of the special events / providing a free beverage / giving away $10 gift certificates
02 sleeping on my left side / has something to do with digestion / the digestive process / helps blood circulation
03 a regular reader of your magazine / without using any chemicals / put ducks into my fields / in front of your rice fields
04 blanket with the checkered pattern / a toy horse in the corner / the round mirror on the wall
05 work at our senior citizen's center / How considerate of you / prepare lunch like I did before / have someone else clean the laundry room
06 Do I get a discount / play games with the robots / the membership discount does not apply
07 gave up participating in it / it's fully healed / I've planned to study abroad / I have to leave before the contest begins
08 go over what we've prepared / that's what I ordered / souvenirs for the party
09 see the preview of the movie / sent by text message / will be given a poster
10 Our company policy doesn't allow us / Which airport should we arrive at / spend hours waiting for a connecting flight
11 stop by the dry cleaner's shop / where the shop is located
12 a big fan of him / Mark the date
13 have all the introductions ready / lend you one of his suits / pretty much have the same build
14 they include his deep knowledge and thoughts / join a philosophy discussion group / develop critical thinking skills
15 has always taken care of his travel bag / old enough to prepare what he needs / without her help
16-17 like delivery by animal / adapted to run over ice and snow / ideally suited to this job

35회 | 2019학년도 대학수학능력시험 고3

• 정답 •
01 ① 02 ① 03 ② 04 ④ 05 ⑤ 06 ② 07 ② 08 ④ 09 ⑤ 10 ④ 11 ③ 12 ④ 13 ④ 14 ⑤ 15 ①
16 ③ 17 ⑤

01 야구 경기 취소 안내

정답률 95% | 정답 ①

다음을 듣고, 남자가 하는 말의 목적으로 가장 적절한 것을 고르시오.
✔ 경기 취소를 공지하려고
② 팬클럽 가입을 권유하려고
③ 경기장 개장을 홍보하려고
④ 웹 사이트 점검을 안내하려고
⑤ 시상식 일정 변경을 사과하려고

M : Attention, Whittenberg Dragons and Westbrook Whales fans.
Whittenberg Dragons와 Westbrook Whales팬들은 주목해 주세요.
This is an announcement about today's game at Estana Stadium.
오늘 Estana 경기장에서 있을 경기에 대한 안내입니다.
Today's baseball game was supposed to begin in twenty minutes.
오늘 야구 경기는 20분 뒤에 시작할 예정이었습니다.
But it started raining one hour ago, and has not stopped.
하지만 한 시간 전에 비가 내리기 시작했고, 멈추지 않았습니다.
According to the forecast, the weather will only get worse.
일기예보에 따르면 날씨는 더 나빠질 뿐이라고 합니다.
Because of this, we have decided to cancel today's game.
이 때문에, 우리는 오늘 경기를 취소하기로 결정했습니다.
Tickets you purchased for today's event will be fully refunded.
오늘 행사 티켓은 전액 환불됩니다.
And information about the make-up game will be updated on our website soon.
그리고 보충 경기에 대한 정보가 곧 우리 웹 사이트에 업데이트 될 것입니다.
Once again, today's game has been canceled due to heavy rain.
다시 한 번 말씀드리면, 폭우로 인해 오늘 경기는 취소되었습니다.
Thank you for visiting our stadium, and we hope to see you again at our next game.
저희 경기장을 방문해 주셔서 감사드리며, 다음 경기에서 다시 뵙기를 바랍니다.

Why? 왜 정답일까?
'Because of this, we have decided to cancel today's game.'와 'Once again, today's game has been canceled due to heavy rain.'에서 남자는 비 때문에 예정되어 있던 야구 경기가 취소되었음을 안내하므로, 남자가 하는 말의 목적으로 가장 적절한 것은 ① '경기 취소를 공지하려고'이다.

- announcement ⓝ 발표, 소식
- forecast ⓝ (일기의) 예보, 예측
- purchase ⓝ 구매, 구입
- be supposed to ~할 예정이다, ~하기로 되어있다
- decided ⓐ 결정한, 분명한
- refund ⓥ 환불하다

02 화학 실험에 대한 조언

정답률 95% | 정답 ①

대화를 듣고, 여자의 의견으로 가장 적절한 것을 고르시오.
✔ 실패한 실험을 분석하면 실험에 성공할 수 있다.
② 과학 수업에서는 이론과 실습이 병행되어야 한다.
③ 과학자가 되기 위해서는 인문학적 소양도 필요하다.
④ 실험 일지는 실험 보고서 작성에 도움이 된다.
⑤ 실험을 할 때마다 안전 교육을 해야 한다.

W : Andrew, you look unhappy. What's wrong?
Andrew, 기분이 안 좋아 보여. 무슨 일이니?
M : Hi, Ms. Benson. I've been trying this chemical reaction experiment again and again, but it's not working.
안녕하세요, Benson 선생님. 전 화학 반응 실험을 몇 번이고 시도해보고 있는데, 효과가 없어요.
W : Why isn't it working?
왜 효과가 없지?
M : I don't know. Maybe I don't have much talent for chemistry.
모르겠어요. 전 아마 화학에 재능이 별로 없나 봐요.
W : Don't be so hard on yourself.
너무 자책하지 마.
M : So what should I do?
그럼 어떻게 해야 할까요?
W : I believe that the path to success is through analyzing failure.
난 성공의 길은 실패를 분석하는 데 있다고 생각해.
M : Analyzing failure? What do you mean?
실패 분석이요? 어떤 말씀이시죠?
W : By examining what went wrong in your experiment, you can do it right.
네 실험에서 무엇이 잘못되었는지를 살펴봄으로써, 너는 그것을 제대로 할 수 있어.
M : Hmm. You mean that even though my experiment didn't work, I can learn something from failure?
흠. 제 실험이 효과가 없었긴 하지만, 실패로부터 무언가를 배울 수 있다는 말씀이세요?
W : Exactly. If you figure out how and why it didn't work, you can succeed at your experiment.
바로 그거야. 만약 어떻게 그리고 왜 그것이 효과가 없었는지 알아내면, 넌 실험에 성공할 수 있어.
M : Now I understand. I'll review my experiment. Thanks.
이제 알겠어요. 실험을 재검토해 볼게요. 고맙습니다.

Why? 왜 정답일까?
'I believe that the path to success is through analyzing failure.'와 'By examining what went wrong in your experiment, you can do it right.'에서 여자는 실패한 실험을 분석

해보면 실험이 왜 잘못되었는지를 알게 되어 다시 제대로 할 수 있게 된다고 이야기하고 있다. 따라서 여자의 의견으로 가장 적절한 것은 ① '실패한 실험을 분석하면 실험에 성공할 수 있다.'이다.

- chemical reaction 화학 반응
- talent ⓝ 재능
- analyze ⓥ 분석하다
- experiment ⓝ 실험
- Don't be so hard on yourself. 너무 자책하지 마.
- succeed at ~에 성공하다

03 골동품 전시회 안내
정답률 95% | 정답 ②

대화를 듣고, 두 사람의 관계를 가장 잘 나타낸 것을 고르시오.

① 모델 – 사진작가
② 기증자 – 박물관 직원
③ 영화 관람객 – 티켓 판매원
④ 인테리어 디자이너 – 건축가
⑤ 고객 – 가구점 직원

[Cell phone rings.]
[전화벨이 울린다.]

W : Hello.
여보세요.

M : Hello, Ms. Monroe. This is John Brown. I'm calling to invite you to a special event.
안녕하세요, Monroe 씨. 저는 John Brown입니다. 특별한 행사에 당신을 초대하려고 전화 드렸습니다.

W : Oh, thank you for calling. What's the event?
오, 전화해주셔서 고맙습니다. 무슨 행사죠?

M : Our museum will hold an exhibition of antique items, including the old pictures and tools you donated, under the theme *Life in the 1800s*.
저희 박물관에서는 *Life in the 1800s*라는 주제로 당신이 기증한 오래된 그림과 도구들을 포함한 골동품 전시회를 열 예정입니다.

W : That's wonderful. When is it?
멋지군요. 그게 언제인가요?

M : It'll be from December 3rd to 7th. And it's all thanks to generous people like you.
12월 3일부터 7일까지예요. 이건 모두 당신처럼 관대한 분들 덕분입니다.

W : It's my pleasure. I want my donation to help people learn about the past.
천만에요. 사람들이 과거에 관해 배우는 데 제 기증품이 도움이 되길 원해요.

M : Thank you. The antique items you donated have really improved our collection.
감사합니다. 기증해주신 골동품들이 저희 소장품의 가치를 정말로 높여주었어요.

W : I'm glad to hear that. I'm looking forward to visiting the exhibition.
말씀을 들으니 기쁘네요. 그 전시회에 꼭 가보고 싶어요.

M : I'll send you the invitation letter soon.
곧 초대장을 보내드리겠습니다.

W : Great. I'll be waiting for it.
좋아요. 기다리고 있을게요.

M : Again, on behalf of our museum, we appreciate your donation.
다시 한 번, 저희 박물관을 대표해서 기증에 감사드립니다.

Why? 왜 정답일까?

'Our museum will hold an exhibition of antique items, including the old pictures and tools you donated, ~'와 **'Again, on behalf of our museum, we appreciate your donation.'**에서 여자가 골동품 기증자이고, 남자가 박물관 직원임을 모두 알 수 있으므로, 두 사람의 관계로 가장 적절한 것은 ② '기증자 – 박물관 직원'이다.

- exhibition ⓝ 전시회
- donate ⓥ 기증하다
- improve ⓥ (~의 가치를) 높여주다, 향상시키다
- on behalf of ~을 대표하여, 대신하여
- antique item 골동품
- generous ⓐ 관대한, 후한, 넉넉한
- collection ⓝ 소장품, 수집품

04 생일 파티 준비
정답률 93% | 정답 ④

대화를 듣고, 그림에서 대화의 내용과 일치하지 않는 것을 고르시오.

M : Mom, I think the backyard is ready for Dad's birthday party.
엄마, 뒷마당에 아빠의 생일 파티를 할 준비가 된 것 같아요.

W : Really? Let's see.
정말? 어디 한번 보자.

M : *[Pause]* 「I hung a screen between the trees.」 ①의 근거 일치
[잠시 멈춤] 전 나무들 사이에 스크린을 걸어놨어요.

W : That's nice.
멋지네.

M : I think he'll enjoy watching our old family videos there.
전 아빠가 그곳에서 오래된 가족 비디오를 보는 것을 좋아할 거라고 생각해요.

W : I'm sure he will. 「Oh, did you buy the heart-shaped cake on the table?」 ②의 근거 일치
분명히 그럴 거야. 오, 탁자 위에 있는 하트 모양의 케이크는 네가 샀니?

M : Yes. I got it from Dad's favorite bakery.
네. 아빠가 제일 좋아하는 빵집에서 샀어요.

W : He'll love it. 「What are the two boxes under the chair?」 ③의 근거 일치
아빠가 좋아하시겠구나. 의자 밑에 있는 상자 두 개는 뭐니?

M : They're gifts from Grandma and Grandpa.
할머니와 할아버지가 주신 선물이에요.

W : How nice of them. Hmm. 「I think the striped mat on the grass is too small.」 We cannot all sit there. ④의 근거 불일치
친절하셔라. 흠. 잔디 위에 있는 줄무늬 매트는 너무 작은 것 같구나. 우린 거기 다 앉을 수 없어.

M : You're right. I'll bring more chairs.
엄마 말이 맞아요. 의자를 더 가져올게요.

W : Good idea. 「And you put the grill next to the garden lamp.」 ⑤의 근거 일치

좋은 생각이야. 그리고 정원 등 옆에 그릴을 놓았구나.

M : Yeah. As you know, Dad loves barbecue.
네. 엄마도 아시다시피, 아빠는 바비큐를 좋아해요.

W : Right. We're almost ready for the party.
그래. 우린 파티 준비가 거의 다 되었구나.

Why? 왜 정답일까?

대화에서 매트에는 줄무늬가 있다고 언급하는데(**I think the striped mat on the grass is too small.**), 그림 속 매트에는 별 무늬가 있다. 따라서 그림에서 대화의 내용과 일치하지 않는 것은 ④이다.

- backyard ⓝ 뒷마당
- ready for ~할 준비가 된
- heart-shaped 하트 모양의

05 과학 박람회 발표
정답률 88% | 정답 ⑤

대화를 듣고, 남자가 여자에게 부탁한 일로 가장 적절한 것을 고르시오.

① 발표 주제 정하기
② 식용 곤충 조사하기
③ 설문 조사 결과 분류하기
④ 사진 촬영하기
⑤ 유인물 배부하기

W : Jim, are you doing a presentation for the science fair?
Jim, 너 과학 박람회에서 발표할 거니?

M : Yes. I'm really nervous because it's my first time presenting in public.
응. 난 사람들 앞에서 발표하는 건 처음이라서 정말 긴장돼.

W : Don't worry. You'll do well. What's the topic?
걱정하지 마. 잘할 거야. 주제가 뭐야?

M : Eating insects as food.
식량으로서 곤충 섭취야.

W : Sounds interesting. Why did you choose that?
재미있겠다. 왜 그걸 골랐어?

M : Because it's a possible solution to future food problems.
그건 미래의 식량 문제에 대한 가능한 해결책이기 때문이야.

W : So what are you going to do in your presentation?
그럼 발표 때 무엇을 할 거야?

M : I'll introduce some insect-based recipes and share my survey results on people's opinions about eating insects.
난 곤충에 기반을 둔 요리법을 소개하고 곤충을 먹는 데 관한 사람들의 의견을 다룬 설문 결과를 공유할 거야.

W : I can't wait to see it. I'll take some pictures for you since it's your first public presentation.
빨리 보고 싶다. 네 첫 공개 발표이니 내가 사진을 좀 찍어줄게.

M : Thank you. But my brother Tom is going to take pictures.
고마워. 하지만 내 동생 Tom이 사진을 찍어줄 거야.

W : Okay. Is there anything I can help you with?
알겠어. 내가 뭐 도와줄 일이 있을까?

M : Sure. Could you help with distributing hand-outs to the audience?
물론이지. 관객들에게 유인물을 배부하는 것을 도와줄래?

W : Yes, I'll do that.
그래, 그렇게 할게.

M : Thank you.
고마워.

Why? 왜 정답일까?

처음으로 공개 발표를 진행하게 된 남자는 여자에게 유인물을 돌리는 일을 도와줄 수 있는지 묻고 있으므로(**Could you help with distributing hand-outs to the audience?**), 남자가 여자에게 부탁한 일로 가장 적절한 것은 ⑤ '유인물 배부하기'이다.

- in public 사람들 앞에서, 공개적으로
- opinion ⓝ 의견, 생각, 여론
- distributing ⓐ 분배의, 배급의, 분포의
- survey ⓝ 설문 조사
- hand-out 유인물
- audience ⓝ 관객, 청중

06 인라인 스케이트 구매
정답률 86% | 정답 ②

대화를 듣고, 남자가 지불할 금액을 고르시오. [3점]

① $120 ② $140 ③ $160 ④ $180 ⑤ $200

W : Good afternoon. What can I help you with, sir?
안녕하세요. 무엇을 도와드릴까요, 손님?

M : I'm looking for inline skates for my twins.
전 제 쌍둥이를 위해 인라인 스케이트를 찾고 있어요.

W : I see. We have beginner skates and advanced skates. A pair of beginner skates is $60 and a pair of advanced skates is $80.
그렇군요. 초보자 스케이트와 상급자 스케이트가 있습니다. 초보자용 스케이트는 60달러이고 상급자 스케이트는 80달러입니다.

M : My boys will start learning next week.
우리 아들들은 다음 주에 배우기 시작할 거예요.

W : Then you need the beginner skates.
그렇다면 초보자용 스케이트가 필요하시군요.

M : Right. I'll buy two pairs in size 13.
네. 13 사이즈로 두 켤레를 살게요.

W : Okay. And I think your sons also need safety equipment.
알겠습니다. 그리고 아드님들은 안전 장비도 필요할 것 같아요.

M : They already have elbow and knee pads. So, they only need helmets. How much are helmets?
아이들은 이미 팔꿈치 보호대와 무릎 보호대를 갖고 있어요. 그러니 그들은 헬멧만 있으면 돼요. 헬멧은 얼마인가요?

W : They originally cost $20 each. But we have a promotion this week. So, you will get a 50 percent discount on each helmet.
원래 그것은 하나에 20달러입니다. 하지만 이번 주에는 판촉 행사가 있어요. 그래서 헬멧 하나당 50퍼센트 할인을 받으시게 됩니다.

M : That's nice. I'll buy two helmets.
좋네요. 헬멧을 두 개 살게요.

W : Do you want anything else?
더 필요하신 건 없으세요?

M : No, that's all. Here's my credit card.
아니요, 그게 다예요. 여기 제 신용카드입니다.

[문제편 p.205]

Why? 왜 정답일까?

대화에 따르면 남자는 쌍둥이 아들들에게 줄 60달러짜리 초보자용 스케이트를 두 켤레 사고, 추가로 20달러짜리 헬멧을 50퍼센트 할인가로 두 개 구입하였다. 이를 식으로 나타내면 '60×2+20×2×0.5=140'이므로, 남자가 지불할 금액은 ② '$140'이다.

- advanced ⓐ 상급의, 고급의
- safety equipment 안전 장비
- promotion ⓝ 판촉, 판매 촉진, 홍보

07 드론 비행 대회 참가

정답률 93% | 정답 ②

대화를 듣고, 여자가 드론 비행 대회에 참가할 수 없는 이유를 고르시오.

① 부모님이 방문하셔서
✔ 취업 면접에 가야 해서
③ 졸업식에 참석해야 해서
④ 파트너를 구하지 못해서
⑤ 드론을 갖고 있지 않아서

[Cell phone rings.]
[휴대전화 벨이 울린다.]

M : Hey, Rebecca. I have good news.
안녕, Rebecca. 좋은 소식이 있어.

W : Hi, Michael. What is it?
안녕, Michael. 그게 뭔데?

M : I saw an advertisement about a drone flying competition. Why don't we enter the competition as a team?
난 드론 비행 대회에 관한 광고를 봤어. 우리 한 팀으로 대회에 참가하는 게 어때?

W : Great! I recently got a new drone as a graduation present. Is there anything we need to enter the competition?
좋아! 나는 최근에 졸업 선물로 새 드론을 받았어. 대회에 참가하는 데 필요한 게 있니?

M : No, all we need is our own drones.
아니, 우리 소유인 드론만 있으면 돼.

W : Good. My new drone flies much faster and longer than the old one. When is the competition?
좋아. 내 새 드론은 예전 것보다 훨씬 빠르고 더 오래 날아. 대회가 언제야?

M : It's next Friday afternoon.
다음 주 금요일 오후야.

W : Friday? I can't make it that day.
금요일이라고? 나 그날은 안 돼.

M : Oh! I forgot. You said that your parents are visiting.
아! 내가 깜박했다. 너희 부모님이 방문하실 거라고 했었지.

W : Actually, they came yesterday.
사실, 그분들은 어제 오셨어.

M : Then, why can't you go?
그럼 왜 못 가?

W : I have to go to a job interview.
취업 면접을 보러 가야 해.

M : I see. Good luck on the interview. I'll try to find another partner.
그렇구나. 면접에 행운을 빌게. 난 다른 파트너를 찾아봐야겠다.

Why? 왜 정답일까?

대화에 따르면 여자는 다음 주 금요일 오후에 취업 면접이 있어 드론 비행 대회에 참가할 수 없다(**I have to go to a job interview.**). 따라서 여자가 드론 비행 대회에 참가할 수 없는 이유로 가장 적절한 것은 ② '취업 면접에 가야 해서'이다.

- advertisement ⓝ 광고
- competition ⓝ 경연대회, 경쟁
- make it (시간 맞춰) 참석하다, 가다, 해내다, 성공하다

08 국제 불꽃놀이 행사

정답률 94% | 정답 ④

대화를 듣고, International Fireworks Festival에 관해 언급되지 않은 것을 고르시오.

① 개최 일시
② 개최 장소
③ 참가국
✔ 주제
⑤ 교통편

M : Honey, what are you looking at?
여보, 뭘 보고 있어요?

W : I'm looking at the International Fireworks Festival website. You know I love fireworks.
International Fireworks Festival 웹 사이트를 보고 있어요. 내가 불꽃놀이를 좋아하는 거 알죠.

M : Okay, then we should go. 「When is it?
좋아요, 그럼 가야겠네요. 그게 언제예요?

W : It's on Saturday, November 24th and starts at 8 p.m.」 ①의 근거 일치 It's also at the same place as last year.
11월 24일 토요일이고 오후 8시에 시작해요. 작년과 같은 장소에서 해요.

M : Ah! 「It'll be held at Green Dove Park again?」 ②의 근거 일치
아! Green Dove 공원에서 다시 열리나요?

W : Yes. And the website says four countries are going to participate this year.
네. 그리고 웹 사이트에는 올해 4개국이 참여할 거라고 나와 있어요.

M : Great. 「Which countries?
좋아요. 어느 나라인가요?

W : Korea, Spain, China and the U.S. will take part.」 ③의 근거 일치
한국, 스페인, 중국, 미국이 참가해요.

M : Our children loved the festival last year. Let's take them again.
우리 아이들은 작년에 그 축제를 좋아했어요. 또 데려가요.

W : Of course. But last year, there were almost no parking spaces available near the park.
물론이죠. 하지만 작년에는 공원 근처에 주차할 수 있는 공간이 거의 없었어요.

M : If we don't drive, 「how should we get there?
운전을 하지 않는다면 우린 어떻게 가야 하죠?

W : The festival provides a free shuttle bus from Town Hall Station.」 ⑤의 근거 일치
이 축제에서 Town Hall 역에서 출발하는 무료 셔틀 버스를 제공해요.

M : Really? Then, let's take the shuttle bus.
정말요? 그럼 셔틀버스를 타죠.

Why? 왜 정답일까?

대화에서 남자와 여자는 International Fireworks Festival에 관해 개최 일시, 개최 장소, 참가국, 교통편을 언급하므로, 언급되지 않은 것은 ④ '주제'이다.

Why? 왜 오답일까?

① 'It's on Saturday, November 24th and starts at 8 p.m.'에서 '개최 일시'가 언급되었다.
② 'It'll be held at Green Dove Park again?'에서 '개최 장소'가 언급되었다.
③ 'Korea, Spain, China and the U.S. will take part.'에서 '참가국'이 언급되었다.
⑤ 'The festival provides a free shuttle bus from Town Hall Station.'에서 '교통편'이 언급되었다.

- firework ⓝ 불꽃놀이, 폭죽
- take part 참가하다, 참여하다
- provide ⓥ 제공하다

09 업사이클 워크숍 개최 안내

정답률 95% | 정답 ⑤

2018 Upcycling Workshop에 관한 다음 내용을 듣고, 일치하지 않는 것을 고르시오.

① 3일간 진행될 것이다.
② 세미나실에서 열릴 것이다.
③ 패션 디자이너가 가르칠 것이다.
④ 모든 재료가 제공된다.
✔ 참가 연령에 제한이 없다.

W : Attention, please.
주목해 주세요.
I'm Jenny Stone, the manager of the community center.
저는 주민 센터 관리자인 Jenny Stone입니다.
I'm going to tell you about the 2018 Upcycling Workshop.
여러분께 2018 Upcycling Workshop에 대해 말씀드리겠습니다.
Upcycling is creative reuse.
업사이클이란 창의적인 재사용입니다.
It gives new life to old objects.
그것은 오래된 물건에 새로운 생명을 줍니다.
「The workshop will last three days, from November 23rd to 25th.」 ①의 근거 일치
워크숍은 11월 23일부터 25일까지 3일간 계속됩니다.
It'll run from 1 to 4 p.m.
오후 1시부터 4시까지 진행될 것입니다.
「The workshop will be held in the seminar room.」 ②의 근거 일치
워크숍은 세미나실에서 열릴 것입니다.
And we have a special treat this time.
그리고 이번에는 특별히 준비한 것이 있습니다.
「The famous fashion designer, Elizabeth Thompson, will teach you in the workshop.」
유명한 패션 디자이너인 Elizabeth Thompson이 워크숍에서 여러분을 가르칠 것입니다. ③의 근거 일치
You'll learn many upcycling methods from her.
여러분은 그녀에게 많은 업사이클 방법을 배우시게 될 겁니다.
For example, you'll remake plastic bags into rugs and old shirts into hats.
예를 들어, 당신은 비닐봉투를 깔개로, 낡은 셔츠를 모자로 개조하게 될 것입니다.
「All materials are provided.」 ④의 근거 일치
모든 재료는 제공됩니다.
And there's no participation fee.
그리고 참가비는 없습니다.
「The workshop is open to people 18 and older.」 ⑤의 근거 불일치
이 워크숍은 18세 이상의 사람들을 대상으로 합니다.
We're looking forward to seeing you.
여러분을 뵙게 되기를 고대합니다.

Why? 왜 정답일까?

'The workshop is open to people 18 and older.'에서 워크숍은 18세 이상의 사람들을 대상으로 한다고 하므로, 내용과 일치하지 않는 것은 ⑤ '참가 연령에 제한이 없다.'이다.

Why? 왜 오답일까?

① 'The workshop will last three days, ~'의 내용과 일치한다.
② 'The workshop will be held in the seminar room.'의 내용과 일치한다.
③ 'The famous fashion designer, Elizabeth Thompson, will teach you in the workshop.'의 내용과 일치한다.
④ 'All materials are provided.'의 내용과 일치한다.

- upcycling ⓝ 새활용
- creative ⓐ 창의적인
- give life to ~에 생명을 주다, 생기를 불어넣다
- object ⓝ 물건
- special treat 특별한 사항, 특별한 대접
- method ⓝ 방법
- participation fee 참가비

10 도마 구매

정답률 93% | 정답 ④

다음 표를 보면서 대화를 듣고, 여자가 구매할 도마를 고르시오.

Cutting Boards at Camilo's Kitchen

	Model	Material	Price	Handle	Size
①	A	plastic	$25	×	medium
②	B	maple	$35	○	small
③	C	maple	$40	×	large
✔	D	walnut	$45	○	medium
⑤	E	walnut	$55	○	large

M : Welcome to Camilo's Kitchen.
Camilo's Kitchen에 오신 것을 환영합니다.

35회

W : Hello. I'm looking for a cutting board.
안녕하세요. 전 도마를 찾고 있어요.

M : Let me show you our five top-selling models, all at affordable prices. Do you have a preference for any material? We have plastic, maple, and walnut cutting boards.
가장 잘 팔리는 다섯 가지 제품을 모두 적당한 가격에 보여드리겠습니다. 선호하시는 재료가 있나요? 플라스틱, 단풍나무, 호두나무 도마가 있습니다.

W : 「I don't want the plastic one because I think plastic isn't environmentally friendly.」
전 플라스틱이 환경 친화적이지 않다고 생각하기 때문에 플라스틱을 원하지 않아요. 근거1 Material 조건

M : I see. What's your budget range?
그러시군요. 예산 범위는 어떠신가요?

W : 「No more than $50.」 근거2 Price 조건
50달러 이상은 안 돼요.

M : Okay. Do you prefer one with or without a handle?
알겠습니다. 손잡이가 있는 것과 없는 것 중에 어느 것이 더 좋으세요?

W : 「I think a cutting board with a handle is easier to use. So I'll take one with a handle.」
손잡이가 달린 도마가 사용하기 더 쉬울 것 같아요. 손잡이가 달린 것으로 사겠어요. 근거3 Handle 조건

M : Then, which size do you want? You have two models left.
그럼 어떤 크기를 원하세요? 두 가지 제품이 남았습니다.

W : Hmm. 「A small-sized cutting board isn't convenient when I cut vegetables. I'll buy the other model.」 근거4 Size 조건
흠. 야채를 자를 때 작은 크기의 도마는 편하지 않아요. 다른 것으로 살게요.

M : Great. Then this is the cutting board for you.
좋아요. 그럼 이게 손님을 위한 도마로군요.

Why? 왜 정답일까?

대화에 따르면 여자는 재료가 플라스틱이 아니면서, 가격은 50달러를 넘지 않고, 손잡이가 달려 있으며, 크기가 작지 않은 도마를 사려고 한다. 따라서 여자가 구매할 도마는 ④ 'D'이다.

- **cutting board** 도마
- **affordable** ⓐ (가격이) 적당한, 알맞은, 저렴한
- **environmentally friendly** 환경 친화적인

11 늦게 귀가하는 딸을 데리러 가기

정답률 92% | 정답 ③

대화를 듣고, 남자의 마지막 말에 대한 여자의 응답으로 가장 적절한 것을 고르시오.

① No. You can't study with us. – 아니요. 당신은 우리와 공부할 수 없어요.
② Okay. I'll do the report by myself. – 알겠어요. 전 보고서를 혼자 쓸게요.
③ Sure. I'll call you when I'm done. – 네. 끝나면 전화 드릴게요.
④ Yes. I'm pleased to join your team. – 네. 당신의 팀에 참여하게 되어 기뻐요.
⑤ Sorry. You have to finish by tomorrow. – 죄송해요. 내일까지는 끝내주셔야 해요.

M : Amy, you said you're going to study at Donna's house tonight, right?
Amy, 너 오늘 밤에 Donna네 집에서 공부할 거라고 했지, 그렇지?

W : Yes, Dad. We have to submit our team report online by midnight.
네, 아빠. 저희는 오늘 자정까지 팀 보고서를 온라인으로 제출해야 해요.

M : I think you'll be quite late. Should I pick you up?
꽤 늦을 것 같구나. 내가 데리러 갈까?

W : Sure. I'll call you when I'm done.
네. 끝나면 전화 드릴게요.

Why? 왜 정답일까?

아버지인 남자는 딸인 여자가 친구네 집에서 팀 보고서를 마치고 돌아오면 늦을 것을 염려하며 데리러 가야 할지 묻고 있다(**Should I pick you up?**). 따라서 여자의 응답으로 가장 적절한 것은 ③ '네. 끝나면 전화 드릴게요.'이다.

12 도로 안전 프로그램 등록

정답률 93% | 정답 ④

대화를 듣고, 여자의 마지막 말에 대한 남자의 응답으로 가장 적절한 것을 고르시오.

① Be careful. The roads are slippery. – 조심하세요. 길이 미끄러워요.
② I agree. The seats are very comfortable. – 동의합니다. 자리가 매우 안락하네요.
③ Wonderful. Let's attend the program together. – 멋지네요. 함께 프로그램에 참석하죠.
④ Great. I'll register my son for the program. – 좋아요. 제 아들을 프로그램에 등록시킬게요.
⑤ I'm sorry. Your son has to wait longer. – 죄송합니다. 아드님은 더 오래 기다리셔야 해요.

W : Thank you for waiting, sir. How can I help you?
기다려주셔서 감사합니다, 손님. 어떻게 도와드릴까요?

M : My son wants to join the road safety program. Are there any seats still available?
제 아들이 도로 안전 프로그램에 참여하고 싶어 합니다. 아직 자리가 있나요?

W : It's your lucky day! Somebody just canceled. So your son can have that seat.
운이 좋으시군요! 방금 어떤 분이 취소하셨습니다. 그러니 아드님이 그 자리에 들어오시면 됩니다.

M : Great. I'll register my son for the program.
좋아요. 제 아들을 프로그램에 등록시킬게요.

Why? 왜 정답일까?

대화에서 남자가 아들이 도로 안전 프로그램에 참여하고 싶어 한다며 자리가 있는지 문의하자, 여자는 마침 다른 사람이 취소했기 때문에 아들이 들어올 자리가 있음을 알려주고 있다(**Somebody just canceled. So your son can have that seat**). 따라서 남자의 응답으로 가장 적절한 것은 ④ '좋아요. 제 아들을 프로그램에 등록시킬게요.'이다.

- **available** ⓐ 이용[사용]할 수 있는
- **cancel** ⓥ 취소하다
- **slippery** ⓐ 미끄러운
- **register A for B** A를 B에 등록시키다
- **comfortable** ⓐ 안락한, 쾌적한

13 약 때문에 운전을 할 수 없는 남자

정답률 93% | 정답 ④

대화를 듣고, 여자의 마지막 말에 대한 남자의 응답으로 가장 적절한 것을 고르시오. [3점]

Man: ______________________________

① Absolutely! You should go and see a doctor.
당연하죠! 당신은 가서 진찰을 받아야 해요.
② No problem. I'll visit you on my business trip.
문제없어요. 출장 중에 당신을 방문할게요.
③ Sure. You can check the directions before driving.
물론이죠. 당신은 운전하기 전에 길을 확인할 수 있어요.
④ Okay. I'll ask my team so I can take the medicine.
알겠어요. 내가 약을 먹을 수 있도록 내 팀원들에게 물어볼게요.
⑤ Right. Taking a trip is a great way to relieve stress.
맞아요. 여행 가는 것은 스트레스를 해소하는 훌륭한 방법이에요.

W : Honey, what did the doctor say about your neck?
여보, 의사가 당신 목에 대해 뭐라고 했어요?

M : She said that it's not too bad. I just need to take these pills and get enough rest.
아주 심하지는 않다고 했어요. 난 그저 이 약을 먹고 충분히 쉬면 돼요.

W : I'm relieved that it's not so serious.
그렇게 심각하지 않아서 다행이에요.

M : But there's a problem. The doctor said I shouldn't drive after taking the medicine. It can make me very sleepy.
하지만 문제가 있어요. 의사가 말하길 약을 먹은 후에 운전을 해서는 안 된대요. 약이 무척 졸릴 수 있대요.

W : Oh, no. What about your business trip on Monday?
오, 이런. 월요일 출장은 어쩌죠?

M : Exactly. I'm supposed to drive my team members since I know the area.
그러니까요. 난 그 지역을 알고 있어서 우리 팀원들을 태워주기로 되어 있어요.

W : You cannot drive. It would be very dangerous.
운전하면 안 돼요. 그건 매우 위험할 수 있어요.

M : Maybe I'll skip the medicine before I drive.
어쩌면 운전하기 전에 약을 건너뛰어야겠어요.

W : Wouldn't it delay your recovery and even make your neck pain worse?
그러면 회복이 지연되고 심지어 목 통증이 더 심해지지 않겠어요?

M : Yeah. I do need to take the medicine regularly.
네. 나는 정말 그 약을 규칙적으로 먹어야 해요.

W : Then one solution would be to see if somebody else in your team can drive instead of you.
그렇다면 한 가지 해결책은 당신 팀 내 다른 누군가가 당신 대신에 운전을 해줄 수 있는지 알아보는 것이겠네요.

M : Okay. I'll ask my team so I can take the medicine.
알겠어요. 내가 약을 먹을 수 있도록 내 팀원들에게 물어볼게요.

Why? 왜 정답일까?

대화에 따르면 남자는 목이 아파 병원에서 약을 받아왔는데 이 약을 먹으면 졸릴 수 있어 운전을 해서는 안 된다. 이 때문에 남자는 예정했던 대로 출장 때 팀원들을 차에 태워갈 수가 없게 되었고, 여자는 남자에게 운전을 대신할 사람이 없는지 알아보도록 제안하고 있다(**Then one solution would be to see if somebody else in your team can drive instead of you.**). 따라서 남자의 응답으로 가장 적절한 것은 ④ '알겠어요. 내가 약을 먹을 수 있도록 내 팀원들에게 물어볼게요.'이다.

- **relieved** ⓐ 다행인, 안도한
- **business trip** ⓝ 출장
- **delay** ⓥ 지연시키다, 늦추다
- **regularly** ad 규칙적으로

14 뮤지컬의 원작 소설 추천하기

정답률 93% | 정답 ⑤

대화를 듣고, 남자의 마지막 말에 대한 여자의 응답으로 가장 적절한 것을 고르시오.

Woman: ______________________________

① I agree. The actors performed well in the musical.
동의해. 배우들은 뮤지컬에서 연기를 잘했어.
② You're right. Let's wait for the reviews of the musical.
네 말이 맞아. 그 뮤지컬에 대한 평을 기다려보자.
③ Good. Now, we should rewrite the script of the musical.
좋아. 이제 우리는 뮤지컬 대본을 다시 써야 해.
④ Great. I need a new musical instrument for our performance.
훌륭해. 난 우리 공연을 위해 새로운 악기가 필요해.
⑤ Thanks. Then, I'll read the novel before I watch the musical.
고마워. 그럼 난 뮤지컬을 보기 전에 소설을 읽어야겠다.

M : Hey, Jessica. You got here early.
Jessica, 일찍 왔네.

W : You too, Mike. What are you reading?
너도, Mike. 무엇을 읽고 있니?

M : I'm reading a magazine article about the musical *Spring Empire*.
뮤지컬 *Spring Empire*에 관한 잡지 기사를 읽고 있어.

W : Oh, *Spring Empire*? I'm going to see it next week. What does the article say?
오, *Spring Empire*? 난 그걸 다음 주에 볼 거야. 기사에는 뭐라고 쓰여 있어?

M : It mentions that the leading actors are geniuses and that the musical is going to be so popular.
주연 배우들은 천재이고 뮤지컬이 아주 인기가 많을 거라고 언급하고 있어.

W : Wow, I really can't wait to see it.
와, 정말 빨리 보고 싶다.

M : Actually, I've seen it already. Since you haven't watched the musical, I recommend you read the original novel first.
사실, 난 그걸 벌써 봤어. 네가 뮤지컬을 보지 않았으니, 원작 소설을 먼저 읽어보길 추천할게.

W : Why do you say that?
왜 그렇게 말하는 거니?

M : The storyline is complicated. In my case, reading the novel first helped me fully understand and better enjoy the musical.
줄거리가 복잡해. 내 경우엔, 먼저 소설을 읽은 것이 내가 뮤지컬을 완전히 이해하고 더 잘 즐길 수 있도록 도와줬어.

W : Then, I need to get a copy of the book.
그럼 책을 한 권 사야겠어.

M : I have one. I can lend it to you if you want.
내게 한 권 있어. 원하면 빌려줄 수 있어.

W : Thanks. Then, I'll read the novel before I watch the musical.
고마워. 그럼 난 뮤지컬을 보기 전에 소설을 읽어야겠다.

Why? 왜 정답일까?

여자가 보려는 뮤지컬을 먼저 본 남자는 여자에게 뮤지컬의 원작 소설을 읽어보라고 권하며(**Since you haven't watched the musical, I recommend you read the original novel first.**) 자신의 책을 빌려주겠다(**I can lend it to you if you want.**)고 말한다. 따라서 여자의 응답으로 가장 적절한 것은 ⑤ '고마워. 그럼 난 뮤지컬을 보기 전에 소설을 읽어야겠다.'이다.

- **mention** ⓥ 언급하다, 말하다
- **leading actor** 주연 배우
- **recommend** ⓥ 추천하다, 권하다
- **original novel** 원작 소설
- **complicated** ⓐ 복잡한
- **fully** ad 완전히, 충분히

[문제편 p.206]

15 자기소개서에 관해 조언해 주기
정답률 72% | 정답 ①

다음 상황 설명을 듣고, Steve가 Cathy에게 할 말로 가장 적절한 것을 고르시오. [3점]

Steve: ____________

✔ You should highlight your volunteer experience as a translator.
너는 번역가로 자원봉사했던 경험을 강조해야 해.
② How about volunteering together for the translation club?
번역 동아리에서 자원봉사를 함께 하는 게 어때?
③ Why don't you help me write a self-introduction letter?
내가 자기소개서 쓰는 것을 네가 도와주면 어떠니?
④ You need to spend more time practicing translation.
넌 번역을 연습하는 데 더 많은 시간을 들일 필요가 있어.
⑤ You'd better become more qualified as a volunteer.
너는 번역가로서 더 자격을 갖추어야 해.

M : Cathy is starting high school and is looking to join a club.
Cathy는 고등학교에 입학해서 동아리에 가입하려 한다.
She's interested in translation and has volunteered as a translator before.
그녀는 번역에 관심이 있고 이전에 번역가로 자원봉사를 한 적이 있다.
So she's happy when she finds a translation club at her school.
그래서 그녀는 학교에서 번역 동아리를 찾고는 기뻐한다.
To enter the club, she must write a self-introduction letter.
동아리에 들어가려면 그녀는 자기소개서를 써야 한다.
However, she's not satisfied with the letter she wrote.
하지만, 그녀는 자신이 쓴 자기소개서에 만족하지 않는다.
She remembers that her older brother Steve has lots of experience writing self-introduction letters.
그녀는 오빠 Steve가 자기소개서를 써본 경험이 많다는 것을 기억한다.
Cathy asks him for advice about her self-introduction letter.
Cathy는 그에게 자기소개서에 대한 조언을 구한다.
Steve thinks the letter doesn't focus enough on what she did as a volunteer translator.
Steve는 그 자기소개서가 그녀가 자원봉사 번역가로서 했던 일에 충분히 초점을 맞추지 못한다고 생각한다.
So Steve wants to suggest to Cathy that she emphasize her volunteer work related to translation.
그래서 Steve는 Cathy에게 번역과 관련된 자원봉사 활동을 강조하라고 제안하고 싶다.
In this situation, what would Steve most likely say to Cathy?
이 상황에서, Steve는 Cathy에게 뭐라고 말할 것인가?

Steve : You should highlight your volunteer experience as a translator.
너는 번역가로 자원봉사했던 경험을 강조해야 해.

Why? 왜 정답일까?

상황에 따르면 번역 동아리에 지원하고자 자기소개서를 쓰고 있는 Cathy에게 오빠인 Steve는 번역과 관련된 봉사활동을 더 강조할 것을 제안하려 한다(**So Steve wants to suggest to Cathy that she emphasize her volunteer work related to translation.**). 따라서 Steve가 Cathy에게 할 말로 가장 적절한 것은 ① '너는 번역가로 자원봉사했던 경험을 강조해야 해.'이다.

- **translation** ⓝ 번역, 통역
- **self-introduction letter** 자기소개서
- **qualified** ⓐ 자격을 갖춘, 자격이 있는

16-17 일상 음식의 예기치 못한 탄생지

W : Hello, students.
안녕하세요.
Previously, we discussed traditional foods in different countries.
학생 여러분, 저번에 우리는 다른 나라의 전통 음식에 대해 논의했습니다.
「Today, I'll talk about surprising birthplaces of everyday foods.」 16번의 근거
오늘은 일상적인 음식의 놀라운 탄생지에 대해 이야기하겠습니다.
「First, people believe the Caesar salad is named after a Roman emperor.」 17번 ①의 근거 일치
첫 번째로, 사람들은 시저 샐러드가 로마 황제의 이름을 딴 것이라고 믿습니다.
But a well-known story is that the name came from a chef in Mexico.
하지만 유명한 이야기에 따르면 그 이름은 멕시코의 한 요리사에게서 유래했습니다.
He created it by putting together some basic ingredients when running out of food.
그는 음식이 떨어져갈 때 몇 가지 기본적인 재료들을 함께 넣어 그것을 만들었습니다.
「Second, bagels are a famous New York food.」 17번 ②의 근거 일치
두 번째로, 베이글은 뉴욕의 유명한 음식입니다.
But they're likely from central Europe.
하지만 그것들은 중부 유럽에서 온 것 같습니다.
A widely repeated story says that they were first made in Vienna to celebrate the defeat of an invading army.
널리 반복되는 이야기에 따르면 그것들은 침략군의 격퇴를 기념하기 위해 비엔나에서 처음 만들어졌다고 합니다.
「Third, many people think kiwis are from New Zealand.」 17번 ③의 근거 일치
세 번째로, 많은 사람들은 키위가 뉴질랜드에서 기원했다고 생각합니다.
It's probably because a small flightless bird from New Zealand has the same name.
뉴질랜드의 날지 못하는 작은 새가 같은 이름을 가지고 있기 때문일 것입니다.
In fact, the food is from China.
사실, 그 음식은 중국에서 왔습니다.
「Last, if there's any country known for potatoes, it's Ireland.」 17번 ④의 근거 일치
마지막으로, 감자로 알려진 나라가 있다면 아일랜드입니다.
That's because crop failures of this food caused extreme hunger in Ireland in the 19th century.
19세기 아일랜드에서 이 음식의 흉년이 극심한 기아를 일으켰기 때문입니다.
However, the food is believed to come from South America.
하지만 이 음식은 남아메리카에서 유래한 것으로 여겨집니다.
Now, we'll watch a short video about these foods.
이제 이 음식에 대한 짧은 비디오를 보도록 하겠습니다.

- **birthplace** ⓝ 탄생지, 출생지
- **be named after** ~의 이름을 따서 짓다
- **ingredient** ⓝ 재료
- **run out of** ~이 다 떨어지다
- **invading army** 침략군
- **crop failure** 흉작
- **misconception** ⓝ 오해, 잘못된 견해
- **spread** ⓥ 전파되다, 퍼지다, 흩뜨리다

16 주제 파악
정답률 73% | 정답 ③

여자가 하는 말의 주제로 가장 적절한 것은?

① why traditional foods are popular – 왜 전통 음식은 인기가 있는가
② misconceptions about organic foods – 유기농 식품에 대한 오해
✔ unexpected origins of common foods – 평범한 음식들의 예기치 못한 기원
④ when foods spread across countries – 음식은 언제 나라를 건너 전파되는가
⑤ importance of eating fresh foods – 신선한 식품을 먹는 것의 중요성

Why? 왜 정답일까?

'**Today, I'll talk about surprising birthplaces of everyday foods.**'에서 여자는 일상 음식의 놀라운 탄생지에 관해 이야기할 것임을 말하므로, 여자가 하는 말의 주제로 가장 적절한 것은 ③ '평범한 음식들의 예기치 못한 기원'이다.

17 언급 유무 파악
정답률 94% | 정답 ⑤

언급된 음식이 아닌 것은?

① Caesar salad – 시저 샐러드
② bagels – 베이글
③ kiwis – 키위
④ potatoes – 감자
✔ buffalo wings – 버팔로윙

Why? 왜 정답일까?

담화에서 여자는 놀라운 탄생지에서 기원한 일상 음식의 예로 시저 샐러드, 베이글, 키위, 감자를 언급하였다. 따라서 언급된 음식이 아닌 것은 ⑤ '버팔로윙'이다.

Why? 왜 오답일까?

① '**First, people believe the Caesar salad is named after a Roman emperor.**'에서 '시저 샐러드'가 언급되었다.
② '**Second, bagels are a famous New York food.**'에서 '베이글'이 언급되었다.
③ '**Third, many people think kiwis are from New Zealand.**'에서 '키위'가 언급되었다.
④ '**Last, if there's any country known for potatoes, it's Ireland.**'에서 '감자'가 언급되었다.

Dictation 35
문제편 207쪽

01 was supposed to begin in twenty minutes / have decided to cancel today's game / due to heavy rain
02 Don't be so hard on yourself / through analyzing failure / review my experiment
03 hold an exhibition of antique items / it's all thanks to generous people / on behalf of our museum
04 the backyard is ready for / buy the heart-shaped cake / How nice of them / the striped mat
05 my first time presenting in public / I can't wait to see it / distributing hand-outs to the audience
06 What can I help you with / your sons also need safety equipment / elbow and knee pads / have a promotion
07 an advertisement about a drone flying competition / all we need is / I can't make it that day
08 at the same place as last year / almost no parking spaces available / provides a free shuttle bus
09 Upcycling is creative reuse / have a special treat / no participation fee
10 all at affordable prices / plastic isn't environmentally friendly / with or without a handle
11 submit our team report / Should I pick you up
12 any seats still available
13 take these pills / shouldn't drive after taking the medicine / Wouldn't it delay your recovery
14 the leading actors are geniuses / I recommend you read the original novel / better enjoy the musical
15 has volunteered as a translator before / has lots of experience writing self-introduction letters / she emphasize her volunteer work
16-17 when running out of food / defeat of an invading army / any country known for potatoes / is believed to come from

| 정답과 해설 |

01 특별 부록 회 | 수능 대비 파이널 모의고사 고3

• 정답 •

01⑤ 02② 03⑤ 04⑤ 05⑤ 06① 07③ 08③ 09③ 10⑤ 11① 12① 13③ 14② 15③ 16④ 17⑤

01 담화의 목적 파악하기 정답 ⑤

W : May I have your attention, please?
잠시 주목해 주시겠습니까?
We appreciate your visiting our place today.
오늘도 저희 장소를 찾아주셔서 감사합니다.
Are you enjoying yourself in the woods of books?
책의 숲에서 즐거운 시간을 보내고 계신가요?
It is now ten to five.
지금 시간은 5시 10분 전입니다.
The Auburn Bookstore will be closing in 10 minutes.
Auburn 서점은 10분 후에 문을 닫습니다.
Please make your final selections and proceed to the checkout registers.
구입할 물건을 결정해서 계산대로 가주시기 바랍니다.
Shoppers with five or less items may pay for their purchases at the stationery department at the back of the store.
5권이나 그 이하의 책을 구매 하실 손님께서는 저희 서점 뒤쪽에 있는 문구 코너에서 계산하셔도 됩니다.
The bookstore is open from 9 a.m. to 5 p.m. on weekdays; 10 a.m. to 4 p.m. on Saturdays; and is closed on Sundays.
저희 서점은 평일 아침 9시부터 오후 5시까지, 토요일에는 오전 10시에서 오후 4시까지 영업을 하고, 일요일은 쉽니다.
We'd appreciate you wrapping up your shopping so that we can close the shop on time.
저희가 서점을 제 시각에 닫을 수 있도록 쇼핑을 마무리해 주시면 감사하겠습니다.
Thank you for shopping with us.
저희 서점에서 쇼핑해 주셔서 감사합니다.

Why? 왜 정답일까?

서점이 문 닫을 시간이 얼마 남지 않아 쇼핑을 마무리 해 줄 것을 부탁하고 있으므로 여자가 하는 말의 목적으로는 ⑤가 적절하다.

- appreciate ⓥ 고맙게 여기다
- selection ⓝ 선택
- proceed ⓥ 나아가다, 진행하다
- checkout register 계산대
- purchase ⓝ 구입
- stationery ⓝ 문구
- wrap up 정리하다, 마무리하다

02 의견 파악하기 정답 ②

M : Jessica, have you made plans for the trip to Jeju Island?
Jessica, 제주도 여행 계획은 세웠니?
W : Yes, Dad. As soon as I unpack in the hotel, I am heading straight to a chocolate factory. After that I am visiting an aquarium. Then I will grab a quick dinner and go to...
네, 아빠. 호텔에 짐을 풀자마자 바로 초콜릿 공장에 갈 거예요. 그 후에 수족관을 방문할 예정이에요. 그다음 간단하게 저녁을 먹고...
M : Hold on. I am already exhausted only listening to your plan.
잠깐만. 너의 계획을 듣기만 해도 나는 벌써 지치는구나.
W : You know, it's not only my first trip to Jeju but it's also my first trip going solo. I want to see as many things as possible there.
있잖아요, 제주도 여행은 처음일 뿐만 아니라 혼자 가는 첫 여행이기도 하잖아요. 저는 그곳에서 가능한 한 많은 것들을 보고 싶어요.
M : I understand, but your trip shouldn't be too demanding. You will be worn out.
이해는 하지만 여행이 너무 힘들면 안 된단다. 너는 지칠 거야.
W : Well, Dad. I only have two days and I can handle the busy schedule.
음, 아빠. 저에겐 고작 이틀밖에 없어요. 그리고 전 바쁜 일정을 소화할 수 있어요.
M : Listen to your Dad this time. The beauty of trip is not to see as many things and visit as many places as possible.
이번에는 아빠 말을 들으렴. 여행의 미는 가능한 한 많은 것을 보고, 많은 곳에 가는 것이 아니란다.
W : It's not? Then what do you think is the true beauty of traveling?
아니라고요? 그러면 진정한 여행의 묘미는 무엇이라고 생각하세요?
M : Your trip begins from the airport. Just looking out the window from the plane, talking with people from different city, and taking in the air in the city you've never been to are all part of the trip.
너의 여행은 공항에서부터 시작된단다. 비행기에서 창밖을 내다보는 것, 다른 도시에서 온 사람들과 이야기하는 것, 그리고 네가 가본 적이 없는 도시의 공기를 마시는 것 모두 여행의 일부야.
W : I got what you mean. I thought I had to do something in particular during the trip.
무슨 말씀이신지 알겠어요. 저는 여행 동안 특별히 무언가를 해야 한다고 생각했어요.
M : So you will revise your plan, won't you?
그래서 너는 너의 계획을 수정할 거잖아, 그렇지?
W : Yes, I will. I promise.
네, 그럴게요. 약속해요.
M : Good, and don't forget to consider the time it takes to move from one place to another.
좋아, 그리고 한 장소에서 다른 장소로 이동하는 데 걸리는 시간을 고려하는 것을 잊지 말렴.

Why? 왜 정답일까?

남자는 여자의 여행 계획을 듣고 너무 빡빡한 일정을 지적하며 여행의 진정한 묘미에 대한 자신의 생각을 말하고 있다. 따라서 남자의 의견으로는 ② '비행기 창 밖을 내다보는 것과 새로운 곳의 공기를 마시는 것도 여행이다.'가 가장 적절하다.

- unpack ⓥ (짐 등을) 풀다
- exhausted ⓐ 기진맥진한
- demanding ⓐ 힘든
- worn out 매우 지친
- revise ⓥ 수정하다, 개편하다

03 대화자의 관계 파악하기 정답 ⑤

W : Excuse me, sir. Did you finish checking my shop for the safety?
실례합니다. 안전을 위해 우리 가게를 점검하는 것이 끝났나요?
M : Almost, but I have a few things to tell you.
거의 끝났습니다. 하지만 몇 가지 말씀 드릴 것이 있습니다.
W : Sure, what are they?
물론이죠. 무엇인가요?
M : First of all, you should secure the exits in case of fire emergency.
우선, 화재 상황에 대비하기 위해 비상구를 확보해야 합니다.
W : Of course. Are there any problems to the exits?
물론이지요. 비상구에 무슨 문제가 있나요?
M : Well, you need to remove some boxes blocking the fire exit.
음, 화재 비상구를 막고 있는 몇몇 상자를 치울 필요가 있습니다.
W : Oh, I'm sorry. I didn't know that. I'll get rid of them right away. We do have fire extinguishers in the passage, which are well maintained.
오, 죄송합니다. 미처 몰랐네요. 즉시 치우도록 하겠습니다. 우리는 복도에 소화기를 잘 관리하고 있습니다.
M : Yes, they are. I wonder if your employees know how to operate them properly.
네, 그렇군요. 당신의 종업원들이 그것들을 적절히 작동하는 방법을 알고 있는지 궁금하군요.
W : Sure. All of us know how to use them. We are educated very often about their usage.
물론이지요. 우리 모두는 그것들을 사용하는 방법을 알고 있습니다. 우리는 그것의 사용에 대해 자주 교육받습니다.
M : Sounds good, and remove the dirt on the exit signs above the doors, so that they can be easily seen from a distance.
좋습니다. 그리고 문 위의 비상구 사인이 멀리서도 잘 보이도록 먼지를 제거하세요.
W : Yes, we will. Thank you for checking our facility for our safety.
네, 그러겠습니다. 안전을 위해 우리 시설을 점검해 주셔서 감사합니다.
M : No problem. Please sign here.
천만에요. 여기에 서명하세요.

Why? 왜 정답일까?

가게 주인과 소방 점검을 하고 있는 검사관과의 대화이므로 두 사람의 관계로는 ⑤의 '가게 주인 – 소방 점검원'이 가장 적절하다.

- safety ⓝ 안전
- secure ⓥ 확실하게 하다, 안전하게 하다
- remove ⓥ 제거하다(= get rid of)
- block ⓥ 막다
- fire exit 소방 비상구
- fire extinguisher 소화기
- properly ad 적절히
- from a distance 멀리서

04 그림 정보 파악하기 정답 ⑤

M : Hi, Christine. Thank you so much for coming.
안녕, Christine. 와줘서 너무 고마워.
W : Hello, Kevin. Thank you for inviting me to the dinner. I think I can already smell something delicious.
안녕, Kevin. 저녁 식사에 나를 초대해줘서 고마워. 벌써 뭔가 맛있는 냄새가 나는 것 같아.
M : Please come and sit. I tried to cook steak but I overcooked it so I changed the menu at the last minute.
와서 앉아. 스테이크를 요리하려고 했는데 내가 너무 태워서 마지막 순간에 메뉴를 바꿨어.
W : That's why there is a steak knife with the curry rice. Curry rice is actually one of my favorite foods.
그래서 카레라이스에 스테이크용 나이프가 있는 거구나. 카레라이스는 사실 내가 가장 좋아하는 음식 중 하나야.
M : I am so glad you like it.
네가 좋아한다니 다행이다.
W : Hey, what's with the lit candle and the bell, by the way?
이봐, 그나저나, 불이 켜진 촛불과 벨은 뭐니?
M : I found this candle and table bell in the kitchen drawer. So I just took them out to make this place look like a restaurant.
이 촛불과 테이블 벨을 부엌 서랍에서 찾았어. 그래서 이 장소를 레스토랑처럼 보이게 하려고 그것들을 꺼냈지.
W : That's funny.
웃기다.
M : Oh, and I was going to place a fork beside your plate but you told me the other day you were good with chopsticks.
아, 그리고 나는 네 접시 옆에 포크를 놓으려고 했는데 지난번에 네가 젓가락질을 잘한다고 말했잖아.
W : Yes, I am perfectly fine with them. Shall we start? My mouth is watering.
응, 젓가락 괜찮아. 먹을까? 군침이 돈다.

Why? 왜 정답일까?

남자가 자신의 집으로 여자를 초대해 저녁 식사를 대접하는 상황이다. 남자는 여자를 위해 카레라이스를 준비했으며 여자가 젓가락질을 잘 한다고 말했던 것을 기억하여 포크는 준비하지 않았다고 말하고 있다. 따라서 ⑤는 대화의 내용과 일치하지 않는다.

- at the last minute 마지막 순간에
- what's with ~ ~는 웬 것이니
- mouth is watering 군침이 돌다

05 부탁한 일 파악하기 정답 ⑤

M : Tiffany, how's life in Korea?
Tiffany, 한국에서의 생활은 어떠세요?
W : Everything is fine. I think all the people here are kind.
모든 게 좋아요. 여기의 모든 사람들은 친절한 것 같아요.
M : I'm glad to hear that. Well, did you buy a cell phone? I know a store which sells a fancy one.
그런 말을 듣게 되어 기쁘군요. 음, 혹시 휴대폰은 구입했어요? 제가 멋진 것을 파는 매장을 알고 있어요.
W : Thanks, but I already bought one. Also, I got a laptop computer and rented a car.
고맙지만, 이미 구입했어요. 게다가 노트북 컴퓨터를 구했고요, 차도 렌트했는걸요.
M : Oh, it sounds perfect. Please let me know if you need any help.
오, 완벽하게 들리네요. 어떤 도움이 필요하면 알려 주세요.
W : Well, Junsoo, I have a problem. I want to move to a new house near the campus.
음, 준수, 저에게 문제가 하나 있어요. 나는 캠퍼스 근처에 새로운 집으로 이사하길 원해요.
M : Have you looked for an ad in the English newspaper?
영자신문의 광고를 살펴보셨어요?
W : I have, but there weren't enough choices there. I want to contact a real estate agency in the local area, but it's hard to find an agent who can speak English.

[문제편 p.211]

네, 하지만 거기에는 고를만한 것이 충분치 않더라고요. 저는 그 지역의 부동산과 연락하기를 원하지만, 영어를 말할 수 있는 부동산 중개인을 찾기가 어려워요.

M : Okay. I'll contact the agency for you. Please tell me the place and the rent range you want.
좋아요. 제가 당신을 위해서 부동산에 연락할게요. 당신이 원하는 장소와 집세 범위를 말해 주세요.

W : Oh, thanks. I really appreciate your help.
오, 고마워요. 당신의 도움에 정말 감사드려요.

Why? 왜 정답일까?

남자가 여자를 위해 할 일로는 ⑤의 '부동산에 대신 전화해 주기'가 가장 적절하다.

- **laptop computer** 노트북 컴퓨터
- **real estate agency** 부동산 중개업소
- **ad** ⓝ 광고(= advertisement)
- **range** ⓝ 범위

06 숫자 정보 파악하기 정답 ①

[Telephone rings.]
[전화가 울린다.]

M : Hello, Amazing Scissors Hair Salon.
여보세요, 어메이징 시저스 헤어 살롱입니다.

W : Hi, this is Kate. I've made an appointment this coming Tuesday at 2.
여보세요, 저는 Kate입니다. 이번 주 화요일 두 시에 예약했어요.

M : Ma'am, can you give me your full name please?
손님, 성함 전체를 말씀해 주시겠어요?

W : It's Katherine Morgan.
Katherine Morgan이에요.

M : *[Typing sound]* Oh, there you are. You are coming in for trimming and highlighting. Is that correct?
[타자 소리] 아, 여기 있군요. 머리 다듬고 염색하시러 오시는군요. 맞나요?

W : Yes, that's right. By the way, I happen to have 10% discount coupon and I want to know if I can use it then.
네, 맞아요. 그런데 제가 마침 10% 쿠폰이 있는데 이걸 그때 사용할 수 있는지 알고 싶어요.

M : You can use the coupon only when your expense is $100 or over. Let me see. Trimming costs $35 and highlighting costs $55. I am afraid, you may not use the coupon this time.
쿠폰은 비용이 100달러이거나 그 이상일 때에만 사용할 수 있어요. 어디 볼까요. 다듬는 비용은 35달러이고 염색 비용은 55달러네요. 아쉽지만 이번에는 쿠폰을 사용할 수 없을 거 같아요.

W : Oh, I see. I will save it for the next time then.
아, 알겠습니다. 그러면 다음을 위해 남겨둘게요.

M : You are still coming in for your hair, though on Tuesday?
그래도 머리 하시러 화요일에 오시는 거죠?

W : Yes, I really need to have my hair trimmed. It looks messy.
네, 머리를 꼭 다듬어야 해요. 머리가 너무 지저분해 보여요.

M : Okay, ma'am. I will see you then.
알겠습니다, 손님. 그때 뵙겠습니다.

Why? 왜 정답일까?

미용실 예약을 한 여자 손님이 쿠폰 사용 가능 여부를 알기 위해 전화 문의를 하고 있는 상황이다. 쿠폰은 지불 금액이 100달러이거나 혹은 그 이상일 때 사용 가능하지만 여자는 머리 다듬기($35)와 염색($55)만 할 예정이라 쿠폰은 다음에 사용하겠다고 말하고 있다. 따라서 여자가 지불할 금액으로 적절한 것은 ①이다.

- **trimming** ⓝ 다듬기, 손질
- **happen to** 마침 ~하다, 우연히 ~하다
- **highlighting** ⓝ 염색
- **messy** ⓐ 지저분한

07 이유 파악하기 정답 ③

W : Hey. Benson. How's your elbow? Are you still in pain?
이봐, Benson. 너의 팔꿈치 좀 어때? 아직도 아프니?

M : No, It's fully recovered, Liz. I am more than ready for the tennis tournament.
아니, 완전히 회복했어, Liz. 나는 테니스 토너먼트를 위한 준비가 충분히 됐어.

W : It's good to hear. Then will you partake in the practice this afternoon?
듣던 중 반가운 소식이다. 그럼 오늘 오후에 연습에 참여할래?

M : No, I am sorry, but I can't today.
아니, 미안하지만 오늘은 안 돼.

W : Why not? Do you have to work on your science project?
왜 안되니? 과학 프로젝트에 집중해야 하니?

M : No, I've already done my part.
아니, 나는 이미 내 역할을 끝냈어.

W : Oh, then I guess you have a test coming up that you need to study for.
아, 그러면 공부해야 할 시험이 다가오고 있나보구나.

M : That was last week. Actually, I am taking my ailing dog to a vet.
그건 지난주였어. 사실 난 아픈 나의 강아지를 동물병원에 데리고 갈 예정이야.

W : Oh, I see. Then will I see you tomorrow at the tennis court?
아, 그렇구나. 그러면 내일 테니스장에서 볼 수 있을까?

M : You bet.
당연하지.

Why? 왜 정답일까?

남자는 팔꿈치는 다 나았지만 아픈 강아지를 데리고 동물병원에 갈 예정이라고 말하고 있다. 따라서 남자가 테니스 연습에 참여할 수 없는 이유로 가장 적절한 것은 ③ '아픈 강아지를 동물병원에 데려가야 해서'이다.

- **partake in** ~에 참여하다
- **ailing** ⓐ 병든, 아픈

08 언급 유무 파악하기 정답 ③

W : Today, we're inviting an expert on a hybrid car to talk with us. Hello, Dr. Jenkins.
오늘 우리와 함께 이야기를 나눌 하이브리드 차에 대한 전문가 한 분을 초대했습니다. 안녕하세요, Jenkins 박사님.

M : Nice to meet you.
반갑습니다.

W : Thank you for coming here. These days, when I see hybrids on the street, I'm fascinated with the fancy design.
와 주셔서 고맙습니다. 요즘 거리에서 하이브리드 차를 볼 때면, 그 세련된 디자인에 저는 매력을 느낍니다.

M : You're right. Most hybrid cars have attractive design. Let me ask you a question. Why do you think people are interested in hybrid cars?
맞아요. 대부분의 하이브리드 차는 멋진 디자인을 갖고 있습니다. 질문 하나만 하죠. 왜 사람들이 하이브리드 차에 관심을 갖는다고 보십니까?

W : Well, it is probably because they can save money on gasoline. Its fuel efficiency is excellent, I heard. Do you have another reason?
글쎄요, 그건 아마도 휘발유 값을 절약할 수 있기 때문이 아닐까요. 그것의 연비는 정말 우수하다고 들었습니다. 다른 이유가 또 있나요?

M : Yeah, there are some other reasons. One of the reasons is that it is eco-friendly. Actually, pollution is getting worse and worse.
네, 다른 이유들도 있지요. 한 가지 이유는 그것이 환경친화적이기 때문입니다. 대기오염이 갈수록 심해지고 있으니까요.

W : I see your point.
무슨 말씀인지 알겠습니다.

M : In fact, I have a hybrid car, too. It could go about 52 miles on a gallon of gas when I'm driving it.
사실, 저도 하이브리드 차를 갖고 있습니다. 제가 운전할 때 1 gallon으로 약 52 mile을 갈 수 있어요.

W : That's really good. But the problem is the price, some people argue. The hybrids are much more expensive to buy than gasoline powered vehicles.
정말 훌륭하네요. 하지만 문제는 가격이라고 몇몇 사람들은 주장합니다. 하이브리드 차가 휘발유차보다 훨씬 비싸다는 것입니다.

M : True. They still cost more than gas-powered vehicles, but they are expected to become less expensive as technology improves.
맞습니다. 아직도 휘발유차보다 구매하기에 비용이 많이 들지요. 그렇지만 기술이 발달할수록 점점 더 싸질 것입니다.

W : Yes, they are. We are grateful that you could share time with us today.
그렇군요. 오늘 시간을 함께 해 주셔서 대단히 감사합니다.

Why? 왜 정답일까?

남자와 여자는 **Hybrid Car**에 대한 여러 정보를 주고받고 있지만 ③의 '주행 시 조용함'에 대해서는 언급하지 않고 있다.

- **expert** ⓝ 전문가
- **fuel efficiency** 연료 효율
- **pollution** ⓝ 오염
- **be fascinated with** ~에 홀리다, 얼을 빼앗기다
- **eco-friendly** ⓐ 환경친화적인
- **grateful** ⓐ 고마워하는

09 세부 정보 파악하기 정답 ③

W : Hello, everyone.
안녕하세요, 여러분.
Welcome to the Peace Charity Marathon homepage.
평화 자선 마라톤 홈페이지에 오신 것을 환영합니다.
With over 100,000 people entering each year, 2 million spectators, huge sums of money raised by charity runners, this is the perfect charity running event.
매년 십 만 명이 넘는 사람들이 참가하고, 2백만 명의 관중들, 자선 대회 경주자들에 의한 모금되는 엄청난 금액으로, 이 대회는 완벽한 자선 경주 행사입니다.
It will take place on riverside road next Saturday.
이 행사는 다음 주 토요일 강변에서 열립니다.
This is a leisurely run and open to anyone aged 12 or over.
이 행사는 여유로운 달리기이며 12살 이상이면 누구나에게 열려 있습니다.
But participants under 15 must be accompanied by an adult aged 18 or over.
하지만 15살 이하 참가자는 반드시 18살 이상 성인이 동반해야 합니다.
It begins at 10 a.m. and ends 4 p.m. and the participants will run different distance according to their hope such as 10km, 20km, and a full course.
오전 10시에 시작해서 오후 4시에 끝나며 참가자들은 희망에 따라 10km, 20km 그리고 정규 코스의 다른 거리를 달리게 됩니다.
You can register online in advance or you can join on the spot before the start of the run.
온라인으로 미리 신청할 수 있으며 시작 전에 현장에서 가입할 수도 있습니다.
As a charity runner, you will be cheered at every corner and it is always nice to see a great mix of nationalities joining in.
자선 대회 경주자로서 여러분은 매 모퉁이마다 환영을 받을 것이며 참가하는 다양한 국적을 보는 것은 항상 즐거운 일입니다.
By running, you can improve your health and help the others in need.
여러분은 뛰면서 건강을 증진시키고 도움이 필요한 다른 사람들을 도울 수 있습니다.
Thank you.
감사합니다.

Why? 왜 정답일까?

오전 10시에 시작해서 오후 4시에 대회가 끝난다고 했으므로 두 번의 경주가 있다는 ③은 내용과 일치하지 않는다.

- **charity** ⓝ 자선
- **take place** 열리다, 발생하다
- **participant** ⓝ 참가자
- **register** ⓥ 등록하다
- **spectator** ⓝ 관중
- **leisurely** ⓐ 여유 있는
- **accompany** ⓥ 동반하다
- **in advance** 미리

10 특정 정보 파악하기 정답 ⑤

M : Welcome to Super Furniture. How can I help you?
Super Furniture에 오신 걸 환영합니다. 무엇을 도와드릴까요?

W : Hi, I am looking for an office chair that goes well with my wooden desk.
안녕하세요, 저는 제 나무 책상과 잘 어울릴만한 사무용 의자를 찾고 있어요.

M : I understand. Is there any particular model you have in mind? If not, I can show you our catalog.
알겠습니다. 염두에 두신 특정한 모델이 있으신가요? 아니시면 저희 카탈로그를 보여드릴 수 있습니다.

W : That would be nice. I am just looking for a comfortable chair that's not too heavy and that's not too costly, either.
그러면 좋을 것 같아요. 저는 너무 무겁지도 않고 너무 비싸지도 않은 편안한 의자를 찾고 있어요.

M : How much are you willing to spend?
얼마를 소비할 의향이 있습니까?

W : I've already spent $250 on the desk, which left me only about $90 in my account.
저는 이미 책상에 250달러를 써서, 제 계좌에는 90달러 정도밖에 남지 않았어요.

M : If that's the case, this model here might be perfect for you.
만약 그러시다면 이 모델이 고객님께 딱 맞을 것 같습니다.

W : Well, I think this one is too heavy for me. I want something under 50 pounds.
음, 이건 저한테 너무 무거운 것 같아요. 저는 50파운드 이하의 것을 원해요.

M : How about this? It will also pair well with your wooden desk and it's under 50 pounds.
이건 어떠세요? 고객님의 나무 책상과도 잘 어울리고 50파운드도 안 됩니다.

W : Yeah, I also like its color, beige. Oh, wait, wait. I almost made a huge mistake. Wheels are necessary. I am sorry, I should've mentioned that sooner.
맞아요, 베이지 색상인 거 또한 좋네요. 앗, 잠시만요. 큰 실수를 할 뻔했네요. 바퀴는 꼭 필요해요. 죄송해요, 제가 좀 더 일찍 말씀드렸어야 했는데.

M : No worries. Then this model must be your ideal office chair but it comes in only two colors, blue and green.
괜찮습니다. 이 모델이 고객님의 이상적인 사무용 의자가 분명한 거 같습니다만 색상은 파란색과 녹색 두 가지 뿐이에요.

W : Oh, either one is fine. I will take it.
오, 둘 중 아무거나 괜찮아요. 이걸로 할게요.

Why? 왜 정답일까?

여자는 가구매장에서 90달러 이하이고, 무게가 50파운드 이하의 바퀴가 있는 사무용 의자를 찾고 있다고 말하고 있다. 여자의 의견을 듣고 남자가 권한 의자는 두 가지 색상(파란색, 녹색)으로만 출시된 모델이라고 하자 여자는 둘 중에 아무거나 괜찮다고 답하고 있으므로 여자가 구매할 의자는 ⑤이다.

- go well with ~와 잘 어울리다
- pair well with ~와 잘 어울리다
- costly ⓐ 값이 비싼
- necessary ⓐ 필수적인

11 짧은 응답 고르기 정답 ①

M : I heard your brother lives in Seattle.
오빠가 시애틀에 산다고 들었는데.

W : Not any more. He moved to Los Angeles recently.
더 이상은 아니야. 그는 최근에 LA로 이사했어.

M : Really? What made him move to a new city?
정말? 왜 그가 새로운 도시로 이사했어?

W : He got a new job there.
그가 거기에서 새로운 직업을 얻었어.

Why? 왜 정답일까?

여자의 오빠가 새로운 도시로 이사한 이유를 묻는 질문에 대한 응답으로는 ①의 '그가 거기에서 새로운 직업을 얻었어.'가 가장 적절하다.

답지 해석

② 물론이지, 그는 거기에서 혼자 살아.
③ 그가 한국을 곧 방문하기를 바래.
④ 이사는 스트레스가 많은 일인 것을 나도 알아.
⑤ 왜 아니겠어? 시애틀은 아름다운 도시야.

- move ⓥ (…으로) 이사하다
- recently ad 최근에
- stressful ⓐ 스트레스가 많은

12 짧은 응답 고르기 정답 ①

W : Kevin, where are you going? It's almost class time.
Kevin, 어디 가니? 수업 시간이 가까웠어.

M : Well, I'm going to return this book in the library.
음, 이 책을 반납하러 도서관에 가는 길이야.

W : Can you be back in time for the class?
수업 시간에 맞게 제 시간에 돌아올 수 있겠니?

M : Don't worry about it. I wouldn't miss it.
걱정마. 나는 수업을 놓치지 않을 거야.

Why? 왜 정답일까?

수업 시간에 늦지 않게 돌아 올 수 있는지를 물어보는 여자의 질문에 대한 남자의 응답으로는 ①의 '걱정마. 나는 수업을 놓치지 않을 거야.'가 가장 적절하다.

답지 해석

② 그래. 나는 수업을 바꾸는 것을 고려 중이야.
③ 안 돼. 그런 경우라면, 나는 연체료를 내야 해.
④ 물론이지. 나는 도서관에서 같이 공부하고 싶어.
⑤ 문제없어. 네가 필요한 책을 내가 대출할 수 있어.

- in time 제 시간에
- late fee 연체료
- check out 대출하다

13 적절한 응답 고르기 정답 ③

W : Hi, Clay. Are you in town for another job interview?
안녕, Clay. 다른 직장 면접으로 시내에 있는 거니?

M : Yes, I'm pretty hopeful this time. I've just finished my second interview with this company.
그래, 이번에는 굉장히 희망적이야. 이 회사에 두 번째 면접을 이제 막 끝냈어.

W : That sounds great. I hope it works out for you. But wasn't it expensive just getting here?
잘 됐구나. 일이 잘 풀려가길 바래. 하지만 여기에 오는 게 비용이 많이 들지 않았니?

M : No, in fact the company is paying all my expenses.
아니, 사실은 회사가 내 모든 비용을 지불하고 있어.

W : How nice!
정말 잘 됐다!

M : They've put me up in a hotel downtown.
그들이 나를 시내에 있는 호텔에 묵게 해줬어.

W : Good for you. How many people are they interviewing?
좋은 일이네. 얼마나 많은 사람들이 면접을 했니?

M : Well, they interviewed 16 the first time, and now four of us were chosen to come back for this interview.
음, 그들이 처음에는 16명을 봤고, 이번 면접에는 그 중에 4명이 다시 오도록 선발됐어.

W : It sounds like you have a good chance to be selected then.
네가 뽑힐 가능성이 높은 것처럼 들리는데.

M : I hope so. The manger told me he would call me on Monday.
그러길 바래. 관리자가 말하기를 월요일에 나에게 전화할 거라고 말했어.

W : I hope it goes well. I'd love it if you came to this area to work.
일이 잘 풀렸으면 좋겠다. 네가 이 지역에서 일하게 되면 정말 좋겠다.

Why? 왜 정답일까?

남자가 두 번째 면접을 끝내고 전화를 기다리는 상황이므로, 이에 대한 여자의 응답으로는 ③의 '일이 잘 풀리길 바래. 네가 이 지역에서 일하게 되면 정말 좋겠다.'가 적절하다.

답지 해석

① 너라면 할 수 있어. 두 번째 면접은 네가 잘 할 수 있을 거야.
② 문제없어. 요즘 호텔에 빈 방이 많아.
④ 행운을 빌어. 나는 네가 관리자로 승진되길 바래.
⑤ 힘내! 16명 중에 선발된 것에 대해 자부심을 갖는 게 좋겠다.

- expensive ⓐ 비싼
- expense ⓝ 비용
- put up 투숙하게 하다; 올리다, 설치하다

14 적절한 응답 고르기 정답 ②

W : Scott, you look tired. Do you have a cold or something?
Scott, 너 피곤해 보인다. 감기라도 걸렸니?

M : No, no cold.
아니, 그런 게 아니야.

W : Then, what's the matter with you?
그러면, 뭐가 문제니?

M : Last night I stayed up late watching American dramas. I've been into them too much recently.
지난밤에 미국 드라마를 보면서 늦게까지 깨어 있었어. 최근에 나는 그것에 너무 빠져 있어.

W : I'm a big fan of them, too. I like romantic comedy genre. What kinds of dramas do you prefer?
나도 그것을 엄청 좋아해. 난 로맨틱 코미디 종류를 좋아해. 넌 어떤 종류의 드라마를 선호하니?

M : I like detective stories. Watching them helps me understand their culture and lifestyles.
나는 탐정 이야기를 좋아해. 그것을 보는 것은 내가 그들의 문화와 생활 방식을 이해하는 데 도움을 줘.

W : You can say that again. Besides, they are fun to watch. I don't know how time flies while I'm watching them.
그렇고말고. 게다가, 그것을 보는 게 재미있어. 미국 드라마를 볼 때면 시간이 어떻게 흘러가는지 모르겠어.

M : Oh, you don't? I also don't know where time goes.
오, 그러니? 나도 시간이 어디로 흘러가는지 모르겠어.

W : It's okay to watch American dramas for fun, but it should not interfere with our studies, I think.
재미로 미국 드라마를 보는 것은 괜찮지만, 그것이 우리의 학업을 방해해서는 안 된다고 생각해.

M : Sure. But I'm worried I'm getting a little addicted to them these days.
물론이지. 하지만 내가 요즘에 그것에 약간 중독되어 가는 것 같아 걱정이야.

W : Be careful about that. We've got to do something about this.
그것에 대해 조심해야 돼. 우리는 이것에 관한 무언가를 해야 해.

M : Right. We need to cut down on them.
맞아. 우리는 그것을 줄일 필요가 있어.

Why? 왜 정답일까?

미국 드라마를 지나치게 시청하는 것에 대해 대책이 필요하다는 여자의 마지막 말에 대한 응답으로는 ②의 '맞아. 우리는 그것을 줄일 필요가 있어.'가 가장 적절하다.

답지 해석

① 물론이야. 나도 미국 드라마를 좋아해.
③ 안 돼. 우리는 그것을 시청할 때 자막이 필요해.
④ 무슨 말인지 알겠어. 너는 그것을 엄청 좋아하는구나.
⑤ 그렇게 생각지 않아. 그것을 보는 것은 많은 이점이 있어.

- stay up late 늦은 시간까지 깨어 있다
- genre ⓝ 유형, 장르
- detective ⓐ 탐정의
- interfere with ~을 방해하다
- addicted ⓐ 중독된
- cut down on ~을 줄이다

15 상황에 적절한 말 고르기 정답 ③

W : Jieun likes reading English books and has confidence to speak English.
지은이는 영어책 읽기를 좋아하고 영어를 말하는 데 자신감이 있다.
Last year she won first place in the English speech contest held in her high school, and she is also willing to take part in other English competitions.
작년에 그녀는 그녀의 고등학교에서 열린 영어 말하기 대회에서 1등상을 받았고 또한 다른 영어 대회에 기꺼이 참여하고자 한다.
Her homeroom teacher, Mr. Lee is proud of her talent and advises her to major in English in university.
그녀의 담임교사인 이 선생님은 그녀의 재능에 대해 자랑스럽게 여기고 그녀에게 대학에서 영어를 전공할 것을 충고한다.
Jieun also wants to study English further, but she's worried that her father wants her to become a lawyer.
지은이도 또한 영어를 좀 더 공부하기를 원하지만, 그녀의 아버지는 자신에게 변호사가 될 것을 원하시는 것이 걱정이 된다.
When she asks Mr. Lee for advice, he says she had better tell her father about what she is really interested in.
그녀가 이 선생님께 조언을 부탁했을 때, 그는 그녀가 정말로 관심 있는 것에 관해 아버지께 말씀드리는 것이 낫겠다고 말한다.
She is encouraged by his words and decides to talk to her father.
그녀는 그의 말에 고무되고 아버지께 말씀드리기로 결심한다.
In this situation, what would Jieun most likely say to her father?
이러한 상황에서, 지은이는 아버지께 무어라고 말할 것 같은가?

Jieun : Dad, I am more interested in English than becoming a lawyer.
아빠, 저는 변호사가 되는 것보다 영어에 더 많은 관심이 있어요.

Why? 왜 정답일까?

아버지를 설득해야 하는 상황이므로 지은이가 아버지에게 할 말로는 ③의 '저는 변호사가 되는 것보다 영어에 더 많은 관심이 있어요.'가 가장 적절하다.

답지 해석

① 선생님께서 저에게 법을 전공하라고 충고하세요.
② 저는 아버지가 훌륭한 변호사인 것이 자랑스러워요.

[문제편 p.212]

④ 저는 선생님께 저의 장래 직업을 수정해 줄 것을 설득할 거예요.
⑤ 저는 에세이 대회보다 말하기 대회에 참가하는 것이 더 좋아요.

- **confidence** ⓝ 자신감
- **take part in** ~에 참가하다
- **major in** ~을 전공하다
- **modify** ⓥ 수정하다
- **be willing to** 기꺼이 ~하다
- **homeroom teacher** 담임교사
- **persuade** ⓥ 설득하다

16-17 장문 듣기

W : Hello, students.
학생 여러분 안녕하세요.
Today we are going to talk about how far we have come with AI.
오늘 우리는 AI와 어디까지 와있는지에 대해 이야기할 것입니다.
AI is replacing human beings very quickly and some scientists insist that in the near future AI take over 80% of human jobs.
AI는 인간을 매우 빠르게 대체하고 있으며 일부 과학자들은 가까운 미래에 AI가 인간 일자리의 80%를 차지할 것이라고 주장합니다.
Today, AI serves coffee and food in a number of restaurants.
오늘날, 인공지능은 많은 식당에서 커피와 음식을 제공합니다.
We also have AI translators, which makes it easier for people to travel around the world without having to learn the local language.
우리는 또한 인공지능 번역기를 갖추고 있어서 사람들이 현지 언어를 배우지 않아도 전 세계를 더 쉽게 여행할 수 있습니다.
AI drivers are on course as the demand for self-driving cars has been picking up for the last 10 years.
지난 10년간 자율주행차에 대한 수요가 증가함에 따라 AI 운전자들은 생겨날 것입니다.
According to some tech experts, professions such as judges and pharmacists will also be replaced one way or another, although many scientists may say otherwise.
많은 과학자들이 다르게 말할 수도 있지만 일부 기술 전문가들에 따르면, 판사와 약사와 같은 직업도 어떤 식으로든 대체될 것입니다.
Then we have to think.
그럼 우리는 생각해 봐야 합니다.
Should we be worried or excited?
우리는 걱정해야 할까요, 아니면 기대해야 할까요?
It is highly possible that our life will be still more convenient with AI doing everything for us from driving to interpreting.
운전에서부터 통역까지 모든 것을 해주는 AI로 인해 우리의 삶이 훨씬 더 편리해질 가능성이 높습니다.
But it will be also very difficult to get yourself a decent job because every time you have a job interview, you will have to prove that you are better than AI.
하지만 면접을 볼 때마다 여러분이 AI보다 낫다는 것을 증명해야 하기 때문에 괜찮은 직업을 얻는 것도 매우 어려울 것입니다.
I am going to show you a short video clip on how well AI performs its task.
AI가 업무를 얼마나 잘 수행하는지에 대한 짧은 동영상을 보여드리겠습니다.

- **replace** ⓥ 대체하다
- **on course** 생겨나다
- **pick up** 증가하다
- **profession** ⓝ 직업
- **one way or another** 어떻게 해서든
- **prove** ⓥ 증명하다
- **take over** 차지하다, 인수하다
- **demand** ⓝ 수요
- **expert** ⓝ 전문가
- **pharmacist** ⓝ 약사
- **decent** ⓐ 괜찮은

16 주제 파악하기 정답 ④

Why? 왜 정답일까?

AI가 어떤 직업군을 대체하고 있고, 미래에 어떤 직업군을 대체할 수 있을지를 이야기하고 있으므로 여자가 하는 말의 주제로는 ④ '인공지능이 직업 면에서 할 수 있는 것'이 가장 적절하다.

답지 해석

① AI가 미래에 얼마나 유용할 수 있는지
② 우리가 AI와 경쟁해야 하는 이유
③ AI가 결코 대체할 수 없는 직업들
⑤ AI가 필요한 다양한 산업

17 언급 유무 파악하기 정답 ⑤

Why? 왜 정답일까?

AI가 대체할 직업의 예로 ⑤ '교사'는 언급되지 않았다.

[문제편 p.212]

특별 부록
02
회 | 수능 대비 파이널 모의고사
고3
| 정답과 해설 |

• 정답 •
01 ⑤ 02 ⑤ 03 ③ 04 ⑤ 05 ② 06 ④ 07 ⑤ 08 ② 09 ③ 10 ③ 11 ② 12 ① 13 ② 14 ③ 15 ⑤ 16 ② 17 ④

01 담화의 목적 파악하기 정답 ⑤

M : We live in a flood of information.
우리는 정보의 홍수 속에 살고 있습니다.
However, the spread of useless and undesirable information can have a harmful effect on human activities.
하지만, 쓸모없고 바람직하지 않은 정보의 확산은 인간의 활동에 해로운 영향을 미칠 수도 있습니다.
For example, vitamin C is one of the essential minerals that treat and prevent some diseases, especially scurvy.
예를 들어, 비타민 C는 몇몇 질병, 특히 괴혈병을 치료하고 예방하는 필수 무기질 중에 하나입니다.
Also, it has been said to be effective on the common cold.
또한 일반 감기에도 효과가 있다고 합니다.
People say routine vitamin C intake can reduce the severity of the common cold.
규칙적인 비타민 C 섭취는 일반 감기의 심각성을 줄일 수 있다고 사람들은 말합니다.
However, relatively large doses of vitamin C may cause indigestion, particularly when taken on an empty stomach.
하지만, 상대적으로 많은 비타민 C의 복용은 특히 빈속에서는 소화불량을 야기할 수 있습니다.
In an experiment, overtaking vitamin C caused nausea, vomiting, diarrhea, flushing of the face, headache, fatigue and disturbed sleep.
실험에서 비타민 C의 과다 섭취는 어지러움, 구토, 설사, 안면 홍조, 두통, 피로, 그리고 수면 장애를 야기했습니다.
Also it was likely to cause some skin rashes on children.
또한 그것은 아이들의 피부 발진을 유발시키는 것 같았습니다.
You may know the saying "Too much is as bad as too little."
여러분은 "지나친 것은 미치지 못한 것만큼이나 안 좋다."라는 속담을 알고 있을 것입니다.
You should remember this saying in taking vitamin C.
비타민 C를 섭취할 때는 이 속담을 기억해야 합니다.

Why? 왜 정답일까?

비타민 C는 적절하게 섭취하면 건강에 유익하나 과다하게 섭취하면 오히려 여러 가지 해를 끼친다는 것을 이야기하고 있으므로, 남자가 하는 말의 목적으로는 ⑤가 가장 적절하다.

- **a flood of information** 정보의 홍수
- **mineral** ⓝ 무기질
- **intake** ⓝ 섭취
- **dose** ⓝ 복용량
- **nausea** ⓝ 어지러움
- **flushing** ⓝ 붉어짐
- **harmful** ⓐ 해로운
- **scurvy** ⓝ 괴혈병
- **severity** ⓝ 심각성
- **indigestion** ⓝ 소화불량
- **diarrhea** ⓝ 설사
- **rash** ⓝ 발진

02 의견 파악하기 정답 ⑤

M : Honey, do you want a fried egg on your rice?
여보, 밥 위에 달걀 프라이 얹어줄까?
W : Yeah, sounds good. Don't throw away the eggshell.
응, 좋아. 달걀껍데기는 버리지 마.
M : Why? What do you want it for?
왜? 왜 달걀껍데기를 원해?
W : I need it when I wash the water bottle. You put crushed eggshells and water in the bottle and briefly shake it. Then the bottle looks brand new.
물병 씻을 때 필요해. 으깬 달걀껍데기와 물을 병에 넣고 잠시 흔들어봐. 그러면 그 병은 완전히 새것처럼 보여.
M : Where did you get such a great tip?
그렇게 좋은 팁을 어디에서 들었어?
W : I read it from a magazine titled "Living & Kitchen".
"Living & Kitchen"이라는 잡지에서 읽었어.
M : Interesting. How does it work?
흥미롭네. 어떻게 작용하는 거야?
W : It said crushed eggshells are rough so they are better at removing debris in the bottle than dish sponges.
으깬 달걀껍데기는 거칠기 때문에 수세미보다 병 안의 잔해를 제거하는 데 더 좋대.
M : That's good to know.
알게 돼서 좋네.
W : Also, eggshells are eco-friendly. I am trying to use less dishwasher detergent these days.
게다가, 달걀껍데기는 친환경적이잖아. 난 요즘 주방 세제를 덜 쓰려고 노력 중이야.
M : I really shouldn't throw away eggshells.
달걀껍데기를 버리면 정말 안 되겠군.
W : Yeah, every time you have eggs for your breakfast, please save eggshells for my later use.
응, 당신이 아침식사로 달걀을 먹을 때마다, 나중에 내가 사용할 수 있도록 달걀껍데기를 남겨놔줘.
M : Sure thing.
물론이야.

Why? 왜 정답일까?

여자는 달걀껍데기의 놀라운 효능에 대한 이야기를 하며, 특히 물병을 씻을 때 주방 세제보다 더 우수한 세정력을 지녔다는 사실에 대해 말하고 있다. 따라서 여자의 의견으로는 ⑤ '달걀껍데기는 주방 세제보다 물병 세척에 탁월하다.'가 가장 적절하다.

- **debris** ⓝ 찌꺼기, 잔해
- **eco-friendly** ⓐ 친환경적인
- **dish sponge** 수세미
- **dishwasher detergent** 주방 세제

03 대화자의 관계 파악하기 정답 ③

W : Good morning, Mr. Smith.
안녕하세요, Smith 씨.

특별 부록 02회

M : Good morning. Ms. Parker.
안녕하세요. Parker 씨.
W : This is your fifth practice with me, right?
저와 함께하는 당신의 다섯 번째 연습입니다, 맞죠?
M : Yes, ma'am. Thanks to you, I feel like I've improved a lot.
네. 덕분에 많이 좋아진 것처럼 느껴져요.
W : Thanks. Please remember 'Practice makes perfect.' Oh, you should fasten your seat belt before you start.
감사합니다. '연습이 완벽을 만든다'는 것을 명심하세요. 오, 출발하기 전에 안전벨트를 매야 합니다.
M : I'm sorry I forgot. Now let's start.
잊고 있었네요. 미안합니다. 자 시작할게요.
W : Good start. I think you have practiced a lot. Why don't you practice parking today?
좋은 출발입니다. 연습을 많이 하신 것 같군요. 오늘은 주차를 연습해 볼까요?
M : I see. Is this spot where we're going to park?
알겠습니다. 이곳이 우리가 주차할 곳인가요?
W : Yes. First, turn the wheels so that the front of the car is closer to the fence.
네. 먼저, 자동차의 앞부분이 울타리에 근접하도록 핸들을 돌리세요.
M : I got it. *[pause]* Am I doing it right?
알겠습니다. *[잠시 중단됨]* 제가 잘 하고 있나요?
W : You're almost perfect. Move slowly and put the car in reverse.
거의 완벽하시네요. 천천히 움직여서 차를 후진시키세요.
M : Okay, I will.
네, 그렇게 할게요.

Why? 왜 정답일까?

운전 강사와 운전을 배우고 있는 수강생과의 대화이므로 두 사람의 관계로는 ③이 가장 적절하다.

- fasten ⓥ 매다
- wheel ⓝ 핸들, 바퀴
- in reverse 후진으로, 거꾸로

04 그림 정보 파악하기 정답 ⑤

M : Hi, Clair. What are you looking at on your cell phone?
안녕, Clair. 핸드폰에 무엇을 보고 있니?
W : Hi, Jacob. It is my family picture taken last week. I paid a lot for this photo shoot.
안녕, Jacob. 지난주에 찍은 우리 가족 사진이야. 이 사진 촬영에 큰 돈 썼어.
M : You did? Let me see. Wow, what a big family you have!
그랬니? 어디 봐. 와, 대가족이구나!
W : Yeah, my grandparents also live with us. Grandma is in a wheelchair. She needs our help. Do you recognize my sister by the way? You've met her once.
응, 할아버지, 할머니도 우리와 같이 사시거든. 할머니가 휠체어를 타셔. 할머니는 우리의 도움이 필요하셔. 그나저나 나의 여동생 알아보겠니? 너는 그녀를 한 번 만난 적이 있어.
M : No, I don't really remember her face, but I remember this man here with glasses.
아니, 그녀의 얼굴은 잘 기억나지 않지만, 여기 안경을 쓴 남자는 기억이 나.
W : He's my Dad.
우리 아빠야.
M : Your Dad? He looks so young. I thought he was your uncle or big brother.
너의 아버지라고? 너무 젊어 보이셔. 난 이분이 너의 삼촌이나 오빠라고 생각했어.
W : He will be happy to hear that because he is trying really hard to look young these days. He said he didn't even grow his beard after the marriage to look younger.
아빠가 그 말을 들으면 무척 기뻐하실 거야. 요즘 젊게 보이시려고 정말 노력하시거든. 아빠가 말씀하시길 더 어려 보이시려고 결혼 이후에는 수염도 안 기르셨대.
M : Why is he so obsessed with his appearance?
왜 그렇게 외모에 집착하시니?
W : My Dad is 8 years older than my Mom and he doesn't want to look far older than Mom.
아빠가 엄마보다 8살이 더 많아서 엄마보다 훨씬 더 늙어 보이고 싶어 하지 않으셔.

Why? 왜 정답일까?

남자와 여자는 여자의 가족사진에 관한 이야기를 나누고 있다. 사진 속 여자의 아버지가 젊어 보인다는 남자의 말에 자신의 아버지가 젊어 보이기 위해 결혼 후 수염을 기르지 않았다고 이야기하고 있으므로 ⑤는 대화의 내용과 일치하지 않는다.

- recognize ⓥ 알아보다
- beard ⓝ 턱수염
- be obsessed with ~에 집착하다
- appearance ⓝ 외모

05 부탁한 일 파악하기 정답 ②

[Telephone rings.]
[전화가 울린다.]
W : Hello.
여보세요.
M : Hello, Erin. It's me, Henry.
안녕, Erin. 나야, Henry.
W : Hi, Henry. What's up?
안녕, Henry. 무슨 일이니?
M : Erin, what are you doing tonight?
Erin, 오늘 밤에 무슨 일하니?
W : Tonight? I have to finish my science paper. Why?
오늘 밤? 과학 보고서를 끝마쳐야 하는데. 왜?
M : Well, I'm thinking about going to a musical with you.
음, 너와 같이 뮤지컬 보러 가는 것을 생각 중이거든.
W : Really? Sounds great. How about tomorrow night? I'll be free then.
정말? 멋지게 들린다. 내일 밤은 어때? 내가 그때는 한가한데.
M : Okay. The musical title is *Lion King*. I will reserve the tickets online in advance.
좋아. 뮤지컬 제목은 '라이온 킹'이야. 내가 온라인으로 먼저 표를 예매할게.
W : Perfect, I can't wait to watch the musical. When does it start?
완벽해. 빨리 그 뮤지컬을 보고 싶다. 언제 시작하니?
M : It starts at eight. Maybe we can have a pizza before the show.
8시에 시작해. 아마 상영하기 전에 우리가 피자를 먹을 수 있을 것 같은데.
W : Good idea. Then let's meet at the Pizza Mall and have pizza together. Let me order for the pizza before you arrive there.
좋은 생각이야. 그러면 피자 몰에서 만나서 같이 피자를 먹자. 네가 거기 도착하기 전에 내가 피자를 주문해 놓을게.
M : All right, thank you. Tomorrow I'll be in the Pizza Mall at seven near the theater.
좋아, 고마워. 내일 극장 근처에 있는 피자 몰에 7시에 있을게.
W : Okay. See you then.
그래. 그때 보자.

Why? 왜 정답일까?

남자는 여자를 위해 뮤지컬 표를 예매하고, 이에 대한 보답으로 여자는 피자를 미리 주문해 놓기로 한다.

- reserve ⓥ 예약하다
- in advance 미리

06 숫자 정보 파악하기 정답 ④

W : Brownies! Cookies! Homemade brownies and cookies for sale!
브라우니 사세요! 쿠키 사세요! 집에서 만든 브라우니와 쿠키가 판매 중입니다!
M : Excuse me. Did you make these cookies yourself?
실례합니다. 이 쿠키를 직접 만드셨나요?
W : Yes, my sisters and I made all of these. We are trying to collect money to help the needy.
물론입니다. 제 자매들과 제가 이 모든 것을 만들었습니다. 불우한 사람들을 돕기 위해 돈을 모으고 있어요.
M : Good girls. How much is this cookie?
착한 소녀들이군요. 쿠키는 얼마예요?
W : They're one dollar each, but if you buy ten cookies, you can have them for eight dollars.
각각 1달러인데요. 10개를 사시면 8달러에 사실 수 있습니다.
M : Okay, I need twenty cookies for my family.
좋아요. 우리 가족을 위해 20개가 필요합니다.
W : In that case, the discounted price is only fifteen dollars.
그런 경우라면, 할인된 가격은 15달러입니다.
M : Good. *[pause]* Oh, is this lemonade also made by you?
좋아요. *[잠시 후]* 오, 이 레몬에이드도 만든 건가요?
W : Of course. We squeezed the lemons and made this drink.
물론입니다. 우리가 레몬을 짜서 음료수를 만들었습니다.
M : Hmm... How much is it?
음…. 얼마인가요?
W : It is three dollars. Would you like some?
3달러입니다. 드릴까요?
M : Well, I'd like to buy two lemonades. Could you wrap all of these up?
음, 2잔 사고 싶네요. 모든 것을 다 포장해 주시겠어요?
W : No problem. Just one moment.
문제없습니다. 잠시만 기다리세요.

Why? 왜 정답일까?

쿠키가 20개에 15달러이고, 레몬에이드가 2잔에 6달러이므로 지불해야 할 총합은 21달러이다.

- homemade ⓐ 집에서 만든
- the needy 불우한 사람들
- squeeze ⓥ 짜다
- wrap up 포장하다

07 이유 파악하기 정답 ⑤

[Cellphone rings.]
[핸드폰이 울린다.]
M : Hey, Judy. I have a news you might be interested in.
이봐, Judy. 네가 관심을 가질 만한 소식이 있어.
W : Hi, Mike. What is it?
안녕, Mike. 뭔데?
M : I saw an advertisement about a cycling competition. Why don't we enter the competition as a team?
사이클 대회에 대한 광고를 봤어. 우리 한 팀으로 참가하는 게 어때?
W : Great! I was about to die of boredom. This is exactly what I needed. Is there anything we need to enter the competition?
잘됐다! 지루해서 죽을 뻔 했는데. 이것이 바로 내가 필요했던 거야. 우리가 대회에 참가하기 위해 필요한 것이 있어?
M : No, all we need is our own cycle and a bike helmet.
아니, 자신의 사이클과 자전거 헬멧만 있으면 돼.
W : Good, I am all set with the gear. When is the competition?
좋아, 난 장비를 다 갖추었어. 대회는 언제야?
M : It's next Friday.
다음 주 금요일이야.
W : Friday? I can't make it that day.
금요일? 나 그날은 안돼.
M : Oh! I forgot. You said you had a job interview that day.
아! 깜박했다. 너 그날 취업 면접 있다고 했다.
W : Actually, it was yesterday and it went pretty well, I think.
사실 어제였는데 꽤 잘한 거 같아.
M : Good for you. Then why can't you come?
잘됐네. 그러면 왜 못 가?
W : I am participating in my niece's graduation.
난 내 조카 졸업식에 참석해야 해.
M : I see. I will have to find another partner.
알겠어. 다른 파트너를 구해야 할 거 같다.

Why? 왜 정답일까?

여자는 사이클 대회에 관심을 보였지만 대화의 후반부에 사이클 대회가 열리는 금요일에는 조카 졸업식에 참석해야 한다고 말하고 있다. 따라서 여자가 사이클 대회에 참가하지 못하는 이유로는 ⑤ '조카의 졸업식에 참석해야 해서'가 가장 적절하다.

- make it 시간 맞춰 가다
- graduation ⓝ 졸업(식)

08 언급 유무 파악하기 정답 ②

[The telephone rings.]
[전화벨이 울린다.]
W : This is the Days Inn. May I help you?
Days 모텔입니다. 도와 드릴까요?
M : Hi, I'm Robin Taylor. Next week, I'm visiting Days Beach with my family.
안녕하세요. Robin Taylor라고 합니다. 다음 주에 가족들과 함께 Days 해변에 가려고 합니다.
W : All right. We are near the beach, and we have a spacious parking lot.
좋습니다. 우리는 해변 근처에 위치해 있고 넓은 주차장을 가지고 있습니다.
M : Good. Do you have a shuttle bus to the airport?
좋아요. 혹시 공항으로의 셔틀 버스가 있나요?

[문제편 p.213]

W : I'm sorry we don't have one, but there is public transportation around here to the airport.
세틀 버스는 없습니다만, 근처에 공항까지의 대중교통이 있습니다.
M : Not bad. Hmm... And I have to use the Internet service during my stay.
괜찮네요. 음…. 머무는 동안 인터넷 서비스를 이용해야 하는데요.
W : Don't worry. You can connect to the Internet through free wireless Wi-Fi in your room.
걱정 마세요. 당신은 객실에서 무료 무선 와이파이를 통해 인터넷에 연결할 수 있습니다.
M : Okay, and I guess you have a swimming pool. My children like swimming.
좋네요. 수영장은 있겠지요. 아이들이 수영을 좋아합니다.
W : Of course. Anyone can swim in the pool at anytime. Also, you can read the newspaper for free in the lobby.
물론입니다. 누구라도 어느 때고 수영을 즐길 수 있습니다. 또한 로비에 있는 무료 신문을 읽을 수도 있습니다.
M : Well, are there any room safes in the rooms?
음, 객실에 금고가 혹시 있나요?
W : I'm afraid not. But you can leave your valuables at the front desk at anytime.
없습니다만, 귀중품을 언제든 프런트 데스크에 맡길 수 있습니다.
M : Okay, I'll call you again after I've decided on the dates.
잘 됐네요. 날짜가 결정되면 다시 전화 드릴게요.
W : Sure. Have a good day.
물론입니다. 좋은 시간되세요.

Why? 왜 정답일까?

두 사람은 Days Inn의 전망에 대해서는 언급하지 않고 있다.

- spacious ⓐ 넓은
- wireless ⓝ 무선
- safe ⓝ 금고
- public transportation 대중교통
- swimming pool 수영장
- valuable ⓝ 귀중품

09 세부 정보 파악하기 정답 ③

M : Welcome.
환영합니다.
Thank you for calling Auburn Stadium located on University Road, between 5th and 6th street.
5번가와 6번가 사이에 University Road에 위치한 Auburn Stadium에 전화 주셔서 감사합니다.
If you are interested in using stadium for your team, press one.
여러분의 팀을 위해 경기장을 사용하는 데 관심이 있으시면 1번을 누르세요.
For information about ticket sales including group sales and season subscriptions, press two.
단체 판매와 시즌 예약을 포함한 모든 티켓 판매에 관한 정보는 2번을 누르세요.
If you want to know information about the Auburn High School Football Games, press three.
Auburn 고등학교 미식축구 경기에 관한 정보는 3번을 누르세요.
For K-pop concert schedules and pricing information this weekend, press four.
이번 주말에 있을 K-pop 콘서트 일정과 가격 정보에 대해서는 4번을 누르세요.
Or for general information, box office operating hours, or accommodations for the disabled, press five.
또는 전체적인 정보, 매표소 운영 시간, 장애인 시설에 대해서는 5번을 누르세요.
To repeat these choices, press nine.
이러한 선택을 반복하시려면 9번을 누르세요.
To speak with a stadium operator, press zero or stay on the line for a moment.
경기장 교환원과 이야기하기 위해서는 0번을 누르시거나 잠시 기다려 주세요.
Thank you.
감사합니다.

Why? 왜 정답일까?

매표소 운영 시간에 관한 사항은 4번이 아니라 5번을 눌러야 하므로 ③은 내용과 일치하지 않는다.

- subscription ⓝ 예약, 기부
- accommodation ⓝ 시설
- box office 매표소
- the disabled 장애인

10 특정 정보 파악하기 정답 ③

M : Ms. Jason, we're going on a business trip to Tokyo next week. Why don't we book flight tickets on this website?
Jason 씨, 우리는 다음 주에 도쿄로 출장을 갈 거예요. 이 웹사이트에서 같이 비행기표를 예약하는 거 어때요?
W : Okay, Mr. Collin. Do you know how much we can spend on the flight?
알겠습니다, Collin 씨. 비행기에 우리가 얼마를 쓸 수 있는지 아시나요?
M : As far as I know, our company policy doesn't allow us to spend more than $500 per ticket.
제가 알기로는 우리 회사 정책은 표 한 장당 500달러 이상 사용하는 것을 허용하지 않습니다.
W : I see. And what about the departure time? I have to take my child to a preschool every morning.
알겠습니다. 그리고 출발 시간은 어떻게 됩니까? 저는 매일 아침 제 아이를 유치원에 데려다줘야 해요.
M : Then our flight has to be the one taking off in the afternoon.
그러면 우리 비행기는 오후에 이륙하는 비행기여야 하군요.
W : That'll be great. Which airport should we arrive at?
그러면 좋을 것 같아요. 우리는 어느 공항에 도착해야 하나요?
M : Haneda airport is closer to the company we're visiting.
하네다 공항이 우리가 방문할 회사와 더 가까워요.
W : No, actually it's not. Look at the presented distance estimation. Narita airport is a little closer to the company.
아니에요. 사실 그렇지 않아요. 제시된 거리 측정치를 보세요. 나리타 공항이 그 회사에서 조금 더 가까워요.
M : Oh, you're right. Wow, look! The tickets to Narita are now on sale. We should hurry and book two round-trip tickets.
아, 맞네요. 와, 보세요! 나리타행 표가 지금 할인판매 중이에요. 우리 서둘러서 왕복 두 장 표를 예매해야 해요.
W : No, these are stopover tickets. I don't want to waste time waiting for a connecting flight.
아니에요, 이것들은 경유 표예요. 저는 연결 항공편을 기다리느라 시간을 낭비하고 싶지 않아요.
M : Me, neither. Let's book the nonstop flight.
저도 그래요. 직항 항공을 예매하죠.
W : Okay. I am on it.
네, 제가 할게요.

Why? 왜 정답일까?

항공편 예매를 위해 남자와 여자가 대화를 나누고 있는 상황이다. 비행기표 값은 한 장당 500달러 이하이고, 여자는 오전보다 오후 출국을 선호한다고 말하고 있으며, 남자와 여자 모두 나리타 공항 직항편을 원하고 있다. 이런 조건에 모두 부합하는 것은 ③이다.

- as far as I know 내가 아는 한
- departure ⓝ 출발
- take off 이륙하다
- estimation ⓝ 측정치
- stopover ⓝ 경유
- policy ⓝ 정책
- preschool ⓝ 유치원
- distance ⓝ 거리
- round-trip ⓝ 왕복
- I am on it. 내가 할게.

11 짧은 응답 고르기 정답 ②

M : Do we have to purchase the bus tickets to Busan in advance?
부산에 가는 버스표를 미리 구입해야 될까?
W : Well, there are a few days left until this Saturday.
음, 이번 토요일까지 며칠 남아 있는데.
M : Don't wait too long. The good ones tend to sell out soon.
너무 오래 지체하지 마. 좋은 표는 금방 매진되기 쉬워.
W : I see. I will buy them online this afternoon.
알겠어. 내가 오늘 오후에 온라인으로 구매할게.

Why? 왜 정답일까?

버스표가 매진되기 쉽다는 남자의 말에 대한 여자의 응답으로는 ②의 '알겠어. 내가 오늘 오후에 온라인으로 구매할게.'가 가장 적절하다.

답지 해석

① 맞아. 오늘 거기에 가는 게 너무 기다려진다.
③ 표가 이미 매진이라는 소식을 듣게 되어 유감이다.
④ 물론이지. 부산은 가장 아름다운 도시 중에 하나야.
⑤ 잘했어. 그것들을 미리 구매한 것은 잘 한 일이야.

- purchase ⓥ 구입하다
- sold out 매진인
- in advance 미리

12 짧은 응답 고르기 정답 ①

W : Why don't they provide us with the products yet?
왜 그들이 상품을 아직 제공하지 않는 거지?
M : I don't know the reason, either. We ordered them last week.
나도 그 이유를 모르겠어. 우리가 지난주에 주문했었는데.
W : Well, what if they can't come in under our schedule?
음, 우리 일정에 맞게 상품이 들어오지 못하면 어떻게 하지?
M : Then we'll have to arrange another supplier.
그러면 우리가 다른 공급자를 준비시켜야지.

Why? 왜 정답일까?

상품이 일정에 맞게 들어오지 못하면 어떻게 할지를 묻는 여자의 질문에 대한 남자의 응답으로는 ①의 '그러면 우리가 다른 공급자를 준비시켜야지.'가 가장 적절하다.

답지 해석

② 우리 일정보다 먼저 물건이 들어와서 기쁘다.
③ 걱정 마. 내가 제 시간에 그 장소에 도착할 수 있어.
④ 사실, 그들로부터 상품을 주문하지 않았어.
⑤ 유감스럽지만, 우리가 지난주에 물건을 주문했어야 했는데.

- provide A with B A에게 B를 공급하다
- arrange ⓥ 준비하다, 조정하다
- what if ~하면 어떡하지?
- on time 제시간에

13 적절한 응답 고르기 정답 ②

W : Ted, did you read the article?
Ted, 그 기사 읽었니?
M : What is it about?
뭐에 관한 기사 말이야?
W : I just read an article that said paid homes for senior citizens have been increasing these days.
요즈음 유료 양로원이 늘어나고 있다는 기사를 이제 막 읽었어.
M : Well, I think it's kind of an unavoidable phenomenon.
음, 피할 수 없는 현상이라고 생각되는데.
W : I don't think so. I don't know why anybody would put their parents in one of those.
그렇게 생각지 않아. 누군가가 자신의 부모님을 왜 그러한 시설에 맡기는지 난 이유를 모르겠어.
M : But what if an old person is sick and can't be taken care of at home?
하지만 나이 드신 분이 아프고 집에 돌봐 줄 수 있는 사람이 없으면 어떡해?
W : When people are sick, they want to be with people they care about in familiar surroundings.
사람들이 아프면, 그들은 친근한 환경에서 그들이 좋아하는 사람들과 같이 있는 것을 원해.
M : I agree, but sometimes that's not realistic.
나도 동의하지만, 때때로 그건 현실적이지 않아.
W : Don't you think that if your parents take care of you when you're young, you have the responsibility to take care of them later on?
네가 어렸을 때 너희 부모님께서 너를 돌봐 주었다면, 나중에 네가 그들을 돌봐 줄 의무가 있다고 생각지 않니?
M : Mary, I see your point.
Mary, 네 말 이해하겠다.
W : I will not put my parents in an old-people's facility.
나는 내 부모님을 양로원에 위탁하지는 않을 거야.

Why? 왜 정답일까?

여자는 양로원에 나이 드신 분을 보내는 것을 반대하고 있으므로 여자의 응답으로는 ②의 '나는 내 부모님을 양로원에 위탁하지는 않을 거야.'가 적절하다.

답지 해석

① 네가 현실에 집중해야 한다고 말하고 싶구나.

③ 부모들이 자신들의 아이들을 돌보는 것은 당연해.
④ 나이 드신 분들은 시골에 사는 게 더 낫다.
⑤ 이러한 시설들이 전국에 확산되어야 한다고 생각해.

- **paid home for senior citizens** 유료 양로원
- **phenomenon** ⓝ 현상
- **realistic** ⓐ 현실적인
- **unavoidable** ⓐ 피할 수 없는
- **surrounding** ⓝ 환경
- **responsibility** ⓝ 의무

14 적절한 응답 고르기 정답 ③

W : Hi! Tom! Are you going to the freshman barbecue party tonight?
안녕, Tom! 너 오늘 밤 신입생 바비큐 파티에 갈 거니?
M : Maybe. Hmm.... Actually, I don't know. All those people... I won't know anyone.
아마도, 음…. 사실은 잘 모르겠어. 모든 사람들… 나는 아무도 몰라.
W : But that's what makes it interesting. Don't you want to make some new friends?
하지만 그게 흥미로운 점이지. 너 새로운 친구들 만들고 싶지 않니?
M : Yes, but I don't think a party is the best way.
만들고 싶지만, 파티가 가장 좋은 방법이라고는 생각 안해.
W : What do you mean, Tom?
무슨 뜻이니, Tom?
M : I've never met a new person I enjoyed talking with at the party.
나는 파티에서 이야기를 나누기를 즐길만한 사람들을 만나 본 적이 없어.
W : Really? I love meeting people at parties in big groups.
정말? 나는 큰 그룹의 파티에서 사람들 만나는 게 좋은데.
M : For me, it's just hard to talk to someone in a big group.
나에게는 큰 그룹에서 사람들에게 말을 걸기가 어려워.
W : Why? You have a lot of choices... there are a lot of people and a lot of possibilities for meeting people.
왜? 너는 선택의 폭이 넓잖아. 많은 사람들과 많은 사람들을 만날 가능성들.
M : But don't you think it's hard to get to know people? It will be so noisy.
하지만, 너는 사람들을 잘 알기가 어려운 것 같지 않니? 많이 시끄러울 거야.
W : So, how do you like to meet people?
그래서 어떻게 사람들을 만나고 싶은 거니?
M : In my case, I prefer to meet people in small groups.
내 경우에는, 작은 그룹에서 사람들을 만나는 게 더 좋아.

Why? 왜 정답일까?

사람들을 어떻게 만나는 것을 좋아하냐는 여자의 질문에 대한 응답으로는 ③의 '내 경우에는, 작은 그룹에서 사람들을 만나는 게 더 좋아.'가 가장 적절하다.

···· 답지 해석

① 이제야 말이 통하는구나. 나는 파티를 매우 좋아해.
② 사실 나는 아버지 차로 파티에 갈 거야.
④ 물론이지, 나는 어디에서나 사람들과 어울리는 것을 좋아해.
⑤ 파티에서 나는 어울릴만한 많은 재미있는 사람들을 만났다.

- **freshman** ⓝ 신입생
- **noisy** ⓐ 시끄러운
- **possibility** ⓝ 가능성

15 상황에 적절한 말 고르기 정답 ⑤

M : Janet and David live next door to each other and have quite a good relationship.
Janet과 David는 옆집에 살고 있고 꽤 좋은 관계를 맺고 있습니다.
This week, Janet is going on a business trip to Taiwan and she is not due back until next week.
이번 주에 Janet은 대만으로 출장을 갈 예정이고, 다음 주에나 돌아올 예정입니다.
She had everything sorted before she leaves for Taiwan except the morning paper that comes every morning.
그녀는 대만으로 떠나기 전에 매일 아침 오는 조간신문을 제외하고 모든 것을 정리했습니다.
She has subscribed to the morning paper for 5 years and cancellation of newspaper subscription is not in her mind.
그녀는 5년째 조간신문을 구독하고 있으며 신문 구독 취소는 염두에 두고 있지 않습니다.
She doesn't want to cancel it just because of a week-long trip but she is also worried that the morning paper might pile up in front of her door to indicate to passersby that she is away and the house is empty.
그녀는 일주일간의 출장 때문에 (구독) 취소를 하고 싶지는 않지만, 그녀는 또한 아침 신문이 그녀의 문 앞에 쌓여 행인들에게 그녀가 집에 없고 집이 비어 있다는 것을 알리게 될까 봐 걱정됩니다.
So she wants to ask a favor of David who already knows about the trip.
그래서 그녀는 출장에 대해 이미 알고 있는 David에게 부탁하고 싶어 합니다.
In this situation, what would Janet most likely say to David?
이런 상황에서 Jenet은 David에게 뭐라고 말할까요?
Janet : Can you take in my morning paper while I am away?
제가 없는 동안 제 조간신문을 받아 주시겠어요?

Why? 왜 정답일까?

여자는 다음 주 대만으로 출장을 가는 동안 조간신문이 배달되어 자신의 문 앞에 쌓일 것을 걱정하고 있다. 따라서 여자가 남자에게 할 말로 가장 적절한 것은 ⑤ '제가 없는 동안 제 조간신문을 받아 주시겠어요?'이다.

···· 답지 해석

① 제가 좋아할 만한 기사를 이메일로 전달해 주시겠습니까?
② 원한다면 제가 없는 동안 제 조간신문을 읽으셔도 됩니다.
③ 신문 배달원이 실제로 매일 오는지 확인해 줄 수 있습니까?
④ 조간신문을 공유하고 비용을 나눠서 내는 게 어때요?

- **sort** ⓥ 해결하다, 정리하다
- **subscribe to** ~을 구독하다
- **passerby** ⓝ 행인
- **morning paper** 조간신문
- **pile up** 쌓이다
- **ask a favor of** ~에게 부탁하다

16-17 장문 듣기

W : Hello, students.
학생 여러분 안녕하세요.
In the last class, we talked about some funny English expressions containing color terms.
지난 수업에서, 우리는 색 용어를 포함한 재미있는 영어 표현에 대해 이야기했습니다.
Today, we will be continuing with a list of funny English expressions and the meanings but this time some expressions related to animals.
오늘 우리는 재미있는 영어 표현들과 그 의미들의 목록을 이어나갈 것이지만 이번에는 동물과 관련된 표현들입니다.
The first one is "horse sense", meaning common sense.
첫 번째는 상식을 의미하는 "horse sense"입니다.
When you agree to someone because his or her statement is so right, you can say "It's horse sense."
누군가의 말이 너무 옳기 때문에 여러분이 그 또는 그녀에게 동의할 때, 당신은 "그것은 상식이야."라고 말할 수 있습니다.
The next expression, "white elephant" means an unwanted item which costs you a lot to keep but you cannot get rid of.
다음 표현인 "white elephant"는 여러분이 보관하는 데 많은 비용이 들지만 없앨 수 없는 원치 않는 물건을 의미합니다.
Another expression, "the black sheep", refers to a troublemaker of a family or a group.
또 다른 표현인 "the black sheep"은 가족이나 집단의 말썽꾸러기를 말합니다.
The last one is "dog eat dog."
마지막은 "dog eat dog"입니다.
When you say "It is a dog eat dog situation," you mean that the competition is so intense and competitive that people will do whatever they can to win or achieve what they want even if it means hurting or harming others.
여러분이 "dog eat dog 상황이다"라고 말하면, 경쟁이 너무 치열하고 경쟁적이어서 사람들이 이기거나 원하는 것을 이루기 위해 그들이 할 수 있는 모든 것을 할 거라는 것을 의미합니다. 심지어 그것이 타인을 다치게 하거나 해를 입히는 것이라도 말이죠.
We will stop here for today and I hope today's lesson helps you broaden your way of speaking English.
오늘은 여기까지 하고, 오늘 수업이 여러분의 영어 말하기 방식을 넓히는 데 도움이 되길 바랍니다.

- **term** ⓝ 용어
- **get rid of** ~을 없애다
- **broaden** ⓥ 넓히다
- **statement** ⓝ 말, 진술
- **intense** ⓐ 격렬한

16 주제 파악하기 정답 ②

Why? 왜 정답일까?

여자는 수업 시간에 동물과 관련된 영어 표현에 대해 이야기하고 있으므로 여자가 하는 말의 주제로는 ② '영어 표현과 의미에 관련된 다양한 동물들'이 가장 적절하다.

···· 답지 해석

① 동물과 관련된 영어 표현의 기원
③ 색깔과 동물들이 어떻게 영어 표현에 등장했는지
④ 왜 동물을 사용해 영어 표현을 만드는 것이 흔한지
⑤ 자주 사용되는 몇몇 영어 관용구의 숨은 뜻

17 언급 유무 파악하기 정답 ④

Why? 왜 정답일까?

동물과 관련된 영어 표현의 예로 ④ '거위'는 언급되지 않았다.

[문제편 p.214]

특별 부록 03 회 | 수능 대비 파이널 모의고사 | 정답과 해설 | 고3

• 정답 •

01 ② 02 ④ 03 ② 04 ② 05 ③ 06 ② 07 ② 08 ① 09 ④ 10 ④ 11 ① 12 ⑤ 13 ① 14 ④ 15 ③ 16 ④ 17 ②

01 담화의 목적 파악하기 정답 ②

M : Hello, everyone. I'm Noah Jones, teacher at Wilton Elementary School.
안녕하세요, 여러분. Wilton 초등학교의 교사인 Noah Jones입니다.
As you are probably already aware, we are in the middle of the flu season.
이미 아마 알고 계시겠지만, 지금은 독감의 계절에 있습니다.
Unfortunately, several of the children have already become ill.
불행히도, 몇몇 아이들이 이미 병에 걸렸습니다.
In order to prevent the spread of infection, we remind the children to continually wash their hands, use good hygiene products, and use tissues to blow their noses.
전염이 확산되는 것을 방지하기 위해, 우리는 아이들에게 꾸준히 손을 씻고, 좋은 위생 제품을 사용하고, 또 코를 풀 때 휴지를 사용하도록 상기시키고 있습니다.
Regrettably, we are now out of tissues in our classroom.
유감스럽게도, 지금 교실에 있는 휴지가 다 떨어지게 되었습니다.
We would be most appreciative if each child could help us out by bringing in at least one box of tissues.
아이들이 각자 휴지를 적어도 한 통씩 가지고 오는 것으로 저희를 도와준다면 매우 감사하겠습니다.
Hopefully, that should take us through to the end of the year.
바라건대, 우리들은 금년 말까지 그것들을 사용하게 될 것입니다.
Thank you in advance for all help you can provide for the children.
여러분이 아이들을 위해 주실 모든 도움들에 대하여 미리 감사드립니다.

Why? 왜 정답일까?

독감이 유행하고 있어 학급의 휴지가 필요하니 학생을 통해서 가져와 달라는 내용이므로 남자가 하는 말의 목적으로는 ②가 가장 적절하다.

- elementary school 초등학교
- infection ⓝ 감염
- hygiene ⓝ 위생
- blow ⓥ 불다
- regrettably ad 유감스럽게
- appreciative ⓐ 고마워하는
- in advance 미리

02 의견 파악하기 정답 ④

W : Good morning, Jacob.
안녕, Jacob.
M : Hi, Kelly. How was your weekend? Did you do anything special?
안녕, Kelly. 주말은 어떻게 보냈어? 뭐 특별한 일이라도 했니?
W : All I did was catch up on my sleep.
밀린 잠을 잔 거밖에 안 했어.
M : Oh, did you sleep in? For how many hours?
오, 늦잠 잤니? 몇 시간 동안이니?
W : Well, I went to bed at 11 at night and slept in until 10 the next morning.
글쎄, 밤 11시에 잠들어서 다음 날 아침 10시까지 늦잠 잤어.
M : But doesn't sleeping too much over the weekend make you more tired?
그렇지만 주말 동안 너무 많이 자는 것이 너를 더 피곤하게 하지 않니?
W : No, it really works for me. I read somewhere that catching up on sleep is helpful.
아니, 나에게는 정말 효과가 있어. 밀린 잠을 자는 것이 도움이 된다고 어디선가 읽었어.
M : Really? I think I should try that too because I've been feeling tired lately.
정말? 나도 한 번 해봐야 할 것 같아, 최근에 너무 피곤했거든.
W : Yeah, you should. It also helps you be more focused during weekdays.
그래, 해 봐. 주중에 더 집중할 수 있도록 도움도 돼.
M : No wonder you look so alive.
어쩐지 너는 생기있어 보이더라.
W : Yes, I can't feel more refreshed. But there is a downside of sleeping in.
응, 이보다 더 상쾌할 수 없어. 하지만 늦잠을 자는 것에 단점이 있어.
M : What is it?
뭔데?
W : You have absolutely no time to meet your friends on weekends.
주말에 친구들을 만날 시간이 전혀 없어.

Why? 왜 정답일까?

여자는 주말에 밀린 잠을 자면 상쾌하고 주중에 더 집중할 수 있다는 자신의 생각을 말하고 있다. 따라서 여자의 의견으로는 ④가 가장 적절하다.

- catch up on sleep 밀린 잠을 자다
- sleep in 늦잠 자다
- refreshed ⓐ 상쾌한
- downside ⓝ 단점

03 대화자의 관계 파악하기 정답 ②

M : Laura, you did a good job. Why don't you come here?
Laura, 잘했다. 이리 와 볼래?
W : Okay, how was my play?
네. 제 플레이가 어땠나요?
M : You were good as usual. You smashed the ball impressively.
평소처럼 잘 했다. 네가 공을 인상적으로 스매싱했어.
W : Thank you, sir. When I served the ball, I tried to remember what you said.
감사합니다. 제가 공을 서브할 때, 코치님이 하신 말씀을 기억하려고 노력했어요.
M : Good. Here is a towel to wipe your face.
잘했다. 여기 얼굴 닦을 수건 있다.
W : Thanks. Well, although I narrowly won this game, I think I need more practice.
고맙습니다. 음, 제가 간신히 경기에 이기긴 했지만, 좀 더 연습이 필요한 것 같아요.
M : Of course. Please, remember, "Practice makes perfect." How about your new racket?
물론이지. "연습이 완벽을 만든다"라는 말을 기억해라. 새 라켓은 어떠니?
W : It is excellent. This racket is lighter than the last one. I like it.
아주 좋아요. 이 라켓이 먼저 것보다 가벼워요. 마음에 들어요.
M : I'm glad you like it.
마음에 든다니 다행이구나.
W : I think there was a little problem in the play when receiving the serve. Well, could you analyze today's game for me?
서브를 받을 때 오늘 경기에서 좀 문제가 있었던 것 같아요. 음, 저를 위해 오늘 경기를 분석해 주실 수 있으세요?
M : No problem. After resting a little bit, let's check the video clip together which recorded your play.
문제없다. 좀 쉰 다음에 이번 경기를 녹화한 비디오 클립을 같이 점검해 보자.
W : I see. Thank you, sir.
네, 알겠습니다. 고맙습니다.

Why? 왜 정답일까?

경기 후에 경기 내용에 대해서 코치와 선수가 이야기를 나누고 있으므로 두 사람의 관계로는 ②가 가장 적절하다.

- smash ⓥ 세게 내리치다
- impressively ad 인상적으로
- wipe ⓥ 닦다
- narrowly ad 간신히
- analyze ⓥ 분석하다

04 그림 정보 파악하기 정답 ②

M : Wow, there are so many pictures hanging on the walls of your house. You must like pictures.
와, 너희 집 벽에 그림이 많이 걸려 있다. 너는 그림을 좋아하는구나.
W : It's my father. He loves collecting pictures of animals, especially dogs and cats.
우리 아버지야. 아버지는 동물들, 특히 강아지와 고양이의 그림을 모으는 것을 좋아하셔.
M : I can tell. I see a lot of dogs and cats in the pictures along with other animals.
알겠네. 그림에서 다른 동물들과 함께 많은 강아지와 고양이가 보여.
W : Yeah, but the funny thing is he never buys pictures of them together in the same frame.
응, 그런데 재밌는 건 아버진 같은 액자에 그들(강아지, 고양이)이 함께 있는 건 절대 구매하지 않으셔.
M : You are right! A dog is with deer and cats are with a hen or a rabbit. Is there any reason?
그렇네! 강아지는 사슴과 있고, 고양이는 닭이나 토끼랑 있네. 이유가 있니?
W : I never asked. I think he just likes pictures that reflect the reality. You know how they are.
물어본 적이 없어. 그냥 아버지는 현실을 반영하는 그림을 좋아하시는 거 같아. 너도 알잖아, 강아지와 고양이가 어떤지.
M : I know. Dogs and cats are believed to not get along well. But look at this picture. A lion with tigers?
알지. 강아지와 고양이는 사이가 좋지 않은 것으로 여겨지잖아. 하지만 이 사진을 봐. 호랑이랑 사자가 같이 있는데?
W : Let's not think too deeply about the reason. It's probably just my father's taste.
이유에 대해 너무 깊게 생각하지 말자. 아마 그냥 아버지의 취향인가 봐.
M : Okay. Which one is your room, anyway?
알겠어. 어쨌든 어떤 방이 네 방이니?
W : Come, my room is this way.
일로 와. 내 방은 이쪽이야.

Why? 왜 정답일까?

여자의 집에 방문한 남자가 여자의 집에 걸려있는 많은 그림을 보고 대화를 나누고 있는 상황이다. 여자는 자신의 아버지가 동물 그림을 수집하는 것을 좋아하지만 강아지와 고양이가 함께 있는 그림은 구매하지 않는다고 설명하고 있다. 따라서 ②는 대화의 내용과 일치하지 않는다.

- reflect ⓥ 반영하다
- get along well 잘 지내다
- taste ⓝ 취향

05 부탁한 일 파악하기 정답 ③

M : Hi, Sharon. You look down. What's the matter?
안녕, Sharon. 우울해 보여. 무슨 일이니?
W : Hi, Billy. Remember my assignment about wildflowers?
안녕, Billy. 야생화에 대한 나의 과제 기억하니?
M : Of course. That's for your biology class, right?
당연하지. 생물학 수업을 위한 거잖아, 맞지?
W : Yeah. I was going to attach some pictures of wildflowers but I couldn't.
응, 야생화 사진을 첨부하려고 했는데 그러지 못했어.
M : I see. Can't you hand in your assignment without the pictures?
그렇구나. 사진 없이 네 과제를 제출하면 안 되니?
W : No, I really need them. I even tried to take pictures of violets, but it is hard to find them in the city like this.
안 돼, 난 사진이 정말 필요해. 심지어 제비꽃 사진을 찍으려고 해봤는데 이런 도시에서는 제비꽃을 찾는 것이 어려워.
M : You know what? My big uncle owns an orchard and grows all types of flowers.
저, 있잖아, 우리 큰아버지가 과수원을 갖고 계시고, 모든 종류의 꽃들을 기르셔.
W : Oh, can you please ask him to take pictures of violets and send them to you?
오, 큰아버지께 제비꽃 사진을 찍어서 너에게 보내달라고 부탁해 줄 수 있니?
M : Well, how about I give you his number and you ask him yourself?
음, 내가 너에게 큰아버지 번호를 주고 네가 직접 여쭤보는 건 어때?
W : What? But I've never met him before. I don't even know him.
뭐라고? 하지만 난 그분을 뵌 적이 없어. 그분을 알지도 못해.
M : Doesn't matter. You will better explain your situation, things like how many pictures you need and why you need them.
상관없어. 사진이 몇 장이나 필요한지, 왜 필요한지 등 네 상황을 네가 더 잘 설명할 거야.
W : You're right. Okay, I will talk to him in person on the phone. Thanks, Billy.
네 말이 맞아. 알겠어, 내가 전화로 직접 그분이랑 이야기해 볼게. 고마워, Billy.

Why? 왜 정답일까?

여자가 생물학 수업을 위한 사진을 구하지 못하자 남자가 자신의 큰아버지가 과수원을 운영한다고 말하며 도움을 주는 상황이다. 대화의 마지막 부분에 남자는 자신의 큰아버지의 전화번호를 줄테니 직접 통화해 보라고 제안하고 있으므로 남자가 여자를 위해 할 일로 가장 적절한 것은 ③ '큰아버지의 전화번호를 알려주기'이다.

[문제편 p.215]

• wildflower ⓝ 야생화
• attach ⓥ 첨부하다, 붙이다
• violet ⓝ 제비꽃
• in person 직접
• biology ⓝ 생물학
• hand in ⓥ 제출하다
• orchard ⓝ 과수원

06 숫자 정보 파악하기 정답 ②

W : Excuse me, how much is this book?
실례합니다만, 이 책은 얼마인가요?
M : Well, as it says, the price is $80.
음, 써져 있다시피, 가격은 80달러입니다.
W : That's too expensive. Well, I heard if I have a bookstore membership, I can get it at a discounted price.
그건 너무 비싸네요. 음, 제가 서점 회원권이 있으면, 할인된 가격에 책을 살 수 있다고 들었는데요.
M : Right. If you join, you'll get a 20% discount off the list price on hardcover best sellers and 10% off our price on almost everything else.
맞습니다. 당신이 가입하시면 하드커버 베스트셀러를 20% 할인해서 살 수 있으며, 그 밖의 거의 모든 것을 10% 할인으로 구입할 수 있습니다.
W : That sounds great. In this case, I can save $8.
좋은 것 같네요. 이 경우에 그러면 8달러를 절약할 수 있네요.
M : You bet.
그렇습니다.
W : How long is the membership valid for?
회원권은 얼마나 오랫동안 효력이 있나요?
M : It lasts for one year.
그것은 일 년 동안 지속됩니다.
W : Good, how much is the membership?
좋네요, 회원권이 얼마입니까?
M : It's only five dollars a year for membership. You can sign up for it now.
일 년에 회원권이 5달러입니다. 지금 가입하실 수 있습니다.
W : Okay. Let me sign up and buy the book now.
알겠습니다. 지금 가입하고 그 책을 구입하겠습니다.

Why? 왜 정답일까?

회원 가입비가 5달러이고, 도서는 10% 할인된 가격인 72달러에 구입하게 되므로 여자가 지불할 금액은 77달러이다.

• discounted price 할인된 가격
• sign up for ~에 가입하다

07 이유 파악하기 정답 ②

M : Honey, Do you still have the receipt for the selfie stick?
여보, 셀카봉 영수증 아직 갖고 있지?
W : The one we bought for this trip? Yeah, I think so.
이번 여행을 위해 산 거? 응, 있을 거야.
M : Where is it? Just tell me where it is, then I will go get it.
어디 있어? 그게 어디 있는지만 말해줘 그러면 내가 가서 가지고 올게.
W : It must be somewhere in my purse. What do you need it for, by the way? Is there anything wrong with the stick?
내 지갑 어딘가에 있을 거야. 그런데, 당신은 그것이 왜 필요해? 셀카봉에 무슨 문제라도 있어?
M : No, it's not that.
아니야, 그런 거.
W : Then why are you returning it?
그러면 왜 반납하려고 해?
M : What? Why would I return the selfie stick that we bought because we needed it.
뭐? 우리가 필요해서 산 셀카봉을 내가 왜 반납하겠어?
W : Oh, isn't it why you want the receipt? To get a refund?
아, 그래서 영수증을 찾는 것이 아니야? 환불 받으려고?
M : No, it's nothing like that. I just saw an ad on TV saying that the store is running a promotion.
아니, 전혀 그런 거 아니야. 방금 TV에서 매장에서 프로모션을 진행한다는 광고를 봤어.
W : A promotion? Then what do we do with the receipt?
프로모션? 그러면 영수증으로 뭘 하는데?
M : The ad said there is a serial number on every receipt issued during the promotion. I want to see if there is really...
광고에 따르면 프로모션 기간 동안 발행되는 모든 영수증에 일련번호가 있대. 보고 싶어서, 정말 있는지...
W : Oh my god! Do we get cash back or what? Run! It is in my purse. Quick!
맙소사! 우리 현금을 돌려받는 거야 아니면 뭐야? 뛰어! 내 지갑 안에 있어. 서둘러!
M : Okay, but don't get your hopes up too high otherwise you will get disappointed.
알겠어. 하지만 너무 기대하지는 마. 그렇지 않으면 실망할 테니.

Why? 왜 정답일까?

남자가 여자에게 영수증의 위치를 물으며 급하게 영수증을 찾고 있는 상황이다. 이유를 묻는 여자에게 남성은 매장의 프로모션에 대해 설명한 후, 영수증의 일련번호를 확인하고 싶다고 말하고 있다. 따라서 남자가 영수증을 찾는 이유로 가장 적절한 것은 ② '영수증에 기재된 일련번호를 확인하려고'이다.

• receipt ⓝ 영수증
• refund ⓝ 환불
• get one's hopes up 기대하다
• purse ⓝ 지갑
• issue ⓥ 발행하다

08 언급 유무 파악하기 정답 ①

W : Hi, Adam. What are you doing?
안녕, Adam. 뭐하고 있니?
M : I'm reading some comments about the Mystery on the Internet.
인터넷에서 Mystery에 관한 의견을 읽고 있어.
W : Mystery? Is it a kind of a novel or something?
Mystery라고? 일종의 소설 같은 거니?
M : Are you kidding? It is a soap opera. How don't you know that? It's very popular these days among teenagers.
농담하니? 그것은 연속극이야. 어떻게 그것을 모를 수가 있어. 그것은 요즈음 십대들에게 아주 인기가 좋아.
W : Oh, I remember someone talked about that.
오, 누군가가 그것에 관해 이야기했던 것이 기억난다.
M : People are crazy about it because the plot is unpredictable, not to speak of the excellent acting by the actors, Kevin and Jennifer.
Kevin과 Jennifer와 같은 배우들의 훌륭한 연기는 말할 것도 없고 그 줄거리가 예측할 수 없어서 사람들이 정말 그것에 대해 열광적이야.
W : So is it going to be on tonight?
오늘 밤에 그것이 방영되니?
M : Yes, it should be starting in about thirty minutes – around 9 : 30 p.m. I can't wait to watch it.
그래. 약 30분 지나면 9시 30분에 시작할거야. 정말 기다려져.
W : What do you think is going to happen this time?
이번에는 무슨 일이 일어날 것 같은데?
M : I'm not sure. Last time the main character was in a trap and he was kind of embarrassed.
확실하지 않아. 하지만 지난번에 주인공이 함정에 빠져서 당황한 상황이었어.
W : Well, judging from the title, there seems to be some mysterious people in the drama.
음, 제목으로 판단해 보면, 그 드라마에는 몇몇 신비로운 사람들이 나올 것 같은데.
M : You can say that again. Almost all the characters in the drama are wrapped in mystery.
그렇고말고. 드라마의 거의 모든 등장인물들이 미스터리에 싸여 있어.

Why? 왜 정답일까?

드라마의 제목, 주요 장면, 출연 배우 그리고 방영 시간에 대한 언급은 있지만, ①의 '배경'에 관한 언급은 하지 않고 있다.

• comment ⓝ 논평, 의견
• unpredictable ⓐ 예측할 수 없는
• judging from ~로 판단하건대
• soap opera 연속극, (멜로) 드라마
• not to speak of ~는 말할 것도 없이

09 세부 정보 파악하기 정답 ④

W : Welcome to Haleakala Ranch Ride!
Haleakala Ranch Ride에 오신 것을 환영합니다!
Ride across the largest working cattle ranch on Maui at the scenic 4,000 feet elevation.
Maui에 그림 같은 4,000 피트 고도에서 가장 크게 운영 중인 소 방목장을 가로질러 말을 타 보세요.
With the panoramic views of Maui and the ocean below you'll see parts of Maui best seen from a horse!
파노라마 같은 Maui의 광경과 아래로는 바다 광경과 더불어 여러분은 말에서 최고로 잘 볼 수 있는 Maui의 지역을 보게 될 것입니다.
Our Haleakala Ranch Ride features over 1.5 hours of historic scenery for an unforgettable experience.
우리의 Haleakala Ranch Ride는 잊지 못할 경험을 위해 역사적인 풍경의 1시간 30분(투어)을 특징으로 합니다.
We offer early morning and afternoon rides at 9 a.m. and 2 p.m.
우리는 오전 9시, 오후 2시의 이른 오전과 오후의 말 타기를 제공합니다.
Due to high demand, we prefer advance reservations.
많은 수요로 인해, 우리는 미리 예약하시는 것을 선호합니다.
Drop-ins may not have a chance to ride horses.
불쑥 들르시는 분들은 말을 탈 기회를 갖지 못할 수도 있습니다.
A refreshment such as soft drinks is provided during the tour.
청량음료와 같은 음식물은 투어 도중에 제공됩니다.
All our tours are guided by friendly experts and you'll feel like you're visiting a friend who owns a horse ranch.
모든 여행은 친절한 전문가가 가이드 합니다. 당신은 말 목장을 가지고 있는 친구의 집을 방문한 것 같은 기분을 느낄 수 있으실 겁니다.
I hope you will have an exciting experience with us!
저희와 함께 신나는 경험이 되시길 바랍니다.

Why? 왜 정답일까?

미리 예약할 것을 선호하며, 불쑥 들른 사람은 말을 못 탈 수도 있다고 했으므로 ④는 내용과 일치하지 않는다.

• cattle ranch 소의 방목장
• scenery ⓝ 풍경
• drop-in ⓝ (예약 없이) 불쑥 들른 사람
• elevation ⓝ 고도, 높이
• unforgettable ⓐ 잊을 수 없는
• refreshment ⓝ 음식물

10 특정 정보 파악하기 정답 ④

M : Welcome to Dominion's Kitchen.
어서오세요, Dominion's Kitchen입니다.
W : Good afternoon. I am looking for a cutting board.
안녕하세요. 저는 도마를 찾고 있어요.
M : Let me show you some of our top-selling models, all at affordable prices. Do you have a preference for material? We have plastic, hard wood and soft wood cutting board.
가장 많이 판매되는 모델 중 몇 가지를 보여드릴게요. 가격도 합리적이에요. 선호하시는 재질이 있으신가요? 플라스틱, 단단한 나무, 부드러운 나무 도마가 있습니다.
W : Anything will do except for the plastic ones. I think plastic isn't environmentally friendly.
플라스틱을 제외하고는 아무거나 좋습니다. 플라스틱은 환경친화적이지 않은 것 같아요.
M : I see. What's your budget range?
그러시군요. 예산 범위가 어떻게 되세요?
W : No more than $70.
70달러 이하요.
M : Okay. Do you prefer one with or without a handle?
알겠습니다. 손잡이가 있는 것이 좋습니까, 없는 것이 좋습니까?
W : Either one is fine but I want the one with a hole. You know, so I can hang it somewhere.
어느 것이든 상관없지만 구멍이 있는 것을 원해요. 어딘가에 걸어둘 수 있게요.
M : We only have two models with a hole, the hard wood one and the plastic one. But the wood one is slightly over your current budget. Will you take the plastic one?
구멍이 있는 모델은 단단한 나무와 플라스틱 두 가지뿐입니다. 하지만 나무 도마는 손님의 현재 예산을 약간 초과하네요. 플라스틱 도마로 하시겠습니까?
W : How much is the wood one?
나무 도마는 얼마예요?
M : It is $75
75달러입니다.
W : I think I will have to tighten the family budget next month. I will take that one.
다음 달에 가계를 조여야 할 것 같네요. 그걸로 할게요.

[문제편 p.215]

Why? 왜 정답일까?

처음에 여자는 도마를 구입하는 예산으로 70달러라고 언급하지만 대화의 후반부에 마음을 바꿔 구멍이 있는 도마를 사기 위해 초반 예산보다 더 비싼 75달러의 도마를 구매하겠다고 말하고 있다. 또한 플라스틱 재질은 싫다고 말하고 있으므로 여자가 구매할 도마로 가장 적절한 것은 ④이다.

- cutting board 도마
- material ⓝ 재료
- budget ⓝ 예산
- tighten ⓥ (바짝) 죄다
- affordable ⓐ 알맞은
- environmentally friendly 친환경적인
- current ⓐ 현재의

11 짧은 응답 고르기 정답 ①

M : Gina, how was 'Eleven' fan meeting yesterday?
Gina, 'Eleven' 팬 미팅은 어땠어?

W : It was a waste of time. I didn't see my favorite singer, Kevin.
시간 낭비였어. 내가 좋아하는 가수인 Kevin을 만나지 못했어.

M : Oh, really? Was he absent from the meeting?
오, 정말? 그가 모임에 빠졌니?

W : Well, he didn't show up.
음, 그가 나타나지 않았어.

Why? 왜 정답일까?

그녀가 좋아하는 가수가 모임에 빠졌냐는 남자의 질문에 대한 응답으로는 ①의 '음, 그가 나타나지 않았어.'가 적절하다.

···· 답지 해석

② 그를 전에 본적이 있니?
③ 맞아, 그가 모임에 참석했어.
④ 아니, 모임은 훌륭했어.
⑤ 그가 따뜻한 태도로 나에게 인사했어.

- fan meeting 팬 미팅
- show up 나타나다
- waste of time 시간 낭비
- greet ⓥ 인사하다

12 짧은 응답 고르기 정답 ⑤

W : Ben, why didn't you come to my party last night?
Ben, 어젯밤 내 파티에 왜 오지 않았니?

M : I'm sorry, Sarah. I had to visit my grandmother at the hospital.
미안해, Sarah. 병원에 계신 할머니를 문안 갔어야 했어.

W : Oh, I'm sorry to hear that. How is she?
오, 그런 소식을 들어 유감이구나. 할머니는 어떠시니?

M : She was not good at one time, but is recovering now
그녀가 한 때 좋지 않았지만, 지금은 회복 중이셔.

Why? 왜 정답일까?

할머니의 안부를 묻는 여자의 말에 대한 남자의 응답으로는 ⑤의 '그녀가 한 때 좋지 않았지만, 지금은 회복 중이셔.'가 가장 적절하다.

···· 답지 해석

① 그녀는 여든 살이지만, 매우 건강하셔.
② 나는 괜찮아. 누구라도 실수할 수 있지.
③ 네가 맞아. 그녀가 너의 파티에 갔어야 했어.
④ 그렇고말고. 의사 선생님은 정말 친절하셨어.

- make a mistake 실수 하다
- recover ⓥ 회복하다

13 적절한 응답 고르기 정답 ①

M : Hello, Mrs. Williams. Can I have a word with you?
안녕하세요, Williams 선생님. 잠시 말씀 좀 나눌 수 있을까요?

W : Oh, hi, Ted. Come on in.
오, 안녕, Ted. 어서 들어와.

M : I'm here to talk to you about the result of the election yesterday.
어제 선거 결과를 선생님께 말씀드리려고 왔어요.

W : Speaking of the election, I was just wondering about the result. How was the election?
선거 이야기가 나왔으니 말인데, 결과에 대해 궁금해 하고 있었어. 선거가 어땠니?

M : The process of the election was not easy, but anyway, I was elected the chairman of our school.
선거의 과정은 쉽지 않았지만, 어쨌든 제가 학교의 회장으로 선출되었습니다.

W : Oh, really? Congratulations. I was worried because I heard there were many competitive candidates in the election.
오, 정말? 축하해. 선거에서 경쟁력 있는 후보자가 많아서 걱정했어.

M : Right, in the beginning, I didn't have much support from my friends.
맞아요, 처음에는 제가 친구들로부터 많은 지지를 받지 못했어요.

W : How did you overcome this obstacle?
어떻게 그 장애를 극복했니?

M : Well, I tried to meet as many students as possible and persuade them to support me.
음, 저는 가능한 한 많은 학생들을 만나려고 노력했고 그들이 저를 지지하도록 설득하려고 했어요.

W : Good effort, Ted.
잘했어, Ted.

M : As a homeroom teacher, your help really encouraged me a lot.
담임 선생님으로서, 선생님의 도움이 저에게 많은 격려가 되었습니다.

W : My pleasure. I think it's lucky for you to be in my class.
천만에. 네가 우리 학급에 있는 것은 행운인 것 같아.

Why? 왜 정답일까?

선거에서 도와줘서 고맙다는 남자의 말에 대한 여자의 응답으로는 ①의 '천만에요. 네가 우리 학급에 있는 것은 행운인 것 같아.'가 가장 적절하다.

···· 답지 해석

② 잘 됐구나. 너는 모든 행사에서 회장을 돕게 될 거야.
③ 힘 내. 다음번에는 친구들로부터 많은 지지를 받을 거야.
④ 천만에요. 선거에서 당신과 경쟁해서 기뻤습니다.
⑤ 걱정마라. 선거에서 지는 것이 실패를 의미하지는 않는다.

- election ⓝ 선거
- candidate ⓝ 후보자
- obstacle ⓝ 장애물
- competitive ⓐ 경쟁력 있는
- support ⓝ 지지
- persuade ⓥ 설득하다

14 적절한 응답 고르기 정답 ④

W : Adam, I want you to clean up the house with me.
Adam, 당신이 나와 함께 집 청소를 했으면 좋겠어요.

M : No problem. Every spring we need to clean up. What should I do first?
좋아요. 매년 봄마다 우리는 청소를 해야죠. 내가 뭘 먼저 할까요?

W : Well, how about cleaning and reorganizing your bookshelf?
음, 당신의 책장을 다시 정리하고 청소하면 어때요?

M : I see. There is a lot of dust on the bookshelf. I haven't cleaned it for some time.
알겠어요. 책장에 먼지가 많네요. 내가 한동안 청소를 안 했어요.

W : Needless to say dust, there are too many old books of yours.
먼지는 말 할 필요도 없고, 오래된 당신 책들이 너무 많아요.

M : Hmm.... It's true, but sometimes I want to read my old books.
음. 사실이지만, 나는 가끔씩 오래된 책들을 읽고 싶어요.

W : As far as I remember, you've not read one of these books since last year.
제가 기억하기로는, 당신은 작년이래로 그 책들을 한 권도 안 읽었잖아요.

M : No, I sometimes enjoy reading a book from them.
아니에요, 저는 가끔 그것들 중에서 책을 읽기를 즐겨요.

W : Honey, the books are taking up too much space. I want you to remove them.
여보, 그 책들이 너무 많은 공간을 차지하고 있어요. 난 치웠으면 좋겠어요.

M : Do you mean I should get rid of them?
내가 그것들을 버려야 한다는 말이에요?

W : Yes, if you don't read them any more, you should throw them out.
그래요, 더 이상 읽지 않는다면 버려야 해요.

M : They look useless to you, but they are precious to me.
그것들은 당신에겐 쓸모없어 보이지만 내게는 소중해요.

Why? 왜 정답일까?

책을 버려야 한다는 여자의 의견에 남자는 반대하고 있으므로 여자의 마지막 말에 대한 남자의 응답으로는 ④의 '그것들은 당신에겐 쓸모없어 보이지만 내게는 소중해요.'가 가장 적절하다.

···· 답지 해석

① 그것들은 제 것이 아니에요. 사실 당신 거에요.
② 물론이죠. 청소는 항상 나를 상쾌하고 즐겁게 해요.
③ 청소 전에 내 오래된 책들을 정리하고 싶어요.
⑤ 알겠어요. 제가 지금부터 좀 더 자주 책장을 청소하도록 할게요.

- clean up 청소하다
- bookshelf ⓝ 책장
- needless to say ~는 말할 것도 없이
- get rid of ~을 제거하다
- reorganize ⓥ 다시 정리하다
- dust ⓝ 먼지
- take up (공간을) 차지하다

15 상황에 적절한 말 고르기 정답 ③

W : Sumi, Heesung and Hyunwoo are classmates and they are having a good time, eating lunch together.
수미, 희성, 현우는 급우이고 점심을 함께 먹으며 즐거운 시간을 보내고 있다.
As they are finishing their meals, Sumi suggests that they go shopping in the department store that was newly opened last weekend.
식사를 끝마쳐갈 때, 수미가 지난 주말에 새로 개장한 백화점에 쇼핑을 하러 가자고 제안한다.
Heesung answers that it is a good idea because this is bargain sale season and he also likes window shopping.
희성은 지금이 바겐세일 기간이고 그도 또한 윈도우 쇼핑을 좋아하기 때문에 좋은 의견이라고 대답한다.
However, Hyunwoo is worried because he won't be able to join them.
하지만 현우는 그가 그들과 합류할 수 없기 때문에 걱정이 된다.
This evening, his father is returning from America and his family including Hyunwoo are supposed to meet him at the airport.
오늘 저녁, 그의 아버지가 미국에서 돌아오시며, 현우를 포함한 그의 가족은 아버지를 공항에서 맞이하기로 되어 있다.
Before long, Hyunwoo should leave here to join his family.
곧, 현우는 가족과 합류하기 위해 이곳을 떠나야 한다.
In this situation, what is Hyunwoo most likely to say to his friends?
이러한 상황에서, 현우는 친구들에게 무엇이라고 말할 것 같은가?

Hyunwoo : I'd love to, but I have a previous engagement.
그러고 싶지만, 난 선약이 있어.

Why? 왜 정답일까?

친구들이 쇼핑을 현우는 아버지를 마중하기 위해 공항에 가야 하는 상황이므로, 현우가 친구들에게 할 말로는 ③의 '그러고 싶지만, 난 선약이 있어.'가 가장 적절하다.

···· 답지 해석

① 나를 공항까지 태워줘서 고마워.
② 물론이지, 너희와 쇼핑하는 것이 정말 좋아.
④ 미안하지만, 지금 미국으로 떠나야 해.
⑤ 좋은 생각이야. 네가 어디를 가든 따라 갈게.

- go shopping 쇼핑하러 가다
- bargain sale 바겐세일
- be supposed to ~하기로 되어 있다
- department store 백화점
- window shopping 윈도우 쇼핑

16-17 장문 듣기

W : Hello, students.
학생 여러분 안녕하세요.
In the previous class, we discussed traditional foods in different countries.
이전 수업에서, 우리는 다른 나라의 전통 음식에 대해 토론했습니다.

특별 부록 03회

[문제편 p.216]

Today, we will talk about surprising birthplace of everyday foods.
오늘 우리는 일상 음식의 놀라운 탄생지에 대해 이야기 할 것입니다.
First, people believe that French fries were first invented in France as the name indicates.
우선, 사람들은 이름에서 알 수 있듯이 프렌치프라이가 프랑스에서 처음 발명되었다고 믿습니다.
But the original fry was born in Belgium, where the locals were particularly fond of fish.
하지만 원래의 감자튀김은 현지인들이 특히 생선을 좋아하던 벨기에에서 생겨났어요.
When the river froze one cold winter, people began to fry potatoes instead of fish and the fry was born.
어느 추운 겨울에 강이 얼었을 때, 사람들은 생선 대신 감자를 튀기기 시작했고 감자튀김이 탄생했어요.
Croissants are a famous French food.
크루아상은 유명한 프랑스 음식입니다.
As a result, people tend to pronounce the word using a French accent.
그 결과, 사람들은 프랑스 억양을 사용하여 그 단어를 발음하는 경향이 있습니다.
But, it was first created in Austria by an Austrian baker.
하지만, 그것은 오스트리아의 한 제빵사에 의해 오스트리아에서 처음 만들어졌습니다.
The baker made a pastry in the shape of Muslim crescent.
그 제빵사는 이슬람교의 초승달 모양으로 페이스트리를 만들었습니다.
Third, many people think kiwis are from New Zealand.
셋째, 많은 사람들은 키위가 뉴질랜드산이라고 생각합니다.
It's probably because New Zealand people are called Kiwis.
그것은 아마 뉴질랜드 사람들이 키위라고 불리기 때문일 것입니다.
In fact, the food is from China.
사실, 그 음식은 중국에서 왔습니다.
Last, seaweed black paper, better known as *Gim* to korean is falsely believed to be Japanese food.
마지막으로, 한국인에게 *김*으로 더 잘 알려진 검은색 해조 종이는 일본 음식으로 잘못 알려져 있습니다.
It is partly due to the fact that Japanese Sushi is more familiar to people around the world than gimbap.
부분적으로 일본 초밥이 김밥보다 전 세계 사람들에게 더 친숙하기 때문입니다.
However, this edible seaweed paper is originally cultivated and consumed in Korea.
하지만, 이 식용 해조 종이는 원래 한국에서 재배되고 섭취됩니다.
Now, we'll look at some pictures of these foods.
이제, 우리는 이 음식들의 사진들을 볼 것입니다.

- **indicate** ⓥ 가리키다, 나타내다
- **be fond of** ~을 좋아하다
- **pronounce** ⓥ 발음하다
- **crescent** ⓝ 초승달
- **seaweed** ⓝ 해조, 미역
- **edible** ⓐ 먹을 수 있는
- **cultivate** ⓥ 재배하다
- **consume** ⓥ 섭취하다, 소비하다

16 주제 파악하기 정답 ④

Why? 왜 정답일까?

여자는 수업 중 일상적인 음식의 놀라운 탄생지에 대해 이야기하고 있으므로 여자가 하는 말의 주제로는 ④ '일상적인 음식의 예상치 못한 기원'이 가장 적절하다.

답지 해석

① 몇몇 음식들이 어떻게 나라들을 가로질러 퍼지는지
② 전통음식이 인기있는 이유
③ 유명한 음식에 대한 오해
⑤ 어떻게 일부 음식들이 그들의 이름을 얻었는지

17 언급 유무 파악하기 정답 ②

Why? 왜 정답일까?

음식의 예상치 못한 기원의 예로 ②의 '나초'는 언급되지 않았다.

[문제편 p.216]

REAL

575만권 수능기출 베스트셀러 2006~2024

리얼 오리지널 BOOK LIST

예비 [고1] 전과목

고등학교 첫 시험 & 3월 대비

- 반 배치 + 3월 [전과목]
- 3월 전국연합 [전과목]

[고1] 전과목

학력평가 & 중간·기말 대비

- 6월 학평+기말고사
- 9월 학평+중간고사
- 11월 학평+기말고사

[고1] 3개년 | 16회

3개년 전국연합 12회+실전 4회

- 국어 영역
- 영어 영역
- 수학 영역

[고1] 3개년 | 12회

3개년 전국연합 모의고사 12회

- 국어 영역
- 영어 영역

[고2] 3개년 | 16회

3개년 전국연합 12회+실전 4회

- 국어 영역
- 영어 영역
- 수학 영역

[고2] 3개년 | 12회

3개년 전국연합 모의고사 12회

- 국어 영역
- 영어 영역

[고1·2] 미니 모의고사

하루 20분 30일 완성 모의고사

- 고1 국어 영역
- 고1 영어 영역
- 고2 국어 영역
- 고2 영어 영역
- 고3 영어 영역

영어 독해 [빈·순·삽]

하루 20분 20일 완성 빈·순·삽

- 기본(고1)
- 완성(고2)
- 실전(고3)

영어 독해

영어 독해 문제만 20회 구성

- 고1 영어 독해
- 고2 영어 독해

평가원 기출 독해만 21회 구성

- 고3 영어 독해

영어 듣기

영어 듣기 문제만 28회 구성

- 고1 영어 듣기
- 고2 영어 듣기

수능기출 35회 + 파이널 3회

- 고3 영어 듣기

[고3] 3개년

3개년 교육청+평가원 [총17회]

- 국어(공통+화작·언매)
- 수학(공통+확통·미적)

수능기출 17회 + 파이널 3회

- 영어 영역(총 20회)

[고3] 수능특강 변형

EBS 수능특강 변형 문제집

- 영어(상)
- 영어(하)

[고3] 5개년

6·9·수능 평가원 기출만 15회

- 국어(공통+화작·언매)
- 영어 영역
- 수학(공통+확통·미적)

[고3] 사탐·과탐

기출 최다 문항 1000제 50회 수록

- 사회·문화
- 생활과 윤리
- 지구과학 I
- 생명과학 I

We are all of us star and deserve to twinkle.

우리는 모두 별이고 반짝일 권리가 있다.

리얼 오리지널 | 수능기출 학력평가 7개년 기출 문제집 38회 [고3 영어 듣기]

발행처 수능 모의고사 전문 출판 입시플라이 **발행일** 2024년 12월 19일 **등록번호** 제 2017-0022호

홈페이지 www.ipsifly.com **대표전화** 02-433-9979 **구입문의** 02-433-9975 **팩스** 02-433-9905

발행인 조용규 **편집책임** 양창열 김유 이혜민 임명선 김선영 **물류관리** 김소희 이혜리 **주소** 서울특별시 중랑구 용마산로 615 정민빌딩 3층

※ 페이지가 누락되었거나 파손된 교재는 구입하신 곳에서 교환해 드립니다. ※ 발간 이후 발견되는 오류는 입시플라이 홈페이지 정오표를 통해서 알려드립니다.

| 리얼 오리지널 |

하루 20분 루틴으로 1등급 Fix!

30일 완성 [미니 모의고사]

하루 20분! 30일 완성으로 국어·영어 1등급 Fix!

하루 20분 30일 완성 | 수능기출 미니 모의고사

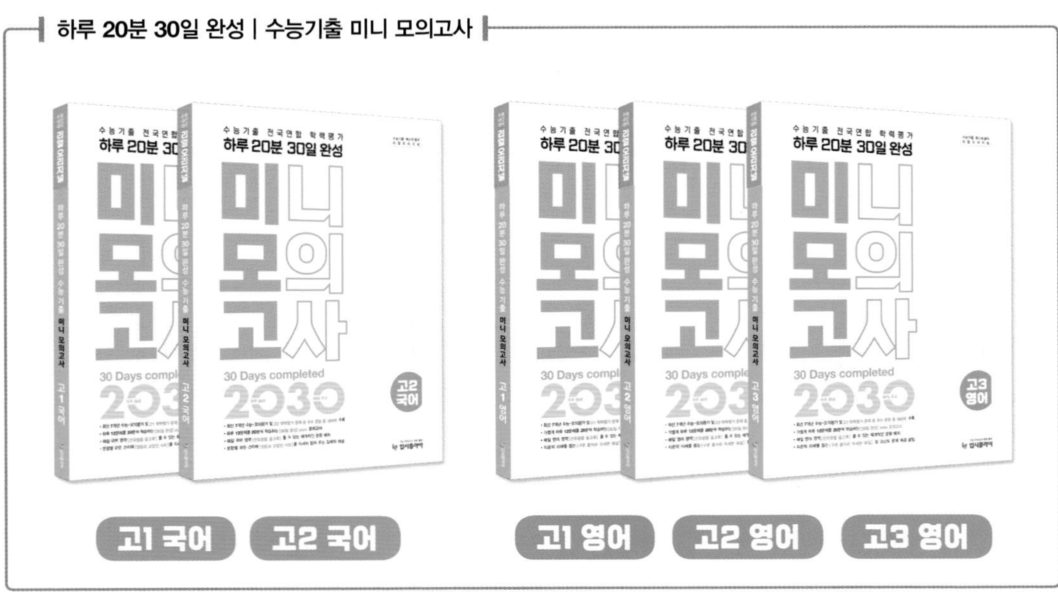

가볍게 *'하루 20분'*
하루 12문제씩 20분을 학습하는
매일 루틴(Routine)은 수능에 대한 감을 잡아주기 때문에
꾸준한 *'수능 대비'*가 가능합니다.

• 수능기출 미니 모의고사 [30일 완성] 특징

- 고1 국어, 고2 국어 | 고1 영어, 고2 영어, 고3 영어
- 최근 7개년 수능기출 학력평가 문제 중 **[우수 문항 선별] 후 총 360문항** 수록
- 매일 정기적인 학습으로 **수능의 감을 잡는 꾸준한 연습**
- **하루 12문제를 20분씩 학습**하는 효율적인 **30일 완성 PLAN**
- 과목별로 **매일 전 유형을 골고루 풀어 볼 수 있는 체계적인 문항 배치**
- **A4 사이즈로 제작**해 간편한 휴대와 편리한 학습